MW01484512

CRIMINAL LAW AND THE AMERICAN PENAL SYSTEM

ASPEN CASEBOOK SERIES

Criminal Law and The American Penal System

Cases and Context

Andrew Manuel Crespo
Morris Wasserstein Public Interest Professor of Law
Havard Law School
Executive Faculty Director
Institute to End Mass Incarceration

John Rappaport
Professor of Law
The University of Chicago Law School

ASPEN PUBLISHING

To contact Customer Service, e-mail customer.service@aspenpublishing.com, call 1-800-950-5259, or mail correspondence/to:

> Aspen Publishing
> Attn: Order Department
> 1 Wall Street
> Burlington, MA 01803

Printed in the United States of America.

1 2 3 4 5 6 7/8/9/0

ISBN 978-1-5438-3510-6

Library of Congress Cataloging-in-Publication Data

Names: Crespo, Andrew Manuel, author. | Rappaport, John, 1980- author.
Title: Criminal law and the American penal system: cases and context / Andrew Manuel Crespo, Morris Wasserstein Public Interest Professor of Law Executive Faculty Director, Institute to End Mass Incarceration Havard Law School; John Rappaport, Professor of Law, The University of Chicago Law School.
Description: First edition. | Burlington: Aspen Publishing, 2025. | Series: Aspen coursebook series | Includes bibliographical references and index. | Summary: "Law school book for the Criminal Law course" — Provided by publisher.
Identifiers: LCCN 2024052734 | ISBN 9781543835106 (hardback) | ISBN 9781543835113 (ebook)
Subjects: LCSH: Criminal justice, Administration of—United States. | Criminal law—United States. | Punishment—United States. | Imprisonment—United States. | LCGFT: Textbooks.
Classification: LCC KF9223.C74 2025 | DDC 345.73/0773—dc23/eng/20241106
LC record available at https://lccn.loc.gov/2024052734

ABOUT ASPEN PUBLISHING

Aspen Publishing is a leading provider of legal education content and digital learning solutions in the United States and globally. Our innovative products and platforms—designed based on best practices in learning science—engage students and enhance outcomes. From textbooks and audiobooks authored by renowned experts to digital platforms and products like LEAF, Connected eBooks, Connected Quizzing, PracticePerfect, and JD-Next, we empower the next generation of legal professionals with innovative, trusted, and accessible resources.

The Aspen Casebook Series, affectionately known as the "red and black" casebooks among law faculty and students, includes hundreds of highly regarded textbooks across more than 80 disciplines. These range from foundational courses like Torts and Contracts to emerging electives such as Sustainability and the Law of Policing. Our study aids, including the popular *Examples & Explanations* series, help law students master complex topics with clarity and confidence.

Aspen's expertise extends to undergraduate education with our Paralegal, Criminal Justice, and Business Law series, offering the same hallmark quality to a broader audience. JD-Next, our groundbreaking online law school prep course and admissions test, provides a realistic preview of law school, equips students with essential skills for academic success, and evaluates their readiness for legal studies.

Aspen Publishing Is Proud to Be a UWorld Company

Since 2003, UWorld has been a global leader in developing high-quality learning tools for students preparing for high-stakes exams. With a commitment to excellence, UWorld has helped millions of students in undergraduate, graduate, and professional programs in fields such as medicine, nursing, finance, and law achieve their academic and career goals.

Founded by Chandra S. Pemmasani, M.D., during his medical residency, UWorld began focusing on medical education and has since expanded into various academic fields, including law. In 2020, UWorld launched its Legal vertical, starting with its comprehensive Multistate Bar Exam (MBE®) Question Bank, followed by the acquisition of Themis Bar Review, which integrated resources to provide a complete bar exam preparation experience. In 2024, UWorld expanded its offerings by acquiring Aspen Publishing, enhancing its suite of legal education products.

Today, UWorld offers an unparalleled range of study materials that blend active learning methods with expert content, ensuring students and educators can access the most effective resources. From bar preparation to law school success, UWorld is committed to supporting the next generation of legal professionals. Learn more at uworld.com.

SUMMARY OF CONTENTS

TABLE OF CONTENTS

Chapter 10   The End of Mass Incarceration: Ideas and Interventions   869

WHY STUDY CRIMINAL LAW?

For the past half-century, Criminal Law has been taught as a standard, introductory doctrinal course in the law school curriculum. Traditionally, students in this course consider the relationship among conceptual building blocks like the law of *mens rea*, *actus reus*, causation, justification, and excuse. They delve deeply into emblematic crimes, such as homicide and sexual assault. They study and unpack doctrines grounded in old English precedents and trace them forward into more recent cases and statutes. And they consider extensions of foundational principles in more complex settings, such as the law of attempt, complicity, and conspiracy. Through all of this, they probe analytic nuances and inconsistencies. But by and large, they are urged to take their subject as it is presented to them: as a system of law, governing a system of punishment.

This approach may have worked well when it was first adopted in the seminal casebooks of the mid-twentieth century. It may even have worked well when it was expanded and refined in the early editions of the leading contemporary casebooks, first authored in the 1960s and 1970s. But as many professors—and even more students—increasingly recognize, that conventional approach does not work today. Indeed, it is scarcely hyperbolic to suggest that this version of Criminal Law, inherited from earlier eras, is at risk of becoming a failed course, animated by a logic and a pedagogy so disconnected from the core issues driving the modern American penal system as to threaten the course's basic grounding in reality.

The problem is not hard to diagnose. Guided by the leading teaching materials of the day, traditional criminal law courses often fail to acknowledge adequately two fundamental and interrelated issues. The first is the stark, glaring, and racially unjust failing of mass incarceration and the related failing of police misconduct and abuse. For half a century, the United States incarcerated more of its own people than any other nation in history or across the globe, in a manner disproportionately burdening Black and Brown men. Massive as that carceral system is, the criminal law casts an even larger shadow outside the prison walls, where communities of color are policed even more intensively than they are incarcerated.

These facts are widely known to today's generation of law students. For the first time in history, students now arrive on campus having lived through not one but two massive, nationwide protests concerning the penal system's operation. Those protests were triggered most immediately by the deaths of two Black men, Michael Brown in 2014 and George Floyd in 2020, at the hands of white police officers. These police killings and the protests that followed underscored the deeper pathologies of the American penal system and immersed incoming law students in a modern vernacular of criminal justice reform.

Then these students arrive on campus and take Criminal Law. And all too frequently, they discover that the course — guided by contemporary casebooks — treats mass incarceration and the problems of police power as at best ancillary topics. Either these subjects are treated as minor themes that supplement a criminal law course focused on moral philosophy, statutory interpretation, and doctrinal nuance, or they are relegated to the course's epilogue or concluding sessions.

Students, and more than a few professors, are rightly frustrated by this disjunction between the defining issues of the modern American penal system and the basic introductory criminal law course. But that disjunction arises not merely from some oversight or failure to update contemporary casebooks to include "current events." Rather, the defect relates to the course's second failure: it does not reflect *current ideas.*

Simply put, Criminal Law *the course* has failed to account for some of the most significant developments of the past two decades in criminal law *the scholarly field.* Central among these developments is the insight, captured by the late Bill Stuntz, that "criminal law *does not drive criminal punishment.*"[1] Rather, as Stuntz observed, the role substantive criminal law plays in the modern penal system "is to empower prosecutors" and police officers, "who are the criminal justice system's real lawmakers."[2]

Stuntz was among the most influential criminal law scholars of the past half-century. But his work offers a warning to those who teach Criminal Law that is too frequently ignored: "Anyone who reads criminal codes in search of a picture of what conduct leads to a prison term," he wrote, "will be seriously misled."[3] In other words, it is impossible to describe — let alone to study, analyze, or critique — the modern American penal system simply by studying the criminal law as it exists "on the books."

And yet, contemporary Criminal Law casebooks continue to insist on precisely this misdirection. They focus students' attention on the intricacies and doctrinal nuances of the criminal codes and interpretive doctrines of one jurisdiction or another, without ever letting students know the rest of

---

1. William J. Stuntz, *The Pathological Politics of Criminal Law,* 100 Mich. L. Rev. 505, 506 (2001).
2. *Id.*
3. *Id.* at 506-507.

the story—that criminal law, as portrayed in these books, does not define how punishment unfolds in America. Law enforcers do.

Critically, these law enforcers exercise their power against the backdrop of a set of overlapping and interacting social hierarchies, which their actions can in turn both shape and reconstitute. As decades worth of scholarship explores, criminal law is both shaped by and perpetually shaping society. To understand criminal law, one must therefore understand its relationship to the history and social hierarchies from which it stems, including along dimensions of race, gender, and class. A course that fails to center these essential concepts will leave students ill-equipped to truly understand, critique, or change the American penal system.

None of this is to say that law—including substantive criminal law—is irrelevant to the modern American penal system. Quite to the contrary, developments in the criminal law were *essential* to the rise of racialized mass incarceration, over-policing, and police abuse. Indeed, the very phrase mass incarceration is frequently accompanied by another watchword of criminal justice reform: overcriminalization. The idea this word captures, which Stuntz and others have so carefully explained, is not that the substantive criminal law stopped governing the American penal system. Rather, the key insight is that the substantive criminal code transformed into a *mechanism* by which *law enforcers* came to govern that system as a law largely unto themselves—exercising vast, largely unchecked, and often problematic discretion that determines who gets punished and how.

Among those law enforcers, prosecutors loom large. And understanding how criminal law shapes their power is essential to understanding the penal system's operation. But prosecutors are not the only state actors empowered to enforce the criminal law. As Alice Ristroph observes, it is the police who "connect crimes to punishments" by supplying "prosecutors, courts, and eventually prisons with persons to punish."[4] For this reason, while discussions of policing are typically relegated to a separate course on constitutional criminal procedure, a truly complete study "of criminal law must address the agents and practices of law enforcement" as an integral component of the course.[5] After all, every stop, frisk, and arrest is supposed to be predicated on an officer's suspicion that the target of such state action violated the substantive penal code. And virtually every criminal conviction starts with an arrest.

In short, to understand the operation of the criminal law, one needs to understand the relationship between that body of law and the key institutional actors it empowers: prosecutors and police officers. This book

---

4. Alice Ristroph, *The Thin Blue Line from Crime to Punishment*, 108 J. Crim. L. & Criminology 305, 306 (2018).

5. *Id.* at 310; *see also id.* at 306 ("Policing is central to the operation of the modern criminal law, and yet, it has long been almost entirely ignored by criminal law theorists.").

accordingly aims to tell the story of criminal law's evolution from a legal framework that defined, cabined, and legitimated law enforcement power to one that has expanded that power in ways that are intimately interlaced with background sociological histories and dynamics. We believe that evolution should be the central story of the first-year course on these topics, and that it is thus important to emphasize the connection *between* the *Criminal Law* and the *American Penal System*.

As its title suggests, that is the story this book tells. Its aims are straightforward: to consider the role that criminal law might serve in a well-functioning and just society, to question how the legitimacy of criminal law might change in societies that are unjust or unequal, to chart the role that law and legal actors played in producing the American penal system's current pathologies, and to invite students to imagine ways in which law and legal actors might go about addressing and redressing those systemic and institutional failings.

Our goal is not to replace this essential and foundational law school class with a political science course or a criminology class. Law and legal analysis, primarily of conventional case materials, continue to anchor this book, much like they anchor many others. But unlike any other book, we situate those familiar materials in a fundamentally different conceptual framework, one that is novel to criminal law casebooks even if it will likely be familiar to both scholars and practitioners in the field.

The course this casebook supports is thus still very much a course *about* criminal law. But it is a course about the role that body of law has played in producing a penal system increasingly seen as flawed or unjust by large segments of society. Our aim, in other words, is not to sever ties with the traditional topics of the criminal law course, but rather to create stronger ties between those topics and the realities of the penal system. As students will see, legal actors — lawyers — have been central players in the evolution of the penal system's pathology. Likewise, students will see that tomorrow's legal actors — the students themselves — will likely play a significant role in identifying pathways toward the system's reform.

ACKNOWLEDGMENTS

The earliest conversations about this book began, many years ago, seated across from Joe Terry. Since then, he and the team at Aspen Publishing and the Froebe Group have been terrifically supportive editors and publishers. We are most especially grateful to Joanne Butler, Jessica Barmack, Patrick Cline, and Corinne Pulicay.

We are fortunate to teach in a vibrant field populated by incredible scholars, many of whom, in their generosity, have engaged in numerous conversations with us about the aims, contours, and execution of this book. We could not adequately capture our gratitude for all of those essential exchanges nor name each interlocutor individually, but we do want to acknowledge specifically those colleagues and friends who took the time to offer substantial written feedback on portions of the project or to indulge our requests for guidance in their areas of expertise. Thank you to Will Baude, Joseph Blocher, Aaron Chalfin, Vincent Chiao, Jessica Clarke, Adam Davidson, Justin Driver, Dan Epps, Chad Flanders, Stephen Galoob, Ben Grunwald, Rachel Harmon, Thea Johnson, Liz Kamali, Emma Kaufman, Erin Kelly, Orin Kerr, Nancy King, Genevieve Lakier, Christopher Lewis, Richard McAdams, Gabe Mendlow, Darrell Miller, Erin Murphy, Alexandra Natapoff, Danny Richman, Anna Roberts, Chris Slobogin, Sonja Starr, Seth Stoughton, Ryan Sakoda, Rachel Sachs, Jocelyn Simonson, Roseanna Sommers, Jeannie Suk Gersen, and Crystal Yang. We are grateful as well to the participants in academic roundtables discussing this project hosted by the University of Minnesota Law School, the Washington University School of Law in St. Louis, the American Bar Association Criminal Justice Section Academics Committee and the American Association of Law Schools Criminal Law Section, Vanderbilt Law School, and the Michigan Journal of Race and Law.

The pages that follow, including all the many endnotes, were produced with the invaluable support of a small army of research assistants, to whom we are so very grateful. At the University of Chicago: Evan Blanchard-Wu, Brian Bornhoft, Rachel Caldwell, Angela Chang, Tawkir Chowdhury, David Doktorman, Ryan Guo, Youssef Mohamed Helmi, Mateus Kaba Aboud, Jonah Klausner, Ben Klein, Ronja Kleinholz, Rachel Linton, Jenna Liu, Grace Masback, Olivia Miller, Alec Mouser, Jacqueline Pecaro, Marissa Piccolo, Shreya Minama Reddy, Sebastian Torero, and Hannah Zobair.

And at Harvard Law School: Sarah Atkinson, Shing-Shing Cao, Jessenia Class, Robert Clinton, Elliott DeRiso, Avery Farmer, Amber Feng, Delaney Herndon, Larson Ishii, Peter Jen, Dasha Kolyaskina, Jack Lubin, Jordan Mulevicz, David Popoola, Alex Ramsey, Parisa Sadeghi, David Sanchez, Will Searcy, Emma Sherry, Marisa Skillings, and Lizzie Wallace. We are especially grateful to David S., Sarah, Shing-Shing, Amber, and Emma for their work captaining our various RA teams over the years.

Our colleagues in the University of Chicago Law School's D'Angelo Law Library and the Harvard Law School Library supported our endless requests to track down sometimes obscure sources with characteristic professionalism and good cheer. The Clerk of Court's Office in Mississippi County, Missouri graciously sent us the audio recording of the proceedings in *People v. Anderson*, which anchors this book's second chapter. And nearly two dozen jurists across the country — including nine state supreme court justices — took the time to respond to our survey asking for help identifying recent cases in their jurisdictions that might serve as valuable teaching materials. We are grateful to Justice Christine Donohue (Pa.), Justice Gary Hill (S.C.), Justice Steve McCullough (Va.), Justice David Nahmias (Ga.), Justice William P. Robinson III (R.I.), Chief Justice Loretta Rush (Ind.), Chief Justice Mary Russell (Mo.), Justice Caleb Stegall (Kan.), Justice David Viviano (Mich.), Judge Terry Crone (Ind.), Judge Anthony Kline (Cal.), Judge Amy Ronayne Krause (Mich.), Judge Thomas Logue (Fla.), Justice James Milkey (Mass.), Justice Mary Mikva (Ill.), Justice Eileen Moore (Cal.), Judge Douglas Nazarian (Md.), Judge Paul Reilly (Wis.), Judge Jerry Tao (Nev.), Judge Diana Terry (Colo.), and Judge Gary Witt (Mo.).

Finally, for their treasured friendship and endless professional guidance and support, Andrew Crespo is grateful to John Manning, Martha Minow, Carol Steiker, John Goldberg, and Daphna Renan — and most of all to Abby Shafroth, Quincy Evans Correa, and Walden Evans Correa, for their bountiful love and infinite smiles. John Rappaport similarly appreciates Jonathan Masur, Richard McAdams, and Tom Miles — and his family, Lynnette Li, Lena Rappaport, and Jonah Rappaport, for their enduring and invaluable support.

A.M.C.
J.R.
January 2025

The authors would like to thank the authors, publishers, and copyright holders who granted permission to reproduce the following excerpted works and images:

EXCERPTS

Abramson, Jeffrey. "Two Ideals of Jury Deliberation." *University of Chicago Legal Forum*, vol. 1998, 1998. University of Chicago Law School. Reprinted with permission.

Bell, Monica. "Police Reform and the Dismantling of Legal Estrangement." *The Yale Law Journal*, vol. 126, Jan. 2017. The Yale Law Journal Company, Inc. Reprinted with permission.

Berlatsky, Noah. "Want to Reduce Mass Incarceration? Fund Public Defenders." *Medium*, Arc Digital, 11 Sep. 2018, medium.com/arc-digital/want-to-reduce-mass-incarceration-fund-public-defenders-f514d1dade38.

Binder, Guyora. "The Culpability of Felony Murder." *Notre Dame Law Review*, vol. 83, no. 3, Jan. 2008. University of Notre Dame Law School. Reprinted with permission.

Bollag, Jordan. "Drug Decriminalization Policies Work—with Properly Funded Treatment Services." *Jacobin*, Aug. 2023. Copyright © 2023 Jacobin.

Buell, Samuel W. *Capital Offenses: Business Crime and Punishment in America's Corporate Age*. W.W. Norton & Company, 2016. Reprinted with permission.

Burrus, Trevor. "How the Drug War Broke Policing." Cato Institute, 15 Jun. 2020, www.cato.org/blog/how-drug-war-broke-policing. Licensed under CC BY-NC-SA 4.0, https://creativecommons.org/licenses/by-nc-sa/4.0/.

Butler, Paul. "Racially Based Jury Nullification: Black Power in the Criminal Justice System." *The Yale Law Journal*, vol. 105, Dec. 1995. The Yale Law Journal Company, Inc. Reprinted with permission.

Caldwell, Matthew. "The End of Public Defenders." *Inquest,* 25 Feb. 2022, inquest.org/the-end-of-public-defenders/. Reprinted with permission.

Capers, Bennett. "Maybe, If . . ." *Inquest*, 25 Jun. 2024, inquest.org/maybe-if/. Reprinted with permission.

Clune, Michael. "Why Decriminalizing Drugs Is a Bad Idea." *The Washington Post*, 10 Apr. 2023. Reprinted with permission.

Cohan, William D. "How Wall Street Banks Stayed out of Jail." *The Atlantic,*
Sep. 2015. Reprinted with permission.

D.C. Bar. "Ethics Opinion 320." Dcbar.org, 2003, www.dcbar.org/for-lawyers
/legal-ethics/ethics-opinions-210-present/ethics-opinion-320.
Reprinted with permission.

Davis, Raeford. "Why I Hated Being a Cop." The Marshall Project, 22 Apr.
2016, www.themarshallproject.org/2016/04/21/why-i-hated-being
-a-cop.

Dvorak, Petula. "Passengers Watched Killing on Metro Car. Should They
Have Intervened?" *The Washington Post,* 9 July 2015. Copyright © 2015
The Washington Post. All rights reserved. Used under license.

Estrich, Susan. "Defending Women." *Michigan Law Review,* vol. 88, no. 6,
1990. University of Michigan Law School. Reprinted with permission.

Farias, Cristian. "On Both Sides of the Gun." *Inquest,* 13 Jul. 2023, https://
inquest.org/on-both-sides-of-the-gun/. Reprinted with permission.

Forman, James. *Locking up Our Own: Crime and Punishment in Black America.*
Farrar, Straus & Giroux, 2017. Reprinted with permission.

Frampton, Thomas Ward. "The Dangerous Few: Taking Seriously Prison
Abolition and Its Skeptics." *Harvard Law Review,* vol. 135, 2022.
Copyright © 2022 The Harvard Law Review Association.

Friedman, Jaclyn. Interview by Colette Perold. Challenging Male Supremacy
Project, http://challengingmalesupremacy.org/wp-content/uploads
/2015/03/Expanding-Consent-excerpt-Jaclyn-Friedman.pdf. Licensed
under CC BY-NC-SA 4.0, https://creativecommons.org/licenses/by-nc
-sa/4.0/deed.en.

Gersen, Jeannie Suk. "Revisiting the Brock Turner Case." *The New Yorker,* 29
Mar. 2023. Condé Nast. Reprinted with permission.

Ghandoosh, Nazgol and Kristen M. Budd. "Incarceration and Crime: A
Weak Relationship." The Sentencing Project, 13 Jun. 2024, www.senten
cingproject.org/reports/incarceration-and-crime-a-weak-relationship/.
Reprinted with permission.

Gilmore, Ruth Wilson, and James Kilgore. "Ruth Wilson Gilmore and James
Kilgore: The Case for Prison Abolition." The Marshall Project, 19 June
2019, www.themarshallproject.org/2019/06/19/the-case-for-abolition.

Glanton, Dahleen. "When the Felony Murder Rule Looms Overhead, A Plea
Deal Isn't Always a Lifeline." Chicago Tribune, 23 Sep. 2019. Copyright
© 2019 Chicago Tribune. All rights reserved. Used under license.

Gornick, Janet C., and David S. Meyer. "Changing Political Opportunity: The
Anti-Rape Movement and Public Policy." Journal of Policy History, vol.
36, no. 3, 1998. Copyright © 1998 Cambridge University Press.

Green, Tewkunzi. "Surviving Everywhere." *Inquest,* 16 Nov. 2021, inquest.
org/surviving-everywhere/.

Gruber, Aya. *The Feminist War on Crime.* University of California Press,
May 2020.

Grunwald, Ben. "Data-Driven Incarceration." *Inquest*, 12 Jan. 2023, https://inquest.org/data-driven-decarceration/. Reprinted with permission.

Hamilton, Olivia. "Nobody Cares if You're Pregnant." *Inside This Place, Not of It*, edited by Robin Levi and Ayelet Waldman. Copyright © 2011 Verso Books.

Hampton, Jean. "Correcting Harms Versus Righting Wrongs: The Goal of Retribution." *UCLA Law Review*, vol. 39, 1992. UCLA School of Law. Reprinted with permission.

Harawa, Daniel. "Trials without Justice." *Inquest*, 21 Sept. 2021, inquest.org/trials-without-justice/. Reprinted with permission.

Hatton, Erin. "Growing Justice." *Inquest*, 9 Sept. 2022, inquest.org/growing-restorative-transformative-justice/. Reprinted with permission.

Henning, Kristin. *The Rage of Innocence: How America Criminalizes Black Youth*. Copyright © 2021 by Kristin Henning. Used by permission of Pantheon Books, an imprint of the Knopf Doubleday Publishing Group, a division of Penguin Random House LLC. All rights reserved.

Herzing, Rachel. "Abolition Is Practical." *Inquest*, 11 July 2023, inquest.org/abolition-is-practical/. Reprinted with permission.

Husak, Douglas N. "Justifications and the Criminal Liability of Accessories." *Journal of Criminal Law & Criminology*, vol. 80, iss. 2, 1989. The Northwestern University Pritzker School of Law. Reprinted with permission.

Jacobs, Anna. "I Don't Know If Anyone in There Ever Used the Word 'Diabetes.'" *Inside This Place, Not of It*, edited by Robin Levi and Ayelet Waldman. Copyright © 2011 Verso Books.

Jayadev, Raj and Pilar Weiss. "Organizing towards a New Vision of Community Justice." *LPE Project*, 9 May 2019, lpeproject.org/blog/organizing-towards-a-new-vision-of-community-justice/. Reprinted with permission.

Johnson, Jason. "'Defund the Police' Led to Lower Standards." *The Wall Street Journal*, 22 Feb. 2023. Copyright © 2023 Dow Jones & Company.

Kaba, Mariame, et al. *No More Police: A Case for Abolition*. Copyright © 2022 The New Press.

Kaba, Mariame. *We Do This 'Til We Free Us*. Haymarket Books, 2021.

Kahan, Dan. "Culture, Cognition, and Consent: Who Perceives What, and Why, in 'Acquaintance Rape' Cases." *University of Pennsylvania Law Review*, vol. 158, 2010. University of Pennsylvania Law School. Reprinted with permission.

Kennedy, Randall. *Race, Crime, and the Law*. Pantheon Books, 1997. Reprinted with permission.

Kerr, Orin. "Sandra Bland and the 'Lawful Order' Problem." *The Washington Post*, 23 Jul. 2015. Reprinted with permission.

Klein, Ezra. "'Yes Means Yes' Is a Terrible Law, and I Completely Support It." *Vox*, 13 Oct. 2014, www.vox.com/2014/10/13/6966847/yes-means-yes-is-a-terrible-bill-and-i-completely-support-it.

Rasmussen, Cameron and Sonya Shah. "Growing Justice." *Inquest*, 9 Sept. 2022, inquest.org/growing-restorative-transformative-justice/. Reprinted with permission.

Rehavi, M., and Sonja Starr. "Racial Disparity in Federal Criminal Sentences." *Journal of Political Economy*, vol. 122, 1 Dec. 2014. University of Chicago Press. Reprinted with permission

Roberts, Dorothy E. "Abolition Constitutionalism." *Harvard Law Review*, vol. 133, 8 Nov. 2019. The Harvard Law Review Association. Reprinted with permission.

Rodríguez, Dylan. "Abolition as Praxis of Human Being: A Foreword." *Harvard Law Review*, vol. 132, Apr. 2019. The Harvard Law Review Association. Reprinted with permission.

Salavieri, Francesca. "I Eventually Made Friends with the Mice." *Inside This Place, Not of It*, edited by Robin Levi and Ayelet Waldman. Copyright © 2011 Verso Books.

Sanderson, Marilyn. "I Wonder if the Staff Consider Us Human at All." *Inside This Place, Not of It*, edited by Robin Levi and Ayelet Waldman. Copyright © 2011 Verso Books.

Schulhofer, Stephen J. *Unwanted Sex: The Culture of Intimidation and the Failure of the Law.* Harvard University Press, Copyright © 1998 by the President and Fellows of Harvard College. Used by permission. All rights reserved.

Shulevitz, Judith. "Regulating Sex." *The New York Times*, 27 Jun. 2015. Copyright © 2015 The New York Times Company. All rights reserved. Used under license.

Sood, Avani Mehta. "Attempted Justice: Misunderstanding and Bias in Psychological Constructions of Criminal Attempt." *Stanford Law Review*, vol. 71, 31 Mar. 2019. Stanford Law School. Reprinted with permission.

Srinivasan, Amia. *The Right to Sex.* Bloomsbury Publishing, 2021. Reprinted with permission.

Stephens, Bret. "The Hard-Drug Decriminalization Disaster." *The New York Times*, 1 Aug. 2023. Copyright © 2023 The New York Times Company. All rights reserved. Used under license.

Stuntz, William J. "The Pathological Politics of Criminal Law." *Michigan Law Review*, vol. 100, iss. 3, 2001. University of Michigan Law School.

Sullum, Jacob. "Did Drug Decriminalization Cause a 'Catastrophe' in Oregon?" Reason.com, 3 Aug. 2023, reason.com/2023/08/03/did-drug-decriminalization-cause-a-catastrophe-in-oregon/. Reprinted with permission from *Reason* Magazine and Reason.com.

Trillin, Calvin. "The Color of Blood." *The New Yorker*, Feb. 2008, www.newyorker.com/magazine/2008/03/03/the-color-of-blood.

Wilson, James Q., and George K. Kelling. "Broken Windows: The Police and Neighborhood Safety." *The Atlantic*, Mar. 1982, www.theatlantic.com/magazine/archive/1982/03/broken-windows/304465/.

Yaffe, Gideon. "A Republican Crime Proposal That Democrats Should Back." *The New York Times*, 12 Feb. 2016. Reprinted with permission.

Zatz, Noah. "The Carceral Labor Continuum." *Inquest*, June 2023, inquest. org/the-carceral-labor-continuum/. Reprinted with permission.

IMAGES

Berkowitz Should Be Convicted of Rape: Agree/Disagree. Chart. From Dan M. Kahan, "Culture Cognition, and Consent: Who Perceives What, and Why, in Acquaintance-Rape Cases," *University of Pennsylvania Law Review*, vol. 158, 2010. University of Pennsylvania Law School. Reprinted with permission.

Berkowitz Should Be Found Guilty of Rape: Percentage Agreeing (1st demographic breakdown). Graph. From Dan M. Kahan, "Culture Cognition, and Consent: Who Perceives What, and Why, in Acquaintance-Rape Cases," *University of Pennsylvania Law Review*, vol. 158, 2010. University of Pennsylvania Law School. Reprinted with permission.

Berkowitz Should Be Found Guilty of Rape: Percentage Agreeing (2nd demographic breakdown). Graph. From Dan M. Kahan, "Culture Cognition, and Consent: Who Perceives What, and Why, in Acquaintance-Rape Cases," *University of Pennsylvania Law Review*, vol. 158, 2010. University of Pennsylvania Law School. Reprinted with permission.

Critical Resistance. *Reformist Reforms vs. Abolitionist Steps to End Imprisonment*, 2021. Chart. criticalresistance.org/wp-content/uploads/2021/08 /CR_abolitioniststeps_antiexpansion_2021_eng.pdf. Reprinted with permission.

Example of an Age-Crime Curve. Graph. From Sampson, Robert J. and John H. Laub, "Life-Course Desisters? Trajectories of Crime among Delinquent Boys Followed to Age 70." *Criminology*, vol. 41, no. 3, Aug. 2003. The American Society of Criminology. Reprinted with permission.

How many years until incarceration in the United States falls to 1970 rates? Graph. From Jacob Kang-Brown, et al., *The New Dynamics of Mass Incarceration*. Vera Institute, Jun. 2018.

Juvenile Convicts at Work in the Fields. Photograph. Library of Congress, www.loc.gov/item/2016818521/.

Lisa Robinson of Washington reacts to Derek Chauvin's murder conviction. Photograph. Copyright © 2021 Alex Brandon/The Associated Press. All rights reserved.

Men in prison working in a field. Photograph. From *The Atlantic*. Copyright © 2015 The Atlantic Monthly Group, LLC. All rights reserved. Used under license.

Number of Adults Under Community Supervision More Than Tripled Over 36 Years. Graph. Pew Research Center, Washington, D.C. (2018),

https://www.pewtrusts.org/-/media/assets/2018/09/probation
_and_parole_systems_marked_by_high_stakes_missed_opportunities
_pew.pdf.

Protestors clash over the Goetz verdict. Photograph. Copyright © 1987 AP. All rights reserved.

Protestors show support for Bernie Goetz. Photograph. Copyright © Rick Maiman/NY Daily News via Getty Images.

Romer, Paul. Homicide and Total Incarceration Rate for the United States (per 100,000 Residents). Graph. 13 June 2014, marroninstitute.nyu. edu/blog/the-great-crime-wave-the-tragedy-of-mass-incarceration. Reprinted with permission.

Schlag, Anne Katrin. Percentage of U.S. Drug Users Who Develop Dependence. Table. From "Percentages of Problem Drug Use and Their Implications for Policy Making: A Review of the Literature." *Drug Science & Law*, vol. 6, 2020. Walter de Gruyter GmbH. Reprinted with permission.

Schlag, Anne Katrin. Percentage of US Respondents Who Have Used Drugs. Table. From "Percentages of Problem Drug Use and Their Implications for Policy Making: A Review of the Literature." *Drug Science & Law*, vol. 6, 2020. Walter de Gruyter GmbH. Reprinted with permission.

U.S. Incarceration and Psychiatric Hospitalization Rates. Graph. From Raphael, Steven and Michael A. Stoll, "Assessing the Contribution of the Deinstitutionalization of the Mentally Ill to Growth in the U.S. Incarceration Rate." *The Journal of Legal Studies*, vol. 42, no. 1, Jan. 2013. University of Chicago Press Journals. Reprinted with permission.

CRIMINAL LAW AND THE AMERICAN PENAL SYSTEM

PART 1

PUNISHMENT AND CRIME: CONCEPTUAL AND EMPIRICAL FOUNDATIONS

The first three chapters of this book lay important conceptual and empirical foundations for the chapters that follow. We begin, in Chapter One, with a comprehensive overview of mass incarceration, describing the history of American prisons, presenting facts and figures that set American incarceration apart from every other penal system of the world, and offering firsthand accounts from people incarcerated within prison walls of the lived reality of American punishment. We conclude this chapter with cases and commentary designed to probe an essential question: What distinguishes criminal law from other substantive domains of law, including private law and civil regulatory law? And we suggest one prominent answer: that criminal law is uniquely the law of punishment and blame.

Understanding criminal law as the law of punishment, in turn, raises its own foundational question: What are the legitimating rationales offered to justify a state's coercive and often painful punishment of its own people? And are there circumstances in which a state might be thought to lose any legitimate claim to such power? These are the core questions of Chapter Two, which explores longstanding philosophical debates related to a trio of justifications offered for state punishment—retributivism, utilitarianism, and expressivism—and which examines philosophical arguments that states that tolerate, ignore, or foster systemic social inequality may lose the moral standing to punish in some or all circumstances.

Finally, Chapter Three begins where Chapter Two leaves off, examining the existing empirical evidence about the root causes of crime, including the robust sociological evidence demonstrating that structural forces such as income and racial inequality are major forces in spurring crime within American society. Chapter Three then asks how the criminal law ought to respond to this sociological reality, with a focus on a set of doctrines, generally known as doctrines of excuse, that sometimes—but only rarely—bar criminal punishment when people violate the criminal law due in part to influences beyond their control.

CHAPTER 1

WHAT IS PUNISHMENT?

Defining the Criminal Law

> "Whatever views one holds about the penal law, no one will question its importance in society. This is the law on which [people] place their ultimate reliance for protection against all the deepest injuries that human conduct can inflict on individuals and institutions. By the same token, penal law governs the strongest force that we permit official agencies to bring to bear on individuals. Its promise as an instrument of safety is matched only by its power to destroy."
>
> Herbert Wechsler, *The Challenge of a Model Penal Code*,
> 65 Harv. L. Rev. 1097, 1098 (1952)

INTRODUCTION

This is a course about American criminal law and the ways in which it constructs a system of punishment—the American penal system. Ask someone to describe that system and you are likely to hear about people and settings that routinely appear on television and in pop culture: police officers patrolling the streets, lawyers objecting in court as their adversaries cross-examine witnesses, people accused of crimes anxiously awaiting a jury's verdict or a judge's sentence. Growing up with this cultural backdrop, students often come to law school with some general idea of the types of conduct that can prompt a criminal prosecution. You may never have heard of some of the phrases common to other foundational courses (*fee simple, efficient breach, diversity jurisdiction*). But you have a sense of what *murder, robbery,* and *rape* are, just as you know it is a crime to shoplift or to possess certain types of drugs. Most people in the United States also have at least some intuition about whether certain types of conduct should be deemed criminal in the first place and about how society ought to respond when people engage in behavior harmful to others. Perhaps most notably, having lived through the birth of the Black Lives Matter movement and a decade's worth of protests over policing and mass incarceration, most Americans also know that a great many people in this country think our approach to defining crimes and to punishing people who commit them is highly problematic and racially unjust.

This course delves deeply into these essential issues. In it, you will study both the laws and the myriad overlapping institutions that together constitute the American penal system. You will examine the ways in which those laws and institutions created a system that many today find untenable, and you will reflect on the extent to which you share that critique. Finally, you will consider how the laws and institutions studied in this course might be changed — to better hold people accountable for harms they cause to others, and to better hold the state itself accountable for the harms it imposes as it attempts to prevent and punish crime.

All of that exploration begins in this initial chapter with an examination of two foundational questions: What *is* the criminal law? And what do we mean by *punishment?*

At the most basic (though, as we will soon see, oversimplified) level, it is tempting to answer both of these questions in a word: *prison.* As a form of punishment, prison sentences dominate our conception of the American penal system. And the prospect of prison is, at least as a rough first cut, a good way of distinguishing the criminal law from other aspects of the legal system. A lot of behavior, after all, is "against the law." Breaching an agreement, for example, might violate the private law of contract, just as parking on the wrong side of the street might violate the local regulatory code in your town. In both instances, if you fail to do what the law says you should do, there will be consequences: breaching a contract can lead to an order to pay civil damages, while regulatory infractions carry fines. In neither instance, though, will someone come and carry you off to prison.

That power to imprison, which social theorist Max Weber described as a form of *state violence,* is one of the most substantial and dangerous powers a government can wield. To Weber, it is a component of what he called the state's monopoly on violence. "The state is considered the sole source of the 'right' to use violence," he wrote, which means that "the relation between the state and violence is an especially intimate one." Consider a person who is grabbed off the street and carried away to a cell. If a private person commits such acts, she is guilty of kidnapping. But when agents of the state do the same thing, we call their action an *arrest,* and we call any subsequent period of incarceration for the person removed from society a *sentence.* To the person on the receiving end, these coercive acts can feel similar, even though the first is a crime while the second is a tool the state uses to respond to conduct it deems criminal.[1]

Criminal law, in other words, is the means by which a society specifies the principal conditions under which the government may lawfully deploy force against its own people — often by incarcerating them. Our examination of the meaning of the terms *criminal law* and *punishment* thus starts with an overview of the history, the present-day scale, and the lived experience of incarceration in America, all of which are taken up in the first section of this chapter.

And yet, salient as incarceration is in discussions of the American penal system, it does not actually work as a *defining* feature of either crime or punishment—because it is both too narrow and too broad. On the one hand, it is too narrow because the penal system routinely punishes people who have committed crimes by imposing penalties on them that do not include incarceration, whether by sentencing them to probation, by levying criminal fines, or by exposing them to formal and informal consequences flowing from the fact of criminal conviction. These noncarceral punishments, which are frequently imposed on people prosecuted for and convicted of lower-level misdemeanor offenses, can have substantial and long-lasting consequences that ought not be sidelined when studying the criminal law. On the other hand, incarceration is too broad a definition for the boundaries of the criminal law, because many thousands of people—including those who are locked up in immigration detention centers, juvenile detention centers, or secured psychiatric institutions—are currently incarcerated in the United States even though they have never been found guilty or in some instances even been accused of criminal wrongdoing.

In short, our legal system frequently imposes punishment without incarceration and frequently imposes incarceration without purporting to punish. The idea that punishment and the criminal law can be *defined* by incarceration thus works only as a rough first approximation. The second and third parts of this chapter explore these added layers of nuance in an effort to arrive at a more precise definition of these foundational ideas.

I.   INCARCERATION

Prisons loom large in the American penal system. In person, their immensity casts an imposing shadow. In courtrooms, they are physically removed, but remain a palpable presence given the threat of incarceration as a punishment for crime. Our goal in this section is to gain a working understanding of this penal institution. Where did the prison come from? What is the scale and composition of the prison population in the United States today? And what are some of the salient features of life within American prisons—of life "on the inside"?

A.   A Brief History of Prisons in America

In the opening pages of *The Oxford History of the Prison*, Norval Morris and David Rothman observe that "institutions of incarceration appear so

monumental in design and so intrinsic to the criminal justice system" that
it is often difficult in the popular imagination "to conceive of a moment
when prisons were not at the core of criminal justice." In the United
States, while prisons were not commonplace in the colonial era or at the
founding, they developed very soon thereafter, in the late 1780s and early
1790s, with the opening of Castle Island prison in Massachusetts, Newgate
prison in New York, and, most famously, the Walnut Street penitentiary
in Philadelphia. As an institution, prisons have changed in some salient
respects since those early days. But the history of American prisons is
marked just as much by a series of failed attempts to transform or reform
the institution — and by the eventual abandonment of many such efforts.
The notes that follow offer a necessarily abbreviated account of this history
from the American founding up through the early 1970s when the modern
era of mass incarceration began, with sources cited in the endnotes offering
more detailed and expansive analyses.[2]

NOTES AND QUESTIONS

1. "A Sanguinary Hue": Punishment in Colonial America. A few months
after the colonies declared their independence from Great Britain, the
Commonwealth of Virginia set out to revise its legal code. To draft its new
penal laws, it turned to the author of the Declaration of Independence and
its future governor, Thomas Jefferson. To modern readers, the code Jefferson proposed will hardly seem enlightened. In gruesome detail, it specified
a set of punishments to be imposed "very directly to limb." For example,
for men convicted of sodomy, Jefferson proposed castration. By contrast,
Jefferson wrote that a woman convicted of sodomy should be punished "by
cutting through the cartilage of her nose a hole of at least one-half inch
diameter." As for anyone convicted of maiming or disfiguring another person, Jefferson proposed maiming and disfiguring the perpetrator in kind,
"or if that cannot be [accomplished] for want of the same [body] part, then
as nearly as may be [achieved by disfiguring] some other part [of his body]
of at least equal value and estimation in the opinion of a jury."[3]

Ultimately, the Virginia legislature declined to adopt Jefferson's suggestions. In fact, as historian Kathryn Preyer recounts, Jefferson himself came
to worry that his eye-for-an-eye approach would be too "revolting to the
humanised feelings of modern times" in post-revolutionary America. This
nod to modernity captures a significant turning point in the country's
approach to punishment. Before the Revolution, the penal law of England
and the colonies had what Jefferson called a "sanguinary hue." Executions
were more common than they are today, particularly in England, where
Parliament expanded the list of capital offenses nearly fivefold between
1688 and 1815. The American colonies executed comparatively fewer

people—a few hundred prior to the Revolution—but punishments on this side of the Atlantic were sanguinary spectacles. "Whipping was an extremely common punishment," historian Lawrence Friedman writes, and branding and mutilation were not unheard of: "Dozens of detached ears," cut from the heads of people convicted of crimes, "litter the record books."[4]

While contemporary punishment remains physically brutal in certain ways, including with respect to capital punishment and to the high levels of violence in modern American prisons, Jefferson's early reference to "the humanised feelings of modern times" accurately captures the significant change that occurred when the colonies stepped forward into independence. Sanguinary punishments quickly fell out of favor, at least with respect to the formal criminal law that applied to free white people. As we will soon see, the story—as with so much else in American law—was very different for Black people, who were frequently and brutally tortured by their enslavers in the antebellum period and who continued to be brutally coerced into penal labor following the Civil War and emancipation. With respect to the *de jure* penal system applicable to white people, however, the late-eighteenth century evolution in penal philosophy was pronounced. Pennsylvania, the Quaker state, led the way by limiting capital punishment to a subset of homicides—a move soon followed by states across the country. By the 1820s, Friedman notes, "whipping and other means of mortifying the flesh fell into disrepute" as formal punishments for crimes, as the sanguinary era of punishment came to an end.[5]

2. "A Remedy for All the Evils of Society": The Birth of the Prison and of a Carceral Ideology. The rapid shift away from punishing the flesh raised an obvious question: If people convicted of crimes were not to be hanged, whipped, branded, or mutilated, how would they be punished? The answer, it turns out, was prison—although perhaps not intentionally so at first. Surveying the early American penal system, Alexis de Tocqueville observed that penitentiaries seemed to have been invented because "People said: *instead of killing the guilty, our laws put them in prison; thus, we have a penitentiary system.*" In other words, as historian David Rothman writes, the prison arose from a move away "from the gallows, rather than any faith in the powers of the penitentiary itself." And yet, the lack of any clear animating rationale did not stop prisons from materializing or from spreading once invented. Pennsylvania was at the forefront, converting a jail on Philadelphia's Walnut Street initially used to hold people awaiting trial into the first American facility intentionally designed as a penitentiary in 1790.* Over the ensuing

---

* Today, the word *prison* is a term of art for an institution that incarcerates people serving sentences typically longer than a year. *Jails* incarcerate people detained while awaiting trial and, sometimes, people serving relatively shorter sentences.

decades, New York, New Jersey, Virginia, Kentucky, Massachusetts, Vermont, New Hampshire, and Maryland constructed their own penitentiaries as well.[6]

Before long, ideology caught up with reality, as the proponents and administrators of the nascent prison system began justifying incarceration as an appropriate response to crime. As historian Lawrence Friedman notes, "New ideas about the *sources* of crime" drove this new carceral ideology.

> People felt that bad company, vice-rotten cities, temptations, [and] weaknesses in the family were producing waves of crime. They located the sources of deviant behavior in society itself, in the environment. This was, of course, quite different from the classic colonial view, which located the source of sin in individual weaknesses, or in the devil and his minions. But if society itself was corrupting, for some people, what was to be done? One solution was a kind of radical surgery: remove the deviant from his (weak and defective) family, his evil community, and put him in "an artificially created and therefore corruption-free environment."[7]

Consistent with this new way of thinking, the early penitentiaries were conceived as sites "of penitence and reformation" and were operated accordingly. As Friedman observes, each of these new penitentiaries was "committed to silence, to a certain amount of isolation; and, more fundamentally, to discipline and regimentation" that forced prisoners to adhere "to the same daily rhythm." To quote Tocqueville, "Moral and religious instruction . . . form[ed] the whole basis of the system."[8]

This new carceral ideology soon gained fervent supporters who proselytized the prison as "the remedy applicable to all of society's ills." Many of these early proponents exhibited a zeal that Tocqueville called "monomania," exemplified well by prison chaplain James Finley who, writing in his journal in 1846, suggested that if we could only "all be put on prison fare, for the space of two or three generations, the world would ultimately be the better for it." "Indeed," Finley went on, "should society change places with the prisoners" and adopt "the regularity, and temperance, and sobriety of a good prison," it would soon see that "the prisoner has the advantage."[9]

3. "A Crisis of Legitimacy." Rosy sentiments notwithstanding, the early prisons were hardly idyllic. In fact, as Friedman notes, "decay set in almost immediately in most prisons—almost as soon as the last brick was laid and the prison opened for business." As a result, historian Rebecca McLennan writes, by as early as 1816, fewer than thirty years after Philadelphia's Walnut Street prison opened its doors, it was "palpably evident" to many observers that "the penitential mode of punishment was caught up in a crisis of legitimacy."[10]

At the root of this decay lay a perennial problem. "Men were sentenced to prison," Friedman writes, "faster than the state built new cells and cellblocks." Prisons thus quickly became "characterized by overcrowding, brutality, and disorder," with corporal punishment akin to torture reemerging as a commonplace (if now only quasi-licit) feature of carceral punishment. As historians note, "it was not uncommon to hang convicts by their thumbs" or to force them to endure "the near suffocation of a shower bath," which today's reader would recognize as a form of waterboarding. Little wonder, then, that when English novelist Charles Dickens visited a Pennsylvania penitentiary a decade after Tocqueville conducted his own tour of American prisons, he condemned the institution he visited as "cruel and wrong," decrying "the immense amount of torture and agony that this dreadful punishment, prolonged for years, inflicts on the sufferers."[11]

By the time of the Civil War, Dickens' condemnation was leveled nationwide. In one of the most well-known reports of the era, Enoch Wines and Theodore Dwight concluded that "there is not a state prison in America in which the reform of convicts is the one supreme object of the discipline," nor "a prison system in the United States" that "would not be found wanting." And yet, as Friedman observes, "there was no going back. Imprisonment was and remained the basic way to punish men and women convicted of serious crimes. The great penitentiaries were not pulled down. There they stood — corrupt and brutal; warehouses for convicts." From its outset the prison system seemed to prove true the words of reformer Samuel Gridley Howe, who observed in the mid-1800s that institutions "so strongly built, so richly endowed . . . cannot be got rid of so easily."[12]

4. The Rhetoric and the Reality of Rehabilitation and Reform. Consistent with Howe's prediction, the waves of criticism that crashed against the prison during its first 150 years set the stage for a series of attempted reforms, but not for the prison's abolition. The first such wave built on the Wines and Dwight report, as reformers in the 1870s pushed to provide prisoners with opportunities for education and to reward their progress toward rehabilitation with early release. Elmira Reformatory was the paragon of this model and inspired a small wave of follow-on programs with its early signs of success. But as Edgardo Rotman writes, these efforts ultimately "did little to halt the deterioration of the country's prisons," with Elmira itself succumbing to rampant overcrowding that overwhelmed and eventually doomed its rehabilitative model. By the end of the nineteenth century, observers were lamenting "the dark ages for America's prisons."[13]

And so the turn of the century saw its own wave of proposed reforms. This time, the focus turned toward therapeutic models popular in the Progressive Era that sought to leverage psychiatric diagnoses and treatments as mechanisms of rehabilitation, "on the assumption that criminal offenders suffered from some form of physical, mental, or social pathology." These reforms brought on classification systems that sorted people into different types of penal institutions, ranging from minimum security facilities to the eventual supermax institutions and "Big Houses" that incarcerated thousands of prisoners at once. As Rotman writes, some reforms in this Progressive Era were salutary: the worst practices of the 1800s fell away as prisoners were now allowed to commingle and communicate with each other and were afforded opportunities to enjoy exercise, recreation, and entertainment and to correspond with the outside world. And yet, like the reforms that came before, the "Progressive prison-reform movement fell considerably short of its goals" and "did not lead to effective treatment" because, once again, there were too many people incarcerated and not enough therapists to treat them all. The maximum-security facilities erected in this era remain permanent fixtures of the prison landscape today, even though the rehabilitative model (as we will discuss further in Chapter Two) did not endure.[14]

By the late 1960s, with the country standing on the cusp of an unprecedented explosion in the prison population, a presidential commission summed up the state of things. "Life in many [penal] institutions," it wrote, was "at best barren and futile, at worst unspeakably brutal and degrading." Nearly 100 years of reform efforts, in other words, constituted "a persistent but ultimately unsuccessful effort to ameliorate" the institution's worst aspects, to the point that some historians argue the reformers did more harm than good, clothing "the prison with the mantle of legitimacy long after the reality of reform had disappeared." Whether one accepts that criticism or not, it is clear that the prison has endured through time, evolving without fundamentally changing. For that reason, many who study its history describe it as "a monument to failure, hallowed only by time."[15]

5. The Business of Bondage. To call the prison system a failure is to accept, at least implicitly, that rehabilitation and reformation were its goals. But as Adam Hirsch observes, an alternative account views prisons as arising not from some benign or beneficent desire to rehabilitate offenders but rather "to advance the fortunes of the ruling elite, helping to entrench their political power, even as the institution served to exploit the labor power of its inmates." Judged against this ulterior motive, critics contend the prison has been not a failure but rather a terrifying success.[16]

At least two aspects of nineteenth-century prison history are cited as powerful examples of carceral exploitation and oppression. The first is the longstanding practice of using prisoners' labor to benefit private industry. The second is the use of the prison as a tool of racial subordination, most especially in the postbellum South.

Take first prison labor. In *The Crisis of Imprisonment,* historian Rebecca McLennan notes that "forced, hard, productive labor was of foundational importance to the penal order" dating back to the 1820s, when prison policymakers first came to see "contractual penal servitude" and "prison labor as a vital source of revenue" that could defray—or even exceed—the operating costs of penal institutions. But public institutions were not the only financial beneficiaries of prison labor. Rather, as McLennan writes, "the practice of selling the labor of convicts to *private* enterprise . . . became widely and deeply entrenched in penal ideology" over the course of the 1800s, such that by the 1880s two thirds of all prisoners "labored away on a daily basis for private interests." In industrial states, these incarcerated labor- ers produced shoes, stoves, saddles, and textiles. In the South and West, they "worked the mines, laid railroad tracks, or tended the fields of com- mercialized agricultural interests." In all events, their labor was "remarkably lucrative" to private industry; manufacturers holding decades-long con- tracts accumulated "vast fortunes through their prison industries."[17]

In the 1930s, private contracting was curtailed by federal legislation. But prison labor continued, as prisons pivoted to a state-use model still employed today that relies on prison labor to produce goods and services for the state itself or for sale by state-owned industries. From the prisoners' perspective, this work likely continues to feel exploitative, given that they are often paid pennies on the hour. Nor has the original private contract- ing system been entirely abandoned. Federal legislation enacted in the late 1970s reopened the door to private-sector employment of prison labor, and multiple private companies now operate everything from underwear assem- bly lines to customer-service call centers within prison walls.[18]

6. "Slavery by Another Name." Insofar as prison labor forces people in bondage to engage in hard labor for virtually no wages, it evokes a parallel institution long known as America's original sin: slavery. It is important not to confound prison labor with the more brutal and dehumanizing institu- tion of chattel slavery, at least with respect to prison labor as it existed in the North before the Civil War. When it comes to the postbellum South, how- ever, historical scholarship shows the extent to which prisons emerged as a tool of racial oppression—a key institution in the effort "to reclaim slav- ery from the destruction of the Civil War" and to reinstitute what historian Douglas Blackmon calls "slavery by another name."[19]

The turning point was emancipation. Prior to the war, there were hardly any Black people in Southern prisons, because almost all of them were enslaved. But that changed when the Thirteenth Amendment com- manded that "[n]either slavery nor involuntary servitude . . . shall exist within the United States." As sociologist Loïc Wacquant observes, emanci- pation "created a double dilemma for southern white society: how to secure anew the labor of former slaves, without whom the region's economy would collapse, and how to sustain the cardinal status distinction between whites and 'persons of color,' i.e. the social and symbolic distance [that Southern whites felt they] needed to prevent the odium of 'amalgamation' with a group [they] considered inferior, rootless, and vile."[20]

The "solution" to that dilemma lay in the South's ability to exploit an opening in the text of the Thirteenth Amendment itself. Slavery was illegal, the Amendment declared, *"except as punishment for crime."* Southern whites quickly leveraged this exception, to the point that in the immediate aftermath of the Civil War, Wacquant writes, "southern prisons turned black overnight." As early as 1871, prisons in Virginia that had scarcely admitted a Black person before the war were more than eighty percent Black; in Georgia, the prison population was nearly ninety percent Black by 1899.[21]

The mechanism of this transformation was straightforward. As Blackmon recounts, starting in the late 1860s and accelerating after the end of Reconstruction, "every southern state enacted an array of interlocking laws essentially intended to criminalize black life." As a result, Wacquant explains, "thousands of ex-slaves were being arrested, tried, and convicted for acts that in the past had been dealt with by [a] master" or for otherwise "refusing to behave as menials and follow the demeaning rules of racial etiquette" in post-Reconstruction society.[22]

Once these freed-then-convicted Black men were sent to prison, they encountered institutions modeled on the slave labor of the antebellum plantation. And like the plantations they replaced, these new labor camps often benefited private owners, who were able to purchase convict labor through the same contract leasing systems that had been prevalent in the North for decades prior to the war. As Blackmon describes,

> By the end of Reconstruction in 1877, every formerly Confederate state except Virginia had adopted the practice of leasing black prisoners into commercial hands. There were variations among the states, but all shared the same basic formula. Nearly all the penal functions of government were turned over to the companies purchasing convicts. In return for what they paid each state, the companies received absolute control of the prisoners. . . . Company guards were empowered to chain prisoners, shoot those attempting to flee, torture any who wouldn't submit, and whip the disobedient — naked or clothed — almost without limit. . . .
>
> In almost every respect — the acquisition of workers, the lease arrangements, the responsibilities of the leaseholder to detain and care for them, the incentives for good behavior — convict leasing adopted practices almost identical to those emerging in slavery in the 1850s.[23]

In fact, the new Southern convict-leasing system was in some ways more brutal than its predecessor. As Edgardo Rotman explains, "The states leased prisoners to entrepreneurs who, having no ownership interest in them, exploited them even worse than slaves." And as Lawrence Friedman recounts, these new brutal overseers "worked black bodies as hard as they could," making "use of 'shackles, dogs, whips, and guns,' [that] 'created a living hell for the prisoners.'" For a great many people, Friedman observes, the ordeal was not survivable.

The mortality rates on these chain gangs were staggering. Two hundred eighty-five convicts were sent to build the Greenwood and Augusta Railroad between 1877 and 1880. Almost 45 percent of them died—and these were young black men in the prime of their lives.

Blackmon reports a similarly staggering death rate in Alabama. The prisoners, he writes, "were routinely starved and brutalized by corporations, farmers, government officials, and small-town businessmen intent on achieving the most lucrative balance between the productivity of captive labor and the cost of sustaining them."[24]

The postbellum Southern prison, in other words, combined economic exploitation with racial oppression. In so doing, Wacquant observes, it "played a major role in the economic advancement of the New South during the Progressive era, as it 'reconciled modernization with the continuation of racial domination.'" The upshot was devastating. As Blackmon describes, a "world in which the seizure and sale of a black man—even a black child—was viewed as neither criminal nor extraordinary had reemerged," not long after the Civil War ended.[25]

The most egregious horrors of the Southern convict-leasing system lasted for decades and would not fully recede until the dawn of World War II. And echoes of the system carry forward into the present day. They are most acutely felt at institutions like Parchman State Penitentiary in Mississippi or Angola State Prison in Louisiana, two former slave plantations that were reborn as prisons after the Civil War. As Whitney Benns writes for *The Atlantic*, images from these prisons "offer visual proof of a truth that America has worked hard to ignore: In a sense, slavery never ended at Angola; it was reinvented."[26]

Juvenile convicts at work in the fields.

Individuals incarcerated at Angola State Prison (2015)

The prison's intertwinement with racial oppression, however, extends beyond images of Black men tilling Southern fields under the watchful eye of armed men on horseback. As we will see in the pages and chapters to come, scholars, historians, jurists, activists, lawyers, and citizens have long criticized the American penal system for imposing unconscionable harm on Black America — a condemnation voiced as forcefully today as it was in earlier eras.

B.   Mass Incarceration by the Numbers

Historians would likely balk at any effort to pick the moment in over two centuries of prison history when "everything changed." But if one were to pick a year, it would likely be 1972 — when a prison population that had been relatively stable for decades started to explode.

The scale of that explosion is unprecedented in human history. Between 1972 and 1998, the American prison population more than quintupled, jumping from a starting point below 200,000 people to more than 1.25 million. By the time it reached its peak in 2009, the prison population in the United States was eight times larger than it had been in 1972 — a per capita increase, accounting for population growth, of five hundred percent.[27]

In recent years, the prison population has started pointing downward, falling substantially in some states. By 2019, it had dropped eleven percent nationwide off its 2009 peak, although local jail populations increased in some states over the same period. Still, because the peak was so high, it is

Figure 1.1   How Many Years Until Incarceration in the United States Falls to 1970 Rates?

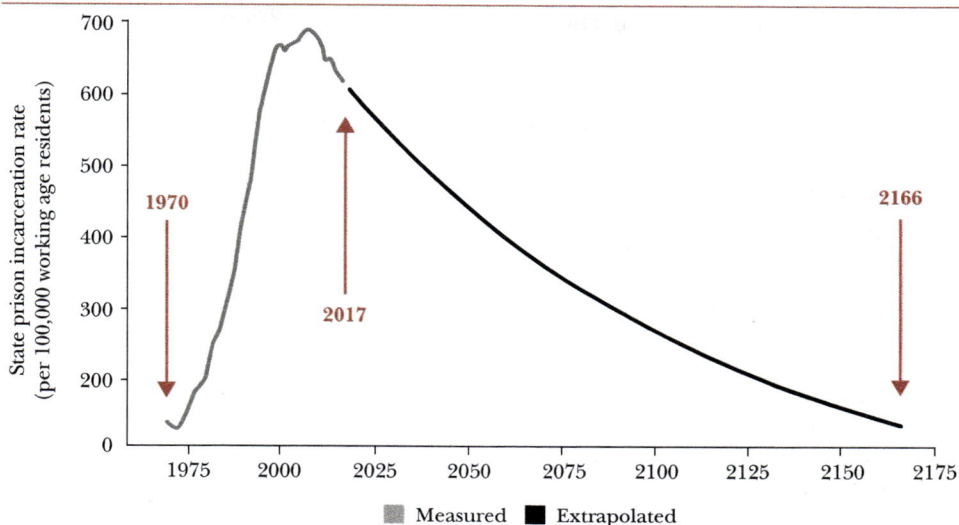

Jacob Kang-Brown et al., Vera Inst. of Just., *The New Dynamics of Mass Incarceration* 6, fig.1 (2018)

not easy to reverse. According to a Vera Institute report published in 2018, if the incarceration rate were to continue falling at the pace it fell through 2017, it would take nearly 150 years to return to 1970 levels.[28]

The phenomenon described above goes by a familiar name: *mass incarceration*. The fact that this phrase is so familiar, however, masks a strange reality. Virtually everyone who studied the American penal system prior to the 1970s failed to see mass incarceration coming. As sociologist Loïc Wacquant observed, in the mid-1970s, "leading analysts of the penal question" were "unanimous in predicting the imminent marginalization of the prison as an institution of social control or, in the worst-case scenario, the long-term stability of penal confinement at a historically moderate level."[29]

The story of how mass incarceration came about is complex and contested. Writing at the crest of the wave and reflecting on mass incarceration's rise, sociologist David Garland observed, "We still do not really know how we got from there to here." In the chapters to come, we will attempt to unpack some of the competing explanations for mass incarceration's rise, focusing on the role that law and lawyers played in creating and perpetuating the current state of affairs. At the outset, though, it is important to have a thorough account of some of the central facts and figures that define mass incarceration itself.[30]

Toward that end, this section gives an overview of some of the most salient and striking data describing mass incarceration in the United States. It bears noting that the underlying data are by their nature dynamic and often hard to collect. Still, it is possible to get a reasonably clear picture, thanks in large part to a set of data sources maintained by the federal government's Bureau of Justice Statistics (BJS) and to the enterprising work of scholars and nonprofits.[31]

NOTES AND QUESTIONS

1. The Largest Carceral System in the History of the World. The United States incarcerates more people than any other country in the known history of the world. In 2018, the average daily population of American prisons and jails topped 2.1 million people.[*] That number exceeds the entire national population of nearly one hundred separate countries. But even this figure fails to capture the system's true scale given that, as Professor John Pfaff notes, the incarcerated "population on any one day reflects only a fraction of those *passing through*" the system. As Professor Ben Grunwald observes, the "dynamic flow of new admissions" is an important data point because the harms incarceration inflicts—on people who are incarcerated, on their families, on their communities—are felt most sharply "at admission or [in] the first few months thereafter," even if people end up rotating through the system relatively quickly. Focusing on this statistic, the data are staggering: In 2018, 10.7 million people were admitted into jails across the country, with an average weekly turnover rate of 54.9 percent.[32]

Translating all this data into lifetime incarceration rates is challenging. But recent survey data indicate that more than one out of every five people in the United States has been incarcerated at some point in their lifetime. Almost *half* of all people in the country (45 percent) have an immediate family member—a parent, a sibling, a partner, or a child—who has spent time in prison or jail.[33]

As these data show, the United States incarcerates a remarkably high proportion of people living within its shores—531 out of every 100,000 people in the country, according to a 2024 report. This rate of incarceration is lower than it was in the peak year of 2009, but still far outstrips almost every other country on the planet, as confirmed by data collected in the annual *World Prison Brief.* The incarceration rate in the United States is between three and eight times higher than the rates in Canada, the United Kingdom, France, and Germany, which are commonly considered among the United States' "peer nations." Just as notably, the incarceration rate in the United States is roughly double or triple that of Russia, Iran, and Saudi Arabia.[34]

---

* As noted earlier (p. 7), *prisons* are institutions that incarcerate people who are serving sentences imposed following a judgment of conviction, typically for longer than a year. *Jails,* by contrast, serve two distinct functions: they incarcerate people serving relatively shorter sentences and people who are being detained while awaiting trial—that is to say, people who have not yet been convicted of anything.

Figure 1.2   Per Capita Incarceration Rates Across the Group of Seven Nations

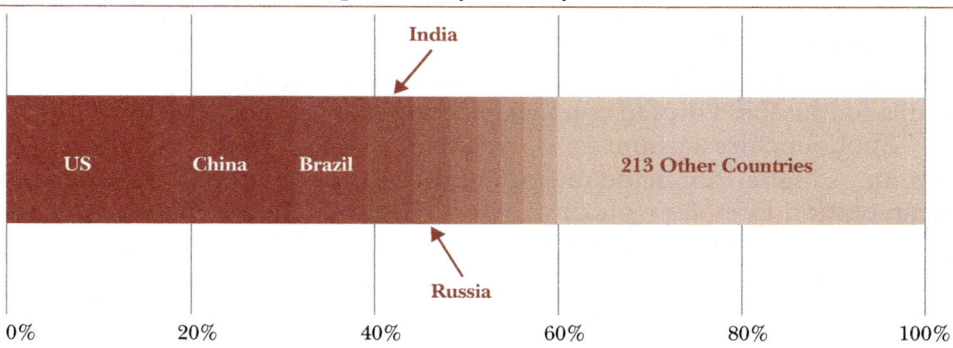

Helen Fair & Roy Walmsley, World Prison Brief, *World Prison Population List* (14th ed. 2024)

Figure 1.3   Global Prison Population by Country

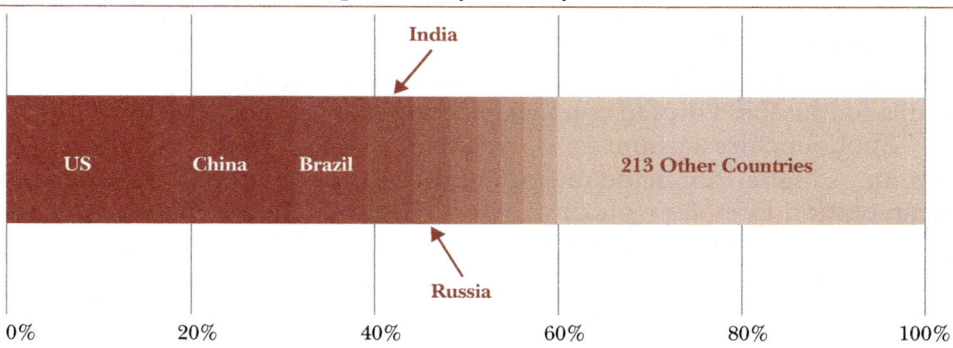

Helen Fair & Roy Walmsley, World Prison Brief, *World Prison Population List* (14th ed. 2024)

All told, the United States, which is home to only five percent of the world's population, incarcerates almost one fifth of the world's prisoners. In absolute terms, the prison population in the United States outstrips the prison populations of both India and China, the two countries with the largest populations on the planet.

2. Comparing Incarceration Rates to Crime. International comparisons raise an important question: Is the United States a global outlier in incarceration because it is a global outlier in crime? More generally, what is the relationship between the incarceration rate and the crime rate?

The answer to this question is complicated. Reliable data are elusive. More fundamentally, crime data are socially constructed — as is the very idea of crime itself. Consider that in some countries it is a crime to engage in blasphemy, heresy, or sex with someone of the same gender, even though such conduct is constitutionally protected in the United States. Still, it is possible to make some reasonably reliable comparisons across time and space by focusing on certain seriously violent or harmful behaviors that are consistently deemed criminal in most if not all countries over much of history. Focusing on these crimes, the best available data indicate that American mass incarceration cannot be explained by abnormally high rates of crime, whether compared to other countries or to earlier periods within the United States itself.

Consider first the international comparison. As Professor Holger Spamann reports, "U.S. crime rates are high relative to peer countries" for at least some types of crime. Specifically, the United States is an outlier with respect to drug use and, especially, homicide. When it comes to homicide, the United States is unique, with a homicide rate that is triple that of other nations in the Organisation for Economic Cooperation and Development (OECD). Still, if we expand our view to examine a broader set of baseline crimes that are "commonly emphasized in the comparative literature as a proxy for *overall* crime," the difference between the United States and other countries essentially disappears. In other words, the data "shows the United States clustered with other industrial countries in crime rate, but head and shoulders above the rest in violent death," a discrepancy that Professors Franklin Zimring and Gordon Hawkins attribute mainly to a substantially higher prevalence of guns in this country (and thus to criminal incidents that are more deadly).[35]

But homicides account for only sixteen percent of the U.S. prison population. A higher homicide rate alone thus cannot explain why American incarceration rates are typically five to six times higher than those of peer nations. Rather, empirical scholars contend that—above and beyond any differences in rates of crime—the United States incarcerates more of its own people than similarly situated countries because it is more punitive:

> [T]he high U.S. imprisonment rate results primarily from much greater lengths of prison sentence by every punitiveness measure we [a]re able to use—years of imprisonment per recorded crime or conviction, or average sentence length given a commitment—than are imposed in other countries. The high American imprisonment rate is also partly explained by comparatively high probabilities of imprisonment given a conviction.[36]

As for the history of crime *within* the United States, the basic conclusion is similar: changes in the crime rate cannot explain the rise or persistence of modern-day mass incarceration. Rather, in the words of the Council of Economic Advisors, "Criminal justice policies, not changes in underlying crime, account for nearly all of the growth in the incarcerated population in recent decades."

This is not to say that the domestic crime rate and the domestic incarceration rate are unrelated. On the contrary, the country's incarceration explosion followed quickly on the heels of a doubling in the national homicide rate. But the homicide rate plateaued around 1974, as the incarceration rate began to climb most steeply, and then fell precipitously—along with the overall crime rate—during the 1990s, even as the incarceration rate continued to climb for another decade and a half.[37]

Figure 1.4 **Homicide and Total Incarceration Rate for the United States (Per 100,000 Residents)**

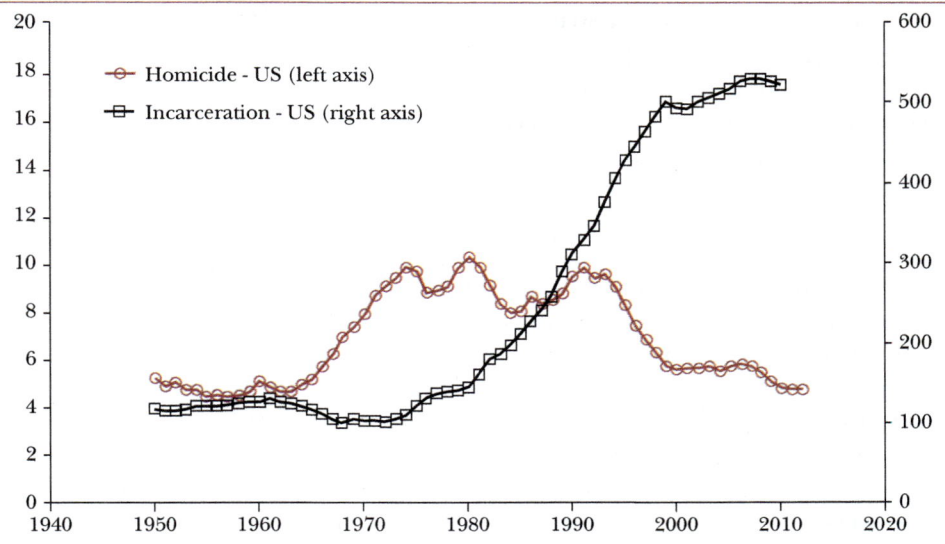

Paul Romer, *Crime Waves and the Tragedy of Mass Incarceration* (2014)

Of course, comparing incarceration rates to crime rates raises a question about whether crime rates fell *because* of mass incarceration — that is to say, a question of whether mass incarceration "worked" when it comes to reducing crime. We will return to this question in later chapters. But we can offer a preview: There is some evidence that, at moderate levels, incarceration reduces crime outside prison. Nevertheless, empirical scholars generally agree on "the low effectiveness of *mass* incarceration."[38]

3. Who Is in Prison? The phrase mass incarceration captures well the enormous and unprecedented scale of the American prison population. But to many critics, it is not just the size of the incarcerated population that makes the system unjust. It is also the composition, which is substantially poorer, dramatically more male, and far more Black than the rest of the country.

Consider race first. Black people are substantially overrepresented in the prison population, where they account for nearly one third of all incarcerated people, compared to 13.4 percent of the U.S. population. The incarceration rate for Black people is five times higher than it is for white people. Hispanics are also overrepresented in the prison population, although the precise extent of that overrepresentation is clouded by unreliable data. We will explore the sources and causes of these racial disparities at length in future chapters, especially Chapters Three, Eight, and Nine.[39]

Focusing on race alone, however, fails to capture the complete demographic portrait of the American prison population, which also skews along other lines. Sex is the most striking differentiating factor, with men constituting 93 percent of the prison population. The prison population is also disproportionately LGBTQ, with 9.3 percent of people incarcerated in male prisons and 42.1 percent of people incarcerated in female prisons identifying as lesbian, gay, or bisexual. As for economic class, the median annual income of people in prison prior to their incarceration is 41 percent lower than for nonincarcerated people, with people in prison disproportionately clustered at the bottom of the income scale.[40]

Combining these various statistics offers an intersectional portrait of the people most impacted by mass incarceration. Black men, especially those who are poor, are sent to prison at rates far outpacing other social groups. Indeed, taking just race and sex into account, empiricists estimate that between a quarter and a third of all Black men will be incarcerated at some point in their lifetimes — an incarceration rate double the rate for Hispanic men and more than six times higher than for white men. Even more striking, though, are the data for Black men without a high school diploma who were born in the late 1970s, as mass incarceration was taking off. Within that cohort of men currently in their mid-40s, more than two thirds (69 percent) will have served time in prison during their lifetimes. Reflecting on this reality, sociologist Bruce Western observes that the now-familiar phrase "mass incarceration" captures more than just "a very high rate of incarceration historically [and] comparatively." It means, Western says, that our incarceration rates are "so socially concentrated that we're no longer incarcerating the individual. We're incarcerating whole social groups."[41]

4. Federalism. Mass incarceration has emerged in recent years as a focal point of national discourse, but talking about it as a national phenomenon can sometimes mask the extent to which penal policy is driven by state and local actors. In fact, while the federal government sends more people to prison than any single state, it still accounts for only eleven percent of the national prison population—just barely edging out California. The states are thus responsible for roughly ninety percent of the national prison population. And importantly, they vary substantially in their incarceration rates. Likewise, states have played different roles in bringing about the recent drop in the national prison population. Given these variations, which replicate over myriad dimensions from prison conditions to wages paid for incarcerated labor, some scholars argue that "there is no single 'criminal justice system,' but instead a vast patchwork of systems."[42]

5. Underlying Crimes and Sentences. Most Americans misunderstand some of the basic facts about the underlying criminal offenses that lead to terms of incarceration. Specifically, recent polling indicates that most Americans think that roughly half of the people in prison were sent there for drug offenses.

That assumption likely arises from the coincidence of the mass incarceration explosion with the so-called War on Drugs in the 1980s (a topic taken up in Chapter Eight). But while drug convictions account for 46.3 percent of the federal prison population, they account for only 14.1 percent of the state prison population, which as noted above dwarfs the federal side.[43]

In truth, incarceration rates are driven not by drugs, but by crimes of violence, which account for 55 percent of all state prison beds—including 14.2 percent of prisoners who are serving time for murder, 13 percent for sexual assault, and 12.4 percent for robbery. This often-overlooked reality raises a challenge for those hoping to reverse or undo mass incarceration. In order to do so, the country would have to dramatically reduce the amount of time that people convicted of violent crimes spend in prison, dramatically reduce the incidence of violent crime itself, or both.[44]

Figure 1.5   Prison and Jail Population by Offense Type

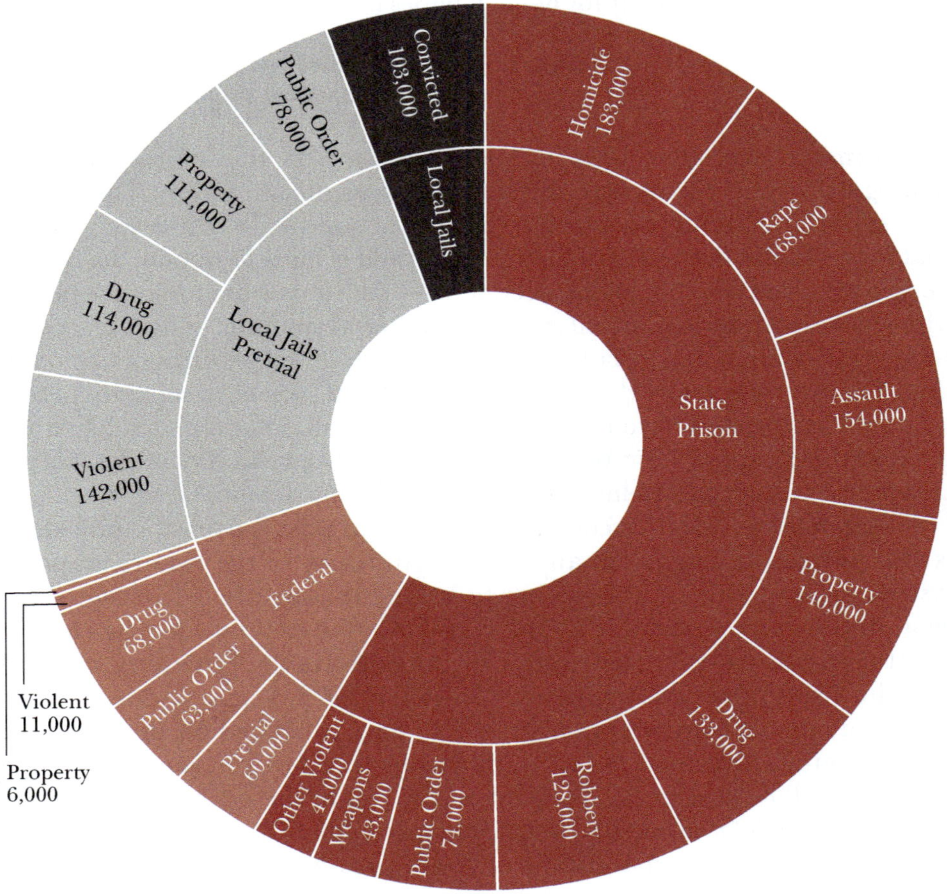

Prison Pol'y Initiative, *Mass Incarceration: The Whole Pie 2024* (2024)

With respect to sentence lengths, it bears noting that violent crimes — like all other crimes — were in fact punished less severely in the United States just a few decades ago. According to a study conducted by the Pew Center on the States, state prison sentences (including sentences for violent offenses) increased on average 36 percent between 1990 and 2009. In some of the most populous states, the increase was even more dramatic, with sentence lengths rising 51 percent in California, 91 percent in Virginia, and 166 percent in Florida.[45]

C.   Life on the Inside

"Outside prison, mass incarceration is measured in numbers, which is understandable, because the numbers are staggering. But after more than 30 years in prison — my entire adult life — I have mass incarceration sewn into my flesh and bones. I can't turn away from it or choose not to know it, and it leaves me with little or no capacity for hope. It buries me. It keeps me from breathing."

Arthur Longworth, *Raised, and Imprisoned, by the State*,
Marshall Project (May 26, 2015)

Numbers can tell us only so much. At their best, they convey the scale, demography, and big-picture dynamics of mass incarceration. They reveal almost nothing, though, about life within a prison's walls. By its very nature, that more qualitative sense of life on the inside is hard to obtain, at least for people who have never been incarcerated — which is true of most of the people who study the American penal system, whether as students or as researchers. Indeed, separation and isolation are among the central features of incarceration. The prison is *designed* to remove people from society, to separate people who are incarcerated from everyone else. As a result, to quote sociologist and prison ethnographer Loïc Wacquant, we have "hypervisibility of the issue of *crime* in US culture and politics" but "total invisibility of *punishment*."[46]

Still, hard as it is to access and assess life in prison from the outside, it is also difficult to engage in any meaningful study of the American penal system without at least attempting to bridge that divide — to understand what imprisonment actually is and what it does to people. Getting close to painful and brutal experiences can be uncomfortable. Emerging from his first site visit to the Los Angeles county jail in 1998, Wacquant described a sense "of embarrassment, of 'dirtiness,' to have infringed on the dignity of human beings by the mere fact of having been there and seen that place, and thus to have treated its denizens as one might the occupants of a zoo." Still, he insisted, "it takes that[;] it is indispensable to go see, touch, feel."[47]

Many of the richest accounts of life in prison are first-hand, intimate, and personal, contained in a growing array of books, essays, radio programs, and podcasts that are authored by incarcerated and formerly incarcerated people. The remainder of this section presents a small slice of this body of work. The underlying accounts themselves are too textured and varied to capture adequately in these pages. Students looking to immerse themselves in these first-hand accounts should go directly to the source.* The goals of the remainder of this section, rather, are threefold: to surface some cross-cutting themes about the prison experience in the United States; to create a point of connection across the prison's dividing line, between authors and readers who may have lived very different lives; and finally, to underscore an essential point running through this course—namely, that prisons are not just institutions of public punishment but also sites of intense and often wrenching lived experiences, affecting millions of people in profoundly life-altering ways.[48]

1. Deprivation, Loss, and Neglect

Jack Henry Abbott, *In the Belly of the Beast* 45-46 (1981): Let us say you are in a cell ten feet long and seven feet wide. That means seventy feet of *floor* space. But your bunk is just over three feet wide and six and a half feet long. Your iron toilet and sink combination covers a floor space of at least three feet by two feet. All tallied, you have approximately forty-seven square feet of space on the floor. It works out to a pathway seven feet long and about three feet wide—the excess is taken up by odd spaces between your commode and wall, between the foot of the bunk and the wall. If I were an animal housed in a zoo, in quarters of these dimensions, the Humane Society would have the zookeeper arrested for cruelty. It is illegal to house an animal in such confines. But I am not an animal, so I do not insist on such rights.

Wilbert Rideau, *In the Place of Justice* 63-64 (2010): It's quiet [in solitary confinement]. Profoundly so. Rain whispers against the open window a few feet away. The only other thing you can hear is your own heart, thumping. I've known men who could not stand this silence, but I've grown accustomed to it. I scratch a fingernail on one of the bars, to reassure myself I haven't gone deaf. I've stood here many nights staring out my second-floor window

---

* For audio productions, consider San Quentin Radio and the podcast *Ear Hustle.* For essays, consider The Marshall Project's *Life Inside* series and the many works published by incarcerated writers at *Inquest.* For poetry, consider R. Dwayne Betts, *Felon: Poems* (2019), and the Free Minds Poetry Blog. For books, consider Wilbert Rideau, *In the Place of Justice* (2011); R. Dwayne Betts, *A Question of Freedom* (2009); Jack Henry Abbott, *In the Belly of the Beast, Letters From Prison* (1991); Jeff Smith, *Mr. Smith Goes to Prison* (2015); *Inside This Place, Not of It: Narratives from Women's Prisons* (Robin Levi & Ayelet Waldman eds., 2011); Jimmy Santiago Baca, *A Place to Stand* (2007); and George Jackson, *Soledad Brother: The Prison Letters of George Jackson* (1970).

at the same scene below, week after week, month after month, year after year . . . after year. Except for the rain, it never changes. . . . This is my reality. Solitude. Four walls, gray-green, drab, and foreboding. Three of steel and one of bars, held together by 358 rivets. Seven feet wide, nine feet long. About the size of an average bathroom or—and my mind leaps at this—the size of four tombs, only taller. . . . This is my life, every minute of the year. I'm buried alive. But I'm the only person for whom that fact has meaning, who feels it, so it's immaterial.*

R. Dwayne Betts, *A Question of Freedom* 14-15 (2009): He had to come back and give me a blanket is what I thought. That's why I didn't yell out to him, didn't remind him that I didn't have sheet or mattress or real blanket. I expected to get a mattress, to be treated as if I deserved not to sleep in a cold cell on a cold slab of concrete in the dead of winter. Although it was cold I peeled my sweater off. When I threw the colorful mess onto the slab of concrete that was my bed, it landed on dried spit.

Days passed and I still had no mattress. It was February and cold, and I hadn't changed my clothes since walking into the jail.

"Deputy! Deputy! Ay, look man, look in this cell. I need a mattress, a pillow. All y'all left me with is this small-ass blanket."

The deputy didn't stop walking, but he looked in my direction.

"How long you been in there?"

He moved along as he asked his question, then stopped and walked back towards me. I thought, if he looks in here he'll be able to see that I smell like I've been living in a puddle of piss and sleeping on cold concrete. "I've been here about three, four days. Deputy, I haven't had a shower, no phone call. This ain't right. You gotta do something for me." I was begging and learning Prison 101. You could beg, but that just made you feel like the time was doing you, like you weren't in control of yourself. Worse than that, you could beg and still not get anything. I didn't get a mattress that day, and after asking for a day or so longer gave up on it. I learned to ignore the night air as it cut into my skin, ignore the indents and ridges of the concrete scraping my face.

Anna Jacobs, *I Don't Know If Anyone in There Ever Used the Word "Diabetes,"* in *Inside This Place, Not of It* 119, 127-129 (Robin Levi & Ayelet Waldman eds., 2011): Usually I'm a real Texas-type girl, you can't beat me down. But I knew something was wrong, it just wasn't anything I could put my finger on. Then, after three or four weeks, my feet started swelling. . . . They were as big as a salad plate. . . . I put in a medical request and saw a physician's assistant. She just said, "Get over it. Get real." . . . I felt so bad,

---

* For more information on solitary confinement, see The Liman Center, *Seeing Solitary,* https://seeingsolitary.limancenter.yale.edu.

I just knew something was really wrong with me, and I was afraid I'd die in prison. . . . I'm on insulin now, but I never got any while I was in there, and no one ever told me what I should or shouldn't eat. . . . The thing about it is, you didn't have a choice anyway. [They] put me on a "diabetic tray," but no one would honor it. . . . The only thing different at breakfast was that they'd give you pancakes with sugar-free syrup. . . . The thing is, in the women's prison, they just don't have any special food for diabetic people. Maybe they do for the men, because I spent one night in a men's prison . . . and they had something like three different menus to pick from for breakfast, lunch, and dinner. . . . Now, I'm not exactly a women's libber, but if they've got that for the men, why don't they have it for the women? And if they're going to call it a diet menu, or a diabetic menu, why isn't it closely monitored? Because the food where I was nearly killed me.

Olivia Hamilton, *Nobody Cares If You're Pregnant,* in *Inside This Place, Not of It* 25, 27-35 (Robin Levi & Ayelet Waldman eds., 2011): I had a friend at Kmart who used to do fake refunds. She'd say a customer was coming in and she was refunding stuff that wasn't really being refunded. So I did it [too]. . . . [W]e really needed the money. I was behind on a lot of bills, and I was trying to catch up. . . . I was sentenced to a year and the judge said, "Hopefully you'll do six months on good behavior. . . ."

My due date was May 24, 2008, just before Memorial Day weekend. A female doctor from the Atlanta Medical Center came to visit me on the 22nd. At that time, I wasn't showing any signs of labor. . . . She said I should be fine through the weekend, and that everything was normal about my pregnancy. Then, on the evening of the 23rd—this was a Friday evening—the guards called me, and they told me to pack my stuff. . . . I got over to the infirmary, and the captain said, "Well, the doctor from the prison says he's going to send you in to be induced . . . [b]ecause your due date is May 24th, and this is a holiday weekend." . . .

They put me in a room and shackled me. I was more upset than anything that the baby just wasn't ready, and I didn't want to be forced. They gave me Pitocin,* but it wasn't working. Later, in the middle of the night, the doctor . . . said, "Well, if you don't move any more by tomorrow, we're going to have to do a c-section." I said . . . "I have never had a c-section in my life. My oldest son was nine pounds—no cuts, no slits, no nothing. And you're going to make me have a c-section?" The next day, the doctor came back and took me in to have the c-section done. A sergeant came in and said, "She needs to be shackled. She's no different from anybody else." I was hurting, and I was tired. I said to the sergeant, "Ma'am, there is no way I need these shackles. I'm not going anywhere; I'm in pain. You've got a guard in my room. And I don't know if you have kids, but this ain't

---

* Pitocin is an intravenous medication commonly used to induce labor.

something fun to have your hands shackled for." . . . The doctor gave me an epidural. I went through with the c-section and finally, the baby came on out. . . . The guard held him up to show him to me. Even then, they never took the shackles off me. . . .

I named the baby Joshua. I wonder about him; does he remember all that we went through? . . . After I left the hospital, my boyfriend picked up the baby and took him home. I guess for me, walking out of that hospital, knowing I was leaving my son—it killed me inside. I felt like I was being punished for the one mistake that I'd made in my life. I just remember looking at my baby, and kissing him, and crying, and not wanting to go. The nurse who was holding him was really hurt too. She asked me, "Do you want to kiss him again?" And I kissed him one last time, and they took me out the door.

2.   Loneliness

Robert K. Wright, *Finding Peace—and Briefly, Freedom—at My Grandfather's Funeral,* Marshall Project (Oct. 10, 2019): The two officers are wearing suits. I am dressed in my state greens, a matching button-up shirt and pants that resemble the pajama sets my grandfather used to wear around the house. I am not allowed to wear anything appropriate to his funeral. I am made to put my incarceration on full display. . . . I see my oldest sister staring at me with what looks like a mixture of fear and sadness. As she walks toward me, she looks to the officers for a sign that it's okay to approach. It must be hard to watch someone you love shackled like some animal. "It's alright," I tell her, "you can hug me." She stands on her toes and wraps her arms around my neck. I take one more look around the room before the guards grab my arm and say it is time to leave. . . . As I'm escorted through the crowd of mourners, I receive hugs and condolences. But I don't really acknowledge them. I'm already preparing myself for a return to captivity. I'm ushered into the back of the van, lay my forehead on the window and let out a long deep breath.

Fernando Rivas, *Being a Prisoner Is Like Being a Ghost,* Marshall Project (Oct. 24, 2019): Going to prison is a lot like dying, only you live on as a ghost, a ghost that regularly haunts your family and friends by phone, letters, cards or email. You lose your corporal reality. You are no longer a member of family or society. You are in what I think of as the Fourth World, a lower rung than the poverty-ridden Third World, a ghetto of the soul. In the beginning I desperately wanted my loved ones to visit me. My pre-prison self still clung to life, there was still a slight pulse in the dying heart. . . . After a few months I changed my mind. My wife and I agreed mutually that it would be too painful to share a life that had been snatched from us, cut short. We'd planned to travel to Europe, to spend time with the grandchildren, to visit family in another state. Holidays, vacations, time together in our final years.

All of that had been wiped out, and we refused to see it replaced with a series of institutionalized visitations.

George T. Wilkerson, *How a Phone Changed My Life on Death Row*, Marshall Project (Oct. 6, 2016): Before I was on death row, I had a way of feeling close to people. Even if I was unable to be physically near them, I had the next best thing: the phone. I'd become so dependent on and attuned to the voices on the other end that I could detect the subtlest emotional shifts, like dipping my finger into water to test its heat. But when I was escorted through death row's red-rimmed doorway, I learned that we had no phone access, except a 10-minute call at Christmas. I felt like an untethered astronaut lost in space, trying to keep from giving in to a panicky madness in the face of too much black.

Jeremy Woody, *The Isolation of Being Deaf in Prison*, Marshall Project (Oct. 18, 2018): None of the staff knew sign language, not the doctors or the nurses, the mental health department, the administration, the chaplain, the mail room. Nobody. In the barbershop, in the chow hall, I couldn't communicate with the other inmates. When I was assaulted, I couldn't use the phone to call the Prison Rape Elimination Act . . . hotline to report what happened. And when they finally sent an interviewer, there was no interpreter. . . . I met several other deaf people while I was incarcerated. But we were all in separate dorms. I would have liked to meet with them and sign and catch up. But I was isolated. They housed us sometimes with blind folks, which for me made communication impossible. They couldn't see my signs or gestures, and I couldn't hear them. They finally celled me with another deaf inmate for about a year. It was pretty great, to be able to communicate with someone. But then he got released, and they put me with another blind person.

Eli Hager, *My Life in the Supermax*, Marshall Project (Jan. 8, 2016): Sometimes . . . you could take a whole toilet paper roll, put it over the drain in your sink or shower, and blow as hard as you could. That would blow the water down the pipes just far enough that the pipes were empty between you and your neighbor's cell. Then you keep holding the toilet paper roll over the drain, you talk into it, and your neighbor can hear what you're saying clearly. It depended on the cell you were in, if the pipes were lined up and all that, but you could usually contact your neighbor this way or even one more inmate down the line.

Byron Case, *The Surprisingly Nomadic Lives of Prisoners*, Marshall Project (Feb. 14, 2019): In nearly two decades down, I've only been able to keep two cellmates for more than a few months. Most of these moves happened because of how prison administrators perceive their facility's population. To them, we're not people trying to live with and around each other, we're items in a warehouse, moved according to spatial and categorical requirements.

R. Dwayne Betts, *A Question of Freedom* 61 (2009): All of it taught me that I was by myself in the cell. Even when I had a cell partner, I was alone with my thoughts. I'd never told my mom this, never told any of my friends. I stopped talking to most of my friends the day the cops clamped cuffs around my wrists. . . . I got letters. Bags of them in the months I spent at the jail, but they all were a one-way conversation. People told me about what went on in their lives and expressed concern about me—I said as little as I could with as many words as possible. I taught myself the secret of survival: learning to do it all alone.

3.   Monotony and the Passage of Time

Diary of Sam Gutierrez, reprinted in Norval Morris, *The Contemporary Prison: 1965–Present*, in *The Oxford History of the Prison: The Practice of Punishment in Western Society* 227, 228 (Norval Morris & David J. Rothman eds., 1995): You asked me to keep a diary for one day. You told me I was not to tell you that things were good or bad—just to tell you exactly what I did and what happened to me through one day. I have never done anything like this before. It is not easy to describe a day of monotony and boredom other than as monotonous and boring.

Before I start on the diary, let me say this: if you expect the usual prison tale of constant violence, brutal guards, gang rapes, daily escape efforts, turmoil, and fearsome adventures, you will be deeply disappointed. Prison life is really nothing like what the press, television, and movies suggest. It is not a daily round of threats, fights, plots, and "shanks" (prison-made knives) — though you have to be constantly careful to avoid situations or behavior that might lead to violence. A sense of impending danger is always with you; you must be careful to move around people rather than against or through them, but with care and reasonable sense you can move safely enough. For me, and many like me in prison, violence is not the major problem; the major problem is monotony. It is the dull sameness of prison life, its idleness and boredom, that grinds me down. Nothing matters; everything is inconsequential other than when you will be free and how to make time pass until then. But boredom, time-slowing boredom, interrupted by occasional bursts of fear and anger, is the governing reality of life in prison.

Jack Henry Abbott, *In the Belly of the Beast* 45-46 (1981): I have experienced everything possible to experience in a cell in a short time—a day or so if I'm active, a week or two if I'm sluggish. I must fight, from that point on, the routine, the monotony that will bury me alive if I am not careful. I must do that, and do it without losing my mind. . . . I have my seven-by-three-foot pathway, and I pace, at various speeds, depending on my mood. I think. I remember. I think. I remember.

Eric Borsuk, *Halfway to Nowhere*, Marshall Project (Feb. 9, 2015): It's hard to remember myself before all this, as a 19-year-old college kid who thought it was a good idea to join some buddies in stealing a first edition of Charles Darwin's "On the Origin of Species" and other rare books and manuscripts from a university library. In prison, you start to forget after a while even why you're there. Who you were, what you wanted—the steady, quotidian punishment grinds it away.

Jerry Metcalf, *After 20 Years in Prison, All I Can Write Is Fantasy*, Marshall Project (Apr. 13, 2017): I wish I were free, but not for the reasons that you, my readers, might think. When I lay in my cell and daydream of freedom, I don't fantasize about women, flashy cars, or what my next crime or crimes might be, as some men in here certainly do. No, I fantasize about how great my life could be if I owned a laptop (and knew how to use it) instead of this ancient typewriter of mine. . . . I dream of what life might be like with the entire world opened up to me. Not only would I be able to reliably write about cell phones and gas pumps, I'd be able to write about anything and everything. I'd be able to use modern technology to write words that might help change other people's lives for the better—because they'd be relatable words, not false ones.

R. Dwayne Betts, *House of Unending*, in *Felon: Poems* 81, 81 (2019)

> Of lockdown, hunger time & the blackened flower—
> > Ain't nothing worth knowing. Prison becomes home;
> The cell: a catacomb that cages and the metronome
> > Tracking the years that eclipse you.

4. Violence

Wilbert Rideau, *In the Place of Justice* 76-77 (2010): Thursdays were "fresh fish" days at Angola, when new inmates joined the general inmate population. . . . [W]e set out on the Walk, an elevated, twelve-foot-wide concrete thoroughfare for foot traffic that ran throughout the sprawling Main Prison complex. . . . Convicts lined it, leaning on the railing and studying the fresh fish. Some were merely curious; others looked for friends or enemies among the new faces; and the predators were there searching out the weak to enslave. Slavery was commonplace at Angola, with perhaps a quarter of the population in bondage. Slaves met many needs in an all-male world shaped by deprivation.

Marilyn Sanderson, *I Wonder If the Staff Consider Us Human at All*, in *Inside This Place, Not of It* 149, 156-157 (Robin Levi & Ayelet Waldman eds., 2011): [I]n prison we can't ever touch anyone. We can't hug, hold hands, or pat each other on the shoulder to comfort each other, because you'll get a write-up for sexual abuse. . . . Of course this is because of all the problems with rape and sexual assault in prison. But that happens more often between staff and inmates than between two inmates. Sexual assault between staff and inmates happens fairly frequently, but it is undercover. . . . A lot of women in prison are very vulnerable, and there are staff members who take full advantage of that.

Jerry Metcalf, *The Everyday Chaos of Incarceration*, Marshall Project (Mar. 1, 2018): I haven't experienced a truly good night's sleep—a sound, comfortable sleep—in two decades. Too much chaos. Too much uncertainty . . . [and] violence, which in prison is the ultimate norm. Over the years, I've been stabbed, cut, clunked, almost raped, and had the crap kicked out of me on numerous occasions. And in self-defense—especially back when I was young and considered "pretty" by the sexual predators—I've been forced to do a number of those things myself.

Jeff Smith, *Mr. Smith Goes to Prison* 141, 156 (2015): The biggest threats in prison don't come from the obvious places—the sex-crazed guy who jumps you in the shower or the muscle hired by the bookie to collect debts. The biggest threat comes from the myriad quotidian interactions that can go horribly wrong, for reasons unfathomable to the uninitiated. There was, for instance, the time an argument in the television room escalated into a fight over whether the TV should be tuned to basketball or women's track. . . . [M]any prisoners viewed violence as a necessary, even desirable tactic for addressing even the smallest conflict, for getting revenge, and for showing that one was not to be fucked with. . . . The ability to emit a credible threat of violence was precisely what ensured that one would rarely have to engage in violence. The most feared guys never touched a soul, because they didn't need to—usually because they were said to have badly mangled somebody who'd crossed them. It was the least feared—and the least connected—guys who always seemed to be beefing over petty matters that escalated when neither side could retreat without losing face. Those with the least stature scrapped tenaciously so as not to lose what little rep they had.

Francesca Salavieri, *As Long as No One Dies on My Shift, I Don't Care What You Do to Each Other,* in *Inside This Place, Not of It* 135, 145 (Robin Levi & Ayelet Waldman eds., 2011): There is such a thing as a "quiet storm." This is a prearranged fight by inmates that other inmates cover up. Most officers allowed this, and they'd say, "As long as no one dies on my shift, I don't care what you do to each other." That was the famous saying in there. Sometimes, just for fun, the officers would take a Blood and a Crip, who are usually held in separate wings, and have them switch their spots, just to watch them fight. I saw three girls get airlifted out.

5. Hierarchy, Power, and Loss of Dignity

Michael J. Moore, *All of Us Inside Have Cried Out*, Marshall Project (July 23, 2020): [A]t the end of May, just about everyone in my living unit was following a breaking story. I . . . watch[ed] the footage of a Black man lying face down in a Minneapolis street, crying for his mother while three cops knelt on top of him — one on his neck. One other stood by, apparently making sure nobody intervened. I found myself thinking of what happened here a few months ago when a corrections officer stepped up behind a seated prisoner in our dining hall and began speaking aggressively to him. . . . [T]he incarcerated man he approached seemed genuinely caught off guard, asking calmly at first what he had done wrong. However, before the man could back away, the corrections officer grabbed him and threw him to the floor. In seconds other guards had him surrounded. They pinned and handcuffed his hands behind his back while his aggressor had a knee pressed into his neck. My fellow prisoner begged them to stop because he couldn't breathe, only to be told to "shut the fuck up."

As I watched a scene that was nearly identical on my television, I couldn't help but relive my anger. Although more than 100 people (including other guards) watched what took place in our dining hall that afternoon, the C.O. still had his job, freedom and continued license to commit violent and potentially deadly assaults at will.

Shane Bauer, *American Prison* **142 (2018):** "Does anybody know why we don't want them to wear individualized clothing?" The assistant warden asks us all. "We want them institutionalized. You guys ever hear that term? We want them *institutionalized* not *individualized.* Is that sort of a mind game? Yup. But you know what? It's worked over the couple hundred years that we've had prisons in this country. So that's why we do it. We don't want them to feel as though they are individuals. We want them, for lack of a better term, to feel like a herd of cattle. We're just moving them from point A to point B, letting them graze in the dining hall and then back go to the barn. Okay?"*

Irma Rodriquez, *You Can Get Accustomed to the Loss of Dignity,* **in** *Inside This Place, Not of It* **203, 207-209 (Robin Levi & Ayelet Waldman eds., 2011):** It's hard to explain how degrading prison is to someone who's never experienced it. You are told when to wake up, when you can bathe, when you can brush your teeth. You stand for twenty minutes waiting for a door to open just so you can walk in a line and go eat. You're given three minutes to shovel down your food and then you're right back in that line, waiting for the door to open so you can go put your stuff away. . . . COs routinely come into our rooms and take our things. . . . You've got three blankets? Trust me, they will take them away. You have a homemade pillow sewn up, they'll take that. You're constantly living on edge.

---

   * This excerpt was written by a journalist who went undercover as a prison guard in 2014.

Jerry Metcalf, *The Everyday Chaos of Incarceration,* **Marshall Project (Mar. 1, 2018):** When I first entered prison, almost everything seemed alien and disgusting. On day one, I was stripped of my clothes alongside a bunch of other men, marched around naked, and issued an ID number. Let's examine that for a minute. I'd been methodically shamed and humiliated, assigned a new form of identification, and then informed that not only was I no longer free, I was effectively the property of the state of Michigan—all in the course of a few minutes. I was stunned. But today, 20 years later, that all seems quite normal to me. "251141, report to your housing unit . . . Hey, 251141, where the hell d'you think you're going? Get over here . . . 251141, you've got mail. . . ."

As for strip searches, well, I've endured hundreds of them. "Bend over and spread your ass cheeks . . . Lift your dick . . . Now your nuts . . . Hold your mouth open with your fingers . . . No, I don't have anything for you to wash your hands with . . . Let me see the bottoms of your feet."

Eli Hager, *My Life in the Supermax,* **Marshall Project (Jan. 8, 2016):** I think most people take it for granted that they are human, but when you get to [prison], you realize that being human isn't a birthright.

6.   Acculturation

R. Dwayne Betts, *Essay on Reentry (for Nicholas Dawidoff),* in *Felon: Poems* 49, 49 (2019):

> Of prison, no one tells you the time
> will steal your memories—until there's
> nothing left but strip searches & the hole
> & fights & hidden shanks & the spades games.

Wilbert Rideau, *In the Place of Justice* 63-64, 73 (2010): I came from that [outside] world, was once a part of it. But it's strange to me now, like a foreign country I've only read about. . . . It's been too long. . . . It's hard to believe that I once experienced a life in that world outside my window. Would I even be able to recognize the neighborhood I grew up in? Are kids playing hooky still shooting craps on those old tombs? Is Old Man Martello still peddling cigarettes three for a nickel to underage smokers? . . . I long to get away from this field of pain and misery. . . . Then I think: Could I fit into that world out there? So much has changed. I was a boy when I left that world. I know nothing of the world that has taken its place. How could I adjust to that world when I couldn't even adjust to the world I knew, the world that shaped me, or misshaped me? Having lived in this jungle for so long, could I function in a civilized world?

Jack Henry Abbott, *In the Belly of the Beast* 4-5, 14 (1981): [We] all hold up like good soldiers and harden ourselves in prison. But if you do that for too long, you lose yourself. Because there is something helpless and weak and innocent—something like an infant—deep inside us all that really suffers in ways we would never permit an insect to suffer. That is how prison is tearing me up inside. It hurts every day. Every day takes me further from my life. And I am not even conscious of how my dissolution is coming about. Therefore, I cannot stop it. . . . I *remember* society, and it is not like prison. I feel that if I ever did *adjust to prison*, I could by that alone never adjust to society.

Malcolm X, *The Autobiography of Malcolm X as Told to Alex Haley* 176 (1965): Any person who claims to have deep feeling for other human beings should think a long, long time before he votes to have other men kept behind bars—caged. I am not saying there shouldn't be prisons, but there shouldn't be bars. Behind bars, a man never reforms. He will never forget. He will never get completely over the memory of the bars. After he gets out, his mind tries to erase the experience, but he can't. I've talked to numerous former convicts. It has been very interesting to me to find that all of our minds had blotted away many details of years in prison. But in every case, he will tell you that he can't forget those bars.

Wilbert Rideau, *In the Place of Justice* 334 (2010): What I don't tell them is that, like other refugees, I bring with me to this free society the vestiges of life under the old regime: constant watchfulness, studying the faces around me, routine examination of the motives of newcomers in my life, and a lingering sense that I should have a witness with me at all times. I can't step out of my ingrained wariness as easily as I shed my prison denims. So despite my newfound liberty, I socialize very little and keep my business to myself. These mind-sets will fade, I hope, but it may take more time than I have.

II.   PUNISHMENT WITHOUT INCARCERATION

Incarceration is the most intense and most severe mode of punishment meted out by the American penal system, short of the death penalty. But it is not the most common. On any given day there are over one million more people serving noncarceral sentences in the United States than there are people in prisons and jails. In other words, for all its enormity and impact, mass incarceration is only one piece—and not even the largest piece—of the broader American penal system. An analysis of that system that focuses solely on incarceration thus "*understates* the reach of the criminal justice system and, in some sense, *misrepresents* the modal criminal justice encounter."[49]

And yet, as Professor Alexandra Natapoff observes, legal scholarship and teaching typically focus solely on the "top of the penal pyramid," where the most serious offenses are put through relatively rigorous adjudication processes and yield the most serious sentences. The cases at the middle and

Figure 1.6   Number of Adults Under Carceral Supervision

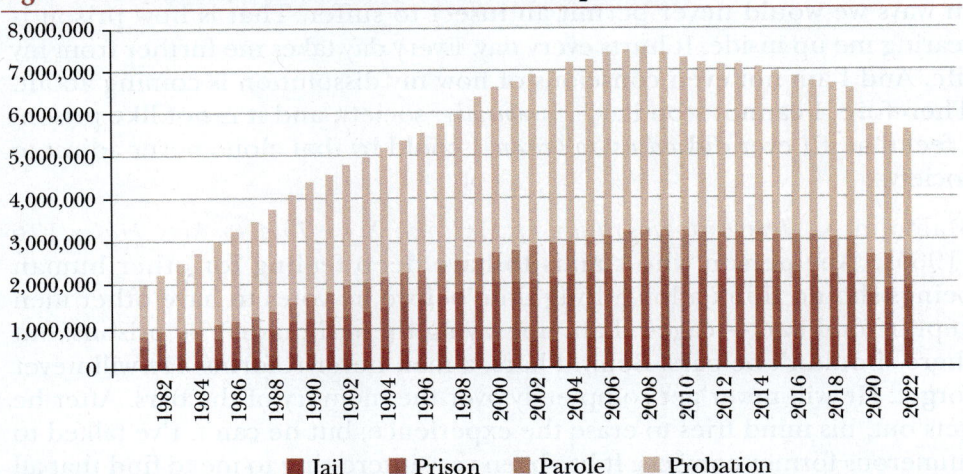

Pew Charitable Trusts, *Probation and Parole Systems Marked by High Stakes, Missed Opportunities* 4 fig.1 (2018)

lower levels of that pyramid involve a wide range of conduct, from trivial infractions like jaywalking to behavior more widely viewed as antisocial like theft or robbery. Criminal codes often authorize incarceration for such behavior but do not require it, leaving judges with discretion to impose a carceral sentence or some other form of punishment such as community supervision or financial penalties. Beyond those direct punishments, the conviction itself, even for relatively minor crimes, will often trigger follow-on consequences ranging from the loss of housing benefits or immigration status to more informal impairments to employability and social standing.[50]

The remainder of this part discusses these various forms of noncarceral punishment, which for millions of people are the true mark of the penal system in the United States.

A.   Community Supervision

NOTES AND QUESTIONS

1. Probation and Parole. Across the full range of criminal sanctions, sentences that include some period of community supervision—either as an alternative or as a supplement to incarceration—are by far the most common. Most often this supervision takes the form of *probation*, which is typically imposed as an alternative to incarceration but can also form part of a blended sentence that includes an initial period of jail or prison time. In either instance, the sentencing judge usually "suspends" a specified term of incarceration that hangs over the sentenced person's head during the term of probation, which can vary substantially in length. During the probationary term, the sentenced person is often ordered to comply with a set of standardized or tailored conditions, ranging from a blanket order not to commit any new offenses to specific orders mandating drug testing, anger management classes, or a curfew. Probation is often supervised, with an assigned probation officer monitoring the defendant's progress and compliance. The probation officer usually has the power to adjust certain terms of probation and can initiate a revocation hearing if the defendant fails to comply with any of the ordered conditions. If a judge concludes the defendant violated the terms of probation, no matter how technical, she generally has the discretion to impose any or all of the previously suspended sentence of incarceration—or instead to return the defendant to a second round of probation, potentially longer than the first.[51]

Parole is functionally similar to probation but always follows a period of incarceration and is typically administered by an executive agency known as the parole board rather than by courts. Parole typically applies in indeterminate sentencing systems, in which a judge sentences a convicted defendant to a range of years rather than to a specific term of incarceration. When a sentenced individual has served the minimum portion of such a sentence, he comes before a parole board which reviews his criminal history and behavior in prison to determine whether to release him into the community, subject to supervision and conditions, the violation of which could be grounds for being sent back to prison.

According to the most recent data, there are roughly 4.4 million people in the United States serving a term of community supervision at any given point in time, 3.6 million of whom are on probation and 878,000 of whom are on parole. In per capita terms, this means that between one and two percent of people in the country are currently under community supervision. As is true of the prison population, these numbers are dramatically higher than they were half a century ago, with the number of people on probation and parole today four to five times higher than in the mid-1970s. Like the prison population, people under community supervision are disproportionately men of color.[52]

2. Supervision as Service, Supervision as Surveillance. Between 1970 and 2000, as mass incarceration was on the rise, scholars noted a shift in the character of community supervision, away from a social worker model aimed at helping people get back on their feet and toward a law enforcement model that monitored them for compliance with conditions. Opponents of this shift pointed to research indicating that rehabilitative programming is more effective at reducing recidivism than pure surveillance programs lacking counseling services. Some studies even indicated that intensive supervision of low-level offenders can lead people to commit more crime, not less. Inspired in part by this research, a more recent trend has been toward a blended form of supervision that combines both models.[53]

As with all aspects of the American penal system, however, community supervision varies substantially in practice, with different models dominating in different agencies or even across individual officers. Some people, particularly those convicted of low-level offenses, may encounter probation officers so overwhelmed by high caseloads that they scarcely have time to monitor anyone. Others are placed in high-intensity programs that can entail regular drug testing, geolocation monitoring via an ankle bracelet, a host of required programs and conditions, and curfews that can sometimes approximate house arrest.[54]

3. Supervision as a Pathway to Incarceration. Community supervision is often described as an alternative to incarceration—a less serious mode of punishment for less serious offenders. But as scholars observe, the truth is that supervision and incarceration "have grown in tandem, sustaining each other in 'feedback loops,'" with "one-half of the people admitted to U.S. jails, and more than one-third of those admitted to prisons," sent there "as a result of revocation from community supervision." Sometimes, these revocations occur when people on probation or parole are accused of committing a new criminal offense. Instead of charging them with a new criminal case, prosecutors can simply move to revoke probation or parole—a process with substantially weaker procedural protections than an actual prosecution. Many revocations, however, are predicated on mere technical violations of release conditions, such as failure to abide by a curfew or to attend prescribed meetings.[55]

As Richard Seiter explains:

> [There is] a trend to violate releasees for minor technical violations, as administrators and parole boards do not want to risk keeping offenders in the community. If these minor violators later commit a serious crime, those deciding to allow them to continue in the community despite technical violations could face criticism. . . . This "risk-free" approach represents an "invisible policy" not passed by legislatures or formally adopted by correctional agencies. However, these actions have a tremendous impact on prison populations, cost, and community stability.[56]

As with incarceration more generally, the upshot of all of these revocations is that the United States is an international outlier with respect to both its high rates of revocation and the overall percentage of people under supervision.

> In 2011, the nationwide probation rate for the U.S. was seven times the average rate among European countries, four times the Canadian rate, five times that in England and Wales, and seven times that in Australia.

No other country for which we have statistical data casts the net of social control through probation as widely as the United States. Community supervision in the U.S. [also] generates enormous inflow to the prisons by transnational standards. In 2011, the average among reporting European states was only 6.3 percent of prison admissions attributable to "recalls" from community supervision—compared with 30 to 40 percent in this country over the past 20 years.[57]

4. Supervision as a Business. Finally, consider the ways in which community supervision—again, like incarceration—can benefit private actors by serving as a source of revenue.

In the past few years, [as] politicians from both major parties have begun to turn against mass incarceration . . . [p]rivate-prison corporations . . . have begun to expand into the "alternatives" industry. . . . Private-probation companies . . . have quietly taken off in recent years, often selling themselves as a cheap way to keep small-time offenders out of jail. In 2010, Judicial Correction Services made the magazine *Inc.*'s list of "the fastest growing private companies in America," for the third year in a row. . . . In return for an exclusive contract with a municipality, companies like Freedom Probation offer their services to courts for free. . . . The industry [thus] aims to shift the financial burden of probation directly onto probationers. Often, this means charging petty offenders—such as those with traffic debts—for a government service that was once provided for free. These probationers aren't just paying a court-ordered fine; they're typically paying an ever-growing share of the court's administrative expenses, as well as a separate fee to the for-profit company that supervises their probation and enforces a payment schedule—a consolidated weekly or monthly set of charges divided between the court and the company. The system is known as "offender-funded" justice.[58]

B. *Fines and Fees*

Preceding sections explored some of the ways in which state and local governments might generate revenue through the penal system—for themselves or for private actors—through practices like convict leasing or the imposition of "user fees" on people sentenced to terms of community supervision. The most common and most direct form of penal revenue generation, however, is also one of the oldest penal sanctions: the fine.

As Lawrence Friedman notes, "the workaday fine, the drudge-horse of criminal justice, was probably the most common form of punishment" in colonial America. Fines, however, were not a central focus of most people studying the modern American penal system—until 2015, when Ferguson, Missouri, became ground zero for a national discussion about the penal system's failings.[59]

The connection between those failings and penal fines crystalized when the U.S. Department of Justice released its investigative report of the Ferguson Police Department:

> Ferguson's law enforcement practices are shaped by the City's focus on revenue rather than by public safety needs. This emphasis on revenue has compromised the institutional character of Ferguson's police department, contributing to a pattern of unconstitutional policing, and has also shaped its municipal court, leading to procedures that raise due process concerns and inflict unnecessary harm on members of the Ferguson community. Further, Ferguson's police and municipal court practices both reflect and exacerbate existing racial bias, including racial stereotypes. Ferguson's own data establish clear racial disparities that adversely impact African Americans. The evidence shows that discriminatory intent is part of the reason for these disparities. Over time, Ferguson's police and municipal court practices have sown deep mistrust between parts of the community and the police department, undermining law enforcement legitimacy among African Americans in particular.[60]

As sociologists Alexes Harris, Heather Evans, and Katherine Beckett document, Ferguson hardly stands alone. Monetary sanctions are a major component of the penal system, "imposed by the courts on a substantial majority of the millions of U.S. residents convicted of felony and misdemeanor crimes each year." As Harris and Beckett further observe, "these penalties supplement rather than replace other punishments, especially confinement. As a result of their widespread imposition (and the rapid expansion of the penal system), millions of mainly poor residents of the United States now possess legal debt [that] tends to grow over time because it is subject to interest and surcharges and often is substantial relative to expected earnings."[61]

The following excerpts shed further light on the scope and nature of this mode of revenue-generating punishment, focusing on the impact fines and fees have on the vast majority of criminal defendants who are indigent.

April D. Fernandes et al., *Monetary Sanctions: A Review of Revenue Generation, Legal Challenges, and Reform*, 15 Ann. Rev. L. & Soc. Sci. 397, 398-401 (2019): The death of Michael Brown and the aftermath in Ferguson, Missouri, was a watershed moment. . . . The resulting Ferguson Report detailed a punitive and racist system . . . that targeted the economically disadvantaged African American residents of Ferguson with numerous and costly court fines and fees. . . .

In 2012, Ferguson reported that it generated approximately $2.2 million in revenues from fines and forfeitures, or approximately $105 per capita. These fines and forfeitures revenues accounted for more than 20% of the city's own-source revenue for that year. [But] Ferguson is not the only municipal government with criminal justice revenues at these extreme levels. In 2012, 355 municipalities (with populations of more than 500 residents) collected at least $100 in fines and forfeitures revenues per capita, and 208 municipalities generated at least 20% of their own-source revenues from fines and forfeitures. Of these, 54 were cities in large central metropolitan areas, 137 were cities in large fringe metropolitan areas, 109 were cities in medium or small metropolitan areas, and 119 were municipalities in rural areas. Criminal justice revenue dependence is a widespread phenomenon, and many municipal governments are at or above the troubling levels reported by the Department of Justice (DOJ) in Ferguson. . . .

Buried deep in state and city statutes, the procedures for assessment, collection, and enforcement of court fines, fees, and costs have been formulated to compensate for increasing budget shortfalls for overexpanded court and incarceration systems . . . [and for] stakeholders . . . far outside the court system, from the public school system to health care. . . . The growing reliance on monetary sanctions revenue [in turn] necessitates collection procedures and practices that range from wage garnishment and tax levies to driver's license suspensions to recoup costs. Because these sanctions were often levied on those who did not have the means to pay, more punitive sanctions, such as arrest warrants and incarceration, were implemented to dually punish and collect on legal debt. Such practices represent increased burdens on . . . the poor and communities of color.

. . . [These] practices foment increased distrust of law enforcement and the criminal justice system [and extend] the time that individuals spend under surveillance. . . . The expanded reach of the monetary sanctions system may be yet another mechanism that prompts individuals with outstanding legal debt to not engage in the formal labor market, financial institutions, and health care systems, among others, or to be locked out of these institutions as a result of legal debt. . . . The acknowledgment of the existence of many Fergusons demands a set of diverse and complex responses to the building and sustaining of these systems that further disadvantage already poor communities and communities of color.

Beth A. Colgan, *Reviving the Excessive Fines Clause*, 102 Calif. L. Rev. 277, 286-293 (2014): The costs of administering the court system—from arrests to prosecution and sentencing—are increasingly borne by the indigent, who make up the vast majority of criminal defendants. Costs charged to the defendant include a wide variety of prosecutorial and administrative activities associated with the justice system, such as the costs related to law enforcement investigations, prosecutors' preparation for trial, issuance of arrest warrants, . . . impaneling of a jury . . . [and even] costs related to the assignment of indigent defense counsel.

. . . In some cases, . . . individuals are ineligible for parole unless they can pay a $60 fee; those who cannot pay the fee remain in prison at a cost to taxpayers of approximately $80 to $110 per day regardless of the defendant's ability to successfully reintegrate into society. . . . In many places, probation terms — and the various payments related thereto — may also be extended as a penalty for failing to pay previously assessed economic sanctions. . . .

Yet another perversion stems from the way in which the collateral consequences of being unable to pay sometimes pushes individuals farther and farther from a point where payment is possible. Low-income individuals with debt from economic sanctions lose out on public benefits for which they may otherwise qualify. For example, one debtor reported that he could not use a [public] housing voucher because it required that he contribute toward his housing costs, but he needed the money he might otherwise use to supplement the housing voucher to pay for his economic sanctions. . . .

Likewise, individuals on probation and parole who miss a payment are excluded from receiving Social Security, food stamps, and Temporary Assistance for Needy Families (TANF). These types of benefits are a lifeline for many low-income families, and without them, debtors may not be able to continue making payments on their economic sanctions or even meet their basic needs.

Katherine Beckett & Alexes Harris, *On Cash and Conviction: Monetary Sanctions as Misguided Policy*, 10 Criminology & Pub. Pol'y 509, 528 (2011): [T]he idea that judges are responsible for sentencing and for the assessment of fees and fines that subsidize court operations is a significant conflict of interest. For these reasons, the National Center for State Courts concluded that the concept of self-supporting courts "is not consistent with judicial ethics or the demands of due process." The American Bar Association also recommends that courts have "a predictable general funding stream that is not tied to fee generation."

Alexes Harris et al., *Drawing Blood from Stones: Legal Debt and Social Inequality in the Contemporary United States*, 115 Am. J. Socio. 1753, 1792 (2010): From a policy perspective, it might be argued that criminal justice costs are appropriately borne by convicted criminals and that victims and governments should be reimbursed for the costs of offenders' felonious behavior. Yet few victims actually receive compensation through court-ordered restitution. Indeed, some might argue that requiring that offenders financially restore victims will inevitably fail and that this approach is a predictably ineffective way of ensuring that crime victims' needs are met. In addition, it is not clear whether government efforts to recoup funds are actually a net gain for the state. Moreover, our data indicate that the widespread imposition of substantial legal debt may encourage antisocial rather than prosocial outcomes. In particular, our respondents reported that possession of legal debt created a disincentive to work and encouraged going on the run. If the policy goal is to improve the lives of victims, recoup state expenditures, and reduce crime, our findings suggest that the imposition of monetary sanctions is very likely a policy failure.

Beth A. Colgan, *Beyond Graduation: Economic Sanctions and Structural Reform*, 69 Duke L.J. 1529, 1535-1536 (2020): In 1976, the Prison Research Education Action Project ("PREAP"), a collective of abolitionist leaders, released an influential publication, *Instead of Prisons: A Handbook for Abolitionists.* In it, they offered a variety of alternatives to incarceration, including the use of restitution and fines. In doing so, the authors pointed favorably to the European "day-fines" model, under which the amount of a fine imposed is determined by multiplying a person's daily income—minus deductions for living expenses and the like—with a penalty unit based on the seriousness of the given offense. The authors deemed the use of graduated economic sanctions transformative because it did not involve incarceration, allowed people to remain and participate in their communities, and presumably decreased the amount of money entering state coffers that would otherwise be used to finance custodial and community supervision.

C. Collateral Consequences

The consequences of a criminal conviction do not end upon release from incarceration, completion of community supervision, or payment of penal debt. Rather, a set of second-order impacts stretches on for years or decades. Termed *collateral consequences*, these follow-on effects can be formal *(de jure)* or informal *(de facto)* and can sometimes last a lifetime.

1. De Jure Collateral Consequences

According to the National Institute of Justice and the American Bar Association, examples of *de jure* collateral consequences are virtually endless. A database compiled by those organizations lists 44,778 discrete statutory limitations and disqualifications that flow from convictions across the fifty states. As the database reports, a criminal conviction can render a person ineligible for various employment licenses ranging from a cosmetology license to a license to do construction work to a license to sell funeral insurance; it can bar access to certain benefits or programs such as food stamps; it can render a person ineligible to be a formal caretaker or guardian for a loved one in need. The notes that follow focus on three collateral consequences that stand out in the academic literature and in policy debates: immigration, loss of housing, and disenfranchisement.[62]

NOTES AND QUESTIONS

1. Immigration. For immigrants and their families, the most severe collateral consequence of a criminal conviction is the prospect of losing lawful immigration status and being deported from the United States. As the

Supreme Court observes, "While once there was only a narrow class of deportable offenses and judges wielded broad discretionary authority to prevent deportation, immigration reforms over time have expanded the class of deportable offenses" to the point that "[t]he 'drastic measure' of deportation or removal is now virtually inevitable for a vast number of noncitizens convicted of crimes." Padilla v. Kentucky, 559 U.S. 356, 360 (2010). Under current law, a person can be stripped of lawful immigration status and deported following conviction for any one of dozens of statutorily enumerated crimes or any one of hundreds more offenses that fall into catch-all categories such as "crimes of violence" or "crimes of moral turpitude." See 8 U.S.C. §1101(43). As scholars, judges, and practitioners have observed, it is often very difficult for lawyers—let alone laypeople—to determine whether a given criminal conviction will in fact trigger immigration consequences. See Padilla, 559 U.S. at 380-382 (Alito, J., concurring) ("[P]rofessional organizations and guidebooks . . . are right to say that 'nothing is ever simple with immigration law[,]' including the determination whether [it] clearly makes a particular offense removable."). Still, the very fact that immigration law and criminal law have become so intertwined—into what some call a melded law of *crimmigration*—means that criminal lawyers and judges, primarily at the state level, are effectively frontline enforcers of the federal immigration system.[63]

    2. Housing. Beyond forcing removal to a different country, criminal convictions can also impact where a person lives in a more local sense. The public housing system, which consists of a partnership between federal and local government agencies, exists to ensure that people with low income have access to shelter. But when it comes to people with a criminal record, the vast majority of whom are poor, local housing authorities often embrace the view espoused a quarter-century ago by President Clinton: "If you break the law, you no longer have a home in public housing, one strike and you're out." President Clinton thought this "one strike" policy "should be the law everywhere in America," and in a series of statutes passed during his administration, Congress moved in that direction. For people convicted of some specific offenses, it banned access to federally funded public housing outright. But it also took steps to grant local public housing authorities the discretion to deny housing to anyone with a criminal record of any kind. According to the advocacy group Human Rights Watch, local public housing authorities used that discretion to adopt "exclusionary policies that deny eligibility to applicants with even the most minor criminal backgrounds." Criminal convictions can also create hurdles to housing for people in the private housing market, as landlords often do not like to rent to people with records—and are free to discriminate against them.[64]

    As Professor Valerie Schneider explains, barring people with criminal records from housing may ultimately be criminogenic, producing more crime rather than less:

Without housing, individuals are more likely to engage in crimes of survival, such as burglary, and are also more likely to seek money through illegal means, such as the drug trade. Additionally, homelessness is a predictor for more minor crimes, as homeless individuals are forced to "live private lives in public spaces," leading to arrests for offenses such as urinating or drinking in public. One study in New York revealed that "a person without stable housing is seven times more likely to re-offend after returning from prison" than a person who has stable housing.[65]

3. "Civil Death." A third and final set of *de jure* consequences of criminal conviction bars people from participating in some of the core aspects of civic life, including running for office, serving on juries, and—most notably—voting. Through these various forms of excommunication "the disenfranchised [are] severed from the body politic and condemned to the lowest form of citizenship," McLaughlin v. City of Canton, 947 F. Supp. 954, 971 (S.D. Miss. 1995), suffering what some refer to as "civil death."[66]

Given the highly skewed racial and socioeconomic demographics of people convicted of crimes, civic disenfranchisement systematically disempowers the people with the least power to begin with. That effect, Professors Jeff Manza and Christopher Uggen argue in their seminal book on the topic, may have been intentional. While acknowledging that individual states establish voter eligibility rules and that there are thus "50 different, often zigzagging stories to be told," Manza and Uggen conclude that "one factor—race—seems to recur again and again." In support of this assertion, they note that felon disenfranchisement laws spiked in two historical waves: one in the North after voting rights expanded to include all white men (irrespective of property ownership) and another in the South after the Civil War and the passage of the Fifteenth Amendment, which effectively extended the right to vote to Black men. That latter wave, Manza and Uggen contend, "cannot be separated from the criminal justice and racial politics in this same period," which sought to entrench racial hierarchy and safeguard white supremacy after the Civil War. Manza and Uggen also use a statistical regression analysis to demonstrate that "[w]hen African Americans make up a larger portion of a state's prison population, that state is significantly more likely to adopt or extend felon disenfranchisement."[67]

This systematic disenfranchisement of poor, disproportionately Black men may alter the outcomes of elections, Manza and Uggen contend. They identify at least one presidential race (Bush-Gore in 2000), seven Senate elections, and four gubernatorial elections between 1978 and 2004 in which a defeated Democrat would likely have won had felons not been disenfranchised.[68]

Professor Pamela Karlan argues that felon disenfranchisement laws call into question the legitimacy of not only the electoral process but also the very criminal laws that produce felony convictions in the first place.

The legitimacy of criminal punishment, at least within our system, depends on the legitimacy of the process that produces and enforces the criminal law. The legitimacy of that process in turn depends on the ability of citizens to participate equally in choosing the officials who represent them in deciding what behavior to outlaw, which individuals to prosecute, and how to punish persons convicted of a crime. Lifetime disenfranchisement of ex-offenders short circuits this process in a pernicious and self-reinforcing way. It is a relic of an era in which exclusion from self-government was the norm for most citizens. Today, it operates primarily to punish. And it punishes not only individual citizens, most of whom have otherwise paid their debt to society and reentered the free world, but the communities which bear the brunt of the criminal laws the political system enacts.[69]

2.   De Facto Collateral Consequences

Criminal convictions are not just legal judgments. As we will explore further in Chapter Two, they are also *social* judgments—expressions of blame and condemnation that carry potentially lifelong consequences for how a person with a criminal record is viewed by fellow members of society. In the words of Chief Justice Earl Warren, "Conviction of a felony imposes a *status* upon a person which not only makes him vulnerable to future sanctions through . . . civil disability statutes, but which also seriously affects his reputation and economic opportunities." Parker v. Ellis, 362 U.S. 574, 593-594 (1960) (Warren, C.J., dissenting). Consider, in this respect, the following four excerpts.

Jason Bost, *After 20 Years, Still Haunted by a Drug Conviction*, Marshall Project (Oct. 26, 2017): [W]hen I signed my daughter up for a summer basketball league and casually mentioned I was available to volunteer, I was thrilled they asked me to coach. . . . But about a week before the season started, I received an email asking me to complete a volunteer coaching form. Immediately, I got a sinking feeling in my stomach, one I had come to know very well over the years. It was the same sickening dread that visited me every time I applied for a job. Sure enough, there was the question on the coaching form. "Have you ever been convicted of a felony?" . . .

As is the case for many of my friends of color, the criminal justice system has since become an ever-present shadow looming over my life. [My] felony conviction was followed by rejection after rejection from jobs I was overqualified for, and even law schools I applied to. Now this: Maybe I couldn't even be a volunteer youth basketball league coach. . . . I also feared I would now have to disclose an aspect of my past to the other parents, teachers and members of my community—people I suspected would probably judge me harshly. I'd worked hard to establish myself as a professional and an equal peer among them and now feared they would view me as they might view many other men of color: as a problem.

Devah Pager, *Marked* 4-5, 36-37 (2007): For each individual processed through the criminal justice system, police records, court documents, and corrections databases detail dates of arrest, charges, conviction, and terms of incarceration. Most states make these records publicly available, often through on-line repositories, accessible to employers, landlords, creditors, and other interested parties. . . . The state in this way serves as a credentialing institution, providing . . . [t]he "credential" of a criminal record . . . [that] constitutes a formal and enduring classification of social status . . . [and that] regulate[s] access and opportunity across numerous social, economic, and political domains. Within the employment domain, the criminal credential has indeed become a salient marker for employers . . . [t]he majority of [whom] claim that they would not knowingly hire an applicant with a criminal background. . . .

Overt social distinctions based on race, gender, national origin, or other ascribed characteristics have become increasingly censured in recent years. . . . [But with] respect to the specific case of the criminal credential, individuals are routinely—and legally—denied access to jobs, housing, educational loans, welfare benefits, political participation, and other key social goods solely on the basis of their criminal background. . . . The legitimacy of these status characteristics is reinforced by assumptions of personal initiative (or personal culpability) in the acquisition of the credential and by the institutional authority with which the credentials are granted or imposed. It is the legitimacy of the credential that gives it its unquestioned influence.

James B. Jacobs, *The Eternal Criminal Record* 163-164, 190-192 (2015): American criminal record policy exceptionalism is illustrated by a comparison with Spain, which, like other continental EU member states, treats criminal records as personal data entitled to privacy protection. Access to police and court records is restricted in order to protect the convicted person's privacy and dignity and to promote rehabilitation. Although Spain's Constitution requires public access to criminal trials, the verdict is not usually announced in open court; rather, the defendant is informed of the judgment in writing, perhaps several weeks after completion of the trial. If there is a published opinion, a government agency first anonymizes the defendant's name and other identifying information. Case files are not available for public inspection. . . .

Transparency of governmental operations and especially court proceedings is a hallmark of American democracy and deeply embedded in American political-legal culture. People have a right to know what is and has occurred in the courts. Justice should be done and should be seen to be done. . . . [But] European countries conceive of an individual's criminal history record as analogous to information about race, religion, health, and sexual orientation. An individual's criminal history is not other people's business.

Amanda Agan & Sonja Starr, Ban the Box, Criminal Records, and Racial Discrimination: A Field Experiment, 133 Q.J. Econ. 191, 192-195 (2018): Tens of millions of Americans—disproportionately including black men—have criminal records, and face resulting barriers to employment access. In an effort to help overcome those barriers, and thereby reduce racial disparities in employment, more than 150 jurisdictions and 25 states have recently passed "Ban the Box" (BTB) laws and policies. The "box" . . . is the question on a job application form asking whether the applicant has been convicted of a crime, which is often accompanied by yes and no checkboxes. BTB prohibits employers from asking such questions on initial job applications or in interviews . . . [and thus] seeks to increase employment of people with criminal records.

. . . We submitted nearly 15,000 fictitious online job applications on behalf of young males to entry-level positions [to test the effects of BTB laws]. [Our first finding] supports BTB's core premise: when employers ask about them, felony convictions are a major employment barrier. Applicants without convictions were 63% more likely to be called back than those with convictions (5.2 percentage points over a baseline of 8.2%). [But our second finding shows that BTB laws also] appear to increase racial discrimination. . . . [B]efore BTB, white applicants received 7% more callbacks than similar black applicants, but after BTB this gap grew to 43%. . . . The post-BTB increase in racial inequality in callback rates appears to come from a combination of losses to black applicants and gains to white applicants. In particular, black applicants without criminal records saw a substantial drop in callback rates after BTB, which their white counterparts did not see. Meanwhile, white applicants with criminal records saw a substantial increase in callbacks, which their black counterparts did not see. This pattern suggests that when employers lack individualized information, they tend to generalize that black applicants, but not white applicants, are likely to have records.

III.   INCARCERATION WITHOUT PUNISHMENT

Just as it is possible—indeed, common—to punish people convicted of crimes without incarcerating them, it is also possible—and again, common—to incarcerate people who have never been convicted or even accused of criminal wrongdoing. These incarcerated individuals are often left out of courses on American criminal law, precisely because they are not governed by it. To say as much, though, begs an important question: What *is* the criminal law, and what separates it from other bodies of law if not the power to incarcerate? As an entry point to this important question, consider the following case.

Kansas v. Hendricks

521 U.S. 346 (1997)

THOMAS, J. In 1994, Kansas enacted the Sexually Violent Predator Act, which establishes procedures for the civil commitment of persons who, due to a "mental abnormality" or a "personality disorder," are likely to engage in "predatory acts of sexual violence." Kan. Stat. Ann. §59-29a01 *et seq.* (1994). The State invoked the Act for the first time to commit Leroy Hendricks, an inmate who had a long history of sexually molesting children, and who was scheduled for release from prison shortly after the Act became law. . . .

. . . Although freedom from physical restraint "has always been at the core of the liberty protected by the Due Process Clause from arbitrary governmental action," Foucha v. Louisiana, 504 U.S. 71, 80 (1992), that liberty interest is not absolute. The Court has recognized that an individual's constitutionally protected interest in avoiding physical restraint may be overridden even in the civil context. . . . Accordingly, States have in certain narrow circumstances provided for the forcible civil detainment of people who are unable to control their behavior and who thereby pose a danger to the public health and safety. We have consistently upheld such involuntary commitment statutes provided the confinement takes place pursuant to proper procedures and evidentiary standards. It thus cannot be said that the involuntary civil confinement of a limited subclass of dangerous persons is contrary to our understanding of ordered liberty.

. . . We have sustained civil commitment statutes when they have coupled proof of dangerousness with the proof of some additional factor, such as a "mental illness" or "mental abnormality." These added statutory requirements serve to limit involuntary civil confinement to those who suffer from a volitional impairment rendering them dangerous beyond their control. The Kansas Act is plainly of a kind with these other civil commitment statutes: It requires a finding of future dangerousness, and then links that finding to the existence of a "mental abnormality" or "personality disorder" that makes it difficult, if not impossible, for the person to control his dangerous behavior. Kan. Stat. Ann. §59-29a02(b) (1994). . . .

. . . The thrust of Hendricks' argument is that the Act establishes criminal proceedings; hence confinement under it necessarily constitutes punishment. He contends that where, as here, newly enacted "punishment" is predicated upon past conduct for which he has already been convicted and forced to serve a prison sentence, the Constitution's Double Jeopardy and *Ex Post Facto* Clauses are violated. We are unpersuaded by Hendricks' argument that Kansas has established criminal proceedings.

The categorization of a particular proceeding as civil or criminal "is first of all a question of statutory construction." Allen v. Illinois, 478 U.S.

364, 368 (1986). We must initially ascertain whether the legislature meant the statute to establish "civil" proceedings. If so, we ordinarily defer to the legislature's stated intent. Here, Kansas' objective to create a civil proceeding is evidenced by its placement of the Act within the Kansas probate code, Kan. Stat. Ann., Art. 29 (1994) ("Care and Treatment for Mentally Ill Persons"), instead of the criminal code, as well as its description of the Act as creating a "*civil commitment procedure*," §59-29a01 (emphasis added). Nothing on the face of the statute suggests that the legislature sought to create anything other than a civil commitment scheme designed to protect the public from harm.

Although we recognize that a "civil label is not always dispositive," *Allen*, 478 U.S. at 369, we will reject the legislature's manifest intent only where a party challenging the statute provides "the clearest proof" that "the statutory scheme [is] so punitive either in purpose or effect as to negate [the State's] intention" to deem it "civil," United States v. Ward, 448 U.S. 242, 248-249 (1980). In those limited circumstances, we will consider the statute to have established criminal proceedings for constitutional purposes. Hendricks, however, has failed to satisfy this heavy burden.

As a threshold matter, commitment under the Act does not implicate either of the two primary objectives of criminal punishment: retribution or deterrence. The Act's purpose is not retributive because it does not affix culpability for prior criminal conduct. Instead, such conduct is used solely for evidentiary purposes, either to demonstrate that a "mental abnormality" exists or to support a finding of future dangerousness. . . . In addition, the Kansas Act does not make a criminal conviction a prerequisite for commitment—persons absolved of criminal responsibility may nonetheless be subject to confinement under the Act. An absence of the necessary criminal responsibility suggests that the State is not seeking retribution for a past misdeed. . . .

Nor can it be said that the legislature intended the Act to function as a deterrent. Those persons committed under the Act are, by definition, suffering from a "mental abnormality" or a "personality disorder" that prevents them from exercising adequate control over their behavior. Such persons are therefore unlikely to be deterred by the threat of confinement. And the conditions surrounding that confinement do not suggest a punitive purpose on the State's part. The State has represented that an individual confined under the Act is not subject to the more restrictive conditions placed on state prisoners, but instead experiences essentially the same conditions as any involuntarily committed patient in the state mental institution. Because none of the parties argues that people institutionalized under the Kansas general civil commitment statute are subject to punitive conditions, even though they may be involuntarily confined, it is difficult to conclude that persons confined under this Act are being "punished."

Although the civil commitment scheme at issue here does involve an affirmative restraint, "the mere fact that a person is detained does not inexorably lead to the conclusion that the government has imposed punishment." United States v. Salerno, 481 U.S. 739, 746 (1987). The State may take measures to restrict the freedom of the dangerously mentally ill. This is a legitimate nonpunitive governmental objective and has been historically so regarded. . . . If detention for the purpose of protecting the community from harm *necessarily* constituted punishment, then all involuntary civil commitments would have to be considered punishment. But we have never so held.

Hendricks focuses on his confinement's potentially indefinite duration as evidence of the State's punitive intent. That focus, however, is misplaced. Far from any punitive objective, the confinement's duration is instead linked to the stated purposes of the commitment, namely, to hold the person until his mental abnormality no longer causes him to be a threat to others. If, at any time, the confined person is adjudged "safe to be at large," he is statutorily entitled to immediate release. Kan. Stat. Ann. §59-29a07 (1994). . . .

Hendricks next contends that the State's use of procedural safeguards traditionally found in criminal trials makes the proceedings here criminal rather than civil. . . . [But] the State's decision "to provide some of the safeguards applicable in criminal trials cannot itself turn these proceedings into criminal prosecutions." *Allen*, 478 U.S. at 372. The numerous procedural and evidentiary protections afforded here demonstrate that the Kansas Legislature has taken great care to confine only a narrow class of particularly dangerous individuals, and then only after meeting the strictest procedural standards. That Kansas chose to afford such procedural protections does not transform a civil commitment proceeding into a criminal prosecution.

Finally, Hendricks argues that the Act is necessarily punitive because it fails to offer any legitimate "treatment." Without such treatment, Hendricks asserts, confinement under the Act amounts to little more than disguised punishment. . . . We have [previously] observed that, under the appropriate circumstances and when accompanied by proper procedures, incapacitation may be a legitimate end of the civil law. Accordingly, the Kansas court's determination that the Act's "overriding concern" was the continued "segregation of sexually violent offenders" is consistent with our conclusion that the Act establishes civil proceedings, especially when that concern is coupled with the State's ancillary goal of providing treatment to those offenders, if such is possible. While we have upheld state civil commitment statutes that aim both to incapacitate and to treat, we have never held that the Constitution prevents a State from civilly detaining those for whom no treatment is available, but who nevertheless pose a danger to others. A State could hardly be seen as furthering a "punitive" purpose by involuntarily confining persons afflicted with an untreatable, highly contagious disease. Similarly, it would be of little value to require treatment as a precondition for civil confinement of the dangerously insane when no acceptable treatment existed. . . .

. . . We therefore hold that the Act does not establish criminal proceedings and that involuntary confinement pursuant to the Act is not punitive. Our conclusion that the Act is nonpunitive thus removes an essential prerequisite for both Hendricks' double jeopardy and *ex post facto* claims.

KENNEDY, J., concurring. . . . Notwithstanding its civil attributes, the practical effect of the Kansas law may be to impose confinement for life. . . . A common response to this may be, "A life term is exactly what the sentence should have been anyway," or, in the words of a Kansas task force member, "SO BE IT." The point, however, is not how long Hendricks and others like him should serve a criminal sentence. With his criminal record, after all, a life term may well have been the only sentence appropriate to protect society and vindicate the wrong. The concern instead is whether it is the criminal system or the civil system which should make the decision in the first place. If the civil system is used simply to impose punishment after the State makes an improvident [judgment] on the criminal side, then it is not performing its proper function. . . .

BREYER, J., dissenting. . . . [O]ne would expect a nonpunitively motivated legislature that confines *because of* a dangerous mental abnormality to seek to help the individual himself overcome that abnormality. . . . Conversely, a statutory scheme that provides confinement that does not reasonably fit a practically available, medically oriented treatment objective, more likely reflects a primarily punitive legislative purpose. . . . [A]s of the time of Hendricks' commitment, the State had not funded treatment, it had not entered into treatment contracts, and it had little, if any, qualified treatment staff. . . . [Moreover,] [t]he Act explicitly defers diagnosis, evaluation, and commitment proceedings until a few weeks prior to the "anticipated release" of a previously convicted offender from prison. Kan. Stat. Ann. §59-29a03(a)(1) (1994). But why, one might ask, does the Act not commit and require treatment of sex offenders sooner, say, soon after they begin to serve their sentences?

An Act that simply seeks confinement, of course, would not need to begin civil commitment proceedings sooner. Such an Act would have to begin proceedings only when an offender's prison term ends, threatening his release from the confinement that imprisonment assures. But it is difficult to see why rational legislators who seek treatment would write the Act in this way—providing treatment years after the criminal act that indicated its necessity.

Henry M. Hart, Jr., *The Aims of the Criminal Law,* 23 Law & Contemp. Probs. 401, 403-404 (1958): Thus far, it will be noticed, nothing has been said about the criminal law which is not true also of a large part of the noncriminal, or civil, law. The law of torts, the law of contracts, and almost every other branch of private law that can be mentioned operate, too, with general directions prohibiting or requiring described types of conduct, and the community's tribunals enforce these commands. What, then, is distinctive about the method of the criminal law?

Can crimes be distinguished from civil wrongs on the ground that they constitute injuries to society generally which society is interested in preventing? The difficulty is that society is interested also in the due fulfillment of contracts and the avoidance of traffic accidents and most of the other stuff of civil litigation. The civil law is framed and interpreted and enforced with a constant eye to these social interests. Does the distinction lie in the fact that proceedings to enforce the criminal law are instituted by public officials rather than private complainants? The difficulty is that public officers may also bring many kinds of "civil" enforcement actions—for an injunction, for the recovery of a "civil" penalty, or even for the detention of the defendant by public authority. Is the distinction, then, in the peculiar character of what is done to people who are adjudged to be criminals? The difficulty is that, with the possible exception of death, exactly the same kinds of unpleasant consequences, objectively considered, can be and are visited upon unsuccessful defendants in civil proceedings.

If one were to judge from the notions apparently underlying many judicial opinions, and the overt language even of some of them, the solution of the puzzle is simply that a crime is anything which is *called* a crime, and a criminal penalty is simply the penalty provided for doing anything which has been given that name. So vacant a concept is a betrayal of intellectual bankruptcy. . . . Moreover, it is false to popular understanding, and false also to the understanding embodied in existing constitutions. By implicit assumptions that are more impressive than any explicit assertions, these constitutions proclaim that a conviction for crime is a distinctive and serious matter—a something, and not a nothing. What is that something?

NOTES AND QUESTIONS

1. Forms and Scale of Civil Detention. As the Court in *Kansas v. Hendricks* makes clear, incarceration and the criminal law do not always go hand in hand. Sometimes, the state incarcerates people—in settings that can look and feel very much like a prison—by invoking its *civil* authority. In fact, according to the Prison Policy Initiative, more than 575,000 of the roughly 2.3 million people incarcerated in the United States in 2018 were not serving a criminal sentence.[70]

The vast majority of people so incarcerated are pretrial detainees. In 2018, 490,000 people were detained in jails on any given day, awaiting resolution of a pending criminal case. These individuals are detained by the penal system. But they have not been convicted of anything and are thus presumed innocent as a matter of law. The idea that an innocent person could be detained for months or even years in exactly the same jail used to incarcerate people convicted of crimes may seem strange. A majority of the Court, however, upheld this form of incarceration on the ground that it "is regulatory, not penal." United States v. Salerno, 481 U.S. 739, 746-747 (1987). "Congress," the majority held, "perceived pretrial detention as a potential solution to a pressing societal problem," namely, "preventing danger to the community," which the Court deemed "a legitimate regulatory goal." *Id.*[71]

After pretrial detention, the next most common form of "regulatory" incarceration in the United States is immigration detention. More than 500,000 people were sent to an immigration detention center in 2019, with roughly 50,000 people detained in such facilities on any given day. In recent years, these facilities captured public attention as activists, lawyers, and members of Congress decried the conditions in which detainees were held — conditions similar to and often worse than those found in jails and prisons. According to Professor César Cuauhtémoc García Hernández, these conditions, when considered alongside Congress' overarching approach to immigration policy, indicate a desire to use immigration detention as a form of punishment for people who have not complied with (civil) immigration laws. The Supreme Court, however, has long treated immigration detention as a form of regulatory confinement.[72]

While pretrial detention and immigration detention are the most substantial forms of noncriminal incarceration in the United States, there are multiple other examples. As noted in *Hendricks*, people who are found to have some form of mental impairment and to be a danger to themselves or others may be civilly committed to an institution against their will. *See* Addington v. Texas, 441 U.S. 418, 428-431 (1979). There are few data about how many people are civilly committed at any given time. But according to the Prison Policy Initiative, at least 22,000 people are currently being detained on grounds that they are criminally insane, incompetent to stand trial, or (like Mr. Hendricks) sexually dangerous. As alluded to in *Hendricks,* states also generally have the authority to hold people infected with communicable diseases in forced quarantine.[73]

Beyond civil commitment, there are also approximately 44,000 juveniles who are currently detained in the United States after having been found delinquent. As the Supreme Court has held, "proceedings involving juveniles [are] 'civil' not 'criminal' and therefore not subject to the [same] requirements which restrict the state when it seeks to deprive a person of his liberty." In re Gault, 387 U.S. 1, 17 (1967). As with immigration detention, however, the conditions of confinement in juvenile detention centers often approximate conditions in a jail or prison—and can sometimes be worse.[74]

Finally, while small in number, prisoners held in what is sometimes called "executive detention" often attract substantial attention, as is true of the roughly 780 people detained by the U.S. government in Guantánamo Bay, Cuba, as enemy combatants over the past two decades, dozens of whom have been incarcerated for nearly twenty years with no prospect of release.[75]

2. What Is the Criminal Law? As the preceding note suggests, labeling a specific form of incarceration "criminal" or "civil" goes beyond semantics. As a matter of well-developed constitutional law, a person prosecuted in a criminal proceeding enjoys certain procedural rights that do not attach to civil proceedings, including the right to a speedy and public trial, the right to be presumed innocent, and—perhaps most importantly—the right not to be convicted unless the government has proven its case beyond a reasonable doubt. These protections are designed to constrain the state's ability to wield the heavy artillery of a penal sanction. But as *Hendricks* and the cases in the preceding note make clear, those protections largely fall away if a statutory proscription or governmental sanction is deemed "civil" as opposed to "criminal." The difference between those two labels and thus the definitional boundary of the criminal law itself is therefore quite significant, which brings us back to Professor Hart's question: What *is* the criminal law?

Confronted with that question in *Hendricks,* the Supreme Court first gestures at an answer that verges on tautology. "We must initially ascertain whether the legislature meant the statute to establish 'civil' proceedings," the Court says, and "[i]f so, we ordinarily defer to the legislature's stated intent." To Professor Hart, this answer comes close to the "intellectual bankruptcy" of saying "simply that a crime is anything which is *called* a crime, and a criminal penalty is simply the penalty provided for doing anything which has been given that name."[76]

Circularity aside, there is also a pragmatic problem with such an approach. Permitting the legislature to determine the boundaries of the criminal law—and thus to determine the boundaries of the Constitution's heightened procedural protections for criminal cases—would essentially render those protections optional. The government, after all, could simply relabel its penal code a civil code. Or it could create a civil code that is a carbon copy of its penal code and thereby give prosecutors the option to choose between the two regimes.§

Perhaps in recognition of this underlying danger, *Hendricks* and the cases that precede it do not, ultimately, rest entirely on legislative labels. Rather, they insist that at least in some instances courts interpreting the Constitution must impose their own framework to define the boundaries of the criminal law. As the Supreme Court notes in a case preceding *Hendricks*, drawing this line "has been extremely difficult and elusive of solution." Kennedy v. Mendoza-Martinez, 372 U.S. 144, 168-169 (1963) (identifying a nonexhaustive list of factors to inform the inquiry). Ultimately, *Hendricks* points to the nub of an answer. The civil commitment statute at issue in that case is a *civil* commitment statute, the Court holds, because "commitment under the Act does not implicate either of the two primary objectives of criminal punishment: retribution or deterrence." The criminal law, in other words, is ultimately distinguishable from all other bodies of law because it alone is the law of *punishment*.

For Professor Hart, this boils down to saying that the uniquely defining feature of criminal law is that it is fundamentally a law of blame:

> What distinguishes a criminal from a civil sanction and all that distinguishes it, it is ventured, is the judgment of community condemnation which accompanies and justifies its imposition. . . . It is not simply any conduct to which a legislature chooses to attach a "criminal" penalty. It is conduct which, if duly shown to have taken place, will incur a formal and solemn pronouncement of the moral condemnation of the community.[77]

Of course, this is not to say that the criminal law is narrow, or that it does not—in its present-day, American form—extend to a wide swath of conduct that does not, or at least *ought not*, incur communal condemnation. On the contrary, the story of how American criminal law came to sweep so broadly and to incarcerate so many is a central theme of this course and of this book. Still, there is an important insight in Professor Hart's attempt to define the substantive core of the criminal law: Unlike any other body of law, the criminal law is unique in that its very purpose is to condemn, usually through the infliction of pain. Or, to return to the insight from Weber that opened this discussion, the criminal law is the primary means by which the state wields its monopoly on violence, against its own people.

---

§. Notably, in some specific subject-matter areas—including securities enforcement, the tax code, and environmental law—the federal government has essentially done just this, creating a system of "parallel enforcement" where the same conduct can be prosecuted civilly, criminally, or both. Some have argued that because this approach "blurs the civil/criminal distinction," it "weakens the constitutional rights that rely on it, by allowing the prosecutor to simply choose at will between the two regimes." David A. Barker, Note, *Environmental Crimes, Prosecutorial Discretion, and the Civil/Criminal Line*, 88 Va. L. Rev. 1387, 1418 (2002).

Framed in these terms, the criminal law's potency and its danger are laid bare. It is the law of imprisonment and the law of mass incarceration, the law of supervision, the law of fines and fees—the law that, alone among others, carries what Herbert Wechsler called the uniquely potent "power to destroy." All of which raises a rather fundamental question with which Hart was centrally concerned: "Why should the good society make use of the method of the criminal law at all?"[78]

That question—*why punish?*—has preoccupied philosophers for centuries, spawning a range of answers that, as *Hendricks* confirms, continue to inform criminal jurisprudence, doctrine, and policy today. The following chapter examines the contours of this longstanding debate.

CHAPTER 2
WHY PUNISH?

"[W]hen we reflect on the punishments inflicted (in our name) on so many of our fellow citizens and on the effects of those punishments on those who suffer them, we cannot but raise the question of legitimacy—of what can justify any practice of criminal punishment."

R.A. Duff, *Punishment, Communication, and Community* xii (2001)

"Examination of the purposes commonly suggested for the criminal law will show that each of them is complex and that none may be thought of as wholly excluding the others. . . . The problem, accordingly, is one of the priority and relationship of purposes as well as of their legitimacy—of multivalued rather than of single-valued thinking."

Henry M. Hart, Jr., *The Aims of The Criminal Law,*
23 Law & Contemp. Probs. 401, 401 (1958)

People v. Anderson

No. 14-MI-CV00243 (Cir. Ct. of Mississippi Cnty. Mo. May 5, 2014) (transcript of oral decision)

BROWN, J. Mr. Anderson, in my twenty-four years on the bench I thought I'd seen everything. Then all of a sudden your case came along and here we are — so I was wrong. I agree with the brief that has been submitted by the Attorney General's office that there are three things that this Court has to consider, three relevant factors. One is the seriousness of the crime you were convicted of and the sentence that you received. In the year 2000, you were convicted of two very serious crimes, and I think the thirteen-year sentence you were given in the year 2000 was not an unreasonable sentence. I think it was a fair sentence. However, the other factor is the clerical error. This clerical error was not your fault. It was not the fault of the sentencing judge in St. Charles County. It was not the fault of the Missouri Supreme Court. This was a unique error that was made and this type of error almost never happens, as evidenced by the fact that I am not aware of this type of a case in modern Missouri history having occurred.

And thirdly, another factor the Court has to consider is how you conducted yourself in the last thirteen years, in between the time you were released by the Department of Corrections and the time you were taken back into custody in July of 2013. . . .

INTRODUCTION

In the early morning hours of July 25, 2013, Cornealious Michael Anderson was asleep in his home in Webster Groves, Missouri, a town just outside of St. Louis and just south of Ferguson. Married and the father of four children, he owned a small construction company and was widely admired in the community. In the words of his friend and business partner, "He doesn't cuss. He doesn't drink. He's a family man."

Anderson's friends and family were thus surprised when, on that July morning, police officers dressed in tactical gear blocked off his street, pounded on his door, swept into his home, and carried him outside.

Anderson was less surprised. Standing on his front lawn in handcuffs, he spoke to his distraught wife over the phone while holding back tears. "Baby I'm sorry," he said. "This is something from thirteen years ago. I thought this was over."

As Judge Brown observed above, Anderson's case is unique — the product of a highly rare and consequential clerical error that resulted in his spending thirteen years free in the community when he was supposed to be in prison. And yet, unusual as Anderson's case is, it presents a lens through which to examine one of the central questions that has animated criminal jurisprudence and legal philosophy for millennia. *Why punish?*

That is the question we will address in this chapter. In the pages to come, you will encounter canonical and contemporary philosophers of criminal law debating some of the leading justifications offered for the penal system's existence. Engaging with these sources, you will consider which, if any, seem most persuasive. And you will consider whether, separate or together, any of them suffice to justify punishment in the United States today.

These abstract ideas will be grounded and enhanced by keeping Mr. Anderson's case in mind. As you read on, ask yourself the question that was before Judge Brown: *Should Anderson serve his sentence, thirteen years after it was imposed?* To grapple with that question, we must first understand what actually happened in Mr. Anderson's case, the details of which are reported in the following edited compilation of stories from the *Riverfront Times*, which were later turned into a podcast episode for *This American Life.*

Jessica Lussenhop

The (Extremely) Long (and Sometimes Forgetful) Arm of the Law

Adapted from the Riverfront Times (Sept. 12, 2013)*

Just after dawn on July 25, a phalanx of vehicles blocked traffic on a quiet residential street in Webster Groves, Missouri. Moments later a team of U.S. marshals piled out, pounded on the door of an unremarkable-looking suburban home and rousted Cornealious "Mike" Anderson from inside. "You've got the wrong guy," blurted the 36-year-old contractor as the marshals, outfitted in tactical gear and helmets, swept his two-story home. The only person inside was two-year-old Nevaeh, Anderson's youngest daughter, asleep in her crib in the master bedroom. A marshal lifted her out, confused and crying, and carried her downstairs.

By now Anderson—still dressed in his pajamas and handcuffed on the front porch—was in a cold sweat. His mother-in-law who lived just down the block arrived minutes later with Anderson's six-year-old son, Jorden. The marshals handed over Nevaeh to her grandmother, and Jorden watched the marshals lead his tearful father away. As officials were still sorting out where to take Anderson, one of the marshal's cell phones began ringing repeatedly. It was Anderson's wife, LaQonna, who'd been alerted of the arrest while away on a business trip. The marshal allowed Anderson a few moments to fill her in. "Baby, I'm sorry," he told her. "This is something from thirteen years ago. I thought that this was over."

* * *

A few hours later Anderson arrived at a facility 100 miles west of St. Louis that accepts new inmates and sorts them for their eventual permanent homes within the Missouri Department of Corrections. He's been there ever since. As he sits in the prison's linoleum-floored visitors center, he chokes up recalling what his children saw that morning seven weeks ago. "I just tell 'em, 'I just got some business to take care of. I'll be home soon.'"

For more than a decade, Anderson was supposed to have been in a Missouri prison cell. Instead, through some kind of massive procedural screwup, he was out walking among us. Finding him would have been a trivially easy task for police. He didn't change his name. He didn't leave town.

---

* The text below includes modest edits to the original, presents some text out of order, and incorporates text from a related article: Jessica Lussenhop, *Cornealious "Mike" Anderson: An Epilogue to the* RFT *Story Featured on* This American Life, Riverfront Times (Feb. 14, 2014).

In fact, he registered his contracting business with the secretary of state to his current address.

But until this summer the Missouri criminal-justice system seems to have simply forgotten about him, thirteen years after he was sentenced for his role in an armed robbery in St. Charles.

Anderson walked out of prison for the first time in June 2000. Ten months after being convicted of the robbery, he was released on bond while his case was being considered on appeal. Most everyone contacted by *Riverfront Times* agrees that Anderson's bond should have been revoked or a warrant issued for his arrest when his appeals concluded and his conviction was affirmed. Bafflingly, neither occurred. Anderson did not conceal that he was released. The very first line of one of his post-conviction filings reads, "Movant is not presently incarcerated." Throughout that brief his address is given as a home in Webster Groves. No one apparently thought anything of this.

Then, earlier this summer, over a decade after Anderson was sentenced, a blip of activity occurred in his dormant file. The Missouri Department of Corrections was preparing for his release — that is, for the release he would have been getting if he had in fact been incarcerated since 2000. The DOC, upon realizing the error, contacted the AG's office and got the ball rolling on the warrant that prompted Anderson's July arrest.

"It's still kind of unclear to me how he fell through the cracks," says Patrick Megaro, Anderson's attorney. "I don't think any of it is attributable to him at all. I think what happened is there was a clerical error, and the Missouri Department of Corrections figured they had a prisoner in their custody. Nobody double-checked."

"Obviously, I don't know what happened, but presumably there was a break in that line of communication," says St. Charles prosecuting attorney Tim Lohmar.

Ever since his arrest, Anderson's family has been seeking information on how this could have happened and how to get him home as soon as possible. They are desperate to avoid the worst-case scenario: He will simply have to serve the remaining thirteen years of his sentence starting now.

***

Since leaving prison in 2000, Anderson has not gotten so much as a speeding ticket. To his friends and family, he is an ideal father, church member and football coach, and bears no resemblance to the 22-year-old who was convicted so many years ago. His business partner and friend Brian Mayer says Anderson was working 70 to 80 hours a week on the company he founded, Anderson Construction and Investment. "He doesn't cuss. He doesn't drink. He's a family man," says Mayer. "The only thing he does is go fishing now and then. I hate that this is going on."

LaQonna Anderson says she knew very little about her husband's past crime until now. A soft-spoken 29-year-old with high cheekbones, she could pass for an even younger woman were the skin under her eyes not ringed with worry. She's not been sleeping or eating properly and has begun to lose weight. Little wonder: She's a suddenly single mother of four with a full-time job as a hotel manager during the day.

"School's starting tomorrow," she sighs one afternoon last month, look-ing across the kitchen table at her twelve-year-old son, JerQon. "A lot of kids have their mom and their dad on the first day. Mike was always there with them on their first day of school." In the room that just weeks earlier swarmed with police, JerQon tries to articulate how his father's absence is affecting him. "He said that I'm the man of the house and keep up with the kids," he says. "Help 'em out and make sure they don't get on momma's nerves."

Anderson's father, Cornealious Michael II, says that while his son may have had some problems in the past, the last thirteen years have proven that he does not deserve to be in prison. "If the point of incarceration is rehabil-itation, the job's already done."

***

On August 15, 1999, a manager at a Burger King in St. Charles placed the day's cash—in total a little over $2,000 in bills and coins—in two bank bags and made the short drive to the Mercantile Bank on West Clay Street. As he put his keys into the night-deposit box, he heard footsteps coming up fast behind him.

"Two black males came running up to my car with hand guns [*sic*] pointing them at me," the victim wrote in his statement to the police. "Told me to drop the bags or they were going to blow my fucken [*sic*] head off."

The manager dropped the money and put up his hands, and the men, their faces concealed, grabbed the cash and ran. After waiting a beat, the manager chased after them behind the bank and watched as they disap-peared into a cluster of low-slung apartment buildings across the street. The victim ran out to busy West Clay Street, hoping to flag down a pass-ing police car, but instead he watched a small blue vehicle race out from inside the apartment village. As it passed, he caught the license-plate num-ber. The plate came back to a 1993 blue Plymouth registered to 22-year-old Cornealious Michael Anderson III.

Police didn't catch up with Anderson for another two months. They eventually found him hiding under a blanket at his girlfriend's apartment. Anderson initially told detectives his car had been stolen and filled out a four-page statement asserting as much. But when the cops threatened to charge his girlfriend with hindering their investigation, Anderson crumbled. "I was there when the robbery took place," he wrote in a new statement. "There was a BB gun being used that was provided by Jay Harris."

Anderson told police that he and Harris were tooling around St. Charles in Anderson's car when Harris noticed bank customers making night deposits. Anderson insisted it was Harris' idea to pull over and rob a man they saw about to drop off his cash. Anderson said Harris pointed the BB gun and that he pointed his hand at the victim as if it were a gun. After they drove off, he ditched the car and called his girlfriend to come pick them up.

"I take full responsibility for my actions and my involvement in this crime," he wrote.

***

Two days after this story first published, we received an e-mail that read: "Just to let you know that I was that victim. Why don't you talk to me and I will tell you how bad it screwed up my life." His name is Dennis—we've agreed to use only his first name.

After the robbery in 1999, Dennis quit his job at Burger King and became increasingly paranoid that the men who'd held him up would find him and try to prevent him from testifying. He had a wife and small children, and he says he made them move more than once. But that didn't seem to calm his nerves. "Once this happened, I shut everything out around me. Didn't care," he says. "I didn't want to be involved in anything. Stayed away from home, stayed away from the kids or the old lady. Would not even come home. Go get shitfaced, pretty much." Eventually, Dennis's marriage broke up.

Now, some thirteen years later, he says he mostly forgot about the robbery—until he read about it in the *Riverfront Times*. "I was sitting there back at work eating my lunch and reading this magazine," he says. "About halfway through I realized they were talking about me." Naturally, he'd just assumed that after the trial, Anderson went to prison. "There are so many cracks he fell through—how could that be possible?" Dennis asks.

In our first conversation Dennis seemed angry at Anderson. But by the time we met him in person, he had a new, more surprising reaction. "I think what really pissed me off is how our government dropped the ball," he says. Anderson "screwed up and he was supposed to pay for it," Dennis said. "Our government screwed up. Who's paying for that? Does he have to pay for that again? Doesn't seem right."

Dennis shared another surprising anecdote—his daughter read the story in a high school class, not knowing that her dad was the victim of the robbery. When she came home and started talking about it, Dennis let her tell him her conclusion—that Anderson should get to go home—before he revealed he was the Burger King manager.

"She sat down at her bed and was like, 'No way,'" says Dennis. "Then she asked me my opinion and I told her pretty much, 'They should let him go.'"

***

Seated at a slightly sticky table in the prison's bright visitation room, Anderson cuts a very different figure than the man in LaQonna's books of family photos of weddings and Christmas mornings. He is dressed in a dingy white T-shirt, gray pants and blue slippers. A scruffy, three-week-old beard grows from his chin. He is sleep deprived and emotionally fragile. He speaks in a soft, earnest baritone voice about his past mistakes. He admits he was "young and dumb" once, trying to fit in with a wilder crowd.

"Yes, I feel responsible. I could have stopped it," he says of the robbery. "A year or two in jail, yeah, I would have done that. I knew that I was there. I knew that something could have been done, but I ran. I was scared. But thirteen years for that? There are guys in here on attempted murder; they've been here for ten years, for taking a life."

Anderson says he has paperwork for a petition for clemency in his cell. Aside from that, he's just waiting and praying that he is released. He has told his wife and family that he won't put them on the visitation list because he doesn't want them to see him inside. He says he does not think about the possibility of having to serve the full sentence.

Still, there are those who say regardless of his good behavior, Anderson has a debt to pay. Prosecuting Attorney Lohmar says that while the circumstances surrounding Anderson's story are "crazy" to him, the situation is cut and dried. "The jury heard the evidence, the judge upheld the sentence," he says. "As unfair as it may seem to he and his family, he's got thirteen years he owes the state. I don't think there's much more to say than that."

Questions: Should Anderson serve his sentence? The State, appealing to a backward-looking theory of punishment, says yes. "Anderson has a debt to pay," the prosecuting attorney insists. "He's got thirteen years he owes the state" for the harm he caused to Dennis and to the broader community. Anderson's father, however, offers a different perspective. Appealing to a forward-looking theory of punishment, he insists that whatever good punishment is supposed to accomplish, "The job's already done." Punishing Anderson will not accomplish anything at this point and will only inflict more harm—on Anderson, his family, and his community.

In broad strokes, these two diverging views track two major branches in the philosophy of punishment. The first, captured by the prosecuting attorney, is commonly known as *retributivism*. This theory justifies punishment

on the idea that a wrongdoer morally deserves to be punished and that
the state has the moral authority, and maybe the duty, to impose such punishment in order to acknowledge and respond to crime. By contrast, the
second philosophy, captured by Anderson's father, is typically known as *utilitarianism* or *consequentialism*. It justifies punishment based on the good—the
utility, the positive consequences—that might come from punishing those
who break the law. For example, punishment might prevent that person
from committing future harm or might deter others from doing so.

The next two sections of this chapter explore these two dominant theories of punishment in turn. We then briefly consider a set of sociologically
grounded theories that attempt to mitigate or resolve some of the tensions
between retributivism and consequentialism. Finally, we turn to a set of critical
theories that ask a common and essential question: What obligations must the
State itself fulfill before it has standing to punish people in the first place—and
what ought to happen when the State fails to meet those obligations?

I.   RETRIBUTIVISM

> "Retributivism is the view that punishment is justified by the moral culpability
> of those who receive it. A retributivist punishes because, and only because,
> the offender deserves it."
>
> Michael S. Moore, *The Moral Worth of Retribution*, in *Responsibility,
> Character, and the Emotions* 179 (Ferdinand Schoeman ed., 1988)

Retributivism is a penal theory grounded in a notion of *moral desert*. It links
the justification for punishment to the prior wrongful conduct of the person
being punished. But beyond this starting point, retributivism encompasses
a number of divergent ideas—some, but not all, of which are embraced
by people who consider themselves "retributivists." As an initial matter, it
is thus important to pull apart the different strands of retributive thought.
Consider this explanation from philosopher J.L. Mackie:

> Within what can be broadly called a retributive theory of punishment, we
> should [first] distinguish negative retributivism, the principle that one
> who is not guilty must not be punished, from positive retributivism, the
> principle that one who is guilty ought to be punished. We can [then] add
> a third principle of permissive retributivism, that one who is guilty may be
> punished. . . . For completeness, we should think also of quantitative vari-
> ants of each principle, that even one who is guilty must not be punished
> to a degree that is out of proportion to his guilt [and] that one who is
> guilty ought to be punished in proportion to his guilt, or may be punished
> in proportion to his guilt.[1]

As Mackie explains, retributivism in its broadest sense encompasses these three main ideas: The innocent should not be punished. The guilty should (or may) be punished. And the degree of punishment should fit the underlying offense. Of these three ideas, the first proposition, what Mackie calls "negative retributivism," is broadly accepted. Few modern philosophers defend punishing people who have done nothing wrong. We will return to this principle later in the chapter when we consider how it interacts with—and constrains—a purely utilitarian theory of punishment. Likewise, Mackie's third principle, sometimes called the *proportionality principle*, is one we will return to repeatedly in future chapters, as much of the criminal law is structured around the idea that people who commit less serious crimes should be punished less severely than people who commit more serious crimes—even if the American penal system does not always live up to this ideal.

The middle principle Mackie identifies, *positive retributivism*, captures what is sometimes called "the core of retributivism." According to this principle, a wrongdoer's moral "desert is not just a constraint on blame and punishment but also provides an important rationale for these attitudes and practices," such that "we *should* blame and punish culpable wrongdoers proportionate to their desert." As Mackie explains, this core idea is "the really controversial issue" in penal philosophy. To see why, consider the various manifestations of the argument set out below.[2]

A.   Strong (Mandatory) Retributivism

Strong retributivists believe the state has a moral obligation—a duty—to punish wrongdoers. Consider the following illustrative excerpts.

Immanuel Kant, *The Philosophy of Law* 194-198 (William Hastie trans., Edinburgh, T.&T. Clark 1887). The right of administering punishment is the right of the sovereign as the supreme power to inflict pain upon a subject on account of a crime committed by him. . . . Punishment can never be administered merely as a means for promoting another good either with regard to the criminal himself or to civil society, but must in all cases be imposed only because the individual on whom it is inflicted has committed a crime. For one man ought never to be dealt with merely as a means subservient to the purpose of another. . . . Against such treatment his inborn personality has a right to protect him. . . . The Penal Law is a categorical imperative; and woe to him who creeps through the serpent-windings of utilitarianism to discover some advantage that may discharge him from the Justice of Punishment. . . . For if Justice and Righteousness perish, human life would no longer have any value in the world. . . . Justice would cease to be Justice, if it were bartered away for any consideration whatever. . . . Even if a Civil Society resolved to dissolve itself with the consent of all its members — as might be supposed in the case of a people inhabiting an island resolving to separate and scatter themselves throughout the whole world — the last murderer lying in the prison ought to be executed before the resolution was carried out. This ought to be done in order that every one may realize the desert of his deeds, and that bloodguiltiness may not remain upon the people; for otherwise they might all be regarded as participators in the murder as a public violation of Justice.

Michael S. Moore, *The Moral Worth of Retribution,* **in** *Responsibility, Character, and the Emotions* 181-182, 212, 214 (Ferdinand Schoeman ed., 1988). Retributivism is a very straightforward theory of punishment: We are justified in punishing because and only because offenders deserve it. Moral culpability ("desert") is in such a view both a sufficient as well as a necessary condition of liability to punitive sanctions. Such justification gives society more than merely a right to punish culpable offenders. . . . For a retributivist, the moral culpability of an offender also gives society the duty to punish. Retributivism, in other words, is truly a theory of justice such that, if it is true, we have an obligation to set up institutions so that retribution is achieved. . . .

Our concern for retributive justice might be motivated by very deep emotions that are nonetheless of a wholly virtuous nature. These are the feelings of guilt we would have if we did the kinds of acts that fill the criminal appellate reports of any state. . . . A moral being *feels* guilty when he or she *is* guilty of past wrongs. . . . We should trust what our imagined guilt feelings tell us. . . . [S]uch guilt feelings typically engender the judgment that we deserve punishment. I mean this . . . in the strong sense that we *ought* to be punished. . . . [W]e should ask whether there is any reason not to make the same judgment about [other people]. If we experience any reluctance to transfer the guilt and desert we would [apply to ourselves to someone else who has committed a crime,] we should examine that reluctance carefully. Doesn't it come from feeling more of a person than [them]? We are probably not persons who grew up [without privilege, so] it may be tempting to withhold from [people who have faced more challenging circumstances] the benefit each of us gives himself or herself: the benefit of being the subjective seat of a will that [is] capable of both choice and responsibility. Such discrimination is a temptation to be resisted, because it is no virtue. It is elitist and condescending toward others not to grant them the same responsibility and desert you grant to yourself. . . . It is a refusal to admit that the rest of humanity shares with us that which makes us most distinctively human, our capacity to will and reason — and thus to be and do evil.

Jean Hampton, *Correcting Harms Versus Righting Wrongs: The Goal of Retribution*, 39 UCLA L. Rev. 1659, 1668, 1686-1687, 1690-1691, 1701-1702 (1992). [M]orality demands of each of us that we respect the dignity of others and of ourselves, and thus reject the way that, for example, a white supremacist would insist on his own superiority over other racial groups, or the way in which a male might relish the idea that he is the intrinsic superior of all women. . . . [R]etribution is a response to a wrong that is intended to vindicate the value of the victim denied by the wrongdoer's action. . . . When we face actions that not merely express the message that a person is degraded relative to the wrongdoer but also try to establish that degradation, we are morally required to respond by trying to remake the world in a way that denies what the wrongdoer's events have attempted to establish, thereby lowering the wrongdoer, elevating the victim, and annulling the act of diminishment. . . .

The more awful the wrong, the larger the purported gulf between wrongdoer and victim, and thus the more substantial and severe the punishment must be in order to defeat the wrongdoer and thereby deny his claim to superiority. . . . From a retributive point of view, punishments that are too lenient are [thus] as bad as (and sometimes worse than) punishments that are too severe. When a serious wrongdoer gets a mere slap on the wrist after performing an act that diminished her victim, the punisher ratifies the view that the victim is indeed the sort of being who is low relative to the wrongdoer. When the American courts, until recently, responded to spousal abusers with light punishment or no punishment at all, they were expressing the view that women were indeed the chattel of their husbands. . . .

Liberals should wish not for a morally neutral state, but for a morally reputable and conscientious one that accepts that it has a role to play in insuring that each of us is accorded the value we ought to have. . . . For how can human autonomy be realized in a society without mutual respect for human worth?

Questions: How do you think Kant, Moore, and Hampton each would rule in Michael Anderson's case? If you think each would say Anderson should serve his sentence, would they explain their rulings differently? And what about Dennis, Anderson's victim? Would it matter to any of these theorists that Dennis thought the state "should let [Anderson] go"? *Should* it matter? Finally, what arguments might you offer based on these accounts to say that Anderson should *not* be punished?

B. Weak (Permissive or Mixed) Retributivism

Not all retributivists endorse a strong form of retributivism, under which the state has a moral obligation — a duty — to punish wrongdoers.

Rather, some argue that even if a person's culpable wrongdoing can *justify* punishment, it does not necessarily *require* such punishment. Consider the following excerpts.

David O. Brink, *Fair Opportunity and Responsibility* 148-149 (2021). Other things being equal, we should blame and punish culpable wrongdoers proportionate to their desert. However, other things are not always equal. This is where predominant retributivism diverges from pure retributivism. Whereas the pure retributivist thinks that desert is the only factor affecting the decision to punish, predominant retributivism recognizes that there can be non-desert-based reasons . . . to punish less than required by desert. Such non-desert factors can include the costs of punishment, the prospects for rehabilitation, evidence of remorse and restitution, and the value of mercy, forgiveness, and reconciliation. . . . Because predominant retributivism allows that desert can compete with non-desert reasons against proportionate punishment, it is a mixed theory of punishment.

Douglas Husak, *Holistic Retributivism*, 88 Calif. L. Rev. 991, 996-998 (2000). Retributivists seemingly suppose that their task is complete when they show that the punishment of culpable wrongdoers is intrinsically good. . . . I can appreciate why retributivists tend to dwell on this part of the story, inasmuch as consequentialists have refused to concede the crucial point: Punishing culpable wrongdoers is intrinsically good. . . . [But] [r]etributivists must show not only that giving culpable wrongdoers what they deserve is intrinsically valuable, but also that it is sufficiently valuable to offset what I will refer to as the drawbacks of punishment—negative values that inevitably are produced when an institution of punishment is created.

Punishment has (at least) three drawbacks that must be addressed by attempts to justify it. The first such drawback is the astronomical expense of our system of criminal justice. . . . These funds might well be used to support any number of other worthy goods: education, transportation, the arts, welfare, and a host of others. . . . The second drawback is that an institution of punishment is susceptible to grave error. . . . When we convict the innocent, lives may be ruined unjustly. When we punish in excess of desert, the quality of lives will be unjustly impaired. . . . We [also] sometimes punish persons for conduct that is not wrongful at all. No one has a precise estimate of how many innocent persons are punished, how many guilty persons are punished in excess of their desert, or how many persons are punished for crimes that should not have been enacted in the first place. But the likelihood that this figure is high should give considerable pause to those retributivists who defend the institution of punishment as a device to attain the intrinsic value of giving persons the punishments they deserve. . . . [Finally,] the third drawback of punishment is the risk that authority will be abused. . . . Recent revelations . . . are only the latest reminders that we frequently require protection from those who are charged to protect us.

Jean Hampton, *Correcting Harms vs. Righting Wrongs: The Goal of Retribution,*
39 UCLA L. Rev. 1659, 1691, 1694-1695 (1992). I take it to be extremely difficult for a society to fashion retributive punishments for serious felons that
simultaneously respect the wrongdoer and defeat him in a way that destroys
his claim to mastery. . . . [P]erhaps the most surprising aspect of the theory of
retribution I have developed [is] that the retributive response need not be in
the form of a punishment to count as retribution. . . . Consider the seemingly
passive and loving response of "turning the other cheek," which certainly cannot count as punishment so defined. Nonetheless, this sort of response, far
from being the opposite of retribution, is actually an instance of it in many
circumstances. Consider the following remarks by St. Paul: "[I]f your enemy
is hungry, feed him; if he is thirsty, give him drink; for by so doing, you will
heap burning coals upon his head." . . . The pain Paul describes comes from
the emotions of humiliation and shame, which kindness can evoke in us when
we are benefited by those whom we have wronged. Such treatment startles us,
prompts us to rethink how our own responses to our benefactor have been so
much uglier than our victim's behavior toward us, and (assuming we have a
decent conscience) makes us ashamed of what we have done. Through that
shame we are humbled. The person we have wronged has defeated us, and
robbed us of our pretense of elevation over him. We are chastened, just as
surely as if we had been punished.

Questions: How would you describe the differences among the views
Brink, Husak, and Hampton articulate above? What arguments for and
against punishing Anderson would you make by drawing on their views
of retributivism? How do those arguments differ from the arguments you
made when drawing on the "pure" form of retributivism in the preceding section? Finally, how do you think these three theorists would rule in
Anderson's case? If you can't tell, is that a problem?

Once you've read the utilitarianism section of this chapter, come back
here and consider whether the arguments you would offer based on the
excerpts above differ from what Kant calls "the serpent-windings of utilitarianism." If your utilitarian arguments differ from those you made here, how
so? If they do not, is that a problem?

C. Retributivism and Mass Incarceration

Notwithstanding the softer and more nuanced versions of retributivism
outlined above, many people continue to see what Professor Alice Ristroph
calls "an edge of righteousness to retributivism." As such, the theory is controversial not only in abstract philosophical debates but also because it is
often associated with the rise of mass incarceration. In part, this association is historical. The 1970s and 1980s saw not only a steep vertical climb in

incarceration rates but also "a steady rise in the popularity of retributivism" in academic circles, a striking reversal of fortune given the philosophy's "near death in the 1950's and 1960's." Of course, as we will see throughout this book, many factors contributed to the rise of mass incarceration, and at least some scholars question whether jurisprudential philosophy has any "impact at all on the actual workings of American justice." But others lay part of the blame for mass incarceration at retributivism's feet. Is this fair? Consider the following two excerpts.[3]

David O. Brink, *Fair Opportunity and Responsibility* 143 (2021). If retributivism were responsible for the ills of mass incarceration, that would be reason to be skeptical of retributivism. But retributivism is not to blame for excesses in the criminal justice system. Retributivism can require accountability and proportionate punishment without requiring or even permitting [overly punitive] penal practices. There's no reason to assume that retributivism supports these practices or opposes criminal law reform. Indeed, it is natural to frame calls for criminal justice reform by saying these aspects of mass incarceration imprison people out of proportion to their deserts. But this justification of reform presupposes, rather than condemns, retributive ideas.

What proportionality clearly requires is *comparative* just deserts. This gives us only *ordinal* information about the magnitude of just deserts until we have *anchors* for the ordinal scale. . . . There is room for disagreement about what quantum of punishment is appropriate for the anchors, especially at the maximum. . . . We also need to distinguish the *length* and *manner* of punishment. We tend to think of punishment in terms of incarceration. But incarceration is only one form punishment can take. . . . It is open to retributivists to think that proportionality requires shorter periods of incarceration and more humane forms of incarceration for many crimes. Indeed, one might think that incarceration should be limited primarily to violent crime and serial offenders and that various kinds of diversionary treatment, such as community service and house arrest, would be appropriate for most forms of non-violent crime and first offenders.

In these ways, one can be a retributivist without endorsing the degree of punitiveness in the current American criminal justice system. Retributivists can and do think that prison conditions, criminalization for non-violent offenses, sentence length, and post-incarceration penalties are disproportionately punitive and violate just deserts.

James Q. Whitman, *A Plea Against Retributivism*, 7 Buff. Crim. L. Rev. 85, 87-103 (2003). Thirty years ago, a new generation of philosophers demanded a criminal law founded on blame — on unembarrassed condemnation where condemnation is warranted. They have made themselves dominant on the American philosophical scene. . . . Before we endorse retributivism, even in its most modest forms, we need some thoughtfully worked-out understanding of its dangers. Why has the age of the renaissance of neo-retributivism also been the age of epochally harsh punishment? . . .

Perhaps the public does in some sense hear what philosophers have to say. But one fears that what they hear are the words "blame," and "condemnation," and that when they hear those words they succumb to the urge toward vengeance. To be sure, all thoughtful philosophers are careful to distinguish retribution from vindictiveness or vengeful ferocity, just as all of them insist on the principle of proportionality. Indeed, our philosophies of retributivism are hedged about at every turn by distinctions and caveats, as they have been for generations. . . . [But] the public is not very good at understanding all the subtle stuff. . . . [T]o the extent retributivist philosophers are heard at all, they are heard in ways that amount to pouring gasoline on the fires of American punishment. . . .

Indeed, if we are honest about it, perhaps we will admit that our neo-retributivism does have a spiritual affinity with our crackdown, much though we may resist the thought. Whatever the subtleties in their philosophy, our retributivists do indeed typically believe in hard looks and hard consequences, just as their fellow citizens do. . . . If retributivism is such an egalitarian philosophy, why does it find so little to say about an American system of punishment that so consistently treats offenders like second-class citizens, and indeed like sub-humans? . . .

These are worries, I contend, that should figure in the night thoughts of any American attracted to retributivism.

II. UTILITARIANISM

> "[L]ook not at the greatness of the evil past, but the greatness of the good to follow. . . . [W]e are forbidden to inflict punishment with any other design, than for correction of the offender, or direction of others."
>
> Thomas Hobbes, *Leviathan* 119 (Michael Oakeshott ed., Collier 1962) (1651)

Retributivism sees punishment as inherently good and perhaps required. Utilitarianism starts from the opposite premise. "[A]ll punishment in itself is evil," says English jurist and philosopher Jeremy Bentham, who along with Italian mathematician and economist Cesare Beccaria is viewed as the modern founder of consequentialist penal philosophy. And because all punishment is evil, it is forbidden—unless "it promises to exclude some greater evil" or to accomplish some greater good.[4]

There is an aspiration to precision in this school of thought. Indeed, part of consequentialism's appeal is that it offers an alternative to the vague intuitionism of retributivism, which suffers from what Professor Göran Duus-Otterström calls "robust uncertainty" when it comes to determining how much punishment is the right amount. By contrast, utilitarianism promises a more reticulated *cost-benefit analysis*. First, we must decide what societal goals punishment is meant to achieve. Next, we measure whether imposing punishment advances those goals and at what cost, to those same goals or any other relevant ones. If punishment maximizes social benefits over social costs—i.e., if it maximizes social welfare—it should be imposed. Otherwise, it should not.[5]

This basic thought process is easy enough to describe. But it is hardly simple to execute, nor is it free of its own underlying normative decisions. Perhaps most fundamentally, we need to decide at the outset what to count as a cost and what to count as a benefit. Likewise, as Professors Dale Whittington and Duncan McRae write, we need to determine "which individuals should be accounted for in this calculation," and thus whose benefits and costs to consider. These choices can be significant, perhaps even determinative. For example, an analysis that ignores or downplays the harms incarceration imposes on the families and friends of people who are incarcerated—either because such costs are deemed irrelevant or because they are too hard to calculate—would underweight the costs of incarceration and thus propose more of it than an alternative analysis that incorporates these harms. Similarly, an analysis that presumes that punishment entails zero benefit for the people being punished runs the risk of underweighting the social value of punishment if that presumption turns out to be unfounded.[6]

Given the central role that costs and benefits play as inputs to the utilitarian analysis, this section begins with an overview of the costs and benefits that economists and others rely upon when evaluating penal policies through a utilitarian lens. It then gives an overview of the three primary mechanisms by which punishment is generally thought to offer social benefits—namely, through its potential *deterrence, rehabilitation,* or *incapacitation* of people who commit crimes. Finally, the section ends by examining mass incarceration through a cost-benefit lens.

A.   Costs and Benefits of Punishment

"The general object which all laws have, or ought to have," Bentham says, "is to augment the total happiness of the community." Accordingly, he goes on, laws must strive "to exclude, as far as may be, every thing that tends to subtract from that happiness." The word *happiness* here represents an all-encompassing idea. For classic utilitarians, it is the "final good at which all human action must aim." In its purest form, utilitarian analysis ought to account for every possible enhancement or diminution of global happiness that a policy or course of action might bring about.[7]

The monumental nature of that undertaking could easily prove paralyzing in practice. As a result, utilitarian analyses of punishment tend to operate within a narrower scope, focusing on some of the significant costs and benefits of punishment that might ultimately influence "the total happiness of the community," albeit without capturing the totality of that idea. Consider this illustrative passage from President Obama's Council of Economic Advisers:

> From an economic perspective, the goal of an efficient criminal justice system is to maximize the safety of citizens and minimize criminal activity while also limiting the direct and indirect costs of criminal justice policies to individuals, communities and the economy. Broadly, debates about the criminal justice system can [thus] be framed as a comparison of the system's societal benefits in terms of *reduced crime* and its societal costs in terms of *direct government spending and collateral consequences for individuals, families and communities.*[8]

One could certainly propose additions to this list of the costs and benefits of punishment. But a penal policy that does not advance social welfare if measured against these conventional metrics will generally be deemed to "fail" the cost-benefit test. Let us thus take a moment to consider these metrics more closely.

NOTES AND QUESTIONS

1. Some Costs: Suffering, Spending, and Community Destabilization. What are the "direct and indirect costs of criminal justice policies to individuals, communities and the economy"?

The cost of punishment to the people being punished should be obvious. Kant forthrightly says that to punish someone is "to inflict pain" upon him. One need only read the first-hand accounts of prison offered in Chapter One — describing material deprivation, loneliness, monotony, and loss of dignity — to see his point. Prison, like other forms of punishment, is frequently *designed* to be painful, or at the least to be very unpleasant. In fact, scholars dating back to Bentham have argued that prison conditions must be worse than conditions of extreme poverty in society, so as not to incentivize poor people to seek out prison in hopes of improving their material conditions (an idea known as the *principle of less eligibility*).[9]

But the costs of punishment extend beyond the pain of incarceration itself. People in prison, for example, often experience violent harm in the form of assaults at the hands of other prisoners or prison guards. Punishment also often has severe consequences for the loved ones of the people who are punished. As sociologist Todd Clear explains, incarceration "breaks families apart, strains their economic resources, weakens parental involvement with children, and leads to emotional and social isolation."[10]

In addition to these individual and family costs, punishment also entails substantial societal costs. For starters, there are the direct *fiscal* costs of maintaining a penal system — the money society spends on punishment. Incarceration alone is quite expensive, as the state must assume the substantial costs of operating prisons. These costs vary by state. But conservative estimates of regular operational costs per individual — excluding the substantial costs of constructing the prisons themselves — ranged in 2015 from a low of roughly $14,000 per year in Alabama to a high of over $64,000 in California. Just a few years later, California projected its annual cost per prisoner would reach $75,560, "enough to cover the annual cost of attending Harvard University and still have plenty left over." As the Department of Education has observed, this statistic is broadly representative of national trends in prison spending and the extent to which such spending outpaces investments in public education.[11]

These costs of incarceration represent just a fraction of total direct spending on the American penal system. As we will see in future chapters, the system's reach is broadest outside the prison walls, where police officers enforce the criminal law through millions of stops, frisks, and arrests, most of which never lead to a term of incarceration. The breadth of policing's footprint is visible in public spending. The United States spends roughly $277 billion per year on police and prisons together, of which only about one third ($90 billion) goes to prison operations. State and federal police forces, including specialized agencies like the Drug Enforcement Agency and the FBI, consume the rest, at a rate of nearly $500 million per day.[12]

Beyond direct public expenditures, the costs of punishment also encompass a broad set of "indirect" costs that utilitarian analysis must consider. For example, as the Council of Economic Advisors explains, "Having a criminal record or a history of incarceration is a barrier to success in the labor market," with limited employment and depressed wages in turn stifling the "ability to become self-sufficient." "Beyond earnings, criminal sanctions can have negative consequences for individual health, debt, transportation, housing, and food security." These costs are borne by the individuals who suffer them directly and also by public and private institutions that may step in to lend assistance.[13]

Finally, and paradoxically, punishment can produce a social-cost feedback loop — by generating more crime. A "growing body of work" demonstrates that incarceration can "increase recidivism" and thus be *criminogenic*. Multiple mechanisms could explain this phenomenon, including the fact that "incarceration, especially at high rates, could disrupt social networks by damaging familial, economic, and political sources of informal social control. The consequence of this damage . . . would be more, not less, crime."[14]

Figure 2.1.   U.S. Spending on Law Enforcement and Corrections, 2021

Parent	Component	Funding
Federal (DHS)	Customs and Border Protection	$15,038,557,000
Federal (DHS)	Coast Guard	$12,844,954,000
Federal (DHS)	Immigration and Customs Enforcement	$7,973,529,000
Federal (DHS)	Transportation Security Administration	$5,017,731,000
Federal (DHS)	Secret Service	$2,438,001,000
Federal (DHS)	Law Enforcement Training Centers	$340,348,000
Federal (DHS)	Aid to state/local police	$1,315,000,000
Federal (DOD)	'1033' transfers to state/local police	$89,318,501
Federal (DOJ)	US Marshals Service	$1,496,000,000
Federal (DOJ)	National Security Division	$117,451,000
Federal (DOJ)	Parole Commission	$13,539,000
Federal (DOJ)	Interagency Drug and Crime	$550,458,000
Federal (DOJ)	Federal Bureau of Investigation	$9,748,686,000
Federal (DOJ)	Drug Enforcement Agency	$2,796,762,000
Federal (DOJ)	Alcohol, Tobacco, and Firearms	$1,483,887,000
Federal (DOJ)	Bureau of Prisons	$7,708,375,000
Federal (DOJ)	Aid to state/local police	$2,443,800,000
Federal (LEG)	Capitol Police	$515,541,000
State/local gov't	Police	$123,046,259,000
State/local gov't	Corrections	$82,175,474,000

Stephen Semler (@stephensemler), X (Jan. 20, 2022, 11:29AM), https://x.com/stephensemler/status/1484216618058235905

2. A Potential Benefit: Crime Control. Against the many costs of punishment outlined above, consequentialist analyses of penal policy typically focus on a single potential benefit: crime prevention. As philosopher Antony Duff explains, crime reduction is by definition a social benefit for consequentialists: "[I]f the law defines as criminal (as for any consequentialist it should) only conduct that causes or threatens harm, reducing the incidence of such conduct will do good by reducing both the incidence and the fear of such harm." Thus, while it is possible that punishment might achieve other social goods, crime prevention is, in conventional practice, the only benefit taken into account in cost-benefit analyses of penal policy.[15]

A substantial body of literature attempts to measure the social costs of crime, in hopes of estimating "the 'bang-per-buck'" of competing approaches to penal policy. Methods for measuring these costs range widely. Some scholars estimate how much people value crime prevention by gauging the amount they pay in real-world transactions to avoid higher risks of victimization. For example, one might measure the differences between home prices in low-crime and high-crime neighborhoods or the difference in wages paid to employees of low-crime and high-crime shifts at a convenience store and then estimate from these differences the monetary value people place on avoiding victimization. Far beyond the penal context, this inductive methodology is used to place a statistical value on human life, which can be calculated by comparing wages across jobs with different workplace fatality rates. This statistical construct in turn drives cost-benefit analyses of various laws and policies—from speed limits that might reduce fatal traffic accidents to penal policies that might reduce homicides. Alternatively, some scholars attempt to measure the costs of crime directly by using surveys that ask people how much they would spend to gain, say, a ten percent drop in the risk of certain types of crime. Finally, some scholars take a bottom-up approach, summing the costs that actually arise when people become victims of crime—including, for example, the money paid for medical and mental health care, the economic loss of stolen or damaged property, lost wages or productivity, and the intangible losses associated with pain and suffering.[16]

Economists Patricio Domínguez and Steven Raphael survey these competing methods and summarize leading studies employing each approach. As they note, no method is perfect. Studies based on real-world transactions, for example, are by necessity indirect—looking at things like housing prices—because "individuals do not directly buy and sell victimization." As a result, these estimates may be confounded by omitted variables or by imperfect information or skewed risk preferences within the markets being used as proxies for crime-avoidance preferences. The survey approach has its own downsides: people may not appreciate the significance of a given percentage-point drop in baseline crime rates or may overstate their willingness to pay for crime avoidance given that they won't actually have to pay what they say they will pay on a survey. Perhaps more fundamentally, because both of these methods use dollars as the metric of individual preferences and measure people's "willingness to pay" for crime avoidance, they systematically "place greater weight on the welfare of the wealthy," who have more money to spend and who spend it more freely than people with lesser means.[17]

Given these divergent modes of measuring the costs of crime, it's unsurprising that estimates vary considerably. Even within a single study, estimates can vary widely depending on the assumptions made to try to surmount the methodological challenges identified above. Even modest differences in the estimated costs of individual criminal events become substantial once aggregated to a societal level. For example, some analyses

Figure 2.2.   Estimates of the Social Cost of Crime, 2014

Real (2015 $Billions)	Mean	Median	Min	Max
Cost of all Crimes by Category				
Murder	110.6	141.0	14.5	215.8
Rape	21.1	21.4	9.7	36.2
Assault	53.0	58.2	11.3	88.6
Robbery	56.0	25.9	4.2	140.9
Burglary	38.2	40.7	3.9	94.6
Larceny	23.1	5.9	2.2	63.5
Vehicle Theft	6.0	5.0	0.9	11.4
Implied Total Cost	307.9	298.0		

Council of Econ. Advisers, *Economic Perspectives on Incarceration and the Criminal Justice System* 35 tbl.1 (2016)

peg the total monetary cost of murder in the United States in 2014 at $14.5 billion dollars, while others put it at $215.8 billion—more than an order of magnitude higher. Likewise, estimates for the societal cost of robbery that same year ranged from a low of $4.2 billion to a high of $140.9 billion.[18]

With margins this wide, determinations of whether a social policy "passes" cost-benefit analysis often turn on which estimate of costs one chooses as a baseline. A great deal thus depends on highly technical methodological choices underlying consequentialist policymaking. This much, however, is clear: Crime is costly. In one of the most cited bottom-up analyses, economist David Anderson estimates the value of risks to life and health caused by crime each year at over a trillion dollars. And as the story of Dennis at the beginning of this chapter makes clear, behind all of these numbers are real people, suffering real harms.[19]

B.   Mechanisms of Crime Control

To say that crime is costly and that crime prevention is a social good does not in itself justify *punishment* as a means of reducing crime. Rather, as Professor Antony Duff observes, there are "many *non*punitive ways of preventing crime—persuasion, education, 'situational crime prevention' for instance, and other measures aimed at removing the causes or occasions of crime." If the overarching utilitarian goal is to maximize social welfare, we should care about the relative effectiveness of these different policy options.[20]

And in fact, economic analyses demonstrate that nonpunitive approaches to crime control are frequently better at reducing or preventing crime than penal sanctions, at least in our current social environment. Consider here the words of the Council of Economic Advisors, which found that "some criminal justice policies, including increased incarceration," are demonstrably less effective than "investments in education" or in policies that expand "legitimate employment opportunities," given the "total costs" of these alternative approaches. Put more simply, even if one assumes that penal sanctions pass a cost-benefit test (on the theory that they yield more social benefit than harm), they do not appear to be particularly *cost-effective*.[21]

We will return to this question of cost-effectiveness at the end of this section, when examining contemporary mass incarceration through a consequentialist lens. And we will return to it again in the following chapter when we explore the broader societal drivers of criminality. Here, though, we focus more narrowly on the specific mechanisms by which punishment might achieve any crime prevention at all — bracketing for now the question of whether using it to do so is efficient or just. In his seminal *Principles of Penal Law*, Jeremy Bentham outlined three such mechanisms that continue to dominate discussions today: *deterrence, rehabilitation*, and *incapacitation*. Let us consider each in turn.

1.   Deterrence: The Basic Theory

Writing in 390 BC, the Greek philosopher Plato insisted that "punishment is not inflicted by a rational man for the sake of the crime that has been committed" but rather "to prevent either the same man or, by the spectacle of his punishment, someone else, from doing wrong again." In "all events," Plato continued, "punishment is inflicted as a deterrent."[22]

The centrality of this argument in penal philosophy was reaffirmed two thousand years later when Bentham called deterrence "the chief end of punishment." Describing what is sometimes called the *hedonistic calculus*, Bentham outlined the basic theory as follows: "When a man perceives or supposes pain to be the consequence of an act," he will "withdraw" from that act if "the apparent magnitude . . . of that pain be greater than the apparent magnitude or value of the pleasure or good he expects to be the consequence of the act." In this respect, Bentham concluded, "every one calculates. Each individual calculates with more or less correctness, according to the degrees of his information, and the power of the motives which actuate him; but all calculate."[23]

In modern times, Bentham's account of deterrence flies under the banner of *rational choice theory*. Spearheaded in the 1960s by American economists led by Gary Becker, this theory holds that "a person commits an offense if the expected utility to him exceeds the utility he could get by using his time and other resources at other activities." A surprising amount is packed into this unassuming assertion. Let's unpack it.[24]

NOTES AND QUESTIONS

1. Utility. For starters, what is *utility*? As used here, utility refers to the total satisfaction an individual derives from an act. This is equivalent to the *net benefit* of the act to the individual — the *benefits* minus the *costs*. When it comes to people contemplating a crime, the kinds of benefits we typically consider in this analysis are wide-ranging. Some are financial, "such as the gains obtained from theft, robbery, insurance fraud, killing a rival drug dealer, etc." Others are more emotional or psychological, "such as the thrill of danger, peer approval, retribution, sense of accomplishment, or 'pure' satisfaction of wants." Importantly, the monetary and psychic benefits of crime are unique to individuals, some of whom will gain more from criminal acts than others.[25]

Likewise, the potential costs of crime are broad and individualized as well. It's important to note, however, that when assessing the utility of a given criminal act, we are focused on the personal costs to the individual who is deciding whether to break the law — not the harms to the victim or society described earlier in this section. Those personal costs can include material ones like "the cost of supplies purchased to commit crimes." Or they can include psychic ones like "guilt, anxiety, fear, dislike of risk, or other emotions associated with committing crime."[26]

On top of all this, and perhaps most relevant when considering the deterrent potential of the criminal law, costs also include the costs associated with "all formal and informal sanctions" imposed on those lawbreakers who are apprehended and sentenced. These sanctions, in turn, can comprise direct costs, like fines or prison time, as well as indirect costs, like social stigma or other collateral consequences.[27]

2. Expected Utility and Bounded Rationality. Next, we must consider what is meant by *expected* utility. The key point here is that individuals make decisions, including the decision to commit a crime, under conditions of uncertainty. They have to make guesses and predictions about the future. Suppose, for example, you are thinking of picking someone's pocket. There is a lot you do not know. Does the person have a wallet? Is there money in it? How much? Will you get caught? What punishment will you receive if you are? The answers to these questions determine both the personal benefits and personal costs of committing the crime. But they are unknown. Your rational calculation must therefore turn on the *potential* benefits and costs—that is, on a prediction of your *expected* utility.*

Importantly, people rarely make these predictive calculations accurately. For one thing, people do not always know what conduct the criminal law proscribes or how severely it punishes different forms of conduct. If most people do not know the details of criminal law doctrine on a given issue, fine-grained distinctions between different legal rules are unlikely to have much effect on their behavior. (We will take up related questions regarding fair notice and ignorance of the law in subsequent chapters.) Separately, some people might misapprehend their chances of getting caught. Psychological biases may also lead people to unduly discount the future pain of a decades-long prison term even when they are aware they could face such punishment. Finally, people may be less likely even to attempt these calculations when it comes to certain expressive or emotionally motivated crimes, as opposed to instrumental ones like theft.[28]

In short, people often exhibit what economists call *bounded rationality*: They calculate risks and rewards, but imperfectly. Consequently, as Professors Paul Robinson and John Darley write, there is reason to hold some "skepticism about the criminal law's deterrent effect—that is, skepticism about the ability to deter crime through the manipulation of criminal law rules and penalties."[29]

3. Opportunity Costs and Inequality.   Finally, what do rational choice theorists mean when they say crime will occur only if its expected utility exceeds that of *other activities*? Note at the outset that rational choice theory predicts an individual will not commit a crime if his expected utility from doing so is negative—that is to say, if the expected costs outweigh the expected benefits. But will he necessarily offend when the expected utility is positive? The answer to that question depends on his alternatives, also known as his *opportunity costs*. After all, a person committing a crime gives up the chance to engage in other, potentially beneficial *legal activity* while he is spending time and effort "planning, performing and concealing the criminal act." If the utility he would receive from that alternative, legal course of action exceeds the utility he'd obtain from crime, the theory predicts he will pursue the legal option.[30]

---

* Relatedly, we can speak of *expected* punishment as a function of sentence length and sentence likelihood: If you face a 50 percent chance of receiving a two-year prison sentence, your *expected* punishment—which is part of your overall expected costs—is one year in prison.

The implications of this last point are significant once we take income inequality into account. As economists of crime observe, "[t]he lower an individual's level of income, the lower is his or her opportunity cost of engaging in illegal activity," as people who "are only able to earn a low wage" will generally not be "giving up substantial legal income" if they turn their energies instead to committing crimes.[31]

Of course, the amount of money a person can earn legally depends on many factors, including "region, rate of unemployment, and IQ" but also "age, sex, race, education, [and] training." For many people, the costs of committing a crime will typically outweigh the benefits. But as philosopher Tommie Shelby explains, for others, the calculus can cut the other way:

> People from all races, classes, and types of neighborhood engage in criminal activity for money, status, power, or amusement. When poor persons from ghettos choose crime, however, they do so under conditions of material deprivation and institutional racism. Thus their criminal activity sometimes expresses something more, or something other, than a character flaw or a disregard for the authority of morality. Some rely on crime to supplement income derived from work, welfare benefits, or private assistance. Others, such as those who have dropped out of the legitimate labor market altogether, who do not qualify for welfare benefits, or who cannot rely on kin support, use crime as their primary source of income.

Hence Becker's observation that "[s]ome persons become 'criminals' . . . not because their basic motivation differs from that of other persons, but because their benefits and costs differ."[32]

4. Specific Deterrence.   Finally, note that rational choice theorists and their critics are often discussing the criminal law's capacity to deter crime in society writ large. The idea here, to recall Plato, is that "the spectacle" of one person's punishment will deter "someone *else* . . . from doing wrong again." Bentham referred to this form of deterrence, "which is applicable to all members of the community," as "general prevention" or *general deterrence*—an idea taken up in the immediately following section. Note though that Bentham distinguished that idea from "particular prevention," also called *specific deterrence*, "which applies to the delinquent himself."[33]

The basic idea of specific deterrence is that a person who is punished will be uniquely deterred from future offending—because the pain of his own prior punishment will be acute, as may be any warning he received that future lawbreaking on his part will be punished more severely on account of his prior criminal record. Some studies isolate and demonstrate the existence of a specific deterrence effect of punishment under certain circumstances, though there is conflicting evidence as to whether and when it is sufficiently large to overcome the criminogenic effects of punishment noted earlier (p. 74).[34]

2.   General Deterrence: The Evidence

Rational choice theory points to certain mechanisms societies might use to try to control crime. As noted above, many of these mechanisms, such as investing in education or public health, are nonpunitive. The choice to use penal mechanisms as opposed to or in addition to these other approaches is an important decision in its own right, which we will take up later in this chapter. For present purposes, though, it bears noting that if one focuses exclusively on the penal system, rational choice theory suggests that actors responsible for drafting and enforcing the criminal law might try to deter crime in a few discrete ways. Specifically, they could try to increase the expected costs of crime to individual offenders—by increasing the likelihood of apprehension, the severity of punishment, or both.[35]

NOTES AND QUESTIONS

1. Likelihood of Apprehension.   Consider first the likelihood of apprehension. The basic intuition that people will shy away from crime when they're likely to get caught animated urbanist Jane Jacobs' famous suggestion that having residents' "eyes on the street" helps to secure vibrant urban spaces.[36]

It also shows up in ethnographic studies, such as this explanation offered in 1991 by an individual who had committed multiple burglaries:

> I don't do this part of town in the summer. Too many kids playing around. But now [in February] the best time to do crime out here is between 8:00 and 9:00 [a.m.] All the mothers are taking the kids to school. I wait until I see the car leave. By the time she gets back, I've come and gone.[37]

Quantitative empiricists seeking to measure the impact of apprehension risk on criminal offending tend to focus on police presence: Does more policing mean less crime? When asking that question, we need to isolate increases merely in police presence from increases in actual arrests, as the latter might depress crime by removing would-be offenders from the community (a topic we'll take up in a moment when discussing incapacitation). If increasing police presence alone depresses crime, that would be meaningful evidence of a deterrence-driven effect.

An increasingly large and sophisticated literature supports the conclusion that this effect is real. In one recent study, for example, economist Steven Mello looks at a 2009 influx in federal grant money for hiring police, which was allocated using an application-score cutoff. Cities just above and just below that cutoff were similarly situated, but only the former got funds to hire more police. When these cities hired more police, they saw crime decline—especially robbery, larceny, and auto theft—with no increase in arrests.[38]

Significantly, the watchful eye need not wear a badge and carry a gun. When Chicago employed community members to monitor certain city blocks during students' travels to and from school, crime on those blocks declined by 18 percent relative to neighboring blocks without monitors. Providing further evidence of the monitors' deterrent effect, the incidence of some crimes *increased* during hours when the monitors were not present and in areas farther from monitored blocks. Quantitative studies also show that increased outdoor lighting—as occurs when new streetlights are installed or during daylight savings time—reduces crime, presumably by increasing the risk of detection.[39]

2. Severity of Punishment. While the crime-reducing impact of increased detection seems well supported, the deterrent effect of increased punishment is less certain. As far back as 1764, Cesare Beccaria asserted that "Crimes are more effectually prevented by the *certainty* than the *severity* of punishment." Centuries later, a series of empirical studies support this view. As reported by Professors Aaron Chalfin and Justin McCrary, "the evidence suggests that the magnitude of deterrence owing to more severe sentencing is not large and is likely to be smaller than the magnitude of deterrence induced by changes in the certainty of capture." They conclude after careful review that "the degree to which offenders are deterred by harsher sanctions remains an open question."[40]

Digging into that empirical debate, some studies suggest that well-publicized and drastic changes in threatened punishment—such as "three strikes" rules that impose severe mandatory sentences for a person's third conviction, no matter how minor the offense—have an appreciable deterrent effect on future offending. As criminologist Paul Cromwell and his colleagues report in their study of burglary:

> When long sentences began to seem inevitable, many of the older, recidivist burglars in our study desisted or took up less serious crime. Some reported getting out of the criminal life entirely, or trying to. One informant told us: "I've been down twice before and the next one could be the 'bitch' [life imprisonment as a habitual offender]. It's not worth it anymore." A larger group reported that they began to participate in less serious crimes. Fearing the consequences of a new felony conviction, many began shoplifting—boosting—a misdemeanor in most jurisdictions. [One] said: "I didn't want to get the bitch so I qui[t] doing burglaries and started shoplifting."[41]

On the other hand, drastic punishments cannot deter people who doubt (rationally or not) that such sentences will actually be imposed. And in fact, most studies that compare young offenders just below the age of criminal majority to older offenders who are just above the line and face harsher sanctions as a result find little evidence of deterrence in the latter group. Likewise, the literature on capital punishment does not find "any credible evidence of deterrence" from the threat of execution. And even in the studies that do find a deterrent effect from heightened punishment, "the *magnitude* of the response is actually quite small once one considers the increase in sentence lengths" associated with policies like the three-strikes laws.[42]

Of course, even if drastic punishments do deter to some degree, that does not in itself mean they are warranted; the high social and personal costs of severe punishment and the possibility that similar benefits could be obtained through nonpunitive means may counsel against such sanctions, as discussed later in this section and in Chapter Three.

3. Rehabilitation

An alternative consequentialist theory of punishment rests not upon deterrence but upon the so-called *rehabilitative ideal.* The basic idea, as Professor Antony Duff describes it, is that penal institutions might "so modify people's dispositions and motives that they will in [the] future refrain from crime willingly—rather than, as with deterrence, doing so reluctantly from fear of punishment." Like deterrence, the rehabilitative ideal has ancient roots, stretching back at least as far as Plato's assertion that "judgment by sentence of law is never inflicted for harm's sake" but rather to make "him that suffers it a better man, or, failing this, less of a wretch." In its most optimistic framing, the rehabilitative ideal echoes Jean-Jacques Rousseau, who said "[t]here is not a single ill-doer who could not be turned to some good."[43]

As a conceptual matter, some argue that rehabilitation is not punishment at all. The point of rehabilitation, after all, is to help people lead more flourishing lives, not to cause them pain. But of course people who are forced to receive such rehabilitation in the form of a prison sentence or community supervision generally do not want such help—they would rather be left alone. Rehabilitative punishment is thus, as Professor Michael Moore writes, "paternalistic in character," which, he argues, prompts some serious objections:

> First, such a paternalistic reform theory allocates scarce societal resources away from other, more deserving groups that want them [such as people who are poor or people who would benefit from mental health treatment. Instead, those resources go] to a group that hardly can be said to deserve such favored status and, moreover, does not want such "benefits." As a simple matter of distributive justice it is difficult to argue that criminals should be favored in the allocation of scarce social resources in these ways. Second, in any political theory according high value to liberty, paternalistic justifications are themselves to be regarded with suspicion. Criminals are not in the standard classes in society for which paternalistic state intervention is appropriate, such as . . . the young, or others whose capacity for rational choice is diminished. . . . Third, such recasting of

punishment in terms of "treatment" for the good of the criminal makes possible a kind of moral blindness that is dangerous in itself. As C.S. Lewis pointed out some years ago, adopting a "humanitarian" conceptualization of punishment makes it easy to inflict treatments and sentences that bear no relation to the desert of the offender. We may do more to others "for their own good" than we ever allow ourselves to do when we see that it is really for our good that we act.[44]

These arguments speak to the potential danger of locking people up "for their own good." It remains possible, however, that rehabilitation advances a broader, societal good.* After all, everyone is better off if people who commit crimes don't commit any more. And notably, while there is evidence that incarceration is criminogenic (p. 74), there is also evidence that certain types of rehabilitative programming—offered within and outside of prison—can help people avoid future offending. Consider the following from Professor Joan Petersilia:

> Rehabilitation programs reduce recidivism if they incorporate proven principles and are targeted to specific offenders. Research demonstrates that offenders who earn a high school equivalency diploma while behind bars are more likely to get jobs after release. Those who receive vocational skills training are more likely to get jobs and higher wages after release. And those who go through intensive drug treatment programs in prison are less likely to relapse outside of it. If we could implement effective programs, we could expect to reduce recidivism by 15 to 20 percent. To put it in concrete terms: About 495,000 of the 750,000 prisoners who will be released this year are likely to be rearrested within three years. With effective programs, we could reduce the number of repeat offenders by nearly 100,000. We could do even better if these efforts were linked to improved services in the community upon release. Such efforts would pay for themselves by reducing future criminal justice and corrections costs. Economist Mark A. Cohen and criminologist Alex Piquero found in a recent study that a high-risk youth who becomes a chronic offender costs society between $4.2 and $7.2 million, principally in police and court outlays, property losses, and medical care. You either pay now or pay later—and you pay a lot more later.

Consistent with Petersilia's analysis, Professors Mark Lipsey and Francis Cullen report that "every meta-analysis of large samples of studies comparing

---

* It is also possible that Moore is wrong to say people who have committed crimes are undeserving of "favored status" in our moral calculus. In a novel rejoinder to conventional wisdom and practice, Professors Christopher Lewis and Benjamin Ewing separately argue that people who recidivate ought to be punished *less* severely than people who are convicted of an offense for the first time—precisely because the burden of a first conviction makes them less culpable the second time around. *See* Christopher Lewis, *The Paradox of Recidivism,* 70 Emory L.J. 1209 (2021); Benjamin Ewing, *Prior Convictions as Moral Opportunities,* 46 Am. J. Crim. L. 283 (2019).

offenders who receive rehabilitation treatment with those who do not has found lower mean recidivism for those in the treatment conditions."[45]

And yet, it is important to recognize that even the most optimistic account suggests only a moderate impact. Effective rehabilitative programs "could reduce the number of repeat offenders by nearly 100,000," Petersilia says, but that would still leave 400,000 people "who will be released this year [and] are likely to be rearrested within three years." The rehabilitative ideal has always struggled against this reality. And perhaps perversely, this very shortcoming has often led policymakers to abandon rehabilitation altogether. As noted in Chapter One, prison reformers throughout American history have attempted to turn prisons into genuine sites of reformation but have not succeeded in embedding the rehabilitative ideal within American penology. Many contemporary scholars trace the ideal's most recent fall, which coincided with the rise of mass incarceration, to an influential article written in 1974 that highlighted the perceived ineffectiveness of rehabilitative efforts. Known as the Martinson Report, the article famously asked "What works?" when it comes to rehabilitation programming, and suggested the answer is "nothing." Martinson's argument was immediately challenged, and Martinson himself later walked back his initial damning assessment. But it was too late. As Professor David Garland reports, the years following his initial report saw "an astonishingly sudden draining away of support for the ideal of rehabilitation."[46]

All of which raises a question: Is the decline of the rehabilitative ideal a good thing or ought we hope for its return? On the one hand, abandoning proven efforts to rehabilitate people could be a net loss for society and those who lose out on beneficial programs. On the other hand, paying lip service to the rehabilitative ideal while failing to fulfill it might justify a set of penal sanctions and practices, up to and including incarceration, that are based on a rehabilitative mirage. Along these lines, consider this passage from the Supreme Court's decision in *Tapia v. United States*, 564 U.S. 319 (2011), in which the Court held that a federal trial judge lacks authority to extend a prison sentence in order to make the person being sentenced eligible for rehabilitative programming:

> For almost a century, the Federal Government employed in criminal cases a system of indeterminate sentencing . . . [that] was premised on a faith in rehabilitation. . . . A convict, the theory went, should generally remain in prison only until he was able to reenter society safely. His release therefore often coincided with "the successful completion of certain vocational, educational, and counseling programs within the prisons." S. Rep. No. 98-225, p. 40 (1983). . . . But this model of indeterminate sentencing eventually fell into disfavor. . . . Lawmakers and others increasingly doubted that prison programs could "rehabilitate individuals on a routine basis" — or that parole officers could "determine accurately whether or when a particular prisoner ha[d] been rehabilitated." S. Rep., at 40. Congress

accordingly enacted the Sentencing Reform Act of 1984 . . . [which states] that "imprisonment is not an appropriate means of promoting correction and rehabilitation." [18 U.S.C. §3582(a).]

. . . [T]he sentencing court here did nothing wrong — and probably something very right — in trying to get Tapia into an effective drug treatment program. But the record indicates that the court may have done more — that it may have selected the length of the sentence to ensure that Tapia could complete [a] 500 Hour Drug Program. "The sentence has to be sufficient," the court explained, "to provide needed correctional treatment, and here I think the needed correctional treatment is the 500 Hour Drug Program." The "number one" thing [the trial judge went on,] "is the need to provide treatment. In other words, so she is in long enough to get the 500 Hour Drug Program." These statements suggest that the court may have calculated the length of Tapia's sentence to ensure that she receive certain rehabilitative services. And that a sentencing court may not do.

4. Incapacitation

The final consequentialist justification for punishment — incapacitation — is often presented as "the least complicated." The basic idea is captured by James Q. Wilson. "Wicked people exist," he says. "Nothing avails except to set them apart from innocent people." Writing in support of the Clinton-era crime bill, columnist Ben Wattenberg infamously put the point even more bluntly: "A thug in prison cannot shoot your sister."[47]

Wattenberg's rhetoric — and particularly his use of the coded and racially charged word *thug* — may strike many as offensive. But the core incapacitationist argument is not without a point. Incarcerating people who have committed crimes makes it difficult for them to hurt people outside of prison. Note, however, that this fact alone does not necessarily mean that incapacitation reduces crime. Rather, the true crime-reducing effects of incapacitation are complicated by the possibility that incarceration simply *relocates*, *postpones*, or perhaps even *stimulates* future crime.[48]

NOTES AND QUESTIONS

1. Relocating Crime. Consider first relocation. Incarceration in and of itself does not stop people from committing crimes. It stops them from committing crimes outside of prison. Incarceration, in other words, might simply shift "the locus of crime from one side of the prison wall to the other." For this reason, Professors Guyora Binder and Ben Notterman argue that it would be better to speak in terms of "'segregation' rather than 'incapacitation' of offenders."[49]

Social scientists who measure "incapacitation effects" sometimes ignore crime within prisons, which Ben Gifford argues is both immoral and illogical. Exposure to crime, he argues, is not "part of the punishment" someone receives when sent to prison, nor should we assume "that prison crime is preferable to crime in the outside world." We must, in other words, account for prison crime itself as a cost of incarceration. And as Gifford goes on to explain, while "available data is scarce, the information we have suggests that crime, especially violent crime, is rampant in prisons and jails."

> That prison rape is common should come as no surprise to those steeped in American popular culture. The potential magnitude of the phenomenon is nevertheless astounding: According to a recent BJS study . . . a full 4% of state and federal prisoners surveyed between 2011 and 2012 reported experiencing at least one incident of sexual victimization in the prior year. . . . Indeed, the Department of Justice (DOJ) concluded [recently] that "more than 209,400 persons were victims of sexual abuse in prisons, jails, and juvenile facilities" in 2008 [and that] "at least 78,500 prison and jail inmates . . . were victims of the most serious forms of sexual abuse."
>
> Even for those who are spared the horrors of sexual abuse, prison is a violent place. A 2004 survey conducted by the BJS found that 32.6% of state prisoners reported being injured since admission, with 15.9% reporting that they were hurt in a fight. More recent studies have suggested an even harsher reality, with some scholars finding that as many as one-third of prison inmates reported being physically assaulted in a six-month period.

Given these statistics, Professor Chris Lewis points out, "decisions about who we incarcerate, and for how long, may dictate *who* gets hurt, and whose rights are violated—but not *whether* people get hurt, or how much."[50]

2. Postponing Crime. Consider next the possibility that incarceration simply postpones criminal offending to a later date. Over ninety-five percent of people sent to prison eventually get released. What happens when they return to the community? If prisons are criminogenic, as multiple studies indicate, people released from prison may actually produce *more* crime in the long run. Incarceration, in other words, would not so much incapacitate crime as borrow against the future—with interest. Indeed, incarceration is likely to produce an enduring downward effect on crime over a person's lifespan only if at least one of two things is true: incarceration successfully rehabilitates people or deters future offending, or it locks them up until they "age out" of criminality, incarcerating them past the age at which they might be likely to engage in further offending after being released. Some lengthy sentences might produce this latter effect. But it is doubtful that American incarceration achieves it in the aggregate.[51]

3. Replacement Effects. As Judge Richard Posner once explained, it is possible that "removing one offender from the pool of offenders[] simply make[s] a career in crime more attractive to someone else, who is balanced on the razor's edge between criminal and legitimate activity and who now faces reduced competition in the crime 'market.'" United States v. Jackson,

835 F.2d 1195, 1199 (7th Cir. 1987) (Posner, J., concurring). The more market-like a given form of criminal behavior (think drug sales), the more likely it is that sending one actor to prison will simply draw someone else in—someone who had not previously been participating in the illicit market. In such a scenario, incarceration is not reducing crime; it is producing new offenders.[52]

Empirical scholars of incarceration acknowledge that replacement effects are real, though their magnitude is difficult to measure. One way to get around this problem is to study the amount of crime that occurs in a place, rather than the amount of crime committed by particular people. Using strategies like these, Professor Shawn Bushway reports, "[t]he best modern estimates for the size of the [incapacitation] effect are modest, in the neighborhood of two to five serious crimes per year" for each individual who is incarcerated. Based on these studies, he goes on, it seems safe to say that "incapacitation is real," in the sense that incarcerating people does cause some reduction in crime outside of prison during the period of incarceration. Whether that reduction is worth its social costs, however, is a separate question—one that must consider the magnitudes of those costs and the reduction in crime itself.[53]

C. Mixed Theory (Again): Retributive Constraints on Utilitarian Means

Each of the mechanisms discussed thus far—deterrence, rehabilitation, incapacitation—holds some promise to prevent future crime. If that reduction is large enough, it could produce so much social benefit that punishment would become attractive from a utilitarian perspective. It is important to note, however, that for most modern utilitarians, overwhelming social benefit alone will not always justify punishment. Rather, just as some retributivist philosophers endorse a "mixed" version of retributivism that embraces some utilitarian principles (pp. 67-69), many utilitarians today recognize some retributive limits on utilitarian analysis.

To appreciate this point, consider a thought experiment suggested by philosopher H.J. McCloskey in the 1960s. McCloskey imagined a sheriff in a southern town faced with a large and bloodthirsty lynch mob that wants to kill a Black man whom it believes—with no basis—committed a murder. The sheriff concludes that if he frames this innocent Black man, he will pacify the mob and save multiple other innocent Black people from being killed. This hypothetical may seem farfetched today, but it would not have been a century ago.[54]

A *pure* utilitarian might well argue that McCloskey's sheriff ought to sacrifice the innocent man—arresting him, prosecuting him, perhaps even executing him—if doing so would save the lives of multiple other people.

As Professor Antony Duff observes, "the aim of efficient crime-prevention could in principle sanction the deliberate 'punishment' of those known to have committed no offense at all . . . for the sake of efficient deterrence," as might plausibly occur if state actors investigating a notorious crime make an example of an innocent person to send a message that crime will not be tolerated.[55]

To a great many people (including Duff), this conclusion is untenable. The state ought not punish an innocent person because doing so "is an *intrinsic* wrong." Indeed, this proposition is the core tenet of *negative retributivism* discussed earlier in this chapter: "one who is not guilty must not be punished." As philosopher J.L. Mackie observes, this principle is "very widely, perhaps universally" accepted, including by utilitarians. As a result, most contemporary utilitarians are not *pure* utilitarians in the absolute sense of the term. Rather, in the words of philosopher H.L.A. Hart, they contend that the "general justifying aim" of punishment is the maximization of social welfare, but, as Duff notes, they view that aim as "constrained by the demands that we punish only those who have voluntarily broken the law, and that the severity of the punishment be proportionate to the seriousness of the crime for which it is imposed." As Duff concludes, "[t]he resulting theory preserves the central consequentialist thought that punishment is justified only if it is a cost-effective way of achieving certain beneficial consequences. But it avoids the familiar objections to *purely* consequentialist accounts by building in side-constraints that preclude the objectionable implications of such accounts."[56]

Questions: Recall Michael Anderson's case. What arguments might a pure or constrained utilitarian offer in favor of making him serve his sentence? What arguments might be advanced against punishing him? How do arguments grounded in the three mechanisms of utilitarian crime-prevention differ from each other in this context? Do they all cut in the same direction? What should a judge do if they do not? Finally, is there empirical information you would like to have—or think you need—to craft or evaluate these arguments? And what ought a judge do if such evidence is unavailable or insufficiently robust?

D.   Mass Incarceration Through the Cost-Benefit Lens

What bottom-line conclusions might cost-benefit analysis yield with respect to the penal policies that have produced mass incarceration? Consider the President's Council of Economic Advisors' assessment, offered in 2016:

> Several economists have performed formal cost-benefit calculations of criminal justice policies. Given the small size of the marginal impact of

incarceration on crime, *most cost-benefit calculations find that the costs of incarceration and sentencing policy outweigh the benefits in the United States,* even though many of these calculations do not consider the added indirect costs related to collateral consequences.

In other words, "[g]iven the total costs, some criminal justice policies, *including increased incarceration, fail a cost-benefit test.*"[57]

Note part of the mechanism driving this conclusion: "the small size of the marginal impact of incarceration on crime." As Professor Shawn Bushway explains, in a society that already incarcerates the individuals who cause the most harm, "the only way to incarcerate more people is to incarcerate offenders who commit fewer crimes." In other words, "[w]hen incarceration rates are high, further incarceration entails incapacitating" people whose "incarceration will yield fewer public safety benefits." The leading study demonstrating this effect, by Rucker Johnson and Steven Raphael, elaborates:

> [W]e find that the effect on crime rates of incarcerating one more inmate has declined drastically over the past quarter century. . . . For 1978–90, we estimate that each additional prison-year served prevented approximately 30 index crimes. For the period 1991–2004, the comparable value is eight. . . . This large decline in the marginal effect of an inmate suggests that the most recent increases in incarceration have been driven by the institutionalization of many inmates who, relative to previous periods, pose less of a threat to society. Indeed, given the much lower crime-abating effects for the most recent period, it is likely the case that for many recent inmates, the benefits to society in terms of crime reduction are unlikely to outweigh the explicit monetary costs of housing and maintaining an additional inmate. Moreover, once we account[] for the additional external costs of incarceration, such as the adverse effects on the families of inmates, the effects on victimizations behind bars, the effects of additional HIV/AIDS infections, and the potential effects on the long-term employment prospects of former inmates, the benefit-cost ratio on the margin is likely to be substantially less than one.[58]

In sum, the Council of Economic Advisors concludes, "given the size of the U.S. incarcerated population, the aggregate crime-reducing impact of increasing incarceration rates is likely to be minimal" and not worth the substantial costs on the other side of the ledger, particularly given the alternative strategies — such as investing in education and employment programs — that data suggest are more cost-effective.[59]

The empirical analyses producing this conclusion are complex. In the face of such complexity, Bentham urged caution before embracing punitive social policies. Legislators, he warned, could get the cost-benefit calculus wrong in either direction, either criminalizing too much or too little in the quest for welfare maximization. But an "error on the maximum side," meaning too much punishment, he warned, "is that to which legislators and men in general are naturally inclined: antipathy, or a want of compassion for individuals who are represented as dangerous and vile, pushes them onward to an undue severity. It is on this side, therefore, that we should take the most precautions, as on this side there has been shown the greatest disposition to err."[60]

And yet, some contemporary observers fear that policymakers today talk the talk of cost-benefit analysis without doing the hard work necessary to get it right. In the words of Professors Paul Robinson and John Darley, consequentialism sometimes appears as "more a style of conversation — 'deterrence speak' — than a true reliance upon deterrence analysis." A leading criminology text argues that this faux consequentialism can mask an almost unthinking punitivism:

> [T]he real risk is . . . a crass and simplistic rational choice theory. In this version, the claim is made that because offenders are rational, they can be "scared straight" by making sure that "crime does not pay." This mindset justifies setting *severe* penalties and increasing costs unendingly until crime is reduced. The logic of this populist version of rational choice is dangerous. If crime does not go down, then this is taken as evidence that even harsher punishments are needed; and if crime does go down, then this is taken as evidence that severity is the key to solving the crime problem. The potential ineffectiveness of severe sanctions thus can never be demonstrated because both failure and success are taken as evidence in favor of their use.[61]

For all their differences, then, utilitarianism and retributivism might share something in common. Despite the nuanced caveats of philosophers and experts in both camps, their words can be heard by policymakers and the broader public as arguments for expanding the scope and severity of American punishment.

III.   A SOCIOLOGICAL THEORY OF PUNISHMENT

The preceding two sections outlined the dominant penal philosophies of retributivism and consequentialism. These competing theories are often framed as irreconcilably divergent approaches. One looks backward to past conduct and grounds punishment in moral desert; the other looks forward to the consequences of punishment and justifies punishment by the social benefit it aims to afford society as a whole. And yet, notwithstanding these differences, theorists dating back at least as far as sociologist Émile Durkheim have argued that the "two opposing theories" can and "must be reconciled."[62]

For Durkheim and others, one route to reconciliation is to consider a broader range of possible functions criminal law might serve in society.

Rather than focus solely on reducing crime, these scholars ask what role it might serve in reinforcing the central sociological bonds that keep a society together. Punishment, on this account, is justified as a tool for expressing and reinforcing a society's shared moral fabric—including, potentially, a thread of retributivism that, as a matter of sociological reality, seems to run through that fabric, whether we want it to or not. This argument, often known as *expressivism*, has a number of prominent proponents, as well as some prominent critics.

A.   *Criminal Law as Expression of Social Values*

Proponents of expressivism argue that punishment reinforces social cohesion by communicating to the members of a society what their shared moral commitments are and by confirming—to everyone—that those commitments remain intact even when they are violated by individual transgressors. Retributive practices, on this view, could be *instrumentally* useful if people in society have, as a matter of psychological reality, a shared and largely inescapable set of retributive instincts. Failure to respect those instincts, the argument goes, could cause people to doubt whether society shares their values, to question the existence of a shared moral commitment, and, eventually, to falter in their own devotion to the law. Acting in accordance with felt retributive instincts might avoid such bad outcomes, and thus yield what Professors Paul Robinson and John Darley call the "utility of desert."

Consider the following excerpts, which explore this expressivist thesis.

Émile Durkheim, *The Division of Labor in Society* 46, 63 (W.D. Halls trans., 1984) (1893). [Punishment's] real function is to maintain inviolate the cohesion of society by sustaining the common consciousness in all its vigour. If that consciousness were thwarted . . . it would necessarily lose some of its power . . . [and] there would result a relaxation in the bonds of social solidarity. The consciousness must therefore be conspicuously reinforced the moment it is met with opposition. The sole means of doing so is to give voice to the unanimous aversion that the crime continues to evoke, and this by an official act, which can only mean suffering inflicted upon the wrongdoer. . . . [T]his suffering is not a gratuitous act of cruelty. It is a sign indicating that the sentiments of the collectivity are still unchanged, that the communion of minds sharing the same beliefs remains absolute. . . . [I]n truth, punishment has remained, at least in part, a work of vengeance. It is said that we do not make the culpable suffer in order to make him suffer; it is none the less true that we find it just that he suffer. Perhaps [this instinct is] wrong, but that is not the question. We seek, at the moment, to define punishment as it is or has been, not as it ought to be.

R.A. Duff, *Punishment, Communication, and Community* 80-82, 89 (2001). The criminal law of a liberal polity, and the criminal process of trial and conviction to which offenders are subjected, are communicative enterprises that address the citizens, as rational moral agents, in the normative language of the community's values. The criminal law . . . speaks to the citizens as members of the normative community. It seeks not just (as might a sovereign) their obedience to its demands, but their understanding and acceptance of what is required of them as citizens. . . . In defining certain kinds of conduct as public wrongs, the law seeks to persuade citizens (those who need persuading) to refrain from such conduct. . . . To say this is not, however, to posit a consequentialist aim for the criminal law or for criminal convictions — to portray them as contingently efficient means to the independently identifiable end of crime-prevention. . . . The aim is not simply that citizens refrain from crime or that offenders refrain from repeating their crimes. . . . It is, rather, that citizens recognize and accept the law's requirements as being justified and refrain from crime for that reason, or that offenders recognize the wrongfulness of their past crimes and refrain from future crimes for that reason. . . .

We can justify punishment in a similar way: as a communicative enterprise focused on the past crime . . . [that looks] to a future aim to which it is related, not merely contingently as an instrumental technique, but internally as an intrinsically appropriate means. We can thus provide a unitary justification of punishment. . . . Punishment will now look both back (as retributivists insist it must) to a past crime as that which merits this response, and forward (as consequentialists insist it must) to some future good that it aims to achieve.

J.L. Mackie, *Morality and the Retributive Emotions*, 1 Crim. Just. Ethics 3, 3, 7-9 (1982). The paradox is that, on the one hand, a retributive principle of punishment cannot be explained or developed within a reasonable system of moral thought, while, on the other hand, such a principle cannot be eliminated from our moral thinking. . . . How, then, are we to resolve the paradox of retribution? It ceases to be puzzling [if] we make the . . . move of saying that moral distinctions are founded on sentiment, not on reason. . . . When we seek to rationalize our moral thinking, to turn it into a system of objective requirements, we cannot make sense of [our focus on] retrospectivity [in punishment]. We either, with the utilitarians, attempt to deny it and eliminate it or to subordinate it to forward looking purposes, or, with their retributivist opponents, try various desperate and incoherent devices, none of which . . . will really accommodate the principle of desert within any otherwise intelligible order of ideas. But if we recognize them simply as sentiments — though socially developed sentiments — we have no difficulty in understanding their obstinately retrospective character.

Paul H. Robinson & John M. Darley, *The Utility of Desert*, 91 Nw. U. L. Rev. 453, 454, 457-458 (1997). [S]ociety ought to assign criminal punishments on essentially just desert grounds . . . [because] a criminal law based on the community's perceptions of just desert is, from a utilitarian perspective, the more effective strategy for reducing crime. . . . The real power to gain compliance with society's rules of prescribed conduct lies not in the threat or reality of official criminal sanction, but in the . . . networks of interpersonal relationships in which people find themselves [and] the social norms and prohibitions shared among those relationships and transmitted through those social networks. . . . The law is not irrelevant to these social and personal forces. Criminal law, in particular, plays a central role in creating and maintaining the social consensus necessary for sustaining moral norms. In fact, in a society as diverse as ours, the criminal law may be the only society-wide mechanism that transcends cultural and ethnic differences. Thus, the criminal law's most important real-world effect may be its ability to assist in the building, shaping, and maintaining of these norms and moral principles. It can contribute to and harness the compliance-producing power of interpersonal relationships and personal morality. . . . Thus, we assert, the criminal law's moral credibility is essential to effective crime control, and is enhanced if the distribution of criminal liability is perceived as "doing justice," that is, if it assigns liability and punishment in ways that the community perceives as consistent with the community's principles of appropriate liability and punishment. Conversely, the system's moral credibility, and therefore its crime control effectiveness, is undermined by a distribution of liability that deviates from community perceptions of just desert.

B. Critiques of the Communitarian Account

The sociological theory described in the preceding section is fundamentally communitarian in character. It grounds punishment's legitimacy in a desire to preserve a collective moral, social, and legal order. But is the premise of this argument correct? That is to say, is it coherent to describe modern American society as a shared communitarian endeavor? And more directly, do people have a shared set of moral instincts with respect to punishment? Consider the following passages:

Jeffrie Murphy, *Marxism and Retribution*, 2 Phil. & Pub. Affs. 217, 240 (1973). [Some theories of punishment presuppose] what might be called a "gentlemen's club" picture of the relation between man and society—i.e., men are viewed as being part of a community of shared values and rules. The rules benefit all concerned and, as a kind of debt for the benefits derived, each man owes obedience to the rules. In the absence of such obedience, he deserves punishment in the sense that he owes payment for the benefits. For, as rational man, he can see that the rules benefit everyone (himself included) and that he would have selected them in the original position of choice.

Now this may not be too far off for certain kinds of criminals — e.g., business executives guilty of tax fraud. . . . But to think that it applies to the typical criminal, from the poorer classes, is to live in a world of social and political fantasy. Criminals typically are not members of a shared community of values with their jailers; they suffer from what Marx calls alienation. And they certainly would be hard-pressed to name the benefits for which they are supposed to owe obedience. If justice, as both Kant and Rawls suggest, is based on reciprocity, it is hard to see what these persons are supposed to reciprocate for.

John Rappaport, *Some Doubts About "Democratizing" Criminal Justice*, 87 U. Chi. L. Rev. 711, 739-740, 743-744 (2020).   [There is a prominent notion] that Americans reside in reasonably cohesive communities that are capable of forming and expressing . . . "community values" and "community views" of justice. Most accounts [along these lines] are nostalgic, even romantic. . . . [But] "We the people" have always been an exclusive bunch. We can imagine idyllic, homogeneous colonial villages[, for example,] only by blinking the women, blacks, and other marginalized groups who did not share in old-world self-governance. . . .

[T]he criminal justice system of colonial America . . . simply did something different from what we need our law to do today. Colonial justice enforced the dominant norms of white Christian men and excluded those who would not conform. It did not attempt to reconcile conflicting views of a heterogeneous populace.

True, . . . work by Professor Paul Robinson and others . . . has found surprising concordance in lay judgments of desert. [But] there is a credible argument that Robinson — and those who rely on his findings — overstate the extent of lay consensus. . . . [And] the consensus Robinson does find concerns only relative, not absolute, blameworthiness. People largely agree, that is, on how to rank offenses in order of severity. But Robinson does not find that people agree on how severely to punish any particular offense, and many others have found that they do not. For a project that envisions aligning criminal punishment with "community views of justice" . . . this distinction matters.

Donald Braman et al., *Some Realism About Punishment Naturalism*, 77 U. Chi. L. Rev. 1531, 1552-1553, 1556 (2010).   [I]s the public really in agreement about the relative seriousness of the vast majority of bad acts committed in the United States? . . . [T]he number of people estimated to be using marijuana in the last year alone exceeded the number of all those estimated to have suffered criminal victimization of any kind. Add prostitution (recent studies find that more than one in six adult males has paid for sex) and you begin to see just how common controversial crimes are. . . . While far harder to estimate, surveys suggest that rates of willful tax evasion—the seriousness of which is also disputed—run as high as 25 percent of the population. . . . [A] third of [survey] participants [believe] smoking marijuana should bring no penalty at all. A similarly large percentage of the population felt the same way about prostitution. [These data] provide enough evidence of public dissensus on these issues to make one wonder how [anyone] can be so confident in their claims that our understandings of wrong acts are so broadly shared and deeply nuanced.

IV. CHALLENGING THE STATE'S AUTHORITY TO PUNISH

As the excerpts in the preceding section from Professors John Rappaport and Jeffrie Murphy highlight, some arguments against a communitarian theory of punishment go beyond the claim that communities are heterogeneous, or even that some segments of a community are excluded from majoritarian decision making. Rather, there is the further claim that in some societies— including the United States—the state itself has created, maintained, or, at the least, tolerated structural inequities that subordinate and oppress the groups who typically bear the brunt of the state's penal sanctions. These circumstances pose the possibility that, to quote Professors Erin Kelly and Göran Duus-Otterström, "punishment might be permissible in an ideal society [but] could well be impermissible in imperfect societies such as ours."[63]

The excerpts that follow begin to examine this essential question, which we will explore in more depth in the next chapter: Does the state have authority to punish when the society it has cultivated is marked by systemic injustice? Consider the following passages.

R.A. Duff, *Blame, Moral Standing and the Legitimacy of the Criminal Trial*, 23 Ratio 123, 136-138 (2010). Theorists and practitioners of criminal justice are often concerned about the possibility of doing penal justice in contexts of serious social injustice. Suppose that the criminal law itself, viewed (as far as this is possible) independently of its social and political context, meets the requirements of justice: it defines as criminal only wrongful kinds of conduct . . . [and] convicts [people] only given certain proof of their guilt. . . . Most importantly, [assume] the criminal law treats all those subject to it (at least formally) as equals: neither in its content nor in its procedures does it discriminate against any group. However, the society's broader social, political and economic structures involve various kinds of serious, systemic injustice. Certain groups (identified by race, class, or income) suffer serious, unjust disadvantages: they are excluded from many rights and benefits that others enjoy in virtue of their membership of the

polity—educational or vocational opportunities, welfare provision, political participation, and so on. It is also (and, of course, non-coincidentally)
true that a large proportion of those who appear in the criminal courts
belong to these groups[.]

[W]e should surely be worried about the justice of convicting and punishing [members of such groups] for their crimes. . . . To put a person on
trial is to call him to answer . . . to his fellow citizens [and] to the polity . . . in
whose name the court acts . . . . But there is more to being a member of such
a community than being answerable to your fellows in its criminal courts.
. . . [T]o be a member is to be entitled to appropriate respect and concern
from one's fellow citizens both collectively and individually . . . . But that
is just what this defendant has not received from his fellow citizens: rather
than being included, as an equal participant, in the rights and benefits of
citizenship, he has been systematically excluded from significant aspects of
them; those who would now call him to account as a fellow citizen have notably failed to treat him as a fellow citizen in their dealings with him outside the
criminal law. But citizenship cannot be divided: that failure to treat him as a
citizen outside the court cannot be dismissed as irrelevant . . . . [I]t would be
reasonable for him to argue that the polity that has failed hitherto to treat
him as a citizen cannot legitimately or with integrity now insist that he must
answer in this court for his wrongdoing. This would not be to deny that he did
wrong, or that he should answer for it (at least to its victims). It would rather
be to deny the standing of this court to call him to answer to this charge.

Victor Tadros, *Poverty and Criminal Responsibility*, 43 J. Value Inquiry 391, 391,
393 (2009). Let us suppose that . . . the state has responsibility for reducing
criminogenic social conditions and that, by perpetuating economic injustice, it has failed adequately to achieve this. To what extent can these two
things undermine the entitlement of the society to hold poor individuals
criminally responsible for what they do? . . . Our right to blame them, it
might be argued, is eroded by the fact that we perpetrated the injustice
. . . even if they are responsible for what they have done. There are different explanations of how our standing to hold others responsible may be
eroded, but [one is] . . . complicity: the fact that one person participates in
the wrong of someone else deprives the one of standing to hold the other
person responsible for the wrong. A person cannot act as judge when he
ought to be a co-defendant. . . . From this we can derive a moral claim that
poor people have for the state to refrain from holding them responsible for
their crimes, even if they are in fact responsible for them. In recognizing
this, we do not . . . regard their actions as either justified or excused. There
may be someone who can hold them responsible for what they have done.
But the person who can do this is not the author of the circumstances that
make their wrongdoing more likely to occur. In holding them criminally
responsible, we perpetrate a kind of injustice against them.

Erin Kelly, *The Limits of Blame: Rethinking Punishment and Responsibility* 168-169 (2018). Individualized blame diverts attention from a relevant acknowledgment of shared responsibility for factors that help to explain why crime is committed. Though a person's choice to commit a crime may have been a morally bad one, limiting our moral attention to that fact is objectionable when institutional and social factors unjustly limit an agent's access to reasonable alternatives. . . . Not only have the state's policies, such as a history of enforced residential segregation by race, contributed to joblessness and enduring poverty; they have undercut the stabilizing social structures and opportunities that help to prevent crime. Under these circumstances, the state's moral failures are obscured by blaming and stigmatizing individual wrongdoers.

Tommie Shelby, *Dark Ghettos* 3, 207-208, 215-220 (2016). The presence of ghettos in American cities is a strong indication that just background conditions do not prevail. . . . The impact of ideological, institutional, and structural racism is deepest in dark ghettos, because racism and neighborhood disadvantage combine to create a uniquely stigmatized subgroup of the black population. . . . [I]t is enormously difficult for the black poor to leave ghettos, because either they cannot afford to move out or residents of nonghetto areas—whether because of racial prejudice, class bias, or narrow self-interest—inhibit the urban poor from joining these more advantaged communities. Many among the black poor are effectively confined to ghetto neighborhoods. . . . A social order that relegates a segment of its citizenry to humiliating forms of exploitation cannot reasonably expect allegiance from that oppressed group. . . . The existence of the dark ghetto—with its combination of racial stigma, neighborhood disadvantage, inadequate schools, fragile families, forced servitude, and shocking incarceration rates—is simply incompatible with any meaningful form of reciprocity among free and equal citizens. . . .

If this conjecture is correct, then when the ghetto poor in the United States refuse to respect the authority of the law qua law, they do not thereby violate the principle of reciprocity or shirk valid civic obligations. . . . The ghetto poor do have duties, natural duties, that are not defined by civic reciprocity and thus are not negated by the existence of even a grossly unjust social order. Among these is the duty not to be cruel. There is a duty to not cause unnecessary suffering. There is a duty of mutual respect: to show due respect for the moral personhood of others. . . . Yet fulfilling one's natural duties to others may nevertheless be compatible with a number of unlawful actions. . . . [T]aking the possessions of others, especially when these others are reasonably well off, may be permissible. Mugging someone at gunpoint does not show sufficient respect for the victim's claim to be free from threats against their person. But shoplifting and other forms of theft might be permissible. . . . [G]iven the advantages of concerted group action, participating in gangs may be a defensible and effective means to secure needed income. Something similar can be said in favor of prostitution, welfare fraud, tax evasion, selling stolen goods, and other off-the-books transactions in the underground economy. . . . My goal is not to mark the precise line between permissible crimes and impermissible ones but only to offer reasons for thinking that not all crimes perpetrated by the ghetto poor are wrong and that condemning criminal transgressions as a violation of civic responsibility is misplaced.

A.   *Abolition*

If it is true, as the theorists above argue, that governments in the United States lack the moral standing to blame some individuals for at least certain criminal conduct, what follows from that conclusion?

One potential answer is that such punishment itself is illegitimate and ought to be abolished. *Penal abolition* is a phrase containing multitudes. In the words of one leading abolitionist scholar, Professor Dorothy Roberts, abolition is an "amorphous" collection "of theories, principles, and strategies" that can sometimes be "hard to pin down." But as Roberts goes on to explain, it is possible to articulate "three central tenets that are common to formulations of abolitionist philosophy."

> First, today's carceral punishment system can be traced back to slavery and the racial capitalist regime it relied on and sustained. Second, the expanding criminal punishment system functions to oppress black people and other politically marginalized groups in order to maintain a racial capitalist regime. Third, we can imagine and build a more humane and democratic society that no longer relies on caging people to meet human needs and solve social problems.[64]

For decades, penal abolition was a topic largely ignored in American criminal law courses. Professor Máximo Langer, who ultimately does not subscribe to abolitionism, argues that this omission is problematic. Even if one disagrees with abolitionist thinking or approaches, he says, there is no denying that abolitionism represents a "powerful social movement and set of ideas" in contemporary American politics and that "it is important to engage in these types of critical discussions to identify the best way forward." Toward that end, we will examine this set of ideas and related practices closely in the final chapter of this book, exploring the contemporary abolitionist movement as well as prominent arguments against this school of thought. We place this discussion at the close of the book not because we think it unimportant but because we see contemporary American penal abolitionism as a response to pathologies that must be diagnosed before delving into potential prescriptions or interventions.[65]

For now, it is enough to observe that abolition is one potential answer to the challenge posed above by Duff, Tadros, Kelly, and Shelby: If a state that has created, perpetuated, or tolerated systemic injustice lacks the moral authority to blame, perhaps it has no legitimate authority to punish at all. And perhaps, as many abolitionist scholars argue, suggesting otherwise is its own form of legitimation and perpetuation of injustice. Consider the passages below from Dylan Rodríguez and Allegra McLeod:

Dylan Rodríguez, *Abolition as Praxis of Human Being: A Foreword*, 132 Harv. L. Rev. 1575, 1576-1577 (2019).   Contemporary reformist approaches to addressing the apparent overreach and scandalous excesses of the carceral state—characterized by calls to end "police brutality" and "mass incarceration"—fail to recognize that the very logics of the overlapping criminal justice and policing regimes systemically perpetuate racial, sexual, gender, colonial, and class violence through carceral power. Thus, in addition to being ineffective at achieving their generally stated goals of alleviating vulnerable peoples' subjection to legitimated state violence, reformist approaches ultimately reinforce a violent system that is fundamentally asymmetrical in its production and organization of normalized misery, social surveillance, vulnerability to state terror, and incarceration. It is within this irreconcilable reformist contradiction that an abolitionist historical mandate provides a useful and necessary departure from the liberal assumption that either the carceral state or carceral power is an inevitable and permanent feature of the social formation.

Allegra McLeod, *Prison Abolition and Grounded Justice*, 62 UCLA L. Rev. 1156, 1207-1208 (2015).   [A]n abolitionist ethic, in virtue of its structural critique of penal practices, is oriented toward displacing criminal law as a primary regulatory framework and replacing it with other social regulatory forms, rather than only or primarily moderating criminal punishment or limiting its scope or focus. . . . More modest reform, in tolerating with relative comfort imprisonment and punitive policing, does not register the need for change with as much urgency.

B.   Inaction as Injustice

And yet, as even some prominent abolitionists acknowledge, a world without prisons poses at least one obvious problem. It struggles, McLeod writes, to address "those instances where imposing punishment remains perhaps necessary, as the lesser of two evils, when someone has committed and continues to pose a great threat of violence to others." As abolitionist Derecka Purnell writes, such violence is itself a critical concern for abolitionist writers and activists because—as we will discuss at length in the next two chapters—it is precisely the members of the most marginalized communities who "are those victims, those survivors of violence."[66]

To some scholars, the concentration of harm in communities suffering from systemic injustice and neglect is itself a potential justification for criminal law enforcement. Consider, in this respect, the following passage from Victor Tadros.

> [F]ailing to hold poor criminals responsible for their crimes might further erode the security of the poor. The poor, by being victims of distributive injustice, are already worse off than they ought to be in security terms. . . . Given that they are victims of economic injustice, the poor are almost certainly more insecure than they ought to be. This will be so for two reasons. First, poverty, or at least poverty which is a consequence of injustice, is almost certainly a cause of an increase in the crime rate, particularly in poor communities. Second, because the poor have less wealth than they ought to have, they have less money to spend on enhancing their security. One advantage of being wealthy is that the wealthy can make themselves more secure from crime, by living in more expensive safer places, by purchasing security alarms and by choosing to go to more expensive restaurants, clubs, and bars where crime is less likely to occur. Therefore, failing to prosecute and convict the offender of a security based offence might compound the injustice done to others who are already victims of injustice. For these reasons, we should not think that the claim of complicity provides an absolute bar on prosecuting the poor for the crimes that they commit. Let us suppose that the state is complicit in the crimes of the poor, by perpetrating economic injustices against them which make them more likely to offend. That provides a reason not to hold the poor responsible for the crimes they commit. But the state must attend not only to the injustices that result from prosecution and conviction but also the injustices that result from a failure to prosecute and convict.[67]

In other words, as Shelby writes, "the state in an unjust society faces a dilemma. Either it can punish those it has no right to punish or it can fail to protect those it has treated unjustly." For some theorists, including Shelby, this dilemma is best resolved by permitting the state "to penalize" at least violent crime, "in order to deter and contain it" and thus to "protect the vulnerable from unjustified harm."[68]

And indeed, in this idea, we arrive at one irreducible justification proffered for the criminal law: protection. As we will see later this book, a legal system that aims to provide such protection can quickly expand beyond that mandate, affording ever greater power to law enforcers. Moreover, as we will consider when we return to discussions of abolitionist and other critical accounts of American criminal law, there are those who argue that safety and security might be achieved through other legal and social frameworks. But before we examine these important issues, we need to engage fully with the implications raised by the social theorists you've just read above, all of whom suggest that the state's authority to punish may be *contingent*—that the legitimacy of using state violence to punish crime may depend in relevant part on what *causes* crime in the first place. We take up that essential question, the root causes of crime, in the next chapter.

Questions: And what of Mr. Anderson? Having considered the various accounts, justifications, and criticisms of punishment offered in this chapter, do you think Mr. Anderson should serve his thirteen-year sentence, or any part of it? Should he be punished in any other way? Has he been punished?

The legal posture of his case, as it came to Judge Brown, was unusual, much like the facts underlying the case itself. Invoking Missouri precedent, Anderson's attorney filed a motion for a declaratory judgment asking Judge Brown to treat the thirteen years that Anderson had been free in the community as if they had been time served in prison, on the theory that it was the state's fault that he had never been taken into custody. Coincidentally, the main case laying out the governing legal framework involved another defendant named Anderson who was *also* accidentally released from prison. *See* Anderson v. Crawford, 309 S.W.3d 863 (Mo. Ct. App. 2010). Interpreting this precedent, Judge Brown concluded that the question of whether to require Michael Anderson to serve his sentence was effectively left to the court's discretion.

On May 5, 2014, after Anderson had been detained for nearly ten months following his arrest, Judge Brown issued the following decision orally from the bench. In the audio recording of his ruling, you can hear a woman, presumably LaQonna Anderson, cry out as the judgment is rendered.

People v. Anderson

No. 14-MI-CV00243 (Cir. Ct. of Mississippi Cnty. Mo. May 5, 2014) (transcript of oral decision)

BROWN, J. . . . Mr. Anderson . . . you have lived an exemplary life. You've been a good father, you've been a good husband, you've been a good tax paying citizen of the State of Missouri. That's something I've got to consider, and I place a lot of weight on that consideration. I suspect the fear of going to prison the last thirteen years has been a mighty powerful influence on your behavior, and may be one of the reasons you've lived such a great life. But I've had people on supervised probation for several years who had a large sentence hanging over their head and they didn't accomplish nearly the things you accomplished, and you weren't on probation. So that leads me to believe that you are a good man and that you are a changed man. That makes a huge difference in my decision today. You are not the man you were fourteen years ago. I don't believe you are. Those are the factors I will consider and that I have considered.

Mr. Anderson . . . I believe that continuing to incarcerate you would serve no purpose. I think it would be a waste of taxpayer dollars. And I think it would unnecessarily punish an obviously rehabilitated man. In the interest of justice, I believe you should be released from the Department of Corrections. . . . I'm not willing to place your fate in the hands of the Parole Board. So, therefore, I think the only way to do this is by granting you credit for time served from the date you were released from the Department of Corrections on June 9, 2000 to the date that you were arrested and returned to custody on July 25, 2013. My order therefore gives you credit, Mr. Anderson for all 4,974 days you were not in custody and as such your sentence will be fully served and satisfied today. . . .

Mr. Anderson . . . in releasing you today, I don't want you to think that this Court in any way excuses you for the crime that you committed many years ago. Once again, I think the sentence that you received in 2000 was fair and just. But I also believe that you're a good man, that you've proven your ability to turn your life around. . . . Go home to your family, Mr. Anderson. Continue to be a good father, a good husband, continue to be a good worker, a good taxpaying member of the State of Missouri. Good luck to you.

WHAT CAUSES CRIME?

"[C]rime is a difficult subject to study, more difficult to analyze into its socio-logical elements, and most difficult to cure or suppress. It is a phenomenon that stands not alone, but rather as a symptom of countless wrong social conditions."

W.E.B. Du Bois, *The Philadelphia Negro: A Social Study*
241-242 (reprt. 1996) (1899)

INTRODUCTION

At the close of the preceding chapter, we encountered philosophers who questioned a key premise of the criminal law that often goes unexamined: the state's right to punish. As Professor Antony Duff asks, is state punishment legitimate when "society's broader social, political and economic structures involve various kinds of serious, systemic injustice"? What if those systemic injustices, in addition to being unfair or wrong, are also *criminogenic*—meaning that they actively spur crime in society?[1]

Some of these philosophers suggested, in various ways, that when socioeconomic forces make criminal offending more likely, that creates a reason not to hold people impacted by those forces responsible for crimes they commit, even if they are still, in some sense, responsible for their actions. The principal purpose of this chapter is to carry forward this critical and provocative inquiry by delving into a related and foundational question: *What causes crime?*[2]

For many generations, criminal law courses did not much engage this question, beginning their analyses instead only at the point when a crime had occurred and focusing solely on whether and how the person charged with committing it should be held accountable. The implicit premise of this approach is that the penal system's job is to react to people who commit crimes—not to understand the circumstances that led up to and may have contributed to their criminal acts. But beyond law school, generations of

105

social scientists have long taken the opposite approach, developing rich theoretical accounts of the causes of criminal behavior. Increasingly, they have subjected those theories to empirical testing. Successful lawyers ought not ignore this body of knowledge. Rather, responsible lawyers should care about how and why criminal defendants arrived at the penal system's doorstep, for at least two reasons.

First, ignoring the causes of crime can lead to a dehumanizing and incomplete perspective on criminal law. Paraphrasing attorney Bryan Stevenson, pretending that a person's criminal act is the only relevant fact about him worth considering reduces his full and complex life to the worst thing he has ever done. Borrowing from retributivists like Immanuel Kant and Michael Moore, one might argue that such an approach denies the individual's "inborn personality" and stems from an implicit assumption that those who study or administer the criminal law are "more of a person" than those punished by it. What is more, as Erin Kelly observed in the preceding chapter, focusing blame exclusively on the individual wrongdoer "diverts attention from a relevant acknowledgment of shared responsibility for factors that help to explain why crime is committed," including potentially "the state's moral failures" in allowing criminogenic social conditions to persist. A failure to grapple with the root causes of crime, in other words, can bias and truncate criminal law's core project of assigning blame and accountability appropriately and proportionately.[3]

Second, and more pragmatically, individual criminal cases, as well as overarching penal policies, are embedded in a social context. Whether litigating within the system or working to improve or transform it, lawyers need to understand the problems the criminal law is trying to solve. One goal the penal system pursues is protecting people from harms caused by others. To engage with or to challenge that system, or to assess the viability of alternatives to it, lawyers must understand what motivates such harmful behavior in the first place.

This isn't always easy to do. But the basic question is also in many ways unavoidable. Indeed, crude and intuitional versions of criminological theory likely float through the minds of legislators as they enact American penal policy and of prosecutors, judges, and jurors as they implement that policy. Put more simply, when presented with a given case, everyone likely has instincts about the extent to which the individual defendant is responsible for his conduct, and about how much blame should be attributed instead to his life circumstances. Just as assuredly, these instincts and intuitions vary from one person to another, supporting varying ideas about how to respond to crime.

To illuminate this point, we begin this chapter with a trio of cases. Together, they present various interacting forces and circumstances that ultimately lead to criminal offending. The point of considering these cases at this stage is not to focus on doctrinal analysis or any technical legal issues they may seem to present. We will devote considerable time to those questions later in this chapter and in the chapters to come. Rather, the point here is to read these cases with three basic questions in mind: Do you think the defendant should be punished? If so, how severely? And, if you had to rank these three individuals in terms of the severity of the sentences they should receive, how would you?

Regina v. Kingston

[1995] 2 AC 355 (HL)*

MUSTILL, L. [I]n March 1992 the respondent Barry Kingston and a man named Penn were jointly indicted on a count of indecent assault on a youth aged 15 years. . . . The relevant facts are simple. [Kingston] was in dispute over business matters with a couple named Foreman [who had employed Kingston for over a decade at a small spa they owned in Brighton, England. The Foremans eventually fired Kingston, who in turn filed a wrongful termination suit against them. His suit was successful, resulting in a substantial damages award of £12,000. In addition to the animosity engendered by this litigation, the Foremans also came to fear that Kingston knew potentially inculpatory information about their business finances and tax history.]

[Eventually, the Foremans reached out to Kevin Penn, an acquaintance of Kingston's known for engaging in shady dealings for profit. The Foremans] employed Penn to obtain damaging information which they could use against the respondent who is a homosexual with paedophiliac predilections.

As part of this plan [Penn schemed to create a scenario that would stir Kingston's latent sexual desires, in hopes of recording him in a compromising situation and then offering that recording to the Foremans as potential blackmail. In furtherance of this plot, Penn befriended a group of local teenage boys. Pretending to be someone who could help the boys break into modeling, Penn arranged a series of photo shoots for some of the boys, none of which was overtly sexual in nature. After laying this foundation over a series of months, Penn moved forward with his blackmail plot, focusing on one of the teenagers in particular.]

Penn invited the youth to his room. According to the evidence given by the youth at the trial he remembered nothing between a time when he was sitting on the bed and when he woke up, still in Penn's room, the following morning. It was the case for the prosecution, which the jury by their verdict

---

* The case excerpt below incorporates additional facts beyond those contained in the written opinion, drawn from Paul H. Robinson, *Criminal Law Case Studies* 199-202 (5th ed. 2015).

on the second count must have accepted, that the boy fell asleep because Penn had secretly given him a soporific drug in a drink.

On the same evening the respondent went to the room where the youth lay unconscious. He and Penn indulged in gross sexual acts with him. As part of the plan Penn made a recording of what was going on, and also took some photographs. . . . Later, this material came into the hands of the police and charges were brought.

At the outset of the trial counsel for the respondent foreshadowed a defence on the lines that as part of the plan Penn had secretly administered drugs not only to the boy but also to the respondent. . . . [T]he general nature of the case is clear enough. In ordinary circumstances the respondent's paedophiliac tendencies would have been kept under control, even in the presence of the sleeping or unconscious boy on the bed. The ingestion of the drug (whatever it was) brought about a temporary change in the mentality or personality of the respondent which lowered his ability to resist temptation so far that his desires overrode his ability to control them. Thus we are concerned here with a case of disinhibition. The drug is not alleged to have created the desire to which the respondent gave way, but rather to have enabled it to be released. The situation is therefore different from that [in] which . . . the drug directly brought about the [harmful] conduct with which he was charged.

William Lee & Madeline Buckley

11-Year-Old 'Yummy' Sandifer Was on the Run for Killing a Teenage Girl. Then He Was Killed by His Own Gang in a Chicago Story That Shocked the Nation 25 Years Ago

Adapted from the Chicago Tribune (Aug. 30, 2019)

Standing just 4-foot-6 and weighing only 68 pounds, [11-year-old Robert "Yummy" Sandifer] was an unlikely triggerman for the Black Disciples street gang. . . . The boy's story—a home life that bred little but anger, a record of more than 30 arrests before reaching his teens—was a reminder of deep cracks in the system that, some argue, have never been repaired.

"There's a lot of Yummy Sandifers out there," said Patrick Murphy, a longtime Cook County public guardian who represented Yummy . . . and is now a Juvenile Court judge. . . . "He might be slightly younger, but there are a lot of young kids out there that the gangs mobilize to do their dirty work for them and it's still going on."

. . . Deborah Dean remembers taking Yummy to church after his family moved into the home behind hers in the early 1990s. This clannish pocket of [the] Roseland [neighborhood of Chicago] was packed with first- and second-generation homeowners willing to lend a hand with parenting responsibilities, especially to struggling neighbors.

But Yummy was something else.

He was the type of boy neighbors hated to see coming down the street. Undersized for his age, he picked fights with boys bigger and smaller. He was good enough with his hands that he could link bicycles end-to-end and steal two at a time. But not so good that he could avoid detection while shoplifting repeatedly at convenience stores. . . .

There were quiet moments with the hardened little boy who still softened for sweets and toys. . . . But those moments never lasted. "Even when I took him to church, he would get into a fight. And my mom would always take him to the back and talk to him and stuff like that, give him some sweets," [Dean] said. [Other neighbors] were far less charitable. "He was a crooked son of a bitch," an exasperated grocer told *Time* magazine. . . .

But few, if any, of his neighbors knew of the terrors he faced in his own household. . . . His small body "bore 49 scars," [a medical report observed]. "Some likely the result of the normal falls and mishaps of youth, but others just as likely evidence of the abuse he suffered at an early age."

Born to a mother with drug issues and a mostly absent father, as a toddler Yummy was removed from his mother's home after he was found with multiple bruises and cord marks on his tiny body, and cigarette burns on his neck, shoulder blade and buttocks.

He spent most of his time in his grandmother's care but was housed in juvenile facilities as he got into more legal trouble. Through it all, he maintained a poor self-image, authorities said.

"Robert is a child growing up without any encouragement and support," an examiner at a state-run shelter wrote in a psychological report. . . . "He is lonely and feels poorly about himself. He has a sense of failure that has infiltrated almost every aspect of his inner self."

"He is caught up in a never-ending cycle of emotional overload and acting out," the report continued. "His anger is so great that his perception of the world is grossly distorted and inaccurate."

Illiterate, lonely and desperate for attention, authorities said the boy took solace as a "shorty," the lowest ranking member of the "8-ball" faction of the Black Disciples, one of the South Side's largest gangs. He had "BDN III," which stood for Black Disciples Nation, tattooed on his right forearm. He was picked up for auto theft, arson, armed robbery and a slew of other crimes. . . .

Yummy joined the Black Disciples during a particularly contentious war with the Gangster Disciples in a largely residential area that put families in the crosshairs. . . . Chicago's gang wars of the 1980s and 1990s were noteworthy for how street gangs—with their complicated hierarchy of members—used young members like Yummy for gang business[, ordering them to commit hits on rival gang members].

On Aug. 28, 1994, authorities said, leaders tasked the boy with shooting rivals. Police soon found a 16-year-old boy bleeding and writhing in pain near 108th Street and Perry Avenue. An officer leaned down and asked: "Who shot you?"

"Yummy shot me," the teen said. "I think his name is Robert."

Before a detective could even retrieve Yummy's mugshot, he was notified of another shooting less than a block away. This time, there were two teens — 14-year-old Shavon Dean, who was dead at the scene, and a 17-year-old boy who said Yummy had shot them both.

. . . [Today, twenty-five years after the fatal shooting, there sits in the 10800 block of South Wentworth Avenue a] peaceful stretch of grass with planters full of herbs and plots of red flowers that serves as a memorial park for Shavon Dean.

The garden became Deborah Dean's labor of love after her daughter was killed. Built in 1994, it remains a place Dean visits weekly to find some peace. She tends to it regularly for her daughter, the aspiring beautician who made things around her more beautiful.

Dean still has dreams of improving the garden. She wants benches installed to replace the makeshift seats she created with planks of wood. She imagines a mural on surrounding structures showing her daughter and other children taken from the neighborhood too early.

The garden is really for all of them, she says, the lost children of Roseland and the rest of the city. . . .

"All my baby wanted to do was go to school and become somebody," Dean said. "She didn't get that chance."

United States v. Murdock

471 F.2d 923 (D.C. Cir. 1972)

BAZELON, C.J. At issue here are much more than technical rules of law devoid of any significance outside a courtroom or law school lecture hall. A racial epithet hurled at appellants by one of their victims touched off an explosion of violence and bloodshed, an explosion that reverberates the traumas of our entire society. We cannot rationally decry crime and brutality and racial animosity without at the same time struggling to enhance the fairness and integrity of the criminal justice system. That system has first-line responsibility for probing and coping with these complex problems.

The tragic events which gave rise to this appeal might possibly have been avoided by various means. Proponents of legislation for the effective control of firearms will find powerful ammunition here. But such measures can never reach the root causes of crime so long as we remain in ignorance of the mental agonies that produce bizarre and violent behavior. Criminal trials . . . compel us to explore these problems, and thereby offer some slight hope that we will learn, in the course of deciding individual cases, something about the causes of crime. . . .

On the evening of June 4, 1968, five men and a woman — all white — walked into a hamburger shop, stood by the take-out counter, and ordered some food. The men were United States Marine Lieutenants in formal dress white uniforms; the woman was a friend of one of them. They noticed three Negro men sitting at the other end of the counter; these were appellants [Gordon] Alexander and [Benjamin] Murdock and one Cornelius Frazier.

[Alexander and one of the Marines, Lieutenant Ellsworth Kramer, engaged in a protracted staring match. Eventually, Alexander approached Kramer, tapped him on the shoulder and said, "You want to come outside and talk about it more?" Kramer responded, "Yes." At that point another of the Marines, Lieutenant William King, injected himself into the exchange and hurled a racial epithet at Alexander, calling him the n-word and a "dirty bastard."]

[Alexander then drew a .38-caliber revolver, cocked it, and pointed into King's chest, saying, "I will show you what I want." The Marines possessed no weapons and, according to their testimony, were not advancing toward Alexander. As they stood there, Murdock drew up to Alexander's left and pulled out his own .38 caliber revolver. A series of shots suddenly rang out. None of the Marines attempted to retaliate; two were fatally wounded. Alexander and Murdock withdrew from the shop, but one of them stuck his arm back into the shop and attempted — unsuccessfully — to fire his weapon several more times.]

. . . Alexander and Murdock were each found guilty of carrying a dangerous weapon, and of four counts of assault with a dangerous weapon. Murdock, in addition, was found guilty of two counts of second-degree murder. . . .

Prior to trial, Murdock filed a notice of intent to rely on the insanity defense. . . . Murdock relied primarily on the testimony of Dr. Williams, a board-certified psychiatrist and professor at Howard University Medical School [who had examined Murdock on two occasions]. . . . According to the testimony of Dr. Williams, Murdock was strongly delusional, though not hallucinating or psychotic; he was greatly preoccupied with the unfair treatment of Negroes in this country, and the idea that racial war was inevitable. He showed compulsiveness in his behavior, emotional immaturity, and some psychopathic traits. Since his emotional difficulties were closely tied to his sense of racial oppression, it is probable that when the Marine in the Little Tavern called him a "black bastard" Murdock had an irresistible impulse to shoot. His emotional disorder had its roots in his childhood, in the Watts section of Los Angeles; particularly important was the fact that his father had deserted his mother, and he grew up in a large family with little money and little love or attention.

Dr. Williams stated firmly that in his view Murdock was suffering from an abnormal mental condition that substantially impaired his behavior controls. But he stated just as firmly that the condition did not amount to a mental illness: "My idea of mental illness is that an individual is out of touch with reality. He has auditory hallucinations, he has delusions, he has mannerisms that set him off as a different individual. He withdraws from society. And his behavior as such is tremendously bizarre. [That sort of behavior] is what I call, what they would call at Johns Hopkins, a major psychosis and a form of mental illness."

. . . [Defense counsel] conceded to the jury that Murdock "did not have a mental disease in the classic sense," *i.e.*, he did not have a psychosis. But, counsel argued, the expert testimony showed that at the critical moment Murdock did not have control of his conduct, and the reason for that lack of control was a deepseated emotional disorder that was rooted in his "rotten social background."

There are clear differences among the cases above. But also note several important commonalities. In each case, the person who committed the crime chose to engage in conduct that caused real, even fatal, harm to others. At the same time, in each case, the defendant's decision occurred within and against the backdrop of a set of circumstances that influenced his choice, making his decision to do harm more likely—perhaps substantially so.

Some of these circumstances were highly *individualized*, residing within the defendant's own body or mind. Robert Sandifer, for example, was only eleven years old when he killed Shavon Dean. As the U.S. Supreme Court has observed, citing considerable scientific literature, juvenile brains are not fully developed, which causes juveniles to have "an underdeveloped sense of responsibility" and to be "more vulnerable or susceptible to negative influences and outside pressures, including peer pressure." Roper v. Simmons, 543 U.S. 551, 569-570 (2005). As for Barry Kingston and Benjamin Murdock, both of their trials featured extensive testimony from mental health experts who portrayed the men as suffering from identifiable psychological afflictions—be they the "delusional" and "psychopathic traits" of Murdock or Kingston's "paedophilia," which would be called "pedophilic disorder" by experts today.[4]

Other relevant circumstances were *situational*, pertaining to the scene in which the harmful conduct unfolded. Consider here the fact that Sandifer was ordered by more senior members of a hierarchical and violent gang to carry out the shootings he committed. Or that Murdock fired his weapon only after being called the n-word and a dirty "Black bastard" during a heated interracial conflict. Or that Kingston molested his teenage victim in the course of a devious blackmail plot in which Kingston himself was drugged against his will.

Finally, beyond the immediate setting, the cases implicate *historical* circumstances of the defendants' lives that likely shaped the defendants' behavior. Those circumstances, in turn, stemmed from broader *sociological* forces that shape the distribution of criminogenic risks in a society. In Sandifer's case, these forces are stark, encompassing myriad examples of deprivation, neglect, and abuse in his young life. Murdock's case offers fewer details of his so-called "rotten social background," but the opinion notes that he grew up without his father "in a large family with little money and little love or attention." As for Kingston, we do not know much about his upbringing or his personal history. We do, however, know that pedophilic disorder is closely linked to cycles of victimization, in which people who engage in sexual conduct with minors have often been victims of similar sexual abuse themselves.[5]

The goal in the remainder of this chapter is to explore the import and interaction of these various potential drivers of crime. We begin, in the chapter's first part, with an examination of some of the leading theories about the causes of crime, along with empirical evidence that supports or undermines them. The chapter's second part then turns from theory and evidence to law. The goal here is to consider how the evidence about root causes of crime does and should intersect with the law of *excuse*. Specifically, we ask: When should criminogenic circumstances outside a person's control lead to a conclusion that the person ought not be punished criminally for harmful actions they have taken? We examine this question first by exploring three classic doctrines gestured at in the cases above: the *insanity defense*, the *involuntary intoxication defense*, and the *infancy defense*. We then compare these three recognized doctrines of excuse to the "rotten social background" theory pressed by Murdock above, a theory generally rejected in American courts.

As a formal matter, these excuse doctrines are typically treated as *defenses* to liability. As such, they have often been taught after introducing concepts central to the idea of liability itself—ideas like *mens rea, actus reus,* causation, and concurrence, which we will introduce in coming chapters. As the discussion in this chapter will show, however, while formally denominated defenses, the doctrines we explore in this chapter can just as easily be understood to concern the fundamental preconditions for liability itself: Who in our society can and cannot be held criminally responsible for their actions? When, how, and why should a person's circumstances factor into the assessment of his culpability for harms he caused to others? Comparing these doctrines shows how the criminal law answers these questions while affording an opportunity to consider how, if at all, various ideas about root causes of crime might influence the liability decision—and why legal actors might resist integrating such insights.

Finally, we conclude the chapter with a section on the relationship between race and crime. Here, we observe that the communities most

harmed by structural racism will also be the communities in which criminogenic social forces are most concentrated. Recognizing as much brings
to the fore a dilemma that undergirds much of this course and frames the
chapters that follow: The communities the penal system destabilizes most
are also the communities most harmed by crime.

I.   CRIME AND SOCIETY

> "Society includes within itself the germs of all the crimes committed, and at
> the same time the necessary facilities for their development. It is the social
> state, in some measure, which prepares these crimes, and the criminal is
> merely the instrument to execute them."
>
> M.A. Quetelet, *A Treatise on Man and the Development of His Faculties*
> 6 (Robert Knox trans., Edinburgh, W. & R. Chambers 1842)

As the cases opening this chapter demonstrate, criminal behavior does not
occur in a vacuum. It occurs within a social context. We saw hints of this
insight in the preceding chapter when studying deterrence and the *rational
choice theory* of crime, which, in economist Gary Becker's words, "assumes
that a person commits an offense if the expected utility to him exceeds the
utility he could get by using his time and other resources at other activities." This theory offers a potential explanation for why the state might seek
to punish someone—the idea being that punishment might, by reducing
"expected utility," shape behavior and, in so doing, deter crime. But it also
implies a theory of crime itself, one in which crime is a product, at least in
part, of situation and circumstance. After all, the extent to which people
will benefit from committing a crime, their likelihood of getting caught,
and the consequences they might experience as a result are all functions of
circumstances that are often outside the individual's control.[6]

Still, while rational choice theory might be read to imply a circumstantial theory of crime, it is often criticized for putting too much weight on
individual agency and too little on the broader societal circumstances that
foster or promote criminal behavior by molding the environment in which
that agency is exercised. The theory says individuals maximize their preferences among available options, but it tends to leave unaddressed questions about how those preferences are formed and options are distributed.
Scholars sensitive to this critique have, as far back as the Progressive Era,
urged researchers "to stop looking for the sources of crime inside of individuals and . . . start looking at the social contexts in which individuals find
themselves." It "is this larger cultural and structural context," they have
observed, "that explains why the commission of burglary and robbery is disproportionately a 'rational choice' for residents in inner-city communities
as opposed to those in middle-class communities."[7]

At the same time, and, as noted at the outset of this chapter, criminal conduct is also a product of individual traits and choices. As Professor Rachel Barkow writes:

> [E]mphasis on structural reform is certainly a better model than the get-tough frame that ignores structural forces. . . . [But there are also] some individuals who, if they know they can act on their self-interest without sufficiently severe consequences, will do so. . . . Greed, lust, boredom, envy, ambition, fear, honor, cruelty, anger-control issues, religion, political ideology, and a host of other individual predilections and dispositions will exist at some level no matter how society is constructed. . . . Conflicts of interest between people will exist even if basic needs are met. Rich people and poor people alike commit crimes. Crimes like bribery, fraud, blackmail, and corruption are crimes of greed and a lust for power, and they will not be eradicated through structural change because they exist under every societal design. We have seen individuals harm each other in every societal arrangement on Earth and throughout history.[8]

Our goal in this part is not to ignore the existence of these individualized drivers of crime. Rather, it is to examine the ways in which social structure and individual attributes combine to form the essential context that shapes individuals' choices, including choices to violate the criminal law. We begin by distilling from the social science literature some of the principal mechanisms through which social forces can exert criminogenic pressure. We then illustrate how these mechanisms might explain the criminogenic nature of social phenomena like income inequality, unemployment, poor education, and exposure to violence—showing *why* and *how* "structural disadvantage" tends to cause crime. Finally, we conclude this part by exploring the relationship between these societal drivers of crime and individual biological and psychological characteristics—including protective characteristics that help explain why most people who encounter structural disadvantage do not offend. Ultimately, combining these insights, we arrive at an integrated *biosocial theory* of crime.

A. *Societal Drivers of Crime*

The United States underwent enormous social and economic change in the early twentieth century: mass industrialization, urbanization, increased immigration, the Great Depression, and the Great Migration of Black Southerners to Northern cities. Alongside this social upheaval, crime became "visibly concentrated among the urban poor."[9]

Scholars and policymakers wanted to know why. In 1942, two sociologists, Clifford Shaw and Henry McKay, offered an observation that would blossom into one of the most enduring and influential sociological theories of crime. Shaw and McKay noticed that the concentration of crime in impoverished urban neighborhoods persisted regardless of which racial or ethnic groups happened to live in those neighborhoods at a given point in time. And people who moved out of these neighborhoods and into lower-crime parts of the city committed fewer crimes once they settled into their new homes. Crime, in other words, seemed to be a function of place—and more specifically, of neighborhood dynamics that occur when people react to challenging conditions and high rates of residential turnover.[10]

1.   Why Neighborhood Dynamics Matter: Institutions, Relationships, and Experiences

In the decades since Shaw and McKay's seminal work, generations of social scientists have posited distinct and also overlapping theories that identify some of the mechanisms through which neighborhood dynamics may be criminogenic. A full accounting of those theories could fill an entire introductory text on criminology, of which there are many. The primer we offer in the following notes is necessarily a stripped-down distillation, aimed at orienting future lawyers to some of the dominant insights in the field. For a deeper dive into the underlying literature, readers may consult the sources collected in the endnotes.

NOTES AND QUESTIONS

1. Institutions. Shaw and McKay argued that poverty and residential turnover drive crime because they weaken conventional institutions of informal social control—schools, churches, community centers, and the like—resulting in what social scientists call *social disorganization.* Socially disorganized communities, the theory goes, lack the tools to constrain harmful behavior, particularly in the neighborhood's youth. Such communities lack, in other words, a sense of "collective efficacy," which sociologist Robert Sampson defines as "social cohesion among neighbors combined with their willingness to intervene on behalf of the common good" when a problem, such as juvenile misbehavior, arises. According to sociologist Ruth Kornhauser, as social cohesion dissipates, so too does the community's ability to reach common ground and form shared understandings about social values. The end result, she says, is an "attenuated communal value system" that is unable to "serve as the basis for effective community control."[11]

Empirical research has strongly supported Shaw and McKay's theory. One study, for example, found that nonprofit organizations focused on controlling violence and building community life substantially reduce violent crime. Involvement with religious institutions, too, is negatively correlated with delinquent behavior. And in a fascinating demonstration of the importance of social cohesion and communal values, a recent study, leveraging evidence from the Great Migration, showed that cities with higher concentrations of Black migrants from the same Southern birth town experience significantly less serious crime even after controlling for a host of social and economic characteristics. The transmission of "anticrime norms" through tight, historically connected social networks was listed among the most plausible explanations for the effect.[12]

2. Relationships. Separately but relatedly, Shaw and McKay argued in their early work that neighborhoods exhibiting social disorganization also tend to foster what they called *criminal traditions,* a set of value and information systems that pass on delinquent norms and practices to successive generations of youth through the everyday process of *social learning.* The basic idea is that deviant behavior—and the moral valence attached to that behavior—is learned from and reinforced by interactions with deviant actors, typically peers. In his famous book *Code of the Street,* sociologist Elijah Anderson argues that, in some disadvantaged urban neighborhoods, value systems that countenance violence and aggression can arise as a cultural adaptation to group-level alienation from mainstream society. With few conventional opportunities available, some young people in these settings pursue respect according to the "code of the street," in which even trivial affronts must be met with force. Meanwhile, some youths whose families teach conventional values are pressured to abide the code of the street out of self-preservation, jeopardizing their paths to mainstream success. Many aspects of social learning theory have received empirical support. Researchers have established, for example, that the number of delinquent friends an adolescent has strongly predicts his likelihood of criminal involvement. Studies have also shown that social learning among individuals can increase total deviance at the neighborhood level, known as a "multiplier" effect.[13]

At the same time, relationships with peers and elders—and the institutions they populate—can also reduce the risk of criminal involvement. Partly this is simply the inverse of the point just made: relationships can teach prosocial behavior and values as well as deviant ones. But there's something more, and different, here too. Attachment to and investment in other people creates what sociologist Travis Hirschi called a "stake in conformity" through a process called *social bonding.* Social bonding matters because it "gives us something to lose through crime." Specifically, criminal offending risks losing the approval of people whose opinions we value and potentially even the freedom to participate alongside them in family life, school activities, work, and more. The more social bonds people have, the more they stand to lose by violating community norms. When community institutions are weak, then, community members lose more than just the potential for self-monitoring and informal norm enforcement mentioned earlier. They also have fewer opportunities to form enduring social bonds that internally motivate them to adhere to conventional norms.[14]

3. Experiences. Layered on top of the preceding two mechanisms, social scientists add an account of the criminogenic effect of stress and strain. On this account, called *strain theory*, crime arises as a maladaptive way to cope with "certain emotional states—most notably frustration-induced anger." The stressors and strains that can produce such frustration are manifold. A lost job, a romantic breakup, the sickness or death of a friend or loved one—all of these and more can create criminogenic strain.[15]

Notably, the criminogenic impact of psychological strain is higher in socially disorganized settings. People with weak social bonds or who associate with deviant peers are more likely to cope with strain through deviant, rather than prosocial, means. At the same time, as noted later in this chapter, communities without adequate social welfare systems and with depressed economic opportunities often lack access to mental health services. The upshot is that strain is both concentrated within and has a heightened criminogenic effect on socially disorganized communities. This, in turn, leads to frequent interactions between angry and frustrated individuals, creating a tinderbox of sorts. As sociologist Robert Agnew put it, these communities "are more likely to select and retain strained individuals" who can't afford to live elsewhere, can't access or afford needed support services, and who in turn "produce strain" for others and "foster criminal responses to strain."[16]

2.   Applying the Theories to Understand Structural Disadvantage

With these theoretical guideposts in hand, including what we learned about rational choice theory in Chapter Two, we can begin to understand *why* structural disadvantage is criminogenic. Consider the following markers of disadvantage, all of which are common in communities suffering from systemic inequality.

NOTES AND QUESTIONS

1. Economic Inequality, Poverty, and Weak Labor Markets. Take first economic inequality. According to Professor Richard McAdams, there is "significant evidence" that the criminogenic effects of income inequality are "real and substantial." As economist Morgan Kelly observes, multiple sociological mechanisms may explain this relationship:

> [1] In the economic [*i.e.*, rational choice] theory of crime, areas of high inequality place poor individuals who have low returns from market activity next to high-income individuals who have goods worth taking, thereby increasing the returns to time allocated to criminal activity. [2] Strain theory argues that, when faced with the relative success of others around them, unsuccessful individuals feel frustration at their situation.

The greater the inequality, the higher this strain and the greater the inducement for low-status individuals to commit crime. [3] Social disorganization theory argues that crime occurs when the mechanisms of social control are weakened. Factors that weaken a community's ability to regulate its members [include] poverty. . . . In this case, inequality is associated with crime because it is linked to poverty: areas with high inequality tend to have high poverty rates.[17]

Unemployment and underemployment, which frequently accompany inequality, also increase crime. Viewed through the lens of rational choice theory, this connection makes sense. When the money to be made from crime exceeds lawful earnings available in the labor market, it is easy to see how rational choices might push someone toward crime. In the words of one man interviewed by criminologists Bruce Jacobs and Richard Wright, "If I had a union job making $16 or $17" per hour, "something that I could really take care of my family with, I think that I could be cool with that [and not commit robberies]." Having a job and coworkers also facilitates social bonding, while job loss and joblessness—and the resulting financial difficulties—can generate substantial criminogenic strain.[18]

Quantitative research consistently confirms that unemployment, job loss, and low wages all increase crime—especially financially motivated crime. One study, for example, finds that young people who leave school during recessions are more likely to commit crime and to experience sustained criminal involvement than similarly situated peers who exit into a strong labor market. Other work shows that people recidivate less when they are released from prison into labor markets with good low-skilled jobs that are open to former offenders, like construction and manufacturing. Job loss itself, separate from the status of joblessness, has also been shown to increase both property *and* violent crime—for both the displaced workers and also their close family members. And wages matter, too: one recent study, echoing earlier research, finds that minimum-wage increases significantly reduce the rate at which people released from prison return, an effect dominated by reductions in income-related crimes like theft.[19]

Consistent with all this research, a robust literature demonstrates that not only economic opportunity but also public assistance, which mitigates the criminogenic effects of unemployment and underemployment, reduces crime. This is true with respect to both direct welfare aid and expanded social safety net programs like nutritional assistance, unemployment insurance, and Medicaid.[20]

2. Struggling Schools. A large body of research has found that high educational attainment, school attendance, and school and teacher quality all mitigate the risk of criminal involvement. One recent study, for example, exploits the rollout of two large-scale educational programs in North Carolina to show that early childhood education reduces adult offending by roughly 20 percent, with effects concentrated in high-poverty counties. Another leverages changes in state compulsory schooling laws, finding that each additional year of high school education reduces subsequent male arrest and incarceration rates by 10-15 percent for both property and violent crimes. As for school quality, research shows that students who win school-choice lotteries to attend better-performing public schools commit significantly less crime in the years after leaving school than comparable students who fare less well in the lotteries. Studies even show that education has an *intergenerational* effect on crime, as children of better-educated parents are less likely to engage in crime.[21]

Here, too, the relationship between education and crime likely operates simultaneously through multiple channels. More and better schooling improves subsequent labor market prospects, raising the opportunity costs of crime and reducing the strains associated with joblessness and underemployment. Schooling can have contemporaneous effects on crime as well. For example, school attendance "incapacitates" children, reducing opportunities to offend, at least insofar as crime is less likely inside school than outside it. It can also mitigate neighborhood disorganization by providing mechanisms of informal social control and social bonds to teachers, coaches, and other prosocial adults. At the same time, a struggling school, much like a socially disorganized neighborhood, can become criminogenic if it brings together at-risk students who negatively influence each other through social learning or expose each other to criminal opportunities.[22]

3. Environmental Design and Urban Blight. Recall Shaw and McKay's central insight: place matters. This turns out to be true not only at the city or neighborhood level, but also on a much smaller scale. Both the built and natural environment on a city block, or even a single lot, can attract or repel crime — things like lighting, landscaping, zoning, upkeep, and vacancy. Dark alleys and vacant lots provide cover for illegal activity, limiting the risk of apprehension and reducing deterrence. Poorly maintained homes and public spaces signal a lack of social capital and collective involvement in community spaces. Residents in such settings are less likely to spend time outside their homes, forming bonds with neighbors and keeping their "eyes upon the street." Disrepair can be stressful, too, a constant reminder of resources needed but not had, or of mounting financial obligations.[23]

Decades of research illustrate these mechanisms at work. One study, for example, randomly allocated temporary streetlights to 40 public housing developments in New York City. These developments experienced significant reductions in serious, nighttime, outdoor crimes compared to similar developments that did not receive lights. They also experienced large declines in arrests, pointing to deterrence as the likeliest mechanism at play. In another randomized controlled trial, researchers "cleaned and greened" vacant lots in a major city, removing trash and debris, planting new grass and trees, and installing low wooden perimeter fences. This treatment significantly decreased overall crime as well as gun violence, burglary, and nuisance. Residents near the cleaned-up lots also reported a 75 percent increase in their use of outdoor spaces.[24]

4. Exposure to Violence. Finally, many studies have found that exposure to violence strongly increases the risk of offending in children and adolescents. One striking study, for example, finds that "being exposed to firearm violence approximately doubles the probability that an adolescent will perpetrate serious violence over the 2 subsequent years." The effects of violence exposure operate through multiple channels. Even more than urban decay, the regular occurrence of violence in a community signals a lack of collective efficacy and an "attenuated community value system." Where that violence is not wholly condemned — or worse yet, is rewarded or perpetrated by individuals who garner peer or community respect — social learning theory predicts that those exposed are more likely to replicate the behavior. Experiencing or witnessing violence also causes psychological strain that can trigger delinquent coping mechanisms. And over time, exposure to violence can even reduce children's "future orientation," leading them to discount the anticipated consequences of their behavior, undermining the law's potential deterrent effect.[25]

B. A Biosocial Theory of Crime

Biosocial criminology, as its name suggests, attempts to explain crime and deviance through the confluence of the sociological risk factors discussed above and biological ones, including genetics and neuroscience. Many contemporary researchers approach this theory with understandable trepidation. As a field, criminology has a pernicious history of deploying biological reasoning to advance an unfounded and racist ideology. That history, criminologist Adrian Raine observes, makes most people "deeply uncomfortable with the implications" of biology talk.[26]

That discomfort and the history behind it should be taken seriously. We begin this section by exploring this history and the perils of biological reasoning — before then examining the merits of a careful, empirically grounded biosocial theory of crime.

1. The Perils of Biological Reasoning

Italian physician Cesare Lombroso, often described as the father of criminology, had Charles Darwin's recently published theory of evolution in mind when, one night in 1870, he discovered a depression on the cranium of a deceased highway robber. This cranial depression, Lombroso knew, was typical of some rodents, which led him to hypothesize that the robber was an evolutionary throwback whose development was arrested at, or possibly had degenerated to, a primitive mental stage. This observation planted the seeds for what became Lombroso's towering 1876 volume, *Criminal Man*. Based on years of study of humans both dead and alive, Lombroso argued that deviance was marked by physical anomalies reminiscent of apes and early humans, including a sloping forehead, large ears, facial and cranial asymmetry, long arms, and bulky jaw bones. While "normal" people might occasionally stray and break the law, Lombroso believed, these "physical markers could be used to identify those whose mental faculties were deficient and who were, as a result, prone to criminality." These "born criminals," according to Lombroso, were society's real menace.[27]

As the following two notes discuss, there were four major problems with Lombroso's theory: It was wrong. It was dangerous. It was popular. And it was enduring.

NOTES AND QUESTIONS

1. The Long Reach of a Discredited Theory. Lombroso presented his work with a flourish, offering reams of purportedly valid data alongside "illustrations of naked, tattoo-speckled bodies" and "creepily malformed faces." Together with his "flamboyant, vivid language," this approach helped his theory spread far and wide. Before long, the broader public encountered it in the pages of popular fiction, with famous writers like Arthur Conan Doyle describing one of his characters — Sherlock Holmes' archnemesis, Professor Moriarty — as a man with a "criminal strain . . . in his blood" and "hereditary tendencies of the most diabolical kind."[28]

But Lombroso's work was as flawed as it was captivating. As later scholars would observe, his central conceptual classifications, like the "born criminal," were so vague that they could "pretty much be interpreted to mean anything," making his theory unfalsifiable. His studies were also not replicable due to "the absence of systematic procedures for gathering and analyzing data" in his work. Perhaps most important, he seldom used suitable control groups, making it virtually impossible for him to establish that any patterns he perceived were due to anything other than chance. In short, Lombroso "did science backward: He started with a conviction" and then "interpreted his data in the way that best supported his preconceived notions."[29]

Eventually, these defects were exposed. In 1913, an English prison medical officer named Charles Goring penned "the definitive refutation of Lombrosian theory." Carefully studying 96 physical features in 3,000 Englishmen convicted of crimes alongside a control group of nonconvicted males, Goring found virtually no statistically significant differences between the two groups. In the words of one modern commentator, Goring's findings proved that there "is no such thing as a physical criminal type."[30]

And yet, Lombroso's legacy endured and even spread, including to America, where it was embraced by leading social scientists at Harvard and Columbia throughout the 1930s, 40s, and 50s. Thus, in the middle of the last century, one could read work by Earnest Hooton, an anthropologist at Harvard University, who argued that "criminals are inferior to civilians in nearly all of their bodily measurements" and who further urged society to sterilize people who are "insane, diseased and criminal."[31]

Hooton's theory was just as unscientific as Lombroso's. As Professor Ronald Akers writes, Hooton "began with the assumption that criminals are biologically inferior" and only counted data in his study confirming that hypothesis, while ignoring available evidence to the contrary. Scholars demonstrated the flaws in Hooton's work as early as 1951. Still, just as occurred with Lombroso's original theory, the false narrative about biological drivers of crime held sway for decades — perhaps in part because the theory supported the political agendas of those outside the academy, who made "efforts to incorporate the alleged biology-crime link into public policy." One such policy was eugenics, reflected in Hooton's advocacy of forced sterilization as a tool to "breed out" deviant traits from the population. Others used the same biological reasoning to advocate harsh criminal punishments, including the death penalty and lengthy prison sentences, on the view that society has a right to defend itself from born criminals — just as it does from wild animals, without "thinking that they are to blame for not having been born lambs."[32]

2. An Enduring Legacy. It was not until the late 1950s that scholars generally abandoned Lombroso's work, as its linkage to the eugenics movement became anathema in the aftermath of the Nazis' brutal, eugenics-based crimes against humanity. Today, social scientists view Lombroso's findings as wrong and his work as thoroughly discredited.[33]

And yet, the core Lombrosian idea continues to lay hold on popular imagination. Where earlier generations had Sherlock Holmes, later audiences had movies like *Scarface* or *The Texas Chainsaw Massacre*, which presented their villains as "criminal by nature." Indeed, research suggests that people today consistently associate certain physical features with deviance and dangerousness. Those associations, in turn, appear to affect criminal justice outcomes, with one physical marker standing out in many people's minds: Blackness. Scholars have found that even today, darker skin and Afrocentric facial features are associated with harsher sanctions for criminal defendants.* This finding is but one example of the enduring legacy of Lombrosian thinking. As contemporary scholars note, Lombroso "injected racism into the new field of criminology" by equating at the outset "white men with civilization and black, brown, or yellow men with 'primitive' or 'savage' societies."[34]

In the decades that followed, many different ethnic groups in the United States were "vilified by allegations that they harbor 'racial instincts' for certain types of criminality," with Italian Americans and American Jews both stigmatized at times as criminal races.† But while this spurious race-crime thesis eventually fell away for so-called "ethnic whites" in the United States, the same cannot be said for Black Americans. Rather, as Professor Randall Kennedy writes, "the term 'Black crime'" has lingered in our vernacular even into the present day, "long after the disappearance of references to 'Jewish crime' or 'Italian crime.'"[35]

3. Tropes About "Black Crime." Much like Lombroso's original theory, the claim that Black people are biologically predisposed to crime was pressed by white supremacists deploying pseudo-science. As historian Khalil Gibran Muhammad writes, arguments in this vein accelerated with "the publication of the 1890 Census," when "prison statistics for the first time became the basis of a national discussion about blacks as a distinct and dangerous criminal population." The data in that census showed disproportionate Black representation in the prison population, which "white social scientists presented . . . as objective, color-blind, and incontrovertible" proof of a distinctly Black form of criminality. As Muhammad goes on to show, these interpretations of the data were themselves stained by white supremacy. Frederick Hoffman, whose seminal tract fueled the false Black-criminality thesis, "combined crime statistics with a well-crafted white supremacist narrative to shape the reading of black criminality while trying to minimize the appearance of doing so." White immigrant crime, for example, was discounted and explained away, while readers were told that, for Black people, "the primary factor" driving crime "is racial inheritance."[36]

---

    * Interestingly, this effect is most pronounced when white defendants have such features.

    † It is worth observing that Cesare Lombroso himself was Jewish. When his biological theory was deployed to suggest that Jews might be predisposed to crime, Lombroso countered in later editions of *Criminal Man* that "Jewish patterns of behavior" in Italy "derived from the historical legacy of persecution rather than from innate racial characteristics," even as he maintained that crime among poor and disempowered Southern Italians was racially based.

The supposed data supporting the Black criminality thesis was, even before the 1890 Census, refuted by "leading scientists," who "slowly recognized that variations within so-called races matched or exceeded those found between them." But just as with Lombroso's own work, the theory's damage far outlasted its discreditation. For one thing, the Black criminality thesis became in part a self-fulfilling prophecy, as law enforcement officers internalized the idea of racial inferiority and criminality — and then shaped their arrest and prosecution practices around that false idea. Thus, as Swedish social scientist Gunnar Myrdal observed, writing in 1944, "probably no group of whites in America have a lower opinion of the Negro people and are more fixed in their views than Southern policemen." To these officers, he went on, "practically every Negro man is a potential criminal," and they "are convinced that the traits are 'racial.'" Driven by these racist ideologies, law enforcement officers disproportionately arrested Black people, which in turn produced more so-called "evidence" of Black criminality.[37]

Nor did these racist tropes disappear with the Civil Rights Era advances of the 1960s. On the contrary, when crime rates increased into the 1980s, familiar tropes about Black crime resurfaced in prominent outlets and at leading universities like Harvard and Johns Hopkins, where some social scientists offered supposed racial differences in intelligence as an explanation for reported racial differences in criminal offending. As one modern criminology text concludes, "the early 1990s saw a restoration of elements of social Darwinism, with suggestions that African Americans . . . were both cognitively and morally inferior by nature and that this inferiority explained much of the crime problem."[38]

This insidious trope was wrong at its inception and remains wrong today. Criminologist Francis Cullen and his colleagues, for example, have shown that, contrary to the claims cited above, the relationship between scores on IQ tests (which purport to measure intelligence) and criminal involvement is, at best, modest and is "dwarfed" by a range of societal factors. Likewise, sociologist Robert Sampson and colleagues found that IQ scores and other individual factors explain very little about variations in violent offending, while societal factors have considerable explanatory power.[39]

Still, the trope of Black criminality persists. Likely, it proves difficult to inter because it purports to explain an unfortunate but real discrepancy in criminal offending rates: As noted prison abolitionist and critical race theorist Paul Butler observes, and as official crime statistics bear out, "African American men commit a disproportionate share of certain serious crimes, including homicide, assault, and robbery." This real discrepancy poses essential questions about how to interpret such data and what meaning to project onto them. We will return to those important questions in the last part of this chapter.[40]

2.   The Merits of a Biosocial Understanding of Crime

The history recounted above helps to explain why biological reasoning is often a third rail in criminology. Many people fear that giving oxygen to ideas with such a track record will legitimate racist or eugenicist tropes or will empower them in the academy, policy circles, or public discourse. Indeed, the reluctance spans conventional political ideologies, as criminologist Adrian Raine explains:

> Conservatives worry that acknowledging biological risk factors for violence will result in a society that takes a soft approach to crime, holding no one accountable for his or her actions. Liberals abhor the potential use of biology to stigmatize ostensibly innocent individuals. Both sides fear any seeming effort to erode the idea of human agency and free will.[41]

And yet, as Raine goes on to explain, "It is growing harder and harder . . . to avoid the mounting evidence" supporting an integrated *biosocial theory* of crime. Indeed, according to one leading contemporary criminological text, "the remarkable progress and rising popularity of biosocial theorizing is so impressive as to signal what may become the major criminological paradigm for the next several decades and beyond."[42]

Raine and his colleague Andrea Glenn report that meta-analysis of "well over 100 behavioural genetics studies with different designs—including twin studies, studies of twins reared apart and adoption studies—have converged on the conclusion that antisocial and aggressive behaviour have a considerable genetic basis." It appears, in other words, that some propensity toward deviance may indeed be inherited—just as Lombroso suggested. Beyond inherited traits, there are myriad other naturally occurring biological risk factors for deviance. Attributes such as low cortisol levels, increased testosterone levels, low resting heart rate, reduced skin conductance activity, reduced functioning in the frontal lobe of the brain, and abnormal amygdala volume and activity have all been shown to impede impulse control, emotional processing, and the ability to learn from rewards and punishment.[43]

Many forces we think of as environmental also operate through biological pathways. The most obvious examples have some sort of chemical or physical component, like early exposure to lead, which has been shown to affect cognitive functioning and aggression, increasing criminal involvement. Even many forces we might think of as purely social in nature turn out to interact with biology—chronic stress and strain during childhood, for example, not only impact behavior directly, but also lastingly alter the body's hormonal stress-response system.[44]

In short, the basic tenet of biosocial criminology appears to be well supported: "Biological traits interact with the social environment to shape human behavior." At the same time, it is critical to appreciate that an individual's biological makeup does not alone *cause* any specific behavior. Rather, it creates "a tendency to respond to environmental factors through general predispositions." Not all people with a given biological risk factor will commit crimes, just as not everyone who grows up in a socially disorganized neighborhood or has delinquent peers will offend.[45]

A central advantage of biosocial theory is its ability to account for precisely this point. What the theory says, at bottom, is that "genetic *and* environmental factors shape the way that biological systems develop and function, and thus affect multiple complex psychological processes that are important in controlling and regulating behaviour and in behaving morally." Some biological risk factors manifest differently in different social environments, while the same social environment might operate "differently for different individuals because of neurological variations." Social and biological influences, in other words, can exacerbate each other's criminogenic effects—or buffer or offset them.[46]

Given this blended, biosocial interaction, the best way to explain crime is likely through the lens of risk factors and protective factors. A risk factor is anything associated with a higher likelihood of criminal offending; a protective factor is anything associated with a lower likelihood. Risk factors exist at multiple biological, individual, and societal levels, from the individual to the family, from peer groups to neighborhoods. Those risk factors are cumulative—the more of them that are present, the greater the likelihood of criminal offending. But risk factors can also be mitigated by protective factors.

With this general overview in mind, we present below some notes reporting evidence on some of the main biosocial interactions that affect propensity to crime.

NOTES AND QUESTIONS

1. Age. The single best predictor of criminal involvement is age. As countless studies show, there is a well-defined "age of offending," with people aging into and out of life phases when they are most likely to engage in crime. Specifically, participation in crime reaches a "peak[] in adolescence followed by a less sharp decline through middle adulthood, with eventual disappearance in the sixties." This relationship, known as the age-crime curve, is "one of the brute facts of criminology." In fact, the age-crime relationship is so powerful that some researchers say the postwar baby boom can help explain why crime rose during the 1960s and 70s—when the Baby Boomers' children moved through adolescence.[47]

Figure 3.1   Example of an Age-Crime Curve

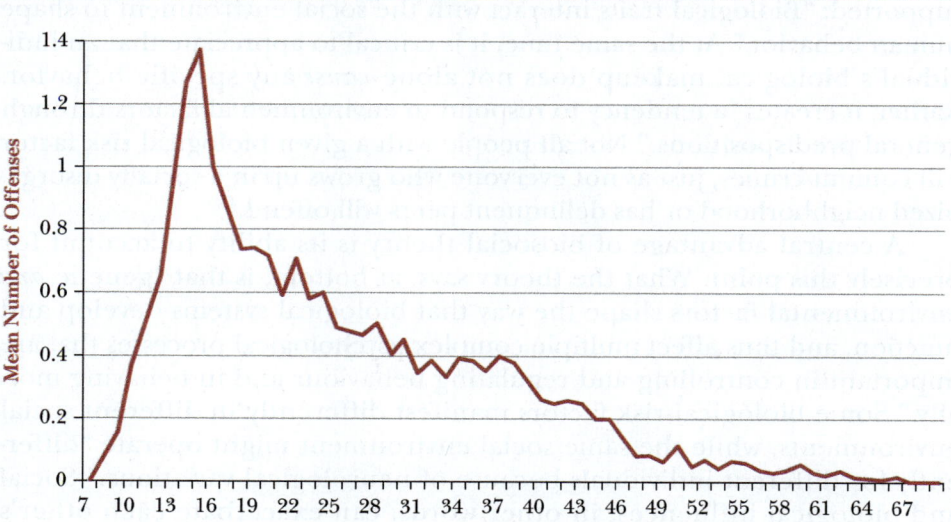

Robert J. Sampson & John H. Laub, *Life-Course Desisters? Trajectories of Crime Among Delinquent Boys Followed to Age 70*, 41 Criminology 301, 312 fig.1 (2003)

The age-crime relationship likely reflects some social factors. Adolescents might be monitored more closely than adults (enabling greater detection of crime) or might have weaker social bonds to encourage conformity. At the same time, few would deny that biology contributes significantly. As the Supreme Court has explained, quoting a research-packed brief from the American Psychological Association, "It is increasingly clear that adolescent brains are not yet fully mature in regions and systems related to higher-order executive functions such as impulse control, planning ahead, and risk avoidance." Miller v. Alabama, 567 U.S. 460, 472 n.5 (2012). Indeed, it now appears that this psychosocial immaturity persists well into an individual's twenties.[48]

2. Sex. As ample research shows, males are far more likely to commit crime—especially violent crime—than females.[*] The male-to-female violent crime ratio is more than 4 to 1. For homicides, it reaches almost 10 to 1.[49]

———————

[*] Much criminological research has overlooked transgender and gender nonbinary individuals. Put differently, the terms "male" and "female," as commonly used in the field, appear to refer both to sex assigned at birth and gender, assuming a world comprising only cisgender, gender binary individuals. Calls for a "queer criminology," however, aim to change this. For an example, see Carrie L. Buist & Emily Lenning, *Queer Criminology* (2016).

As with the age-crime curve, some of this gap is likely socially con-structed. Boys are socialized differently from girls from an early age, raised and taught by society to adopt different behaviors and attitudes. Likewise, parents may give boys more freedom to associate with delinquent peers. It is unlikely, though, that biology is absent in male offending. Recent research has found that biological factors including testosterone levels and resting heart rate partly explain the gap between the sexes. And in fact, differences in physically aggressive behavior have been observed as early as infancy.[50]

What is less clear is the extent to which, given these sociological and biological differences, female offending is driven by the same factors as male offending. Put another way, it is unclear how well "general" crimino-logical theories (which focus on men) can explain female offending at all. Surprisingly little research tackles female crime. Lombroso himself applied his evolutionary perspective to female offenders, arguing that (like male offenders) they were biological throwbacks marked by physical stigmata such as moles and masculine facial features. It would take another 75 years before feminist criminologists in the United States would look into the question of female offending again. In the midst of second-wave feminism, theories emerged predicting that, as women gained social equality, their offending would come to resemble that of men. Around the same time, research also began to demonstrate that both the patterns of and pathways to violent offending seem to vary between men and women—women more often kill intimate relations, for example. This work has led to the develop-ment of a "gendered" theory of crime that accepts certain general deter-minants of criminal involvement but adds that gendered concerns—such as gender norms, physical strength, and sexuality—mediate how crimino-genic forces influence the nature and incidence of offending.[51]

3. Brain Development and Function. Perhaps the clearest example of biosocial criminology comes from studying the ways brain development and function affect people's propensity to commit crime. The most prominent finding may come from the many studies documenting how lead exposure increases violent behavior; new evidence suggests air pollution may do the same. As scientists have shown, these environmental toxins damage the brain's prefrontal cortex, which regulates behavior and is one of the body's main drivers of impulse control. Drawing on this finding, some criminolo-gists point to environmental legislation mandating unleaded gasoline as a major driver in the crime drop of the 1990s.[52]

Similar biological mechanisms are at play when the brain is injured in other ways. The U.S. Supreme Court, for example, once blocked the exe-cution of a man named Lawrence Jefferson who had been convicted of a violent murder. When he was two years old, Jefferson had suffered a serious traumatic brain injury when a car ran over the top of his head. The result-ing brain damage caused him to experience "emotional dullness, restless or aggressive characteristics, impulsiveness, temper outbursts, markedly diminished impulse control, impaired social judgment, and transient outbursts of rage" that were "totally inconsistent with his normal behavioral pattern." Jefferson v. Upton, 560 U.S. 284, 286 (2010) (per curiam) (cleaned up). More subtly, but still consequentially, studies have shown that impaired fetal and infant development related to poor maternal health during pregnancy, birth complications, and infant malnutrition—all of which have sociological underpinnings—can impact brain development in criminogenic ways. One prominent theory contends that neuropsychological deficits along the lines described above separate the relatively small group of individuals who never "age out" of crime from the much larger group whose deviance is principally limited to their adolescent years.[53]

Finally, and perhaps most controversially, modern criminologists suggest that certain neuropsychological factors less severe than brain damage can nonetheless cause "individuals to pursue short-term gratification without consideration of the long-term consequences of their acts." Traditionally labeled *self-control theory*, this account of crime initially attributed an individual's ability to refrain from antisocial behavior to sociological factors, including the extent to which parents and other adult authority figures monitor and correct deviant behavior, primarily during early childhood but also later into adolescence. But neuroscientific studies have now begun to demonstrate that genetics, too, play a role in individual self-control. Likewise, interaction between sociological stressors and biological processes can influence self-control. Researchers have found, for example, that prefrontal brain function is altered in some children facing intense socioeconomic challenges in ways similar to the effects of brain damage. Exposure to violence, discussed above, also impairs self-control.[54]

As for the implications of these findings, empirical research confirms that self-control robustly predicts crime. One study, which followed 1,000 children from birth to age 32, found that childhood self-control—measured as early as 3 to 5 years old by researcher-observers and later teachers, parents, and the children themselves—predicted criminal offending even after controlling for intelligence and social class. In a separate cohort of 500 sibling pairs, the sibling with lower self-control at age 5 was significantly more likely to engage in antisocial behavior by early adolescence, despite shared family background.[55]

II.   POTENTIAL APPLICATION WITHIN THE CRIMINAL LAW

"Criminal trials . . . compel us to explore [and thus] offer some slight hope that we will learn, in the course of deciding individual cases, something about the causes of crime."

United States v. Alexander, 471 F.2d 923, 926
(D.C. Cir. 1972) (Bazelon, C.J.)

As the preceding section demonstrates, crime is influenced by many factors beyond individual choices and decisions. A person's biology, upbringing, interpersonal relationships, neighborhood dynamics and institutions, and exposure to societal harms like poverty and violence all play substantial roles in spurring crime. As sociologist W.E.B. Du Bois writes in the quote opening this chapter, crime "is a phenomenon that stands not alone, but rather as a symptom of countless wrong social conditions."[56]

And yet, as Professor David Sklansky observes, criminal law and the logics and practices of the American penal system often seem to operate on a different premise, with criminology and criminal law like two fields passing in the night, if not drifting apart. The result, Sklansky writes, is that "lawmakers have increasingly tended to treat criminal violence," if not crime itself, "as characterological instead of situational."[57]

This tendency to individualize — to treat crime as primarily, if not exclusively, a product of personal choices divorced from societal forces — is present throughout various aspects of substantive criminal law, as will be evident in many of the chapters that follow. Our goal in this section is to put this disconnect front and center by focusing on one area within the criminal law where one might expect the sociological drivers of crime to be most relevant: the legal doctrines of excuse. These doctrines exculpate individuals who have done something wrong, but under conditions or circumstances the law deems to relieve them of criminal liability. Our focus here will be on four doctrines, three of which are recognized but narrow, and one of which was urged on courts decades ago but never taken up. Throughout our study of these doctrines, our goal will be to ask why and when the law deems certain people eligible for punishment, how the law can or should interact with sociological understandings of crime, and why the legal system might be reluctant to incorporate insights from the sociology of crime.

A. *The Insanity Defense*

Finger v. State

27 P.3d 66 (Nev. 2001)

BECKER, J. In April of 1996, appellant Frederick Finger was . . . accused of murdering his mother, Franziska Brassaw, by stabbing her in the head with a kitchen knife. . . . [A]t the time of his arraignment, the district court denied Finger's request to enter a plea of "not guilty by reason of insanity" as that plea had been abolished by the 1995 Nevada Legislature. Subsequently, Finger entered a plea of guilty but mentally ill to a charge of second-degree murder. The district court convicted Finger of second-degree murder and sentenced him to serve life in prison with minimum parole eligibility after ten years.

[W]e conclude that Nevada's current statutory scheme would permit an individual to be convicted of a criminal offense under circumstances where the individual lacked the mental capacity to form the applicable intent to commit the crime, a necessary element of the offense. . . .

FACTS

[On April 10, 1996, at approximately 4:00 a.m., Finger's neighbor Jeff Jordan woke to the sound of a woman screaming. Finger soon pounded on Jordan's door, shouting, "Someone killed my mother! She's hurt real bad! I think she might be dead!" Jordan called 911. When the police arrived, Finger was standing outside, some distance down the block. Police officers approached Finger, who fled. When the officers caught up with Finger, they saw he was covered in blood. Finger announced that "someone beat my mother and killed her" and "the Mexican guy who lives in her house killed her." Jose Rivera, who lived with Finger and Brassaw, let the police into the house, where they discovered Brassaw's body. Rivera, who had no blood on his clothes, told the police he'd been awakened by the sound of a fight and opened his door to see Brassaw staggering as if injured. He then barricaded himself until the noise died down. Another neighbor told the police he'd been awakened by the sound of Finger's voice outside his window; Finger was holding an object and mumbled, "I framed my mother." This neighbor led the police to a bloodied kitchen knife not far from where Finger had been standing. Finger was arrested for murder.]

Finger has an extensive history of mental illness. He was first determined to be mentally ill in 1972 at the age of seventeen. Finger has been diagnosed as suffering from schizophrenia, manic depressive disorder with homicidal and suicidal tendencies, intermittent explosive disorder and paranoia. Finger periodically suffers from visual and auditory hallucinations. In addition, Finger had a long history of violence and co-dependency with his mother and had been institutionalized in mental health facilities several times due to delusions and attacks on his mother or other members of his family.

Upon interviewing Finger, it was immediately apparent to defense counsel that Finger was of questionable mental capacity. Counsel sought psychiatric evaluations. Two of the three evaluations concluded that Finger was unable to aid in his own defense. Based upon the evaluations, the district court committed Finger to the Lakes Crossing Center for the Criminally Insane until such time as he was found competent to participate in judicial proceedings.

In the course of these evaluations, Finger gave two different versions of what happened to his mother. The first version was consistent with his statements to the police. Finger claimed that Rivera had killed his mother, but could not give a coherent explanation for the blood on his clothes or his possession of the knife. The second version was an admission that he had stabbed his mother because she had been plotting to kill him and he decided to kill her before she had the opportunity to carry out her plot.

On December 18, 1996, Finger was deemed competent [for trial]. . . . Finger requested permission from the district court to enter a plea of not guilty by reason of insanity. . . . Based upon the district court's denial of his request . . . and, by inference, his ability to raise insanity as a complete defense to the murder charge, Finger determined that there were no issues to be resolved by a trial. Therefore, Finger entered his plea of guilty but mentally ill . . . [and] was convicted of second-degree murder. . . .

DISCUSSION

. . . In 1995 the Legislature abolished the plea of "not guilty by reason of insanity" and created a new plea of "guilty but mentally ill." . . . [A]n individual pleading "guilty but mentally ill" is still subject to the same punishment as an individual who enters an unconditional plea of guilty or is found guilty upon trial. In the case of guilty but mentally ill defendants, however, the district court may suggest that the prison system provide certain types of treatment to the convicted individual. . . .

HISTORICAL PERSPECTIVE

For hundreds of years, societies recognized that insane individuals are incapable of understanding when their conduct violates a legal or moral standard, and they were therefore relieved of criminal liability for their actions. Such individuals did not escape responsibility for their actions; they were still locked away, but in asylums, not prisons.

This concept of treating individuals differently based upon their mental capacity is called legal insanity. It recognizes that a "crime" involves something more than just the commission of a particular act, it also involves a certain mental component. This mental component is usually referred to as the *mens rea* of a crime, or criminal intent. The term "*mens rea*" refers to the mental state of a person at the time of the commission of the criminal act. Most serious crimes, either at common law or by statute, require a particular degree of *mens rea,* or criminal intent, to be proven as a material element of the offense. This is usually demonstrated by the use of such words as "knowingly," "willfully," or "deliberately." Where a person is unable to form the required criminal intent, the *mens rea,* that person is considered to be legally insane.

The American Bar Association has researched and documented centuries of references to this idea.

> As early as the sixth century B.C., commentary on the Hebrew scriptures distinguished between harmful acts traceable to fault and those that occur

without fault. To those ancient scholars, the paradigm of the latter type of act was one committed by a child, who was seen as incapable of weighing the moral implications of personal behavior, even when willful; . . . insane persons were likened to children.

ABA Criminal Justice Mental Health Standards 324 (1989).

Although the general concept of legal insanity in relation to criminal culpability is centuries old, the definition of what constitutes legal insanity and how it should be presented to a jury under the American legal system is not so ancient. It first became a topic of intense legal discussion as a result of a singular instance in English history. In 1843, Daniel M'Naghten attempted to assassinate the prime minister of Britain. M'Naghten suffered from a paranoid delusion. He believed that the prime minister was conspiring to kill him. As a result of this delusional belief, M'Naghten determined that he would kill the prime minister before the prime minister could act against M'Naghten. M'Naghten shot at the prime minister's carriage, killing the prime minister's secretary, a passenger in the carriage. M'Naghten was acquitted of the crime based upon the definition of insanity which was given to the jury in the judge's instructions.

The acquittal was met with public outrage. Queen Victoria and the House of Lords summoned the judges of the common-law courts to answer questions regarding the concept of insanity and its relationship to moral and criminal culpability. Fourteen of the fifteen justices agreed that the instructions given to the jury were improper and that M'Naghten should not have been acquitted. The judges then endorsed the following definition of legal insanity, which has become known as the M'Naghten rule.

> The jurors ought to be told . . . that every man is to be presumed to be sane, and to possess a sufficient degree of reason to be responsible for his crimes, until the contrary be proved to their satisfaction; and that to establish a defence on the ground of insanity, it must be clearly proved that, at the time of the committing of the act, the party accused [was] laboring under such a defect of reason, from disease of the mind, as not to know the nature and quality of the act he was doing; or, if he did know it, that he did not know he was doing what was wrong.

M'Naghten's Case, 8 Eng. Rep. 718, 10 Cl. & Fin. 200, 209 (1843).

M'Naghten created a very strict guideline for determining insanity. The fact that a person had mental health problems did not necessarily mean that he or she could meet the M'Naghten test for insanity. In order to be considered legally insane under M'Naghten, a defendant must labor under a delusion so great that he is incapable of appreciating his surroundings. This delusion must do one of two things: (1) rob the defendant of the ability to understand what he is doing; or (2) deprive the defendant of the ability to appreciate that his action is wrong, that is, not authorized by law. For example, persons who think that they are shooting at a target shaped like a human being would meet the first factor of the standard. They would not understand the nature and quality of their act (*i.e.,* shooting at a person, not a target). Similarly, persons who thought they were soldiers in the middle of a battlefield and that the individuals they were killing were enemy forces would meet the second factor of *M'Naghten.* Such persons would know they were shooting and killing human beings, but would not understand that it was wrong because of their delusional belief they were in the middle of a war. . . .

Using this standard, the English common-law judges then concluded that M'Naghten was not legally insane because, even if his delusion were true and the prime minister was conspiring to kill M'Naghten, this would not entitle M'Naghten to take the law into his own hands and hunt down the prime minister.

While such severe delusional states do exist, they are not the kind of mental illness most commonly encountered in the criminal justice system. In the past one hundred and fifty years, few defendants with mental health problems have been acquitted based upon the legal insanity test set forth in *M'Naghten.*

Beginning in the early 1900s, some legal scholars and mental health professionals began to advocate for an expanded definition of legal insanity. They felt the M'Naghten rule was too limited and that people with severe mental illnesses were being improperly convicted of crimes. The M'Naghten rule looks only to the cognitive condition of the defendant's state of mind. That is, the ability of the defendant to perceive reality and make rational choices based upon that perception. If you can form the criminal intent to do an act, then the reasons why you think you must do the act are irrelevant. Advocates for change believed that individuals who suffered from partial delusions, such as a conspiracy complex, should not be subject to criminal incarceration, but should be committed to a treatment facility for the mentally ill. Although such individuals had the mental capacity to form the required *mens rea* or criminal intent, advocates argued that these individuals could not control their acts and that to handle such individuals through the criminal justice system was inhumane. This is referred to as the "volitional" component of legal insanity.

This advocacy resulted in some courts adopting a new standard for legal insanity, the irresistible impulse test. Under this theory, a defendant is legally insane if he or she suffers from a mental condition that creates overwhelming compulsions urging her to commit the illegal acts. For example, if a person was under a delusion that God wanted certain people killed and, based upon hearing the voice of God, that individual immediately began killing people around them, then that person would be legally insane under the irresistible impulse test, but not under the M'Naghten standard. The individual knew that he was killing human beings and that he was not authorized by law to take a human life, but he could not resist what he perceived to be the will of God and acted under the impulse of his delusion.

[In later years, some scholars and policymakers proposed a third approach that was ultimately adopted by the American Law Institute (ALI). Under this test,] a person is not responsible for criminal conduct committed during a time when, as a result of a severe mental disease or defect, that person lacks substantial capacity either to appreciate the criminality of his or her conduct or to conform his or her conduct to the requirements of law. . . . To be considered legally insane under the ALI [approach], a person does not have to be totally incapacitated, as with the M'Naghten rule, but they must have a substantial impairment of their mental capacity. . . .

The trend to expand the definition of legal insanity [exemplified by both the volitional component and the substantial capacity test] continued into the early 1980s. It ceased, however, as a result of John Hinckley's acquittal in the attempted assassination and shooting of President Ronald Reagan. Hinckley asserted the insanity defense, alleging he was under an irresistible compulsion brought on by a mental disease or defect. Hinckley would not have been able to assert his defense under the M'Naghten rule, but was successful in convincing a jury that he was legally insane under the lesser standards . . . that governed his trial.[2]

In response to the *Hinckley* case, many jurisdictions made changes to their laws regarding the concept of legal insanity. . . . [T]wo new approaches to dealing with mentally ill defendants were considered. The first [approach created a new form of verdict by which] a person can be found guilty, but mentally ill, of a criminal offense. It was originally intended as an additional verdict or plea, not as a replacement for the insanity defense. It gives the criminal justice system an alternative to either finding mentally ill persons guilty of a criminal offense or totally acquitting them of any criminal liability.

This allows states to maintain a stricter definition of insanity, but still provide for a verdict with different penalty implications for persons with mental health conditions that did not rise to the level of legal insanity. It has sometimes been described as . . . the rule of diminished capacity. In such a case, the state mandates different treatment for such individuals [following their convictions] than would be accorded to them under a more traditional finding of guilt. Thus a jury would be less inclined, out of sympathy for the defendant's mental condition, to improperly acquit a defendant because they would have another option.

---

2 Hinckley was obsessed with actress Jodie Foster and presidential assassins. He attempted to kill President Reagan in an effort to gain her attention and secure a place in history. While his thought process was clearly irrational, Hinckley knew that he was shooting at a human being and that such an action was illegal, indeed Hinckley intended to commit murder [to impress Foster].

The second [approach] developed after *Hinckley* involved [narrowing] the definition of legal insanity . . . to include only the first part of the M'Naghten rule. . . . [Under this approach, as] long as a defendant can appreciate the nature and quality of his act, he is not legally insane and is capable of forming the necessary *mens rea.* Therefore, the person who thought he was shooting at a target would still be legally insane, but the individual who believes he is killing an enemy soldier would not qualify as insane under the law. Under this approach, because the latter individual is capable of recognizing he was killing a human being, he possesses the requisite intent to kill. . . .

As can be seen from the above discussion, federal and state laws regarding the insanity defense cover a broad spectrum of theories with respect to the treatment accorded to a mentally ill defendant. They are the product of society's continuing struggle over the need to protect the public from the actions of such individuals versus our recognition that a [severely] mentally ill individual may not possess the same level of culpability as a person who has no mental health problems.

Nevada law and the 1995 amendments

Prior to . . . 1995 . . . Nevada courts applied the [full] M'Naghten rule. . . . [I]n rare instances where individuals were found to be not guilty by reason of insanity, they were immediately committed to a mental health facility. They would only be released if a judge determined that they were no longer mentally ill and that they were not a danger to themselves or others. . . . [Following] the Hinckley decision [Nevada did not adopt any] new procedures or laws regarding legal insanity. Such actions were not necessary since Nevada already adhered to a very narrow view of legal insanity.

In 1995, at the urging of the Nevada District Attorney's Association, the Nevada Legislature considered several amendments to the laws involving the insanity defense. . . . The prosecutors believed that too many courts were allowing defendants to present evidence of mental health problems and argue for an insanity acquittal even when that evidence did not relate to, or support, a M'Naghten defense. Instead such evidence appeared to be more aligned with concepts of the irresistible impulse [or other] theories of legal insanity which were not recognized under Nevada law. . . .

[In response], the Legislature determined to abolish the concept of legal insanity as a defense to culpability. . . . Finger argues that due process requires [the state to show] a person not only intends to do the specific act, but also understands the act is wrong because it is not permitted by law. . . .

The history of American jurisprudence reflects that . . . the concept of legal insanity, that a person is not culpable for a criminal act because he or she cannot form the necessary *mens rea,* is . . . a fundamental principle. . . . Congress, even in the face of the public outrage following the

Hinckley trial, refused to completely abolish the concept of legal insanity, recognizing that culpability is a prerequisite to a criminal prosecution. While courts and scholars may debate what standard or definition should apply in determining what constitutes legal insanity . . . all have agreed that due process requires that a defendant be able to present evidence and argue that he or she lacked the *mens rea* to commit the criminal act. . . .

We conclude that legal insanity is a well-established and fundamental principle of the law of the United States. It is therefore protected by the Due Process Clause[] of . . . the . . . Nevada Constitution[]. . . . Thus the provisions of [the 1995 law] abolishing the insanity defense are unconstitutional and unenforceable. . . .

CLARIFICATION OF M'NAGHTEN

Because of the confusion over the application of *M'Naghten* evidenced in the legislative hearings [in 1995], we take this opportunity to clarify our previous case law. To qualify as being legally insane, a defendant must be in a delusional state such that he cannot know or understand the nature and capacity of his act, or his delusion must be such that he cannot appreciate the wrongfulness of his act, that is, that the act is not authorized by law. So, if a jury believes he was suffering from a delusional state, and if the facts as he believed them to be in his delusional state would justify his actions, he is insane and entitled to acquittal. If, however, the delusional facts would not amount to a legal defense, then he is not insane. . . .

This is a very narrow standard. Unless a defendant presents evidence that complies with this standard, he or she is not entitled to have the jury instructed on the issue of insanity. . . .

We understand that few people will qualify as legally insane under the M'Naghten rule. However, the adoption of a more expansive definition of legal insanity is not required by the . . . Nevada Constitution[] and is therefore a legislative, not a judicial prerogative.

APPLICATION TO FINGER

[Finger reasonably believed that under the 1995 law, which we today hold unconstitutional, he] would have been prohibited from arguing legal insanity as defined by *M'Naghten*. . . . He is therefore entitled to withdraw his plea of guilty but mentally ill, enter a plea of not guilty in accordance with this opinion and proceed to trial. On the limited record presented to us, it appears that Finger killed his mother because of his delusional belief that she was conspiring with others to kill him and he needed to kill her before she could carry out her scheme. If this was his delusional belief, Finger would not qualify as legally insane. This is because there is no evidence that, in his delusion, he believed he was in imminent danger which, if true, would justify self-defense.* However, we are mindful of the fact that the record is incomplete. Finger never fully developed his expert testimony on the record. Therefore, there may be additional evidence to support a M'Naghten defense. We therefore remand this matter to the district court for further proceedings consistent with this opinion. . . .

NOTES AND QUESTIONS

1. A Choice of Tests. As the *Finger* court explains, "federal and state laws regarding the insanity defense cover a broad spectrum of theories with respect to the treatment accorded to a mentally ill defendant." Today, some states follow the *M'Naghten* test, a stringent standard that deems the defendant insane only if he committed a crime while operating "under such a defect of reason, from disease of the mind, as not to know the nature and quality of the act he was doing; or, if he did know it, that he did not know he was doing what was wrong." Others add to this the "irresistible impulse" test, which recognizes that insanity can stem not only from impairments to *cognitive* or *moral capacity* (as in *M'Naghten*), but also to *volitional capacity*. A defendant is excused under this test if a qualifying mental condition overwhelmingly compelled him to break the law. And others take a still more expansive view that does not require *total* impairment of cognitive, moral, or volitional capacity, but rather a lack of *substantial capacity* along any of these dimensions.

As *Finger* also explains, some states have moved in the opposite direction, limiting or even abolishing the insanity defense. The *Finger* court invalidated Nevada's attempt to do so under the state's constitution. The federal Constitution, however, may impose no such limitation, giving states virtually free rein to shape the insanity defense as they see fit.[58]

2. "Disease of the Mind." Success on an insanity plea requires proving not only the right kind and degree of impairment under state law, but also a causal connection between the impairment and a "disease of the mind." The law is surprisingly unclear on what qualifies as a "disease of the mind." But as the *Finger* court explains, the fact that a person has "mental health problems" is not itself enough, given the breadth of accepted mental-health-related diagnoses. Within this universe, all courts seem to agree that some types of psychosis will suffice to provide a predicate for an insanity defense; the doctrinal dispute is mainly over what else should count. Severe post-traumatic stress disorder, for example, and multiple personality disorder (i.e., dissociative identity disorder) both have been the basis for successful

---

* Editor's Note: In order to claim self-defense, a person must typically be in immediate danger of physical harm; harm that is more temporally removed is not enough. We will discuss this aspect of self-defense doctrine in detail in Chapter Four.

insanity defenses. The temporary effects of intoxication, by contrast, as well as the bodily compulsion experienced during substance use withdrawal, do not qualify as "diseases of the mind."[59]

   3. Diminished Capacity. As the *Finger* court indicates, some states separately permit what is called a *diminished capacity* defense. Though similarly founded upon evidence of some abnormal mental condition, the diminished capacity defense differs significantly from the insanity defense. In fact, diminished capacity is often pled by defendants who suffer from some mental abnormality that does not qualify as a "disease of the mind" for purposes of insanity or does not inhibit their capacity to understand the nature of their actions or their wrongfulness. Instead, a defendant pleading diminished capacity argues that his mental condition prevented him from forming the *mens rea* required for conviction of the crime with which he's been charged. In practice, the issue arises most frequently in first-degree murder cases. As you will learn in Chapter Four, many states require the prosecution to prove an especially heightened degree of *mens rea* for this offense (known as *premeditation* or *deliberation*). It is possible to form an intent to kill without having this added degree of *mens rea*. It is thus also possible to have a mental condition that substantially interferes with one's ability to premeditate, while not necessarily impeding the ability to form a criminal intent. Evidence of diminished capacity typically leads to conviction of a lesser crime (such as second-degree murder) but not to total exculpation.

   4. Competency and Civil Commitment. The insanity defense is distinct from two other legal doctrines concerning the intersection of mental health conditions and the criminal law. The first concerns a defendant's *competency to stand trial.* Recall that, in *Finger*, the trial court initially accepted expert views that "Finger was unable to aid in his own defense." Based on that finding, the court ordered Finger to be sent to a psychiatric institution "until such time as he [could be] found competent to participate in judicial proceedings." Here, the court was invoking a rule of federal constitutional law holding that "a person whose mental condition is such that he lacks the capacity to understand the nature and object of the proceedings against him, to consult with counsel, and to assist in preparing his defense may not be subjected to a trial." Drope v. Missouri, 420 U.S. 162, 171 (1975). This inquiry focuses on the defendant's mental capacity at the time of trial, not the time of the offense. And the prohibition on proceeding to trial lasts only so long as the defendant remains unable to understand the nature of the proceedings or to participate in his defense. As in *Finger*, a court may detain an incompetent defendant at a psychiatric facility in hopes of restoring his competency to stand trial, though he "cannot be held more than the reasonable period of time necessary to determine whether there is a substantial probability that he will attain that capacity in the foreseeable future." Jackson v. Indiana, 406 U.S. 715, 738 (1972). In certain circumstances, a defendant may be forcibly medicated in an effort to restore his competency to stand trial. *See* Sell v. United States, 539 U.S. 166 (2003). In Finger's case, he was ultimately deemed competent to stand trial, which is why the case against him was able to proceed.

Separately, individuals suffering from certain mental health conditions can be *civilly committed*. As discussed in Chapter One, civil commitment is a form of involuntary confinement distinct from criminal punishment. As the Supreme Court held in *Kansas v. Hendricks* (p. 47), civil commitment statutes do "not establish criminal proceedings" and the "involuntary confinement" they authorize is deemed "not punitive." 521 U.S. 346, 369 (1997). A person need not be accused of any crime to be civilly committed. Anyone who "is mentally ill and . . . requires hospitalization for his own welfare and protection of others" could be civilly confined in a mental health facility against his will. Foucha v. Louisiana, 504 U.S. 71, 75-76 (1992). There is, though, a direct link between the insanity defense and civil commitment: A defendant who prevails on an insanity defense will be acquitted of criminal charges but, in nearly every state, will face automatic civil commitment proceedings. In most states, there are no limits to the duration of that commitment — it can last longer than the maximum prison sentence for the offense charged, if not indefinitely. Most states provide some mechanism for regular judicial review to see whether commitment remains appropriate. But this is no guarantee of release. After being found not guilty by reason of insanity and civilly committed following his attempted assassination of President Reagan, John Hinckley stayed in an institution for 35 years, even though his doctors had declared his mental illness in full remission after 15.[60]

5. Asylums and Prisons. Prisons and psychiatric institutions have long been intertwined. Indeed, one of the foundational works of American prison history is David Rothman's book *The Discovery of the Asylum*, which explores the carceral system's roots in a set of institutions including what would today be called sites of civil detention. These institutions are now formally distinct: the word *prison* means something distinct from the words *asylum* or *psychiatric hospital*. But the interrelationship between the institutions remains, as both continue to house overlapping segments of society.[61]

In 1939, British psychiatrist Lionel Penrose advanced a now-famous "balloon theory" that posited a near-perfect overlap in those populations. Squeeze down on one of the two institutions, he predicted, and the other will balloon in size. On a facial level, that dynamic appears to describe the United States during the twentieth century. At mid-century, the inpatient psychiatric hospitalization rate was three times the incarceration rate. This state of affairs prompted the deinstitutionalization movement of the 1960s and 70s that aimed to shrink substantially the number of people who were

Figure 3.2   U.S. Incarceration and Psychiatric Hospitalization Rates

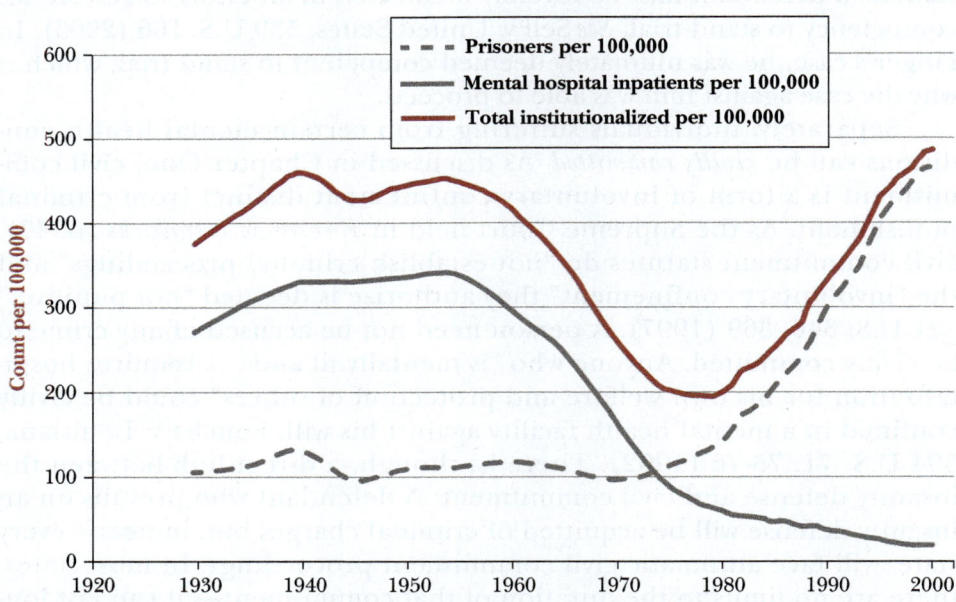

Steven Raphael & Michael A. Stoll, *Assessing the Contribution of the Deinstitutionalization of the Mentally Ill to Growth in the U.S. Incarceration Rate*, 42 J. Legal Stud. 187, 188 fig.1 (2013)

civilly committed. By the end of the century, that population had significantly fallen — and prisons were larger by a long shot.[62]

A closer examination, though, reveals a more complicated set of dynamics. As the authors of the leading study put it, "the 1950 demographic composition of the mental hospital population differs considerably from the 2000 demographic composition of prison and jail inmates." The type of people who are in prison now, in other words, are largely not the same type of people who were in mental hospitals in a previous era. That said, there is evidence of a direct pipeline from mental hospitals to carceral facilities toward the end of the twentieth century, with the deinstitutionalization movement likely causing four to seven percent of the prison boom in the century's last two decades. "While this is a relatively small contribution to the prison population growth overall," the same study explains, it does suggest "that a sizable portion of the mentally ill behind bars would not have been incarcerated in years past."[63]

Regardless of how we got here, there can be no doubt that, today, mental illness is prevalent in American jails and prisons. At least half of incarcerated individuals report having mental health problems or symptoms indicative of mental illness. The rate of *severe* mental illness in jails and prisons is nearly five times that of the general adult population. In fact, these penal institutions are frequently among the country's largest mental health institutions, with Chicago's Cook County Jail "considered the largest mental-health facility in the nation."[64]

At the same time, popular concerns that individuals with mental illness are dangerous do not track existing evidence. The best estimates find that only four percent of violent acts in the United States are directly attributable to serious mental illness. One study reports that people with mental illness are less likely than the general population to be seriously violent. If anything, the evidence indicates that people suffering from mental illness experience a significantly elevated risk of being the victims of violence, not the perpetrators.[65]

Rather than violence, a huge number of people with mental illness are incarcerated for crimes of poverty and need. Many of them are arrested repeatedly for things like retail theft (to find necessities), breaking and entering (to find shelter), or drug possession (to self-medicate). For many of these individuals, the door to jail is a revolving one. Unsurprisingly, given these realities, a growing body of research finds that access to health care — especially mental health care and substance abuse treatment — reduces crime in the community.[66]

6. *A Narrow Defense.* Recall the *Finger* court's pronouncement that "few people will qualify as legally insane." That seems especially true in states (like Nevada) that have embraced a narrow version of the defense, and doubly true in states like Kansas and Arizona that have gone even further, limiting their insanity tests to cognitive and moral incapacity, respectively. But even in states adopting broader versions of the test, the insanity defense very rarely succeeds. According to one report, only 0.008 percent of felony cases in which the state disputes the defendant's attempt to raise an insanity defense end with a verdict of not guilty by reason of insanity.[67]

Given the prevalence of mental illness in jails and prisons, it is worth considering why the insanity defense is applied so narrowly. Part of the reason is surely a concern that malingering defendants are feigning mental illness to escape responsibility for their crimes. Fiction across centuries is full of such tales, from Odysseus and Hamlet in classic literature on through the defendants portrayed by Edward Norton in *Primal Fear* and Jack Nicholson in *One Flew over the Cuckoo's Nest*. In real life, the so-called Hillside Strangler, Kenneth Bianchi, pleaded insanity and convinced multiple psychiatrists that he had multiple personalities before his ruse was revealed. And in perhaps the most notorious example of malingering in the criminal context, Vincent Gigante, boss of the Genovese crime family for almost 25 years, feigned insanity for decades, frequently wandering the streets of Greenwich Village in his bathrobe and slippers, mumbling to himself.[68]

At a deeper level, though, the real issue may not be too many feigned mental illnesses but too many real ones. Roughly 20 percent of Americans

(53 million) live with some mental illness, while roughly 6 percent (14 mil-lion) have a serious mental illness that substantially interferes with major life activities. Notably, the majority of people suffering from such condi-tions do not receive mental health services or medication. There are many reasons people who might benefit from treatment don't seek it, including denial or a commitment to self-help. But among those who do want assis-tance, roughly half cite financial barriers as a reason for not obtaining it. The deinstitutionalization movement that began in the 1960s, kickstarted by the Community Mental Health Act of 1963, was designed to shift care from state-run asylums to community-based mental health centers. Yet congressional funding never came for that transformation, and to this day many communities are unable to provide the care their residents need.[69]

The end result is a large gap between society's mental health needs and the mental healthcare it provides. And when people fall through that crack, they often find their way into the penal system. "When people do not receive the care they need, they become symptomatic," explains Nneka Jones Tapia, a psychologist and former warden of Cook County Jail. Often, she goes on to note, their symptomatic "behaviors look criminal. And we have done an excellent job of criminalizing people with mental illness." Put more simply, the penal system presently functions in part as a means of con-trolling societal mental health issues—using arrests, court supervision, and incarceration to manage a problem that might otherwise be treated as a public health issue. A more robust insanity defense would make it harder to use the criminal law this way.[70]

B. Intoxication

United States v. F.D.L.

836 F.2d 1113 (8th Cir. 1988)

GIBSON, J. F.D.L. and R.L.R. appeal from an adjudication of delin-quency . . . following the district court's determination that defendants were guilty of committing involuntary manslaughter on an Indian reser-vation. . . . On appeal, both F.D.L. and R.L.R. allege that the district court erred in rejecting their defense claim of temporary insanity by reason of involuntary intoxication. . . .

On Monday, January 27, 1986, the frozen body of Loren Lyons was dis-covered in the back seat of his car, which was stuck in the snow off a road in Redlake, Minnesota. Lyons had died of hypothermia.

On the previous Friday night, F.D.L., R.L.R. and Connie Lussier, R.L.R.'s fifteen-year-old half-sister, after drinking several beers, went to [a] gas station in the "back of town" area of Redlake. There they met Lyons, who had also been drinking, and asked him for a ride. Lyons agreed. . . . [After some time,] Lyons pulled his car to the side of the road and rolled two marijuana cigarettes. Connie Lussier saw Lyons sprinkle a white powder on the marijuana. R.L.R., who was riding in the seat next to Lyons, did not see the white powder. There was testimony that the white powder Connie Lussier saw sprinkled on the marijuana was probably phencyclidine (commonly known as PCP or angel dust). . . . [T]he defendants and Connie Lussier testified they felt unusually "high" after smoking the marijuana.

The group drove around Red Lake for another twenty minutes or so, when Lyons stopped the car so the defendants could urinate. [A fight broke out in which F.D.L. and R.L.R overpowered Lyons.] Connie Lussier testified the beating lasted fifteen minutes. After the fight, Lyons was unconscious. F.D.L. and R.L.R. lifted Lyons into the car and put him in the back seat. They could hear him breathing and snoring, and didn't think they had hurt him badly. . . . F.D.L. and R.L.R. continued to drive, with Lyons in the back seat of the car. After dropping off Connie at the home of Sheldon Bailey, R.L.R. lost control of the car as he fumbled for a cigarette. The road was icy, and the car slid into a ditch and became embedded in a snow bank.

Leaving the motor and heater running, and a door ajar to prevent carbon monoxide poisoning, the defendants abandoned the car and walked about one-half mile to the home of Sheldon Bailey. R.L.R. walked that distance without his winter coat and testified that he didn't remember feeling cold. . . .

Over the weekend several people, including F.D.L., walked past Lyons' car in the ditch. No one observed until Monday that Lyons was in it. Temperatures in the area sank from eight degrees above zero on Friday night to twenty-six degrees below on Sunday night and Lyons froze to death.

On appeal, F.D.L. and R.L.R. . . . argue that the trial court improperly rejected their claims of temporary insanity due to involuntary intoxication. . . . The Fifth Circuit has stated: "The concept of criminal responsibility in the federal courts is a congeries of judicially made rules of decision based on common law concepts." United States v. Lyons, 731 F.2d 243, 247 (5th Cir. 1984) (en banc). The practice of relieving a defendant of criminal responsibility, because of involuntary intoxication, extends back to the earliest days of common law.

The courts dealing with this issue, nearly all of them state courts, have defined involuntary intoxication in essentially the same terms as insanity. Like insanity, involuntary intoxication diminishes the culpability of a crime. The defendant is excused from criminality because intoxication affects the ability to distinguish between right and wrong. Thus, the mental state of an involuntarily intoxicated defendant is measured by the test of legal insanity. . . . These cases all require a finding that there has been involuntary ingestion of an intoxicant, usually through trickery, and that the defendant was unable to appreciate the nature and quality or wrongfulness of his acts.

There are facts in this record to support a finding that R.L.R. and F.D.L. were involuntarily intoxicated because, unknown to them, PCP had been added to their marijuana cigarettes. There was testimony that PCP is commonly added to marijuana cigarettes; that PCP was a problem on the reservation; and that PCP was added to the cigarettes smoked by the defendants. Additionally, testimony established that R.L.R. walked a considerable distance without his coat in extremely cold weather, conduct that is at least consistent with the anesthetic effects of PCP. . . .

The findings of the district court, however, are sufficient to dispose of the involuntary intoxication defense, as they reject its second element, namely, that the defendants were unable to appreciate the nature and quality or wrongfulness of their acts. The district court found that at the time of the acts resulting in Lyons' death, the defendants were capable of knowing and did know, that their conduct was a threat to his life and they were able to foresee the consequences of their acts. These findings establish that R.L.R. and F.D.L. were able to appreciate the nature and quality or wrongfulness of their acts. Thus, the converse of the second element of the involuntary intoxication defense is established. . . . Accordingly, we reject the argument of F.D.L. and R.L.R. that the district court erred in refusing to accept the defense of involuntary intoxication.

Additionally, even if the district court believed that PCP was added to the marijuana, it may have determined the intoxication was not involuntary, but voluntary. R.L.R. and F.D.L. had voluntarily consumed beer and smoked marijuana cigarettes. Any intoxication resulting from this activity would be no defense. . . . In a factually similar case, *People v. Velez*, 221 Cal. Rptr. 631 (Cal. Ct. App. 1985), the defendant raised the defense of involuntary intoxication after smoking a marijuana cigarette unaware it contained PCP. The Court in holding the defendant *voluntarily* intoxicated as a matter of law noted,

> [A] reasonable person has no right to assume that a marijuana cigarette furnished to him at a social gathering will not contain PCP; nor may such a person assume such a marijuana cigarette will produce any predictable intoxicating effect. Absent these assumptions, defendant cannot contend he was involuntarily intoxicated, because he has no right to expect the substance he consumed was other than what it was nor that it would produce an intoxicating effect different from the one it did.

Id. at 638. . . .

We affirm the judgment of conviction.

NOTES AND QUESTIONS

1. **Kingston *Redux.*** The rule stated in *F.D.L.* is the general one: involuntary intoxication excuses criminal conduct only if its effects rise to the heights of temporary insanity. Partly on this rationale, when the House of Lords considered the case of Barry Kingston described at the beginning of this chapter, it rejected his argument that he sexually assaulted his victim only because he himself had been involuntarily drugged:

> [T]here is an instinctive attraction in the proposition that a retributory system of justice should not visit penal consequences on acts which are the ultimate consequence of an event outside the volition of the actor. . . . [But the jury's guilty verdict implies] that whatever drug [Kingston] may have taken had not had such an effect on his mind that he did not intend to do what he did. . . . [N]or was it suggested that the effect of the drug was to produce a condition of temporary insanity. . . . In ordinary circumstances [Kingston's] paedophilic tendencies would have been kept under control, even in the presence of the unconscious or sleeping boy on the bed. The ingestion of the drug . . . brought about a temporary change in the mentality or personality of [Kingston] which lowered his ability to resist temptation so far that his desires overrode his ability to control them. Thus we are concerned here with a case of disinhibition. The drug is not alleged to have created the desire to which [Kingston] gave way, but rather to have enabled it to be released.

Regina v. Kingston [1995] 2 AC 355 (HL) 363-364. On this view, the individual who has been drugged is no different from one who, for whatever reasons beyond his control, has little willpower. Accordingly, a defendant's claim "that he would not have committed the crime had he been sober is no defense," explains a leading treatise, "any more than one's claim that he would not have committed a crime of violence had he been a less excitable or pugnacious person, or a crime of theft had he been of a less acquisitive nature."[71]

The House of Lords added a litany of pragmatic reasons for declining to expand the involuntary intoxication defense to cover cases like Kingston's:

> Before the jury could form an opinion on whether the drug might have turned the scale witnesses would have to give a picture of the defendant's personality and susceptibilities, for without it the crucial effect of the drug could not be assessed; pharmacologists would be required to describe the potentially disinhibiting effect of a range of drugs whose identity would [sometimes] be unknown. . . . Much more significant would be the opportunities for a spurious defense. . . . The defendant would only have to assert, and support by the evidence of well-wishers, that he was not the sort of person to have done this kind of thing, and to suggest an occasion when by some means a drug might have been administered to him. . . .

Id. at 376-377. Are you persuaded? The House of Lords noted that it would find a way to confront these pragmatic difficulties "if that is what the interests of justice require," but that justice made "no such demands" in Kingston's case. Do you agree?[72]

2. The Meaning of "Involuntary." There can be little dispute that, in a scenario like *Kingston*—in which Penn "secretly administered" drugs to Kingston—Kingston's ingestion of the drugs and subsequent intoxication were "involuntary." But not every case is so clear. Involuntary intoxication also occurs when an individual is forced—for example, by threat of serious physical harm—to consume liquor or drugs or does so pursuant to medical advice. A few states also treat as involuntary so-called "pathological intoxication," which happens when the defendant knew what substance he was taking but experienced an unanticipated and grossly excessive reaction to it. A grayer area exists when the defendant's intoxication results from the combined effects of an involuntarily ingested substance and a voluntarily ingested illegal intoxicant. Hence the *F.D.L.* court's suggestion that F.D.L. and R.L.R.'s intoxication from PCP may have been, for legal purposes, voluntary after all.[73]

Then there is the question of addiction. When an individual who suffers from alcoholism or substance abuse disorder experiences an overwhelming compulsion to consume alcohol or drugs, then does so and becomes intoxicated as a result, is this involuntary intoxication? The law's response is clear: no. Indeed, while states may not punish addiction itself, *see* Robinson v. California, 370 U.S. 660 (1972) (p. 785), "most jurisdictions have held that an irresistible compulsion to consume intoxicants caused by a physiological or psychological disability does not render the ensuing intoxication involuntary." See v. State, 757 S.W.2d 947, 950 (Ark. 1988) (collecting cases). In considering whether this rule makes sense, note that an estimated 40 to 60 percent of addiction vulnerability is genetic, and that a huge number of people who use illegal drugs like heroin began with prescription opioids. But consider, also, the implications of the contrary rule.[74]

3. Voluntary Intoxication. Involuntary intoxication has been recognized as an excuse because, as with insanity stemming from a "disease of the mind," there is "no immoral or blameworthy stigma attached to the condition." People v. Low, 732 P.2d 622, 627 (Colo. 1987). The same has never been thought true of *voluntary intoxication*. Rather, an enduring line of thinking holds that "one who has voluntarily impaired his own faculties should be responsible for the consequences." Montana v. Egelhoff, 518 U.S. 37, 50 (1996). Some states embrace this view fully and forbid any defensive use of evidence of voluntary intoxication, hoping this will "deter[] drunkenness or irresponsible behavior while drunk." *Id.* Note that around 30 percent of people in prison report having consumed alcohol at the time of their offense and almost 40 percent report having used drugs.[75]

In states that do allow it, the defense of voluntary intoxication typically resembles the defense of diminished capacity: evidence of voluntary intoxication can be offered to argue that the defendant lacked the capacity to form the specific degree of *mens rea* required for conviction of the crime with which he's been charged, often resulting in conviction of a related but lesser offense. As with diminished capacity, this issue arises most frequently in connection with crimes that require the state to prove an especially elevated *mens rea*, such as first-degree murder. Some states restrict the defense to such cases.[76]

C. *Infancy*

In every state, youth — or *infancy*, as the legal doctrine is known — places some wrongdoers beyond the criminal law's reach. The notes that follow discuss this doctrine and the legal system's response to youth criminality.

NOTES AND QUESTIONS

1. The Infancy Defense. In discussing the rationale for the insanity defense, *Finger* previewed the rationale for the infancy allowance as well: the law's desire to distinguish "between harmful acts traceable to fault and those that occur without fault." In fact, the *Finger* court explains, "the paradigm of the latter type of act was one committed by a child, who was seen as incapable of weighing the moral implications of personal behavior, even when willful." Protection was then extended by analogy to defendants who are insane.

The common law developed a crisp framework to administer the infancy defense. It entirely "precluded criminal prosecution for children under the age of seven, and created a rebuttable presumption of incapacity for children seven to fourteen." Gammons v. State, 696 P.2d 700, 701 (Ariz. 1985). Children older than fourteen were held to have the same criminal capacity as adults. Some states continue to follow this basic common law framework today. In these states, to overcome the presumption of incapacity for children in the middle age range, "the surrounding circumstances must demonstrate . . . that the [child] knew what he was doing and that it was wrong." Adams v. State, 262 A.2d 69, 72 (Md. Ct. Spec. App. 1970). Notice, perhaps unsurprisingly, the strong parallel between this test and the *M'Naghten* test for insanity.[77]

2. Juvenile Delinquency. Most states have moved away from the common law's tripartite, discretionary framework. In these jurisdictions, children below a prescribed cutoff age cannot be criminally prosecuted as adults and are subject instead only to proceedings in the juvenile court system. Juvenile courts deal with various matters concerning minors, including cases involving *delinquent acts* that would be crimes if committed by an adult. The stated goal of delinquency proceedings is rehabilitation — helping troubled children mature into stable and law-abiding adults. Partly for this reason, juvenile court proceedings are relatively informal, bearing some, but not all, of the procedural trappings of adult criminal court. *Compare* In re Gault, 387 U.S. 1 (1967) (affording juveniles rights to due process, counsel, and against self-incrimination), *with* McKeiver v. Pennsylvania, 403 U.S. 528 (1971) (no right to a jury). Juvenile court proceedings are often closed to the public and the child's name is generally kept out of the public record. A child found to be delinquent may be committed to a juvenile detention facility, technically a form of civil commitment, but in some instances little different from prison for children. Detention must end when the juvenile court loses jurisdiction over the youth — which can be as late as age 21 — though many states allow a "blended sentence" that combines a term of juvenile detention with a subsequent adult prison term.[78]

About half the states impose no minimum age for juvenile delinquency charges, which means that a child of any age can be arrested and brought to court for delinquency proceedings. Among those that do place limits, the threshold can be as low as seven. In recent years, several states have raised this minimum age; New York, for example, went from seven years old to twelve and North Carolina from six to ten. While the juvenile system is intended to support the children who pass through it, juvenile courts and detention facilities have been subjected to intense and ongoing criticism for decades. According to critics, contact with the system harms, rather than improves, children's life outcomes and disproportionately burdens youth of color, due in part to racialized perceptions of deviance and violence. Readers interested in learning more about these issues may consult the sources cited in the notes.[79]

3. Trying Children as Adults. The infancy defense has long been subject to exceptions for particularly serious crimes. The common law's presumption of incapacity for children between seven and fourteen frequently gave way when a child had committed a particularly atrocious act. Many modern statutes incorporate similar rules. Where cases are assigned to criminal court based on the charges alone, with no consideration of the child's needs, the system's rehabilitative ideal becomes difficult to discern. Fear of juvenile violent crime and the accompanying turn to a general deterrence rationale has resulted in more and younger children being tried as adults in criminal court.[80]

As one example of how these schemes work, New York permits criminal prosecution of fourteen-year-olds for serious crimes like kidnapping and rape and of thirteen-year-olds for murder; for most other crimes, the line is drawn at seventeen or eighteen years old. Nationwide, one can find examples of ten- and eleven-year-olds being tried as adults for murder. Indeed, even in states that have, in response to concerted public pressure, recently raised their minimum age for criminal responsibility, carve-outs for violent crimes remain.[81]

4. Fear of the Black Child. Many critics contend that race is a dominant factor in how juvenile delinquency is perceived, defined, and addressed. Consider in this regard the excerpt below.

Kristin Henning, *The Rage of Innocence: How America Criminalizes Black Youth* 13-16 (2021). Forty years of adolescent self-report studies from the University of Michigan and the Centers for Disease Control confirm that youth of all races and ethnicities admit involvement in risky, irresponsible, and even dangerous behaviors. In 2018, 58.5 percent of high school teenagers surveyed in the United States reported that they had tried alcohol by the 12th grade, 42.9 percent had been drunk, and 49 percent had tried marijuana. More than 39 percent reported having had sex, and within that group 13.8 percent reported that they had used no protection to prevent pregnancy. Nothing in this data collection suggests that Black youth are inherently more reckless, impulsive, or dangerous than white youth. In fact, notwithstanding some differences in the type of drug, type of weapon, or age at the onset of such behaviors, white youth report risky behaviors at rates similar to—and sometimes higher than—Black and Hispanic youth.

All of these behaviors arise out of the same impulsive, short-sighted features of adolescence that are common among youth of all races. Yet we don't treat youth of all races the same. Poor Black youth who experiment with drugs and alcohol in public spaces like a park or a street corner are more visible—and appear more dangerous—than wealthier white youth who use drugs in the privacy of their own homes and clubhouses. Black youth who have greater access to more stereotypically frightening drugs like crack are demonized as violent criminals, while white youth who can afford more expensive drugs like powder cocaine are excused as impulsive and experimenting teens. Teachers and counselors who are inundated with negative images and faulty narratives about Black youth in poor, urban schools are less likely to tolerate and forgive adolescent misconduct than teachers who work with white youth in rural or wealthy communities. And police officers who are vulnerable to racial bias and stereotypes in fast-paced and stressful encounters with youth make snap judgments and racialized assumptions about what they see and how they will respond.

At every stage of the juvenile legal system, Black youth are treated more harshly than white youth. Despite years of evidence that white youth use drugs at the same rates as Black youth or higher, 19 percent of all drug cases referred to U.S. juvenile courts in 2018 involved Black youth. This data is notable when we consider that only 15 percent of youth in the juvenile-court age range that year were Black. Black youth also accounted for 35 percent of all juvenile arrests for any crime in 2018 and 40 percent of all cases in which the youth was sent to a detention facility to await trial or sentencing. Black youth accounted for 39 percent of all cases formally processed in a juvenile court, 37 percent of all cases in which the youth was found guilty, and more than 51 percent of youth whom a judge transferred from juvenile court to be tried as an adult. After they were found guilty, Black youth accounted for more than 41 percent of all cases in which the youth was placed in secure or nonsecure residential settings. . . .

So if the science and the data tell us that white youth act a lot like Black youth, then why don't we treat Black youth the same? The answer is simple: We don't see Black children as children.

D.   "Rotten Social Background"

Recall from the beginning of this chapter the case of Benjamin Murdock, who was prosecuted for shooting and killing a marine after a racially charged altercation in which Murdock was called racial slurs including the n-word. Murdock argued that his challenging childhood and upbringing had impaired his impulse control. On appeal from his conviction for second-degree murder, Murdock contested the trial court's decision to give the following jury instruction:

> We are not concerned with a question of whether or not a man had a rotten social background. We are concerned with the question of his criminal responsibility. That is to say, whether he had an abnormal condition of the mind that affected his emotional and behavioral processes at the time of the offense.

Murdock, 471 F.2d at 959. The court of appeals rejected Murdock's claim over a now-canonical dissent by Chief Judge Bazelon, who wrote:

> It may well be that the trial judge was motivated by a reasonable fear that the jury would reach its decision on the basis not of the law but of sympathy for the victims of a racist society. Nevertheless, I think that the quoted instruction was reversible error. It had the effect of telling the jury to disregard the testimony relating to Murdock's social and economic background and to consider only the testimony framed in terms of "illness." . . .
>
> [W]e sacrifice a great deal by discouraging Murdock's responsibility defense. If we could remove the practical impediments to the free flow of information we might begin to learn something about the causes of crime. We might discover, for example, that there is a significant causal relationship between violent criminal behavior and a "rotten social background." That realization would require us to consider, for example, whether income redistribution and social reconstruction are indispensable first steps toward solving the problem of violent crime.

Id. at 960, 965 (Bazelon, C.J., dissenting).

Bazelon's opinion did not carry the day, in Murdock's case or in the long run of American law. No jurisdiction has ever recognized a defendant's "rotten social background" or what later became called "severe environmental deprivation" (SED) as a valid basis for criminal exculpation. But Bazelon's argument in favor of such a defense did spark a passionate academic debate over whether and how the administration of the criminal law ought to account for societal drivers of crime. The legal system's decision to reject the defense, in other words, was deliberate and considered—and remains illuminative.

NOTES AND QUESTIONS

1. Arguments Favoring the Defense. Scholars who argued in favor of a poverty-based defense along the lines Judge Bazelon proposed in *Murdock* offered two principal arguments that will by now be familiar.

The first, Professor Michele Gilman explains, asserts that socioeconomic deprivation "can cause a defendant to commit a crime, thereby diminishing his responsibility, similar to a defense of diminished capacity or insanity." As Professor Norval Morris put the point (in now-outmoded language):

> Why not permit the defense of dwelling in a Negro ghetto? Such a defense would not be morally indefensible. Adverse social and subcultural background is statistically *more* criminogenic than is psychosis; like insanity, it also severely circumscribes the freedom of choice. . . .

Indeed, for Morris the poverty-driven defense flows *a fortiori* from the logic of the insanity defense: "You argue that insanity destroys, undermines, diminishes a man's capacity to reject what is wrong and adhere to what is right. So does the ghetto—more so."[82]

Separately, there is an argument for the defense that echoes the theories of social standing advanced by Professors Antony Duff, Victor Tadros, Erin Kelly, and Tommie Shelby at the close of the preceding chapter. As Professor Gilman again explains, the defense can be "justified with regards to social forfeit theory, which holds society morally responsible for its socioeconomic failures." In Bazelon's words, "it is simply unjust to place people in dehumanizing social conditions, to do nothing about those conditions, and then to command those who suffer, 'Behave—or else!'" The "law should not convict unless it can condemn."[83]

2. Theoretical Objections. Professor Stephen Morse, who debated with Bazelon in law reviews, offered one of the most comprehensive objections to the proposed defense. In philosophical terms, Morse rejects the idea that poverty or deprivation truly *causes* people to commit crimes. For him, such an argument is overly deterministic and elides the role individual agency plays in producing criminal acts.

> [W]e are all the victims of various pressures affecting our choices. All environments affect choices and make some choices easy and some choices

hard. The pressure on a person to break the law is certainly greater if all his friends and neighbors do it than if they do not. On the average, it will be harder for the person who lives in a "criminogenic" subculture to obey the law than for the person who lives in a crime-free subculture. We are not very surprised if the slum kid turns to crime. We are more surprised if the suburban kid does. Yet it is clear that the environment is not all-determinative: it interacts with intrapersonal factors. The majority of persons in the most criminogenic subculture are law-abiding, and there are members of law-abiding subcultures who break the law.

A person's behavior is a matter of harder choices and easier choices. But behavior *is* a matter of choice. . . . [And] where there is choice, it is both moral and respectful to the actor to hold the actor responsible. . . .[84]

Morse does not deny that there are *some* circumstances in which an individual's capacity to make genuinely free choices are so constrained as to warrant exculpation. He accepts, for example, that the conventional insanity defense is legitimate and justified to ensure that people are not punished for harms they could not avoid causing. Even "the law-and-order adherent," he writes, accepts that compulsion is an excusing condition. Morse "does not wish to punish the offender" if he "is convinced that a choice to offend is sufficiently unfree."[85]

The problem, in Morse's view, is that "there is no reason to believe that most people subjected to SED are acting under compulsion when they commit criminal acts." In other words, Morse writes, he is "simply not convinced that those Judge Bazelon considers unfree are, in fact, faced with sufficiently hard choices to justify acquittal." And, he goes on, for those who truly *are* suffering "from sufficiently impaired behavioral controls, then the insanity defense is the only doctrinal vehicle for raising such a claim."[86]

Of course, as Morse acknowledges, the insanity defense often will not apply in situations where a person's *social background* compels their antisocial behavior, because the doctrine requires a mental disorder. Morse considers this limitation unfortunate and contemplates expanding the insanity doctrine to cover such cases: "If we think that substantially impaired behavioral controls should mitigate or excuse, then the criminal law should develop a generic excusing condition for this situation that would be available to all defendants who might suffer from such impairments through no fault of their own." Still, the central point for Morse is that the defense should be framed in terms of compulsion, not deprivation:

> SED may be a risk factor for impaired behavioral controls, [but] an SED defense would be over-and-underinclusive . . . because many SED sufferers do not suffer from such problems and many non-SED sufferers may have such difficulties. . . . [Indeed,] it seems patronizing and demeaning to claim that all victims of SED are impaired human beings.[87]

3. Practical Challenges and Political Problems. Morse also responds to the argument that systemic injustice and other societally generated drivers of crime strip the state of the moral authority to punish.

> [A]n SED defense is not the appropriate means to achieve broad social justice in our moral and political culture. Advocates want nothing less than a massive transformation of our social structure. This is a political proposal, and it should be addressed by political institutions, especially the legislatures . . . which can provide and implement redistributional and other allegedly welfare-enhancing policies. In contrast, the primary purposes of criminal justice are to achieve retributive justice and social safety. An SED defense would do neither. The defense might indirectly increase social safety if jurors routinely accepted it, if society was consequently transformed, if severe deprivation was thereby diminished, and if crime vastly decreased as a result. But this is a pipedream.

In part this argument rests on a sharp distinction between the domains of law and politics. Morse seems to imply that law and legal actors like prosecutors and judges ought not be concerned with pursuing "broad social justice in our moral and political culture." That premise of Morse's argument is, of course, debatable.[88]

But Morse's rejoinder is also in part an argument about practicalities. He doubts that recognizing a deprivation defense would actually lead to social changes that address the root drivers of crime. Notably, Judge Bazelon shared some of this skepticism in his dissenting opinion in *Murdock*:

> If we were to facilitate Murdock's defense, as logic and morality would seem to command, so that a jury might acquit him because of his "rotten social background" rather than any treatable mental illness, the community would have to decide what to do with him. . . .
>
> Acquitting a defendant like Murdock and returning him to the street might . . . protect our integrity. But it would probably be . . . difficult to obtain public support for, or even unfriendly acquiescence in, Murdock's release. . . . It could be said, after all, that acquittal would result not in spite of Murdock's dangerousness, but precisely because of it. Thus, while there may be no reason in logic why Murdock could not be returned to the street, as a practical matter that is probably an unfeasible result.

Murdock, 471 F.2d at 961, 963 (Bazelon, C.J., dissenting).

What, then, Bazelon wondered, would or should society do when confronted with someone like Murdock, who may pose a danger to the society that made him dangerous in the first place? Anticipating Tadros' observation at the close of the preceding chapter that "failing to hold poor criminals responsible for their crimes might further erode the security of the poor," Bazelon considered this problem to be a dilemma implicating "profound moral and legal questions." *Id.* at 964.[89]

Plainly, [a] [h]ospital would find it difficult to justify holding Murdock on the grounds that he was insane in any conventional sense. None of the psychiatrists who testified at trial . . . suggested that his "sanity" had ever been lost. Nevertheless, Murdock may well be dangerous. . . .

The options that would permit us to acquit Murdock but hold him in custody nonetheless . . . [would require] an expansion of the boundaries of the civil commitment doctrine. We could strive to limit the expansion by applying the new rationale only to persons who have undergone a criminal trial and been acquitted [based on their rotten social background]. But as a practical matter it seems very unlikely that the expansion could be so confined. The new rationale would permit—perhaps demand—that all persons who are rendered dangerous by a "rotten social background" should be preventively detained. . . .

We cannot escape the probability, if not absolute certainty, that every effort to diminish the class of persons who can be found criminally responsible will produce a concomitant expansion in the class of persons who can be subjected to involuntary civil commitment. The implications in this context are staggering. The price of permitting Murdock to claim the benefit of a logical aspect of the responsibility doctrine may be the unleashing of a detention device that operates, by hypothesis, at the exclusive expense of the lowest social and economic class.

Id. at 961, 964.

Questions: Considering the competing views above, how would you decide Murdock's case? Should he be entitled to raise an exculpatory defense, similar in kind to the insanity defense, based on his prior life circumstances? Should such a defense prevail on the facts of his case? If you answer yes to both of these questions, what if anything should happen to Murdock if he is found "not guilty by reason of social deprivation"? Finally, why do you think the legal system has uniformly rejected the arguments in favor of such a defense?

III.   RACE AND CRIME

Consider finally and once again the question of race. As noted earlier, criminology's entwinement with eugenics and white supremacy cast a long shadow over biosocial criminology. For similar reasons, it is often difficult to talk openly and candidly about the relationship between race and crime in the United States. As sociologist Elliott Currie notes, people working to end racial injustices in the penal system sometimes "bury the subject" for fear that mentioning it will reinforce "longstanding stereotypes about black people and crime," which continue to be deployed in "service of racist and regressive social policies." Some scholars, motivated by similar concerns, go a step further, either denying that racial differences in criminal offending exist or arguing that any such reported differences can be explained wholly by "police bias and the alleged invalidity of official crime statistics."[90]

To be sure, there is some truth to these contentions. Official statistics on race and crime are often based on arrests, which consistently show racial differentials. Half of all murder and robbery arrests are of African Americans, for example, and Black people are overrepresented in arrests for some other crimes as well. But arrest data measure the activity of two groups of people: those being arrested and those doing the arresting. As such, arrest rates have police discretion, and with it the potential for racialized police bias, baked into them. And multiple studies — not to mention ample lived experience — confirm that racial biases in policing, against Black people in particular, are real, substantial, and pervasive.[91]

At the same time, it is not plausible to assert that police biases account for *all* of the apparent racial differences in criminal offending. Clear-eyed scholars writing from the heartland of the ideological left are among the most direct critics of such claims, describing them as a form of "subterfuge" that should "strain credulity." In the words of legal scholar and prison abolitionist Paul Butler, "there is no evidence" that police bias alone can explain the fact that "African American men commit a disproportionate share of certain serious crimes, including homicide, assault, and robbery."[92]

The essential question, then, is why these differentials exist. The discussion in this chapter offers an answer. In American society, all the many sociological drivers of crime disproportionately affect communities of color, especially Black communities. As a result, one should *expect* to see higher rates of crime in precisely these communities. Not because their residents are "born criminals" or because they have some inherent disregard for the law. But rather because society has long shown insufficient regard for them.

This is not a new idea. W.E.B. Du Bois made the point in 1899, writing in *The Philadelphia Negro* about the central role economic exclusion played in fomenting differences between Black and white criminal offending. Fifty years later, Clifford Shaw and Henry McKay argued that while rates of delinquency for Black boys were "higher than the rates for white boys" in the neighborhoods they studied,

> it cannot be said that they are higher than rates for white boys in comparable areas, since it is *impossible* to reproduce in white communities the circumstances under which Negro children live. Even if it were possible to parallel the low economic status and the inadequacy of institutions in the white community, it would not be possible to reproduce the effects of segregation and the barriers to upward mobility.[93]

Today, this constellation of disadvantages — low socioeconomic status, weakened social institutions, and a lack of upward social mobility, all reinforced by persistent segregation and discrimination — goes by a familiar phrase: *systemic racism*. And as sociologists Robert Sampson and William

Julius Wilson have documented, the phenomenon is real. Governmental policy and private discrimination, they write, have "combined to concentrate urban black poverty and family disruption in the inner city" to such a degree that "the 'worst' urban contexts in which whites reside are considerably better than the average context of black communities." Indeed, echoing Shaw and McKay, Sampson and Wilson write that today, "even given the same objective socioeconomic status, blacks and whites face vastly different environments in which to live, work, and raise their children." According to any one of the sociological theories of crime outlined in this chapter, these racialized differences in neighborhood context should lead us to expect corresponding racial differences in criminal involvement.[94]

Empirical work also consistently finds that racial segregation explains neighborhood rates of violence above and beyond explanations grounded in economic disadvantage. As sociologist Elliott Currie explains, "segregation matters because it is a marker for many other adversities—a kind of shorthand for the whole range of historical and current patterns of deliberate discrimination and disinvestment that have profoundly shaped black life in America" and that aren't captured by standard measures of economic disadvantage. And, he goes on to note, "for blacks who do manage to move up the social and economic ladder, segregation creates barriers to residential mobility, making it harder for them to escape violent surroundings despite their socioeconomic success." At the same time, other studies have found that "when white men are exposed to the same level of structural impediments as black men, white men are more likely to commit homicide than black men," suggesting that perhaps "black masculinity is not a cause of disproportionate violence by black men but rather, in some instances, a protector against it."[95]

In short, sociological theories of crime not only anticipate that crime will be concentrated in racially marginalized communities, they help us understand why. Sampson, Wilson, and Hannah Katz capture the point well: "What drives crime (and other human behaviors)," they write, "remains rooted in fundamental historical and structural conditions that are differentially experienced by racial groups." Put more simply, in the words of Elliott Currie, "more than a century's worth of research shows that the racial disparity in violence is not a symptom of community failure: it is a symptom of social injustice." Indeed, it would be surprising if a society marked by systemic racism did *not* see social harms concentrated among the most vulnerable communities—including the harms associated with criminal offending itself.[96]

Understood in this light, efforts to ignore or minimize the reality of racial differentials in crime are not benevolent gestures of racial enlightenment. They are a way of shutting one's eyes to a significant aspect of racial oppression itself. Our goal in the chapters that follow is to avoid such an approach—to embrace the complex harms of both crime and the penal system's response to it, with an informed understanding throughout of the role society itself plays in spurring and fomenting crime. With this understanding in mind, we turn in the next chapter to study the criminal law of violence.

REVISITING THE CASES

Think back to the trio of defendants whose stories began this chapter: Barry Kingston, Robert Sandifer, and Benjamin Murdock. Which of them, if any, would you vote to convict? How would you rank the severity of their crimes? The appropriate punishments? What factors would you consider in selecting punishments other than the nature of the crimes for which they were being tried?

For Kingston, how do you weigh the fact that, under ordinary circumstances, he had control over his sexual urges and would not have acted upon them even when presented with an opportunity to do so? Would the origins of his pedophilic disorder make a difference to your analysis? For example, would you assess his liability differently if you were told that his disorder was inherited? Or resulted from childhood abuse? What if he had a brother who suffered the same abuse but did not develop pedophilic disorder? And do you agree with the House of Lords' analysis of Kingston's involuntary intoxication defense? Should Kingston have such a defense if he's tried in a jurisdiction that recognizes substantial volitional impairment as a type of insanity?

As you read, in some states 11-year-old Sandifer could be tried as an adult for murder. How would you go about deciding whether he should be? What might be the downstream effects on gang-related crime if individuals like Sandifer are tracked to the juvenile courts? Either separately, or in conjunction with his age, what weight would you give to Sandifer's upbringing and the violence he endured as early as toddlerhood?

Do you agree that Murdock was not insane, even temporarily? Supposing we accept Dr. Williams' testimony that Murdock was "strongly delusional" and had an "irresistible impulse to shoot" after the marine called him a "black bastard"? Does it matter what definition of insanity is employed? Does it make sense to deny Murdock the defense because his impairments stemmed from an "emotional disorder" with "roots in his childhood, in the Watts section of Los Angeles," rather than from a "disease of the mind"?

PART 2

AMERICAN CRIMINAL LAW: CONTENT, USAGES, AND EXPANSION

The next five chapters of this book present and examine the core substantive content of American criminal law. The first three of these chapters (Chapters Four, Five and Six) each focuses on a set of criminal offenses that are traditionally called *mala in se* crimes, meaning crimes that are considered, in virtually all societies, to involve inherently harmful and wrongful conduct. Chapter Four discusses the law of violence, with a focus on criminal homicides. Chapter Five discusses the law of sexual coercion and sexual violence, with a focus on sexual assault. And Chapter Six discusses the law of property-related offenses, with a focus on the law of theft and on white-collar and corporate crime.

Our goals in these chapters are threefold.

First, we aim to build a nuanced and sophisticated understanding of the basic conceptual and doctrinal features of American criminal law writ large, which apply across a wide range of offenses. We provide a brief overview of these core concepts here, along with a roadmap of where you can expect to see them elaborated in the pages to come. In particular, *criminal liability*, meaning the formal legal finding that a person is guilty of a crime, typically involves the following key conceptual building blocks:

- *Actus reus.* Also known as the *guilty act* requirement, the *actus reus* requirement holds that for criminal liability to attach, a criminal defendant must have engaged in some *legally prohibited conduct*. In the American legal system, these legal prohibitions are codified in penal statutes. Sometimes the proscribed conduct is stated generically, such as the "killing of a human being." 18 U.S.C. §1111. Other times it is stated more specifically, such as engaging "in the business of importing, manufacturing, or dealing in explosive materials without a license." 18 U.S.C. §842(a)(1). In all events, the state must prove that every component of the proscribed act was committed by the defendant (or, as we will discuss in Chapter Seven, by someone acting in concert with the defendant). As a general rule, the proscribed act must also result from the defendant's volitional physical actions, a principle sometimes called the *voluntary act* requirement; under this rule, a sleepwalker or a person whose body is physically overpowered and literally forced to act in a certain way has not committed an *actus reus*. We will examine the *actus reus* requirement in detail in Chapter Five when exploring the various approaches states adopt in defining the conduct that constitutes sexual assault. And we will explore in Chapter Seven the narrow set of circumstances in which criminal liability can attach when a person *fails* to take certain action, also known as an *omission*.

- *Mens rea.* Also known as the *guilty mind* or *culpability* requirement, the *mens rea* requirement refers to two related ideas. First, as we have already seen in Chapter Three, criminal liability typically requires a showing that a person acted with moral blameworthiness, which may be present or absent based on the person's mental state and intentions when engaging in prohibited conduct. Second, criminal statutes often distinguish between different *levels* or *degrees* of culpable mental states. For liability to attach for a specific offense, the state must show that the defendant had the requisite degree of culpability for that crime. We will examine *mens rea* in detail in Chapter Four when exploring the different mental states associated with different forms and degrees of criminal homicide. Later in Chapter Four we will also explore the narrow set of circumstances, generally known as *strict liability*, in which criminal liability can attach even in the absence of any culpable mental state. We will return to this idea in Chapter Five when discussing mistakes of fact and in Chapter Six when studying strict liability in the context of regulatory crimes.

- *Concurrence.* The principle of concurrence holds that for criminal liability to attach, a person's guilty mind and guilty action must exist at the same time. Thus, a person who intends to kill someone in June, abandons that intention in July without ever having acted on it, and then later causes the person's death entirely by accident in August is not guilty of murder—because the guilty intention and the fatal act lack concurrence.

- *Causation.* For some criminal offenses, criminal liability attaches only if a specific harmful result occurs. For example, a person cannot be convicted of murder unless someone—the alleged victim—has in fact died. Without that specific result, the crime has not occurred. The *causation* requirement holds, moreover, that the defendant's guilty action must have been what caused the legally proscribed result. This requirement entails two related ideas, which are also covered in detail in most required torts classes. The first idea, known as *but-for causation* or *cause in fact*, holds that the defendant's guilty action must have been an actual cause of the result. A person who intends to kill someone, fires a bullet at them, and misses, is not guilty of murder if the intended victim is at that moment fatally struck by lightning. The second idea, known as proximate causation, holds that, under certain circumstances, a person's guilty action may become so attenuated from the resulting harm as to sever the chain of causation and negate criminal liability. We will examine *proximate causation* further in Chapter Four when exploring limitations to the felony murder doctrine.

- *Justification & Excuse.* Finally, for criminal liability to attach, a criminal defendant must generally have acted without justification or excuse. A justification occurs when the defendant's conduct, even though harmful and perhaps intentionally undertaken, is nonetheless authorized and desirable in the eyes of the law because it serves some identifiable social good. We will examine the concept of justification in detail in Chapter Four when exploring the law of self-defense and again in Chapter Six when exploring the law of necessity. An excuse, by contrast, occurs when a person's illegal and culpable action is not socially desirable (and thus not justified) but nonetheless occurs under conditions that the law considers inappropriate for criminal punishment. We already encountered multiple doctrines of excuse in Chapter Three, and we will return to this concept in Chapter Four when examining the law of self-defense.

As to our second core goal in this part of the book, beyond providing a firm grounding in the substantive and doctrinal content of criminal law and the conceptual building blocks just described, we aim to examine the ways in which criminal law both grows out of and also shapes or reinforces underlying societal forces across a range of dimensions, including those pertaining to race, sex, and class. We explore these interconnections in each of the chapters to come, with a principal (but not exclusive or exhaustive) focus on race in Chapter Four, on sex in Chapter Five, and on class in Chapter Six.

Finally, in each of the chapters of this part, we will begin to explore how substantive criminal law shapes institutional power, affording discretion and decisionmaking authority to different sets of actors. This last theme comes to the fore in the last two chapters of this part, where we examine criminal law's transition from a mechanism for holding people accountable for misconduct to a tool that law enforcement actors use to try to solve crimes or prevent future ones. Put another way, these chapters examine the *instrumental* uses of criminal law as a device that can help to expand proactive law enforcement power. We will encounter this set of ideas first in the context of examining doctrines of *group liability* in Chapter Seven, and then again in examining the law of *attempt* and the law of *possession* in Chapter Eight.

One final note: Criminal law in the United States is highly variable from one state to another. Specific doctrinal nuances and sometimes even higher-level approaches to defining criminal liability can hold sway in one state while being rejected in another (as the study of the insanity defense in Chapter Three has already shown). Our aim in the chapters to follow is not to map out with precision where each state stands on a given doctrinal issue or to catalog their distinctly nuanced formulations. Rather, throughout this book, we aim to provide a foundational understanding of some core conceptual and doctrinal features that structure American criminal law, recognizing that the phrase "American criminal law" is itself something of an abstraction insofar as even the most expert criminal lawyers need to look up the codes and doctrines in their local jurisdictions to understand what "the criminal law" is in any given context. The following pages will equip you with the necessary foundation from which such future research can progress, by providing an account of common aspects of the general criminal law across jurisdictions and of some of the major fault lines along which jurisdictions diverge.

CHAPTER 4

HOMICIDE AND THE CRIMINAL LAW OF VIOLENCE

"We rely on law to sort out good violence from bad violence, and bad violence from worse violence—to determine when it matters that an act is violent, how much it matters, and in what way."

David Alan Sklansky, *A Pattern of Violence* 32 (2021)

INTRODUCTION

This chapter explores the law of interpersonal violence, with a particular focus on the law of homicide.

For many decades, the decision to start a criminal law course's examination of substantive doctrine with homicide went largely unquestioned. In fact, homicide was often the paradigmatic example of a criminal offense and the only one studied in detail. This traditional focus was somewhat curious, given that the underlying body of eighteenth and nineteenth century law did not, as Professor David Sklansky reports, "treat violent crime as a separate, especially serious category." Indeed, Sklansky goes on, "references to 'violent crime' did not become common in American discourse until the 1970s." Likewise, as Professor Alice Ristroph observes, criminal law casebooks in the early 1900s tended to emphasize property crimes like theft and embezzlement over violent ones.[1]

The shift in classroom focus came with the publication, in 1940, of an influential casebook written by Jerome Michael and Herbert Wechsler, chief reporter for the Model Penal Code, which later became a powerfully influential criminal law text (p. 171). In parallel with that work to reframe American criminal law, Wechsler, through his casebook with Michael, also aimed to reframe how the law would be taught—including by moving the law of homicide to the center of the class. According to Ristroph, that decision was conceptually consequential: It advanced "the view that criminal law is uniquely necessary and important because it is the only adequate response to a unique set of gravely injurious behaviors." Eight decades later, Sklansky observes, this account of criminal law's core purpose remains a dominant theme: "Responding to violence is often described today as the chief mission, the central justification, of criminal law."[2]

But this violence-centering account can distort important realities. As sociologist Patrick Sharkey reports, only one in five Americans has ever been physically harmed or threatened with harm during a crime, and homicides in particular represent only a tiny fraction of American crime. The FBI's Uniform Crime Reports show a yearly average of approximately 5 homicides per 100,000 people in the United States over the past two decades— compared to roughly 2,000 thefts, 600 burglaries, 300 stolen cars, 270 assaults, 120 robberies, and 40 rapes. Even during the worst years of deadly violence recorded, from roughly the 1970s through the 1990s, the national homicide rate fluctuated between 8 and 10 killings per 100,000 people, orders of magnitude lower than other forms of crime.[3]

Given these background statistics, a criminal law course focused intensely on homicide, or even on violence more generally, risks skewing our understanding of what the criminal law and the penal system actually do. In particular, Ristroph argues, it risks obscuring "the many ways in which criminal law operates to subordinate individuals who have *not* inflicted great harm upon others," including the masses of people arrested, prosecuted, and often incarcerated for property crimes, possessory drug offenses, and low-level misdemeanors. Nor, Ristroph contends, is the problem limited to the classroom. Given the role that lawyers play in shaping penal policy, an undue emphasis on homicide in law school may "have contributed affirmatively to the collection of phenomena commonly labeled mass incarceration" by training future lawyers and policymakers to "trust and embrace criminal law" and to "buttress support for criminal legal interventions" in their careers.[4]

Recognizing these concerns, we treat the law of homicide as the starting point for our discussion of American criminal law, not the end point or even the focal point. Our overarching goal is to study some of the most important and potentially troubling aspects of the American penal system, including the ways it affects people accused of *non*violent conduct. We will examine these themes closely in Chapters Six, Eight, and Nine. Moreover, even within this initial exploration of truly violent crime, we aim to examine and critically assess how the criminal law operates as an extension of underlying social forces and hierarchies—including those related to race, class, gender, and sexuality. Our intention, in other words, is neither to position violent crime as a focal concern nor to present the law of homicide in some romanticized or idealized form, as an uncomplicated or entirely welcome form (in Wechsler's words) of "protection against all the deepest injuries that human conduct can inflict on individuals."[5]

Still, given the concerns laid out by Ristroph and others, one might wonder why we begin with homicide at all. There are countless offenses one could study first when learning about the criminal law. We have chosen to start with the law of homicide and to study it closely because we believe an alternative approach—one that downplayed the significance of violence in America—would itself distort reality and, in its own way, minimize deep racial injustice.

The reason for this conclusion stems from what might at first seem paradoxical. The American penal system is often condemned as racist and unjust not only because it imposes too much punishment—too many convictions, too many prison sentences—but also too little, particularly when Black people are the victims of violent crimes. This duality is starkly evident when Black people are killed by the police, a form of violence this chapter covers in detail. Consider the movement and the very phrase *Black Lives Matter*. Members of this movement have offered powerful critiques of the carceral state, often forwarding what Professor Amna Akbar describes as "a decarceral agenda rooted in an abolitionist imagination." And yet, the phrase "Black Lives Matter" was born not from a decarceral impulse but from a carceral one—from a desire to see *more* prosecutions and convictions when Black people are killed by police, with hopes of expressing through formal state sanctions that Black lives do in fact matter and that people who violently take them away will be punished. "Black Lives Matter" is thus a phrase chanted in fervent frustration when police officers who kill Black people are not charged with or are acquitted of murder. Likewise, it is sometimes shouted in jubilation when they are, on rare occasion, convicted.[6]

Lisa Robinson of Washington reacts on Tuesday, April 20, 2021, upon learning that former Minneapolis police officer Derek Chauvin was convicted of murder for killing George Floyd.

These decisions to charge, acquit, or convict all occur within the legal framework we will study in this chapter: the law of homicide. But the dualism and tensions described above — in which certain communities are simultaneously over-punished and under-protected — are not confined to police killings. On the one hand, the criminal law's approach to violent crime fuels mass incarceration. More than half the people currently incarcerated in the United States are serving time for offenses labeled violent, with the most severe sentences (including for murder convictions) disproportionately landing on Black and Latino men. More fundamentally, as we discuss in detail in this chapter, the law of homicide rests on certain foundational conceptions of reasonableness and violence that are themselves inflected with ideas about race, gender, sexuality, and class, with race playing "a particularly strong role in determining how violence is perceived and assessed."[7]

On the other hand, the worry that violence against Black people too often goes unpunished also extends beyond police killings, which account for only a fraction of the violent deaths inflicted on people of color each year. Deaths at the hands of community members are more common and are also racially skewed. Most violent crime is intraracial. And given the criminogenic nature of concentrated disadvantage discussed in Chapter Three, that violence tends to proliferate in poor urban communities, often communities of color. As Sharkey and Professor Robert Sampson write, violence in the United States is thus "divided by place" and also by race, "with sharply uneven distributions across the nation's neighborhoods, towns, and cities." The upshot, as sociologist Elliott Currie reports, is that a young Black man in the United States today is fifteen times more likely to die from violence than his white counterpart. This violence takes "more years of life from black men than cancer, stroke, and diabetes combined." In parts of the country where violence is the worst, more than 40 people per 100,000 are killed each year, a rate unmatched in most of the world. The result, writes Currie, is "one of the most fundamental inequalities imaginable: a radical disparity in the very prospect of survival itself." And the societal consequences of these killings extend far beyond the individual lives lost.[8]

This racialized aspect of violent crime — in which people of color are overrepresented among both victims and perpetrators — is often considered an impolitic, perhaps even taboo topic to broach. As we discussed at the close of Chapter Three, this reluctance to engage directly with the racialized reality of violence in America is understandable but ultimately misguided. The fact that racial disparities in homicides exist does not mean the blame for violence lies with the communities suffering from it. Rather, as sociologists Adaner Usmani and John Clegg observe, before one can "blame individuals, one must make the additional, nonobvious argument that they are responsible for the antecedent causes of their crime." The overwhelming evidence points to a more complex dynamic. As Currie notes, and as Chapter Three elaborated in detail, "more than a century's worth of research shows that the racial disparity in violence is not a symptom of community failure: it is a symptom of social injustice."[9]

But to many people directly impacted by this racialized violence, society's indifference goes beyond its failure to reckon with the antecedent causes of crime. It extends to a perceived indifference to the violence that erupts. This indifference is felt most acutely when murders, particularly of Black people, go unsolved—which happens often, as the *Washington Post* reported in 2018:

> In the past decade, police in 52 of the nation's largest cities have failed to make an arrest in nearly 26,000 killings. . . . In more than 18,600 of those cases, the victim . . . was black. Black victims, who accounted for the majority of homicides, were the least likely of any racial group to have their killings result in an arrest . . . . While police arrested someone in 63 percent of the killings of white victims, they did so in just 47 percent of those with black victims. . . . In almost every city surveyed, arrests were made in killings of black victims at lower rates than homicides involving white victims.[10]

As the authors of this report observe, police chiefs consistently assert that "they work just as hard to solve black murders" and that their "investigations are often hampered by reluctant witnesses. But residents and community leaders in many cities remain skeptical that police are doing all they can to solve black homicides." This skepticism echoes a narrative long espoused by scholars, activists, and community members alike:

> Black Americans have long contended that the criminal justice system devalues black lives by allowing black killings to go unpunished. In 1892, anti-lynching activist and journalist Ida B. Wells urged black families to purchase guns to "be used for that protection which the law refuses to give."
>
> For many, the belief that police don't value black lives was reinforced in 2012, when police in Sanford, Florida, did not immediately arrest neighborhood watchman George Zimmerman after he shot and killed Trayvon Martin, a black 17-year-old, as he walked home from a store.
>
> Zimmerman was later arrested and charged, but his acquittal in 2013 planted the seeds of the Black Lives Matter movement.[11]

Viewing this history in context, leading voices in today's movement for racial justice see what Ibram X. Kendi calls "a straight line between black people being outraged loudly about police officers being able to shoot and kill people and being able to get away from it and black people quietly wondering when that homicide in their neighborhood is going to be solved."[12]

On this account, the fact that certain neighborhoods are simultaneously over-policed and under-protected is really no paradox at all. Rather, as Professor Alexandra Natapoff argues, these parallel injustices can be seen as "twin symptoms of a deeper democratic weakness of the criminal system: its non-responsiveness to the needs of the poor, racial minorities, and the otherwise politically vulnerable. . . . Official disregard of crime is part of this dynamic, as are mass imprisonment, excessive sentences, and racially skewed enforcement practices."[13]

To Currie, this dual disregard for Black life calls to mind what W.E.B. Du Bois once called society's "peculiar indifference":

> We find it easier to understand this connection when the hand that holds the gun that kills a young black man is that of a white police officer. When the hand belongs to another young black man, the connection is less direct and less transparent. But it is no less real. Our inability or unwillingness to recognize that connection represents a failure of the moral as well as the sociological imagination and helps to perpetuate a level of preventable trauma and needless suffering that has no counterpart anywhere in the developed world.[14]

We thus open our study of American criminal law by examining the law of violence. We aim neither to overemphasize the significance of criminal violence in America nor to downplay the urgent and often racialized problem it poses. Organizationally, the chapter proceeds through four principal parts. We start with the role that mental state plays in assigning criminal liability. Next, we consider circumstances in which liability attaches even in the absence of a culpable mental state, as occurs in the context of the felony murder doctrine. We then consider the concepts of justification and excuse, in turn, by studying the law of self-defense and police use of force.

I. THE ROLE OF MENTAL STATES IN ASSIGNING CRIMINAL LIABILITY

> "For hundreds of years the books have repeated with unbroken cadence that *Actus non facit reum nisi mens sit rea.*"
>
> Francis Bowes Sayre, *Mens Rea*, 45 Harv. L. Rev. 974, 974 (1932)

The Latin maxim quoted above is a tenet of Anglo-American criminal law stretching back to the *Laws of Henry I* written in 1115. Its most famous translation comes from William Blackstone: "an unwarrantable act without a vicious will is no crime at all." In its Latin rendering, the phrase provides two of the core building blocks of criminal liability, which generally arises when a person commits an *actus reus* (a guilty act) with *mens rea* (a culpable state of mind). With respect to criminal homicides, the *actus reus* element is typically straightforward: any action that causes the death of another person will suffice. In this chapter, we will thus focus our attention on the concept of *mens rea*, leaving a more detailed study of *actus reus* to Chapter Five.[15]

Broadly speaking, *mens rea* stands for the idea that criminal liability requires a guilty mind. At this level of generality, *mens rea* is roughly a synonym for what Professor Francis Sayre calls "general moral blameworthiness." Understood as such, the *mens rea* requirement has many exceptions. For one, criminal law sometimes attaches liability when people do not act with a guilty mind—when they lack *mens rea*—as with strict liability offenses discussed later in this chapter and in Chapter Six. Separately, it also punishes people for acts that are not obviously blameworthy—things like smoking marijuana or spitting on the sidewalk—which are often referred to as *mala prohibita,* regulatory, or public-order offenses. We will explore these sorts of crimes in future chapters.[16]

Here, our initial focus is on a narrower and more technical meaning of the phrase *mens rea,* one that aims to distinguish among different *levels* of mental culpability. These gradations of *mens rea* emerged slowly over time, as expositors of the criminal law strove for clearer accounts of the different degrees of blameworthiness. Unfortunately, clarity was not always the end result. With different courts writing opinions in different states at different points in time, the law of *mens rea* grew increasingly marked by "disparity and confusion," as different jurisdictions (and sometimes different courts within one jurisdiction) offered competing "definitions of the requisite but elusive mental element." Morissette v. United States, 342 U.S. 246, 252 (1952).

With varying degrees of success, scholars and lawmakers have attempted over the past half-century to organize this area of law by enumerating discrete and clearly defined mental states. Much of that work was driven by the Model Penal Code (MPC), which offered a precisely tiered hierarchy of culpability. Written over a span of years and adopted in 1962, the Model Penal Code was authored by a group of scholars and jurists known as the American Law Institute who hoped to clarify criminal law's traditional common law framework inherited from England and adapted over time by courts across the United States. As its name suggests, the Model Penal Code was a forward-looking document—a *model* of what the criminal law could be rather than a *restatement* of what it was. The ALI had produced restatements of other fields of law, many of which continue to influence fields like contract, torts, and property. But precisely because the criminal law before the adoption of the MPC had been so disorganized, its core principles could not easily be catalogued. Instead, the MPC drafters promised "a systematic re-examination" of criminal law, with a goal of "articulating legislative issues, analyzing possible solutions and appraising the competing values and considerations which a legislative choice should weigh."[17]

Drafted primarily by academics, the MPC is not formally law anywhere, but it has had considerable influence. Thirty-four states ultimately revised their penal codes in its wake, some adopting large portions of the MPC outright and others embracing its basic vocabulary and conceptual approach (though none adopted it wholesale). Even in systems that did not adopt the code, like the federal system, judges and lawyers often turn to its framework and commentaries for guidance. The code thus generally operates as its drafters intended, as "a treatise on the major problems of the penal law and their appropriate solutions from which future legislation, adjudication and administration may be able to draw aid."[18]

At the same time, there remain many states that do not engage directly with the MPC and that thus continue to define their law of *mens rea* by grappling with common law terms and concepts that stretch back centuries. As we will see in the pages that follow, the differences between these two approaches—the common law approach and the more modern MPC approach—are real, but also ought not be overstated. In both regimes, expositors of the criminal law attempt to differentiate among different levels of mental culpability within two large categories of crimes: those that are committed *intentionally* and those that are committed *unintentionally*. The following pages thus aim to illuminate some basic and common aspects of the general law of *mens rea,* using the crime of homicide as a guiding example across these two general categories. We begin with homicides that are committed intentionally.

A. *Intentional Homicide*

Under traditional common law formulations, murder is an unlawful killing committed with *malice,* sometimes called *malice aforethought.* As we will see in this chapter, such malice can manifest in various ways: A defendant could act with callous disregard for how his risky behavior might unintentionally harm others; malice could also be supplied by a defendant's killing someone in the course of committing some other felony. We will return to these theories of malice in later sections. In this section, we focus on a more straightforward way of demonstrating malice: unlawfully killing another person *intentionally* or, in the language of the Model Penal Code, with the *purpose* of causing their death.

Within this domain of intentional killings, many jurisdictions using the traditional common law framework further identify two dividing lines, premeditation and provocation, that distinguish three different types of intentional homicide: first-degree murder, which is defined as an intentional, premeditated killing; second-degree murder, which is defined as an intentional but not premeditated killing; and voluntary manslaughter, which is defined as an intentional killing committed under mitigating circumstances, most commonly, under circumstances of provocation. Some states use additional dividing lines. For example, in many states, a homicide might be classified as first-degree murder based on the status of the victim, the status of the perpetrator, or the method of causing death. But these statutory divisions are typically layered on top of the basic divisions set out above. And as we will see, the Model Penal Code also divides intentional homicides into two separate, tiered offenses—murder and manslaughter—eschewing the concept of premeditation but adhering to a concept akin to (but distinct from) provocation.[19]

In this section, we will explore these dividing lines in more detail. But first, we consider a more fundamental question: Why divide intentional homicides into discrete offenses at all?

NOTES AND QUESTIONS

1. A Brief History of Dividing Death. In each of the three offenses described above—first-degree murder, second-degree murder, and manslaughter—a person unlawfully takes another human life. In so doing, she violates a fundamental precept of virtually all known moral, religious, and legal codes: thou shalt not kill. For centuries, Anglo-American criminal law did not complicate matters much beyond that. A person who unlawfully killed another was guilty of a single offense (murder) and was subject to a single penalty: execution. The options, in other words, were acquittal or the gallows. As Professor Elizabeth Papp Kamali explains, as far back as medieval England, this unmitigated severity yielded a large number of acquittals, perhaps because jurors confronting cases in the "grey area lying between . . . two extremes" felt "great pause in handing down a guilty verdict" with its accompanying death sentence. Over time, that merciful impulse to treat less egregious killings less severely—and a countervailing desire to avoid the full exculpation of an acquittal where an unlawful killing had occurred—drove English jurists to carve out from murder the new offense of manslaughter, which lay within the grey area Kamali describes and which did not require execution.[20]

Centuries later, in 1794, Pennsylvania became the first jurisdiction to further divide the offense of murder into degrees, in similar hopes of confining capital punishment. As the Model Penal Code's commentaries explain:

> [Pennsylvania's] statute provided that "all murder, which shall be perpetrated by means of poison, or by lying in wait, or by any other kind of willful, deliberate, and premeditated killing, or which shall be committed in the perpetration, or attempt to perpetrate any arson, rape, robbery or burglary shall be deemed murder in the first degree; and all other kinds of murder shall be deemed murder in the second degree." The thrust of this reform was to confine the death penalty, which was then mandatory on conviction of any common-law murder, to homicides judged particularly heinous. Other states followed the Pennsylvania practice until at one time the vast majority of American jurisdictions differentiated degrees

of murder and the term "first-degree murder" passed into common parlance.[21]

2. *The Proportionality Principle: Justifications and Limits.* As the foregoing note indicates, intentional homicide was subdivided into discrete crimes in furtherance of a broader principle of *proportionality*, which is frequently cited as a core feature of American criminal law. The basic idea is both simple and familiar: the punishment should fit the crime. As noted in Chapter Two, this principle has a grounding in retributive theories of punishment, which hold "that even one who is guilty must not be punished to a degree that is out of proportion to his guilt."[22]

Proportionality can also be supported on utilitarian grounds. If all punishment is evil and must be justified by some greater good, as Jeremy Bentham says, then any *excess* punishment (beyond that necessary to serve the greater good) is by definition unwarranted. Likewise, a utilitarian who is focused on deterring harmful conduct might propose a scale of graduated punishments to induce someone who contemplates multiple offenses to stop at the least harmful one. This is called *marginal deterrence.* As Bentham writes:

> When thieves break into a house, they may execute their purpose in different manners: by simply stealing, by theft accompanied with bodily injury, or murder, or incendiarism. If the punishment is the same for simple theft, as for theft and murder, you give the thieves a motive for committing murder, because this crime adds to the facility of committing the former, and the chance of impunity when it is committed.
>
> The great inconvenience resulting from the infliction of great punishments for small offences, is, that the power of increasing them in proportion to the magnitude of the offence is thereby lost.[23]

The proportionality principle is invoked time and again in American criminal law. At sentencing, judges are often empowered to impose a punishment within a statutory range and are urged to do so in a manner that is proportionate to the underlying offense and other features of the defendant's blameworthiness. Likewise, when setting those initial statutory ranges, legislatures are supposed to arrange crimes proportionately to one another. Indeed, as we will discuss further in Chapter Nine, the Supreme Court has held that "[t]he concept of proportionality is central to the Eighth Amendment," which contains within its ban on cruel and unusual punishments "the precept of justice that punishment for crime should be graduated and proportioned to [the] offense." Graham v. Florida, 560 U.S. 48, 59 (2010).

And yet, as we will see in later chapters, American criminal law often honors the proportionality principle only in the breach. As noted in Chapter One, legislatures across the country have enacted penalty regimes far harsher than can be found in other countries, suggesting a potential lack of proportionality relative to *external* benchmarks. The Supreme Court, meanwhile, has upheld those severe sentencing laws against constitutional challenge, even when they seem to lack any *internal* proportionality across offenses. For example, the Court has validated lengthy sentences up to and including life in prison, leveled under three-strikes laws against prior offenders, for crimes as minor as stealing a set of golf clubs. *See, e.g.,* Ewing v. California, 538 U.S. 11 (2003) (p. 829).

3. The Proportionality Principle: Challenges in Application. Before understanding how the proportionality principle might sometimes fail in American criminal law, we must try to understand how it might conceivably operate in the first place. What dividing lines *should* a legal system use to differentiate one crime from another? Consider as an entry point to this discussion the facts of *State v. Forrest,* 362 S.E.2d 252 (N.C. 1987). The North Carolina Supreme Court described the key facts as follows:

> On 22 December 1985, defendant John Forrest admitted his critically ill father, Clyde Forrest, Sr., to Moore Memorial Hospital. Defendant's father, who had previously been hospitalized, was suffering from numerous serious ailments . . . . By the morning of 23 December 1985, his medical condition was determined to be untreatable and terminal. Accordingly, he was classified as "No Code," meaning that no extraordinary measures would be used to save his life, and he was moved to a more comfortable room.
>
> On 24 December 1985, defendant went to the hospital to visit his ailing father. No other family members were present in his father's room when he arrived. While one of the nurse's assistants was tending to his father, defendant told her, "There is no need in doing that. He's dying." . . . The nurse's assistant noticed that defendant was sniffing as though crying and that he kept his hand in his pocket during their conversation. She subsequently went to get the nurse. When the nurse's assistant returned with the nurse, defendant once again stated his belief that his father was dying. The nurse tried to comfort defendant, telling him, "I don't think your father is as sick as you think he is." Defendant, very upset, responded, "Go to hell. I've been taking care of him for years. I'll take care of him." Defendant was then left alone in the room with his father.
>
> Alone at his father's bedside, defendant began to cry and to tell his father how much he loved him. His father began to cough, emitting a gurgling and rattling noise. Extremely upset, defendant pulled a small pistol from his pants pocket, put it to his father's temple, and fired. He subsequently fired three more times and walked out into the hospital corridor, dropping the gun to the floor just outside his father's room.
>
> Following the shooting, defendant, who was crying and upset, neither ran nor threatened anyone. Moreover, he never denied shooting

his father and talked openly with law enforcement officials. Specifically, defendant made the following oral statements: "You can't do anything to him now. He's out of his suffering." "I killed my daddy." "He won't have to suffer anymore." "I know they can burn me for it, but my dad will not have to suffer anymore." "I know the doctors couldn't do it, but I could." "I promised my dad I wouldn't let him suffer."

Id. at 253-254. The defendant argued that on these uncontested facts there was insufficient evidence to find him guilty of first-degree premeditated murder. And he further argued that the trial court's jury instructions were erroneous because they did not explicitly tell the jury that it could acquit him of murder altogether and convict him instead of manslaughter on the ground that he killed his father in "the heat of passion," given his "highly emotional state" and the fact that "he was overwhelmed by the futile, horrible suffering before him." *Id.* at 255.

In a divided opinion, the North Carolina Supreme Court rejected both arguments. It acknowledged that it had "held on numerous occasions that, under certain circumstances, one who kills another human being in the 'heat of passion,' produced by adequate provocation sufficient to negate malice, is guilty of manslaughter rather than murder." *Id.* at 256. But it noted that it had also "narrowly construed" that doctrine, limiting it to circumstances in which a defendant is provoked by "an assault or threatened assault" or similar affronts. *Id.* By contrast, the court held, in this case "the seriously ill deceased did nothing to provoke defendant's action," given that he "was lying helpless in a hospital bed when defendant shot him four separate times." *Id.* at 258. As to premeditation, the court held "that there was substantial evidence that the killing was premeditated," given the "defendant's own statements following the incident," in which he "stated that he had thought about putting his father out of his misery because he knew he was suffering" and "had promised his father that he would not let him suffer." *Id.*

Writing in dissent, Chief Justice Exum sharply disagreed with the majority's holding:

> Almost all would agree that someone who kills because of a desire to end a loved one's physical suffering caused by an illness which is both terminal and incurable should not be deemed in law as culpable and deserving of the same punishment as one who kills because of unmitigated spite, hatred or ill will. Yet the Court's decision in this case essentially says there is no legal distinction between the two kinds of killing. Our law of homicide should not be so roughly hewn as to be incapable of recognizing the difference. . . .
>
> The difference, legally, between the two kinds of killings hinges on the element of malice, the former being without, and the latter with, malice. The absence of malice, however, does not mean the killing is justified

or excused so as not to be unlawful; it means simply that the killing is mitigated so as not to be murder but manslaughter. . . .

The trial court . . . in effect, precluded the jury from considering at
all defendant's reasons for killing his father on the issue of whether he
acted with malice. . . . Ordinarily this kind of error calls for a new trial.

Id. at 260.

The diverging views within the court carried serious implications.
Once Mr. Forrest was convicted of first-degree murder, he faced a *mandatory* life sentence. Had he been convicted instead of second-degree murder or manslaughter, he would have faced a presumptive minimum of just
15 years. And yet, as *Forrest* also shows, while the significance of these dividing lines can be enormous, deciding where to draw them can be complicated, with judges forming sharply different conclusions on the same set
of facts. Which opinion in *Forrest* has it right? To engage that question, we
need to understand better the key dividing lines at issue — *premeditation*
and *provocation*.[24]

1. Premeditation: Distinguishing Degrees of Intentional Murder

Commonwealth v. Jordan

65 A.3d 318 (Pa. 2013)

McCaffery, J. . . . During a period of approximately six weeks in the fall
of 2007, Appellant committed six armed robberies of retail food shops
in North Philadelphia. . . . [At] approximately 10:30 a.m. on October 31,
2007, Appellant returned to the Dunkin' Donuts shop that was the site of
his first robbery, and again demanded money from the employees at gunpoint. While this final robbery was in progress, Officer Charles Cassidy, who
was dressed in his police uniform, parked his car in front of the shop and
opened its front door. As the officer was about to enter the shop, Appellant
turned toward the officer, took two steps in his direction, pointed a gun at
him, and shot him in the forehead at close range. Appellant immediately
fled from the scene, stopping to bend over to take the fallen officer's service
revolver. . . . At trial, [defense] counsel's defense strategy was to argue that
Appellant had fired his gun in a "panicky reaction" when Officer Cassidy
interrupted the robbery in progress. . . .

[In reviewing] the legal sufficiency of the evidence to support [the]
first-degree murder conviction . . . we determine whether the evidence presented at trial and all reasonable inferences derived therefrom, viewed in
the light most favorable to the Commonwealth as verdict-winner, are sufficient to establish all the elements of first-degree murder beyond a reasonable doubt.

There are three elements of first-degree murder: (1) a human being was unlawfully killed; (2) the defendant was responsible for the killing; and (3) the defendant acted with malice and a specific intent to kill. As set forth in the third element, first-degree murder is an intentional killing, *i.e.*, a "willful, deliberate and premeditated killing." 18 Pa. Cons. Stat. §2502(a), (d). "Premeditation and deliberation exist whenever the assailant possesses the conscious purpose to bring about death." Commonwealth v. Drumheller, 808 A.2d 893, 910 (Pa. 2002). The law does not require a lengthy period of premeditation; indeed, the design to kill can be formulated in a fraction of a second. Commonwealth v. Earnest, 21 A.2d 38, 40 (Pa. 1941) ("Whether the intention to kill and the killing, that is, the premeditation and the fatal act, were within a brief space of time or a long space of time is immaterial if the killing was in fact intentional, willful, deliberate and premeditated."). Specific intent to kill as well as malice can be inferred from the use of a deadly weapon upon a vital part of the victim's body. Whether the accused had formed the specific intent to kill is a question of fact to be determined by the jury.

Based on our review of the certified record in the case before us, we conclude that the evidence was sufficient to support Appellant's first-degree murder conviction. . . . A surveillance camera captured the robbery and murder on videotape. . . . The videotape showed Appellant entering the front door of the Dunkin' Donuts, pushing a customer to the side while holding a gun, glancing over his shoulder when Officer Cassidy came to the front door, and turning around to face the front door and the officer. Then, as revealed by the video, Appellant took two steps in Officer Cassidy's direction, raised his gun, and aimed it toward Officer Cassidy, who remained near the front door. The officer immediately fell, and Appellant fled through the front door, past the fallen officer; as Appellant was fleeing, he bent over and picked up the officer's service revolver from the ground. The crime scene investigator who had studied the scene of the murder and viewed the surveillance videotape, testified that Appellant had been approximately three feet from Officer Cassidy at the time of the shooting.

The above-summarized evidence is sufficient to establish all three elements of first-degree murder, *i.e.*, that Appellant had formulated the specific intent to kill Officer Cassidy and had fatally acted on that intent. . . .

State v. Guthrie

461 S.E.2d 163 (W. Va. 1995)

CLECKLEY, J. The defendant, Dale Edward Guthrie, appeals the . . . jury verdict . . . finding him guilty of first degree murder. . . . [T]he defendant was sentenced to serve a life sentence . . . .

It is undisputed that on the evening of February 12, 1993, the defendant removed a knife from his pocket and stabbed his co-worker, Steven Todd Farley, in the neck and killed him. The two men worked together as dishwashers at Danny's Rib House in Nitro and got along well together before this incident. On the night of the killing, the victim [and other coworkers] were joking around while working in the kitchen of the restaurant. The victim was poking fun at the defendant who appeared to be in a bad mood. He told the defendant to "lighten up" and snapped him with a dishtowel several times. Apparently, the victim had no idea he was upsetting the defendant very much. The dishtowel flipped the defendant on the nose and he became enraged.

The defendant removed his gloves and started toward the victim. Mr. Farley, still teasing, said: "Ooo, he's taking his gloves off." The defendant then pulled a knife from his pocket and stabbed the victim in the neck. He also stabbed Mr. Farley in the arm as he fell to the floor. Mr. Farley looked up and cried: "Man, I was just kidding around." The defendant responded: "Well, man, you should have never hit me in my face." The police arrived at the restaurant and arrested the defendant. He was given his *Miranda* rights. The defendant made a statement at the police station and confessed to the killing.[1] The police officers described him as calm and willing to cooperate.

---

1. The confession, which was read to the jury, stated, in part:

I arrived at work, at 4:00 o'clock, and was looking forward to another evening of work, I was looking forward to it, because I do enjoy working at Danny's Rib House. Upon my arrival at work I immediately observed the verbal and physical aggression of Mr. Farley. During the evening of work I heard him calling certain employee's [sic] "Boy" and during the evening he referred to me as "Boy" "many times, I did and said nothing, continuing my work, letting it pass. He was really loud, and obnoxious, as I'm sure many employee's [sic] noticed. As the evening was coming to a close Mr. Farley walked very close by me and said "that I had an 'attitude problem.'" It was verbal, I let it pass, continuing my work. After bringing some dishes to the cook, I walked back to the dishwasher to begin drying off some dishes, Mr. Farley approached me and made a sarcastic comment about me being a quiet person, he walked ever closer, to me until he was in my face, as I was trying to carry out my responsibilities. After all these things were said, and even though he was exhibiting physical aggression by coming up to my face, and putting forth what I interpreted to be a challenge, again I did nothing, continuing to carry out my responsibilities. Standing a few inches from my face he took his wet dishrag and hit me once, on the forearm, I did nothing continuing my work. Standing in the same area, he hit me again on the forearm, obviously wanting a confrontation, I gave him none, continuing my work. Standing in the same place he hit me, hard, two times in the face, it really hurt, it was soaking wet, and it stung, as he brought it to bear upon my face, at that moment I thought he was going to go further and hit me, so I reached in my right pants pocket, and retrieved my lock blade knife, that I use for skinning rabbits and squirrells [sic] during hunting season. I swung at Mr. Farley with my right hand in which was my knife, he backed up, so I didn't swing twice, he slowly sunk to [the] floor, I ran to the front of the restaurant and yelled out, call the ambulance. All I came to work for, was to work, and carry out my obligations, having ill will toward no one, and I still have none, but I feel I had the right to respond, finally, to this act of aggression that was perpetrated against me, I do not exhibit aggressive, violent behavior but I felt I had no alternative, or recourse.

It is also undisputed that the defendant suffers from a host of psychiatric problems. He experiences up to two panic attacks daily and had received treatment for them . . . for more than a year preceding the killing. He suffers from chronic depression (dysthymic disorder), an obsession with his nose (body dysmorphic disorder), and borderline personality disorder. The defendant's father shed some light on his nose fixation. He stated that dozens of times a day the defendant stared in the mirror and turned his head back and forth to look at his nose. His father estimated that 50 percent of the time he observed his son he was looking at his nose. The defendant repeatedly asked for assurances that his nose was not too big. This obsession began when he was approximately seventeen years old. The defendant was twenty-nine years old at the time of trial.

The defendant testified he suffered a panic attack immediately preceding the stabbing. He described the attack as "intense"; he felt a lot of pressure and his heart beat rapidly. In contrast to the boisterous atmosphere in the kitchen that evening, the defendant was quiet and kept to himself. He stated that Mr. Farley kept irritating him that night. The defendant could not understand why Mr. Farley was picking on him because he had never done that before. Even at trial, the defendant did not comprehend his utter overreaction to the situation. In hindsight, the defendant believed the better decision would have been to punch out on his time card and quit over the incident. However, all the witnesses related that the defendant was in no way attacked, as he perceived it, but that Mr. Farley was playing around. The defendant could not bring himself to tell the other workers to leave him alone or inform them about his panic attacks. . . .

SUFFICIENCY OF THE EVIDENCE

First, the defendant strives to persuade us that the record in this case does not support the verdict of guilty of first degree murder beyond a reasonable doubt. . . . [O]ur authority to review is limited. . . . It is possible that we, as an appellate court, may have reached a different result if we had sat as jurors. However, . . . it does not matter how we might have interpreted or weighed the evidence. Our function when reviewing the sufficiency of the evidence to support a criminal conviction is to examine the evidence admitted at trial to determine whether such evidence, if believed, is sufficient to convince a reasonable person of the defendant's guilt beyond a reasonable doubt. Thus, the relevant inquiry is whether, after viewing the evidence in the light most favorable to the prosecution, any rational trier of fact could have found the essential elements of the crime proved beyond a reasonable doubt. . . .

The essential facts of this case — those that the jury was unquestionably entitled to find — are rather simple: The defendant became irritated with the "horseplay" of the victim; when the victim in jest hit the defendant with a wet dishtowel on his nose, the defendant became angry and drew a four-inch-long lock blade knife from his pocket and stabbed the victim fatally in the neck. After the defendant was confronted with his deed, he made a statement that could be interpreted to mean he was not remorseful but, to the contrary, was unconcerned about the welfare of the victim. . . . There is no doubt what inferences and findings of fact the jury had to draw in order to convict the defendant of first degree murder. The jury must have believed that: (1) The "horseplay" provocation was not sufficient to justify a deadly attack; (2) the defendant was under no real fear of his own from being attacked; (3) the stabbing was intentional; and (4) the time it took the defendant to open his knife and inflict the mortal wound was sufficient to establish premeditation.

The difficult factual question must have been the mental state of the defendant at the time of the stabbing. The evidence was somewhat conflicting on this point. . . . After reviewing the record, this Court has some doubt as to whether this is a first degree murder case; . . . [but we] do not find the evidence so weak as to render the verdict irrational. A rational jury may well have found the defendant guilty of some lesser-included crime without violating its oath; but, drawing all favorable inferences in favor of the prosecution, a rational jury could also convict [of first degree murder].

JURY INSTRUCTIONS

. . . The jury was charged in this case on the offenses of first and second degree murder and the lesser-included offenses of voluntary and involuntary manslaughter. . . . The purpose of instructing the jury is to focus its attention on the essential issues of the case and inform it of the permissible ways in which these issues may be resolved. If instructions are properly delivered, they succinctly and clearly will inform the jury of the vital role it plays and the decisions it must make. "Without [adequate] instructions as to the law, the jury becomes mired in a factual morass, unable to draw the appropriate legal conclusions based on the facts." State v. Miller, 459 S.E.2d 114, 127 (W. Va. 1995). This is, in essence, what the defendant argues in this case, *i.e.*, the instructions were inadequate and failed to inform the jury of the difference between first and second degree murder. More precisely, the defendant asserts the trial court's instructions regarding the elements of first degree murder were improper because the terms wilful, deliberate, and premeditated were equated with a mere intent to kill.

The jury was instructed [as follows]:

"[T]o constitute a willful, deliberate and premeditated killing, it is not necessary that the intention to kill should exist for any particular length of time prior to the actual killing; it is only necessary that such intention should have come into existence for the first time at the time of such killing, or at any time previously . . . . [T]o constitute a 'premeditated' murder an intent to kill need exist only for an instant. . . . [W]hat is meant by the language willful, deliberate and premeditated is that the killing be intentional."

The linchpin of the problems that flow from these instructions is the failure adequately to inform the jury of the difference between first and second degree murder. Of particular concern is the lack of guidance to the jury as to what constitutes premeditation and the manner in which the instructions infuse premeditation with the intent to kill. . . . The source of the problem in the present case stems from language in *State v. Schrader*, 302 S.E.2d 70 (W. Va. 1982), [where] we stated: ". . . The achievement of a mental state contemplated in a statute such as ours can immediately precede the act of killing. Hence, what is really meant by the language 'willful, deliberate and premeditated' . . . is that the killing be intentional." *Id.* at 75. . . .

While many jurisdictions do not favor the distinction between first and second degree murder, . . . we do not have the judicial prerogative to abolish the distinction between first and second degree murder and rewrite the law of homicide for West Virginia. . . .[22] [W]e believe within the parameters of our current homicide statutes the *Schrader* definition of premeditation and deliberation is confusing, if not meaningless. To allow the State to prove premeditation and deliberation by only showing that the intention came "into existence for the first time at the time of such killing" completely eliminates the distinction between the two degrees of murder. Hence, we feel compelled in this case to attempt to make the dichotomy meaningful by making some modifications to our homicide common law.

Premeditation and deliberation should be defined in a . . . way to give juries both guidance and reasonable discretion. Although premeditation and deliberation are not measured by any particular period of time, there must be some period between the formation of the intent to kill and the actual killing, which indicates the killing is by prior calculation and design. . . . This means there must be an opportunity for some reflection on the intention to kill after it is formed. The accused must kill purposely after contemplating the intent to kill. Although an elaborate plan or scheme to take life is not required, . . . *Schrader*'s notion of instantaneous

---

22. . . . [D]efining premeditation in such a way that the formation of the intent to kill and the killing can result from successive impulses grants the jury complete discretion to find more ruthless killers guilty of first degree murder regardless of actual premeditation. History teaches that such unbridled discretion is not always carefully and thoughtfully employed, and this case may be an example. In 1994, the Legislature raised the penalty for second degree murder to ten-to-forty years (from five-to-eighteen years), making it less important to give juries the unguided discretion to find the aggravated form of murder in the case of more ruthless killings, irrespective of actual premeditation. The penalties are now comparable.

premeditation and momentary deliberation is not satisfactory for proof of first degree murder. . . .

Thus, there must be some evidence that the defendant considered and weighed his decision to kill in order for the State to establish premeditation and deliberation under our first degree murder statute. This is what is meant by a ruthless, cold-blooded, calculating killing. Any other intentional killing, by its spontaneous and nonreflective nature, is second degree murder.[24]

. . . To the extent that the *Schrader* opinion is inconsistent with our holding today, it is overruled. . . . [We] now approve as a proper instruction under today's decision[:]

> "The jury is instructed that murder in the first degree consists of an intentional, deliberate and premeditated killing which means that the killing is done after a period of time for prior consideration. The duration of that period cannot be arbitrarily fixed. The time in which to form a deliberate and premeditated design varies as the minds and temperaments of people differ, and according to the circumstances in which they may be placed. Any interval of time between the forming of the intent to kill and the execution of that intent, which is of sufficient duration for the accused to be fully conscious of what he intended, is sufficient to support a conviction for first degree murder."

State v. Hatfield, 286 S.E.2d 402, 410 n.7 (W. Va. 1982). . . . Reversed and remanded.*

WORKMAN, J., concurring. I concur with the holding of the majority, but write this separate opinion to reiterate that the duration of the time period required for premeditation cannot be arbitrarily fixed. . . . Given the majority's recognition that these concepts are necessarily incapable of being reduced formulaically, I am concerned that some of the language in the opinion may indirectly suggest that some appreciable length of time must

---

24. As examples of what type of evidence supports a finding of first degree murder, we identify three categories: (1) "planning" activity—facts regarding the defendant's behavior prior to the killing which might indicate a design to take life; (2) facts about the defendant's prior relationship or behavior with the victim which might indicate a motive to kill; and (3) evidence regarding the nature or manner of the killing which indicate a deliberate intention to kill according to a preconceived design. The California courts evidently require evidence of all three categories or at least extremely strong evidence of planning activity or evidence of category (2) in conjunction with either (1) or (3). *See* People v. Anderson, 447 P.2d 942 (Cal. 1968). These examples are illustrative only and are not intended to be exhaustive.

* Editor's Note: The court considered the possibility that the instructional error in Mr. Guthrie's case was harmless given its separate conclusion that the evidence was in fact sufficient to support a first-degree murder conviction. The court ultimately reversed the conviction, however, due to a separate constitutional error in the proceedings not discussed in the excerpted opinion above. It therefore did not need to decide the harmlessness issue.

pass before premeditation can occur. . . . Accordingly, it is necessary to make abundantly clear that premeditation is sufficiently demonstrated as long as "[a]ny interval of time, no matter how short that interval is, lapses between the forming of the intent to kill and the execution of that intent." *See Hatfield*, 286 S.E.2d at 410.

NOTES AND QUESTIONS

1. Defining Premeditation. Most American jurisdictions use some version of the premeditation-deliberation formula to separate first- and second-degree murder. But as the *Jordan* and *Guthrie* cases show, the meaning of the words premeditation and deliberation remains unsettled, sometimes to the point of confusion. Speaking over a century after Pennsylvania first defined first-degree murder by reference to premeditation, Justice Benjamin Cardozo thought the concept "much too vague to be continued in our law." Reflecting candidly on his own experience as a state court judge, he added, "I am not at all sure that I understand it myself after trying to apply it for many years and after diligent study of what has been written in the books." Writing nearly another century later, Professor Kimberly Ferzan echoed Cardozo's frustration, describing "the doctrinal terrain" as "a state of chaos," with "profound confusion about the moral and conceptual questions surrounding premeditation."[25]

One axis of disagreement tracks the dispute between the *Jordan* and *Guthrie* courts regarding the minimum amount of time in which premeditation can occur. Courts also disagree about whether premeditation and deliberation are actually one concept or two. Consider Nevada, where the state supreme court has vacillated between insisting (in 1981) that premeditation and deliberation each must be proven beyond a reasonable doubt, to stating (in 1992) that they mean the same thing, to then returning (in 2000) to the view that "deliberation is a distinct element of *mens rea* for first-degree murder." Byford v. State, 994 P.2d 700, 714 (Nev. 2000).[26]

As noted in Chapter Three, the premeditation-deliberation requirement (whatever its precise formulation) can also encompass questions about the defendant's mental ability to plan and reason clearly about her actions. If circumstances are such that a defendant has *diminished capacity* to engage in premeditation, a first-degree conviction may be legally barred. As the discussion in Chapter Three observes (p. 140), defendants may argue diminished capacity where they acted under some abnormal mental condition not rising to the level of insanity. *See, e.g.*, State v. Stewart, 719 S.E.2d 876, 885 (W. Va. 2011) (holding that, "in cases involving Battered Woman's Syndrome, evidence that a defendant meets the profile of the syndrome is admissible to explain to the jury how domestic abuse may affect a defendant's reasoning, beliefs, perceptions, or behavior," which "is relevant because it may negate an essential element of the crime charged, such as premeditation, malice or intent"). Similarly, the defense of *voluntary intoxication* (p. 148) may be available to a defendant who, due to the intoxicating effects of drugs or alcohol, lacked the ability to premeditate the crime. *See, e.g.,* State v. Skidmore, 718 S.E.2d 516, 522 (W. Va. 2011).

   2. Proving Premeditation. Related to the questions of definition described above, premeditation also poses challenges of proof. Consider, for example, *People v. Oros*, 917 N.W.2d 559 (Mich. 2018). There, the Michigan Supreme Court applied what it calls the "second look" doctrine, which strives to clarify the temporal aspect of premeditation by specifying that "the interval between initial thought and ultimate action should be long enough to afford a reasonable man time to subject the nature of his response to a 'second look.'" People v. Morrin, 187 N.W.2d 434, 449 (Mich. Ct. App. 1971). On its face, this formulation sounds like *Guthrie*, and Michigan precedent had applied the doctrine to invalidate a first-degree murder conviction where "there was no basis for the jury to conclude that the defendant had adequate time for a 'second look.'" *Oros*, 917 N.W.2d at 567. Yet, in *Oros*, the court also emphasized language in its precedents stating that "the minimum time necessary to exercise this [second-look] process is incapable of exact determination," adding that it could be as short as "a 'brief moment of thought' or a 'matter of seconds.'" *Id.* at 566.

   Applying this standard to the facts at hand, the court upheld the first-degree murder conviction of a man who claimed he was attacked by a woman whose apartment he had entered in a failed attempt to perpetrate a scam. According to the defendant, the woman "struck him over the head with a coffee mug, knocking him to the ground, and climbed on top of him with 'a huge knife in her hand'"; he eventually made his way out from beneath her and stabbed her to death. *Id.* at 567. The prosecution disputed these facts. But it is not clear that the factual dispute mattered, as the court's opinion contains the following passage:

> [I]t is reasonable to infer that defendant had the opportunity for a "second look" during the period of time that elapsed when he flipped the victim over to position her face down on the floor, climbed onto her back, and then continued to stab her. It took thought and reflection to flip the victim over, permitting an inference that defendant acted with both premeditation and deliberation. Moreover, the location and depth of the victim's stab wounds support an inference that defendant thought about, measured, and evaluated his options. Many of the stab wounds were anywhere from 2 to 5 inches deep, which would indicate the amount of force used to not only plunge the knife into the victim's body, but also to retract it. Given the amount of effort expended for these particular stab wounds, it was reasonable for the jury to infer that sufficient time existed

between each stab wound to allow defendant the opportunity to take a "second look."

Id. at 569. The court's analysis drew a dissent, which criticized its "blow-by-blow account" for failing "to identify any evidence from which to infer that the defendant thought about his intent to kill before deciding to act." *Id.* at 574 (McCormack, J., dissenting). "In so holding," the dissent, echoing *Guthrie*, argued that the court "treats premeditation, deliberation, and intent to kill as fungible — thereby collapsing the distinction between first- and second-degree murder." *Id.* at 570.

Reasonable minds can differ as to whether the *Oros* majority overturned Michigan's second-look doctrine, as the dissent implies. It is clear, however, that the majority's approach affords wide discretion to the trier of fact: "it is within the province of the fact-finder," the majority held, "to determine whether there was sufficient time for a reasonable person to subject his or her action to a second look." *Id.* at 566 (majority opinion).

In an effort to give jurors some guideposts for that determination, a number of courts have embraced a set of factors first identified by the California Supreme Court in *People v. Anderson*, 447 P.2d 942 (Cal. 1968), and recited above in note 24 of the *Guthrie* opinion (p. 183). In *Anderson*, the court considered a brutal murder of a ten-year-old girl by her mother's partner. Applying what came to be known as the *Anderson* factors, the court held that the evidence was insufficient to support a conviction for first-degree murder.

> It is well established that the brutality of a killing cannot in itself support a finding that the killer acted with premeditation and deliberation. . . . [W]e find that the only evidence of (1) defendant's behavior prior to the killing which could be described as "planning" activity related to a killing purpose was defendant's sending the victim's brother on an errand and apparently returning home alone with the decedent. Such evidence is highly ambiguous in terms of the various inferences it could support as to defendant's purpose in so behaving. The evidence of (2) defendant's prior behavior with the victim (alleged sexual molestation . . .) is insufficient to support a reasonable inference that defendant had a "motive" to kill the girl, which could in turn support an inference that [his] striking [her repeatedly] with the machete was the result of a "preconceived design" and "forethought." Finally, the evidence of (3) the manner of killing (brutal hacking) does not support a reasonable inference of deliberately placed blows, which could in turn support an inference that the act of killing was premeditated rather than "hasty and impetuous."

Id. at 947, 952.

3. Problematizing Premeditation. Some people who study the law of premeditation contend that the challenges of both definition and application described above are inescapable, because the very idea of using premeditation to identify the worst murderers does not make any sense. For some critics, the problem is that the concept of premeditation is *unintelligible,* insofar as it inherently collapses into the idea of intent. Justice Cardozo suggested as much when he said that "[i]f intent is deliberate and premeditated whenever there is choice, then in truth it is always deliberate and premeditated, since choice is always involved in the hypothesis of the intent." To others, using premeditation to define first-degree murder is *impractical:* Even if one tries to separate intent from premeditation by focusing on the concept of reflection, Professor Kimberly Ferzan writes, most "rational agents will often have to further deliberate as to how to kill," such that in practice it will be the "extraordinarily rare individual who will not engage in some additional exercise of deliberation in intention formation or intention execution." Finally, and perhaps most fundamentally, even if one can both define and coherently apply a body of law that treats premeditation and deliberation as an intelligible dividing line, it is not clear that this is the *right* metric by which to separate out the worst murders. The problem, as Ferzan observes, is that premeditation "appears to be both over- and under-inclusive in capturing the most culpable actors."[27]

> It is overinclusive because it reaches individuals who kill with good reason (mercy killers) but whose actions are nevertheless neither justified nor excused by the criminal law. [E]ven if one believes that active euthanasia is properly criminalized . . . one may still reject that these killers are among the worst killers. . . . Additionally, premeditation captures those who take a long time to decide to kill because they may truly value the life they end, rather than fully identifying with their killings.
>
> Premeditation appears underinclusive because it does not capture those who give little thought to their killings. If thoughtless killers are as culpable as premeditating ones, then the law should not draw any distinction. Indeed, *People v. Anderson* is an infamous example of premeditation's underinclusiveness. . . . As one commentator notes[,] "The butchering of a child for reasons of sexual frustration and rage represents an extreme challenge to the value of human life. It ranks high on any intuitive scale of wrongdoing, and may explain why many appellate courts have been so reluctant to take premeditation seriously—it leads to decisions like *Anderson.*"[28]

For an alternative view, consider a recent defense of premeditation offered by Justice Caleb Stegall, writing for the Supreme Court of Kansas:

> [H]ow does an intentional act differ from a premeditated one? . . . I see a freshly baked chocolate chip cookie and I eat it. There is a fair chance I ate it intentionally—that is, I possessed the requisite mental condition of purpose, aim, and objective—but without premeditation.

In ordinary language, it might be said that I ate the cookie "without a second thought." This doesn't mean I ate it on accident. It means I did not engage in a cognitive moment of reflection or pondering. It was an "impulse" decision. . . .

Alternatively, perhaps I saw the cookie, decided to eat it, and as I reached for it, an internal, cognitive brake was engaged that essentially asks—"Is eating the cookie really what you want to do before dinner?" My thought processes have now entered a phase of conscious deliberation. . . . At this point, I can override that cognitive brake and eat the cookie anyway; or, I may alter my intended behavior once the process of "reflection" and "thinking over" has played itself out. The temporal space required to complete that process may be very short—a mere hesitation, perhaps, as my hand hovers over the cookie and I complete the internal double-check. We all are familiar with that cognitive sensation, and we all have likely learned to recognize it in others when we see it—to discern the "hesitation" that goes along with "having a second thought." This is premeditation.

Premeditated murder is a more serious crime with a more serious penalty precisely because society and law have recognized for centuries that overriding an internal cognitive brake—that is, choosing the intended act after reflection—is a factual element that makes the crime factually worse. . . . "A deterrent rationale generally motivates the distinction—if an action is premeditated or planned, it can be deterred." Nita A. Farahany, *Law and Behavioral Morality*, 52 Nomos 115, 126 (2012). So a person "who not only aims at evil, but takes time and consideration to achieve this evil, appears particularly culpable." Kimberly Kessler Ferzan, *Plotting Premeditation's Demise*, 75 Law & Contemp. Probs. 83, 95 (2012).

State v. Stanley, 478 P.3d 324, 335 (Kan. 2020).[29]

4. Adjudicating Premeditation. In *Guthrie,* the court describes its decision to separate first- and second-degree murder in part as a means of limiting jury discretion. Justice Cardozo similarly saw an ill-defined account of premeditation as conferring "a privilege [on] the jury to find the lesser degree when the suddenness of the intent, the vehemence of the passion, seems to call irresistibly for the exercise of mercy." For Cardozo, there was nothing wrong with affording juries such discretion. "I have no objection," he said, "to giving them this dispensing power," so long as it is "given to them directly and not in a mystifying cloud of words." Professor Michael Mannheimer, by contrast, takes a different view: "unbridled jury discretion to decide to convict of a crime that paves the way for the death penalty, on the one hand, or one that is punishable only by little more than a dozen years in prison, on the other, verges on lawlessness. Such overly broad discretion can lead to unpredictable, inconsistent, undesirable, and even indefensible results."[30]

This debate hints at a more fundamental tension over the role of juries in the adjudication of guilt. We will see that tension arise repeatedly in the pages and chapters to come, typically revolving around the same basic questions: Should the law prize jury discretion, in hopes of tailoring just outcomes to the particularities of each case? Or should it cabin such discretion, in hopes of avoiding disparate outcomes and implicit (or explicit) biases?

Treating the premeditation debate as a debate over jury power, however, assumes that Cardozo and *Guthrie* are right in thinking that jurors are especially or primarily empowered by a regime that eliminates the distinction between first- and second-degree murder. Is this right? Note that the Michigan Supreme Court in *Oros* purported to adhere to an alternative legal framework (the second-look doctrine) but suggested that *this* approach affords maximal discretion to jurors: "it is within the province of the factfinder to determine whether there was sufficient time for a reasonable person to subject his or her action to a second look." *Oros*, 917 N.W.2d at 566.

Questions: As between the *Jordan* and *Guthrie* regimes, which do you think empowers juries more? Are there any other institutional actors empowered by either approach? What about by the approach in *Anderson*?

2. Malice and Provocation: Distinguishing Murder from Manslaughter

Girouard v. State

583 A.2d 718 (Md. 1991)

COLE, J. In this case we are asked to reconsider whether the types of provocation sufficient to mitigate the crime of murder to manslaughter should be limited to the categories we have heretofore recognized, or whether the sufficiency of the provocation should be decided by the factfinder on a case-by-case basis. Specifically, we must determine whether words alone are provocation adequate to justify a conviction of manslaughter rather than one of second degree murder.

The Petitioner, Steven S. Girouard, and the deceased, Joyce M. Girouard, had been married for about two months on October 28, 1987, the night of Joyce's death. Both parties, who met while working in the same building, were in the army. They married after having known each other for approximately three months. The evidence at trial indicated that the marriage was often tense and strained, and there was some evidence that after marrying Steven, Joyce had resumed a relationship with her old boyfriend, Wayne.

On the night of Joyce's death, Steven overheard her talking on the telephone to her friend, whereupon she told the friend that she had asked her first sergeant for a hardship discharge because her husband did not love her anymore. Steven went into the living room where Joyce was on the phone and asked her what she meant by her comments; she responded, "nothing." Angered by her lack of response, Steven kicked away the plate of food Joyce had in front of her. He then went to lie down in the bedroom.

Joyce followed him into the bedroom, stepped up onto the bed and onto Steven's back, pulled his hair and said, "What are you going to do, hit me?" She continued to taunt him by saying, "I never did want to marry you and you are a lousy fuck and you remind me of my dad."[1] The barrage of insults continued with her telling Steven that she wanted a divorce, that the marriage had been a mistake and that she had never wanted to marry him. She also told him she had seen his commanding officer and filed charges against him for abuse. She then asked Steven, "What are you going to do?" Receiving no response, she continued her verbal attack. She added [falsely] that she had filed charges against him in the Judge Advocate General's Office (JAG) and that he would probably be court martialed.

When she was through, Steven asked her if she had really done all those things, and she responded in the affirmative. He left the bedroom with his pillow in his arms and proceeded to the kitchen where he procured a long handled kitchen knife. He returned to Joyce in the bedroom with the knife behind the pillow. He testified that he was enraged and that he kept waiting for Joyce to say she was kidding, but Joyce continued talking. She said she had learned a lot from the marriage and that it had been a mistake. . . .

After pausing for a moment, Joyce asked what Steven was going to do. What he did was lunge at her with the kitchen knife he had hidden behind the pillow and stab her 19 times. Realizing what he had done, he dropped the knife and went to the bathroom to shower off Joyce's blood. Feeling like he wanted to die, Steven went back to the kitchen and found two steak knives with which he slit his own wrists. He lay down on the bed waiting to die, but when he realized that he would not die from his self-inflicted wounds, he got up and called the police, telling the dispatcher that he had just murdered his wife.

When the police arrived they found Steven wandering around outside his apartment building. Steven was despondent and tearful and seemed detached, according to police officers who had been at the scene. He was unconcerned about his own wounds, talking only about how much he loved his wife and how he could not believe what he had done. Joyce Girouard was pronounced dead at the scene. . . .

. . . Girouard was convicted, at a [bench] trial . . . , of second degree murder and was sentenced to 22 years incarceration, 10 of which were suspended. . . . We granted certiorari to determine whether the circumstances

---

1. There was some testimony presented at trial . . . that . . . her father . . . had impregnated her when she was fourteen, the result of which was an abortion. . . .

of the case presented provocation adequate to mitigate the second degree murder charge to manslaughter.

Petitioner [argues] that the provocation to mitigate murder to manslaughter should not be limited only to the traditional circumstances of: extreme assault or battery upon the defendant; mutual combat; defendant's illegal arrest; injury or serious abuse of a close relative of the defendant's; or the sudden discovery of a spouse's adultery. Petitioner argues that manslaughter is a catchall for homicides which are criminal but that lack the malice essential for a conviction of murder. [He further] argues that the trial judge did find provocation (although he held it inadequate to mitigate murder) and that the categories of provocation adequate to mitigate should be broadened to include factual situations such as this one.

The State counters by stating that although there is no finite list of legally adequate provocations, . . . there are some concededly provocative acts that society is not prepared to recognize as reasonable. Words spoken by the victim, no matter how abusive or taunting, fall into a category society should not accept as adequate provocation. According to the State, if abusive words alone could mitigate murder to manslaughter, nearly every domestic argument ending in the death of one party could be mitigated to manslaughter. . . .

Initially, we note that the difference between murder and manslaughter is the presence or absence of malice. Voluntary manslaughter has been defined as "an *intentional* homicide, done in a sudden heat of passion, caused by adequate provocation, before there has been a reasonable opportunity for the passion to cool." Cox v. State, 534 A.2d 1333, 1335 (Md. 1988).

There are certain facts that may mitigate what would normally be murder to manslaughter. For example, we have recognized as falling into that group: (1) discovering one's spouse in the act of sexual intercourse with another; (2) mutual combat; (3) assault and battery. There is also authority recognizing injury to one of the defendant's relatives or to a third party, and death resulting from resistance of an illegal arrest as adequate provocation for mitigation to manslaughter. . . .

In order to determine whether murder should be mitigated to manslaughter we look to the circumstances surrounding the homicide and try to discover if it was provoked by the victim. . . . For provocation to be "adequate," it must be "calculated to inflame the passion of a reasonable man and tend to cause him to act for the moment from passion rather than reason." Carter v. State, 505 A.2d 545, 572 (Md. Ct. Spec. App. 1986). The issue we must resolve, then, is whether the taunting words uttered by Joyce were enough to inflame the passion of a *reasonable* man so that that man would be sufficiently infuriated so as to strike out in hot-blooded blind passion to kill her. Although we agree with the trial judge that there was needless provocation by Joyce, we also agree with him that the provocation was not adequate to mitigate second degree murder to voluntary manslaughter.

Although there are few Maryland cases discussing the issue at bar, those that do hold that words alone are not adequate provocation. Most recently, in Sims v. State, 573 A.2d 1317 (Md. 1990), we held that "[i]nsulting words or gestures, no matter how opprobrious, do not amount to an affray, and standing alone, do not constitute adequate provocation." That case involved the flinging of racial slurs and derogatory comments by the victim at the defendant. That conduct did not constitute adequate provocation.

[Some courts have held] that words can constitute adequate provocation if they are accompanied by conduct indicating a present intention and ability to cause the defendant bodily harm. Clearly, no such conduct was exhibited by Joyce in this case. While Joyce did step on Steven's back and pull his hair, he could not reasonably have feared bodily harm at her hands. This, to us, is certain based on Steven's testimony at trial that Joyce was about 5′1″ tall and weighed 115 pounds, while he was 6′2″ tall, weighing over 200 pounds. Joyce simply did not have the size or strength to cause Steven to fear for his bodily safety. Thus, since there was no ability on the part of Joyce to cause Steven harm, the words she hurled at him could not . . . constitute legally sufficient provocation. . . .

[W]ith no reservation, we hold that the provocation in this case was not enough to cause a reasonable man to stab his provoker 19 times. Although a psychologist testified to Steven's mental problems and his need for acceptance and love, we agree with the Court of Special Appeals speaking through Judge Moylan that "there must be not simply provocation in psychological fact, but one of certain fairly well-defined classes of provocation recognized as being adequate as a matter of law." Tripp v. State, 374 A.2d 384, 392 (Md. Ct. Spec. App. 1977). The standard is one of reasonableness; it does not and should not focus on the peculiar frailties of mind of the Petitioner. That standard of reasonableness has not been met here. . . . [S]ocial necessity dictates our holding. Domestic arguments easily escalate into furious fights. We perceive no reason for a holding in favor of those who find the easiest way to end a domestic dispute is by killing the offending spouse.

We will leave to another day the possibility of expansion of the categories of adequate provocation to mitigate murder to manslaughter. The facts of this case do not warrant the broadening of the categories recognized thus far.

Brown v. United States

584 A.2d 537 (D.C. 1990)

NEWMAN, J. Ava Brown appeals her conviction for malicious destruction of property stemming from an incident in which Brown smashed the front windows and door of her mother's home in an effort to get inside and take possession of her runaway son, who was then staying at his grandmother's home. . . . We reverse the conviction.

I.

On Friday September 16, 1988, Lamar Brown, Ava Brown's twelve-year old son, ran away from home. His grandmother, Ava Brown's mother, Joylette Young, found him on a street on September 23 and took him home with her . . . . Young testified that she did not notify Brown that she had found Brown's son because Brown had no telephone and the boy insisted that he did not wish to return to his mother's home.

Ava Brown searched unsuccessfully for her son for ten days. She contacted the police and the Youth Division and talked to friends and neighbors. On Monday September 26th, sometime after 8:00 p.m., she contacted a friend of Lamar's named Antoine and asked him if he knew Lamar's whereabouts. Antoine told Brown that Lamar had been picked up from an area playground by his grandmother, Ms. Young.

At about 9:40 that evening, Ava Brown, with her other son, Javan, in tow, appeared at the front door of her mother's home seeking her son. Ms. Young told Brown that she could not have the boy, because Brown had been physically and mentally abusing him and he did not want to return home with her. Brown insisted that she be allowed to come in and get the boy. Young refused. Brown picked up a wrought iron chair from the front porch and began smashing windows and the front door in an attempt to gain entry, destroying three windows, curtains, blinds, and the panes in a fifteen light door in the process. . . .

Young called the police and then left the house via the basement with Lamar in an attempt to reach Young's car while Brown was occupied breaking through the front door. As the pair reached Young's car, they were observed by Lamar's younger brother, Javan, who called out to Lamar to come to him and his mother. Brown left the porch in an attempt to stop them, but was restrained by neighbors and held on the ground until the police arrived.

At trial, Brown conceded all elements of the charge except malice, arguing that she had been provoked by (1) her mother's earlier threats to institutionalize the boy to remove him from her care and (2) her mother's refusal to allow her access to her son after a ten-day search for the boy. Concerning the former point, Brown was prevented by the court from testifying about the alleged threats on grounds that, as a matter of law, Brown's motivations for trying to enter the house were irrelevant. . . . Concerning the latter point, the court said to the jury:

> You're instructed that as a matter of law it is not adequate provocation, justification, or excuse to damage or destroy property if somebody is not doing something that you think they should be doing, such as in this case,

not turning over the defendant's son. As a matter of law, that is not sufficient justification or excuse to thereupon start destroying property.

II.

Although provocation is a matter usually connected with the law
of homicide, we have held that the malice required . . . as an element of
the charge of malicious destruction of property is the same as the malice
required to make out a case of murder. "[M]alice in the legal sense imports
the absence of all elements of justification, excuse or recognized mitigation."
Charles v. United States, 371 A.2d 404, 411 (D.C. 1977). Thus, provocation
is a proper defense to the charge of malicious destruction of property, and
we look to the doctrine of provocation as it has developed in the context of
homicide . . . to guide us in deciding this case.

Under the common law, the doctrine of provocation developed . . .
fixed categories of conduct by the victim, paradigms of misbehavior, which
the law recognized as sufficiently provocative to mitigate what would otherwise be malicious conduct by the defendant. Familiar examples of these
categories of provocative conduct by the victim are adultery and assault. . . .
In addition, rules were developed to keep certain types of conduct outside
the fixed categories, and thus away from the jury, such as insulting words
and gestures unaccompanied by other conduct. Thus, under the common
law, there grew up a process of pigeon-holing provocative conduct.

But the domination of provocation doctrine by fixed categories of recognized conduct has long been questioned by a number of commentators
and courts. . . . Culminating in the formulation adopted in the Model Penal
Code, the modern view has turned away from the rigid common law rules
of fixed categories of conduct and toward the broader conception of provocation embodied in the phrase "extreme mental or emotional disturbance
for which there is reasonable explanation or excuse." Model Penal Code
§210.3. Under this view, if there is evidence of extreme emotional distress,
it is left to the trier of fact to determine whether, under the circumstances,
there is a reasonable "explanation or excuse" for the defendant's conduct.
Id. at 61.[16]

The view expressed in the Model Penal Code has been said to have
been anticipated by a 19th century decision of the Michigan Supreme
Court, *Maher v. People*, 10 Mich. 212 (1862). Maher was charged with assault
with intent to kill his wife's lover. On the day of the assault, he followed
the pair to the woods, observed them enter the woods, waited for them to

---

16. *See also* Wayne R. LaFave & Austin W. Scott, *Criminal Law* §76 at 574 (1972) ("[T]here
seems to be a growing realization that what might or might not cause a loss of self control in a
reasonable Englishman of a century ago might not necessarily produce the same reaction in the
reasonable Anglo-American of today.").

emerge, and then followed his victim to a saloon. Just before entering the saloon, he was told by an acquaintance that the two had intercourse the day before. Maher then entered the saloon and fired a shot at his victim's head, wounding and nearly killing him. . . .

[A]s the Supreme Court of Michigan formulated it, provocation may be any set of circumstances that would naturally arouse passion in and dominate the reason of an ordinary person and which, in the jury's view, did so with regard to the defendant in the case at hand. In reversing Maher's conviction, the court offered as its rationale for adopting this flexible standard "the almost infinite variety of facts presented by the various cases as they arise," *id.* at 222, and concluded that "the law cannot with justice assume, by the light of past decisions to catalogue all the various facts and combinations of facts which shall be held to constitute reasonable or adequate provocation." *Id.* at 222-223. . . . Judge Manning, writing in dissent in *Maher*, took the [common law] view that "the cause of provocation must occur in the defendant's presence," *id.* at 228, referring of course to the adulterous act. . . .

Defense counsel [in Brown's case] strove to get his evidence of provocation before the jury. Initially, he attempted to present the theory that Brown was provoked by Young's refusal to turn over her son. This theory was thwarted by the trial court's ruling that, as a matter of law, Young's refusal to turn over Brown's son was inadequate provocation. We disagree. We cannot say that an ordinary, reasonable person, after searching for her son for ten days only to learn that he was staying with her own mother and that her own mother had not only failed to inform her of her son's whereabouts but also refused to return the boy to the custody of his own parent, could not have been so impassioned by these circumstances as to lose her self-control and, acting without reflection, destroy windows and a door in an attempt to get into her mother's house and retrieve her lost son. . . . Brown was denied the opportunity to present evidence on this issue by the trial court's ruling that Brown's testimony concerning [the] alleged threats [to institutionalize Brown's son] and Brown's motives in attempting to enter the house to prevent them from taking place was irrelevant. This limitation on the introduction of evidence, as well as the jury instructions implementing this ruling, each constitute reversible error. *Reversed and remanded.*

NOTES AND QUESTIONS

1. Killing Without Malice. In the language of the common law, manslaughter is defined as an unlawful killing without the element of *malice aforethought* essential to murder. As we will see, some manslaughters (like some murders) are committed unintentionally, when criminally risky behavior causes a death. This is often called *involuntary manslaughter.* Separately, manslaughter convictions can arise when a doctrine that would otherwise fully exculpate a defendant applies only partially to the facts at hand, as occurs in cases of imperfect self-defense discussed later in this chapter. In the world of intentional homicides, however, manslaughter most commonly occurs when a person wrongfully kills under circumstances the law treats as *mitigating* culpability and reducing the grade of the crime. As with premeditation, defining those mitigating circumstances can be challenging. As a general rule, courts focus on two key issues: whether the killing was *provoked* or committed by someone who was otherwise experiencing *extreme emotional distress*; and whether, if provoked, the person who killed nonetheless had time to *cool off* prior to committing the homicide. The next two notes address these issues.

2. Provocation vs. Extreme Emotional Distress. As the *Brown* opinion recounts, American jurisdictions historically have split between those that confine adequate bases of provocation to specific categories and those that take a more holistic, case-by-case approach. The MPC embraces the holistic school of thought, stating that "[c]riminal homicide constitutes manslaughter when [it] would otherwise be murder [but] is committed under the influence of extreme mental or emotional disturbance for which there is a reasonable explanation or excuse." Model Penal Code §210.3(1)(b). In its most expansive interpretations, this language may not even require a provocative triggering event immediately preceding the homicide. Consider *State v. White*, 251 P.3d 820 (Utah 2011), in which a woman was charged with attempted murder for driving her car into her ex-husband's office in an effort to run him over. The Utah Supreme Court described the relevant facts as follows:

> Brenda and Jon White were married for eleven years. Both parties admit the marriage was difficult and that talk of divorce was common. According to Ms. White, Jon was addicted to pornography and suggested that Ms. White participate in "sexual threesomes" with him and his co-worker. Ms. White further alleges that during the marriage Jon was having an affair with another woman. These behaviors caused Ms. White to experience feelings of great anxiety, anger, and agitation, and they eventually led to the couple's divorce.
>
> Following the divorce, Ms. White's stress increased. She struggled financially to support her two daughters and, as a result of having to work more hours, saw less of her children. Throughout this period of time, Ms. White claims that Jon began to withdraw from the children and failed to pay child support. Jon canceled Ms. White's medical insurance, which left her unable to pay for medication she needed to treat her anxiety and depression. . . . Because of her financial troubles, Ms. White attempted to refinance the home, but learned that she would not be able to complete the refinancing process without Jon's assistance and signatures.

On April 26, 2006, Brenda went to Jon's office to speak to him about refinancing the house. . . . Jon walked out to the parking lot with Brenda. Brenda asked Jon to sign a quit-claim deed to the marital home, but Jon refused to do so until Brenda took his name off the two mortgages encumbering the property. The conversation escalated in intensity and Brenda became extremely upset. She climbed into her vehicle and turned on music with the lyrics, "I want to kill you; I want to blow you away." During the song, she joined her hands together to mimic a gun and pointed her fingers at Jon. She then told Jon he was a "parasite" and that she was going to wipe him off the earth. Jon went back into the office, and Brenda drove away.

That same afternoon, around 4:30 p.m., Ms. White returned to Jon's workplace to again discuss refinancing the home. When she arrived, . . . [she] observed him talking on a cell phone—a cell phone that she claims Jon had repeatedly denied owning. Ms. White testified that at that moment she was overcome with all the anger, agitation, loss, grief, and disappointment she had experienced throughout her relationship and the divorce. Ms. White claims at that point, her emotions took over and she lost all self-control.

As she watched Jon talk on his cell phone, Ms. White drove her vehicle toward him, accelerating quickly. When Jon heard tires screeching, he jumped between two parked cars, over a small cement wall, and back into his office building. Ms. White continued to follow Jon, driving her car through the building's double glass doors. After entering the lobby with her car, Ms. White struck Jon twice with her vehicle. Jon flew over the hood of the car and landed on the ground, injuring his left leg.

Id. at 822-823.

The intermediate appellate court affirmed the trial court's refusal to give an "extreme emotional distress" instruction, holding "that a highly provocative, contemporaneous trigger is required for Defendant's reaction to qualify as extreme emotional distress" and that "Mr. White's use of a cell phone that he had previously denied possessing" was "not sufficiently provocative." State v. White, 206 P.3d 646, 648, 654 (Utah Ct. App. 2009). But the state supreme court reversed:

> The extreme emotional distress defense was generally enacted by states in response to the unworkable nature of the heat of passion defense. *See* State v. Bishop, 753 P.2d 439, 469-70 (Utah 1988). The defense was meant to "substantially enlarge the class of cases that might be reduced to manslaughter" and "to do away with categories of adequate provocation which had developed in the cases." *Id.* . . . [A] person acts under the influence of extreme emotional distress when "he is exposed to extremely unusual and overwhelming stress" that would cause the average reasonable person under the same circumstances to "experience a loss of self-control,"

and "be overborne by intense feelings, such as passion, anger, distress, grief, excessive agitation, or other similar emotions." *Id.* at 471. . . . [U]nlike the former "heat of passion" defense, [the extreme emotional distress defense may be available where] "a significant mental trauma has affected a defendant's mind for a substantial period of time, simmering in the unknowing subconscious and then inexplicably coming to the fore." People v. Shelton, 385 N.Y.S.2d 708, 715 (Sup. Ct. 1976). . . .

[W]hen a person reacts to a situation, that reaction cannot be viewed in isolation. Rather, a reaction to an event must be evaluated in its broader context. This context is relevant, maybe essential, to acquiring an accurate picture of the past experiences and emotions that give meaning to that reaction. Those past experiences must be taken into account . . . . [W]e find no language in our precedent that requires [a] triggering event be contemporaneous with the defendant's loss of self-control. A close temporal tie between provocation and the criminal act was necessary under the "heat of passion" formulation because manslaughter was not available if there was time for the defendant to "cool off." No such requirement exists to assert the extreme emotional distress defense.

White, 251 P.3d at 826-828.

3. Cooling Off. As the preceding note indicates, states that adhere to the traditional common law approach to manslaughter typically require that a sufficiently provocative act occur close in time to the subsequent homicide. When too much time intervenes, these courts will conclude that this "cooling off period" negates any mitigating effect the initial provocation may have had. Consider *State v. Henson,* 197 P.3d 456 (Kan. 2008). In that case, a group of men were drinking outside an auto repair shop after a day of hard work. The men started talking about boxing and, in the course of that conversation, one of them, Toriana Henson, pointed at another, Randy Davis, and said "the bigger they are, the harder they fall." Upon hearing this, Davis apparently felt threatened and immediately punched Henson, knocking him unconscious for approximately ten minutes. When Henson came to, he left the auto shop and went to his house where he cleaned the blood from his face and retrieved a pistol. Returning to the auto repair shop about 20 to 30 minutes after being punched, Henson walked into the garage where Davis and others were sitting. He pointed the gun at Davis, said "What's up now, Randy?" and then shot him in the head. The state supreme court affirmed the trial court's refusal to give a voluntary manslaughter instruction and quoted an earlier nineteenth-century opinion with similar facts, *State v. Yarborough,* 18 P. 474 (Kan. 1888), to explain why:

The law carefully distinguishes between a sudden transport of passion, which springs instantaneously from what it allows as a sufficient provocation, and which prompts to an immediate act of violence, and a purpose of revenge, which usually follows such passion. In the first case, in condescension to the frailty of our nature the law allows the provocation to extenuate a homicide committed at the instant, from murder to manslaughter. In the other, the provocation furnishing an incentive to revenge, so far from extenuating the crime, is a circumstance to be looked to as evidence of malice; and especially would this be so if the prisoner, in consequence of the provocation, had made threats against the life of the deceased.

Henson, 197 P.3d at 464.

4. Reasonableness and the Challenge of Individualization. Notwithstanding some notable differences, a common thread runs through the doctrinal frameworks described so far. Stated in the language of the common law, as in *Girouard*, mitigation from murder to manslaughter turns on whether the surrounding circumstances of a homicide would "inflame the passion of a *reasonable* man." The MPC similarly defines manslaughter as "a homicide . . . committed under the influence of extreme mental or emotional disturbance for which there is a *reasonable* explanation or excuse." *See* Model Penal Code §210.3 (emphasis added). Finally, the cooling-off doctrine insists on a murder conviction, as opposed to a manslaughter conviction, when an otherwise-provoked "defendant has killed after a period of reflection and deliberation during which a *reasonable* person's passions would have cooled." State v. Soto, 34 A.3d 738, 745 (N.H. 2011) (emphasis added).

Reasonableness, in short, is the touchstone. On some level, this seems strange. After all, as Professor Stephen Morse observes, "Reasonable people do not kill no matter how much they are provoked." Defining manslaughter as occurring only when "an ordinary person would kill under the circumstances" would therefore seem to all but eliminate the mitigating effect of the doctrine. When the California Supreme Court was asked to adopt precisely such a definition in *People v. Beltran*, 301 P.3d 1120 (Cal. 2013), it thus refused. In so doing, it offered the following clarification about the focus of the reasonable-person inquiry:

> [S]ociety expects the average person not to kill, even when provoked. As Professor Dressler stated, we punish a person who kills in the heat of passion or upon provocation because "he did not control himself as much as he should have, or as much as common experience tells us he could have, nor as much as the ordinarily law-abiding person would have." Joshua Dressler, *Rethinking Heat of Passion: A Defense in Search of a Rationale*, 73 J. Crim. L. & Criminology 421, 467 (1982). . . . Such a killing is not justified but understandable in light of "the frailty of human nature." Maher v. People, 10 Mich. 212, 219 (1862). The killing reaction therefore is the extraordinary reaction, the unusual exception to the general expectation that the ordinary person will not kill even when provoked.

Adopting a standard requiring such provocation that the ordinary person of average disposition would be moved to kill [thus] focuses on the wrong thing. The proper focus is placed on the defendant's state of mind, not on his particular act. To be adequate, the provocation must be one that would cause an emotion so intense that an ordinary person would simply react, without reflection. . . . Framed another way, provocation is not evaluated by whether the average person would act in a certain way: to kill. Instead, the question is whether the average person would react in a certain way: with his reason and judgment obscured.[31]

Id. at 1130.

This explanation helps to clarify "the proper focus" of the reasonable-person test. But it does not supply much guidance as to how the test should be *applied* in the course of determining (to quote *Beltran*) "whether the average person would react in a certain way." More specifically, it does not answer a fundamental question that arises time and again in criminal law and in American law more generally whenever the reasonable-person conceit is deployed. Who *is* the reasonable person? And more to the point: How much should we imagine the hypothetical reasonable person to share certain relevant characteristics with the actual human being standing accused of a crime?

Canvassing a sizable scholarly literature on these fundamental questions, Professor Jonathan Witmer-Rich describes them as presenting "a longstanding conceptual puzzle" that many scholars have suggested simply "cannot be answered." As Witmer-Rich explains, at some level the "reasonable person" *must* share some basic attributes with the individual standing trial:

[T]he "reasonable person" must be a person who has just experienced what the defendant experienced. Asking whether a "reasonable person" would have become extremely provoked at the sight of his child being sexually assaulted presupposes that the reasonable person is a parent who has a child, and the reasonable person has just witnessed that child being sexually assaulted.[32]

But, as Professor Victoria Nourse explains, there are problems with individualizing the reasonable person both too much *and* too little. On the one hand, if we individualize too much, "the law acquires the characteristics of the defendant" and "appears to prefer the defendant to the rest of society." Indeed, in its most extreme form, a maximally individualized reasonable-person test collapses into a purely subjective one. To some that may seem desirable. But consider that a purely subjective approach will struggle to deny mitigation in cases where it seems unwarranted. For example, as Witmer-Rich notes, if we encounter a white supremacist who becomes "extremely angry at the sight of an inter-racial couple kissing in public," we would not want the law to ask whether "a reasonable racist person" would have been provoked by such conduct. Such an approach would treat the racist killing as less bad *because* the killer was a racist, which seems both morally wrong and socially corrosive. Nourse continues:

> [T]he law will be perceived, not simply by defendants, but by the law-abiding, as endorsing claims of violence based on "reasonable" emotions that amount to what the law, in other places, would declare to be sexist or racist. In a world in which the law embraces these emotions as reasonable, critics have a right to fear that the law has upended itself and, in effect, changed the relation between citizens and their government.[33]

And yet, perhaps paradoxically, a more objective, less individualized approach can yield injustices of its own. Consider the following passage from Professors Dan Kahan and Martha Nussbaum:

> The facts of social variation warn us that we must ask, "Whose ideas of reasonableness?" When we are asking about anger, for example, do we look for our norm of reasonableness to the [Inuit peoples] or to the ancient Romans, or to some critical norm that transcends both cultures? If the answer is that we should look to our fellow-citizens and define the emotion and its norms as they do — by no means an obvious answer, since we might have good reasons to think some prevailing norms unreasonable — we still must ask, which fellow citizens, and why those?

Kahan and Nussbaum's questions raise the possibility that a putatively "objective" reasonable-person test is in fact not objective at all but is instead simply substituting one subjective judgment for another — the subjectivity of the jury for the subjectivity of the defendant. After all, if the law does not tell a jury who the reasonable person is (including by suggesting that the reasonable person is someone like the defendant), then it invites the jury to graft onto the reasonable person a set of societal preconceptions that will naturally tend to track dominant social hierarchies. The notes that follow explore these issues in greater detail as they arise within the specific context of manslaughter's provocation doctrine.[34]

5. A Gendered Past. As the cases in this section reflect, prosecutions implicating the law of manslaughter often involve intimate-partner violence. Defined generally as sexual violence, stalking, physical violence, or psychological aggression by a romantic or sexual partner, intimate-partner violence is experienced by approximately one-third of both women and men in the United States during their lifetimes, according to the Centers for Disease Control and Prevention. The impact of such violence, however, is markedly more severe for women, 25 percent of whom report that intimate-partner violence has caused them to fear for their safety, to need medical care or assistance from law enforcement, or to miss at least one day of work or school — a rate more than double that reported by men. This gender discrepancy, moreover, grows starker as the violence worsens. In 2010, of the 2,310 women killed by a known assailant, more than half were killed by a former or current romantic partner, compared to only 5.6 percent of 5,471 male victims. And yet, critics have long argued that the criminal law of homicide, rather than protecting women in the face of such harms, reinforces "cultural values that condone masculine violence," and in so doing ultimately devalues women's lives.[35]

The law's failure to protect women's interests, critics point out, has deep historical roots. At common law, married women were the property and subjects of their husbands. Blackstone famously reported that "if the feme kills her baron, it is regarded by the laws as a much more atrocious crime" than if a husband kills his wife, "as she not only breaks through the restraints of humanity and conjugal affection, but throws off all subjection to the authority of her husband" and commits "a species of treason."* In like fashion, the law viewed adultery—by a wife—as an affront to a husband's authority. As Professor Elizabeth Rapaport explains, the basic logic here, embodied in the common law of provocation, analogizes adultery to assault, albeit one in which "[t]he blow administered to the husband is moral, not physical."

> Within the patriarchal conception of marriage, any challenge to masculine control—adulterous behavior or inclinations, contesting household authority, leaving—is an assault on both legitimate prerogatives and the very masculinity of the husband. Traditionally, violence to reassert possession or punish defiance has been considered legitimate masculine behavior. . . . It was not pain and anger at betrayal, which either the husband or wife may feel, that mitigated culpability at classical common law; rather, it was the defense of masculinity and its prerogatives and the legitimacy of violence as a vehicle of male control of the family.[36]

Indeed, in some jurisdictions, this patriarchal logic was taken to its extreme. As Professor Cynthia Lee explains, "A husband's observation of his wife in the act of adultery was thought to be such a grievous injury and affront to the husband that several states, including Georgia, Texas, Utah, and New Mexico, [once] deemed the husband's killing of an adulterous wife or her lover a justifiable homicide—not a crime at all." At the same time, women who killed their cheating husbands could not claim provocation. Rather, the law simply "expected a dutiful wife to accept her philandering husband's misbehavior," holding that if she "killed her unfaithful husband or his lover, she was a murderer."[37]

---

* 1 William Blackstone, *Commentaries* *445 n.35. Blackstone went on to observe that the law condemned a wife who killed her husband "to the same punishment as if she had killed the king. . . . [F]or every species of treason . . . the sentence of women was to be drawn and burnt alive." *Id.*

Nor was provocation's gendered legacy limited to cases involving adultery. Rather, as Lee further notes, the doctrine's gendered account of male and female behavior and emotion carries over to each of the common law categories described in the leading cases above:

> If we look carefully at the early common law categories of legally adequate provocation, it becomes apparent that they were created with the hot-blooded man in mind. Men were thought more likely than women to be subjected to an aggravated assault or battery. Men were thought more likely than women to be involved in mutual combat. They were also thought more likely than women to respond with violence to a serious crime committed against a close relative.[38]

6. A Gendered Present. The MPC expressly and intentionally broke from the common law's categorical approach to provocation doctrine. As the *White* opinion observes, this reform substantially enlarged "the class of cases that might be reduced to manslaughter" and thus extended the historical trend of mitigating penal sanctions in cases of homicide.

This effort to mitigate penal severity was lauded by many liberal reformers. But the MPC drafters expanded leniency by injecting "a larger element of subjectivity" into manslaughter's governing standard, insisting that reasonableness "be determined from the viewpoint of a person in the actor's situation under the circumstances as he believes them to be." Model Penal Code and Commentaries §210.3 cmt. 3 at 49-50. According to Emily Miller, this more subjective approach may have exacerbated the doctrine's tendency toward gendered injustice: By granting jurors "greater latitude to give voice to their own prejudices," which frequently are grounded in "cultural norms biased in favor of men," the MPC may have "entrenched patterns of masculine violence against women."[39]

Professor Victoria Nourse's systematic analysis of cases spanning fifteen years validates Miller's concern:

> If life tells us that crimes of passion are the stuff of sordid affairs and bed side confrontations, [an analysis of the MPC's] reform tells us that the law's passion may be something quite different. . . . Reform has permitted juries to return a manslaughter verdict in cases where the defendant claims passion because the victim left, moved the furniture out, planned a divorce, or sought a protective order. Even infidelity has been transformed under reform's gaze into something quite different from the sexual betrayal we might expect—it is the infidelity of a fiancée who danced with another, of a girlfriend who decided to date someone else, and of the divorcée found pursuing a new relationship months after the final decree. In the end, [the MPC's] reform has transformed passion from the classical adultery to the modern dating and moving and leaving. And because of that transformation, these killings, at least in reform states, may no longer carry the law's name of murder.

Nourse concludes that, in an "upside-down" sort of way, "the common law approach toward the provocation defense, deemed an antique by most legal scholars, provides greater protection for women than do purportedly liberal versions of the defense."[40]

7. A Feminist Critique, a Feminist Defense. Given the injustices that can and do occur under both the categorical common law approach and the more flexible MPC framework, some feminist critics argue that the problem is with provocation doctrine itself. The claim, on this view, is that sexist application of the doctrine is inescapable. After all, the argument goes, in a male-dominated sociolegal community, one would expect the people writing and applying the laws—legislators, judges, prosecutors, and juries—to embody a certain set of perspectives even as they purport to apply objective tests couched in gender-neutral language, like "reasonableness." To quote Professor Catharine MacKinnon, a sexist state "will appear most relentless in imposing the male point of view when it comes closest to achieving its highest formal criterion of distanced aperspectivity. When it is most ruthlessly neutral, it will be most male . . . ."[41]

Building on this critique, some have called for the abolition of the provocation doctrine altogether. As Miller writes:

> Because what is "reasonable" cannot be determined without reference to value systems biased in favor of men, the only truly egalitarian approach is abolition. The value of human life must trump the law's sympathy for the defendant's response. By virtue of its brutal discrimination against women under both the common law and MPC, the defense of voluntary manslaughter no longer has a place in American penal law.[42]

Others, however, contend that abolishing the provocation doctrine—and thus treating all unlawful intentional killings as murder—would work its own social injustice. Perhaps counterintuitively, some of that injustice may actually hurt *women.* Professor Aya Gruber explains:

> One of provocation critics' most persistent assumptions is that the defense inequitably favors male over female defendants. They assert the doctrine excuses only masculine violence provoked by affronts to male dignity. . . . Accordingly, commentators reason that male defendants must benefit disproportionately from the defense. . . . If anything, the opposite is true. Women defendants are more successful at defending against murder charges than men, just as they are more successful in defending against most crimes and obtaining favorable sentences. . . . In fact, one might argue that certain proposals to ratchet up punishment in intimate homicide cases could disproportionately burden women. Unlike male killers, who largely kill in nonintimate settings, female killers generally slay intimates (lovers, family members, and children). Thus, a legal change directed toward reducing leniency in intimate homicides increases severity

in the one realm where women are most likely to be murder defendants, leaving untouched the nondomestic homicides perpetrated nearly exclusively by men.[43]

More fundamentally, Gruber argues that attempts to cast the provocation doctrine as either good or bad for women contravene what Professor Martha Minow calls "the basic feminist insight into the variety of women's positions and interests." Some women are undoubtedly victims of male violence, Minow says, but others "are the mothers, daughters, or sisters of men facing retributive justice," while others still "are the victims of other women's violence." Building on this point, Gruber contends that the traditional feminist critique of provocation doctrine actually embraces a form of gender stereotyping. It treats men who commit intimate-partner killings as "presumptiv[e] abusers who acted in accordance with their controlling behavior patterns, whereas women intimate killers are presumptively passive responders to subordination by a violent man." According to Gruber, this account leaves people out: "sympathetic male defendants, who might be unfairly burdened by narrow provocation laws; undeserving female defendants, who might be unfairly benefitted by broad provocation laws; or any male victims. In the feminist script, these characters simply do not exist (or are so negligible that they do not merit mention)."[44]

Taking these points together, Gruber ultimately defends modern provocation doctrine against its feminist critique by invoking feminism itself. But her defense of provocation doctrine goes beyond feminism to defend manslaughter's mitigating impulse on its original terms — as an effort to scale back punitive excess in a penal system defined by severe punishment, and thus to cabin laws that "significantly burden subordinated defendants, exacerbate mass incarceration, and bolster the penal state."

> Sexist wife killers are not the only defendants who might benefit from provocation. According to Department of Justice statistics, from 1980 to 2008, male-on-female intimate killings comprised less than 10 percent of all homicides. After examining the demographic information, I have concluded elsewhere that "the group most likely to be burdened by the elimination or limitation of the provocation defense is young men of color accused of non-intimate homicides and facing murder charges in one of the most punitive systems on earth."[45]

Gruber further argues:

> One might reply that even one sexist defendant who succeeds in his provocation defense is unacceptable and cite the facts of a particular heinous case to support this contention. However, all legal rules operate within a cultural milieu and occasionally produce undesirable results. Pointing to an unwanted result is but part of the argument. There must be another part of the equation articulating the threshold at which production of

unsatisfactory results requires legal reform. Otherwise, the progressive feminist position on provocation is indistinguishable from the tough-on-crime, conservative tactic of exposing individual cases of leniency toward "monstrous" offenders as a ground to dismantle the entire system of criminal defense protections.[46]

8. Gay and Trans Panic. Manslaughter doctrine's intersection with embedded masculinity norms surfaces in another set of cases, in which defendants raise arguments colloquially known as the "gay panic" or "trans panic" defense. Here, men accused of killing gay or transgender people argue that their homicidal actions should be mitigated to manslaughter because, they say, a sexual or romantic interaction with a gay or transgender person can be severely emotionally disturbing. The argument has roots in a psychological diagnosis coined by Edward Kempf in the 1920s that identified intense feelings of anxiety in closeted gay men when their attraction to other men came into open conflict with prevailing anti-gay or anti-trans societal norms. Building on this idea, gay and trans panic defenses are sometimes invoked by closeted gay or trans people themselves who are accused of killing LGBTQ victims in circumstances that "outed" or appeared to out the killer. The defense is also invoked by men who identify as straight and cisgender and who contend they were provoked by unwanted sexual advances from gay or trans people. In either instance, Professor Cynthia Lee observes, the argument rests on "dominant norms of masculinity," which hold that men "are supposed to be interested in women, not men," and "are supposed to be the sexual aggressors, not the ones aggressed upon." In her article, Lee describes the killing of a trans woman named Islan Nettles as emblematic of scenarios in which these arguments are invoked:

> On August 17, 2013, James Dixon was walking on Frederick Douglass Boulevard in Harlem with some friends when he spotted Islan Nettles, an attractive transgender woman. Dixon crossed the street and began chatting with Nettles, asking her for her name and where she was from. Soon he heard his friends mocking him for flirting with Nettles, saying, "that's a guy." Dixon's demeanor suddenly changed. Angrily, Dixon demanded to know if Nettles "was a man" before punching and knocking her to the ground. Dixon's attack "left the 21-year-old African American comatose, her face battered beyond recognition." Nettles died five days later from head injuries she suffered after hitting the concrete . . . . In explaining why he punched Nettles, Dixon told police, "I just didn't want to be fooled" . . . . His explanation echoes a familiar theme of trans panic that suggests that by holding herself out as female, the transgender woman culpably tries to trick straight men into having sex with her. It reinforces the trope of the transgender female as a deceitful interloper, trying to pass as female in order to capture unwitting

heterosexual men. Dixon's comments also suggested Nettles was at fault for her own death, even though Dixon was the one who initiated the conversation, and it appears that she did nothing to provoke the attack except for being a transgender woman. . . . The underlying impetus for Dixon's loss of self-control seems to have been Dixon's fear of being seen as gay. . . . Dixon may have felt it especially important to prove that he was not attracted to Nettles because just a few days earlier, he had hit on two other transgender women, and his friends had mocked him for doing so.[47]

While there are no comprehensive statistics on violent victimization of gay and trans people, available data indicate that they experience disproportionately high rates of violence in the United States. Against this backdrop, calls to eliminate the gay and trans panic defenses through targeted legislation have gained traction in recent years, with over ten states passing such legislative bans since 2014. Under these laws, reasonableness is expressly defined to exclude the so-called gay or trans panic response. Prior to such statutory interventions, a handful of courts had issued opinions similarly barring gay panic arguments.[48]

9. Mere Words and Racial Slurs. Just as the reasonable-person test imports social norms concerning gender and sexuality, it can, and frequently does, import similar norms regarding race. We will delve deeply into the ways in which violence and reasonableness are racially perceived and constructed later in this chapter when studying self-defense, a doctrine that bears many conceptual parallels to the law of provocation. For present purposes, we can observe one specific way in which race and reasonableness are intertwined by revisiting this holding from the *Girouard* opinion that opened this section: "words alone are not adequate provocation." Commonly referred to as the "mere words" rule, this once-absolute doctrine has softened over time to permit a manslaughter conviction when words convey information about underlying events (such as an affair or assault on a loved one) that would themselves constitute adequate provocation under the law if observed directly. But it generally holds firm when the words at issue don't convey information but instead are purely "insulting or abusive."[49]

Should this categorical limitation apply, as the *Girouard* court held, to "the flinging of racial slurs"? It is difficult, if not impossible, to answer that question by asking how a reasonable person would or should respond to such words without first envisioning that reasonable person's race. Nowhere is this more apparent than when it comes to "the nuclear bomb of racial epithets" in the United States: the n-word. As journalist J Wortham notes in the podcast *Still Processing*, that most infamous of slurs draws its power in part from the way it "has been wielded throughout time" as a tool to "limit and reduce and diminish and humiliate and really render a person into nothingness." As Wortham goes on to emphasize, the word's power is closely tied to its historical association with violence:

> It comes from a place of having to fight for your worthiness, and it also comes from a direct historical experience of people who were called that word and their life hung in the balance. . . . Like, someone is saying that word to you, you know that they're also willing to probably kill you, right?[50]

Understanding the word this way, it is harder to separate it from a physical assault or a threat of physical violence, both of which have long been deemed sufficient to mitigate a fatal response from murder to manslaughter. Indeed, Professor Richard Delgado argues, the impact of a racial epithet can itself be physiological. "Immediate mental or emotional distress is the most obvious direct harm caused by a racial insult," Delgado writes, which "can cause mental, emotional, or even physical harm to [its] target, especially if delivered in front of others."[51]

Taking these considerations together, Professor Randall Kennedy argues that the mere-words rule should be discarded, along with other categorical restrictions on provocation doctrine. "It should be up to a jury," he says, "to determine whether, in fact, a defendant lost control of himself or herself" when confronted with a racial slur. Professor Cynthia Lee takes the opposite position, arguing that "[t]he law should discourage violence in response to verbal provocations," no matter how offensive the provocation may be. As Lee notes, her position is the dominant one in American courts today, which tend to withhold manslaughter instructions in racial epithet cases, although with some exceptions.[52]

But as Lee also notes, the law was not always so opposed to treating verbal insults as a source of mitigation. In the mid-nineteenth century, courts declined to apply the mere-words rule when an enslaved Black person insulted a white man. A case captioned *The State v. Jarrott, a slave*, 23 N.C. 76 (1840), expressly grounds this asymmetrical approach in white supremacy:

> [I]t cannot be conceded that the same matters which would be deemed in law a sufficient provocation to free a white man, who had committed a homicide, in a moment of passion, from the guilt of murder, will have the same effect, when the party slain is a white man, and the offender a slave. . . . Among equals, the general rule is, that words are not, but blows are, a sufficient provocation. [But] there might be words of reproach, so aggravating when uttered by a slave, as to excite the temporary fury which negatives the charge of malice. This difference in the application of the same principle, arises from the vast difference which exists, under our institutions, between the social condition of the white man and of the slave; in consequence of which difference, what might be felt by one as the grossest degradation, is considered by the other as but a slight injury. And from the same cause, it must necessarily follow, that some acts, which

> between white persons are grievous provocations, when proceeding from a white person to a slave—whose passions are, or ought to be tamed down to his lowly condition—will not, and cannot be so regarded. The degrees of homicide are indeed to be ascertained by common law principles; but the principles themselves are necessarily, in their application, accommodated to the actual conditions of human beings in our society.

Id. at 82.

Sitting with the language above, one may be struck by two somewhat competing reactions. First, of course, is a sense of justified revulsion at a legal opinion so nakedly asserting the racial superiority of white people over Black people. Second, and perhaps uncomfortably, one can recognize in *State v. Jarrott* a mode of argument about reasonableness and the criminal law that many today (including in the notes above) invoke in support of greater equity. Indeed, the argument advanced by Kennedy and others that racial slurs should be permitted to mitigate a homicide when leveled against racial minorities echoes in form the assertion in *Jarrott* that the criminal law's application should be "accommodated to the actual conditions of human beings in our society." More specifically, the argument that racial slurs are uniquely harmful when leveled against racial minorities might be thought to rest on the "vast difference which exists, under our institutions, between the social condition" of white people and Black people today, "in consequence of which difference, what might be felt by one as the grossest degradation, is considered by the other as but a slight injury." Put more simply, the n-word means something very different when used by a white person against a Black person, precisely because of their racial positions.

To note as much is not to excuse the *Jarrott* court or validate its logic. Far from it. Rather, the idea is to try to pinpoint where exactly the injustice of the opinion's reasoning lies. The real issue may be not *whether* the law should acknowledge and account for hierarchies of oppression in society but rather *how* it should do so—by aggravating and validating them or by attempting to mitigate and undermine them.

B. Unintentional Homicide

Not all homicides are intentional. Some are not even criminal. Imagine a fatal car accident in which a person darts into the road, leaving the driver little time to swerve. This death is a homicide: one person (the driver) killed another. But it is not a *criminal* homicide. Rather, it's a tragic accident in the truest sense of the word. And as Professor Francis Shen observes, "it seems to be a human universal that we generally do not punish truly accidental acts, but only culpable ones."[53]

But to say that this incident was *truly* an accident is to acknowledge that not all accidents are created equal. In fact, some are hard to describe as "accidents" at all, even if we acknowledge they were unintentional.

Our intuitions about the fatal car crash, for example, would almost surely change if we learned that the driver sped through a red light. And they would change all the more if we learned that he was racing down city streets with another car, or that he was drunk. In these latter examples, the driver could and likely would be prosecuted for the resulting homicide even if he did not mean for anyone to die. Indeed, he potentially could be convicted of multiple different criminal homicides, ranging from negligent homicide, to involuntary manslaughter, to murder.

The imposition and grading of criminal liability in the context of these unintended deaths turns on the idea of *culpable risk*. Engaging in conduct that generates harmful risk in the world, including a risk of death, can be a crime, with the severity of that crime turning on the *amount* of risk, the *context* surrounding the risk, the *materialization* of the risk, and potentially on a person's *awareness* of the risk when she acts. Unfortunately, judicial opinions and statutes are not always precise in their treatment of these issues. Many jurisdictions continue to employ fuzzy concepts and language dating back to the early common law, when ideas like criminal "recklessness" that form key parts of contemporary criminal law were not yet fully developed. As the Supreme Court explained in *Voisine v. United States*, 579 U.S. 686 (2016),

> Recklessness was not a word in the common law's standard lexicon, nor an idea in its conceptual framework . . . . The common law traditionally used a variety of overlapping and, frankly, confusing phrases to describe culpable mental states—among them, specific intent, general intent, presumed intent, willfulness, and malice. Whether and where conduct that we would today describe as reckless fits into that obscure scheme is anyone's guess . . . .

Id. at 697-698.

One of the most significant innovations of the Model Penal Code was its clarification of the law of *mens rea* in this respect. The statutory framework that it sets out to define culpable mental states can be intimidating on first encounter. But it provides the clearest conceptual roadmap to modern criminal law's approach to these issues and is particularly helpful in understanding how the law deals with unintentional crimes. We thus begin this section with the relevant MPC provisions, followed by a case applying them in the context of an unintentional killing.

Model Penal Code Excerpts

Section 210.1 – Criminal Homicide.

(1) A person is guilty of criminal homicide if he purposely, knowingly, recklessly or negligently causes the death of another human being.

(2) Criminal homicide is murder, manslaughter or negligent homicide.

Section 210.2 – Murder.

(1) Except as provided in Section 210.3(1)(b), criminal homicide constitutes murder when:

(a) it is committed purposely or knowingly; or

(b) it is committed recklessly under circumstances manifesting extreme indifference to the value of human life. Such recklessness and indifference are presumed if the actor is engaged or is an accomplice in the commission of, or an attempt to commit, or flight after committing or attempting to commit robbery, rape or deviate sexual intercourse by force or threat of force, arson, burglary, kidnapping or felonious escape.

(2) Murder is a felony of the first degree. . . .

Section 210.3 – Manslaughter.

(1) Criminal homicide constitutes manslaughter when:

(a) it is committed recklessly; or

(b) a homicide which would otherwise be murder is committed under the influence of extreme mental or emotional disturbance for which there is reasonable explanation or excuse. The reasonableness of such explanation or excuse shall be determined from the viewpoint of a person in the actor's situation under the circumstances as he believes them to be.

(2) Manslaughter is a felony of the second degree.

Section 210.4 – Negligent Homicide.

(1) Criminal homicide constitutes negligent homicide when it is committed negligently.

(2) Negligent homicide is a felony in the third degree.

Section 2.02 – General Requirements of Culpability.

(1) **Minimum Requirements of Culpability.** Except as provided in Section 2.05,* a person is not guilty of an offense unless he acted purposely, knowingly, recklessly or negligently, as the law may require, with respect to each material element of the offense.

(2) **Kinds of Culpability Defined.**

(a) **Purposely.** A person acts purposely with respect to a material element of an offense when:

(i) if the element involves the nature of his conduct or a result thereof, it is his conscious object to engage in conduct of that nature or to cause such a result; and

(ii) if the element involves the attendant circumstances, he is aware of the existence of such circumstances or he believes or hopes that they exist.

(b) **Knowingly.** A person acts knowingly with respect to a material element of an offense when:

---

* Editor's Note: Section 2.05 concerns strict liability offenses and is discussed *infra* p. 508.

(i) if the element involves the nature of his conduct or the attendant circumstances, he is aware that his conduct is of that nature or that such circumstances exist; and

(ii) if the element involves a result of his conduct, he is aware that it is practically certain that his conduct will cause such a result.

(c) **Recklessly.** A person acts recklessly with respect to a material element of an offense when he consciously disregards a substantial and unjustifiable risk that the material element exists or will result from his conduct. The risk must be of such a nature and degree that, considering the nature and purpose of the actor's conduct and the circumstances known to him, its disregard involves a gross deviation from the standard of conduct that a law-abiding person would observe in the actor's situation.

(d) **Negligently.** A person acts negligently with respect to a material element of an offense when he should be aware of a substantial and unjustifiable risk that the material element exists or will result from his conduct. The risk must be of such a nature and degree that the actor's failure to perceive it, considering the nature and purpose of his conduct and the circumstances known to him, involves a gross deviation from the standard of care that a reasonable person would observe in the actor's situation.

(3) **Culpability Required Unless Otherwise Provided.** When the culpability sufficient to establish a material element of an offense is not prescribed by law, such element is established if a person acts purposely, knowingly or recklessly with respect thereto.

(4) **Prescribed Culpability Requirement Applies to All Material Elements.** When the law defining an offense prescribes the kind of culpability that is sufficient for the commission of an offense, without distinguishing among the material elements thereof, such provision shall apply to all the material elements of the offense, unless a contrary purpose plainly appears.

(5) **Substitutes for Negligence, Recklessness and Knowledge.** When the law provides that negligence suffices to establish an element of an offense, such element also is established if a person acts purposely, knowingly or recklessly. When recklessness suffices to establish an element, such element also is established if a person acts purposely or knowingly. When acting knowingly suffices to establish an element, such element also is established if a person acts purposely.

(6) **Requirement of Purpose Satisfied if Purpose Is Conditional.** When a particular purpose is an element of an offense, the element is established although such purpose is conditional, unless the condition negatives the harm or evil sought to be prevented by the law defining the offense.

(7) **Requirement of Knowledge Satisfied by Knowledge of High Probability.** When knowledge of the existence of a particular fact is an element of an offense, such knowledge is established if a person is aware of a high probability of its existence, unless he actually believes that it does not exist.

(8) **Requirement of Wilfulness Satisfied by Acting Knowingly.** A requirement that an offense be committed wilfully is satisfied if a person acts

knowingly with respect to the material elements of the offense, unless a purpose to impose further requirements appears.

(9) **Culpability as to Illegality of Conduct.** Neither knowledge nor recklessness or negligence as to whether conduct constitutes an offense or as to the existence, meaning or application of the law determining the elements of an offense is an element of such offense, unless the definition of the offense or the Code so provides.

(10) **Culpability as Determinant of Grade of Offense.** When the grade or degree of an offense depends on whether the offense is committed purposely, knowingly, recklessly or negligently, its grade or degree shall be the lowest for which the determinative kind of culpability is established with respect to any material element of the offense.

Section 1.13 – General Definitions.

. . .

(9) **"element of an offense"** means (i) such conduct or (ii) such attendant circumstances or (iii) such a result of conduct as (a) is included in the description of the forbidden conduct in the definition of the offense; or (b) establishes the required kind of culpability; or (c) negatives an excuse or justification for such conduct; or (d) negatives a defense under the statute of limitations; or (e) establishes jurisdiction or venue.

(10) **"material element of an offense"** means an element that does not relate exclusively to the statute of limitations, jurisdiction, venue, or to any other matter similarly unconnected with (i) the harm or evil, incident to conduct, sought to be prevented by the law defining the offense, or (ii) the existence of a justification or excuse for such conduct.

People v. Hall
_____

999 P.2d 207 (Colo. 2000)

BENDER, J. . . . While skiing on Vail mountain, Nathan Hall flew off of a knoll and collided with Allen Cobb, who was traversing the slope below Hall. Cobb sustained traumatic brain injuries and died as a result of the collision. The People charged Hall with felony reckless manslaughter.

. . . The court [below] held that Hall's conduct did not involve a substantial risk of death because any risk created by Hall had a less than fifty percent chance of causing another's death. . . . The court ruled that when viewed in the light most favorable to the People, the facts showed that Hall was "skiing too fast for the snow conditions" . . . [and] that while such conduct may involve a substantial risk of injury, a person of ordinary prudence and caution would not infer that skiing too fast for the conditions creates at least a fifty percent chance of death. Thus, the court held that the prosecution failed to meet its burden [and affirmed the trial court's dismissal of the charges for lack of probable cause]. . . .

DISCUSSION

. . . With the exception of strict liability crimes, a person is not subject to criminal sanctions unless the prosecution establishes that, in addition to committing a proscribed act, the person acted with the culpable mental state required for the particular crime. . . . In the past, courts and legislatures developed a variety of definitions for different mental states, creating confusion about what the prosecution had to prove in a criminal case. . . . In order to eliminate the confusion created by this variety of ill-defined mental states, the Model Penal Code suggested that criminal codes articulate and define the specific culpable mental states that will suffice for criminal liability. As part of a complete revision of Colorado's criminal code in 1971, the General Assembly followed the Model Penal Code's suggestion and adopted a provision specifically defining four culpable mental states: "intentionally," "knowingly," "recklessly," and "criminal negligence." . . . To be convicted of any crime other than a strict liability crime, a defendant must act with one of these four culpable mental states, depending on the statutory definition of each particular crime. . . .

To demonstrate that Hall committed the crime of manslaughter, the prosecution must provide sufficient evidence to show that the defendant's conduct was reckless. . . . As Colorado's criminal code defines recklessness, "A person acts recklessly when he consciously disregards a substantial and unjustifiable risk that a result will occur or that a circumstance exists." Thus, in the case of manslaughter, the prosecution must show that the defendant's conduct caused the death of another and that the defendant: (1) *consciously disregarded* (2) a *substantial* and (3) *unjustifiable risk* that he would (4) *cause the death of another.* We examine these elements in detail.

SUBSTANTIAL AND UNJUSTIFIABLE RISK

To show that a person acted recklessly, the prosecution must establish that the person's conduct created a "substantial and unjustifiable" risk. The district court . . . relied on an erroneous definition of a "substantial and unjustifiable" risk. Whether a risk is substantial must be determined by assessing both the likelihood that harm will occur and the magnitude of the harm should it occur. . . . [W]hether a risk is unjustifiable must be determined by assessing the nature and purpose of the actor's conduct relative to how substantial the risk is. . . . [T]he risk must be of such a nature that its disregard constitutes a gross deviation from the standard of care that a reasonable person would exercise.

A risk does not have to be "more likely than not to occur" or "probable" in order to be substantial. A risk may be substantial even if the chance that the harm will occur is well below fifty percent. Some risks may be substantial even if they carry a low degree of probability because the magnitude of the harm is potentially great. For example, if a person holds a revolver with a single bullet in one of the chambers, points the gun at another's head and pulls the trigger, then the risk of death is substantial even though the odds that death will result are no better than one in six. As one court remarked, "If the potential of a risk is death, that risk is always serious. Therefore, only *some likelihood* that death will occur *might create* for most people a 'substantial and unjustifiable' risk." State v. Standiford, 769 P.2d 254, 263 n.9 (Utah 1988) (emphasis added). Conversely, a relatively high probability that a very minor harm will occur probably does not involve a "substantial" risk. . . .

Whether a risk is substantial is a matter of fact that will depend on the specific circumstances of each case. Some conduct almost always carries a substantial risk of death, such as engaging another person in a fight with a deadly weapon or firing a gun at another. In such instances, the substantiality of the risk may be evident from the nature of the defendant's conduct . . . .

Other conduct requires a greater inquiry into the facts of the case to determine whether it creates a substantial risk of death. . . . A court cannot generically characterize the actor's conduct (e.g., "driving a truck") in a manner that ignores the specific elements of the conduct that create a risk (e.g., driving a truck with failing brakes on a highway). For example, "installing a heater" carries little risk under normal circumstances. However, the Connecticut Supreme Court held that improperly wiring a 120-volt heater to a 240-volt circuit, failing to use a lock nut to connect the heater to the circuit breaker, and using other faulty installation techniques creates a substantial risk of "catastrophic fire" and death. *See* State v. Salz, 627 A.2d 862, 865, 869-871 (Conn. 1993). . . .

As well as being substantial, a risk must be unjustifiable in order for a person's conduct to be reckless. Whether a risk is justifiable is determined by weighing the nature and purpose of the actor's conduct against the risk created by that conduct. If a person consciously disregards a substantial risk of death but does so in order to advance an interest that justifies such a risk, the conduct is not reckless. For example, if a surgeon performs an operation on a patient that has a seventy-five percent chance of killing the patient, but the patient will certainly die without the operation, then the conduct is justified and thus not reckless even though the risk is substantial.

In addition to the separate analyses that are applied to determine whether a risk is both "substantial" and "unjustified," the concept of a "substantial and unjustifiable risk" implies a risk that constitutes a gross deviation from the standard of care that a reasonable law-abiding person would exercise under the circumstances. . . . A substantial and unjustifiable risk must constitute a "gross deviation" from the reasonable standard of care in order to justify the criminal sanctions imposed for criminal negligence or reckless conduct, as opposed to the kind of deviation from the reasonable standard of care that results in civil liability for ordinary negligence.[12]

Whether a risk is substantial and unjustified is a question of fact. Hence, at trial, the trier of fact must determine whether the facts presented prove beyond a reasonable doubt that the risk was substantial and unjustified. . . .

CONSCIOUS DISREGARD

In addition to showing that a person created a substantial and unjustifiable risk, the prosecution must demonstrate that the actor "consciously disregarded" the risk in order to prove that she acted recklessly. A person acts with a conscious disregard of the risk created by her conduct when she is aware of the risk and chooses to act despite that risk. In contrast to acting "intentionally" or "knowingly," the actor does not have to intend the result or be "practically certain" that the result will occur, he only needs to be "aware" that the risk exists. . . .

Although recklessness is a less culpable mental state than intentionally or knowingly, it involves a higher level of culpability than criminal negligence. Criminal negligence requires that, "through a gross deviation from the standard of care that a reasonable person would exercise," the actor fails to perceive a substantial and unjustifiable risk that a result will occur or a circumstance exists. An actor is criminally negligent when he should have been aware of the risk but was not, while recklessness requires that the defendant actually be aware of the risk but disregard it. Thus, even if she should be, a person who is not actually aware that her conduct creates a substantial and unjustifiable risk is not acting recklessly.

A court or trier of fact may infer a person's subjective awareness of a risk from the particular facts of a case, including the person's particular knowledge or expertise. For example, a court may infer a person's subjective awareness of the risks created by firing a gun from the facts that the person served an extended tour of duty in the military as a rifleman and machine gunner and was instructed by both the army and his father not to point a gun at another person. A court may infer from a person's extensive training and safety instruction that the person understood the risks of fire and other "catastrophic dangers" created by the "slipshod" installation of a baseboard heater. *See Salz*, 627 A.2d at 869-870.

---

12. We note that both criminal negligence and recklessness require that the actor's conduct involve a "gross deviation" from the standard of care that a reasonable person would exercise under the circumstances in each case. Thus, the same risk will suffice for either criminally negligent or reckless conduct. However, the standards are sufficiently distinct to justify unequal penalties because in the case of reckless conduct *the actor must be aware of the risk* he creates, while criminally negligent conduct requires only that he failed to perceive the risk.

In addition to the actor's knowledge and experience, a court may infer the actor's subjective awareness of a risk from what a reasonable person would have understood under the circumstances. . . . [T]he court may consider the perspective of a reasonable person in the situation and with the knowledge and training of the actor. Although a court can infer what the defendant actually knew based on what a reasonable person would have known in the circumstances, a court must not confuse what a reasonable person would have known in the circumstances with what the defendant actually knew. Thus, if a defendant engaged in conduct that a reasonable person would have understood as creating a substantial and unjustifiable risk of death, the court may infer that the defendant was subjectively aware of that risk, but the court cannot hold the defendant responsible if she were actually unaware of a risk that a reasonable person would have perceived. . . .

APPLICATION

. . . Like other activities that generally do not involve a substantial risk of death, such as driving a car or installing a heater, "skiing too fast for the conditions" is not widely considered behavior that constitutes a high degree of risk. However, we hold that the specific facts in this case support a reasonable inference that Hall created a substantial and unjustifiable risk that he would cause another's death.

Several witnesses stated that Hall was . . . travelling too fast for the conditions, at an excessive rate of speed, and that he was out of control. [One witness, Buck Allen, who was himself a judge,] said that Hall passed him on the slope travelling three times faster than Allen, himself an expert skier. [Another witness] presented testimony that Hall was a ski racer, indicating that Hall was trained to attain and ski at much faster speeds than even skilled and experienced recreational skiers. The witnesses said that Hall was travelling straight down the slope at such high speeds that, because of his lack of control, he would not have been able to stop or avoid another person. . . . [T]he nature of Cobb's injuries and other facts of the collision support the inference that Hall was skiing at an inordinately high speed when he struck Cobb. . . .

In addition to Hall's excessive speed, Hall was out of control and unable to avoid a collision with another person. All the witnesses said Hall was not traversing the slope and that he was skiing straight down the fall line. Hall was back on his skis, with his ski tips in the air and his arms out to his sides to maintain balance. Allen said that Hall was bounced around by the moguls on the slope rather than skiing in control and managing the bumps. Hall admitted . . . that he first saw Cobb when he was airborne and that he was unable to stop when he saw people below him just before the collision. . . . [A] reasonably prudent person could have concluded that

Hall was unable to anticipate or avoid a potential collision with a skier on the trail below him.

While skiing ordinarily carries a very low risk of death to other skiers, a reasonable person could have concluded that Hall's excessive speed, lack of control, and improper technique for skiing bumps significantly increased both the likelihood that a collision would occur and the extent of the injuries that might result from such a collision, including the possibility of death . . . .

We next ask whether a reasonable person could have concluded that Hall's creation of a substantial risk of death was unjustified. To the extent that Hall's extremely fast and unsafe skiing created a risk of death, Hall was serving no direct interest other than his own enjoyment. Although the sport often involves high speeds and even moments where a skier is temporarily out of control, a reasonable person could determine that the enjoyment of skiing does not justify skiing at the speeds and with the lack of control Hall exhibited. Thus, a reasonable person could have found that Hall's creation of a substantial risk was unjustifiable.

In addition to our conclusion that a reasonable person could have entertained the belief that Hall's conduct created a substantial and unjustifiable risk, we must ask whether Hall's conduct constituted a "gross deviation" from the standard of care that a reasonable law-abiding person (in this case, a reasonable, law-abiding, trained ski racer and resort employee) would have observed in the circumstances.

As we noted, the nature of the sport involves moments of high speeds and temporary losses of control. However, the General Assembly imposed upon a skier the duty to avoid collisions with any person or object below him.[14] Although this statute may not form the basis of criminal liability, it establishes the minimum standard of care for uphill skiers and, for the purposes of civil negligence suits, creates a rebuttable presumption that the skier is at fault whenever he collides with skiers on the slope below him. A violation of a skier's duty in an extreme fashion, such as here, may be evidence of conduct that constitutes a "gross deviation" from the standard of care imposed by statute for civil negligence. . . .

[W]e next ask whether a reasonably prudent person could have entertained the belief that Hall consciously disregarded th[e] risk. Hall is a trained ski racer who had been coached about skiing in control and skiing safely. Further, he was an employee of a ski area and had a great deal of skiing experience. Hall's knowledge and training could give rise to the

---

14. Colo. Rev. Stat. §33-44-109(2) states:

Each skier has the duty to maintain control of his speed and course at all times when skiing and to maintain a proper lookout so as to be able to avoid other skiers and objects. However, the primary duty shall be on the person skiing downhill to avoid collision with any person or objects below him.

reasonable inference that he was aware of the possibility that by skiing so fast and out of control he might collide with and kill another skier unless he regained control and slowed down.

In addition to inferring Hall's awareness of the risk from Hall's training and experience, a reasonable person with expert training and knowledge of skiing may have realized that skiing at very high speeds without enough control to stop or avoid a collision could seriously injure or kill another skier. A reasonable expert and experienced skier also might understand that in view of his duties under section 33-44-109, he must maintain enough control to avoid collisions with skiers below him on the slope. Thus, both Hall's subjective knowledge and the awareness that a reasonable person with Hall's background would have had support the inference that Hall consciously disregarded the risk he created by acting despite his awareness of the risk.

Although the risk that he would cause the death of another was probably slight, Hall's conduct created a risk of death. Hall's collision with Cobb involved enough force to kill Cobb and to simulate the type of head injury associated with victims in car accidents. Even though it is a rare occurrence, the court heard testimony that two skiers in the past eleven years died on Vail mountain alone from skier-to-skier collisions. . . .

Thus, interpreting the facts presented in the light most favorable to the prosecution, we hold that a reasonably prudent and cautious person could have entertained the belief that Hall consciously disregarded a substantial and unjustifiable risk that by skiing exceptionally fast and out of control he might collide with and kill another person on the slope. . . . Thus, we remand this case to the district court for trial.

People v. Hall methodically applies the MPC framework to an unintentional homicide. In so doing, it both clarifies that framework and foregrounds questions the framework raises. The following notes address some of those questions. We begin with questions that probe conceptual ambiguities in the law of unintentional crimes and progress to those that raise deeper normative issues about how we understand and punish risky behavior in a society that exposes people to harmful risks in different, and often unequal, ways.

NOTES AND QUESTIONS

1. Distinguishing Negligence from Recklessness. Most unintentional crimes involve one of two mental states under the MPC: recklessness or negligence. In this respect, the MPC offers a more precise framework than the common law approach, which many jurisdictions continue to follow. Consider this illustrative excerpt from *State v. Torres*, 495 N.W.2d 678 (Iowa 1993):

> This court has described what recklessness is in the context of involuntary manslaughter cases: . . . "Culpable conduct should require proof of recklessness, that is, conduct evidencing either a willful or wanton disregard for the safety of others. Ordinarily, such conduct should be conscious and intentional, creating an unreasonable risk of harm to others, where such risk is or should be known to defendants." State v. Kernes, 262 N.W.2d 602, 605 (Iowa 1978).

Id. at 681. The *Torres* opinion goes on to quote Professor William Prosser's *Handbook of the Law of Torts* to elaborate on the meaning of recklessness: "The usual meaning assigned to 'wilful,' 'wanton' or 'reckless,' according to taste as to the word used, is that the actor has intentionally done an act of an unreasonable character in disregard of a risk known to him or so obvious that he must be taken to have been aware of it, and so great as to make it highly probable that harm would follow."[54]

Question: How does this definition of recklessness differ from the MPC's definition?

2. Distinguishing Degrees of Risk. The *Hall* court observes that, under the MPC's framework, "the same risk will suffice for either criminally negligent or reckless conduct." More specifically, the MPC defines both recklessness and negligence as entailing a "substantial" degree of risk, the assumption of which constitutes a "gross deviation" from the standard of care that a reasonable, law-abiding person would observe under the circumstances.* This formulation is meant to capture conduct that is more extreme and thus more culpable than the *ordinary negligence* standard employed in the law of torts. That lesser standard imposes civil liability when a person engages in conduct that entails merely an "unreasonable risk of harm." Most states embrace this distinction between civil and criminal negligence, though many permit criminal liability to attach at the lower civil standard for at least some offenses.[55]

The MPC and most states also recognize a degree of risk *higher* than recklessness. This zone of *recklessness-plus* separates out a distinctly serious class of unintentional homicides and classifies them as murder. In jurisdictions that use the traditional common law vocabulary, this higher degree of recklessness is often called "depraved heart murder," a nod to Blackstone's

---

    * Technically, the MPC's negligence provision defines the point of reference as a "reasonable" person, while its recklessness provision points to a "law-abiding" person. The Code's official commentaries do not suggest that any meaningful distinction is meant by this difference, and courts often treat the terms interchangeably, asking, as in *Hall*, whether a person's "conduct constituted a 'gross deviation' from the standard of care that a reasonable law-abiding person . . . would have observed."

statement that malice aforethought, whether express or implied, is the "dictate of a wicked, depraved, and malignant heart." Contemporary courts often state the common law test as follows:

> Implied malice may include killings where there is no intent to kill, such as a killing . . . evidencing a depraved heart. [T]he elements of implied malice that will support a charge of murder under a depraved heart theory are met when: (1) The killing resulted from an intentional act, (2) [t]he natural consequences of the act are dangerous to human life, and (3) [t]he act was deliberately performed with knowledge of the danger to, and with conscious disregard for, human life.

State v. Herrera, 364 P.3d 1180, 1183 (Idaho 2015). The MPC captures a similarly aggravated form of recklessness when it defines a criminal homicide as murder if "it is committed recklessly under circumstances manifesting extreme indifference to the value of human life." Model Penal Code §210.2(1)(b).[56]

   3. Distinguishing Quantitative vs. Qualitative Conceptions of Risk. Note that, with respect to each of the tiers of risk just described, courts are typically reluctant to define the relevant threshold in quantitative, probabilistic terms. This reluctance is not universal, though. Consider again *State v. Torres,* 495 N.W.2d 678 (Iowa 1993), where the state supreme court reversed an involuntary manslaughter conviction of a man who, during an episode of domestic violence, swept a lamp to the floor and caused it to shatter. His wife soon slipped and fell onto a shard of the broken lamp in a manner that fatally severed her femoral artery. Describing the fall as "a tragic, freak accident," the court went on to hold that in order for a person's conduct to be reckless or negligent, "the danger must be so obvious from the facts that the actor knows or should reasonably foresee that harm will probably— *that is, more likely than not*—flow from the act." *Id.* at 681-682 (emphasis added). Concluding that the prosecution had failed to show that the woman's death "would probably—not possibly—have happened" as a result of the husband's breaking of the lamp, the court deemed the evidence insufficient to support a conviction. *Id.* at 682.

   More commonly, courts take the impressionistic approach laid out in *Hall,* which leaves largely undefined the risk threshold for each tier of unintentional crime. In these states, to quote the *Hall* opinion, a "risk may be substantial even if the chance that the harm will occur is well below fifty percent," though sometimes "a relatively high probability that a very minor harm will occur" will not amount to a substantial risk. As the MPC drafters forthrightly acknowledged in embracing this impressionistic method, it is transparently indeterminate.

> Some standard is needed for determining how substantial and how unjustifiable the risk must be in order to warrant a finding of culpability. There

is no way to state this value judgment that does not beg the question in the last analysis; the point is that the jury must evaluate the actor's conduct and determine whether it should be condemned.

Model Penal Code and Commentaries §2.02 cmt. 3 at 237.

Question: How does the decision to leave the governing risk thresholds unspecified impact the institutional power of the various actors in the adjudicatory process, including prosecutors, juries, and judges?

4. Distinguishing Knowledge from Recklessness: Results. As the preceding notes explain, recklessness and negligence each comes into play when a person engages in conduct that entails a *risk* of harm. Whether that harm will materialize is genuinely uncertain at the time the person acts—but if it does, he is liable, because creating the risk was culpable.

Knowledge is different. As the MPC defines it, a person acts with knowledge that his actions will cause harm if he is "aware that it is *practically certain*" harm will result. Model Penal Code §2.02(2)(b)(ii) (emphasis added). In the words of the U.S. Supreme Court, "A person who injures another knowingly, even though not affirmatively wanting the result, still makes a deliberate choice with full awareness of consequent harm." Borden v. United States, 593 U.S. 420, 426 (2021). Of course, the practical certainty the MPC describes is not the same as an absolute certainty. One might argue it is impossible to know with true certainty that an action will cause a specific result, such as death. Some people survive a gunshot wound to the head, for example. And yet, shooting someone in the head seems different in kind from merely engaging in conduct that entails a substantial and unjustifiable *risk* of harm. One could reasonably regard death as a "practically certain" outcome of such a shooting.*

And in fact, at common law, a person was generally presumed to *intend* the natural consequences of his actions. Following that presumption, "[c]ommon-law authorities included in the notion of intent to kill [those cases that involved a mere] awareness that the death of another would result from one's actions, even if the actor had no particular desire to achieve such a consequence." Model Penal Code and Commentaries §210.2 cmt. 1 at 14. Knowledge and intent, in other words, were assimilated into one another. The MPC, in contrast, recognizes intent (or purpose) only where the actor actually has the "conscious object" to cause the prohibited result. Model Penal Code §2.02(2)(a)(i). Importantly, though,

---

* Note, however, that according to some studies, between five and ten percent of people who are shot in the head survive. *See, e.g.,* Silky Chotai & Khoi D. Than, *Gunshot Wound Head Trauma,* Am. Ass'n Neurological Surgeons, https://www.aans.org/Patients/Neurosurgical-Conditions-and-Treatments/Gunshot-Wound-Head-Trauma (reporting that "[g]unshot wounds to the head are fatal about 90 percent of the time, with many victims dying before arriving to the hospital").

it deems both purpose and knowledge sufficiently culpable for murder liability. *See id.* §210.2(1)(a).[*]

As to the threshold between a risk that will be deemed reckless and the practical certainty required for knowledge, this is not always an easy line to draw. Consider, for example, the case of *State v. Jenkins*, 840 A.2d 242 (N.J. 2004). In that case, the defendant, Kendall Jenkins, was sitting on a park bench when he recognized a man walking by, Arthur Thomas, as someone who had testified against him in a prior murder trial (in which Jenkins was acquitted). Jenkins "went after Thomas, picked up a brick, and slammed it into the back of his head. Reeling from the blow, Thomas fell down a flight of stairs and landed headfirst on the concrete below." *Id.* at 246. Thomas died, and Jenkins was convicted of murder. On appeal, Jenkins argued that the trial court had erred in refusing to allow the jury to consider the lesser charge of manslaughter on a recklessness theory. As the New Jersey Supreme Court summarized it:

> The trial court apparently looked at the definition of murder and reasoned that because defendant intentionally struck Thomas in the head with a brick and because Thomas died, defendant purposely or knowingly caused [Thomas'] death. Finding no evidence of anything other than an intentional act that ultimately resulted in death, the court concluded that a jury could not rationally find the existence of mere reckless conduct. In essence, the court determined murder to be the only form of homicide at issue because it concluded that defendant either purposely or knowingly killed the victim.

Id. at 251. But this, the New Jersey Supreme Court held, elided the "pivotal question," namely, "whether the jury could have concluded that defendant hit the victim without conscious knowledge that death was a high probability but, instead, with reckless disregard of the possibility or probability that death would occur." *Id.* at 252. Focusing on that question, the Court held:

> [T]he proper inquiry in distinguishing murder from . . . manslaughter relates to defendant's state of mind as to the risk of death. . . . [Here,] the facts indicate that the jurors . . . could have rationally concluded that defendant struck the victim not knowing that [it] would result in the

---

[*] One might wonder, then, why the MPC differentiates *purpose* from *knowledge* at all. As the Code's commentaries explain, the distinction "is inconsequential for most purposes of liability." Model Penal Code and Commentaries §2.02 cmt. 1 at 234; *see also* Borden v. United States, 593 U.S. 420, 426 (2021) ("We have characterized the distinction between the two as 'limited,' explaining that it 'has not been considered important' for many crimes." (quoting United States v. Bailey, 444 U.S. 394, 404 (1980))). But it matters in some contexts, such as the doctrines of group liability we will discuss in Chapter Seven. These doctrines dictate that "a true purpose to effect [a] criminal result is requisite for liability." Model Penal Code and Commentaries §2.02 cmt. 1 at 234.

victim's death. . . . The expert [autopsy] testimony indicating that it was not defendant's blow but rather the subsequent fall to the pavement that caused Thomas's death provides significant support for [such a view]. That being the case, the trial court was obligated to instruct on manslaughter . . . as well as murder.

Id.

Compare this analysis to *State v. Raines*, 606 A.2d 265 (Md. 1992), in which the defendant, a drunk passenger in a car driving down the highway, fired a gunshot into the driver side window of an adjacent tractor-trailer. Upholding a first-degree murder conviction, the court wrote:

> There is a critical distinction between the facts of this case and [one in which a person] . . . shoots in the general direction of a passing passenger train or vehicle on the highway. [There,] a person may or may not be in the path of the bullet. On the other hand, Raines shot at the driver's window of a tractor-trailer being driven on a highway. He knew someone was behind the window. Raines's actions in directing the gun at the window, and therefore at the driver's head on the other side of the window, permitted an inference that Raines shot the gun with the intent to kill.

Id. at 270.

Notably, even properly instructed jurors sometimes struggle to grasp the difference between knowledge and recklessness. In a study on hundreds of mock jurors, scholars presented a range of factual scenarios that were designed to track the MPC's various culpable mental states. They found that in most instances the jurors "behaved as the MPC assumes they would," with one notable exception: jurors struggled "to differentiate between knowing and reckless conduct, even with the benefit of jury instructions." Professor Sherry Colb argues that the problem here is not with the jurors but rather with a central ambiguity in the law itself.

> For you to know that your behavior is virtually certain to cause death, two things must logically be true: (1) you believe that your behavior under the circumstances will almost certainly cause death, *and* (2) your behavior under the circumstances will in fact almost certainly cause death. . . . To be consciously aware that one's behavior is extremely risky, it must be the case that (1) one believes that one's conduct is extremely risky *and* that (2) one's conduct is in fact extremely risky. . . . In trying to decide whether a defendant has acted with knowledge or recklessness, there are accordingly four possible combinations: (1) certainty in belief and certainty in fact; (2) high risk in belief and high risk in fact; (3) certainty in belief and high risk in fact; and (4) high risk in belief and certainty in fact. If we assume that the jury can somehow figure out on its own that knowledge and recklessness each entail two separate elements, then the jury will see that combination #1 readily qualifies the defendant's conduct as

"knowing," and combination #2 readily qualifies it as "reckless." But what is the jury to make of combinations #3 and #4?[57]

5. Alternative Theories of Liability. One might think the lack of clarity described above would make it hard for prosecutors to pursue cases in which the underlying facts about the defendant's mental state are unclear. But prosecutors generally are not forced to choose which version of a potentially ambiguous set of events to present to the jury. Rather, they can urge the jury to view a single event as having unfolded in different ways—and to convict on any theory.* Consider again *State v. Herrera*, 364 P.3d 1180 (Idaho 2015). In that case, the defendant argued that he accidentally shot his girlfriend in the head during an argument. The evidence showed that the gun used in the homicide was unloaded but that a single round remained in the chamber. According to the defendant, "at the moment he picked the gun up out of the drawer, he did not believe there was a round in the chamber." *Id.* at 1182. And yet, he "gave varying accounts of what exactly caused the gun to discharge." *Id.* At first, he told the police that when he was trying to unload the gun it just "went off and hit her in the head." *Id.* But later at trial he claimed that he "began to lift the gun to point it at himself," at which point his girlfriend "grabbed the barrel of the gun and pulled it and it went off." *Id.* The prosecution also presented forensic evidence showing that the gun was pressed against the girlfriend's forehead when it fired and expert testimony that the gun could not fire without the trigger being pulled.

On these facts, the prosecution charged Mr. Herrera with three offenses: second-degree murder, voluntary manslaughter, and involuntary manslaughter. And with respect to the murder charge, it expressly argued in the alternative that the jury could conclude "that Herrera acted with malice either because he intentionally shot Stephanie or acted with such extreme indifference to her life that he had an abandoned and malignant heart." The jury convicted Herrera of second-degree murder and the state supreme court upheld the verdict on the unintentional homicide theory.[58]

6. Distinguishing Knowledge from Recklessness: Conduct. The notes above explore the sometimes-blurry line between knowledge and recklessness with respect to the likely results of a person's conduct. A separate issue arises when the defendant lacks subjective awareness about his actual conduct itself. Consider *United States v. Jewell*, 532 F.2d 697 (9th Cir. 1976). In this case, Charles Jewell drove into the United States in a truck carrying 110 pounds of marijuana within a hidden compartment. Mr. Jewell testified that he did not know there was marijuana in the truck and the court of

---

* A separate question arises as to whether a defendant can be sentenced to cumulative punishments under such circumstances. We discuss this issue in Chapter Nine (p. 809).

appeals concluded that a jury could have believed him. But the court also concluded that the facts showed Jewell "deliberately avoided positive knowledge of the presence of the contraband to avoid responsibility in the event of discovery." *Id.* at 699. As the MPC's drafters observe, "[w]hether such cases should be viewed as instances of acting recklessly or knowingly presents a subtle but important question." Model Penal Code and Commentaries §2.02 cmt. 9 at 248. Specifically, how should the law treat people whose *lack of knowledge* about a potentially culpable act is itself intentional? Many courts embrace an approach commonly known as the *willful blindness* doctrine, which ascribes a knowing *mens rea* to someone who consciously avoids learning the true nature of his potentially illegal conduct. As the Supreme Court has explained, lower courts "articulate the doctrine of willful blindness in slightly different ways" but generally "appear to agree on two basic requirements: (1) the defendant must subjectively believe that there is a high probability that a fact exists and (2) the defendant must take deliberate actions to avoid learning of that fact." Global-Tech Appliances, Inc. v. SEB S.A., 563 U.S. 754, 768 (2011). We will return to the willful blindness doctrine in Chapter Eight (p. 666)

7. Distinguishing Competing Accounts of the Conduct. Sometimes, the view one takes of the consequences likely to flow from a person's conduct turns on how one characterizes the underlying conduct itself. In *Hall,* the court wrote that it "must inquire beyond the general nature of the defendant's conduct and consider the specific conduct in which the defendant engaged." But this approach is not always easy to apply in practice. Consider once again *State v. Torres,* 495 N.W.2d 678 (Iowa 1993). The majority opinion in that case described the essential facts as follows:

> Brenda slapped Jimmy. He responded in kind. During the altercation he beat her about the face and head and tore her shirt and bra from her body, leaving her in her underpants. He then turned to the nightstand between the waterbed and the doorway and, with a sweeping motion, cleared everything off the top of it. Among the things that went crashing to the floor was a large glass lamp and a telephone. The lamp shattered, littering the floor and doorway with large and small pieces of glass. Jimmy said he was leaving and walked out the bedroom door, kicking the large broken lamp as he left.
>
> Brenda then cried out to Jimmy that "she was cut." Jimmy turned back and saw Brenda lying on her side somewhere between the bed and the doorway. Blood was gushing profusely from a cut in her left groin area. Unknown to Jimmy and Brenda, her wound was mortal. In the fall she had severed her left femoral artery and vein.

Id. at 679-680.

To the majority, these facts supported a conviction for an assault (based on the beating). It thus upheld Mr. Torres's conviction and 180-day sentence for that charge. But the evidence, it held, did not support a homicide conviction:

> Here the critical act was sweeping the lamp off the table, an act that by itself is not highly dangerous or unlawful. . . . For the State to establish recklessness, Jimmy . . . would have had to know or foresee that the lamp would probably break when he swept it off the table. The evidence is that the lamp had fallen before and had not broken. During [a] scuffle between the police and Jimmy, a lamp identical to the lamp that was broken was knocked to the floor but did not break. Second, Jimmy would have had to know or foresee that Brenda would probably follow him, fall, and impale herself in a vital area of the body on a piece of glass that was more than four feet away from her. We think it is unreasonable to expect Jimmy to have known or to have foreseen the chain of events that ultimately led to Brenda's death. The record suggests to us a tragic, freak accident.

Id. at 682. The dissenting judge, however, took a different view of the case.

> According to the majority the case is about a broken lamp and the "freak accident" that followed. It is not. This case is about reckless conduct that the district court aptly described as "the final act in an episode of domestic violence." . . . [The] autopsy indicated that Brenda Torres had recently been struck on the right side of her mouth, most likely with the defendant's fist. . . . She had recently been struck on the left cheek with a patterned object, possibly a watchband. She suffered a recent bruise on the right chin, and a recent blow to the left chin. She suffered contusions about the lower neck area. In addition, Brenda Torres had been struck several times about the scalp area with a blunt, rectangular object. . . . [According to our precedents], an activity's "inherent risk to others" is only one — and not necessarily the decisive — factor. The defendant's conduct must also be assessed in light of "the activity he or she engaged in at the relevant time." State v. Kernes, 262 N.W.2d 602, 605 (Iowa 1978). This broadening of the zone of danger is in keeping with the statutory proscription against "the commission of an act *in a manner* likely to cause death or serious injury." Iowa Code §707.5(2) (emphasis added). Because the majority focuses so narrowly on the single act of breaking a lamp, it is not surprising that it finds "the act" insufficient to establish the requisite recklessness under the statute. I believe its analysis is faulty in [that] it wholly ignores *the manner* in which the act was performed, that is, the context in which a reasonable fact finder could conclude that Torres' act was reckless. . . . I would affirm Torres' conviction for involuntary manslaughter.

Id. at 682-684 (Neuman, J., dissenting).

8. Distinguishing Defendants Based on Moral Luck. Note a feature common to all of the cases described thus far: the defendant's liability turns on whether the risk inherent in his dangerous behavior actually materializes. But whether that happens is often beyond his control. Consider Mr. Hall, the skier in the case that opens this section. When he launched into the air, he did not know whether someone was in his path below. And in fact, as the court acknowledged, the most likely scenario when someone takes a risky jump on the slopes is that he lands on the ground, without hurting anyone else. Were that to have happened here, Mr. Hall would have continued on his way down the mountain—without ever having committed a crime, let alone a criminal homicide.

This raises a question about why liability should turn on the seeming happenstance that a harmful risk materialized in one instance and not another. To make the point crisp, imagine a person walking along a highway overpass tossing rocks into the lanes of traffic below, without looking or caring how they land. Such a person could potentially be convicted of depraved-heart murder if the rock happens to smash into a windshield and cause a fatal crash. By contrast, if the rock simply hits the pavement, liability shrinks substantially and may even evaporate.* Crucially, the person's conduct *and* mental state are identical in the two situations, with his liability seemingly turning on an element of moral luck beyond his control. Why should the outcome of that moral coin flip matter, let alone matter *so much*?

This issue arises in various contexts, including, as we will see in later chapters, the law of attempt. Consider two competing answers to the question. The first, offered by James Fitzjames Stephen, takes a sociological view:

> [I]t seems to me that it would be rather pedantic than rational to say that each had committed the same offence, and should subjected to the same punishment. [O]ne has had the bad luck to cause a horrible misfortune, and to attract public attention to it, and the other the good fortune to do no harm. Both certainly deserve punishment, but it gratifies a natural public feeling to choose out for punishment the one who actually has caused great harm, and the effect in the way of preventing a repetition of the offence is much the same as if both were punished.[59]

H.L.A. Hart, by contrast, acknowledges the societal impulse that Stephen centers—but argues the criminal law should resist it, not indulge it.

---

* Some jurisdictions reduce this liability gap in certain contexts by attaching criminal liability to purely risky behavior, independent of resulting harm. Reckless driving statutes are a prime example. Some jurisdictions take the concept further by creating a general offense of "reckless endangerment," though typically the offense is treated less seriously than risky behavior that results in actual harm. *See* Model Penal Code §211.2; *see, e.g.*, People v. Feingold, 852 N.E.2d 1163, 1164, 1168-1169 (N.Y. 2006) (finding liability for reckless endangerment where defendant's suicide attempt resulted in a gas explosion).

No doubt there is often an inclination to treat punishment like compensation and measure it by the outcome alone. There may even at times be public demand that this be done. . . . But there seems no good reason for adopting this misassimilation as a principle or to stigmatise as "pedantic" the refusal to recognize that the difference made by "bad fortune" and "good luck" to the outcome of the very same act justifies punishing one and not the other.[60]

9. Distinguishing Differently Situated Individuals. How should we think about criminalizing risk when the risk itself—and the justifications for assuming it—look different to people in different social contexts? This question echoes one encountered earlier, in the law of provocation, where we examined competing arguments about whether and how to individualize the "reasonable person." With respect to unintentional crimes, reasonableness again assumes a central conceptual role. The MPC, for example, determines whether a risk is "substantial and unjustifiable" by examining it "from the point of view of the actor's perceptions, i.e., to what extent he was aware of risk, of factors relating to its substantiality and of factors relating to its unjustifiability." Model Penal Code and Commentaries §2.02 cmt. 3 at 238. The jury, in other words, is supposed to ask whether the defendant's actions were "a gross deviation from the standard of care that a reasonable person would observe *in the actor's situation.*" Model Penal Code §2.02(2)(d) (emphasis added).

Sometimes, considering the actor's situation can make the actor seem more culpable. Recall the *Hall* court's decision to evaluate that case from the perspective of "a reasonable, law-abiding, trained ski racer and resort employee . . . [who] had a great deal of skiing experience." Assessing the facts through that lens, the court held that "Hall's knowledge and training could give rise to the reasonable inference that he was aware of the possibility that by skiing so fast and out of control he might collide with and kill another skier unless he regained control and slowed down."

In other cases, a nuanced consideration of social context might cut in the other direction—if courts are able to see it. Consider, in this vein, the following case.

State v. Williams, 484 P.2d 1167 (Wash. Ct. App. 1971). Defendants, husband and wife, were charged . . . with the crime of manslaughter for negligently failing to supply their 17-month child with necessary medical attention, as a result of which he died . . . . The defendant husband, Walter Williams, is a 24-year old full-blooded Sheshont Indian with a sixth-grade education. His sole occupation is that of laborer. The defendant wife, Bernice Williams, is a 20-year-old part Indian with an 11th grade education. At the time of the marriage, the wife had two children, the younger of whom was a 14-month son. Both parents worked and the children were cared for by the 85-year-old mother of the defendant husband. The defendant husband assumed parental responsibility with the defendant wife to provide clothing, care and medical attention for the child. Both defendants possessed a great deal of love and affection for the defendant wife's young son. . . .

Parental duty to provide medical care for a dependent minor child was recognized at common law and characterized as a natural duty. . . . On the question of the quality or seriousness of breach of the duty, at common law, in the case of involuntary manslaughter, the breach had to amount to more than mere ordinary or simple negligence—gross negligence was essential. In Washington, however, [our statutes] supersede both voluntary and involuntary manslaughter as those crimes were defined at common law. Under these statutes the crime is deemed committed even though the death of the victim is the proximate result of only simple or ordinary negligence. . . . If such negligence proximately causes the death of the victim, the defendant, as pointed out above, is guilty of statutory manslaughter. . . .

Timeliness in the furnishing of medical care [accordingly] must be considered in terms of "ordinary caution." The law does not mandatorily require that a doctor be called for a child at the first sign of any indisposition or illness. The indisposition or illness may appear to be of a minor or very temporary kind, such as a toothache or cold. If one in the exercise of ordinary caution fails to recognize that his child's symptoms require medical attention, it cannot be said that the failure to obtain such medical attention is a breach of the duty owed. In our opinion, "a reasonable amount of discretion is vested in parents, charged with the duty of maintaining and bringing up infant children; the standard is at what time would an ordinarily prudent person, solicitous for the welfare of his child and anxious to promote its recovery, deem it necessary to call in the services of a physician." People v. Pierson, 68 N.E. 243, 244 (N.Y. 1903).

It remains to apply the law discussed to the facts. . . . Because of the serious nature of the charge against the parent and step-parent of a well-loved child, and out of our concern for the protection of the constitutional rights of the defendants, we have made an independent examination of the evidence . . . .

Dr. Gale Wilson, the autopsy surgeon and chief pathologist for the King County Coroner, testified that the child died because an abscessed tooth had been allowed to develop into an infection of the mouth and cheeks, eventually becoming gangrenous. This condition, accompanied by the child's inability to eat, brought about malnutrition, lowering the child's resistance and eventually producing pneumonia, causing the death. Dr. Wilson testified that in his opinion the infection had lasted for approximately 2 weeks, and that the odor generally associated with gangrene would have been present for approximately 10 days before death. He also expressed the opinion that had medical care been first obtained in the last week before the baby's death, such care would have been obtained too late to have saved the baby's life. Accordingly, the baby's apparent condition between September 1 and

September 5, 1968 became the critical period for the purpose of determining whether in the exercise of ordinary caution defendants should have provided medical care for the minor child.

The testimony concerning the child's apparent condition during the critical period is not crystal clear, but is sufficient to warrant the following statement of the matter. The defendant husband testified that he noticed the baby was sick about 2 weeks before the baby died. The defendant wife testified that she noticed the baby was ill about a week and a half or 2 weeks before the baby died. The evidence showed that in the critical period the baby was fussy; that he could not keep his food down; and that a cheek started swelling up. The swelling went up and down, but did not disappear. In that same period, the cheek turned "a bluish color like." The defendants, not realizing that the baby was as ill as it was or that the baby was in danger of dying, attempted to provide some relief to the baby by giving the baby aspirin during the critical period and continued to do so until the night before the baby died. The defendants thought the swelling would go down and were waiting for it to do so; and defendant husband testified, that from what he had heard, neither doctors nor dentists pull out a tooth "when it's all swollen up like that."

There was an additional explanation for not calling a doctor given by each defendant. Defendant husband testified that "the way the cheek looked, and that stuff on his hair, they would think we were neglecting him and take him away from us and not give him back." Defendant wife testified that the defendants were "waiting for the swelling to go down," and also that they were afraid to take the child to a doctor for fear that the doctor would report them to the welfare department, who, in turn, would take the child away. "It's just that I was so scared of losing him." They testified that they had heard that the defendant husband's cousin lost a child that way.

The evidence showed that the defendants did not understand the significance or seriousness of the baby's symptoms. However, there is no evidence that the defendants were physically or financially unable to obtain a doctor, or that they did not know an available doctor, or that the symptoms did not continue to be a matter of concern during the critical period. Indeed, the evidence shows that in April 1968 defendant husband had taken the child to a doctor for medical attention.

In our opinion, there is sufficient evidence . . . that applying the standard of ordinary caution, i.e., the caution exercisable by a man of reasonable prudence under the same or similar conditions, defendants were sufficiently put on notice concerning the symptoms of the baby's illness and lack of improvement in the baby's apparent condition in the period from September 1 to September 5, 1968 to have required them to have obtained medical care for the child. The failure so to do in this case is ordinary or simple negligence, and such negligence is sufficient to support a conviction of statutory manslaughter.

10. Distinguishing Between Individuals and the State. To some readers, the court's opinion in *Williams*, issued by a panel of judges that did not include any Native Americans, will betray a failure of the empathy necessary to assess risk and its justifications from "the actor's situation." After all, the parents in *Williams* offered a justification for their course of conduct. They worried that if they took their child to the doctor, "the Welfare Department would take the baby away." This was not an irrational fear. They heard it had happened to a relative and may have seen it in other families in the Native American community. Indeed, a few years after the *Williams* decision was issued, Congress investigated this phenomenon and found that 25 to 35 percent of Native American children across the country were being taken from their parents by child welfare officers, purportedly acting in "the best interests of the child." Often, these state agencies acted with direct support from the federal Bureau of Indian Affairs. Eventually, Congress enacted the Indian Child Welfare Act to address these practices, giving tribal authorities primary responsibility over Native American child custody matters. More recently, scholars and activists have criticized state agencies nationwide on the ground that they separate families and ultimately harm children, in the name of children's safety, with harms concentrated among Black children and families.[61]

Against this backdrop, it is possible to criticize the *Williams* decision as lacking compassion for people in a position of social weakness. As Oliver Wendell Holmes once put the point, criminal codes "do not merely require that every man should get as near as he can to the best conduct possible for him. They require him at his own peril to come up to a certain height. They take no account of incapacities . . . ." Accordingly, "[i]f they fall on any one class harder than another, it is on the weakest."[62]

Yet framing the problem this way misses a broader point. As Professor Victoria Nourse argues, "the intellectual focus on the individual tends to divert us from the state's role" in creating the conditions that can lead to harm in the first instance. Nourse views *Williams*, and the standard criticism of its reasoning, as exemplifying this misdirection.

> [T]his is a case taught in almost every criminal law course in the country . . . . The standard question presented is about individualization: do we take account of the defendants' background? Their education? The fact that they live on a reservation?
>
> . . . [This] conventional focus on the characteristics of the Williams defendants tends to occlude the role of the state by embedding it within the mind of the reasonable person. . . .
>
> But is this the only place where these facts belong? Is it really a "liberal" theory of the criminal law that asks us whether these people are "like us"? Isn't there a real problem here in that the state was taking away babies because they thought these parents "lesser" in some way? My point

is not that these facts exonerate, but that they raise important questions about something more than how we "describe" the Williamses' individual minds, psychology, or background. One need not go further than the entrapment defense to recognize that a just relation between a citizen and state may require that the state acknowledge its own participation in crime and that such participation recommends leniency or mitigation. . . .

Protecting defendants is not the same as describing them; protecting them means enforcing a just relation between the state and the defendant. Currently, our only option in a crudely descriptive, hyperindividualistic world appears to be to pathologize defendants, to render them sick, insane, or somehow subject to special rules for special classes. The poor town drunk, poor battered woman, and the poor ill-educated Native American: they are sick and all good liberals should have compassion. But this kind of condescension, however wrapped up in kindness, risks blindness to oppressive relations. The problem with individualization is not simply that some excuses may be abused; the problem with individualization is that it may not be enough to protect individuals from a world of real inequality and bias—inequality and bias that do not exist simply in the minds or bodies of defendants.[63]

C.   Felony Murder

We opened our study of *mens rea* with the suggestion that this component of American criminal law reflects a commitment to proportionality. The entire hierarchy of mental states—from purpose and knowledge down through recklessness and negligence—represents an effort to link the severity of criminal punishment to the degree of culpability associated with wrongful conduct. We now close our study of *mens rea* by examining a doctrine that challenges this commitment: the felony murder rule.

Generally stated, *felony murder* is a doctrine that can render a person guilty of murder—including first-degree murder—if a death occurs while he is committing some other felony, such as robbery or arson. By treating the separate, predicate felony as the trigger for murder liability, the doctrine allows a murder conviction of someone who did not knowingly or even recklessly cause another person's death. Imagine, for example, an individual who, while committing an armed robbery, slips on ice and drops his gun in a manner that causes it to discharge, killing the robbery victim. Clearly this person is guilty of a robbery. But a murder? The principles of *mens rea* outlined thus far would struggle to classify this unintended death among the very worst homicides. But under the felony murder doctrine, it could be first-degree murder.

To many observers, this outcome seems unjust, precisely because it contravenes the proportionality principle and the approach to culpability outlined in this chapter. And, in fact, the felony murder doctrine is frequently maligned, to the point that one leading scholar calls it "one of the most widely criticized features of American criminal law."[64]

As with every aspect of criminal law, efforts to unpack the debate over this doctrine are complicated by the fact that there is no *one* felony murder rule. Rather, there are dozens across the various states, some harsher than others. As the cases and discussion below show, this jurisdictional variation leads to debates, at the most basic level, over what "the" felony murder rule even *is*. Is it a form of strict liability that renders *mens rea* irrelevant for a certain category of homicides? Or is it a unique form of negligence liability that treats risky conduct as especially bad when it takes the form of an independent, serious offense?[65]

The answers to these questions can shape how one views the doctrine and its potential defects. Our goal in this section is not to delve deeply into all the many doctrinal twists and turns of the felony murder rule as it has been defined and applied across states and over time. Rather, our aim is to trace the doctrine's broad outlines with two specific points in mind. First, we show how — in nearly all its manifestations — the felony murder rule stands in tension with the graded approach to culpability that has animated the law of *mens rea* thus far. And second, we highlight how the doctrine creates institutional power, enhancing the ability of prosecutors to determine case outcomes by changing the calculus of plea negotiations.

We begin with an outline of the doctrine's parameters, as captured in the two cases that follow.

People v. Stamp

82 Cal. Rptr. 598 (Cal. Ct. App. 1969)

COBEY, J. . . . Defendants Koory and Stamp, armed with a gun and a blackjack, entered the rear of the building housing the offices of General Amusement Company . . . . Stamp, the one with the gun, went into the office of Carl Honeyman, the owner and manager. Thereupon Honeyman, looking very frightened and pale, emerged from the office in a "kind of hurry." He was apparently propelled by Stamp who had hold of him by an elbow.

The robbery victims were required to lie down on the floor while the robbers took the money and fled out the back door. As the robbers, who had been on the premises 10 to 15 minutes, were leaving, they told the victims to remain on the floor for five minutes so that no one would "get hurt."

Honeyman, who had been lying next to the counter, had to use it to steady himself in getting up off the floor. Still pale, he was short of breath, sucking air, and pounding and rubbing his chest. As he walked down the hall, in an unsteady manner, still breathing hard and rubbing his chest, he said he was having trouble "keeping the pounding down inside" and that his heart was "pumping too fast for him." A few minutes later, although still looking very upset, shaking, wiping his forehead and rubbing his chest, he was able to walk in a steady manner into an employee's office. When the police arrived, almost immediately thereafter, he told them he was not feeling very well and that he had a pain in his chest. About two minutes later, which was 15 to 20 minutes after the robbery had occurred, he collapsed on the floor. At 11:25 he was pronounced dead on arrival at the hospital. The coroner's report listed the immediate cause of death as heart attack.

The employees noted that during the hours before the robbery Honeyman had appeared to be in normal health and good spirits. The victim was an obese, 60-year-old man, with a history of heart disease, who was under a great deal of pressure due to the intensely competitive nature of his business. Additionally, he did not take good care of his heart.

[At trial, expert witnesses] testified that although Honeyman had an advanced case of atherosclerosis, a progressive and ultimately fatal disease, there must have been some immediate upset to his system which precipitated the attack. It was their conclusion in response to a hypothetical question that but for the robbery there would have been no fatal seizure at that time. The fright induced by the robbery was too much of a shock to Honeyman's system. . . .

Appellants' contention that the evidence was insufficient to prove that the robbery factually caused Honeyman's death is without merit. . . . A review of the facts as outlined above shows that there was substantial evidence of the robbery itself, that appellants were the robbers, and that but for the robbery the victim would not have experienced the fright which brought on the fatal heart attack.

Appellants' contention that the felony-murder rule is inapplicable to the facts of this case is also without merit. Under the felony-murder rule of section 189 of the Penal Code, a killing committed in either the perpetration of or an attempt to perpetrate robbery is murder of the first degree. This is true whether the killing is wilfull, deliberate and premeditated, or merely accidental or unintentional, and whether or not the killing is planned as a part of the commission of the robbery. . . .

The doctrine presumes malice aforethought on the basis of the commission of a felony inherently dangerous to human life. This rule is a rule of substantive law in California and not merely an evidentiary shortcut to finding malice as it withdraws from the jury the requirement that they find either express malice or the implied malice which is manifested in an intent to kill. Under this rule no intentional act is necessary other than the attempt to or the actual commission of the robbery itself. When a robber enters a place with a deadly weapon with the intent to commit robbery, malice is shown by the nature of the crime.

There is no requirement that the killing occur, "while committing" or "while engaged in" the felony, or that the killing be "a part of" the felony, other than that the few acts be a part of one continuous transaction. Thus the homicide need not have been committed "to perpetrate" the felony. . . .

The doctrine is not limited to those deaths which are foreseeable. Rather a felon is held strictly liable for *all* killings committed by him or his accomplices in the course of the felony. As long as the homicide is the direct causal result of the robbery the felony-murder rule applies whether or not the death was a natural or probable consequence of the robbery. So long as a victim's predisposing physical condition, regardless of its cause, is not the *only* substantial factor bringing about his death, that condition, and the robber's ignorance of it, in no way destroys the robber's criminal responsibility for the death. So long as life is shortened as a result of the felonious act, it does not matter that the victim might have died soon anyway. In this respect, the robber takes his victim as he finds him. . . .

The judgment [of conviction for first-degree murder] is affirmed.

State v. Harding

528 S.W.3d 362 (Mo. Ct. App. 2017)

PAGE, J. Ricky Harding appeals his conviction after a jury trial for felony murder . . . . In the early morning hours of May 25, 2014, Daughter awoke to the sound of an argument between her Mother and Defendant. She peeked out of her bedroom into the living room, saw Defendant screaming at her Mother, and saw her Mother crying. Daughter listened to the argument, and when she later peeked out again, she saw her Mother grab Defendant's gun from between the couch cushions. Defendant stood and moved for the gun. Daughter saw her Mother hunch over, hiding the gun between her legs, with Defendant behind her Mother struggling for control of the weapon. Daughter hid behind her door, and then heard a shot. . . .

Paramedics arrived and transported Mother to the hospital. Having lost too much blood to be resuscitated, Mother died. Defendant arrived, agitated and argumentative, at the hospital sometime thereafter. He was arrested outside the emergency room, and was charged with second degree felony murder . . . . [Defendant, a prior felony offender, knew it was illegal for him to possess a firearm.]

. . . Defendant argues the evidence was insufficient to establish that Victim's death was caused as a result of him being a felon in possession of a firearm. . . . Absent this alleged error, Defendant maintains he would not have been convicted of felony murder . . . . We disagree. . . .

"A person commits the offense of [felony murder] if he or she . . . commits or attempts to commit *any* felony, and, in the perpetration or the attempted perpetration of such felony . . . another person is killed as a result of the perpetration or attempted perpetration of such felony . . . ." Mo. Rev. Stat. §565.021.1(2). "[T]he practical effect of the felony-murder rule [is that it] permits the felonious intent necessary to a murder conviction to be shown by the perpetration of or attempt to perpetrate a felony." State v. Rumble, 680 S.W.2d 939, 942 (Mo. 1984) (en banc).

"The plain and ordinary meaning of '*any*' as used in Section 565.021 indicates our legislature intended that *every* felony could serve as an underlying felony for the purpose of charging a defendant with second degree felony murder. Nowhere does the statute limit the felony to be used in charging under this statute to any particular type of or specific felony, i.e., inherently dangerous, as some other states have done." State v. Bouser, 17 S.W.3d 130, 139 (Mo. Ct. App. 1999).

Here, Defendant was charged with felony murder in connection with the commission of the class D felony of unlawful possession of a firearm . . . . [I]t is not disputed that Defendant illegally obtained and possessed a 1911 Colt .45 Pistol — prohibited by [his prior] burglary conviction — through the events of the night in question. . . .

However, we must also apply a "foreseeability-proximate cause" concept to the underlying felony when determining a person's responsibility for a felony-murder killing. "A defendant may be responsible for any deaths that are the natural and proximate result of the crime unless there is an intervening cause of that death." State v. Burrage, 465 S.W.3d 77, 80 (Mo. Ct. App. 2015). To test causation, Missouri courts will often look at the underlying felony, generally, as well as at the facts of the particular case. A death is foreseeable if the underlying felony and killing were a part of a continuous transaction, "closely connected in time, place and causal relation." State v. Manuel, 443 S.W.3d 669, 677 (Mo. Ct. App. 2014). It is inconsequential that a defendant's conduct was not the immediate cause of death, but is sufficient if the conduct "was a contributing proximate cause of death." *See* State v. Scroggs, 521 S.W.3d 649 (Mo. Ct. App. 2017). . . .

Whether a person's death can be a natural and proximate cause of a violation of the felon-in-possession law in order to support a charge of felony murder appears to be a matter of first impression in Missouri. Although not controlling, several other states have confronted this issue. . . . In *Ford v. State*, 423 S.E.2d 255, 256 (Ga. 1992), as the defendant — a prior felon — attempted to unload a firearm while in his apartment, the weapon discharged, sending a bullet through the floor into the apartment below, where it struck and killed the victim. The defendant was charged with felony-murder predicated on a violation of Georgia's felon-in-possession law, because, like Missouri, Georgia's felony-murder statute did not restrict which felonies could underlie a felony-murder charge. After defendant's conviction by a jury, the Georgia Supreme Court reversed, finding the felony of felon-in-possession was not "dangerous per se," nor were the "attendant circumstances" in this matter sufficient to create "a foreseeable risk of death." *Id.*

[By contrast, in] *Hines v. State*, 578 S.E.2d 868 (Ga. 2003), the defendant—a former felon—spent the day consuming large amounts of alcohol while concurrently hunting turkey with his friends. Late in the day, the defendant shot a fellow-hunter when the defendant "took an unsafe shot at dusk, through heavy foliage, at a target eighty feet away that he had not positively identified as a turkey." In *Hines*, unlike *Ford*, the Georgia Supreme Court upheld the defendant's conviction of felony murder predicated on its felon-in-possession law, because "under the circumstances . . . the defendant's illegal possession of a firearm created a foreseeable risk of death." *Id.*

Similar to Georgia, Missouri's felony-murder law applies to all felonies, and also allows for the circumstances of the case to guide whether the death is the "natural and proximate result of the commission of the underlying felony." *Scroggs*, 521 S.W.3d at 656. Thus, Missouri's felon-in-possession law is sufficient to *charge* a defendant with felony-murder, but the underlying facts dictate whether Missouri's felon-in-possession law is sufficient to *convict* a defendant of felony-murder.

. . . [W]e may only review the underlying circumstances to determine whether the murder was foreseeable and a proximate cause of the underlying felony. In this case, we hold a rational juror could have found Defendant's unlawful possession of the firearm to be a foreseeably proximate cause of Victim's death, as the facts of this case indicate a causal link between Defendant's possession and Victim's death. Defendant purchased the stolen gun "off the street" and kept it loaded in a couch cushion where anyone could access it, including the young children residing in the home. Defendant was aware he was barred from possessing the pistol, yet knowingly introduced the firearm into the home where he and Victim were prone to frequent domestic disputes. On the night of Victim's death, Defendant left the firearm tucked between two couch cushions, for anyone—including Defendant—to easily access. Victim and Defendant engaged in a lengthy verbal altercation, culminating in a physical fight for control of the pistol. Victim ended up hunched over the gun, hiding it between her legs. The weapon discharged, and the bullet injured Victim's femoral artery, ultimately causing her death. It is the fault of Defendant that this weapon became a part of the altercation that resulted in Victim's death—i.e., his felony-possession was closely connected in time, place and causal relation to her death—and therefore completely foreseeable that such an incident would occur.

Therefore, the trial court did not err in entering judgment for the felony-murder charge predicated on the felony of unlawful possession of a weapon. . . .

NOTES AND QUESTIONS

1. A Form of Strict Liability? Criticism of the felony-murder doctrine often starts from the premise that it imposes *strict liability*, as the *Stamp* opinion expressly states. That phrase, employed both in criminal law and in the civil law of torts, refers to liability that "is not based upon any intent of the defendant to do harm" or "upon any negligence." In other words, strict liability imposes consequences on a person even when the harm he causes—in this case, death—is a "merely accidental" consequence of his actions, to quote *Stamp*.[66]

It may seem strange to describe a death caused in the course of a separate felony as an "accident." Indeed, much of the debate over the felony murder doctrine turns on whether thinking of such deaths as "accidental" is ever appropriate. There are, however, some cases in which the term may be apt. Consider the facts of *Hines v. State*, 578 S.E.2d 868 (Ga. 2003), which is discussed in the *Harding* opinion above:

> While hunting, Robert Lee Hines mistook his friend Steven Wood for a turkey and shot him dead. . . . Taken in the light most favorable to the jury's verdict of guilty, the evidence at trial showed that, late in the afternoon of April 8, 2001, Hines and some of his friends and relatives went turkey hunting. They split into two groups, with Hines and his friend Randy Stoker hunting together in one area, and the victim, the victim's wife, and Hines's son hunting in a different area, approximately one-fourth mile away. As the sky was growing dark, Hines heard a turkey gobble, "saw it fan out and shot." Hines's shot went through heavy foliage and hit the victim approximately eighty feet away. Immediately thereafter, the victim's wife screamed, "You shot Wood." Hines and his son went for help, but the victim died before help could arrive.

Id. at 871.

As noted in the *Harding* opinion, the jury convicted Mr. Hines of felony murder, predicated on his unlawful possession of a gun (the hunting rifle) that he was barred from carrying by a prior felony conviction. The opinion upholding Hines's conviction drew a dissent, which objected to the disproportionate punishment that followed.

> The death in this case is clearly a tragic incident . . . . But the sanction of life in prison for murder should be reserved for cases in which the defendant's moral failings warrant such punishment. . . . Hines will be serving the same punishment—life in prison—as an arsonist convicted of felony murder who firebombed an apartment that he knew was occupied, causing the death of two young children, and the same punishment as an armed robber convicted of felony murder who entered a store with a firearm and shot and killed a store employee. . . . I [cannot] agree with

subjecting so many hunters to the possibility of spending life in prison
when they do not fastidiously follow proper hunting procedures and accidentally shoot a fellow hunter.

Id. at 875-876 (Sears, J., dissenting). The dissenting judge thought Hines
may have "engaged in negligent hunting practices," given that he had been
drinking and was hunting at dusk. *Id.* at 875. But it is not clear these facts
rise to the level of criminal negligence; and if they don't, Hines's murder
conviction would appear to rest on a form of strict liability.

It bears noting that strict liability is not a concept wholly foreign to
criminal law. On the contrary, as we will see in Chapter Six, states have a
long history of enacting penal offenses, often known as *regulatory* or *public
welfare* offenses, in which "the guilty act alone makes out the crime" without
any requirement of proving *mens rea.* Morissette v. United States, 342 U.S.
246, 256 (1952). For example, some statutes make it a strict liability crime
to sell contaminated food. Under these laws, a person can be convicted of
such an offense even if he took special care to sell food that was safe and
even if no reasonable person would have had any reason to think the food
at issue was tainted. But while strict liability crimes like these exist, they have
been confined to a "limited class of offenses," precisely because they contravene the general requirement that criminal punishment requires a culpable mental state. *Id.* at 258. Courts have identified various factors to help
mark the permissible boundaries of this class of offenses, chief among them
being the penalty attached: strict liability is generally confined to minor
offenses.*

**2. The Inherently Dangerous Felony Requirement: A Form of Per Se (or Presumed)
Negligence (or Recklessness)?** Defenders of the felony murder doctrine do not
disagree in principle with the critiques outlined above. On the contrary,
they acknowledge that it is possible to find "egregious cases" in which the
doctrine has been applied to create severe injustices. But they also contend
that those extreme cases are fewer and farther between than the doctrine's
critics suggest, and that "there are both good and bad versions of the felony
murder doctrine."[67]

Notably, in the eyes of these defenders, the "good" versions of the felony murder rule do not really impose strict liability at all. Rather, by cabin-
ing the rule in various ways, the argument goes, these less sweeping versions
of the doctrine are better understood as resting liability on a presumption
that the defendant's conduct (the predicate felony) entailed culpably risky

---

* The Model Penal Code, for example, prohibits strict liability for offenses with penalties
higher than a monetary fine. Model Penal Code §2.05 & note. Not all states go so far, but they
do all view strict liability as inappropriate when penalties are severe. To quote the U.S. Supreme
Court, "punishing a violation as a felony is simply incompatible with the theory of the [strict lia-
bility] public welfare offense." Staples v. United States, 511 U.S. 600, 618 (1994).

behavior. Two doctrinal limitations in particular, both alluded to in the lead cases above, can be seen as functionally recasting felony murder into a form of negligence liability: the inherently dangerous felony rule and the proximate cause requirement.[68]

Consider the former first. Most states hold that "[i]n order to apply the felony-murder doctrine, the underlying felony must be one which is inherently dangerous to human life." State v. Smallwood, 955 P.2d 1209, 1214 (Kan. 1998). Technically speaking, a felony murder doctrine cabined by this limitation still imposes a form of strict liability: as the *Stamp* court explains, it "presumes malice aforethought on the basis of the commission of a felony inherently dangerous to human life" and thus "withdraws from the jury" any need to find that the defendant knowingly, recklessly, or negligently caused a person's death. At the same time, the inherently dangerous felony limitation does conceptual work similar to a negligence requirement, so long as the phrase "inherently dangerous" identifies felonies carrying a certain amount of fatal risk. Defined as such, Professor Guyora Binder argues, the very fact that a predicate felony is dangerous would seem to "imply culpability with respect to a result element that has no explicit culpability attached."[69]

And indeed, this is precisely how the phrase "inherently dangerous" is often defined. Consider, for example, the states of Georgia and California, which define inherently dangerous felonies, respectively, as those that "by their nature or by the attendant circumstances, create a foreseeable risk of death," Ford v. State, 423 S.E.2d 255, 256 (Ga. 1992), or that carry "a high probability that death will result," People v. Patterson, 778 P.2d 549, 558 (Cal. 1989). Classic examples are robbery, rape, arson, burglary, and kidnapping. According to Professor Binder and Professor Mark Kelman, this definition substantively tracks the foreseeable-risk idea at the heart of negligence liability, and thus simply creates "a per se negligence rule that achieves the same aims" as the more familiar "negligence standard."[70]

Indeed, one could construct a doctrinal framework in which *recklessness*, complete with its subjective risk-awareness requirement, is also presumed when certain inherently dangerous felonies are committed. Consider in this context the approach adopted by the MPC. In preparing that framework, the Code's drafters began by condemning the "essential illogic" of felony murder doctrine. It is a tenet of criminal law, they wrote, that "[l]esser culpability yields lesser liability, and a person who inadvertently kills another under circumstances not amounting to negligence is guilty of no crime at all." Model Penal Code and Commentaries §210.2 cmt. 6 at 36. They went on to argue that the "felony-murder rule contradicts this scheme. It bases conviction of murder not on any proven culpability but on liability for another crime. [But the] underlying felony carries its own penalty [so] the additional punishment for murder is therefore gratuitous . . . ." *Id.*

Given this criticism, one might expect the MPC's drafters to have simply abandoned the doctrine. And indeed, the Code's primary drafter, Professor Herbert Wechsler, wrote that abolition of the rule was the drafters' first choice. But "such a course was thought to be impolitic, given the weight of prosecutive opposition." As a result, the final version of the code reads as follows:

> [C]riminal homicide constitutes murder when . . . it is committed reck-lessly under circumstances manifesting extreme indifference to the value of human life. Such recklessness and indifference are presumed if the actor is engaged or is an accomplice in the commission of, or an attempt to commit, or flight after committing or attempting to commit robbery, rape or deviate sexual intercourse by force or threat of force, arson, bur-glary, kidnapping or felonious escape.

Model Penal Code §210.2(1).[71]

Questions: How does the MPC provision above differ from the "per se negligence" approach that Professors Binder and Kelman suggest is at work in the inherently dangerous felony doctrine? How does it differ from the more standard "extreme indifference to the value of human life" method of establishing murder liability in cases of unintentional homicide that do not implicate the felony murder doctrine?

3. Proximate Cause: Foreseeability as Culpability? In contrast to *Stamp*, *Harding* makes clear that Missouri law does not contain an inherently dangerous felony limitation. Rather, as the opinion states, "*every* felony could serve as an underlying felony for the purpose of" applying Missouri's felony murder doctrine. The opinion does, however, suggest an alternative (and commonplace) limitation on the doctrine's reach: "we must . . . apply a 'foreseeability-proximate cause' concept to the underlying felony," the court explains.[72]

Proximate cause is a famously elusive concept, with various formulations employed to describe its operation. The idea plays a major role in the law of torts and is covered in detail in that course, though the most recent Restatement of Torts deems the phrase misleading and prefers "scope of liability." In the context of the felony murder doctrine, a leading criminal law treatise summarizes the proximate cause requirement this way:

> In felony-murder cases as well as other homicide cases, it is often said that the death must have been the "natural and probable consequence" of the defendant's conduct. When death has occurred only as a consequence of some intervening act following the defendant's conduct (as is frequently the case in the felony-murder context), the issue is frequently put in terms of whether the intervening cause was "foreseeable" (as distinguished from actually "foreseen").

> . . . [C]ourts have drawn the perimeters of [proximate] cause more closely when the intervening cause was a mere coincidence (i.e., where the defendant's act merely put the victim at a certain place at a certain time, and because the victim was so located it was possible for him to be acted upon by the intervening cause) than when it was a response to the defendant's prior actions (i.e., a reaction to conditions created by the defendant). Foreseeability is required as to the former, but in the latter instance the question is whether the intervening act was abnormal—that is, whether, looking at the matter with hindsight, it seems extraordinary.[73]

As the foregoing passage indicates, the proximate cause doctrine—like the law of negligence and recklessness—focuses on risk, by asking whether the harm (here, a death) was a natural, probable, and/or foreseeable consequence of the defendant's felonious actions. Indeed, the basic conceptual similarity between the two doctrines comes through when one lays the passage above side-by-side with cases addressing liability for unintended homicides that do not implicate the felony murder doctrine. Recall, for example, *State v. Torres*, where the court held that liability for an unintentional homicide requires that "the danger must be so obvious from the facts that the actor knows or should *reasonably foresee* that harm will *probably* . . . flow from the act." 495 N.W.2d at 681 (emphasis added). Given this similarity, some scholars argue that a felony murder rule cabined by a proximate cause requirement—like a felony murder rule cabined by an inherently dangerous felony limitation—is functionally imposing a form of negligence liability, not strict liability. In the words of Professor Binder, "If 'causing' a result means foreseeably bringing it about, it entails culpability with respect to that result." In fact, some contend that "courts hostile to [the] strict liability species of murder" have built up the proximate cause doctrine for this very reason and have thus "introduced a culpability requirement through the back door of causation." Model Penal Code and Commentaries §210.2 cmt. 6 at 34.[74]

Still, it is important to be clear that, strictly as doctrinal matter, proximate cause and *mens rea* are discrete elements of the analysis. Formally speaking, the felony murder doctrine "permits the felonious intent necessary to a murder conviction to be shown by the perpetration of or attempt to perpetrate a felony," as the *Harding* court says, and thus "presumes malice aforethought on the basis of the commission of a felony," in the words of *Stamp*. The foreseeability analysis under proximate cause is thus *not* a question of *mens rea*. As a result, the risk-foreseeability analysis under the proximate cause heading can be and often is different from what it would be under the negligence or recklessness headings.

For example, it is possible—because the two risk analyses are formally independent—to have a lower risk threshold in one context than in another, and thus to sweep in a broader swath of unintended harms.

Compare, for example, the *Harding* and *Torres* cases themselves. Both involve domestic disputes that ended in unintended and fatal femoral artery wounds that were not directly inflicted by the defendants' own hands. In *Torres*, the resulting death is described as a "tragic accident" beyond the reach of criminal homicide liability, while in *Harding* the result is described as "completely foreseeable." One way to reconcile these cases is to identify factual differences that render the fatal outcome in *Harding* more foreseeable than the fatal outcome in *Torres*. But another is to entertain the possibility that "foreseeability" means something different—and less demanding—when deployed in the proximate cause analysis for felony murder than when deployed in the negligence and recklessness analyses for negligent homicide and manslaughter.[75]

4. Proportionality and Culpability, Revisited: Does Motive Matter? The basic argument presented by the doctrine's defenders, as summarized in the preceding two notes, is that felony murder is not actually a form of strict liability but rather a species of negligence liability. Note, however, that this argument alone does not answer one of the primary objections to the doctrine—that it imposes disproportionately severe penalties on relatively less culpable actors. In *People v. Aaron*, 299 N.W.2d 304 (Mich. 1980), the Michigan Supreme Court put the objection this way:

> The felony-murder rule's most egregious violation of basic rules of culpability occurs where felony murder is categorized as first-degree murder. All other murders carrying equal punishment require a showing of premeditation, deliberation and willfulness while felony murder only requires a showing of intent to do the underlying felony. Although the purpose of our degree statutes is to punish more severely the more culpable forms of murder, an accidental killing occurring during the perpetration of a felony would be punished more severely than a second-degree murder requiring intent to kill, intent to cause great bodily harm or wantonness and willfulness.

Id. at 317.

To meet this objection, it is not enough to observe that the felony murder doctrine might be understood (functionally) as imposing a form of negligence liability. Rather, one needs to make the further claim that, in the set of cases falling within the rule, individuals who behave negligently and cause another's death have committed an *especially wrongful* form of homicide—a form of *aggravated* negligence properly assimilated into murder. Consider the following argument in support of such a view, from one of the doctrine's chief academic defenders.

Guyora Binder, *The Culpability of Felony Murder*, 83 Notre Dame L. Rev. 965, 967-968, 970-971, 1034-1036 (2008). How can merely negligent homicide deserve punishment as murder? Because the felon's additional depraved purpose aggravates his culpability for causing death carelessly. . . . We justify speeding a critically injured patient to a hospital; we condemn the same behavior in the context of drag racing or flight from arrest. As a society, we . . . are quicker to condemn failure to provide medical care to a child if motivated by cruelty or indifference than if motivated by religious conviction. And, most pertinently, we regard the risk of death associated with robbery as less acceptable than the greater risk of death associated with resisting robbery. Thus, we evaluate action based not only on its expected danger, but also on the moral worth of its motives. This principle that guilt depends on reasons for action justifies aggravating homicide liability on the basis of a felonious motive. A bad enough motive can make even a negligent killing culpable enough to merit murder liability. . . .

[Opponents of the felony murder rule embrace a] narrowly cognitive view of culpability that prevails in contemporary criminal law theory. According to this view, culpability is purely a function of the expectation of harm attributable to an actor at the time he or she acts. Thus, the actor's purposes, motives, meanings, and values are irrelevant. In particular, such goals as completing a rape, demeaning a victim because of her race, or intimidating political opponents are irrelevant to culpability for a killing. All that matters is the death and the expectation of causing it. This cognitive conception of culpability reflects a restrictive view of the role of criminal law in a liberal state—as opposing harmful conduct, but taking no sides in disagreements about values. . . . Actors can be blamed for their choices, but not for the values that guide choice. . . .

By contrast to cognitive theory's aspiration to value neutrality, an expressive conception of culpability overtly defines action as culpable insofar as it expresses a commitment to unworthy values. . . . On this view, conduct is culpable if done for reasons reflecting a lack of proper regard for others' welfare, autonomy, or equal citizenship. . . . In the case of a hate crime, a diffuse wrongful aim (to subordinate a group) changes the normative meaning and aggravates the wrong of causing harm intentionally. In the case of felony murder, a more precise wrongful aim (e.g., to expropriate property, to violate sexual autonomy, to destroy a building) changes the normative meaning and aggravates the wrong of causing harm negligently. Why should the criminal law consider the offender's ends in negligently imposing a fatal risk? Because imposing such a risk for an evil purpose expresses reprehensible values.

5. The Merger Doctrine. Even states that employ broad versions of the felony murder doctrine generally recognize a need to limit the doctrine's reach with respect to a subset of potential predicate crimes—namely, crimes that are themselves violent assaults less than murder. Absent such a limitation, the felony murder rule would render nearly every homicide a murder, because nearly every homicide would be committed in the course of some lesser felony offense, like felony assault or manslaughter. To guard against this collapse, states employ a doctrine of *merger*. Under this rule, certain felonies that are closely bound up in the homicide itself cannot serve as predicates for application of the felony murder rule. In *State v. Jones*, 155 A.3d 492 (Md. Ct. Spec. App. 2017), Maryland reversed its precedent rejecting the merger doctrine and joined the great majority of states that embrace the rule:

> A common limitation of the application of the felony-murder doctrine is the merger doctrine. The merger doctrine, first conceived in the nineteenth century, bars the application of the felony-murder doctrine whenever the underlying felony is an integral element of the homicide. In other words, to support a charge of felony murder, the underlying felony must be independent of the homicide. . . .
>
> [As Chief Judge Cardozo once explained, applying the felony-murder rule without a merger limitation] "would mean that every homicide, not justifiable or excusable, would occur in the commission of a felony, with the result that intent to kill and deliberation and premeditation would never be essential." People v. Moran, 158 N.E. 35, 36 (N.Y. 1927). [The Supreme Court of California has similarly observed that applying the felony-murder doctrine without such a limitation] "extends the operation of that rule 'beyond any rational function that it is designed to serve.' To allow such use of the felony-murder rule would effectively preclude the jury from considering the issue of malice aforethought in all cases wherein homicide has been committed as a result of a felonious assault—a category which includes the great majority of all homicides. This kind of bootstrapping finds support neither in logic nor in law." People v. Ireland, 450 P.2d 580, 590 (Cal. 1969). . . .
>
> "[A]pplication of the felony-murder rule to felonious assaults would . . . frustrate the Legislature's intent to punish certain felonious assaults resulting in death (those committed with malice aforethought, and therefore punishable as murder) more harshly than other felonious assaults that happened to result in death (those committed without malice aforethought, and therefore punishable as manslaughter)." People v. Hansen, 885 P.2d 1022, 1028 (Cal. 1994).
>
> With these considerations in mind, we find good and sufficient cause in favor of overruling *Roary v. State*, 385 Md. 217 (2005), which held that first-degree assault was a viable predicate for . . . felony murder. [That holding] is wrong in that it expands unwisely felony murder and elevates practically all shooting deaths in Maryland to second-degree felony murder, thereby effectively eliminating the crime of manslaughter.

Id. at 500, 504-505, 507.

Distinguishing between predicate felonies that will and will not merge into the homicide is not always straightforward. The touchstone inquiry, though, often turns on whether the predicate felony entailed a harm distinct from the ultimately fatal violence. In *People v. Burton*, 491 P.2d 793 (Cal. 1971), the Court explained the reasoning behind this approach:

> [T]here is a very significant difference between deaths resulting from assaults with a deadly weapon, where the purpose of the conduct was the very assault which resulted in death, and deaths resulting from conduct for an independent felonious purpose, such as robbery or rape, which happened to be accomplished by a deadly weapon and therefore technically includes assault with a deadly weapon. Our inquiry cannot stop with the fact that death resulted from the use of a deadly weapon and, therefore, technically included an assault with a deadly weapon, but must extend to an investigation of the purpose of the conduct.

Id. at 801.

6. Liability for Deaths Caused by Others. The cases we have seen in this chapter mostly apply the felony murder doctrine to make a single defendant liable for murder based on his own actions. It bears noting, though, that the felony murder doctrine can also make one felon liable for a murder caused by someone else. Most commonly, this occurs in the case of co-felons who, acting together, jointly commit the predicate offense. As the Supreme Court of Pennsylvania has explained, courts in such cases often endorse "the application of the felony-murder rule to co-felons who do not, in fact, cause the death," if the death was caused by one of the other participants in the felony. Commonwealth v. Allen, 379 A.2d 1335, 1339 (Pa. 1977). Multiple states provide for the same outcome by statute. This application of the felony murder doctrine overlaps with, and in some instances doctrinally draws upon, a separate set of criminal law concepts regarding group liability, including doctrines of accomplice liability and conspiracy liability discussed in Chapter Seven. We will return to this aspect of felony murder doctrine and compare it to complicity and conspiracy doctrines in that chapter (p. 607).[76]

It bears noting that some jurisdictions apply the felony murder doctrine to hold a person liable for deaths caused by people *uninvolved* in the underlying felony, or perhaps even by people (like police officers) who were actively resisting or attempting to thwart the underlying felony. Jurisdictions are split over this application of the felony murder doctrine. A substantial majority apply the doctrine only where the fatal act was committed by a co-felon, but a number of states take the opposite approach, as captured in the case below.[77]

People v. Hernandez, 624 N.E.2d 661 (N.Y. 1993). This appeal raises the question whether a conviction of felony murder under Penal Law §125.25(3) should be sustained where the homicide victim, a police officer, was shot not by one of the defendants but by a fellow officer during a gun battle following defendants' attempted robbery. . . . Defendants Santana and Hernandez conspired to ambush and rob a man who was coming to a New York City apartment building to buy drugs. The plan was to have Santana lure him into the building stairwell where Hernandez waited with a gun. In fact, the man was an undercover State Trooper, wearing a transmitter, and backed up by fellow officers. Once the Trooper was inside the building, Hernandez accosted him and pointed a gun at his head. A fight ensued during which the officer announced that he was a policeman, pulled out his service revolver and began firing. In the confusion, Hernandez, still armed, ran from the building into a courtyard where he encountered members of the police back-up unit. They ordered him to halt. Instead, he aimed his gun at one of the officers and moved toward him. The officers began firing, and one, Trooper Joseph Aversa, was fatally shot in the head. . . . The evidence at trial did not establish who killed Aversa, but the People concede that it effectively eliminated the possibility that either defendant was the shooter. . . .

Some 30 years ago, this Court affirmed the dismissal of a felony murder charge on the grounds that neither the defendant nor a cofelon had fired the weapon that caused the deaths. *See* People v. Wood, 167 N.E.2d 736 (N.Y. 1960). . . . At the time, the relevant provision of [our] former Penal Law defined murder in the first degree as "[t]he killing of a human being . . . by a person engaged in the commission of, or in an attempt to commit a felony." . . . In 1965, the Legislature revised the felony murder statute by removing th[at] language that had been dispositive in *Wood* and replacing it with a provision holding a person culpable for felony murder when, during the commission of an enumerated felony or attempt, either the defendant or an accomplice "causes the death of a person other than one of the participants." Thus, this appeal raises the question of whether *Wood* remains good law despite the recasting of the Penal Law. . . .

The People . . . premise their argument on the established construction of the term "causes the death," which . . . has been construed to mean that homicide is properly charged when the defendant's culpable act is "a sufficiently direct cause" of the death so that the fatal result was reasonably foreseeable. In the People's view the evidence here meets that standard. They contend that it was highly foreseeable that someone would be killed in a shootout when Hernandez refused to put down his gun and instead persisted in threatening the life of one of the back-up officers. . . .

In response, defendants assert that *People v. Wood,* though decided on narrow statutory grounds, states a rule that was followed for centuries at common law and one that has been embraced by a significant number of jurisdictions. . . . Some courts have held that when the victim or a police officer or a bystander shoots and kills, it cannot be said that the killing was in furtherance of a common criminal objective. Others have concluded that under such circumstances the necessary malice or intent is missing. . . . Still other courts have . . . asserted that no deterrence value attaches when the felon is not the person immediately responsible for the death, or have contended that an expansive felony murder rule might unreasonably hold the felons responsible for the acts of others—for instance, when an unarmed felon is fleeing the scene and a bystander is hit by the bad aim of the armed victim.

. . . Defendants' position . . . assumes that the Legislature intended an unusually narrow construction of the word "causes" even though New York homicide decisions had defined causality more expansively. . . . The Legislature could easily have written . . . the limitation endorsed by defendants—as it did [when specifying that the felony murder doctrine in our state does not apply] to the death of a cofelon—but it chose not to do so. [As to] the relevant common law . . . [v]ariations on the felony murder doctrine were widespread in American jurisprudence, with liability turning on such factors as whether the victim was one of the felons, whether the felons initiated the gun battle and whether the deceased had been used as a shield by defendant.

. . . Unlike defendants and those courts adopting the so-called agency theory, we believe New York's view of causality, based on a proximate cause theory, to be consistent with fundamental principles of criminal law. Advocates of the agency theory suggest that no culpable party has the requisite *mens rea* when a nonparticipant is the shooter. We disagree. The basic tenet of felony murder liability is that . . . the presence or absence of the requisite *mens rea* is an issue turning on whether the felon is acting in furtherance of the underlying crime at the time of the homicide, not on the proximity or attenuation of the death resulting from the felon's acts. Whether the death is an immediate result or an attenuated one, the necessary *mens rea* is present if the causal act is part of the felonious conduct.

No more persuasive is the argument that the proximate cause view will extend criminal liability unreasonably. . . . New York law is clear that felony murder does not embrace any killing that is coincidental with the felony but instead is limited to those deaths caused by one of the felons in furtherance of their crime. [C]riminal liability will adhere only when the felons' acts are a sufficiently direct cause of the death. When the intervening acts of another party are supervening or unforeseeable, the necessary causal chain is broken, and there is no liability for the felons. Where a victim, a police officer or other third party shoots and kills, the prosecution faces a significant obstacle in proving beyond a reasonable doubt to a jury that the felons should be held responsible for causing the death. . . .

In short, our established common-law rules governing determinations of causality . . . provide adequate boundaries to felony murder liability. The language of Penal Law §125.25(3) evinces the Legislature's desire to extend liability broadly to those who commit serious crimes in ways that endanger the lives of others. That other States choose more narrow approaches is of no moment to our statutory scheme. Our Legislature has chosen not to write those limitations into our law, and we are bound by that legislative determination.

. . . . [I]t was highly foreseeable that when Hernandez continued toward the officer with his gun drawn that shots would be fired and someone might be hit. Foreseeability does not mean that the result must be the most likely event. Undoubtedly, in planning the robbery, defendants did not anticipate that their victim would be a State Trooper or that a back-up unit would be on the scene. Yet, it was foreseeable that police would try to thwart crime, and Hernandez was aware that police were on the scene at the point he resisted arrest and remained armed. [I]t is simply implausible for defendants to claim that defendants could not have foreseen a bullet going astray when Hernandez provoked a gun battle outside a residential building in an urban area.

7. Systemic Consequences: Does Felony Murder Doctrine Matter? The discussion to this point tees up an important practical question. "For the vast majority of cases," the MPC drafters observed, "it is probably true that homicide occurring during the commission or attempted commission of a felony is murder independent of the felony-murder rule." Model Penal Code and Commentaries §210.2 cmt. 6 at 37. Data substantiating this assertion are hard to come by. But its reasoning is straightforward: "If a defendant undertakes a dangerous felony, he probably has exhibited the extreme recklessness or malice aforethought necessary for a conviction of murder." If the felony murder rule is in practice (if not in form) tracking other existing criminal doctrines imposing homicide liability, up to and including murder, how much of a difference does the rule actually make in the world? One answer, suggested by the MPC drafters, is "not very much."[78]

And yet, focusing solely on the similarity among fact patterns that might support convictions under these doctrines fails to account for the way most convictions are produced: through plea bargaining. We will discuss plea bargaining at length in Chapter Nine. For now, it is enough to observe that a prosecutor can substantially increase her plea bargaining leverage by raising the defendant's potential sentence, his odds of conviction, or both. The felony murder rule does both. As the Supreme Court has explained in a different context, "[t]he purpose and obvious effect of doing away with the requirement of a guilty intent is to ease the prosecution's path to conviction." Morissette v. United States, 342 U.S. 246, 263 (1952). In the felony murder context, that glide path typically runs to the highest homicide charge available. Moreover, even when felony murder doctrine is cabined to fact patterns involving negligent, reckless, or grossly reckless conduct, it operates differently from unintentional homicide doctrine. In Professor Binder's words, if the felony murder doctrine approximates negligence liability, it does so by creating "a *per se* negligence rule" that replaces "a discretionary negligence standard" under which the task of assessing the substantiality and unjustifiability of risk is left to the jury's discretionary judgment. Put more simply, the felony murder doctrine relieves the prosecution of the burden of proving *to the jury* that the defendant acted recklessly or negligently in causing a death. This makes it easier to secure a conviction, potentially for a very high sentence, and thus easier to extract a guilty plea.[79]

Taking these various dynamics together, the doctrine opens up the possibility for prosecutorial tactics like those deployed against a group of teenagers charged with first-degree murder in Illinois in 2008. According to newspaper reports, this group of teenagers broke into a house planning to steal the owner's guns. As the reports continue, the teenagers took special care to make sure no one would get hurt during the burglary, which they "had meticulously planned."

> They knew the homeowner, who was supposed to be in the hospital that night. . . . To make sure no one was home, they knocked on the door and threw a rock through the window. The coast was clear, so the youngest boys, ages 14, 15 and 16, went in. The 18-year-old [Moore] waited in the car. What the boys didn't know was that a friend of the homeowner was asleep inside. As the boys crept into the bedroom, he woke up, grabbed a gun from the dresser drawer and fired.[80]

The bullet struck and killed one of the teenagers, a fourteen-year-old named Travis Castle. All three surviving teenagers were charged with Castle's murder under what a local reporter called "a controversial Illinois law known as the felony murder rule," which exposes people to "murder charges if someone dies during the commission of certain felonies—even if the suspect in the underlying crime does not have a murder weapon or was not immediately present when the death occurred." And like the vast majority of criminal defendants, each of the teenagers pled guilty to lesser offenses. The following excerpt, which focuses on the oldest of the three defendants, describes the plea bargaining tactics used in this case, and many others.[81]

Dahleen Glanton, *When the Felony Murder Rule Looms Overhead, A Plea Deal Isn't Always a Lifeline*, Chi. Trib. (Sept. 23, 2019). At the age of 18, Cody Moore had to make the most important decision of his life. He was involved in a residential burglary in which a 14-year-old accomplice was shot and killed. Though Moore waited in the car, he and two other teenagers were charged with first-degree murder in their friend's death.

Initially, prosecutors charged Moore with residential burglary, a suitable penalty for what he did. But they later upped the charge to first-degree murder, setting the stage for a plea agreement that ultimately would land Moore behind bars for a much longer period than the burglary charge allowed.

Moore's case highlights the complicated and unfair practice of overcharging suspects under the Illinois felony murder rule and using it as leverage to alleviate the uncertainty and other costs of trying a case in court. While plea bargains are a fundamental tool within our judicial system, they take on an element of high-pressure bargaining in Illinois when the felony murder rule is applied. Teenagers, in particular, are likely to accept any terms when facing the threat of life in prison. . . . Moore had to weigh the carrot prosecutors were dangling in front of him against the grim future of life behind bars. Would he risk the next 20 years to life without the possibility of parole? Or would he plead guilty to lesser charges of home invasion and involuntary manslaughter in exchange for a sentence of 30 years and possibly be out in 15? He took the deal.

II. LAWFUL VIOLENCE: JUSTIFYING AND EXCUSING HARM

To this point, we have examined scenarios in which the law uniformly treats harming another human being as wrong — or at the very least, in cases of true accidents, as regrettable. But are there scenarios in which the law might actually endorse intentional violence?

As the quotation from Professor David Sklansky opening this chapter suggests, the answer is yes: "We rely on law to sort out good violence from bad." Within the criminal law, "good violence" refers to violence that is deemed *justified.* Justification bars criminal liability because justified conduct is not morally wrongful under the circumstances in which it is committed. It is not blameworthy, and therefore is not punished. But justifications are not the only bases for a defense. Sometimes violence is not "good," and thus not justified, but is nonetheless beyond criminal law's punishment because it is *excused.* As we saw in Chapter Three, with excuses the defendant's harmful act is, in the words of H.L.A. Hart, "something which is deplored, but the psychological state of the agent when he did it exemplified one or more of a variety of conditions which are held to rule out . . . public condemnation and punishment." Excuses thus exculpate the defendant without endorsing his conduct.[82]

In the pages that follow, we will explore the concepts of justification and excuse through the lenses of two settings in which these dividing lines are routinely confronted: self-defense and police use of force. We begin with self-defense.

Parker v. United States

155 A.3d 835 (D.C. 2017)

EASTERLY, J. Tameka Parker appeals her conviction, following a bench trial, for simple assault. She argues that the evidence was insufficient to disprove her claim of self-defense. . . . As there was no basis for the trial court to reject Ms. Parker's claim of self-defense, we reverse.

I. FACTS

Early one evening in June 2014, Ms. Parker walked out of her home where she lived with her three children. She was about to get into a friend's car, when she heard Mr. Powell yell from across the street that he "should go over and smack the shit out of that bitch." When Ms. Parker asked to whom he was speaking, Mr. Powell crossed the street and came onto her property, positioned himself so that he and Ms. Parker were face-to-face, and said, "bitch, you." Mr. Powell's "aggressive" approach indicated to Ms. Parker that "he was trying to fight her," and Mr. Powell asked her "do you want that smoke," a question Ms. Parker understood as a threat to shoot her.

Mr. Powell's mother crossed the street with him, and several of his brothers joined them on Ms. Parker's property; the family surrounded her friend's car and yelled insults at Ms. Parker. They called her a "dirty bitch" and accused her of being "hot," i.e., "working with the police." "There were a lot of them," and Ms. Parker "feared for her life."

When he was less than two feet away from her, Mr. Powell spit in her face. Ms. Parker . . . "really was scared" once Mr. Powell spit on her, because she "didn't know what he was going to do next." She spit back.

At about that time, unbeknownst to Ms. Parker, a police officer arrived. While sitting in his car, the officer saw Mr. Powell face-to-face with Ms. Parker, surrounded by approximately ten people, all standing near a car and yelling at each other. The officer could not hear what they were saying, but he saw Ms. Parker spit on Mr. Powell. When he spoke to her at the scene, she explained (because the officer had not seen the entire encounter and in particular, had not seen Mr. Powell spit on Ms. Parker) "that she wouldn't just spit on him for no reason, that he spit on her first." The officer then arrested Ms. Parker for simple assault.

At trial, . . . Ms. Parker testified . . . that she spit on Mr. Powell but claimed she was acting in self-defense. . . . Ms. Parker repeatedly testified that she was afraid of Mr. Powell. On direct, Ms. Parker was asked what she believed was going to happen at the time she spat back at Mr. Powell and she said, "I thought he was going to hit me, honestly that was the next thing. I was fearing for my life. I am scared for my life, like I didn't know what they were going to do." On cross-examination, she specifically denied being angry: "I wasn't angry. I was scared for my life. I was more scared than anything." . . .

The government argued in closing that . . . the evidence established that Ms. Parker was "very angry," "indignant," and "offended by what she states that the complainant did to her." The government further asserted that Ms. Parker had not "expressed a fear of imminent bodily injury. What she has expressed is being angry at this complainant and not liking this complainant." . . .

The trial court . . . acknowledged that "every person has the right to use a reasonable amount of force in self-defense if one, she actually believes she is in imminent danger of bodily harm and if two, she has reasonable grounds for that belief." The court . . . nonetheless concluded that Ms. Parker's self-defense claim failed because of what it perceived to be Ms. Parker's motive in responding to Mr. Powell:

> It is eminently reasonable that . . . she would feel herself in imminent danger and I find that she did, but in order for self-defense to apply she has to use a reasonable amount of force in self-defense. Using a reasonable amount of force is not because she is angry or indignant or outraged or because of injustice . . . . [T]he government has proven on this record that the spitting occurred not for reasons of self-defense but for those other reasons. . . . I directly asked, why did you spit on him. [She replied:] I spit in his face because he came on my property and he spit on me first and there is street justice in that. That is fine in a sense, . . . but it is not fine when it comes to the law of the District of Columbia . . . .

The court concluded that "for all these reasons the government had proved beyond a reasonable doubt that Ms. Parker committed the offense of simple assault and did not spit on Mr. Powell as an act of self-defense."

II. ANALYSIS

When a defendant "presents any evidence that she acted in self-defense," the government assumes the burden of proving, beyond a reasonable doubt, that she did not. *See* Williams (Shirley) v. United States, 90 A.3d 1124, 1128 (D.C. 2014). . . . As a preliminary matter, we question whether the record supports the court's finding that Ms. Parker acted out of a purely retributive motive. . . . Instead, at most, the evidence supports only a determination that Ms. Parker was motivated to spit on Mr. Powell by a mixture of fear and anger.[15]

---

15. Evidence that a defendant has mixed emotions, however, will not defeat a claim of self-defense. . . . [T]he proper inquiry is whether the defendant believed she was in imminent danger, not whether she was or was not fearful. Moreover, as humans rarely experience one emotion at a time, it is only to be expected that, in a situation where a person might need to act in self-defense, she will experience some mix of fear and anger or indignation or vindictiveness. Thus, if the government could carry its burden to disprove a claim of self-defense simply by establishing that a defendant who actually and reasonably believed she was in imminent danger also experienced other emotions or had mixed motives, self-defense claims would be severely curtailed, if not eliminated entirely.

We need not decide whether the trial court made a factfinding error, however, because the trial court's focus on motive begs a more fundamental question of law: if the government fails to disprove that a defendant reasonably believed that she was in imminent danger of bodily harm, can it still carry its burden to rebut a claim of self-defense by showing that there was another motive guiding the defendant's action? For the reasons discussed below, we conclude that . . . it cannot.

"The essence of the self-defense situation is a reasonable and bona fide belief of the imminence of bodily harm."[16] Kinard v. United States, 96 F.2d 522, 526 (D.C. Cir. 1938). . . . If there is evidence that the defendant actually and reasonably believed herself to be in imminent danger of bodily harm . . . the inquiry proceeds to the amount of force employed. . . . "[I]n a situation where the evidence establishes that self-defense would otherwise be justified," the government can rebut a self-defense claim only if it proves that a defendant used "excessive force." Williams v. United States, 90 A.3d 1124, 1128 (D.C. 2014). But distinguishing what constitutes excessive force from a "reasonable amount of force" is not a wholly objective inquiry; the factfinder must take into account evidence of the defendant's mental state under the circumstances.

> The claim of self-defense is not necessarily defeated if, for example, more knife blows than would have seemed necessary in cold blood are struck in the heat of passion generated by the unsought altercation. A belief which may be unreasonable in cold blood may be actually and reasonably entertained in the heat of passion.

Inge v. United States, 356 F.2d 345, 348 (D.C. Cir. 1966). The question is thus whether the defendant's use of force is "a proportionate reaction to the threat that she perceived" while in the heat of the moment. *Ewell*, 72 A.3d at 130. . . .

Under this construct—where the first inquiry is whether a defendant actually and reasonably believed she was in imminent danger of bodily harm and the second inquiry is whether, taking this belief into account, she employed excessive force—motive is not an additional, separate consideration. If the government has not disproved that a defendant actually and reasonably believed she was in imminent danger of bodily harm, we accept that she acted out of that belief. . . . [C]laims of self-defense rise or fall on

---

16. The requisite level of reasonably perceived danger is different, depending on whether the defendant employed deadly or nondeadly force: "where an accused, claiming self-defense, uses deadly force, he must—at the time of the incident—actually believe and reasonably believe that he is in imminent peril of death or serious bodily harm; whereas one utilizing nondeadly force must show that he reasonably believed that some harm was imminent." Ewell v. United States, 72 A.3d 127, 131 (D.C. 2013). [Editor's Note: Deadly force is generally defined as force that creates a substantial risk of death or serious bodily harm, whether or not that risk materializes.]

determinations of whether the defendant reasonably believed herself to be in imminent danger of bodily harm or used excessive force. . . .

In Ms. Parker's case, the trial court as the factfinder concluded that Ms. Parker actually and reasonably believed she was in imminent danger of bodily harm from Mr. Powell. At that point the only question left for the trial court was whether Ms. Parker had employed excessive force. Ms. Parker obviously did not use more force than was reasonable under the circumstances. Thus the court should have determined that Ms. Parker acted in self-defense and acquitted her of assault. . . .

FERREN, J., concurring. . . . Our dissenting colleague [argues] that despite an unequivocal, conclusive finding that appellant believed herself to be in imminent danger of bodily harm . . . the government can disprove the defense by satisfying the court that an additional motive negated her belief, and that the force employed was weak, not defensive. . . . [T]he dissent relies . . . on appellant's spitting—a "predictably ineffectual," "tit-for-tat act of retaliation"—to . . . [argue] that appellant did not "actually" and "reasonably" believe that the weak force used—her spitting—would be enough to protect her against "imminent bodily harm."

. . . I cannot agree that appellant's spitting can disqualify her from claiming self-defense because of its presumed weakness as a response to the neighbor who spit at her first. Appellant's response was "a proportionate reaction to the threat that she perceived." Ewell v. United States, 72 A.3d 127, 130 (D.C. 2013). . . . I cannot believe . . . that ineffectual force can be deemed unreasonable simply because it is too lame rather than excessive. . . . [I]f appellant had whacked her assailant rather than spit on him, there would have been little, if any, basis for questioning whether a self-defense instruction . . . was available in this case. Indeed, our dissenting colleague seems to agree. But apparently the trial court rejected self-defense not because appellant lacked the belief of imminent bodily harm required to justify self-defense but, at least in part, because the court believed that the defensive response was too lame—a curious concern because the forbidden response, unreasonable force, is force too violent, not too weak . . . .

THOMPSON, J., dissenting. . . . [W]hat was missing each time from appellant's explanation of why she spit on Powell was any statement to the effect that she spit on him in an effort to protect herself from harm. Appellant had every opportunity to respond, "I spit on Powell to make him and his family go away" or "to make them stop bothering me," or something to that effect, but she gave no such response. . . . Nor did appellant describe her act of spitting on Powell as a merely reflexive action. . . .

[The trial] court found that appellant's motive in spitting on Powell was to effect "street justice" (i.e., retribution, revenge, or retaliation), and was not at all to defend herself. . . . [It further] reasoned that appellant could not have reasonably thought that her spitting at Powell would extricate her from danger, i.e., cause Powell and his family to leave her alone.[6] . . .

In numerous cases involving claims of self-defense, this court has said the following or its equivalent: "One who is defending against an assault charge, who is claiming self-defense, *must have honestly and reasonably believed* that he was in imminent peril of death or serious bodily harm, and *that his response was necessary to save himself.*" Travers v. United States, 124 A.3d 634, 639 (2015). [The emphasized language indicates that a] person acts *in self-defense* only when her action is an effort to save or protect herself or to fend off harm. . . . And while it may be difficult to prove that "there was another motive guiding the defendant's action," *ante,* if the credited evidence proves that such other motive(s) alone, and not defense of self, was the defendant's reason for using force, the government will have met its burden to rebut the defendant's claim of self-defense. . . .

[I]n focusing only on whether the defendant feared imminent bodily harm and whether she used excessive force, the majority opinion gives short shrift to the rule that, even as to non-deadly force, "the right of self-defense is a law of necessity, arising only when the necessity begins, and equally ends with the necessity." Harper v. United States, 608 A.2d 152, 154 (D.C. 1992). [T]he opinion does damage to the principle that none of us is entitled to "take redress into our own hands." State v. Ouellette, 37 A.3d 921, 926 n.2 (Me. 2012). [T]he majority's holding [offers] a new pronouncement that takes advantage of the unusual facts of this case to abandon the principle that a valid claim of self-defense also requires *a belief by the defendant that the force she used was necessary to protect herself* from imminent danger. I do not understand on what authority my colleagues believe they are free to renounce that principle.

———————————

The deliberate use of force against another person, including force as minimal as spitting, is usually a crime. If fatal, the crime is homicide. At the other end of the spectrum, it could be a relatively minor offense, like the misdemeanor simple assault at issue in *Parker.* In either scenario, however, the doctrine of *self-defense* precludes criminal liability when an individual

---

6. I suspect the trial judge would have had no trouble concluding that appellant had acted in self-defense if she had, for example, grabbed a stick and brandished it at Powell and his family members, or if she had pulled out a can of pepper spray and let them have it. Both of those actions are, at least arguably, more aggressive actions than spitting, and our public policy surely is not to encourage an escalation of aggressive conduct. But, as a policy matter reflected in the common law, we tolerate a victim's violent actions designed to stop a first aggressor's assaultive action, and do not tolerate a victim's violent actions that amount to nothing more than tit-for-tat acts of retaliation . . . .

uses force to protect herself against harm threatened by someone else. Self-defense is a staple of criminal litigation. According to one famous study of criminal courts in Chicago, roughly 30 percent of all defendants contesting charges for crimes of violence invoke self-defense.[*] Analogous defenses exist when force is used to protect another person or, in some cases, property.[83]

What is the legal basis for this extraordinary privilege to use violence against an attacker? Consider two explanations. The first is a *rights-based account*: Every person has a right to bodily autonomy and an accompanying right to protect that autonomy. The right to use defensive force, on this view, is thus *pre-political* in the sense that, to quote Blackstone, it is a "primary law of nature" that precedes the formation of political society and cannot be "taken away by the law of society." Note that this account challenges Max Weber's idea, introduced in Chapter One, that the state has an absolute monopoly on violence. Rather, the rights-based account of self-defense holds that people have a freestanding right to use defensive violence that the state cannot take away.[84]

An alternative account holds firm the state's monopoly on violence. On this view, the state delegates the authority to use defensive force to individuals, who can then use "state force" defensively in certain circumstances. The lawful defender stands in the shoes of the state, so to speak, as something like a temporary police officer. As Professor Alice Ristroph explains, this *state-power account* of self-defense treats the doctrine as a mechanism "by which political institutions share — or refuse to share — their discretionary power, including the power to use violence."[85]

As a descriptive matter, court opinions explaining self-defense sometimes gesture at the rights-based account. But as the remainder of this chapter shows, they also carefully regulate — and at times strictly confine — the circumstances in which defensive force is tolerated. The state, in other words, acts as if its monopoly on violence is indeed absolute, with the permitted (or delegated) domains of violent self-help bounded by the criminal law itself.

The remainder of this section examines those doctrinal bounds. In so doing, we will explore a series of questions that structure self-defense doctrine. First, *why* does the state sometimes permit nonstate actors to use violence at all? Second, *how* does the state decide whose bodily security — or even whose life — to protect when a conflict among multiple people could cause serious harm to any one? Third, in what ways does the state's

---

[*] Most jurisdictions, like the *Parker* court, require the prosecution to prove beyond a reasonable doubt that the defendant was *not* acting in self-defense, although the defendant may first have to point to some evidence indicating that self-defense was plausibly at issue. A minority of jurisdictions, in contrast, treat self-defense as an *affirmative defense* the defendant must prove by a preponderance of the evidence. *See* 1 Barbara E. Bergman et al., *Wharton's Criminal Evidence* §2:10 (15th ed. 2021).

authorization to use violence change when it flows not to a private actor but to an *agent of the state,* as occurs when the police use force against civilians? And finally, under what circumstances does the state *excuse* violence even while recognizing it as wrongful?

A. *Why Permit Defensive Violence? Justification, Necessity, and Imminence*

Understanding defensive force as a limited delegation of the state's own monopoly on violence raises a fundamental paradox that shapes this body of law: Lawful defensive force commonly involves violence that the state itself could not directly inflict.

In part, this is a paradox of process. Consider a person acting in self-defense who kills his aggressor. Viewed as delegated state action, such a killing is akin to a summary execution, inflicting death without any hearing or neutral determination of culpability. Understood as such, it seems a clear denial of due process. A defendant charged with a capital offense is—for good reason—entitled to multiple rounds of judicial review before the state may execute its ultimate sentence. But as the Supreme Court has observed, "The use of deadly force . . . frustrates the interest of the individual, and of society, in judicial determination of guilt and punishment." Tennessee v. Garner, 471 U.S. 1, 9 (1985).

The paradox is substantive as well, as individuals acting in lawful self-defense can use violence in ways forbidden to the state altogether. Indeed, while incarceration can be understood as a *form* of state violence, the Constitution prohibits formal corporal punishment like the body blows permitted under self-defense. *See* Jackson v. Bishop, 404 F.2d 571 (8th Cir. 1968). Likewise, self-defense doctrine licenses deadly force to repel nonfatal attacks, like sexual assault, that cannot legally give rise to a death sentence. *See* Coker v. Georgia, 433 U.S. 584 (1976) (prohibiting capital punishment for rape). And while 23 states have abolished capital punishment altogether, each of them permits individuals to kill an attacking wrongdoer under certain circumstances.

Why does the law allow these anomalies? The basic answer is that defensive force is a *second-best* means of preventing wrongful harm when the *first-best* means of prevention—calling the police or other public safety officials—isn't possible. The premise here is that the law prefers to *prevent* wrongful harm ex ante rather than *punish* it ex post. As we will see in later chapters, the impulse to use the criminal law preventively can lead to expansive doctrines of liability and highly contested forms of "proactive policing." In the context of defensive force, however, preventing a wrongful, potentially fatal attack seems clearly preferable to letting the victim die and punishing the wrongdoer after the fact. As Blackstone puts it, "the future process of law is by no means an adequate remedy for injuries accompanied with force."[86]

Note two important implications of this reasoning. First, to say that the law prefers prevention to punishment is to say that self-defense often operates as a doctrine of *justification*: "what is done is regarded as something which the law does not condemn," and may even regard with "commendation rather than blame." A justification-oriented account of defensive force dominates much of the scholarship and jurisprudence on the doctrine and is the initial focus of the discussion in this chapter. We will also see, though, that it is possible for the doctrine to operate as an excuse, as occurs when the use of defensive violence "is deplored, but the psychological state of the agent when he did it" takes "public condemnation and punishment" off the table.[87]

Second, casting defensive force as a "second-best" mode of protection means that defensive force is justified only when it's truly necessary. This principle of *necessity* drives most of modern self-defense doctrine, which developed before standing police departments existed and thus before official state protection could be summoned for aid. Today, hundreds of thousands of law enforcement officers work in cities and towns across the country. But even still, the police are not omnipresent — and rightly so. Given this reality, defensive force may sometimes be the only way for an individual to avoid victimization.

In what circumstances, then, is defensive force deemed necessary under the criminal law? In large part, self-defense doctrine gives us a temporal answer. Self-defense is authorized only when the threat of violence is *imminent*, meaning, in the words of a leading treatise, "almost immediately forthcoming." Thus, as the *Parker* court tells us, "[t]he essence of the self-defense situation is a reasonable and bona fide belief of the imminence of bodily harm." *Parker*, 155 A.3d at 845. This imminence requirement is the law's way of funneling people toward the law's presumed first-best option of protection, by forcing them to call the police when time permits. But is it *fair* to require people to call the police whenever time would allow? Consider the following cases.[88]

State v. Schroeder

261 N.W.2d 759 (Neb. 1978)

BOSLAUGH, J. . . . Mark Schroeder[] appeals from a sentence . . . for assault with intent to inflict great bodily injury. . . . The assault took place in a cell at the Reformatory Unit near Lincoln, Nebraska. The defendant was confined in the cell with three other prisoners, one of whom was Gary Riggs, the victim.

The defendant was 19 years of age at the time of the offense. Riggs was 24 years of age. Riggs had a reputation among the other prisoners for sex and violence and the defendant was afraid of Riggs. In its brief the State concedes that Riggs had unquestionably placed the defendant in a position of general subservience.

The evidence shows that the defendant and Riggs had been gambling and that the defendant owed Riggs approximately $3,000. Riggs had threatened to make a "punk" out of the defendant by selling the debt to some other prisoner. A punk is defined in the record as a prisoner who commits homosexual acts with other prisoners. . . .

On the day before the incident, the defendant and the other two prisoners in the cell submitted a written request that Riggs be moved to another cell. On the night the assault occurred . . . [t]he defendant testified Riggs said that he might walk in his sleep that night and "collect some of this money I got owed to me tonight."

The defendant went to bed about 10 p.m. but, apparently, was unable to sleep because of what Riggs had said. The defendant got up about 1 a.m., and stabbed Riggs in the back with a [makeshift] knife. Riggs was asleep at the time but awakened when he was stabbed. When Riggs tried to remove the knife from his back, the defendant struck Riggs in the face several times with a metal ashtray. The guard was called and Riggs was taken to the hospital. . . .

[T]he use of deadly force may be justifiable if the actor believes such force is necessary to protect himself against sexual intercourse compelled by force or threat. The defendant's evidence was such that the jury could have found that the defendant believed he would be forced by Riggs to submit to sodomy if he did not kill or disable Riggs that night. . . .

The State . . . contends that the defense was not applicable because there was no specific and imminent threat of injury to the defendant. Riggs was asleep when the defendant stabbed him and Riggs had made no overt act or assault upon the defendant. Section 28-836(1), R.R.S. 1943, provides that the use of force may be justifiable if the actor believes that such force is immediately necessary for the purpose of protecting himself against the use of unlawful force by the other person on the present occasion.

The rule in this state has been that in order to excuse or justify a killing in self-defense the defendant must have reasonably believed that his life was in imminent danger or that he was in imminent danger of suffering great bodily harm. The present statutory requirement is that the actor believe such force is immediately necessary to protect himself against the use of unlawful force by the other person on the present occasion. Although the term "present occasion" may have relaxed somewhat the former requirement of imminent danger, the present statutory requirement is essentially the same requirement as existed prior to the enactment of section 28-836, R.R.S. 1943.

The problem in this case is that there was no evidence to sustain a finding that the defendant could believe an assault was imminent except the threat that Riggs had made before he went to bed. The general rule is that words alone are not sufficient justification for an assault. There is a very real danger in a rule which would legalize preventive assaults involving the use of deadly force where there has been nothing more than threats. We conclude that the trial court did not err in refusing to instruct the jury as requested by the defendant. . . .

CLINTON, J., dissenting. . . . In this case the defendant was faced with a threat by Riggs that he would "collect some of this money I got owed to me tonight." The defendant could not be expected to remain awake all night, every night, waiting for the attack that Riggs had threatened to make. The defendant's evidence here was such that the jury could have found the defendant was justified in believing the use of force was necessary to protect himself against an attack by Riggs "on the present occasion."

   . . . Forcible sodomy is surely a great wrong to the victim. Our statute recognizes the common law rule that one may use deadly force to protect oneself from a forcible sexual assault. The evidence would justify the conclusion and permit the jury to find that defendant could not have waited and protected himself by the use of deadly force. With the weapon which was available to him, he seemingly could not have exercised such deadly force had he waited. . . . That weapon may have been inadequate to protect him had he waited until the actual assault commenced.

   [Opinion of WHITE, J., dissenting, omitted.]

Commonwealth v. Sands, 553 S.E.2d 733 (Va. 2001): A jury convicted the defendant, Victoria Shelton Sands, of the first degree murder of her husband, Thomas Lee Sands. . . . [Thomas severely beat his wife for over a decade, eventually on a daily basis. Victoria repeatedly said she wanted a divorce but Thomas always responded by beating her and threatening to kill her and her family if she ended their relationship. At one point, in July of 1998, he kept her hostage in their residence for three weeks. A month later, Victoria asked her parents for help contacting the police, but soon after her mother spoke with law enforcement, both parents were injured in an automobile accident that sent them to the hospital. The defendant was afraid to take any further action without her parents' support.]

   [On the morning of August 23, 1998,] a neighbor observed the defendant walk out of her kitchen door onto the back porch with a gun in her hand. . . . The defendant's husband . . . followed her onto the back porch where . . . [he] seized the gun that the defendant had been carrying, and . . . fired two shots into the ground near her. . . . Soon thereafter, the defendant's aunt, Sallie Hodges, arrived at the house. . . . Thomas would not allow [Victoria] to leave with Hodges. He kept pacing the floor and pointing his finger at Hodges, while stating, "I'll kill you and your whole family. . . . I've knocked off a few and I can knock off a few more." . . . Around 10:00 p.m., the defendant telephoned Hodges and asked her to come over and get the couple's son. . . . The defendant testified that she wanted her son out of the house because she "sensed" that her husband was going to kill her.

[Later that night, Victoria called her sister-in-law, Angela Shelton, and asked her to come to the house. When Shelton arrived, Victoria pulled up her shirt, revealing serious injuries. She then "started shaking really, really bad, and her eyes got real wild eyed," according to Shelton. Victoria then said, "He's evil. He is gonna kill me." At that point, Victoria ran to retrieve the gun, and went to the bedroom] where she shot her husband five times while he was lying in bed, watching television. . . . After shooting her husband, the defendant walked back to the kitchen, put the gun on a bar, and telephoned "911." . . .

We agree that the defendant reasonably believed that she was in danger of serious bodily harm or death. Nevertheless, . . . [e]ven when viewed in the light most favorable to the defendant, the evidence fails to reveal any overt act by her husband that presented an imminent danger at the time of the shooting. . . . While we do not doubt the defendant's genuine fear for her life or minimize the atrocities inflicted upon her, we cannot point to any evidence of an overt act indicating imminent danger . . . when she shot him five times while he reclined on the bed. . . . Thus, the defendant was not entitled to an instruction on self-defense.

KOONTZ, J., dissenting. In my view, the pattern of brutalizing acts committed upon Sands over the preceding twenty-four hours, coupled with the repeated threats to kill her, [made] a self-defense instruction appropriate. Although the victim was reclining in bed at the moment of the killing, a jury could have concluded that Sands's belief that she nevertheless remained in imminent danger of death or serious bodily harm was reasonable under the circumstances. [T]he victim "would intermittently watch television in the bedroom for short periods of time, but always returned to the assault upon his wife." There is no evidence that this pattern would not continue. . . .

Ha v. State, 892 P.2d 184 (Alaska Ct. App. 1995): [The defendant, Xi Van Ha, immigrated from Vietnam and worked as a fisherman. One night, while socializing, he encountered Buu Van Truong, who was described as "drunk" and as having "a reputation for violence." As the night went on, Buu began attacking Ha, first with his fists and then with a hammer, while screaming, "I'm going to kill you, and I will strike you until you die!" Another fisherman managed to disarm Buu and escort Ha away safely.] That night, Ha could not sleep. He feared that Buu was bound to return and kill him as he had promised. . . . He lay awake on his bunk throughout the night, with [a] rifle at his side, "the voice of Mr. Buu . . . resounding in his ears." . . .

Shortly after noon [the next day], Ha went to where he believed Buu was working. When he discovered that Buu was not there, Ha sat down for a while to wait for him. . . . Ha spotted Buu returning from a grocery store, carrying a bag of groceries. . . . Ha pulled out his rifle and ran towards Buu from behind. Ha repeatedly shot Buu in the back, firing the rifle thirteen times until he had emptied the weapon of ammunition. Buu . . . died immediately. . . . Ha was indicted and tried for first-degree murder. . . .

. . . Ha argues that, because of his cultural background and his poor command of English, he felt that it would be useless to go to the police for help and that he had "no viable alternatives" to killing Buu. [But] Ha had ample opportunity to inform others of his conflict with Buu and to seek their assistance. . . . [E]ven assuming that Ha believed it would be pointless to speak with any of these people about Buu's threats, this does nothing to establish that Buu posed an imminent danger to Ha or that Ha could have reasonably believed that Buu posed such a danger. . . . Ha also appears to argue that Vietnamese culture teaches that all police are corrupt, that one can expect no help from the authorities, and that people must take the law into their own hands to resolve personal disputes. Assuming for purposes of argument that Ha's characterization of Vietnamese culture is accurate . . . , this still does not establish that Ha reasonably believed that Buu posed an imminent danger to him. To the extent that Ha might be arguing that the law of self-defense should make exceptions for people whose culture encourages vendettas, killings to assuage personal honor, or preemptive killings to forestall future harm, we reject Ha's argument. . . .

NOTES AND QUESTIONS

1. Imminent Threats vs. Imminent Responses. The three cases above each entails what one might call a "preemptive strike" against a genuinely dangerous aggressor. Could such action ever be justified, given the imminence requirement reaffirmed in each opinion? The answer may turn on whether the requirement is "couched in terms of the immediate *need to use force,*" as it is described in some states, or instead as focusing on "the threat of imminent *attack* by another," the more common statutory and doctrinal framing. *State v. Buggs,* 806 P.2d 1381, 1384 (Ariz. Ct. App. 1990). In *State v. Buggs,* the Arizona Court of Appeals explored the subtle but potentially significant difference between these two approaches with this hypothetical:

Suppose A kidnaps and confines D with the announced intention of killing him one week later. D has an opportunity to kill A and escape each morning as A brings him his daily ration. Taken literally, the *imminent* [threat] requirement would prevent D from using deadly force in self-defense until A is standing over him with a knife [at the end of the week], but that outcome seems inappropriate. The proper inquiry is not the immediacy of the threat but the immediacy of the response necessary in defense. If a threatened harm is such that it cannot be avoided if the intended victim waits until the last moment, the principle of self-defense must permit him to act earlier—as early as is required to defend himself effectively.

Id. Is this what the *Schroeder* dissent had in mind when arguing that Schroeder's "weapon may have been inadequate to protect him had he waited until the actual assault commenced"?

Ultimately, it is unclear this difference in framing amounts to "any practical distinction in the application of the law," as the *Buggs* court itself observed. *Id.* In that case, the defendant claimed he faced an imminent threat after being assaulted at a bar by men he believed to be members of the Crips gang. Immediately following the assault, he went into an alley near the bar, armed himself with a gun, and returned to the bar's parking lot where he opened fire on the men who had just attacked him. When asked why he acted this way, he said: "Because I know the Crips, I know what they do. You have to get them before they get you. . . . [T]hey all holding a gun. So, you want to stay alive the best thing to do is get them when you see them." Rejecting this argument, the court held that "[t]he defendant's action was not immediately necessary to prevent the harm he feared." *Id.*

> While we agree that a victim's past acts and reputation for violence will often be relevant on the question of the reasonableness of a defendant's use of force in self-defense, it would be inappropriate in a case such as this to dispense with or dilute the requirement that one may resort to deadly force only if it is necessary to prevent immediate harm. The defendant's "self-defense" in this case was nothing other than a "preemptive strike" against the men he feared. While there may be some circumstances imaginable that would allow for a defense based on that concept, this case does not present them.

Id. at 1385.

> *2. Necessity Without Imminence?* Note some common threads that run through *Schroeder, Sands, Ha,* and *Buggs.* First, the defendants in all four cases were *technically* able to alert the authorities—the police or a prison guard—to the threat, in the sense that they had the time and means to do so. None of them faced a threat like an "uplifted knife," which makes "[d]etached reflection" impossible. Brown v. United States, 256 U.S. 335, 343 (1921). And yet, each defendant nonetheless faced real—some might say overwhelming—obstacles to seeking help and preventing the harm they faced. And crucially, those obstacles look different when viewed from the perspectives and experiences of people who hold less power in American society.

A legal system with insufficient awareness of or regard for those perspectives may not fully appreciate just how substantial the obstacles may have been. Sometimes, this blind spot can influence the law's assessment of how much risk of harm people must assume before they can use defensive force. Consider that in *Schroeder*, *Sands*, and *Buggs*, the courts essentially tell the defendants to wait until the risk of death at the hands of more powerful assailants materializes. Criticizing this implicit admonition to face one's fears head on, Professor Cynthia Gillespie argues that the law "over many centuries has come to embody masculine assumptions about the circumstances that entitle a person to act in self-defense."[89]

Beyond assumptions of masculinity, the doctrine also has clear assumptions about the role of police in society. Adopting a "police-centric" view of criminal law, the premise in much of self-defense doctrine is that calling the police is *good* and *preferred*—indeed, *required*. What happens, then, to people who, perhaps with good reason, don't feel they can rely upon the police for help? Is the "first-best" option of calling the police something we ought to demand of these defendants? Likewise, what if the state is unable or unwilling to protect its citizens from danger, as the materials in the introduction to this chapter suggest may be the case in many communities across the country?

Pushing back on the suggestion that such considerations ought to make a difference, Professor Fiona Leverick argues that the imminence requirement serves a purpose beyond funneling people toward law enforcement assistance.

> It also serves to restrict the availability of self-defence to situations where the threatened harm is likely actually to materialize. If a threat of harm is not imminent, it is more difficult to know with any degree of certainty whether the harm would have occurred and whether the accused could have saved her life *simply by doing nothing* (and thus preserving the life of the potential aggressor). By requiring imminence of harm, the law tries to ensure that the defensive response of the accused was genuinely necessary, thus avoiding the killing of an aggressor wherever this is reasonably possible.[90]

In other words, perhaps Thomas Sands never would have killed Victoria. Perhaps the prison authorities—who apparently ignored Schroeder's request to move Riggs to a different cell—would have prevented Riggs from hurting Schroeder. Or maybe Riggs would have decided not to carry out his threatened rape. Should the law require Sands and Schroeder to refrain from striking first because their aggressors *might* not have ever carried out their threats?

In the end, regardless of how you answer these questions, what's important to see is that these *are* the questions self-defense law is resolving in each of these cases. Through the answers it gives, the law determines who is worthy of the right to claim protection. The question here arises in the context of the imminence requirement, the validity of which has been described by some as the "central debate in the theory of self-defense." But as we will see, determining who ought to survive a violent encounter is something the doctrine of self-defense does time and again.[91]

B.   Deciding Whom to Protect

As the preceding discussion of the imminence requirement suggests, the law of self-defense frequently decides who deserves protection when violence looms—and, by implication, who bears the risk of potentially deadly force. Put more bluntly, self-defense doctrine often determines who should live and who should die, or suffer some other woeful fate. That choice is inescapably fraught. It is also inevitably made against the backdrop of sociological power structures and systemic biases that inform how different lives are valued, and thus which lives matter most when violence erupts. What is more, reflecting these same social influences, the law sometimes elevates the defender's dignity, property rights, or sexual autonomy above the aggressor's right to life.

Beyond the imminence cases discussed above, three doctrinal corollaries to the general self-defense rule confront these vexing issues: the initial-aggressor doctrine, the retreat doctrine, and the castle doctrine. This section explores these three doctrines in turn. But first we consider some supposedly "easy" cases, in which the right to self-defense (including deadly self-defense) is firmly established, in order to understand why the law ever chooses a defender's interests over the aggressor's life.

1.   The "Easy" Cases

Consider the following "easy" cases of deadly self-defense.

1. **Gunslinger Aggressor:** A pulls a gun from his waistband and says he will kill D. D draws his own gun and fatally shoots A.
2. **Child Aggressor:** A, an eight-year-old child, pulls a gun from his waistband and says he will kill D. D draws his own gun and fatally shoots A.
3. **Sexual Aggressor:** A kidnaps D and tells D he will not let D leave until D has sex with him. D draws a gun and fatally shoots A.

Most, if not all, jurisdictions would hold the use of defensive force lawful in each of these three cases. But why? If we assume human lives are of equal value, necessity alone cannot answer this question because it cannot explain why the defender is justified in taking the aggressor's life. Put another way, necessity tells us why the defender can use force instead of relying on the state to provide safety *if* the aggressor's life may indeed be taken at all. But it doesn't tell us *why* the aggressor's life may be taken in the first place. Large literatures explore this question, with answers tracking two familiar lines first discussed in Chapter Two—one focused on rights, the other on deterrence.[92]

A rights-based account of self-defense justifies the decision to elevate the defender's interests over the aggressor's by invoking the idea of *forfeiture*. The starting premise here is that all individuals possess a right to life that is self-evident, fundamental, and worthy of respect to the extent possible. The theory of forfeiture explains when that right gives way by focusing on the aggressor's "unjust threat to the life of another that cannot be avoided by any reasonable means." As Professor Fiona Leverick explains, by infringing the fundamental rights of someone else, the aggressor "temporarily forfeits her [own] right to life." Note, though, that the temporary nature of forfeiture raises questions over when, if ever, the aggressor might see her right to life restored, rendering a subsequent use of force by the initial defender a violation of the aggressor's rights. These issues inform the initial-aggressor doctrine discussed below.[93]

In contrast to a rights-based account, one can also understand self-defense in consequentialist terms. On this view, the doctrine deters violent crime and reduces the overall amount of suffering in society. The idea here is simple. As Professor Richard Brandt writes, "awareness by a potential aggressor that force against him is legitimate is itself a deterrent factor" because he knows his violent aggression could end in his own state-sanctioned death. Notice that this theory is also an empirical one—either self-defense makes the world less violent or it doesn't. Unfortunately, we have little evidence in either direction. Nor is the idea obviously correct. On the one hand, surely the prospect of deadly defensive force deters *some* would-be aggressors. On the other hand, it might encourage some aggressors to use greater force than they otherwise would have in order to overwhelm the victim before he can defend himself. The most we can say is that it's possible authorizing self-defense reduces overall societal violence and that, if it does, it may be justified on consequentialist grounds. This is not to say, however, that the broadest imaginable authorization would be best. Indeed, we will soon examine a body of empirical research suggesting that extending the justification too far causes more violence than it prevents.[94]

The forfeiture and deterrence theories undergird self-defense doctrine. But do they fully answer the "easy" cases? The first case, the Gunslinger Aggressor, seems straightforward: the aggressor poses an unjust threat to the defender's life and so temporarily forfeits his own right to life; likewise, permitting defensive force against him could deter others like him from committing similar acts. The other cases, though, present enduring challenges.

Consider the Child Aggressor. Children are generally not legally responsible for their actions. How, then, can we say the child forfeited her right to life by drawing a gun? One response, Professor Leverick suggests, might be that "forfeiture is based not on fault but on the *conduct* of the aggressor." Is this satisfying? At the same time, children are likely not deterrable by the threat of defensive force because "their immaturity, recklessness, and impetuosity [all] make them less likely to consider potential" consequences of their actions. Miller v. Alabama, 567 U.S. 460, 472 (2012). Reflecting these difficulties, some argue that killing the Child Aggressor is *not* justified but instead is merely excused.[95]

Finally, the Sexual Aggressor case is challenging because the aggressor has not threatened to *kill* his victim.* As noted earlier, the Constitution holds "that a sentence of death is grossly disproportionate and excessive punishment for the crime of rape and is therefore forbidden by the Eighth Amendment as cruel and unusual punishment." Coker v. Georgia, 433 U.S. 584, 592 (1977). In the language of the forfeiture theory, one might argue that the same holds true with respect to deadly defensive force, insofar as the Sexual Aggressor has not threatened to extinguish someone's life. Of course, this conclusion is not self-evident, as one could view rape as a denial of humanity similar in meaning — and culpability, for forfeiture purposes — to a threat to life.[96]

The point in raising these questions is not to suggest that the doctrinal answers to these easy cases are wrong (or that they are right). Rather, it is simply to observe that even in the easiest cases, self-defense doctrine confronts, and resolves, hard questions. Those questions get harder once we move beyond the easy cases to consider a trio of circumstances in which American jurisdictions are sharply divided over who deserves the law's protection when violence erupts.

2.   Who Caused the Necessity?

The easy cases above all involve an innocent defendant who uses force to stop an entirely unexpected attack. But sometimes the defendant plays some part, even a minor one, in contributing to the situation in which defensive force is used. In these cases, the law must decide whether and when the defendant's contribution to the trouble might strip away her right to lawful self-defense. At the same time, it must determine whether and when a person who has lost the right to protect his own life may recover it. In practice, these questions turn many self-defense cases into what Professor Margaret

---

* Most self-defense statutes authorize deadly defensive force against a threat of serious bodily harm, including threats of rape, which are also sometimes expressly enumerated as grounds for deadly defensive force. *See, e.g.,* Ala. Code §13A-3-23(a)(3); Del. Code Ann. tit. 11 §464(c); *see also* Model Penal Code §3.04(2)(b).

Raymond describes as "a dance of shifting privileges, in which each actor can in turn acquire and lose the right to respond with force to unlawful force exerted against him." In this section, we explore three related concepts the law employs to sort and resolve these cases, the outcomes of which vary widely from state to state.[97]

a.   Initial Aggression

The initial-aggressor doctrine follows directly from basic principles of self-defense. If one person wrongfully attacks another, the person being attacked can respond with force. That force is justified self-defense and therefore lawful. A necessary corollary of this rule is that the *initial aggressor*, now facing *lawful* force, has no right to use defensive force in response. The key becomes identifying who the initial aggressor is in any given conflict. As the following case and notes show, this is not always clear. There are also circumstances in which an initial aggressor may *recover* the right to self-defense, as the following opinion also explores. (Note that while this case arose from the military court system, ordinary criminal law concepts apply.)

United States v. Behenna

71 M.J. 228 (C.A.A.F. 2012)

STUCKY, J. [First Lieutenant Michael Behenna was found guilty of murder and sentenced to dismissal from the military, twenty-five years of confinement, and forfeiture of all pay and allowances.] We granted review . . . to determine whether the military judge provided complete and accurate self-defense instructions . . . . We hold that, although the military judge's instruction on escalation was erroneous, it was harmless beyond a reasonable doubt because escalation was not in issue. Moreover, contrary to Appellant's arguments, withdrawal also was not in issue. . . .

I.

In September 2007, Appellant was assigned to Bayji, Iraq, an area north of Baghdad. . . . During his deployment, Appellant learned of information linking Ali Mansur, the deceased in this case, to a group . . . believed to be responsible for attacks on Coalition Forces. . . .

On April 21, Appellant's platoon was patrolling Salaam Village . . . [when] an explosive device was detonated near the vehicles. Appellant saw several individuals in his platoon injured or killed by the blast. A draft intelligence information report issued on April 27 stated that Mansur was likely a member of the group that was operating out of Salaam Village. After the report was issued, Mansur was apprehended for interrogation . . . .

Appellant read the report of Mansur's interrogation and only found information regarding Mansur's job and background . . . . Appellant asked that Mansur be reinterrogated based on his belief that Mansur had information on insurgents operating out of Salaam Village, who Appellant believed were responsible for the April 21 attack. Appellant did not participate in the second interrogation, and although Mansur provided information willingly, the interrogator told Appellant that Mansur was being deceptive.

After the second interrogation, Appellant was ordered to return Mansur to [a nearby village]. Appellant continued to believe that Mansur had information regarding the April 21 attack and the group operating out of Salaam Village . . . . On the day that Mansur was to be released, Appellant went with an interpreter [referred to by the parties as Harry] to retrieve Mansur from his cell. Appellant told Mansur, "I'm going to talk to you later on today. There is [sic] three pieces of information that I want from you. If I don't get that information today, you will die today." Appellant admitted the scare tactic was unauthorized but claimed his intent was only to frighten Mansur into providing information.

[While transporting Mansur,] Appellant ordered his platoon to take the desert route . . . because he wanted "to talk to Ali in a remote, secure location." On the desert route, Appellant saw a culvert; he ordered the platoon to stop . . . . Appellant, Harry, and Mansur immediately started walking towards the culvert. . . . [Before entering the] culvert, Appellant told Mansur he wanted the information he had asked about earlier that day. Mansur responded that he did not know anything.

Appellant then moved Mansur into the culvert and cut off his shirt and told [another soldier] to cut off his pants and underwear. . . . Appellant ordered Mansur, who was then naked and unbound, to sit on a rock or piece of concrete inside the culvert. Mansur continued to claim ignorance, so Appellant pointed a loaded pistol at him to frighten him into providing the information. . . .

As soon as Appellant pulled out his pistol, Harry stepped outside the culvert because he was afraid of the ricochet. . . . Once Harry was outside the culvert, Appellant again asked for the information and stated that if Mansur did not tell him what he wanted to hear that he would die. Mansur said something, and Harry looked at Appellant to translate, and then two shots were fired. Harry testified that everything happened quickly, that he was surprised by the gunshots, and that he did not see exactly what happened before the shots were fired. . . .

Appellant's testimony was mostly consistent with that of the other witnesses, although he did elaborate on what occurred before he fired his pistol. He testified that he pointed his pistol at Mr. Mansur and told him that "this was his last chance to tell the information or he would die." Appellant testified he heard Mr. Mansur say something in Arabic that was different than his previous responses, so he looked over to Harry for interpretation.

While looking at Harry, Appellant testified that he heard a piece of concrete hit over his left shoulder. He turned towards Mansur and saw him reaching for the pistol; the distance between them was only two or three feet. He took a step or two to his left, towards the entrance of the culvert, to create distance between him and Mansur, and then fired two shots into Mansur. Mansur was shot once in the head and once in the chest; the order of the shots was a contested issue. Appellant stated that everything happened fast and that he fired the shots because he "was scared Mansur was going to take his weapon." Appellant insisted throughout his testimony that he never intended to kill Mansur; he just wanted to scare him for information.

. . . Harry later asked Appellant why he had shot Mansur, and Harry testified that Appellant said "Ali Mansur planted explosives twice on a specific road and the explosive that went off in the Salaam Village, he had a hand into this too. He was part of this operation." [Evidence introduced at trial also indicated that, after shooting Mansur, Appellant ordered another soldier to give him a grenade, which he then detonated near Mansur's body.]

During trial, the defense provided unrebutted testimony from two experts in the field of forensics. [Both experts opined that Mansur was standing when he was shot and that the chest wound was inflicted first.]

II.

. . . The right to act in self-defense . . . is not absolute. Initial aggressors . . . lose the right to act in self-defense. However, an initial aggressor . . . regains the right to act in self-defense if the other party escalates the degree of force, or if the initial aggressor . . . withdraws in good faith and communicates that intent to withdraw. With these principles in mind, we turn our attention to the instructions in this case.

. . . Appellant's claim of error is in regard to the following instruction on losing and regaining the right to act in self-defense:

> . . . If you are convinced beyond a reasonable doubt that the accused, without provocation or other legal justification or excuse, assaulted Ali Mansur then you have found that the accused gave up the right to self-defense. *However, if you have a reasonable doubt that the accused assaulted Ali Mansur, was provoked by Ali Mansur, or had some other legal justification or excuse, and you are not convinced beyond a reasonable doubt that Ali Mansur did not escalate the level of force,* then you must conclude that the accused had the right to self-defense, and then you must determine if the accused actually did act in self-defense.

. . . [The] emphasized portion of the instruction is an erroneous statement of law. Specifically, the military judge linked the lawful use of force with the issue of escalation with the conjunction "and." . . . This is an inaccurate statement of law because Appellant would have had the right to self-defense if his original use of force had been lawful — it was provoked, justified, or otherwise excusable (i.e., Appellant was not an initial aggressor) — *or* if Mr. Mansur had escalated the level of force.

Having found that the instruction was erroneous, we must test for prejudice. . . . We begin by noting that Appellant was not in an active battlefield situation, that Mansur was not then actively engaged in hostile action against the United States or its allies, and that there were no other military exigencies in play. . . . [T]he events that transpired in the culvert do not implicate the unique aspects of military service in a manner that requires us to apply other than basic criminal law concepts. . . .

Even when viewed in the most favorable light, Appellant's own testimony about the events that transpired in the culvert demonstrate that he was the initial aggressor because he brought about the situation that resulted in his killing of Mansur. Appellant deviated from his assigned duty to return Mansur to his home, without authority, to take him to a remote culvert in the desert, far from any active hostilities for further unauthorized interrogation.

More importantly, Appellant then stripped the detainee naked and forced him to sit on a rock while Appellant, in full combat attire with a loaded pistol, interrogated him. Appellant also told Mansur . . . that he was going to die unless he provided specific information. Although we are mindful that Mansur was a detainee, it is evident that Appellant's use of force in the culvert before the shooting — the critical moment in reviewing this issue — was unauthorized and excessive. [T]here is no evidence on which a rational member could rely to conclude that Appellant was not the initial aggressor.

The next question is whether a rational member could have found that Appellant regained the right to act in self-defense as a result of either Mansur's escalating the conflict or Appellant's withdrawing in good faith. Under our case law, Mansur could not have escalated the level of force in this situation, as Appellant had already introduced deadly force. Even assuming for a moment that Mansur could have escalated the level of force, we conclude that a naked and unarmed individual in the desert does not escalate the level of force when he throws a piece of concrete at an initial aggressor in full battle attire, armed with a loaded pistol, and lunges for the pistol. This is especially so when the initial aggressor "had every opportunity to withdraw from the confrontation and there was no evidence he either attempted or was unable to do so." Furthermore, nothing in Appellant's testimony indicated that he clearly manifested an intent to withdraw or that Mr. Mansur prevented Appellant from withdrawing. . . .

Ultimately, even if we assume that Mansur lunged for Appellant's pistol and Appellant feared that Mansur would use the pistol if he was able to seize it, because Appellant was the initial aggressor, and because there was no evidence to support a finding of escalation or withdrawal, a rational member could have come to no other conclusion than that Appellant lost the right to act in self-defense and did not regain it. As such, withdrawal was not in issue and the erroneous instruction on escalation was superfluous. . . . For this reason, Appellant is not entitled to relief.

EFFRON, J., dissenting. . . . Under the majority view, Appellant did not have the right to defend himself, notwithstanding evidence that a person suspected of supporting the enemy rose up and reached for Appellant's weapon during an interrogation. The majority takes the position that Appellant, by virtue of conducting an unauthorized interrogation that used improper techniques, including pointing a pistol at the suspect and using threatening words, did not have the right to defend himself when his life was threatened.

I respectfully disagree . . . . Under the majority's approach, the panel should not have had the opportunity to consider factual issues raised by Appellant's testimony, including whether the interrogation techniques amounted to the use of force likely to produce death or grievous bodily harm, whether Appellant intended to use the interrogation techniques as a pretext for killing Ali Mansur, or whether Appellant reasonably apprehended that Ali Mansur rose up and reached for Appellant's weapon for the purpose of killing Appellant. These issues, however, were matters for resolution by a court-martial panel, not this Court.

If the Government accuses a member of the armed forces of conducting an improper and abusive interrogation, the [law] provides ample authority to hold that person accountable in a court-martial. Such accountability, however, does not require the servicemember to sacrifice the right of self-defense; nor does it deprive the servicemember of the right to have the panel decide whether, as a matter of fact, the circumstances justified the use of force to save the servicemember's life from an attack by a person suspected of supporting the enemy. . . .

NOTES AND QUESTIONS

1. Escalation. The *Behenna* court says an initial aggressor recovers the right to self-defense if the respondent "escalates the degree of force." This rule extends from first principles if one views a disproportionate or excessive response to an initial act of aggression as itself an *unlawful* use of force, which is precisely what self-defense doctrine protects against. On this understanding, the escalation rule permits the initial aggressor to defend against this unlawful, excessive reaction to his wrongful but milder opening act. (It follows that if the initial aggressor's opening salvo involves *deadly* force, escalation falls out of the analysis; as the *Behenna* court says, a respondent like "Mansur could not have escalated the level of force in this situation, as [the initial aggressor] had already introduced deadly force.")

Note, however, that *Behenna* articulates the minority rule. Most states do not allow initial aggressors to recover the right to self-defense even when met with disproportionate (and thus seemingly unlawful) force. Does this make sense? The initial aggressor was clearly wrong to attack or threaten the respondent. But is requiring him to suffer deadly force or to risk prison (if he injures or kills the escalating respondent) an appropriate sanction for that wrong?[98]

2. Withdrawal. As *Behenna* explains, the other circumstance in which an initial aggressor recovers the right to self-defense, recognized by most states, is when he "withdraws in good faith" from the encounter "and communicates that intent to withdraw." The idea here is straightforward. By withdrawing openly and in good faith, the initial aggressor ends the encounter and resets the parties' respective moral positions. If the respondent now attacks the initial aggressor, the respondent, who is no longer acting out of necessity, becomes the initial aggressor for a *new* encounter—and the former initial aggressor (now himself the respondent) may justifiably defend himself. This *pas de deux* is a crisp example of the "dance of shifting privileges" that Professor Raymond ascribes to self-defense doctrine. But is it good policy? As Professor Leverick notes, without reliable data, the rule's utility is speculative at best, as one could predict either more or less overall violence to result:

> If we deny the defence to the accused who starts the trouble . . . even where [she] communicates her withdrawal from the conflict, this might act as a disincentive to violence and aggression in society. . . . [On the other hand,] if an initial aggressor is permitted to plead self-defence provided that she ceases her attack and communicates this to her victim, this provides a very clear incentive for her to do so. If that incentive is not in place, she has every reason for continuing to use violence rather than withdrawing.[99]

In applying the withdrawal rule, courts disagree over whether *actual* notice of withdrawal is necessary or only *reasonable efforts* to give notice. Which is the better rule? Suppose an initial aggressor dazes the respondent, rendering the respondent unable to recognize the aggressor's good-faith withdrawal. Should the initial aggressor be permitted to use defensive force if the respondent pursues him? *See* People v. Button, 39 P. 1073, 1075-1076 (Cal. 1895) (no). What if the respondent is dazed instead because he was drinking excessively? The most common approach in this case seems to require only reasonable efforts. *See, e.g.*, State v. Muhammad, 757 S.W.2d 641, 643 (Mo. Ct. App. 1988).

3. Defining Aggression: The Killing of Trayvon Martin. The majority and dissent in *Behenna* did not primarily divide over questions of escalation or withdrawal. Rather, they disagreed about whether Behenna's unauthorized interrogation of Mansur made Behenna the initial aggressor in the first place. Such disagreement is not uncommon, even though the answer to the question will often be dispositive.

Consider the prosecution in 2013 of George Zimmerman, who killed Trayvon Martin, a Black teenager, in a gated community in Sanford, Florida and then claimed he acted in self-defense. This case captured national attention for at least two reasons. First and foremost, it was — at the time — the latest in a long line of killings of unarmed Black people in which the killer was not ultimately convicted. To many people, this fact, combined with Martin's young age, made the case a powerful example of systemic racism, and particularly of the "fear and disdain for Black youth" that Professor Kristin Henning documents. As President Barack Obama said days after Zimmerman's acquittal, if Trayvon Martin had been "a white male teen . . . from top to bottom, both the outcome and the aftermath might have been different." Viewed from a decade's remove, it seems clear today, as noted in this chapter's introduction, that Zimmerman's acquittal "planted the seeds of the Black Lives Matter movement."[100]

Beyond crystalizing the role race plays in the administration of the criminal law, the case was also significant in the way it pushed the law of self-defense and its various corollary doctrines into the national discourse. The public discussion at the time focused mostly on one such doctrinal corollary, Florida's controversial "Stand Your Ground" law, which relates to the duty to retreat taken up later in this chapter. But as Henning notes, that focus was curious given that Zimmerman's defense team intentionally "avoided that debate by arguing that Zimmerman was pinned in by Trayvon" at the moment of the fatal shot and thus "had no opportunity to retreat, making Stand Your Ground irrelevant to the case." As a legal matter, the initial-aggressor doctrine was far more important to the case's outcome — and its application more controversial.[101]

As some readers will know, Zimmerman testified that he became suspicious of Martin as soon as he saw Martin walking home from a 7-Eleven convenience store through the gated community Zimmerman was patrolling as a volunteer neighborhood watchman. Martin was talking on the phone with his friend Rachel Jeantel at the time. According to Jeantel, Martin became nervous that Zimmerman was watching him and began to run. Ignoring a 911 dispatcher's instructions, Zimmerman pursued Martin — while armed — and a confrontation ensued, ending in Zimmerman shooting Martin to death.[102]

Zimmerman and the prosecution disputed how the physical confrontation began. But even accepting Zimmerman's contention that Martin punched him first, who was the initial aggressor in the overall encounter? Under Florida law, Zimmerman was the initial aggressor if he used or threatened force against Martin. *See* Gibbs v. State, 789 So.2d 443, 445 (Fla. Dist. Ct. App. 2001). Could a reasonable jury have found that Martin reasonably understood Zimmerman's armed pursuit as an implicit threat of force — and therefore that Martin was acting in self-defense when he (according to Zimmerman) punched Zimmerman first?

The jury at Zimmerman's trial was not given a chance to decide this question because the trial court rejected the state's request to give an initial-aggressor instruction that would have put this issue to the jury. Professor Alafair Burke writes that "[l]osing the initial aggressor instruction may have been the moment the state lost its case." And that may well be. Note, though, that Florida law at the time embraced a variant of the escalation rule: An initial aggressor could regain the right to self-defense if the respondent's force was "so great" that the aggressor "reasonably believes" he "is in imminent danger of death or great bodily harm" and that he "has exhausted every reasonable means to escape such danger other than the use of force which is likely to cause death or great bodily harm to the assailant." Fla. Stat. §776.041(2)(a).[103]

Questions: How does the escalation rule just stated differ from the escalation rule described in *Behenna*? Could a reasonable jury have found that, even if he was the initial aggressor, Zimmerman later satisfied these conditions, given evidence in the record that Martin was on top of Zimmerman, punching him in the head, when Zimmerman shot him?

b. Provocation

Unlike the initial-aggression doctrine, the *provocation* doctrine comes into play when a person invites or otherwise brings about a violent affray *without* using or threatening force. Instead, in the classic example, the provocateur goads the respondent by word or action into an attack — and then defends himself against that aggression. Even though the respondent lashes out first, the provocateur's involvement in causing the trouble can sometimes be enough to strip away his right to self-defense.

Notice that, unlike the initial-aggressor rule, the provocation rule does not follow directly from first principles. Merely goading or taunting someone is not unlawful and is certainly not unlawful *force*. Why, then, does the provocateur forfeit self-defense? Professor Kimberly Kessler Ferzan explains it this way:

> A provocateur creates the risk that another person will harm him by engaging in conduct that he knows may produce a violent response, either because it will anger the respondent or otherwise give him a reason to engage in violent conduct. Having created this risk of harm to himself, he forfeits his moral complaint when this very risk materializes. It is true that this conduct is insufficient to justify the respondent's behavior, but sometimes, there are just two wrongdoers.[104]

There is widespread agreement over the basic provocation principle that, to invoke the privilege of self-defense, a defendant must be "free from fault" in bringing about the conflict. *See, e.g.,* Commonwealth v. Spotz, 84 A.3d 294, 316 n.16 (Pa. 2014). But states diverge significantly over what kinds of "fault" matter.

At one end of the spectrum, some say the provocateur forfeits the right to self-defense only if he provoked the respondent *with the purpose of inflicting death or serious bodily harm*—in particular, if the provocation was an artifice designed to make the provocateur's subsequent use of deadly force appear to be "defensive." An old English precedent known as *Mason's Case* exemplifies this approach. Mason's Case (1756) 168 Eng. Rep. 66. There, the defendant Richard Mason verbally goaded his brother William and taunted him with a cudgel. As William drew near, Richard dropped the cudgel on the floor. William picked it up and struck Richard with it twice on the shoulder, at which point Richard produced a sword he had been concealing and fatally stabbed William. The judges rejected Richard's claim of self-defense, pointing to evidence that Richard had approached William seeking revenge for past slights. That William struck Richard with the cudgel was immaterial, as those blows "were plainly . . . sought [by Richard], that he might execute the wicked purpose of his heart, with some colour of excuse."[105]

Few, if any, states would allow a defendant like Richard Mason to claim self-defense, though a handful would permit him the use of *nondeadly* defensive force. Indeed, many states push further, withholding the self-defense right whenever the defendant provokes the respondent *with the purpose to cause any affray,* regardless of whether his ultimate plan is to inflict death or serious bodily harm.[106]

Further still along the spectrum are cases in which the defendant did not *intentionally* provoke an affray but still engaged in some wrongdoing—legal, moral, or both—that foreseeably had that effect. Here the states diverge again. One approach is exemplified by *Barker v. State,* 477 S.W.3d 583 (Ky. 2015). There, the defendant harbored a grudge against a man named Zachary Scarpellini. Acting on that grudge, he travelled to Scarpellini's apartment at night carrying a knife and loaded gun and surreptitiously tried to slash Scarpellini's tires. When Scarpellini learned this was happening, he armed himself and went out to confront the defendant, chasing him down the street. An altercation ensued during which the defendant fatally shot Scarpellini. On appeal, the Kentucky Supreme Court found "virtually no evidence" to support the state's theory that the defendant had provoked Scarpellini by coming to Scarpellini's home and trying to slash his tires. *Id.* at 587. Indeed, the court wrote that the defendant "participated in a wrongdoing which *sought to avoid direct confrontation with the victim*" because he acted "[u]nder cover of night and [was] hiding behind a vehicle to go undetected." *Id.* (emphasis added). The court added, "we have difficulty imagining a provocation where the defendant does not seek out—or, at the very least, encounter—the victim." *Id.*

Compare this holding to *Marquardt v. State*, 882 A.2d 900 (Md. Ct. App. 2005). There, the defendant, Joseph Marquardt, was concerned for the wellbeing of his pregnant wife, who was addicted to drugs and had gone missing for two days. Upon learning that his wife was at the apartment of a man named Robert Lambert, the defendant grabbed a baseball bat and went to that location. When he arrived, he used the bat to smash a panel on the apartment's front door near the lock and started to let himself in. As Marquardt opened the door, Lambert jumped up and started running toward him. Marquardt testified at trial that he saw something in Lambert's hand and "wasn't going to take a chance," so he hit Lambert in the head with the bat. *Id.* at 910. The blow sent Lambert to the hospital and caused permanent deafness in his left ear. Marquardt argued that he was entitled to a self-defense instruction because "he did not bring the bat with him with the intention of fighting anyone." *Id.* at 926. The trial court refused to give the instruction and the Court of Appeals affirmed:

> Here, appellant admitted breaking into Lambert's apartment with a baseball bat. Although appellant may have only brought the bat to gain entrance to the apartment and not to physically injure anyone, he provoked the conflict by breaking into Lambert's home.

Id. at 927.

Finally, at the farthest end of the provocation spectrum, courts sometimes deny the right of self-defense to a person whose only "fault" is *voluntarily coming toward a foreseeable confrontation*. The logic here echoes the principle in tort law of assumption of risk: a person who voluntarily comes toward danger might be thought (in Professor Ferzan's words above) to have created a "risk of harm to himself" and thus forfeited "his moral complaint when this very risk materializes." Imagine, for example, a person who attends the funeral service of a fallen soldier wearing a t-shirt reading "Thank God for Dead Soldiers" as a means of protesting the fact that the U.S. military enlists gay servicemembers. The Westboro Baptist Church has infamously protested at 600 military funerals in even more disruptive ways. *See* Snyder v. Phelps, 562 U.S. 443 (2011) (holding such protests constitutionally protected). If the grieving father of the dead soldier were to rush at this protestor, threatening to punch him, should the protestor be allowed to beat the father up to repel the attack? Or might we instead view the protest itself as an initial act of provocation?

Note that it is impossible to answer this question without resolving some basic and fundamental questions about a free society. As the Westboro example suggests, this is an inherently normative and oftentimes fraught undertaking. As the case that follows shows, it is also inevitably informed by underlying social judgments about who is entitled—or ought to be entitled—to go where they like and do what they please.

As you will see, the case below involves an attempted lynching of a Black man on the streets of Washington, DC. Though the case itself is a century old, it remains good law, cited with approval by courts in the nation's capital as recently as 2015. On four occasions, the opinion uses an infamous racial slur, the n-word, each time quoting trial testimony that described the lynch mob's actions. Following the consistent example of judges and lawyers today, "many of them liberal luminaries," we present the opinion as it was written—and the underlying testimony as it was delivered—having "concluded that, in legal matters, direct and accurate reporting of the facts is a key facet of rendering justice," and that in this case in particular the lynch mob's words and actions are an essential component of the analysis. We caution, however, that there is a meaningful difference between reading this word and hearing it spoken aloud, and that it is thus "also much different to say it than it is to write it," a point that bears emphasis when preparing for and engaging in class discussion.[107]

Laney v. United States

294 F. 412 (D.C. Cir. 1923)

VAN ORSDEL, J. . . . The indictment charged the defendant [William Laney] with the crime of murder in the first degree, growing out of the killing of one Kenneth Crall, during a race riot in Washington on July 21, 1919.* The defense interposed was self-defense . . . [but] in our opinion, viewing the evidence in the most favorable aspect, self-defense does not enter into the case.

Defendant testified as follows:

On the night of the 21st of July, 1919, I went to the theater with Mattie Burke . . . . On my return to 617 Massachusetts avenue, as I got to the corner where the Home Savings Bank is located, a large crowd that was there started to yelling 'Catch the nigger.' and 'Kill the nigger.' and started to chase me. I ran ahead of them down Massachusetts avenue. When I got near to 617 Massachusetts avenue, I pulled out my gun and the crowd stopped chasing me. I went into the back yard, and while trying to fix the safety on my gun it went off. I then put the gun in my pocket and went to the front again, intending to go back to my place of employment. The mob was attacking a house across the street, and were coming both ways

---

* Editor's note: Mr. Laney was represented by a defense team including William Lepré Houston, "one of Washington, D.C.'s finest African-American attorneys" and the father of Charles Hamilton Houston, "widely recognized as the architect of" *Brown v. Board of Education,* 347 U.S. 483 (1954). José Felipé Anderson, *The Criminal Justice Principles of Charles Hamilton Houston: Lessons in Innovation,* 35 Balt. L. Rev. 313, 313, 317 (2006).

on Massachusetts avenue . . . . While I was in the areaway between 617 and 619, the mob came across from the south side of the street, firing and hollering 'Let's kill the nigger.' The mob was firing at me, and I shot in the direction towards Seventh street. I fired to protect my life. I fired three shots. My pistol had eight bullets in it at first. There were four bullets in it when it was taken by the officials; three bullets having been fired in the front yard and one in the back yard.

The witness Mattie Burke testified . . . as follows:

Later [Mr. Laney] came running back, with a mob chasing him, throwing sticks and stones at him, hollering 'Catch the nigger!' I think Mr. Laney had his gun in his hand while he was running, but I did not see him do anything with it. He ran into the areaway between 615 and 617. The crowd, consisting of 100 or more men, then started after a house on the opposite side of the street. At that time William Laney went into the back yard and tried his gun. I was with him in the back yard at the time. Then we came out to the front again. After attacking the house on the opposite side of the street, the mob gathered in the car track as though they were coming toward 617, and then Laney fired his gun. After Laney had escaped through the back way, the crowd began to break into the house, and then I escaped myself over the back fence, and I did not see any more.

It is clearly apparent from the above testimony that, when defendant escaped from the mob into the back yard of the Ferguson place, he was in a place of comparative safety, from which, if he desired to go home, he could have gone by the back way, as he subsequently did. The mob had turned its attention to a house on the opposite side of the street. According to Laney's testimony, there was shooting going on in the street. His appearance on the street at that juncture could mean nothing but trouble for him. Hence, when he adjusted his gun and stepped out into the areaway, he had every reason to believe that his presence there would provoke trouble. We think his conduct in adjusting his revolver and going into the areaway was such as to deprive him of any right to invoke the plea of self-defense . . . .

It is a well-settled rule that, before a person can avail himself of the plea of self-defense against the charge of homicide, he must do everything in his power, consistent with his safety, to avoid the danger and avoid the necessity of taking life. If one has reason to believe that he will be attacked, in a manner which threatens him with bodily injury, he must avoid the attack if it is possible to do so, and the right of self-defense does not arise until he has done everything in his power to prevent its necessity. In other words, no necessity for killing an assailant can exist, so long as there is a safe way open to escape the conflict . . . .

[One is not, however,] required to retreat when he is assailed in a place where he has a right to be, unless by so doing an affray can be clearly avoided. He may stand upon his rights, and resist the attack to the extent apparently necessary to avoid death or great bodily harm. Likewise one may defend his domicile or his property to the extent of taking life, when necessary in defense of his property, or to protect himself or those in his charge from death or bodily injury. Beard v. United States, 158 U.S. 550 (1895) . . . .

In the present case the defendant was neither acting in defense of his property nor attempting to avoid an affray. His going out into the areaway leaves but one inference to be drawn, namely, that he knew his presence there would cause trouble.

Nor was he in a place where, under the circumstances, he had a right to be. If conditions on the street had been normal, he would have had the right to elect that way to go home; but he had no right to go there with another way equally available, if by so doing it would invite an affray, which would almost inevitably result in the taking of life. . . .

NOTES AND QUESTIONS

1. Coming to the Trouble: Comparing Laney to Kyle Rittenhouse. In its logic and holding, *Laney* rests directly on principles of white supremacy. The court indicates that it was the lynch mob, not Laney, who "had a right to be" on the street that night. Likewise, it holds that it was Laney who provoked the mob—with his presence on that street, meaning, effectively, with his Blackness. It is striking, given all this, to see *Laney* cited with approval by some contemporary courts without any suggestion that its reasoning or holding is problematic. *See, e.g.*, Andrews v. United States, 125 A.3d 316 (D.C. 2015).

Still, is it possible that the core principle in the case—stripped of its racist application—has merit? Put more directly, why shouldn't we require people to avoid violent and potentially fatal confrontations whenever possible? Recall the Westboro hypothetical earlier. Or consider the controversial prosecution and acquittal of Kyle Rittenhouse, a white, conservative teenager who went to a Black Lives Matter protest armed with an AR-15 semi-automatic weapon—which he ultimately used to shoot multiple people, two fatally, in what he later said was self-defense. At trial, one of the people Rittenhouse shot, Gaige Grosskreutz, testified that he had pointed a gun at Rittenhouse. As Professor Ronald Sullivan explains, that testimony created "a textbook case of an imminent threat," which meant that "[p]rovocation was the prosecution's best chance at securing a conviction." Sullivan lays out that provocation argument:

> Rittenhouse, the argument runs, is morally blameworthy for coming to a chaotic situation with a gun and a design to engage in private law enforcement. The jury charge reads, "[a] person who engages in unlawful conduct of a type likely to provoke others to attack, and who does provoke an attack, is not allowed to use or threaten the use of force in self-defense

against the attack." Arguably, Rittenhouse's conduct fits the definition of provocation. Counterarguments assert that Rittenhouse's intent on possessing the gun was defensive. It was for protection. He did not brandish the weapon to anyone and, absent that, provocation becomes a hard case to make. The jury, obviously, credited the latter argument . . . .

Note that the version of the provocation doctrine articulated here in support of convicting Rittenhouse is the same one articulated in *Laney*: coming to a chaotic situation with a gun. Professor Sullivan observes that, "as a matter of law," the jury's decision to acquit was "not unreasonable," even if it defied "the moral intuitions of the many who objected to the verdict." Do you agree?[108]

2. Recovering the Right. Imagine that when the conflict involving Kyle Rittenhouse first began, he had put down his AR-15 and raised his hands in the air, and only then had Gaige Grosskreutz pulled a gun on him. If we assume Rittenhouse provoked the initial confrontation by coming to the trouble, should he be able to recover the right to self-defense by withdrawing from the conflict openly and in good faith? Most states say yes: as is true of initial aggressors, a provocateur who withdraws from a conflict can use defensive force if the respondent continues to attack.*

Is there a reason to treat initial aggressors and provocateurs differently for these purposes? Professor Ferzan argues there is, because compared to initial aggressors, provocateurs "are less able to unring the provocative bell": "When an aggressor stops an attack, there is no need to defend. When a provocateur incites anger and rage, there is no way to undo the damage."[109]

Consider in this context *United States v. Peterson*, 483 F.2d 1222 (D.C. Cir. 1973). In that case, Charles Keitt and two friends drove in Keitt's car to an alley behind the house of Bennie Peterson, the defendant, and tried to steal the windshield wipers from Peterson's wrecked car. While Keitt was doing this, Peterson emerged, and the men argued vigorously. Peterson then went back into the house, retrieved a gun, and came back outside; while Peterson was inside, Keitt and his companions went back to their car and were about to leave. And then:

> Upon his reappearance in the yard, Peterson paused briefly to load the pistol. "If you move," he shouted to Keitt, "I will shoot." He walked to a

---

* *See, e.g.*, Ariz. Rev. Stat. Ann. §13-404(B)(3); Iowa Code §704.6(3)(b). Many states, however, distinguish *among* provocateurs, providing that those who provoke an attack as a purposeful ruse to justify their own violence can never recover the right, while other, less culpable provocateurs can. *See, e.g.*, 720 Ill. Comp. Stat. §5/7-4(b); Kan. Stat. Ann. §21-5226(b). Similar to the escalation doctrine discussed above, some states also permit a provocateur to recover the self-defense right if his provocation is answered with deadly force. *See, e.g.*, Mont. Code Ann. §45-3-105(2)(a); Wis. Stat. §939.48(2)(a).

point in the yard slightly inside a gate in the rear fence and, pistol in hand, said, "If you come in here I will kill you." Keitt alighted from his car, took a few steps toward Peterson and exclaimed, "What the hell do you think you are going to do with that?" Keitt then made an about-face, walked back to his car and got a lug wrench. With the wrench in a raised position, Keitt advanced toward Peterson, who stood with the pistol pointed toward him. Peterson warned Keitt not to "take another step" and, when Keitt continued onward shot him in the face from a distance of about ten feet. Death was apparently instantaneous.

Id. at 1225-1226. As the *Peterson* case illustrates, self-defense scenarios can be very fluid. Who started the trouble here? If Keitt provoked the encounter by coming to Peterson's house to steal from him, did he then withdraw by getting back into his car? Was that enough to "unring the bell" of provocation, resetting the scene and putting Peterson at fault for approaching Keitt with the gun?

c.   Unclean Hands

Finally, in an approach related to but distinct from both the initial-aggressor doctrine and the provocation doctrine, some states deny the self-defense privilege whenever a defendant engages in a crime causally related to the harm he inflicts in an ensuing confrontation—even if that crime did not actually provoke the respondent. Indiana law, for example, provides that defensive force is not justified if the defendant "is committing or is escaping after the commission of a crime." Ind. Code §35-41-3-2(g)(1). This law was dispositive in *Mayes v. State*, 744 N.E.2d 390 (Ind. 2001), in which the defendant fatally shot his girlfriend Mary, allegedly in self-defense, with an unlicensed firearm. The Indiana Supreme Court upheld Mayes's murder conviction, reasoning that "the jury could have concluded that but for Mayes' possession of the unlicensed handgun, Mary would still be alive because Mayes' unlicensed handgun was required, by law, to be kept at his dwelling, on his property, or at his fixed place of business." *Id.* at 394; *see also* Dawkins v. State, 252 P.3d 214, 218-219 (Okla. Crim. App. 2011) (denying self-defense to defendant based on possession of an illegally modified firearm).

Does this approach make sense? Consider that it is a federal crime for an individual with a felony conviction to possess a firearm. *See* 18 U.S.C. §922(g). This restriction touches roughly 13 percent of all adult males and one-third of Black adult males. Does *Mayes* therefore imply that millions of people—disproportionately Black—lack the right to self-defense whenever a firearm is necessary to secure it? How can this be squared with the Supreme Court's Second Amendment pronouncements on the crucial role of firearms in personal self-defense? *See, e.g.*, McDonald v. City of Chicago, 561 U.S. 742, 767-778 (2010).[110]

More broadly, does an unclean hands approach imply that anyone involved in criminal activity forfeits the right of self-defense? The Ohio

Court of Appeals suggested as much in *State v. Robinson*, 726 N.E.2d 581 (Ohio Ct. App. 1999), which held that a person guarding a drug stash house cannot claim self-defense if violent intruders come and try to steal the drugs. "Such a rule," a dissenting judge pointed out,

> would preclude a purchaser of drugs from asserting self-defense if the seller attacked him or her, and foreclose a prostitute from asserting the defense if the case involved a brutal attack by a customer. Likewise, an investment banker who was embezzling funds could not assert a self-defense claim if attacked by an irate client; nor could a mechanic defend himself or herself if attacked by a customer while rolling back an odometer.

Id. at 589 (Painter, J., concurring in part and dissenting in part).[111]

3.   The Duty to Retreat

The initial aggressor in an altercation typically must withdraw, or retreat, to regain his right to self-defense. But why shouldn't *everyone* have a duty to retreat before harming another person in self-defense? Doesn't the very idea of *necessity* imply such a rule — that if harm can be avoided by running away, it should be? Early British common law endorsed this view, at least as concerns deadly defensive force. "[T]he law requires," wrote Blackstone, "that the person, who kills another in his own defence, should have retreated as far as he conveniently or safely can, to avoid the violence of the assault, before he turns upon his assailant." But a majority of American jurisdictions have, over time, come to disagree.[112]

Culverson v. State
_____
797 P.2d 238 (Nev. 1990)

YOUNG, C.J. Samuel Culverson was convicted by a jury of first degree murder and sentenced to two terms of life imprisonment without possibility of parole for killing Michael Smith. [On the day in question, Culverson and Smith had been sitting in Culverson's car along with two other men. When the conflict broke out, Smith exited the car and pointed a gun at Culverson, who shot Smith in response. Eyewitnesses disagreed over who had initiated the conflict.] Smith died from four bullet wounds from Culverson's gun. The police found a pellet gun next to Smith's body. . . .

Culverson contends that the district court erroneously informed the jury that he had a duty to retreat before he could act in self-defense. Specifically, Culverson objects to Instruction No. 19 which states:

> In this case even if you should believe from the evidence that the deceased commenced the encounter in question and was the first to offer violence, but further believe from the evidence, beyond a reasonable doubt, that

the defendant could, by making a reasonable effort, have avoided or safely withdrawn from it, and thereby avoided further trouble, and that he made no effort to do so, but voluntarily entered into and continued the encounter and shot and killed the deceased, then the killing of the deceased is not excused or justified on the ground of self-defense.

The leading Nevada case which deals with the duty to retreat is *State v. Grimmett*, 112 P. 273 (Nev. 1910). In *Grimmett*, the victim, while standing behind a bar, took a gun from a drawer and fired one shot at the defendant who immediately fired two shots killing the victim. This court held:

> The law is well established that where a person, without voluntarily seeking, provoking, inviting, or willingly engaging in a difficulty of his own free will, is attacked by an assailant, and it is necessary for him to take the life of his assailant to protect his own, then he need not flee for safety, but has the right to stand his ground and slay his adversary.

Id. Culverson contends that *Grimmett* stands for the proposition that Nevada does not require a person to retreat when he reasonably believes that he is about to be attacked with deadly force. We agree. First, we note that a rule requiring a non-aggressor to retreat confers a benefit on the aggressor and a detriment on the non-aggressor. Second, it is often quite difficult for a jury to determine whether a person should reasonably believe that he may retreat from a violent attack in complete safety. Thus, a rule which requires a non-aggressor to retreat may confuse the jury and lead to inconsistent verdicts. We believe that a simpler rule will lead to more just verdicts.

One reason that has been given to support the no duty to retreat rule is that the non-aggressor should be able to avoid the appearance of cowardice. We do not believe this is a valid reason to support the rule we now adopt. However, the reasons cited amply support the rule that a non-aggressor need not retreat if he reasonably believes he is about to be seriously injured or killed.

Therefore, we hold that a person, who is not the original aggressor, has no duty to retreat before using deadly force, if a reasonable person in the position of the non-aggressor would believe that his assailant is about to kill him or cause him serious bodily harm. . . .

Accordingly, we reverse Culverson's conviction for first degree murder and remand this matter to the district court for a new trial.

ROSE, J., concurring. . . . [I]n considering the duty to retreat in the face of deadly force, I would require a non-aggressor to retreat if he or she could do so in complete safety. This differs somewhat from the majority's position that a non-aggressor does not have to retreat, even though he or she could do so with complete safety, if a reasonable person in his or her position would believe that death or serious bodily harm is about to be inflicted upon him or her. . . .

Other states are divided on the issue of whether a defendant has a duty to retreat. The majority of jurisdictions hold that a defendant who was not the initial aggressor is not required to retreat before using deadly force against someone whom he reasonably believes is about to kill or seriously injure him. A significant minority of states have adopted the rule that a defendant must retreat, if he can safely do so, when threatened with deadly force. . . .

[Like the majority, I do not believe] it is cowardly to walk away safely from a[n] attacker rather than to kill him or her. . . . Rather, I believe that:

> A really honorable man, a man of truly refined and elevated feeling, would perhaps always regret the apparent cowardice of a retreat, but he would regret *ten times more*, after the excitement of the contest was past, the thought that he had the blood of a fellow-being on his hands.

Joseph H. Beale, Jr., *Retreat from a Murderous Assault*, 16 Harv. L. Rev. 567, 581 (1903) (emphasis added). The policy of saving one human life, even if it is that of an aggressor, outweighs the interest an individual might have in avoiding the appearance of cowardice.

The person who retreats can usually rely upon the state to punish the aggressor for his or her actions. [The majority nonetheless adopts a contrary rule, citing administrability concerns. But a] jury is required to make many difficult decisions and it is perfectly capable of determining whether a reasonable person should know that he or she could retreat without using deadly force. . . . [S]elf-defense is measured by necessity. There is no necessity to use deadly force if a defendant may retreat in complete safety.

For the preceding reasons, I believe the better rule would be that a person who has a reasonable belief that he or she is about to be killed or seriously injured has the duty to retreat, rather than use deadly force against his aggressor, if as a reasonable person he or she should know that a retreat can be made with *complete safety*. Whether a person should reasonably know that he or she can retreat with complete safety will be determined after examination of the totality of circumstances surrounding the attack, including but not limited to, the immediate excitement which is caused by the attack. As Justice Holmes stated, "detached reflection cannot be demanded in the presence of an uplifted knife." Brown v. United States, 256 U.S. 335, 343 (1921).

NOTES AND QUESTIONS

1. Nondeadly Force. As the *Culverson* court observes, most U.S. states do not impose a duty to retreat. Yet even jurisdictions that do impose the duty require retreat only if the defender uses deadly force. No state, in other words, requires retreat before using *nondeadly* defensive force. Does it make sense to require retreat only before the use of deadly force? In what sense is *any* defensive force necessary when safe retreat is possible? In a well-known opinion, one court candidly acknowledged that "it might be argued that a safe retreat should be taken if thereby the use of *any* force could be avoided." State v. Abbott, 174 A.2d 881, 885 (N.J. 1961). Still, the court rejected this view, noting only that the "position never has been accepted." *Id.*[113]

2. The Ascent of the "True Man" Principle. Early American criminal law tracked British common law in requiring a person claiming self-defense to retreat "to the wall" before turning to defensive violence. In practice, both the British rule and its American heir permitted some exceptions; retreating until literally boxed in by a wall was rarely required. Still, as *Culverson* explains, the predominant rule in the U.S. today abandons the duty to retreat altogether. In these states, even the more modest duty to retreat *at all* is not imposed, although in some of these states an untaken opportunity to retreat may still weigh against the defendant when determining whether deadly force was truly necessary.[114]

The move away from the duty to retreat began in the late nineteenth century, as U.S. states started to embrace the principle that "a true man, who is without fault, is not obliged to fly from an assailant, who, by violence or surprise, maliciously seeks to take his life or do him enormous bodily harm." Erwin v. State, 29 Ohio St. 186, 199-200 (1876). One court famously wrote that this "true man" rule, as it came to be known, better reflects "the tendency of the American mind." Runyan v. State, 57 Ind. 80, 84 (1877). The Oklahoma Court of Criminal Appeals emphasized this point, writing that retreat "to the wall" is "not the law in free America."

> Here the wall is to every man's back. It is the wall of his rights; and when he is at a place where he has a right to be, and he is unlawfully assailed, he may stand and defend himself . . . .

Fowler v. State, 126 P. 831, 833 (Okla. Crim. App. 1912).

Much has been written about what drove this legal change. Some accounts emphasize "concern for the values of masculine bravery in a frontier nation" rife with novel and violent threats. Another points to the spread of firearms, which make retreat considerably riskier. Most recently, historian Caroline Light argues that the "true man" rule served to empower white men, who disproportionately benefited from its application, "just as the preeminence of white patriarchal power was being challenged by abolitionists and suffragists."[115]

Regardless of the underlying social forces driving the change, courts explained the move away from the duty by citing the twin justifications supporting self-defense itself. First, the "true man" rule was said to vindicate the defender's autonomy and dignitary rights. The *Culverson* court rejects the idea that avoiding cowardice justifies the "true man" rule, but plenty of earlier decisions embraced this rationale. *See, e.g., Abbott,* 174 A.2d at 884

("[T]he advocates of no-retreat say the manly thing is to hold one's ground, and hence society should not demand what smacks of cowardice."). Second, the "true man rule" was also said to deter violence by "letting the would-be robber, murderer, ravisher, and such like, know that their lives are, in a measure, in the hands of their intended victims." *Erwin,* 29 Ohio St. at 200. As such, the argument goes, it is the rule "best calculated to protect and preserve human life." *Id.*

Of course, while many states jettisoned the duty to retreat, a strong minority did not. These states embraced a different conception of honor, captured most eloquently by Professor Joseph Beale's argument, quoted in the *Culverson* concurrence, that a "really honorable man" avoids bloodshed. Anticipating a more modern locution, the Alabama Supreme Court (writing in 1892) put the point more bluntly. "[N]o balm or protection is provided for wounded pride or honor in declining combat . . . . Such thoughts are trash, as compared with the inestimable right to live." Springfield v. State, 11 So. 250, 252 (Ala. 1892). Channeling a state-power account of self-defense, defenders of the retreat rule hold that "the proper and sufficient remedy is not a trial of strength but rather a complaint to the police. If this foregoes a private sanction that might operate as a deterrent to aggressors, it does so in reliance on the adequacy of the public sanctions and does so only when the highest value is at stake."[116]

But what if "public sanctions" are inadequate? As noted in the introduction to this chapter, a *Washington Post* investigation determined that, of nearly 55,000 homicides in 55 cities over the past decade, almost 50 percent did not result in an arrest—a rate that climbed much higher when the victim was Black or Latino. If we insist that people retreat before defending themselves with deadly force, who benefits and who is harmed?[117]

3. The "Stand Your Ground" Revolution. Since just 2005, 26 states have revised their self-defense statutes by enacting what have become known as "Stand Your Ground" laws, which eliminate any duty to retreat before using deadly force, even if safe retreat is available. In many states, these statutes largely confirmed preexisting doctrine. The "true man" principle was already the majority position before 2005 and only a handful of states have actually eliminated the duty to retreat since then. That said, some of the new laws included additional measures designed to strengthen the right to self-defense, such as immunity from prosecution for defendants who make a prima facie showing of self-defense. The upshot of such provisions is "that the issue can be raised in a pretrial setting in an effort to avoid any trial, 'an additional procedural hurdle that no other criminal prosecution has.'"[118]

In the wake of Trayvon Martin's death at the hands of George Zimmerman, reformers across the country began working to repeal these new Stand Your Ground laws. The effort was spurred by President Barack Obama, who said days after Zimmerman's acquittal that "we might want to examine those kinds of laws," which send a message to "our communities that someone who is armed potentially has the right to use those firearms even if there's a way for them to exit from a situation," a message that he said undermines the "peace and security and order that we'd like to see." But how much impact do these laws really have? Even putting aside the fact that most of them reaffirmed preexisting law, it is worth pausing to consider whether repealing them—and reinvigorating the duty to retreat—would actually make a difference in case outcomes.[119]

A crucial point here is that even in states that retain the duty to retreat, retreat is required only if the defender "*knows* that he can avoid the necessity of using such force *with complete safety.*" *Abbott*, 174 A.2d at 885 (quoting Model Penal Code §3.04(2)(b)(ii)). As one court elaborates:

> One who is wrongfully attacked need not risk injury by retreating, even though he could escape with something less than serious bodily injury. It would be unreal to require nice calculations as to the amount of hurt, or to ask him to endure any at all. And the issue is not whether in retrospect it can be found the defendant could have retreated unharmed. Rather the question is whether he knew the opportunity was there, and of course in that inquiry the total circumstances including the attendant excitement must be considered.

Id. at 885-886.

How many cases can satisfy this standard? If one takes the words *know* and *complete* seriously, the answer may be "very few." Indeed, while Trayvon Martin's killing fueled public outrage over Florida's Stand Your Ground statute, the statute in the end seems not to have been relevant to the case. The jury's acquittal indicates that they had at least reasonable doubt about the testimony of prosecution witnesses that Zimmerman, rather than Martin, was on top when Zimmerman fired his gun. Given that, there was also reasonable doubt as to Zimmerman's ability to retreat from Martin with complete safety. In other words, even if Florida had retained a duty to retreat, that duty likely would not have required Zimmerman to retreat under the circumstances.

4. The Impact of "Stand Your Ground" Laws. While the facial difference between the "true man" rule and the duty to retreat may be slight on paper, a recent systematic review of 32 social science studies finds that Stand Your Ground laws alter people's behavior in the world—by *increasing* levels of violence in society. These findings rebut claims from supporters of the statutes that Stand Your Ground laws protect the public from violent crime. To the contrary, the studies show that enactment of the laws was associated with either no change or small increases in homicide, aggravated assault, and robbery. In some settings, the increase in violence was more substantial: seven Florida-based studies showed 24 percent to 45 percent increases in homicide. While some of the additional homicides may have been justified, the evidence suggests that most of them were not.[120]

As is true of violent crime more generally, the impacts here fall disproportionately along racial lines. One study finds that, among adolescents, the increase in homicide victimization following enactment of Florida's Stand Your Ground law was concentrated among Black victims. At the same time, self-defense claims under Florida's Stand Your Ground law are denied more often when the victim of defensive force is white, especially when the defender is not. This is consistent with other accounts showing that when women, people of color, and gender-nonconforming people have attempted to stand their ground, they have often been prosecuted and convicted, suggesting, Professor Light argues, that "white masculinity define[s] the exclusive contours of 'true manhood.'"[121]

What might explain the seemingly significant impact of these statutes, given the minimal facial distinction between Stand Your Ground and duty to retreat? One possibility is that a meaningful number of cases actually fall into the narrow gap between the two rules. Consider *State v. Smiley*, 966 So. 2d 330 (Fla. 2007), in which Florida's Stand Your Ground law conceivably could have changed the outcome in a case where a taxi driver shot a man who left the cab but then turned and flashed a knife. As one juror put it, the defendant cab driver, Mr. Smiley, "had a lot of chances to retreat and to avoid an escalation . . . . He could have just gotten in his cab and left."[122]

Another, more plausible, explanation is that application of Stand Your Ground laws extends beyond their formal terms. In 2012, for example, a grand jury in Louisiana declined to indict a man who, after an argument, fired at an SUV full of teenagers as it drove away, killing one. The sheriff defended the shooter to the press, saying that he had "decided to stand his ground" and that, for all he knew, someone might have jumped out of the car with a gun. Nothing in Louisiana's Stand Your Ground law authorized shooting at people as they flee. "At the same time," as one commentator wrote, "we have to accept that the law can be misconstrued by the very people meant to enforce it." Similarly, while Florida's Stand Your Ground law appears to have been *technically* irrelevant to the analysis of the Zimmerman case, the jury may have weighed it when acquitting him, according to an account one of the jurors gave after the case concluded.[123]

In short, law matters not only because of the rules it prescribes to resolve disputes in court but also because of what it communicates, to its enforcers and to the public. In a duty-to-retreat jurisdiction, the law teaches that one *must* retreat before using deadly defensive force—unless there is any uncertainty about whether retreat can be safely accomplished. In a Stand Your Ground jurisdiction, by contrast, the lesson is simply that retreat is unnecessary, maybe even disfavored. Even if these messages differ only slightly in substance, they frame the critical issue in opposite ways. Stand Your Ground jurisdictions effectively put a thumb on the scale in favor of deadly defensive force, which can influence both prosecutor and jury decisions in close cases. And it can shade other crucial choices made in the jury's shadow, such as whether to plead guilty instead of trusting a self-defense claim at trial—and, perhaps, whether to pull the trigger in the first place.[124]

4. The Castle Doctrine

Even in jurisdictions that have resisted the "true man" principle, "[i]t is not now and never has been the law that a man assailed in his own dwelling is bound to retreat." People v. Tomlins, 107 N.E. 496, 497 (N.Y. 1914). Rather, a person assailed in his house "may stand his ground and resist the attack. He is under no duty to take to the fields and the highways, a fugitive from his own home." *Id.* This principle, known as the "castle exception" to the duty to retreat, draws inspiration from the common-law adage that "a man's house is his castle." But *why* do we have the castle doctrine and what are its bounds? Consider the following case and notes.[125]

Commonwealth v. Daniels

301 A.2d 841 (Pa. 1973)

EAGEN, J. Joseph Daniels, the appellant, was convicted in a nonjury trial of two charges of voluntary manslaughter. . . . The prosecution stemmed from the stabbing of Perry Kellam and Dempsey Wilson shortly before midnight on January 23, 1971, in the hallway of an apartment house in which Daniels resided in Philadelphia. . . . Reading the record in a light most favorable to the Commonwealth, the following facts emerge.

Shortly before midnight Daniels was playing cards with four female friends in his fourth-floor apartment when he answered a knock on the door and was confronted by Wilson, Kellam and two other men. Wilson demanded immediate payment of a debt of $7.00 that Daniels allegedly owed him. Daniels denied the debt, told the men to leave and closed the door. Three or five minutes later there was another knock or kicking on the door and Daniels went to the kitchen and placed a butcher knife in one of his pockets. When he opened the door Daniels was again confronted by the same four men, but this time Kellam did most of the talking. When Daniels again denied the debt, Kellam invited him outside. Kellam then drew his hand back and Daniels observed "something like brass knuckles on his hand with a fork sticking out." Daniels kicked Kellam and he fell down a nearby stairs. Kellam then started back up the stairs and Daniels "met him halfway." Daniels pulled the knife and stabbed Kellam and the latter fell down. When Kellam tried to get up Daniels stabbed him again. Daniels then ascended the stairs and upon finding Wilson standing in the doorway of his apartment he stabbed him in the chest. Wilson then ran down a hallway and Daniels ran behind him and stabbed him in the back.

In view of the proof . . . we agree with the appellant that the conviction based on the death of Kellam may not stand as a matter of law. The Commonwealth's own proof establishes this stabbing was committed in self-defense. The stabbing of Wilson, however, is another matter.

The killing of another human being without justification or excuse is felonious homicide. But a killing is not felonious . . . if it is committed in self-defense. The following conditions must be satisfied before one can successfully invoke the defense of self-defense: (1) the slayer must have been free from fault in provoking or continuing the difficulty which resulted in the killing; (2) the slayer must have reasonably believed that he was in imminent danger of death, great bodily harm, or some felony, and that there was a necessity to kill in order to save himself therefrom; (3) the slayer must not have violated any duty to retreat or avoid the danger.

It is clear that Daniels was without fault in provoking the altercation here involved. The Commonwealth argues however, that after initially repelling the four aggressors by kicking Kellam down the stairs, Daniels then became the aggressor by meeting him "halfway" when he started up the stairs again. We are not so persuaded.

The staircase involved was located immediately outside the door leading to Daniels' apartment and consisted of eight steps leading to a landing located midway between the 4th and 3rd floors. The record is unclear as to how many steps Kellam fell, but assuming he fell to the described landing he was not far removed from Daniels at any relevant time. When Kellam started up the stairs again brandishing a bent fork, Daniels certainly had reasonable grounds to believe he was in imminent danger of death or great bodily harm, and since he was in his own dwelling house, there was not duty to retreat. Where a man is dangerously assaulted or feloniously attacked in his own dwelling house by one not a member of his household, he need not retreat, but may stand his ground and meet deadly force with deadly force to save his own life, or to protect himself from great bodily harm. The fact that Daniels descended the steps part way to better repel the attack did not, under the circumstances, render him the aggressor in the relevant sense. . . .

The circumstances surrounding the stabbing of Wilson . . . differ substantially. While Daniels lacked culpability in provoking the fight, he was the one responsible for continuing it once Wilson began to flee. This is evidenced by Daniels' own statement:

> I don't know what happened to Kellam after that because I turned around quickly and went back up the stairs, Wilson was still in front of my door, he was making an effort at me, and I stabbed him, he ran down the hall and I came right behind him, I think I stabbed him again, he said "Joe don't kill me," and thats [sic] when I stopped.

In the situation where the original assailant attempts to flee and is pursued by his intended victim, the assailant becomes the assaulted. Here once Wilson attempted to flee from Daniels and the latter continued the altercation by pursuing him, Daniels then became the aggressor and was not acting in self-defense.

The judgment of sentence imposed for the killing of Wilson is affirmed. The judgment of sentence imposed for the killing of Kellam is reversed.

MANDERINO, J., concurring and dissenting. . . . The majority attempts to compartmentalize a single episode in which the appellant reasonably feared aggression from four men in the hallway outside appellant's apartment.

Appellant was sitting at home minding his own business, when four aggressive men knocked at his door. They leave the first time, but return shortly thereafter. Appellant, who had several visitors in his apartment, reasonably stepped into the hall rather than expose his visitors to the four aggressive intruders. One of them brandishes a dangerous weapon, another came at the appellant. In the course of the entire episode, appellant stabs two of the men. . . . An episode, such as that which occurred in this case, cannot be broken up. At the time appellant stabbed Wilson, two of the group of four men were still in the hallway outside appellant's apartment. What was the appellant to do when a second man came at him after he had already found it necessary, in self-defense, to stab the first man? He could hardly have been expected to leave the second man alone while there were still present in the hallway the third and fourth members of the gang. How would the appellant know what these two men would do, or what weapons they had? The majority analyzes the factual situation as though there were four unrelated aggressors. There was actually one single aggressor which can fairly be called a gang and as long as the gang was threatening, the appellant had a right to defend himself.

The majority not only splits up the episode as though a computer were at hand, but it relies on the appellant's statement that he stabbed Wilson as he ran down the hall. Wilson was not running toward a customary exit. Why would a reasonable man think Wilson was retreating permanently? Wilson could easily have turned back toward the appellant and continued his aggression, particularly since two members of the gang were still there.

What happened in this case could happen to any citizen who is minding his own business, sitting at home with friends. Four aggressors with weapons arrive and start something endangering appellant's life. Within a few minutes, in self-defense, appellant stabs two of them. How can we possibly justify one killing and not the other? The appellant's judgment of sentence should be reversed as to both Kellam and Wilson.

POMEROY, J., concurring and dissenting. I agree with the Court that the killing by the appellant Daniels of Dempsey Wilson cannot as a matter of law be regarded as justified under a claim of self-defense. I am unable to agree, however, that the killing of Perry Kellam — appellant's first victim — can and should be so regarded. . . .

. . . [T]o show that a killing was in self-defense . . . "the slayer must have reasonably believed that he was in imminent danger of death, great bodily harm, or some felony, and that there was a necessity to kill in order to save himself therefrom." Commonwealth v. Johnston, 263 A.2d 376 (Pa. 1970). Accepting the view that appellant was acting in self-defense when he left his apartment, knife in hand, to confront Kellam, it escapes me how, particularly at the appellate level, it can be said *as a matter of law* that Daniels entertained a reasonable belief that he was in imminent danger of death and that there was a necessity to kill in order to save himself when his assailant *had been once stabbed, had fallen down, and was trying to get up.* The judge who was acting as fact finder did not so interpret the evidence presented to him; I see no basis for this Court to do so.

. . . My greater concern with the Court's decision, however, is that it assumes, without a word of discussion, that the common hallway of an apartment house is a no-retreat area for purposes of our law of self-defense.

The law of this Commonwealth, as i[s] well known, is that when faced with an assault of deadly force while in his own home or in his place of business, a man need not retreat but may stand his ground and meet the attack with deadly force of his own. My research reveals that we have never considered the question of whether common hallways or stairways of apartment houses are no-retreat areas . . . .

In a society that has come increasingly to live in apartments abutted by common hallways and staircases, the question implicit in this case assumes particular significance were we to consider it with the care which it warrants. Were we to agree, as I am satisfied we should, that one faced with an assault of deadly force while in an apartment hallway must retreat to his own apartment (if by doing so he could reduce the risk to his own life), then obviously appellant here could not establish self-defense in rushing in an aggressive manner from a no-retreat area (doorway of an apartment) *into* a retreat area. . . .

NOTES AND QUESTIONS

1. Why Not Retreat? The basic rule announced in *Daniels* is common across U.S. jurisdictions: even where retreat is otherwise required, that obligation is lifted in the home — and sometimes in other places, too.[*] Two

---

* Some states include vehicles or workplaces, for example, as well as the area immediately outside the home; others do not. *Compare, e.g.,* Conn. Gen. Stat. §53a-19(b) (workplace treated like dwelling); Fla. Stat. §776.013(2)(a) (occupied vehicle treated like dwelling), *with, e.g.,* People v. Aiken, 828 N.E.2d 74, 78 (N.Y. 2005) (doorway of home not treated like dwelling).

justifications typically surface for this rule. First, retreating from the home might just trade one danger for another. "There are many lonely ranches, miles away from any help or any safe place of retreat," wrote the Wyoming Supreme Court in a classic statement of the point; "[t]hat any man or woman so situated must first look about for means of escape before they can defend themselves against impending danger is not the law." Palmer v. State, 59 P. 793, 796 (Wyo. 1900). Second, home is said to be the last sanctuary—a place to retreat *to*, not *from*. A person attacked in her home, Professor Fiona Leverick writes, has a right "to remain in her home simply on the basis that it *is* her home and her source of shelter." Note that in this context, to say that the householder has a right to remain in her home is to say that she may lawfully kill to vindicate that right, even when she could have avoided killing by retreating.[126]

The disturbing case of *State v. Smith*, 876 N.W.2d 310 (Minn. 2016), puts this point in sharp relief. Byron Smith, a 64-year-old man, had been the victim of multiple burglaries in the fall of 2012; during one of those burglaries, some guns he owned were stolen. After speaking with one of his neighbors, Smith came to suspect that a different neighbor was the culprit—and that this person was "watching Smith's house to see when he came and went." *Id.* at 317. With these suspicions in mind, Smith apparently decided to set a trap. Specifically, after seeing the suspected neighbor drive by his home, Smith "moved his vehicle from his garage, which faced the street, and parked it several blocks away." *Id.* He then walked back to his house "through his backyard, which faced the river, instead of approaching the main entry of his house from the street." *Id.*

Upon reentering his house, Smith "went down to his basement and turned on a digital audio recorder." *Id.* The opinion describes his subsequent actions as follows:

> He sat down in an upholstered reading chair facing the side of the basement stairwell . . . [armed with] a nine-shot revolver . . . [and a] loaded mini-14 rifle. Smith's outdoor video surveillance system was running. In the adjacent basement workroom was a screen showing pictures from four security cameras placed around the exterior of Smith's home.
>
> [Smith's audio recorder captured him saying, "In your left eye." And then, "I realize I don't have an appointment but I would like to see one of the lawyers here." These statements were made while Smith was alone in the house, as if he was rehearsing things he would say later.]
>
> At 12:33 p.m., Nicholas Brady approached Smith's house, looked into the windows, and tried the doorknobs. Smith heard the doorknobs rattling, saw a shadow in front of the picture window in the basement, and listened as Brady walked across the deck. Then glass broke upstairs, which was the sound of Brady breaking and entering through Smith's bedroom window. Brady approached the basement stairs. Below, Smith sat waiting.

> As Brady descended the stairs, Smith saw Brady's feet, his knees, and then his hip. Smith shot Brady in the chest with the rifle. Smith later told investigators that he had not seen Brady's hands when he fired. Smith shot Brady a second time. Brady tumbled down to the basement floor, face up. Three seconds later, at close range, Smith shot the groaning Brady [again]. The bullet went through Brady's hand and then through the side of his head. Smith said to Brady, "You're dead."

Roughly eight minutes later, Haile Kifer entered Smith's house, calling for Brady. Smith shot Kifer as she descended the basement stairs, then shot her five more times, once by her left eye, killing her.

Upon arrest, Smith told the police that, for the past month, he'd felt "very threatened" and, when he heard footsteps on the stairs, he believed the burglars had returned. *Id.* at 320. He added, "I figured they're willing to use guns if they steal guns and I decided that I've got a choice of either shooting or being shot at." *Id.*

The jury convicted Smith of first-degree murder after concluding he "did not use reasonable force." As the local sheriff put the point, "We understand and respect that [the] right [to self-defense] exists, but what happened in this case went further. The law doesn't permit you to execute somebody when there's no possible way the crime can continue." On this logic, though, Smith should have been acquitted — indeed, perhaps not even arrested — if he had shot Brady and Kifer each only once, even if those shots had been fatal. Several academics and experienced attorneys said that, on those slightly altered facts, Smith's right to use deadly defensive force in his own home was clearly established under Minnesota law.[127]

2. Presuming Grave Danger. Many of the recent Stand Your Ground statutes take the castle doctrine a step further. In addition to eliminating the duty to retreat when attacked inside the home, these laws *presume* that a householder is justified in using deadly defensive force against an intruder. Wisconsin's statute, for example, provides that, if an individual uses deadly defensive force,

> the court may not consider whether the actor had an opportunity to flee or retreat . . . and shall presume that the actor reasonably believed that the force was necessary to prevent imminent death or great bodily harm . . . if . . . [t]he person against whom the force was used was in the actor's dwelling . . . after unlawfully and forcibly entering it, the actor was present in the dwelling, . . . and the actor knew or reasonably believed that the person had unlawfully and forcibly entered the dwelling.

Wis. Stat. §939.48(1m)(ar).[128]

Consider the statute's implications in the context of one incident, from March 2012 in Wisconsin, in which the police broke up a house party at which 20 or so young people, many underage, were drinking. Some of the partygoers fled, including Bo Morrison, a 20-year-old Black man, who ran and hid between a refrigerator and a dresser in the enclosed porch of a nearby house belonging to Richard Kind. Kind, who is white, had called the police to report the noisy gathering, heard noises from the back of his house, retrieved his gun, and went to investigate. Shortly after Kind entered the dark porch, he noticed Morrison stand up and asked him what he was doing. Morrison, who was unarmed, raised his hand and took a step forward, at which point Kind fired a single, fatal shot. Kind was never charged in Morrison's death — and likely could not have been, given the statute quoted above.[129]

3. Whose Castle? As historian Caroline Light observes, the castle doctrine "originated at a time when women and nonwhite people were largely excluded from the rights, protections, and immunities, of full citizenship." Its principal import was thus that it "exempted white, property-owning men from the prohibitions circumscribing the use of defensive violence." To what extent do these effects persist today? Many commentators continue to view the castle doctrine as affording special treatment to society's privileged classes. But as Professor Benjamin Levin points out, "home invasions generally take place in low-income, urban areas, which are disproportionately inhabited by citizens of color and where police response time may be greater than in more privileged areas." If that is right, he argues, "the doctrine may in fact benefit underprivileged people more than it victimizes them."[130]

4. The Cohabitant Exception. One of the most controversial aspects of the castle doctrine is whether it applies when the aggressor is not an intruder but rather a cohabitant of the defender's home. A majority of states say there is no duty to retreat from the home even when attacked by a cohabitant, but some states have gone the other way.[131]

As a matter of logic, the answer is not obvious. Some argue that if a person "is a lawful occupant, he has the right to remain in the house, and that right is not lessened or destroyed by the fact that he enjoys his right in common with another or with others." State v. Phillips, 187 A. 721, 721 (Del. 1936). That said, the idea that the home is the refuge to which we are supposed to retreat suggests the doctrine ought not apply "among members of a family, all lawfully on the premises and all lawfully claiming the home as their ultimate sanctuary." Conner v. State, 361 So. 2d 774, 775 (Fla. Dist. Ct. App. 1978).

But here, again, more interesting than the doctrine itself are the social forces that have shaped — and are shaped by — the doctrine. The castle doctrine's archetype is the household patriarch repelling an unlawful intruder, a far cry from a private, intrafamilial dispute. Reflecting this distinction, the Connecticut Supreme Court famously concluded the doctrine was clearly not "intended to sanction the reenactment of the climactic scene from 'High Noon' in the familial kitchens of this state." State v. Shaw, 441 A.2d 561, 566 (Conn. 1981).

And yet, while the cohabitant exception was initially motivated by a desire to discourage family violence, its effects may have been to facilitate precisely that, and thus have troubled generations of commentators. Simply put, "[i]mposing a duty to retreat from the home" when a person is being attacked by someone else in the household "may adversely impact victims of domestic violence." Weiand v. State, 732 So. 2d 1044, 1052 (Fla. 1999). As noted earlier in this chapter, the harms of such violence fall disproportionately on women.

As Professor Jeannie Suk Gersen observes, the early common law recoiled from "the unsettling phenomenon of wives killing husbands at home," precisely because "the idea of a wife killing her husband represented a threat not only to a human life, but to the notion of [her] being a subject who is governed" by the castle's king. The cohabitant rule arguably facilitates this patriarchal power dynamic when it comes to battered women, as it tells them they must try to escape their advancing abuser if they can, even if that requires fleeing the home. In recognition of this dynamic, several states in the 1990s began to abandon the exception, and, Suk Gersen writes, "explicitly grounded their doctrinal shifts on a sympathetic understanding of the dynamics of DV and its victims." This reorientation may have saved some women's lives. But as Suk Gersen concludes, it may have done so at the cost of framing a battered woman as "a supplicant who had to prove she was disempowered and coerced in order not to be punished for defending her life."[132]

C.   Law Enforcement Use of Force

To this point, we have examined how criminal law regulates and defines defensive force as a slice of the state's monopoly on violence delegated to private actors. Things look different, though, when the state deploys its violent powers directly—including through its official agents, the police.

Different does not necessarily mean wrong. As legal philosopher Jonathan Quong puts it, "[l]egitimate political institutions have functions that individuals do not, and as a result, they may have justifications for the use of force . . . that private individuals may lack." The criminal law agrees, and thus grants police officers authority that encompasses but also extends beyond the power to use defensive force enjoyed by civilians. Specifically, it casts aside certain restrictions on defensive force that apply to private individuals. And it authorizes violence in additional scenarios that don't involve defensive force at all.[133]

This latter use of *non*defensive violence would ordinarily be a crime. But as Professor Rachel Harmon explains, it is central to the very meaning of policing.

> If someone pushed you against a wall and took everything from your pockets, you would report a robbery. If you saw someone grab your neighbor from his driveway, tie his hands behind his back, throw him into a car, and drive away, you would report a kidnapping. And if you saw the neighbor killed while struggling to escape, you would report a murder.

When the police do these things, however, their actions are often lawful. Indeed, Harmon adds, "[t]he very thing that makes a police officer a police officer is that states authorize actions that might be criminal under different circumstances."[134]

Of course, Quong's initial observation — that *legitimate* political institutions *may* have justifications for the use of force — is conditional in at least two important respects. First, the starting premise that the relevant political institutions here (the police) are legitimate is not self-evidently or universally true. In fact, it is actively contested within and by many communities across the country, for reasons we will soon explore.

Second, the authorization to use state violence is not absolute. Violence may be justified, or may not, depending on the circumstances. In other words, such force operates within legal limits. Criminal law is not the only or even the most important source of those limits. The most familiar alternative is the Fourth Amendment, which renders unconstitutional any police use of force that effects an unreasonable "seizure" of a civilian. Over the course of decades, volumes of U.S. Supreme Court opinions have defined the word "seizure" and expounded on the word "unreasonable." We will discuss aspects of this body of law in detail in Chapter Nine; it is also typically covered in a separate course on criminal procedure.

Sometimes state criminal codes track the substance of Fourth Amendment opinions, equating unconstitutionality with criminality. But sometimes they don't. As a result, in any given case, police violence might be unconstitutional but not criminal or, more rarely, criminal but not unconstitutional. Our focus in this section is on those circumstances in which substantive criminal law exposes police officers to or shields them from criminal prosecution, with a goal of examining these issues both descriptively and critically. We begin by studying the doctrinal frameworks that define the lawful bounds of police violence. We then take stock of the problem of police violence in society and consider the role that criminal law does and should play in addressing that problem.

1. Criminal Liability for Police Use of Force

Substantive criminal law doctrines pertaining to police use of force can be difficult to trace — precisely because police officers are rarely prosecuted or convicted for using violence, including in cases where that violence seems potentially unlawful. As a result, pertinent appellate opinions, the bread and butter of law school courses like this one, are few and far between. The following opinion is one of the few we found that discusses explicitly how police authority to use force differs from that afforded private individuals.

Commonwealth v. Asher

31 N.E.3d 1055 (Mass. 2015)

BOSTFORD, J. This case concerns the beating of an unarmed civilian by the defendant Jeffrey Asher, a police officer who responded to another officer's request for assistance with a traffic stop in Springfield. The defendant was charged with assault and battery by means of a dangerous weapon . . . . At trial, the defendant contended . . . that the beating was justified based on the need for self-defense and defense of others present. The jury found him guilty of both charges. We affirm the convictions.

Background. . . . Based on the evidence presented at trial, the jury could have found the following. On the evening of November 27, 2009, Officer Michael Sedergren and Lieutenant John Bobianski of the Springfield police department were on patrol in a cruiser when they observed a black Honda Civic automobile dragging its muffler and causing sparks to fly behind it. The officers stopped the vehicle, and Bobianski spoke to the driver, Malika Barnett. While Bobianski was speaking to Barnett, Sedergren observed Barnett's companion, Melvin Jones, who was the sole passenger in the vehicle (and the victim in this case), slide toward the floor in the right front passenger's seat and stuff something in his waistband. Concerned that the victim could be hiding a weapon or other contraband, Sedergren requested assistance over the police radio from Officer Theodore Truoiolo and the defendant, who were together on patrol that night in a separate vehicle.

Once Truoiolo and the defendant arrived, all four officers approached the Honda, with two officers on each side of the vehicle.[1] Truoiolo and Sedergren went to the passenger's side and asked the victim to step out of the vehicle so that they could conduct a patfrisk[*] of him. . . . At the officers' instruction, the victim moved to the rear of the vehicle and placed his hands on the trunk. Truoiolo then began patting the victim's outer garments to check for weapons. When Truoiolo reached the victim's front right pants pocket, Truoiolo felt a hard object no bigger than his palm.[2]

---

1. The victim in this case was a black male. All four officers involved in the incident were white males.

* Editor's Note: "Patfrisk" is a term used, seemingly uniquely, in Massachusetts to describe a police tactic more commonly called a "frisk" or, sometimes, "stop and frisk." We discuss this tactic and the legal doctrines governing its use in detail in Chapter Nine.

2. On cross-examination, Officer Theodore Truoiolo admitted that the object in the victim's pants pocket could not have been a gun, and that Truoiolo never indicated to the other officers that the victim might be armed.

Truoiolo squeezed the object and yanked the victim toward himself; as he did so, the victim threw his elbow and forearm into Truoiolo's chest and tried to run away.

Sedergren caught the victim around the neck about five feet from the vehicle, but the victim continued to try to run, and the two men ended up against the side of the hood of the second police cruiser. Truoiolo then grabbed hold of the victim's collar and right shoulder, while Sedergren had the victim in a "choke hold type maneuver" and was on top of the victim's back. At this point, the victim was bent forward over the hood of the police cruiser, with his head facing the windshield and his legs spread apart. The defendant, having seen the victim try to run, went over to the cruiser where the victim was lying spread eagle. The defendant was unable to see the victim's hands, but in response to a statement of Sedergren's, the defendant began to hit the victim repeatedly around his head with a flashlight.[3] . . . [T]he defendant swung the flashlight at the victim fourteen or more times. At least three strikes made contact with the victim's head and upper body.

The victim continued to move after the first strikes to his head. The officers were shouting commands such as, "don't move" and, "give us your hands," but they did not state that the victim was under arrest. Eventually, Truoiolo cuffed the victim's right hand but could not reach the victim's left hand because of where Sedergren was positioned. The defendant, realizing that many of his blows were hitting the hood of the cruiser rather than the victim's upper body, moved down and delivered three hard blows with the flashlight to the victim's upper leg. Then, in response to another statement from Sedergren, the defendant hit the victim behind his left knee.[4] Following that blow, the victim fell to the ground with the officers on top of him. The defendant continued to hit the victim as he was lying still on the ground, this time around the victim's upper body and his feet. Eventually, the officers rolled the victim to the side while he lay on the ground and finished handcuffing him, and then Truoiolo reached into the victim's pocket and pulled out the hard object that he had felt earlier, a small bag that was determined to contain "crack" cocaine and marijuana. The victim had no weapons on his person, and no weapons were found in the vehicle.

---

3. The exact words that Officer Michael Sedergren used were somewhat in dispute. Sedergren testified that he said, "He's got my fucking gun, smash him"; the defendant testified that Sedergren said, "He's got my gun, hit him, hit him."

4. Sedergren testified that he called for the defendant to strike the victim again after Sedergren heard Truoiolo say that the victim was "going for his waist." However, as previously noted, Truoiolo knew that the victim did not have a gun in his waistband, and Truoiolo gave no indication to the other officers following the patfrisk that the victim might be armed. Truoiolo admitted on cross-examination that any possible threat of deadly force against the officers was neutralized by the time that Truoiolo handcuffed the victim's right hand.

The victim was taken by ambulance to Baystate Medical Center [with severe injuries to his head, which caused lasting vision loss]. . . .

DISCUSSION

. . . [T]his case was fundamentally about the reasonableness of a police officer's use of force against a civilian; therefore, the judge's instructions should have acknowledged the defendant's status and explained that, as a police officer, the defendant would have been justified in using force in connection with his official duties . . . as long as such force was necessary and reasonable. . . .

In addition, the defendant raises legitimate concerns with respect to the judge's instruction on self-defense. . . . [T]he judge referenced a defendant's obligation to do "everything reasonable in the circumstances to avoid physical combat before resorting to force" including considering "avenues of escape that were reasonably available." . . . We agree with the defendant that a police officer has an obligation to protect his fellow officers and the public at large that goes beyond that of an ordinary citizen, such that retreat or escape is not a viable option for an on-duty police officer faced with a potential threat of violence. . . . Furthermore, while it is appropriate to require a police officer to do "everything reasonable in the circumstances to avoid physical combat before resorting to force" against a civilian, the question must be whether the defendant *as a police officer* had reasonable options available other than to use force—not whether a similarly situated civilian would have had other options.

In sum, the judge's instructions to the jury were erroneous in two respects: (1) they failed to acknowledge, particularly in connection with the claim of self-defense, that the defendant was a police officer and that he was entitled to use force in carrying out his official duties if and to the extent such force was necessary and reasonable; and (2) the self-defense instruction included an erroneous statement that the defendant had a duty to retreat if possible under the circumstances. We turn, then, to the question whether the errors were prejudicial to the defendant. . . .

Considering the jury instructions as a whole . . . we conclude that the errors were not prejudicial. At trial, the defendant admitted to hitting the victim repeatedly with the flashlight, the victim clearly sustained significant injuries, and the only issue was whether the defendant's acts were justified. The record as a whole presents extremely strong evidence that the defendant did not strike the victim in the manner that he did in self-defense and in defense of his fellow officers. The video recording of the beating showed three officers surrounding a single victim, who was bent over the hood of a car as the defendant struck him repeatedly with a flashlight. Sedergren, who was on top of the victim's back and was holding him around the neck, weighed between 250 and 260 pounds at the time of the incident;

the victim, by comparison, weighed about 165 or 170 pounds. None of the officers saw the victim's hand on Sedergren's gun. Moreover, based on the officers' positioning around the victim, it was implausible if not impossible that the victim could have reached the gun, because it was holstered on the right side of Sedergren's body, where Truoiolo was. . . . [T]he video recording also belied the defense's theory, because although an officer can be heard on the recording yelling "smash him in the knees," . . . there was no audible statement or reference regarding a gun.

Furthermore, . . . the judge explained that whether a defendant was justified in using force . . . depended upon what a reasonable person would have done in the circumstances that were presented *to the defendant*. . . . Even in the absence of a specific instruction on the defendant's status as a police officer, it was clear to the jury that he was, in fact, an officer, and that at the time of the incident, he was involved in a traffic stop as part of his official duties. Moreover, . . . the defendant introduced evidence concerning the "continuum" of force that police officers are trained to use in responding to an individual who presents varying degrees of threatening behavior or resistance. We presume that the jury . . . evaluated the defendant's claims of self-defense and defense of others from the perspective of what a reasonable police officer would have done in the circumstances presented to him or her.

Finally, . . . [even] if the judge had charged the jury that the defendant was entitled to use such force as was necessary and reasonable to carry out his official duties, the addition of this instruction would not have had an effect on the verdicts. The force that the defendant used here . . . was extreme and went beyond that which was necessary for the accomplishment of any of the defendant's responsibilities as a police officer that night. Even if the defendant believed at one point that the victim was trying to grab Sedergren's gun, that danger would have completely dissipated by the time the victim was on the ground; yet even then, the defendant continued to strike the victim. In these circumstances, assuming the jury had been instructed properly about the defendant's police officer status, the jury reasonably could not have found that the beating was justified. . . .

NOTES AND QUESTIONS

1. Initial Aggression and Provocation. The self-defense privilege is generally unavailable to someone who starts the trouble by launching or provoking the initial attack. But police officers sometimes have no choice other than to initiate a violent encounter, as part of their job is to arrest people. Indeed, one might say that the power to arrest "is a condition precedent to the state's entire system of law enforcement," given that most people would not go to jail or face prosecution voluntarily. Tennessee v. Garner, 471 U.S. 1, 10 (1985). And as the Supreme Court has long recognized, "the right to make an arrest . . . necessarily carries with it the right to use some degree of physical coercion or threat thereof." Graham v. Connor, 490 U.S. 386, 396 (1989).

As these opinions make clear, "police have the unique power to initiate violence — like knocking down the door of a private home in the middle of the night — that other people don't." When the police break into a house this way, they often do so in full tactical gear with guns drawn, a highly provocative act that occurs countless times a year when officers execute legally valid search warrants. Likewise, police conduct millions of weapons searches each year, like the "patfrisk" mentioned in *Asher*. Each of those encounters is a highly intrusive physical act: "A thorough search must be made of the [suspect's] arms and armpits, waistline and back, the groin and area about the testicles, and entire surface of the legs down to the feet." Terry v. Ohio, 392 U.S. 1, 17 n.13 (1968). And yet, these provocative and aggressive actions are part and parcel of policing itself. For this reason, as Professor Cynthia Lee notes, statutes on police use of force generally "do not contain an initial aggressor limitation."[135]

But what if the officer's initial actions are not themselves a *lawful* exercise of police authority, as in the case of an arrest without probable cause? Or what if the circumstances are cloudy? Consider the infamous raid in which police officers killed Breonna Taylor. The Constitution requires police officers to knock and announce themselves as law enforcement officials before executing a search warrant. As the Supreme Court has explained, this requirement exists for "the protection of human life and limb, because an unannounced entry may provoke violence in supposed self-defense by the surprised resident." Hudson v. Michigan, 547 U.S. 586, 594 (2006). In Taylor's case, it is not clear the officers ever announced their presence before forcing their way into Taylor's apartment shortly after midnight. Taylor's boyfriend, Kenneth Walker, did not know the intruders were police and fired one shot at them in self-protection, just as the *Hudson* Court feared might occur. The officers returned fire, killing Taylor and sparking a renewed wave of national protests over police killings of unarmed Black people.[136]

Walker was prosecuted for the single shot he fired at the armed men he thought were breaking into his house. Those charges were dismissed a year later. But they raise an important question. How should we evaluate the attempted use of defensive force by civilians — and police responses to that defensive force — when police officers initiate violence in ways that are at best only questionably legal? At common law, civilians had the right to resist an unlawful arrest, which could in turn render the officer's response to such resistance unlawful. *See, e.g.,* Bad Elk v. United States, 177 U.S. 529 (1900). This position lost ground in the mid-twentieth century. Still, 13 states retain the right to resist today, and some even authorize the civilian to use deadly force against the officer. *See, e.g.,* State v. McGowan, 557 S.E.2d 657, 659

(S.C. 2001) ("[A] person has a right to resist an unlawful arrest even to the extent of taking the life of the aggressor if it be necessary in order to regain his liberty.").[137]

2. Duty to Retreat. As we learned earlier, many states (albeit a minority) require an individual to retreat before using deadly defensive force if it is possible to do so safely. When it comes to police use of force, however, the *Asher* court states the longstanding and uniform rule: "[R]etreat or escape is not a viable option for an on-duty police officer faced with a potential threat of violence." Here, too, the logic of the rule flows from the power to arrest itself, which could easily be frustrated if the police were required to run away anytime someone tried to resist an arrest with violence. Indeed, the Commentaries to the MPC insist that "[t]here can be no controversy" on this point, as "public policy demands" that police functions like making an arrest or executing a court order "be performed and that, if forcible resistance is encountered, it be overcome." Model Penal Code and Commentaries §3.04 cmt. 4(c) at 57.[138]

In recent years, however, the concept of *de-escalation* has emerged as a focal point for police reform. Officers are being trained and encouraged to de-escalate altercations whenever possible rather than to "overcome" any "forcible resistance." As noted by the President's Task Force on 21st Century Policing during the Obama Administration, this approach can sometimes involve retreating:

> In traditional police culture, officers are taught never to back down from a confrontation, but instead to run *toward* the dangerous situation that everyone else is running away from. However, sometimes the best tactic for dealing with a minor confrontation is to *step back*, call for assistance, [and] de-escalate . . . .[139]

Of course, to say that retreat and de-escalation can be more effective or just police tactics is not the same as saying the police should be *criminally* liable if they opt instead to press forward with force. Should the criminal law impose such liability?

One scenario in which issues of retreat and necessity frequently arise is when a civilian is armed with a knife or blunt instrument but not a gun. In 2017, for example, officers approached Scout Schultz, a 21-year-old student at Georgia Tech, outside a dormitory on campus. The officers were responding to a call about an individual with a knife. They saw Schultz carrying a multitool with a small blade, which was not extended, and which the officers repeatedly asked Schultz to drop. Schultz did not drop the tool but instead walked slowly toward the officers, arms down, saying, "Shoot me." As Schultz moved toward officer Tyler Beck, Beck fired a single, fatal shot into Schultz's chest. A video of the incident is widely available. Among other things, it reveals no bystanders at risk from Schultz.

The prosecutor declined to charge Beck in Schultz's death, deeming the shooting justified.[140]

Professor Frank Zimring points out that, across six years of nationwide data, people "who brandish knives and rush at police or who waive blunt objects as they lurch toward an officer *never* caused a death of an officer." "One wonders," Zimring continues, "whether such weapons should really be considered deadly weapons when police in uniform are the targets." If not, "then the hundreds of killings each year by officers responding to the brandishing of such weapons" might not actually "be necessary to protecting the lives of American police." Indeed, in the UK and Germany, where civilian firearms are scarce, fatal police-civilian interactions register in the single digits. These figures, Zimring argues, "provid[e] reassurance that failing to kill those who use weapons other than guns against police is not an indicator of increased risk to police lives."[141]

In 2020, California revised its penal code in an effort to accommodate the competing principles just discussed. The new statute, California Penal Code §835a, first reaffirms that a police "officer who makes or attempts to make an arrest need not retreat or desist from their efforts by reason of the resistance or threatened resistance of the person being arrested." *Id.* §835a(d). It goes on, however, to specify that "'retreat' does not mean tactical repositioning or other deescalation tactics." *Id.* In other words, the failure to use "tactical repositioning or other deescalation tactics" *does* inform the ultimate determination of whether an officer used "objectively reasonable force," as California law requires. *Id.* §835a(b).

3. Proportionality. For a private citizen, self-defense is generally lawful only if it is proportional. Roughly speaking, force may be used to defend against force, and deadly force against deadly force. But the police frequently use force to perform duties that are not defensive at all, such as forcing a suspect to submit to a search or arrest. Are the police required to use proportional force when effectuating those aims? And what would proportional mean in this context?

States disagree on the circumstances in which the criminal law prohibits the use of deadly force to effect an arrest. No state authorizes deadly force to arrest a misdemeanor suspect, but the treatment of felony suspects varies considerably.

In a 1985 decision called *Tennessee v. Garner*, 471 U.S. 1 (1985), the Supreme Court held that an officer violates the Fourth Amendment when he uses deadly force to prevent the escape of a fleeing felony suspect unless such force "is necessary to prevent the escape and the officer has probable cause to believe that the suspect poses a significant threat of death or serious physical injury to the officer or others." *Id.* at 3. Later, in *Graham v. Connor*, 490 U.S. 386 (1989), the Court indicated that the test for excessive force is a more general "test of reasonableness" that "is not capable of precise definition," but which considers such factors as "the severity of the crime at issue, whether the suspect poses an immediate threat to the safety of the officers or others, and whether he is actively resisting arrest or attempting to evade arrest by flight." *Id.* at 396.

The states, however, are not required to criminalize every unconstitutional act. As a historical matter, many states did choose to conform their criminal codes to the Fourth Amendment's limitations, turning a Fourth Amendment violation into a crime. But other states have criminalized less than the full scope of conduct prohibited by the Fourth Amendment. In some states, for example, it is not a crime for an officer to use deadly force to stop a fleeing felony suspect whether or not there is probable cause to believe the suspect is armed and dangerous.

Consider in this context the fatal encounter that occurred in Ferguson, Missouri, in the summer of 2014, when a white police officer named Darren Wilson shot and killed Michael Brown, an unarmed Black teenager. Alongside the police killing of Eric Garner, another unarmed Black person, just weeks earlier, the shooting of Michael Brown—and the protests that followed when prosecutors declined to charge Wilson with a crime—sparked the national Black Lives Matter movement. The highly controversial decision not to file charges was later reinforced when the Civil Rights Division of the U.S. Department of Justice also declined to prosecute Wilson for the same incident, releasing a detailed report describing its investigation and its reasoning.[142]

Much of the debate over these decisions centered on whether Wilson reasonably feared for his life or safety when he fired at Brown. That inquiry turns on questions such as whether Brown's hands were up when Wilson shot him and how much distance separated the two men. But it turns out that Wilson had a separate defense to state murder charges under Missouri law: If he reasonably believed that deadly force was necessary to *arrest* Brown, he could not be prosecuted for the homicide.

On this latter question, the evidence was less ambiguous. Prior to the fatal encounter, Brown had taken a pack of cigarillos from a nearby convenience store without paying, prompting a police dispatcher to put out a call for officers to respond to a "stealing in progress." Wilson was answering that call when he encountered Brown, who matched the description of—and indeed was—the suspect. Putting aside the question of whether Brown's subsequent actions during the encounter threatened Wilson's safety, they do seem to show that Brown was unwilling to submit to arrest:

> Wilson and other witnesses stated that [when Wilson attempted to exit his police cruiser] Brown then reached into the SUV through the open driver's window and punched and grabbed Wilson. This is corroborated by bruising on Wilson's jaw and scratches on his neck, the presence of Brown's DNA on Wilson's collar, shirt, and pants, and Wilson's DNA on Brown's palm.[143]

As a trio of commentators would later explain, if the grand jury tasked with deciding whether to file murder charges against Wilson "believed . . . that Brown had no intention to surrender, then, under Missouri law, they could not vote to indict." In other words, these authors argued, while many "have blamed the prosecutors or the bias of the grand jurors" for failing to seek justice in this case, "the decision more likely reflect[ed] the failure of the law to properly calibrate the permissible use of deadly force by police officers when they attempt to arrest a suspect."[144]

Following Brown's death, Missouri narrowed this defense, immunizing use of deadly force to effect an arrest only when the suspect poses a threat of serious physical injury to the arresting officer or others. *See* Mo. Rev. Stat. §563.046(3).

2. The Problem of Police Violence

In the summer of 2014, as noted above, the nascent Black Lives Matter movement burst into the national consciousness when white police officers killed two unarmed Black people, Michael Brown and Eric Garner, over the span of just a few weeks in two different cities. Though sparked by those deaths, the national protests that followed were fueled by generations of simmering resentment flowing from similar instances of police violence tracing back over decades — through famous names like Amadou Diallo and Rodney King and through countless others known only to families and local communities.[145]

Six years later, the world watched as Minneapolis police officer Derek Chauvin knelt on the neck of George Floyd, another Black man, for over nine minutes, purportedly arresting him for tendering a counterfeit $20 bill. Floyd's brutal murder sent 15 to 26 million people to the streets in the United States, and many more worldwide — turning Black Lives Matter into what some have called the largest social movement in American history.[146]

The list of our nation's historic injustices against African Americans is long. Even so, according to Professor Paul Butler,

> nothing since slavery — not Jim Crow segregation, not forced convict labor, not lynching, not restrictive covenants in housing, not being shut out of New Deal programs like Social Security and the GI Bill, not massive resistance to school desegregation, not the ceaseless efforts to prevent African Americans from voting — nothing has sparked the level of outrage among African Americans as when they have felt under violent attack by the police.[147]

In this section, we present evidence about the frequency and distribution of police violence in the United States. The section that follows explores the role that criminal prosecution does and ought to play in quelling that violence.

NOTES AND QUESTIONS

1. The Scale of Police Violence. Law enforcement in the United States is thoroughly decentralized, with roughly 18,000 distinct law enforcement agencies employing over 750,000 sworn officers at the federal, state, county, and city levels. Across all these many police departments, there is no central repository for use-of-force data, nor any general requirement that agencies capture data on use of force or make them public. Congress ordered the Attorney General to collect and report data on excessive force almost 30 years ago, but that simply never happened. And while the FBI launched a new effort in 2019, few agencies have submitted data in response. Other government data sources, such as the Center for Disease Control and Prevention's National Vital Statistics System, have been shown to underestimate the incidence of police violence by more than half. All this makes it incredibly difficult to assess how, when, where, and against whom the police are using force.[148]

The best available data have been compiled by journalists and activists in the government's stead, with a focus on police *fatalities.* These data show that, in each year since 2015, police officers have killed about 1,000 people. This is a large number: Police use of force is among the leading causes of death for young men in the United States and the U.S. rate of police killings is massive by international standards.[149]

The total number of police *shootings* — both fatal and nonfatal — is likely much higher. Again, there are no official statistics, but credible estimates put the total number at two to three times the number of fatal shootings, meaning that roughly one-third to one-half of police shootings are deadly.[150]

Good data are even scarcer for so-called "less lethal" force — things like Tasers, pepper spray, and batons. Here, data are typically available only from individual agencies that volunteer it, and many don't. Using data on hospital admissions, one team of researchers estimated that police encounters involving "less lethal" force led to over 50,000 hospital visits in 2012 alone, not counting an estimated 4,200 bites by police dogs. A large majority of the injuries were caused by blows with the body or blunt objects. There is some evidence that police violence has become more salient in recent years not because it's getting worse but rather because societal responses to it — including the Black Lives Matter protests themselves — have intensified.[151]

2. The Distribution of Police Violence. Of course, what makes this issue so explosive is not only the amount of harm the police inflict, but also the distribution of that harm, particularly across racial groups. Black and Hispanic men are 2.5 and 1.3 times more likely to be killed by the police than their white peers, respectively. The risk is highest for Black men, who face

1-in-1,000 lifetime odds of being killed by the police. According to one study, "across a large proportion of counties, individuals who were shot by police had a higher median probability of being *unarmed* black individuals than being *armed* white individuals." And the Black-white disparity for "less lethal" force is, if anything, at least as large.[152]

What is somewhat less clear is the point in the chain of events leading up to a violent police-civilian interaction at which these disparities arise—and, in particular, what role racial bias plays in causing them. One possibility is that the police are more likely to use force against Black people than white people during similar interactions, either due to racial animus, racialized fear, or implicit bias. But an alternative explanation could be that the disparity in use of force reflects an underlying disparity in interaction rates. On this account, Black men are harmed by the police more often than others because they interact with the police more frequently. Indeed, some data show that the proportion of all force incidents that involve Black men is similar to the proportion of police-civilian interactions that involve Black men.[153]

The latter story is sometimes offered to argue that the police are not biased in the critical decision of whether to use force once a given interaction is underway. But this conclusion doesn't necessarily follow, for a somewhat subtle reason. Studies show that racial bias likely affects who gets stopped by the police in the first place—either because some individual officers discriminate against Black people or because structural biases drive policy-level decisions about where the police are sent. Any such biases will skew the populations of people being stopped and arrested along racial lines, in a way that makes it *less* likely that Black people who are stopped are engaged in any criminal activity. That is, if the police are biased in favor of stopping Black people (relative to white people), they are employing a lower threshold of suspicion before initiating interactions with Black people. As a result, more of the Black people stopped will be doing nothing wrong. This means that equal rates of police violence across the two groups supports the conclusion that anti-Black bias is at play *in the decision to use force.* Absent such bias, we would expect force to be used less often against Black people, because Black people stopped by the police are less frequently engaged in illegal activity.[154]

3. Communal Consequences of Police Violence. The effects of racialized police violence—especially unjustified violence—reach far beyond the physical harms inflicted, and beyond the direct victims and their families. One recent study, for example, found that living in close proximity to police killings led to lower GPAs, elevated levels of emotional disturbance, and reduced rates of graduation and college enrollment for high school students in Los Angeles. The effects were concentrated in Black and Hispanic students and were largest when unarmed people of color were killed.

Another study found that police killings of unarmed Black people, specifically, are associated with more poor mental health days among Black people generally (but not white people) in the following month or two. We will return to the community-level and racialized impacts of police maltreatment in Chapter Nine.[155]

3.   Accountability and the Criminal Law

As noted in the introduction to this chapter, the phrase "Black Lives Matter" was a call to prosecute and convict police officers accused of killing Black people — to show them and the world that Black lives really do matter, in the face of police violence that often sends the opposite message. In the broader context of institutionalized police behavior, criminal prosecutions of individual officers play relatively little part in societal efforts to tackle the problem of police violence. On one level, this is not surprising. If police violence is a product of structural forces, it will require a layered response in which multiple policymakers collaborate to change police behavior. Indeed, undue focus on individual accountability could reinforce the idea that the structural problems themselves do not exist — that police violence is, to quote a common phrase, the product of "a few bad apples." Still, when the police kill, calls for individual accountability often ring loudly. And commentators and activists alike have debated whether prosecutors' approach to police violence ought to change, raising the question: How much criminal prosecution of police officers who kill should we want? Consider that question as you read the following notes.

NOTES AND QUESTIONS

1. The Infrequency of Police Prosecutions. Police officers are rarely charged with crimes for on-duty conduct, even in cases that shock the public conscience. Even fewer are convicted or serve any prison time. No charges were filed, for example, against the officers who took the lives of Michael Brown, Eric Garner, Tamir Rice, or Stephon Clark; those who killed Freddie Gray, Rekia Boyd, and Philando Castile were acquitted. The convictions of Derek Chauvin for the murder of George Floyd, Jason Van Dyke for the murder of Laquan McDonald, and Michael Slager for the murder of Walter Scott are notable in their rarity. Extrapolating from data discussed earlier, police officers likely shot and killed around 15,000 people between 2005 and 2020; but by one count only 121 officers were arrested for murder or manslaughter for on-duty killings during that span of time and only 44 were convicted, often of a lesser charge.[156]

2. "The Prosecution Team." There are multiple, overlapping explanations for why police prosecutions are so rare and so seldom successful. First and foremost, the local criminal prosecutors with authority to bring charges have close relationships with and depend heavily upon their local police departments. It's the police who track down suspects and gather the evidence needed to secure their convictions. Likewise, it is the police who are positioned to have the biggest impact on public perceptions of local crime rates—even though the head prosecutor is often the only law enforcement leader who stands for election. Taking these dynamics together, it is clear that the police are "an integral part of the prosecution team." *E.g.*, Mastracchio v. Vose, 274 F.3d 590, 600 (1st Cir. 2001). Suffice to say, prosecuting members of the team can cause serious tensions, as numerous progressive prosecutors who have promised greater police accountability in recent years have seen firsthand.[157]

One possible way to overcome this challenge is to bring in prosecutors who aren't on the same team. New Jersey, for example, recently authorized the appointment of independent prosecutors in certain cases involving police defendants—though the practice in most states is still to have the local prosecutor's office spearhead prosecutions for alleged violations of state law.[158]

Federal prosecutors are another option. In fact, the U.S. Department of Justice has a dedicated team of prosecutors within its Civil Rights Division who focus specifically on police misconduct cases. Their jurisdiction flows from 18 U.S.C. §242, which criminalizes the "willful[l]" deprivation of civil rights, including the right not to be subjected to police brutality. The four officers involved in the death of George Floyd, for example, were indicted under this law. Overall, however, federal prosecutions of the police are exceedingly rare. Partly this is a matter of limited resources; only the most egregious police abuses rise to the level of federal investigation. But it may also in part be because the Supreme Court has interpreted §242 to require prosecutors to prove that the police acted with "a purpose to deprive a person of a specific constitutional right." Screws v. United States, 325 U.S. 91, 101 (1945) (plurality opinion). As Judge Paul Watford writes, "[i]t's never been entirely clear how the government is supposed to go about proving this element of the offense," but the "one thing everyone agrees on" is that "*Screws* has made it harder for the government to win convictions, even in cases where the defendants obviously acted in bad faith." The George Floyd Justice in Policing Act of 2020 would have substituted this standard with the more traditional *mens rea* requirement that the police acted "knowingly or recklessly," but the bill did not pass.[159]

3. Blue Walls and Bills of Rights. Beyond potential prosecutor loyalties, police officers also enjoy procedural protections unavailable to other criminal suspects that make it more difficult to build a case against them. Often secured by union contracts or special statutes, these packages of protections are generally referred to as police officer "bills of rights." Police in some jurisdictions, for example, cannot be interrogated until 48 hours after arrest and are permitted to review inculpatory evidence before submitting to an interview. Moreover, once the case goes to trial, police officers often make credible witnesses in their own defense. In part this is because they are professionally trained to *be* witnesses and often have ample experience testifying in the same courthouse in the trials or hearings of people they have arrested. In some communities, the officers' professional stature and authority may further bolster them in the eyes of juries and judges. Finally, the widespread "blue wall of silence," an informal code under which officers conceal each other's misdeeds, can hobble prosecutions by blocking prosecutors' access to crucial testimony — including testimony from officers who may be the only surviving witnesses to a fatal police shooting.[160]

In recent years, some states have begun to revise the law on some of these procedural issues. Maryland, for example, recently repealed its Law Enforcement Officer Bill of Rights, putting police defendants on closer-to-level footing with other criminal suspects. Of course, as noted earlier in this section, the substantive criminal law itself often insulates police use of force — including deadly force — from criminal liability altogether. Prosecutors, in other words, might not always be declining to charge officers who've committed crimes; rather, police conduct that shocks members of the public may not actually be criminal in the first place.[161]

4. The Case for More Prosecutions. Should prosecutors pursue criminal charges against police officers more often? Some think so, for multiple reasons. First, tracking a retributivist argument, is the claim that officers need to be held accountable. The same bills of rights that often impede prosecutions can render employment sanctions unavailable, while robust doctrines of immunity and broad indemnification policies protect officers from civil liability when they are sued. Even when officers are fired, which is rare, they are often reinstated through labor arbitration or find jobs at other departments. Criminal prosecutions, proponents argue, are the most appropriate response to violent and unlawful police behavior — and sometimes seem like the only legal response within reach. Then there is deterrence and incapacitation. Research has consistently shown that a small number of officers commit a grossly disproportionate amount of misconduct. Prosecuting those officers may be the best way to pluck them off the street—and send an important message to others. Finally, from an expressivist perspective, even those who may generally champion more lenient approaches to criminal justice might underscore the unique impact on affected communities when agents of the state itself cause serious harm. Frequently, these community members *want* criminal prosecution of officers who hurt and kill—and believe that failure to prosecute degrades not just the lives of those lost, but of everyone else in the community as well.[162]

5. Problematizing Police Prosecutions from the Right: Policing Is Hard. Other commentators reject the call for more aggressive prosecution of the police. While the police wield unparalleled power to inflict harm, the argument goes, they also take on substantial personal risk. In a nation with more guns than people, we rely on them to resolve our most volatile situations. Some other occupations may have higher accident and fatality rates, but there is likely none with higher rates of intentional, assaultive violence. By one count, roughly 10 percent of officers are assaulted on the job each year. Moreover, just as with killings *by* the police, Professor Zimring documents, "the rate at which American police are killed in attacks is . . . much higher in the United States than elsewhere." Given all these risks, not to mention the split-second tactical decisions officers must make, some argue it is simply unfair to prosecute officers who err, except in the most egregious cases.[163]

What is more, the threat of criminal liability may well discourage some new entrants into the profession, potentially decreasing the quality of officers over the long run. Law enforcement leaders already assert that it's never been harder to recruit good candidates. Likewise, the threat of criminal liability for actions taken on the job may drive existing officers to find ways to spend less time actively policing. To the extent policing itself is a public good, discouraging *good* policing is a social loss. From this perspective, it is better to use milder, non-penal mechanisms like employment sanctions or civil liability to keep officers in line. Indeed, as we learned in Chapter Two, sanctions that are swift and certain, but relatively light, may achieve greater deterrence than the distant threat of criminal punishment — and possibly with lower risk of scaring people away from the profession.[164]

6. Problematizing Police Prosecutions from the Left: Don't Level Up, or Ignore the Real Issue. Still other commentators see calls for aggressive prosecution of the police as a species of *progressive carceralism* that ultimately reflects the same punitive impulses that gave rise to mass incarceration. These voices recognize and are deeply troubled by the double standards inherent in a system that harshly punishes everyone whom the police arrest but goes light on the police themselves. Still, the better course, these thinkers urge, is to treat all defendants more like police defendants. Rather than taking procedural protections away from police suspects, we should give those same protections to everyone else. More fundamentally, rather than prosecute *more* police, we should prosecute *fewer* civilians. Indeed, one might worry that the impulse toward more punishment for the police could be particularly damaging to the effort to end mass incarceration precisely because, as noted in the introduction to this chapter, the same people are sometimes working for both causes. It is not impossible to advocate abolition of prisons and also greater use of them for police, but there is at least some tension in such a position.[165]

A final critique maintains that the focus on individual prosecutions obscures the underlying structural and cultural forces that feed the police-violence problem. "It creates scapegoats that may satisfy society's moral outrage," Professor Barbara Armacost observes, "while deflecting attention away from the institutional structures that lie at the root of the problem of police brutality." Even if "a relatively small number of repeat offenders per-petrat[e] a large majority of incidents of police violence," as the data show, Armacost argues that police officers still "act within the constraints of a very powerful organizational culture that significantly influences and constrains their judgments and conduct." Thus, the repeat-offender phenomenon says as much, if not more, she argues, about that culture and the "formal and informal norms and expectations that create the environment in which the brutal acts [are] allowed to continue" as it does about the offenders them-selves. All of this suggests, Armacost concludes, that "no legal strategy that ignores the power of the police organization will have any lasting success in addressing police brutality."[166]

In the following excerpt, Mariame Kaba and Andrea Ritchie, two lead-ing voices with respect to police abolition, discuss these questions in the context of the killing of Breonna Taylor, discussed earlier in this chapter (p. 305)

Mariame Kaba & Andrea J. Ritchie, *We Want More Justice for Breonna Taylor Than the System That Killed Her Can Deliver*, in Mariame Kaba, *We Do This 'Til We Free Us* 63, 64-66 (2021). As prison-industrial complex abolition-ists, we want far more than what the system that killed Breonna Taylor can offer — because the system that killed her is not set up to provide justice for her family and loved ones. . . . [U]ltimately we must choose to support collective responses that align with our values. We can't claim the system must be dismantled because it is a danger to Black lives and at the same time legitimize it by turning to it for justice. As Angela Y. Davis points out, "we have to be consistent" in our analysis and not respond to violence in a way that compounds it. We need to use our radical imaginations to come up with new structures of accountability beyond the system we are working to dismantle.

This is neither a popular nor easy position to take. It's really, really hard. People who have been or seen their loved ones arrested, prose-cuted, incarcerated, and killed for the slightest infraction — or none at all — want the system to act fairly by arresting, prosecuting, and incar-cerating those who harm and kill us. People who have consistently been denied protection under the law desperately want the law to live up to its promises. . . . [T]here is no question Breonna's family is enti-tled to accountability — including immediate termination of the officers involved in her killing, and banning them from any future position that would allow them to carry a weapon or hold a position of power that can be abused in the way they abused it in Breonna's case. They are also entitled to a process through which the officers must hear and be accountable to their pain, know the full value of the life they took, and make amends to our collective satisfaction. . . . Breonna's family—and all of us—are . . . entitled to more than an individualized response to what is a systemic problem.

D.   *Self-Defense as Excuse*

Sometimes, the criminal law refuses to impose liability when a person uses defensive force even if there was no justified reason to harm or kill the person injured by the defendant. Here, the defendant escapes conviction not because he did what the law considers the right thing, but rather because he could not reasonably have been expected to behave differently under the circumstances. His actions, in other words, are *excused.* As Professor George Fletcher explains, "[a] justification speaks to the rightness of an act; an excuse, to whether the actor is accountable for the concededly wrongful act."[167]

As we have seen, a number of classic doctrines operate exclusively as excuses, including the doctrines of insanity, intoxication, and infancy that we studied in Chapter Three. In each of these settings, it is clear the defendant's conduct was wrong, even though a disability of mind or circumstance renders him undeserving of criminal sanction. Self-defense, by contrast, is a hybrid. Sometimes it works as a justification, as in the case of a defender who protects himself against an unlawful aggressor. But other times it shields those who did something wrongful but understandable. The key here is once again the concept of reasonableness. To quote one leading treatise, self-defense is permissible when a person "*reasonably believes* (a) that he is in immediate danger of unlawful bodily harm from his adversary and (b) that the use of such force is necessary to avoid this danger." If the defender's belief is accurate, his conduct is justified, because he really *was* in danger. But a "reasonable belief" can also be *inaccurate:* you might reasonably believe you are in danger even though really you are not. In that case, your defensive use of force is excused, though not justified. The concept of "reasonableness" thus takes on enormous importance, as the cases and notes in this section make plain.[168]

Students sometimes wonder why criminal law professors insist on teaching the distinction between justification and excuse when it seems to make so little practical difference. After all, a valid defense of whichever type results in the defendant's acquittal. To be fair, the distinction has some

practical implications when one gets down in the weeds.* But the basic
question is a good one, and two responses stand out. First, justification and
excuse *communicate* different messages to the individuals involved. As legal
philosopher John Gardner explains:

> Criminal lawyers . . . tend to take it for granted that any doctrine that
> serves to acquit the accused, and therefore to avert the adverse normative
> consequences of her action, is as good as any other so far as the accused is
> concerned . . . . [But this] implies that nobody who is tried in the criminal
> courts has . . . any self-respect. . . . The self-respecting person aspires to
> live up to the proper standards for success in and fitness for the life she
> leads, and holds herself out to be judged by those standards. It follows
> that . . . a self-respecting person wants . . . it to be the case [first] that her
> actions were not truly wrongful, or if they were wrongful, that they were
> at any rate justified, or if they were not justified, that they were at any rate
> excused.[169]

The law's communicative message speaks in similar fashion to those harmed
by the defendant. There is a big difference, for example, between being
told that your loved one is dead because *he* was in the wrong and the defendant rightfully killed him with justified force, or being told instead that your
loved one should still be here — that his death was a terrible mistake, and
no fault of his own.

Second, it is valuable to distinguish excuses from justifications to better understand why the law acquits those whose conduct is merely excusable. One answer, favored by Jeremy Bentham, is that excuses kick in when
conduct is undeterrable and punishment would be nothing but a pointless
cruelty. The threat of criminal punishment will not influence an individual
who is insane, for example, so Bentham argues nothing is lost by declining
to punish his crimes. The legal philosopher H.L.A. Hart disagrees, arguing
that Bentham's claim neglects general deterrence. After all, Hart argues,
"if the law contained no [excuses], many people who now take a chance in
the hope that they will bring themselves, if discovered, within these exempting provisions would in fact be deterred." Eliminating excuses, in other
words, could "maintain the efficacy of threats [of punishment] for others
at its highest." Still, Hart defends excuses on different grounds: Sometimes,
he observes, we find ourselves in dire circumstances that we cannot predict, prevent, or control that impel us to violate the law. The function of
excuses, Hart argues, is to assure us the law will afford some grace if we are
so unlucky.[170]

---

* For example, the distinction between justification and excuse may have implications
for the liability of third parties: it may be permissible to assist someone engaged in a justified
act, like legitimate self-defense, but not an excused act, like a robbery committed by someone who is insane. *See* George P. Fletcher, *Rethinking Criminal Law* 760-762 (Oxford Univ.
Press 2000) (1978).

We now turn to examining how self-defense and police use of force each can function as an excuse under certain circumstances — including when the defendant may reasonably but *mistakenly* believe force is needed.

People v. Goetz

497 N.E.2d 41 (N.Y. 1986)

WACHTLER, C.J. A Grand Jury has indicted defendant on attempted murder, assault, and other charges for having shot and wounded four youths on a New York City subway train after one or two of the youths approached him and asked for $5. The lower courts, concluding that the prosecutor's charge to the Grand Jury on the defense of justification was erroneous, have dismissed the attempted murder, assault and weapons possession charges. We now reverse and reinstate all counts of the indictment.

The precise circumstances of the incident giving rise to the charges against defendant are disputed, and ultimately it will be for a trial jury to determine what occurred. We feel it necessary, however, to provide some factual background to properly frame the legal issues before us. Accordingly, we have summarized the facts as they appear from the evidence before the Grand Jury. We stress, however, that we do not purport to reach any conclusions or holding as to exactly what transpired or whether defendant is blameworthy. The credibility of witnesses and the reasonableness of defendant's conduct are to be resolved by the trial jury.

On Saturday afternoon, December 22, 1984, Troy Canty, Darryl Cabey, James Ramseur, and Barry Allen boarded an IRT express subway train in The Bronx and headed south toward lower Manhattan. The four youths rode together in the rear portion of the seventh car of the train. Two of the four, Ramseur and Cabey, had screwdrivers inside their coats, which they said were to be used to break into the coin boxes of video machines.

Defendant Bernhard Goetz boarded this subway train at 14th Street in Manhattan and sat down on a bench towards the rear section of the same car occupied by the four youths. Goetz was carrying an unlicensed .38 caliber pistol loaded with five rounds of ammunition in a waistband holster. The train left the 14th Street station and headed towards Chambers Street.

. . . Canty approached Goetz, possibly with Allen beside him, and stated "give me five dollars." Neither Canty nor any of the other youths displayed a weapon. Goetz responded by standing up, pulling out his handgun and firing four shots in rapid succession. The first shot hit Canty in the chest; the second struck Allen in the back; the third went through Ramseur's arm and into his left side; the fourth was fired at Cabey, who apparently was then standing in the corner of the car, but missed, deflecting instead off of a wall of the conductor's cab. After Goetz briefly surveyed the scene around him, he fired another shot at Cabey, who then was sitting on the end bench of the car. The bullet entered the rear of Cabey's side and severed his spinal cord.

All but two of the other passengers fled the car when . . . the shots were fired. . . . The conductor . . . went into the car where the shooting occurred and saw Goetz sitting on a bench, the injured youths lying on the floor or slumped against a seat, and two women who had apparently taken cover, also lying on the floor. Goetz told the conductor that the four youths had tried to rob him.

While the conductor was aiding the youths, Goetz headed towards the front of the car. The train had stopped just before the Chambers Street station and Goetz went between two of the cars, jumped onto the tracks and fled. Police and ambulance crews arrived at the scene shortly thereafter. Ramseur and Canty, initially listed in critical condition, have fully recovered. Cabey remains paralyzed, and has suffered some degree of brain damage.

On December 31, 1984, Goetz surrendered to police in Concord, New Hampshire . . . . Later that day . . . he made two lengthy statements, both of which were tape recorded with his permission. In the statements . . . Goetz admitted that he had been illegally carrying a handgun in New York City for three years. He stated that he had first purchased a gun in 1981 after he had been injured in a mugging. Goetz also revealed that twice between 1981 and 1984 he had successfully warded off assailants simply by displaying the pistol.

According to Goetz's statement, the first contact he had with the four youths came when Canty, sitting or lying on the bench across from him, asked "how are you," to which he replied "fine." Shortly thereafter, Canty, followed by one of the other youths, walked over to the defendant and stood to his left, while the other two youths remained to his right, in the corner of the subway car. Canty then said "give me five dollars." Goetz stated that he knew from the smile on Canty's face that they wanted to "play with me." Although he was certain that none of the youths had a gun, he had a fear, based on prior experiences, of being "maimed."

Goetz then established "a pattern of fire," deciding specifically to fire from left to right. His stated intention at that point was to "murder the four youths, to hurt them, to make them suffer as much as possible." When Canty again requested money, Goetz stood up, drew his weapon, and began firing, aiming for the center of the body of each of the four. Goetz recalled that the first two he shot "tried to run through the crowd but they had nowhere to run." Goetz then turned to his right to "go after the other two." One of these two "tried to run through the wall of the train, but he had nowhere to go." [Cabey] "tried pretending that he wasn't with the others" by standing still, holding on to one of the subway hand straps, and not looking at Goetz. Goetz nonetheless fired his fourth shot at him. He then ran back to the first two youths to make sure they had been "taken care of." Seeing that they had both been shot, he spun back to check on the latter two. Goetz noticed that the youth who had been standing still was now sitting on a bench and seemed unhurt. As Goetz told the police, "I said 'you seem to be all right, here's another,'" and he then fired the shot which severed Cabey's spinal cord. Goetz added that "if I was a little more under self-control I would have put the barrel against his forehead and fired." He also admitted that "if I had had more bullets, I would have shot them again, and again, and again."...

Penal Law article 35 . . . permits the use of force . . . in defense of a person . . . . Penal Law §35.15(1) sets forth the general principles governing all such uses of force: "[A] person may . . . use physical force upon another person when and to the extent he *reasonably believes* such to be necessary to defend himself . . . from what he *reasonably believes* to be the use or imminent use of unlawful physical force by such other person."

Section 35.15(2) sets forth further limitations on these general principles with respect to the use of "deadly physical force": "A person may not use deadly physical force upon another person under circumstances specified in subdivision one unless (a) He *reasonably believes* that such other person is using or about to use deadly physical force . . . or (b) He *reasonably believes* that such other person is committing or attempting to commit a kidnapping, forcible rape, forcible sodomy or robbery."*. . .

Because the evidence . . . included statements by Goetz that he acted to protect himself from being maimed or to avert a robbery, the prosecutor correctly chose to [instruct the Grand Jury to consider the question of self-defense]. . . . When the prosecutor had completed his [instruction], one of the grand jurors asked for clarification of the term "reasonably believes." The prosecutor responded by instructing the grand jurors that they were to consider the circumstances of the incident and determine "whether the defendant's conduct was that of a reasonable man in the defendant's situation." It is this response by the prosecutor — and specifically his use of "a reasonable man" — which is the basis for the dismissal of the charges by the lower courts. . . . [B]ecause section 35.15 uses the term *"he* reasonably believes," the appropriate test, according to [the Appellate Division], is whether a defendant's beliefs and reactions were "reasonable *to him.*" Under that reading of the statute, a jury which believed a defendant's testimony that he felt that his own actions were warranted and were reasonable would have to acquit him, regardless of what anyone else in defendant's situation might have concluded. Such an interpretation defies the ordinary meaning and significance of the term "reasonably" in a statute, and misconstrues the

---

* Editor's Note: New York law defines "deadly physical force" in a typical way, as "force which, under the circumstances in which it is used, is readily capable of causing death or other serious physical injury." N.Y. Penal Law §10.00(11). In other words, physical force need not *actually cause* serious physical injury, let alone death, to be considered deadly force; what matters is that it is *capable* of causing such harm.

clear intent of the Legislature, in enacting section 35.15, to retain an objective element as part of any provision authorizing the use of deadly physical force.

Penal statutes in New York have long codified the right recognized at common law to use deadly physical force, under appropriate circumstances, in self-defense. These provisions have never required that an actor's belief as to the intention of another person to inflict serious injury be correct in order for the use of deadly force to be justified, but they have uniformly required that the belief comport with an objective notion of reasonableness. . . .

The plurality below agreed with defendant's argument that the change in the statutory language from "reasonable ground," used prior to 1965, to "he reasonably believes" in Penal Law §35.15 evinced a legislative intent to conform to [a] subjective standard [of belief]. This argument, however, ignores the plain significance of the insertion of "reasonably." . . . "Believes" by itself requires an honest or genuine belief by a defendant as to the need to use deadly force. Interpreting the statute to require only that the defendant's belief was "reasonable to *him*," as done by the plurality below, would hardly be different from requiring only a genuine belief; in either case, the defendant's own perceptions could completely exonerate him from any criminal liability.

We cannot lightly impute to the Legislature an intent to fundamentally alter the principles of [self-defense] to allow the perpetrator of a serious crime to go free simply because that person believed his actions were reasonable and necessary to prevent some perceived harm. To completely exonerate such an individual, no matter how aberrational or bizarre his thought patterns, would allow citizens to set their own standards for the permissible use of force. . . .

Goetz also argues that the introduction of an objective element will preclude a jury from considering factors such as the prior experiences of a given actor and thus, require it to make a determination of "reasonableness" without regard to the actual circumstances of a particular incident. This argument, however, falsely presupposes that an objective standard means that the background and other relevant characteristics of a particular actor must be ignored. To the contrary, we have frequently noted that a determination of reasonableness must be based on the "circumstances" facing a defendant or his "situation." Such terms encompass more than the physical movements of the potential assailant. . . . [T]hese terms include any relevant knowledge the defendant had about that person. They also necessarily bring in the physical attributes of all persons involved, including the defendant. Furthermore, the defendant's circumstances encompass any prior experiences he had which could provide a reasonable basis for a belief that another person's intentions were to injure or rob him or that the use of deadly force was necessary under the circumstances.

Accordingly, a jury should be instructed to consider this type of evidence in weighing the defendant's actions. The jury must first determine whether the defendant had the requisite beliefs under section 35.15, that is, whether he believed deadly force was necessary to avert the imminent use of deadly force or the commission of one of the felonies enumerated therein. If the People do not prove beyond a reasonable doubt that he did not have such beliefs, then the jury must also consider whether these beliefs were reasonable. The jury would have to determine, in light of all the "circumstances," as explicated above, if a reasonable person could have had these beliefs.

The prosecutor's instruction . . . to determine whether, under the circumstances, Goetz's conduct was that of a reasonable man in his situation was thus essentially an accurate charge. . . . It will now be for the petit jury to decide whether the prosecutor can prove beyond a reasonable doubt that Goetz's reactions were unreasonable and therefore excessive. . . .

Accordingly, . . . the dismissed counts of the indictment [should be] reinstated.

NOTES AND QUESTIONS

1. A Cause Célèbre. Bernie Goetz shot Troy Canty, Darryl Cabey, James Ramseur, and Barry Allen on December 22, 1984. At the time, Goetz, a white man, was 37. The four people he shot were Black and between the ages of 18 and 19. Dubbed the "subway vigilante," Goetz quickly gained significant popular support, fueled by fear, frustration, and fury over the high and still-rising violent crime rates plaguing American cities at the time, including New York — and by a sense that the government was doing nothing about it. As political scientist James Q. Wilson drolly observed, "There are no more liberals on the crime and law-and-order issue in New York because they've all been mugged."[171]

A citywide poll weeks after the shooting found that 52 percent of New Yorkers supported Goetz's actions, while 28 percent did not. Those figures varied somewhat by race, but not as much as contemporary readers might expect: 45 percent of Black respondents supported Goetz, while 33 percent did not; for white respondents, the numbers were 56 percent and 26 percent. Many Black leaders privately felt torn. They too were fed up with high rates of crime, including crime committed by young people; and, as Professor Lillian Rubin writes in her book on the *Goetz* case, they recognized that the impact of that crime fell "much more heavily on their own black community than on the white one." Yet they couldn't shake the "nagging question": did Goetz shoot "*because* the youths were black? Is that at least partly what the celebration is all about?"[172]

Protestors show support for Bernie Goetz

Support for Goetz was not limited to New York City. Rubin writes that "[t]alk-show hosts from coast to coast report[ed] being swamped with callers wanting to congratulate the new American hero" and newspapers were buried by letters of support. It didn't matter that little was known about the case at this point—people were "less concerned with the exact events . . . than with the concept that *someone somewhere* had chosen to fight back." Goetz was thus, in a sense, "the symbolic embodiment of everyone's fantasies. He's the man who acts instead of talks, the guy who's mad as hell and isn't going to take it anymore." Even among those who did not support Goetz, there was a "certain sympathetic understanding" that put "feelings and intellect at war."[173]

In mid-January of 1985, parts of Goetz's confession tapes were leaked. Many in the public now heard for the first time the violent, noxious statements reported in the Court of Appeals' opinion above. They also learned that Goetz had used two illegal hollow-point bullets and had told the police that he wished he had gouged Troy Canty's eyes out with his keys. Nevertheless, a subsequent nationwide poll found that two-thirds of respondents sympathized with Goetz and opposed indicting him for attempted murder. And, indeed, on January 25, 1985, the initial grand jury to consider the case declined to charge Goetz with either assault or attempted murder, indicting him on only weapons charges instead. Though consistent with public opinion at the time, the grand jury's decision surprised many, and questions soon surfaced about the district attorney's handling of the case. Meanwhile, Goetz, emboldened by the development, increasingly took to the limelight to plead his cause.[174]

In late February, detailed, written reports of Goetz's police interviews were made public, further underscoring the cold-bloodedness of his actions, and public sentiment began to change. Goetz's neighbors also surfaced vile, racist views Goetz had volunteered at a community meeting a few years prior. The more people learned these things about Goetz, the less they liked him, especially in the Black community. A series of polls in March showed Black-white approval gaps above 20 percent. The police commissioner, a Black man named Benjamin Ward, publicly criticized the grand jury's decision not to indict on more serious charges and Black activists called for a federal civil rights prosecution — a plea rebuffed by then-U.S. Attorney Rudolph Giuliani, who deemed the shootings motivated by "fear, not race."[175]

On March 27, a second state grand jury indicted Goetz for attempted murder and assault. Goetz moved to dismiss the indictment, a procedural option available in New York courts but not in many other states. That motion initiated the litigation that culminated in the Court of Appeals' opinion above. Released on July 8, 1986, that opinion set Goetz on a path to trial.

2. The Trial and the Verdict. Trial began in December 1986. Three hundred New Yorkers were summoned to court as potential jurors. The process of voir dire produced a jury with ten white and two Black members, eight men and four women. Six of the jurors reported having been crime victims.[176]

Much of the trial focused on the timing and sequencing of the shots Goetz fired. The prosecution argued, consistent with Goetz's own statement to police and the testimony of one eyewitness, that Goetz's fourth shot missed Darrell Cabey, and that Goetz fired the fifth shot while standing over him. The defense, by contrast, argued that the fourth shot hit Cabey and the fifth shot missed. "If the jury thought that Goetz was on automatic pilot," the defense reasoned, "they would tend to see all five firings as beats in one stanza of self-defense. If they would be willing to acquit for the first shot injuring Troy Canty, then they would be inclined to acquit on the final shot that paralyzed Darrell Cabey." Eight independent eyewitnesses testified, consistent with this version, that the five shots sounded in rapid succession. None of these witnesses remembered a pause before the final bang and none saw Goetz standing over Cabey.[177]

On June 16, 1987, the jury acquitted Goetz on all of the major charges. According to multiple accounts, including a book written by Mark Lesly, who served as a juror in the case, the jury apparently agreed that "the way in which Canty got almost nose-to-nose with Goetz meant that he had invaded Goetz's space in a potentially hostile manner." And given evidence indicating that the youths were operating as a group, Lesly reports, the jury thought Goetz had reasonably believed the foursome "represented a danger . . . and the implication of a threat." The jury further seemed to conclude that it was not unreasonable for Goetz to think this perceived threat could not be repelled simply by brandishing the gun; facing a group in the narrow confines of a moving train, Lesly writes, "the gun could have been wrested away and perhaps used against him."[178]

Finally, on the critical issue of Cabey's shooting, Lesly reports that the jury had doubt over whether Goetz really had paused and fired at Cabey from close range. In other words, they discounted Goetz's own contrary statements to the police—in which he admitted telling Cabey, "you seem to be all right, here's another"—as they had no way of being certain whether these were the words of a "man with a score to settle" or "of a frightened, confused, bitter man . . . and the manifestations of internal turmoil, guilt, self-deprecation, self-directed rage." The jurors' doubts were bolstered by the district attorney's concession during closing argument that, "[i]n all probability, the defendant uttered these words only to himself and probably not even mouthing the words, but just saying them in his own mind as he squeezed the trigger that fifth time."[179]

The case, however, was not just about these factual details. Like many criminal prosecutions, the jury also engaged in what Professor George Fletcher calls a "moral interpretation" of whether the shooting was reasonable "in a moral sense," a judgment that "does not lend itself to easy proof." In fact, Fletcher goes on to argue, "the pivotal issue of reasonableness did not lend itself to any proof at all" but turned instead "on background assumptions about the *kinds of people* who confronted each other that Saturday afternoon in the subway."

> If the prosecution could establish that Goetz was basically an eccentric, irresponsible person, the jury would be more likely to believe that he behaved unreasonably in the shooting. If the defense could establish that the "gang of four" were lawless "predators," the jury would be more inclined to believe that they were about to rob and assault Goetz and that his response, therefore, was reasonable under the circumstances.[180]

Whatever the rationale, the jury's verdict did little to settle public opinion. Many Black leaders viewed the outcome as a blow to race relations—a verdict that would have been unthinkable if the racial roles of Goetz and the people he shot had been reversed. Nevertheless, a Gallup poll reported strong majority support for the verdict among New Yorkers: 83 percent among whites, 78 percent among Hispanics, and 45 percent among Black city dwellers. Goetz was eventually sentenced to one year in jail for possessing an unlicensed firearm. He was released after eight months. Nearly a decade later, a civil jury—also considering whether Goetz had acted reasonably under the circumstances—found Goetz liable and awarded Cabey $43 million in damages. Asked about the judgment in 2004, however, Goetz remarked, "I don't think I've paid a penny on that."[181]

Protestors clash over the Goetz verdict

3. Subjectivity vs. Objectivity. In the proceedings producing the appellate opinion above, Goetz argued that lawful self-defense requires only a genuine, *subjective* belief in the need to use defensive force—anything more, he insisted, is unrealistic and unfair. His logic, echoed by others, is that there simply "are no reasonable people under conditions in which death or severe bodily harm are believed imminent." Any expectation of reasonable behavior in such conditions is "neurologically unrealistic" and ignores the human instinct for "fight or flight." More fundamentally, even if some people could act reasonably when facing an imminent threat of death, one might argue that "it is simply unjust to punish someone who thinks—however fancifully—that the circumstances warrant his using deadly force." Rather, true culpability on this view "consists in a state of consciousness, in a state of mind, in choosing to do evil, in knowingly pitting oneself against the interests and rights of others."[182]

For generations of lawyers, *Goetz* is remembered for its rejection of this subjective-belief approach and its insistence that the defendant's belief be both subjectively reasonable and *objectively reasonable.* The Court of Appeals broke no new ground on this point, which had been the prevailing rule in New York and elsewhere for centuries. But make no mistake: while the objective-reasonableness requirement may sound like a significant hurdle compared to the wholly subjective alternative considered in *Goetz*, it still permits acquittal on "self-defense" grounds if a defendant mistakenly perceives a threat that isn't there—as long as the mistake was "reasonable."[183]

4. Individualization, Revisited. In reaffirming the requirement of objective reasonableness in self-defense doctrine, the court in *Goetz* highlights a question we first encountered when studying the law of provocation earlier in this chapter—namely, a question about how objective reasonableness ought to be understood. In its purest form, objective reasonableness might mean, as Goetz feared, that the "background and other relevant characteristics of a particular actor must be ignored"—that he is to be judged, instead, against the actions of a generic "reasonable man." But few, if any, jurisdictions employ such an extreme approach. Most, like New York, hold that "a determination of reasonableness must be based on the 'circumstances' facing a defendant or his 'situation.'"[184]

What, then, counts as part of the defendant's "circumstances" or "situation"? The *Goetz* court answered the question this way: "any relevant knowledge the defendant had" about the potential assailant; "any prior experiences he had which could provide a reasonable basis for a belief that another person's intentions were to injure . . . him or that the use of deadly force was necessary under the circumstances"; and "the physical attributes of all persons involved, including the defendant." Goetz had no "relevant knowledge" about the youths he shot, who were strangers to him, but the Court of Appeals' decision may have looked different if the opposite had been true.[185]

The jury did hear, however, that, in 1981, Goetz had been mugged by three young men in the subway and suffered a serious, lasting injury to his knee. Is that a prior experience that "could provide a reasonable basis for a belief" that the youths "were to injure or rob him or that the use of deadly force was necessary under the circumstances"? If so, were the two occasions on which he "successfully warded off assailants simply by displaying the pistol" also relevant? Note that, in a post-trial newspaper column, one of the jurors wrote that the prior mugging had moved her toward acquittal: "What is reasonable for [Goetz]," she explained—given his prior victimization—"might not be reasonable for me."[186]

The relevance of "the physical attributes of all persons involved, including the defendant," seems straightforward in some cases. Suppose, for example, the defendant is a frail and elderly woman and the potential assailant is an NFL linebacker who approaches with fists clenched. Or vice versa. Surely these considerations inform the reasonableness of the defendant's belief in the need to use defensive force, especially deadly force, to ward off the attack? Goetz was frequently described as "slight," though he was bigger than each of the youths in 1984. Still, one of the jurors, himself a martial arts expert, opined that Goetz would not have fared well in hand-to-hand combat with any of the youths, let alone all of them together. What are the implications of jurors making these sorts of judgments? Are they unavoidable, even if the court instructs the jurors not to make them?[187]

5. Imperfect Self-Defense. What about defendants who hold a genuine but *unreasonable* belief in the need to use defensive force? Typically, they're out of luck — self-defense is simply unavailable. *See, e.g.,* Hill v. State, 979 So.2d 1134, 1135 (Fla. Dist. Ct. App. 2008) (per curiam). For *fatal* defensive force, however, some states recognize something called "imperfect self-defense" that mitigates murder down to manslaughter. *See, e.g.,* Wilson v. State, 30 A.3d 955, 960 (Md. 2011); 18 Pa. Cons. Stat. §2503(b). The MPC adopts a similar approach for both fatal and nonfatal defensive force, allowing punishment for a negligence offense (like negligent homicide) when the defendant was negligent in forming his unreasonable belief, and a recklessness offense (like manslaughter) when he was reckless in forming that belief. Only a few states have followed the MPC's approach.[188]

1. Reasonableness and Race

As the *Goetz* case demonstrates, the reasonableness of a defendant's use of defensive force often intersects with underlying societal ideas about race, gender, sexuality, and class, with race, according to Professor David Sklansky, playing "a particularly strong role in determining how violence is perceived and assessed."[189]

Sometimes, the defendant will attempt to inject his own race or ethnicity into the analysis by arguing that he reacted to a perceived threat in a manner consistent with his cultural background. As we saw earlier in this chapter, this argument was rejected in *Ha.* That rejection is typical across courts. Indeed, as one court put it, "the standard of the reasonable man, the person of ordinary temper, is employed precisely to avoid different applications of the law . . . to defendants of different races, creed, color, sex or social status." Gonzales v. State, 689 S.W.2d 900, 903 (Tex. Crim. App. 1985) (en banc).[190]

But while the law may deem race irrelevant to the formal analysis of self-defense, it is harder to remove race from the minds of the people deciding a case — including the prosecutors who file charges, the lawyers who craft defense strategies, and the jurors who deliver a verdict. Here, the race or ethnicity of the defendant's *putative assailants* often looms large, raising the possibility that determinations of whether a defendant's fear was "reasonable" will be driven at least partly by racist stereotypes. At Goetz's trial, for example, no explicit mention was made of the race of the parties involved. Yet surely it was never far from the surface. "Goetz's legal team," observes one commentator, "took full advantage of racially charged imagery and code words." Among other things, Goetz's counsel displayed "blown-up pictures of the four youths . . . in their street garb looking self-confident and ready for action." Later, they staged a reenactment of the altercation using — for no legally relevant reason — four young Black men, "fit and muscular, dressed in T-shirts," to stand in for the four youths.[191]

As the *Goetz* example highlights, the concern over racial stereotyping is most acute when the target of defensive force is a Black male. Contemporary social science research documents prevalent implicit bias in American society that includes "the stereotypical association of black males with aggression and crime." Those stereotypes can cause people to perceive certain actions as dangerous when taken by a Black male but innocuous when taken by someone else. This bias can operate in the moments preceding an affray or upon review by actors in the penal system. In particular, one might worry, as Professor Cynthia Lee writes, that "jurors may perceive ambiguous actions" taken by Black males "as more hostile than they actually are" and "may more readily believe the defendant's claim that he honestly and reasonably believed he needed to act in self-defense." Stereotypes of Asian Americans as martial artists and young Latinos as gang members, Lee further reports, can have similar effects.[192]

Some argue these racialized inferences are rational, citing statistics showing uneven crime rates across racial groups. We discuss these statistics at length in Chapter Three. Even assuming their truth, however, they provide little help when it comes to answering the question that really matters in a self-defense case, because the reasonableness assessment is not a comparative exercise across different societal groups. If it were, it would be reasonable for any given person to fear *all men*, given that men commit violent offenses far more often than women. The reason this logic fails is that the proportion of all men who commit violent crimes is still quite small. The same is true for Black men. Indeed, because most violent crime is intraracial, Lee observes, "a White person is more than four times as likely to be killed by another White person than by a Black person." In other words, to quote Professor Paul Butler, "if you see a black man behind you in the street, your rational, evidence-based assumption should be that he presents no threat. He is literally hundreds of times more likely to be on his way to work, school, or the movies than he is to rob, rape, or murder you." As Professor Jody Armour concludes, reasoning from comparative race-based crime statistics ultimately "threatens to undermine the rational determination of how long the defendant should have waited for the stranger to clarify his intentions before resorting to deadly force," and thus whether the defendant was objectively reasonable in acting as he did.[193]

Notably, as Lee emphasizes, race often cuts the other way in self-defense cases when the person invoking self-defense "belongs to a racial group whose members are perceived as violent and dangerous" and the *putative assailant* is white. In this context, "jurors may be less willing to believe the defendant's claim of self-defense." Indeed, for much of our history, Black people attempting to use self-defense against white violence suffered punishment by juries of white men or, worse yet, mob violence and lynching. While times have changed in some respects, these old ways of thinking still linger. Consider, for example, the prosecution of John White, a 53-year-old

Black man who shot and killed one of five white teenagers who came to his home, lobbing racial epithets, to confront his son over a spurious accusation of sexual assault. In a case that drew the attention of national civil rights groups, the jury ultimately rejected White's claim of self-defense and convicted him of manslaughter. He was sentenced to serve between two and four years in prison but was released early when New York Governor David Patterson commuted his sentence. The following excerpt offers further discussion of White's case, including explicit mention of the racial slurs described above which, as in the case of *Laney* earlier in this chapter (p. 280), are retained in the text that follows.[194]

Calvin Trillin, *The Color of Blood*, New Yorker (Feb. 24, 2008). According to a study released a few years ago, Long Island is the single most segregated suburban area in the United States. The residents of 40 Independence Way — John and Sonia White and their youngest son, Aaron — are African-American and so are their next-door neighbors, but the black population of Miller Place is less than one-half of one per cent. . . . [Their son] Aaron was able to spend his senior year at Miller Place High School, which takes pride in such statistics as how many of its students are in Advanced Placement history courses. Aaron, an erect young man who is likely to say "sir" when addressing one of his elders, graduated in June of 2005. He was one of four black students in the class. . . .

[At a high school party, a girl named] Jennifer, who was then fifteen, told her brother that, because of a past incident, she felt frightened in Aaron's presence. Dano Cicciaro, . . . who thought of himself as a protective older brother to Jennifer, handled the situation smoothly, saying to Aaron something like "It's nothing personal, but you'll have to leave." . . . [But when Dano later] learned exactly why Jennifer felt uncomfortable around Aaron, she later testified, "he freaked out." While in an Internet chat room with a couple of other boys, Jennifer told Dano, Aaron had posted a message saying that he wanted to rape her. . . . Dano wanted to confront Aaron immediately. It didn't matter that Aaron denied having posted the message. It didn't matter that the posting had taken place nine months before and that Jennifer's real older brother, Craig, had actually forgotten about it. In court many months later, Jennifer [explained that she] eventually learned that the offending message had not, in fact, been sent by Aaron — it had grown out of something said on a MySpace account set up in Aaron's name as a prank . . . .

On the evening of August 9th, when Jennifer told Dano about the rape posting, there were other elements involved. A lot of beer had been consumed. It was late in the evening, a time when the teen-age penchant for melodrama tends to be in full flower. Dano was filled with what Paul Gianelli, one of John White's defense attorneys, called "a warped sense of chivalry" and Dano's godfather, Gregg Sarra, preferred to characterize as "valor, protecting a woman, honor." For whatever reason, Dano Cicciaro and four of his friends were soon heading toward the Whites' house . . . .

What happened when they got there remains a matter of sharp dispute. There is no doubt that the boys were displaying no weapons when they got out of their cars, although one of them, Joseph Serrano, had brought along a baseball bat that remained in the back seat of the Mustang. There is no doubt that John White emerged from his garage carrying a pre-Second World War Beretta pistol that he kept there—part of an inheritance from his grandfather that had also included, White later said, "rifles and shotguns and a lot of advice." Aaron was a few steps behind him, carrying a 20-gauge shotgun. There is no doubt that Dano "slapped" or "whacked" or "grabbed" the Beretta. There is no doubt that, before [the fatal shot that killed Dano], there had been shouting and foul language from both sides. The tenor of the conversation, the defense team eventually maintained, could be surmised from the tape of a 911 line that the boys did not realize was open as they rushed their friend to a Port Jefferson hospital . . . . [T]he voice of Joseph Serrano, sitting in the back seat with his bleeding friend and his baseball bat, comes through clearly: "Fucking niggers! Dano, I'll get 'em for you, Dano." . . .

Suffolk County is a place where a good number of residents are active or retired law-enforcement officers, and where even a lot of residents who aren't own guns—a place where it is not surprising to come across a plaque that bears the picture of a pistol and the phrase "We Don't Dial 911." . . . Judging by comments posted online in response to *Newsday* articles, public opinion seemed muddled by the conflict between two underpinnings of life in Suffolk County—a devotion to the sanctity of private property, particularly one's home, and an assumption that the owner of the property is white. . . .

[S]ome of White's strongest supporters—people like Lucius Ware, the president of the Eastern Long Island branch of the N.A.A.C.P., and Marie Michel, a black attorney who joined the defense team—believed that if a white homeowner in Miller Place had been confronted late at night by five hostile black teen-agers there would have been, in Marie Michel's words, "no arrests, no indictment, and no trial." The homeowner would have been judged to have had "a well-founded fear," they thought, and if the justice system dealt with the incident in any way it would have been to charge the boys with something like breach of the peace or aggravated harassment ("What were they doing in that neighborhood at that time of night?"). For that matter, these supporters would argue, would Dano have "freaked out" if the male accused of wanting to rape Jenny Martin hadn't been black? Wouldn't teen-agers spoiling for a fight have dispersed if a white father walked out of the house, with or without a gun, and told them in no uncertain terms to go home? . . .

[At trial,] John White testified that, believing the young men had come to harm his family, he backed them off his property with [his grandfather's] old pistol. . . . He described Dano Cicciaro and his friends as a lynch mob shouting, among other things, "We could take that skinny nigger mother-fucker." Recalling that evening, White said, "In my family history, that's how the Klan comes. They pull up to your house, blind you with their lights, burn your house down. That's how they come." . . .

In its decision in the case of Bernard Goetz, the white man who in 1984 shot four young black men who had approached him on the subway demanding money, the New York Court of Appeals, the highest court in the state, ruled that justification could have a subjective as well as an objective component—fears raised by the defendant's past experiences, for instance. By bringing up the history that White's family had with the Klan, the defense team raised a subjective component of justification, along with the objective component of home protection. "We are all products of our past," Paul Gianelli said of his client during one of the breaks in the trial. "He brought to that particular evening who he is." The defense was making a case for, among other things, the power of race memory. . . .

In his summation, the prosecutor asked a series of questions as a way to illustrate how White's behavior had deviated from the behavior of a reasonable person. . . . Race, [he] said, was being used to distract the jurors from the simple fact that by walking down the driveway with a loaded pistol John White, a man intimately familiar with firearms, had engaged in conduct that had recklessly caused the death of Dano Cicciaro. [The prosecutor's closing argument] followed that of Frederick K. Brewington, a black attorney, active in black causes on Long Island, who was [White's lawyer]. "Race has so much to do with this case, ladies and gentlemen, that it's painful," Brewington told the jury: Dano Cicciaro and his friends thought they had a right to go to John White's house and "terrorize his family with impunity and arrogance" because of "the false racial privilege they felt empowered by." In Brewington's argument, John White thought, " 'Once they see I have a gun they'll back off' . . . but they did not take 'the skinny old nigger' seriously." . . . . Joseph Serrano's slur on the 911 tape [was, according to Brewington] a mirror of the boys' true feelings. "What we do under cover of darkness sometimes comes to light," he said. . . .

[T]wo weeks [after John White was convicted], a crowd of several hundred people, almost all of them black, . . . gathered on a cold Saturday afternoon in front of the criminal-court building in Riverhead. . . . The guilty verdict had made White the sort of hero all too familiar in the race memory of African-Americans—someone held up as an example of the unjustly treated black man. On the podium were black officeholders, speakers from the spectrum of black organizations on Long Island, and two people who had come from Manhattan—Kevin Muhammad, of Muhammad Mosque

No. 7, and Al Sharpton. A lot of N.A.A.C.P. people were in the audience, and so were a lot of people from Faith Baptist Church. Various speakers demanded a retrial, or called for the resignation of the district attorney, or pointed out the difference in how white homeowners in similar situations have been treated, or called for the young white men involved to be indicted. . . . There were chants like "No Justice — No Peace" and, loudest of all, "Free John White."

2.   Reasonableness and Gender

Multiple self-defense doctrines, including the imminence requirement and the cohabitant exception to the castle doctrine, may disadvantage individuals enmeshed in abusive relationships, which disproportionately impact women. The objective-reasonableness requirement can introduce gender bias as well. In the words of Professor Elizabeth Schneider, "sexual stereotypes of women and the male orientation built into the law prevent judges and jurors from appreciating" the "circumstances" and "perceptions" of women who use defensive force, especially deadly force. Should courts take gender into account when assessing the reasonableness of the defendant's defensive acts? Consider this question as you read the following case.[195]

State v. Wanrow

559 P.2d 548 (Wash. 1977) (en banc)

UTTER, J. [Yvonne Wanrow was convicted by a jury of second-degree murder. On the afternoon of August 11, 1972, Wanrow and her two children were staying at the home of Wanrow's friend, Shirley Hooper. Hooper had asked Wanrow to come to her house because Hooper was afraid of her neighbor, the decedent William Wesler. Specifically, the women's children had informed Hooper that Wesler had recently molested Hooper's young daughter and tried to abduct Wanrow's young son. Hooper also suspected that Wesler had tried to break into her bedroom by cutting a hole in her window screen. Hooper called the police and requested that Wesler be arrested, but the police stated, "We can't, until Monday morning." Hooper was urged by the police officer to go to the police station Monday morning and "swear out a warrant."]

That evening, Ms. Hooper called the defendant and asked her to spend the night with her in the Hooper house. At that time she related to Ms. Wanrow the facts we have previously set forth. The defendant arrived sometime after 6 p.m. with a pistol in her handbag. The two women ultimately determined that they were too afraid to stay alone and decided to ask some friends to come over for added protection. The two women then called the defendant's sister and brother-in-law, Angie and Chuck Michel. The four adults did not go to bed that evening, but remained awake talking and watching for any possible prowlers. There were eight young children in the house with them. At around 5 a.m., Chuck Michel, without the knowledge of the women in the house, went to Wesler's house, carrying a baseball bat[,] . . . [and] accused Wesler of molesting little children. Mr. Wesler then suggested that they go over to the Hooper residence and get the whole thing straightened out. . . .

The testimony as to what next took place is considerably less precise. It appears that Wesler, a large man who was visibly intoxicated, entered the home and when told to leave declined to do so. A good deal of shouting and confusion then arose, and a young child, asleep on the couch, awoke crying. The testimony indicates that Wesler than approached this child, stating, "My what a cute little boy," or words to that effect, and that the child's mother, Ms. Michel, stepped between Wesler and the child. By this time Hooper was screaming for Wesler to get out. Ms. Wanrow, a 5'4" woman who at the time had a broken leg and was using a crutch, testified that she then went to the front door to enlist the aid of Chuck Michel. She stated that she shouted for him and, upon turning around to reenter the living room, found Wesler standing directly behind her. She testified to being gravely startled by this situation and to having then shot Wesler in what amounted to a reflex action. . . .

Reversal of respondent's conviction is . . . required by a . . . serious error committed by the trial court. . . . In the opening paragraph of instruction No. 10, the jury, in evaluating the gravity of the danger to the respondent, was directed to consider only those acts and circumstances occurring "at or immediately before the killing." This is not now, and never has been, the law of self-defense in Washington. On the contrary, the justification of self-defense is to be evaluated in light of all the facts and circumstances known to the defendant, including those known substantially before the killing. . . . Respondent's knowledge of the victim's reputation for aggressive acts was gained many hours before the killing and was based upon events which occurred over a period of years. Under the law of this state, the jury should have been allowed to consider this information in making the critical determination of the "degree of force which . . . a reasonable person in the same situation . . . seeing what (s)he sees and knowing what (s)he knows, then would believe to be necessary." State v. Dunning, 506 P.2d 321, 322 (Wash. Ct. App. 1973). . . .

The second paragraph of instruction No. 10 contains an equally erroneous and prejudicial statement of the law. That portion of the instruction reads:

> However, when there is no reasonable ground for the person attacked
> to believe that *his* person is in imminent danger of death or great bodily

> harm, and it appears to *him* that only an ordinary battery is all that is
> intended, and all that *he* has reasonable grounds to fear from *his* assailant,
> *he* has a right to stand *his* ground and repel such threatened assault, yet
> *he* has no right to repel a threatened assault with naked hands, by the use
> of a deadly weapon in a deadly manner, unless *he* believes, *and has reason-
> able grounds* to believe, that *he* is in imminent danger of death or great
> bodily harm.

In our society women suffer from a conspicuous lack of access to training in
and the means of developing those skills necessary to effectively repel a male
assailant without resorting to the use of deadly weapons. Instruction No. 12
does indicate that the "relative size and strength of the persons involved"
may be considered; however, it does not make clear that the defendant's
actions are to be judged against her own subjective impressions and not
those which a detached jury might determine to be objectively reasonable.
The applicable rule of law is clearly stated in *State v. Miller*, 250 P. 645, 645
(Wash. 1926):

> If the appellants, at the time of the alleged assault upon them, as reason-
> ably and ordinarily cautious and prudent men, honestly believed that they
> were in danger of great bodily harm, they would have the right to resort to
> self-defense, and their conduct is to be judged by the condition appearing
> to them at the time, not by the condition as it might appear to the jury in
> the light of testimony before it.

The second paragraph of instruction No. 10 not only establishes an
objective standard, but through the persistent use of the masculine
gender leaves the jury with the impression the objective standard to
be applied is that applicable to an altercation between two men. The
impression created—that a 5'4" woman with a cast on her leg and using
a crutch must, under the law, somehow repel an assault by a 6'2" intoxicated man without employing weapons in her defense, unless the jury
finds her determination of the degree of danger to be objectively reasonable—constitutes a separate and distinct misstatement of the law and,
in the context of this case, violates the respondent's right to equal protection of the law. The respondent was entitled to have the jury consider
her actions in the light of her own perceptions of the situation, including those perceptions which were the product of our nation's "long and
unfortunate history of sex discrimination." Frontiero v. Richardson,
411 U.S. 677, 684 (1973). Until such time as the effects of that history are eradicated, care must be taken to assure that our self-defense
instructions afford women the right to have their conduct judged in
light of the individual physical handicaps which are the product of sex
discrimination. To fail to do so is to deny the right of the individual
woman involved to trial by the same rules which are applicable to male
defendants. . . .

NOTES AND QUESTIONS

1. Subjectivity and Individualization, Revisited. Reading the *Wanrow* opinion, one might think the court adopted a purely subjective standard of reasonableness, particularly when the court says "that the defendant's actions are to be judged against her own subjective impressions and not those which a detached jury might determine to be objectively reasonable." In an analysis of the case, however, Professor Donna Coker and Lyndsay Harrison push back on this reading. The "significance of the decision for American criminal law," they write, "lies in a crucial nuance about the standard for self-defense—the principle that the opposite of the erroneous 'reasonable man standard' is *not* what people think of as a 'subjective' standard." The *Wanrow* opinion, they note, "expressly stated that the jury was to determine the 'degree of force which . . . a reasonable person in the same situation'" would have used. "What the *Wanrow* court recognized was that an instruction that encouraged jurors to judge a female defendant's reasonableness vis-à-vis a male standard of conduct and belief was not an 'objective' standard, but a particularized male standard." In other words, Coker and Harrison argue, "the Court replaced a standard that appeared to be objective but was in fact quite biased with a standard that might be mistaken for subjective but was in fact far less biased than its predecessor." And in so doing, they conclude, the opinion put "feminist theory into action to fight gender bias in the criminal justice system, and marked the beginning of what came to be called 'women's self-defense work.'"[196]

Without necessarily discounting this argument, some contend that *Wanrow*'s move is ultimately unnecessary because traditional criminal law standards already instruct jurors to consider the defendant's situation. If applied faithfully, these commentators contend, that standard can resolve women's self-defense claims fairly. In fact, there is some evidence that juries are *more* lenient when assessing self-defense claims made by women—especially young, conventionally attractive women.[197]

2. Wanrow and Anti-Indian Sentiment. As Coker and Harrison observe, "Wanrow's now-famous case enters law school textbooks on the issue of what constitutes a fair trial for *women*. . . . But race and racism were as important to the fair trial question in *Wanrow* as were gender and sexism." Wanrow, they explain, was Native American; Wesler was white. As Coker and Harrison go on to write, when the case was heard on appeal,

> [h]undreds of Native Americans sat on the floor and crowded around the back of the courtroom . . . . Many of the supporters had come by caravan . . . . In Spokane, Washington, where Wanrow's trial took place, much of the white population harbored racist attitudes regarding Native Americans. Furthermore, anti-Indian sentiment was at a fever pitch at the time of Wanrow's trial because of the widespread publicity

accompanying the concurrent American Indian Movement (AIM) occupation of Wounded Knee [protesting] government mistreatment of Native Americans . . . . [Wanrow's cause was] taken up by AIM members who spread the word [of her prosecution] through Native American newspapers and gatherings, participated in events to raise funds for her defense, and provided her with support. It was [later] promoted by feminists across the country, several of whom drove to Washington to organize popular support for her defense among non-Indians [and] were able to raise funds for her defense and to draw national attention to her case, and that of other women who claimed they acted in self-defense in killing a male attacker.[198]

3. Battered Woman Syndrome. In *Wanrow*, the defendant's relationship to the male decedent was attenuated; he was her friend's next-door neighbor. The more common setting for considering self-defense through a gendered lens, by contrast, is in cases of domestic abuse. Consider a defendant who suffers from "battered woman syndrome," a situation in which a regular pattern of abuse by an intimate partner creates in the battered woman "low self-esteem and a 'learned helplessness,' i.e., a sense that she cannot escape from the abusive relationship she has become a part of." State v. Leidholm, 334 N.W.2d 811, 819 (N.D. 1983). Ought that history of abuse be part of the self-defense analysis? Specifically, should the jury be asked whether a "reasonable battered woman" would have acted as the defendant did? Scholars have long debated this question. Some herald opinions that answer it in the affirmative as feminist advances that bend the law to be more protective of women in the face of a longstanding history in which police and prosecutors ignored spousal abuse—and in which the law once openly permitted it. Others worry this approach patronizes women. In the words of Professor Anne Coughlin, the logic seems to be that women are not "capable of abiding by criminal prohibitions," which appears to deny "that women have the same capacity for self-governance that is attributed to men." In evaluating these competing arguments, consider the following excerpt of an article by Professor Susan Estrich, and the case that follows.[199]

Susan Estrich, *Defending Women*, 88 Mich. L. Rev. 1430, 1434-1437 (1990). If the defender is young or crippled or blind, we should not expect him to behave like a strapping, sighted adult. On the other hand, if the reasonable person has all of the defender's characteristics, the standard loses any normative component and . . . would give free rein to the short-tempered, the pugnacious, and the foolhardy who see threats of harm where the rest of us would not . . . . [When navigating these tensions in the context of battered women, we are forced to ask a few questions. First, did] she believe that she was in imminent danger of death or serious bodily harm?

. . . [And, second, is evidence of her abuse] also relevant to and probative of the determination of the "reasonableness" of that belief[?]

In this context, "reasonableness" can have two possible meanings. First, a woman's choice may be "reasonable," even if it conflicts with our own (or a mythical other's) assessment of the situation, if the woman is indeed right, or probably right, or at least more likely right than us, in her assessment. To the extent that her experience as a battered woman, and the syndrome from which she suffers, makes her a better judge than us of the seriousness of the situation she actually faces, there should be no question that such evidence is not only relevant, but also highly probative. . . . The special knowledge — of the [woman's expert witness] and of the woman herself — of the cycles of domestic violence can be understood as casting additional and needed light on this rather well-established form of inquiry. Does the woman know something we don't about the risk she faces? Does she, and her expert, foresee that a serious beating is imminent where you and I would simply not recognize the danger? If the answer is yes, then the jury should know it as well, and take it into account. . . .

But what of the woman who shoots her husband while he is sound asleep, and not, by anyone's account, about to do anything? What of the woman who faces a beating, but not — even within her own or her expert's description of the cycles of violence — serious bodily harm? Put aside the woman who has tried to escape in the past and been beaten for it, or who has called the police and been rebuffed, or who would be leaving her young children defenseless if she left. In these cases, properly applied, the retreat requirement cannot be met with the necessary "complete safety." But what of the woman who has never tried any of these alternatives? What of the woman who could walk out the back door and into a neighbor's house?

In such cases, the "reasonableness" inquiry, and the evidence of battered woman's syndrome, does not really go to the rightness of the woman's belief in the need for deadly force. It is, instead, a request to abandon the limits on self-defense out of empathy for the circumstances of the defender and disgust for the acts of her abuser. We can find her belief in the imminence of danger "reasonable" only by deciding that these standards mean less in the home than outside it, mean less when applied to cruel husbands who torment defenseless wives than to others.

On its face, that is a very uncomfortable request . . . . The unfairness, as I see it, is not that such women may be punished for "overreacting," but that Bernhard Goetz — a white, male New York subway rider — does so much worse, ignores the rules so much more blatantly, and is exculpated for it. In theory, vigilante men are not acting in self-defense; yet in practice, they seem to fare much better before juries and grand juries.

Lalchan v. United States

282 A.3d 555 (D.C. 2022)

McLEESE, J. [The defendant, Dianna Lalchan,] shot and killed her husband, Christopher Lalchan. Ms. Lalchan fired three bullets, one of which hit a wall and one of which hit the floor. When the final bullet was fired, Mr. Lalchan was facing Ms. Lalchan and moving forward. That bullet, which was fatal, hit Mr. Lalchan in the back of the head. Mr. Lalchan was near to the floor when he was struck by that bullet. Ms. Lalchan was some distance away from Mr. Lalchan at the time of the fatal shot.

The dispute at trial was whether Ms. Lalchan acted with premeditated and deliberate malice or instead acted either in lawful self-defense or in good-faith but unreasonable self-defense. The United States argued that Ms. Lalchan murdered Mr. Lalchan, mainly for financial and personal reasons surrounding their potential divorce. In support of that argument, the United States relied on the fact that Mr. Lalchan had been shot in the back of the head. The United States also elicited evidence that Ms. Lalchan was the breadwinner in the relationship and was worried about having to pay Mr. Lalchan alimony and splitting their property after their divorce. The United States also elicited evidence that Ms. Lalchan had realized during the marriage that she was attracted to women, and she was concerned that Mr. Lalchan would tell Ms. Lalchan's conservative family about that.

Ms. Lalchan testified that she shot Mr. Lalchan because she feared for her life. In support of that testimony, Ms. Lalchan introduced the following evidence. Early in their relationship, Mr. Lalchan became angry and smashed items such as Ms. Lalchan's laptop. Mr. Lalchan's violent behavior later escalated to shoving and slapping. The abuse culminated in Mr. Lalchan strangling Ms. Lalchan on several occasions. The first two times Mr. Lalchan strangled Ms. Lalchan occurred during arguments. Before he strangled her, Mr. Lalchan's demeanor would suddenly change: he became quiet, shut down emotionally, and focused intently on stopping himself from exploding. Ms. Lalchan described that change as "like the Hulk" (the Marvel Comics character) when he is trying to hold himself back. In two of the incidents, Mr. Lalchan strangled Ms. Lalchan until she passed out. Mr. Lalchan strangled Ms. Lalchan a third time about two months before the shooting. In that incident, Mr. Lalchan lifted Ms. Lalchan by the neck with one hand while holding a gun with the other. Mr. Lalchan threw Ms. Lalchan into a wall and hit her with the gun. After that incident, Ms. Lalchan began looking into getting a divorce.

On the night of the shooting, the Lalchans were arguing about the possibility of divorce. Mr. Lalchan threw a bicycle, punched a television, grabbed his gun, and threatened to commit suicide. Ms. Lalchan got the gun and put it down, but the argument continued. Mr. Lalchan raised a mop handle over his head, threatening Ms. Lalchan with it. Ms. Lalchan grabbed the mop handle, and the two tussled over it. Eventually, Ms. Lalchan let Mr. Lalchan know that "this was it" and that he would not have any more chances. Mr. Lalchan said, "Do I need to shut you up?" He then shut down like he had before and came at Ms. Lalchan. Fearing that Mr. Lalchan might kill her, Ms. Lalchan grabbed the gun and shot Mr. Lalchan.

. . . Dr. Mary Ann Dutton, a clinical psychologist specializing in domestic violence, testified as a defense expert. In brief, she testified . . . that "Battered Woman Syndrome" is a legal term, not a diagnosis of a psychological disorder. She also discussed a number of common misconceptions that people have about women who have been battered, including that such women are usually unemployed, meek, and financially dependent. Dr. Dutton testified that intimate-partner violence commonly escalates over time. Battered women often do not leave or report abuse, because they are embarrassed, fear that such steps might make the abuse worse, or hope that things will improve. Battered women who try to leave the relationship are at particularly high risk, facing a risk of abuse approximately four times greater than that faced by women who remain in the relationship. A woman who has previously been strangled is seven times more likely to be killed than a woman who has not previously been strangled.

Dr. Dutton further testified that people who have suffered intimate-partner violence learn to identify cues indicating that violence is about to occur, such as a look or a tone of voice. Over time, such cues can become all that is needed to put people who have suffered life-threatening abuse in fear for their lives. Such cues can cause an automatic response leading the person to fight back or flee.

The jury acquitted Ms. Lalchan of first-degree murder and second-degree murder but found her guilty of voluntary manslaughter while armed and possession of a firearm during a crime of violence.

Ms. Lalchan asked the trial court to instruct the jury that, in determining whether Ms. Lalchan acted in lawful self-defense, the jury should consider whether Ms. Lalchan acted as a "reasonable woman with a history of trauma and the effects of battery." The trial court denied the motion, concluding that the evidence that Ms. Lalchan suffered effects from prior battery could be considered in determining whether Ms. Lalchan subjectively perceived danger but had no bearing on whether Ms. Lalchan's perception was objectively reasonable. . . .

We conclude that the trial court's ruling was incorrect. . . . The "right of self-defense, and especially the degree of force [that a person] is permitted to use to prevent bodily harm, is premised substantially on the [person's] own reasonable perceptions of what is happening." Fersner v. United States, 482 A.2d 387, 391 (D.C. 1984). Such perceptions may include "an enhanced sense of peril based on personal knowledge that the attacker has committed prior acts of violence." Id. We have [in prior cases recognized that expert testimony relating to battered woman's syndrome may be introduced by the prosecution to explain the actions of an abused woman in the prosecution of her abuser]. We see no basis for a different conclusion where, as in the present case, a defendant is relying on such evidence in support of a claim of self-defense. *See* Parker v. United States, 155 A.3d 835, 852 (D.C. 2017) (Ferren, J., concurring) ("[I]n the case of a 'battered spouse' defense, a wife's misperception that her husband was imminently threatening her life might justify a finding that her stabbing him was reasonable under the circumstances.").

In denying the requested instruction, the trial court indicated that the instruction would be contrary to this jurisdiction's prohibition of diminished-capacity defenses. We disagree. We have formulated the concept of diminished capacity in a variety of ways. One common thread in those formulations is that diminished-capacity defenses rely on the idea that the defendant suffers from a mental "abnormality" that falls short of legal insanity. In the present case, however, Dr. Dutton made clear that she was not testifying that Ms. Lalchan was suffering from a mental abnormality or illness. Rather, Dr. Dutton explained that persons who have been subjected to intimate-partner abuse can learn, both consciously and unconsciously, to perceive signs that such abuse may be coming, just as children can learn to sense from facial cues that their parents are very upset with them. Persons who have been subjected to intimate-partner abuse also can develop automatic responses to such signs, through the process of conditioned learning. These are ordinary human reactions, not an abnormal mental state or disorder. Dr. Dutton's testimony thus did not run afoul of [our jurisdiction's] prohibition on introducing evidence of diminished capacity. . . .

In our view, the instructions as a whole did not adequately explain to the jury that the objective reasonableness of Ms. Lalchan's conduct could be understood in light of the effects of any prior abuse on Ms. Lalchan's perceptions at the time of the incident. . . . We hold that a specific instruction on the effect that intimate-partner violence can have on reasonable perceptions of danger was required in the circumstances of this case. *See, e.g.,* Smith v. State, 486 S.E.2d 819, 823 (Ga. 1997) ("We take this opportunity to announce the rule that when a battered person syndrome self-defense claim has been properly established, the court should give specific jury instructions on justification by self-defense which are tailored to explain how the defendant's experiences as a battered person affected that defendant's state of mind at the time of the killing."). . . . Ms. Lalchan's sole defense was that she shot Mr. Lalchan in self-defense. The acquittals indicate that the jury accepted that Ms. Lalchan may have acted out of a subjective fear of injury, rather than with premeditation or unmitigated malice. The guilty verdict on manslaughter, however, indicates that the jury concluded that Ms. Lalchan did not have an objectively reasonable fear of injury. For the reasons we have explained, the denial of the requested instruction left the jury without adequate guidance about the potential relevance of Dr. Dutton's testimony to that issue.

3.   Reasonableness and Resistance

In popular discourse, robust conceptions of self-defense — from Stand Your Ground laws to the castle doctrine — are often associated with politically conservative viewpoints. But as the preceding sections indicate, robust accounts of self-defense have also been championed by those advocating politically liberal positions, including the idea that the doctrine should account for "race memory," as the N.A.A.C.P. advocates argued in the case of John White, or that it should account for feminist theories of violence, as reflected in debates over battered woman syndrome. More broadly, marginalized groups that have often found themselves on the losing side of litigation over self-defense have a long history of appealing to "self-help," including armed self-help, in the absence of state protection — arguments that resonate with some of the broader themes of self-defense discussed in this chapter.

NOTES AND QUESTIONS

1. Defense as Liberation.   Consider, for example, civil rights activist Ida B. Wells, who in the late nineteenth century argued that "a Winchester rifle should have a place of honor in every black home," as "the only times an Afro-American who was assaulted got away has been when he had a gun and used it in self-defense."[200]

Consistent with Wells's message, a recent empirical study found that, across the Jim Crow South, fewer lynchings occurred where Black people had greater access to firearms. As historian Caroline Light observes, a similar relationship between Black victimization and firearm access persisted into the Civil Rights Era, as Black paramilitary organizations formed in opposition to a Southern society "stubbornly resistant to the full inclusion and citizenship of African Americans." While many today remember the nonviolent civil disobedience work of Dr. Martin Luther King Jr. and others during the Civil Rights Era, Light argues that "the armed support of Black paramilitary organizations was critical to the advances of the modern civil rights movement."[201]

Light maintains that these liberatory organizations successfully "drew on existing ideals of self-defense while challenging their white supremacist foundations." And as she notes in the following excerpt, an array of contemporary organizations follow their path on behalf of their varied constituents.[202]

Caroline Light, *Stand Your Ground: A History of America's Love Affair with Lethal Self-Defense* 4-6, 149 (2017): Beginning in the 1970s, around the same time that women's self-defense classes were gaining popularity, the National Rifle Association began a special effort to reach out to women with messages of empowerment and personal safety. The group Women in the NRA (WINRA) emerged in the 1970s with the promise of "new programs, new approaches, new opportunities" designed specifically for female gun enthusiasts [and] offered a booklet . . . to educate women on "effective self-defense techniques." . . .

Today the spread of perceived insecurity, as well as a lack of faith in the protective powers of the government and local police, transcends ideological boundaries, with members of targeted minority groups also arming themselves against criminal threats. A recent example is the National African American Gun Association (NAAGA), established in 2015 to "expose, educate, and motivate as many African American men and women to go out and purchase a Firearm for Self-Defense and to take training on proper gun use." Described on the website as a "civil rights organization," the NAAGA emphasizes the need for Black self-protection in a nation that—in spite of popular appeals to color blindness—disproportionately subjects people of color to sustained violence and exclusion. The organization sees itself as part of a long legacy of Black armed self-defense whose antecedents include the Buffalo Soldiers, the Tuskegee Airmen, the Deacons of Defense, and the Black Panther Party (BPP). Jews for the Preservation of Firearms Ownership (JPFO) similarly appeals to historic discrimination and violence in its efforts to expose the "racist roots of 'gun control,'" which the JPFO characterizes as "victim-disarmament." The JPFO website features a "genocide chart," which contains statistics on all "victims of disarmament," from the Armenian genocide and Nazi Holocaust to the mass murder of Tutsi in Rwanda in the 1990s. For the JPFO and NAAGA, historic racism and antisemitism—which have featured government and police complicity—justify the present accumulation of firearms for minority communities. . . .

[Similarly, the] Pink Pistols were founded in 2000 in response to police and civilian violence against gay, lesbian, and gender nonconforming individuals to empower members to channel their "ammosexuality" by learning how to defend themselves with lethal weapons. Like NAAGA and JPFO, the group's mission is preventative as well as reactive. According to founding member Gwendolyn S. Patton, "We teach queers to shoot, then teach the world that we have done it."

2. Armed While Black. At the same time, Light observes, Black gun ownership, in particular, can be fraught with danger. The same racial stereotypes that present Black people as a threat shape how guns are perceived in the hands of Black owners. Perhaps no case illustrates the point more clearly than Philando Castile's:

[T]hirty-two-year-old Philando Castile of Minnesota explained to the police who pulled him over for a broken taillight that he was carrying a

concealed firearm for which he had a permit. As he tried to extract his
license from his pocket, the police opened fire through his car window,
killing him in front of his girlfriend and four-year-old child. In this case, it
did not matter that Castile was a law-abiding citizen following the principles of armed citizenship, or that he was complying peaceably with police
orders; in the eyes of the police who killed him, his blackness excluded
him from the category of "law-abiding citizenship."

As Light concludes, "This is not the first time this has happened, and it
likely will not be the last." The officer who killed Castile was acquitted of all
charges.[203]

4.   Reasonableness and Law Enforcement Use of Force

Just as self-defense can function as either a justification or an excuse,
so too can law enforcement use of force. A police officer who *correctly* concludes that force is needed for self-defense or to carry out her duties is
justified in using force; an officer who *reasonably but mistakenly* believes such
force is needed is *excused* from criminal responsibility. And so, just as with
self-defense, an officer who reasonably but mistakenly believes a suspect
is reaching for a gun is exculpated not because he did the right thing but
because the law does not expect him to have acted differently under the
circumstances. The police and media often refer to both types of incidents colloquially as involving "justified" force, but this is imprecise as a
criminal law matter — and it is useful to see how different the two scenarios are.

How often do these mistakes happen? To get a very rough sense, we
can start by examining data on the frequency with which the police shoot
unarmed individuals. The sources mentioned earlier in this chapter report
that around 20 percent of individuals shot by the police are completely
unarmed. Nearly another 30 percent are armed with something other than
a firearm, such as a blade or blunt instrument. Given that virtually all officer
deaths in intentional attacks result from the use of a firearm, this suggests
that roughly half of all people shot by the police posed no real lethal threat
to the officers who shot them.[204]

There are significant racial disparities in the pool of unarmed individuals killed by the police. In three separate studies, roughly half of all
unarmed people shot by the police were Black. Given background population statistics, this means that unarmed black people are nearly eight times
more likely to be shot by the police than white people. To put the point differently, Black people who were fatally shot by the police in 2015 were twice
as likely as white people to be unarmed, and twice as likely to be mistaken as
armed with a gun.[205]

These disparities likely result partly from the same racial stereotypes
that shape ordinary civilian perceptions of threat. Consider the following

reflections on how these stereotypes interact with the law's reasonableness requirement in the ordinary case.

Cynthia Lee, *Murder and the Reasonable Man* 179-180 (2003): The police officer does not consciously decide to use deadly force because of the suspect's race, but the suspect's race nonetheless influences the officer. Racial stereotypes may alter the officer's perception of danger, threat, and resistance to authority. A simple question, "Officer, why am I being stopped?" may be perceived as behavior challenging the officer's authority when asked by someone who is Black. Police officers may also "see" danger more readily when dealing with a person of color. . . .

It is hard to feel punitive toward someone who sincerely believed he was acting in self-defense. The law, however, requires that officers who claim self-defense must have more than just an honest belief in the need to act in self-defense. The officer's belief must also be reasonable or, as the courts have held, one that a reasonably prudent officer in the same situation would have held.

The reasonableness requirement can be helpful and problematic at the same time. On the one hand, the reasonableness requirement operates as a check on the officer's subjective beliefs. It ensures some objective standard against which the officer's personal beliefs are to be measured so that an officer's completely unfounded and irrational fears cannot [excuse] actions that injure innocent citizens. On the other hand, the reasonableness requirement provides a way in which social attitudes and biases can influence the legal determination regarding the validity of police use of force. Racial stereotypes can make an officer's use of deadly force seem reasonable, when in the absence of such stereotypes the officer's actions would appear unjustified. If stereotypes encourage police officers to use deadly force against certain members of the community and not others, it is necessary to critically examine whether it is appropriate to call the officer's belief in the need to use force reasonable.

Professor Lee has encouraged legislation that turns on the reasonableness of the officer's *actions*, not just the reasonableness of his *beliefs*, which, she maintains, "ends up being an inquiry into the reasonableness of the officer's fear of the suspect." This would include considerations such as whether the officer attempted to deescalate the situation or, instead, acted to increase the risk of a deadly confrontation. Lee would also allow for an "imperfect" defense that mitigates murder to manslaughter when an officer's belief in the need to use deadly force was sincere but unreasonable. What do you think of Lee's proposal? How much difference would you expect it to make?[206]

CHAPTER 5

SEXUAL ASSAULT

"Rape is a crime of gender inequality."

Catharine MacKinnon, *Rape Redefined*,
10 Harv. L. & Pol'y Rev. 431, 431 (2016)

"Sex, which we think of as the most private of acts, is in reality a public thing. The roles we play, the emotions we feel, who gives, who takes, who demands, who serves, who wants, who is wanted, who benefits, who suffers: the rules for all this were set long before we entered the world."

Amia Srinivasan, *The Right to Sex* xii (2021)

INTRODUCTION

Few if any topics in the study of criminal law are more fraught or more challenging to teach, study, or discuss than the law of sexual assault. Sexual violence and conversations about how to address it are at once salient and submerged in society, a point captured well by the now-famous rallying cry *#MeToo*. That phrase stands in for a watershed moment in American politics and culture. Just consider the words that often follow it: the *#MeToo* movement, the *#MeToo* generation, the *#MeToo* era. And yet, the words themselves — *me, too* — are meant to draw attention to the fact that sexual violence often seems, or is made to be, invisible. As explained by Tarana Burke, the community organizer and activist who originated the phrase a decade before it entered broad usage, "me too" is meant to "show the world how widespread and pervasive sexual violence is," and "to let other survivors know they are not alone." When actress Alyssa Milano popularized the phrase in 2017, she echoed the idea that sexual violence too often goes overlooked, writing that she hoped to "give people a sense of the magnitude of the problem."[1]

This contradiction, in which sexual violence is both pervasive and peripheral, emphasized and ignored, has long shaped the development of the law of rape as well, and the ways in which it is taught. Consider a sobering set of statistics. According to a national survey published by the Centers for Disease Control and Prevention, nearly 9.5 million women in the United States (7.6 percent of all U.S. women) were victims of sexual violence in 2017. The same survey shows that a staggering 67.8 million women (54.3 percent) have been victimized by sexual violence at some point in their lives, the vast majority before turning twenty-five years old. To be clear, men are also victims of sexual violence, especially though by no means exclusively in prison. But the gender disparities in sexual violence are substantial, as captured in the figures below.[2]

Figure 5.1.   Lifetime Reports of Sexual Violence – U.S. Women

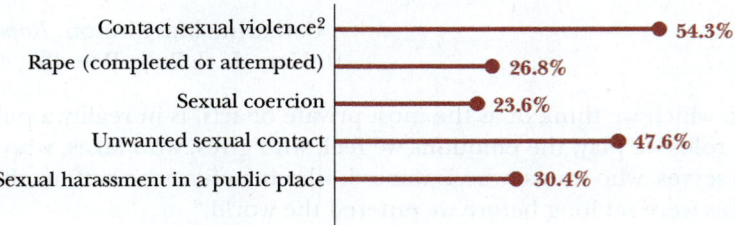

Lifetime Reports of Sexual Violence—U.S. Women, National Intimate Partner and Sexual Violence Survey, 2016/2017 Annualized Estimates[1]

[1] All percentages are weighted to the U.S. adult population.
[2] Contact sexual violence includes rape, sexual coercion, and/or unwanted sexual contact.

Kathleen C. Basile et al., Ctrs. for Disease Control & Prevention, *The National Intimate Partner and Sexual Violence Survey: 2016/2017 Report on Sexual Violence* 4 fig.1 (2022)

Figure 5.2.   Lifetime Reports of Sexual Violence – U.S. Men

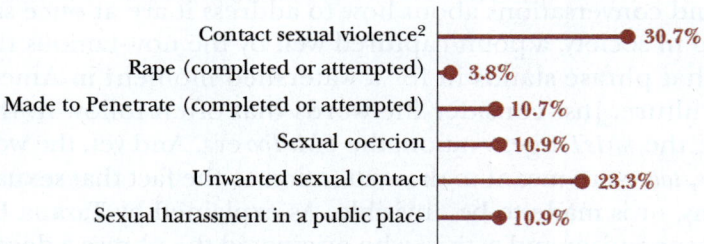

Lifetime Reports of Sexual Violence—U.S. Men, National Intimate Partner and Sexual Violence Survey, 2016/2017 Annualized Estimates[1]

[1] All percentages are weighted to the U.S. adult population.
[2] Contact sexual violence includes rape, being made to penetrate, sexual coercion, and/or unwanted sexual contact.

Kathleen C. Basile et al., Ctrs. for Disease Control & Prevention, *The National Intimate Partner and Sexual Violence Survey: 2016/2017 Report on Sexual Violence* 4 fig.2 (2022)

At the same time, prosecutions for these harms are relatively rare. According to the federal Bureau of Justice Statistics, fewer than one quarter of sexual assaults are ever reported to the police. Of those that are, the vast majority do not lead to prosecution or punishment. One study finds that for every 100 rape cases reported to law enforcement, only thirty-three are ever referred to prosecutors, of which only half result in criminal charges. Of those, only half again result in a conviction and a prison sentence. These data generally track a congressional report published three decades ago, which found that ninety-eight percent of rape victims "never see their attacker caught, tried and imprisoned."[3]

Reflecting on this stark reality, Michelle Bowdler penned a book in 2020 with a provocative title, asking *Is Rape a Crime?* Of course, in a specific and legalistic sense the answer to that question is clear. Rape has been a crime for centuries. Historically, it was a capital offense, punishable by death. It continues to be prosecuted every day in courts across the country, with people convicted of rape or sexual assault currently constituting about fourteen percent of the national prison population.[4]

But in a broader sense, Bowdler's question captures real and sharp disjunctions in the way our society thinks about, talks about, and approaches sexual violence. These disjunctions exist between our formal laws and the ways they are applied by legal institutions, between those laws and the social norms they are meant to reflect or shape, and among views within our polity about what sexual norms are or should be in the first place.

Sitting atop these cross-cutting currents, it should be no surprise that the meaning of the word *rape* as a legal term of art is often in flux and long has been. As historian Estelle Freedman explains, "*rape* is a legal term that encompasses a malleable and culturally determined perception of an act." Reflecting that malleability, the word's legal meaning has changed repeatedly over history, with some dramatic changes over the span of just the past half-century. This malleability continues into the present, as shown by the wide variation across jurisdictions and settings in what the law prohibits when it comes to sexual conduct.[5]

None of this variation is accidental. On the contrary, it can be traced directly to politics. Feminist organizers, activists, and scholars worked for decades and continue working today to change the laws governing gender justice in the United States, including the criminal laws and penal system practices that determine how sexual assault is defined, prosecuted, proven, and punished. Those efforts have at times succeeded in changing the criminal law in identifiable and significant ways. They have also met regular resistance, and at times have drawn backlash — including from feminists who resist carceral approaches to gender justice.

The history of the law of sexual assault, in short, traces an arc and raises a set of questions described well by philosopher and feminist scholar Amia Srinivasan:

> [This is] a story of the mobilization of the law in service of gender justice. But it's a history that also points to the limits of the law. Where precisely those limits are — the point beyond which the law must cease trying to guide culture, but instead wait impatiently for it — is a question not of principle, but of politics.[6]

It is impossible to study this topic without centering those politics in the conversation. Indeed, as Srinivasan's words above suggest, those politics and their interrelationship with law *are* the conversation — one that asks what our social norms around sex and gender equality are and ought to be, and what role law ought to play in both reacting to and shaping gender justice in society.

As Professor Jeannie Suk Gersen writes, these questions are as urgent and pressing today as they have ever been, for society writ large and for law students in particular. "Now more than ever," she writes, "it is critical that law students develop the ability to engage productively and analytically in conversations about sexual assault."[7]

At the same time, there is no denying that these conversations (and the reading materials required to engage in them) can be challenging to confront. In a sense, that is true of so much of what we study in this course. Murder, drug addiction, homelessness, incarceration, police violence, racism—all of these topics can be difficult to discuss, and each could be traumatic for people directly impacted. Still, rape seems different in kind. As the statistics cited above (and additional statistics on college sexual assault in particular) make clear, sexual violence and investigations into allegations of sexual violence have undoubtedly touched the lives of a large number of the people reading these words and preparing to discuss these issues in class. As law professor James Tomkovicz writes, we cannot "ignore the possibility that the classroom dialogue about sexual assault causes personal anguish to a certain number of victims of the crime," even if other survivors might be harmed by ignoring the topic or minimizing its import. More broadly, there is simply no denying that conversations about sexual violence and gender justice can be fraught. Lived experiences and perspectives on the subject can be strongly influenced not only by our differing genders, but by cultural, political, and ideological differences as well. Again, that is true of so much in the study of law. But with this topic the fault lines can sometimes seem particularly sharp.[8]

For all of these reasons, some students (and some professors) urge that the topic of sexual assault be avoided altogether in the introductory criminal law course. And in fact that was once the way of things. As Professor Suk Gersen explains, just a few decades ago, "rape law was not taught in law schools, because it wasn't considered important or suited to the rational pedagogy of law-school classrooms." That choice was itself sharply criticized, most especially by feminist scholars who rejected not only the minimization of sexual violence but also the implicit and sexist assumption that "rape just cannot be discussed within the rational space of the law school classroom because women will just get too emotional, too hysterical even." It was only through the concentrated efforts of a pioneering generation of feminist legal scholars that things began to change, until "eventually the topic became a major part of most law schools' mandatory criminal-law course."[9]

The words of one of those early scholars, Professor Susan Estrich, herself a survivor of sexual assault, ring true today much as they did when she wrote them thirty years ago:

> There's a debate going on in America as to what is reasonable when it comes to sex. Turn on the radio and you will hear it. To silence that debate

in the classroom is to remove the classroom from reality, and to make ourselves irrelevant. It may be hard for some students, but ultimately the only way to change things—and that's usually the goal of those who find the discussions most difficult—is to confront the issues squarely . . . .[10]

Our goal in this chapter is to do precisely that—to approach these discussions with care and sensitivity while engaging honestly and directly with the many hard questions this topic has long posed. To structure that discussion, the chapter is divided into three main parts that together share three overarching themes: to understand the dynamic relationship between formal laws and fluctuating social norms; to understand how institutional actors impact and sometimes impede legal reform efforts; and to understand the ways in which reform efforts shift to new horizons over time, setting the stage for future battles.

Organizationally, the chapter's three parts unfold as follows: The first focuses on different ways of defining the conduct, or *actus reus*, proscribed by the criminal offense of rape. The second turns to questions related to *mens rea*, with a focus on issues that arise when a person accused of sexual assault claims to have mistakenly believed he was engaging in consensual sex. Finally, the third part confronts the challenges inherent in assessing the credibility of competing factual accounts in this context.

I. ACTUS REUS

"Sex can be coerced in a multitude of ways that the law tolerates and sometimes tacitly encourages."

Stephen Schulhofer, *Unwanted Sex* ix-x (1998)

Rape is sometimes imagined or described as an explosion of sexual violence. In the words of Professor Aviva Orenstein, the typical rapist on this view is "a sex-crazed, deviant sociopath" who uses "extreme force to violate his victim." For much of history, this idea of rape as violence anchored the criminal law's definition of the offense, which treated physical force as an inherent and essential element of the crime. Without physical violence, the law held, there was no rape.[11]

But while violent stranger rapes undeniably happen and are undeniably traumatic, they are not the most common form of sexual assault. The vast majority of victims are assaulted by someone they know, often someone they know well. According to a leading survey, more than half of female rape victims are raped by an acquaintance while an additional forty percent are raped by an intimate partner. These encounters can, but often do not, involve extreme physical violence. Rather, as Professor Stephen Schulhofer wrote in a foundational study of the law of rape, sex can be coerced in many different ways: "by overt brutality, by physical intimidation, by the coercive effects of status, power, or authority," or "by the manipulative abuse of trust." Crucially, he went on, many of these forms of coercion are not legally defined as rape. Indeed, some of them are not crimes at all.[12]

In this respect, the law of rape differs from the law of homicide studied in the preceding chapter. There, we did not dwell on the *actus reus* of the offense, as any action that causes the death of another person will suffice. When it comes to sexual assault, however, defining the conduct that constitutes a rape — or that differentiates degrees of sexual assault from one another — is a central focus of the criminal law, and raises questions of longstanding debate.

At the heart of that debate is a disagreement over what rape *is*. Is it mainly a crime of violence, in which one person uses superior physical strength or threats of harm to overpower and attack someone else? Or is it mainly a crime of domination and subordination, in which one person violates another's bodily and sexual autonomy by causing her to have sex that she does not want? Clearly there can be overlap between these two different accounts. But just as clearly, they are not the same thing. Indeed, much of the modern history of the law of rape involves efforts to move the law from the first account of rape to the second.

In this opening part of the chapter, we will study that ongoing legal evolution. We begin by exploring — and critiquing — a historical and still prevalent doctrinal approach that considers physical force or threats of physical force to be the *sine qua non* of sexual assault. Situating this doctrinal framework in its historical and contemporary context, we will surface a set of assumptions underlying this approach, including assumptions about what makes for "good" and "bad" sex and a related set of assumptions about the credibility of women.

We will then turn to an alternative legal framework in which the *actus reus* of rape is defined instead simply as sex that is *nonconsensual*. Here, we will observe how feminist law reforms redefined the *actus reus* of rape in many jurisdictions over a span of years. And we will explore some of the challenging questions this new approach raises when it comes to defining with specificity the *actus reus* of the offense. We will also explore questions concerning the meaning of consent itself, including questions about the preconditions necessary for treating explicit expressions of consent as valid or invalid.

Finally, we conclude this part by studying some of the harms that may arise when criminal liability for sexual assault expands. In particular, we will examine a longstanding debate about the role criminal law should play in driving social change. And we will contextualize that debate by studying a set of systemic racial injustices that have long shaped the ways in which sexual assault laws are implemented in practice. Surfacing these racial injustices raises a broader set of questions about the dangers that might flow from using carceral systems to promote gender justice, a theme that recurs throughout the chapter.

A.   *Physical Force and Resistance*

Commonwealth v. Berkowitz

609 A.2d 1338 (Pa. Super. Ct. 1992), aff'd, 641 A.2d 1161 (Pa. 1994)*

FACTUAL BACKGROUND

In the spring of 1988, appellant [Robert Berkowitz] and the victim were both college sophomores at East Stroudsburg State University, ages twenty and nineteen years old, respectively. They had mutual friends and acquaintances. On April nineteenth of that year, the victim went to appellant's dormitory room. What transpired in that dorm room between appellant and the victim thereafter is the subject of the instant appeal.

During a one day jury trial . . . the victim gave the following account during direct examination by the Commonwealth. At roughly 2:00 on the afternoon of April 19, 1988, after attending two morning classes, the victim returned to her dormitory room. There, she drank a martini to "loosen up a little bit" before going to meet her boyfriend, with whom she had argued the night before. Roughly ten minutes later she walked to her boyfriend's dormitory lounge to meet him. He had not yet arrived.

Having nothing else to do while she waited for her boyfriend, the victim walked up to appellant's room to look for Earl Hassel, appellant's roommate. She knocked on the door several times but received no answer. She therefore wrote a note to Mr. Hassel, which read, "Hi Earl, I'm drunk. That's not why I came to see you. I haven't seen you in a while. I'll talk to you later." She did so, although she had not felt any intoxicating effects from the martini, "for a laugh."

After the victim had knocked again, she tried the knob on the appellant's door. Finding it open, she walked in. She saw someone lying on the bed with a pillow over his head, whom she thought to be Earl Hassel. After lifting the pillow from his head, she realized it was appellant. She asked appellant which dresser was his roommate's. He told her, and the victim left the note.

Before the victim could leave appellant's room, however, appellant asked her to stay and "hang out for a while." She complied because she "had time to kill" and because she didn't really know appellant and wanted

---

* Editor's Note: The facts presented here are from the intermediate appellate court opinion; the legal analysis is from the state supreme court opinion. For consistency and ease of reading, minor nonsubstantive edits have been made to the text without further notation.

to give him "a fair chance." Appellant asked her to give him a back rub but she declined, explaining that she did not "trust" him. Appellant then asked her to have a seat on his bed. Instead, she found a seat on the floor, and conversed for a while about a mutual friend. No physical contact between the two had, to this point, taken place.

Thereafter, however, appellant moved off the bed and down on the floor, and "kind of pushed" the victim "back with his body. It wasn't a shove, it was just kind of a leaning-type of thing." Next appellant "straddled" and started kissing the victim. The victim responded by saying, "Look, I gotta go. I'm going to meet my boyfriend." Then appellant lifted up her shirt and bra and began fondling her. The victim then said "no."

After roughly thirty seconds of kissing and fondling, appellant "undid his pants and he kind of moved his body up a little bit." The victim was still saying "no" but "really couldn't move because" appellant . . . "was over [her]." Appellant then tried to put his penis in her mouth. The victim did not physically resist, but rather continued to verbally protest, saying "No, I gotta go, let me go," in a "scolding" manner.

Ten or fifteen more seconds passed before the two rose to their feet. Appellant disregarded the victim's continual complaints that she "had to go," and instead walked two feet away to the door and locked it so that no one from the outside could enter.[2]

Then, in the victim's words, appellant "put me down on the bed. It was kind of like—he didn't throw me on the bed. It's hard to explain. It was kind of like a push but no." She did not bounce off the bed. "It wasn't slow like a romantic kind of thing, but it wasn't a fast shove either. It was kind of in the middle."

. . . . [T]he victim did not physically resist in any way while on the bed because appellant was on top of her, and she "couldn't like go anywhere." She did not scream out at anytime. . . . [According to the victim's testimony, once] appellant was inside her, the victim began saying "no, no to him softly in a moaning kind of way because it was just so scary."

After about thirty seconds, appellant pulled out his penis and ejaculated onto the victim's stomach. Immediately thereafter, appellant got off the victim and said, "Wow, I guess we just got carried away." To this the victim retorted, "No, we didn't get carried away, you got carried away." The victim then quickly dressed, grabbed her school books and raced downstairs to her boyfriend who was by then waiting for her in the lounge. Once there, the victim began crying. Her boyfriend . . . called the police.

Defense counsel's cross-examination elicited more details regarding the contact between appellant and the victim before the incident in

---

2. The victim testified that she realized at the time that the lock was not of a type that could lock people inside the room.

question. The victim testified that roughly two weeks prior to the incident, she had attended a [seminar lecture that] had discussed the average length and circumference of human penises. After the seminar, the victim and several of her friends had discussed the subject matter of the seminar over a speaker-telephone with appellant and his roommate Earl Hassel. The victim testified that during that telephone conversation, she had asked appellant the size of his penis. According to the victim, appellant responded by suggesting that the victim "come over and find out." She declined.

When questioned further regarding her communications with appellant prior to the April 19, 1988 incident, the victim testified that on two other occasions, she had stopped by appellant's room while intoxicated. During one of those times, she had laid down on his bed. When asked whether she had asked appellant again at that time what his penis size was, the victim testified that she did not remember.

Appellant took the stand in his own defense and offered an account of the incident and the events leading up to it which differed only as to the consent involved. According to appellant, the victim had begun communication with him after the school seminar by asking him of the size of his penis and of whether he would show it to her. Appellant had suspected that the victim wanted to pursue a sexual relationship with him because she had stopped by his room twice after the phone call while intoxicated, laying down on his bed with her legs spread and again asking to see his penis. He believed that his suspicions were confirmed when she initiated the April 19, 1988 encounter by stopping by his room (again after drinking), and waking him up.

Appellant testified that, on the day in question, he did initiate the first physical contact, but added that the victim warmly responded to his advances by passionately returning his kisses. He conceded that she was continually "whispering no's," but claimed that she did so while "amorously passionately" moaning. In effect, he took such protests to be thinly veiled acts of encouragement. When asked why he locked the door, he explained that "that's not something you want somebody to just walk in on you doing."

According to appellant, the two then laid down on the bed, the victim helped him take her clothing off, and he entered her. He agreed that the victim continued to say "no" while on the bed, but carefully qualified his agreement, explaining that the statements were "moaned passionately." According to appellant, when he saw a "blank look on her face," he immediately withdrew and asked "is anything wrong, is something the matter, is anything wrong." He ejaculated on her stomach thereafter because he could no longer "control" himself. . . .

After hearing both accounts, the jury convicted appellant of rape and indecent assault. . . .

LEGAL ANALYSIS

The crime of rape is defined as follows:

> A person commits a felony of the first degree when he engages in sexual intercourse with another person not one's spouse: (1) by forcible compulsion; (2) by threat of forcible compulsion that would prevent resistance by a person of reasonable resolution; (3) who is unconscious; or (4) who is so mentally deranged or deficient that such person is incapable of consent. 18 Pa. C.S.A. § 3121.

. . . "The force necessary to support a conviction of rape need only be such as to establish lack of consent and to induce the victim to submit without additional resistance. The degree of force required to constitute rape is relative and depends on the facts and particular circumstance of the case." Commonwealth v. Rhodes, 510 A.2d 1217, 1226 (Pa. 1986).

In regard to the critical issue of forcible compulsion, the complainant's testimony is devoid of any statement which clearly or adequately describes the use of force or the threat of force against her. In response to defense counsel's question, "Is it possible that when Robert lifted your bra and shirt you took no physical action to discourage him," the complainant replied, "It's possible." When asked, "Is it possible that Robert was not making any physical contact with you aside from attempting to untie the knot in the drawstrings of your sweatpants," she answered, "It's possible." . . . She agreed that appellant's hands were not restraining her in any manner during the actual penetration, and that the weight of his body on top of her was the only force applied. She testified that at no time did appellant verbally threaten her. The complainant did testify that she sought to leave the room, and said "no" throughout the encounter. As to the complainant's desire to leave the room, the record clearly demonstrates that the door could be unlocked easily from the inside, that she was aware of this fact, but that she never attempted to go to the door or unlock it.

As to the complainant's testimony that she stated "no" throughout the encounter with appellant, we point out that, while such an allegation of fact would be relevant to the issue of consent, it is not relevant to the issue of force. In *Commonwealth v. Mlinarich*, 542 A.2d 1335 (Pa. 1988) (plurality opinion), this Court sustained the reversal of a defendant's conviction of rape where the alleged victim, a minor, repeatedly stated that she did not want to engage in sexual intercourse, but offered no physical resistance and was compelled to engage in sexual intercourse under threat of being recommitted to a juvenile detention center. . . .

Moreover, we find it instructive that in defining the related but distinct crime of "indecent assault," . . . the Legislature did not employ the phrase "forcible compulsion" but rather chose to define indecent assault as "indecent contact with another . . . *without the consent of the other person.*" The phrase "forcible compulsion" is explicitly set forth in the definition of rape . . . , but the phrase *"without the consent of the other person,"* is conspicuously absent. The choice by the Legislature to define the crime of indecent assault utilizing the phrase "without the consent of the other" and to not so define the crime of rape indicates a legislative intent that the term "forcible compulsion" . . . be interpreted as something more than a lack of consent. . . .

Reviewed in light of the above described standard, the complainant's testimony simply fails to establish that the appellant forcibly compelled her to engage in sexual intercourse as required under 18 Pa.C.S. § 3121. Thus, even if all of the complainant's testimony was believed, the jury, as a matter of law, could not have found appellant guilty of rape. . . .

As to the indecent assault charge . . . [t]he evidence described above is clearly sufficient to support the jury's conviction of indecent assault. "Indecent contact" is defined as "[a]ny touching of the sexual or other intimate parts of the person for the purpose of arousing or gratifying sexual desire, in either person." 18 Pa.C.S. § 3101. Appellant himself testified to the "indecent contact." The victim testified that she repeatedly said "no" throughout the encounter. Viewing that testimony in the light most favorable to the Commonwealth as verdict winner, the jury reasonably could have inferred that the victim did not consent to the indecent contact. Thus, the evidence was sufficient to support the jury's verdict finding appellant guilty of indecent assault.*

State v. Jones

299 P.3d 219 (Idaho 2013)

JONES, J. [Russell] Jones, Craig Carpenter, and the victim, A.S., were long-time friends. Carpenter and A.S. were engaged and had children together but, unbeknownst to Carpenter, Jones and A.S. had been sexually involved for approximately four years. On May 22, 2008, after spending the night together in Jackpot, Nevada, A.S. and Jones drove back to Idaho and decided they would end their affair. But despite this, they returned to A.S.'s apartment and engaged in consensual sex that morning.

Afterwards, A.S. went to the bathroom and then returned to the bedroom, where Jones was looking at pornographic material on the computer. Jones sat next to A.S. on the bed and started touching her. [S]he responded

---

* Editor's Note: At the time of this decision, indecent assault was defined in Pennsylvania's criminal code as a misdemeanor in the second degree, carrying a maximum punishment of two years in prison. Rape, by contrast, was a felony in the first degree, carrying a maximum punishment of twenty years in prison. In this case, Berkowitz was initially sentenced to serve between one and four years in prison on the rape count and a concurrent term of six to twelve months on the indecent assault count. *See* 609 A.2d at 1341-1342.

by telling him that "I thought we had decided that the time before was the last time and it wasn't going to happen anymore."

[According to A.S.'s testimony, at that point she was laying on her stomach and "Jones got behind me. I wasn't sure what he was doing, and I got up on my elbows to see what he was doing, and he was undoing his pants. I told him, no, that I wasn't going to do this." Jones pressed his body against A.S., whose arms were already beneath her body. Jones moved A.S.'s underwear to the side and had intercourse with her, while she yelled at him and told "him to stop and please quit."]

After Jones eventually left, A.S. contacted the Boise State University Women's Center. She told a counselor that she had been raped and was advised to call the police, which she did not do.

Thereafter, A.S. continued to be in contact with Jones and subsequently went to Jackpot with him again. On May 27, Jones went to A.S.'s apartment to watch movies. . . . At the time, A.S. was taking an antihistamine for a bee sting and a prescription anti-anxiety medication, both of which caused her to feel drowsy. As a result of her drowsiness she laid down on the living room couch and started to "drift off." Jones went into the living room, sat next to her, and started stroking her hair. A.S. testified that after he "grabbed a handful of hair and pulled" hard enough to hurt her, she was nonresponsive in hopes that "if she just laid there and didn't move he would leave her alone." [Jones continued to touch A.S., forcefully grabbing her breast and then putting his fingers inside her vagina. Jones then pushed A.S.'s legs apart and began to have intercourse with her.] In response, A.S. "just froze," and testified that she was "paralyzed" with fear.

. . . Based on the May 22 incident in the bedroom (Count I) and the May 28 incident on the couch (Count II), Jones was charged with two counts of forcible rape. . . . Jones moved for a directed verdict at the close of evidence, alleging that the State failed to prove: (1) that A.S. resisted sexual intercourse and (2) that her resistance was overcome by force. The district court denied the motion, and the jury convicted Jones of both counts of forcible rape. He was sentenced to concurrent 25-year sentences, with five years determinate for each. . . .

The Idaho Code defines forcible rape "as the penetration, however slight, of the oral, anal or vaginal opening with the perpetrator's penis accomplished with a female [who] resists but her resistance is overcome by force or violence." . . . The term "resistance" is not defined in the rape statute and there is no legislative history to provide guidance. Thus, we begin our review by considering the common law. "At common law, a state had to prove beyond a reasonable doubt that the woman resisted her assailant to the utmost of her physical capacity to prove that an act of sexual intercourse was rape." Michelle J. Anderson, *Reviving Resistance in Rape Law*, 1998 U. Ill. L. Rev. 953, 962. Thus, under the utmost-physical-resistance standard, "verbal resistance was simply inadequate to prove anything." *Id.* at 992.

The utmost-resistance requirement, beyond producing some severely inequitable results at trial,[5] proved to be nearly impossible to establish. [According to Professor Michelle Anderson,] even "if a woman struggled to the utmost of her physical capacity until doing so appeared futile to her, and only then acquiesced to the rapist's advances, she . . . was not raped." *Id.* at 964. Thus, the utmost-resistance standard has since been abandoned to varying degrees. . . .

This Court . . . clarified the meaning of the resistance requirement in *State v. Andreason*, 257 P. 370 (Idaho 1927), [where we explained that] "the importance of resistance by the woman is simply to show two elements of the crime—the assailant's intent to use force in order to have carnal knowledge, and the woman's nonconsent." *Id.* at 371.

. . . Given the plain language of Idaho's forcible rape statute and Idaho's well-established case law regarding resistance, we hold the statute does not require that rape victims resist to their utmost physical ability and that verbal resistance is sufficient . . . . Based on the evidence before it, the jury certainly had sufficient basis to find that on May 22, A.S. resisted Jones' advances. She testified that she "kept yelling at him and pleading for him to stop and please quit, and he just kept ignoring her."

. . . The next issue before us is the meaning of "force or violence" overcoming resistance [as set out in our statute] . . . . [A]s stated by the Washington Court of Appeals in *State v. McKnight*, 774 P.2d 532, 535 (1989)[:] "The force to which reference is made in forcible compulsion 'is not the force inherent in the act of penetration but the force used or threatened to overcome or prevent resistance by the female.' [It must be] more than that which is normally required to achieve penetration." . . . Based on the plain language of [our own rape] statute we hold that [the same] standard applies in Idaho. [A contrary holding] would effectively render the force element moot. Force would *always* be present and never have to be proven, so long as there was sexual intercourse. Generally speaking, "it is incumbent upon a court to give a statute an interpretation which will not render it a nullity." Hecla Mining Co. v. Idaho State Tax Comm'n, 697 P.2d 1161, 1165 (Idaho 1985). . . .

[Here, the] jury had sufficient evidence before it to conclude beyond a reasonable doubt that Jones used force that overcame A.S.'s resistance [during the initial incident on May 22]. This is because Jones used more

---

5. This is exemplified by the outcome in *Brown v. State*, 106 N.W. 536 (Wis. 1906). [There, the victim testified that she "tried as hard" as she could "to get away" from her assailant and that she "screamed as hard" as she could, but that her assailant told her "to shut up" and "held his hand on [her] mouth until [she] was almost strangled." *Id.* at 537.] Despite this, the Court held that the victim had not sufficiently resisted, because she only yelled "let me go" once, her screams were inarticulate, and she failed to resist with "hands and limbs and pelvic muscles." *Id.* at 538.

force than is inherent in the sexual act. . . . As A.S. testified, Jones "leaned forward" and she "was pushed down" [and] "couldn't get up"; he "leaned forward to where his body was pushing on" hers, pinning her hands underneath her so she could not turn around; and he removed her underwear to the side. Jones argues that all these actions were merely incidental to the act of intercourse. But Jones' use of his body weight to trap A.S.'s hands under her, and effectively forestall any struggle, seems in particular less "incidental" to sex and far more like force employed to overcome her resistance. Thus, a jury could well have found beyond a reasonable doubt that Jones used force to overcome A.S.'s resistance during the incident on May 22. . . .

We hold that there is insufficient evidence to support a charge of forcible rape based on Count II. By her own admission, A.S. "didn't respond" physically, or even verbally, to Jones' advances on May 28—she "just froze." Idaho's forcible rape statute expressly requires resistance. Satisfying this element with inactivity strains the definition of resistance, essentially nullifying the resistance requirement. Though studies have shown that "freezing up" is indeed a legitimate, understandable reaction of victims of sexual assault, this Court has no authority to jettison the resistance requirement—modifying this State's statutes is the Legislature's province alone. As the statute is plainly written, some quantum of resistance is required, and A.S. did not resist Jones' advances on May 28. There was insufficient evidence on the element of resistance to support the conviction of forcible rape on Count II so we need not consider the issue of force. The conviction on Count II is accordingly reversed.

NOTES AND QUESTIONS

1. Force and Resistance. The opinions above were written two decades apart, one in 1994 and the other in 2013. But they take similar approaches to defining the *actus reus* of rape. That crime occurs, both opinions hold, when a sexual aggressor uses or threatens to use physical force, above and beyond the force "inherent in the sexual act," to physically overpower someone into sex. Absent such physical overpowering, the sex—even if clearly unwanted—is not considered rape under this framework.

Courts applying this approach often purport to focus on the defendant's actions, asking whether the defendant used force severe enough under the law to constitute a rape. But as the opinions above show, courts will often focus as much if not more on the victim's behavior, asking whether she *resisted*, or, more accurately, whether she resisted enough or in the right way. Thus, in *Berkowitz*, the court deems it relevant and seemingly dispositive that the woman did not scream, did not try to leave the room, and "took no physical action to discourage" Berkowitz's advances. Indeed, the court defines "force" in reference to the woman's resistance: "The force necessary to support a conviction of rape," it says, is force that would "induce the victim to submit without additional resistance."

In *Jones*, the focus on the victim's actions is even more explicit because the governing statute expressly requires a victim to resist for an encounter to be classified as a rape. The *Jones* court thus reverses the defendant's conviction on the second count of rape because the victim "didn't respond physically" to his aggressive advances. As for the initial encounter, where the victim clearly did resist, the defendant's physical aggression constituted a rape only because it was severe enough "to overcome her resistance" and "effectively forestall any struggle."

As these opinions indicate, whether formally stated in terms of *force* or in terms of *resistance*, the legal framework is functionally the same. As one legal scholar puts it, "If the law makes force an element of rape, then so is resistance."[13]

2. Rape Culture. In her groundbreaking book *Real Rape*, Professor Susan Estrich writes that opinions like the ones above, focusing as they do on the woman's actions, read "not as a judgment that the man acted reasonably, but as a judgment that the woman victim did not." Estrich does not use the phrase *rape culture* to describe this focus, but others would. Asked to define that phrase, author Kate Harding offered this response:

> [I]t's a culture where we blame victims, where we disbelieve victims. . . . It's a culture where we always identify with the person who's accused of rape instead of identifying with the victim. . . . Immediately the suspicion falls on the person who reported the rape. It's a culture where we believe a lot of rape myths, such as, "She was asking for it." If you're drinking, if you're in a certain part of town, if you're wearing a certain outfit, people are going to say outright that you deserved to be raped.[14]

And indeed, some reactions to the *Berkowitz* opinion when it was issued were explicit in this regard. Professor Camille Paglia, for example, expressed shock and outrage that Berkowitz had been prosecuted in the first place — because, in her words, a woman who "goes into the room of a man who's in bed and sits on the floor with her breasts sticking up [is] sending a signal." Implicitly, the signal that Paglia imagines the woman in *Berkowitz* to have sent is that, despite repeatedly saying the word "*no,*" she wanted to have sex with Berkowitz.[15]

3. "Good Sex." Of course, if the woman in *Berkowitz* had in fact wanted to have sex with Berkowitz — if their sex had been consensual — he would not have committed a crime. Under prevailing legal theories and societal norms, mutually desired sex between consenting adults is generally considered a good thing. At a basic biological level, societies (species, really) have a procreative interest in self-perpetuation, which typically requires sex. But as Professor Schulhofer writes, the notion that sex can be both a personal and a social good goes well beyond procreation. A commitment to sexual autonomy, he argues, requires the conclusion that law should "protect our freedom to seek emotional intimacy and sexual fulfillment with willing partners." In the words of Professor Martha Chamallas, it is precisely these mutually gratifying sexual encounters, which "have pleasure or intimacy as their purpose," that come the "closest to the egalitarian ideal of good sex."[16]

Many feminists have long championed this idea that there is such a thing as *good sex* worth celebrating or protecting. Indeed, it is a central component of the so-called sexual revolution of the 1960s, 70s, and 80s, during which, Professor Elisa Glick writes, "pro-sex feminists argued, persuasively," that treating "women as disempowered actors" when it comes to sex "fails to see women as sexual subjects in their own right." As anthropologist Carol Vance explains, these feminists

> demanded better birth control and abortion on demand, while savaging ideologies of love and romance that left them infantile and desperate. . . . They laid claim to a new language of their bodily desire, rejecting the idea that sex is something that is done to women. They rejected the prescriptive orgasm (vaginal, during penetration only) in favor of an explosion of clitoral and other pleasures. They agitated for lesbian rights, producing lyrical descriptions of women loving each other in ways that were not only nurturing but electric and juicy. They ridiculed and protested patriarchal sex advice books, meat-market beauty pageants, and male-dominated gynecology. Feminists set up alternative clinics and self-help networks, which empowered women with sexual knowledge and care. Their educational tools included vibrators, Betty Dodson's *Liberating Masturbation*, and *Our Bodies, Ourselves*. Motivating all these actions was a passionate commitment to women's sexual freedom — a freedom we had not seen or known yet but which we were determined to think through and make possible.

Writing in 2021 and looking back on multiple waves of feminism over decades, Professor Amia Srinivasan concludes that "contemporary feminism [with] its insistence on women's right to sexual pleasure . . . has largely taken up the pro-sex perspective," although, she adds, "many feminists still feel the pull of an older, more circumspect approach to sex" (as we will explore later in this chapter).[17]

4. The Meaning of "No." If one accepts the idea that there is such a thing as good sex, one challenge societies confront when regulating sexual encounters is to draw lines that separate good sex, bad sex, and criminal sex. It is in this regard that the force requirement set out in *Berkowitz* and *Jones* is often criticized as sexist and misogynist. The core problem, according to critics, is that the requirement conclusively substitutes force and resistance for consent itself. In the words of one opinion embracing the approach, "lack of consent is generally *established through* proof of resistance or by proof that the victim failed to resist because of fear." State v. Rusk,

424 A.2d 720, 726 (Md. 1981) (emphasis added). Likewise, in *Berkowitz*, the court notes that the force element in the Pennsylvania rape statute serves "to establish lack of consent."

But as noted at the outset of this part, most sexual violence does not involve a violent, physically overpowering stranger. Rather, as Professor Michelle Anderson writes:

> The typical rape in the United States does not happen in an alley-way. It most often happens in the victim's own home or in the home of a friend, relative, or neighbor. The typical rape is not launched by a stranger. Acquaintances and intimate partners commit the vast majority of rapes. . . . The typical rape involves no knives, guns, or other weapons. . . . [It] does not involve valiant physical resistance on the part of the victim. Frozen in fright, many women cry or remain passive in the face of a sexual attack.[18]

On this factual premise, the fundamental problem critics identify with the force requirement is that it defines as "not rape" what for most women is the archetypical experience of sexual subordination. In the words of Professor Dorothy Roberts, "If rape is violence as the law defines it (weapons, bruises, blood) then what most men do when they disregard women's sexual autonomy is not rape." Indeed, in *Berkowitz*, there was direct evidence, independent of any facts relating to force or resistance, that showed the woman did not consent. In the court's words, she "stated 'no' throughout the encounter." By deeming that fact irrelevant to the defendant's rape charge, the court—like all courts embracing the force requirement—rejects the idea that "no means no" when defining the crime of rape.[19]

   5. A Patriarchal Past: Force as Part of Sex? To begin to understand why the law in some jurisdictions defines rape this way, it will help to situate the force requirement within its historical context. The Oxford English Dictionary defines the word *patriarchy* to mean a "form of social organization" marked by the "predominance of men in positions of power and influence in society, with cultural values and norms favouring men." It is, the dictionary says, a form of "government or rule by a man or men."[20]

   By any account, the early Anglo-American society from which modern rape law descends was a patriarchal society. In his famous *Commentaries on the Laws of England* written in the 1760s, William Blackstone described the "very being or legal existence of the woman" as being "suspended during the marriage, or at least [a]s incorporated and consolidated into that of the husband." Pursuant to this principle and the related law of coverture—which considered married women the legal property of their husbands—married women were prohibited from voting or from owning property. And echoing this common law history, American society from the time of the founding on into the twentieth century "did not perceive women as equals, and did not recognize women's rights." Dobbs v. Jackson Whole Women's Health, 597 U.S. 215, 373 (2022) (Breyer, Sotomayor, Kagan, JJ., dissenting).[21]

Consistent with this view, women also lacked "any control over their bodies." *Id.* For married women, this lack of bodily autonomy was evident in the *spousal exception* to rape law, which made it legally impossible for a husband to rape his wife. As Professor Leigh Bienen explains, legal authorities endorsing the doctrine believed that "the wife's promise to obey meant that the husband had a right to sexual intercourse with the wife upon all occasions." In other words, as Professor Michelle Anderson writes, "The rape of a married woman by her husband was not a transgression at all because a man was allowed to treat his chattel as he deemed appropriate."[22]

In this sociolegal context, historian Estelle Freedman writes, "the requirement of female chastity" was "critical" to the social order. Precisely because rape in this era was understood as "a transgression against the man who owned the woman as his property," as Anderson writes, *all* sex with an unmarried woman and *all* extramarital sex with a married woman was verboten. As Freedman explains, "prospective husbands sought virginal brides," which meant that virginity "had calculable worth when fathers negotiated marriages for their daughters." A woman "sullied through sexual relations before marriage" would find that her "reputation was ruined." At the same time, extramarital sex with a married woman "represented the appropriation of a husband's sole access to his wife, compromising his paternity," which meant that a "wife, too, had to be beyond reproach." Indeed, *consensual* sex outside of marriage was often a crime: women who engaged in it could be accused of fornication and punished by whipping.[23]

In short, at the time when much of rape law was developed, sex outside of marriage was socially and legally unacceptable, even if a woman desired it. Of course, sex outside of marriage still happened. And the way in which it happened — that is to say, the prevailing sex norms of the time — were inevitably shaped by these background norms of chastity, in complicated and (to modern readers) uncomfortable ways. As Freedman explains, the background norm that unmarried sex was wrong or even criminal created a "thin line between what was then considered coercive, rather than consensual sex." For their part, "Men often employed some level of aggression when they approached women sexually." And it was widely assumed — at least by the men writing rape laws at the time — that women "require as part of ordinary 'love play' aggressive overtures by the man." The assumption, in other words, was that women regularly pretended to refuse sex that they actually desired, and that they even "enjoyed forceful sexual intercourse."[24]

Consistent with this understanding, one can find many examples of literature from this era echoing Lord Byron's satiric poem *Don Juan*, in which Byron reimagines Don Juan not as a womanizer but as a man routinely seduced by women. Describing what is imagined to be a consensual romantic encounter, Byron writes this line of verse: "A little still she strove, and much repented, and whispering 'I will ne'er consent,' consented." Originating as it did in this context, the force requirement in rape law can be understood, at least in part, as an attempt by (male) lawmakers to solve what they perceived to be a challenge inherent in the sexual norms of the time. More controversially, it is possible some women, operating under the internalized morality of those same patriarchal sex norms, may have thought themselves required to exhibit chastity, such that women were expected to demur sex while men were expected to show some amount of aggression in pursuing it, even when the sex was mutually desired. In all events, the fact that prevailing sociolegal norms defined "normal" sex as sometimes entailing a degree of aggression, force, or resistance gives relevant context to formal legal definitions of rape that required *overpowering* force and *substantial* resistance—as the force requirement demands.[25]

6. A Patriarchal Past: Force as Proof of "True" Nonconsent? The social norms described above might also explain a related aspect of the force requirement's origins, which we will consider again at the end of this chapter when examining questions of proof and credibility. Simply put, in the words of Professor Richard Klein, "[t]here clearly was a connection between concerns about women fabricating rape charges and the requirement that to convict someone of rape, it must be shown that the victim fought and struggled to the utmost." "[H]ow else," Klein imagines early lawmakers asking themselves, "would it be known that the woman hadn't really desired the intercourse?"[26]

Tracing this fear of false rape accusations back to early common law authorities, Professor Susan Estrich highlights the famous English Lord Chief Justice Matthew Hale, who once wrote that rape is a charge "easily to be made and hard to be proved." Hale's clear implication, Estrich explains, is that if women "are spurned in the relationship or caught in the act and forced to explain, we call it 'rape.'" Professor Patricia Falk sums up the critique more pointedly, writing that "American jurisdictions added the force requirement to supply external evidence of nonconsent, probably because of rampant, sexist distrust of rape victims."[27]

Here again, Professor Anne Coughlin urges modern readers to understand rape law "not in isolation, but in conjunction with the fornication and adultery prohibitions with which it formerly resided" and which provide relevant context.

> Far from being positively valued and protected, the exercise of sexual autonomy was something [in this older era that was] discouraged, even criminalized. Since legal institutions were assigned the task of enforcing both the rape laws and the fornication and adultery laws, it would not be surprising to discover that appellate judges and, presumably, other law enforcement officials found ways to enlist rape doctrine to detect and

discipline [consensual] sexual transgressions . . . in which the man and the woman were accomplices. . . . By unearthing our ancestors' belief that all nonmarital intercourse should be criminalized, we may begin to understand, even as we reject, the inclination of courts to approach rape complaints with deep suspicion.[28]

7. A Patriarchal Present? Of course, as Coughlin says explicitly above, even if a historical understanding of patriarchal sex norms might help to partially explain the force requirement's legal origins, that history does not necessarily justify the requirement's continued existence. On the contrary, Coughlin writes, "if we now are prepared to agree that fornication," i.e., consensual sex outside of marriage, "no longer should be criminalized" given "contemporary constitutional guarantees [and] contemporary moral and political judgments . . . then there appears to be no justification for adhering to a definition of rape that treats the rapist's victim as a lawbreaker who must plead for an excuse from criminal responsibility." The force requirement, in other words, can be understood — and is understood by many legal scholars today — as what Professor Richard Klein calls a modern-day continuation of "age-old prejudices and unfair, pervasive doubts about the credibility of any woman who claimed to have been raped."[29]

But are these societal views about force and consent truly relegated to the age-old past? Consider the following excerpt.

Dan M. Kahan, *Culture, Cognition, and Consent: Who Perceives What, and Why, in Acquaintance-Rape Cases*, 158 U. Pa. L. Rev. 729, 731-734, 774, 776-777, 783-784 (2010). Does "no" always mean "no" to sex? . . . According to critics, the traditional and still dominant common law definition of rape . . . which requires proof of "force or threat of force" . . . is founded on antiquated expectations of male sexual aggression and female submission. Defenders of the common law reply that the traditional definition of rape sensibly accommodates contemporary practices and understandings — not only of men but of many women as well. The statement "no," they argue, does not invariably mean "no" but rather sometimes means "yes" or at least "maybe."

. . . In both law journals and law school classrooms, that debate is frequently brought into sharp focus — and sharp contention — by examination of a controversial case, *Commonwealth v. Berkowitz*. In an experimental study [conducted in 2009], a large and diverse national sample of [1,500] adults reviewed the key facts in *Berkowitz*, including the uncontested fact that the victim in the case repeatedly said "no" immediately before and during intercourse with the defendant. The subjects then indicated whether they believed the victim consented to sex or could reasonably have been understood to have done so by the defendant. . . .

[W]hen individuals of diverse cultural values are exposed to the same sources of evidence — eyewitness statements, expert opinions, and even videotaped recordings of key events—they can hear and see very different things. The study found that exactly this dynamic is at work when individuals consider the evidence in a case like *Berkowitz*. The question whether the putative victim in that case effectively conveyed consent or the lack of it depends on the answer to another question—who is being asked. Individuals who adhere to a largely traditional cultural style, one that prescribes highly differentiated gender roles and features a commitment to hierarchical forms of authority and social organization more generally, are highly likely to believe that "no" did not mean "no" in *Berkowitz*. In contrast, persons who subscribe to a more egalitarian cultural style that denies the legitimacy of hierarchical forms of social organization, including those founded on gender, are much more likely to perceive that the complainant did not consent and that the defendant knew that. . . .

[Notably, gender] mattered much less than culture—or, more accurately, mattered only in conjunction with it. Overall, women were no more or less likely to favor conviction [for Berkowitz] than were men. However, women who subscribed to the hierarchical cultural style—particularly older women who did—were more inclined to form a pro-defendant view of the facts. . . . Those who subscribe to traditional gender norms conceive of saying "no" but meaning "yes" as a strategy some women use to evade the stigma that these norms visit on women who engage in casual sex. . . .

[As to the survey's results,] a relatively large majority—72%—agreed that "[b]y saying 'no' several times, [the woman in *Berkowitz*] made it clear to [Berkowitz] that she did not consent to sexual intercourse." Nevertheless, majorities also agreed that "if [she] had really meant not to consent to sexual intercourse" she "would have tried to push [him] off of her" (66%) and "would have tried to leave the dormitory room" (63%). . . . Overall, then, the responses seem to indicate ambivalence, stemming from the absence of physical resistance, about whether [her] "no" communicated lack of consent. Indeed, 40% of the subjects, across conditions, indicated that they agreed that "[d]espite what she said or might have felt after, [she] really did consent to sexual intercourse with [him]."

[As to whether Berkowitz should have been found guilty of rape,* 57% of the subjects said yes, while 43% said no, with the following intensity levels and demographic breakdowns:]

---

* Editor's Note: As indicated earlier in this excerpt, the ultimate question of liability turns in part on whether a jury thought Berkowitz reasonably could have understood the woman to have consented, a question distinct from whether she actually consented. We will explore this question in detail in the next part of this chapter when examining *mens rea*.

Berkowitz Should Be Found Guilty of Rape

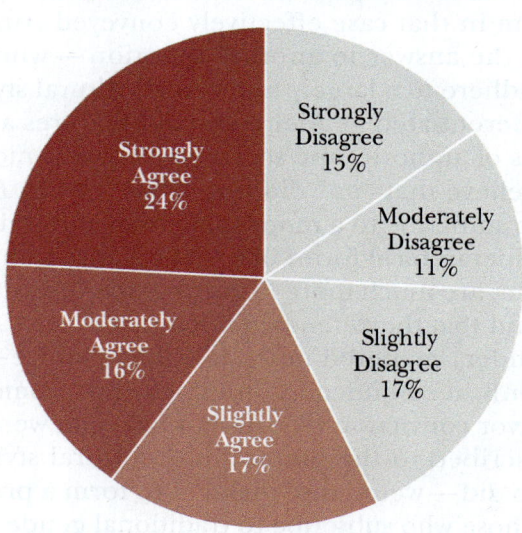

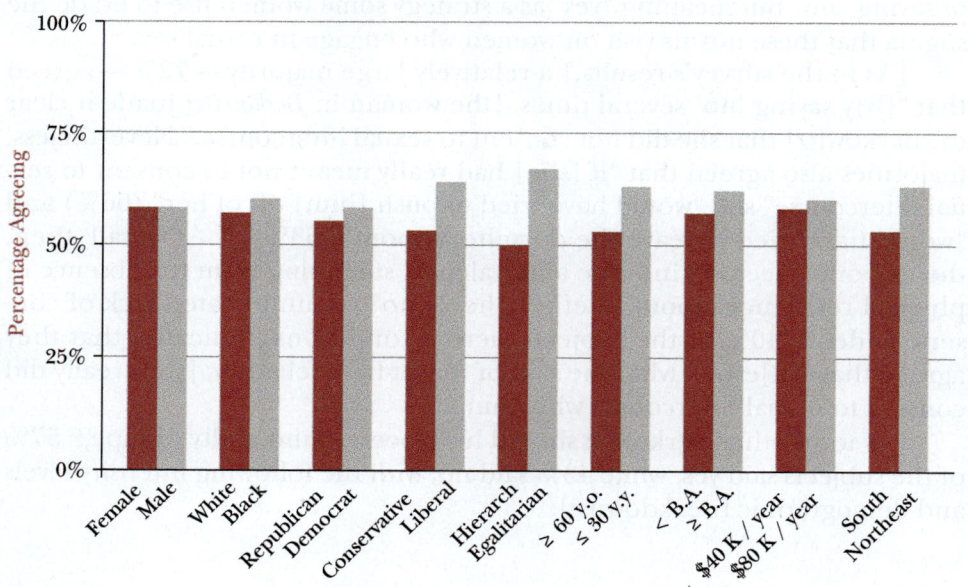

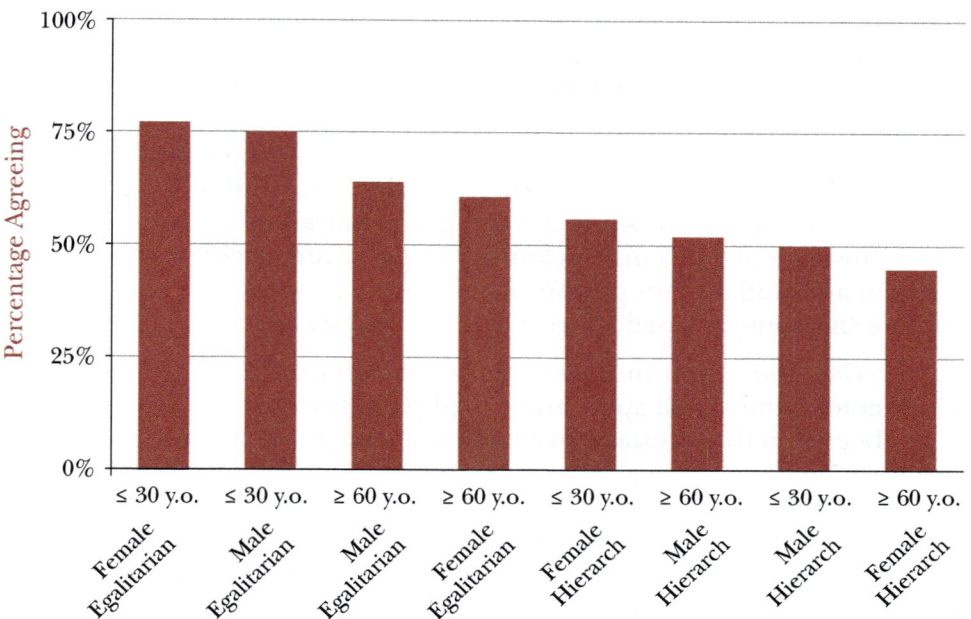

8. State of the Law. According to Professor David Bryden, "[v]irtually all modern rape scholars want to modify or abolish the force requirement as an element of rape." But as Professor Kahan wrote in the preceding note, at least as of 2010, the force requirement provided the "still dominant" definition of rape in the United States. A year later, in 2011, Professors John Decker and Peter Baroni conducted a comprehensive survey and concluded that only seventeen states had abandoned the force or resistance requirements with respect to "sexual penetration offenses."[30]

Somewhat more recently, the American Law Institute attempted to catalog the current state of the law. As it reported in 2021, "[a]ny summary of current law is necessarily approximate" given that "the definition of required force and the operational significance of such force vary widely" across jurisdictions. Adding to this complexity, "[s]ome statutes do not *seem* to require proof of force at all, but [then] define nonconsent by referring to force and resistance"; meanwhile, in "other states, statutory language nominally imposes a strong force requirement, but courts interpret or apply that language in ways that diminish or minimize the degree of force actually required."[31]

With those caveats, the Institute ultimately found that "[m]ost jurisdictions take force of some sort into account in defining or grading their adult felony sex offenses." Specifically, eleven states "still require proof of a significant degree of physical force" or "require resistance unless it would be futile or likely to result in injury" as an element of "the *least serious* of the adult felony sex offenses," meaning that serious criminal liability of any sort requires a showing of significant force or resistance. In addition, a number of states retain a force requirement but "define it broadly to include not just physical force but circumstantial coercion or intimidation" or "require only a slight showing of force or restraint (such as pressure applied against a victim's hands or body parts)." Finally, at the other end of the spectrum, seventeen states punish as a felony "sexual penetration solely on the basis of the absence of consent," meaning without a force requirement, while thirteen additional states punish such conduct as a misdemeanor. We will explore this consent-based approach in the next section.[32]

9. Coercion. Even in jurisdictions that retain the traditional force requirement, the actual application of physical force by the defendant has never been strictly necessary. Instead, the *threat of force* has also sufficed to sustain a rape conviction. In many states, this is clear on the face of the penal code. As we saw in *Berkowitz*, for example, Pennsylvania's rape statute covers sex procured through "forcible compulsion" or the "threat of forcible compulsion." 18 Pa. Cons. Stat. §3121(a). Other states have reached the same position by judicial decision. *See, e.g.*, State v. Penland, 472 S.E.2d 734, 742 (N.C. 1996) (interpreting statute's "by force and against the will" requirement to include "threats" of force). That said, the state's burden in overcoming the force requirement by pointing to threats of force is a "demanding one," a leading treatise explains. The threat must typically be so grave that the victim fears death or great bodily harm, sufficient to preclude resistance to the sexual act.[33]

Beyond threats of serious physical violence, some jurisdictions allow additional forms of coercion to overcome the force requirement, often employing a concept known as *constructive force*. Constructive force, the North Carolina Supreme Court explains, encompasses "fear, fright, or coercion" and "is demonstrated by proof of threats or other actions by the defendant which compel the victim's submission to sexual acts." State v. Etheridge, 352 S.E.2d 673, 682 (N.C. 1987). So, in *Commonwealth v. Caracciola*, 569 N.E.2d 774, 775 (Mass. 1991), the Massachusetts Supreme Judicial Court found the force requirement satisfied where the defendant falsely told the victim that he was a police officer and threatened to arrest her "for more things than he was planning on" unless she had sex with him. Sometimes, the constructive force doctrine is also held to support criminal liability when a defendant engages in "the imposition of psychological pressure on one who, under the circumstances, is vulnerable and susceptible to such pressure." Benyo v. Commonwealth, 568 S.E.2d 371, 373 (Va. Ct. App. 2002). We will return to the question of pressure and vulnerability later in this chapter when examining the role of power imbalances in sexual assault law (p. 391).[34]

B. *Sex Without Consent*

In re M.T.S.

---

609 A.2d 1266 (N.J. 1992)

HANDLER, J. Under New Jersey law a person who commits an act of sexual penetration using physical force or coercion is guilty of second-degree sexual assault. The sexual assault statute does not define the words "physical force." The question posed by this appeal is whether the element of "physical force" is met simply by an act of non-consensual penetration involving no more force than necessary to accomplish that result.

That issue is presented in the context of what is often referred to as "acquaintance rape." The record in the case discloses that the juvenile, a seventeen-year-old boy, engaged in consensual kissing and heavy petting with a fifteen-year-old girl and thereafter engaged in actual sexual penetration of the girl to which she had not consented. There was no evidence or suggestion that the juvenile used any unusual or extra force or threats to accomplish the act of penetration.

. . . On Monday, May 21, 1990, fifteen-year-old C.G. was living with her mother, her three siblings, and several other people, including M.T.S. and his girlfriend. A total of ten people resided in the three-bedroom townhome at the time of the incident. M.T.S., then age seventeen, was temporarily residing at the home with the permission of C.G.'s mother; he slept downstairs on a couch. C.G. had her own room on the second floor. At approximately 11:30 p.m. on May 21, C.G. went upstairs to sleep after having watched television with her mother, M.T.S., and his girlfriend. When C.G. went to bed, she was wearing underpants, a bra, shorts, and a shirt. At trial, C.G. and M.T.S. offered very different accounts concerning the nature of their relationship and the events that occurred after C.G. had gone upstairs. The trial court did not credit fully either teenager's testimony.

C.G. stated that earlier in the day, M.T.S. had told her three or four times that he "was going to make a surprise visit up in her bedroom." She said that she had not taken M.T.S. seriously and considered his comments a joke because he frequently teased her. She testified that M.T.S. had attempted to kiss her on numerous other occasions and at least once had attempted to put his hands inside of her pants, but that she had rejected all of his previous advances.

C.G. testified that on May 22, at approximately 1:30 a.m., she awoke to use the bathroom. As she was getting out of bed, she said, she saw M.T.S., fully clothed, standing in her doorway. According to C.G., M.T.S. then said that "he was going to tease [her] a little bit." C.G. testified that she "didn't think anything of it"; she walked past him, used the bathroom, and then returned to bed, falling into a "heavy" sleep within fifteen minutes. The next event C.G. claimed to recall of that morning was waking up with M.T.S. on top of her, her underpants and shorts removed. She said "his penis was into her vagina." As soon as C.G. realized what had happened, she said, she immediately slapped M.T.S. once in the face, then "told him to get off her, and get out." She did not scream or cry out. She testified that M.T.S. complied in less than one minute after being struck; according to C.G., "he jumped right off of her." She said she did not know how long M.T.S. had been inside of her before she awoke.

C.G. said that after M.T.S. left the room, she "fell asleep crying" because "she couldn't believe that he did what he did to her." She explained that she did not immediately tell her mother or anyone else in the house of the events of that morning because she was "scared and in shock." According to C.G., M.T.S. engaged in intercourse with her "without [her] wanting it or telling him to come up to her bedroom." By her own account, C.G. was not otherwise harmed by M.T.S.

At about 7:00 a.m., C.G. went downstairs and told her mother about her encounter with M.T.S. earlier in the morning and said that they would have to "get him out of the house." While M.T.S. was out on an errand, C.G.'s mother gathered his clothes and put them outside in his car; when he returned, he was told that "he better not even get near the house." C.G. and her mother then filed a complaint with the police.

According to M.T.S., he and C.G. had been good friends for a long time, and their relationship "kept leading on to more and more." He had been living at C.G.'s home for about five days before the incident occurred; he testified that during the three days preceding the incident they had been "kissing and necking" and had discussed having sexual intercourse. The first time M.T.S. kissed C.G., he said, she "didn't want him to, but she did after that." He said C.G. repeatedly had encouraged him to "make a surprise visit up in her room."

M.T.S. testified that at exactly 1:15 a.m. on May 22, he entered C.G.'s bedroom as she was walking to the bathroom. He said C.G. soon returned from the bathroom, and the two began "kissing and all," eventually moving to the bed. Once they were in bed, he said, they undressed each other and continued to kiss and touch for about five minutes. M.T.S. and C.G. proceeded to engage in sexual intercourse. According to M.T.S., who was on top of C.G., he "stuck it in" and "did it [thrust] three times, and then the fourth time he stuck it in, that's when she pulled him off of her." M.T.S. said that as C.G. pushed him off, she said "stop, get off," and he "hopped off right away."

According to M.T.S., after about one minute, he asked C.G. what was wrong; she replied with a back-hand to his face. He recalled asking C.G. what was wrong a second time, and her replying, "how can you take advantage of me or something like that." M.T.S. said that he proceeded to get dressed and told C.G. to calm down, but that she then told him to get away from her and began to cry. Before leaving the room, he told C.G., "I'm leaving . . . I'm going with my real girlfriend, don't talk to me . . . I don't want nothing to do with you or anything, stay out of my life . . . don't tell anybody about this . . . it would just screw everything up." He then walked downstairs and went to sleep.

. . . M.T.S. was charged with conduct that if engaged in by an adult would constitute second-degree sexual assault of the victim . . . . Following a two-day trial on the sexual assault charge, M.T.S. was adjudicated delinquent. After reviewing the testimony, the court concluded that the victim had consented to a session of kissing and heavy petting with M.T.S. The trial court did not find that C.G. had been sleeping at the time of penetration, but nevertheless found that she had not consented to the actual sexual act. Accordingly, the court concluded that the State had proven second-degree sexual assault beyond a reasonable doubt. On appeal, following the imposition of [a suspended sentence] the Appellate Division determined that the absence of force beyond that involved in the act of sexual penetration precluded a finding of second-degree sexual assault. It therefore reversed the juvenile's adjudication of delinquency . . . .

The New Jersey Code of Criminal Justice defines "sexual assault" as the commission "of sexual penetration" "with another person" with the use of "physical force or coercion." An unconstrained reading of the statutory language indicates that both the act of "sexual penetration" and the use of "physical force or coercion" are separate and distinct elements of the offense. Neither the definitions section of [the statute] nor the remainder of the Code of Criminal Justice provides assistance in interpreting the words "physical force." . . . The State would read "physical force" to entail any amount of sexual touching brought about involuntarily. A showing of sexual penetration coupled with a lack of consent would satisfy the elements of the statute. The Public Defender urges an interpretation of "physical force" to mean force "used to overcome lack of consent." That definition equates force with violence and leads to the conclusion that sexual assault requires the application of some amount of force in addition to the act of penetration.

. . . [Because] the statutory words "physical force" do not evoke a single meaning that is obvious and plain . . . the court seeks the underlying intent of the legislature, relying on legislative history and the contemporary context of the statute. With respect to a law, like the sexual assault statute, that "alters or amends the previous law or creates or abolishes types of actions, it is important, in discovering the legislative intent, to ascertain the old law, the mischief and the proposed remedy." Grobart v. Grobart, 74 A.2d 294 (N.J. 1950). . . .

The provisions proscribing sexual offenses found in the Code of Criminal Justice became effective in 1979, and were written against almost two hundred years of rape law in New Jersey. . . . Under traditional rape law, in order to prove that a rape had occurred, the state had to show both that force had been used and that the penetration had been against the woman's will. Force was identified and determined not as an independent factor but in relation to the response of the victim, which in turn implicated the victim's own state of mind. . . . [This approach] squarely placed on the victim the burden of proof and of action. Effectively, a woman who was above the age of consent had actively and affirmatively to withdraw that consent for the intercourse to be against her will. . . .

The presence or absence of consent often turned on credibility. . . . Courts and commentators historically distrusted the testimony of victims, "assuming that women lie about their lack of consent for various reasons: to blackmail men, to explain the discovery of a consensual affair, or because of psychological illness." Cynthia A. Wicktom, Note, *Focusing on the Offender's Forceful Conduct: A Proposal for the Redefinition of Rape Laws*, 56 Geo. Wash. L. Rev. 399, 401 (1988). . . . The resistance requirement had another untoward influence on traditional rape law. . . . The amount of force used by the defendant was assessed in relation to the resistance of the victim. . . . Resistance, often demonstrated by torn clothing and blood, was a sign that the defendant had used significant force to accomplish the sexual intercourse. Thus, if the defendant forced himself on a woman, it was her responsibility to fight back, because force was measured in relation to the resistance she put forward. Only if she resisted, causing him to use more force than was necessary to achieve penetration, would his conduct be criminalized. . . .

. . . Critics [of traditional rape law] shared a central premise: that the burden of showing non-consent should not fall on the victim of the crime. . . . Similarly, with regard to force, rape law reform sought to give independent significance to the forceful or assaultive conduct of the defendant and to avoid a definition of force that depended on the reaction of the victim. Traditional interpretations of force were strongly criticized for failing to acknowledge that force may be understood simply as the invasion of "bodily integrity." Susan Estrich, *Rape*, 95 Yale L.J. 1087, 1105 (1986). In urging that the "resistance" requirement be abandoned, reformers sought to break the connection between force and resistance. . . .

. . . The new statutory provisions covering rape [adopted by our legislature] were formulated by a coalition of feminist groups assisted by the National Organization of Women (NOW) National Task Force on Rape. . . . Since th[is] 1978 reform, the Code has referred to the crime that was once known as "rape" as "sexual assault." The crime now requires "penetration," not "sexual intercourse." It requires "force" or "coercion," not "submission" or "resistance." It makes no reference to the victim's state of mind or attitude, or conduct in response to the assault. . . . It emphasizes the assaultive character of the offense by defining sexual penetration to encompass a wide range of sexual contacts, going well beyond traditional "carnal knowledge."[2]

. . . The Legislature's concept of sexual assault and the role of force was significantly colored by its understanding of the law of assault and battery. As a general matter, criminal battery is defined as "the unlawful application of force to the person of another." 2 Wayne LaFave & Austin Scott, *Criminal Law*, § 7.15, at 301 (1986). The application of force is criminal when it results in either (a) a physical injury or (b) an offensive touching. *Id.* at 301-302. Any "unauthorized touching of another [is] a battery." Perna v. Pirozzi, 457 A.2d 431 (N.J. 1983). Thus, by eliminating all references to the victim's state of mind and conduct, and by broadening the definition of penetration to cover not only sexual intercourse between a man and a woman but a range of acts that invade another's body or compel intimate contact, the Legislature emphasized the affinity between sexual assault and other forms of assault and battery. . . . We are thus satisfied that an interpretation of the statutory crime of sexual assault to require physical force in addition to that entailed in an act of involuntary or unwanted sexual penetration would be fundamentally inconsistent with the legislative purpose to eliminate any consideration of whether the victim resisted or expressed non-consent.

. . . Because the statute eschews any reference to the victim's will or resistance, the standard defining the role of force in sexual penetration must prevent the possibility that the establishment of the crime will turn on the alleged victim's state of mind or responsive behavior. We conclude, therefore, that any act of sexual penetration engaged in by the defendant without the affirmative and freely-given permission of the victim to the specific act of penetration constitutes the offense of sexual assault. Therefore, physical force in excess of that inherent in the act of sexual penetration is not required for such penetration to be unlawful. The definition of "physical force" is satisfied if the defendant applies any amount of force against another person in the absence of what a reasonable person would believe to be affirmative and freely-given permission to the act of sexual penetration.

Under the reformed statute, permission to engage in sexual penetration must be affirmative and it must be given freely, but that permission may be inferred either from acts or statements reasonably viewed in light of the surrounding circumstances. Persons need not, of course, expressly announce their consent to engage in intercourse for there to be affirmative permission. Permission to engage in an act of sexual penetration can be and indeed often is indicated through physical actions rather than words.

---

2. The reform replaced the concept of carnal abuse, which was limited to vaginal intercourse, with specific kinds of sexual acts contained in a broad definition of penetration: "Sexual penetration means vaginal intercourse, cunnilingus, fellatio or anal intercourse between persons or insertion of the hand, finger or object into the anus or vagina either by the actor or upon the actor's instruction."

Permission is demonstrated when the evidence, in whatever form, is sufficient to demonstrate that a reasonable person would have believed that the alleged victim had affirmatively and freely given authorization to the act. . . . Although it is possible to imagine a set of rules in which persons must demonstrate affirmatively that sexual contact is unwanted or not permitted, such a regime would be inconsistent with modern principles of personal autonomy. . . .

Today the law of sexual assault is indispensable to the system of legal rules that assures each of us the right to decide who may touch our bodies, when, and under what circumstances. The decision to engage in sexual relations with another person is one of the most private and intimate decisions a person can make. Each person has the right not only to decide whether to engage in sexual contact with another, but also to control the circumstances and character of that contact. No one, neither a spouse, nor a friend, nor an acquaintance, nor a stranger, has the right or the privilege to force sexual contact.

. . . We acknowledge that cases such as this are inherently fact sensitive and depend on the reasoned judgment and common sense of judges and juries. The trial court concluded that the victim had not expressed consent to the act of intercourse, either through her words or actions. We conclude that the record provides reasonable support for the trial court's disposition. Accordingly, we reverse the judgment of the Appellate Division and reinstate the disposition of juvenile delinquency for the commission of second-degree sexual assault.

1. Defining Consent

In jurisdictions that follow the approach taken in *M.T.S.*, consent plays a critical role in defining the crime of sexual assault. Yet the concept of consent itself is amenable to many meanings and may be implemented in many ways. The following notes explore some of the complexity surrounding the derivation and definition of consent in this context.

NOTES AND QUESTIONS

1. Statutory Interpretation. The statute at issue in *M.T.S.* defines sexual assault "as the commission 'of sexual penetration' 'with another person' with the use of *'physical force or coercion.'*" Many courts would read the highlighted words to establish a force requirement. And in fact, the *M.T.S.* court acknowledges that "[a]n unconstrained reading of the statutory language indicates that both the act of 'sexual penetration' and the use of 'physical force or coercion' are separate and distinct elements of the offense."

But the court ultimately holds that "physical force in excess of that inherent in the act of sexual penetration is not required" to establish criminal liability under the statute. In so doing, it adopts what is sometimes called the *intrinsic force* approach, whereby a statutory force requirement is deemed satisfied by the act of penetration alone — or, for statutes that criminalize nonpenetrative sexual contact, by any such contact. The upshot of this approach, as the *M.T.S.* court makes clear, is that a sexual assault occurs whenever one person causes another to engage in *unwanted* or *non-consensual* sex. As the court holds, "any act of sexual penetration engaged in by the defendant without the affirmative and freely-given permission of the victim to the specific act of penetration constitutes the offense of sexual assault."

As a matter of statutory interpretation, the intrinsic force approach invites some criticism. Consider the following passage from *State v. Jones* where the court defends a contrary holding, sometimes called the *extrinsic force* approach, in a portion of its opinion only partly excerpted above:

> The primary justification for the extrinsic force standard seems to be textual. . . . [Our statute] defines forcible rape as "penetration, however slight," "[w]here [a woman] resists but her resistance is overcome by force or violence." Were we to construe "force" as encompassing the act of penetration itself, it would effectively render the force element moot. Force would always be present and never have to be proven, so long as there was sexual intercourse. Generally speaking, "it is incumbent upon a court to give a statute an interpretation which will not render it a nullity." Hecla Mining Co. v. Idaho State Tax Comm'n, 697 P.2d 1161, 1165 (Idaho 1985). Thus, in order to give full effect to the complete text of the statute, we adopt the extrinsic force standard. . . . We must work within the confines of the statute as written.

299 P.3d 219, 228-229 (Idaho 2013).

Of course, the textualist argument set forth above concerns the proper role of *courts* in construing legislative enactments. As the *Jones* court goes on to observe, it remains fully within the prerogative of legislatures to define sexual assault in terms of nonconsent—including by repealing preexisting force requirements. *See id.* at 230 ("[M]odifying this State's statutes is the Legislature's province . . . .") And a number of state legislatures have taken such steps, including New Jersey, which codified the holding of *M.T.S.* by statute years after the opinion was issued.[35]

2. Affirmative Consent. The *M.T.S.* court establishes that, in New Jersey, consent is the dividing line between lawful and criminal sexual encounters. But how is consent itself defined? Here again is some of the relevant language from the opinion:

> [P]ermission to engage in sexual penetration must be affirmative and it must be given freely, but that permission may be inferred either from

acts or statements reasonably viewed in light of the surrounding circumstances. Persons need not, of course, expressly announce their consent to engage in intercourse for there to be affirmative permission. Permission to engage in an act of sexual penetration can be and indeed often is indicated through physical actions rather than words. Permission is demonstrated when the evidence, in whatever form, is sufficient to demonstrate that a reasonable person would have believed that the alleged victim had affirmatively and freely given authorization to the act. . . . Although it is possible to imagine a set of rules in which persons must demonstrate affirmatively that sexual contact is unwanted or not permitted, such a regime would be inconsistent with modern principles of personal autonomy . . . .

Questions: Under the language above, what must a prosecutor prove to satisfy the *actus reus* element of the offense? What facts may the prosecutor draw upon to satisfy that burden? What facts could a defense attorney invoke to rebut the prosecutor's assertion? Is this the right place to draw the line? On this last question, consider the following excerpts.

Aya Gruber, *Consent Confusion*, 38 Cardozo L. Rev. 415, 416-419, 429-431 (2016). The slogans are ubiquitous: Only 'Yes' Means 'Yes.' Got Consent? Consent is Hot, Assault is Not. Ask First! . . . [And yet,] consent is far from clear. The urgent question is "Got Consent?," but people have wildly different conceptions about when to answer, "I do." Some will say that sexual consent is present when parties are mentally willing to have sex. However, there are a variety of views about what constitutes a consensual mental state, ranging from enthusiastic to grudging, from hedonistic to instrumental, from sober to quite inebriated. Others argue that focusing on internal willingness puts victims on trial; thus, sexual consent should be about what the parties say and do. Even here, there is considerable variability on what constitutes performative consent. Some hold that engaging in sexual activity without protest, or with weak protest, communicates consent. Others insist that consent be "affirmatively" or "positively" expressed. To complicate matters, affirmative consent, depending on who you ask, runs the gamut from nonverbal foreplay to "an enthusiastic yes."

. . . . What has caused so much confusion? In short, decades ago, feminist reformers [e]ffected the shift from defining rape as forced sex to defining it as unconsensual sex, in an effort to broaden liability for bad sexual behavior. However, even this shift proved unsatisfying to many activists who contended that biased or mistaken decision-makers misapplied the standard . . . by, for example, finding subtly coerced agreement valid, invariably deriving willingness from silence, or allowing the defendant too much leeway to interpret any behavior as consent. To reduce the risk of bad calls, [some] reformers advocate for affirmative consent.

Affirmative consent [proposals] direct decision-makers to focus on what complainants do or say, and not on what they intend. . . . [And they treat] only *certain* . . . external manifestations [as within] the world of communicative performances that make sex permissible. [Even so, the] meaning of "affirmative consent" [itself] is not uniform, and can range from narrow communicative prescriptions (contract, verbal yes) to any behavior that conveys internal agreement (foreplay, acquiescence). . . . The below categories of affirmative consent are culled from the vast amount of criminal law, educational policy, scholarship, media commentary, and internet discussion regarding affirmative consent. Here is a spectrum . . . from more sex-regulatory/prosecutorial to less sex-regulatory/lenient:

More Regulatory

- A signed contract
- An enthusiastic yes
- A verbal yes
- Stop, seek, and obtain permission
- Words and/or conduct that clearly and contemporaneously convey agreement
- Words and/or conduct (including omissions) that, in context, convey agreement (i.e., ordinary external manifestations)

Less Regulatory

Maura Lerner, *National Group Hopes to Stir Talk with Its Sex Contracts*, Star Tribune (July 9, 2015). Alison Berke Morano knew that the idea of a written contract, titled "YES! We agree to have SEX!" would get people talking. And laughing. But as co-founder of the Affirmative Consent Project, she couldn't be more pleased. Morano's group has launched a national campaign encouraging colleges to adopt "affirmative consent" policies, which state that students could face disciplinary action for sexual encounters unless both participants give explicit consent. As part of the campaign, Morano and her group created "consent kits," which include both a condom and a written contract that students can sign ("On this date . . . we agree to have consensual sex . . . ."). Morano admits that she doesn't expect everyone to actually sign such a document. And it's certainly not required by any college . . . . But Morano sees the contract as a way to make a point about having sex: Are they sure the feeling is mutual? "We hope that people will just look at it," she said. "Maybe it slows them down for a tenth of a second. They look at each other and say, 'We're sure, right?'"

Jaclyn Friedman in Colette Perold, Challenging Male Supremacy Project, *Expanding Consent: An Interview with Jaclyn Friedman* (n.d.). I think most people are familiar with the concept "no means no," and that's not an accident.

A lot of activists worked a lot of decades to get the concept of "no means no" into the mainstream consciousness. "No means no" is to say that when a person says "no" to a sexual encounter or a sexual advance, you ought to stop. . . . I don't think it's a fully universally accepted concept unfortunately. But the problem with "no means no," as important as it is, is that it doesn't go far enough. [M]ost of the time when we're talking about "no means no," we're talking about men needing to listen to women's "no's." And when we leave it there, it underlines all of the sort of diseased ideas about sex and sexuality that we have in our culture, which is that women are the keeper of the "no," women want to say "no," women don't like sex, only bad women give it up, and men only want "yes." It leaves all of those messed up dynamics in place. So "yes means yes" is about suggesting that none of us can have a complete independent sexuality — a full healthy sexuality — unless we have access to "yes" and "no" equally. . . .

[T]he corollary to ["no means no"] that you hear very often is, "Well, she didn't say no." That leaves . . . a very blurry area where a lot of people do things that they know their partner isn't into or doesn't want, but will do anyway because they can "get away with it." And what we're saying is that those things are still sexual assault and rape. Unless you have enthusiastic consent, which is more than just the absence of "no," consent is not complete. When all you're relying on is the absence of "no" to equal consent, you leave out coercion, you leave out the possibility that someone is panicked or terrified, or even that the person is confused in the moment about what they want and isn't given the space to figure it out. A healthy sexual encounter — one that is free of coercion or violence — requires enthusiastic consent, which means it's your responsibility to make sure your partner is having a great time. Not just that they're willing or will let you, but that they really are excited about doing whatever it is you want to do with them.

Cal. Educ. Code §67386. In order to receive state funds for student financial assistance, the governing board of [every college and university in the state] shall adopt a policy [that] shall include . . . [a]n affirmative consent standard in the determination of whether consent was given by both parties to sexual activity. "Affirmative consent" means affirmative, conscious, and voluntary agreement to engage in sexual activity. It is the responsibility of each person involved in the sexual activity to ensure that the person has the affirmative consent of the other or others to engage in the sexual activity. Lack of protest or resistance does not mean consent, nor does silence mean consent. Affirmative consent must be ongoing throughout a sexual activity and can be revoked at any time. The existence of a dating relationship between the persons involved, or the fact of past sexual relations between them, should never by itself be assumed to be an indicator of consent.

3. Drawing Lines While Defining Crimes: The Model Penal Code Revision Debate. The California statute excerpted above is not a criminal statute. It exists within the state's educational code and requires, as a condition of state funding, that every college and university in the state incorporate the legislated definition of consent into university codes and policies—including disciplinary codes that can lead to sanctions such as suspension or expulsion. Such punishments can of course have serious consequences. But they are typically much less severe than the penalties associated with a criminal conviction, which can include both incarceration and required enrollment in national sex-offender registries. All of which raises a question: What lines should the *criminal law* draw when it comes to defining consent?

This question constantly comes before policymakers and jurists authoring and engaging with sexual assault laws. In recent years, it was also at the center of a contested effort within the American Law Institute, which considered various approaches in the course of proposing amendments to the antiquated rape provisions of the original 1962 Model Penal Code. While members of the ALI generally agreed that the original text needed updating, there was sharp disagreement over what should take its place. The following excerpts and the subsequent text give an overview of that debate.[36]

Am. L. Inst., Model Penal Code: Sexual Assault and Related Offenses, Discussion Draft No. 2, at 1-6 (April 28, 2015)

Section 213.0 – Definitions

. . . "Consent" means a person's positive agreement, communicated by either words or actions, to engage in a specific act of sexual penetration or sexual contact. . . .

"Sexual contact" means any touching of any body part of another person, whether clothed or unclothed, by any body part, body fluid, or object . . . for the purpose of sexual gratification, sexual humiliation, sexual degradation, or sexual arousal. . . .

"Sexual penetration" means any act involving penetration, however slight, of the anus or vulva by any object or body part, unless done for bona fide medical, hygienic, or law enforcement purposes; or direct contact between the mouth or tongue of one person and the anus, penis, or vulva of another person. . . .

Section 213.1 – Forcible Rape

. . . An actor is guilty of Forcible Rape, a felony of the second degree, if he or she knowingly or recklessly: uses physical force, physical restraint, or an implied or express threat of physical force, bodily injury, or physical restraint to cause another person to engage in an act of sexual penetration . . . .

Section 213.2 – Sexual Penetration Against the Will or Without Consent

. . . An actor is guilty of Sexual Penetration Against the Will, a felony of the third degree, if he or she knowingly or recklessly engages in an act of sexual penetration with a person who at the time of such act has expressed by words or conduct his or her refusal to consent to the act of sexual penetration; a verbally expressed refusal establishes such refusal in the absence of subsequent words or actions indicating positive agreement. . . .

An actor is guilty of Sexual Penetration Without Consent, a misdemeanor, if the actor knowingly or recklessly engages in an act of sexual penetration with a person who at the time of such act has not given consent to such act. . . .

Section 213.6 – Criminal Sexual Contact

. . . An actor is guilty of Criminal Sexual Contact Without Consent, a petty misdemeanor, if the actor knowingly or recklessly engages in sexual contact without consent . . . .

Judith Shulevitz, *Regulating Sex*, N.Y. Times (June 27, 2015). [T]hough most people think of "yes means yes" as strictly for college students, it [may] actually [be] poised to become the law of the land. . . . Codes and laws calling for affirmative consent proceed from admirable impulses. . . . [J]ust as you wouldn't take a precious object from someone's home without her permission, you shouldn't have sex with someone if he hasn't explicitly said he wants to. And if one person can think he's hooking up while the other feels she's being raped, it makes sense to have a law that eliminates the possibility of misunderstanding. . . .

Perhaps the most consequential deliberations about affirmative consent are going on right now at the American Law Institute [where] more than 4,000 law professors, judges and lawyers [have] been thinking about how to update the [model] penal code for sexual assault, which was last revised in 1962. When [the discussion draft excerpted above] circulated in the weeks before the institute's annual meeting . . . some highly instructive hell broke loose. In a memo that has now been signed by about 70 institute members and advisers . . . readers have been asked to consider the following scenario: "Person A and Person B are on a date and walking down the street. Person A, feeling romantically and sexually attracted, timidly reaches out to hold B's hand and feels a thrill as their hands touch. Person B does nothing, but six months later files a criminal complaint. Person A is guilty of 'Criminal Sexual Contact' under [the] proposed [revisions]."

Far-fetched? Not as the draft is written. . . . The obvious comeback to this is that no prosecutor would waste her time on such a frivolous case. But that doesn't comfort signatories of the memo, several of whom have pointed out to me that once a law is passed, you can't control how it will be used. For instance, prosecutors often add minor charges to major ones (such as, say, forcible rape) when there isn't enough evidence to convict on the more serious charge. They then put pressure on the accused to plead guilty to the less egregious crime.

. . . It's important to remember that people convicted of sex crimes may not only go to jail, they can wind up on a sex-offender registry, with dire and lasting consequences. Depending on the state, these can include notifying the community when an offender moves into the neighborhood;

restrictions against living within 2,000 feet of a school, park, playground or school bus stop; being required to wear GPS monitoring devices; and even a prohibition against using the Internet for social networking. . . .

Stephen J. Schulhofer, the law professor who co-wrote the [proposed] model penal code [revisions], told me that he and his co-author have already recommended that the law do away with the more onerous restrictions that follow from being registered as a sex offender. . . . [And, he says, the] case for affirmative consent is "compelling" [because] being raped is much worse than having to endure that awkward moment when one stops to confirm that one's partner is happy to continue. Silence or inertia, often interpreted as agreement, may actually reflect confusion, drunkenness or "frozen fright," a documented physiological response in which a person under sexual threat is paralyzed by terror. To critics who object that millions of people are having sex without getting unqualified assent and aren't likely to change their ways, he'd reply that millions of people drive 65 miles per hour despite a 55-mile-per-hour speed limit, but the law still saves lives. As long as "people know what the rules of the road are," he says, "the overwhelming majority will comply with them." He understands that the law will have to bring a light touch to the refashioning of sexual norms, which is why the current draft of the model code suggests classifying penetration without consent as a misdemeanor, a much lesser crime than a felony.

[Still, others disagree.] "It's an unworkable standard," says the Harvard law professor Jeannie C. Suk. "It's only workable if we assume it's not going to be enforced, by and large." But that's worrisome too. Selectively enforced laws have a nasty history of being used to harass people deemed to be undesirable, because of their politics, race or other reasons.

Nonetheless, it's probably just a matter of time before "yes means yes" becomes the law in most states. Ms. Suk told me that she and her colleagues have noticed a generational divide between them and their students. As undergraduates, they're learning affirmative consent in their mandatory sexual-respect training sessions, and they come to "believe that this really is the best way to define consent, as positive agreement," she says. When they graduate and enter the legal profession, they'll probably reshape the law to reflect that belief.

Debate over the ALI's proposed revisions continued for a number of years. In April of 2022, the Institute advanced its final proposed draft, which appears poised to be adopted. The proposal changed in meaningful respects from the initial draft excerpted above. Perhaps most notably, the definition of consent was changed to read as follows:

"Consent" . . . means a person's willingness to engage in a specific act of sexual penetration . . . or sexual contact. Consent may be express or it may be inferred from behavior—both action and inaction—in the context of all the circumstances. . . . Consent may be revoked or withdrawn any time before or during the act of sexual penetration, oral sex, or sexual contact. A clear verbal refusal—such as "No," "Stop," or "Don't"—establishes the lack of consent or the revocation or withdrawal of previous consent. Lack of consent or revocation or withdrawal of consent may be overridden by subsequent consent given prior to the act of sexual penetration . . . or sexual contact.[37]

The definition of sexual contact, which was directly criticized in the hand-holding example quoted in the *New York Times* article above, was amended to read as follows:

"Sexual contact" means any of the following acts, when the actor's purpose is the sexual arousal, sexual gratification, sexual humiliation, or sexual degradation of any person: (i) touching the clothed or unclothed genitalia, anus, groin, breast, buttocks, or inner thigh of any person with any body part or object; or (ii) touching any body part of any person with the clothed or unclothed genitalia, anus, groin, breast, buttocks, or inner thigh of any person; or (iii) touching any clothed or unclothed body part of any person with the ejaculate of any person.[38]

With these changes, the proposed provisions treat "Sexual Assault in the Absence of Consent" as a felony with the *actus reus* element satisfied "when the actor engages with another person in, or causes another person to engage in, submit to, or perform, an act of sexual penetration . . . and the other person does not consent to that act." The offense is punishable by up to three years, or by up to five years if "the other person has, by words or actions, expressly communicated unwillingness to submit to or perform the act, or the act is so sudden or unexpected that the other person has no adequate opportunity to express unwillingness before the act occurs." The proposed provisions continue to define as a petty misdemeanor—punishable by up to six-months incarceration—a crime now called "Offensive Sexual Contact," the *actus reus* of which is satisfied when a person "engages in an act of sexual contact with another person or causes another person to submit to or perform an act of sexual contact; and the other person did not consent to that act."[39]

4. Current State of the Law. It is too soon to tell whether or how the proposed ALI revisions might impact sexual assault law across U.S. jurisdictions. It is possible, however, to glean a snapshot of the current state of the law with respect to affirmative consent as of the revision project's near conclusion. In a detailed survey conducted in 2016, the reporters of the ALI project identified twenty-one states that "punish penetration in the absence of consent" as a felony or a misdemeanor "and require either affirmative consent or circumstances akin to contextual consent," by which the reporters mean something like the ALI's own final proposal (quoted above) that consent "be inferred from behavior—both action and inaction—in the context of all the circumstances." The remaining states either do not primarily define sexual assault in terms of consent or do not define consent.

As to the approaches taken across the twenty-one states that treat non-consent as the essential element, the reporters offer the following overview:

> Many media accounts identify "affirmative consent" with a requirement of express verbal permission or even (perhaps sarcastically) with an electronic "consent app" or written contract; such accounts often go on to suggest that advocates of affirmative consent support that standard as a legal requirement. No American jurisdiction adopts such a standard for criminal law purposes; applying this definition, the count of affirmative-consent jurisdictions is zero.
>
> The Reporters identified in American law three roughly grouped formulations of a consent requirement—language emphasizing "affirmative permission," "positive cooperation" and the like; language describing "express or implied acquiescence"; and language defining consent as a matter of conduct that communicates willingness or assent as judged under the totality of the circumstances. The first surely counts as a conception of "affirmative" consent, and the second arguably does as well; the third[, which mirrors the ALI's own proposed "context of all circumstances" approach,] does not. . . .

The reporters go on to write that, of these twenty-one states, thirteen adopt one of the first two formulations described above and thus "go even further than the [ALI's proposed] contextual consent standard . . . by imposing punishment in the absence of a more explicit form of agreement or permission."[40]

2. Preconditions to Consent

The preceding section examined debates, in jurisdictions that define sexual assault as sex without consent, about where legal lines defining consent should be drawn. But the law has also long identified scenarios in which lawful consent is simply not possible—either because of characteristics of the participants in the encounter or because of surrounding coercive forces or power dynamics. Put another way, the law has always identified circumstances in which even an explicitly stated "yes" or a conceded desire for intercourse from all parties does *not* translate to a lawfully consensual sexual act.

But here again, the precise circumstances in which such sex ought to be deemed sexual assault are contested, and can produce different rules across jurisdictions. The notes that follow examine these issues across a range of scenarios. We begin with cases in which expressions or manifestations of consent are obtained through deception and cases in which a person's capacity to consent may be impaired due to alcohol or drugs. We then consider certain categorical rules prohibiting sex based on the age, disability, or status of the actors, before concluding with an examination of the relationship between consent and power differentials more broadly.

NOTES AND QUESTIONS

1. Deception. When should the law criminalize sexual conduct where one party consents after having been lied to by the other? As a general matter, most jurisdictions distinguish between what the law sometimes calls "fraud in the factum," which refers to deceptions about the nature of the physical action at issue, and "fraud in the inducement," which refers to the use of deception to get another person to consent to a sexual act. The prevailing state of the law is that the former deception can give rise to criminal liability for sexual assault, but the latter cannot.[41]

Under this approach, a gynecologist who inserts his fingers or his penis into a woman while falsely telling her he is inserting a medical instrument is guilty of sexual assault. *See, e.g.,* People v. Ogunmola, 238 Cal. Rptr. 300 (Cal. Ct. App. 1987). But the same doctor—or even a man only pretending to be a doctor—would not be guilty if he had sex with a woman after procuring consent by telling her, again falsely, that she "contracted a dangerous, highly infectious and perhaps fatal disease" and that the only remedy would be to have sex with him after he "had been injected with a serum which would cure [her]." Boro v. Superior Court, 210 Cal. Rptr. 122, 123 (Cal. Ct. App. 1985).[42]

Applying the same line of reasoning, some courts have held that it is not sexual assault to trick someone into having sex by pretending to be someone else. In *People v. Hough*, 607 N.Y.S.2d 884 (N.Y. Crim. Ct. 1994), for example, the court granted a motion to dismiss a sexual assault charge where the defendant had sex with his twin brother's girlfriend after tricking her into believing he was his twin. Some states, the court noted, have statutes that vitiate consent "where [a] defendant achieved the sexual intercourse by impersonating the woman's *husband.*" *Id.* at 886 (emphasis added). But this rule, the court held, generally does not extend to cases where a man "procures . . . consent by impersonating the female's boyfriend," a scenario governed instead by the default rule that fraud in the inducement does not undermine consent. *Id.* at 885.

These cases and others like them draw considerable criticism. "The real-life victims of rape-by-deception," Professor Patricia Falk writes, "experience multiple physical, psychological, and emotional harms." Consider one notorious case from 2014 in which, as Professor Roseanna Sommers reports, a woman was

in a relationship with a man who had lied to her about nearly everything: his name, his profession, his backstory, and his reasons for needing to borrow money. It was not until the pair was engaged and [the woman] was pregnant that she happened upon her fiancé's wallet and discovered his true identity. A quick web search revealed that he was a scam artist who had fathered thirteen children by six women, and that one of his former fiancées had written a book about his exploits . . . .

As Sommers goes on to write, the stunned woman ultimately "had an abortion and called the police," hoping "her ex-fiancé would be prosecuted for a sex crime." But in New Jersey, where these incidents occurred, "as in the vast majority of states, it is not sexual assault to con someone into having sex."[43]

Given the harm caused in scenarios like these, some scholars have called for legal reform. As Professor Sommers observes, the "canonical view" in *other* areas of law is that "material deception vitiates consent." Someone who gains consent to enter a house by pretending to be a utility worker, for example, has committed a trespass; so too, lying to obtain someone else's money is considered "theft by deception." Professor Susan Estrich argues that sex should be treated the same way, with consent deemed nonexistent whenever obtained by a "misrepresentation of material fact," where the truth would have caused the other person not to consent to having sex. A number of scholars agree, arguing that the law's differential treatment of sex is emblematic of misogynist rape exceptionalism, whereby, as Sommers summarizes it, a man's "right to seduce" through deceit is treated "as part of ordinary male sexual aggression," while women's interests are trivialized and demeaned—with some judges seemingly considering such women "so gullible, so naïve, and so stupid" as to "get what they deserve."[44]

And yet, many scholars—including a number of feminist rape-law reformers—are unwilling to expand liability on this issue along the lines Estrich and others advocate. Professor Deborah Tuerkheimer, for example, argues that there "are plenty of names for people who" trick others into having sex, but " 'rapist' is not among them." Rather, she says, consent in such circumstances "was obtained; it cannot be discounted solely by virtue of its imperfection." Notably, as Professor Sommers' research shows, Professor Tuerkheimer's view tracks broadly and deeply held public understandings of consent. Based on original surveys of scores of people presented with dozens of consent-by-deception scenarios—including multiple scenarios involving sex obtained by clearly material deceptions—Sommers finds that "laypeople largely agree that coercion and incapacitation invalidate consent, [but] believe that deception does not."[45]

One upshot of these findings, Sommers concludes, is that policymakers' resistance to expanding criminal liability in sex-by-deception cases "may be influenced not (just) by patriarchal sexual moralism or sexist attitudes toward women but also by the commonsense understanding of consent," which bears "a remarkable parallel" to the extant "legal distinction between 'fraud in the factum' . . . and 'fraud in the inducement.' " Of course, as

Sommers observes, "surveying the public tells us what people think; it does not necessarily tell us what is morally right or what the law should be." But to date, at least, the criminal law has generally tracked the historical dividing line, while occasionally broadening liability to address certain egregious frauds in the inducement—including cases of impersonation or false medical diagnoses or treatments. The ALI's proposed revisions to the Model Penal Code track this basic approach. Explaining that decision, the ALI reporters emphasize "society's willingness to tolerate artifice and deception as methods of sexual seduction."

> Individuals commonly lie about their age, occupation, job prospects, marital status, involvement with others, parenthood status, and whether they are interested in a serious relationship. And people pervasively lie about the state of their affection for the other party. Empirical research has not yet established how frequently the phrase "I love you" is uttered untruthfully in an effort to gain sexual favor, but the number is undoubtedly high enough to make criminal punishment of that behavior an unnerving prospect.[46]

2. Impaired Consent. The drafters of the 1962 Model Penal Code describe alcohol and drugs as "common ingredients of the ritual of courtship." Model Penal Code and Commentaries §213.1 cmt. 5 at 315. "The traditional routine of soft music and wine" as well as "the modern variant of loud music and marijuana," they write, imply "some relaxation of inhibition." *Id.* But, they go on to caution, "[w]ith continued consumption, relaxation blurs into intoxication and insensibility," raising a critical question for sexual assault law: when should intoxication be deemed to vitiate an individual's consent to sexual acts? *Id.*[47]

Jurisdictions divide on this question in meaningful ways and along multiple axes. All hold that a person who has sex with an *unconscious* victim is guilty of sexual assault. As the original MPC drafters observe, "the degree of required incapacitation" necessary to constitute unconsciousness "is extreme." *Id.* at 319. But so long as that standard is met, the MPC drafters continue, "[i]ntercourse with an unconscious [person] was an established specie of rape" both "at common law" and "in every jurisdiction" they had surveyed at the time. *Id.* Indeed, sex with an unconscious person constitutes sexual assault even in jurisdictions that adhere to the force requirement, with courts holding (some might say straining to hold) that when a victim is unconscious the force intrinsic in penetration is sufficient to meet the force requirement, even though it would not otherwise be so.[48]

A more complicated question arises when the degree of intoxication is less extreme, impairing a person's capacities without rising to the level of unconsciousness or complete incapacitation. In some states, a person who has sex with someone in such a condition is culpable only if he administered the intoxicating substance to the victim without the victim's knowledge and thereby "impaired the victim's power to appraise or control" her actions or her response to the defendant's advances—conduct sometimes referred to as "spiking" or "roofieing." Colo. Rev. Stat. Ann. §18-3-402(4)(d). Absent such conduct, sex with a conscious but intoxicated person is not a crime in these states.[49]

Other states' rape laws reach further, covering cases in which the defendant takes advantage of the victim's intoxication even though he did not bring it about. In these jurisdictions, the primary legal question turns on the degree of intoxication the law will treat as vitiating consent. *People v. Smith*, 120 Cal. Rptr. 3d 52 (Cal. Ct. App. 2010), provides an illustrative example of one state's approach. There, a woman became voluntarily intoxicated after taking medication and consuming several drinks at a bar. The defendant brought her to a hotel across the street, where the clerk judged her to be "very, very out of it, very very intoxicated." *Id.* at 53. The defendant returned to the hotel later that night and had sex with the victim. Upholding his rape conviction, the California Court of Appeal explained that rape occurs under California law when the victim is "so intoxicated that she cannot . . . exercise reasonable judgment" in deciding whether to consent. *Id.* at 55. In such circumstances, the court held, "the issue is not whether the victim actually [*i.e.,* verbally or outwardly] consented to sexual intercourse, but whether he or she was capable of exercising the degree of judgment a person must have in order to give legally cognizable consent." People v. Giardino, 98 Cal. Rptr. 2d 315, 321 (Cal. Ct. App. 2000). But as one leading treatise reports, other states use different formulations, with some focusing not on the intoxicated person's ability to form consent but rather on her ability to apprise the nature of her conduct, to communicate her lack of consent, or to resist.[50]

A final question concerns the scenario in which both people in a sexual encounter are voluntarily intoxicated. In particular, does a criminal defendant's own intoxication mitigate his liability? In general, the answer is no. As we learned in Chapter Three (p. 148), some states reject the defense of voluntary intoxication for all forms of criminal liability, on the theory that "one who has voluntarily impaired his own faculties should be responsible for the consequences." Montana v. Egelhoff, 518 U.S. 37, 50 (1996). But even those states that recognize voluntary intoxication as a defense to some crimes generally reject its application to the crime of rape.[51]

Note, however, a challenge that arises when both actors are impaired. As the reporters of the proposed MPC revisions observe, some commentators argue that "when both the accused and the complainant are intoxicated," liability should be mitigated or removed because "to hold otherwise would be to find that although two people, both heavily intoxicated, engaged in sexual activity, only one person is held responsible for those choices." In fact, the reporters go on to note, "[e]mpirical evidence suggests that . . . when both parties were intoxicated at the time of the sexual act, lay persons and jurors tend to discount the culpability of the actor and impute culpability to the complainant." Ultimately, the reporters propose exempting sexual assault from the otherwise applicable MPC rule that intoxication defenses are available for knowing or purposeful mental states, leaving it instead to each state to decide this question for itself.[52]

3. Age. Every jurisdiction deems minors below a certain age categorically incapable of giving valid consent, and criminalizes sexual acts with such children. This offense is commonly known as *statutory rape*. In most states, the age cutoff falls between 16 and 18 years old. Most states also include a close-in-age exception, defining, as a leading treatise puts it, "a range of age differences between the . . . participants inside of which sexual intercourse is lawful" notwithstanding their youth. Vermont, for example, deems it a crime to engage in a sexual act with a child under the age of 16 *unless* the child is at least 15 years old and the defendant is less than 19 years old. Vt. Stat. Ann. tit. 13, §3252(c).[53]

Traditionally, statutory rape laws imposed strict liability with respect to the defendant's awareness of the minor's age. It was no defense, in other words, if the defendant mistakenly believed the minor was above the age cutoff set by law. Beginning in the 1960s, however, some states began to adopt a defense of reasonable mistake as to age, and over a third of states embrace such a defense today. *See, e.g.*, Me. Stat. tit. 17-A, §254(2) ("It is a defense . . . that the actor reasonably believed the other person is at least 16 years of age."). We will return to this question of strict liability in the next part of this chapter, when discussing the *mens rea* for sexual offenses.[54]

4. Disability. Sex with a mentally disabled individual can also constitute rape, regardless of actions such a person may take that could appear to indicate consent. The reasoning for this categorical rule parallels the reasoning with respect to statutory rape. As the commentary to the original MPC says, a person can be "incapable of meaningful consent for reasons other than immaturity," including where they are "mentally incompetent to understand the significance of the sexual act." Model Penal Code and Commentaries §213.1 cmt. 1 at 276. As with intoxication, however, there is little consensus as to what sort of incapacity the state must prove. Some states describe a victim who is incapable of appraising the nature of the sexual acts. *See, e.g.*, Colo. Rev. Stat. Ann. §18-3-402(1)(b). Others refer to someone incapable of giving consent. *See, e.g.*, Ala. Code §13A-6-61(a)(2).

Note that part of the challenge in drawing this line stems from what the ALI, in its revision project, calls an "underlying tension" between two competing goals:

> concern for protecting persons with a mental impairment from exploitation and abuse, which points toward setting the baseline for capacity to

consent at a relatively high level of mental and social functioning, versus setting such a high standard that many such persons will be precluded from experiencing sexual intimacy and sexually fulfilling relationships, even with peers who pose no danger to them.

The proposed ALI revisions navigate this tension by creating a safe harbor similar to the "close in age" exception in some statutory rape laws. Under the proposed revisions, liability attaches when a person has sex with someone whose "intellectual, developmental, or mental" disability or illness renders them "substantially incapable" of understanding the sexual activity involved or their right to withhold consent, unless the accused defendant has a "similarly serious disability." This exception, according to the drafters, "safeguards the right of disabled and mentally ill persons to engage sexually with peers in situations less fraught with the risk of exploitation" while also avoiding the complication that could arise (as in the case of two intoxicated people) where the law would say that "both parties are 'victims' and 'actors.' "[55]

5. Status. Extending the logic and concern over exploitation seen in the preceding notes, criminal statutes consistently regard certain groups of people in society as categorically disempowered, such that it is per se sexual assault when sex occurs between them and those who hold power over them. As of a 2011 survey, forty-two states had enacted such statutes. Connecticut law, for example, punishes prison guards who have sex with people "in custody" under their "supervisory or disciplinary authority." Conn. Gen. Stat. Ann. §53a-71(a)(5). This prohibition applies even if the incarcerated person expressly consents to having sex with a guard. Similar statutes prohibit doctors or therapists from sleeping with their patients and high school teachers from sleeping with their students, even if the student is of legal age. *See, e.g., id.* §§53a-71(a)(6)-(8); N.J. Stat. Ann. §2C:14-2(c)(5). "The legislative purpose of these rules," according to a leading treatise, "is to extend the same protection afforded minors to certain other individuals whose relationship is such that meaningful consent is not possible."[56]

6. Power. How far should the law go in prohibiting sex between people whose different social positions might entail power imbalances or hierarchies? As Professor Stephen Schulhofer writes, "A prison guard's power clearly prevents an inmate from choosing freely whether to accept or refuse a sexual proposal, but do we say the same about a college professor and a nineteen-year-old student in his course? If so, do we also say the same about a corporate-vice president and a junior executive working in another division?" The following excerpts explore these questions.[57]

Stephen J. Schulhofer, *Unwanted Sex* 14, 168-171, 184 (1998). Suppose that Sally and her boss, Bill, are working late together on a project for an important client. When they are ready to leave the office, Bill asks Sally to drive home with him and come up to his apartment for a drink. . . . His eyes and his smile make clear, in a respectful way, that he finds Sally intelligent and attractive and that he wants a chance to know her personally. Sally may be just as strongly attracted to Bill as he is to her. She may be delighted by the prospect of having a sexual relationship with him. Still, Bill's [invitation] can pose serious problems. He has enormous power to affect her career, whether he mentions it or not. And Sally would know that a decision to turn him down cannot help but color his feelings about her. So Sally might feel under pressure to accept, whether she really wants to or not. [What's more, Bill's invitation may signal that he sees Sally] not only in her professional role but potentially in a sexual one. Not everyone would find that message upsetting. . . . But for many women, too long accustomed to being treated as sex objects and little else, it can be especially important to know that at work they are seen exclusively as competent professionals. . . . [Finally, it is important to recognize] that because of women's physical and economic vulnerability, a sexual advance in an unexpected context can arouse anxiety [and] even fear that the proposition is a prelude to the use of force.

[E]xisting laws do not bar bosses . . . from making sexual demands on their subordinates. So far as current law is concerned, there is still "no harm in asking," even when the asking is done by a supervisor who completely controls a woman's professional future. . . . Standards are urgently needed to identify the kinds of sexual liaisons that should be entirely off limits. But it is equally important to avoid overkill. We should not subject freely chosen relationships to an extensive regime of legal regulation . . . . It remains essential to respect the freedom of every competent adult to seek intimacy with a genuinely willing partner. . . . [I]f sexual interaction is ruled legally out of bounds every time one of the parties has any possible source of power over the other, our opportunities to find companionship and sexual intimacy will shrink dramatically. To create a legal barrier to every relationship not formed on the purely neutral ground of the singles bar or the church social would be pathetic and absurd. . . . In practice, a ban on supervisor-subordinate sex could rule out, at many firms, a large portion of the potential relationships [and require] employees to date people outside the firm . . . . But the job site is often one of the most sensible places to seek a potential partner.[58]

Amia Srinivasan, *The Right to Sex* 126-131 (2021). In 2010, Yale became the first U.S. university to impose a blanket prohibition on relationships between faculty and undergraduate students. . . . [M]any other U.S. universities quickly followed . . . invariably justify[ing] these prohibitions by citing the difference in power between teacher and student—a difference, they say, that casts doubt on the meaningfulness of the student's consent.

The expansion of campus sexual harassment policies to cover consensual faculty-student relationships is part of the legacy of the women's liberation movement[, which successfully pushed courts to recognize sexual harassment in employment and educational settings as a cognizable cause of action under federal civil rights laws]. Yet as soon as this expansion began, some feminists denounced it as a profound betrayal of their principles. To deny that women students could consent to sex with their professors, they argued, inverted the rapist's logic of "no means yes" into the moralizing logic "yes means no." Were women university students not adults? Were they not entitled to have sex with whom they pleased? Did such policies not play into the hands of the resurgent religious right, which was all too keen to control women's sex lives? . . . It is, no doubt, sometimes the case that women students consent to sex they don't really want because they are afraid of what will happen if they don't — a bad grade, a lackluster recommendation, being ignored by their supervisor. But there are also many women students who consent to sex with their professors out of genuine desire. . . . To insist that the power differential between professor and student precludes consent is either to see women students, like children, as intrinsically incapable of consent to sex — or to see them as somehow incapacitated by the dazzling force of the professor. And which professor is really *that* good?

But this is not to say that genuinely wanted teacher-student sex is unproblematic. Imagine a professor who happily accepts the infatuated attentions of his student, takes her out on dates, has sex with her, makes her his girlfriend, perhaps as he has done with many students before. The student has consented, not out of fear. Are we really prepared to say that there is nothing troubling here? . . . Is it too sterile, too boring to suggest that instead of sleeping with his student, this professor should have been — *teaching* her?

7. Sexism. Professor Amia Srinivasan situates her analysis of sex between university students and professors against the backdrop of a broader and longstanding debate within feminism between two competing ideas. On the one hand, there are voices (like those Srinivasan highlights) who resist a "virtuous and moral sexuality" that treats women "like children" and insists that even their express, perhaps enthusiastic yeses mean no. As Srinivasan explains, an important theme in feminism is the notion that we should "take women at their word." Indeed, some would argue that if a "woman says she enjoys" certain types of sex, "we are required . . . to trust her," for "a feminism that trades too freely in notions of self-deception is a feminism that risks dominating the subjects it presumes to liberate."[59]

And yet, feminism from its inception has been thoroughly attentive to and arrayed against structural power imbalances in society, including most obviously patriarchy and sexism. That focus, Srinivasan observes, forces an interrogation of "the ethics of sexual relationships inflected by large differentials of power," all of which leads many feminists — building in large part on the groundbreaking work of Professor Catharine MacKinnon—to ask two provocative questions: When a person has sex with someone who is relatively and meaningfully more powerful, is true consent really possible? And, in a patriarchal society, are all women relatively powerless compared to men, such that consent itself is always an illusion? The following excerpts further consider these ideas.[60]

Robin West, *Sex, Law, and Consent,* in *The Ethics of Consent: Theory and Practice* 236 (Franklin G. Miller & Alan Wertheimer eds., 2010).   Heterosexual women and girls, married or not, consent to a good bit of unwanted sex with men that they patently don't desire [for any number of reasons:] to avoid a hassle or a bad mood the endurance of which wouldn't be worth the effort, to ensure their own or their children's financial security, to lessen the risk of future physical attacks, to garner their peers' approval, to win the approval of a high-status man or boy, to earn a paycheck or a promotion or an undeserved A on a college paper, to feed a drug habit, to survive, or to smooth troubled domestic waters. Women and girls do so from motives of self-aggrandizement, from an instinct for survival, out of concern for their children, from simple altruism, from friendship or love, or because they have been taught to do so. But whatever the reason, some women and girls have a good bit of sex a good bit of the time that they patently do not desire.

Catharine A. MacKinnon, *Toward a Feminist Theory of the State* 174-178 (1989).   Consent is supposed to be women's form of control over intercourse. . . . The law of rape presents consent as free exercise of sexual choice under conditions of equality of power without exposing the underlying structure of constraint and disparity. . . . The age line under which girls are presumed disabled from consenting to sex, whatever they say, rationalizes a condition of sexual coercion which women never outgrow. . . . [It] defines those above the age line as powerful, whether they actually have power to consent or not. The vulnerability girls share with boys—age—dissipates with time. The vulnerability girls share with women—gender—does not. . . . When sex is violent, women may have lost control over what is done to them, but absence of force does not ensure the presence of that control. . . . If sex is normally something men do to women, the issue is less whether there was force than whether consent is a meaningful concept.

Catharine A. MacKinnon, *Feminism, Marxism, Method, and the State: Toward Feminist Jurisprudence,* 8 Signs 635, 646-647 (1983).   The point of defining rape as "violence not sex" or "violence against women" has been to separate sexuality from gender in order to affirm sex (heterosexuality) while rejecting violence (rape). The problem remains what it has always been: telling the difference. The convergence of sexuality with violence . . . is recognized by rape survivors [who] see the rape in intercourse. The uncoerced context for sexual expression becomes as elusive as the physical acts come to feel indistinguishable. Instead of asking, what is the violation of rape, what if we ask, what is the nonviolation of intercourse? . . . Perhaps the wrong of rape has proven so difficult to articulate because the unquestionable starting point has been that rape is definable as distinct from intercourse, when for women it is difficult to distinguish under conditions of male dominance.

Andrea Dworkin, *Intercourse* 59, 79-83, 158-159 (1997). There is the nearly universal conviction — or so it appears — that sex (fucking) is good and that liking it is right: morally right; a sign of human health; nearly a standard for citizenship. . . . The current argument between the Right and the Left is not about the nature of fucking as such. It is strictly about whether or not this good thing is good outside marriage or between persons of the same gender . . . . [But intercourse is also] commonly written about and comprehended as a form of possession or an act of possession, during which, because of which, a man inhabits a woman, physically covering her and overwhelming her . . . . He has her, or, when he is done, he has had her. . . . The act itself, without more, is the possession. There need not be a social relationship in which the woman is subordinate to the man, a chattel in spirit or deed . . . . There need not be an ongoing sexual relationship in which she is chronically, demonstrably, submissive or masochistic. The normal fuck by a normal man is taken to be an act of invitation and ownership undertaken in the mode of predation: colonializing, forceful (manly) or nearly violent . . . .

Intimate, raw, total, the experience of sexual possession for women is real and literal, without any magical or mystical dimension to it: getting fucked and being owned are inseparably the same; together, being one and the same, they are sex for women under male dominance as a social system. . . . Intercourse occurs in a context of a power relation that is pervasive and incontrovertible. The context in which the act takes place, whatever the meaning of the act itself, is one in which men have social, economic, political, and physical power over women. Some men do not have all those kinds of power over all women; but all men have some kinds of power over all women; and most men have controlling power over what they call *their* women — the women they fuck. The power is determined by gender, by being male. Intercourse as an act often expresses the power men have over women. Without being what society recognizes as rape, it is what society — when pushed to admit it — recognizes as dominance.

Stephen J. Schulhofer, *Unwanted Sex* 53, 86 (1998). The argument that inequality of any sort involves coercion leads in short order to the conclusion that virtually all heterosexual sex is coercive. . . . Perspectives like these still ring true for many women today, as the wide impact of MacKinnon's work attests. And even those who consider her claims of present-day coercion exaggerated must acknowledge her basic point: culture, education, and social pressures unquestionably influence our values, our priorities, and the kinds of things we want. And external forces can make us reluctantly forgo what we want; in this respect economic, social, and psychological power bears important similarities to physical duress.

The large problem in the work of MacKinnon [and] Dworkin . . . is not that their views about the importance of social power are false. Rather, the problem is that these views draw no distinctions, accept no boundaries, and thus seem not to acknowledge the possibility of acceptable forms of sexual intimacy between men and women. . . . [B]y collapsing the distinctions *between* kinds of social pressure, feminism of this sort doesn't advance the effort to draw workable legal lines. Sometimes this strand of feminism even seems to impede the legal reform effort, because it tends to obliterate differences between the kinds of pressure that society will inevitably tolerate and the kinds that it might plausibly forbid.

Amia Srinivasan, *The Right to Sex* 82-83 (2021). Since the 1980s, the wind has been behind a feminism which does not moralize about women's sexual desires, and which insists that acting on those desires is morally constrained only by the boundaries of consent. . . . In this sense, the norms of sex are like the norms of capitalist free exchange. What matters is not what conditions give rise to the dynamics of supply and demand—why some people need to sell their labor while others buy it—but only that both buyer and seller have agreed to the transfer. It would be too easy, though, to say that sex positivity represents the co-option of feminism by liberalism. Generations of feminists and gay and lesbian activists have fought hard to free sex from shame, stigma, coercion, abuse, and unwanted pain. . . .

[Feminist author Ellen Willis writes that] it is "axiomatic that consenting partners have a right to their sexual proclivities, and that authoritarian moralism has no place" in feminism. And yet, she goes on, "a truly radical movement . . . must look beyond the right to choose, and keep focusing on the fundamental questions. Why do we choose what we choose? What would we choose if we had a real choice?" . . . One might feel that Willis has given with one hand and taken away with the other. But perhaps she has given with both. Here, she tells us, is a task for feminism: to treat as axiomatic our free sexual choices, while also seeing why, as "anti-sex" and lesbian feminists have always said, such choices, under patriarchy, are rarely free. What I am suggesting is that, in our rush to do the former, feminists risk forgetting the latter.

8. Prostitution. The competing ideas in the preceding note confront each other acutely and concretely with respect to one issue thoroughly governed by the criminal law: prostitution. As Professors Jody Miller and Martin Schwartz write, women who engage in prostitution are among the most vulnerable to assault and yet are also among the most invisible when it comes to studying or prosecuting sexual violence. "Their unique position as women who openly sell sex to men makes prostitutes face a conglomeration of rape myths even stronger than those faced by other women," they write. As a result, many who study prostitution conclude that "prostitutes can be raped with impunity" because police officers and prosecutors are unlikely to pursue criminal charges—even though research in the United States and across the globe "consistently documents the high level of violence against prostituted women, including physical and sexual assaults by both pimps (persons, generally men, who benefit from the earnings of prostitutes) and customers." Some studies find that 70 percent or more of women engaged in prostitution have been raped by customers. And as compared to cisgender women, studies show that trans women who are sex workers face an even higher risk of violence.[61]

At the same time, prostitution itself is almost universally criminalized in the United States, meaning that people who sell sex to others can be prosecuted for that offense. According to one study, in 2011 over 44,000 people nationwide were prosecuted for prostitution, nearly 70 percent of whom were women. Whether or not such conduct should be a crime, however, sparks serious debate. Some argue that prostitution is a form of oppression and violence, such that prosecuting people who engage in it is akin to prosecuting victims—an argument most forcefully advanced when minors engaging in prostitution are prosecuted, as occurred 760 times in 2011. Others argue that prostitution is a social vice that is inherently immoral and corrosive of social norms. *See, e.g.,* United States v. Bitty, 208 U.S. 393, 401 (1908) (describing "women who, for hire or without hire, offer their bodies to indiscriminate intercourse with men" as exhibiting "hostility to the idea of the family" and to "that reverent morality which is the source of all beneficent progress in social and political improvement"). Still others, echoing the sexual autonomy arguments of the preceding note, argue that prostitution can be and often is a form of consensual sexual activity between two adults—and that, as a familiar slogan goes, "sex work is work" that ought not be denigrated, let alone criminalized. As Professor Amia Srinivasan puts the point, "If a woman says she enjoys . . . being paid to have sex with men, or engaging in rape fantasies, or wearing stilettos—and even that she doesn't just enjoy these things but finds them emancipatory, part of her feminist praxis—then we are required, many feminists think, to trust her." Consider the following excerpts, which further explore these arguments.[62]

Catharine A. MacKinnon, *Prostitution and Civil Rights,* 1 Mich. J. Gender & L. 13, 13-14 (1993). Women in prostitution are denied every imaginable civil right in every imaginable and unimaginable way, such that it makes sense to understand prostitution as consisting in the denial of women's humanity, no matter how humanity is defined. . . . In prostitution, women are tortured through repeated rape and in all the more conventionally recognized ways. Women are prostituted precisely in order to be degraded and subjected to cruel and brutal treatment without human limits; it is the opportunity to do this that is exchanged when women are bought and sold for sex. . . . The point of prostitution is to transgress women's personal security. Every time the woman walks up to the man's car, every time the man walks into the brothel, the personhood of women—not that secure in a male dominated society to begin with—is made more insecure.

Michelle Madden Dempsey, *Sex Trafficking and Criminalization: In Defense of Feminist Abolitionism*, 158 U. Pa. L. Rev. 1729, 1746, 1748-1750, 1769-1771 (2010). [F]or the sake of argument, [let's] concede that people can genuinely consent to selling sex, that their consent negates any wrongful harm they might experience, [that] in fact some people do consent[, and that prostitution can be genuinely valuable for some people]. Note that these concessions are entirely consistent with the [fact that] many prostituted people do experience substantial harm in prostitution. Indeed, in light of these concessions, we might refine that [point] as follows: many prostituted people experience substantial harm in prostitution, though some do not. The fact that some people do not experience harm does not, of course, diminish the urgency or importance of the fact that many do. . . . On this account, we can understand the . . . claim that "violence is intrinsic to prostitution" to mean that violence occurs within the practice of prostitution (i.e., within the very performance of the commercial sex act). And of course it does. . . .

[F]eminist abolitionism advocates the abolition of sex trafficking and prostitution. These goals, of course, are not unconnected. . . . From a feminist-abolitionist view . . . abolition of prostitution is instrumentally valuable to the abolishment of sex trafficking, and the abolishment of sex trafficking is both intrinsically valuable and instrumentally valuable in creating a post-patriarchal society. . . .

One controversial way in which feminist abolitionists have sought to achieve their goals is through the criminalization of the purchase of sex. At first glance, this approach may seem overly broad: . . . Why not simply focus on the traffickers and leave the buyers alone? . . . Once we abolish sex trafficking, we might very well be left with innocuous or even valuable forms of prostitution—but given the concessions above, that result should not be a matter of regret, right? . . .

Well, no . . . . [T]he market dynamics of purchasing sex render buyers complicit in the harm prostituted people suffer at the hands of traffickers and abusive pimps. . . . [T]he point of criminalizing the purchase of sex . . . is to prevent harm to . . . prostituted people. . . . [T]he buyer is responsible for causing harms to prostituted women not because he [inevitably and in all cases] directly inflicts the harm through his act of prostitute-use, but because his purchase of sex [inevitably] generates demand for the commercial sex market, which thereby encourages the trafficking and abusive pimping that often supplies this market.

Amia Srinivasan, *The Right to Sex* 151-154 (2021). Once we take it as given that under current economic conditions many women will be compelled to sell sex, and that under current ideological conditions many men will buy it, the most important question remaining is: what can we do to strengthen the hand of women in this bargain? Nicole Shulze, a sex worker in Cologne, told the Guardian: "I think every city should have a secure space for sex workers to work, to rest . . . because there's prostitution in every city."

The feminist debate about sex work very often involves a tension . . . . At the level of the symbol, . . . [t]he prostitute is the perfected figure of women's subordinate status, just as the john is the perfected figure of male domination. Their sexual transaction, defined by inequality and often accompanied by violence, stands in for the state of sexual relations between women and men more generally. Seen this way, the prostitute calls out to be saved, the john to be punished . . . for the good of all women. Anti-prostitution feminists propose to answer this call [by] making the buying, and sometimes also the selling, of sex illegal.

But the criminalization of sex work does not, on the whole, help sex workers, much less "save" them. . . . [S]ex workers have long been telling us that legal restrictions on sex work make their lives harder, more dangerous, more violent, and more precarious. When prostitution is criminalized, as in most of the U.S., sex workers are raped by johns, and by the police, with impunity. . . . When buying but not selling is illegal . . . johns demand increased privacy for their transactions with sex workers, forcing women to take greater risks to make the same money. Under none of these criminalizing regimes are sex workers, as a class, better off. . . .

Symbolism, of course, matters: patriarchy establishes itself at the level of words and signs, not just bodies. But the demands of the symbolic can be in tension with those of real women who must pay their bills, feed their children, and sometimes are assaulted by the men to whom they sell sex. For sex workers themselves, the choice between men's punishment and their own survival is all too clear.

Joseph J. Fischel, *Is There a Constitutional Right to Sex Work?*, Boston Rev. (Feb. 1, 2022). [T]he argument for the constitutional protection of sex work is worth expounding, not only in the hopes of appealing to a future judiciary, but also in the service of a more expansive politics of sexual freedom. . . . Several sex workers or sex worker collectives have challenged anti-prostitution laws in lower courts, claiming that if, according to [the U.S. Supreme Court's decision in] Lawrence v. Texas, 539 U.S. 558 (2003) (p. 790), the Constitution protects gay sex from criminalization, then it should protect commercial sex too. No court has yet agreed, but the courts' rejections have been anchored in misunderstandings of sex work and mischaracterizations of sex workers — in a word, whorephobia. [By] whorephobia [I mean the] observation that our default, stubborn cultural presumption — a presumption baked into law — is that sex workers are morally unworthy, or, worse, morally toxic. . . . Crudely, [it is a view that] commercial sex is quick and dirty and hookers are interchangeable. [But as multiple ethnographies of sex work attest,] [c]ommercial sex is not necessarily any longer or any shorter than noncommercial sex[;] the relationship between a client and sex worker may go on for days, months, or years, just like noncommercial relationships. . . . [A]s a function of several broad political, economic, and cultural transformations, "the defining features of modern street prostitution (the prostitute as public, and therefore disreputable woman; the exchange of cash for expedient sexual release as ideological antithesis to private-sphere sex and love) have become increasingly muted. In their place has emerged a brave new world of commercially available intimate encounters that are subjectively normalized for sex workers and clients alike."

. . . So what then are the right, good, and constitutional parameters of our sexual liberty? What decisions about sex — our sexual practices, sexual partners, and the conditions of our sexual exchange — ought to be protected from state and police interference? State courts have held that *Lawrence*'s liberty extends to a right to fornicate (to have nonmarital sex). What makes sex for money so patently different? Why does the presence of money mean the absence of rights? . . . So often we are told that prostitutes are symbols and victims of patriarchy. But what is more patriarchal: a woman selling sex, or public authorities disallowing her to do so?[63]

C. Law and Social Change

Throughout this chapter, we have seen reformers and activists turn to the criminal law as a tool they hope will foster broad social change. Note here a difference between this account of criminal law and others encountered thus far. Rather than use the law to punish and deter *rare* conduct broadly recognized as harmful (as in, for example, the case of criminal homicides), here advocates of expanded criminal liability hope to curtail *widespread* behavior precisely because large segments of society do *not* recognize it as being as harmful or as wrongful as the advocates contend it truly is. Recall here Professor Kahan's study, excerpted earlier in this chapter (p. 366), which showcased deep cultural divisions about sexual consent and which found that for large segments of contemporary society, "no . . . does not invariably mean 'no' but rather sometimes means 'yes' or at least 'maybe.'" Against this cultural backdrop, the goal of rape-law reform, often on reformers' own account, is to use criminal law to uproot entrenched patriarchal norms and practices in an effort to speed along far-reaching and fundamental societal shifts.

Framed as such, the rape-law reform movement raises a number of challenging questions. First there is a question of efficacy. Are these legal reforms *successful* at changing social norms and practices? Here, many scholarly accounts are pessimistic. "When people so often disagree about what 'consent' or 'force'" means, Professor Stephen Schulhofer writes, "the rape law of statutes and court decisions often appears irrelevant or meaningless. Social attitudes are tenacious, and they can easily nullify the theories and doctrines found in the law books." Empirical studies seem to confirm this assessment. Writing in 2008 and surveying multiple studies spanning decades, Professor Richard Klein concludes that "analysis of the impact of [myriad rape law] reforms has shown that the expected gains have not been achieved" with respect to "either the reporting rates of victims or the responses to the reports by the criminal justice system. The one positive finding," Klein says, is that people "ultimately convicted of rape were somewhat more likely to receive prison sentences than had previously been the case," though even this, he notes, "may just be reflective of the overall toughening of our sentencing laws."[64]

If rape-law reform has been at best only partially successful in achieving its aims, two further questions come to the fore. In terms of diagnosis, why have reforms fallen short? And in terms of assessment, what *ought* the role of criminal law be in this context? The notes that follow explore these issues further. They begin with a historical account of the rape-law reform movement and offer different scholarly assessments of the reasons for its shortfalls. They then present contrasting views on the use of legal sanctions to advance social change — a debate over what is sometimes called *carceral feminism*. And they situate that debate within a concrete discussion of sentencing and punishment severity, with a focus on the prosecution of Stanford student Brock Turner and the subsequent recall of the judge who sentenced him.

NOTES AND QUESTIONS

1. The Rape-Reform Movement. Rape-law reform did not occur in a vacuum. Take the pathbreaking case of *M.T.S.*, which in 1992 eliminated the force requirement in New Jersey and replaced it with a non-consent regime. The court's analysis was heavily influenced by the fact that the state legislature had substantially revised New Jersey's rape statute in the late 1970s in response to organizing and lobbying efforts from local and national feminist organizations. In fact, the opinion recounts, the revised statute's "provisions . . . were formulated by a coalition of feminist groups assisted by the National Organization of Women (NOW) National Task Force on Rape."

That task force was an outgrowth of two intertwined movements: the feminist movement and the anti-rape movement. As Professor Vicki Rose wrote in 1977, the "first stirrings of the anti-rape movement were apparent during the late 1960s" as "women began to meet in consciousness-raising groups and organize to act on other issues." Through this network, Professor Rose Corrigan writes, activists came to see rape and the fear of rape "as a key element of women's subjugation," which in turn made sexual violence "a focal point of women's thinking about issues of power, sexuality, and gender inequality." Ultimately, this organizing spurred the formation of multiple advocacy groups dedicated to ending sexual violence—the pillars of the anti-rape movement.[65]

The history of that movement fills volumes, charting not only its rise and successes but also its ebbs and setbacks. The following two excerpts offer a partial overview.

Janet C. Gornick & David S. Meyer, *Changing Political Opportunity: The Anti-Rape Movement and Public Policy*, 10 J. Pol'y Hist. 367, 375-377, 379-380, 383, 386 (1998). Although rape was appropriately the concern of many women, it was more radical feminist activists who first devoted sustained energy to it. . . . This radical wing of the women's movement . . . exhibited an explicit local community orientation . . . [and] initially devoted a good deal of attention to building consciousness and community at the grassroots level. . . . In the safety of these groups, many women revealed that they had been raped, and the frequency of these revelations led to a recognition among activists that, as Csida and Csida wrote, "Rape was not an isolated act of violence—that it really was the ultimate sexist act—the definitive ripoff of female by male—and that it occurred far more frequently than any one realized."

Activists began to fight back with direct-action tactics at the local level. In 1970, radical feminists on the West Coast, outraged by the tale of a topless dancer raped at a bachelor party, picketed the wedding with placards declaring the groom a rapist. The New York Radical Feminists (NYRF), after learning that one of their members had been raped while hitchhiking, sponsored a "Speak-Out on Rape" [in 1971 that] drew an overflow crowd of more than three hundred and considerable press attention [and that] was later recognized as the emergence of a war against rape. The Speak-Outs spread, and activists distributed reports of them widely, effectively putting the issue at the top of the political agenda for many feminists.

. . . [Many] women who had been raped described the poor treatment that they received from a range of public institutions. . . . Prosecutors and judges required them to substantiate their claims with kinds of evidence not required for other crimes, and their personal lives were subject to public scrutiny, such that many women felt they were interrogated more aggressively by police and prosecutors, and with more suspicion, than were the alleged rapists. [And] conviction rates for rape were very low. . . .

Feminist anti-rape activists proffered multiple goals, some directly addressing problems faced by individual women: (1) to provide direct services to women who had been raped and (in most communities) to advocate for them as they negotiated local health and criminal justice institutions; (2) to teach women how to avoid and resist rape, and to assist them in doing so; and (3) to encourage (or to force) local institutions—hospitals, police departments, and prosecutors' offices—to be more responsive to women who have been raped in their home communities. . . . Organizations that were primarily liberal feminist in their orientation chose to focus on reforming rape laws at the state level in order to increase conviction rates and to protect women from additional post-rape trauma. More radical groups called for far-reaching social change and, ultimately, the end of sexual violence aimed systematically at women; some of the more radical groups also joined with their liberal counterparts in the legal reform efforts. . . .

Activists sought to raise the profile of rape as an issue and to alter public perceptions of its incidence, circumstances, and effects. . . . [Their efforts yielded a] rapid increase in public attention . . . . Between 1970 and 1974, the number of [*New York Times*] stories about rape rose more than sixfold, from eight (1970) to fifty-three (1974). . . . This was followed by organized efforts aimed at statutory reform across the fifty states . . . . In their reform efforts they focused on the need for four basic legal changes: (1) broadening the definition of rape to include a range of hostile sexual behavior; (2) limiting the need for victims to demonstrate vigorous physical resistance in order to secure convictions; (3) eliminating corroboration requirements that formerly required the testimony of witnesses; and (4) adding "shield" laws that restricted the defendant's use of the victim's past sexual conduct as evidence. . . .

Between 1970 and 1979, forty-nine of fifty states reformed their rape laws [to varying degrees]; thirty states reformed their laws in 1975 alone. Across the country, feminist anti-rape activists, often in coordination with the NOW Task Forces and more mainstream women's organizations such as the League of Women Voters, actively lobbied state legislatures to press for statutory reform. A diverse set of observers—including federal government researchers and legal analysts—attribute the wave of reform largely to the demands of local feminist activists. . . . By the mid-1970s, the anti-rape movement lived in a world quite different from the one in which the Speak-Outs had taken place in 1971.

Leigh Bienen, *Rape III - National Developments in Rape Reform Legislation,* 6 Women's Rts. L. Rep. 170, 171-172 (1980). As of 1980, every state has considered, and most states have passed, some form of rape reform legislation. The reform legislation has usually been lobbied through state legislatures by a coalition of feminists and law-and-order groups. The articulated purposes of the new laws are to increase the number of rape convictions and to ensure that the interests of victims are respected in the criminal justice process. . . . Rape reform legislation, nevertheless, is still controversial. The vast majority of state legislators are male; and the legislative committees where the drafting and amending processes occur are often, if not always, controlled by older, more conservative men. . . . In every state which has passed some form of rape reform legislation, the particular compromise between legislators and lobbyists reflected the balance between the political pressures exerted by reformers and the legislature's perception of the need for reform. In some states, reform efforts were demonstrably more successful than in others.

2. Hurdles and Shortfalls. For all the successes described in the preceding note—including the passage of rape-law reforms nationwide over a span of just a few years—the anti-rape movement also suffered setbacks and, by most accounts, did not fully realize its goals. As with all social movements, no single account explains the full scope of the movement's successes or failures. But the excerpts that follow offer a series of perspectives on why and how the anti-rape movement fell short, taking into account both internal and external challenges.

Janet C. Gornick & David S. Meyer, *Changing Political Opportunity: The Anti-Rape Movement and Public Policy,* 10 J. Pol'y Hist. 367, 386, 388-389 (1998). The early 1970s clearly brought the anti-rape movement a series of remarkable victories . . . . By the end of the decade, however, partly a result of its successes, the movement had stalled and declined sharply. . . . The movement's decline took place on several fronts.

First, [feminist rape crisis centers, which] increased from approximately twenty-five in 1973 to nearly four hundred by late 1976, [were] quickly diluted as [sites of radical organizing as they] abandoned some of the characteristic practices—including most of their social change work—that tied them to the feminist movement. [This happened] in large part because centers pursued newly available public monies [that] required more conventional organizational structures and highly developed service delivery systems. Centers formed after the end of 1973 rarely adopted the feminist collective organizational structure and, importantly, devoted a greater share, sometimes even all, of their resources to direct service rather than to social-change work. . . . After about 1975, the anti-rape movement mobilized fewer and fewer women, largely because the role of the rape-crisis-center volunteer had shifted to services and no longer served as a means to recruit activists. . . .

[Separately,] as the movement's message that rape was an enormous problem became widely accepted, many of the anti-rape movement's original claims—for example, that rape was linked to rigid sex-role stereotyping and to women's subservient position in society—were soon overwhelmed by less comprehensive interpretations of the causes of rape and by a focus on traditional models of crime prevention. In other words, many mainstream political institutions embraced *some* of the political concerns of the anti-rape activists while jettisoning the movement's original radical claims. . . . [F]eminist activists no longer enjoyed a monopoly on the issue of combating rape, and other institutions fighting against rape did not share feminist concerns apart from acting against rapists.

Stephen J. Schulhofer, *Unwanted Sex* 29-40, 93-97 (1998). [In the 1970s] antirape activists [who] pressed for extensive change in statutes and standards of judicial interpretation . . . divided sharply over tactics and strategy. All the reformers understood that a man's failure to obtain genuine consent was the essence of the offense. But reformers worried that statutes making consent a formal issue at trial would focus attention on the dress, behavior, and sexual experience of the victim and might encourage defense attorneys to argue, even in cases involving physical violence, that the victim had encouraged the man's attentions. . . . [N]early all the feminist reformers of the 1970s concluded that the best course was [instead] to eliminate from the statutes all references to the victim's consent and to focus instead on the conduct of the assailant. . . . This meant renewing the emphasis on "forcible compulsion" as the gist of the offense. . . . [F]orce remained the central concept in these statutes, and it was almost always described in terms suggesting physical violence. . . .

[But n]ot all the reformers accepted the strategy of stressing force rather than consent. . . . In [some] states, progressive judges . . . sought to bridge the many gaps in existing rape law by unusual innovations in legal doctrine. . . . [Consider the opinion in *M.T.S.* (p. 371), issued over a decade after the initial legislative reform push, where the court's] solution was to read into the statute a limitation that had not been explicit before, a requirement of *nonconsent*. . . . Somewhat ironically, the outcome [brought] the tactics of rape reform full circle. New Jersey, like many states, had revised its statutes in the late 1970s to eliminate all reference to victim consent and to focus instead on the forcible character of the defendant's conduct. The hope — soon dashed — was that an emphasis on force rather than on consent would cut through the difficulties of proof and facilitate effective enforcement. With *M.T.S.*, the New Jersey Supreme Court rewrote its statute to take just the opposite approach, emphasizing consent and making proof of force superfluous.

However debatable as statutory interpretation, the New Jersey approach . . . makes clear that a man who engages in sexual intercourse, knowing that he doesn't have the permission of the woman, has indeed committed a crime. . . . Yet the New Jersey approach . . . suffers from one major limitation. . . . [W]hat protection does [it] offer to women who do not say "no," who instead acquiesce in a man's demands — for any wide variety of reasons? . . . [By not clearly answering this question, *M.T.S.* yields] a conceptual and practical muddle. It does nothing to indicate what kinds of inducements are permissible and what kinds of pressures will invalidate consent. If the answers are left to the good sense of judges and juries, [the approach] will do nothing to alter the conflicting, subjective judgments that have traditionally produced extremely cautious administration of the law of rape. . . . [One New Jersey prosecutor, interviewed in 1997, five years after *M.T.S.* was decided,] notes that after *M.T.S.*, as before, "juries find it hard to believe, in the absence of traditional physical force or demonstrations of it, that there was an absence of consent."

Dan M. Kahan, *Culture, Cognition, and Consent: Who Perceives What, and Why, in Acquaintance-Rape Cases*, 158 U. Pa. L. Rev. 729, 732-734 (2010). People who share formative identities tend to apprehend facts in a similar way in part because they are likely to be drawing on common life experiences when interpreting the significance of various events. But more importantly, such individuals face strong psychological pressure to fit their perceptions of how the world does work to their shared appraisals of how the world should work: forming beliefs at odds with their core values exposes them to dissonance and risks putting them in conflict with others whose opinions of them affect both their material and emotional well-being. . . .

The influence of culture on individuals' perceptions of fact is much stronger . . . than other factors that might be expected to affect the result in a case . . . [including] the legal definition of rape. [In our study (p. 366) based on the facts of *State v. Berkowitz* (p. 353),] [s]ubjects who were instructed to apply a standard reflecting one or another "reform" definition of rape were not more likely to convict than were subjects instructed to apply the traditional common law definition — or than those who were not supplied with any definition of rape at all. Subjects who were [explicitly] instructed that rape includes sex when a woman says "no" — regardless of what she might have meant to convey or what the man understood her to be communicating — were slightly more likely to convict. But the size of this increase was relatively small compared to the impact of cultural predispositions on subjects who received this or any other definition of rape. . . . [In other words,] legal definitions have relatively little impact on how actual cases are likely to be decided.

Katharine K. Baker, *Why Rape Should Not (Always) Be a Crime*, 100 Minn. L. Rev. 221, 223, 249, 279 (2015). A law that defines rape as nonconsensual sex may get the theory of rape right, but it ignores the overwhelming practical difficulty of proving non-consent to an act for which there are no witnesses, no extrinsic evidence, and often no particular reason to think that the act was not consensual. This problem applies to a huge amount of sexual misconduct . . . . If behavior is not punished criminally because it cannot be proved, then the public's understanding of criminal behavior will not change. [Separately,] [t]ough-on-rapists measures enacted in the 1990s [like the creation of the federal sex offender registry] reflect an understanding of rapists as profoundly deviant and distinctly criminal. [But this] pathological view of rape rejects the feminist insight at the core of much rape reform, which was that male appropriation of sex is common-place and completely understandable given heterosexual scripts and norms of sexual pursuit. . . . When notification and registration laws validate the idea that rapists are uniquely dangerous it becomes much harder for every-one, from judge to juror to prosecutor to victim, to see the boy next door as a rapist. . . . [In short,] the criminal law has been unable to prosecute as rape a tremendous amount of non-consensual sex because it is too difficult to prove beyond a reasonable doubt [and] because the law's treatment of rape sends profoundly inconsistent messages about who rapists are and how bad rape is.

David Bryden & Sonja Lengnick, *Rape in the Criminal Justice System*, 87 J. Crim. L. & Criminology 1194, 1214, 1221-1223, 1228-1229 (1997). The single most important reason why most rapists are not punished is the failure of victims to report the crime to the police, or their later refusal to cooperate as a prosecution witness. . . . Scholars have advanced several reasons for victims' failure to report. Some rape victims are too upset, or too embarrassed at the prospect of answering a stranger's intimate ques-tions about the incident, or so ashamed that they do not want anyone, even their friends, to know about it. Sometimes the victim fears retaliation by her assailant. In other cases, she wishes to conceal some aspect of her own behavior — drug use, for example — immediately prior to the rape. . . . In some acquaintance rape cases, the victim does not report the rape because she blames herself or does not regard the crime as a "real rape." In other acquaintance cases, . . . the victim's decision about whether to report the crime is often affected by the responses of her family [especially where the perpetrator is a relative]. She also may be swayed by the perceived expec-tations of her social group concerning the appropriate behavior of vic-tims. Sometimes the victim does not report because she wishes to maintain her relationship with the offender. One study found that 39% of rape vic-tims date their attacker after the rape. This is much less surprising than it sounds, because many rapes are perpetrated by lovers. . . .

[T]he evidence, although mixed, suggests that rape reporting rates are generally unresponsive to changes in a particular jurisdiction's rape law, even when those changes signal a desire to reduce victim blaming in rape trials. . . . [T]he emotional rigors of a rape trial are due largely to intracta-ble realities: the law's delay; the unpleasantness of having to relive a horrify-ing and extremely intimate experience; fear, even apart from sexual history questions, of cross-examination, or of media publicity; and embarrassment about the rape itself or about surrounding circumstances that inevitably will be revealed during the trial.

3. The Case for More Law. In view of the shortfalls described above, some advocate doubling down on the law-reform strategy on the view that reforms to date have not gone far enough. As Professor Aya Gruber explained earlier in this chapter (p. 378), the push to define the *actus reus* of sexual assault in terms of affirmative consent is an example of this approach, as "many activists" saw prior law reform efforts, like *M.T.S.*, as leaving too much room for "biased or mistaken decision-makers" to continue to under-regulate unwanted sex. As the reporters of the MPC revision project observe, this impulse to press for stronger criminal law is present across rape-law reform debates, which often include "strong arguments for criminalizing sexual conduct that until now much of society has tolerated or not even seen as abusive."[66]

The following pair of excerpts, from the MPC revision reporters and from columnist Ezra Klein, explore the complex dynamics at play when using legal sanctions to shape social attitudes — from a perspective largely sympathetic to such an approach. The note that follows offers a set of more critical assessments.

Am. L. Inst., Model Penal Code: Sexual Assault and Related Offenses, Prelim. Draft No. 5, at 15-16 (Sept. 8, 2015). Because criminal law is the site of the most afflictive sanctions that public authority can bring to bear on individuals, it necessarily must and will reflect prevailing social norms. But for the same reason, it must often be called upon to help shape those norms by communicating effectively the conditions under which commonplace or seemingly innocuous behavior can be unacceptably abusive or dangerous. Nearly all law-reform efforts addressed to the sexual offenses are met at some point by the objection that they go beyond social standards currently accepted by a good many law abiding citizens. . . . [But] [w]here deeply felt injuries are not yet fully appreciated by the general public, the criminal law may at times properly carry the burden of insuring that appropriate norms of interpersonal behavior are more widely understood and respected.

Ezra Klein, *"Yes Means Yes" Is a Terrible Law, and I Completely Support It*, Vox (Oct. 13, 2014). California's "Yes Means Yes" law (p. 380), is a terrible bill.* But it's a necessary one. It tries to change, through brute legislative force, the most private and intimate of adult acts. It is sweeping in its redefinition of acceptable consent; two college seniors who've been in a loving relationship since they met during the first week of their freshman years, and who, with the ease of the committed, slip naturally from cuddling to sex, could fail its test. Defenders of the bill argue that the lovers have nothing to worry about; the assault will never be punished, because no complaint will ever be brought. Technically, that's true. But this is as much indictment as defense: if the best that can be said about the law is that its definition of

---

* Editor's Note: As noted earlier (p.380), the California law is not a penal statute; but arguments similar to those Klein advances can and have been made in support of expanding criminal liability with respect to sexual conduct.

consent will rarely be enforced, then the definition should be rethought. It is dangerous for the government to set rules it doesn't expect will be followed.

But [the] law is a necessarily extreme solution to an extreme problem. Its overreach is precisely its value. Every discussion of the Yes Means Yes law needs to begin with a simple number: A 2007 study by the Department of Justice found that one in five women is the victim of an attempted or completed sexual assault while in college. One. In. Five.

. . . If the Yes Means Yes law is taken even remotely seriously it will settle like a cold winter on college campuses, throwing everyday sexual practice into doubt and creating a haze of fear and confusion over what counts as consent. This is the case against it, and also the case for it. Because for one in five women to report an attempted or completed sexual assault means that everyday sexual practices on college campuses need to be upended, and men need to feel a cold spike of fear when they begin a sexual encounter. . . .

The Yes Means Yes law is trying to change a culture of sexual entitlement. . . . For that reason, the law is only worth the paper it's written on if some of the critics' fears come true. Critics worry that colleges will fill with cases in which campus boards convict young men (and, occasionally, young women) of sexual assault for genuinely ambiguous situations. Sadly, that's necessary for the law's success. It's those cases — particularly the ones that feel genuinely unclear and maybe even unfair, the ones that become lore in frats and cautionary tales that fathers e-mail to their sons — that will convince men that they better Be Pretty Damn Sure. . . . A culture where one-in-five women is assaulted isn't going to be dislodged with a gentle nudge. [It] won't fall without a fight. Ugly problems don't always have pretty solutions.

4. The Case Against Carceral Feminism. Sociologist Elizabeth Bernstein coined the term *carceral feminism* in 2007 to describe the instinct among feminist activists, evident in the notes above, to try to use police, prosecutions, and prisons as tools of gender justice. But as Professor Aya Gruber describes, "not all feminist theories invoke or support criminal law." On the contrary, she argues, "the feminist war on crime is a feminist civil war," and it has raged for decades. On Gruber's telling, the carceral feminist view "is ingrained in contemporary thinking." But it is not without serious opposition within contemporary feminism, from anticarceral feminists including Gruber herself. Consider the excerpts below, from Gruber and from Professor Amia Srinivasan.[67]

Aya Gruber, *The Feminist War on Crime* 1-7, 44-45, 170-171 (2020). When I was a law student and an aspiring criminal lawyer, I always felt mired in a feminist defense attorney dilemma. On the one hand, I was intimately familiar with the harms of sexual assault and firmly believed that gender crimes reflected and reinforced women's second-class status. On the other,

I was involved in public defense and anti-incarceration work and had come to regard the prison as a primary site of violence, racism, and degradation in society. I [entered my career with] dread at the prospect of defending batterers and rapists.

[But that] sense quickly abated after I became a public defender and witnessed firsthand the prosecutorial machine processing domestic violence and sexual assault cases. I felt [instead] a sense of disillusionment that the feminist movement I so admired played such a distinct role in broadening and legitimizing the unconscionable penal state. . . . [W]omen's criminal law activism had not made prosecution and punishment more feminist. It had made feminism more prosecutorial and punitive. . . . In past decades, feminists were rightly concerned about gender violence, and they made philosophical and strategic choices about how to address it. These were hard choices. . . . But it becomes clear that [t]heir reform agendas expanded police and prosecutorial power, emphasized criminals' threat to vulnerable women, diverted scarce resources to law enforcement, and ultimately made many feminists soldiers in the late twentieth-century war on crime. . . . By the close of the millennium, the stalwart suit-wearing SVU prosecutor who throws the book at rapists had replaced the bra-burner as the symbol of women's empowerment. . . .

To be sure, it is natural, even instinctive, to advocate more criminal enforcement in the face of rape crisis statistics and stories of abuser impunity. There is a deeply ingrained American punitive impulse, originating from the media and government's relentless focus on horrific criminality, that leads even progressive incarceration critics to advocate for strict prosecution of those whom they see as the worst of the worst (corporate CEOs, white supremacists). However, in the rush to punish bad apples, real and imagined, we tend to forget that the criminal system is culturally ordered, technocratic, and beholden to specific political forces. . . .

Today, second-wave feminism is remembered—fondly or regretfully—for its contributions to policing, prosecution, and punishment. The prosecutorial achievements of second-wave feminism are numerous and include mandatory arrest and no-drop prosecution for domestic violence, criminalization of nonforcible sex, and prosecution-favoring evidentiary rules. . . . This increased concentration of criminal authority in the intimate realm has had profound effects. Since the 1980s, the population of sex offenders in prison has exploded, even as rape offending has precipitously declined. . . . [And] [f]eminists' more than century-long battle against abusers and rapists is far from over. As with the war on terror, there is an endless supply of frightening bad guys who inspire fear and loathing and have symbolic political meaning. The feminist penal regimes implemented in the 1980s and 1990s are now entrenched institutions overseen by prosecutors, advocates working for the courts, administrators, and for-profit actors with vested interests in their continued survival. . . .

Interestingly, some of the most ardent prison critics remain untroubled by this. They proceed as if there were a carve-out to the mass incarceration critique for sexual misconduct — including, or perhaps especially, intoxicated sex or sex without affirmative consent — even though there is no such carve-out for aggravated assault, drug dealing, or even murder. When it comes to these serious but nonsexual crimes, many feminists are willing to exercise empathy for offenders, look to structural causes, and reject state violence as the solution. The exception for sexual offenses is so taken for granted that few feel the need to mention it or stray from the presumption that sex offenders are just a small minority of those swept up in mass incarceration. However, the reality according to a 2015 Bureau of Justice Statistics report on the U.S. prison population is that sex offenders, at 12.4 percent, constitute a higher percentage of prisoners than burglars and nonsexual assaulters (both approximately 10 percent) and nearly as high a percentage as *all* drug offenders (15.7 percent). But because of the silent exception made for sexual offenses, mass incarceration concerns have not diminished political and popular support for carceral feminist activism as it moves ahead full throttle with new criminalization proposals.

Amia Srinivasan, *The Right to Sex* 159-163, 170-171 (2021). [C]arceral "solutions" tend to make things worse for the women who are already worst off. This is because carceral feminism invites the wielding of the state's coercive power against the women who suffer most from gendered violence — poor women, immigrant women, women of color, low-caste women — as well as the men with whom their lives are fatefully entwined. At the same time, the carceral approach fails to address those social realities — poverty, racism, caste — that lie at the root of most crime, and which make certain groups of women particularly susceptible to gendered violence. . . .

In 1984, bell hooks wrote about the tendency of the women's liberation movement to focus solely on what women could be said to have in common. "It was a mark of race and class privilege," [hooks wrote,] "that middle-class white women were able to make their interests the primary focus of the feminist movement and employ a rhetoric of commonality that made their condition synonymous with 'oppression.'" . . . Carceral approaches to gender justice tend to presuppose a subject who is a "pure" case of women's "common oppression," uncomplicated by such factors as class and race. . . . [But] the belief that incarceration is the way to deal with domestic violence does not take into account the women whose fates are bound up with the men who perpetrate it: the women who are financially dependent on the men who [abuse] them, and who have a large stake in how the men in their community are treated by the police, courts, or prisons. . . . When feminists embrace carceral solutions — cops on the street, men sent to prison — it gives cover to the governing class in its refusal to tackle the deepest causes of most crime [including] poverty [and] racial domination. . . .

The feminists of Me Too appear, on the whole, to have a great deal of faith in the coercive powers of the state. . . . They champion the move to stricter notions of sexual consent both in the law and on university campuses and have denounced critics of these developments as rape apologists. It is hard to blame them. For centuries men haven't only assaulted and degraded women, but have used the state's coercive apparatus to enforce their right to do so. Is it not time women got to wield some of that same power[?] Except that once you have started up the carceral machine, you cannot pick and choose whom it will mow down. . . . This is not to say there are not difficult choices to be made. There are poor women who want to see their abusive partners in prison . . . . Some opponents of carceralism think that no one deserves to be punished, that violence must never be met with violence. But feminists need not be saints. They must only, I am suggesting, be realists. Perhaps some men deserve to be punished. But feminists must ask what it is they set in motion, and against whom, when they demand more policing and more prisons.

5. *Severity of Punishment.* The debate between carceral and anticarceral feminists plays out not only with respect to the scope of criminal liability but also with respect to the severity of punishments imposed on people convicted of sexual assault. Interestingly, in the early days of the anti-rape movement, even those legal reformers who favored broader criminal liability often opposed severe punishment for pragmatic and strategic reasons—and sometimes argued for lowering sex-offense penalties across the board. Writing in 1992, Professor Lynne Henderson put the point this way:

> Feminists are caught in a bind . . . . Because all rape is a form of soul murder, a life-threatening and life-damaging experience, proportionality would seem to demand heavy penalties. . . . Practically, however, a patriarchal society will not tolerate imposition of heavy penalties on large numbers of men for raping women, at least in the short term. [So] feminists might have to accept a shorter, and not a longer, base term than proportionality suggests.

And in fact, this was the early position of many feminist groups. The National Organization of Women, for example, adopted a resolution in 1974 drafted by its National Rape Task Force that called for "a general lowering of penalties, except in gang rapes, to fit the severity of the crime, thus making convictions more possible."[68]

More recently, however, advocates who favor expanded use of criminal law to address sexual misconduct generally tend to favor serious punishments as well—and to criticize prosecutors or judges perceived as too soft on sexual offenders. No case in recent memory captures this dynamic more clearly than that of Brock Turner, a Stanford University undergraduate convicted in 2016 of digitally penetrating an unconscious woman named Chanel Miller. Turner was sentenced to six months incarceration, three years of probation, and lifetime sex-offender registration. (California, where Turner was sentenced, was one of two states that required lifetime registration at the time.) The prosecution had requested a sentence of six years incarceration. Following the sentencing, Stanford Law School professor Michele Dauber launched a campaign to remove the sentencing judge, Aaron Persky, from the bench via a statewide recall vote. The California legislature also swiftly passed new statutes creating mandatory minimum sentences for sexual assault and expanding the definition of sexual assault.[69]

The recall campaign, which made national news and ultimately succeeded in ousting Judge Persky, prompted intense debate over the role criminal punishments ought to play in the pursuit of gender justice — a debate echoing the broader debates over carceral feminism discussed above. The following excerpts offer a set of different perspectives on the Turner case and its aftermath.[70]

People's Sentencing Memorandum, Ex. 16, People v. Turner, No. B1577162 (Cal. Super. Ct. May 27, 2016) (Chanel Miller's victim impact statement). Your Honor, if it is all right, for the majority of this statement I would like to address the defendant directly.

You don't know me, but you've been inside me, and that's why we're here today. On January 17th, 2015 [I woke up] in a gurney in a hallway. I had dried blood and bandages on the backs of my hands and elbow. . . . A deputy explained I had been assaulted. . . . When I was finally allowed to use the restroom, I pulled down the hospital pants they had given me, went to pull down my underwear, and felt nothing. I still remember the feeling of my hands touching my skin and grabbing nothing. I looked down and there was nothing. The thin piece of fabric, the only thing between my vagina and anything else, was missing and everything inside me was silenced. I still don't have words for that feeling. . . .

On that morning, all that I was told was that I had been found behind a dumpster, potentially penetrated by a stranger, and that I should get retested for HIV because results don't always show up immediately. But for now, I should go home and get back to my normal life. Imagine stepping back into the world with only that information. . . . I had scratches and bandages on my skin, my vagina was sore and had become a strange, dark color from all the prodding, my underwear was missing, and I felt too empty to continue to speak. . . .

I was not ready to tell my boyfriend or parents that actually, I may have [been] raped behind a dumpster, but I don't know by who or when or how. If I told them, I would see the fear on their faces, and mine would multiply by tenfold, so instead I pretended the whole thing wasn't real. I tried to push it out of my mind, but it was so heavy I didn't talk, I didn't eat, I didn't sleep, I didn't interact with anyone. . . .

One day, I was at work, scrolling through the news on my phone, and came across an article. In it, I read and learned for the first time about how I was found unconscious, with my hair disheveled, long necklace wrapped around my neck, bra pulled out of my dress, dress pulled off over my shoulders and pulled up above my waist, that I was butt naked all the way down to my boots, legs spread apart, and had been penetrated by a foreign object by someone I did not recognize. This was how I learned what happened to me, sitting at my desk reading the news at work. . . .

And then it came time for him to testify. This is where I became revictimized. . . . My family had to see pictures of my head strapped to a gurney full of pine needles, of my body in the dirt with my eyes closed, dress hiked up, limbs limp in the dark. And even after that, my family had to listen to your attorney say, the pictures were after the fact, we can dismiss them. To say, yes her nurse confirmed there was redness and abrasions inside her, significant trauma to her genitalia, but that's what happens when you finger someone, and he's already admitted to that. . . . To listen to him attempt to paint a picture of me, the seductive party animal, as if somehow that would make it so that I had this coming for me. . . .

You have dragged me through this hell with you, dipped me back into that night again and again. You knocked down both our towers, I collapsed at the same time you did. Your damage was concrete; stripped of titles, degrees, enrollment. My damage was internal, unseen, I carry it with me. You took away my worth, my privacy, my energy, my time, my safety, my intimacy, my confidence, my own voice, until today. . . . If you think I was spared, came out unscathed, that today I ride off into sunset, while you suffer the greatest blow, you are mistaken. Nobody wins. We have all been devastated, we have all been trying to find some meaning in all of this suffering. . . .

Had Brock admitted guilt and remorse and offered to settle early on, I would have considered a lighter sentence, respecting his honesty, grateful to be able to move our lives forward. Instead he took the risk of going to trial, added insult to injury and forced me to relive the hurt as details about my personal life and sexual assault were brutally dissected before the public. . . . The probation officer's recommendation of a year or less in county jail is a soft timeout, a mockery of the seriousness of his assaults, and of the consequences of the pain I have been forced to endure. . . . As this is a first offence I can see where leniency would beckon. On the other hand, as a society, we cannot forgive everyone's first sexual assault or digital rape. . . . The consequences of sexual assault need[] to be severe enough that people feel enough fear to exercise good judgment even if they are drunk, severe enough to be preventative.

Bridget Read, *Rape Culture Is on the Ballot in California: Inside the Movement to Recall Judge Aaron Persky*, Vogue (May 23, 2018). "I think when people hear 'campus rape,' some people, they have a mental picture that's probably wrong, but it's really wrong in this case," Michele Dauber, a Stanford law professor and sociologist, said to me, as we walked over . . . toward the crime scene . . . . "Whatever comes into your mind when you hear campus rape, this is not it," Dauber continued. "This is the stranger-danger-in-the-bushes scenario that your mother warned you about."

. . . Dauber—a tenured law professor at Stanford, a family friend of [Miller's], and an outspoken critic of Stanford's sexual assault disciplinary process—and a group of like-minded supporters [have] come together over one shared goal: to recall Judge Persky. . . . [T]he movement against Persky marks the first judicial recall, in any state, to make it on a ballot in 36 years. (The last successful judicial recall in California was in 1932.) For Dauber and the other volunteers who have spearheaded the effort, a vote for or against recall is a vote for or against the way that American society has normalized sexual violence against women, which is to say it's a vote against rape culture itself.

Critics of Persky's sentencing say that he clearly identified with Turner as a white man . . . and as a former Stanford athlete . . . . [He] sentenced Turner within the bounds of the probation report, which suggested "a moderate county jail sentence" [but] recall supporters believe that report was also biased toward Turner, and that the judge should have made a better final call. . . . "[Persky] saw a young man with a bright future," said Dauber. "He didn't see what was before him. He saw, instead, an image that was untrue and refracted through the lens of bias and privilege."

According to Stanford graduate student Emma Tsurkov, a research assistant of Dauber's who closely followed the trial, Persky's sentencing of Turner was . . . an unconscionable message to send to survivors. "That's what was really, really devastating and discouraging," Tsurkov said, "because it means that no one takes sexual assault seriously. No one can be trusted to actually address this issue. No one can be trusted to protect the bodily autonomy of women."

Judith Levine, *The Problem of Punishment*, Boston Rev. (June 16, 2016). [A]fter an excruciating year awaiting trial, after the hell of the trial itself, [Chanel Miller's statement at Brock Turner's sentencing shows that she] held out hope that an apology would come. . . . She wanted Brock Turner to name the harm he did. She just wanted him to get it. . . . [But] state-administered retribution . . . cannot accomplish what Turner's victim wanted: that her assailant understand and take responsibility for the harm he did to her and to the trust and peace of the community. The adversarial criminal system won't allow that transformation. No defense attorney permits a client to apologize to the victim; that would be an admission of guilt. On the other side, prosecutors are usually hostile to non-criminal resolutions. Convictions get them elected. . . . [But] [t]here is another way.

The practices that fall under the rubric of "transformative" or "restorative" justice support survivors' healing while creating a space for offenders to be accountable for their actions and take steps to lessen the chances they will harm again. . . . They give victims a platform to speak bitterness; they engage broader circles in deciding just and useful restitution; and critically, they seek to bring the harm-doer back into the community and help him embrace the values he has transgressed.* It is assumed that everyone is potentially redeemable. . . . What is the appropriate way to hold a sexual assailant accountable? There's no single answer. But one thing we know is that what we're doing — caging and surveillance — does not work. . . .

[T]here's lots of "poor me" in [Turner's own statement at his sentencing hearing]. He can't sleep or concentrate; he torments himself. He shakes uncontrollably. And so on. But his suffering is also remorseful. "I can never forgive myself for imposing trauma and pain on [Chanel Miller]. It debilitates me to think that my actions have caused her emotional and physical stress that is completely unwarranted and unfair." He writes: "I am the sole proprietor of what happened on the night that these people's lives were changed forever." Might this be a man on the verge of getting it? We may never know.

Aya Gruber, *The Feminist War on Crime* 182 (2020). [P]ublic defenders and other incarceration critics regarded the recall movement with a deep-seated sense of unease. The Santa Clara County public defender Sajid Khan noted "the countless defendants who have suffered relatively harsh sentences in our state [who] fall below any headline" and authored a letter, signed by 116 defenders, opposing recall. Punishing the jurist, it stated, would "deter other judges from extending mercy and instead encourage them to issue unfairly harsh sentences for fear of reprisal." . . . Fifty-three of the 180 Stanford Law School 2016 graduates penned an open letter to Professor Dauber, asking her to halt the recall effort. Several of the drafters had been involved in opposing California's three-strikes laws and highlighted their efforts to convince "judges like Aaron Persky to grant early release to men and women serving life in prison because the people of California once believed that our clients' mistakes made them irredeemable." They implored, "If we demand that Judge Persky immediately hand over his gavel for acting on his empathy for this defendant, how can we credibly assure any other judge that her hand need not waver when the human circumstances of a case seem to call for compassion?"

Jeannie Suk Gersen, *Revisiting the Brock Turner Case*, New Yorker (Mar. 29, 2023). The retired judge LaDoris Cordell, a feminist who, in the nineteen

---

* Editor's Note: For more on restorative justice, see Chapter Ten (p. 926).

eighties, became the first Black woman judge appointed in Northern California and, later, an elected superior-court judge in the same county as Persky, participated in a campaign against the recall. She said, at the time, "I'm opposed to it because I believe this recall is terrible for racial justice." She and others believed that it would make judges less independent and, in particular, more afraid to be lenient. Such reluctance would breed more punitiveness and harm Black and Latino defendants, who are severely over-represented in the criminal justice system.

That debate inspired two political scientists, Sanford C. Gordon of New York University and Sidak Yntiso of the University of Chicago, to study . . . whether the recall campaign changed judges' behavior, and how it affected racial disparities in the sentences that judges imposed. [Their study] relied on data from nearly twenty thousand sentences issued by more than a hundred and fifty California judges, between 2015 and 2018. They found that, immediately after the public announcement of the Persky-recall campaign, judges began imposing sentences that were roughly thirty per cent longer on average, across the board. Those increases maintained pre-existing racial disparities. In other words, even though the Persky-recall campaign aimed to raise consciousness about white privilege, the additional years in prison were disproportionately imposed on Black and Hispanic people. And, even though the campaign focused on sexual assault, the study found that the increased sentence lengths were primarily driven by nonsexual crimes, and possibly by nonviolent crimes.[*]

[Prosecutors] also used the notoriety of Turner's sentencing to successfully advocate for mandatory minimum prison sentences for defendants convicted of sexual assault. A California state lawmaker who sponsored the bill told the Times that "it took the lax sentence in the Brock Turner case that drew international scorn to get this done." If that law had been in place when Turner was sentenced, he would have received a minimum of three years in prison. . . . Notably, Dauber, who led the anti-Persky recall campaign, did not support the mandatory-minimum legislation. Dauber told me that she "felt that tying the hands of all California judges in response to the bias of one judge was wrong," especially "given the research showing the relationship between mandatory minimums and mass incarceration."

D. Race

The law of sexual assault has a troubling racial history. During slavery and forward into the Jim Crow era, intense racial purity panics over Black

---

[*] Editor's Note: For the study, see Sanford C. Gordon & Sidak Yntiso, *Incentive Effects of Recall Elections: Evidence from Criminal Sentencing in California Courts*, 84 J. Pol. 1947 (2022).

men assaulting—or even having consensual sex with—white women not only undergirded criminal laws and legal practices but also fomented extra-legal racial violence. As anti-lynching activist Ida B. Wells reported in a compendium of lynchings, at least 150 Black men were lynched between 1892 and 1894 for allegedly raping or attempting to rape white women. Others were killed for simply expressing romantic interest in white women, as in the case of William Brooks who was lynched on May 23, 1894 for asking a white woman to marry him. Indeed, sex between Black people and white people was illegal in many states, even when consensual, into the mid-1900s.[71]

At the same time, Professor Angela Davis writes, the "fictional image of the Black man as rapist has always strengthened its inseparable companion: the image of the Black woman as chronically promiscuous. For once the notion is accepted that Black men harbor irresistible and animal-like sexual urges," Davis concludes, "the entire race is invested with bestiality." For Black women, these racist promiscuity tropes left many victims of sexual assault ignored by law enforcement actors. They were, Professor Amia Srinivasan writes, "unrapeable" in the face of "white domination."[72]

This section explores the legacy of these racialized accounts of sexual violence. We begin with *McQuirter v. State*, an Alabama appellate court case written in 1953 that Professor Bennett Capers calls "one of the most troubling" cases concerning the law of rape. As Capers goes on to say in the excerpt following the opinion, *McQuirter* is troubling not only for the history it reflects but for the ongoing connections it holds to the present. The notes that follow explore that history and some of its present-day implications.

McQuirter v. State

63 So.2d 388 (Ala. Ct. App. 1953)

PRICE, J. Appellant, a Negro man, was found guilty of an attempt to commit an assault with intent to rape . . . . About 8:00 o'clock on the night of June 29, 1951, Mrs. Ted Allen, a white woman, with her two children and a neighbor's little girl, were drinking Coca-Cola at the "Tiny Diner" in Atmore. When they started in the direction of Mrs. Allen's home she noticed appellant sitting in the cab of a parked truck. As she passed the truck appellant said something unintelligible, opened the truck door and [began to exit the vehicle].

Mrs. Allen testified appellant followed her down the street and when she reached Suell Lufkin's house she stopped. As she turned into the Lufkin house appellant was within two or three feet of her. She waited ten minutes for appellant to pass. When she proceeded on her way, appellant came toward her from behind a telephone pole. She told the children to run to Mr. Simmons' house and tell him to come and meet her. When appellant saw Mr. Simmons he turned and went back down the street to the intersection and leaned on a stop sign just across the street from Mrs. Allen's home. Mrs. Allen watched him at the sign from Mr. Simmons' porch for about thirty minutes, after which time he came back down the street and appellant went on home. . . .

Mr. Clarence Bryars, a policeman in Atmore, testified that appellant stated after his arrest that he came to Atmore with the intention of getting him a white woman that night. Mr. W. E. Strickland, Chief of Police of Atmore, testified that appellant stated in the Atmore jail he didn't know what was the matter with him; that he was drinking a little; . . . that he didn't have any money and he sat in the truck and made up his mind he was going to get the first woman that came by and that this was the first woman that came by. He said he got out of the truck, came around the gas tank and watched the lady and when she started off he started off behind her; that he was going to carry her in the cotton patch and if she hollered he was going to kill her. . . .

Appellant, as a witness in his own behalf, testified [that earlier in the evening he had] parked the truck near the "Tiny Diner" and rode to the . . . colored section [of town known as the "Front"] in a cab. Appellant came back to the truck around 8:00 o'clock and sat in the truck cab for about thirty minutes. He decided to go back to the "Front" to look for [a friend]. As he started up the street he saw prosecutrix and her children. He turned around and waited until he decided they had gone, then he walked up the street toward the "Front," [where he] stayed about 25 or 30 minutes, and came back to the truck. He denied that he followed Mrs. Allen or made any gesture toward molesting her or the children. He denied making the statements testified to by the officers. He testified he had never been arrested before and introduced testimony by two residents of Monroeville as to his good reputation for peace and quiet and for truth and veracity.

. . . Under the authorities in this state, to justify a conviction for an attempt to commit an assault with intent to rape the jury must be satisfied beyond a reasonable doubt that defendant intended to have sexual intercourse with prosecutrix against her will, by force or by putting her in fear. . . . In determining the question of intention the jury may consider social conditions and customs founded upon racial differences, such as that the prosecutrix was a white woman and defendant was a Negro man.

After considering the evidence in this case we are of the opinion it was sufficient to warrant the submission of the question of defendant's guilt to the jury, and was ample to sustain the judgment of conviction.*

Bennett Capers, *The Unintentional Rapist*, 87 Wash. U. L. Rev. 1345, 1346, 1348-1349, 1351 (2010). When it comes to rape, the case law is replete with troubling cases, but one of the most troubling is McQuirter v. State. . . . Part

---

* Editor's Note: McQuirter's sentence in the case was a $500 fine, the equivalent of roughly $5,800 today.

of the trouble . . . has to do with the court's endorsement of the means by which the jury was permitted to find the requisite intent to commit rape: "In determining the question of intention the jury may consider social conditions and customs founded upon racial differences, such as that the prosecutrix was a white woman and defendant was a Negro man." . . . But the racial issues go beyond this overt remark. There are also the racialized mores. For example, the court, in identifying the white witnesses, uses the address "Mr." or "Mrs." No titles are allowed either McQuirter or the identified black witnesses. (There are gender issues as well, to be sure; that the prosecutrix is referred to by her husband's full name, a common practice in the 1950s, is but one example.) The opinion [also] takes for granted, and in doing so adds legitimacy to, the notion of racialized spaces. That McQuirter had stopped in the white part of town, and that there existed the " 'Front,' the colored section," is taken as a given. That McQuirter's walking alone on the same street as Mrs. Ted Allen, "a white woman," was an encroachment upon her space, is also taken as a given. Even McQuirter, in his testimony, understood that the proper thing to do once he saw Mrs. Ted Allen was to "turn[] around and wait[] until . . . they had gone."

Space is racialized, and so is sex. By sex, I am not referring to gender here. I am referring to actual sex. It is not only the possibility of non-consensual sex that is being policed; what is also rendered illicit is even the possibility of interracial consensual sex. What is at risk is not just sexual intercourse, but its natural precursor, social intercourse. All of these are troubling issues.

[W]hen I teach *McQuirter*, many students respond by attempting . . . to de-trouble the case . . . in one of two ways . . . . [Some posit] that it really was McQuirter's intent to rape Mrs. Ted Allen, in which case the guilty verdict was a just one. [Others assume] that, whether or not McQuirter intended to rape Mrs. Ted Allen, the significance of the case is entirely historical—a vestigial relic of how easy it was to bring rape charges against black men in the South, at least where there was a white "victim."

For me, *McQuirter* is not so easily cabined. It is not so easily dismissed. . . . I am a black man living in a country where encounters with overt racism are now rare, but where encounters with unacknowledged and implicit biases about race and sexuality are a daily occurrence. In 1950s Alabama, I could easily have been McQuirter. Now, when I go on solitary evening strolls in the predominantly white neighborhood where I live, I am not afraid that I will be arrested, prosecuted, and convicted of "attempt to commit assault with the intent to commit rape." But I do know that to many unaccompanied women, my race and gender prefigure me as a potential rapist. To many unaccompanied women, I am still McQuirter.

NOTES AND QUESTIONS

1. Punishing Black Men. Before the American civil war, punishment for rape fell disproportionately on Black men accused of raping white women. As compared to white men convicted of rape, Black men disproportionately received life sentences. And with respect to capital punishment, of "174 men known to have been executed for criminal charges related to a rape between 1700 and 1820," historian Sharon Block reports, "142 — more than 80 percent — were identified as being of African descent." That "number is especially striking," Block continues, given "that whites outnumbered blacks in every region" throughout this period. "The only more conspicuous racial disparity," she concludes, "related to the victims of criminally prosecuted sexual assaults: approximately 95 percent of them were white."[73]

The eradication of slavery did little to change these racial patterns. As noted earlier, lynchings of Black men for alleged sexual offenses against white women reached what Professor Aya Gruber describes as "epidemic levels" in the Reconstruction Era, when this form of racial terror served as "a prime mechanism for maintaining slavery-era conditions." Things were little better in the courts. In Virginia, for example, 45 Black men, but not a single white man, were executed for rape in the first half of the twentieth century. As Professor Crystal Feimster explains, southern white culture of this time portrayed Black men as "beastly and unable to control their sexual desires," and essentially "defined rape as a crime committed by black men against white women."[74]

Against this backdrop, consider the following excerpt from an amicus brief authored by Ruth Bader Ginsburg and her colleagues at the ACLU in *Coker v. Georgia*, a 1977 case that held the death penalty unconstitutional as a penalty for the rape of an adult woman.

Brief Amici Curiae of the American Civil Liberties Union et al., Coker v. Georgia, 433 U.S. 584 (1977). Historically rape was seen as a crime of property. The person aggrieved by rape was not the woman herself, but rather her father or husband because his property had been violated. . . . In the South, this property tradition was particularly pernicious. White women were recognized as the possessions of white men, but were valued more highly than slaves — persons owned explicitly under the law as chattel. The value of a slave lay in his/her capacity to toil and to reproduce, but the worth of a white woman was determined by her chastity, purity and exclusivity. In this view, rape was particularly injurious to a white woman because it undermined her worth, and thus hindered her ability to marry or lowered her value as the exclusive sexual property of her husband. . . .

White men alone had sexual access to white women. Rape of white women by black men threatened the white man's status by decreasing the value of his sexual possession, and by jeopardizing the "purity" of his race, and it was therefore necessary to take extreme measures to prevent this result. Lynching was one such measure; a double standard of justice for weighing rape by white men and by black men was another; and the death penalty for rape—particularly when perpetrated by blacks—was yet a third.

The Georgia courts early defined a double standard of justice for rape law. In 1851, the Georgia Supreme Court . . . allowed a jury to infer intent to commit rape when the evidence showed only an assault committed by a negro man upon a white woman. In *Dorsey v. State*, 480 34 S.E. 135, 136, 137 (Ga. 1899), the Georgia Supreme Court explained that [a Black man's] race might properly be considered "to rebut any presumption that . . . his intention was to obtain the consent of the female [before having] sexual intercourse with her." . . . This separate standard for rape committed by black men was [also] reflected in Georgia's penalty structure. In 1816, the Georgia penal code expressly provided that rape committed by a white man would be punished by a term of imprisonment of not more than twenty years, and attempted rape by not more than five years, but that slaves and "free persons of color" were to be put to death for the crimes of rape or attempted rape on a free white female. . . .

In practice, that [penalty disparity] persisted long after official statements of it were removed from the law books. A study of the death sentences for rape imposed over a 20-year period in 11 Southern States shows that "among 1,265 cases in which the race of the defendant and the sentence are known, nearly seven times as many blacks were sentenced to death as were whites" and that "black defendants whose victims were white were sentenced to death approximately eighteen times more frequently than defendants in any other racial combination of defendant and victim." Wolfgang & Riedel, *Race, Judicial Discretion and the Death Penalty*, 407 Annals Am. Acad. Pol. & Soc. Sci. 119, 129-130 (1973).

In sum, the death penalty for rape is an outgrowth of both male patriarchal views of women no longer seriously maintained by society, and gross racial injustice created in part out of that patriarchal foundation.

2. Abandoning Black Women. For Black women victimized by sexual violence, rape law has often offered little protection. "During slavery," Professor Angela Harris writes, "the rape of a black woman by any man, white or black, was simply not a crime." For white men, whose legal immunity was deemed obvious, prosecutions never made the law books. One study "found no reported cases . . . in which a white was prosecuted for the rape or attempted rape of a black woman, free or slave." As for Black men, courts often adopted the approach exhibited by the Mississippi High Court of Errors and Appeals in *George v. State*, 37 Miss. 317 (1859). There, the indictment of a Black man accused of raping an enslaved Black girl was dismissed after defense counsel successfully argued that the "crime of rape does not exist in this State between African slaves" because "their intercourse is promiscuous" and "to be regulated by their owners." *Id.* at 320. Likewise, in *Commonwealth v. Mann*, 4 Va. 210 (Va. Gen. Ct. 1820) (per curiam), the court dismissed an indictment against a Black man "because it is no where in the Indictment stated, that *Mary M'Causland,*" the alleged victim, "was a *white* woman." *Id.* at 210. As for those "few places where the rape of a Black woman was technically criminalized," Professor Jeffrey Pokorak notes that "rules of procedure prevented Black women from testifying about their victimization." In fact, as late as 1918, the Florida Supreme Court maintained an explicitly racist presumption that a woman testifying against a man is "chaste" provided that she is "of the Caucasian race." Dallas v. State, 79 So. 690, 691 (Fla. 1918). No such presumption applied to women of what the court called "another race that is largely unmoral." *Id.*[75]

Professor Amia Srinivasan argues that these longstanding historical prejudices are not confined to a distant past, and present multiple challenges for Black women today.

Amia Srinivasan, *The Right to Sex* 13-14 (2021). A study conducted by the center on Poverty and Inequality at Georgetown Law found that Americans of all races tend to see black girls as more sexually knowing and less in need of nurture, protection, and support than white girls the same age. . . . The reality is that black girls and women, in the contemporary U.S. and as compared with white women, are particularly susceptible to certain forms of interpersonal violence . . . .

There is a disturbing genius at work in the white mythology about black sexuality. By portraying black men as rapists and black women as unrapeable . . . the white mythos produces a tension between black men's quest to exonerate themselves and black women's need to speak out against sexual violence, including the violence perpetrated against them by black men. . . . Black women who speak out against black male violence are blamed for reinforcing negative stereotypes of their community and for calling on a racist state to protect them. At the same time, the internalization of the sexually precocious black girl stereotype means that black girls and women are seen by some black men as asking for their abuse. Responding in 2018 to decades of well-documented allegations of rape and abuse, R. Kelly's team issued a statement saying that they would "vigorously resist this attempted public lynching of a black man who has made extraordinary contributions to our culture." Kelly's team did not address the fact that almost all his accusers were black.

3. Data on Race and Prosecutions. Contemporary data show that race continues to condition the penal system's response to sexual assault. Recall Justice Ginsburg's observation back in 1977 (p. 421) that "black defendants whose victims were white" received severe punishments, up to and including death sentences when capital punishment for rape was still lawful, at rates dramatically exceeding "any other racial combination of defendant and victim." According to a systematic review of the academic literature from 1961 to 2016, a similar dynamic remains evident in the data. Looking at cases where "a black defendant was convicted of assaulting a white victim [or] a stranger," the authors find that "black defendants received harsher sentences" than white ones.[76]

The same review, however, reports a more nuanced dynamic when the defendant and alleged victim are of the same race, as is true for most victim-based crimes, for sexual offenses and more broadly. Here, white defendants were more likely to be convicted and "were then more likely to receive harsher and longer sentences as compared to defendants of color." One study within the review posits a few possible explanations for the more lenient treatment of Black defendants in sexual assault cases. First, "prosecutors might be using their discretion to compensate for police bias that leads to discriminatory arrests of minorities for sexual assault. For example, police could be arresting minorities with less evidence of sexual assault, or their arrest charges could be overly severe, resulting in downgrading by the prosecutor." Alternatively, and consistent with the preceding note, it may be that Black female victims are devalued—a conclusion supported by the fact that "the majority of African-American sex offenders" nationwide "were serving time for victimizing White women," even though Black women have a lifetime incidence of rape virtually identical to white women and even though most sexual assault is intraracial.[77]

II.   MENS REA

"[W]omen are . . . violated every day by men who have no idea of the meaning of their acts to women. To them, it is sex."

Catharine A. MacKinnon, *Feminism, Marxism, Method, and the State: Toward Feminist Jurisprudence*, 8 Signs 635, 652-653 (1983)

What should happen if one participant in a sexual encounter believes—or claims to have believed—that the other person consented when that was not actually the case? In the absence of an expressly verbal "yes means yes" rule, which no jurisdiction currently adopts, the possibility for such misunderstandings is real. Should criminal liability attach when they occur? Would exculpating individuals in such circumstances invite defendants to say they thought they had consent even when they knew, or perhaps should have known, they did not?

As a legal matter, these questions implicate the *mens rea* of sexual assault. As we learned in Chapter Four, the *mens rea* requirement can entail different degrees of culpable mental states, ranging from negligence, to recklessness, to knowledge or purpose. It can also be eliminated altogether by imposing strict liability. In the context of sexual assault, the essential question becomes what mental state ought to attach to a defendant's awareness of certain key attendant circumstances. In a statutory rape prosecution, *how sure* should the law require someone be that the person they are having sex with is of legal age? In cases of intoxication, *how sure* should the law require someone be that the person they are having sex with is not unduly impaired? Most fundamentally, *how sure* should the law require someone be that the sex they are having is in fact consensual?

Commonwealth v. Fischer

721 A.2d 1111 (Pa. 1998)

BECK, J. . . . Appellant, an eighteen year-old college freshman, was charged with [sexual assault] in connection with an incident that occurred in a Lafayette College campus dormitory. The victim was another freshman student appellant met at school.

At trial, both the victim and appellant testified that a couple of hours prior to the incident at issue, the two went to appellant's dorm room and engaged in intimate contact. The victim testified that the couple's conduct was limited to kissing and fondling. Appellant, on the other hand, testified that during this initial encounter, he and the victim engaged in "rough sex" which culminated in the victim performing fellatio on him. According to appellant, the victim acted aggressively at this first rendezvous by holding appellant's arms above his head, biting his chest, stating "You know you want me," and initiating oral sex.

After the encounter, the students separated and went to the dining hall with their respective friends. They met up again later and once more found themselves in appellant's dorm room. While their accounts of what occurred at the first meeting contained significant differences, their versions of events at the second meeting were grossly divergent. The victim testified that appellant locked the door, pushed her onto the bed, straddled her, held her wrists above her head and forced his penis into her mouth. She struggled with appellant throughout the entire encounter and warned him that "someone would look for her" and "someone would find out." She also told him that she was scheduled to be at a mandatory seminar and repeatedly stated that she did not want to engage in sex, but her pleas went unheeded.

According to the victim, appellant forced his hands inside a hole in her jeans and penetrated her with his fingers. He then placed his penis inside the torn jeans, removed it and ejaculated on her face, hair and sweater. Thereafter, he turned her over onto her stomach, pulled down her underpants and attempted to penetrate her anally. Throughout the incident, appellant made various statements to the victim, including "I know you want it," "I know you want my dick in your mouth" and "Nobody will know where you are." When the victim attempted to leave, appellant blocked her path. Only after striking him in the groin with her knee was the victim able to escape.

Appellant characterized the second meeting in a far different light. He stated that as he led the victim into his room, she told him it would have to be "a quick one." As a result, appellant figured that their sexual liaison would be brief. Thereafter, according to appellant, he began to engage in the same type of behavior the victim had exhibited in their previous encounter. Appellant admitted that he held the young woman's arms above her head, straddled her and placed his penis at her mouth. He testified that at that point he told her "I know you want my dick in your mouth." When she replied "no," appellant answered "No means yes." After another verbal exchange that included the victim's statement that she had to leave, appellant again insisted that "she wanted it." This time she answered "No, I honestly don't." Upon hearing this, appellant no longer sought to engage in oral sex and removed himself from her body. However, as the two lay side by side on the bed, they continued to kiss and fondle one another.

Appellant admitted to touching the victim's genitalia and to placing his penis inside the hole in her jeans. According to appellant, the victim enjoyed the contact and responded positively to his actions. At some point, however, she stood up and informed appellant that she had to leave. When appellant again attempted to touch her, this time on the thigh, she told him she was "getting pissed." Before appellant could "rearrange himself," so that he could walk the victim to her class, she abruptly left the room.

At trial, both sides presented evidence to support their positions. Appellant's college friends testified that after the first encounter, but before the second, appellant showed them bite marks on his chest that he had received from the victim during the first encounter. Numerous character witnesses testified on appellant's behalf. . . . Medical personnel testified to treating the victim on the night in question. Many of the victim's friends and classmates described her as nervous, shaken and upset after the incident.

Defense counsel argued throughout the trial and in closing that appellant, relying on his previous encounter with the victim, did not believe his actions were taken without her consent. Presenting appellant as sexually inexperienced, counsel argued that his client believed the victim was a willing participant during their intimate encounters. In light of his limited experience and the victim's initially aggressive behavior, argued counsel, appellant's beliefs were reasonable. . . .

The jury returned a verdict of guilty [and the appellant] was sentenced to two to five years in prison. On direct appeal, he retained new counsel [and now] argues that trial counsel provided ineffective assistance in failing to request a jury charge on the defense of mistake of fact. Specifically, appellant claims that counsel should have asked the court to instruct the jurors that if they found appellant reasonably, though mistakenly, believed that the victim was consenting to his sexual advances, they could find him not guilty.

The standard of review for ineffectiveness challenges is clear. . . . Counsel cannot be deemed ineffective for failing to pursue a baseless claim. Further, the quality of counsel's stewardship is based on the state of the law as it existed at time of trial; counsel is not ineffective if he fails to predict future developments or changes in the law.

[The Commonwealth relies primarily on *Commonwealth v. Williams*, 439 A.2d 765 (Pa. Super. 1982).] The facts [of that case] established that the victim accepted a ride from the appellant on a snowy evening in Philadelphia. Instead of taking the young woman to the bus station, appellant drove her to a dark area, threatened to kill her and informed her that he wanted sex. The victim told Williams to "go ahead" because she did not wish to be hurt. [Williams argued] that the trial court erred in refusing to instruct the jury "that if the defendant reasonably believed that the prosecutrix had consented to his sexual advances that this would constitute a defense to the rape . . . charge." This court rejected Williams's claim and held:

> . . . . The charge requested by the defendant is not now and has never been the law of Pennsylvania. . . . *If the element of the defendant's belief as to the victim's state of mind is to be established as a defense to the crime of rape then it should be done by our legislature which has the power to define crimes and offenses. We refuse to create such a defense.*

The Commonwealth insists that under *Williams*, appellant was not entitled to the instruction he now claims trial counsel should have requested.

In response, appellant makes two arguments. First, he argues that the "stranger rape" facts of *Williams* were far different from those of this case, making the case inapplicable. Second, he maintains that the law with respect to rape and sexual assault has changed significantly over the last decade [in ways that make] a mistake of fact instruction in a date rape case a necessity for a fair trial. . . .

Less than one year after [this court's] *Berkowitz* decision, the legislature amended the sexual assault law by adding a definition for forcible compulsion. [The new statute continues to require "compulsion" as an element of sexual assault, but now defines compulsion to include the use "of physical, intellectual, moral, emotional or psychological force, either express or implied."] It is this broader definition, argues appellant in this case, that prompts the necessity for a mistake of fact jury instruction in cases where such a defense is raised. According to appellant: "The language of the present statute inextricably links the issues of consent with *mens rea*. To ask a jury to consider whether the defendant used 'intellectual or moral' force, while denying the instruction as to how to consider the defendant's mental state at the time of alleged encounter is patently unfair to the accused."

Appellant's argument is bolstered by the fact that the concept of "mistake of fact" has long been a fixture in the criminal law. The concept is codified in Pennsylvania and provides, "Ignorance or mistake as to a matter of fact, for which there is reasonable explanation or excuse, is a defense if the ignorance or mistake negatives the intent, knowledge, belief, recklessness, or negligence required to establish a material element of the offense." The notion that one charged with sexual assault may defend by claiming a reasonable belief of consent has [also] been recognized in other jurisdictions. *See In re M.T.S.*, 609 A.2d 1266, 1279 (N.J. 1992). . . .

Appellant's insistence that *Williams* should be disregarded in light of the legislature's broader and more complex definition of forcible compulsion is echoed by the Subcommittee [on Model Jury Instructions]:

> In the opinion of the Subcommittee there may be cases . . . where a defendant might non-recklessly or even reasonably, but wrongly, believe that . . . a non-resisting female is consenting. An example might be "date rape" resulting from mutual misunderstanding. The boy does not intend or suspect the intimidating potential of his vigorous wooing. The girl, misjudging the boy['s] character, believes he will become violent if thwarted; she feigns willingness, even some pleasure. In our opinion the defendant in such a case ought not to be convicted of rape.

. . . . Despite appellant's excellent presentation of the issues, [our case law precludes] relief in this case. . . . We are keenly aware of the differences between *Williams* and this case. Most notable is the fact that Williams and his victim never met before the incident in question. Here, appellant and the victim not only knew one another, but had engaged in intimate contact just hours before the incident in question. It is clear however, that the *Williams* court's basis for denying the jury instruction was its conclusion that the law did not require it and, further, that the judiciary had no authority to grant it. Even if we were to disagree with those conclusions, we are powerless to alter them.

Even if we decide that we are persuaded by appellant's arguments . . . we face a second barrier. Because this appeal raises ineffective assistance of counsel, we are required to find that appellant's trial lawyer made a mistake [by failing] to argue for a change in the law [as set out in *Williams*]. . . . This, of course, is not possible. We simply cannot announce a new rule of law and then find counsel ineffective for failing to predict same. . . . The relief appellant seeks represents a significant departure from the current state of the law. Despite its compelling nature, it cannot be the basis for an ineffective assistance of counsel claim.

Judgment of sentence affirmed.

People v. Sojka

126 Cal. Rptr. 3d 400 (Cal. Ct. App. 2011)

SIGGINS, J. Appellant John Sojka was convicted by a jury of one count of attempted rape by force. He argues that the trial court failed to instruct the jury that he could not be guilty of attempted rape if he reasonably but mistakenly believed the victim consented to intercourse. We agree that the trial court should have instructed on Sojka's mistaken belief in the victim's consent, and that its failure to do so was prejudicial. . . .

Sojka met the victim early one evening in a bar when she was delivering some posters promoting a musical production. The two struck up a conversation and Sojka bought her a beer. One beer led to another and a bit later the two left and went to another bar where they socialized with other patrons, continued drinking, and played pool until about midnight. Over the course of the evening Sojka and the victim were friendly and mildly amorous with one another. They left the bar and Sojka offered to give the victim a ride home. He says that once the two got into his car, they kissed and caressed each other for about 15 minutes. The victim doesn't remember doing so, but recalled being affectionate with Sojka and not at all apprehensive about him. He was feeling good about her, and thought the two might have sex.

Their accounts of what happened once they arrived at the victim's apartment are starkly different. The victim says that she used the bathroom. When she came out, Sojka was completely naked and forced himself on her. She was shocked and froze, but when he did not relent she said "no" and told him not to touch her. Sojka kept advancing on the victim. He removed her clothes, was kissing her all over, digitally penetrated her vagina, performed oral sex on her and tried to force her to perform oral sex on him. She was objecting and resisting the entire time, but did not scream. When Sojka climbed on top of her and attempted intercourse, he finally began to heed the victim's pleas to stop. He again tried to get her to perform oral sex on him, but eventually got up and moved away. He put on his clothes and left the apartment.

Sojka, on the other hand, testified that after the victim came out of the bathroom, the two started kissing, removed each other's clothes and dropped to the floor. He fondled her and performed oral sex on her. She seemed excited, and was moaning a little bit like she was enjoying their foreplay. She did not complain, resist or act like she wanted him to stop. When Sojka climbed on top of the victim to initiate sexual intercourse, she pushed him and yelled at him to stop. He got up, put his clothes on and left the apartment.

The victim was initially in shock and apprehensive about reporting the incident to police. She spent some time talking to her boyfriend and her best friend on the phone, showered and slept for a few hours before calling

911 shortly after 5:00 a.m. She was taken to the hospital by police and examined by a nurse practitioner. She had injuries that were consistent with the story she told to the nurse practitioner about her nonconsensual sex with Sojka. But, with the possible exception of some "fingertip" bruising around one of the victim's knees, all of her injuries could also have arisen from consensual sex. An expert also testified that a woman with the victim's physical characteristics who had consumed the amount of alcohol she reportedly consumed between 5:00 p.m. and midnight would have had approximately a .20 percent blood alcohol level at the time of the assault.

The jury could not reach verdicts on [multiple charges accusing Sojka of forced oral copulation and digital penetration but] Sojka was convicted of attempted rape. . . . He was sentenced to . . . three years in prison. . . .

In *People v. Mayberry*, 542 P.2d 1337 (Cal. 1975), our Supreme Court held that a defendant who entertains a reasonable and good faith, but mistaken, belief that a victim voluntarily consented to intercourse does not have the wrongful intent necessary to be convicted of rape. . . . This defense has both a subjective and objective component. In order to satisfy the subjective component, the defendant "must adduce evidence of the victim's equivocal conduct on the basis of which he erroneously believed there was consent." People v. Williams, 841 P.2d 961, 965 (Cal. 1992). To satisfy the objective component, the defendant must show his belief regarding consent was formed in circumstances society will tolerate as reasonable. When warranted by the evidence, it is error for the court to decline an instruction on the effect of a defendant's reasonable and honest belief in the victim's consent. . . .

Here, the Attorney General argues that because Sojka and the victim gave starkly different accounts of the sexual activity that occurred between them, and the victim was so clear that she resisted Sojka at all turns, there was no basis to conclude the victim's conduct was equivocal. Moreover, says the Attorney General, because Sojka argued that he stopped his advances when the victim rejected his attempt to have intercourse there was no evidence that he misinterpreted the victim's conduct. We disagree on both counts.

We disagree with the Attorney General's first premise because one can only conclude the victim was unequivocally resistant to intercourse by completely disregarding Sojka's testimony. That is not the law. . . .

[As to] the Attorney General's second point . . . it is the events that led to the victim's rejection of Sojka's advance, not her rejection or his cessation, that are material to his possible mistaken belief. Just because he stopped when she said no to intercourse does not make all that went before irrelevant or immaterial to the issue of consent. Sojka testified that it seemed to him the victim was enjoying their foreplay and their sexual activity was mutual. The prosecutor in closing acknowledged that the victim had been affectionate and physically intimate with Sojka. Given the events that occurred over the course of the evening, and Sojka's testimony of what occurred in the victim's apartment, the jury should have been instructed on Sojka's reasonable good faith, but mistaken, belief in her consent to sexual intercourse. . . . If the trial court had a concern that the victim's equivocal conduct or acquiescence in sexual conduct arose only after Sojka overcame her will, the jury could have been further instructed "that a reasonable mistake of fact may not be found if the jury finds that such equivocal conduct on the part of the victim was the product of 'force, violence, duress, menace, or fear. . . .'" *Id.* at 968.

. . . [In closing argument, the prosecution told the jury] that what Sojka was thinking was "irrelevant. Whether he thinks she is consenting is irrelevant, ladies and gentlemen. It is actual consent that's involved here. Did she consent is the issue. Not whether he imagined that she did." . . . The failure to instruct on the potential effect of Sojka's good faith but mistaken belief was prejudicial [and the conviction is reversed].

NOTES AND QUESTIONS

1. Mistaken Consent. In *Fischer*, the court upheld the defendant's conviction even though his jury did not have an opportunity to consider his mistake of fact defense. Because the case was examined through the lens of an ineffective assistance of counsel claim, the court did not directly decide whether the trial court should have permitted the defense. Some courts, however, hold outright that a defendant simply cannot argue he was mistaken as to consent in a sexual assault prosecution. *See, e.g.,* Commonwealth v. Lopez, 745 N.E.2d 961 (Mass. 2001); State v. Reed, 479 A.2d 1291 (Me. 1984). But other states go the other way, adopting an approach in line with the *Sojka* opinion above.

Which approach is more appropriate? Consider the following excerpts.

Catharine A. MacKinnon, *Feminism, Marxism, Method, and the State: Toward Feminist Jurisprudence,* 8 Signs 635, 651-654 (1983). Rape, like many crimes and torts, requires that the accused possess a criminal mind (mens rea) for his acts to be criminal. The man's mental state refers to what he actually understood at the time or to what a reasonable man should have understood under the circumstances. The problem is this: the injury of rape lies in the meaning of the act to its victims, but the standard for its criminality lies in the meaning of the same act to the assailants. Rape is only an injury from women's point of view. It is only a crime from the male point of view, explicitly including that of the accused. . . . What this means doctrinally is that the man's perceptions of the woman's desires often determine whether she is deemed violated. . . . But men are systematically conditioned not even to notice what women want. They may have not a glimmer of women's indifference or revulsion. . . . [I]n whose interest is a law that allows one person's conditioned consciousness to contraindicate another's experienced violation? . . .

But the deeper problem is the rape law's assumption that a single, objective state of affairs existed, one which merely needs to be determined by evidence, when many (maybe even most) rapes involve honest men and violated women. When the reality is split—a woman is raped but not by a rapist?—the law tends to conclude that a rape *did not happen.* To attempt to solve this by adopting the standard of reasonable belief without asking, on a substantive social basis, to whom the belief is reasonable and why—meaning, what conditions make it reasonable—is one-sided: male-sided.

Stephen J. Schulhofer, *Unwanted Sex* **51, 63 (1998).** It might seem too obvious for discussion that consent means consent in the mind of the person who is supposed to be giving it—in this case, the woman. But in a criminal case, the court must decide whether the defendant is at fault. That question—at least as typically posed—returns attention to the man's perspective. . . . The question that should be controlling—what did the woman herself mean?—gets transformed into a question about what he thought she meant. . . .

The core of the problem in assessing consent is not the exceptionally insensitive man who thinks a woman's "no" really means she is burning with desire for him. What makes the gender gap so troublesome is that widely shared assumptions often make it "reasonable" for him to think this. A reasonableness standard gives no content to the requirement of consent and simply allows all the difficult, culturally contentious issues to be resolved case by case, behind closed doors, by police, prosecutors, and juries. [But the] very existence of strongly held but sharply contrasting beliefs, even among women, makes clear that few problems in rape enforcement can be solved by relying on judgments about reasonableness. It is simply not possible, in the present state of American sexual relationships, to have an objective standard of "reasonable" conduct.[78]

Dan M. Kahan, *Culture, Cognition, and Consent: Who Perceives What, and Why, in Acquaintance-Rape Cases,* **158 U. Pa. L. Rev. 729, 783 (2010).** [In our survey (p. 366) based on the facts of *Commonwealth v. Berkowitz* (p. 353),] sixty-three percent [of respondents thought] that "[Berkowitz] believed that [the woman] consented to sexual intercourse," and 46% agreed that "given all the circumstances, it would have been reasonable for [him] to believe [she] consented to sexual intercourse."

Douglas N. Husak & George C. Thomas III, *Date Rape, Social Convention & Reasonable Mistakes,* **11 Law & Phil. 95, 123, 125 (1992).** A single physical rejection (for example, [a woman] moves [a man's] hand from her leg) following hours of intense foreplay obviously presents a very different picture of nonconsent than repeated physical and verbal rejections, delivered in an emotional and frightened manner. At some point along this spectrum, it is no longer reasonable for [the man] to think that [the woman] has consented. . . . [Social conventions defining consent provide] the vehicle through which [a man] interprets the words or actions of [a woman]. Until we more fully understand the social convention about consent to have sex, any judgment about the reasonableness of a mistake about consent is fragile. . . .

[T]he evidence suggests a convention [may now exist that could] produce somewhat frequent mistakes of fact about a woman's consent. If so, and if the reformers succeed in restricting or eliminating the mistake-of-fact defense, some men will be convicted of rape even though they had reason to believe that consent had been given. Some might welcome this result. [O]ne might believe that it is more important to seek to change the social convention or to send a symbolic message than to do justice in an individual case. But if one believes that the criminal law should seek to apply the just result in particular cases, men whose belief in consent is consistent with the social convention seem unlikely candidates for convictions of a serious felony.

Amia Srinivasan, *The Right to Sex* 20-22 (2021). How many men are truly unable to distinguish between wanted and unwanted sex, between welcome and "gross" behavior, between decency and degradation? . . . It is true that women have always lived in a world created by men and governed by men's rules. But it is also true that men have always lived alongside women who have contested these rules. For much of human history their dissent has been private and unsystematic: flinching, struggling, leaving, quitting. More recently it has been public and organized. Those who insist that men aren't in a position to know better are in denial of what men have seen and heard. Men have chosen not to listen because it has suited them not to do so, because the norms of masculinity dictate that their pleasure takes priority, because all around them other men have been doing the same. The rules that have really changed, and are still changing, do not so much concern what is right or wrong in sex: women have been telling men the truth about that, one way or another, for a very long time. [What has] really changed . . . is that they can no longer be confident [that] no consequences will follow.

2. Strict Liability. Note that to reject a mistake of fact defense as to consent is in effect to adopt a strict liability rule. A defendant in such a regime will be guilty of sexual assault if he has sex with someone who did not consent, *no matter how reasonable it might have been* to think otherwise. Recall the debates about strict liability encountered in the context of the felony murder rule (p. 233). Does strict liability seem more appropriate in the context of a sexual offense? If so, ought it apply to other attendant circumstances beyond consent, such as a person's age or state of intoxication? Consider the following cases.

Garnett v. State, 632 A.2d 797 (Md. 1993). Maryland's "statutory rape" law prohibiting sexual intercourse with an underage person [reads as follows]: "A person is guilty of rape in the second degree if the person engages in vaginal intercourse with another person . . . who is under 14 years of age and the person performing the act is at least four years older than the victim." . . .

Raymond Lennard Garnett is a young retarded man. At the time of the incident in question he was 20 years old. He has an I.Q. of 52. His guidance counselor from the Montgomery County public school system, Cynthia Parker, described him as a mildly retarded person who read on the third-grade level, did arithmetic on the 5th-grade level, and interacted with others socially at school at the level of someone 11 or 12 years of age. Ms. Parker added that Raymond attended special education classes and for at least one period of time was educated at home when he was afraid to return to school due to his classmates' taunting. Because he could not understand the duties of the jobs given him, he failed to complete vocational assignments; he sometimes lost his way to work. As Raymond was unable to pass any of the State's functional tests required for graduation, he received only a certificate of attendance rather than a high-school diploma.

In November or December 1990, a friend introduced Raymond to Erica Frazier, then aged 13; the two subsequently talked occasionally by telephone. On February 28, 1991, Raymond, apparently wishing to call for a ride home, approached the girl's house at about nine o'clock in the evening. Erica opened her bedroom window, through which Raymond entered; he testified that "she just told me to get a ladder and climb up her window." The two talked, and later engaged in sexual intercourse. Raymond left at about 4:30 a.m. the following morning. On November 19, 1991, Erica gave birth to a baby, of which Raymond is the biological father.

. . . At trial, the defense twice proffered evidence to the effect that Erica herself and her friends had previously told Raymond that she was 16 years old, and that he had acted with that belief. The trial court excluded such evidence as immaterial, explaining: "[T]he only two requirements as relate to this case are that there was vaginal intercourse, and that Ms. Frazier was under 14 years of age and that Mr. Garnett was at least four years older than she. . . . The victim's representation as to her age and the defendant's belief, if it existed, that she was not under age, what amounts to what otherwise might be termed a good faith defense, is in fact no defense to what amounts to statutory rape. It is in the Court's opinion a strict liability offense."

. . . Raymond [argues] that the criminal law exists to assess and punish morally culpable behavior [and] says such culpability was absent here. He asks us either to engraft onto [the statute] an implicit *mens rea* requirement, or to recognize an affirmative defense of reasonable mistake as to the complainant's age [on the ground] that it is unjust, under the circumstances of this case . . . to brand him a felon and rapist.

. . . Statutory rape laws are often justified on the "lesser legal wrong" theory or the "moral wrong" theory; by such reasoning, the defendant acting without *mens rea* nonetheless deserves punishment for having committed a lesser crime, fornication, or for having violated moral teachings that prohibit sex outside of marriage. Maryland has no law against fornication. It is not a crime in this state. . . . If the perpetrator participates in a mutual act of sexual intercourse, believing his partner to be beyond the age of consent, with reasonable grounds for such belief . . . he has not consciously taken any risk. Instead he has subjectively eliminated the risk by satisfying himself on reasonable evidence that the crime cannot be committed. If it occurs that he has been misl[e]d, we cannot realistically conclude for such reason alone the intent with which he undertook the act suddenly becomes more heinous. . . .

We think it sufficiently clear, however, that Maryland's second degree rape statute defines a strict liability offense that does not require the State to prove *mens rea;* it makes no allowance for a mistake-of-age defense. The plain language of [the statute] viewed in its entirety, and the legislative history of its creation lead to this conclusion. . . . This interpretation is consistent with the traditional view of statutory rape as a strict liability crime designed to protect young persons from the dangers of sexual exploitation by adults, loss of chastity, physical injury, and, in the case of girls, pregnancy. The majority of states retain statutes which impose strict liability for sexual acts with underage complainants. . . . Any new provision introducing an element of *mens rea,* or permitting a defense of reasonable mistake of age, with respect to the offense of sexual intercourse with a person less than 14, should properly result from an act of the Legislature itself, rather than judicial fiat. Until then, defendants in extraordinary cases, like Raymond, will rely upon the tempering discretion of the trial court at sentencing.

Commonwealth v. Blache, 880 N.E.2d 736 (Mass. 2008). On August 17, 2000, the complainant, who was twenty-six years old, went out with a female friend to a bar. . . . Before leaving home at around 7 p.m., the complainant smoked marijuana and took an antianxiety medication called Klonopin. She had not eaten any food all day. The complainant had "a couple" of alcoholic drinks at the first bar she visited, and drank "a lot" at a second bar, where she spent the latter part of the evening. Between 11:30 p.m. and midnight, the complainant [became] "very drunk," and she had only intermittent memories of the remainder of the evening. When the group left the bar shortly before it closed, the complainant was "causing a scene," was argumentative, had difficulty walking, and fell twice.

The complainant's friend took her keys to drive her . . . to [his] house in Methuen [where she] continued to behave belligerently. She attempted to leave . . . but drove her truck into [the] fence and then backed up into the house itself, at which point [the friend] telephoned the police [and] told them he needed assistance with an unwanted and very intoxicated female guest. Before the police arrived, the complainant returned to the house and "passed out" for some time.

The Methuen police dispatched the defendant, Officer David Blache, to respond to the call. . . . When the defendant arrived, the complainant woke up [but] was "still drunk" . . . . The defendant spent about forty-five minutes at the house gathering information for an accident report and arranging for the complainant's truck to be towed. During this time, according to [multiple witnesses,] the complainant exhibited sexually aggressive behavior toward the defendant. She touched him, tried to kiss him and "grab his crotch," asked him if he wanted to have sex with her, licked the windows of his police cruiser, and pulled down her pants to show the defendant her genitals. Witnesses also testified that at this time she was still drunk; she slurred her speech; and she pulled down her pants and began to urinate in the street . . . . [T]he defendant . . . allowed the complainant to sit in the front seat of his cruiser because she was cold; after she twice turned on the cruiser's lights and siren, he transferred her to the back seat.

[T]he defendant obtained permission from police headquarters to transport [the complainant to her] home . . . because she did not have enough money to pay for a taxi. [According to the complainant,] the next thing she remembered was the car pulling up next to a dumpster. Once the car stopped, [she testified that] the defendant opened the driver's side rear door, pulled down [her] pants, and vaginally raped her in the back seat of the cruiser. She testified that she told him she "didn't want to do that," and tried to kick the defendant and the partition between the front and rear seats, but she was unable to open the opposite door because there was no interior handle. She further testified that the defendant then drove her home, and when he dropped her off he warned her that the police have a "code of silence" and they would not believe her.

The defendant also testified at trial. He admitted having intercourse with the complainant, but he claimed that it was consensual and occurred at her house. According to the defendant, he dropped the complainant at home and cleared the call with headquarters, then he knocked on her door and asked to use her bathroom. He testified that when he emerged from the bathroom, the complainant was completely naked; they embraced, she performed oral sex on him, and they had consensual intercourse on her couch.

Although the complainant did not remember making any telephone calls after she returned home, the prosecutor played recordings of two 911 calls she placed to the Haverhill police. Additionally, [one of her friends] testified that he answered two calls from the complainant . . . about one-half hour after the complainant had left with the defendant. In the first call, she said in a "bragging" or "sarcastic" tone, "Tell Dave [[(the friend whose fence she drove into)]] thanks for the best fuck of my life," and hung up. In the second call, a few minutes later, she said, "Tell Dave I'm going to go for the whole rape thing," and hung up.

[A] vaginal swab taken from the complainant as part of [a rape kit] examination contained sperm cells [that] matched a blood sample submitted by the defendant. Sperm was also detected in a stain on the zipper area of the defendant's uniform pants but not in the back seat of the cruiser. The complainant's blood was drawn at 7:30 a.m. . . . . [A] toxicology expert testified that [based on extrapolation,] the complainant's blood alcohol level at 2:30 to 3 a.m. would have been between 0.176 and 0.24 per cent, a level that typically causes disorientation, loss of judgment, impaired perception, lethargy, imbalance, slurred speech, loss of memory, impaired comprehension, and confusion.

. . . . It is a matter of common knowledge that there are many levels of intoxication, and the fact of intoxication, by itself, does not necessarily mean that the individual in question is incapable of deciding whether to assent to a sexual encounter. The question instead is whether, as a result of the complainant's consumption of drugs, alcohol, or both, she was unable to give or refuse consent. . . .

[There must] also be proof that the defendant knew or should have known of the complainant's incapacity to consent. . . . Massachusetts has not recognized the "defense" of mistake of fact in rape cases generally. But . . . a primary rationale for [that] rule [is that] in cases where the complainant has the capacity to consent[, our state's law requires a showing of the] use of force or threat of bodily injury [to establish the crime of rape.] [P]roof of that element of force should negate any possible mistake as to consent. [H]owever, in [cases of incapacity] the prosecution is not required to prove the use of force[, so] the possibility of a defendant's reasonable mistake about the complainant's consent could increase, creating the potential for injustice if no instruction concerning the defendant's honest and reasonable belief as to the complainant's consent were given.

The judge's instructions in this case . . . failed to address the issue of the defendant's awareness of the complainant's possible incapacity. [At a] retrial, if the complainant's capacity to consent is again at issue, the defendant will be entitled to an instruction that, in order to sustain a conviction on a theory of incapacity to consent, the Commonwealth must prove that the defendant knew or reasonably should have known that the complainant's condition rendered her incapable of consenting.

3. Recklessness or Negligence. Among the states that recognize a mistake of fact defense, two distinct approaches have emerged. The first embraces a negligence standard, permitting liability when the defendant reasonably should have known that consent to sex was lacking. Some states have set the bar higher, requiring the state to prove that the defendant was at least reckless with respect to the nonexistence of consent—meaning that he was *aware* of the risk that consent was absent. *See, e.g.,* Reynolds v. State, 664 P.2d 621 (Alaska Ct. App. 1983); State v. Koonce, 731 S.W.2d 431 (Mo. Ct. App. 1987). This recklessness standard is thought by its adherents "to protect the defendant against conviction . . . where the circumstances regarding consent are ambiguous." *Reynolds,* 664 P.2d at 625.

The arguments for one or the other standard mirror debates about negligence and recklessness in the criminal law more broadly. "The traditional argument against negligence liability," Professor Susan Estrich observes, "is that punishment should be limited to cases of choice, that it is unjust to punish a man for his stupidity and ineffective in deterrence terms. According to this view, a man should be held responsible only for what he does knowingly, or purposely, or at least aware of the risks involved." And yet, Estrich continues, turning to the arguments in favor of a negligence rule, "[t]he man who has the inherent capacity to act reasonably but fails to has, through that failure, made a blameworthy choice for which he can justly be punished." The negligent man charged with rape is the man "who could have done better but did not; could have paid attention, but did not." Negligence liability thus "provides an additional motive to men to 'take care before acting,'" Estrich argues. Such a rule, moreover, would parallel the law of criminal homicide, which "has long punished unreasonable action which leads to the loss of human life as manslaughter." The harm associated with sexual violation "is sufficiently great," Estrich concludes, "to justify negligence liability for rape as for killing."[79]

III.   CONFRONTING CREDIBILITY

> "I know two men who were, I am fairly confident, falsely accused of rape. . . . I know many more than two women who have been raped."
>
>   Amia Srinivasan, *The Right to Sex* 1-2 (2021)

If the law broadly prohibits unwanted sex—adopting, for example, an affirmative consent *actus reus* and strict liability with respect to the defendant's *mens rea*—the primary remaining defense strategy for lawyers representing people accused of sexual assault will be factual. Despite what the complaining witness may have subsequently told police, prosecutors, or the jury, skilled defenders will argue, at the time of the alleged incident she consented. The rape allegation, they will say, is false. In fact, in most of the cases we have seen in this chapter, some version of this dynamic has been evident. Recall how many times an opinion's recitation of the facts presented competing versions of the underlying events—a so-called "he said, she said" exchange, in which he said she said yes.

For lawyers tasked with litigating and adjudicating cases in a system dedicated to due process and dependent on the adversarial presentation of facts, this inescapable aspect of sexual assault prosecutions can present a challenge. "Some men are falsely accused of rape," Professor Amia Srinivasan writes; "there is nothing to be gained by denying it." According to the National Registry of Exonerations, which tracks people who have been fully exonerated after having spent time in prison, eleven percent of all exonerations recorded since 1989 have been of people falsely convicted of sexual assault. Consistent with the history and racial legacies discussed earlier (p. 417), these convictions are disproportionately concentrated among Black defendants. "Fifty-nine percent of sexual assault exonerees are Black," researchers report, a statistic that suggests "innocent Black people are almost eight times more likely than white people to be falsely convicted of rape." And for every person who is formally exonerated, there are more who were falsely convicted but cannot establish their innocence.[80]

And yet, as Professor Srinivasan goes on to say, "false accusations are rare." Surely they are less common than the instances in which a false-allegation defense is advanced. Still, that defense can sometimes succeed in exculpating people who are in fact guilty in part because it trades on some of the very myths, tropes, or biases that have long invited jurors—of all genders—to doubt the veracity of women, especially women who act in certain ways or who come from certain backgrounds. Recall here Kate Harding's definition of rape culture (p. 361) as "a culture where we always identify with the person who's accused of rape instead of identifying with the victim" and where "the suspicion falls on the person who reported the rape. It's a culture where we believe a lot of rape myths . . . ."[81]

For these reasons, anti-rape activists have long worked to cabin and combat challenges to women's credibility in sexual assault prosecutions. As we have seen (p. 403), one of the main goals of the 1970s rape-law reform effort was to enact rape shield laws that limited defense lawyers' ability to question complaining witnesses, in an effort to bar what advocates called the "second victimization" of cross-examination at trial. More recently, activists of the #MeToo era have popularized another rallying cry that captures the core of the argument: #BelieveWomen.[82]

A challenge, perhaps uniquely felt by lawyers, is how to square these important efforts with some key tenets of the criminal legal system. In the United States, as in many other countries, "[t]he principle that there is a presumption of innocence in favor of the accused is the undoubted law, axiomatic and elementary, and its enforcement lies at the foundation of the administration of our criminal law." Coffin v. United States, 156 U.S. 432, 453 (1895). Consistent with that principle, Americans frequently quote with approval William Blackstone's famous assertion that "it is better that ten guilty persons escape, than that one innocent suffer."[83]

Ought this precept apply when the accusation is rape? Or should the procedural and constitutional safeguards that generally apply to criminal prosecutions be relaxed or eliminated in this context? Consider the case and materials that follow.

State v. Stephen F.

188 P.3d 84 (N.M. 2008)

BOSSON, J. This appeal implicates two competing interests—an accused's constitutional right to confront witnesses against him, and the State's interest, as expressed in our rape shield statute and corresponding rule of evidence, in protecting those witnesses from unwarranted intrusions on their privacy. . . .

On the night in question, Stephen F., who was then fifteen, and B.G., who was sixteen, engaged in sexual intercourse. Stephen, a long-time friend of B.G.'s brother, was spending the night at her family's house, as he often did. B.G., Stephen, and her brother shared an alcoholic beverage while they watched a movie in her bedroom. After initially leaving her bedroom to sleep on the living room couch, Stephen came back to her room and, according to B.G., forced her to engage in oral, vaginal, and anal sex. Stephen then left her room, and spent the rest of the night in the living room. In the morning, B.G. told her mother that Stephen had raped her.

There is no dispute that Stephen and B.G. engaged in sexual intercourse. Stephen's sole defense was that B.G. consented, and then fabricated the rape allegation to avoid being punished by her parents. Stephen based his defense on B.G.'s deposition testimony. During the deposition, B.G. explained that her parents are opposed to premarital sex because of their deeply held religious convictions. Significantly, B.G. also explained that she had previously been punished when her parents learned from her brother that she had engaged in consensual sex with someone else. To establish a motive to lie about the present event, Stephen wanted to cross-examine B.G. about this prior incident.

[Evidentiary] Rule 11-413 provides: "evidence of the victim's past sexual conduct, opinion evidence thereof or of reputation for past sexual conduct shall not be admitted unless, and only to the extent that the court finds, that evidence of the victim's past sexual conduct is material and relevant to the case and that its inflammatory or prejudicial nature does not outweigh its probative value." . . . Stephen argued that he had a right under the Sixth Amendment to the United States Constitution . . . to cross-examine B.G. and reveal her motive to lie. The trial court . . . prohibited Stephen from cross-examining B.G. or any other witness, such as her parents, about the prior sexual encounter, finding "specifically that the prejudicial aspects of this would greatly outweigh the probative value." . . .

A defendant's "right to confront and to cross-examine is not absolute and may, in appropriate cases, bow to accommodate other legitimate interests in the criminal trial process." Chambers v. Mississippi, 410 U.S. 284, 295 (1973). However, a court's decision to restrict a defendant's ability to confront a witness, even when based on legitimate state interests, "calls into question the ultimate integrity of the fact-finding process and requires that the competing interest be closely examined." *Id.* . . . Thus, "[a] defendant's right of confrontation—with its protection of the right to cross-examine, test credibility, detect bias, and otherwise challenge an opposing version of facts—is a critical limitation on the trial court's discretion to exclude evidence a defendant wishes to admit." State v. Johnson, 944 P.2d 869, 876 (N.M. 1997). . . .

[In this case, the trial court allowed the defense] to question B.G. and her family about their religious convictions . . . . [But by] limiting Stephen's cross-examination to B.G.'s religious convictions [alone], the trial court effectively foreclosed Stephen's ability to establish a motive for B.G. to fabricate the rape allegation. To establish that motive, Stephen needed to show that B.G. had a reason to fear punishment. To do so, it was necessary that Stephen have the ability to [show] that she had been punished previously. [B]ecause he was limited to questioning B.G. solely about her family's religious convictions, Stephen's argument that B.G. had a motive to lie became groundless and ineffective.

. . . . Our conclusion is supported by *Davis v. Alaska*, 415 U.S. 308 (1974) . . . . Just as in the instant appeal, the trial court [in that case] allowed the defendant to question the witness about his bias [to testify in a way that helped the state], but without the benefit of backing up the defendant's theory of bias with [evidence from] the witness's juvenile record [showing that the witness was on probation and could face punishment if he displeased the authorities. A state statute made juvenile records confidential, but the] U.S. Supreme Court [nonetheless] concluded that the limited cross-examination that the court permitted ran afoul of the defendant's constitutional right to confront witnesses against him. . . .

Similarly, in this case, . . . to ensure that Stephen had the opportunity to effectively cross-examine B.G., he should have been allowed to challenge B.G.'s allegation that he raped her. He could only do so with her testimony and the testimony of her parents about the consequences that resulted from her prior consensual sexual experience. By prohibiting Stephen from so doing, the trial court deprived the jury of vital information and had the effect of stripping Stephen of his only defense.

NOTES AND QUESTIONS

1. Rape Culture as Law. Rape shield laws were enacted in part to combat a set of legal rules that once operated in the opposite direction, expressly instructing jurors to regard women with skepticism and to scrutinize their allegations of rape more closely than other criminal accusations. As discussed earlier in this chapter (p. 365), the force requirement itself was premised in part on the prevailing assumption that women frequently fabricated rape charges to exact revenge when scorned or to exculpate themselves when caught engaging in consensual extramarital sex. But the law of evidence made the point even more explicitly. Consider, by way of illustration, a portion of the court's opinion in *In re M.T.S.* (p. 371) not previously excerpted:

> [A] host of evidentiary rules and standards of proof distinguished the legal treatment of rape from the treatment of other crimes. Many jurisdictions held that a rape conviction could not be sustained if based solely on the uncorroborated testimony of the victim. Often judges added cautionary instructions to jury charges warning jurors that rape was a particularly difficult charge to prove. Courts in New Jersey allowed greater latitude in cross-examining rape victims and in delving into their backgrounds than in ordinary cases. Rape victims were required to make a prompt complaint or have their allegations rejected or viewed with great skepticism. Some commentators suggested that there be mandatory psychological testing of rape victims.

609 A.2d 1266, 1272-1273 (N.J. 1992). As the reporters of the MPC revision project note, most American jurisdictions have done away with these evidentiary rules, though a handful still employ corroboration requirements or cautionary instructions in cases in which a complainant's testimony exhibits "material inconsistencies," is "inherently incredible," or involves "other special circumstances" such as mental impairments.[84]

2. #BelieveWomen and Due Process. How ought we think of the relationship between efforts to combat longstanding sociolegal skepticism of rape victims on the one hand and the legal system's presumption of innocence and commitment to due process on the other? Consider the following excerpts.

Michelle J. Anderson, *Diminishing the Legal Impact of Negative Social Attitudes Toward Acquaintance Rape Victims*, 13 New Crim. L. Rev. 644, 657 (2010). [R]ape law traditionally insisted that the sexual history of a woman who alleged that she was raped was relevant to the truth of her allegation. A chaste woman was considered more likely to have resisted the defendant's sexual advances and to have lodged a legitimate claim of rape. By contrast, an unchaste woman was considered more likely to have succumbed willingly to the defendant's sexual advances and to have lied about it later. . . . Embedded within rape law, therefore, was an informal, though powerful, normative command that women must maintain an ideal of sexual abstinence to obtain legal protection, an implicit chastity requirement . . . [that enforced] moral judgments on women's sexual lives. . . . Women deserve to have the criminal law vindicate them when they are raped, even if they have been previously unchaste or promiscuous with the defendant or with others. By engaging in significant sexual behavior, a woman should not have to assume the risk that men will violate her sexual autonomy. It should not matter whether a woman is a virgin or a so-called "whore" before the law: she deserves to be treated with legal respect, regardless of her sexual past.

Susan Estrich, *Palm Beach Stories*, 11 Law & Phil. 5, 11-14 (1992). No myth is more powerful in the tradition of rape law than the myth of the lying woman: the spurned lover who seeks revenge; the deflowered virgin who refuses to assume responsibility for her sexual activities; the vicious and spiteful woman who would lie about a rape charge. Of course, women do on occasion fabricate rape charges—and when it happens, it is trumpeted on tabloid television. . . . But no study has ever found that women lie about rape any more frequently than men lie about other crimes. . . . Still, this male rape fantasy of being falsely charged with rape lives on. . . . [And] [p]recisely because it is all but impossible these days to argue successfully that no means yes, or that . . . stupidity as to consent should serve as a defense, men charged with rape, and those who defend them, have few options but to argue the incredibility of the woman victim. [T]he argument has appeal, I think, because many people, including many prosecutors and judges, remain ambivalent about the expansion of rape liability: unwilling to continue to afford men the privilege of aggression, but also chary with their sympathy for women who should know better. So the old myths of the lying woman are reasserted. . . . Thus, we face a new stage in the changing realities of rape law—a final battle, one hopes, in the effort to expand liability to include date rape and acquaintance rape. The debate is less and less about what counts as force, or what is required to prove nonconsent. Today's debate, on the radio, in the newspaper, and in the courtroom, is about when women should be believed.

Bennett Capers, *Real Women, Real Rape*, 60 U.C.L.A. L. Rev. 826, 855-856, 858-859, 863-864, 866, 871 (2013). On one level, rape shield laws communicate that a complainant's sexual history with other individuals is irrelevant . . . a sentiment that many advocates of rape shield laws would support. But rape shield laws also communicate . . . that sexual history matters so much that it must be concealed, corseted, and locked away. Put differently, removing sexual history from the courtroom does more than simply render sexual history irrelevant. It privileges chastity, or something like chastity. Indeed, by pushing for rape shield laws, feminists have inadvertently legitimized the very chastity requirement they found so troubling. . . . Rape shield law's contribution to the feminist agenda is not the subversion of the law's preference for good girls but rather a sleight of hand . . . . The complainant, by virtue of the rape shield laws, becomes a woman without a sexual past—a virtual virgin, a virgin anew, or at least a good girl anew. . . .

[But there is] a related problem with rape shield laws. . . . While young, demure, white women may fit easily into the stock type of the victim, the damsel in distress, or the good girl, and thus receive some benefit from rape shield's protections, women who do not fit this description are likely to find jurors applying different default assumptions. . . . [J]urors in a case involving an Asian complainant may view her as "exotically sexual [and] willingly submissive," while jurors in a case involving a Hispanic woman may view her as hot blooded, "wanton and promiscuous" . . . . [O]ur law's history of treating black women as negligible is so long [and even today] stereotypes about black women and their sexuality continue to affect juror decision-making. . . . [T]he expressive message of rape shield laws is likely ineffective when it comes to other victims as well: older women, single women, overweight women, poor women, working women, unattractive women, gay or transgender women, and even male victims. . . . [R]ape shield laws might be good for cardboard cutout women, ideal women, imaginary women, and women who can play the part, but not for the rest of us.

Aya Gruber, *The Feminist War on Crime* 138-141 (2020). Criminal litigation is undoubtedly stressful to victims. From rape exams to subpoenas and cross-examinations, victims endure unpleasant, adversarial, time-consuming processes . . . . The most aggressive assaults on defendants' due process rights will not fully eradicate litigation's costs to victims, and the fact that rapists face long jail terms means that even the most conservative pro-incarceration jurists cannot make rape trials rubber stamps. . . . [A]ttorneys must test the credibility of every witness, even if people generally tell the truth in court. Prosecutors and defenders "impeach" adverse witnesses [in every criminal case] by probing their pre- and post-event behavior, bringing up contradictory statements, highlighting memory failures, and the like. The rape victim is the prime prosecution witness to the crime. It would be defense malpractice not to ask questions like "If he raped you, why did you tell your boyfriend nothing happened?"; "How do you remember the rape when you were too drunk to remember any other details of the night?"; and "Why did you keep hanging out with a rapist?" No doubt, feminists look at these questions as "rapey," victim-blaming inquisitions. However, if rape trial processes stray from typical credibility testing only for rape victims, it amounts to a presumption that rape complaints are invariably true, otherwise known as a presumption of guilt.

Amia Srinivasan, *The Right to Sex* 5, 9-11 (2021). In 2007, Carolyn Bryant admitted that she had lied, fifty-two years earlier, when she said that a fourteen-year-old black boy named Emmett Till had grabbed and sexually propositioned her—a lie that spurred Bryant's husband, Roy, and his brother to abduct, bludgeon, shoot, and kill Till. . . . For many women of color, the mainstream feminist injunction "Believe women" and its online correlate #IBelieveHer raise more questions than they settle. Whom are we to believe, the white woman who says she was raped, or the black or brown woman who insists that her son is being set up? Carolyn Bryant or Mamie Till?

Defenders of "men's rights" like to say that "Believe women" violates the presumption of innocence. But this is a category error. The presumption of innocence is a legal principle: it answers our sense that it is worse, all else being equal, for the law to wrongly punish than to wrongly exonerate. It is for this reason that in most legal systems the burden of proof rests with the accuser, not the accused. "Believe women" is not an injunction to abandon this legal principle [but rather] a political response to what we suspect will be its uneven application. . . . [It] operates as a corrective norm, a gesture of support for these people—women—whom the law tends to treat as if they were lying. . . . The presumption of innocence does not tell us what to believe. It tells us how guilt is to be established by the law: that is, by a process that deliberately stacks the deck in favor of the accused. Harvey Weinstein had a right to the presumption of innocence when he stood trial. But for those of us not serving on his jury, there was no duty to presume him innocent or to "suspend judgment" before the verdict was in. . . . [T]he norms of law do not set the norms of rational belief.

CHAPTER 6

THEFT, NECESSITY, AND WHITE-COLLAR CRIME

"[T]o achieve proper self-development—to be a person—an individual needs some control over resources in the external environment."

Margaret Jane Radin, *Property and Personhood*,
34 Stan. L. Rev. 957, 957 (1982)

INTRODUCTION

The ability to acquire, produce, and sell property is a central element of life in a modern capitalist society. And law is central to property itself. It defines the boundaries of ownership interests, the rights that flow from them, the means by which they are generated, and the manner in which they can be transferred.

All of this and more is covered in another class: Property (of course). But criminal law plays an important, complementary role, in several ways. Most directly, it is the enforcement mechanism for a number of property rights. Someone who takes another person's property without permission has committed the crime of theft; someone who enters another person's property without permission has committed the crime of trespass. Criminal law also does work to bolster the integrity of the markets in which property is exchanged. Someone who lies in an effort to manipulate that market might be guilty of fraud; someone who seeks to gain an unfair advantage in public markets by using nonpublic information might be guilty of insider trading; competitors who collude to inflate market prices might be guilty of price fixing. Finally, the institutions and systems of criminal law enforcement—including police, prosecutors, and prisons—can themselves be conceived in part as economic actors. Someone who is arrested, convicted, and sent to prison by such actors will be removed from the free labor market and transferred into a separate, penal labor market; upon conviction, that person will often be required to pay money to the state in the form of criminal fines that (much like taxes) could be used to fund large portions of local government operations; and the conviction will mark its recipient within the free labor market as ineligible for some future forms of employment.

In these respects, the relationship between criminal law and the economy underscores a theme seen in prior chapters. Criminal law is produced by the society that enacts it and can thus both reflect and reinforce existing social hierarchies. As we have seen in prior chapters, some of these hierarchies are organized along racial and gender lines. Socioeconomic class, as we will see in this chapter, plays a similar and oftentimes compounding role.

Our goal in these pages is not to delve deeply into the doctrinal definitions and frameworks of the myriad property-based and financial crimes on the books across jurisdictions, topics that are generally covered in advanced classes on federal criminal law or white-collar crime. Rather, our goal is to examine in broad strokes the ways in which criminal law and the penal system interact with people accused of property-related and financial crimes in two different strata of the country's socioeconomic system: the bottom, and the top. We begin in Part I with an introduction to the law of theft, with a focus on how this law relates to conditions of poverty. We then turn in Part II to the law of necessity, with a focus on arguments that economic necessity ought to be a defense to criminal liability. Finally, we conclude in Part III with a discussion of white-collar crime and doctrines related to criminal liability for corporations and corporate officers.

I.   PUNISHING THEFT

"There is no better way to understand the relation between the development of capitalist legal institutions and the changing contours of the right of property than by studying the cases of those charged with stealing."

Michael E. Tigar, *The Right of Property and the Law of Theft*,
62 Tex. L. Rev. 1443 (1984)

People convicted of property crimes—including theft, fraud, burglary, and robbery—account for approximately one fifth of the incarcerated population. At the same time, looking at the incarcerated population as a whole, more than half of people in prison earned less than $38,000 per year before being incarcerated. To put this number in perspective, the federal Bureau of Justice Statistics has found that "82 percent of felony defendants in large state courts" are too poor to afford a lawyer. Consider these statistics while reading the case and materials that follow.[1]

People v. Johnson
160 N.E.3d 31 (Ill. 2019)

THOMAS, J. . . . . Defendant was charged . . . with one count of burglary and one count of retail theft. The burglary count alleged that on July 22,

2014, defendant, "without authority, knowingly entered a building of Wal-Mart . . . with the intent to commit therein a theft." The retail theft count alleged that defendant stole from Walmart various items of merchandise with a total value of less than $300.

The evidence presented at trial, including eyewitness testimony and video surveillance footage, showed that defendant and an accomplice entered the Walmart's vestibule area, placed two backpacks on top of a coin-exchange machine, and then entered the store. Inside, a customer observed the two men walking around with what looked like clothes in their hands and "veering off" when approached. Eventually, the two men returned to the vestibule area separately, each retrieving one of the backpacks from the top of the coin-exchange machine. They then met near some vending machines outside the building. The customer, who was by this time in the parking lot, saw defendant keeping a lookout as the other man removed items from his shirt and pants and stuffed them into one of the backpacks.

As the customer called the police, defendant and the other man returned to the vestibule, again placed their backpacks on top of the coin-exchange machine, and then reentered the store. Defendant later returned to the vestibule area alone, retrieved one of the backpacks from the coin-exchange machine, and exited the store. By this time, three police officers had arrived. [One] officer asked defendant if he had stolen items from Walmart, and defendant admitted that he had. The officers then escorted defendant to the store manager's office, where defendant removed from his backpack or person 14 purchasable items of girl's clothing with a total retail value of $76.91. Defendant stated that he had taken the items to give to his daughter. . . .

The jury returned verdicts finding defendant guilty of burglary and not guilty of retail theft. At sentencing, it was determined that burglary is generally a Class 2 felony with a sentencing range of 3 to 7 years but defendant was subject to a sentencing range of 6 to 30 years due to his criminal history. Defendant's lengthy criminal history included three separate convictions for robbery in 1987, burglary in 1992, separate theft and burglary convictions in 1994, resisting a peace officer in 1998, residential burglary in 1999, possession of cannabis in 2006, a conviction in 2007 for altering a lottery ticket for which he was sentenced to five years in prison in Iowa, convictions for assault and resisting a peace officer in 2009, and another resisting a peace officer conviction in 2012. The prosecutor noted that by his calculations defendant had been sentenced to 36 years in prison in all since 1987, yet he was only 44 years old at the time of sentencing in the present case. The prosecutor argued that defendant had never led a law-abiding life and that he continually commits offenses when he is released . . . . The State therefore recommended a 15-year, extended-term sentence. The trial court considered defendant's lengthy criminal history and the conduct involved in the instant offense, including its nonviolent nature, and sentenced defendant to eight years in prison.

. . . [Our] burglary statute provides for two possible ways to commit the crime of burglary: (1) by entering without authority and with the intent to commit a felony or theft or (2) by remaining without authority and with the intent to commit a felony or theft. In the present case, defendant was charged with and convicted of the first type of burglary—burglary by unauthorized entry. For over 100 years, Illinois case law has recognized that entering a retail store with the intent to commit a theft amounts to the crime of burglary. . . .

[T]he evidence here—which showed that defendant and an accomplice placed two backpacks on a coin-exchange machine in the Walmart vestibule, entered the store proper, and a short time later returned to retrieve the backpacks in order to stuff merchandise into them—was . . . sufficient to prove that defendant entered the store with the intent to commit a theft. And, if it is in fact the case that defendant had the intent to commit a theft when he entered the Walmart, then . . . it must necessarily follow that his entry was "without authority" within the meaning of . . . the burglary statute.

. . . The mere fact that a person commits a theft after entering a store will not establish that he intended to commit a theft upon entry. Rather, there would have to be some other evidence—even if circumstantial—supporting a finding that the defendant entered the premises with the required intent. *Compare* People v. Smith, 637 N.E.2d 1128 (Ill. Ct. App. 1994) (finding evidence sufficient to support element of entry with intent to commit a theft where the defendant entered clothing store with plastic bag used to hide stolen coat and police found in his car the wire cutters used to remove coat from rack), *with* People v. Durham, 623 N.E.2d 1010 (Ill. Ct. App. 1993) (reversing burglary conviction of the defendant who stole men's suit where he carried nothing into store that would indicate an intent to commit a theft and his conduct was that of a normal shopper browsing items). Thus, there is no reason to think that [our holding] will transform all (or even a substantial number of) retail thefts into burglaries. . . . Given the difficulty of proving a defendant's intent at the moment he or she enters a store, it is more probable that the vast majority of suspects will have to be charged only with retail theft because the State has insufficient evidence of intent at entry. . . .

[D]efendant [nonetheless] makes a broad and vague argument that the legislature . . . intended for acts of shoplifting to be prosecuted and punished under the retail theft statute rather than the burglary statute. While it is true that the legislature intended acts of retail theft to be prosecuted under the retail theft statute, defendant's argument misses the point. His alleged act of shoplifting *was* prosecuted under the retail theft statute. He was convicted of burglary, by contrast, for his distinct act of entering a store with the intent to shoplift. The two crimes contain different elements and address distinct harms. Burglary requires an intent to commit a theft upon entry and is complete upon the moment of entry whether or not any theft

actually occurs, whereas retail theft requires that the defendant take possession of merchandise with the intent of permanently depriving the merchant
of the item without paying full retail value. Defendant's argument also rests
on the mistaken premise that the harm caused by shoplifting and the harm
caused by entering a store with the intent to shoplift are measured in the
same way—by the value of the items a person steals or intends to steal. But,
as noted above, a person who enters a store with the intent to steal is at least
arguably more culpable than a person who steals after entering innocently.
Although defendant may disagree with the assessment of the relative culpability posed by his conduct or the risk presented by it, it is the legislature's
role to declare and define conduct constituting a crime and to determine
the nature and extent of the punishment for it.

. . . [W]e have scoured the legislative history and debate surrounding
the enactment of the retail theft statute and can find nothing that would
support defendant's argument. We have only found that the retail theft statute was enacted for the purpose of combating the growing problem of retail
theft in Illinois. And the legislative debate suggests that the idea behind the
law was to give greater tools to merchants and law enforcement to fight the
problem, not to help the retail thief. . . .

THEIS, J., dissenting. At issue is whether a person who enters a retail establishment during regular business hours, remains within areas of the store
that are open to the public, and shoplifts $77 worth of children's clothing
may properly be convicted of burglary by entry . . . .

In Illinois, the crime of retail theft was created in 1975. One of the
senators who introduced the bill described it as "the work product of over
a year of evaluation and study to react to the very serious problem of retail
theft." 79th Ill. Gen. Assem., Senate Proceedings, May 7, 1975, at 97 (statements of Senator Harris). . . . A representative who opposed the bill insisted
that "people who are responsible for retail theft" generally were "not constant, arrogant criminals." 79th Ill. Gen. Assem., House Proceedings, June
11, 1975, at 114 (statements of Representative Duff). Rather, referencing
Jean Valjean, he suggested that retail thieves were "youngsters in stores" or
"poor people who steal bread" and was hesitant to overly penalize them. Id.
The retail theft statute ultimately passed [over this objection] with broad
support.

The legislature has continually refined the retail theft statute. In 1986,
the General Assembly amended the definition of retail theft to include
attempting to return unpaid merchandise for a refund or for credit. The
following year, the statute was amended to provide that "a person who uses
or possesses with the intent to use any theft detection shielding device or
any theft detection device remover with the intent to permanently deprive a
merchant of retail merchandise commits retail theft." 85th Ill. Gen. Assem.,
House Proceedings, June 16, 1987, at 102 (statements of Representative

Barnes). A representative noted that "many attorneys" had recommended the amendment to ensure that "anybody that goes into a store with the intent to steal the merchandise can be found guilty." *Id.* . . .*

Despite the General Assembly's efforts to craft a measured response to the problem of retail theft, the majority would uphold the burglary conviction of a shoplifter [who] entered the store while it was open, and [who] did not exceed the scope of his authority as a member of the public to be there. Accordingly, I would find that the defendant's entry was not "without authority" and that his conduct amounted to retail theft, not burglary. *See* People v. Bradford, 50 N.E.3d 1112, 1120 (Ill. 2016) ("[A]n individual who enters a building lawfully, shoplifts merchandise within areas which are open to the public, then leaves during business hours, is guilty of ordinary retail theft.").

To appreciate why the defendant's conduct was not burglary, we must remember why burglary has been criminalized. Legislatures have "singled out burglary because of its inherent potential for harms to persons." Quarles v. United States, 139 S. Ct. 1872, 1879 (2019). That is, "burglary is dangerous because it creates the possibility of a violent confrontation between the offender and an occupant, caretaker, or some other person who comes to investigate." *Id.*; *cf.* MPC §221.1, Explanatory Note (Am. Law Inst. 1985) (noting that the "crime of burglary reflects a considered judgment that especially severe sanctions are appropriate for criminal invasion of premises under circumstances likely to terrorize occupants"). . . . By contrast, a person who enters Walmart with a backpack is not likely to destabilize the store's operations, and a shoplifter's mere presence within the store is unlikely to result in a violent confrontation. The majority is correct when it notes that burglary and retail theft "contain different elements and address distinct harms." However, the harm that the burglary statute protects against — the likelihood of a dangerous confrontation between the offender and a person who comes to investigate — does not exist with the average shoplifter. . . .

The retail theft statute already criminalizes the act of taking merchandise from a retail establishment without paying for it. There is no justifiable basis for penalizing a shoplifter as a burglar. . . . [B]urglary is always at least a Class 2 felony, while a first-time retail thief who shoplifts items valued at less than $300 is charged with a Class A misdemeanor. Under the majority's rationale, the legislature intended for a person who enters a store with the intent to steal $77 worth of clothing to be charged with a felony, while the

---

* Editor's Note: A single defendant could be prosecuted and convicted for each of the various theft-related crimes discussed in this opinion. For a detailed discussion about how the filing of multiple charges related to a single criminal event impacts criminal prosecutions, see Chapter Nine (p. 812).

person who *actually* steals $77 worth of clothing is charged with a misdemeanor. . . . It would be entirely absurd to punish a person's simple entry into a store that is open to the public more severely than a person's act of shoplifting from that store. . . .

Although the majority stresses that the defendant's "act of shoplifting *was* prosecuted under the retail theft statute," it omits the fact that he was acquitted of retail theft. The jury did not find beyond a reasonable doubt that the defendant stole merchandise from the store, and for the reasons noted above, burglary should not be used as a substitute for prosecuting shoplifters.

NOTES AND QUESTIONS

1. Shoplifting. As both *Johnson* opinions make clear, the Illinois legislature enacted a suite of criminal statutes over a series of years that were designed to address "the growing problem of retail theft in Illinois." In passing the retail theft statute, the legislature pointed to "the substantial burden placed upon the economy of this State resulting from the rising incidence of retail theft." Ill. Rev. Stat. 1975, ch. 38, ¶ 16A-1. In more recent years, many retailers insist the problem has only worsened and is national in scope. The *New York Times* called shoplifting "the nation's most expensive crime," the costs of which are "ultimately passed on to consumers through higher-priced goods." In the wake of the pandemic, several major retailers including Walgreens and Target blamed retail theft for store closures in urban areas. Even more cited theft as an explanation for declining profits.[2]

Skeptics have pushed back on retailers' claims. One investigative journalist, for example, found that crime was higher at stores that Target kept open than at nearby stores that were closed. And analysts from investment bank William Blair suggested that retailers were "exaggerating the impact of theft to disguise their poor business performance," and that "store closures enacted under the cover of [retail theft] relate to underperformance of these locations."[3]

It is difficult to arbitrate these claims in the absence of reliable data, especially since "every era since the 1870s has experienced a supposed shoplifting 'epidemic,'" as Professor John Rappaport writes. The "most commonly cited figure," according to NPR, comes from an annual survey conducted by the National Retail Federation, a lobbying group, which, in 2023, reported retail-theft losses of $40 billion nationwide, or $110 million every day. As a percentage of sales, however, the same survey shows that losses have "barely changed in the past decade." Because "companies do not share data on goods stolen" and "individual stores often don't report incidents to the police," NPR concludes, we are left "only to guess at the true scale of the problem."[4]

2. Criminal Law and Market Bypass. Shoplifting, like many other forms of theft, is a prototypically economic crime. Some people who engage in it do so to obtain items they need but cannot afford. Some shoplift for other reasons, including thrill seeking, peer pressure, or a sense that it is a petty or harmless offense. But even in these latter scenarios, the fact remains that the offense revolves around an economic relationship. The person who shoplifts obtains a good that is being offered for sale in the market-place—and the benefits of that good—without tendering to the seller any compensation. He has, in other words, through deception or other means, reduced the item's price to $0, without the seller's consent. From an economic perspective, everyone has an incentive to pay the lowest price possible for a good, which means that theft is often economically attractive. Zero dollars is a good price. According to economic analyses of criminal law, one of the law's important functions is to counteract this incentive to steal by preventing the end run on market exchanges that theft entails, as Judge Richard Posner explains in the excerpt that follows.

Richard A. Posner, *An Economic Theory of the Criminal Law,* 85 Colum. L. Rev. 1193, 1195 (1985). The major function of criminal law in a capitalist society is to prevent people from bypassing the system of voluntary, compensated exchange . . . . [T]he market is, virtually by definition, the most efficient method of allocating resources. Attempts to bypass the market will therefore be discouraged by a legal system bent on promoting efficiency.

If I covet my neighbor's car, it is more efficient to force me to negotiate with my neighbor—to pay him his price—than it is to allow me to take his car subject to being required by a court to pay the neighbor whatever the court decides the car is worth. If I happen to have no money but want a car, it would be inefficient to let me just take a car. Indeed, unlike the first case, this transfer cannot possibly improve the allocation of resources—that is, it cannot move resources from a less to a more valuable employment—because value is a function of willingness to pay. Since I am unwilling (because unable—but it does not matter why) to pay my neighbor's price for the car, it follows that the car would be less valuable in an economic sense in my hands than in his. The car might, of course, confer more utility (pleasure, satisfaction) on me than on my neighbor, but there is a difference between utility in a broad utilitarian sense and value in a (perhaps narrow) economic sense, where value is measured by willingness to pay for what is not yours already, or willingness to accept payment for what is yours. [Note also that] if I am allowed to take the car I will have an incentive to expend resources on taking it and my neighbor will have an incentive to expend resources on preventing it from being taken, and these expenditures considered as a whole, yield no social [benefit].

The role of the criminal law in discouraging market bypassing is obscured by the fact that the market transaction that the criminal bypasses is [often] not a transaction with his victim. If someone steals my car, normally it is not because he wants *that* car and would have bought it from me if the criminal law had deterred him from stealing it. He steals to get money to use in buying goods and services from other people. The market transaction that he bypasses is the exchange of his labor for money in a lawful occupation. But it is still market bypassing. . . .

[Still,] this does not explain why there is a criminal law, given that there is a law of torts [that could deter economic crimes by requiring civil defendants to repay ill-gotten gains and perhaps even pay punitive damages]. . . . In cases where tort remedies, including punitive damages, are an adequate deterrent because they do not strain the potential defendant's ability to pay, there is no need to invoke criminal penalties [and] no social gain from using a criminal sanction. . . . [C]riminal sanctions generally are reserved, as theory predicts, for cases where the tort remedy bumps up against a solvency limitation. [In such cases, the] optimal damages that would be required for deterrence would so frequently exceed the offender's ability to pay that public enforcement and nonmonetary sanctions such as imprisonment are required. This means that the criminal law is designed primarily for the nonaffluent; the affluent are kept in line, for the most part, by tort law. This may seem to be a left-wing kind of suggestion ("criminal law keeps the lid on the lower classes"), but it is not. It is efficient to use different sanctions depending on an offender's wealth.[5]

3. Criminal Law as a Labor Market Institution. Judge Posner's economic analysis explicitly states that "criminal law is designed primarily for the nonaffluent," meaning the poor. To Posner, this is a feature, not a bug. Criminal sanctions, he argues, are socially inefficient and undesirable; and so, echoing Bentham (p. 71), he says they should be avoided where possible. For the affluent, Posner says, criminal sanctions are largely avoidable because deterrence can be achieved through civil damages, including punitive damages. But for the poor, who cannot afford to pay such sanctions, Posner argues that other forms of deterrence—notably, prison—are the only available tool for avoiding market bypass.

Of course, the nonaffluent are also the most likely to lack access to the market goods they need to live full and healthy lives, or perhaps even the basic goods they need to survive. As a result, the nonaffluent are not only the group that criminal law is designed to deter from theft and other economic crimes; they are also the ones most likely to be driven toward such conduct by economic forces. In this respect, some argue, criminal law is a tool that not only protects the integrity of economic markets and exchanges, but also reinforces and perpetuates inequality between socioeconomic classes. Consider the following excerpts.

Ivan Jankovic, *Labor Market and Imprisonment*, 8 Crime & Soc. Just. 17, 17-20 (1977). [T]heories, as well as practice, of punishment reflect prevailing

ideologies which are, in turn, partly determined by economic requirements of concrete systems of material production. So, for example, societies
plagued by shortages of labor (e.g., sixteenth century Germany) develop
ideologies which emphasize man's duty to work (the Protestant ethic);
those faced with an oversupply of labor (e.g., nineteenth century England)
resort to ideologies which make work one's right to be fought for in the
labor market (the laissez faire of liberal capitalism). . . .

One of the most striking features of capitalist economies is that they
are always faced with an oversupply of labor. . . . [C]apitalist economies
need to maintain a permanent reserve of surplus labor which can at short
notice be coupled with newly invested capital. This reserve army of labor
is created not by fiat or from any ulterior motives but by the technological
processes essential to capitalism. . . . [C]apital has a tendency to move into
new areas of production, likely at first to be labor-intensive, offering higher
potential profits. When these areas are mechanized, the [labor surpluses
reemerge]. The reserve army of labor, then, is a necessary condition for the
rapid movement of capital [from one area of innovation to the next].

A reserve army of labor also places an effective limit on economic
demands of employed workers. The very existence of an army of unemployed persons reminds the employed laborer of his expendability. An economist who argues that "minimum" unemployment is unavoidable in a "free"
society, formulates this point with a disarming frankness: "The labor market
should never be so tight that workers have no incentive to be on their toes."

Two main components of the state's effort to support, and thus control, the surplus population are the social welfare system and the criminal
justice system. Given the persistence and the magnitude of the surplus population in advanced capitalist countries, imprisonment may serve to contain
a fraction of it and to manipulate its size.

Devah Pager, *Marked* 28-30 (2007). Whereas once prisoners represented
only a tiny fraction of the population, today the United States houses
enough inmates to staff an entire global fast food empire. . . . The more
than 600,000 inmates released each year could fill every one of the fast-food
job openings created annually nearly five times over. . . . The large flow of
individuals into and out of the prison system has complex effects, simultaneously concealing and creating inequalities in the labor market. . . .

[With respect to concealment, sociologist Bruce Western and his colleagues have shown that incarcerated people are] invisible to our official
indicators of social and economic wellbeing . . . . Government employment statistics typically limit their analyses to noninstitutionalized civilian
workers. Monthly reports of unemployment and labor force participation
inform us of the health of our economy but ignore the large and growing
numbers of the working-age population that sit idle in our prisons and jails.
If we considered the more than two million inmates in our employment

estimates, our conclusions about the state of the economy would grow steadily less optimistic. Indeed, Western and his colleagues reestimated national unemployment rates, employment-to-population ratios, and earnings with inmates counted among the nonworking. Their new estimates suggest that our official labor force statistics substantially underestimate rates of joblessness and economic inequality. In fact, while the free-market capitalism of America is often touted as the source of its low unemployment rates compared to those of Western Europe, this research suggests that the differential is largely a function of penal intervention. Adjusted estimates of joblessness, taking into account the prison population, indicate that U.S. employment rates are in fact much closer to those of Europe. Prison can thus be thought of as a "labor-market institution," disproportionately removing individuals from the bottom of the socioeconomic hierarchy who would likely otherwise be counted among the unemployed. . . .

[As for exacerbation of inequality, people returning from prison after release] face significant legal and social barriers to finding employment. . . . Several studies of local or state inmate populations report that between 75 and 80 percent of parolees remain jobless up to a year after release from prison. More controlled studies, following large samples over time and comparing them to otherwise similar individuals who have never been incarcerated, also show serious economic penalties following spells of incarceration. Sociologists Robert Sampson and John Laub, for example, using a rich set of longitudinal data from an early cohort of juvenile delinquents, find that incarceration has a strong and significant negative effect on later job stability, even after controlling for alcohol use, criminal activity, and prior criminal history. Using longitudinal data on a more recent cohort of men, Bruce Western estimates that incarceration is associated with a 10 percent drop in wages and a flatter earnings trajectory than that of similarly skilled men who did not experience incarceration. . . . Long after an individual completes his prison term, the labor market costs of incarceration continue to register.[6]

Bruce Western & Katherine Beckett, *How Unregulated Is the U.S. Labor Market? The Penal System as a Labor Market Institution*, 104 Am. J. Socio. 1030, 1031 (1999). U.S. incarceration lowers conventional measures of unemployment in the short run by concealing joblessness . . . but it raises unemployment in the long run by damaging the job prospects of ex-convicts after release . . . . This argument [indicates] that incarceration has lowered the [reported] U.S. unemployment rate, but it also implies that sustained low unemployment in the future will depend on continuing expansion of the penal system.

Bruce Western & Becky Pettit, *Black-White Wage Inequality, Employment Rates, and Incarceration*, 111 Am. J. Socio. 553, 553-554, 573-574 (2005). Inequality between black men and white men is often measured by wage differences in the civilian labor force. However, comparisons of wage earners may inaccurately describe the relative economic status of black men. . . . The growth of the U.S. penal system through the 1980s and 1990s removed an ever-growing fraction of young, low-skill black men from the noninstitutional population. By 1999, over 40% of young black male high school dropouts were in prison or jail compared to 10.3% of young white male dropouts. High incarceration rates have the effect of concealing poor young men in conventional labor force statistics . . . [such] that labor force statistics for black men cannot be taken at face value. . . . [Reported] improvements in black relative wages are not substantially because of improvements in the market position of black workers. Instead, jobless rates increased among black low-wage workers, and incarceration rates increased among young black workers, removing those with little earnings power from standard labor market accounts [and creating sampling biases in economic data that inflated Black relative earnings by between 7% and 20% among working-age men, and by as much 58% among young men].

4. Prison Labor. The preceding note discusses how criminal law and the penal system interact with the labor market outside of prison. But prisons themselves also contain an internal labor market, composed of prison labor. We explored some of the history of prison labor in Chapter One (p. 10), including in the postbellum South where, according to historian Douglas Blackmon, prison labor reconstituted a form of "slavery by another name" (p. 11). The excerpts that follow build on that discussion, tracing the evolution, modern manifestations, and current-day implications of prison labor.

Rebecca McLennan, *The Buried Roots of Carceral Labor,* Inquest (May 16, 2023). In certain key respects, today's carceral state operates much as the South's convict lease camps and chain gangs operated—that is, as variants of slavery (if not of the chattel variety) and as constitutionally sanctioned instruments of racist social control. In neither era are prisoners meaningfully compensated for their work; in neither is the work voluntary. . . .

[But the] history of forced penal servitude in North America long precedes the Civil War. . . . [I]n the 1820s, following a series of large-scale penitentiary uprisings and the nation's first major recession, many state legislatures enacted tough new laws; built new, fortress-like prisons; and mandated forced labor for prisoners. By 1865 in California, Illinois, Massachusetts, New York, and almost every other non-southern state, tens of thousands of men routinely endured not only forced penal labor but a fully elaborated system of penal *servitude*—that is, a system in which almost all the prisoner's legal and de facto liberties were suspended . . . . Thus, decades before ex-slaveholders enacted the Black Codes and instituted the criminal surety system (often cited in scholarly and activist literature as an origin point for our carceral labor system), northern states had stripped convicted offenders of almost all their rights and sold their labor power to private interests. . . . The overwhelming majority of the tens of thousands of people subjected to contractual penal servitude each year were either young, poor, native-born northern men or else poor immigrant men from Ireland, Germany, England, Scotland, or Western Europe. Immigrants made up anywhere from a quarter to half of all northern prisoners. The vast majority were white. . . . [These i]mprisoned men were very much part of the North's political economy, producing millions of dollars of goods that were sold on the open market. . . . By the mid-1880s, whether toiling on a plantation in Texas or a coal mine in Tennessee, a twine-making workshop in Massachusetts or an oven factory in New York, prisoners were driven and disciplined by private interests whose pursuit of profit was practically unconstrained.

Erin Hatton, *Forced Laborers*, Inquest (May 9, 2023). Few Americans realize that about half of people incarcerated in the United States are working at any given time, and most work for a significant portion of their sentences. . . . [T]here are four types of jobs in U.S. prisons (not counting work in informal or illicit economies behind bars). Common across all four types is the absence of the rights and protections that define free-world labor: no minimum wage, no overtime, no unemployment, no workers' compensation, no social security, no occupational health and safety protections, and no right to form unions and collectively bargain.

The first category of work is facility maintenance . . . . In these roles, incarcerated people work to keep the prison running; they sustain its operations. The vast majority of incarcerated workers perform this type of labor: cooking and serving food in mess halls; cleaning dorms, bathrooms, schoolhouses, hospitals, and recreation yards; cutting lawns and shoveling snow; fixing electrical and plumbing systems; painting walls and washing windows. Because wages for this work are invariably minimal—ranging from no pay at all in many southern states to $2 per hour in Minnesota and New Jersey—this form of labor saves prison operators untold sums of money by supplanting free-world, full-wage workers.

The second category[, which accounts] for just under 5 percent of state and federal prisoner employment[, captures incarcerated people who] produce a wide range of goods and services for sale to government agencies: office furniture and filing cabinets; road signs and license plates; uniforms, linens, and mattresses for prisons and hospitals; wooden benches and metal grills for public parks; even body armor for military and police. . . . On average, state and federal prisoners earn $.33–1.41 per hour for this work.

The third category of incarcerated labor is for private-sector companies that set up shop inside U.S. prisons. Such jobs employ just .3 percent of the U.S. prison population. These are the highest-paid prison jobs because private-sector companies are legally obligated to pay "prevailing wages" in order to avoid undercutting non-prison labor. However, incarcerated workers do not actually receive these "prevailing wages" [because their pay is] subject to many deductions and fees, which are capped at a whopping 80 percent of gross earnings. In other words, U.S. prisons seize most of the workers' wages in these jobs. . . .

The final category is work that occurs outside of the prison, through various labor arrangements such as work-release programs, outside work crews, and work camps. . . . In prison work crews, incarcerated workers leave the prison or jail facility during work hours to perform public works, or "community service" jobs, such as fighting fires and cleaning highways, park grounds, and abandoned lots. Such workers typically return to prison at the end of the workday, unless their labor — as in the case of wildfires — is far from the prison; in those cases, they are typically housed in prison-like facilities, such as fire camps.[7]

Noah Zatz, *The Carceral Labor Continuum,* Inquest (June 1, 2023). [C]arceral labor is not a problem confined to the prison . . . . [Consider] the economic value of the goods and services produced by [prison] labor. This value is most recognizable when the organization obtaining carceral labor (resisting, for now, the label "employer") sells those products. . . . The crucial insight here is that [these products] are interchangeable [with products made in the free market]. Historically, this point has been central to the politics of organized labor's engagement with carceral labor: If products are interchangeable, so are the workforces creating them. The capacity of the prison to brutally exploit incarcerated people [thus] provides a weapon that can be wielded against "free labor," by substituting carceral production at lower wages and greater control. Or by threatening to do so if non-incarcerated workers demand too much. . . .

[At the same time,] a carceral labor continuum links together a wide array of situations where non-incarcerated people work under threat of future incarceration. . . . [P]arole or probation conditions mean that not getting or keeping a job may trigger (re)incarceration, and the obligation to pay criminal fines and fees legally entails an obligation to earn the money with which to pay — or face incarceration. . . . Broadening out further, we can include economic obligations that originate outside the criminal legal system but are carcerally enforced. Child support enforcement quite explicitly involves duties to work (in order to pay) under threat of jail via civil contempt or criminal nonsupport.

5. Fines and Fees. In addition to familiar punishments like incarceration and probation, people convicted of crimes are routinely required to pay fines and fees as a component of their sentence, an issue that gained national attention following the U.S. Department of Justice's investigative report on the Ferguson Police Department discussed in Chapter One

(p. 38). According to one recent survey, "the average debt incurred for court-related fines and fees" among respondents "was $13,607." The report further notes that sixty-three percent of respondents said that "family members on the outside were primarily responsible for court-related costs associated with conviction," of whom "83% were women." Given the low socioeconomic status of most criminal defendants, court-imposed fines and fees often translate into long-term debt that individuals carry and must try to pay during probation or upon release from prison—often under threat of incarceration or reincarceration. According to researcher Abby Shafroth,

> the enforcement methods governments use to collect criminal justice debt have the paradoxical effect of making it harder for those who owe to earn a living and thus to pay the debt, trapping them and their families in poverty. Suspending driver's licenses until a debt is paid off, requiring frequent appearances at debt-related status hearings, subjecting people to arrest for nonpayment, and precluding criminal record expungement until payment is made are just a few examples of collection methods that make it harder for people to work and to achieve financial stability. This problem is particularly acute for the formerly incarcerated [who] face significant barriers to obtaining employment and getting back on their feet. . . . [C]riminal justice debts that burden people leaving prison create a barrier to successful reentry, contributing to cycles of incarceration.[8]

6. *Class-ifying Theft.* If the foregoing analyses of criminal law's economic functions hold true, one should expect to see differences in how theft-related crimes are treated or conceptualized based not just on the conduct at issue, but on the socioeconomic status of the defendant. There is some evidence this is the case. Consider, for example, Professor John Rappaport's observation, drawing on a large-scale, nationally representative survey, that "middle-class individuals are most likely to shoplift." Given the statistics cited earlier showing that the vast majority of people prosecuted for crimes are poor, it seems shoplifting may be predominantly committed by middle-class offenders, but predominantly punished against poor defendants.[9]

What might explain this socioeconomic discrepancy? One way to interrogate that question is to think about another form of conduct analogous to theft that may occur even more frequently than shoplifting: sharing passwords for streaming services. According to one recent survey, thirty-seven percent of people who pay for access to a streaming service share their password with someone they don't live with (most commonly, with their mother, but also frequently with friends). The people on the receiving end avoid paying an average of $15 per month to the streaming service. Netflix, which dominates the streaming market with more than 260 million subscribers, reports that "more than 30 million U.S. and Canadian households are using a shared password to access its content." For many years, Netflix looked the other way, allowing "generous out-of-home password sharing because it helped get users hooked on the service." But as competition in the streaming market increased, the company came to view the sharing as a serious economic problem "creating revenue growth headwinds."[10]

Netflix itself has some technical capacity to restrict password sharing, and recently took steps to do so—which resulted in a substantial rebound in subscriptions and revenue. But imagine it had taken an additional approach. What if, using its internal data showing who was accessing its site from multiple households on a single password, it had requested assistance from law enforcement actors? As Professor Orin Kerr has written, if "Ann gives Bob her Netflix username and password and tells Bob to feel free to use Ann's account," that "can amount to criminal theft of service." It is also possible that Bob's unauthorized access to the site (from Netflix's perspective) may amount to a violation of the federal Computer Fraud and Abuse Act, which can carry steep mandatory penalties for every login.[11]

Questions: Assuming that accessing Netflix via a shared password is a crime, ought people be prosecuted for it? If so, which offenders? If not, why not? Should the same arguments and analyses apply to people accused of shoplifting? Why or why not?

II.   ECONOMIC NECESSITY

"Anyone who has two shirts should share with the one who has none, and anyone who has food should do the same."

Luke 3:11

How ought the criminal law respond to crimes of subsistence committed in circumstances of severe deprivation? Ought there be a defense for someone who trespasses in the face of homelessness, or who steals in the face of starvation? Consider the following cases.

Commonwealth v. Magadini

52 N.E.3d 1041 (Mass. 2016)

HINES, J. The defendant, David Magadini, was convicted by jury on seven counts of criminal trespass, each based on the defendant's presence, in 2014, in privately-owned buildings where he was the subject of no trespass orders. . . . [T]he defendant requested a jury instruction on the defense of necessity, asserting that his conduct was justified as the only lawful alternative for a homeless person facing the "clear and imminent danger" of

exposure to the elements during periods of extreme outdoor temperatures. The judge denied the request, concluding that the defendant had
legal alternatives to trespassing available. As to each conviction, the judge
imposed concurrent sentences of thirty days in a house of correction. . . .

In 2014, the defendant was charged with trespassing on three properties in Great Barrington — Barrington House, Castle Street, and SoCo
Creamery. Barrington House is a mixed-use building with several different restaurants, an enclosed atrium, and apartments above the businesses.
Castle Street is a three-story building with retail establishments, offices,
and apartments. SoCo Creamery is an ice cream shop. The defendant was
barred from each property by no trespass orders. . . .

[Six of the charges pertain to instances in February, March, and April in
which the defendant was found at either Barrington House or Castle Street
in the evening, nighttime, or morning hours on days variously described as
"cold," "very cold," and "cool." The police typically found the defendant]
lying in a hallway by a heater . . . . The seventh charge was based on conduct that occurred on June 10, 2014, when the defendant entered SoCo
Creamery, ignored requests by the clerk to leave the premises, and used the
bathroom for ten to fifteen minutes. . . .

The defendant, a lifelong resident of Great Barrington, became homeless after he moved out of his parents' home in 2004. . . . He planned to
return to his parents' home, but he was unable to do so because the "land-
lord," who "wanted [the defendant] out," refused to allow it. After leaving
his parents' home, he generally lived outside year-round, but during the
winter months, he tried to "find a more sheltered area" from the "ice and a
snow storm." During the cold weather, the defendant used blankets, gloves,
and scarves to try to stay warm, but when the weather was "so severe that it
was not possible," he would seek shelter in private buildings.

For a two- to three-month period in the winter of 2007, the defendant
stayed at [a] local homeless shelter . . . . Three days before he began staying
there, he had gone to that shelter at approximately 3 a.m. following a blizzard. He was refused entry, and he stayed on the porch for about an hour
before being asked to leave. A few days later, he spoke with someone from
the shelter, and he was allowed to stay for a few months before he was told
to leave because of "certain issues." Therefore, the defendant had no other
place to stay in Great Barrington. For a period of "three to four years," he
lived outdoors, first at Stanley Park and later at the outdoor gazebo behind
the Great Barrington Town Hall, where he had been living at the time of
the trespass incidents. He considered the gazebo his home and registered
to vote from that address.

At the time of the trial, the defendant was a sixty-seven year old unemployed college graduate. He had worked in the past, but he was not employed
at the time he was charged with the trespassing offenses. The defendant
had attempted to obtain an apartment almost "every week for about seven

years." Although he had money to pay for an apartment depending on the day, he explained that it was very difficult to find an apartment in Great Barrington because of the upfront fees. . . . He was aware of a homeless shelter in Pittsfield, but he did not consider renting lodging or staying at a homeless shelter outside of Great Barrington. He testified, "I was born here and I intend to stay here." He does not have a driver's license.

. . . The common-law defense of necessity "exonerates one who commits a crime under the 'pressure of circumstances' if the harm that would have resulted from compliance with the law . . . exceeds the harm actually resulting from the defendant's violation of the law." Commonwealth v. Kendall, 883 N.E.2d 269, 272 (Mass. 2008). As such, the necessity defense may excuse unlawful conduct "where the value protected by the law is, as a matter of public policy, eclipsed by a superseding value." *Id.*

For a defendant to be entitled to a necessity defense instruction, he or she must present "some evidence on each of the four underlying conditions of the defense," *id.* at 273: "(1) a clear and imminent danger, not one which is debatable or speculative"; (2) [a reasonable expectation that his or her action] will be effective as the direct cause of abating the danger; (3) there is no legal alternative which will be effective in abating the danger; and (4) the Legislature has not acted to preclude the defense by a clear and deliberate choice regarding the values at issue." *Id.* at 272-273. . . .

The judge focused only on the third element . . . rul[ing] that the defendant had other available legal alternatives, "motels, and hotels, the police station," and that the evidence was lacking on the defendant's inability to "rent a hotel room on these isolated evenings." We conclude that the judge erred in ruling that the defendant failed to meet his burden. . . . [But b]efore we address the third element, we review the first element, "clear and imminent danger," because the Commonwealth contends that the defendant failed to meet the foundational requirement for this element as to the seventh offense, which occurred on June 10, 2014.

There appears to be little question that the weather conditions on the dates of the offenses in February and March presented a "clear and imminent danger"[9] . . . to a homeless person. . . . Moreover, the timing of each of those incidents, in the early morning or late evening hours when the defendant was either sleeping or lying down, suggests the dangerousness of the circumstances where sleeping may place one in the same position for an extended period and, thus, increases the potential harm from the weather. [T]he Commonwealth concedes that the defendant met his burden of

---

9. [A] report of the National Coalition for the Homeless [notes] that "life-threatening cases of hypothermia do not require extreme temperatures; indeed, they often occur when the ambient temperature is between thirty-two degrees Fahrenheit and forty degrees Fahrenheit."

demonstrating a "clear and imminent danger" for these six incidents[, including the one in April].

[T]he defendant did not meet his burden to show a "clear and imminent danger" for the incident on June 10, where the evidence showed only that he had to use the bathroom.[11] Accordingly, we do not include the incident on June 10 in our analysis . . . of the availability of "legal alternatives" to trespass.

[S]atisfaction of the third element requires a defendant to demonstrate that he "made himself aware of any available lawful alternatives, 'or showed them to be futile in the circumstances.' " *Id.* at 273. . . . This does not require a showing that the defendant has exhausted or shown to be futile all conceivable alternatives, only that a jury could reasonably find that no alternatives were available.

The parties agree that this issue is governed by the *Kendall* case, but disagree as to its application. In *Kendall*, the defendant had driven while intoxicated to the hospital so that he could take his girl friend for medical treatment of a serious head wound. He was charged with operating a motor vehicle while under the influence of liquor and requested an instruction on the defense of necessity because he and his girl friend did not have telephones from which they could call 911. [We] affirmed the judge's decision to deny the defendant's request because the record was "devoid of evidence that the defendant made any effort to seek assistance from anyone prior to driving a motor vehicle while intoxicated." *Id.* at 274. Further, the evidence demonstrated that at least one neighbor, who lived [nearby], was home at the time of the incident, that there was a fire station approximately one hundred yards from that neighbor's home, and that the defendant and his girl friend had just left a Chinese restaurant within walking distance from the defendant's home. . . . Three dissenting justices disagreed [with our holding], concluding that the defendant had met his burden because his conduct was not unreasonable in light of the "risk of failure" from the available alternatives; and therefore, weighing the propriety of defendant's choice should have been given to the jury. *Id.* at 275-276 (Cowin, J., dissenting).

Here, the defendant's evidence was sufficient to meet his burden . . . . [T]here is at least "some evidence" that the defendant lacked effective legal alternatives to trespass during cold days and nights. The defendant testified that he stayed at an outdoor gazebo "pretty much" year round, that in 2007 he was told to leave the only local homeless shelter and had previously been denied entry to the shelter in the middle of the night following a blizzard, that no other places "want [him] in their facility," that

---

11. Trial counsel asked the clerk present at the time the defendant entered the store whether the defendant said that his entry was "an emergency and that he really needed to use the bathroom"; she responded, "No, he didn't say anything to me." . . .

he was unable to rent an apartment despite repeated attempts, and that there was nowhere besides public parks where he could stay. . . .

The Commonwealth argues that the defendant failed to meet his burden because he presented no evidence that he was unable to rent an apartment outside of Great Barrington, that he was unable to gain entry to the Pittsfield shelter, and that he would still be excluded from the local homeless shelter in 2014. The Commonwealth's argument is unavailing. We do not require an actor facing a "clear and imminent danger" to conceptualize all possible alternatives. So long as the defendant's evidence, taken as true, creates a reasonable doubt as to the availability of such lawful alternatives, the defendant satisfies the third element. . . .

Additionally, we note that the options proposed by the Commonwealth do not appear to be effective alternatives on the record before us. Where the only local homeless shelter had previously denied the defendant entry at 3 a.m. following a blizzard and had later told him he had to leave, the law does not require the defendant to continue to seek shelter there in order to demonstrate that doing so is futile. Moreover, the defendant's conduct is viewed at the time of the danger, and actions that the defendant could have taken to find shelter before the dangerous condition arose do not negate the conclusion that there were no lawful alternatives available at the time of his unlawful conduct.[13]

. . . Moreover, we are not prepared to say as a matter of law that a homeless defendant must seek shelter outside of his or her home town in order to demonstrate a lack of lawful alternatives. Our law does not permit punishment of the homeless simply for being homeless. Once the foundational requirements are met, the necessity defense allows a jury to consider the plight of a homeless person against any harms caused by a trespass before determining criminal responsibility.[16] . . .

Because we conclude that the judge erred in denying the defendant's request for a jury instruction on the defense of necessity for the trespassing charges that occurred in February, March, and April, 2014, we vacate those

---

13. As the level of harm that could arise from the unlawful conduct increases, so does the requirement for considering lawful alternatives. We recognize that the defendant's conduct may not have been appreciated by owners, managers, and residents of the private buildings in which the defendant sought cover, but there was no evidence that the defendant's presence did, or had the potential to, cause physical harm to any persons. Accordingly, the requirement to consider alternatives may be viewed more leniently where the potential harm was only property-related than it would be viewed where the unlawful conduct . . . had the potential to harm both persons and property. The doctrine of necessity has its roots in the notion that "the law deems the lives of all persons far more valuable than any property." United States v. Ashton, 24 F. Cas. 873, 874 (C.C.D. Mass. 1834).

16. Allowing a defendant to defend his trespassing charges by claiming necessity will not, of course, condone all illegal trespass by homeless persons. It simply allows a jury of peers to weigh the "competing harms" to determine criminal responsibility. . . .

six convictions and remand for a new trial. We affirm the conviction stemming from conduct that occurred on June 10, 2014.

People v. Fontes

89 P.3d 484 (Colo. App. 2003)

GRAHAM, J. . . . Defendant was arrested after he presented a false identification card to a convenience store clerk and attempted to cash a forged payroll check in the amount of $454.75. . . . The court refused defendant's request for a choice of evils instruction, and it also refused to let him present any evidence that his concern for his children's welfare compelled his crimes. . . .

Choice of evils is a statutory defense applicable when the alleged crimes were necessary as an emergency measure to avoid an imminent public or private injury that is about to occur by reason of a situation occasioned or developed through no conduct of the actor and which is of sufficient gravity to outweigh the criminal conduct. The defendant must offer proof of the sudden and unforeseen emergence of a situation requiring his or her immediate action to prevent an imminent injury. [The defense] provides a legal justification for otherwise criminally culpable behavior. A defendant who asserts [the] defense admits the doing of a charged act, but seeks to justify the act on grounds deemed by law to be sufficient to avoid criminal responsibility. A defendant who has a reasonable legal alternative as a means to avoid the threatened injury is foreclosed from asserting a choice of evils defense. Moreover, a defendant who seeks to assert a choice of evils defense must offer evidence that the criminal conduct at issue did not exceed that reasonably necessary to avoid the impending injury . . . .

As part of his offer of proof, defendant indicated that his three children, who ranged in age from sixteen months to eleven years, suffered from serious health problems. On the date the crimes occurred, the children had not eaten for more than twenty-four hours, and three different food banks had turned down defendant's requests for food. Defendant feared that a lack of food would exacerbate his children's health problems and lead to malnutrition and death.

The trial court refused to give a choice of evils instruction, finding that defendant failed to establish an imminent threat of injury to his children and that he did not show that he could not have pursued other legal alternatives for obtaining food. We perceive no error.

While we are not without sympathy for the downtrodden, the law is clear that economic necessity alone cannot support a choice of crime. Although economic necessity may be an important issue in sentencing, a choice of evils defense cannot be based upon economic necessity.

Further, Colorado law requires that the defendant show a direct causal connection between the action taken and the harm sought to be prevented. Here, the trial court properly ruled by implication that the causal link was absent. This ruling finds support in the record from the circumstances of forgery and the relatively large amount of the forged instrument.

We conclude that defendant's offer of proof did not entitle him to assert a choice of evils defense, and the trial court did not err by refusing to give a choice of evils instruction to the jury and by refusing to allow defendant to use the theory as a general defense.

NOTES AND QUESTIONS

1. The Necessity Defense. The necessity defense is not limited to circumstances involving economic need. Rather, as the *Magadini* court makes clear, it "exonerates one who commits a crime under the 'pressure of circumstances' if the harm that would have resulted from compliance with the law . . . exceeds the harm actually resulting from the defendant's violation of the law." In the words of the drafters of the Model Penal Code, the defense "affords a general justification for conduct that would otherwise constitute an offense."

> Under this [principle] property may be destroyed to prevent the spread of a fire. . . . Mountain climbers lost in a storm may take refuge in a house or may appropriate provisions. Cargo may be jettisoned or an embargo violated to preserve the vessel. . . . A developed legal system must have better ways of dealing with such problems than to refer only to the letter of the particular prohibitions, framed without reference to cases of this kind.

Model Penal Code & Commentaries §3.02 cmt. 1 at 9-10.

As the MPC's commentary states, the necessity defense is generally classified as a justification, not an excuse.* In this respect, it bears a resemblance to self-defense, which is sometimes described as "a part of the law of necessity." It is worth noting, however, that self-defense is doctrinally understood to be a "narrower justificatio[n]" than the general necessity defense, *id.* at 11-12, that "has attained relatively fixed rules," as discussed in detail in Chapter Four. If a self-defense claim fails under those fixed rules, many jurisdictions will hold that the defendant "is precluded from justifying his use of force under the general provision for competing harms" set out in the necessity doctrine. State v. Crocker, 506 A.2d 209, 212 (Me. 1986). *But see* Bowen v. State, 162 S.W.3d 226, 229-230 (Tex. 2005) ("[S]elf-defense's statutorily imposed restrictions do not foreclose necessity's availability").[12]

---

* For additional discussion of the distinction between justifications and excuses, see Chapter Four (p. 317).

There is also a broader debate about whether necessity doctrine can ever be invoked in cases of homicide. A number of states say no, citing the sanctity of human life. The MPC, however, urges the opposite view.

> [R]ecognizing that the sanctity of life has a supreme place in the hierarchy of values, it is nonetheless true that conduct that results in taking life may promote the very value sought to be protected by the law of homicide. Suppose, for example, that the actor makes a break in a dike, knowing this will inundate a farm, but taking the only course available to save a whole town. . . . [H]e can rightly point out that the object of the law of homicide is to save life, and that by his conduct he has effected a net saving of innocent lives.

"Net saving" is a critical phrase in the preceding passage, as the MPC drafters insist that the "life of every individual must be taken . . . to be of equal value." The "numerical preponderance in the lives saved compared to those sacrificed" thus becomes the critical issue in the analysis. In cases in which a defendant's actions prevent *less* harm than they cause—whether with respect to homicide or more generally—the justification is not available, though it is possible such a defendant may still be able to invoke the defense of *duress*, which is discussed in Chapter Seven (p. 558).[13]

2. Economic Necessity. If the necessity defense is properly understood, per the discussion above, as broadly applicable when a defendant's actions avoid a more serious harm, how ought one understand the categorical holding in *Fontes* that the "defense cannot be based upon economic necessity," as in cases of poverty, starvation, or homelessness? The *Fontes* approach is adopted by multiple jurisdictions. Is there an argument that, to quote the MPC commentary, "mountain climbers lost in a storm may take refuge in a house or may appropriate provisions," but a homeless person caught in a storm may not do the same? Consider the following argument, forthrightly stated by a British court that, like *Fontes*, rejected the application of the necessity defense to cases of economic need:

> If homelessness were once admitted as a defence to trespass, no one's house could be safe. Necessity would open a door which no man could shut. . . . Each man would say his need was greater than the next man's. The plea would be an excuse for all sorts of wrongdoing. So the courts must, for the sake of law and order, take a firm stand. They must refuse to admit the plea of necessity to the hungry and the homeless; and trust that their distress will be relieved by the charitable and the good.

Borough of Southwark v. Williams (1971) 2 All E.R. 175, 179.[14]

3. What Is a Need? In those jurisdictions that do recognize the necessity defense in cases of economic necessity, what counts as a need? Recall that in *Magadini*, the court overturned six of Magadini's convictions but upheld the seventh, which arose from his entering an ice cream shop, against the wishes of its owner, because "he had to use the bathroom." Implicit in the court's opinion is a view that this need to relieve himself did not count as "clear and imminent danger." Do you agree? What if the same conditions that made it effectively impossible for Magadini to sleep anywhere in the town also made it impossible for him to use a toilet? More broadly, where ought courts or lawmakers draw lines regarding the things that count as necessities in modern society? Ought a person be able to steal internet access for purposes of applying for a job? Should a person be permitted to steal hygiene products, or make up?

Consider, in this respect, the transcript below of a sentencing hearing for a woman sick with cancer who was accused of shoplifting such sundries, along with baby wipes and other items.

Commonwealth v. Menser

No. CP-38-CR-2022-2018 (Ct. of Common Pleas of Lebanon Cnty. Pa. Jan. 22, 2020) (transcript of oral decision)

Mr. Feeman:	Good morning, Your Honor. May it please the Court . . . . My client is 36 years of age. She has a 10th grade education but did obtain her GED. She is the mother of three children. She's married. She's currently receiving disability and unable to work due to her physical and mental conditions as we outlined in the Sentencing Memorandum . . . . Your Honor, . . . my client is currently struggling with Stage IV cancer.
The Court:	I thought it was Stage I. The report said Stage I basal cell.
Mr. Feeman:	Only for the one part of her cancer. The cancer has —
The Defendant:	That's just for my uterus. That's why they want to do the hysterectomy.
The Court:	Okay.
Mr. Feeman:	She's currently scheduled to meet with her oncologist later this morning for a preoperation examination. And that is to be — the operation then is to be set today and to be scheduled in the immediate future. I know, Your Honor, my client's record is not exactly best. The prior record score —
The Court:	The best? 14 prior thefts.
The Defendant:	I'm not going to lie on oath, but a lot of the times that — I'm not saying none of them were me. But a lot of times I was with my kid's dad, he would be putting stuff in my kid's diaper bag.
The Court:	Oh, for God's sake. Don't even go there. Wait until we read the Affidavit of Probable Cause of this. It's horrible. I think you might want to be quiet. . . .

Mr. Feeman:	Thank you, Your Honor. What we're asking for in this case is a period of house arrest.
The Court:	How can we even do that? The [recommended] mitigated range is 3 to 6 months. This doesn't even allow house arrest. There's no RS [restorative sanction, i.e., minimally restrictive] component in this [recommended sentence report from the probation department]. The minimum up to the standard range is 6 months, but keep going.
Mr. Feeman:	We believe that sentencing her to house arrest would allow her to continue to treat—
The Court:	We can always do furloughs. Didn't stop her from stealing 14 times, her medical conditions prior—not this time. Because wait until we read this Affidavit of Probable Cause, knocked my socks off. Keep going.
Mr. Feeman:	Additionally, Your Honor, with the house arrest, it not only would allow her to treat, but continue to take care of her children and—
The Court:	Well, that's something she should have thought about 14 times ago. . . . You don't quit stealing. . . . All right. What do you want to tell me, ma'am?
The Defendant:	I don't even go in stores. I don't want to be in a store.
The Court:	Then why do you keep going in and stealing?
The Defendant:	I haven't been in the store since the last time I ever been caught with—
The Court:	You've been caught.
The Defendant:	—was stealing, which I wasn't even done with my shopping. They said because I had it in my child—I had my baby with me. I had a baby in the stroller while I couldn't push a cart and the stroller, and they said that I was stealing. I wasn't even done shopping. And I had money in my food card. I said I'm not even done shopping, how is that stealing? I didn't leave the store, I'm not done.
The Court:	Yeah. No, wait a minute. You were in the van when the police stopped—I'll read this Affidavit of Probable cause.
The Defendant:	Van?
The Court:	Yes. Let's read it because this is what you pled guilty to. "Your Affiant is Officer Shaun McGuire of the Palmyra Police . . . . On Thursday 9/20/18 I was on duty, in uniform, operating a marked patrol car, working the 1600 to 2400 shift. At approximately 1833 hours . . . I met with James Maldonado who's the Loss Prevention Officer with Weis Market . . . to report a retail theft that

occurred at approximately 1140 hours. . . . Maldonado provided video showing a white female stealing cosmetic products. I reviewed this video and it shows that . . . a white Dodge van . . . pulls in front of Weis Markets. A white female with brown hair, wearing a black sweat-shirt, maroon tank top, floral pants, a medical boot on her right foot and a black shoe on her left exits the van and enters the store. The woman was later identified as Ashley Menser . . . .

Menser is seen concealing numerous items into her red bag that she brought into the store, checking out at register 8, only paying for one gallon of ice tea, and exiting the store with her red bag that is fully visible, full of items that can be seen through the open top. The items that were stolen by Menser that were able to be identified by Weis personnel after watching the video include 3 Maybelline SuperStay foundations ($12.48 each), 1 Maybelline Satin Liquid ($9.99), 2 L'Oreal touch-on highlights ($12.00 each), one Paul Mitchell Super Skinny Serum ($21.99), 1 Kandoo baby wipes, 11 ounces of Village candle ($10.99) totaling $109.63. With sales tax it would have been $116.08.

. . . Menser admitted to stealing two boxes of hair color but she threw them in the dumpster by McDonald's. I informed Menser that she would be charged for Retail Theft and she said that she only told me that she stole the hair color to 'piss me off' in an attempt to discourage me from completing the investigation."

Now that's what the Affidavit of Probable Cause says. House arrest?

The Defendant:	I'll die in jail with cancer.
The Court:	Well, no, you won't because we'll give you a furlough to get whatever medical treatment is done. But listen, I can't protect Weis—look at this record. Let's talk about your record now. Okay. Let's talk about your record.

There's—first Retail Theft [as] a juvenile. Okay, you're dumb, it's 2000, 20 years ago. We'll wipe that one off. But adult Retail Theft '02, 2 years later when you were . . . 18 . . . . You got guilty fines and costs. But you don't listen. [In 2008] they sentenced you for two separate Retail Thefts on the same date and you got 6 months probation. But you didn't listen and then . . . you got caught for another Retail Theft and you got 23 months of probation, which was concurrent. But you don't stop there. And by the way, I'm not reading the other crimes that were non-theft related. The sixth theft that I marked was [in 2009]. You got 8 days in prison. And obviously that didn't impress you much because [months later] you get a Retail Theft . . . and you get 12 months probation. . . . You get another Retail Theft in [2011]. That's number 8 that I counted. You get 22 months probation. [Y]ou get another Retail Theft [in 2017] and a DUI, they gave you 2 years intermediate punishment . . . . And it just doesn't stop. [In 2018] you get another . . . [and] the same day you get another sentence for 23 months [intermediate punishment] but it's a different Retail Theft. There's several.

The Defendant: At that time I was struggling with drugs too.

The Court: Okay. Ashley, you know you don't — you sure don't struggle stealing stuff.

The Defendant: In my addiction —

The Court: You don't struggle stealing stuff. You seem to be able to — you are more than medically and physically and psychologically capable of going in to Weis and stealing stuff all the time and other places.

The Defendant: No, I won't no more.

The Court: . . . And now your lawyer bevies me with all this stuff about medical conditions and this and that and this and that. Here's what's ironic with all of it, if I was to buy that, I'm disabled, if she had all these medical conditions, why in the name of goodness was she walking around in Weis throwing hair color, nail things. Not nothing like baby food or something you would feed your child, right?

Mr. Feeman: Right.

The Court: Baby wipes is the closest we can get to, Kandoo wipes. Everything is cosmetic stuff that you don't need and you're stealing it. And then to make that admission to the Trooper. You don't care. You don't care and we cannot protect our merchants from you going right out on your way to some medical appointment and stealing again. Ma'am, it's all I can do not to send you to the state [prison], and maybe I should do that.

The Defendant: I don't even want to go in stores anymore.

The Court: Maybe I should do that because they have good medical provisions.

The Defendant: I just don't — I won't do — I won't do my medical.

The Court: And 6 months is the minimum I can even live with because this is — if I count right, and I hope I'm right, I

	don't want to miscount. There were 13 priors, so this is number 14.
Mr. Feeman:	You are correct, Your Honor.
The Court:	Okay. And I read all the medical stuff. And . . . by the way, ma'am, I had cancer on my tongue, they cut it out. I saw that. I was not insensitive to that. But it doesn't stop you from stealing.
The Defendant:	I haven't went in stores since the last time.
The Court:	Oh, yeah. You're like the drunk that tells me on the fifth or sixth DUI I haven't had a drink since the last time I was arrested. Well, I got to look at a prior record. I got to look at ranges. I've got to look at a lot of things. And I got to look at a lady that's 36 years old and has the capability right now of walking in and stealing more stuff because she isn't getting the message, and we've tried. We've tried. We've done intermediate punishment. We've done probation. We've done re-sentencing, it doesn't work. It doesn't work. District Attorney, anything?
Mr. Baker:	Your Honor, we're asking for restitution to Weis in the amount $109.63. But I think the Court is—I think the Commonwealth and the Court are on the same page here. It's her eighth Retail Theft overall. [S]o we are asking for incarceration because frankly I don't know what else to do in this case. It's clear she can't be in the community.
The Defendant:	I don't want to go to no stores any more.
The Court:	I've reviewed the pre-sentence investigation report. I've read this case carefully. I've gone back and forth and back and forth. Should I consider house arrest because of her medicals? No. It didn't stop you from stealing all these times. It is flagrant thefts. Just almost—and, you know, I didn't include the fraud or food stamp fraud. . . .
The Defendant:	I'm not even going to be able to take care of my cancer any more. I'm just going to let it kill me.
The Court:	Well, you know what, there are other people and there are other things. You should have thought about that on the last 13 times you stole. All right. I've reviewed the pre-sentence investigation report. This is an egregious, even though the amount is not large, this is a serial thief who will not stop. Who has serious problems. It is a felony. She doesn't have any remorse. She—I haven't seen anything that would lead me to not impose the sentence. I'm cognizant of the . . . medical facility care that the State provides. Accordingly, I'm going to impose the

following sentence consistent with the guideline ranges, and it is as follows:

Count I, Retail Theft, pay the cost of prosecution, and I find she has the ability to pay $10.00 on this fine. Pay the cost of prosecution, a fine of $10.00, and be incarcerated . . . in the State Correctional Facility for an indeterminate period of time, the minimum of which shall be 10 months, the maximum of which will be 7 years . . . .

The Defendant: My mental health. All my medicals, what about all my medicines? My Suboxone I've been on? I don't even go into stores.

The Court: Sheriff, take her and set her over there.

The Defendant: Please, I don't want to go to jail.

The Court: 7 and one-fourth months . . . . The Court urges the State Correctional Facility in light of the Defendant's apparent possible physical conditions, to promptly as possible, move her to a state facility that has adequate medical treatment for her issues. In addition, the Defendant shall pay restitution of $109.63 to Weis Markets at . . . a rate determined by Probation Services. Restitution payments shall commence immediately unless otherwise directed and is to be paid before fines and costs. . . .

The Defendant: . . . What about my mental health?

The Court: . . . They'll get—they'll get your medicines to you.

The Defendant: No. I'm on sustain health medications.

The Court: No, no. You're not ordering—you're not dictating the terms any more. You should have thought about that before. Sheriff, remove her from the courtroom. I'm not going to listen to that. . . . And . . . no contact with Weis Market.

Questions: Should the necessity defense be available to a defendant like Menser? More broadly, do you think the legal system—the prosecutor, the judge, the defense lawyer, the legislature—handled her case appropriately? If not, what should have been done differently by any of these actors?

4. Necessity and Protest. How ought the necessity defense apply when people intentionally break the law to help others harmed by socioeconomic conditions? Should a good Samaritan be permitted to open a safe injection site for users of illegal drugs? More broadly, should individuals who break the law as an act of civil disobedience be permitted to invoke the necessity defense, on the ground that their actions are necessary to avoid the greater harms of the conduct they seek to halt through their protest? Consider the following two cases and the excerpt that follows.

Commonwealth v. Leno

616 N.E.2d 453 (Mass. 1993)

ABRAMS, J. Massachusetts is one of ten States that prohibit distribution of hypodermic needles without a prescription. . . . In June, 1991, the defendants were arrested and charged with sixty-five counts of unauthorized possession of hypodermic needles and fifty-two counts of unauthorized possession of syringes. Each defendant also was charged with one count of distributing an instrument for the administration of a controlled substance.[4] The defendants told the police they were exchanging clean syringes and needles for dirty, possibly contaminated, ones to prevent the spread of AIDS.

Defendant Leno is a fifty-five year old grandfather, who had been addicted to alcohol, cocaine, heroin, or various pills from age twelve to forty-five. At the time of trial, he was in his tenth year of recovery from addiction; his health insurance covered his treatment. Leno learned of needle exchange programs from a National AIDS Brigade lecturer. Leno worked for needle exchange programs in Boston, in New Haven, Connecticut, and in New York City. Leno started a needle exchange program in Lynn in September, 1990, after realizing that "in my own back yard people were dying of AIDS and this particular service was not offered to them." Leno testified that he believed that by providing clean needles to addicts he was helping to stem the spread of AIDS, he was helping addicts, especially the homeless, to reach recovery, and that he was not helping addicts continue their habit. Defendant Robert Ingalls said that he is fifty-three years old and works as a landscaper. He joined Leno in operating a needle exchange program in Lynn as a matter of conscience: "I would have had a hard time with my conscience if I didn't do it . . . . It's sort of an irresistible opportunity for me, if you can save a life."

The two defendants legally purchased new sterile needles over-the-counter in Vermont. The defendants were at a specific location on Union Street in Lynn from 5 p.m. to 7 p.m. every Wednesday evening in 1991 until they were arrested June 19. They accepted dirty needles in exchange for clean needles; they exchanged between 150 and 200 needles each night, for fifty to sixty people. The defendants did not charge for the service or for the materials.

---

4. The police also confiscated several plastic bleach bottles filled with used, dirty syringes and needles. The police, fearing contracting AIDS by touching or counting these instruments, did not charge the defendants with possession of them. The police seized a number of packets containing information on drug treatment centers, the spread of AIDS, the sterilization of needles, and the hazards of sharing needles; the police also seized packages of condoms and small bottles of bleach and of water. The defendants were distributing these items along with clean needles.

The defendants offered expert testimony on AIDS and needle exchange programs. Doctor Ernest Drucker of the Montefiore Medical Center in the Bronx, who is also a professor of epidemiology at Einstein College of Medicine and an authority on the treatment of drug users and the relationship between intravenous drug use and AIDS, stated that: the sharing of needles by infected drug users transmits the AIDS virus; the mortality rate of persons diagnosed with human immunodeficiency virus (HIV) ten years ago is very high, in that fewer than five per cent still are alive; there is no cure for AIDS; studies of needle exchange programs revealed no evidence that such programs cause people who are not drug addicts to become addicts, but that evidence indicates that needle exchange programs bring some addicts into drug and AIDS treatment programs who would not otherwise be there; he could not think of any harmful effects caused by needle exchange programs, and no studies found harmful effects; needle exchange programs save lives; and AIDS accounts for three times as many deaths as all other drug-related causes, such as overdosing, combined.

Elaine O'Keefe, director of the AIDS Division of the New Haven (Connecticut) health department, which has run a needle exchange program for several years, said that the program has shown only positive results. She noted that: a Yale University research study found that the program had significantly reduced needle sharing and produced an estimated reduction of 33% in incidence of new infections among program participants . . . . [According to O'Keefe, the] needle exchange program is saving the lives of "drug users, sexual partners, mostly women, and children who are born of them."

Kathleen Gallagher, director of the AIDS surveillance program of the Massachusetts Department of Public Health, testified that AIDS is a very serious epidemic in Massachusetts and elsewhere, that the AIDS fatality rate is "essentially 100%," that so far more than 5,000 people in Massachusetts were diagnosed as having AIDS, and that many more are infected by HIV but are still asymptomatic. In 1991, 31% of new AIDS cases were intravenous drug users. When sexual partners and children were included, 38% of AIDS cases were associated with intravenous drug use. Fifty percent of Massachusetts women with AIDS contracted the disease through intravenous drug use.

Brian Condron, research director for the Massachusetts Legislature's joint committee on health care, stated that the Legislature had considered repeal of the prescription requirement and needle exchange legislation for several years, with different branches and committees giving approval of some of the bills at different times. The Legislature had not repealed the prescription requirement by the time of trial.

The defendants do not deny that they violated the provisions of the statutes restricting the possession and distribution of hypodermic needles; rather, they contend that the judge's refusal to instruct the jury on the defense of necessity was error. We disagree.

. . . The defendants' argument is that, in their view, the prescription requirement for possession and distribution of hypodermic needles and syringes is both ineffective and dangerous. The Legislature, however, has determined that it wants to control the distribution of drug-related paraphernalia and their use in the consumption of illicit drugs. That public policy is entitled to deference by courts. Whether a statute is wise or effective is not within the province of courts. "It is not for this court to judge the wisdom of legislation or to seek to rewrite the clear intention expressed by the statute." Mellor v. Berman, 454 N.E.2d 907, 913 (Mass. 1983). "Our deference to legislative judgments reflects neither an abdication of nor unwillingness to perform the judicial role; but rather a recognition of the separation of powers and the 'undesirability of the judiciary substituting its notions of correct policy for that of a popularly elected Legislature.'" Commonwealth v. Lammi, 435 N.E.2d 360, 361 (1982).

. . . The defendants argue that the increasing number of AIDS cases constitutes a societal problem of great proportions, and that their actions were an effective means of reducing the magnitude of that problem; they assert that their possession, transportation and distribution of hypodermic needles eventually will produce an over-all reduction in the spread of HIV and in the future incidence of AIDS. The defendants' argument raises the issue of jury nullification, not the defense of necessity. We decline to require an instruction on jury nullification. "We recognize that jurors may return verdicts which do not comport with the judge's instructions. We do not accept the premise that jurors have a right to nullify the law on which they are instructed by the judge, or that the judge must inform them of their power." Commonwealth v. Fernette, 500 N.E.2d 1290, 1298 n.23 (1986).

United States v. Schoon

971 F.2d 193 (9th. Cir. 1992)

BOOCHEVER, J. . . . On December 4, 1989, thirty people, including appellants, gained admittance to the IRS office in Tucson, where they chanted "keep America's tax dollars out of El Salvador," splashed simulated blood on the counters, walls, and carpeting, and generally obstructed the office's operation. After a federal police officer ordered the group, on several occasions, to disperse or face arrest, appellants were arrested. At a bench trial, appellants proffered testimony about conditions in El Salvador as the motivation for their conduct. They attempted to assert a necessity defense, essentially contending that their acts in protest of American involvement in El Salvador were necessary to avoid further bloodshed in that country. While finding appellants motivated solely by humanitarian concerns, the court nonetheless precluded the defense as a matter of law . . . .

A district court may preclude a necessity defense where "the evidence, as described in the defendant's offer of proof, is insufficient as a matter of law to support the proffered defense." United States v. Dorrell, 758 F.2d 427, 430 (9th Cir. 1985). . . . The district court denied the necessity defense on the grounds that (1) the requisite immediacy was lacking; (2) the actions taken would not abate the evil; and (3) other legal alternatives existed. . . .

Necessity is, essentially, a utilitarian defense. . . . What all the traditional necessity cases have in common is that the commission of the "crime" averted the occurrence of an even greater "harm." In some sense, the necessity defense allows us to act as individual legislatures, amending a particular criminal provision or crafting a one-time exception to it, subject to court review, when a real legislature would formally do the same under those circumstances. For example, by allowing prisoners who escape a burning jail to claim the justification of necessity, we assume the lawmaker, confronting this problem, would have allowed for an exception to the law proscribing prison escapes.

. . . [C]ivil disobedience seeks first and foremost to bring about the repeal of a law or a change of governmental policy, attempting to mobilize public opinion through typically symbolic action. . . . Thus, the most immediate "harm" this form of protest targets is the *existence* of the law or policy. However, the mere existence of a constitutional law or governmental policy cannot constitute a legally cognizable harm. There may be, of course, general harms that result from the targeted law or policy. Such generalized "harm," however, is too insubstantial an injury to be legally cognizable. . . . Thus, as a matter of law, the mere existence of a policy or law validly enacted by Congress cannot constitute a cognizable harm. If there is no cognizable harm to prevent, the harm resulting from criminal action taken for the purpose of securing the repeal of the law or policy necessarily outweighs any benefit of the action.

[Separately, protest is] unlikely to abate the evil precisely because the action is indirect. Here, the IRS obstruction, or the refusal to comply with a federal officer's order, are unlikely to abate the killings in El Salvador, or immediately change Congress's policy; instead, it takes another *volitional* actor not controlled by the protestor to take a further step; Congress must change its mind.

A final reason the necessity defense does not apply to these . . . cases is that legal alternatives will never be deemed exhausted when the harm can be mitigated by congressional action. . . . Because congressional action can *always* mitigate this "harm," lawful political activity to spur such action will always be a legal alternative. . . .

The real problem here is that litigants are trying to distort to their purposes an age-old common law doctrine meant for a very different set of circumstances. What these cases are really about is gaining notoriety for a cause — the defense allows protestors to get their political grievances discussed in a courtroom. . . . Because these attempts to invoke the necessity defense "force the courts to choose among causes they should make legitimate by extending the defense of necessity," *id.* at 432, and because the criminal acts, themselves, do not maximize social good, they should be subject to a *per se* rule of exclusion.

Martin Luther King, Jr., *Letter from Birmingham Jail* (Apr. 16, 1963). . . . You deplore the demonstrations taking place in Birmingham. But your statement, I am sorry to say, fails to express a similar concern for the conditions that brought about the demonstrations. I am sure that none of you would want to rest content with the superficial kind of social analysis that deals merely with effects and does not grapple with underlying causes. . . .

In any nonviolent campaign there are four basic steps: collection of the facts to determine whether injustices exist; negotiation; self purification; and direct action. . . . You may well ask: "Why direct action? Why sit ins, marches and so forth? Isn't negotiation a better path?" You are quite right in calling for negotiation. Indeed, this is the very purpose of direct action. Nonviolent direct action seeks to create such a crisis and foster such a tension that a community which has constantly refused to negotiate is forced to confront the issue. It seeks so to dramatize the issue that it can no longer be ignored. My citing the creation of tension as part of the work of the nonviolent resister may sound rather shocking. But I must confess that I am not afraid of the word "tension." I have earnestly opposed violent tension, but there is a type of constructive, nonviolent tension which is necessary for growth. Just as Socrates felt that it was necessary to create a tension in the mind so that individuals could rise from the bondage of myths and half truths to the unfettered realm of creative analysis and objective appraisal, so must we see the need for nonviolent gadflies to create the kind of tension in society that will help men rise from the dark depths of prejudice and racism to the majestic heights of understanding and brotherhood. The purpose of our direct action program is to create a situation so crisis packed that it will inevitably open the door to negotiation. I therefore concur with you in your call for negotiation. . . .

I hope you are able to see the distinction I am trying to point out. In no sense do I advocate evading or defying the law. . . . That would lead to anarchy. One who breaks an unjust law must do so openly, lovingly, and with a willingness to accept the penalty. I submit that an individual who breaks a law that conscience tells him is unjust, and who willingly accepts the penalty of imprisonment in order to arouse the conscience of the community over its injustice, is in reality expressing the highest respect for law.

III. WHITE-COLLAR CRIME

"A corporate prosecution is like a battle between David and Goliath. One would normally assume that federal prosecutors play the role of Goliath [as it] is hard to think of federal prosecutors as the little guy in any fight. Yet they may play the role of David when up against the largest and most powerful corporations in the world."

Brandon Garrett, *Too Big to Jail* 1 (2014)

Criminal law is not a tool for prosecuting economic crimes solely at the bottom of the socioeconomic ladder. Misconduct within and related to corporate settings—often called white-collar crime—can cause major harm, and can be criminally prosecuted. Indeed, as we will see in this section, criminal law has special doctrines of liability that apply only to corporations and corporate officers. But as we will also see, on a practical level, prosecutions of corporate actors often look very different from prosecutions for so-called "street crime." For in this setting, unlike virtually all others, the defendant may be more powerful than the government prosecuting the case.

We begin this part with an overview of some of the unique challenges associated with prosecution in the corporate setting. We then discuss in the following two sections a set of criminal law doctrines that outline the scope of liability in this context.

A. *Prosecution in the Corporate Setting*

The following excerpts give an overview of some of the unique challenges facing prosecutions of corporate actors, along multiple dimensions. The issues raised here will help frame the discussions of criminal liability doctrine in the two sections that follow.

William D. Cohan

How Wall Street Banks Stayed Out of Jail

Atlantic (Sept. 2015)

On May 27, [2015,] in her first major prosecutorial act as the new U.S. attorney general, Loretta Lynch unsealed a 47-count indictment against nine FIFA officials and another five corporate executives. She was passionate about their wrongdoing. "The indictment alleges corruption that is rampant, systemic, and deep-rooted both abroad and here in the United States," she said. "Today's action makes clear that this Department of Justice intends to end any such corrupt practices, to root out misconduct, and to bring wrongdoers to justice."

Lost in the hoopla surrounding the event was a depressing fact. Lynch and her predecessor, Eric Holder, appear to have turned the page on a more relevant vein of wrongdoing: the profligate and dishonest behavior of Wall Street bankers, traders, and executives in the years leading up to the 2008 financial crisis. How we arrived at a place where Wall Street misdeeds go virtually unpunished while soccer executives in Switzerland get arrested is murky at best. But the legal window for punishing Wall Street bankers for fraudulent actions that contributed to the 2008 crash has just about closed. It seems an apt time to ask: In the biggest picture, what justice has been achieved?

Since 2009, 49 financial institutions have paid various government entities and private plaintiffs nearly $190 billion in fines and settlements . . . . That may seem like a big number, but the money has come from shareholders, not individual bankers. (Settlements were levied on corporations, not specific employees, and paid out as corporate expenses — in some cases, tax-deductible ones.) In early 2014, just weeks after Jamie Dimon, the CEO of JPMorgan Chase, settled out of court with the Justice Department, the bank's board of directors gave him a 74 percent raise, bringing his salary to $20 million.

The more meaningful number is how many Wall Street executives have gone to jail for playing a part in the crisis. That number is one. (Kareem Serageldin, a senior trader at Credit Suisse, is serving a 30-month sentence for inflating the value of mortgage bonds in his trading portfolio, allowing them to appear more valuable than they really were.) By way of contrast, following the savings-and-loan crisis of the 1980s, more than 1,000 bankers of all stripes were jailed for their transgressions.

At an event at the National Press Club last February, Holder said the virtual absence of convictions (or even prosecutions) this time around did not result from a want of trying. "These are the kinds of cases that people come to the Justice Department to make," he said. "The inability to make them, at least to this point, has not been as a result of a lack of effort." Preet Bharara, the U.S. attorney for the Southern District of New York, [has similarly argued that the evidence] does not show clear misconduct by individuals. It's possible that Bharara is correct about that: Wall Street bankers make it their daily business to figure out ways to abide by the letter of the law while violating its spirit. And to be sure, much of the behavior that led to the crisis involved recklessness and poor judgment, not fraud. But even so, in light of various whistle-blower allegations — and the size of the settlements agreed to by the banks themselves — this explanation strains credulity. The Justice Department's ethos regarding Wall Street, and the *way* the department went about its business, appear to be a large part of the story.

Any narrative of how we got to this point has to start with the so-called Holder Doctrine, a June 1999 memorandum written by the then-deputy attorney general warning of the dangers of prosecuting big banks — a variant of the "too big to fail" argument that has since become so familiar. Holder's memo asserted that "collateral consequences" from prosecutions — including corporate instability or collapse — should be taken into account when deciding whether to prosecute a big financial institution. That sentiment was echoed as late as 2012 by Lanny Breuer, then the head of the Justice Department's criminal division, who said in a speech at the New York City Bar Association that he felt it was his duty to consider the health of the company, the industry, and the markets in deciding whether or not to file charges.

In the aftermath of the crash, the Justice Department did not refrain from prosecutions altogether. In 2009, the U.S. attorney for the Eastern District of New York tried two Bear Stearns hedge-fund managers — Ralph Cioffi and Matthew Tannin — who had effectively run their $1.6 billion fund into the ground in the spring of 2007, an event that many believe was the canary in the coal mine of the financial crisis. But a jury acquitted the two men in November 2009. Added to the general fear that the economy was extraordinarily fragile, the unexpected acquittal seemed to put a deep freeze on Wall Street prosecutions for close to three years.

. . . A team led by Benjamin Wagner, the U.S. attorney for the Eastern District of California, investigated alleged wrongdoing at JPMorgan Chase. . . . [His] investigation was typical of the Justice Department's approach: hoover up hundreds of thousands of pages of e-mails and documents, interview current and former employees about their business practices, and use the findings as a cudgel to extract a financial settlement. Wagner and his team drafted — but did not file — a complaint against the firm in September 2013 that reportedly detailed how JPMorgan Chase . . . knowingly packaged shoddy mortgages into securities that did not meet its credit standards and then sold them off to investors. As part of its investigation, Wagner's team had deposed Alayne Fleischmann, a JPMorgan Chase banker turned whistle-blower, who'd told the team about what was going on. She had also detailed how, before the crash, her warnings about continuing to package up the bad mortgages into securities and sell them off as investments had gone unheeded by her superiors. After sharing her concerns with her boss in a 13-page letter, Fleischmann had been marginalized and then fired. (Disclosure: JPMorgan Chase also fired [Cohan, the author of this piece], as a managing director, in 2004, and [he was later] in litigation with the bank resulting from a soured investment . . . made in 1999.)

In November 2013, as part of a deal that kept Wagner's complaint from becoming public — and the specifics of Fleischmann's revelations from being widely disseminated — JPMorgan Chase agreed to a $13 billion settlement with various federal and state agencies, then the largest of its kind. Holder heralded the settlement as an important moment of accountability for Wall Street. But extracting large settlements paid with shareholders' money is not the same as bringing alleged wrongdoers to justice. Instead of presenting a detailed picture of JPMorgan Chase's misdeeds—as would have happened had Wagner's complaint been filed and the matter adjudicated in court—the government and the bank negotiated an anodyne 11-page "Statement of Facts" that glossed over many of the details of the behavior Fleischmann was trying to stop, and did not name any JPMorgan Chase bankers.

The Justice Department reached agreements with other Wall Street banks, among them Citigroup and Bank of America, using a similar playbook: Threaten public disclosure of behavior that looks criminal and then, in exchange for keeping it sealed, extract a huge financial settlement. No one individual, or group of individuals, is held accountable. No predawn raids of Park Avenue apartments are made. No one gets arrested. No one gets publicly shamed. . . . [And] the message that their behavior was unacceptable goes undelivered. Instead a very different message is being sent: for financiers, justice is just a check someone else has to write.

James Kwak

America's Top Prosecutors Used to Go After Top Executives. What Changed?

N.Y. Times (July 5, 2017)

Since the turn of the century, changes in the political landscape, the defense bar, the courts and most important the Justice Department have undermined both the ability and the resolve of America's top prosecutors to go after corporations or their executives. . . .

This [newly] solicitous attitude toward corporations was part of a larger cultural shift in the business and legal world. Defending executives became an increasingly lucrative practice for elite law firms, which recruited star prosecutors from the Justice Department. Corporations accused of misconduct lawyered up, offering extensive internal investigations but erecting imposing defenses around individual executives. Banks cultivated plausible deniability, their internal oversight systems too feeble to pin responsibility on any individual; Goldman executives used the abbreviation LDL—"let's discuss live"—to hide their traces. Prosecutors and regulators [facing these tactics] could either negotiate a modest settlement and declare victory or take on the daunting task of bringing actual people to trial—with the significant risk of losing. [As a result,] "A symbiotic relationship developed between Big Law and the Department of Justice," [reporter Jesse] Eisinger writes. Corporations got off paying symbolic penalties, defense firms raked in huge fees, and prosecutors earned P.R. victories—as long as everyone played along.

Increasingly, the prosecutors and the defense attorneys on opposite sides of the table are the same people, just at different points in their careers. Conducting a criminal investigation of an executive isn't just risky;

in addition to jeopardizing a future partnership at a prestigious law firm, perhaps most important, it incurs "social discomfort," especially for the well-mannered overachievers who now populate the Justice Department. No one wants to be a class traitor, especially when the members of one's class are such nice people.

In the eyes of the elite establishment, businesses are now job creators and pillars of the community. Executives who bend the rules are "good people who have done one bad thing," in the words of one S.E.C. lawyer reluctant to bring charges against individuals. Prosecutors no longer punish lawbreakers, but instead make corporations promise to behave better in the future—in the end amounting to "at most a tollbooth on the bankster turnpike," as the longtime S.E.C. attorney Jim Kidney lamented. . . . After decades in which Wall Street masters of the universe were lionized in the media and popular culture, star investment bankers—rich, usually white men in nice suits—just don't match the popular image of criminals. . . .

[Meanwhile, the Justice Department has become] increasingly staffed by intelligent, status-seeking, conformist graduates of the nation's top law schools—all of whom ha[ve] friends on Wall Street and in the defense bar. In that environment, the easy choice [i]s to play along . . . . As Upton Sinclair might have written were he alive today: It is difficult to get a man to understand something, when his résumé depends upon his not understanding it.

There's just one problem. While the "unelected permanent governing class" may have been willing to look the other way when highly paid bankers wrecked the economy, many of the workers who lost their jobs and families who lost their homes were not. Outside the Beltway, the fact that the Wall Street titans who blew up the financial system suffered little more than slight reductions in their bonuses only reinforced the perception that the "system" is "rigged"—with the consequences we know only too well.[15]

Jennifer Arlen

Removing Prosecutors from the Boardroom: Limiting Prosecutorial Discretion to Impose Structural Reforms

Prosecutors in the Boardroom 62, 68-70
(Anthony S. Barkow & Rachel E. Barkow eds., 2011)

The DOJ did not always encourage prosecutors to refrain from indicting firms whose employees clearly had committed criminal violations—quite the contrary. At one point, prosecutors targeted corporations. Yet this more aggressive approach to corporate prosecution was not effective at inducing firms to take the most basic actions needed to deter corporate crime. . . .

To deter corporate crime, the government must ensure that the individuals tempted to commit crimes expect to be punished. . . . Federal authorities cannot effectively deter corporate crime . . . because . . . federal authorities often will be unable either to detect corporate crimes or to identify and sanction those responsible with sufficient regularity. Given the complex, far-reaching, and often decentralized nature of the modern publicly held firm, corporate crimes usually are hard to detect. They can remain hidden for years, even forever. Moreover, even when the government does detect wrongdoing, it may be unable to identify and punish the individuals responsible because corporate crimes often involve actions by many people, and often the person who committed the physical act that constitutes the crime is not the person who made the decision to commit it. As a result, many perpetrators of corporate crime could reap large rewards safe in the knowledge that the government would not be able to convict them.

Alexander Dyck et al.

Who Blows the Whistle on Corporate Fraud?

65 J. Fin. 2213, 2240-2245 (2010)

[E]mployee whistleblowers face significant costs. . . . Many of the individuals [interviewed in our study] are quoted as saying, "If I had to do it over again, I wouldn't." Employees clearly have the best access to information. Few, if any, frauds can be committed without the knowledge and often the support of several employees. . . . In 37% of the cases [we examined], the whistleblower conceals his identity. This is a clear sign that the expected reputational costs exceed the expected reputational benefits of whistleblowing. This impression is confirmed by the data on the cases in which the identity of the whistleblower was revealed. . . . [I]n 82% of the[se] cases, the whistleblower was fired, quit under duress, or had significantly altered responsibilities. In addition, many employee whistleblowers report having to move to another industry and often to another town to escape personal harassment. The lawyer of James Bingham, a whistleblower [against Xerox], sums up Jim's situation as follows: "Jim had a great career, but he'll never get a job in Corporate America again."

Samuel W. Buell

Capital Offenses

146-151 (2016)

In some instances, a firm practically pays its workers to break the law and then hides evidence of the crime. . . . Suppose [a] whistleblower at Walmart . . . called the SEC or the FBI anonymously and said, "Walmart has been paying massive bribes in Mexico, you need to look into it." . . . If you were the prosecutor initially assigned to this, and were told by your supervisor to figure out whether Walmart violated the [Foreign Corrupt Practices Act, a federal criminal statute] against bribing foreign officials, what might you do?

. . . Walmart is really, really big. As in any white collar case, the evidence that will allow you to figure out what happened is going to consist of paper and electronic records and people telling you what happened at their work. And not much else. . . . [Y]ou can pretty much forget real-time informants and tapes. . . .

You certainly have the power to start subpoenaing documents from Walmart and calling its employees into the grand jury for questioning under oath . . . . You might even be able to cobble together enough facts, together with your anonymous tip, to persuade a judge to let you go into Walmart's offices in Arkansas with a search warrant and dig around in the company's documents. But where would you even begin? Would you subpoena Walmart for every document it has about Mexico? Would you start marching hundreds of employees who might know something about the Mexico operation into the grand jury one at a time? To review those millions of documents and handle all those witnesses will take at least months and probably years. The task will require a large team of prosecutors and investigators. All the while, you'll be playing something like the game of Battleship, blindly asking questions and groping around in the documents, trying to guess where the evidence of crime might be tucked away inside the giant company. You will get little help from Walmart's personnel, who will view you and the investigation (correctly) as adversary cops on a mission to imprison someone.

These problems stand in the way of big corporate investigations. Volkswagen, for example, has disclosed that in its internal investigation of the company's cheating on emissions laws, its outside law firm gathered 102 terabytes (the equivalent of 50 million books) of data. . . . The Department of Justice and other federal enforcement agencies could not conduct corporate criminal investigations this way unless Congress multiplied their budgets and personnel by at least ten. Even then, maybe only a dozen really big cases could be seriously pursued in any year.[16]

B. Corporate Liability

The preceding section identifies various challenges facing corporate prosecutions. Some are cultural, as in James Kwak's account of the revolving door between prosecutorial offices and defense firms and of the broader tendency to view white-collar crime as less serious than "conventional" crime, even when the societal harms are substantial. But other challenges are tied to the power and sophistication of large corporate defendants, who may have the resources to go toe to toe with the Department of Justice and the savvy to make an investigation or prosecution as complex and costly as possible. With respect to these latter challenges, substantive criminal law can try to level the playing field—by creating doctrines of liability unique to the corporate context. One of those doctrines, discussed in this section, applies directly to the corporation itself, which can in certain circumstances be held liable for crimes committed by its employees.

United States v. Hilton Hotels Corp.

467 F.2d 1000 (9th Cir. 1972)

BROWNING, J. This is an appeal from a conviction under an indictment charging a violation of section 1 of the Sherman Act, 15 U.S.C. § 1.

Operators of hotels, restaurants, hotel and restaurant supply companies, and other businesses in Portland, Oregon, organized an association to attract conventions to their city. To finance the association, members were asked to make contributions in predetermined amounts. Companies selling supplies to hotels were asked to contribute an amount equal to one per cent of their sales to hotel members. To aid collections, hotel members, including appellant [Hilton Hotels], agreed to give preferential treatment to suppliers who paid their assessments, and to curtail purchases from those who did not.

The jury was instructed that such an agreement by the hotel members, if proven, would be a per se violation of the Sherman Act. . . . [We agree that] the conduct involved here was of the kind long held to be forbidden without more. "Throughout the history of the Sherman Act, the courts have had little difficulty in finding unreasonable restraints of trade in agreements among competitors, at any level of distribution, designed to coerce those subject to a boycott to accede to the action or inaction desired by the group or to exclude them from competition." Barber, *Refusals to Deal Under the Federal Antitrust Laws*, 103 U. Pa. L. Rev. 847, 872-873 (1955). . . .

Appellant's president testified that it would be contrary to the policy of the corporation for the manager of one of its hotels to condition purchases upon payment of a contribution to a local association by the supplier. The manager of appellant's Portland hotel and his assistant testified that it was the hotel's policy to purchase supplies solely on the basis of price, quality, and service. They also testified that on two occasions they told the hotel's purchasing agent that he was to take no part in the boycott. The purchasing agent confirmed the receipt of these instructions, but admitted that, despite them, he had threatened a supplier with loss of the hotel's business unless the supplier paid the association assessment. He testified that he violated his instructions because of anger and personal pique toward the individual representing the supplier.

Based upon this testimony, appellant requested certain instructions bearing upon the criminal liability of a corporation for the unauthorized acts of its agents. These requests were rejected by the trial court. The court instructed the jury that a corporation is liable for the acts and statements of its agents "within the scope of their employment," defined to mean "in the corporation's behalf in performance of the agent's general line of work," including "not only that which has been authorized by the corporation, but also that which outsiders could reasonably assume the agent would have authority to do." The court added:

> A corporation is responsible for acts and statements of its agents, done or made within the scope of their employment, even though their conduct may be contrary to their actual instructions or contrary to the corporation's stated policies.

Appellant objects only to the court's concluding statement.

Congress may constitutionally impose criminal liability upon a business entity for acts or omissions of its agents within the scope of their employment. Such liability may attach without proof that the conduct was within the agent's actual authority, and even though it may have been contrary to express instructions. . . .

Legal commentators have argued forcefully that it is inappropriate and ineffective to impose criminal liability upon a corporation, as distinguished from the human agents who actually perform the unlawful acts, particularly if the acts of the agents are unauthorized. But . . . the strenuous efforts of corporate defendants to avoid conviction, particularly under the Sherman Act, strongly suggests that Congress is justified in its judgment that exposure of the corporate entity to potential conviction may provide a substantial spur to corporate action to prevent violations by employees . . . .

Complex business structures, characterized by decentralization and delegation of authority, commonly adopted by corporations for business purposes, make it difficult to identify the particular corporate agents responsible for Sherman Act violations. At the same time, it is generally true that high management officials, for whose conduct the corporate directors and stockholders are the most clearly responsible, are likely to have participated in the policy decisions underlying Sherman Act violations, or at least to have become aware of them.

Violations of the Sherman Act are a likely consequence of the pressure to maximize profits that is commonly imposed by corporate owners upon managing agents and, in turn, upon lesser employees. In the face of that pressure, generalized directions to obey the Sherman Act, with the probable effect of foregoing profits, are the least likely to be taken seriously. And if a violation of the Sherman Act occurs, the corporation, and not the individual agents, will have realized the profits from the illegal activity.

In sum, identification of the particular agents responsible for a Sherman Act violation is especially difficult, and their conviction and punishment is peculiarly ineffective as a deterrent. At the same time, conviction and punishment of the business entity itself is likely to be both appropriate and effective. For these reasons we conclude that as a general rule a corporation is liable under the Sherman Act for the acts of its agents in the scope of their employment, even though contrary to general corporate policy and express instructions to the agent.

Thus the general policy statements of appellant's president were no defense. Nor was it enough that appellant's manager told the purchasing agent that he was not to participate in the boycott. The purchasing agent was authorized to buy all of appellant's supplies. Purchases were made on the basis of specifications, but the purchasing agent exercised complete authority as to source. He was in a unique position to add the corporation's buying power to the force of the boycott. Appellant could not gain exculpation by issuing general instructions without undertaking to enforce those instructions by means commensurate with the obvious risks. . . .

Model Penal Code Excerpt

Section 2.07. Liability of Corporations, Unincorporated Associations and Persons Acting, or Under a Duty to Act, in Their Behalf

(1) A corporation may be convicted of the commission of an offense if . . . the commission of the offense was authorized, requested, commanded, performed or recklessly tolerated by the board of directors or by a high managerial agent acting in behalf of the corporation within the scope of his office or employment.

. . . .

(4) As used in this Section . . . "high managerial agent" means an officer of a corporation or an unincorporated association, or, in the case of a partnership, a partner, or any other agent of a corporation or association having duties of such responsibility that his conduct may fairly be assumed to represent the policy of the corporation or association.

NOTES AND QUESTIONS

1. Corporate Personhood. In the wake of campaign finance decisions like the U.S. Supreme Court's ruling in *Citizens United v. Federal Election Commission*, 558 U.S. 310 (2010), the notion that "corporations are people" has become politically contested. As a legal matter, however, the idea of corporate personhood stretches back to before the founding of the country. William Blackstone, writing his famous treatise on the English common law, described corporations as "artificial persons" that provide a "necessary" means of facilitating collaborative investment among individuals over time. "[P]ersons in their natural capacities," Blackstone wrote, referring to human beings, have only "rights [that] die with the person," but corporations have "perpetual succession" that amounts to "legal immortality." As a result, Blackstone argued, corporations usefully allow "a series of individuals, one after another," to coordinate, amass property, and exercise legal rights over time—and indeed, in perpetuity.[17]

In the U.S. federal system, where the most complex corporate prosecutions today take place, the idea of corporate personhood is codified in the first section of the U.S. Code, which says that whenever the word "person" is used in a federal statute it "include[s] corporations, companies, associations, firms, partnerships, societies, and joint stock companies, as well as individuals." 1 U.S.C. §1. By virtue of this statutory definition, Professor Brandon Garrett writes, "a corporation can be prosecuted for just about any crime that an individual can be prosecuted for," though in practice corporations tend to be "prosecuted for crimes likely to take place in a business setting, such as accounting fraud, banking fraud, environmental violations, foreign bribery, money laundering, price fixing, securities fraud, and wire fraud."[18]

   2. Which Agents? *Hilton Hotels* establishes the accepted rule of corporate liability in federal courts, which is sometimes referred to as *respondeat superior* liability. As the opinion says, a corporation is liable under this approach "for the acts of its agents in the scope of their employment," with agents here referring, at minimum, to all of the employees of the corporation. By contrast, the MPC's default rule of corporate liability is narrower, applying only to a subset of agents whom the Code terms "high managerial agents." Consider the following case, which explores the boundaries of that term of art in a state that follows the MPC's general approach.

State v. Cmty. Alternatives Mo., Inc., 267 S.W.3d 735 (Mo. Ct. App. 2008). Defendant is a corporation. Defendant's management chain includes a chief executive officer, regional vice presidents, and regional directors. Defendant operates more than 30 group homes, including Turtle Creek Group Home at Bolivar, Missouri (Turtle Creek). Its management chain for the operation of the group homes is divided into three divisions—North, Central, and South. Each division is headed by an executive director, an associate director, and a program coordinator. Turtle Creek is part of defendant's South division. . . .

   Mary Collura was lead staff person for two of the group homes in the South division, Turtle Creek and Forest Ridge. Lead staff person is a management position. Collura was entrusted with the care, safety, health, and well-being of the residents of Turtle Creek. Collura's responsibilities included managing residents' medical care and supervising the staffs at Turtle Creek and Forest Ridge. Collura attended management meetings with [the associate director of the division]. She also performed training for the direct support staff for multiple homes within the South division. She gave job evaluations, disciplined support staff, and had authority to write checks on residents' accounts to buy personal items for them. She was provided a company credit card for use in purchasing supplies.

   Mary Collura had authority to take residents to the doctor when necessary. She was responsible for getting residents to their appointments on time and for maintaining residents' prescriptions and refills. Her duties included ensuring that residents' medical care was properly documented and relaying medical information regarding residents to case managers with the Department of Mental Health.

Gary Oheim was a resident of Turtle Creek from February 2001 until his death on January 30, 2002. He was mentally retarded and suffered from cerebral palsy. He was confined to a wheel chair. He could not move himself. He had to be repositioned often to prevent bedsores from developing. [Collura was made aware that Oheim had developed bedsores but did not communicate this information to his doctors when taking him for appointments, and at times took steps to prevent the doctors from discovering the bedsores. Defendant corporation was convicted of criminal neglect of Oheim based on Collura's conduct.]

[Under our statute,] " 'High managerial agent' means an officer of a corporation or any other agent in a position of comparable authority with respect to . . . the supervision in a managerial capacity of subordinate employees." The plain language of the statute [covers] a person authorized to act in behalf of a corporation who has managerial authority to supervise subordinate employees, comparable to a corporate officer . . . . It is the function within a corporate structure that must be considered, not merely job titles.

In this case, defendant operated many facilities, or business units, under a single corporate ownership. Each business unit had personnel responsible for the care of the residents at its facility. This court does not perceive the legislative intent that fostered enactment of [our statute] to have been to treat large corporations with numerous operating units different from those that operate a single or a few business units. . . .

Mary Collura managed and supervised the employees responsible for providing patient care. She determined what medical care would be afforded Gary Oheim pursuant to the business structure prescribed by defendant. She was defendant's "lead staff person" at Turtle Creek. She supervised staff at Turtle Creek. The support staff at Turtle Creek responsible for direct care-giving to residents reported to Collura. . . . Collura was the only manager who was regularly present at Turtle Creek. There was evidence that Collura's corporate supervisor, Lisa Martin, visited Turtle Creek only about once a month, although Martin testified that she tried to visit Turtle Creek once a week. . . . In the capacity in which she supervised subordinate employees, the evidence was sufficient to permit the jury to find Mary Collura was an agent in a position of comparable authority as an officer of the corporation.

Scott, J., concurring in part and in result. Defendant claims Ms. Collura's supervisory authority as lead person over two of its facilities was not comparable to that of its corporate officers. . . . [T]he flexibility of modern corporate laws and structures could enable "branch managers" to exercise authority comparable to that of a corporate officer, at least within their sphere of influence and with respect to their subordinate employees. To the extent a corporation authorized or permitted branch managers to so act, it would seem appropriate to impute corporate criminal responsibility arising from or relating to those actions. That said, I reject the State's arguments to the extent they suggest that any manager who supervises subordinate employees could be deemed a [high managerial agent]. I believe this interpretation could extend corporate criminal liability far beyond our legislature's intent.

   3. Debating Corporate Liability. When large, publicly traded companies are prosecuted, the executives and managers may bear the brunt of any public opprobrium, and could face career consequences. But if the company's business takes a hit, its shareholders will also be harmed—including ordinary members of the public who invest retirement funds in the company through mutual funds, pension funds, and other standard investment devices. "In most cases," the Model Penal Code drafters write, "these shareholders have not participated in the criminal conduct and lack the practical means of supervision of corporate management to prevent misconduct by corporate agents." Model Penal Code and Commentaries §2.07 cmt. 2(c) at 335. They are, in other words, innocent bystanders. And beyond these shareholders, Professor Albert Alschuler observes, "innocent employees, creditors, customers, and communities sometimes feel the pinch too" when a company they depend upon is prosecuted. For all these reasons, the MPC drafters write, corporate punishment "ought not to be authorized except where [it] clearly may be expected to accomplish desirable social purposes." *Id.* at 336. What are those social purposes? And do they justify criminal sanctions? Consider the following excerpts.[19]

Daniel R. Fischel & Alan O. Sykes, *Corporate Crime*, 25 J. Legal Stud. 319, 320-321 (1996). [C]orporations cannot be imprisoned; they can only be forced to pay money damages. The essential question, then, is whether the criminal law has any useful role to play in setting the damages that firms must pay for the wrongful acts of their agents. This in turn is really two questions: (1) when should the government rather than private parties sue for damages, and (2) in those cases where the government is the preferred plaintiff, when should the action be criminal rather than civil? The answers to these two questions are, respectively, sometimes and never. Although there are cases where government fines and penalties make sense, the civil liability system is better suited to calculate appropriate fines and penalties for organizational defendants. At best, the case for corporate criminal liability must rest on the need to correct some deficiency in the system of civil liability. But a close look at the cases reveals no such deficiency most of the time. Instead, corporate criminal liability is often heaped on top of substantial civil liability in circumstances where there is no reason to believe that civil liability alone would not produce appropriate deterrence. The result is overdeterrence ex ante, and an excessive investment of resources in litigation ex post.

Dan M. Kahan, *Social Meaning and the Economic Analysis of Crime*, 27 J. Legal Stud. 609, 618-619 (1998). [A]ccording to the punishment critics, [deterrence of corporate misconduct] can always be achieved at less cost through civil than through criminal liability. This is so, in part, because criminal fines, unlike (properly calibrated) civil damages, are not tied to expected social harm: fines come in statutorily fixed amounts that are likely either to under- or (more likely, according to the critics) overdeter corporate misconduct. Civil liability is also more efficient because it avoids criminal law's costly procedural protections, including the jury-trial right and the beyond-a-reasonable-doubt standard of proof. Finally, civil is better because it imposes less stigma, which is an inherently wasteful means of inflicting disutility on a corporate wrongdoer: "no one receives a corporation's lost reputation, whereas someone—the government or a private party—receives the cash fine."

Lawrence Friedman, *In Defense of Corporate Criminal Liability*, 23 Harv. J.L. & Pub. Pol'y 833, 857-858 (2000). But deterrence and efficiency are not the only interests in play. There is also the interest in expressive retribution, which provides reason enough not to dispense entirely with corporate criminal liability. Absent the possibility of criminal liability, corporations would escape moral condemnation for wrongdoing, and the retributive import of criminal liability to the community would be lost. For under a civil liability regime for the corporation qua corporation, there would be no moral condemnation equivalent to a criminal conviction: if found civilly liable, a corporation might be deemed negligent, or perhaps reckless, but no statement, in the form of a conviction, would attest to the proper valuation of the persons or goods [that were harmed]. In the end, the financial liability imposed would come to be viewed, by both the corporation and the community, merely as a cost of doing business. . . . Thus corporate exemption from criminal liability would tend to undermine the condemnatory effect of criminal liability on individuals in respect to similar conduct—and, ultimately, to diminish the moral authority of the criminal law as a guide to rational behavior.

Samuel W. Buell, *Capital Offenses* 151-153 (2016). Criminalizing corporations isn't only a way to impose responsibility for harms . . . [n]or is it just a way to deter crime . . . . It's also—indeed, has become mainly—a way to get corporations to help the government gather evidence. If you say to Walmart's lawyers that you're likely to charge the company itself with any [crimes] you discover by its employees unless the company helps you investigate the case, barriers around Walmart's evidence will fall away. . . . The company's management doesn't want you holding a press conference to say

Walmart is a bad corporate citizen . . . . Most of all, Walmart's top managers really don't want the company charged as a criminal. That would deal a blow to the company's reputation, and therefore their reputation as well. A criminal charge also might prevent Walmart from carrying on parts of its business, including selling things to the government, because of laws barring convicted felons from some industries and contracts.

[But] Walmart's executives and lawyers [also] control two things that will speed up your investigation. First, they have a bigger budget. They can hire lots of worker-bee lawyers to swarm Walmart and collect the relevant documents and witnesses. They can fly their . . . employees to you to be interviewed and testify. And their tech people can digitize and search the company's documents. Second, Walmart bosses have the power to fire Walmart employees [and can thus] require their employees, as a condition of remaining at Walmart, to "cooperate" in any criminal investigation. . . .

[For all these reasons,] the government has come to rely heavily on corporate liability for investigating corporate crime. Prosecutors trade liability for policing [conducted by the corporation itself].

Sara Sun Beale, *Is Corporate Criminal Liability Unique?*, 44 Am. Crim. L. Rev. 1503, 1506 (2007). Criminal liability should not be the only remedy, but the hammer of corporate criminal liability should remain in the toolkit of responses to serious corporate misconduct . . . . Nor should prosecutors have less leverage than usual in dealing with the best educated, most sophisticated, and most well represented class of defendants. [It's true] that excessive sanctions have real and terrible costs not only for defendants, but equally serious collateral costs. This is just as true in the case of drug offenses as it is in the case of the criminal conviction of a corporation. . . . The collateral impact of harsh federal sentencing, especially for drug offenses, is felt most starkly in some segments of the community, particularly the African-American community. . . . Thus corporate and white collar scholars and commentators have put their fingers on a problem all right: our sentencing laws have ratcheted up time and time again, with serious collateral effects. This is true across the board . . . . These terrible collateral costs, whether they are imposed on employees and shareholders or children and communities, should be seriously considered in reviewing the current costs of the federal sentencing laws.

4. The Corporate Death Penalty. In 2001, following the exposure of widespread fraud at an energy company called Enron, the Department of Justice filed criminal charges against a company named Arthur Andersen, which was then one of the largest accounting firms in the country and which had been Enron's accountant. Arthur Andersen was convicted of facilitating Enron's fraud by destroying incriminating documents, and while the conviction was later overturned by the Supreme Court, the damage by then had been done: Arthur Andersen's business collapsed between the time it was indicted and the time it was convicted. As Gabriel Markoff writes, this episode soon came to be cited in support of the "unquestioned dogma that a criminal indictment alone can easily destroy even a large, powerful corporation." But that conclusion, Markoff argues, is too quick, at least when it comes to large, publicly traded corporations. In a comprehensive review of fifty-four prosecutions of such companies between 2001 and 2010, Markoff finds that all but five remained actively traded following their prosecutions or were "acquired by another company under favorable circumstances that did not implicate a business failure." The remaining five "suffered fates that could reasonably be described as business failures," though even here, Markoff writes, "none of the companies could reasonably be said to have suffered a business failure because of their convictions."[20]

    5. *Deferred Prosecution Agreements.* Given the fears of collateral harms associated with corporate prosecutions, a now-common approach among federal prosecutors is to pursue what are called *deferred prosecution agreements* (DPAs) or *nonprosecution agreements* (NPAs). As their names suggest, these are agreements *not* to prosecute a corporate defendant so long as the corporation agrees to comply with certain conditions for a set period of time. According to the U.S. Justice Department, these agreements "occupy an important middle ground between declining prosecution and obtaining the conviction of a corporation." The agreements "help restore the integrity of a company's operations and preserve [its] financial viability," the Department writes, while also facilitating "prompt restitution and other compensation for victims." Some scholars, however, offer a more skeptical or critical view. Consider the following excerpts.[21]

Brandon Garrett, *Too Big to Jail* 48 (2014). [I]t is not always clear what prosecutors get in exchange for offering leniency to some of the world's largest companies. The terms of these agreements often lack any rigorous structural reforms. Most [do] require the creation of some kind of compliance program (63 percent, or 160 of 255 [agreements reviewed]), but only a quarter called for independent monitors to supervise compliance, and fewer required evaluating the effectiveness of compliance. More typically, prosecutors ask the company to hire new compliance employees (35 percent, or 88 of 255 agreements), but almost one third did not mention implementing a compliance program at all (31 percent, or 78 of 255 agreements). The agreements were short-lived, lasting for an average of just over two years. It is doubtful that a large company's culture can be reformed in so little time. Despite the genuine ambition of the new approach, reading the terms of these agreements tells us something quite unsettling about how large corporate prosecutions are actually resolved.

Lisa Kern Griffin, *Inside-Out Enforcement,* in *Prosecutors in the Boardroom* 110, 110-111 (Anthony S. Barkow & Rachel E. Barkow eds., 2011). The increasing use of DPAs between the federal government and corporate defendants provides a key mechanism for regulation by prosecutors. . . . They offer corporations an intermediate sanction that averts some of the collateral consequences of indictment and conviction, but they require in exchange full cooperation with the investigation and remedial measures after settlement. . . . [T]here are significant advantages to [this] outsourcing in light of the resource constraints and complexity of corporate criminal investigations . . . . To negotiate and sustain a DPA, corporations must remove legal and informational barriers between the government and their employees. In effect, prosecutors enlist the target corporation as a co-enforcer. [But w]hen they do so, prosecutors cede some discretionary authority to corporations to identify culpable employees and affect the course of the investigation. The result can be ad hoc targeting of individual defendants. In addition, DPAs are less visible than adjudication, which detracts from both the coherence of the government's enforcement strategy and the accountability of prosecutors. . . . Reliance on these intermediaries in the private sector [thus] raises both quality-control issues about the evidence and some of the concerns about capture that regulators confront in civil enforcement.

Jennifer Arlen, *Removing Prosecutors from the Boardroom: Limiting Prosecutorial Discretion to Impose Structural Reforms*, in *Prosecutors in the Boardroom* 62, 63 (Anthony S. Barkow & Rachel E. Barkow eds., 2011). Prosecutors generally should not use DPAs . . . to induce firms to adopt structural reforms, such as compliance programs, because compliance program design involves difficult judgments about when and where to centralize decision making and to collect and channel information. Industries and firms vary enormously as to whether, and in what areas, the compliance benefits of decision-making centralization and oversight exceed the costs. Prosecutors rarely have sufficient experience working in any business, much less adequate industry-specific expertise, to make these decisions reliably. By contrast, civil federal regulatory authorities are more likely to have this expertise, at least with respect to the industries they regulate. In addition, prosecutors are subject to little, if any, external oversight when they intervene in internal corporate affairs. Moreover, prosecutors' offices do not have a formal process for assembling and evaluating data on different compliance programs and monitoring plans to assess their effectiveness. By contrast, regulatory agencies are subject to greater oversight [and] have the information gathering abilities needed to assess compliance decisions.

Gabriel Markoff, *Arthur Andersen and the Myth of the Corporate Death Penalty: Corporate Criminal Convictions in the Twenty-First Century*, 15 U. Pa. J. Bus. L. 797, 800-801 (2013). DPAs supposedly allow the DOJ to efficiently enforce the law and obtain monetary restitution for victims while also permitting companies to avoid criminal conviction and the resulting . . . expense, stigma, and other collateral consequences that accompany a criminal conviction. [But DPAs] are highly controversial in many respects. Criticism of these agreements runs the gamut. Some scholars, particularly members of the law and economics movement, argue that DPAs can often constitute extreme abuses of prosecutorial discretion. Other scholars decry DPAs as a means of letting corporate criminals escape with a slap on the wrist. And others advocate for specific reforms while accepting DPAs as a legitimate tool. Unfortunately, in spite of the great volume of commentary on the matter, there is little to no empirical proof that DPAs are effective at deterring or otherwise preventing corporate crime, and there is anecdotal evidence of DPAs failing spectacularly at preventing corporate recidivism. While a few scholars have performed invaluable empirical studies of DPAs by laboriously gathering them and documenting their attributes, the question of whether DPAs "work" has not been answered.

C.   *Strict Liability and Corporate Officer Liability*

Every action undertaken by a corporation—including every allegedly criminal act—is in truth undertaken by one or more human beings. As a result, every case against a corporate defendant could in principle be a prosecution of someone within the corporation as well. Indeed, as the preceding section makes clear, corporate liability is derivative of employee liability; for a corporate defendant to be guilty, there typically *must* be some human being who is also guilty (though that person generally need not be prosecuted, or even identified).[22]

In prosecutions of such individual defendants, ordinary rules of criminal law generally apply. But they are supplemented by an interlocking pair of doctrines. The first is one we encountered before when studying the felony murder doctrine in Chapter Four and mistake of fact in Chapter Five: *strict liability*. The doctrine's roots are in white-collar crime, where it operates to eliminate the *mens rea* requirement for a broad set of public welfare offenses often termed *regulatory crimes*. These crimes are not unique to corporate settings, but they are concentrated there. And within that context, an additional doctrine, known as the *responsible corporate officer doctrine*, can make certain high-level officers within a corporate structure personally liable for crimes committed within the corporation. The two doctrines can operate in tandem, as seen in the cases that follow.

United States v. Dotterweich

320 U.S. 277 (1943)

FRANKFURTER, J. This was a prosecution . . . charging Buffalo Pharmacal Company, Inc., and Dotterweich, its president and general manager, with violations of . . . the Federal Food, Drug, and Cosmetic Act. The Company [purchased pharmaceuticals] from their manufacturers and shipped them, repacked under its own label, in interstate commerce. . . . [The Act] prohibits "The introduction or delivery for introduction into interstate commerce of any . . . drug . . . that is adulterated or misbranded." . . . Three counts went to the jury—two, for shipping misbranded drugs in interstate commerce, and a third, for so shipping an adulterated drug. The jury disagreed as to the corporation [but] found Dotterweich guilty on all three counts. . . .

The [Act] was an exertion by Congress of its power to keep impure and adulterated food and drugs out of the channels of commerce. . . . The purposes of this legislation thus touch phases of the lives and health of people which, in the circumstances of modern industrialism, are largely beyond self-protection. Regard for these purposes should infuse construction of the legislation if it is to be treated as a working instrument of government and not merely as a collection of English words. The prosecution to which Dotterweich was subjected is based on a now familiar type of legislation whereby penalties serve as effective means of regulation. Such legislation dispenses with the conventional requirement for criminal conduct—awareness of some wrongdoing. In the interest of the larger good it puts the burden of acting at hazard upon a person otherwise innocent but standing in responsible relation to a public danger. And so it is clear that shipments like those now in issue are "punished by the statute if the article is misbranded (or adulterated), and that the article may be misbranded (or adulterated) without any conscious fraud at all. It was natural enough to throw this risk on shippers with regard to the identity of their wares." United States v. Johnson, 221 U.S. 488, 497, 498 (1911).

. . . Nothing is clearer than that [this] legislation was designed to enlarge and stiffen the penal net . . . . This purpose was unequivocally avowed by the two committees which reported the bills to the Congress. The House Committee reported that the Act "seeks to set up effective provisions against abuses of consumer welfare . . . ." And the Senate Committee explicitly pointed out that the new legislation . . . "must strengthen and extend th[e] law's protection of the consumer." . . .

Whether an accused shares responsibility in the business process resulting in unlawful distribution depends on the evidence produced at the trial . . . . The offense is committed . . . by all who do have such a responsible share in the furtherance of the transaction which the statute outlaws, namely, to put into the stream of interstate commerce adulterated or misbranded drugs. Hardship there doubtless may be under a statute which thus penalizes the transaction though consciousness of wrongdoing be totally wanting. Balancing relative hardships, Congress has preferred to place it upon those who have at least the opportunity of informing themselves of the existence of conditions imposed for the protection of consumers before

sharing in illicit commerce, rather than to throw the hazard on the innocent public who are wholly helpless.

. . . To attempt a formula embracing the variety of conduct whereby
persons may responsibly contribute in furthering a transaction forbidden
by an Act of Congress, to wit, to send illicit goods across state lines, would
be mischievous futility. In such matters the good sense of prosecutors, the
wise guidance of trial judges, and the ultimate judgment of juries must be
trusted. Our system of criminal justice necessarily depends on "conscience
and circumspection in prosecuting officers," Nash v. United States, 229 U.S.
373, 378 (1913), even when the consequences are far more drastic than they
are under the provision of law before us. For present purpose it suffices to
say that . . . the District Court properly left the question of the responsibility
of Dotterweich for the shipment to the jury, and there was sufficient evidence to support its verdict.

[Opinion of MURPHY, J., dissenting, omitted.]

United States v. Park

421 U.S. 658 (1975)

BURGER, C.J. . . . Acme Markets, Inc., is a national retail food chain with
approximately 36,000 employees, 874 retail outlets, 12 general warehouses,
and four special warehouses. Its headquarters, including the office of the
president, respondent Park, who is chief executive officer of the corporation, are located in Philadelphia, Pa. [T]he Government charged Acme
and respondent with violations of the Federal Food, Drug and Cosmetic
Act [alleging] that the defendants had received food that had been shipped
in interstate commerce and that . . . they caused it to be held in a building
accessible to rodents and to be exposed to contamination by rodents.

. . . The evidence at trial demonstrated that in April 1970 the Food
and Drug Administration (FDA) advised respondent by letter of insanitary
conditions in Acme's Philadelphia warehouses. In 1971 the FDA found
that similar conditions existed in the firm's Baltimore warehouse. An FDA
consumer safety officer testified concerning evidence of rodent infestation and other insanitary conditions discovered during a 12-day inspection
of the Baltimore warehouse in November and December 1971. He also
related that a second inspection of the warehouse had been conducted in
March 1972. . . .

The Government also presented testimony by the Chief of Compliance
of the FDA's Baltimore office, who informed respondent by letter of the
conditions at the Baltimore warehouse after the first inspection. There was
testimony by Acme's Baltimore division vice president, who had responded
to the letter on behalf of Acme and respondent and who described the steps
taken to remedy the insanitary conditions discovered by both inspections.

The Government's final witness, Acme's vice president for legal affairs and assistant secretary, identified respondent as the president and chief executive officer of the company and read a bylaw prescribing the duties of the chief executive officer. He testified that respondent functioned by delegating "normal operating duties," including sanitation, but that he retained "certain things, which are the big, broad, principles of the operation of the company," and had "the responsibility of seeing that they all work together."

. . . Respondent was the only defense witness. He testified that, although all of Acme's employees were in a sense under his general direction, the company had an "organizational structure for responsibilities for certain functions" according to which different phases of its operation were "assigned to individuals who, in turn, have staff and departments under them." He identified those individuals responsible for sanitation, and related that upon receipt of the . . . FDA letter, he had conferred with the vice president for legal affairs, who informed him that the Baltimore division vice president "was investigating the situation immediately and would be taking corrective action and would be preparing a summary of the corrective action to reply to the letter." Respondent stated that he did not "believe there was anything he could have done more constructively than what he found was being done." . . . Respondent was asked about and . . . admitted receiving[] the April 1970 letter addressed to him from the FDA regarding insanitary conditions at Acme's Philadelphia warehouse. He acknowledged that . . . as Acme's chief executive officer he was responsible for "any result which occurs in our company."

. . . The rule that corporate employees who have "a responsible share in the furtherance of the transaction which the statute outlaws" are subject to the criminal provisions of the Act was not formulated in a vacuum. United States v. Dotterweich, 320 U.S. 277, 284 (1943). [Our cases] reflected the view both that knowledge or intent were not required to be proved in prosecutions under its criminal provisions, and that responsible corporate agents could be subjected to the liability thereby imposed. Moreover, the principle had been recognized that a corporate agent, through whose act, default, or omission the corporation committed a crime, was himself guilty individually of that crime. The principle had been applied whether or not the crime required "consciousness of wrongdoing," and it had been applied not only to those corporate agents who themselves committed the criminal act, but also to those who by virtue of their managerial positions or other similar relation to the actor could be deemed responsible for its commission.

In the latter class of cases, the liability of managerial officers did not depend on their knowledge of, or personal participation in, the act made criminal by the statute. Rather, where the statute under which they were prosecuted dispensed with "consciousness of wrongdoing," an omission or failure to act was deemed a sufficient basis for a responsible corporate agent's liability. It was enough in such cases that, by virtue of the relationship he bore to the corporation, the agent had the power to prevent the act complained of.

. . . [T]he Court has reaffirmed the proposition that "the public interest in the purity of its food is so great as to warrant the imposition of the highest standard of care on distributors." Smith v. California, 361 U.S. 147, 152 (1959). . . . Thus *Dotterweich* and the cases which have followed reveal that in providing sanctions which reach and touch the individuals who execute the corporate mission—and this is by no means necessarily confined to a single corporate agent or employee—the Act imposes not only a positive duty to seek out and remedy violations when they occur but also, and primarily, a duty to implement measures that will insure that violations will not occur. The requirements of foresight and vigilance imposed on responsible corporate agents are beyond question demanding, and perhaps onerous, but they are no more stringent than the public has a right to expect of those who voluntarily assume positions of authority in business enterprises whose services and products affect the health and well-being of the public that supports them.

. . . The duty imposed by Congress on responsible corporate agents is, we emphasize, one that requires the highest standard of foresight and vigilance, but the Act, in its criminal aspect, does not require that which is objectively impossible. The theory upon which responsible corporate agents are held criminally accountable for causing violations of the Act permits a claim that a defendant was powerless to prevent or correct the violation to be raised defensively at a trial on the merits. If such a claim is made, the defendant has the burden of coming forward with evidence, but this does not alter the Government's ultimate burden of proving beyond a reasonable doubt the defendant's guilt, including his power, in light of the duty imposed by the Act, to prevent or correct the prohibited condition. . . .

. . . Turning to the jury charge in this case, it is of course arguable that isolated parts can be read as intimating that a finding of guilt could be predicated solely on respondent's corporate position. But . . . [r]eading the entire charge satisfies us that the jury's attention was adequately focused on the issue of respondent's authority with respect to the conditions that formed the basis of the alleged violations. Viewed as a whole, the charge did not permit the jury to find guilt solely on the basis of respondent's position in the corporation; rather, it fairly advised the jury that to find guilt it must find respondent "had a responsible relation to the situation," and "by virtue of his position had authority and responsibility" to deal with the situation. . . . We conclude that, viewed as a whole and in the context of the trial, the charge was not misleading and contained an adequate statement of the law to guide the jury's determination.

[Opinion of STEWART, J., dissenting, omitted.]

United States v. MacDonald & Watson Waste Oil Co.

933 F.2d 35 (1st Cir. 1991)

CAMPBELL, J. . . . MacDonald & Watson, a company with offices in Johnstown, Rhode Island, was in the business of transporting and disposing of waste oils and contaminated soil. MacDonald & Watson operated a disposal facility on land in Providence, Rhode Island, known as the "Poe Street Lot," . . . under [a] permit [that] authorized the disposal at the lot of *liquid* hazardous wastes [but not] *solid* hazardous wastes . . . . At the Rhode Island administrative hearing held when [the permit was procured], appellant [Eugene K.] D'Allesandro, president [and owner] of MacDonald & Watson, testified that . . . he would be the manager of the facility there. . . . [Notwithstanding the permit's restrictions, MacDonald & Watson disposed of a large amount of solid hazardous waste at the Poe Street Lot for a company called Master Chemical Co. The waste consisted of soil contaminated with the chemical toluene.] . . .

D'Allesandro . . . contends that his conviction under [the Resource Conservation and Recovery Act (RCRA)], §3008(d)(1), must be vacated because the district court incorrectly charged the jury regarding the element of knowledge in the case of a corporate officer. Section 3008(d)(1) penalizes "Any person who . . . *knowingly* transports or causes to be transported any hazardous waste identified or listed under this subchapter . . . to a facility which does not have a permit. . . ." [T]he prosecutor conceded that the government had "no direct evidence that Eugene D'Allesandro actually knew that the Master Chemical shipments were coming in," i.e., were being transported to the Poe Street Lot under contract with his company. The prosecution did present evidence, however, that D'Allesandro was not only the President and owner of MacDonald & Watson but was a "hands-on" manager of that relatively small firm. There was also proof that . . . D'Allesandro's subordinates had contracted for and transported the Master Chemical waste for disposal at that site. The government argued that D'Allesandro was guilty of violating §3008(d)(1) because, as the responsible corporate officer, he was in a position to ensure compliance with RCRA and had failed to do so even after being warned by a consultant on two earlier occasions that other shipments of toluene-contaminated soil had been received from other customers, and that such material violated [the] permit. . . .

The seminal cases regarding the responsible corporate officer doctrine are *United States v. Dotterweich*, 320 U.S. 277 (1943), and *United States v. Park*, 421 U.S. 658 (1975). These cases concerned misdemeanor charges under the Federal Food, Drug, and Cosmetic Act, relating to the handling or shipping of adulterated or misbranded drugs or food. The [statutory] offenses alleged in [those cases] failed to state a knowledge element, and the Court found that they, in fact, dispensed with a *scienter* requirement, placing "the burden of acting at hazard upon a person otherwise innocent but standing in responsible relation to a public danger." *Dotterweich*, 320 U.S. at 277. The Court in *Park* clarified that corporate officer liability in that situation requires only a finding that the officer had "authority with respect to the conditions that formed the basis of the alleged violations." But while *Dotterweich* and *Park* thus reflect what is now clear and well-established law in respect to public welfare statutes and regulations lacking an express knowledge or other *scienter* requirement, we know of no precedent for failing to give effect to a knowledge requirement that Congress has expressly included in a criminal statute. Especially is that so where, as here, the crime is a felony carrying possible imprisonment of five years and, for a second offense, ten.

The district court, nonetheless, applied here a form of the responsible corporate officer doctrine established in *Dotterweich* and *Park* for *strict liability* misdemeanors, as a substitute means for proving the explicit knowledge element of this RCRA felony. As an alternative to finding actual knowledge, the district court permitted the prosecution to constructively establish defendant's knowledge if the jury found the following: (1) that the defendant was a corporate officer; (2) with responsibility to supervise the allegedly illegal activities; and (3) knew or believed "that the illegal activity of the type alleged occurred." [T]he third element did not necessitate proof of knowledge of the Master Chemical shipments charged in the indictment, but simply proof of earlier occasions when D'Allesandro was told his firm had improperly accepted toluene-contaminated soil.

Contrary to the government's assertions, this instruction did more than simply permit the jury, if it wished, to infer knowledge of the Master Chemical shipments from relevant circumstantial evidence including D'Allesandro's responsibilities and activities as a corporate executive. . . . Instead, the district court charged, in effect, that proof that D'Allesandro was a responsible corporate officer would conclusively prove the element of his knowledge of the Master Chemical shipments. . . . We have found no case, and the government cites none, where a jury was instructed that the defendant could be convicted of a federal crime *expressly requiring knowledge as an element*, solely by reason of a conclusive, or "mandatory" presumption of knowledge of the facts constituting the offense. . . .

[T]he district court erred by instructing the jury that proof that a defendant was a responsible corporate officer, as described, would suffice to conclusively establish the element of knowledge expressly required under §3008(d)(1). Simply because a responsible corporate officer believed that on a prior occasion illegal transportation occurred, he did not necessarily possess knowledge of the violation charged. In a crime having knowledge as an express element, a mere showing of official responsibility under

Dotterweich and *Park* is not an adequate substitute for direct or circumstantial proof of knowledge.

NOTES AND QUESTIONS

1. Crime Without Fault. The statute at issue in *Dotterweich* and *Park* was conspicuously silent as to one of the essential features of criminal liability — *mens rea*. The Court thus had to determine how best to construe that statutory silence. And it opted, given the regulatory, public welfare nature of the statute at hand, to read the statute as doing away with a *mens rea* requirement altogether. As a result, even an entirely accidental mislabeling of pharmaceuticals will give rise to criminal liability under the Act. So too a rodent infestation that might occur despite a defendant's best efforts to avoid it. Such is the nature of strict liability.

Of course, in interpreting the statute this way, the Court pushed against one of the foundational tenets of criminal law, examined in Chapter Four — namely, that a culpable mental state is a prerequisite of criminal blame and punishment. While *Dotterweich* and *Park* relax that requirement in the context of public welfare offenses with modest penalties, the Court has elsewhere been reluctant to dispense with the *mens rea* requirement. State courts, meanwhile, have adopted various tests to demarcate the circumstances in which strict liability will apply. Consider the following cases.

Morissette v. United States, 342 U.S. 246 (1952). On a large tract of uninhabited and untilled land in a wooded and sparsely populated area of Michigan, the Government established a practice bombing range over which the Air Force dropped simulated bombs at ground targets. These bombs consisted of a metal cylinder about forty inches long and eight inches across, filled with sand . . . . [T]he range was known as good deer country and was extensively hunted. . . .

[The defendant Morissette works as a fruit stand operator, trucker, and scrap iron collector. In December of 1948, he] went hunting in this area but did not get a deer. He thought to meet expenses of the trip by salvaging some of these casings. He loaded three tons of them on his truck and took them to a nearby farm, where they were flattened by driving a tractor over them. After expending this labor and trucking them to market in Flint, he realized $84. . . . The loading, crushing and transporting of these casings were all in broad daylight, in full view of passers-by, without the slightest effort at concealment.

When an investigation was started, Morissette voluntarily, promptly and candidly told the whole story to the authorities, saying that he had no intention of stealing but thought the property was abandoned, unwanted and considered of no value to the Government. He was indicted, however, on [a] charge [of stealing government property]. . . . The Court of Appeals . . . ruled that this particular offense requires no element of criminal intent. This conclusion was thought to be required by the failure of Congress to express such a requisite . . . .

[The Court of Appeals' holding would] sweep out of all federal crimes, except when expressly preserved, the ancient requirement of a culpable state of mind. . . . The contention that an injury can amount to a crime only when inflicted by intention is no provincial or transient notion. It is as universal and persistent in mature systems of law as belief in freedom of the human will . . . . A relation between some mental element and punishment for a harmful act is almost as instinctive as the child's familiar exculpatory "But I didn't mean to" . . . .

[Accordingly, as the states] codified the common law of crimes, even if their enactments were silent on the subject, their courts assumed that the omission did not signify disapproval of the principle but merely recognized that intent was so inherent in the idea of the offense that it required no statutory affirmation. Courts, with little hesitation or division, found an implication of the requirement as to offenses that were taken over from the common law. . . .

However, [some] offenses belong to a category of another character, with very different antecedents and origins. . . . The industrial revolution multiplied the number of workmen exposed to injury from increasingly powerful and complex mechanisms, driven by freshly discovered sources of energy, requiring higher precautions by employers. Traffic of velocities, volumes and varieties unheard of came to subject the wayfarer to intolerable casualty risks if owners and drivers were not to observe new cares and uniformities of conduct. Congestion of cities and crowding of quarters called for health and welfare regulations undreamed of in simpler times. Wide distribution of goods became an instrument of wide distribution of harm when those who dispersed food, drink, drugs, and even securities, did not comply with reasonable standards of quality, integrity, disclosure and care. Such dangers have engendered increasingly numerous and detailed regulations which heighten the duties of those in control of particular industries, trades, properties or activities that affect public health, safety or welfare.

While many of these duties are sanctioned by a more strict civil liability, lawmakers, whether wisely or not, have sought to make such regulations more effective by invoking criminal sanctions . . . . This has confronted the courts with a multitude of prosecutions, based on statutes or administrative regulations, for what have been aptly called "public welfare offenses." These cases do not fit neatly into any of such accepted classifications of common-law offenses, such as those against the state, the person, property, or public morals. . . . Also, penalties commonly are relatively small, and conviction does no grave damage to an offender's reputation. Under such considerations, courts have turned to construing statutes and regulations which make no mention of intent as dispensing with it and holding that the guilty act alone makes out the crime. This has not, however, been without expressions of misgiving. . . . [Still,] for diverse but reconcilable reasons, state courts converged on the same result, discontinuing inquiry into intent in a limited class of offenses against such statutory regulations. . . .

Neither this Court nor, so far as we are aware, any other has undertaken to delineate a precise line or set forth comprehensive criteria for distinguishing between crimes that require a mental element and crimes that do not. We attempt no closed definition, for the law on the subject is neither settled nor static. The conclusion reached in [*Dotterweich*] has our approval and adherence for the circumstances to which it was there applied. A quite different question here is whether we will expand the doctrine of crimes without intent to include those charged here. Stealing, larceny, and its variants and equivalents, were among the earliest offenses known to the law that existed before legislation; they are invasions of rights of property which stir a sense of insecurity in the whole community and arouse public demand for retribution, the penalty is high and, when a sufficient amount is involved, the infamy is that of a felony, which, says Maitland, is "as bad a word as you can give to man or thing." . . . The Government asks us . . . radically to change the weights and balances in the scales of justice. The purpose and obvious effect of doing away with the requirement of a guilty intent is to ease the prosecution's path to conviction, to strip the defendant of such benefit as he derived at common law from innocence of evil purpose, and to circumscribe the freedom heretofore allowed juries. Such a manifest impairment of the immunities of the individual should not be extended to common-law crimes on judicial initiative.

State v. Yishmael, 456 P.3d 1172 (Wash. 2020). Admission to the practice of law requires years of graduate level study either with a practicing lawyer or at a law school. It requires passage of a rigorous bar examination on a wide range of topics. . . . By contrast, the unlawful practice of law often causes harm without any of the protections for malpractice by lawyers. Because these harms are predictable, the unlawful practice of law is a crime. . . .

Naziyr Yishmael, who is not an attorney, advised clients that they could "homestead" in apparently abandoned properties and, after a period of time, acquire title through adverse possession. After some of his clients were arrested for taking up residence in other people's houses, he was charged with and convicted of misdemeanor unlawful practice of law. . . . He contends the jury was improperly instructed that the unlawful practice of law is a strict liability offense. . . .

As our society has become more and more complicated, our legislatures have created more strict liability offenses as a matter of policy. Generally, legislatures create strict liability offenses to protect the public from the harms that have come with modern life by putting the burden of care on those in the best position to avoid those harms. . . . [The analysis at issue] turns, ultimately, on whether the legislature intended to create a strict liability crime. . . . In this case, unfortunately, we have found no helpful legislative history. [Accordingly, we look to] eight nonexclusive considerations to help us determine whether the legislature intended to create a strict liability offense[:]

> (1) the background rules of the common law, and its conventional *mens rea* element; (2) whether the crime can be characterized as a "public welfare offense" created by the Legislature; (3) the extent to which a strict liability reading of the statute would encompass seemingly entirely innocent conduct; (4) and the harshness of the penalty. Other considerations include: (5) the seriousness of the harm to the public; (6) the ease or difficulty of the defendant ascertaining the true facts; (7) relieving the prosecution of difficult and time-consuming proof of fault where the Legislature thinks it important to stamp out harmful conduct at all costs, "even at the cost of convicting innocent-minded and blameless people"; and (8) "the number of prosecutions to be expected."

State v. Bash, 925 P.2d 978, 983 (Wash. 1996). . . . Taken together, [our analysis of each of these factors leads] us to the conclusion that unlawful practice of law, as charged here, is a strict liability crime. The trial court did not err in so finding.

   2. Limiting Strict Liability. Strict liability is not without controversy. The drafters of the Model Penal Code, for example, viewed the Code's provisions as waging "a frontal attack on absolute or strict liability in the penal law." Model Penal Code and Commentaries §2.05 cmt. 1 at 282. Under their approach, strict liability applies only to statutes in which "a legislative purpose to impose absolute liability . . . plainly appears" or, alternatively, to offenses classified under the MPC as "violations." A "violation," in turn, is defined as a low-level civil infraction that "does not constitute a crime" and that can be punished only by a fine. Model Penal Code §§2.05(1) & 1.03(5). In all other cases, the MPC provides that if a statute is silent with respect to *mens rea*, it should be construed as containing a recklessness requirement. *See id.* §2.02(3)-(5). Some courts are more exacting, holding that in circumstances where strict liability does not apply, legislative silence should be interpreted to "require that the defendant *know* the facts that make his conduct illegal." Staples v. United States, 511 U.S. 600, 605 (1994) (emphasis added).

   How should we understand efforts to cabin strict liability? As the Court in *Morissette* wrote, strict liability can operate as a tool "to ease the prosecution's path to conviction" and "to strip the defendant of" protection. In *Morissette*, where the defendant was a fruit vendor accused of petty theft, the Court clearly meant these observations as criticism. But in the context of corporate prosecutions, some view these same aspects of the doctrine as beneficial features—while others maintain in this context the criticism that strict liability gives prosecutors too much power. In recent years, statutory efforts to cabin strict liability and restore a *mens rea* requirement have prompted vigorous debate, and strange bedfellows. On the one hand, Professor Benjamin Levin reports, the reform proposal "has been supported by both conservative activists and criminal defense attorneys," alongside a coalition comprising the conservative Heritage Foundation and the liberal ACLU. At the same time, Levin observes, the reforms have been "opposed by politicians and commentators on the left who believe that it would operate as a shield against prosecutions for financial and environmental crime." Consider the following excerpts offering views on different sides of this debate.[23]

Matt Ford, *Could a Controversial Bill Sink Criminal-Justice Reform in Congress?*, Atlantic (Oct. 26, 2017). A bill drafted by a group of Senate Republicans earlier this year would tweak the mens rea requirement in federal statutes, adding a default rule for juries to find criminal intent for federal offenses that don't explicitly have an intent standard. . . . But some Senate Democrats fear the measure is far too sweeping and could be a back-door attack on federal health and environmental regulations that police corporate behavior. Rhode Island Senator Sheldon Whitehouse, a member of the Judiciary Committee, told me earlier this week that he wouldn't support a [r]eform bill if it included the change to mens rea. "It would turn me into a warrior against it," he emphasized. Chuck Schumer, the Democratic leader in the Senate, would also oppose such a bill, a spokesman confirmed.

Other Senate Democrats criticized a similar measure that passed the House during the last criminal-justice-reform push. . . . Illinois Senator Dick Durbin, a longtime supporter of [criminal justice] reform, said that version of the mens rea proposal "should be called the White Collar Criminal Immunity Act." . . . Massachusetts Senator Elizabeth Warren said in a speech the following month that the House proposal would "make it much harder for the government to prosecute hundreds of corporate crimes—everything from wire fraud to mislabeling prescription drugs." Negotiations over criminal-justice reform ultimately collapsed that summer as the presidential election entered its final stretch.

But with the campaign over, stakeholders in both parties want to give it another go. . . . Groups as disparate as the ACLU, the Heritage Foundation, the NAACP, and the Koch family's foundations have teamed up in recent years to build a grand coalition for reform. But this unusual display of bipartisanship still hasn't bridged every ideological gulf, as the brewing battle over mens rea exemplifies.

Whitehouse suggested to me that Koch-affiliated organizations may be interested in mens rea reform—and even criminal-justice reform as a whole—because of Koch Industries' past run-ins with environmental regulators. Charles and David Koch are influential donors for Republican candidates and help fund a wide array of conservative and libertarian nonprofit groups.

"It's an open question to what extent the Koch brothers and their operatives, in participating in the sentencing-reform conversations, had in mind all along that at a critical juncture they would try to jam their mens rea proposal into the mix," he told me. "I would hope that that was not true, but I strongly suspect that it was."

. . . "[This is] a category in which the public-health and safety concerns are so serious that you set out a criminal penalty as a boundary with the notion that corporations should stand well back from that boundary as part of protecting people from harm, whether it's chemical emissions or benzene leaks or whatever it is," Whitehouse explained.

Some Democrats indicated they'd be open to a more limited approach on intent standards. The office of Vermont Senator Patrick Leahy, another Democrat on the Judiciary Committee, said any mens rea reform would need to be narrowly tailored, not comprehensive and retroactive. Whitehouse said he'd be willing to discuss a version that focused on "crimes in which an individual human defendant was the target," but that other senators hadn't taken him up on the offer yet.

As for how many of his colleagues would reject a bipartisan sentencing bill with mens rea reform in it, "I haven't done a whip count on that," Whitehouse told me. "I doubt very much that I'm alone on this subject, and I think I'd be even less alone if I had the chance to make the case to my caucus if it came down to this."

Gideon Yaffe, *A Republican Crime Proposal That Democrats Should Back*, N.Y. Times (Feb. 12, 2016). These days, it's practically unheard-of for those on the left to embrace ideas promoted by the likes of the Koch brothers and the conservative Heritage Foundation. But it would be a shame if partisan distrust kept Democrats from supporting a proposal [to] require proof of what lawyers call "mens rea"—literally, a guilty mind[—in more federal prosecutions. O]ver the years, exceptions to the principle have become common because mens rea requirements have not been consistently detailed in laws. . . . Congress is now considering a measure . . . that would require that mens rea be proven in many more cases. For instance, a law making it a crime to mislabel drugs would automatically be interpreted as criminalizing knowing mislabeling. The measure would not affect statutes that make clear that no mental state need be shown for guilt—for example, laws criminalizing sex with minors.

. . . Democrats, however, oppose the mens rea provision on the ground that it would weaken efforts to prosecute corporate executives whose companies have caused harm. . . . But . . . strengthening mens rea requirements will also help poor and minority people. Consider a New York law banning "gravity knives"—folding knives that open with a flick of the wrist—that lacks mens rea protections. The statute does not require proof that a defendant knew her knife was a gravity knife, much less that gravity knives are banned in the state. As a result, the law has been used by the police in New York City to pick up thousands of people, most of them minorities, even if they had the knives for innocent purposes. And in Baltimore, Freddie Gray died in a police van after being arrested for violating a very similar statute that also lacked a mens rea requirement.

The Justice Department opposes the proposed mens rea measure on the ground that it would have prevented convictions of corporate executives whose products caused harm. But it is entirely possible that the government could have proven mens rea had it been required to try. Furthermore, criminal conviction is not the only way to make corporations pay for their harms: Tort liabilities and civil penalties are not constrained by mens rea requirements. . . .

The greatest impact of the federal legislation might be in encouraging changes at the state level, where poor and minority defendants are most frequently prosecuted. Ohio and Michigan have already passed mens rea reform laws. And in the wake of federal legislation, other states, including New York, would likely follow their lead. Democrats should push for even more sweeping changes to unjust "felony murder" laws, which permit murder convictions for anyone participating in a felony in which someone dies, even if no one involved could have been expected to foresee that happening. We know that adolescents are far less aware than adults of the risks their conduct involves, but since felony murder does not require proof of mens rea, adolescent defendants can't offer evidence of their distorted perceptions of risk.

For liberals, the right's proposal offers a chance to strike a blow for justice for ordinary people. No one should be convicted of a crime—or even stopped by the police—without evidence of a criminal state of mind.

Benjamin Levin & Kate Levine, *Redistributing Justice*, 124 Colum. L. Rev. 1531, 1534, 1539, 1556-1558, 1575-1576, 1581-1582 (2024). Increasingly, many progressive commentators criticize mass incarceration and treat criminal legal institutions as objectionable responses to social problems. Nevertheless, these anticarceral commitments often have their limits. Despite the prevalence of increasingly radical rhetoric on the left, many progressives continue to make exceptions and favor criminal solutions when presented with particularly sympathetic victims or particularly unsympathetic defendants. . . . It's tempting to view these carveouts as one-off exceptions to a general opposition to criminal punishment—a random assortment of areas in which anticarceral commitments give way, or in which principle falls in the face of inconsistency (or even hypocrisy). . . . [But really they are] an attempt to redistribute from relatively powerful defendants to weaker or marginalized victims. . . .

Intuitively, financial and economic crimes might be one of the more straightforward fits for a redistributive frame. "White-collar" crime has long been an area in which scholars and commentators have focused on inequality and the perceived impunity of the powerful. . . . Against this backdrop, many progressives and leftists have turned to criminal law as a means of disciplining capital, responding to the immorality (or, at least, amorality) of the marketplace, and curbing the perceived lawlessness of the wealthy. . . . Progressive lawmakers have opposed a number of criminal justice reform bills — particularly so-called "mens rea reform" statutes — because of the possibility that they might aid defendants charged with white-collar crimes. . . .

[But w]hy should we think that the people who are prosecuted or punished will actually be white, wealthy, or powerful? [A] 2000 FBI report on white-collar crime enforcement stated that three times more economic crimes were committed at convenience stores (129,749) than at banks (38,364). The mean amount stolen or counterfeited in white-collar incidents was $9,254.75, the median was $210, and the mode was $100. That is, advocacy geared at white-collar crime enforcement appears just as likely to lead to more check fraud prosecutions as it is to mean a focus on executives at the nation's biggest banks. . . . Indeed, a recent study by legal economist Stephanie Holmes Didwania [reports that] "financial crime prosecutions disproportionately involve people who are low-income and people who are Black."

. . . [More fundamentally, a]rguments don't belong exclusively to the activists who use them. They can be deployed by people with very different politics and goals. Claiming that prison is the right or the best solution to one social problem invites the question of why it wouldn't be just as desirable in another area. . . . Empowering or expanding the carceral state poses significant risks for the population at large—and particularly for marginalized communities. In a system marked by discretion, giving new tools and more power to police and prosecutors in one area means that police and prosecutors have more power—full stop.

3. Corporate Officers and the Duty to Act. Dotterweich and *Morissette* are fundamentally cases about *mens rea* and strict liability. But *Park* and *MacDonald & Watson Waste Oil Co.* are not. In *Park* it was already clear that the statute at issue permitted strict liability; that was the holding of *Dotterweich*. And in *MacDonald & Watson Waste Oil Co.* the statute expressly required knowledge as its *mens rea* element, which meant strict liability was off the table. As Professor Kimberly Ferzan writes, many courts, consistent with the holding in *MacDonald & Watson Waste Oil Co.*, "have recognized that, when the underlying statute is *not* strict liability, then the responsible corporate officer doctrine does not supplant the underlying *mens rea* requirement."[24]

What, then, does the doctrine do? In a word, it creates a special path to establishing a corporate officer's *actus reus* for a given offense. As explained earlier (p. 162), the *actus reus* requirement holds that for criminal liability to attach, a criminal defendant generally must have engaged in some legally prohibited conduct. There is, however, a narrow set of circumstances in which criminal liability can attach when a person fails to take certain action, also known as an *omission*. In these special instances, the law holds that some people have special duties to act in order to protect others. Parents, for example, have a duty to protect their children, such that a failure to do so — what would normally be an unpunishable omission — can be deemed culpable.

Understood against this backdrop, the responsible corporate officer doctrine creates a similar framework for high-level corporate officers with respect to their customers and the broader public. In Professor Ferzan's words, the "doctrine is nothing more than the recognition that corporate officers and employees contractually undertake to protect the public, and the doctrine does nothing more than to recognize that, having engaged in this contractual undertaking, the defendants can be liable for omissions [when] they fail to perform that duty." We will discuss the law of omissions in more detail at the beginning of the next chapter.[25]

CHAPTER 7

GROUP LIABILITY

"It's about time law enforcement got as organized as organized crime."

Rudolph Giuliani, quoted in Peter Stoler et al.,
The Sicilian Connection, Time (Oct. 15, 1984)

"The pawns, man, in the game, they get capped quick. They be out the game early."

D'Angelo Barksdale in *The Wire*
(HBO television broadcast June 16, 2002)

INTRODUCTION

In Chapter Six, we examined the doctrine of corporate liability and observed that, in some cases, it can be used to hold a corporate entity comprising many people liable for criminal misconduct that one or more of those people undertook on the corporation's behalf. As a prosecutorial tool, this form of liability can apply in circumstances in which it might otherwise be practically or doctrinally difficult to impose liability on the individuals directly. In this chapter, we will continue our study of group liability by examining a commonly employed pair of doctrines: *complicity* and *conspiracy*.

Technically, the legal frameworks governing these two doctrines are distinct. Complicity is a theory of liability, not a stand-alone offense. One cannot be guilty of complicity; rather, complicity is a theory by which liability for a crime may attach. Conspiracy, in contrast, is both a theory of liability and a stand-alone offense. The two doctrines also have distinct *actus reus* requirements and different ways of conceptualizing when and why one person in a group should be punished for harms he did not personally cause and did not intend others in the group to cause. And yet, notwithstanding these doctrinal distinctions, complicity and conspiracy both deal with the same basic challenges and have parallel ways of addressing them. Our goal in this chapter is to study these two doctrines side by side, as close cousins.

The aim is not to probe the doctrinal distinctions between them simply for the intellectual exercise but rather to see how the law of conspiracy grows the seeds of liability the law of complicity sows.

At the same time, we aim to explore the institutional pressures that drive this expansion in liability. Specifically, we note an important distinction between the group conduct at issue in this chapter and the group conduct at issue in corporate liability: Here, the actors we study have not chosen to incorporate themselves formally into a state-chartered entity, for obvious reasons. Sometimes, the groups at issue have formed spontaneously and are ephemeral. Other times, they are more organized and enduring—but exist for the purpose of committing crimes. In either instance, there is no separate legal entity that can be targeted directly for prosecution, which means a prosecutor cannot simply indict "the conspiracy" itself. The challenge law enforcement actors confront is thus how to hold potentially sophisticated groups of actors liable for potentially serious harms, and how to overcome the tactics those groups might employ to avoid detection and prosecution for their harmful behavior.

One approach is to create more robust and severe doctrines of liability in order to put pressure on different members of the group. As we will see, that is the path the law has often followed. And as we will further observe, it is a path that can be fraught itself, with serious risk of imposing its own distinct form of harm.

We begin the discussion below by setting an important conceptual baseline regarding the law's treatment of criminal liability involving multiple people. Put simply, the law generally does not require one person to take any affirmative action to *prevent* another person from causing harm or from breaking the law. This principle (and its limited exceptions) is embodied in the law of *omissions*, which holds more generally that people do not usually have any obligation to take affirmative actions to prevent harm in the world. With that baseline in place, we then turn to the converse factual pattern: circumstances in which a person takes *some* action—potentially very minor—that encourages or facilitates criminal actions by someone else. We examine the law's treatment of these scenarios first by studying the law of complicity, with a focus on identifying both the set of actions that can make one person liable for criminal wrongdoing committed by someone else and the states of mind required for such liability to attach. Finally, we identify the ways in which the law of conspiracy expands liability outward—into more complex scenarios and to a broader set of actors—with important consequences.

Throughout the chapter, we will pay attention not only to the conceptual and doctrinal frameworks governing these interrelated bodies of law, but also to the institutional law enforcement practices those doctrines facilitate, most especially with respect to the use of confidential informants and undercover agents.

I. FAILING TO ACT

Pope v. State

396 A.2d 1054 (Md. 1979)

ORTH, J. Joyce Lillian Pope was found guilty [of one count of] child abuse . . . . We remand . . . for the entry of a judgment of acquittal . . .

THE EVIDENCE

The evidence . . . established that Demiko Lee Norris, three months old, died as a result of physical injuries inflicted by his mother, Melissa Vera Norris. The abuse by the mother occurred over a period of several hours on a Sunday morning at Pope's home and in Pope's presence.

Pope's involvement in the events . . . began . . . when she and Melissa, with the child, were driven home by Pope's sister . . . from a service held at the Christian Tabernacle Church. When they arrived at Melissa's grandparents' home, where Melissa was living, Melissa refused to enter the house, claiming that it was on fire, although in fact it was not. During the evening, Melissa had sporadically indicated mental distress. She would at times seem caught up in a religious frenzy with a wild look about her, trying to preach and declaring that she was God. She would as quickly resume her normal self without ever seeming to notice her personality transitions.

Pope agreed to take Melissa and the child into her home for the night because she did not want to put them "out on the street" . . . . [Pope] bought food and diapers for the baby. That evening Pope cleaned and dried the baby and inquired of Melissa about a bad rash he had. Melissa slept in Pope's bedroom. Pope kept the baby with her in the living room, telling Melissa: "You can go to sleep . . . I'll watch the baby. . . ." She explained in her testimony: "And I don't know why it was just, just a funny feeling that I had, you know, and ever since the baby was there I just kept it close to me for some reason." . . .

. . . Throughout the [next] day Melissa "changed back and forth." When Melissa was "herself" she took care of her child. When Melissa thought she was God, Pope undertook the maternal duties. Pope watched the child "like it was my own," because "I felt maybe (Melissa) could (hurt the child) when she confessed she was God. . . ."

. . . [On] Sunday, at about 4:30[am], . . . [Melissa's] episodes of "changing to God" became more pronounced. She stomped and gestured as she strode back and forth, putting crosses on doors and demanding the departure of the evil which she claimed to see. . . . Calling out that Satan had hidden in the body of her son, Melissa began to verbally exorcise that spirit and [to violently] abuse the child . . . [all while] acting like she did not know that Pope was present. . . . Pope did nothing. She admitted that she knew at some point that Melissa was hurting the baby and was "fearful, amazed and shocked at the 'unbelievable' and 'horrible' thing that was happening."

Melissa's frenzy diminished. [Pope's sister] Angela came to the house to take them to church. . . . Angela asked [Pope] what was wrong, and Pope said: "It's Melissa, the baby. . . ." Pope, Melissa and Angela . . . proceeded to the church [where] . . . the child was given . . . to Mother Dorothy King for her prayers. She discovered that the baby's body was cool and sent for ambulance assistance. Police and rescue personnel arrived and determined that the child was dead. There was expert medical testimony that the child had died sometime during the period of fifteen minutes to several hours after it was injured. The medical expert expressed no opinion as to whether the child could have been successfully treated if the injury had been reported sooner.

The police questioned Melissa in Pope's presence. Pope did not contradict Melissa's denial of abusing the child. In fact, Pope, in response to inquiry by the police, said that the baby did not fall, and told them that she had not seen Melissa strike the baby. She explained this untruth in subsequent statements to the police: "It was her body in the flesh, but it wasn't her, because it was something else."[4] . . .

THE CRIME OF CHILD ABUSE

[The statute in operation at the time of the events in this case reads: "Any parent, adoptive parent or other person who has the permanent or temporary care or custody or responsibility for the supervision of a minor child under the age of eighteen years who causes abuse to such minor child shall be guilty of a felony . . . ." A separate statutory provision defines the word "abuse" to mean "any physical injury or injuries sustained by a child as a result of cruel or inhumane treatment or as a result of malicious act or acts . . . ."]

Applying the rules of statutory construction, we [have held that] . . . "[i]n making it an offense for a person having custody of a minor child to 'cause' the child to suffer a 'physical injury,' the Legislature did not require that the injury result from a physical assault upon the child or from any physical force initially applied by the accused individual; it provided instead, in a more encompassing manner, that the offense was committed if physical injury to the child resulted either from a course of conduct constituting 'cruel or inhumane treatment' or by 'malicious act or acts.'" State v. Fabritz, 348 A.2d 275, 280 (Md. 1975). We [thus held] that the failure of [a] mother to seek or obtain any medical assistance for her child, although the need

---

4. The mother, charged and tried separately from Pope, was found to be not responsible for her criminal conduct at the time of the commission of the offense, and, therefore, not guilty by reason of insanity.

therefor was obviously compelling and urgent, caused the child to sustain bodily injury additional to and beyond that inflicted upon the child by reason of the original assault by another. The act of omission by the mother "constituted a cause of the further progression and worsening of the injuries which led to (the child's) death; and that in these circumstances (the mother's) treatment of (the child) was 'cruel or inhumane' within the meaning of the statute and as those terms are commonly understood." *Id.* at 281. . . .

[But] *Fabritz* did not go to the class of persons to whom the statutory proscription applies, as the accused there was a "parent," the victim's mother, expressly designated in the statute. [The statute also covers any person who has "temporary care or custody or responsibility for the supervision of a minor child."] . . . In *Bowers v. State*, 389 A.2d 341 (1978), we . . . [rejected] the contention that the statute was vague and therefore constitutionally defective for the reason that it . . . was too indefinite to inform a person who is not a parent or adoptive parent of a child whether he comes within the ambit of the statute. . . . [Construing first the phrase "permanent or temporary care," we held that this is synonymous with a person's being *in loco parentis* with respect to a child.] "The term 'in loco parentis,' according to its generally accepted common law meaning, refers to a person who has put himself in the situation of a lawful parent by assuming the obligations incident to the parental relation without going through the formalities necessary to legal adoption. It embodies the two ideas of assuming the parental status and discharging the parental duties." Niewiadomski v. United States, 159 F.2d 683, 686 (6th Cir. 1947). . . .

[But the phrase] "responsibility for the supervision of" is not bound by certain of the strictures required for one to stand in place of or instead of the parent. . . . "Responsibility" in its common and generally accepted meaning denotes "accountability," and "supervision" emphasizes broad authority to oversee with the powers of direction and decision. . . . Absent a court order or award by some appropriate proceeding pursuant to statutory authority, we think it to be self-evident that responsibility for supervision of a minor child may be obtained only upon the mutual consent, expressed or implied, by the one legally charged with the care of the child and by the one assuming the responsibility. In other words, a parent may not impose responsibility for the supervision of his or her minor child on a third person unless that person accepts the responsibility, and a third person may not assume such responsibility unless the parent grants it. So it is that a baby sitter temporarily has responsibility for the supervision of a child; the parents grant the responsibility for the period they are not at home, and the sitter accepts it. . . . On the other hand, once responsibility for the supervision of a minor child has been placed in a third person, it may be terminated unilaterally by a parent by resuming responsibility, expressly or by conduct. The consent of the third party in such circumstances is not required; he may not prevent return of responsibility to the parent. But, of course, the third person in whom responsibility has been placed is not free to relinquish that responsibility without the knowledge of the parent. For example, a sitter may not simply walk away in the absence of the parents and leave the children to their own devices.

Under the present state of our law, a person has no legal obligation to care for or look after the welfare of a stranger, adult or child. "Generally one has no legal duty to aid another person in peril, even when that aid can be rendered without danger or inconvenience to himself. A moral duty to take affirmative action is not enough to impose a legal duty to do so." W. LaFave & A. Scott, *Criminal Law* 183 (1972). . . . Ordinarily, a person may stand by with impunity and watch another being murdered, raped, robbed, assaulted or otherwise unlawfully harmed. "He need not shout a warning to a blind man headed for a precipice or to an absentminded one walking into a gunpowder room with a lighted candle in hand. He need not pull a neighbor's baby out of a pool of water or rescue an unconscious person stretched across the railroad tracks, though the baby is drowning, or the whistle of an approaching train is heard in the distance." *Id.* . . .

In the face of this status of the law we cannot reasonably conclude that the Legislature, in bringing a person responsible for the supervision of a child within the ambit of the child abuse law, intended that such responsibility attach without the consent criteria we have set out. Were it otherwise, the consequences would go far beyond the legislative intent. For example, a person taking a lost child into his home to attempt to find its parents could be said to be responsible for that child's supervision. Or a person who allows his neighbor's children to play in his yard, keeping a watchful eye on their activities to prevent them from falling into harm, could be held responsible for the children's supervision. Or a person performing functions of a maternal nature from concern for the welfare, comfort or health of a child, or protecting it from danger because of a sense o[f] moral obligation, may come within the reach of the act. In none of these situations would there be an intent to grant or assume the responsibility contemplated by the child abuse statute, and it would be incongruous indeed to subject such persons to possible criminal prosecution.

THE SUFFICIENCY OF THE EVIDENCE

. . . . Pope's lack of any attempt to prevent the numerous acts of abuse committed by the mother over a relatively protracted period and her failure to seek medical assistance for the child, although the need therefor was obviously compelling and urgent, could constitute a cause for the further progression and worsening of the injuries which led to the child's death. In such circumstances, Pope's omissions constituted in themselves cruel and inhumane treatment within the meaning of the statute. It follows that

Pope would be guilty of child abuse if her status brought her within the class of persons specified by the statute. It being clear that she was neither the child's parent nor adoptive parent, and there being no evidence sufficient to support a finding that she had "the permanent or temporary care or custody" of the child as that status was construed in *Bowers v. State*, so as to be in loco parentis to the child, the sole question is whether she had "responsibility for the supervision of" the child in the circumstances. If she had such responsibility the evidence was legally sufficient to find her guilty of child abuse as a principal in the first degree.

The State would have us translate compassion and concern, acts of kindness and care, performance of maternal functions, and general help and aid with respect to the child into responsibility for the supervision of the child. The crux of its argument is that although Pope was not under any obligation to assume responsibility for the supervision of the child at the outset, "once she undertook to house, feed, and care for (the mother and child), she did accept the responsibility and came within the coverage of the statute." But the mother was always present. Pope had no right to usurp the role of the mother even to the extent of responsibility for the child's supervision. We are in full accord with the view of the Court of Special Appeals that it could not "in good conscience hold that a person who has taken in a parent and child is given the responsibility for the child's supervision and protection even while the child is in the very arms of its mother." Pope v. State, 382 A.2d 880, 890 (Md. Ct. Spec. App. 1978). It would be most incongruous that acts of hospitality and kindness, made out of common decency and prompted by sincere concern for the well-being of a mother and her child, subjected the Good Samaritan to criminal prosecution for abusing the very child he sought to look after. And it would be especially ironic were such criminal prosecution to be predicated upon an obligation to take affirmative action with regard to abuse of the child by its mother, when such obligation arises solely from those acts of hospitality and kindness.

The evidence does not show why Pope did not intervene when the mother abused the child or why she did not, at least, timely seek medical assistance, when it was obvious that the child was seriously injured. Whether her lack of action was from fear or religious fervor or some other reason is not clearly indicated. . . . Pope's conduct, during and after the acts of abuse, must be evaluated with regard for the rule that although she may have had a strong moral obligation to help the child, she was under no legal obligation to do so unless she then had responsibility for the supervision of the child as contemplated by the child abuse statute. She may not be punished as a felon under our system of justice for failing to fulfill a moral obligation, and the short of it is that she was under no legal obligation. In the circumstances, the mother's acquiescence in Pope's conduct was not a grant of responsibility to Pope for the supervision of the child, nor was Pope's conduct an acceptance of such responsibility. . . . We hold that the evidence was not sufficient in law to prove that Pope fell within that class of persons to whom the child abuse statute applies. Thus it is that the judgment of the trial court that she was a principal in the first degree in the commission of the crime of child abuse was clearly erroneous and must be set aside.

The mental or emotional state of the mother, whereby at times she held herself out as God, does not change the result. We see no basis in the statute for an interpretation that a person "has" responsibility for the super-vision of a child, if that person believes or may have reason to believe that a parent is not capable of caring for the child. There is no right to make such a subjective judgment in order to divest parents of their rights and obliga-tions with respect to their minor children, and therefore, no obligation to do so.[15]

[Opinion of ELDRIDGE, J., concurring in part and dissenting in part, omitted.]

NOTES AND QUESTIONS

1. Failure to Intervene. The *Pope* case sets forth a widely accepted prop-osition of American criminal law: People generally have no legal obligation to take affirmative steps to save others in harm's way. Failure to take such steps will thus not give rise to criminal liability. One justification offered for such an approach is that it can be costly—perhaps even dangerous—to save other people from danger, and that these costs should therefore not be lightly imposed. Consider the following two excerpts:

Petula Dvorak, *Passengers Watched Killing on Metro Car. Should They Have Intervened?*, Wash. Post (July 9, 2015). What should they have done? What would you have done? There's a young man being brutally slaughtered—punched, stabbed 30 or 40 times, stomped and repeatedly kicked in the head—in a Red Line Metro car, in the middle of a holiday afternoon, in the nation's capital, in front of almost a dozen witnesses. Yet no one on the train confronted the guy who was killing 24-year-old Kevin Joseph Sutherland right before the passengers' eyes.

This tragedy has become a litmus test online, where the Internet is full of heroes and the heroic ways they claim they would have dealt

---

15. This State has enacted a comprehensive scheme, surrounded by safeguards, for determining whether a person is suffering from a mental illness or mental disorder so as to make it necessary or advisable for the welfare of the person so suffering or for the safety of the persons or property of others that the mentally ill person receive care and treatment. It would be unthinkable to impose such a determination on an ordinary individual at the risk of criminal prosecution. Not even the "reasonable man," so often called upon by the law, has the expertise to make such a judgment.

with the attacker. Police charged 18-year-old Jasper Spires in the bloody Independence Day killing; they say he may have been high when he allegedly tried to rob Sutherland. And here's one more detail to factor into your equation: Spires is described in a police affidavit as 5-foot-5 and 125 pounds. So, not exactly a huge guy.

There were 10 or so other passengers in car No. 3045, and the online second-guessers have been filled with derision for their lack of intervention. Critics have cited the so-called bystander affect — the bigger the crowd, the less likely it is that someone will intervene when a crime is being committed — and lamented what the entire episode says about our country. Never mind that the police always urge witnesses to avoid confronting armed criminals.

On Reddit, which bills itself as "the front page of the Internet" and where this was heavily debated, there were lots of brave, anonymous people. . . . Even my babysitter, the formidable Miss Teresa, thought she would have sprung into action. "I would yell at him," she boomed when she arrived at our house this week. "People in this country don't yell at each other enough. I would've yelled at him. How could they just let that happen without saying anything?". . . .

Sure, it would have been risky to step in on a knife attack. There are plenty of mourners who wish their family members had not risked their lives to save others. But it makes a lot of us uncomfortable to think we would have cowered instead of confronting Sutherland's killer. We live in a country that celebrated the passengers on United Flight 93 who resisted Sept. 11, 2001, hijackers and may have saved hundreds of lives at the Capitol or the White House. . . .

[One man, Dylan Rawls, who had previously intervened in a violent altercation, likely saving the victim's life, reflected on his own actions in that incident.] "I've gone over that night a million times in my head. I've thought: 'That was really dumb. I wasn't thinking,'" he said. "But that's what happened. I wasn't thinking. Had I stopped, thought about it, weighed the pros or cons, had I had time to react, I might've scared myself out of helping."

. . . All week long, he has been thinking about those bystanders on the Metro. What would he have done? . . . [He] is not sure. And he's a little exasperated with the armchair heroes and their takedown of the witnesses. "I didn't want people to be so harsh," he said. "You really don't know unless you're there."

Daniel B. Yeager, *A Radical Community of Aid: A Rejoinder to Opponents of Affirmative Duties to Help Strangers*, 71 Wash. U. L.Q. 1, 15 (1993). In the case of witnesses to crimes, danger — real or imagined — and fear of retaliation account for some failures to intervene or notify authorities. In addition, because emergencies are, for most of us, exotic, a bystander's lack of opportunity for planning and rehearsal and the difficulty of quickly selecting the appropriate type of intervention might make her assistance less likely. . . . The presence of other bystanders may [also] reduce each potential rescuer's individual sense of responsibility to the imperiled, and increase the probability of free-riding. Each is lulled into a state of "pluralistic ignorance," which induces multiple bystanders to interpret others' nonaction as a sign of no danger. Despite the apparent incentive that risk-sharing would provide to potential co-intervenors, because of social inhibitions that arise in groups, people are more prone to respond to another's distress when alone than when accompanied by other witnesses.

Bystanders thus face a "choice of nightmares": fail to intervene and experience the empathic distress of watching another human being suffer, the guilt of failing to live up to a minimal threshold of decency, and the shame of having that failure witnessed by others; or, intervene and risk retaliation by an assailant, the ridicule and derision of nonintervening bystanders, and the threat of being mistaken for the cause of the harm. Moreover, the victim may spurn, attack, or become completely dependent on the rescuer, while the legal system may enlist the rescuer as a witness subject to innumerable encounters with police, lawyers, and judges.

2. Failure to Rescue. The American rule is not limited to scenarios in which one person refuses to stop another from causing harm — or even to scenarios in which rendering aid to a person in peril would be costly or dangerous. Rather, as the *Pope* court observes, "Generally one has no legal duty to aid another person in peril, even when that aid can be rendered without danger or inconvenience to himself. A moral duty to take affirmative action is not enough to impose a legal duty to do so." This rule barring criminal liability for omissions is controversial, given its implications, as reflected in the reasoning and holding of *Pope*: just as a bystander "need not pull a neighbor's baby out of a pool of water . . . though the baby is drowning," Pope had no obligation to rescue Demiko Norris from harm. In fact, the rule is controversial enough to have been abandoned by many other countries, the notable exceptions being jurisdictions in the Anglo-American legal tradition. In the excerpt below, Professor John Kleinig explores the rationales underlying such an approach.

John Kleinig, *Good Samaritanism*, 5 Phil. & Pub. Affs. 382, 382, 388, 389, 402, 403 (1976). [Proponents of Good Samaritan laws concede] that a rich man who lets a beggar die at his feet is morally worse than some [people] for whom severe punishment was prescribed [based on their criminal conduct]. [But they argue that it is too hard to determine where] "we can draw the line." How rich is rich enough, and how much can be required? If it takes a thousand rupees to save the beggar's life, should the rich man be required to provide it? . . .

On the surface [this] looks like a problem of legal draftsmanship. . . . It does nothing to show that if Good Samaritan legislation is introduced, unreasonable sacrifices of welfare and interests will be demanded of Samaritans. As is the case with Good Samaritan provisions in those countries that already have them, the Samaritan will be required only to take reasonable steps to give or procure aid for the imperiled person. Judgments of reasonableness are not impossible of determination, and are the bread and butter of the courts. Good Samaritan legislation would be no exception in this respect. Moreover, if Good Samaritan laws are restricted to cases in which someone is in grave danger, the argument that the courts are already overburdened with cases will count more readily against certain other existing legislation than Good Samaritan legislation.

However, I think another, rather different fear underlies . . . opposition to Good Samaritan legislation. Made explicit by [some] writers, it is basically the fear that Good Samaritan legislation will substantially diminish freedom. In a culture steeped in individualism, nothing produces more hysteria than measures which encroach on individual liberty. "You owe me nothing; I owe you nothing. You stay out of my way, and I'll stay out of yours." That is an extreme expression, but it constitutes an important thread within the Anglo-American sociomoral fabric. And Good Samaritan legislation threatens to snap it.

3. Exceptions to the Rule. The American rule is not without exceptions, as noted in *Jones v. United States*, 308 F.2d 307 (D.C. Cir. 1962):

> There are at least four situations in which the failure to act may constitute breach of a legal duty. One can be held criminally liable: first, where a statute imposes a duty to care for another; second, where one stands in a certain status relationship to another [as in the cases of parents with respect to their children, spouses with respect to their partners, and innkeepers or ship captains with respect to their guests or passengers]; third, where one has assumed a contractual duty to care for another; and fourth, where one has voluntarily assumed the care of another and so secluded the helpless person as to prevent others from rendering aid.

Id. at 310. The second exception, for example, supported the manslaughter convictions of the defendants in *State v. Williams* (p. 229), who failed to obtain medical attention for their 17-month-old child, who perished as a result. But as the *Pope* opinion shows, the default no-duty rule holds considerable sway even in cases where a statute might be construed to create an affirmative duty to rescue.

II.   COMPLICITY

A.   *Actus Reus: Encouragement and Aid*

Pope v. State
_____

   396 A.2d 1054 (Md. 1979)

ORTH, J. [The facts of this case are set forth earlier in this chapter.] The trial court found Pope guilty of the crime of child abuse as a principal in the first degree, and alternatively, as a principal in the second degree. A principal in the first degree is the one who actually commits a crime, either by his own hand, or by an inanimate agency, or by an innocent human agent. . . . Pope was actually present when the felony was committed, but, we have determined, she was not a perpetrating actor. She would be a principal in the second degree if she aided or abetted in the commission of the crime. The principal in the second degree differs from the principal in the first degree in that he does not do the deed himself or through an innocent agent but in some way participates in the commission of the felony by aiding, commanding, counseling or encouraging the actual perpetrator.[16]

   Unless he contributed actual aid it is necessary that his approval should be manifested by some word or act in such a way that it operated on the mind of the perpetrator. Even the secret acquiescence or approval of the bystander is not sufficient to taint him with the guilt of the crime.

> Counsel, command or encouragement may be in the form of words or gestures. Such a purpose "may be manifested by acts, words, signs, motions, or any conduct which unmistakably evinces a design to encourage, incite, or approve of the crime." Promises or threats are very effective for this purpose, but much less will meet the legal requirement, as where a bystander merely emboldened the perpetrator to kill the deceased. . . . One may also encourage a crime by merely standing by for the purpose of giving aid to the perpetrator if necessary, provided the latter is aware of this purpose. Guilt or innocence of the abettor . . . is not determined by the quantum of his advice or encouragement. If it is rendered to induce another to commit the crime and actually has this effect, no more is required. R. Perkins, *Criminal Law* 659 (2d ed. 1969).

_____

   16. The principal in the second degree differs from the accessory before the fact only in the requirement of presence. "The principal in the second degree must be present at the perpetration of the felony, either actually or constructively, whereas the accessory before the fact must be absent. In other words . . . the same aid, command, counsel, or encouragement which will make a principal in the second degree of one who is present (actually or constructively) at the time a felony is committed, will make him an accessory before the fact if he is absent." R. Perkins, *Criminal Law* 658-659 (2d ed. 1969).

. . . When the evidence here is viewed in the light of these criteria, it is patent that it was not legally sufficient to prove that Pope was a principal in the second degree. She neither actually aided the mother in the acts of abuse nor did she counsel, command or encourage her. The Court of Special Appeals pointed out the facts relied on by the trial court—that the events took place in Pope's home, that Pope responded to the commands of the mother, namely that she looked when told to look and came when called, . . . and that she failed to interfere or question the mother's activity, even when the mother appeared rational—were simply not enough to meet the test. . . .

The evidence certainly showed that Pope "witnessed a terrible event" and that she "stood by" while the mother killed the child. But the culpability for her conduct during the abuse of the child must be determined strictly within the law or else the basic tenets of our system of justice are prostituted. There is an understandable feeling of outrage at what occurred, intensified by the fact that the mother, who actually beat the child to death, was held to be not responsible for her criminal acts. But it is the law, not indignation, which governs. The law requires that Pope's conviction of the felony of child abuse be set aside.

NOTES AND QUESTIONS

1. Aiding and Abetting. The terminology in *Pope v. State* reflects an older approach to describing the law of complicity that distinguished among principals in the first degree, principals in the second degree, accessories before the fact, and accessories after the fact. Modern statutes generally refer to the direct perpetrators themselves simply as *principals*, rather than principals in the first degree. And they combine the middle two categories: instead of distinguishing between those who were and were not present at the scene of the offense, modern usage deems anyone who offers sufficient aid or encouragement before or during a criminal act—and has sufficient *mens rea* (as discussed below)—to be an *accomplice*, also known as an *accessory* or an *aider and abettor*.

An accomplice is guilty of the same substantive offense as the principal. Thus, a person who assists a murder is not charged with or convicted of "complicity to commit murder" but is instead guilty simply of "murder," just like the principal. As a result, accomplices are generally exposed to the same penalty as principals, although judges may take the accomplice's role in the offense into account when imposing a sentence.

Those who offer to help a principal escape or avoid punishment after a crime has been completed are still treated separately, either as accessories after the fact or under more modern statutes that criminalize "hindering" apprehension or prosecution. These statutes set out a separate offense, with punishment typically lower than what the principal can receive.

2. Encouraging Crime. Although states use a variety of terms to describe the *actus reus* of complicity, many of them boil down to the notion that the accomplice has encouraged—through words or actions—the principal's offense. As the *Pope* court wrote, "the quantum of . . . encouragement" the accomplice offers is typically irrelevant to his guilt. Still, there must be a way to distinguish acts that constitute "encouragement" from those that do not. This has proved to be a considerable challenge. Consider the following cases.

State v. Conde

787 A.2d 571 (Conn. App. Ct. 2001)

LAVERY, C.J. The defendant, Martin Conde, appeals from the judgment of conviction, rendered after a jury trial, of murder as an accessory. . . .

Late in the evening on February 15, 1996, the victim, Anthony DeJesus, also known as "Dejon," was standing in his former mother-in-law's kitchen . . . when he was gunned down in a hail of bullets fired into the house from points outside. . . . DeJesus, at the time of his death, was a member of the Waterbury chapter of the Nietas, a gang with roots in Puerto Rico's prison system.[*] The defendant at that time was the local president of the Nietas. DeJesus had worked for the defendant selling drugs.

DeJesus formerly had been a member of the local chapter of the Latin Kings, a larger gang whose members tended to be younger than those of the Nietas. Both gangs operated in the south end of Waterbury and made money selling drugs. The relationship between the two gangs was cooperative rather than antagonistic; at some time prior to the events in question, they had entered into a peace treaty.

About one and one-half weeks prior to DeJesus' killing . . . a conversation took place between the defendant and two high ranking members of the Latin Kings. Those members were Ricky Lespier (Ricky) . . . and Jose Dupree (Red). . . . Ricky and Red expressed anger to the defendant regarding a recent incident in which DeJesus had disrespected Red. . . . Ricky told the defendant that he wanted something done because he believed that DeJesus' actions were wrong. The defendant also expressed anger at DeJesus because DeJesus owed him money. The defendant said he wanted DeJesus dead, and told Ricky and Red to "go ahead and kill him." . . .

[At trial, the prosecution also presented testimony from Enrique Adorno, who] was associated with the Nietas for eight years [and] was

---

[*] Editor's Note: The opinion uses the word *nietas* to describe a group called La Asociación ÑETA. The Spanish word "nieta" means "granddaughter" and is not generally used to describe the ñetas. The opinion above maintains the opinion writer's spelling.

"president of discipline." . . . Sometime in the winter of 1996, prior to DeJesus' death, Adorno witnessed the defendant and DeJesus arguing over money, apparently because DeJesus had been selling drugs independently. The defendant told DeJesus that he was tired of waiting for his money. At a party subsequent to DeJesus' murder, the defendant confided in Adorno that he had been involved in the murder and, specifically, that "he and this Latin King guy Red said to do Dejon." . . .

Discussion. The defendant . . . argues that the court improperly conveyed to the jurors that they could find him guilty as an accessory to murder on the basis of his "nonactions," without instructing further that nonaction could be the basis of a conviction only if the defendant had a legal duty to act. . . .

The court charged the jury regarding accomplice liability as to murder as follows:

> . . . . The criminal responsibility of an accessory is . . . as follows: A person acting with the mental state required for the commission of an offense . . . who solicits, requests, commands, importunes or intentionally aids another person to engage in conduct which constitutes an offense shall be criminally liable for such conduct, and may be prosecuted and punished as if he were the principal offender.
>
> . . . Solicit means to order or direct. Importune means to demand or urge. Aid means to assist. And in the course of the definition of assisting, you may take into account the broad range of actions *or nonactions* which are or may not be assistance. . . . Assistance also means help or support. . . .

. . . The defendant claims . . . there was insufficient evidence to show that he intentionally aided the killers of DeJesus . . . . "To justify a conviction as an accessory, . . . [m]ere presence as an inactive companion, passive acquiescence, or the doing of innocent acts which may in fact aid the principal must be distinguished from the criminal intent and community of unlawful purpose by one who knowingly and willingly assists the perpetrator of the offense in the acts which prepare for, facilitate, or consummate it." State v. McClendon, 743 A.2d 1154, 1157 (Conn. App. Ct. 2000).

. . . [T]he defendant's claim that accessory liability may not be based on nonaction where there was no duty to act completely misrepresents the . . . theory pursuant to which he was convicted. In addition, we reject the defendant's argument that passive behavior can never be the basis of a finding of accessory liability, particularly where that behavior is accompanied by a communicated assurance of passivity. . . .

The defendant's claim of insufficiency of the evidence rests on an inaccurate premise. He characterizes his participation in DeJesus' murder as merely declining to protect the victim and argues the general legal principle that one cannot be held criminally responsible for failure to act where there is no duty to act. The idea that one may be guilty as an accessory for failing to fulfill his duty to act is a recognized theory of accessory liability . . . . [But] it is not the theory that the state presented at the defendant's trial. The state argued instead that the defendant's preapproval of the murder was an assurance that the Nietas would not retaliate if DeJesus were killed and, thus, was a form of "intentional aid" . . . . It is of no consequence, therefore, that the defendant was under no duty to protect DeJesus.

We turn then, to the proper issue for our review, which is whether nonaction ever may amount to "intentional aid" . . . . Although our courts have consistently held that one cannot be liable as an accessory on the basis of his "mere presence" at a crime scene or "passive acquiescence" to the commission of a crime, the case law nonetheless establishes that passive behaviors engaged in with the intent to facilitate the commission of a crime are sufficient to support a finding of accessory liability. . . . *See, e.g.,* State v. Fuller, 754 A.2d 207 (Conn. App. Ct. 2000) (defendant aided perpetrator by accompanying him during assault, murder and failing to summon medical assistance for victim). In a case with a similar dynamic to the one at hand, the Maine Supreme Judicial Court held that a wife's statement, "I won't give you any problem," spoken to her husband when she learned that he planned to kill her mother, was an "assurance of non-interference" that "went beyond mere condonation or passive acquiescence" such that the wife was responsible as an accomplice for her mother's murder. State v. Doody, 434 A.2d 523, 529-530 (Me. 1981). . . .

[W]e conclude that the jury had before it sufficient evidence to convict the defendant of murder as an accessory. . . . [A member of the defendant's gang testified about] the power and authority that the president of [the] gang could wield, and of his ability to order beatings or killings. He [further] testified that one of the "rules" of gangs was that they typically offered protection to their members and opined that if a member of one gang harmed, assaulted or murdered a member of a different gang, retaliation or "war" would be the result. Adorno . . . reiterated that gangs offer protection to their members and engage in retaliatory actions when members are harmed. . . .

Given that testimony, the jury had before it sufficient evidence to conclude that the defendant had facilitated DeJesus' murder by counseling and advising the leadership of the Latin Kings that if they went ahead with the murder, no retaliatory action would be forthcoming. From the testimony regarding gang hierarchy and dynamics, and the defendant's position of power, the jury reasonably could have inferred that the Nietas would have retaliated had the Latin Kings not sought permission and approval for the killing first, and, therefore, that lack of permission and approval would have deterred them from proceeding with the killing. In assuring the Latin Kings' leadership that killing DeJesus would not disrupt the peace treaty between the gangs, cause a war and thereby disturb the lucrative drug trade that the two groups shared, the defendant provided a powerful incentive for the Latin Kings to commit the murder. The evidence was sufficient to show that the defendant had provided an assurance of noninterference that went far beyond passive acquiescence or mere condonation, and the jury, therefore, properly could find beyond a reasonable doubt that he intentionally aided in the commission of DeJesus' murder. . . . The judgment is affirmed.

State v. Ulvinen

313 N.W.2d 425 (Minn. 1981)

OTIS, J. . . . Carol Hoffman, appellant's daughter-in-law, was murdered late on the evening of August 10th or the very early morning of August 11th by her husband, David Hoffman [who was appellant's son]. . . .

Appellant's relationship with her daughter-in-law had been a strained one. She moved in with the Hoffmans on July 26, two weeks earlier to act as a live-in babysitter for their two children. Carol was unhappy about having her move in and told friends that she hated [appellant], but she told both David and his mother that they could try the arrangement to see how it worked.

On the morning of the murder [appellant] told her son that she was going to move out of the Hoffman residence because "Carol had been so nasty to me." In his statement to the police David reported the conversation that morning as follows:

> A. Sunday morning I went downstairs and my mom was in the bedroom reading the newspaper and she had tears in her eyes, and she said in a very frustrated voice, "I've got to find another house." She said, "Carol don't want me here," and she said, "I probably shouldn't have moved in here." And I said then, "Don't let what Carol said hurt you. It's going to take a little more period of readjustment for her." Then I told mom that I've got to do it tonight so that there can be peace in this house. . . .
>
> Q. Dave, will you tell us exactly what you told your mother that morning, to the best of your recollection?
>
> A. I said I'm going to have to choke her tonight and I'll have to dispose of her body so that it will never be found. That's the best of my knowledge.
>
> Q. What did your mother say when you told her that?
>
> A. She just—she looked at me with very sad eyes and just started to weep. I think she said something like "it will be for the best." . . . I think she said, again I'm not certain, that it would be the best for the kids.

. . . It is well-settled in this state that presence, companionship, and conduct before and after the offense are circumstances from which a person's participation in the criminal intent may be inferred. The evidence is undisputed that appellant was asleep when her son choked his wife. She took no active part in the [aftermath of the homicide] but came upstairs to intercept the children, should they awake, and prevent them from going into the bathroom. . . .

[Our aiding and abetting statute] implies a high level of activity on the part of an aider and abettor in the form of conduct that encourages another to act. Use of terms such as "aids," "advises," and "conspires" requires something more of a person than mere inaction to impose liability as a principal. The evidence presented to the jury at best supports a finding that appellant passively acquiesced in her son's plan to kill his wife. The jury might have believed that David told his mother of his intent to kill his wife that night and that she neither actively discouraged him nor told anyone in time to prevent the murder. Her response that "it would be the best for the kids" or "it will be the best" was not, however, active encouragement or instigation. There is no evidence that her remark had any influence on her son's decision to kill his wife. [Our statute] imposes liability for actions which affect the principal, encouraging him to take a course of action which he might not otherwise have taken. The state has not proved beyond a reasonable doubt that appellant was guilty of anything but passive approval. However morally reprehensible it may be to fail to warn someone of their impending death, our statutes do not make such an omission a criminal offense. . . . She did not offer advice on how to kill his wife, nor offer to help him. She did not plan when to accomplish the act or tell her son what to do to avoid being caught. She was told by her son that he intended to kill his wife that night and responded in a way which, while not discouraging him, did not aid, advise, or counsel him to act as he did. Where, as here, the evidence is insufficient to show beyond a reasonable doubt that appellant was guilty of active conduct sufficient to convict her of first degree murder . . . her conviction must be reversed.

[Opinion of YETKA, J., concurring, omitted.]

1.   Defining Encouragement

Conde discusses a case, *State v. Doody*, 434 A.2d 523 (Me. 1981), with facts quite similar to those in *Ulvinen*. Whereas Ulvinen told her son that killing his wife "will be for the best," Doody told her husband she wouldn't "give [him] any problem" if he killed her mother. Yet Ulvinen's conviction was reversed, while Doody's was affirmed. Are these cases distinguishable on the facts? If they are, what does that tells us about the line that separates culpable encouragement from nonculpable passive acquiescence? If you cannot distinguish the cases on the facts, consider what this implies about the legal rules the various courts are applying. The pair of notes that follow elaborate on the governing framework.

NOTES AND QUESTIONS

1. Mere Presence. Sometimes a defendant's alleged encouragement is nonverbal. Courts here seem to agree that "mere presence" at the scene of a crime is insufficient to turn a bystander into an accomplice. In *Buchanan v. State*, 316 So.3d 619 (Miss. 2021), for example, the Supreme Court of Mississippi overturned the aggravated assault conviction of a man who was riding in the back seat of an SUV when one of the vehicle's other occupants committed a drive-by shooting. There was no evidence, the court said, that the defendant fired any shots or knew, when he got into the car, that the shooting was planned. Nor was it significant that the defendant made no attempt to leave the group after the shooting, given the risks that doing so might have entailed.

Nevertheless, many courts find defendants liable based on evidence of little beyond mere presence. As the *Pope* court explained, accessory liability can attach to someone who is "merely standing by for the purpose of giving aid to the perpetrator if necessary, provided the latter is aware of this purpose." Consider *In re T.J.W.*, 294 A.2d 174 (D.C. 1972), in which a juvenile was found to have aided and abetted robbery and assault. Although the state had not shown he "actively participated in the assault and robbery," he was present during the crime, fled with the principals, and was later arrested alongside them. *Id.* at 176. "[P]erhaps most significant," the appellate court wrote, is that he "did not, at any time, avail himself of opportunities to withdraw from the scene of the criminal activity," as he easily could have done, and thus "by his continued presence he gave tacit approval and encouragement." *Id.* Many similar cases dot the court reports. *See, e.g.*, Creek v. U.S., 324 A.2d 688 (D.C. 1974); State v. Gervais, 394 A.2d 1183 (Me. 1978).

2. Aiding Crime. One cannot *encourage* another's crime without somehow communicating that encouragement—by words or actions—to the principal actor. That said, an individual who intentionally *aids* the commission of a crime is complicit in that crime even if the principal is wholly unaware of the assistance. This happened in the well-known case of *Tally v. State*, 15 So. 722 (Ala. 1894), which involved a rather extraordinary set of facts. As told by Professor Leo Katz:

> There lived in the Alabama town of Scottsboro, circa 1893, a married man named Robert C. Ross, who entered into an affair with an unmarried young woman named Ann Skelton. This Ann Skelton had four intemperate brothers, who blamed Ross for seducing their sister and resolved to kill him. . . . [Ross] drove his horse-drawn coach to the nearby town of Stevenson, there expecting to catch the train to Chattanooga [to escape to safety]. He never made it onto the train: The Skelton brothers had learned of his whereabouts, managed to catch up with him in front of the train depot, and finished him off in a hail of bullets.

The killing became a *cause célèbre* in Alabama [but not] because of any of the facts . . . described so far . . . . The Skelton brothers had a second sister, who happened to be married to a prominent Alabama judge, one John B. Tally. Tally had learned about the Ross affair and apparently approved of the way the Skeltons were about to deal with it. . . . While Ross was traveling to Stevenson and the Skelton brothers were chasing him there, one of Ross's cousins found out what was going on and decided to send a warning telegram to Stevenson telling Ross "Four men on horseback with guns following. Look out." Judge Tally happened to see this cousin of Ross just as he was leaving the telegraph office and easily guessed what he must have been doing there. Tally thereupon decided he would try to prevent the warning telegram from reaching Ross. He did so by mailing a telegram of his own to the telegraph operator of Stevenson, whom he knew. Tally's telegram read: "Don't let the party warned get away. Say nothing. . . ." Both telegrams arrived in Stevenson, and Ross never got his warning. Whether that was on account of Tally's request, or because there simply wasn't time enough to get it to him, was unclear.[1]

The Supreme Court of Alabama held that Tally was liable for Ross's murder under the law of complicity if either of two conditions was met: First, if "his vigil at Scottsboro to prevent Ross from being warned of his danger was by preconcert with [the Skeltons], or at least known to them, whereby they would naturally be incited, encouraged and emboldened — 'given confidence' — to the deed." *Id.* at 738. Such "preconcert" would constitute encouragement of the crime. Second, and *independently*, Tally would be liable if he "contributed to Ross' death, in point of physical fact, by means of the telegram he sent." *Id.* The court held that these actions would constitute aid, and affirmed Tally's liability on this second basis.

Either encouragement or aid will satisfy the *actus reus* requirement of complicity, and in many cases the same conduct could be characterized in either way. When an accomplice furnishes a weapon, for example, he both emboldens the principal to commit the crime and aids him by providing a tool to do so. Here, nothing turns on the distinction between encouragement and aid drawn by the *Tally* court. The critical point from *Tally* is simply that the principal's awareness of the accomplice's actions, while necessary for *encouragement* to occur, is not essential to the conclusion that the accomplice has *aided* the principal's commission of the crime.

2.   Complicity and Causation

As the *Pope* opinion explains, even slight degrees of encouragement or aid will typically suffice as the *actus reus* of accomplice liability. But what about the *impact* of the accomplice's words or actions on the principal's crime? Consider the following notes.

NOTES AND QUESTIONS

1. But-For Causation and the Materiality of Encouragement or Aid. The *Pope* court wrote that, for encouragement to constitute complicity, there must be evidence that it "operated on the mind of the perpetrator." Similarly, *Ulvinen* explained that the law "imposes liability for actions which affect the principal," overturning the defendant's conviction in part because there was "no evidence that her remark had any influence on her son's decision to kill his wife." And *Tally* required that the judge's actions have "contributed to Ross' death, in point of physical fact."

Does this mean the state must prove that the accomplice's actions *caused* the principal to commit the crime in the traditional sense? The *Tally* court said no:

> The assistance given . . . need not contribute to the criminal result in the sense that but for it the result would not have ensued. . . . It is quite enough if the aid merely rendered it easier for the principal actor to accomplish the end intended by him and the aider and abettor, though in all human probability the end would have been attained without it. If the aid in homicide can be shown to have put the deceased at a disadvantage, to have deprived him of a single chance of life which but for it he would have had, he who furnishes such aid is guilty, though it cannot be known or shown that the dead man, in the absence thereof, would have availed himself of that chance.

15 So. at 738-739.

For a dramatic display of this principle, consider the famous English case of *Wilcox v. Jeffery* (1951) 1 All E.R. 464 (KB). Wilcox, a professional music critic, attended a concert by renowned American saxophonist Coleman Hawkins, who was visiting the UK and who, Wilcox knew, had not obtained a legally required work visa. Wilcox was convicted of aiding and abetting Hawkins' violation of the immigration laws. The appellate court affirmed:

> The appellant attended this concert as a spectator. He paid for his ticket. Mr. Hawkins went on the stage and delighted the audience by playing the saxophone. The appellant did not get up and protest in the name of the musicians of England that Mr. Hawkins ought not to be here competing with them and taking the bread out of their mouths or the wind out of their instruments. It is not found that he actually applauded, but he was there having paid to go in, and, no doubt, enjoying the performance, and then, lo and behold, out comes his magazine with a most laudatory description, fully illustrated, of this concert. . . .
>
> The appellant . . . must, therefore, be held to have been present, taking part, concurring, or encouraging, whichever word you like to use for

expressing this conception. It was an illegal act on the part of Hawkins to play the saxophone or any other instrument at this concert. The appellant clearly knew that it was an unlawful act for him to play. He had gone there to hear him, and his presence and his payment to go there was an encouragement. He went there to . . . get "copy" for his newspaper. It might have been entirely different, as I say, if he had gone there and protested, saying: "The musicians' union do not like you foreigners coming here and playing and you ought to get off the stage." If he had booed, it might have been some evidence that he was not aiding and abetting. If he had gone as a member of a *claque* to try to drown the noise of the saxophone, he might very likely be found not guilty of aiding and abetting. In this case it seems clear that he was there, not only to approve and encourage what was done, but to take advantage of it by getting "copy" for his paper. . . .

Suppose that Wilcox had fallen ill that morning and missed the festivities. Surely the show would have gone on without him. This is another way of saying that Wilcox's paid attendance at the concert was *not* a but-for cause of the illegality—and yet, his conviction as an accomplice stands.[2]

2. *Proximate Causation and Human Agency.* The *Wilcox* and *Tally* opinions indicate that an accomplice's aid or encouragement need not be the but-for cause of the principal's conduct for the accomplice to be held liable. But what about *proximate* causation? On a traditional, blackletter view, it would be impossible to consider an accomplice the proximate cause of the principal's crime because the principal's decision to commit the crime would be deemed an independent act of his own free will, and thus an intervening cause. The principal's own decision to act would thus break the chain of proximate causation between the accomplice's words or deeds and the principal's offense.

Some argue that the very purpose of complicity doctrine is to solve this human-agency conundrum and establish liability for accomplices despite the absence of traditional causation. In the words of Professor Sanford Kadish:

> [W]hen we seek to determine the responsibility of one person for the volitional actions of another the concept of [causation] is not available to determine the answer. . . . [O]ur conception of human actions as controlled by choice will not allow that to work. . . . Some alternative doctrine is needed, therefore, which imposes liability on the actor who is to blame for the conduct of another, but which does so upon principles that comport with our perception of human actions. This is the office of the doctrine of complicity.

Other scholars question whether human free will poses a meaningful challenge to viewing one person as the cause of another's crime. As Professor Joshua Dressler puts it: "Certainly based on a common-sense understanding of causation, it is sensible to claim that when I offer a huge fortune to another person to kill my wife, and he takes my money and performs the deed, I have 'caused' her death." Indeed, some scholars who embrace this view go so far as to argue that complicity doctrine is entirely superfluous, because ordinary causation principles, properly understood, can support direct liability for anyone whom traditional complicity doctrine would deem an accomplice.[3]

Regardless of one's views on these conceptual debates, the common law established a reasonably clear standard—albeit one that can be difficult to apply—for the required causal relationship between the accomplice's actions and the principal's crime. In the words of the *Tally* court: "It is quite enough if the aid merely rendered it easier for the principal actor to accomplish the end intended by him and the aider and abettor, though in all human probability the end would have been attained without it." The question, in other words, is only whether the accomplice's words or actions, when uttered or done, *could* have mattered to the outcome, not whether it turns out they *did* matter. So, for example, one who lends tools for use in a burglary is still an accomplice even if the principal finds and uses better tools at the crime scene. *See* State v. Tazwell, 30 La. Ann. 884 (1878). Only if it is entirely clear that the defendant's actions *could not* have made a difference has the defendant typically escaped liability. A defendant who shouts words of encouragement at a principal who cannot hear, for example, is traditionally not liable as an accomplice. *Cf.* Hicks v. United States, 150 U.S. 442, 450 (1893).[4]

3. Weak Causation and the Challenge of Culpability. Where the causal connection between accomplice and principal is strong—perhaps the accomplice pays the principal to kill the accomplice's nemesis—the case for punishing the accomplice seems intuitive. But why would the law impose punishment when the causal connection is weak, or perhaps even nonexistent? Why impose liability in *Tazwell*, for example, when the principal doesn't use the burglary tools lent to him by the putative accomplice?

It may be possible to understand complicity liability under such circumstances as an effort to punish an accomplice not because of his impact on what *the principal* did, but instead because of what *the accomplice* did himself. He is punished because he promoted, or at least tried to promote, a crime. On this logic, some states have done away with the requirement of any causal relationship whatsoever between the accomplice's words or deeds and the principal's crime. The Model Penal Code exemplifies this approach, stating that "[a] person is an accomplice of another person in the commission of an offense if . . . he . . . aids or agrees or *attempts to aid* such other person in planning or committing it." §2.06(3) (emphasis added). This would cover the case of the deaf principal in the preceding note, as any case in which the defendant attempts to encourage or aid the principal gives rise to liability, even if the defendant demonstrably fails. A healthy handful of states have adopted this approach, though it remains the minority rule.[5]

As the MPC provision reflects, the approach in these states is analogous to the law of attempt, which we study in the following chapter. Both doctrines sometimes punish people who don't cause actual harm, either because the harm never manifests (as in attempt) or because the defendant doesn't cause it (as in complicity).* As we will see for attempt in Chapter Eight, and for complicity in the section that follows, what best justifies punishment in both situations is the defendant's *purposeful* decision to promote criminal behavior. As Judge Learned Hand wrote about complicity doctrine nearly a century ago, to impose liability the law demands that the defendant "seek by his action" to make a crime succeed. United States v. Peoni, 100 F.2d 401, 402 (2d Cir. 1938). It is to this aspect of the doctrine—the accomplice's intentions, or *mens rea*—that we now turn.[6]

B.   Mens Rea: *Knowingly Versus Intentionally Facilitating Crime*

People v. Lauria

59 Cal. Rptr. 628 (Cal. Ct. App. 1967)

FLEMING, J. In an investigation of call-girl activity [the police focused their attention on three] prostitutes actively plying their trade on call, each of whom was using Lauria's telephone answering service, presumably for business purposes.

On January 8, 1965, Stella Weeks, a policewoman, signed up for telephone service with Lauria's answering service. Mrs. Weeks, in the course of her conversation with Lauria's office manager, hinted broadly that she was a prostitute concerned with the secrecy of her activities and their concealment from the police. She was assured that the operation of the service was discreet and "about as safe as you can get." It was arranged that Mrs. Weeks need not leave her address with the answering service, but could pick up her calls and pay her bills in person.

On February 11, Mrs. Weeks talked to Lauria on the telephone and told him her business was modelling and she had been referred to the answering service by Terry, one of the three prostitutes under investigation. She complained that because of the operation of the service she had lost two valuable customers, referred to as tricks. Lauria defended his service and said that her friends had probably lied to her about having left calls for

---

* The connections between attempt and complicity will tighten when we encounter a unique provision of the Model Penal Code that imposes *attempt* liability on individuals who try to promote crimes that do not ultimately occur. *See* Model Penal Code §5.01(3) (p. 648).

her. But he did not respond to Mrs. Weeks' hints that she needed customers in order to make money, other than to invite her to his house for a personal visit in order to get better acquainted. In the course of his talk he said "his business was taking messages."

On February 15, Mrs. Weeks talked on the telephone to Lauria's office manager and again complained of two lost calls, which she described as a $50 and a $100 trick. On investigation the office manager could find nothing wrong, but she said she would alert the switchboard operators about slip-ups on calls.

On April 1 Lauria and the three prostitutes were arrested. Lauria complained to the police that this attention was undeserved, stating that Hollywood Call Board had 60 to 70 prostitutes on its board while his own service had only 9 or 10, that he kept separate records for known or suspected prostitutes for the convenience of himself and the police. When asked if his records were available to police who might come to the office to investigate call girls, Lauria replied that they were whenever the police had a specific name. However, his service didn't "arbitrarily tell the police about prostitutes on our board. As long as they pay their bills we tolerate them." In a subsequent voluntary appearance before the Grand Jury Lauria testified he had always cooperated with the police. But he admitted he knew some of his customers were prostitutes, and he knew Terry was a prostitute because he had personally used her services, and he knew she was paying for 500 calls a month.

. . . Here the People attempted to establish [Lauria's liability] by showing that Lauria, well aware that his codefendants were prostitutes who received business calls from customers through his telephone answering service, continued to furnish them with such service. This approach . . . poses the question of the criminal responsibility of a furnisher of goods or services who knows his product is being used to assist the operation of an illegal business. Under what circumstances does a supplier become [liable for furthering] an illegal enterprise by furnishing goods or services which he knows are to be used by the buyer for criminal purposes?

The two leading cases on this point face in opposite directions. In *United States v. Falcone,* 311 U.S. 205 (1940), the sellers of large quantities of sugar, yeast, and cans were absolved from [liability for moonshining committed by] distillers who bought from them, while in *Direct Sales Co. v. United States,* 319 U.S. 703 (1943), a wholesaler of drugs was convicted of [violating] the federal narcotic laws by selling drugs in quantity to a codefendant physician who was supplying them to addicts.[*] . . . [In] *Falcone,* the sellers' knowledge

---

* Editor's Note: *Falcone* and *Direct Sales* both involved conspiracy charges but the question they confronted arises in complicity cases as well. Lauria himself was charged with and convicted of conspiracy in the present case. But the opinion and analysis above are cited in conspiracy and complicity cases without distinction. *See, e.g.,* United States v. Fountain, 768 F.2d 790, 798 (7th Cir. 1985) (discussing *Lauria* in complicity analysis); *cf.* 2 Wayne R. LaFave, *Substantive Criminal Law* §13.2(d) (3d ed. 2017 & Supp. 2023) (same).

of the illegal use of the goods was insufficient by itself to make the sellers [liable along] with the distillers who bought from them. . . . [But in] *Direct Sales,* the conviction of a drug wholesaler . . . was affirmed on a showing that it had actively promoted the sale of morphine sulphate in quantity and had sold codefendant physician, who practiced in a small town in South Carolina, more than 300 times his normal requirements of the drug, even though it had been repeatedly warned of the dangers of unrestricted sales of the drug. The court contrasted the restricted goods involved in *Direct Sales* with the articles of free commerce involved in *Falcone:*

> All articles of commerce may be put to illegal ends[.] But all do not have inherently the same susceptibility to harmful and illegal use. This difference is important for two purposes. One is for making certain that the seller knows the buyer's intended illegal use. The other is to show that by the sale he intends to further, promote and cooperate in it. . . .

While *Falcone* and *Direct Sales* may not be entirely consistent with each other in their full implications, they do provide us with a framework for the criminal liability of a supplier of lawful goods or services put to unlawful use. Both the element of *knowledge* of the illegal use of the goods or services and the element of *intent* to further that use must be present. . . .

Proof of *knowledge* is ordinarily a question of fact and requires no extended discussion in the present case. The knowledge of the supplier was sufficiently established when Lauria admitted he knew some of his customers were prostitutes and admitted he knew that Terry, an active subscriber to his service, was a prostitute. In the face of these admissions he could scarcely claim to have relied on the normal assumption an operator of a business or service is entitled to make, that his customers are behaving themselves in the eyes of the law. . . . On this record we think the prosecution is entitled to claim positive knowledge by Lauria of the use of his service to facilitate the business of [prostitution].

The more perplexing issue in the case is the sufficiency of proof of *intent* to further the criminal enterprise. The element of intent may be proved either by direct evidence, or by evidence of circumstances from which an intent to further a criminal enterprise by supplying lawful goods or services may be inferred. Direct evidence of participation, such as advice from the supplier of legal goods or services to the user of those goods or services on their use for illegal purposes . . . provides the simplest case. When the intent to further and promote the criminal enterprise comes from the lips of the supplier himself, ambiguities of inference from circumstance need not trouble us. But in cases where direct proof of complicity is lacking, intent . . . must be derived from the sale itself and its surrounding circumstances. . . .

In the case at bench the prosecution argues that since Lauria knew his customers were using his service for illegal purposes but nevertheless continued to furnish it to them, he must have intended to assist them in carrying out their illegal activities. . . . Essentially, the People argue that knowledge alone of the continuing use of his telephone facilities for criminal purposes provided a sufficient basis from which his intent to participate in those criminal activities could be inferred. In examining precedents in this field we find that sometimes, but not always, the criminal intent of the supplier may be inferred from his knowledge of the unlawful use made of the product he supplies. Some consideration of characteristic patterns may be helpful.

1. Intent may be inferred from knowledge, when the purveyor of legal goods for illegal use has acquired a stake in the venture. For example, in *Regina v. Thomas*, 2 All Eng. 181, 342 (1957), a prosecution for living off the earnings of prostitution, the evidence showed that the accused, knowing the woman to be a convicted prostitute, agreed to let her have the use of his room between the hours of 9 p.m. and 2 a.m. for a charge of £3 a night. The Court of Criminal Appeal refused an appeal from the conviction, holding that when the accused rented a room at a grossly inflated rent to a prostitute for the purpose of carrying on her trade, a jury could find he was living on the earnings of prostitution.

In the present case, no proof was offered of inflated charges for the telephone answering services furnished the codefendants.

2. Intent may be inferred from knowledge, when no legitimate use for the goods or services exists. . . . In *Shaw v. Director of Public Prosecutions*, A.C. 220 (1962), the defendant . . . published a directory consisting almost entirely of advertisements of the names, addresses, and specialized talents of prostitutes. Publication of such a directory, said the court, could have no legitimate use and serve no other purpose than to advertise the professional services of the prostitutes whose advertisements appeared in the directory. The publisher could be deemed a participant in the profits from the business activities of his principal advertisers. Other services of a comparable nature come to mind: the manufacturer of crooked dice and marked cards who sells his product to gambling casinos; the tipster who furnishes information on the movement of law enforcement officers to known lawbreakers. In such cases the supplier must necessarily have an intent to further the illegal enterprise since there is no known honest use for his goods.

However, there is nothing in the furnishing of telephone answering service which would necessarily imply assistance in the performance of illegal activities. Nor is any inference to be derived from the use of an answering service by women, either in any particular volume of calls, or outside normal working hours. Night-club entertainers, registered nurses, faith healers, public stenographers, photographic models, and free lance substitute employees, provide examples of women in legitimate occupations whose employment might cause them to receive a volume of telephone calls at irregular hours.

3. Intent may be inferred from knowledge, when the volume of business with the buyer is grossly disproportionate to any legitimate demand, or when sales for illegal use amount to a high proportion of the seller's total business. In such cases an intent to participate in the illegal enterprise may be inferred from the quantity of the business done. For example, in *Direct Sales*, the sale of narcotics to a rural physician in quantities 300 times greater than he would have normal use for provided potent evidence of an intent to further the illegal activity. In the same case the court also found significant the fact that the wholesaler had attracted as customers a disproportionately large group of physicians who had been convicted of violating [federal narcotics laws]. . . .

No evidence of any unusual volume of business with prostitutes was presented by the prosecution against Lauria.

. . . [Notwithstanding the above, there are also] cases in which it cannot reasonably be said that the supplier has a stake in the venture or has acquired a special interest in the enterprise, but in which he has been held liable as a participant on the basis of knowledge alone. . . . In *Regina v. Bainbridge*, 3 All Eng. 200 (1959), a supplier of oxygen-cutting equipment to one known to intend to use it to break into a bank was convicted as an accessory to the crime. . . . It seems apparent from [cases like this] that a supplier who furnishes equipment which he *knows* will be used to commit a serious crime may be deemed from that knowledge alone to have intended to produce the result. . . . For instance, we think the operator of a telephone answering service with positive knowledge that his service was being used to facilitate the extortion of ransom, the distribution of heroin, or the passing of counterfeit money who continued to furnish the service with knowledge of its use, might be chargeable on knowledge alone with participation in a scheme to extort money, to distribute narcotics, or to pass counterfeit money. . . .

Logically, the same reasoning could be extended to crimes of every description. Yet we do not believe an inference of intent drawn from knowledge of criminal use properly applies to the less serious crimes classified as misdemeanors. The duty to take positive action to dissociate oneself from activities helpful to violations of the criminal law [is] far stronger and more compelling for felonies than it is for misdemeanors or petty offenses. In this respect, as in others, the distinction between felonies and misdemeanors, between more serious and less serious crime, retains continuing vitality. . . . With respect to misdemeanors, we conclude that positive knowledge of the supplier that his products or services are being used for criminal purposes does not, without more, establish an intent of the supplier to participate in the misdemeanors. . . . [W]e do not decide . . . that in all cases of felony[,] knowledge of criminal use alone may justify an inference of the supplier's intent to participate in the crime [as decision] on this point is not compelled, and we leave the matter open. . . .

When we review Lauria's activities in the light of this analysis, we find no proof that Lauria took any direct action to further, encourage, or direct the call-girl activities of his codefendants and we find an absence of circumstance from which his special interest in their activities could be inferred. Neither excessive charges for standardized services, nor the furnishing of services without a legitimate use, nor an unusual quantity of business with call girls, are present. The offense which he is charged with furthering is a misdemeanor, a category of crime which has never been made a required subject of positive disclosure to public authority. Under these circumstances, although proof of Lauria's knowledge of the criminal activities of his patrons was sufficient to charge him with that fact, there was insufficient evidence that he intended to further their criminal activities. . . .

In absolving Lauria of complicity . . . we do not wish to imply that the public authorities are without remedies to combat modern manifestations of the world's oldest profession. Licensing of telephone answering services under the police power, together with the revocation of licenses for the toleration of prostitution, is a possible civil remedy. The furnishing of telephone answering service in aid of prostitution could be made a crime. . . . Other solutions will doubtless occur to vigilant public authorities if the problem of call-girl activity needs further suppression.

NOTES AND QUESTIONS

1. Knowing vs. Intentional Aid. Lauria considers the issue of *mens rea* for accomplice liability. The answering services Lauria provided clearly aided the illegal sex work in which some of his customers (the principals) were engaged. And Lauria clearly knew this to be the case. But Lauria successfully argued that he was not an accomplice because the state had not proven that he provided answering services for the *purpose* of aiding the illegal activity. The state offered no direct proof of such intent, nor did it prove any circumstances permitting an inference of such intent based on Lauria's knowledge.

The premise of the court's opinion—that accomplice liability generally requires intent to facilitate the principal's crime—has been subject to significant debate and evolution. Early cases required only *knowledge* of the principal's crime, not an intent to facilitate it. But over time, most jurisdictions came to insist on intent, which a majority of states require today. Still, the issue is not entirely settled. The *Lauria* court, for example, expressed openness to a bifurcated approach in which knowledge suffices for serious crimes but intent is required for minor ones. *See* United States v. Fountain, 768 F.2d 790 (7th Cir. 1985) (adopting this approach). Another oft-discussed proposal would permit accomplice liability for all levels of offense on proof of knowledge while strengthening the *actus reus* requirement to demand *substantial* facilitation of the principal's crime.[7]

It is important to see what is at stake in the choice of *mens rea* standard. As the *Lauria* example shows, extending accomplice liability to cover knowing facilitation of crime could increase the deterrent force of the law, insofar as it would expand the net of criminal liability to cover a greater range of actors and scenarios. A knowledge rule would also punish additional behavior that seems clearly blameworthy. As the Fourth Circuit once wrote, "One who sells a gun to another knowing that he is buying it to commit a murder [should] hardly escape conviction as an accessory to the murder by showing that he received full price for the gun." Backun v. United States, 112 F.2d 635, 637 (4th Cir. 1940).

On the flipside, as Professor Andrew Simester notes, "by narrowing the scope of criminalization we allow more citizens to get on with their day-to-day lives." In this respect, Simester adds, the intent requirement's narrowing approach navigates a tension inherent in the criminal law more generally: "Ordinary citizens must not only be shielded from the misconduct of others; they need also to be shielded from the state, which should not impede their ordinary, quotidien activities." As Professor Kadish writes, the prevalence across states of the purpose requirement over the knowledge requirement reflects a judgment that broader criminal liability, in this context, would be too burdensome: "A pall would be cast on ordinary activity if we had to fear criminal liability for what others might do simply because our actions made their acts more probable."[8]

2. Determining the Scope of Intention. In jurisdictions that insist an accomplice must intend to facilitate the principal's crime, the accomplice will still be liable only for conduct that falls "within this purpose." Model Penal Code and Commentaries §2.06 cmt. 6(b) at 311. But determining the boundaries of that intention can be tricky. And in certain cases, as Professor Kadish observes, the lines can get blurred, as there is sometimes "a strong pull toward viewing the actions of the primary party as in some sense fairly attributable to the secondary actor, even though he did not," strictly speaking, "intend the primary actor to commit them." Kadish identifies two paradigmatic examples in which courts routinely give in to this pull.[9]

First, in some cases, the defendant intends to facilitate wrongful conduct that could constitute any number of discrete criminal offenses, depending on the specific actions the principal ultimately ends up completing. Here, the defendant does not know, and thus cannot intend to facilitate, the principal's *specific* criminal actions. But most courts would hold the defendant responsible as an accomplice for the principal's eventual crimes so long as the principal's conduct is, as the Model Penal Code Commentaries put it, "fairly envisaged in the purposes of the association" between the two actors. Model Penal Code and Commentaries §2.06 cmt. 6(b) at 311. Kadish gives an example:

[A] person who drives a gang of terrorists to their destination knowing they intend some terrorist activity is liable for any crime of terrorism they commit, even if he did not know the particular crime they would commit. It is enough that what they eventually did was within his contemplation as one of the possibilities; it is enough that in this sense he intended their action.

This example contrasts with cases in which "the principal commits a crime wholly different from the one the secondary party intended—robs a person he was instructed to assault, for example," or "uses a knife when all the secondary party intended was an unarmed assault." Many courts would be reluctant to impose accomplice liability on these secondary actors for these separate and more aggravated crimes, because they were not fairly envisaged within the wrongful conduct the putative accomplice meant to encourage.[10]

Second, Kadish identifies a related but distinct set of cases in which the defendant intends to encourage a very specific crime—murder, for example—but does not intend the specific method of committing the crime ultimately used by the principal. As Kadish explains, here too the defendant will be guilty as an accomplice regardless of the specific means that may be employed by the principal in committing the intended offense, as long as they are "fairly envisaged in the purposes of the association." Model Penal Code and Commentaries §2.06 cmt. 6(b) at 311. The intent requirement, in other words, "does not mean . . . that the precise means used in the commission of the crime must have been fixed or contemplated" by the defendant in advance. *Id.* Thus, if a defendant hands the principal a gun and says "please kill my boss," he will be guilty as an accomplice even if the principal commits the crime by poisoning the victim, rather than shooting him. As Kadish writes, "[t]he intention required is that the principal should commit the acts constituting the crime, not that he should use the means intended by the accomplice."[11]

3. *Substantive Crimes of Facilitation.* At the close of its opinion, the *Lauria* court observed that, even though Lauria was not liable for prostitution as an accomplice, the state had other weapons in its arsenal if it wanted "to combat modern manifestations of the world's oldest profession" by going after those who facilitate "call-girl activity." The court suggested, for example, that a non-criminal, regulatory solution might put pressure on those in Lauria's position. It also noted that the "furnishing of telephone answering service in aid of prostitution could be made a crime." In other words, even though furnishing answering services knowing that they are being used to facilitate illegal sex work does not make one an accomplice to the sex work, the legislature is free to create a new criminal prohibition that covers this conduct independently.

Many jurisdictions have pursued this approach in either or both of two forms. First, some jurisdictions have enacted a general prohibition on criminal facilitation that requires a *mens rea* lower than intent and provides an alternative to accomplice liability. New York, for example, makes it a crime to aid in the commission of a felony when the defendant believes "it is probable that he is rendering aid to a person who intends to commit a crime." N.Y. Penal Law §115.00. The gravity of this facilitation offense rises with the severity of the underlying crime. *See, e.g.*, N.Y. Penal Law §115.01; *see also* Ariz. Rev. Stat. §13-1004. Nevertheless, no matter the underlying crime, facilitation remains a *separate offense*, not a means of holding the defendant responsible for a crime someone else carries out. Suppose, for example, that *D* gives *P* a club, which *P* uses to hit *V*. If the prosecutor believes that *D intended* to facilitate *P*'s battery of *V*, she can charge *D* with aiding and abetting battery; if she concludes instead that *D* merely believed it *probable* that *P* would batter *V*, criminal facilitation is the more appropriate charge.

Second, some legislatures have passed laws aimed at specific kinds of assistance, or assistance of specific kinds of crimes. The most salient example from recent times is the federal crime sanctioning anyone who "knowingly provides material support or resources to a foreign terrorist organization" or for use in enumerated terrorism-related offenses. 18 U.S.C. §2339B(a)(1); *see* §2339A. Notice that, in this statute, Congress balanced a watered-down *mens rea* requirement not only against the severity of the underlying crimes, as the *Lauria* court contemplated, but also against the substantiality of the aid, demanding "material" support before imposing liability. That said, the material support requirement has not been especially stringent in practice. In *Holder v. Humanitarian Law Project*, 561 U.S. 1 (2010), the Supreme Court held that training members of designated terrorist organizations in "how to use humanitarian and international law to peacefully resolve disputes," for example, constituted "material support" that violated the statute. *Id.* at 14.

C.   Mens Rea: *Liability for Unintended Harm Caused by Others*

In the preceding section we observed that the *mens rea* of complicity is typically purpose. This is true when, as is often the case, the *actus reus* of the crime is defined solely in terms of prohibited *conduct*. But sometimes, crimes are defined not just by prohibited conduct but also by a prohibited *result*. These crimes are committed only when the proscribed result follows from the defendant's conduct. Homicide, for example, is committed only when the defendant's actions cause a specific result: someone's death. By contrast, the *actus reus* of the crime at issue in *Lauria*—prostitution—is established whenever the defendant engages in the prohibited conduct of exchanging sex for money, without regard to any consequences that might follow from that act.

The distinction between conduct and results can be slippery, but it is firmly entrenched in the law. And importantly, the distinction has doctrinal ramifications when it comes to applying the law of complicity. In most jurisdictions, as the following cases discuss, an accomplice must act purposefully with respect to aiding or encouraging the principal's prohibited conduct but may not need to purposefully intend any prohibited results of that conduct.[12]

Riley v. State

60 P.3d 204 (Alaska Ct. App. 2002)

MANNHEIMER, J. [Richard Riley was convicted of two counts of first-degree assault. On the night of the incident at issue, a group of people were partying around a bonfire on the banks of the Tanana River near Fairbanks, Alaska. At some point during the evening, Riley and another person, Edward Portalla, began recklessly shooting firearms in the general direction of the partygoers. The evidence was unclear as to whether Riley and Portalla were aiming at the people, or were instead merely trying to shoot out the tires of some cars located midway between the shooters and the partygoers. Two of the people near the bonfire were hit by bullets and seriously wounded. Riley and Portalla were each charged with two counts of first-degree assault, which under Alaska law applies when a defendant recklessly causes serious physical injury by means of a dangerous instrument.]

The State faced a problem in prosecuting Riley and Portalla for first-degree assault: the physical evidence . . . did not reveal which of the defendants' weapons had fired the wounding shots. . . . Thus, with respect to each victim, the State could prove that the wound was inflicted by one of the two defendants, but the State could not easily prove which one.

. . . [T]he jurors were instructed that, with regard to each count of first-degree assault, they should decide whether Riley acted as a "principal" (*i.e.*, by firing the wounding shot) or, if they could not decide beyond a reasonable doubt which man fired the shots, they should decide whether Riley acted as an "accomplice" (*i.e.*, by [encouraging] Portalla to fire the wounding shot). The jurors found Riley guilty as an accomplice in the wounding of both victims.

Riley argues that his convictions for first-degree assault are flawed because the jurors were misinstructed regarding the elements of accomplice liability. The alleged flaw concerns the culpable mental state that must be proved when the State alleges a defendant's complicity in another person's crime. . . . He contends that his jury instruction . . . failed to clearly inform the jurors that the State was obliged to prove that Riley intended to have Portalla inflict serious physical injury on the victims (and not simply that Riley acted recklessly [by encouraging Portalla to shoot a gun while aware of] the *possibility* that Portalla's conduct would cause this result). . . .

Discussion. Under [Alaska law], a defendant is legally accountable for another person's conduct if the defendant "aids or abets the other in planning or committing the offense" and if the defendant does so "with the intent to promote or facilitate the commission of the offense." Riley was convicted of first-degree assault under the theory that, acting with the intent to promote or facilitate Portalla's commission of first-degree assault, he aided or abetted Portalla to engage in the conduct that resulted in the wounding of the victims. . . . The question is: What did the legislature mean when they required proof that the accomplice acted with the intent to promote or facilitate "the offense"?

When the underlying offense requires proof of the defendant's intention to cause a particular result (for example, first-degree murder . . . , a crime that requires proof of an intent to cause death), the phrase "intent to promote or facilitate the commission of the offense" seems to offer little trouble. Because the principal must intend to cause death, any accomplice to first-degree murder must likewise intend to cause death. But what if the underlying offense is defined in terms of an *unintended* result? For example, a person commits second-degree murder . . . by unintentionally causing a death while engaged in conduct "manifesting an extreme indifference to the value of human life." . . . When the underlying crime is defined in terms of an unintended result, what does [the law] mean by the phrase "intent to promote or facilitate the commission of *the offense*"?

In *Echols v. State*, 818 P.2d 691 (Alaska Ct. App. 1991), this Court interpreted the complicity statute in the context of a prosecution for first-degree assault, [the crime at issue here]. We held that even though a person could be convicted of first-degree assault as a principal upon proof that they acted recklessly with respect to the prohibited result, a person could not be convicted as an accomplice unless the State proved a different, higher culpable mental state. Specifically, we held that whenever the underlying crime requires proof of a particular result, the statutory requirement that an accomplice "intend to promote or facilitate the commission of the offense" means that the State must prove that the defendant acted "intentionally" with respect to this prohibited result.

[T]his construction of the statute . . . leads to counter-intuitive results in situations like the one presented in Riley's appeal. For example, let us assume that Riley and Portalla engaged in the same conduct (jointly firing weapons into a crowd) but, through misfortune, one of their victims was killed. Let us further assume that the State believed that it was impossible to prove, beyond a reasonable doubt, that this death was intended, so the State charged both defendants with manslaughter. And finally, let us assume that the evidence linking the homicide to either Riley's or

Portalla's personal conduct was so inconclusive that it was impossible to say, beyond a reasonable doubt, which of them was the principal and which the accomplice.

Under the rule of *Echols*, neither Riley nor Portalla can be convicted of manslaughter in this hypothetical situation. The State can prove that both defendants acted recklessly with respect to the possibility that their conduct would cause human death, and this culpable mental state would be sufficient to establish the *principal's* guilt of manslaughter. But the State can not prove . . . which of the defendants was the principal. This means that the State will have to prove both defendants' guilt under a complicity theory. And *Echols* holds that, to prove guilt under a complicity theory, the State has to prove that the defendants acted with the intent to kill. In effect, *Echols* says that, under these circumstances, the State has to prove the defendants guilty of first-degree murder (intentional taking of human life) or the defendants will escape criminal liability for the homicide. . . .

Echols has not found favor among legal scholars. . . . And, indeed, *Echols* represents a distinctly minority view on this issue. This is not to say that other states impose accomplice liability without proof of *mens rea*. . . . It is universally acknowledged that accomplice liability can not be based solely on the fact that a person's words or actions *had the effect* of encouraging or assisting another to commit a crime. The government must also prove, at a minimum, that the accomplice provided the encouragement or assistance with knowledge of the other person's criminal design. Many common-law decisions and many complicity statutes (such as Alaska's) require the government to prove, not only that the defendant knew of the other person's criminal design, but also that the defendant intended to further that criminal design. . . .

But here we reach the critical question: If a defendant provides aid or encouragement to another, acting not only with knowledge of the other person's intention to engage in unlawful or dangerous conduct, but also with the intent to promote or facilitate that unlawful or dangerous conduct, can the defendant be held accountable as an accomplice for a crime arising from the unintended consequences of that conduct? At common law, the answer is "yes."

The rule at common law is that when a person purposely assists or encourages another person to engage in conduct that is dangerous to human life or safety, and unintended injury or death results, it does not matter which person actually caused the injury or death by their personal conduct. Any participant can be convicted of assault or manslaughter (or any similar crime involving proof of an unintended result) so long as the government can prove that the participant acted with the culpable mental state required for the underlying crime — "recklessness," "criminal negligence," "extreme indifference to the value of human life," etc. For example, . . . if two drivers engage in an unlawful race on a public highway, thus encouraging each other to drive recklessly, both will be guilty of man-slaughter if one of them strikes and kills a third person. . . .

[This common law rule is echoed in the Model Penal Code, upon which] Alaska's complicity statute is based. . . . [Specifically, MPC §2.06(3) reads as follows:]

> A person is an accomplice of another person in the commission of an offense if . . . with the purpose of promoting or facilitating the commission of the offense, he . . . aids or agrees or attempts to aid [the] other person in planning or committing it. . . .

[T]his provision is immediately followed by §2.06(4), a section which addresses the legal issue at the heart of this appeal[:]

> When causing a particular result is an element of an offense, an accomplice in the conduct causing [that] result is an accomplice in the commission of that offense if he acts with the kind of culpability, if any, with respect to that result that is sufficient for the commission of the offense.

. . . [T]he Model Penal Code commentary explains that §§2.06(3) and 2.06(4) were intended to be read together: §2.06(3) defines the *conduct* for which an accomplice can be held accountable, while §2.06(4) clarifies that, when that conduct produces a result prohibited by law, the accomplice's culpable mental state with respect to that result (and, thus, the accomplice's guilt or innocence, or the accomplice's degree of guilt) must be evaluated separately from anyone else's culpable mental state. . . . Rejecting the notion that an accomplice should be held accountable for any and all objectively foreseeable results of the principal's conduct, . . . the Model Penal Code codified the rule that even though several defendants are accountable for the same criminal conduct under §2.06(3), each defendant's level of culpability with respect to the results of that conduct must be assessed separately, based on each individual's culpable mental state:

> Subsection (4) makes it clear that complicity in conduct causing a particular criminal result entails accountability for that result so long as the accomplice is personally culpable with respect to the result to the extent demanded by the definition of the crime. Thus, if the accomplice recklessly endangers life by rendering assistance to another, he can be convicted of manslaughter if death results, even though the principal actor's liability is at a different level. In effect, the homicidal act is attributed to both participants, with the liability of each participant measured by his own degree of culpability toward the result.

Model Penal Code and Commentaries §2.06 cmt. 7 at 321. . . .

When we examine court decisions from states that have complicity statutes modeled after §2.06(3) of the Model Penal Code . . . , we find that the great majority have . . . interpreted their statutes in conformity with the Model Penal Code commentary. In particular, with respect to offenses that

involve a resulting injury or death, these courts hold that accomplice liability requires proof (1) that the accomplice intended to promote or facilitate another's unlawful or dangerous *conduct,* and (2) that the accomplice
acted with the culpable mental state specified in the underlying statute with
respect to the resulting injury or death. Thus, these courts uphold accomplices' convictions for unintended criminal homicides — *e.g.,* "extreme
indifference" murder or reckless manslaughter — based on proof that the
accomplice, acting with the culpable mental state required for the underlying crime, purposely encouraged or aided another person to engage in
conduct that posed a substantial and unjustifiable danger to human life. . . .

It is true, as we pointed out in *Echols,* that our criminal code contains
a provision . . . based on Model Penal Code §2.06(3), but it does not contain a provision based on Model Penal Code §2.06(4). . . . In *Echols,* we took
this omission to mean that the drafters of Alaska's criminal code disagreed
with the principle of Model Penal Code §2.06(4), and that they wanted
to require a higher culpable mental state — "intentionally" — whenever a
defendant was prosecuted under a complicity theory.

But . . . [t]he two sections were intended to complement each
other: subsection (3) describes the circumstances in which one person
can be held accountable for another person's *conduct,* and subsection
(4) explains that, even though two or more people may be accountable for
the conduct constituting an offense, each person's *culpable mental state* must
be evaluated separately. Although the drafters of our criminal code did not
explain why they did not codify Model Penal Code §2.06(4), it does not
make sense to interpret their decision as an indication that they wanted to
restrict accomplice liability to instances where the accomplice acted "intentionally" with respect to a result. . . . It now appears to us more likely that
the drafters of Alaska's code failed to include a provision based on Model
Penal Code §2.06(4) because they considered it superfluous. . . .

In conclusion: The Model Penal Code was written to impose accomplice liability for crimes involving unintended injury or death if the accomplice intentionally promotes or facilitates the *conduct* that produces the
injury or death, even though the accomplice did not intend this result.
Among the states that have complicity statutes based on the Model Penal
Code, most courts have interpreted their statutes this way. The reasons that
we gave in *Echols* for interpreting [Alaska law] differently do not withstand
analysis. . . .

Thus, Riley could properly be convicted of first-degree assault . . . either
upon proof that he personally shot a firearm into the crowd or (alternatively) upon proof that, acting with intent to promote or facilitate Portalla's
act of shooting into the crowd, Riley solicited, encouraged, or assisted
Portalla to do so. These are alternative ways of proving that Riley was
accountable for the *conduct* that inflicted the injuries. The government
was also obliged to prove that Riley acted with the culpable mental state

specified by the first-degree assault statute. But regardless of whether Riley acted as a principal or an accomplice, the applicable culpable mental state remained the same: recklessness as to the possibility that this conduct would cause serious physical injury. . . .

[Because the jury's verdict establishes this recklessness finding], we affirm Riley's two convictions for first-degree assault.

NOTES AND QUESTIONS

1. **Mens Rea** *for Results.* As the *Riley* court explains, some jurisdictions continue to apply the rule of *Echols*, which the defendant in *Riley* unsuccessfully attempted to invoke. Under that rule, the accomplice must act with purpose with respect to both the principal's conduct and the results of that conduct, even if the principal could be liable for acting only recklessly or negligently with respect to the prohibited results. Courts adopting this approach sometimes contend that to hold otherwise would require embracing "a logical impossibility," given the strangeness of saying "that the accused *intended* to aid an *unintentional* act." Commonwealth v. Roebuck, 32 A.3d 613, 614 (Pa. 2011). Contemporary courts, however, generally reject this logic and follow the approach set out in *Riley* and the MPC.

While the *Riley* court's reasoning is clear, the facts of the case are somewhat unusual. The prosecution could not tell which actor was the principal and which was the accomplice, because there was no way to determine whose bullets hit the victims and whose missed. Moreover, there is at least an argument (potentially a strong one) that shooting bullets toward a crowd of people might constitute a *knowing* or even a *purposeful* homicide. *See* United States v. Wright, 594 F.3d 259 (4th Cir. 2010). But the *Riley* court's holding applies across fact patterns. Consider the following example.

Desai v. State, 398 P.3d 889 (Nev. 2017). Desai was the original founding member and managing partner of the Endoscopy Center of Southern Nevada and other ambulatory surgical centers (collectively, the clinic) in Las Vegas. Desai made all decisions regarding the clinic, including the ordering and use of supplies and scheduling of patients. He was also in charge of the certified registered nurse anesthetists.

On July 25, 2007, the clinic's first patient of the day informed Desai that he had hepatitis C before his procedure began. Later that day, Michael Washington had a procedure performed at the clinic. Washington was later diagnosed with hepatitis C. On September 21, 2007, the clinic's first patient of the day informed a nurse that he had hepatitis C before his procedure began. Later that day, Sonia Orellana Rivera, Gwendolyn Martin, Patty Aspinwall, Stacy Hutchinson, and Rodolfo Meana had procedures performed at the clinic. All five patients were later diagnosed with hepatitis C. Meana . . . eventually died as a result of the disease.

After learning that multiple patients contracted hepatitis C at the clinic, the Southern Nevada Health District initiated an investigation [and] concluded that the outbreak was the result of the clinic's nurse anesthetists [reusing] vials of propofol after injecting a patient . . . . Desai, along with Ronald Lakeman and Keith Mathahs, who were both nurse anesthetists at the clinic, were [each indicted on multiple charges of recklessly and (separately) negligently endangering their patients in a manner that caused serious bodily harm].

. . . According to a CDC medical officer, unsafe injection practices result when a nurse anesthetist administers to a patient one dose of propofol using a needle and syringe and places that same syringe back into a vial of propofol—even if the needle is changed—which is then later used on a second patient. There is a risk that any blood in the syringe from the first patient will be transferred to the propofol vial that is later used on a second patient.

When the State questioned Mathahs about reentering a propofol vial in order to redose a patient, Mathahs testified that he would replace the needle before reentering the vial. Mathahs further testified on direct examination as follows:

[STATE]:	Are you aware that there is at least a risk of potential contamination even changing out the needle in that situation?
[MATHAHS]:	Yes, there is.
[STATE]:	Did you ever express your concerns about doing this to Dr. Desai?
[MATHAHS]:	Yes.
[STATE]:	What was his response?
[MATHAHS]:	It's to save money, just go ahead and do it.
[STATE]:	So he instructed you to do it even though you made him aware of the risk?
[MATHAHS]:	Yes.
. . .	
[STATE]:	So you expressed—just so we're clear, in whatever words, you expressed that there was a risk in doing that to Dr. Desai and he ordered you to do it anyway and you did it.
[MATHAHS]:	Yes.

. . . Mathahs [also] testified that Desai checked the disposal containers and, if he found any unused propofol remaining in the syringes or vials of propofol, he would yell at the responsible nurse anesthetist for being wasteful. Mathahs "guess[ed]" that Desai wanted any unused propofol to be used on a subsequent patient and testified that he would likely be fired if Desai found a discarded vial still containing propofol. . . .

Viewing the evidence adduced at trial in a light most favorable to the prosecution, we conclude . . . that the State presented sufficient evidence for the jury to find that Desai possessed the necessary intent to aid and abet in the endangerment crimes, and we thus affirm Desai's convictions for these crimes.

2. **Mens Rea** *for Circumstances of the Crime.* Sometimes the critical question concerns the defendant's *mens rea* not with respect to the unintended results of the principal's conduct, but rather the circumstances surrounding that conduct. Consider a statute that makes it a crime to intentionally kill a police officer. Now suppose that *A* intentionally offers principal *P* a gun, intending that *P* will use the gun to kill *V*, who is a police officer. And suppose further that while principal *P* knows that *V* is a police officer (and in fact wants to kill *V* because *V* is a police officer), *A* does not know that *V* is a police officer (and does not care). If *P* intentionally shoots and kills *V*, should *A* be guilty under this statute as an accomplice?

Surprisingly, the Model Penal Code is silent on this question, opting to maintain "deliberate ambiguity as to whether the purpose requirement extends to circumstance elements of the contemplated offense." Model Penal Code and Commentaries §2.06 cmt. 6(b) at 311 n.37. Courts around the country have split on the issue. *Compare, e.g.,* Commonwealth v. Harris, 904 N.E.2d 478 (Mass. App. Ct. 2009) (an accomplice to statutory rape, which imposes strict liability with respect to the minor's age, can be liable without knowledge of age), *with, e.g.,* State v. Bowman, 656 S.E.2d 638 (N.C. Ct. App. 2008) (accomplice must have had knowledge of age).

3. Divergent Culpability: Greater and Lesser Offenses. A premise of the holdings in *Riley* and *Desai* is that factual circumstances could arise in which a principal and an accomplice have *different degrees* of culpability with respect to the potential outcomes of their actions. Consider an alternative version of *Desai* in which the nurses still acted recklessly (because they knew there was a risk that reusing vials would infect patients) but the doctor-supervisor acted *intentionally.* Imagine, for example, that the doctor had a personal vendetta against the patients and instructed the nurses to reuse the vials "to save money" while secretly intending to infect and kill the patients for revenge. In such a scenario, if the patients die, the nurses (the principals) are likely guilty of involuntary manslaughter due to their recklessness. But might the doctor be guilty of a more serious offense, like premeditated murder?

Courts and commentators frequently say yes. For example, in *People v. McCoy,* 24 P.3d 1210 (Cal. 2001), the California Supreme Court held that "[i]f the mens rea of the aider and abettor is more culpable than the actual perpetrator's, the aider and abettor may be guilty of a more serious crime than the actual perpetrator." Drawing on Shakespeare, the court offered the following illustration:

[A]ssume someone, let us call him Iago, falsely tells another person, whom we will call Othello, that Othello's wife, Desdemona, was having an affair, hoping that Othello would kill her in a fit of jealousy. Othello does so without Iago's further involvement. In that case, depending on the exact circumstances of the killing, Othello might be guilty of manslaughter, rather than murder, on a heat of passion theory. Othello's guilt of manslaughter, however, should not limit Iago's guilt if his own culpability were greater. Iago should be liable for his own acts as well Othello's, which he induced and encouraged. But Iago's criminal liability, as Othello's, would be based on his own personal mens rea. If, as our hypothetical suggests, Iago acted with malice, he would be guilty of murder even if Othello, who did the actual killing, was not.

Id. at 1216-1217.

By the same logic, an accomplice could be guilty of a lesser offense than the principal. Imagine, for example, that an office manager with no medical training directed the nurses in *Desai* to reuse vials in order to cut down on costs. There, the accomplice (the office manager) may have been acting at most negligently with respect to the risk of hepatitis infections. But the principals (the nurses, with medical training) were acting more culpably, because they were aware of the risk of infection and thus reckless. Under the logic of *McCoy*, the office manager could be guilty as an accomplice of a lesser offense than the principals, because "she is liable for her mens rea, not the other person's." *Id.* at 1214. "Aider and abettor liability is premised on the combined acts of all the principals, but on the aider and abettor's own mens rea." *Id.* at 1215. Legal scholars who have studied the question closely generally agree with these results.[13]

Note though that these results are in some tension with the idea, sometimes described as a "a central axiom of complicity liability," that complicity doctrine is *derivative,* with the accomplice's guilt rising and falling with that of the principal. Embracing this idea, it is often said that an accomplice cannot be guilty of a crime "when the State fails to establish that the principal committed the crime." People v. Chirchirillo, 913 N.E.2d 635 (Ill. App. Ct. 2009). For example, in *People v. Chirchirillo,* the defendant and a woman named Tiffany set out to steal a gun from another person's home in hopes of selling the gun for drug money. The defendant, who had previously been convicted of a felony, opened the window to the home. Tiffany, who had no prior criminal record, then entered the house and stole the gun, which the defendant never touched. It was clear that both individuals were guilty of burglary. But the court overturned the defendant's conviction, premised on accomplice liability, for being a felon in possession of a firearm. The "defendant could not be held accountable for aiding Tiffany in that offense when it was never established that *Tiffany* was a convicted felon." *Id.* at 644 (emphasis added). And because Tiffany was not guilty, the court

held, neither was the defendant: a "charge based on [complicity] must necessarily flow from the principal crime at issue." *Id.* at 641 (quoting People
v. Hicks, 693 N.E.2d 373 (Ill. 1998)); *see also* State v. Hayes, 16 S.W. 514 (Mo.
1891). Yet as Professor Kadish observes, if the accomplice's liability truly
"derives from that of the principal, the liability of an accomplice could not
exceed that of the principal," as the *McCoy* court and many others permit.[14]

    4. Divergent Culpability: The Principal's Defenses. A similar issue arises
with respect to defenses. If a principal has a valid defense to an alleged
crime, can the accomplice still be held liable? Some courts give different
answers depending on the nature of the defense, though this approach is
not without criticism. Consider the following case and excerpt.

United States v. Lopez, 662 F. Supp. 1083 (N.D. Cal. 1987). This case
involves the alleged escape of two federal prisoners. Defendant Ronald
McIntosh disappeared on October 28, 1986, during an unescorted transfer
from F.C.I. Pleasanton to the federal prison at Lompoc. [A week later, he]
landed a helicopter in the Pleasanton recreation yard . . . and flew off with
defendant Samantha Lopez. Federal authorities apprehended them ten
days later in a Sacramento shopping mall where they were buying a set of
wedding rings.

    [The defendants argued that Lopez was facing credible threats to her
safety inside the prison prior to her escape. At trial, McIntosh argued that
if the jury were to conclude that those threats justified Lopez's escape, it
should find him not guilty of aiding and abetting her escape. The government, by contrast, contended that McIntosh could be convicted of aiding and abetting Lopez' escape even if Lopez succeeded on her necessity
defense.]

    The general rule is that a defendant can be convicted of aiding and
abetting even if the principal is not identified or convicted; however, an
aider and abettor may not be held liable absent proof that a criminal
offense was committed by a principal. "The fact that the principal need
not be identified or convicted has never been thought to obviate the need
for proof showing that an underlying crime was committed by someone."
United States v. Powell, 806 F.2d 1421, 1424 (9th Cir. 1986).

    This Court must therefore determine whether Lopez committed a
criminal offense if her [necessity] defense succeeds. This determination
requires an examination of the theoretical distinctions between two categories of defenses: justification and excuse. . . . Justification defenses are those
providing that, although the act was committed, it is not wrongful. For
example, a forest fire is burning toward a town of 10,000 residents. An actor
burns a field of corn located between the fire and the town in order to set
up a firebreak. . . . Burning the field avoided a greater societal harm; therefore, the act is not a crime. When a defense is categorized as an excuse,
however, the result is that, although the act is wrongful, the actor will not

be held accountable. . . . Thus, an insane person who robs a bank will be excused from liability. . . .

The classification of a defense as a justification or an excuse has an important effect on the liability of one who aids and abets the act. A third party has the right to assist an actor in a justified act. Therefore, a third party could not be held liable for aiding and abetting the arson described in the hypothetical above. In contrast, a sane getaway driver could be convicted of aiding and abetting an insane person's bank robbery. Excuses are always personal to the actor. . . .

[T]he defense asserted by Lopez, under the facts of this case, most nearly resembles necessity, which is a justification to the alleged crime. In the present case, Lopez' claim is not that the alleged threats overwhelmed her will so that her inability to make the "correct" choice should be excused. Instead, Lopez claims that she, in fact, did make the correct choice. She contends she violated the law to avoid the greater societal harm of being killed or seriously injured. . . . Accordingly, if the jury finds Lopez not guilty of escape by reason of her necessity defense, her criminal act will be justified. A justified action is not wrongful; therefore, the prerequisite to imposing liability on McIntosh as an aider and abettor will not be satisfied. No criminal offense will have been committed by a principal. McIntosh is therefore entitled to his requested jury instruction.

Douglas N. Husak, *Justifications and the Criminal Liability of Accessories*, 80 J. Crim. L. & Criminology 491, 494-499, 517-519 (1989). Suppose that *V* threatens to bloody the nose of one of *D1*'s children unless *D1* burglarizes *X*'s house. Unable to accomplish this result alone, *D1* explains his predicament to *D2*, his sympathetic friend. *D2* proposes to lend a ladder to *D1*, so that he can enter the house through a second story window. . . . [Many] commentators . . . would determine whether *D2* has a defense by first identifying what *kind* of defense *D1* possesses. . . . According to this school of thought, if *D2*'s assistance is to be allowed, an argument would have to establish that *D1*'s conduct is "objectively right," and therefore justified.

A number of problems lurk behind this deceptively simple approach. . . . [For starters, it] is noteworthy that *D2* cannot *know* whether he has a *right* to assist *D1* unless he knows that *D1* has a justification for his apparent violation of law. . . . [But] frequently *D2 cannot* know what type of defense *D1* possesses; therefore, he must *guess* whether *D1* has a justification or an excuse. . . . [For example, if *D2* arrives on the scene of an affray between *D1* and *V* not knowing how the violence started, *D2* may not know whether *D1* is entitled to act in self-defense, has a claim of only imperfect self-defense, or lacks any defense at all.] It is peculiar for a theory to assign or withhold rights from parties from an "omniscient" point of view, requiring information that could not be available to the parties who must choose. . . . A person must be permitted to act on the basis of information available to him at the moment of decision. . . .

More importantly, the moral argument in favor of allowing assistance from *D1* whenever *D1* is [legally] justified crumbles when "justification" is construed as "permissible" rather than as "commendable." . . . There is a great deal of difference between conduct that a system of norms should tolerate and not punish or condemn, as opposed to conduct that is worthy of praise and emulation. . . . If *D1*'s conduct were commendable, it is plausible to suppose that the law should not *dis*courage, and might actually *en*courage, assistance from others, notwithstanding the fact that *D1*'s conduct apparently violates a criminal law. But these results do not follow if *D1*'s conduct is merely tolerable. The law need not encourage, and might actively discourage, assistance with conduct that it is willing to permit. . . .

Armed with these insights, it is instructive to return to [our opening] hypothetical. . . . Presumably, *D1* should not be required to sacrifice his son's interest for that of *X*. Whether *D2* should be permitted to assist depends upon whether his friendship to *D1* qualifies as a "special, role differentiated relationship" [sufficient to overcome his otherwise applicable duty to be impartial as between *D1* and *X*]. To ask this question is not to answer it, but rather to indicate the direction in which the solution to many problems of accessorial liability is to be found. The answer is *not* a simple function of the proper classification of *D1*'s defense as a justification or an excuse. What is required in addition to categorizing *D1*'s defense is a theory of special relationships between accessories, principals, and potential victims.[15]

5. Overpowering Accomplices: The Duress Defense. As the preceding excerpt suggests, circumstances may arise in which efforts to get another person to commit a crime can move beyond mere encouragement into something more coercive. At some point, if that coercion becomes serious enough, the person pushed into committing the offense may be relieved of liability. Threats of violence are a classic example. If one person tells another, "You should rob that store; and if you don't, I will hurt your child," the person making the coercive threat should presumably be guilty of the resulting robbery. But the coerced principal might escape liability under a classic doctrine of excuse known as the *duress defense*. Consider the following case.

United States v. Contento-Pachon, 723 F.2d 691 (9th Cir. 1984). . . . The defendant-appellant, Juan Manuel Contento-Pachon, is a native of Bogota, Colombia and was employed there as a taxicab driver. He asserts that one of his passengers, Jorge, offered him a job as the driver of a privately-owned car. [But when the two met to discuss the position, i]nstead of a driving job, Jorge proposed that Contento-Pachon swallow cocaine-filled balloons and transport them to the United States. Contento-Pachon . . . was told not to mention the proposition to anyone, otherwise he would "get into serious trouble." Contento-Pachon testified that he did not contact the police because he believes that the Bogota police are corrupt and that they are paid off by drug traffickers.

Approximately one week later, Contento-Pachon told Jorge that he would not carry the cocaine. In response, Jorge mentioned facts about Contento-Pachon's personal life, including private details which Contento-Pachon had never mentioned to Jorge. Jorge told Contento-Pachon that his failure to cooperate would result in the death of his wife and three year-old child. . . .

Contento-Pachon agreed to take the cocaine into the United States. . . . He was informed that he would be watched at all times during the trip, and that if he failed to follow Jorge's instruction he and his family would be killed. . . . When he arrived at the customs inspection point in Los Angeles, Contento-Pachon consented to have his stomach x-rayed. The x-rays revealed a foreign substance which was later determined to be cocaine.

Duress. There are three elements of the duress defense: (1) an immediate threat of death or serious bodily injury, (2) a well-grounded fear that the threat will be carried out, and (3) no reasonable opportunity to escape the threatened harm. Sometimes a fourth element is required: the defendant must submit to proper authorities after attaining a position of safety.[*] . . .

The element of immediacy requires that there be some evidence that the threat of injury was present, immediate, or impending. "[A] veiled threat of future unspecified harm" will not satisfy this requirement. R.I. Recreation Ctr., Inc. v. Aetna Cas. & Surety Co., 177 F.2d 603, 605 (1st Cir. 1949). The district court found that the initial threats were not immediate because "they were conditioned on defendant's failure to cooperate in the future and did not place defendant and his family in immediate danger." [But the evidence] presented on this issue indicated that the defendant was dealing with a man who was deeply involved in the exportation of illegal substances. Large sums of money were at stake and, consequently, Contento-Pachon had reason to believe that Jorge would carry out his threats. Jorge had gone to the trouble to discover that Contento-Pachon was married, that he had a child, the names of his wife and child, and the location of his residence. These were not vague threats of possible future harm. According to the defendant, if he had refused to cooperate, the consequences would have been immediate and harsh.

---

[*] Editor's Note: Many jurisdictions impose additional requirements and limitations. For example, duress typically cannot excuse the intentional killing (or attempted killing) of an innocent third person. *See, e.g.,* People v. Gafken, 990 N.W.2d 826, 828-830 (Mich. 2022) (acknowledging the traditional rule barring duress as a defense to murder but holding it inapplicable to depraved-heart murder).

. . . The district court [separately] found that because Contento-Pachon was not physically restrained prior to the time he swallowed the balloons, he could have sought help from the police or fled. [But] Contento-Pachon explained that he did not report the threats because he feared that the police were corrupt. The trier of fact should decide whether one in Contento-Pachon's position might believe that some of the Bogota police were paid informants for drug traffickers and that reporting the matter to the police did not represent a reasonable opportunity of escape.

If he chose not to go to the police, Contento-Pachon's alternative was to flee. We reiterate that the opportunity to escape must be reasonable. To flee, Contento-Pachon, along with his wife and three year-old child, would have been forced to pack his possessions, leave his job, and travel to a place beyond the reaches of the drug traffickers. A juror might find that this was not a reasonable avenue of escape. Thus, Contento-Pachon presented a triable issue on the element of escapability.

. . . The government argues that the defense also requires that a defendant offer evidence that he intended to turn himself in to the authorities upon reaching a position of safety. . . . [T]here seems little difference between the third basic requirement that there be no reasonable opportunity to escape the threatened harm and the obligation to turn oneself in to authorities on reaching a point of safety. Once a defendant has reached a position where he can safely turn himself in to the authorities he will likewise have a reasonable opportunity to escape the threatened harm. That is true in this case. Contento-Pachon claims that he was being watched at all times. According to him, at the first opportunity to cooperate with authorities without alerting the observer, he consented to the x-ray. We hold that a defendant who has acted under a well-grounded fear of immediate harm with no opportunity to escape may assert the duress defense, if there is a triable issue of fact whether he took the opportunity to escape the threatened harm by submitting to authorities at the first reasonable opportunity.

6. The Innocent or Irresponsible Agent Doctrine. Notice that if Jorge's coercion of Contento-Pachon shields Contento-Pachon from liability under a duress defense, and if Jorge's liability must derive from Contento-Pachon's importation of drugs, a strange result might follow: Jorge might not be held liable for drug trafficking, even though he appears to be the more culpable actor. To avoid the possibility of this strange result, the common law developed the *innocent agent doctrine*, which is captured in §2.06(2)(a) of the Model Penal Code. This Code section states that "[a] person is guilty of an offense if[,] acting with the kind of culpability that is sufficient for the commission of the offense, he causes an innocent or irresponsible person to engage in such conduct." This is one way to understand the path to liability for Jorge: Jorge caused Contento-Pachon to engage in the illegal conduct, and Contento-Pachon is arguably innocent, insofar as he was coerced.

Alternatively, if "innocent" seems an inapt description of Contento-Pachon's behavior, we would reach the same result if we thought of Contento-Pachon as instead simply a defendant with an excuse—the excuse of duress—and applied the rule of *Lopez*.[16]

There are cases, however, where excuse is not at issue, and where the innocent agent doctrine is paramount. Sometimes, for example, a defendant commits a crime by tricking or manipulating another person into breaking the law, rather than coercing her. Suppose, for example, that *D* is standing inside of a store and wants to steal a candy bar. To do so, he surreptitiously slips the candy bar into the pocket of an unsuspecting customer standing nearby. The customer then exits the store without paying for the candy—and indeed without ever knowing that the candy bar was in her pocket. Outside the store, *D* surreptitiously removes the candy bar from the customer's pocket and goes along his way. Here, the customer is factually innocent of theft. She lacked the *mens rea* for the offense and did not even engage in a voluntary act of taking the candy. But again, *D* has not directly committed the crime of shoplifting either: he did not remove property from the store. If *D*'s potential liability derives from the responsibility of the person who did—the customer—it would seem *D* cannot be held liable. The innocent agent doctrine prevents this result.

Note that a similar result would follow under the parallel "irresponsible" agent doctrine if, rather than sliding the candy bar into the pocket of an unsuspecting customer, our defendant encouraged a nine-year-old child to steal the candy. As described in Chapter Three, most states apply a doctrine of infancy under which criminal liability simply cannot attach to nine-year-old children. In states that classify infancy as an excuse-based doctrine and that also apply *Lopez*, the defendant would be liable for the child's shoplifting even without an irresponsible agent rule. But in states where either of those premises does not hold, the irresponsible agent doctrine fills the gap, ensuring liability for those who use people beyond the reach of criminal punishment, like children or people who are legally insane, as tools of criminality.

D. *Undercover Agents*

"Intelligence—the most detailed information obtainable on the background and activities of suspected criminals—is essential to all law enforcement. It is even more important to successful action against racketeers."

> Statement by Att'y Gen. Robert F. Kennedy to
> the Permanent Subcomm. on Investigations of
> the Senate Gov't Operations Comm. (Sept. 25, 1963)

"Never rat on your friends, and always keep your mouth shut."

> Jimmy Conway in *Goodfellas*
> (Warner Bros. Pictures & Irwin Winkler Productions 1990)

How should the law respond when the state itself is directly complicit in criminal activity because informants or undercover agents participated as principals or accessories? In this section, we will see how the criminal law facilitates the use of informants, undercover agents, and other undercover tactics. We will also consider the rationales for and critiques of these tactics, while exploring some of the narrow limitations on their use flowing from the defense of entrapment.

1.   Liability in Cases of Feigned Principals and Accomplices

State v. Peterson

772 P.2d 513 (Wash. Ct. App. 1989)

COLEMAN, C.J. Wade Peterson appeals from his conviction for one count of manufacturing or possessing a controlled substance with intent to manufacture or deliver. Peterson assigns error to the accomplice liability instruction submitted to the jury. . . .

On March 26, 1985, August Weiss contacted Snohomish County detectives to inform them about a clandestine methamphetamine (speed) laboratory he was operating in their jurisdiction. Weiss told him he was a "cook," *i.e.*, a chemist, in the laboratory and that he had recently been injured in a laboratory mishap. Weiss said the accident had caused him to come forward and inform on the operation in order to turn over a new leaf.

The detectives accompanied Weiss to the residence of . . . Wade Peterson, where the laboratory had been operating for several days. The detectives were posing undercover as Weiss's "security." [Weiss proceeded to cook methamphetamine.] The officers furnished police department glassware and a controlled substance, P2P, to facilitate the process. [Peterson was] present during the manufacture, and Peterson actively assisted Weiss. . . . Peterson was charged [as an accomplice to Weiss] with . . . possession with intent to manufacture or deliver. . . .

The only issue presented in this appeal is whether the trial court erred by submitting to the jury an instruction on accomplice liability where the principal upon whose "crime" the accomplice liability was predicated was a police informer acting in concert with the police.

Appellant argues that it was error for the court to give an accomplice liability instruction in this case because accomplice liability requires a showing that the principal committed the charged crime and the only principal in the crime of possession with intent to manufacture was Weiss. Appellant argues that because Weiss was an informant, he lacked the requisite criminal intent to support a showing that he "committed the crime." We are not persuaded by appellant's argument.

. . . Conviction for accomplice liability is improper where there is no proof that a principal "actually committed the crime." State v. Nikolich,

241 P. 664 (Wash. 1925). But in order to establish accomplice liability "the State need not prove that the principal and accomplice share the same mental state." State v. Bockman, 682 P.2d 925 (Wash. Ct. App. 1984). The State only needs to show "the accomplice's general knowledge of [the principal's] substantive crime." State v. Rice, 683 P.2d 199, 203 (Wash. 1984).

. . . The evidence here establishes that Weiss committed the substantive crime of manufacturing a controlled substance with the intent to manufacture or deliver. The crime here did not require an intent to do more than the proscribed act. It required only manufacture or possession with intent to manufacture or deliver. Thus, although Weiss in effect had the permission of the police to manufacture the speed and arguably did so without a mens rea of criminal purpose, he nonetheless "committed the crime" for purposes of being a principal to support liability under the accomplice liability statute.

While the authorities may have chosen not to prosecute Weiss in exchange for his cooperation, no prosecution of a principal is required to establish an accomplice's liability as such. There was substantial evidence that appellant aided Weiss in the manufacture of the speed. Accordingly, it was not error to give the accomplice liability instruction in this case. The judgment of the trial court is affirmed.

Vaden v. State, 768 P.2d 1102 (Alaska 1989). . . . In November 1983, a horse wrangler employed by [Vaden] . . . informed Fish and Wildlife Protection officers of illegal hunting methods allegedly used by Vaden while guiding a foreign hunter. . . . John Snell, an undercover agent for the Alaska Department of Fish & Game posing as a hunter, contracted for guiding services from Vaden. . . . During the hunt Snell shot and killed four foxes from Vaden's aircraft. The season on foxes was closed at that time. Vaden provided Snell with the shotgun used to shoot the foxes, and maneuvered the aircraft so Snell could shoot the foxes. The fox carcasses were then transported to Anchorage by Vaden.

Vaden was convicted, as an accomplice [to Snell], on four counts of taking foxes from an aircraft and four counts of taking foxes during closed season. . . .

Vaden appealed his convictions, contending that no illegal acts were committed by Snell and thus no criminal liability could attach to Vaden for "aiding and abetting" or transportation of illegally taken game . . . . The court of appeals concluded that Snell had "committed the offense" of taking foxes from the air out of season, but that Snell had a personal [public authority] defense [that] Vaden would not be able to avail himself of . . . .

It is not necessary to decide whether an undercover agent in these circumstances may [indeed] utilize a public authority justification defense. As the court of appeals concluded, [any such] defense is personal to the undercover agent and not transferable to the accomplice. . . . Because the accomplice's state of mind is the focus, defenses of entrapment, duress and heat of passion are not imputed to the accomplice.

NOTES AND QUESTIONS

1. Private vs. Public Undercovers. In each of the preceding cases, the person who directly committed the alleged criminal offense did so with the state's blessing, in order to catch an unsuspecting accomplice. In *Peterson*, the undercover actor was a private citizen operating in concert with law enforcement. In *Vaden*, a law enforcement officer committed the illegal act directly. But this distinction does not matter. In both cases, the court considers the unsuspecting accomplice complicit in the undercover principal's actions, albeit by different modes of reasoning. In *Peterson*, the court appears to hold that the undercover principal was himself technically guilty and that the accomplice's liability flowed from that guilt, even though the undercover principal would never be prosecuted—and was likely granted formal immunity—by the state actors with whom he was cooperating. In *Vaden*, by contrast, the court suggests that the undercover principal may *not* have been subject to any criminal liability himself but affirms the defendant's conviction on the theory that any defenses available to undercover law enforcement actors do not transfer to their unwitting accomplices. The result under either chain of logic is the same: The state is permitted to build cases against people it suspects of engaging in or disposed to criminal activity by sending state agents to participate in and perhaps even directly commit criminal offenses with them.

2. Facilitating Crime. As Professor Alexandra Natapoff writes in a leading book about undercover law enforcement practices, reliance on undercover tactics like those used in the preceding cases "by definition requires the toleration of crime." Consider *Vaden*. The State of Alaska criminalized shooting and killing foxes out of season, presumably to protect the fox population from human predation. And yet, the State itself sent one of its agents to kill these protected foxes, in direct contravention of that law.[17]

Or consider *Peterson*. Manufacturing methamphetamine is both illegal and dangerous, with meth lab explosions sometimes proving fatal to participants and bystanders alike. Indeed, a "mishap" at the very meth lab at issue in *Peterson* had injured the informant Weiss, who was so shaken up by the experience that he turned himself in to the police and confessed to cooking meth. Rather than arrest Weiss, the State sent him back to the lab alongside undercover police officers, who brought "police department glassware and a controlled substance, P2P, to facilitate the process" of cooking more meth—notwithstanding the risk of another dangerous mishap. As Professor Natapoff goes on to write, this practice of letting known criminal actors walk away in exchange for information and even facilitating their criminality to enhance their informational value[] flips the law enforcement endeavor on its head. . . . In effect, snitching is the universal loophole to every substantive criminal law. It is as if each code provision read: "Here is the crime. Here is the punishment. Unless you cooperate."[18]

3. Solving Crime. Why might the criminal law tolerate a world in which officers sworn to uphold the law instead encourage others to break it—or break it themselves, in close collaboration with criminal actors? The obvious answer is that these tactics are useful, maybe even essential, to law enforcement. Consider the words of the U.S. Court of Appeals for the Ninth Circuit in a case highlighted by Professor Natapoff:

> [O]ur criminal justice system could not adequately function without information provided by informants . . . . [I]t is a well-known phenomen[on] that the higher-ups in criminal enterprises attempt to insulate themselves from detection and exposure by having their unlawful schemes carried out by others. Without informants, law enforcement authorities would be unable to penetrate and destroy organized crime syndicates, drug trafficking cartels, bank frauds, telephone solicitation scams, public corruption, terrorist gangs, money launderers, espionage rings, and the likes. In the words of Judge Learned Hand, "Courts have countenanced the use of informers from time immemorial; . . . it is usually necessary to rely upon them or upon accomplices because the criminals will almost certainly proceed covertly." United States v. Dennis, 183 F.2d 201, 224 (2d Cir. 1950).

United States v. Bernal-Obeso, 989 F.2d 331, 334-335 (9th Cir. 1993); *see also* N. Mariana Islands v. Bowie, 243 F.3d 1109, 1123-1124 (9th Cir. 2001) ("Without accomplice cooperation and testimony, many killers, terrorists, rapists, swindlers, white collar and corporate criminals, corrupt public officials, and others would have escaped their just fates."); United States v. Kaminski, 703 F.2d 1004, 1010 (7th Cir. 1983) ("Undercover police work in general . . . is an unattractive business, but that is the nature of the beast . . . ."). The implicit logic here runs from necessity to legality. To extend Professor Anna Lvovsky's observation, it as if courts are saying that informants make for "good enforcement, and good enforcement must be . . . permissible enforcement."[19]

While relying on informants and undercover agents "is sometimes the only way to get information about well-insulated, high-level criminals," the doctrinal holdings from *Vaden* and *Peterson* apply more broadly, including in settings where such tactics are not necessary but, in Professor Natapoff's words, simply promote "law enforcement efficiency, or even mere convenience." Indeed, Natapoff reports that "criminal informant use is everywhere in the American legal system." As one example, "about 20 percent of all federal offenders and 45 percent of federal drug defendants cooperate in some way." And these figures do not include the approximately 30,000 confidential informants who work for the FBI and the Drug Enforcement Administration but are never prosecuted.[20]

4. Informant Credibility and Bias. While recognizing its importance, courts and commentators alike have criticized the widespread use of criminal informants. Some find it inherently unseemly or delegitimating to exchange lenience for assistance or information. *See, e.g.,* United States v. Singleton, 144 F.3d 1343, 1347 (10th Cir. 1998) ("The judicial process is tainted and justice cheapened when factual testimony is purchased, whether with leniency or money."). Professor Richard McAdams elaborates on this concern:

> . . . [U]ndercover operations impose significant costs. A partial list includes the undermining of trust in a society permeated by police spies, the corrupting influence that portraying criminals has on the police agents who carry it out, the potential for violence erupting out of efforts to foment crime, the exploitative recruiting of vulnerable individuals into the dangerous life of a confidential informant, and the public's loss of respect for state agents who engage in deception, betrayal, and the exploitation of human weakness. One might particularly doubt the benefit of undercover operations if one questions, rather than assumes, the value of the prohibitions these operations seek to enforce. Undercover operations are frequently used to enforce "victimless" criminal prohibitions— particularly drug offenses—that are themselves contestable.[21]

Of course, not everyone subscribes to such a critical view. But even those more sanguine about the propriety of using informants often recognize the risks inherent in permitting police to rely upon such individuals. One prominent risk relates to the widely shared fear that informants are inherently biased, and often unreliable. As Professor Andrew Manuel Crespo writes:

> [T]he typical informant cooperates with law enforcement in exchange for a tangible benefit. Sometimes that benefit is money, but usually it is lenient treatment with respect to the informant's own criminal behavior. The informant thus frequently has a strong motive to fabricate or embellish evidence: "a pound of another's flesh will spare [his] own."

And in fact, substantial evidence suggests that false information from confidential informants is a serious problem. Professor Natapoff summarizes reports indicating that nearly half of documented wrongful convictions in capital cases arise from false informant testimony, making "snitches the leading cause of wrongful convictions in U.S. capital cases." More anecdotally, she quotes former narcotics agent John Madinger, who once wrote that in his twenty-five years in law enforcement, having worked with "hundreds of informants," he believed that "exactly one of them was completely truthful, and there is no way to be 100% sure about him."[22]

At the same time, while informants' motive and tendency to fabricate information is widely acknowledged, Crespo cites scholarly literature demonstrating that, Madinger notwithstanding, "law-enforcement actors are predisposed to believe that their informants are telling the truth." In part, this is a function of cognitive biases and unconscious affinity. Natapoff quotes one prosecutor who says:

> You are not supposed to, of course. . . . But you spend time with this guy, you get to know him and his family. You like him. . . . [T]he reality is that the cooperator's information often becomes your mind set. . . . [T]he danger is that because you feel all warm and fuzzy about your cooperator, you come to believe that you do not have to spend much time or energy investigating the case and you don't.[23]

5. Law Enforcement Discretion and Bias. In addition to concerns related to informant credibility and bias, some courts and commentators identify a parallel risk arising from the discretion afforded in this arena to law enforcement actors themselves, who are "engaged in the often competitive enterprise of ferreting out crime." Johnson v. United States, 333 U.S. 10, 14 (1947). This reality may affect the conduct of secretive investigations in multiple ways.

For one thing, undercover officers may face incentives to run up the scorecard against their investigatory targets. A dissenting opinion in *Vaden,* written by Justice Burke, captures some of this concern:

> . . . [T]he potential for abuse inherent in law enforcement methods such as those employed in the case at bar is substantial. Once an agent has succeeded in persuading an individual to take some substantial act in furtherance of his general criminal scheme, the ultimate liability of the targeted defendant, if any, will depend upon which . . . crimes the agent *chooses* to commit in order to secure convictions against his criminal "accomplice."
>
> In this case, Officer Snell shot four foxes. Vaden, as pilot of the plane from which they were shot, was charged with four separate criminal counts of taking foxes from the air out of season. Had Snell opted to shoot a fifth fox, one more count could have been added to Vaden's indictment. In my view, it is clearly inconsistent with due process principles, and manifestly unjust, that the ultimate criminal liability of a defendant should be made to depend upon the good aim and/or the good intentions of the police officer charged with securing his arrest.

768 P.2d at 1111-1112 (Burke, J., dissenting).

Professor Natapoff expresses similar concerns about the use of confidential informants, analogizing it to "an enormous unregulated market in which the government is authorized to pressure and reward anyone it chooses, in almost any way it pleases, in exchange for almost anything it wants." This discretion, Natapoff adds, is frequently exercised "in secret and without accountability." To be clear, such secrecy is often a prerequisite to using informants at all. As Crespo observes, most people involved in illegal activity "will not come forward" with information about others exposed to prosecution "if they perceive a risk that their identities might be revealed." Indeed, as he further notes, "prosecutors will often dismiss a case" against the target of an investigation "rather than reveal a confidential source's identity."[24]

Still, while secrecy regarding the use of informants may be inescapable, some fear it "invites official deceit and even corruption" in service of zealous law enforcement. After all, the people in the best position to check such abuses are others within the law enforcement team—namely, prosecutors. But according to Professor Clifford Zimmerman, "Prosecutors willingly accept and proffer informant testimony without a critical eye, in part because they are not constrained to act otherwise" and in part because, much like the police, "they have an inherent conflict of interest" stemming from their professional incentives.[25]

6. Racial Disparities. Unchecked discretion often opens the door for biases, implicit and explicit, to shape law enforcement practices. Frequently, such biases fall along racial lines, as has been the case with police use of confidential informants in numerous settings. Consider, for example, Professor Alison Siegler and William Admussen's account of a widely used law enforcement tactic involving fake drug stash houses:

> Soon after Leslie Mayfield moved to the Chicago suburbs to escape the violence of the city and got a job at LG Electronics, a coworker mounted a campaign to rope him into robbing a drug stash house containing over a million dollars' worth of drugs. Little did Leslie know that the man nagging him to commit a crime was an informant for the Bureau of Alcohol, Tobacco, Firearms and Explosives (ATF). For a time, Leslie was able to resist the informant's overtures. But after Leslie took a loan from the informant to fix his broken-down car, Leslie felt he had little choice but to commit the robbery to repay the debt. . . .
>
> Every fake stash house operation follows the same basic playbook: an informant working for the ATF or the Drug Enforcement Agency (DEA) approaches someone like Leslie—a person of color in dire financial straits—offers him an enticing jackpot, and then introduces the target to an undercover agent who describes a heavily guarded house to induce him to bring along friends and guns. Federal prosecutors and agents intentionally set a fictional drug amount that will trigger a high

mandatory penalty, while the inducement to bring guns triggers an additional and consecutive mandatory penalty. As a result, defendants typically face a mandatory minimum sentence of fifteen to twenty-five years in prison. When the targets gather to execute the law enforcement-led "robbery," federal agents arrest them. . . . These operations have more than quadrupled since 2004.

Nationwide, federal law enforcement agencies have overwhelmingly targeted people of color to commit these fabricated crimes. In Chicago, from 2011 to 2013, only one individual out of the fifty-seven charged by the ATF in a stash house operation was white. In the past decade of stash house cases in New York, none of the 179 defendants charged were white. In Los Angeles, one agent testified that fifty-five out of sixty stash house defendants indicted were people of color. A 2014 review by *USA Today* of stash house cases nationwide found that "[a]t least 91% of the people agents have locked up using those [stash house] stings were racial or ethnic minorities."[26]

As Professors Elizabeth Hinton and Anna Lvovsky separately observe, the disparities described above are common to drug stings more generally and indeed to undercover policing of various types of suspected crime. In Lvovsky's words, "From drug stings targeting poor and Black neighborhoods, to antiterrorism operations that cast indiscriminate suspicion on Muslim communities, to prostitution arrests trading on race- and gender-based stereotypes about likely buyers and sellers of sex, undercover work has long perpetuated the most abiding disparities of American policing."[27]

Nor is the problem limited to discriminatory targeting. As Professor Natapoff observes, if the use of criminal informants is concentrated in low-income neighborhoods of color, social network effects will cause those racial disparities to snowball:

Snitches tend to snitch on the people with whom they live and interact. When police rely on informants to direct new investigations, police resources will naturally be channeled back into the communities from which the informants come. This phenomenon has special significance for heavily policed urban communities . . . [and] suggests that the use of informants is part of the reason why communities of color are overrepresented in drug enforcement efforts. For example, the San Diego Search Warrant Project concluded that [while] Black and Latinx people represent less than one-third of the San Diego population, over 80 percent of all warrants—and 98 percent of all warrants seeking cocaine—targeted Black and Latinx households. The majority of those warrants turned up no evidence, while two-thirds of warrants directed at white homes produced contraband. One reason for the disparity is that 80 percent of warrants were based on confidential informants. Because informants tend to give information about individuals in their own racial groups, the study hypothesized that disproportionate arrests of African American and Latinx people would lead to disproportionate — and inaccurate — targeting of Black and Latinx homes.[28]

2.   Entrapment

In both *Peterson* and *Vaden,* the undercover actor was the principal in the crime. Weiss cooked the drugs, Snell shot the foxes. But as the fake stash house cases above reflect, the roles are frequently reversed. Often, state informants or undercover agents act as *feigned accomplices* who encourage private individuals to commit crimes.

That encouragement can sometimes be persistent and intense. Consider *United States v. Staufer,* 38 F.3d 1103 (9th Cir. 1994). In that case, the defendant, Mark Staufer, was "experiencing serious financial difficulties. He had almost no money to his name, was living in a garage because he could not afford to pay rent, and had a number of outstanding bills that he was unable to pay." *Id.* at 1105. He also had a friend, Scott, who was secretly working for the government as a confidential informant. Scott himself had been convicted of federal drug crimes. *Id.* He was facing a sentence of more than ten years in prison, which he hoped to avoid serving by helping the government build cases against other people. *Id.* At the direction of his handler, an undercover DEA agent, Scott repeatedly approached Staufer, "always encouraging him to sell drugs." *Id.* Staufer at first refused, but Scott persisted. At one point, Scott was contacting Staufer "so frequently at his job that his supervisor was upset with him." *Id.* When these entreaties proved unfruitful, Scott and the DEA agent leaned into the financial angle, offering "to pay more money than they initially had [offered] to pay when Staufer expressed reluctance." *Id.* Ultimately, Staufer agreed to procure 10,000 doses of LSD in exchange for $8,000. Credible evidence at trial indicated that this was Staufer's first time selling drugs, save for one prior instance in which "he had obtained 25 or 30 doses of LSD for $15" and "given some of it to friends who had given him $8 in return." *Id.*

In an effort to avoid liability, Staufer attempted to invoke the *entrapment defense,* which serves as one of the few potential constraints on the role informants and undercover agents may play in facilitating crime. But the defense is limited. In Staufer's case, it did not work. As the court there held, "Staufer admitted at trial that in the past he had sold small quantities of LSD. . . . [He thus] failed to carry his burden of making it 'patently clear' that he lacked the predisposition to engage in an illegal act, and [a] jury reasonably could have found against him on his entrapment defense." *Id.* at 1108. The following case and notes explore this doctrine in detail.[29]

United States v. Cromitie
_____
   727 F.3d 194 (2d Cir. 2013)

NEWMAN, J. [The defendant, along with three other men, was] convicted of planning and attempting to carry out domestic terrorism offenses involving a plot to launch missiles at an Air National Guard base at Stewart Airport in Newburgh, NY, and bomb two synagogues in the Bronx. . . . We reject the defendants' claims of entrapment as a matter of law . . . [and] therefore affirm.

BACKGROUND

All the charged offenses resulted from an elaborate sting operation conducted by the FBI using an undercover informant . . . [named] Shahed Hussain. . . . Hussain is a Pakistani national . . . . In 2003, Hussain was convicted of fraud . . . . To avoid being deported, . . . Hussain became a paid informant of the FBI and started working in the lower Hudson Valley. . . . Hussain's goal was to "locate disaffected Muslims who might be harboring terrorist designs on the United States." . . .

During a period of several months, Hussain cultivated a friendship with [James] Cromitie, . . . "an impoverished man[]" who sustained himself by committing petty drug offenses for which he had repeatedly been caught and convicted. In addition, he worked a night shift at a local Walmart store, earning less than $14,000 per year.

[During the summer and fall of 2008, Cromitie and Hussain spoke on numerous occasions. After Cromitie at one point expressed hate for Jews and Americans, Hussain, at the FBI's instruction, told Cromitie that he represented a Pakistani organization called Jaish-e-Mohammed (JeM), which Cromitie then expressed a desire to join. Over time, Cromitie expressed interest in putting "a team together" and making a "plan." When Cromitie's commitment wavered, Hussain offered him cash and other valuables.]

[Late in 2008, Hussain suggested that the men "pick a target." Cromitie proposed Stewart Airport, from which, Hussain had told him, military planes carried arms to the Middle East. In early 2009, Hussain bought Cromitie a camera and took him to conduct surveillance at Stewart Airport. A few months later, Cromitie introduced Hussain to three men; the group of four discussed with Hussain an additional plan to bomb two synagogues in the Bronx. In early May, Hussain, Cromitie, and two of Cromitie's recruits traveled to a warehouse where the FBI stored three fake bombs and two fake missiles. Hussain instructed the defendants in how to use the weapons. The group conducted further surveillance and finalized their plans. On May 20, the men gathered to execute the plan. Cromitie placed the fake bombs outside the synagogues while the other defendants acted as lookouts. All of the defendants were arrested and convicted of various crimes and sentenced to 25-year mandatory minimum terms.]

DISCUSSION

"A valid entrapment defense has two related elements: government inducement of the crime, and a lack of predisposition on the part of the defendant to engage in criminal conduct." Mathews v. United States, 485 U.S. 58, 63 (1988). "Predisposition, the principal element in the defense of entrapment, focuses upon whether the defendant was an unwary innocent or, instead, an unwary criminal who readily availed himself of the opportunity to perpetrate the crime." *Id.* "The fact that officers or employees of the Government merely afford opportunities or facilities for the commission of the offense does not defeat the prosecution." Jacobson v. United States, 503 U.S. 540, 548 (1992). . . . [On the other hand,] "[w]hen the criminal *design* originates, not with the accused, but is conceived in the mind of the government officers, and the accused is by persuasion, deceitful representation, or inducement lured into the commission of a criminal act, the government is estopped by sound public policy from prosecution therefor." Sorrells v. United States, 287 U.S. 435, 445 (1932).

. . . Judge Learned Hand . . . postulated . . . three circumstances, any one of which would . . . establish[] a defendant's predisposition [and thus defeat the entrapment defense]: "an existing course of similar criminal conduct; the accused's already formed *design* to commit the crime or similar crimes; [or] his willingness to do so, as evinced by ready compl[ia]nce." United States v. Becker, 62 F.2d 1007, 1008 (2d Cir. 1933). . . . There is normally little controversy as to what constitutes prior "similar criminal conduct." "Ready compliance" is usually indicated by the promptness of a defendant's agreement to commit an offense. . . . What is meant by a pre-existing "design" is more problematic. . . .

When used as one of the three means of showing predisposition, we think "design" must take its meaning from the context of the type of criminal activity comprising the specific offenses a defendant has committed. With respect to a category as varied as terrorist activity, the requisite design in the mind of a defendant may be broader than the design for other narrower forms of criminal activity. In view of the broad range of activities that can constitute terrorism, especially with respect to terrorist activities directed against the interests of the United States, the relevant prior design need be only a rather generalized idea or intent to inflict harm on such interests. A person with such an idea or intent can readily be found to be "ready and willing to commit the offence charged, whenever the opportunity offered."

[We now apply this two-pronged test to the facts of this case.]

(a) INDUCEMENT

. . . Hussain's efforts to persuade Cromitie constituted inducement. As the District Court . . . forcefully stated, "I believe beyond a shadow of a doubt that there would have been no crime here except the government instigated it, planned it, and brought it to fruition." The record fully supports this statement. Hussain's efforts to persuade Cromitie to commit the charged offenses persisted throughout the eleven-month period from their initial meeting until the arrest. In addition to proposing specifics of the planned attacks and supplying bombs and missiles, Hussain's inducements included offers of $250,000, a barber shop at a cost of $70,000, a BMW, and an all-expense-paid, two-week vacation to Puerto Rico for Cromitie and his family. . . .

(b) PREDISPOSITION

With respect to the three means of proving predisposition, it is clear that Cromitie had not engaged in a course of similar conduct prior to the Government's inducement, nor did he readily agree to committing the charged offenses. Thus, the issue becomes whether, prior to inducement, he had an "already formed *design* to commit the crime or similar crimes." *Becker,* 62 F.2d at 1008.

On the first day that Hussain met Cromitie, Hussain quotes Cromitie as saying, "I want to do something to America." The potentially ominous meaning of these words was considerably clarified by Cromitie's immediately preceding statement that he wanted "to die like a shahid, a martyr," and the fact that, as he said them, he pointed his right index finger in the air in a gesture Hussain testified is used "by somebody in radical Islam" to "mean taking an oath in front of Allah to do take part of [*sic*] crime or Jihad act they want to do." The jury was entitled to think that wanting to die like a martyr, coupled with wanting to do something to America, meant a willingness to be a suicide bomber, even though Cromitie never planned to sacrifice his own life.

Fully indicating that Cromitie's initial statements to Hussain revealed a pre-existing design to commit terrorist acts against the interests of the United States are these later statements:

—As early as July 8, 2008, Cromitie told Hussain that he wanted to join JeM, which he believed was a terrorist organization in Pakistan. . . .

—When asked, "Have you ever thought about doing something here?" Cromitie answered, "I have been wanting to do that since I was 7." . . .

—When Hussain said, "Let's pick a target," Cromitie suggested "Stewart Airport." . . .

Cromitie's recorded words [also] explained his motives for what he wanted to do:

—"They taking down our Islamic countries. What do we do to make that stop? So, we start taking something down here."

—"They air force planes bringing 'em troops over there [Afghanistan] to do damage to us. So, if they don't have the planes to carry 'em over there, you can't do too much damage." . . .

These recorded statements, all of which were independent of any inducement, gave indisputable meaning to Cromitie's initial ominous, though somewhat generalized, words about wanting to "do something to America" and "die like a shahid, a martyr." The later statements also gave the jury ample basis for believing Hussain when he testified about what Cromitie had said to him during their first unrecorded conversation. . . .

It is true that during the many months of Hussain's persuasion, Cromitie's commitment to the terrorism plot was not unwavering. . . . [But d]espite moments of wavering, which do not preclude a finding of predisposition, Cromitie revealed his willingness, indeed his eagerness, to commit acts of terrorism through his own recorded statements. Two examples stand out. Referring to the initial conversation with Hussain, Cromitie recalled in a recorded conversation, "You already knew I was like that. It wasn't you who was talking to me, I talked to you about it. When we first met in the parking lot, I talked to you about it." And contemplating that "on the day of judgment" Allah would say that Hussain had enticed him, Cromitie said he would answer, "No! You [Allah] gave me my own will. I did that on my own."

From everything that Cromitie said, the jury was entitled to find that he had a pre-existing "design" and hence a predisposition to inflict serious harm on interests of the United States, even though Government officers afforded him the opportunity and the pseudo weapons for striking at specific targets. . . . The . . . judgments of convictions and sentences of all four defendants are affirmed.*

JACOBS, C.J., concurring in part and dissenting in part . . . . I respectfully dissent in part because James Cromitie was entrapped as a matter of law. . . . In my view, there was no evidence of an "already formed design." At the outset, Cromitie told of wanting to "do something to America" and "die like a martyr," but this big talk does not amount to a design — to *do* what? — never mind one that was "already formed." The design here was entirely formed by the government, and fed to Cromitie. He liked it, but he didn't form it.

The term "already formed design" is defined away by the majority: it is "only a rather generalized idea or intent to inflict harm on" the interests of the United States. . . . [But] the "generalized idea" of an act is not a disposition to do it[.] [E]ntrapment is the very process of mobilizing a generalized idea that otherwise would remain an idle thought. Thus the majority opinion renders entrapment untenable as a defense. . . .

The term "already formed design" takes meaning from its company, appearing in a series of three related ways to show predisposition: commission of the offense in the past, the ready willingness to do it then and there, or a formed design, which looks to the future. Existence of a formed design matters only if it cannot be shown that the defendant had already

_____

* Editor's Note: The court held that analogous evidence supported the jury's rejection of the entrapment defense, on grounds of predisposition, for the other three defendants.

done analogous acts or had given ready assent. The three can operate as alternatives only if they are understood to be of comparable predictive force. There is great predictive force in a showing of past criminal acts along the same lines. Similarly, a ready acceptance bespeaks a complete absence of qualm or inhibition, and likewise shows that the defendant's will and disposition did not run counter to the act and did not need to be overcome.

The predictive force of a formed design is sufficient on its own only if a course of conduct is already so well advanced in the defendant's mind that one can be sure (beyond a reasonable doubt) it was not planted by an agent provocateur. Perhaps this is why we have never before found sufficient evidence to prove that the accused had an already formed design without there also being sufficient evidence of a relevant criminal history or of ready assent to the government's proposal.

It therefore is not enough to infer a formed design to commit an act of terror from a sense of grievance or an impulse to lash out. These disquiets are common, and in most people will never combust.

With this in mind, there is scarce evidence of any "already formed design" on the part of Cromitie. . . . The majority opinion relies heavily . . . on post-inducement acts and statements that do not reflect the defendant's state of mind *before* the initial inducement, and therefore do not bear on predisposition. Cromitie did what he was induced to do, and seemed happy doing it, but that cannot suffice; otherwise the induced act would always evidence the predisposition to do it. . . . Wanting to "die like a martyr" and "do something to America" is not a formed design, and certainly not "preparation," United States v. Sherman, 200 F.2d 880, 882 (1952). These are wishes, not designs. One amounts to no more than the boastful piety of a foolish man;[4] the other could be banter in any faculty lounge.

NOTES AND QUESTIONS

1. Entrapment and Domestic Terrorism. The *Cromitie* case, which became the subject of an HBO documentary called *The Newburgh Sting*, is merely one of roughly 1,000 post-9/11 cases involving allegations of terrorism. Many of those cases also involved allegations of entrapment. *See, e.g.*, United States v. Hammadi, 737 F.3d 1043 (6th Cir. 2013); United States v. Lakhani, 480 F.3d 171 (3d Cir. 2007); United States v. Siraj, 468

---

4. En route to the terror site, the government agent directed Cromitie to assemble the bombs; but he couldn't figure it out. . . . At the site, the government agent directed him to hide the bombs in the trunk of the car; but he couldn't get the trunk open, so he put them in the back seat. The government agent then directed him to arm the bombs, but as they drove away from the supposed car-bomb parked in front of the synagogue, Cromitie exclaimed "holy s***, I forgot to turn it on." . . .

F. Supp. 2d 408 (E.D.N.Y. 2007). While systematic data do not exist, one study estimated that roughly 35 percent of post-9/11 terrorism prosecutions had "four or more core indicators" of entrapment based on the case law. To date, no defendant prosecuted for a terrorism-related offense has been acquitted based on the defense.[30]

   2. The Rise and Limits of Entrapment. As the U.S. Court of Appeals for the Seventh Circuit explained in the case of Leslie Mayfield, the Chicago man induced to "rob" a fake drug stash house, "[e]ntrapment is a relative newcomer to the catalog of criminal defenses." United States v. Mayfield, 771 F.3d 417, 424 (7th Cir. 2014) (en banc). According to a leading treatise, criminal law traditionally placed "no limits upon the degree of temptation to which law enforcement officers and their agents could subject those under investigation." Indeed, early judicial decisions treated claims of government inducement dismissively, likening defendants to Eve in the Garden of Eden:

> Even if inducements to commit crime could be assumed to exist in this case, the allegation of the defendant would be but the repetition of the plea as ancient as the world, and first interposed in Paradise: "The serpent beguiled me and I did eat." That defence was overruled by the great Lawgiver, and . . . this plea has never since availed to shield crime or give indemnity to the culprit, and it is safe to say that under any code of civilized, not to say christian ethics, it never will.

Bd. of Comm'rs of Excise of Onondaga Cnty. v. Backus, 29 How. Pr. 33, 42 (N.Y. Gen. Term 1864).[31]

   As "law enforcement professionalized" in the late nineteenth century, however, and the federal criminal law began to expand into more areas of daily life, law enforcement agencies developed and deployed "techniques of artifice and deception in the pursuit of criminals" with greater fervor and frequency. *Mayfield*, 771 F.3d at 424. Prohibition above all, explains Professor Rebecca Roiphe, "institutionalized the federal wing of law enforcement while simultaneously increasing the scope and creativity of its undercover tactics," all while "linking municipal police to [its] broad national agenda." Courts confronted with these increasingly invasive tactics grew uncomfortable and began to cast about for theories that might limit the state's excesses. Eventually, coalescing around the Supreme Court's Prohibition-era decision in *Sorrells v. United States*, 287 U.S. 435 (1932), they settled on the general approach applied in *Cromitie*, which has changed little in the intervening century.[32]

   Still, while the doctrine was initially created to constrain deceptive law enforcement tactics, those who have attempted to study the frequency of its use today describe it as a defense that is rarely raised and very rarely succeeds. The doctrine is also frequently limited to nonviolent or relatively less serious offenses, further circumscribing its practical utility. *See, e.g., id.* at

451; *see also* Model Penal Code §2.13 (entrapment unavailable "when causing or threatening bodily injury is an element of the offense charged and the prosecution is based on conduct causing or threatening such injury to a person other than the person perpetrating the entrapment").[33]

3. *Defining Predisposition.* Much of the debate between the majority and dissent in *Cromitie* concerns the majority's attempt to establish predisposition by reference to Cromitie's acts and statements postdating Hussain's efforts to ply him. The dissent complains that "[t]he majority opinion relies heavily . . . on post-inducement acts and statements that do not reflect the defendant's state of mind *before* the initial inducement, and therefore do not bear on predisposition." The majority, for its part, maintains that Cromitie's later acts and statements "gave indisputable meaning to Cromitie's initial ominous, though somewhat generalized, words about wanting to 'do something to America.'" The majority, in other words, purports to use Cromitie's post-inducement words and actions to illuminate and clarify his pre-inducement disposition.

The majority's approach should not be taken to confuse the settled proposition that "the relevant question [i]s whether the defendant was predisposed *prior to* the government's initial contact." *Mayfield*, 771 F.3d at 430. The Supreme Court made this clear in *Jacobson v. United States*, upholding the entrapment defense of a defendant who ordered child pornography through the mail after "26 months of repeated mailings and communications from Government agents and fictitious organizations . . . waving the banner of individual rights and disparaging the legitimacy and constitutionality of efforts to restrict the availability of sexually explicit materials." 503 U.S. 540, 550-552 (1992). The Court held:

> Petitioner's ready response to [the Government's] solicitations [to buy] cannot be enough to establish beyond reasonable doubt that he was predisposed, prior to the Government acts intended to create predisposition, to commit the crime of receiving child pornography through the mails. The evidence that petitioner was ready and willing to commit the offense came only after the Government had devoted 2 1/2 years to convincing him that he had or should have the right to engage in the very behavior proscribed by law. Rational jurors could not say beyond a reasonable doubt that petitioner possessed the requisite predisposition prior to the Government's investigation and that it existed independent of the Government's many and varied approaches to petitioner.

Id. at 553.

4. *Inducement.* As the *Cromitie* court explains, the entrapment defense examines not only the defendant's predisposition but also the government's conduct, which must rise to the level of inducement. Doctrinally, that term of art "means more than mere government solicitation of the crime; the fact that government agents initiated contact with the defendant, suggested the crime, or furnished the ordinary opportunity to commit it is insufficient to show inducement." *Mayfield*, 771 F.3d at 434. Rather, what inducement requires is

> government solicitation of the crime *plus* some other government con-
> duct that creates a risk that a person who would not commit the crime if
> left to his own devices will do so in response to the government's efforts.
> The "other conduct" may be repeated attempts at persuasion, fraudulent
> representations, threats, coercive tactics, harassment, promises of reward
> beyond that inherent in the customary execution of the crime, pleas based
> on need, sympathy, or friendship, or any other conduct by government
> agents that creates a risk that a person who otherwise would not commit
> the crime if left alone will do so in response to the government's efforts.

Id. at 434-435. As Professor Ronald Allen put the point, inducement requires conduct that "exceed[s] real world market rates, which includes both financial and emotional markets."[34]

This understanding of inducement holds important implications for what is perhaps the most common form of undercover law enforcement activity: drug stings designed to apprehend street-level sellers and buyers of illegal narcotics. The tactic can unfold from either side of the transaction. In a technique commonly known as *buy-and-bust*, undercover agents pose as the customers, purchase narcotics from unwitting sellers, and then arrest them. Alternatively, in a tactic called a *reverse sting* or (confusingly) a *reverse buy*, the undercovers pose as sellers and arrest those who purchase from them. Note that in both instances, the undercover actor has simply "initiated contact with the defendant, suggested the crime, or furnished the ordinary opportunity to commit it," which, as *Mayfield* notes, "is insufficient to show inducement." *Id.* at 434. The entrapment defense is thus generally off the table with respect to these widespread tactics in the War on Drugs. *See, e.g.*, Bailey v. People, 630 P.2d 1062 (Colo. 1981) (en banc) (buy-and-bust); State v. Agrabante, 830 P.2d 492 (Haw. 1992) (reverse sting).

5. *Inducement Alone.* While the two-pronged doctrinal test set out in *Cromitie* is followed in federal courts and most states, a minority of jurisdictions (and the Model Penal Code in §2.13) collapse the inquiry into a single step. In these states, the doctrinal inquiry does not formally consider the defendant's predisposition but rather rises and falls solely on a showing of inducement. Still, as Professor Louis Michael Seidman observes, "[i]n virtually every case, the [two] tests produce the same results, and those results turn on the defendant's predisposition." Indeed, the definition of inducement set forth in the preceding note incorporates the concept of predisposition when it defines inducement as conduct "that creates a risk that *a person who would not commit the crime if left to his own devices* will do so in response to the government's efforts." *Mayfield*, 771 F.3d at 435 (emphasis added).[35]

6. Entrapment and Due Process. Entrapment doctrine originated in state courts and was later codified in about half the states. Much of the intervening doctrinal development occurred in federal courts, where entrapment is presumed to be an artifact of legislative intention. Across these settings, the defense — like so much else in substantive criminal law — is subject to legislative control. Congress and state legislatures are free to modify the defense or even to abolish it entirely.[36]

That said, the Supreme Court has suggested, and various lower courts have held, that in cases involving outrageous government conduct, an entrapment-like defense is compelled by the Due Process Clause of the U.S. Constitution, and may even be available to a defendant who would be considered predisposed to commit a crime and thus ineligible for the conventional entrapment defense. *See* United States v. Russell, 411 U.S. 423 (1973); Hampton v. United States, 425 U.S. 484 (1976); United States v. Twigg, 588 F.2d 373 (3d Cir. 1978). Still, this defense is more demanding than the entrapment defense and, where recognized, applies in only the rarest of cases. The *Vaden* court, for example, rejected Vaden's claim of outrageous government conduct on the ground that the defense is limited to cases in which the government "engineered and directed the criminal enterprise from start to finish." 768 P.2d at 1108.

A leading treatise speculates that there may be other fact patterns that could constitute outrageous government conduct, including cases where government agents encourage "violence or threat of violence against innocent parties," infiltrate "political organizations to suggest the commission of crimes," exploit "a sexual relationship," or offer "such extraordinarily large financial inducements as to bring about a coercive situation." But courts tend to view the doctrine skeptically. The First Circuit, for example, writes that "the doctrine is moribund" insofar as "courts have rejected its application with almost monotonous regularity." United States v. Santana, 6 F.3d 1, 4 (1st Cir. 1993). The Sixth Circuit, meanwhile, suggests the doctrine is a chimera. "In this circuit, we have never applied the 'outrageous government conduct' defense, and have stated that 'there are . . . strong reasons for concluding that such a defense simply does not exist. . . .'" United States v. Al-Cohan, 610 F.3d 945, 952 (6th Cir. 2010).[37]

III. CONSPIRACY

> "[W]e are mindful that the conspiracy doctrine is inherently subject to abuse and that the government frequently uses conspiracy to cast a wide net that captures many players. Thus, we must be careful to guard against guilt by association, to 'scrupulously safeguard each defendant individually, as far as possible, from loss of identity in the mass.'"
>
> United States v. Evans, 970 F.2d 663, 668 (10th Cir. 1992)
> (quoting Kotteakos v. United States, 328 U.S. 750, 776 (1946))

A.   Agreeing to Commit a Crime

Unlike complicity, conspiracy is both a theory of group liability and a substantive offense. A person accused of being in a criminal conspiracy will thus be charged with the crime of conspiracy itself, and may also separately be charged with substantive crimes committed by co-conspirators. We will return to the group liability component of conspiracy doctrine later in this section. For present purposes, it is important to note that, as a substantive offense, conspiracy is what is often called an *inchoate* offense. The crime is complete when a person forms an *agreement* to commit a crime with someone else, not when that other crime, called the *object crime*, is actually committed. As a result, it is possible for a person to be guilty of conspiring to commit a crime even if the object crime never ultimately occurs. In this respect, conspiracy bears certain similarities to the crime of *attempt*, which we will explore in detail in Chapter Eight.

An essential question at the outset of any conspiracy case is whether an agreement to commit a crime exists. As the first lead case below explains, "[w]ithout an agreement, there is no conspiracy." United States v. Loveland, 825 F.3d 555, 557 (9th Cir. 2016). Examining the contours and nature of the agreement also helps to determine the conspiracy's *scope:* Who is in the conspiracy, and what exactly have they conspired to do? These questions will become especially important when we turn to the group liability component of conspiracy doctrine, as conspiracies with broader scopes will cast wider nets of liability. As an entry point to this discussion, consider the following two cases, which respectively examine two classic conspiracy models: the "chain link" conspiracy and the "hub and spoke" conspiracy.

United States v. Loveland

825 F.3d 555 (9th Cir. 2016)

KLEINFELD, J. . . . Conspiracy means an agreement to commit a crime, not commission of the crime. Though that might sound less serious to a layman, lawyers know that the conspiracy charge affects much about trial and sentencing, all to the advantage of the prosecution. A conspiracy charge imposes one substantial disadvantage to the prosecution: the prosecution must prove the existence of the agreement beyond a reasonable doubt. The agreement can be explicit or tacit, and can be proved by direct or circumstantial evidence, including inferences from circumstantial evidence, but it still has to be proved. Without an agreement, there is no conspiracy. . . .

FACTS

The government charged twelve defendants with conspiracy to possess with intent to distribute methamphetamine. . . . The indictment [charges some of the defendants] with possession with intent to distribute, but not Loveland. For Loveland, the government took it upon itself, by its charging decision, to prove conspiracy or nothing.

The evidence showed that during the relevant period the lead defendant, Jesus Guadalupe Sanchez, imported about two pounds of methamphetamine per month to Idaho from Mexico, Arizona, or California, which he bought for $10,000 a pound. He and his coconspirators resold the methamphetamine to a number of buyers, typically in one- or two-ounce lots, for about $1,200 per ounce. As might be expected in a felonious trade, many of the buyers were regulars, not strangers. Some of the regulars got caught, and one made a recorded purchase for law enforcement in order to get a better deal on sentencing. Several of the others pleaded guilty and testified in exchange for benefits.

At Loveland's jury trial, three of the coconspirators testified to repeated sales to Loveland of two ounces at a time, each time for $2,400. And each time, Loveland paid cash on delivery. There was testimony that the quantities he bought were too much for a person to consume himself without getting sick, so the jury could reasonably infer that Loveland bought the methamphetamine partly or entirely for resale. Two of the coconspirators had different arrangements with Sanchez. [One] paid more . . . per ounce . . . and had an explicit agreement with Sanchez to resell the drugs he bought. [Another] sometimes was "fronted" the methamphetamine, which means he did not have to pay cash on delivery, and would instead pay for his inventory after he resold it. For Loveland, though, it was cash on the barrelhead every time — no discounts, no credit, and no agreement about what he would do with the drugs. . . .

ANALYSIS

. . . Conspiracy is an agreement to commit a crime, and the intent to commit the underlying offense. We assume for purposes of decision that Loveland intended to commit the crime of possession of methamphetamine for purpose of distribution. And we assume for purposes of decision that the Sanchez group knew Loveland was probably reselling the methamphetamine they sold to him, because the quantity exceeded what he could use himself. But Loveland's intent to possess for purpose of distribution and the Sanchez group's sales to him do not add up to conspiracy. The Sanchez group has to have agreed with Loveland, expressly or tacitly, that Loveland should resell the methamphetamine in order for them to have conspired together.[*]

We have a long line of decisions directed at the problem of distinguishing between sale of an illegal substance and conspiracy of the seller with the buyer for the buyer to resell. [In] *United States v. Lennick*, 18 F.3d 814 (9th Cir. 1994), [we] held that the evidence was insufficient to support a conviction for conspiracy to distribute narcotics, where . . . there was no evidence that [a distributor] had agreed with the people to whom he sold or gave the drugs that they should distribute it to others. . . . The case before us is stronger for the government than *Lennick* on the facts because in *Lennick*, arguably, the quantities were too small to support an inference that Lennick knew his distributees would redistribute. But we worded our holding broadly: "To show a conspiracy, the government must show not only that Lennick gave drugs to other people knowing that they would further distribute them, but also that he had an agreement with these individuals to so further distribute the drugs."

. . . [In contrast to *Lennick*,] *United States v. Ramirez*, 714 F.3d 1134 (9th Cir. 2013), . . . was a stronger case for the government than this one. Ramirez's buyer collected money from the government undercover agent while Ramirez was nearby and brought the money immediately to Ramirez. Ramirez exchanged the methamphetamine immediately, which the go-between immediately delivered to the undercover agent. In three out of four of the sales proved, the undercover agent and Ramirez were in sight of each other. [And unlike in *Lennick*, the facts of *Ramirez* involved repeated sales of "escalating" quantities of methamphetamine.] Nevertheless, we held that there was insufficient evidence of conspiracy between Ramirez and the go-between.

A fortiori, the Sanchez group's sales to Loveland, with no involvement in Loveland's resales, does not suffice to establish a conspiracy [as no] one from the Sanchez group observed or was told what Loveland was doing with the methamphetamine. . . . Of course, like any element, the agreement may be proved by direct evidence or circumstantial evidence. And the agreement can be explicit or tacit. But the agreement has to be there. A relationship of mere seller and buyer, with the seller having no stake in what the buyer does with the goods, shows the absence of a conspiracy, because it is missing the element of an agreement for redistribution. . . .

---

[*] Editor's Note: The conspiracy charge in this case centers on whether there was an agreement between Sanchez and Loveland that Loveland would resell the drugs he purchased from Sanchez *to other people*. Under a doctrine known as the *Gebardi* rule, Loveland could not be deemed to have been in a conspiracy with Sanchez to distribute drugs *to Loveland himself* (as occurred each time Loveland bought from Sanchez). As the Supreme Court later explained the rule, "where a statute treats one side of a bilateral transaction more leniently, adding to the penalty of the party on that side for facilitating the action by the other would upend the calibration of punishment set by the legislature." Abuelhawa v. United States, 556 U.S. 816, 820 (2009).

We are unable to see how in this case any reasonable juror could conclude beyond a reasonable doubt that the Sanchez group had an agreement, even tacit, with Loveland, for Loveland to resell the methamphetamine. Though the Sanchez group might assume that Loveland was reselling the methamphetamine that he bought from them, he could have flushed it down the toilet for all they cared, since they already had his money. As for future sales, they had no hold on him. Loveland was free to shop elsewhere. Their stake in his enterprise was no different from a big-box store's stake in a convenience store's financial success from the resale of individually packaged peanuts purchased by the carton from the big-box store. The big-box store ordinarily has no agreement with the convenience store owner regarding his resales. As the Seventh Circuit said in *United States v. Colon*, "Every seller to a distributor has a stake in the distributor's activities; a person who buys for resale will not enrich his seller if his resale business dries up." 549 F.3d 565, 568 (7th Cir. 2008). However, we share the Seventh Circuit's skepticism that "'regular' purchases on 'standard' terms can transform a customer into a co-conspirator." *Id.* at 567. There was no evidence of an agreement, so the evidence was insufficient to support Loveland's conspiracy conviction. Therefore, we reverse the judgment and vacate Loveland's conviction and sentence.

United States v. Kenny

645 F.2d 1323 (9th Cir. 1981)

NELSON, J. . . . Kenny was the proprietor of a now-defunct firm in San Diego known as Ocean Market Consultants ("OMC"). OMC provided a variety of research, technical writing and document preparation services to government and industrial clients in the area. The remaining defendants were civilian employees at the Naval Electronics Laboratory Center ("NELC") at nearby Point Loma. During the time period covered by the indictment, appellant Parker was the supervisor of NELC's Security Systems Programs Office, a section internally designated "Code 1500." Appellant Oelberg, along with defendants Warren and Lab, worked under Parker as members of the Code 1500 staff. . . . Oelberg, Lab, and Warren shared adjoining offices at NELC, a few doors away from Parker's office, during most of their employment there. All four of these Code 1500 employees worked closely together and frequently signed for each other on NELC contracting documents. . . .

[OMC obtained a substantial quantity of business from NELC, primarily through contracts billed on a "time and materials" basis.] Navy records showed total payments to OMC totaling approximately $1.5 million between 1972 and 1976. The evidence indicated that many of these contracts and tasks were false in various respects, resulting in overcharges to the Navy, and consequent illicit profits to Kenny and OMC, of substantial sums of money. The evidence further indicated that in consideration for the issuance and approval of the fraudulent contracts and tasks, Kenny paid cash and check bribes to the defendants employed in Code 1500, as well as furnishing them with other items of value.

Parker, in his role as head of Code 1500, set the stage for [these] illegal activities by arranging for the Navy to award three major contracts to OMC. . . . The prosecution presented evidence showing that a group of tasks issued by Parker to OMC, totaling nearly $158,000, was largely fraudulent. In one case, involving a $58,000 contract to produce manuals for a pair of information-gathering devices on Navy submarines, the . . . manuals called for were not appropriate at that point in time and [were never received]. . . . Although the record does not disclose the exact nature of any arrangement Kenny and Parker may have had, the Government brought out a number of questionable facts indicating kickbacks or bribery. . . .

[The investigatory thread that ultimately led to the defendant's prosecution and convictions did not begin with the kickbacks and bribery just described. Rather, it began with an investigation into a separate moonlighting business called Self-Control Systems or "SCS," which was operated by Oelberg, Warren and Lab. Kenny occasionally did business with this separate moonlighting company and paid for materials or services supplied to SCS using funds from OMC.] . . .

In early 1973, [acting on a tip,] Navy officials and the FBI began inquiries into [OMC] and SCS. The complaint about SCS was referred to Parker, in his capacity as supervisor of Code 1500. . . . Witnesses testified that in late February or early March 1973, Kenny ordered his bookkeeping employees to gather [records related to SCS] on the OMC premises, which he removed. One of the employees testified that Kenny told her that Parker had called and alerted him to the official investigation.

Parker, meanwhile, called Lab back from Washington to a March 5th meeting with Oelberg and Warren to discuss the investigation. He told them that the FBI and the Navy were investigating SCS, and told Lab in the presence of the others that "if this investigation gets into OMC's books" he would kill him. Parker testified that at the meeting, he was aware that Kenny had helped SCS in both marketing advice and art/design work. He testified that he "chewed them out royally" and told the three that he did not want them doing business with Kenny because he was a government contractor. . . . After the meeting, Parker ordered Oelberg and Warren to gather all SCS material and store it in Parker's home. Two days later, he allowed them to reclaim the material, stating that he had "killed" the investigation. . . .

The prosecution presented evidence to show that Lab, Oelberg and Warren had all engaged in fraudulent activities during this time period. Lab, as a Government witness, testified at length about an . . . incident in which he and Warren agreed to issue a phony contract in the amount of $25,000 to Kenny, so that Kenny could meet obligations on a $75,000 line of credit secured by OMC invoices, many of which were false. . . .

MULTIPLE VERSUS SINGLE CONSPIRACY

The appellants . . . argue that, at most, separate conspiracies involving NELC defendants transacting individually with Kenny were shown. Both Parker and Oelberg claim substantial prejudice to their respective defenses as a result, owing to the danger of "guilt by association" in a joint trial with Kenny, as well as the inadmissibility of large portions of Lab's testimony against them if they were not co-conspirators.

It is true that if the indictment charges jointly tried defendants with participation in a single conspiracy, but the evidence reveals multiple, discrete conspiracies, such a variance of proof may be so prejudicial as to require reversal. Reversal is called for "if the variance between the indictment and the proof affects the substantial rights of the parties." United States v. Friedman, 593 F.2d 109, 116 (9th Cir. 1979). . . .

The conspiracy alleged here takes the form of a wheel, with one central hub—Kenny—dealing with the "spokes"—the other defendants—in individual transactions. See Kotteakos v. United States, 328 U.S. 750 (1946). Without more, we agree that such a fact pattern may suggest at most a cluster of separate conspiracies, rather than the "concert of action, all the parties working together understandingly, with a single design for the accomplishment of a common purpose" found in a single conspiracy. United States v. Monroe, 552 F.2d 860, 862-63 (9th Cir. 1977). To follow the wheel metaphor, establishing a single conspiracy in a case such as this generally requires that the Government supply proof that the spokes are bound by a "rim"; that is, the circumstances must lead to an inference that some form of overall agreement exists.

The nature of that "rim" defies precise statement, but general principles are well established. The evidence must show that each of the defendants was involved. A meeting of the minds must be demonstrated. Mere association and activity with a conspiracy is insufficient. However, a formal agreement between the conspirators is not necessary. The agreement may be inferred from the defendants' acts pursuant to the fraudulent scheme or other circumstantial evidence. "The government need not show direct contact or explicit agreement between the defendants. It is sufficient to show that each defendant knew or had reason to know of the scope of the conspiracy and that each defendant had reason to believe that their own benefits were dependent upon the success of the entire venture." United States v. Kostoff, 585 F.2d 378, 380 (9th Cir. 1978). Once the existence of a conspiracy has been established, evidence of only a slight connection is necessary to convict a defendant of knowing participation in it.

In applying the foregoing legal standard to this case, we view the question of whether a single conspiracy has been proved, rather than multiple conspiracies, as essentially that of sufficiency of the evidence. . . . In the instant case, this Court would have to be able to say that *no* rational trier of fact could have found a single conspiracy on this evidence before we could disturb the jury's finding, implicit in its guilty verdict, that a single conspiracy had been proved.

We are persuaded, in reviewing the evidence presented below, that it amply supports a finding of a single conspiracy. The wheel, as it were, has been adequately "rimmed." In particular, we feel that the events surrounding Self Control Systems and the 1973 investigation provide a substantial basis for the inference that "each defendant knew or had reason to know of the scope of the conspiracy and that each defendant had reason to believe that their own benefits were dependent on the success of the entire venture." At the time the Navy investigation began, Kenny removed [SCS] records from OMC, Parker had SCS materials gathered and stored at his house, and the other defendants executed insincere statements that they had no dealings with outside contractors that would generate any conflict of interest with Navy work. The defendants' actions strongly suggest both an awareness of improper dealings between OMC and the NELC defendants, and a belief that an investigation of OMC must be avoided at all costs, lest it reveal past wrongdoing and jeopardize future schemes. The evidence indicates that illicit activities continued after the 1973 investigation, after the Navy investigation had been "killed" by Parker. The jury had sufficient evidence from which to find a single conspiracy.

NOTES AND QUESTIONS

1. Chains vs. Wheels. As the preceding cases demonstrate, the question of whether a conspiracy exists intertwines with the question of whom the putative conspiracy comprises. In a distribution conspiracy like the one at issue in *Loveland*, the alleged co-conspirators have a sequential relationship to one another, with each person's role forming a different link in the distribution chain. That metaphor of a chain can be useful in thinking through whether a common agreement exists among the various actors. As the U.S. Court of Appeals for the District of Columbia Circuit once explained:

> The existence of a chain helps us determine both the unlawful objective and the conspirators' intent. . . . [E]ach link in the chain may rely upon the other links in furtherance of the common interest. The street dealer relies upon his supplier; the supplier relies upon *his* supplier; and so on. The existence of such a "vertically integrated, loose-knit combination," United States v. Bynum, 485 F.2d 490, 495-496 (2d Cir. 1973), may raise the inference that each conspirator has agreed with the others (some

whose specific identity may be unknown) to further a common unlawful objective, e.g., the distribution of narcotics.

United States v. Tarantino, 846 F.2d 1384, 1392-1393 (D.C. Cir. 1988). Of course, as *Loveland* itself shows, even in a chain relationship there must be proof that the alleged "last link" is in fact agreeing to further distribute the drugs, as opposed to merely purchasing them for uses that are detached from those contemplated by agreements further up the chain.

In contrast to a chain conspiracy, a "wheel"-shaped conspiracy "is by its nature less likely to support the conclusion that the parties had a community of interest," rather than a series of overlapping but ultimately discrete bilateral agreements. For this reason, courts, like the *Kenny* court above, insist that "[f]or a wheel conspiracy to exist those people who form the wheel's spokes must have been aware of each other and must do something in furtherance of some single, illegal enterprise. Otherwise the conspiracy lacks 'the rim of the wheel to enclose the spokes.'" United States v. Levine, 546 F.2d 658, 663 (5th Cir. 1977). As one leading treatise summarizes, courts sometimes turn to a totality of the circumstances analysis to help determine whether a rim is present, looking to factors including the overlap in personnel and activity among the alleged co-conspirators, the overlap in time and location of participation, the similarity in the methods of operation, and the degree of shared purpose and interdependence necessary for the overall operation to succeed.[38]

2. Agreements vs. Overt Acts. At common law, an agreement to commit an unlawful act was the sole *actus reus* element for a conspiracy offense. *See, e.g.,* Mulcahy v. The Queen (1868) 3 LRE & I. App. 306, 317 ("When two agree to carry it into effect, the very plot is an act in itself . . . punishable if for a criminal object. . . ."). Some American jurisdictions adhere to the common law approach, particularly in circumstances where the underlying object of the conspiracy is a serious offense. *See, e.g.,* Model Penal Code §5.03(5). But when conspiracy was codified in the United States, many jurisdictions added a second requirement, known as the *overt-act requirement.* Consider, for example, the federal conspiracy statute, 18 U.S.C. §371, which reads:

> If two or more persons conspire either to commit any offense against the United States, or to defraud the United States . . . and one or more of such persons do *any act to effect the object of the conspiracy,* each shall be fined under this title or imprisoned not more than five years, or both.

In this statute, the word "conspire" is understood to contain within it the agreement element, to which the statute adds the overt act requirement via the language highlighted above. Note that the requirement is not that each member of the conspiracy must commit an overt act. So long as "one or more" of them does so, the requirement is satisfied.

As the Supreme Court once explained, "The function of the overt act in a conspiracy prosecution is simply to manifest 'that the conspiracy is at work'" and is not merely a plot "resting solely in the minds of the conspirators." Yates v. United States, 354 U.S. 298, 334 (1957). Consistent with this understanding, conduct sufficient to constitute an overt act can be only a small incremental action beyond the formation of the agreement itself. Consider the following case.

United States v. Bertling, 510 F.3d 804 (8th Cir. 2007). A jury found brothers Vincent Bertling and Karl Raymond Bertling guilty of one count of conspiracy to corruptly endeavor to influence, obstruct and impede justice . . . . [At the time in question, Vincent was in jail awaiting trial on separate charges related to his possession of drugs and firearms. Vincent learned that two individuals, Joanna and David Gillaspie, were expected to be witnesses against him in that case.] That same day, Vincent spoke with his brother, Karl, on a telephone from jail. At the beginning of the conversation, both parties were informed that the conversation would be recorded. Within the first minute of the conversation, Vincent told Karl that Joanna and David would be testifying against him. The following exchange then occurred:

Karl: Oh, man, ohhh. Alright, it's time to get a murder on[.]
Vincent: Huh?
Karl: I said it's time to get a murder on[.]
Vincent: Something.
Karl: Um hum. Yeah. I got an enforcer.

Immediately after these statements, Vincent told Karl that Joanna lived at her grandmother's house, further described as a lime-green house on G Street. Vincent also said that he thought Joanna worked at the Wal-Mart in South Sioux, but Karl corrected him and said she worked at Qwest. . . . This exchange all occurred within the first four minutes of the conversation. Finally, three minutes later, Vincent again mentioned Joanna and said that "it's Joanna that's trying to get me in trouble." After this, the brothers continued to talk about apparently unrelated matters for another eight minutes before the call terminated. . . .

[The jury convicted both men of conspiracy, finding that the phone conversation itself contained within it multiple overt acts in furtherance of the conspiracy.] Vincent and Karl argue [that] the overt acts that the jury found to be in furtherance of the conspiracy were at most specifications of the agreement, not overt acts in furtherance of it. However, any further discussions of how to achieve the purpose of the agreement can be overt acts in furtherance of the agreement. The conspiratorial agreement was established when Vincent responded to Karl's statement that it was time for a murder by saying, "something." In the remaining conversation, Vincent and Karl discussed information necessary to find and murder or intimidate the witnesses, including Karl's statement that he had an enforcer, Vincent's description of where Joanna lived, and their discussion of where Joanna worked. We see no reason why these plans and arrangements cannot constitute overt acts in furtherance of the conspiracy simply because they were contained in the same phone conversation in which the conspiracy was also established. We are aware of no cases, and defendants cite none, that support the proposition that overt acts must occur at a time separate from the formation of a conspiracy.

3. Agreeing with Purpose. Earlier in this chapter, we discussed the *mens rea* requirement for complicity liability with respect to the conduct that an accomplice encourages or assists a principal to commit. Specifically, we saw in *People v. Lauria* (p. 538), that to be guilty as an accomplice a person must aid or encourage someone else to commit a crime with the *purpose* of bringing such a crime about. *Lauria* also discussed the circumstances in which an accomplice's purpose could be inferred from her knowledge that the principal intends to commit a crime when the accomplice has a special interest in the principal's success. When it comes to conspiracy doctrine, this same basic inquiry repeats itself. Technically, the question arises in the context of examining what, exactly, the alleged co-conspirators agreed to do: Did they *agree* to commit a crime? Or did one person simply acquiesce to or refrain from thwarting the criminal plans of another? Put another way, the *actus reus* of conspiracy (agreement) subsumes within it an inquiry into the co-conspirators' mental states, because an agreement—to borrow from classic contract law—is best understood as a "meeting of the minds."

In examining whether a set of alleged co-conspirators' minds have met, conspiracy law generally follows the same doctrinal framework set out in *Lauria*. Indeed, as noted earlier, *Lauria* itself was a conspiracy case. For an additional example of this doctrinal framework being applied to an alleged conspiracy, consider the following case.

Commonwealth v. Camerano, 677 N.E.2d 678 (Mass. App. Ct. 1997). In order to convict Antonio Camerano, the defendant, of conspiracy to possess marihuana with intent to distribute it, the Commonwealth was bound to prove that Camerano had agreed with his tenant, Robert Howell, to cultivate, cure, process, and sell marihuana. . . . For $200 a month, Howell had arranged to rent [from Camerano] land on which [Howell] pitched his house trailer and on which, some time after the initial rental arrangement, he built his garden enclosure. . . .

Howell's garden enclosure was not a conventional greenhouse. The structure was twenty-eight feet wide, thirty feet long, and about eighteen feet high. The sides were of plywood nailed on a frame of two-by-fours and two-by-sixes. As noted, the structure was open to the sky. It had no windows and its single door was padlocked. That padlock the police pried off. Inside, they found 107 marihuana plants, twelve to fifteen feet high. Howell later said the marihuana plants were his. . . .

Here, the prosecution is quite right in pointing out that the jurors need not have believed Camerano when he testified that he did not know what marihuana smelled like and thought Howell was growing tomatoes and flowers in the enclosure. . . . The jury were entitled to infer that the very nature of the locked structure announced to Camerano that something unlawful was going on inside it. That leaves the government with having proved no more than awareness that Howell was growing contraband, not having proved beyond a reasonable doubt an agreement to further that undertaking. . . . There is no evidence that $200 per month was an untoward rent for parking a trailer, nor that Howell had used water in an amount that was unusual and had reflected itself in a higher than normal water bill received by Camerano. No key to the enclosure was found on Camerano's person or in his house, which the police had searched thoroughly. Nothing in the evidence suggested that Camerano used marihuana or would in some other manner share in the success, such as it might be, of Howell's operation. Even Camerano's presence was limited; he was away each working day at his job as a security guard. Awareness may translate to acquiescence but not to "affirmative acquiescence." *See* Commonwealth v. Beneficial Fin. Co., 275 N.E.2d 33, 69 (Mass. 1971). . . .

An agreement to participate in the illicit enterprise might be inferred from evidence such as conversations, writings, unusual rent, unusual water consumption, activity suggesting concurrence with the enterprise, or possession or constructive possession of the contraband. No evidence of that sort is present and the motion for a required finding of not guilty should have been allowed.

4. Feigned Conspirators. Earlier in this chapter, we saw that complicity doctrine accommodates undercover law enforcement tactics by attaching criminal liability even in circumstances where a state agent works with an unsuspecting defendant to commit a crime, as in the case of a feigned principal or accomplice. Modern conspiracy doctrine often follows a similar approach. Specifically, under the Model Penal Code and the majority of jurisdictions that have followed its lead, a defendant can be convicted of participating in a conspiracy *unilaterally.* As one court explains, "Under this unilateral approach to conspiratorial liability, a person may be guilty of conspiracy even though the other party to the criminal agreement is an undercover police officer or police informant who has no intention of actually committing a crime." State v. Roldan, 714 A.2d 351, 355 (N.J. 1998). There need not, in other words, be a *true* agreement between the parties. Rather, the defendant, in the words of the MPC drafters, is guilty if he acts "in the belief that the other party was with him." Model Penal Code and Commentaries §5.03 cmt. 2(b) at 400.

This modern approach "departs from the traditional notion of conspiracy as an entirely bilateral" agreement in which *both* co-conspirators must genuinely agree to commit a crime. State v. Del Fino, 495 A.2d 60, 62 (N.J. 1985). Notably, that older approach remains the law in a number of jurisdictions, including in federal courts. *See, e.g.,* United States v. Makhimetas, 991 F.2d 379, 383 (7th Cir. 1993) ("The elements of the crime [of conspiracy] are not satisfied unless one conspires with at least one true co-conspirator").[39]

5. "The Darling of the Modern Prosecutor's Nursery." As the foregoing notes indicate, conspiracy bears many conceptual similarities to complicity. Indeed, agreeing to commit a crime with someone else could be seen as *encouraging* that other person to commit a crime, such that in many cases a person who conspires to commit a crime will also aid and abet that crime.

And yet, notwithstanding this conceptual connection, prosecutors are likely to charge conspiracy if they have a plausible basis to do so, as opposed to or in addition to relying on a complicity theory of liability. The reason for this is stated crisply in *Loveland*: "the conspiracy charge affects much about trial and sentencing, all to the advantage of the prosecution." 825 F.3d at 557.

With respect to sentencing, the fact that conspiracy is a standalone offense allows prosecutors to threaten conspirators with longer prison terms than would be available if the defendants were charged only with the underlying object crime. *See* United States v. Wylie, 625 F.2d 1371, 1379 (9th Cir. 1980) ("[C]onsecutive sentences can be imposed after convictions for conspiracy and the underlying substantive offense."). Indeed, in some jurisdictions the punishment for conspiracy could be higher than the punishment for the object crime itself. Cases in which conspiracy penalties actually exceed the penalties for the object crime are rare, however, as many states follow the MPC approach, which caps the penalty for a conspiracy charge at the highest penalty authorized for any of the conspiracy's object crimes.[40]

Beyond potential sentencing consequences, there are other formal and informal prosecutorial advantages associated with a conspiracy charge. Formally, conspiracy prosecutions can be brought in any locale where the conspiracy operated, which means the "Government may, and often does, compel one to defend at a great distance from any place he ever did any act because some accused confederate did some trivial and by itself innocent act in the chosen district." Krulewitch v. United States, 336 U.S. 440, 452-453 (1949) (Jackson, J., concurring). Likewise, co-conspirators' statements in furtherance of the conspiracy are generally deemed not to be hearsay, a rule that substantially expands the universe of potentially incriminating evidence available to the prosecution. *See, e.g.,* Fed. R. Evid. 801(d)(2)(E). Finally, and less formally, there is the ever-present risk—particularly in long and complex conspiracy trials—that the jury will not be able to parse out who was really in an agreement with whom. As Justice Jackson in

Krulewitch observes, this risk puts the defendant in a conspiracy trial in "an uneasy seat."

> There generally will be evidence of wrongdoing by somebody. It is difficult for the individual to make his own case stand on its own merits in the minds of the jurors who are ready to believe that birds of a feather are flocked together. If he is silent, he is taken to admit it and if, as often happens, co-defendants can be prodded into accusing or contradicting each other, they convict each other. . . .

336 U.S. at 454 (Jackson, J., concurring). Taken together, these various tactical advantages combine to make a conspiracy charge the "darling of the modern prosecutor's nursery." Harrison v. United States, 7 F.2d 259, 263 (2d Cir. 1925). But they pale in comparison to the facet of conspiracy law that gives prosecutors the most leverage of all and that is most widely criticized: As a super-charged doctrine of vicarious liability, conspiracy law can make a person liable for crimes committed by others in a potentially sprawling and far-flung web of actors, even when he never intended those crimes to occur and perhaps never even knew the crimes were a possibility. It is to this final issue we turn next.

B.   *Vicarious Liability for Crimes of Co-Conspirators*

State v. Bridges

628 A.2d 270 (N.J. 1993)*

HANDLER, J. Defendant in this case was convicted by a jury of conspiracy and several substantive crimes, including murder, which were committed in the course of carrying out the conspiracy. . . . On September 2, 1988, defendant, Bennie Eugene Bridges, attended a birthday party with some fifty to sixty young people for sixteen-year-old Cheryl Smith in the basement of her home in Roebling, New Jersey. At about 12 a.m., Bridges had an argument with another guest, Andy Strickland. Shortly after the heated exchange, Bridges left the party, yelling angrily into the basement that he would soon return with his "boys." . . . [Bridges drove to Trenton and asked co-defendants Keith Bing and Eddie Rolle] to return to the party with him because he expected a confrontation. The two co-defendants agreed to accompany Bridges to the party in Roebling. On the way to the party . . . [the two] co-defendants told Bridges that they were carrying guns "so [the partygoers will] stay back." According to Bridges, the guns were necessary "to intimidate the majority of the boys at the party."

---

* Editor's Note: Portions of this opinion have been reordered from the original.

Bridges and his companions returned to the party at approximately 2 a.m. . . . The trio entered the basement, and Bridges began to argue again with Strickland. Defendant said he would not leave the house until he "fucked somebody up." John Raspberry, a friend of Strickland, interceded and agreed to fight. A crowd then gathered to watch Bridges and Raspberry begin their fight . . . . Bing shouted to the crowd, "Nobody jump in," and Rolle warned, "Nobody here is Superman." A witness testified that the statement by Rolle was meant to imply that nobody in the crowd was bullet-proof.

During the fight Bridges was able to get on top of Raspberry, at which point either Strickland or another member of the crowd pulled defendant off and struck him in the head. At the same time, a member of the crowd struck Bing in the face. Bing immediately drew a .22 caliber revolver, and Rolle pulled out a .32 caliber revolver. Rolle pointed the gun at the crowd and then fired it into the air. Numerous shots were then fired into the crowd as the onlookers tried to flee. Shawn Lockley was shot in the chest and died at the scene; Paul Suszynski was injured by a bullet in the shoulder.

. . . The State charged Bridges with conspiracy to commit the crimes of possession of a weapon for an unlawful purpose; conspiracy to possess a weapon without a permit; and conspiracy to commit aggravated assault, as well as those substantive crimes. . . . In addition, the State charged defendant with murder, the lesser crime of aggravated manslaughter, and possession of a defaced firearm "by being legally accountable for the conduct of a co-conspirator whose acts are the natural and probable consequences of the conspiracy." [Bridges was convicted after trial of the conspiracy counts, the assault counts, the unlawful possession of a firearm counts, and murder, and was sentenced] to a term of life imprisonment with a thirty-year period of parole ineligibility. . . .

The provision of the New Jersey Code of Criminal Justice that posits criminal liability on the basis of participation in a conspiracy is silent with respect to its culpability requirement. It provides: "A person is legally accountable for the conduct of another person when . . . [h]e is engaged in a conspiracy with such other person." N.J. Stat. Ann. §2C:2–6b(4).

. . . [T]he basic principles of the substantive law concerning co-conspirator liability in this State [hold] a conspirator responsible for all criminal acts committed in furtherance of the conspiracy. . . . [Our approach is] strongly influenced by the United States Supreme Court's decision in *Pinkerton v. United States,* 328 U.S. 640 (1946). The Supreme Court in *Pinkerton,* dealing with the liability of co-conspirators, extended the settled law concerning liability for an overt act to all substantive acts "committed by one of the conspirators in furtherance of the unlawful project," that is, "acts done in execution of the enterprise." *Id.* at 647. Significantly, the Supreme Court added:

A different case would arise if the substantive offense committed by one of the conspirators was not in fact done in furtherance of the conspiracy, did not fall within the scope of the unlawful project or *was merely a part of the ramification of the plan which could not be reasonably foreseen as a necessary or natural consequence of the unlawful agreement.* But as we read this record, that is not the case.

Id. at 647-648. The general rule of co-conspirator liability that [derives] from *Pinkerton* is that so long as a conspiracy is still in existence, "an overt act of one partner may be the act of all without any new agreement specifically directed to that act," provided the substantive act could "be reasonably foreseen as a necessary or natural consequence of the unlawful agreement." State v. Stein, 360 A.2d 347, 359 (N.J. 1976).

The Appellate Division majority reasoned that *Pinkerton* was not designed to "read out of vicarious liability the element of intent vis-a-vis the substantive offense." It . . . thus interpreted *Pinkerton* to prescribe a requirement of subjective foreseeability of the criminal consequences as a basis for vicarious co-conspirator liability. That understanding of *Pinkerton* is not supported. Although the [rule], uttered as *dictum,* in *Pinkerton* has been subject to criticism, it has not been disputed that it purported to impose vicarious liability on each conspirator for the acts of others based on an objective standard of reasonable foreseeability. . . . [I]t was understood that the liability of a co-conspirator under the objective standard of reasonable foreseeability would be broader than that of an accomplice, where the defendant must actually foresee and intend the result of his or her acts. . . .

The dissent suggests that a standard of such breadth . . . eliminates any requirement of culpability [and] is inconsistent with the Code and would offend due process. The Legislature, however, in fashioning the Code provisions for imposing vicarious liability on a co-conspirator, did not eliminate all requirements of culpability. That is evident from a clear understanding of the standard derived from *Stein* and *Pinkerton* and from other provisions of the Code itself. . . .

[T]he *Stein* Court's understanding that its standard for imposing liability on a co-conspirator was subject to limitations is reflected in the Court's application of that standard. . . . The defendant in *Stein* was a Trenton attorney who suggested to an "underworld figure" that a particular home would be a good target for a burglary because the residents kept large amounts of cash on hand. About a year after the defendant's last conspiratorial discussion with the "underworld figure," [individuals associated with that figure broke into the residence in question. Stein] was not at the scene and did not participate. The police arrived while the robbery was in progress, [at which point the robbers] took the homeowner's wife and daughter hostage in an attempt to escape. During the ensuing high-speed chase, the robbers crashed into a road block and critically injured two police officers. The mother and daughter, however, were freed. . . .

[T]he original conspiracy [in *Stein*] contemplated a burglary and theft of a household. The Court found that the armed robbery [committed in the course of the burglary] was within the scope of the conspiracy to steal currency from the victim's home. Moreover, the Court considered the assault on the wife as the robbers entered the home "clearly a foreseeable event in the course of an unlawful invasion of the house for criminal purposes by armed men," and therefore not too remote from the conspiracy for defendant to be held vicariously liable. In contrast, the Court found that the defendant[, who was not present when the robbery occurred and who had last spoken to the actual robbers many months earlier, when he encouraged them to steal from the house,] was not liable for the kidnapping of the occupants and the ensuing assaults of the pursuing police officers, concluding that, under the circumstances, it would be unreasonable for a factfinder to find beyond a reasonable doubt that those crimes were necessary or natural consequences of the conspiracy.

Stein's practical limitation of the reasonably foreseeable standard is also evident from its reliance on the early case of *People v. Payne*, 194 N.E. 539 (Ill. 1935). The defendant there conspired to commit a robbery. In a role analogous to that of the defendant in *Stein*, the defendant in *Payne* showed the four co-conspirators the targeted house and claimed that its residents kept a large amount of cash on hand. Also, like the defendant in *Stein*, the defendant in *Payne* did not accompany the co-conspirators on the actual robbery and was thus not present when the four murdered the homeowner during the attempt. The *Payne* court affirmed the defendant's conviction for murder, observing that "it might reasonably be anticipated that an attempted robbery would meet with resistance, during which the victim might be shot." *Id.* at 543.

[Other cases have] addressed conspiratorial liability for consequential acts committed outside the [conspiracy's] originally-intended scope. [Such cases] hold that a conspirator may be held responsible for reasonably foreseeable but originally unintended substantive crimes if the relationship between the conspirator and the substantive crime is not too attenuated. . . . Significantly, the *Stein* case directly addressed the issue of criminal responsibility of a conspirator for the commission of offenses "having some causal connection with the conspiracy but not in the contemplation of the conspirator." 360 A.2d at 359. That is the issue in this case. In resolving that issue, *Stein* formulated a standard for vicarious criminal liability of a co-conspirator based on objective foreseeability that is circumscribed by the requirement that the substantive crime be closely connected to the conspiracy. . . .

We appreciate the concern of the [dissent], that such a standard of vicarious liability for conspirators differs from that of accomplices. Although conspirator liability is circumscribed by the requirement of a close causal connection between the conspiracy and the substantive crime, that standard concededly is less strict than that defining accomplice accountability. It is, however, evident that the Legislature chose to address the special dangers inherent in group activity and therefore intended to include the crime of conspiracy as a distinctive basis for vicarious criminal liability. The legislative history supports the conclusion that the liability for conspirators was intended to be broader than other measures of criminal accountability for vicarious crimes. Accordingly, we conclude, and now hold, that a co-conspirator may be liable for the commission of substantive criminal acts that are not within the scope of the conspiracy if they are reasonably foreseeable as the necessary or natural consequences of the conspiracy.

We fully appreciate that the application of a standard based on this holding will be difficult and complicated because it is necessarily fact-sensitive. Consequently, trial courts must endeavor to explain to juries, as part of their instructions, that when determining criminal liability under that standard, they should consider whether the commission of the substantive crime is actually beyond the scope of the original conspiracy, and if so, whether it is objectively foreseeable or reasonably to be anticipated that the substantive crime would be committed in view of the obvious risks surrounding the attempts to execute the conspiracy, and whether the substantive crime occurred or was committed in a manner that was too far removed or too remote from the objectives of the original conspiracy. Those considerations should enable a jury to determine whether the commission of substantive crimes not within the scope of the conspiracy are reasonably foreseeable as the necessary or natural consequences of the conspiracy and constitutes a just basis for imposing criminal liability on a conspirator for the commission of those crimes. . . .

According to the [court of appeals majority below], Bridges could have foreseen that Bing or Rolle would recklessly fire their handguns, but could not have foreseen that one of the two co-defendants "would either purposely or knowingly cause death or serious injury" to any of the partygoers. . . .

The jury found beyond a reasonable doubt that Bridges had conspired with Bing and Rolle to commit fourth-degree aggravated assault, possess firearms for an unlawful purpose, and possess firearms without a permit. The facts show that after an argument at a party, Bridges angrily threatened those at the party that he was going to retrieve his companions from Trenton. Bridges in fact did travel from Roebling to Trenton and back, returning to the party at 2 a.m. Further, Bridges knew that his cohorts, acquaintances Bing and Rolle, had loaded guns, and even admitted to thinking the guns were necessary. In light of those facts, the jury does not appear to have unreasonably convicted on the fourth-degree aggravated-assault and weapons charges, because those substantive crimes were the direct object of the conspiracy.

The conspiracy did not have as its objective the purposeful killing of another person. Nevertheless, the evidence discloses that the conspiratorial plan contemplated bringing loaded guns to keep a large contingent of young hostile partygoers back from a beating of one of their friends, and that it could be anticipated that the weapon might be fired at the crowd. Also inferable from the evidence is that hostilities might escalate in the course of carrying out that conspiracy. Thus, defendant traveled far and wide to find people on the streets of Trenton at 12:30 a.m. who would back him up in his fight. And Bridges did not balk when the co-conspirators [revealed they were carrying] loaded guns. Further, in the course of carrying out the conspiracy, just prior to Bridges' street fight at the scene, Rolle warned the crowd that "Nobody here is Superman," which was thought to imply that nobody in the hostile crowd could stop a bullet. Yet, Bridges did not back off of his intention to "fuck somebody up."

From that evidence a jury could conclude that a reasonably foreseeable risk and a probable and natural consequence of carrying out a plan to intimidate the crowd by using loaded guns would be that one of the gunslingers would intentionally fire at somebody, and, under the circumstances, that act would be sufficiently connected to the original conspirat[ori]al plan to provide a just basis for a determination of guilt for that substantive crime. . . .

O'HERN, J., concurring in part and dissenting in part. . . . An interpretation of the provisions of the Code of Criminal Justice that would allow a sentence of life imprisonment to be imposed on the basis of the negligent appraisal of a risk that another would commit a homicide, conflicts with the internal structure of the Code. . . . If we assume, as the majority does, that Bridges did not intend that Shawn Lockley be killed, he could not have been convicted . . . as an accomplice to the murder. "Because of a moral intuition about holding one accountable for the wrongdoing of another the extent of accomplice liability has been defined carefully in our Code of Criminal Justice." State v. Weeks, 526 A.2d 1077, 1079-1080 (N.J. 1987). Under the Code, "By definition an accomplice must be a person who acts with the *purpose* of promoting or facilitating the commission of *the* substantive offense for which he is charged as an accomplice." State v. White, 484 A.2d 691, 694 (N.J. 1984). [Nor could Bridges] have been found guilty of conspiracy to commit murder. A person is guilty of a conspiracy to commit an offense only if "*with the purpose* of promoting or facilitating its commission he" or she agrees with another person that they will "engage in conduct which constitutes such crime" or agrees to aid such person "in the planning or commission of such crime." N.J. Stat. Ann. §2C:5-2a (emphasis added).

. . . The Code establishes a carefully-measured grid of criminal responsibility. . . . It presents a complete and carefully structured system that fits punishments to the crimes committed. Thus, one who causes the death of another with the knowledge or purpose to kill will be guilty of murder and can be sentenced to death in certain circumstances or to life imprisonment with a minimum of thirty years without parole. . . . The manslaughter offenses require a finding that an actor causing death has exhibited a reckless disregard for human life. When that recklessness is in disregard of a *probability* that death may occur, the offense is aggravated manslaughter and carries a penalty of up to thirty years in prison. When the proof shows reckless disregard of a possibility of causing death, the offense is reckless manslaughter and carries the penalty of a first-degree crime, up to twenty years in prison. Except for one form of vehicular homicide, *no negligent homicide* exists under New Jersey law, much less a crime of negligent murder.

In describing the purposes of the Code, Dean Robert E. Knowlton explained that one of its main goals was "to achieve greater individual justice through a closer relation between guilt and culpability, requiring workable definitions of the various culpability factors." *Comments upon the New Jersey Penal Code*, 32 Rutgers L. Rev. 1, 2 (1979). . . . The Court has contradicted those principles of justice by making one such as defendant more likely to be found guilty of murder than one charged as an actual conspirator, or as an accomplice to murder, or even as one who attempted murder. In each of those cases, one would have to intend the killing to be convicted of murder. The members of a criminal combination can be prosecuted under one of three theories: as a principal in the crime, as an accomplice to the crime, or as one who conspired to commit the crime. Most often, the conspirator's act will be further removed in time from the criminal act than that of the principal or accomplice. Yet the Court penalizes the conspirator more severely than the principal or accomplice, each of whom would have to have a specific intent, at least knowledge, and in the case of an accomplice, the actual purpose to commit the completed crime. . . .

In a long series of cases, we have attempted to seek rational and proportional punishment for crimes. This case is an example of the most extreme sort—life imprisonment with no possibility of parole for thirty years on the basis of a negligent mental state. The *Pinkerton*-type rule accepted by the Court "may implicate a person, on the basis of negligence or stupidity, in very serious offenses which he never contemplated or agreed, expressly or by implication, to have perpetrated." Peter Buscemi, Note, *Conspiracy: Statutory Reform Since the Model Penal Code*, 75 Colum. L. Rev. 1122, 1152 (1975).

United States v. Alvarez

755 F.2d 830 (11th Cir. 1985)

KRAVITCH, J. On December 2, 1982, in a run-down motel in the Little Havana section of Miami, Florida, a cocaine deal turned into tragedy when a shoot-out erupted between the dealers and two undercover special agents from the Bureau of Alcohol, Tobacco, and Firearms (BATF). During the shoot-out, one of the BATF agents was killed and the other agent, along with two of the cocaine dealers, was seriously wounded . . . . All of the [seven] appellants were convicted of conspiracy to possess with intent to distribute cocaine and possession with intent to distribute cocaine [and five of them were convicted of murder of a federal agent. We focus our analysis here on appellant Portal].

FACTS

[Undercover agents Rios and D'Atri contacted appellants Concepcion and Portal and told them they wished to purchase three kilograms of cocaine. Concepcion answered that the cocaine was available at a price of $49,000 per kilogram. The four men met at the Hurricane Motel in Miami.]

Concepcion and the two agents entered the motel office, while Portal remained outside. Surveillance agents stationed near the motel observed Portal acting as a "lookout." The agents saw Portal closely watching passing cars and pedestrians, and noticed a handgun-shaped bulge on Portal's left side, under his shirt.

[The agents were taken to a room within the motel, where they waited for over an hour for the drugs to be delivered. Inside] D'Atri noticed [another appellant, named Simon,] who was partially seated on and resting against the armrest of a couch, looking out the window and nervously fidgeting with the leather pouch that was suspected to contain a weapon. . . . D'Atri heard the surveillance and backup agents arrive at the door of the motel office. Suddenly, Agent Rios shouted, "No," and D'Atri heard a gunshot. [O]ut of the corner of his eye, D'Atri saw Simon and Agent Rios engaged in a struggle. D'Atri heard another gunshot, and he turned to help Agent Rios. D'Atri lunged at Simon, but, as he reached Simon, he felt tremendous pain in his forehead and left arm. [In the ensuing shootout, Agent Rios was killed by a bullet to his head, which ballistics determined to have been fired by one of the conspirators in the apartment.]

DISCUSSION

. . . Under *Pinkerton*, each member of a conspiracy is criminally liable for any crime committed by a coconspirator during the course and in furtherance of the conspiracy, unless the crime "did not fall within the scope of the unlawful project, or was merely a part of the ramifications of the plan which could not be reasonably foreseen as a necessary or natural consequence of the unlawful agreement." Pinkerton v. United States, 328 U.S. 640, 647-648 (1946). . . . We conclude that, although [Portal's murder conviction] may represent an unprecedented application of *Pinkerton*, such an application is not improper.

. . . The application of the *Pinkerton* doctrine to a particular set of facts ultimately is for the jury to decide. . . . Upon reviewing the record, we find ample evidence to support the jury's conclusion that the murder was a reasonably foreseeable consequence of the drug conspiracy alleged in the indictment. In making this determination, we rely on two critical factors. First, the evidence clearly established that the drug conspiracy was designed to effectuate the sale of a large quantity of cocaine. The conspirators agreed to sell Agents Rios and D'Atri three kilograms of cocaine for a total price of $147,000. . . . [This] drug conspiracy was no nickel-and-dime operation; under any standards, the amount of drugs and money involved was quite substantial.

Second, based on the amount of drugs and money involved, the jury was entitled to infer that, at the time the cocaine sale was arranged, the conspirators must have been aware of the likelihood (1) that at least some of their number would be carrying weapons, and (2) that deadly force would be used, if necessary, to protect the conspirators' interests. We have previously acknowledged the "nexus" between weapons and drugs and we have also recognized that weapons have become "tools of the trade" for those involved in the distribution of illicit drugs. United States v. Montes-Cardenas, 746 F.2d 771, 776-777 (11th Cir. 1984). . . . In light of these observations, and in view of the amount of drugs and money involved in the instant case, the jury's inference was both reasonable and proper.

In our opinion, these two critical factors provided ample support for the jury's conclusion that the murder was a reasonably foreseeable consequence of the drug conspiracy alleged in the indictment. . . . Because we find that the evidence in this case was more than sufficient to allow a reasonable jury to conclude that the murder was a reasonably foreseeable consequence of the drug conspiracy alleged in the indictment, we hold that the court did not err by submitting the *Pinkerton* issue to the jury.

[Portal argues that, even if the murder was reasonably foreseeable, his murder conviction nevertheless should be reversed because the murder was sufficiently distinct from the intended purposes of the drug conspiracy and his individual role in the conspiracy was sufficiently minor.] We are not persuaded.

It is well established that, under the *Pinkerton* doctrine, "[a] co-conspirator is vicariously liable for the acts of another co-conspirator even though he may not have directly participated in those acts, his role in the crime was minor, or the evidence against a co-defendant more damaging." United States v. Gagnon, 721 F.2d 672, 676 (9th Cir. 1983). . . . We acknowledge that the instant case is not a typical *Pinkerton* case. Here, the murder of Agent Rios was not within the originally intended scope of the conspiracy, but instead occurred as a result of an unintended turn of events. We have not found, nor has the government cited, any authority for the proposition that all conspirators, regardless of individual culpability, may be held responsible under *Pinkerton* for reasonably foreseeable but originally unintended substantive crimes.[25] Furthermore, we are mindful of the potential due process limitations on the *Pinkerton* doctrine in cases involving attenuated relationships between the conspirator and the substantive crime.

Nevertheless, these considerations do not require us to reverse the murder conviction[] of Portal . . . for we cannot accept [his] assessment of [his] individual culpability. . . . Portal served as a look-out in front of the Hurricane Motel during part of the negotiations that led to the shoot-out, and the evidence indicated that he was armed. . . . The evidence that Portal was carrying a weapon demonstrated that he anticipated the possible use of deadly force to protect the conspirators' interests. . . .

We find . . . that the relationship between [Portal] and the murder was not so attenuated as to run afoul of the potential due process limitations on the *Pinkerton* doctrine. We therefore hold that *Pinkerton* liability for the murder of Agent Rios properly was imposed on [Portal], and we decline to reverse [his] murder conviction[] on this ground.[27]

NOTES AND QUESTIONS

1. **Pinkerton*'s Breadth.** In *Pinkerton v. United States*, 328 U.S. 640 (1946), two brothers, Walter and Daniel Pinkerton, conspired to sell bootleg liquor without paying federal taxes. "The proof showed that Walter alone committed the substantive crimes. There was none to establish that Daniel participated in them, aided and abetted Walter in committing them, or knew that he had done so. Daniel in fact was in the penitentiary, under sentence for other crimes, when some of Walter's crimes were done." *Id.* at 648 (Rutledge, J., dissenting in part). Nonetheless, on the basis of the underlying agreement to commit tax fraud, Daniel was convicted not only of conspiracy but of the substantive offenses committed by Walter.

On these facts, holding Daniel liable for Walter's crimes represents at most only a modest expansion of the mode of liability at issue in complicity

---

25. . . . At trial in the instant case, the government's attorney argued that *Pinkerton* liability for Agent Rios' murder properly could be imposed on all of the conspirators, and expressed the view that prosecutorial discretion would protect truly "minor" participants . . . from liability for the far more serious crimes committed by their coconspirators. We do not find this argument persuasive. In our view, the liability of such "minor" participants must rest on a more substantial foundation than the mere whim of the prosecutor.

27. Although our decision today extends the *Pinkerton* doctrine to cases involving reasonably foreseeable but originally unintended substantive crimes, we emphasize that we do so only within narrow confines. Our holding is limited to conspirators who played more than a "minor" role in the conspiracy, or who had actual knowledge of at least some of the circumstances and events culminating in the reasonably foreseeable but originally unintended substantive crime.

cases. As the *Pinkerton* Court explained, "The unlawful agreement contemplated precisely what was done. It was formed for the purpose. The act done was in execution of the enterprise." *Id.* at 647 (majority opinion). The *Pinkerton* Court, in other words, held Daniel vicariously liable for Walter's commission of the conspiracy's object crimes, the very crimes Daniel had intended that they would commit.

As the *Alvarez* court would later explain, this application of what has come to be known as *Pinkerton* liability is both the narrowest and the least controversial. A slightly broader application of the doctrine extends the co-conspirator's liability to "cases in which the substantive crime is not a primary goal of the alleged conspiracy, but directly facilitates the achievement of one of the primary goals." 755 F.2d at 850 n.24. For example, in a drug conspiracy, the participants may not have directly agreed to possess unregistered firearms, but that "substantive crime is squarely within the intended scope of the conspiracy," insofar as firearms are essentially tools of the trade for many drug conspiracies. *Id.* In this respect, conspiracy liability is again not much broader than complicity liability, given that (as noted earlier in this chapter) an accomplice is typically liable for any crimes "fairly envisaged in the purposes of [her] association" with the principal. Model Penal Code and Commentaries §2.06 cmt. 6(b) at 311.

But *Pinkerton* liability often goes further. In a paragraph of dicta that on its face imposes *limits* on conspiracy's vicarious liability, the Supreme Court sowed the seeds of *Pinkerton*'s breadth. That paragraph, quoted in *Bridges* above, reads as follows:

> A different case would arise if the substantive offense committed by one of the conspirators was not in fact done in furtherance of the conspiracy, did not fall within the scope of the unlawful project, or was merely a part of the ramifications of the plan which could not be reasonably foreseen as a necessary or natural consequence of the unlawful agreement.

Treating this paragraph as defining the scope of co-conspirators' vicarious liability, many courts in *Pinkerton*'s wake have developed the broad view of *Pinkerton* reflected in *Bridges* and *Alvarez* above: co-conspirators are vicariously liable for the actions of any member of the conspiracy that are reasonably foreseeable consequences of the unlawful agreement. When courts and lawyers speak of *Pinkerton* liability, they are often referring to this broad standard.[41]

2. Pinkerton's Point of Reference: A Conspiracy to Do What? As the portions of *Alvarez* quoted in the preceding note suggest, it is possible to imagine *Pinkerton* liability as expanding outward in concentric circles, starting with the object crime, extending to crimes that "directly facilitate" the object crime, and then applying most broadly to any crimes that are "reasonably foreseeable consequences" of the conspiracy. Understood as such, it becomes clear that the scope of *Pinkerton* liability bears a direct relation-ship to the scope of the conspiracy itself, along two dimensions: *What* did the conspirators agree to do? And *who* exactly is part of the conspiracy? The broader the conspiracy along either or both of these dimensions, the more sweeping *Pinkerton* liability will be.

Consider first the question of what the conspirators agreed to do. In practice, the burden is on the state to articulate, in the charging document, the object of the alleged conspiracy by specifying the crime or crimes the defendants allegedly agreed to commit. *See* United States v. Schramm, 75 F.3d 156, 163 (3d Cir. 1996) ("In cases which involve a conspiracy charge, the illegal object of the conspiracy is an essential element of the offense and must be included in the indictment."). The critical question for trial, then, is whether the state can prove that the defendant "entered into an agreement and knew that the agreement had the specific unlawful purpose charged in the indictment." *Id.* at 159.

Depending on the facts and circumstances, it may be in the prosecu-tion's interest to define the object of the conspiracy broadly or narrowly. On the one hand, if the conspiracy's object is defined broadly, *Pinkerton* will have a longer reach: more crimes will facilitate or be reasonably foresee-able consequences of the conspiracy. This allows the prosecutor to file or threaten to file a larger set of charges against each alleged co-conspirator. On the other hand, by charging broadly, the state may make its own case harder to prove. This is because, to obtain a conviction, the state must prove that the defendant had at least a general awareness of the conspir-acy's breadth and intended to advance its broad objectives. United States v. Evans, 970 F.2d 663, 670 (10th Cir. 1992). The broader the alleged object of the conspiracy, the harder this may be to do, particularly with respect to more minor players who may not know or be invested in the conspiracy's wider-ranging aims.

At the same time, narrowly specified conspiracies present their own advantages and disadvantages for the state. Sometimes the state wants to define the object of the conspiracy narrowly to trigger certain special rules or penalties. For example, under a given statutory scheme, a conspiracy to import drugs may carry higher penalties than a more generally defined conspiracy to smuggle contraband. Yet just as it can be difficult to prove that the defendant understood the expanse of a broadly alleged conspir-atorial object, it can also be difficult to prove that he contemplated a very narrow and specific objective. In *United States v. Idowu*, 157 F.3d 265 (3d Cir. 1998), for example, the government charged the defendant with conspir-acy to possess with intent to distribute more than a kilogram of heroin, an offense carrying a mandatory minimum sentence of 10 years in prison. 21 U.S.C. §§841, 846. The Third Circuit overturned the defendant's convic-tion, determining that, even though the defendant knew he was involved in "some form of illicit activity, . . . there was an absence of evidence that [he] knew the subject matter of the transaction was the purchase of more than one kilogram of heroin." 157 F.3d at 268-270.

As the U.S. Court of Appeals for the First Circuit later explained in a similar case:

> A drug conspirator need not know all of the details of the conspiracy, but it is hard to imagine how someone furnishing a peripheral service to a drug conspiracy could be deemed to "join" that conspiracy unless he knew *both* that the drug conspiracy existed and that the peripheral service being furnished was designed to foster the conspiracy. Both points are critical. No one can join a conspiracy without knowledge of its existence — the gravamen is an *agreement* to commit an offense. And even with knowledge that a conspiracy exists, one who allegedly "joins" only by furnishing some peripheral service can hardly be deemed to have "agreed" to conspire through his conduct unless he has the aim to forward or assist the conspiracy.

United States v. García-Torres, 280 F.3d 1, 4 (1st Cir. 2002).

Taking these points all together, two important features of *Pinkerton* liability emerge. First, the advantages and disadvantages of describing a given conspiracy broadly or narrowly are factually and contextually contingent. A particular approach might benefit the prosecution in one case, but an alternative might be better in another. And second, the prosecutor, as the author of the charging instrument, gets to choose how the conspiracy will be defined in each case — and can tailor that definition to maximize her tactical position.

3. Pinkerton's Point of Reference: A Conspiracy with Whom? As noted earlier in this chapter, *Pinkerton* liability also puts renewed focus on the question of who is deemed to be in a conspiracy. Recall the wheel and chain-link conspiracies discussed at the beginning of this section. In the case of the former, if the wheel is held to be "rimmed," such that all of the relevant actors are deemed to be in a single conspiracy with one another, that could substantially increase the number of people whose crimes can be attributed to one another, and thus substantially expand the universe of *Pinkerton* liability for each individual actor. Likewise, if a person at the retail end of the chain (someone like Mr. Loveland) is held to be in an unbroken line of conspiracy with the potentially heavier-hitting defendants at the manufacturing and importing end of the chain, that last-link defendant could be on the hook for a slew of serious substantive crimes committed by such individuals, including but not limited to trafficking in substantially larger quantities of contraband. In short, the force of *Pinkerton* liability for any given defendant can vary substantially depending on where the conspiratorial lines among the actors are drawn. Consider, in this context, the following two excerpts.

Alex Kreit, *Vicarious Criminal Liability and the Constitutional Dimensions of Pinkerton*, 57 Am. U. L. Rev. 585, 621-622 (2008). The well-known case *Anderson v. Superior Court*, 177 P.2d 315 (Cal. 1947), [is] frequently cited by *Pinkerton* critics as an example of how a broad application of the doctrine can result in potentially unbounded vicarious liability. . . . The defendant in *Anderson* referred pregnant women who were seeking an abortion to a doctor in exchange for a fee for each woman on whom [the doctor] performed the procedure. The doctor had a similar arrangement with sixteen other individuals and all were jointly indicted for conspiracy as well as, vicariously, for every abortion performed by the doctor. Anderson challenged her indictment on the ground that each agreement between the doctor and the referring party was a separate conspiracy. The court rejected this claim and held that there was a single conspiracy, likening it to a business with a "common design" in which each party plays a role in an ongoing enterprise. Accordingly, it found that Anderson could be held vicariously liable for *all* of the abortions performed in furtherance of the conspiracy, including abortions based on referrals by other defendants in which she played no part.

The result in *Anderson* demonstrates how applying *Pinkerton* based on a court's definition of a conspiracy, rather than each defendant's individual agreement or actions, can divorce liability from personal guilt. First, though the defendant may have been able to foresee that the doctor was performing other abortions in general, there is no indication she could have foreseen the extent of his business or any particular abortion apart from the ones that resulted from her referrals. By holding her liable for all of the doctor's abortions based on the scope of the "conspiracy" defined from the perspective of its ringleader, the doctor, the court in effect made the defendant strictly liable for the size of the operation without regard to what may have been foreseeable to her. . . . Similarly, and perhaps more importantly in this case, the defendant's actions did not have a causal relationship with any of the abortions that resulted from referrals by other women. Those abortions may have furthered the broadly defined "conspiracy" from the perspective of the doctor, but had at most a "tenuous," circumstantial relationship with the defendant's agreement and conduct. Anderson did not directly benefit from, or contribute to, the abortions resulting from referrals to the doctor by other women. . . . In short, as the drafters of the Model Penal Code observed, applying the *Pinkerton* test to a broadly defined conspiracy, without regard to each defendant's knowledge of the breadth of the conspiracy, separates vicarious liability from a defendant's culpability and makes him strictly liable for potentially "thousands of additional offenses of which he was completely unaware and which he did not influence at all." Model Penal Code §2.06 cmt. 6(a) at 307 (1985).

United States v. Evans, 970 F.2d 663 (10th Cir. 1992). A conspirator "need not know of the existence or identity of the other members of the conspiracy or the full extent of the conspiracy," United States v. Metro. Enters., 728 F.2d 444, 451 (10th Cir. 1984), but he or she must have a general awareness of both the scope and the objective of the enterprise to be regarded as a coconspirator. This is not to say, however, that a defendant may be convicted of a conspiracy that defies common sense simply because he or she possesses a general awareness of the breadth of its illegal activities. For example, at oral argument, the government suggested that a drug dealer who knows that his supply can be traced to the Medellín cartel has joined a vast conspiracy with the members of the cartel to distribute crack illegally for profit. Under such an approach, a small-time drug dealer could be held responsible for all of the drugs originated by the cartel for sentencing purposes, resulting in a guaranteed life sentence. Such an approach would pervert the concept of conspiracy. Mere knowledge of illegal activity, even in conjunction with participation in a small part of the conspiracy, does not by itself establish that a person has joined in the grand conspiracy.

Questions: Note the test articulated by the *Evans* court above. Now apply that test to the two cases, including the drug conspiracy described in *Evans* itself: Did the person referring women to the abortion provider in *Anderson* "have a general awareness of both the scope and the objective of the enterprise"? Does "a drug dealer who knows that his supply can be traced to the Medillin cartel" have a "general awareness of both the scope and the objective of the enterprise"? If the answer to either of these questions appears to be yes, what does that suggest about the reach of *Pinkerton* liability for each of these individuals? Would such an application of *Pinkerton* "pervert the concept of conspiracy"? If so, what alternative doctrinal formulations or rules would address that problem?

4. **Pinkerton's *Cognates: The* Luparello *Doctrine.*** While *Pinkerton* is often criticized as opening the door to excessively broad applications of vicarious liability, it bears noting that other criminal doctrines previously discussed (in this chapter and elsewhere) can create similarly broad vicarious liability rules. Some jurisdictions, for example, take a different approach to *accomplice* liability from the approach set out earlier in this chapter. A lead case capturing this alternative model is *People v. Luparello*, 231 Cal. Rptr. 832 (Cal. Ct. App. 1987), which held that accomplices are responsible not only for conduct they purposely aid or encourage, but also for the "criminal harms they have naturally, probably and foreseeably put in motion." *Id.* at 849. This standard tracks the *Pinkerton* standard itself and, some scholars argue, may stretch even more broadly than *Pinkerton* liability, at least in jurisdictions where the latter has been cabined or narrowed (as discussed in the notes below). As of 2008, 20 states appeared to follow the *Luparello* approach to accomplice liability.[42]

5. *Pinkerton's Cognates: The Felony Murder Rule.* As previously discussed in Chapter Four, the felony murder doctrine also echoes conspiracy liability in certain respects, insofar as the doctrine can make a person liable for deaths caused by a co-felon, who will typically also be both an accomplice and a co-conspirator in the underlying predicate felony. Generally speaking, there is "[n]o distinction . . . between principals and aiders and abettors for purposes of felony murder liability. Only intent to commit the underlying felony need be proved." Prophet v. United States, 602 A.2d 1087, 1095 (D.C. 1992). Put another way, once it is clear that a person has committed the predicate felony—including as an accomplice—the felony murder doctrine applies, meaning that "all accomplices are culpable for the resulting death." West v. United States, 499 A.2d 860, 866 (D.C. 1985).

Of course, as described in Chapter Four, felony murder doctrine is generally subject to principles of proximate causation. But notably, in defining the boundaries of felony murder's proximate causation requirement, many states echo the liability formula in *Pinkerton* itself, holding "that homicide is properly charged when the defendant's culpable act is 'a sufficiently direct cause' of the death so that the fatal result was reasonably foreseeable." People v. Hernandez, 624 N.E.2d 661, 663 (N.Y. 1993). Some states go so far as to hold that "where the underlying felony is one inherently dangerous to human life, such as burglary, the foreseeability requirement is established as a matter of law." State v. Gleason, 88 P.3d 218, 229 (Kan. 2004); *see also* State v. Mickens, 123 S.W.3d 355, 370 (Tenn. Crim. App. 2003) (holding that the defendant was not entitled to a "natural and probable consequence" instruction otherwise required for vicarious liability because in a felony murder case the requirement is satisfied by the fact of the predicate felony).

Given this close connection between *Pinkerton* liability and felony murder liability as applied to co-felons, it will come as no surprise that critics of one doctrine tend to be critics of the other. Consider, for example, the late Chief Justice Gants of Massachusetts, who cited his state's prior rejection of *Pinkerton* liability as a reason to reject the felony murder rule as well, which the court did.

Commonwealth v. Brown, 81 N.E.3d 1173 (Mass. 2017) (Gants, C.J., concurring). [T]he United States Supreme Court in *Pinkerton v. United States* . . . held that a defendant may be found guilty of substantive offenses committed by his coconspirator in furtherance of the conspiracy, even if he did not participate directly in the commission of those substantive offenses. We no longer adhere to this *Pinkerton* theory of accomplice liability. [Rather, under] our common law of joint venture liability, a defendant is criminally responsible for a crime committed by an accomplice [or coconspirator] only where the defendant knowingly participates in the crime with the intent required to commit it. But until now, we have retained one exception: under our common law of felony-murder, a defendant was still vicariously responsible for all the acts of his or her accomplices that resulted in death committed during the course of the felony. The consequence of this exception was that, if an accomplice shot and killed a victim during the commission of an armed robbery, the defendant was guilty of felony-murder even if he or she sat outside in the getaway vehicle and had implored the accomplices to hurt no one in committing the crime. However, if the accomplice committed the same shooting but the victim survived, the defendant sitting in that getaway vehicle would have been guilty only of the underlying armed robbery, not of the shooting. "Only where a dangerous felony resulted in death did we adopt a principle that we otherwise had 'firmly rejected' — that a person who knowingly participates in one crime as part of a joint venture is 'ipso facto also guilty' of all other crimes committed by an accomplice in furtherance of the joint venture." Commonwealth v. Tejeda, 41 N.E.3d 721, 727 (Mass. 2015). . . . It is time for us to eliminate the last vestige of [this] abandoned principle and end . . . our common law of felony-murder. Doing so means that criminal liability for murder in the first or second degree will be predicated on proof that the defendant acted with malice or shared the intent of a joint venturer who acted with malice.

> *6. Pinkerton's Limits: Abandonment and Renunciation.* While *Pinkerton* liability is generally very broad, there are some doctrinal limitations. One pertains to the conspiracy's duration and the means by which individual members can exit the agreement. Generally speaking, conspiracy is a continuing offense, which means the conspiracy is deemed in effect until its objectives have been fully accomplished or abandoned by *every* member of the conspiracy. As a result of this rule, a person who initially joins a conspiracy but then becomes a dormant or passive member could find himself liable for future substantive crimes committed by other conspirators. Recall in this context *State v. Stein*, 360 A.2d 347 (N.J. 1976), discussed in the *Bridges* opinion above. In that case, the defendant was charged with and convicted of offenses committed by other conspirators over a year after he last took any active role in the conspiracy.
>
> An individual can, however, terminate his association with a conspiracy — and thus cut off his vicarious liability for future acts of former co-conspirators — under the *abandonment* doctrine, sometimes also called *withdrawal.* Typically, this doctrine requires a person seeking to exit a conspiracy to either disclose the conspiracy to law enforcement or clearly communicate his withdrawal to his co-conspirators. As one court recently described the rule, withdrawal "requires more than implied dissociation. It must be sufficiently clear and delivered to those with authority in the conspiracy such that a jury could conclude that it was reasonably calculated to make the dissociation known to the organization. Simply not spending time

with coconspirators is not enough to satisfy this standard." United States v. Randall, 661 F.3d 1291, 1295 (10th Cir. 2011).

Finally, going one step beyond abandonment, many states follow the lead of the MPC, which embraces a *renunciation* defense under which a person is not guilty of the conspiracy charge itself if, "after conspiring to commit a crime, [he] thwarted the success of the conspiracy, under circumstances manifesting a complete and voluntary renunciation of his criminal purpose." Model Penal Code §5.03(6). Note that the defendant must *actually* thwart the conspiracy to establish renunciation; unsuccessful attempts to do so do not suffice.

7. **Pinkerton*'s* Limits: "In Furtherance of."** Recall the *Alvarez* case from the start of this section. There, the court of appeals described itself as "*extend[ing]* the *Pinkerton* doctrine to cases involving reasonably foreseeable but originally unintended substantive crimes," including crimes committed "as a result of an unintended turn of events." As noted above, this approach represents the maximal reach of *Pinkerton* liability. But not all courts have taken *Pinkerton* this far. The U.S. Court of Appeals for the Tenth Circuit, for example, expressly distances itself from *Alvarez* and defines conspiracy liability in a more limited way. Specifically, the court insists that a defendant is vicariously liable only for the crimes of a co-conspirator that are both reasonably foreseeable and also "committed in furtherance of the conspiracy." United States v. Cherry, 217 F.3d 811, 817 (10th Cir. 2000). Note that these are, conceptually, two distinct requirements. As one California appellate court explained while rejecting the in-furtherance-of limitation, "a natural and probable consequence of a conspiracy need not be an act in furtherance of the conspiracy; it simply must be a reasonably foreseeable consequence of the intended crime." People v. Zielesch, 101 Cal. Rptr. 3d 628, 636 (Cal. Ct. App. 2009) (cleaned up).

For an example of a scenario in which this distinction can make a meaningful difference, consider another California case, *People v. Brigham*, 265 Cal. Rptr. 486 (Cal. Ct. App. 1989), which is summarized as follows in a law review article about *Pinkerton* liability by Professor Matthew Pauley:

> In *People v. Brigham*, the defendant, an experienced hit man, and an acquaintance named Bluitt, armed with automatic weapons, set out in a car to find and kill a man named Chuckie. They saw a teenager on the street and defendant said to Bluitt, "That is Chuckie." Bluitt responded, "we're gonna get him." As the car got closer to the teenager, however, the defendant recognized that he was not Chuckie, and so warned Bluitt, saying, "man, that is not Chuckie, man." Bluitt ignored this, saying again "we're gonna get him" and directed the driver to stop. Appellant and Bluitt got out of the car and walked up to the teenager, a fourteen-year-old named Barfield. When they got closer, defendant said to Bluitt, "Don't do it. It ain't cool. That's not the dude, man. Come on." But Bluitt rejected

the defendant's advice, saying he wanted to let people know "we [are] serious." Bluitt fired twice, hitting and killing Barfield.

At trial, the prosecution argued and the jury found that the defendant knew that Bluitt was "hardheaded" and erratic, and, as such, he could reasonably have foreseen that Bluitt, once set in motion, might very well kill someone other than the assigned target, even if told not to do so. The defendant was convicted of first-degree murder. The Court of Appeal affirmed, pointing out that the defendant "was an experienced assassin or hit man as was Bluitt" and they "had worked together in the past." Defendant admitted that he knew Bluitt was "hardheaded," and the court said that "one who is hardheaded may be foreseeably and irrationally difficult to dissuade or control once embarked upon a criminal enterprise." Even if the killing of Barfield did not further the parties' original criminal conspiracy to kill Chuckie, [the court held] "it was nonetheless a foreseeable result . . . of . . . the original . . . agreement to kill Chuckie."[43]

8. Pinkerton's Limits: Due Process. While the *Alvarez* court "extend[ed]" *Pinkerton* as described in the preceding note, it also recognized that, at some point, stretching *Pinkerton* too far might violate the due process rights of a defendant being punished for crimes other people committed. The court therefore limited liability for "reasonably foreseeable but originally unintended substantive crimes . . . to conspirators who played more than a 'minor' role in the conspiracy, or who had actual knowledge of at least some of the circumstances and events culminating in the reasonably foreseeable but originally unintended substantive crime." Other courts have reasoned similarly, permitting *Pinkerton* liability for unintended crimes—if at all—only when the defendant played more than a minor role in the conspiracy or, much the same thing, when the defendant's connection to the substantive crimes was not too attenuated. *See, e.g.,* United States v. Chorman, 910 F.2d 102 (4th Cir. 1990); United States v. Moreno, 588 F.2d 490 (5th Cir. 1979); United States v. Johnson, 886 F.2d 1120 (9th Cir. 1989).

In *United States v. Castaneda,* 9 F.3d 761 (9th Cir. 1993), for example, the defendant occasionally relayed phone messages for her husband, who was involved in trafficking narcotics. Based on this "slight" and "passive" participation in her husband's affairs, she was convicted of conspiracy to distribute drugs. *Id.* at 766-767, 771. Several members of the conspiracy—not the defendant's husband—were also convicted of using firearms while possessing drugs with the intent to distribute them. Under *Pinkerton,* the defendant was convicted of these offenses as well. The Ninth Circuit reversed the defendant's firearm convictions. "[D]ue process constrains the application of *Pinkerton* where the relationship between the defendant and the substantive offense is slight," the court explained, and given the defendant's "lack of participation in the conspiracy and her lack of involvement with the predicate offenses"—the drug possession crimes—"the due process line ha[d] been crossed." *Id.* at 766, 768. Courts and commentators have cited *Castaneda* approvingly, but the Supreme Court has not weighed in on where the line is to be drawn. *See, e.g.,* United States v. Walls, 225 F.3d 858 (7th Cir. 2000); United States v. Collazo-Aponte, 216 F.3d 163 (1st Cir. 2000).[44]

9. Pinkerton's Defense. The limitations described in the preceding notes are not applied uniformly across jurisdictions. As a result, the sweep of conspiracy liability depends not only on how the prosecution defines the breadth of the underlying conspiratorial agreement in the charging document, but also on how the *Pinkerton* standard itself is defined and circumscribed by the relevant courts. Still, this doctrinal variation notwithstanding, *Pinkerton* liability remains a powerful tool for prosecutors. Even in its narrower manifestations, prosecutors armed with this doctrine can threaten relatively peripheral actors in a criminal group (the small fish) with severe punishments based on more serious conduct committed by more culpable actors at the conspiracy's core (the big fish).

To opponents of the doctrine, this technique of squeezing the little fish is morally offensive. To quote Justice O'Hern's dissenting opinion in the *Bridges* case that opens this section, these critics contend that the doctrine "has contradicted those principles of justice" by which a penal system "fits punishments to the crimes committed" and strives to achieve "a closer relation between guilt and culpability." For this and other reasons, "*Pinkerton* doctrine has never been the darling of criminal law scholars."[45]

But the doctrine is not without its defenders, one of the most prominent of whom is Professor Neal Katyal, who makes a case for *Pinkerton* precisely because of — rather than in spite of — its "information extraction" potential, along with other consequentialist aspects of the doctrine. The following excerpt presents the crux of Katyal's argument.

Neal Kumar Katyal, *Conspiracy Theory,* 112 Yale L.J. 1307, 1372-1375 (2003). The editors of the *Harvard Law Review* proclaimed in 1959 that "[n]o court which has taken the *Pinkerton* approach has offered an adequate rationale for convicting a conspirator for the crimes of his associates." More recently, George Fletcher has claimed that while vicarious liability "might make some sense in the field of torts . . . it is patently absurd to think of conspirators controlling each other's acts." Such views have led to the conventional wisdom that *Pinkerton* liability is some sort of criminal monster.

Nevertheless, a broad range of evidence suggests that conspirators often do influence, in profound ways, each other's behavior, not simply through their direct commands but also by their mere presence. This level of influence, in a world where criminal law looked only to commissions, would probably not justify *Pinkerton.* But [an] information-based paradigm yields a different answer because it calibrates liability on the basis of [evidence] as well as activity level. *Pinkerton* should not be condemned before assessing its information-extraction function. Without it, there would be less flipping, and with less flipping, more coercive law enforcement techniques would be necessary. . . .

The benefits of *Pinkerton* are not limited only to information extraction. In addition to punishing crimes of diffusion, the doctrine also increases precontractual uncertainty about the sanction. Under *Pinkerton*, a criminal takes her chances when she joins a conspiracy, in that she is liable for all the crimes that are within the scope of the organization. Greater liability will deter some from joining the conspiracy, and it will also make the [agreement] tougher to strike. Because people are less likely to know the full extent of their liability under *Pinkerton*, moreover, uncertainty increases and the conditions for trust thus diminish. . . .

Furthermore, just as vicarious liability in torts will produce more monitoring, so too will *Pinkerton*. Here, the major reason why is that the increasing amounts of leverage will result in more instances of cooperation with law enforcement. In the lawful entity context, vicarious liability may force corporations to take wasteful precautions. This is, however, exactly the result we want when the organization is an unlawful one. Monitoring will be driven by the climate of uncertainty about loyalty, so that more monitoring begets less trust, and less trust begets more monitoring. Like a romantic couple where one party suspects the other of infidelity and begins tracking the other's movements, the acts of monitoring themselves may contribute to a cycle of distrust, thereby eliminating many advantages of joint activity.

Yet there are reasons not to punish all members of a conspiracy equally. *Pinkerton* creates a strong incentive for someone not to join in a conspiracy at all, for any conspirator can be liable for the multitude of crimes carried out by the conspiracy. But for those who do join, it could generate negative substitution effects. If one will be held liable for the drug dealing of leaders even when the person is a small fry, the person might as well try to be a leader or ratchet up her activity level. This is a serious challenge, but there are three competing considerations. First, *Pinkerton* only attacks actions that were reasonably foreseeable within the scope of the agreement, and therefore creates incentives to reduce that scope. Second, other provisions in federal law, such as the sentencing enhancements for organizers, leaders, and managers, and the reductions for minimal and minor participants, produce marginal deterrence. *Pinkerton* increases the punishment base, but the degree of liability within that base differs markedly due to one's role in the offense. Third, . . . the withdrawal defense provides clear incentives for participants to minimize their conduct and to weaken group identity, and thereby promotes marginal deterrence. . . .

This defense of *Pinkerton* . . . is confined to its functional justification. Unfair discrimination in the way the doctrine is applied, if any, may very well be a reason to reject *Pinkerton* or to take other mitigating steps. Yet some level of unfairness will always be present in the criminal justice system. Unfortunately, innocents will be punished wrongly, and the less culpable will be found liable at times for more than they should. And, if further study shows that *Pinkerton* is applied unfairly in a great number of cases, then the advantages of the doctrine outlined above, particularly in preventing the formation of conspiracies, will have to be weighed against these costs. But, a precondition to this balancing is to understand the function of *Pinkerton*, in terms of providing an ex post mechanism to extract information and an ex ante incentive for conspiracies to adopt inefficient practices.

CHAPTER 8

PREVENTING HARM:
The Law of Attempt and Possession

"[A]n ounce of prevention is worth a pound of cure."

Benjamin Franklin, *On Protection of Towns from Fire*,
Penn. Gazette (Feb. 4, 1735)

INTRODUCTION

In the preceding chapter, we began to see that criminal law can serve instrumental purposes beyond its conventional retributive and utilitarian functions. This is a body of law that does more than assign blame, allocate punishment, and potentially shape the future behavior of private citizens. It is also a tool that facilitates the work of prosecutors and police officers. In the context of the law of complicity and especially conspiracy, we saw that one major instrumental value of criminal law is its *information-forcing* function. Together, these doctrines make it possible for law enforcement actors to pressure minor players in an illicit network into flipping on people closer to the conspiracy's heart. They then facilitate deploying those newly minted confidential informants within the criminal network to gain information about ongoing criminal activity. They can even help law enforcement set up undercover sting operations, in which state actors actively encourage or manufacture new crimes, all with a goal of catching targeted suspects and facilitating their arrest and prosecution.

In this chapter, we turn our focus to a related but distinct instrumental function of the criminal law. Sometimes, law enforcement actors leverage criminal law to try to *prevent* the harms associated with criminal activity from ever taking place. We first encountered this idea of harm prevention in Chapter Four when we studied the law of self-defense. That doctrine encourages people to protect themselves against unlawful aggression, the basic idea being that it is better to prevent a criminal attack than wait to prosecute an unlawful aggressor after the fact. We saw the idea again in the inchoate offense of conspiracy, which permits the state to intervene long before a conspiracy's object crimes are committed. But the notion of harm prevention has broader, arguably universal application, captured well by Benjamin Franklin's famous adage quoted above: "[A]n ounce of prevention is worth a pound of cure."

Thirty years after Franklin wrote that phrase to encourage his neighbors to guard against residential fires, Cesare Beccaria penned a version of the aphorism for the criminal law: "It is better to prevent crimes[] than to punish them." Stated as such, it is hard to argue against harm prevention as a guiding principle. Some crimes can hurt people. A just society should want to minimize such pain — and prevent it where possible. And yet, putting the goal of prevention front and center within the penal system works a fundamental shift in how we think about the roles of law enforcement and criminal law in society. Operating within this framework, the police exist not just to investigate crimes and arrest people who commit them. Their job is also to stop those crimes from taking place. Indeed, if prevention is more important than reaction, society may well view this proactive, preemptive mode of policing as law enforcement's most important function. And if criminal law itself is understood, instrumentally, as a tool that law enforcement can use to do its job, we can expect an emphasis on prevention to influence the substantive criminal law itself.[1]

In this chapter, we begin exploring this shift to a preemptive law enforcement orientation, setting the stage for much of the remainder of the book and course. Our immediate goals here are to understand, question, and critique two key doctrinal mechanisms through which criminal law operates preemptively. We begin with the law of attempt, an inchoate offense that allows the state to arrest, prosecute, and punish people who have not caused any harm in the world or committed any preexisting crime — but who have taken at least some steps toward potentially doing so. Next, we turn to the law of criminal possession, which bears many similarities to the law of attempt but also raises new and complicated questions and challenges. We explore those issues by focusing on the two items people are most commonly prosecuted for possessing: drugs and guns.

I.   ATTEMPT

"[A]ttempt doctrine is a way to expand the scope of criminal liability previously established by independently defined offenses. This expansion of liability is not driven primarily by a determination that preparation for a crime is

... blameworthy, but rather by a determination that sometimes it is appropriate for enforcers to intervene even though they cannot establish a violation of some preexisting statute."

Alice Ristroph, *The Curriculum of the Carceral State*,
120 Colum. L. Rev. 1631, 1676 (2020)

Much like conspiracy, attempt is a standalone offense. In most jurisdictions, it is codified in its own statute, separately from the substantive offenses in the penal code. A person can thus be prosecuted for and convicted of attempt directly. But the crime is also inextricably intertwined with its object. It is unintelligible, in other words, to say that a defendant has been charged with "attempt" without specifying what crime she is accused of having attempted. It is thus common in the criminal law's parlance to refer to a case as involving a charge of attempted murder, attempted rape, or attempted theft. These charges are not the same as charges for murder, rape, or theft. Attempt statutes, for example, typically carry lower sentences than those prescribed for the completed crimes. But the underlying crime nonetheless plays an essential role in understanding the law of attempt, in at least two key respects. First, with respect to *mens rea*, a person typically cannot be guilty of attempting to commit a crime unless she *intends* to commit that crime. Second, with respect to *actus reus*, a person cannot be guilty of attempting to commit a crime unless she takes steps that cross a certain threshold toward the commission of the crime. This part addresses these two aspects of attempt liability in turn.[2]

A.   Mens Rea

Jones v. State

689 N.E.2d 722 (Ind. 1997)

SHEPARD, C.J. A jury found Curtis Lashun Jones guilty of murder, and not guilty of attempted murder. The trial court ... sentenced him to sixty-five years in prison. In this direct appeal, Jones raises two issues: (1) Whether there was sufficient evidence ... to support the conviction for murder; and (2) Whether the verdicts of not guilty on the attempted murder charge and guilty on the murder charge are inconsistent and irreconcilable. Neither of these claims warrants relief, so we affirm.

FACTS

Shortly before 12:45 a.m. on June 16, 1995, Curtis Jones and his friend Troy Phinezy walked to [a home] in Fort Wayne. Both were carrying firearms. . . . Jones walked around to the front of the home [and] fired at least four shots in rapid succession into the window and open door of the home, where fifteen to twenty people were socializing. Three of the bullets struck

Troy Williams, who bled to death. Another bullet struck Latrail Gamble in the arm, injuring but not killing him. Phinezy and Jones ran away, and the police arrived about fifteen minutes later. . . . Jones, who was a gang member, [later told a] friend that he had fired the shots because he was tired of rival gang members killing his friends.

[Jones was charged with one count of murder for the death of Williams and one count of attempted murder for the nonfatal shooting of Gamble. The jury convicted on the murder count but acquitted on the attempted murder count.]

ANALYSIS

Jones first claims the State presented [insufficient] evidence on the [*mens rea*] element of [the murder charge], observing that none of those who testified said Jones had ever declared that he had intended to kill Williams. Additionally, Jones essentially argues that because the evidence apparently was insufficient to prove that he attempted to kill Gamble, it must also have been insufficient to prove that he intentionally killed Williams.

. . . To convict [someone of murder under Indiana law, he "must either have a conscious objective to kill another or be aware of a high probability that his conduct will result in the death of that other individual." Burkhalter v. State, 397 N.E.2d 596, 598 (Ind. 1979)]. Here, the evidence indicates that Jones fired at least four shots in rapid succession from a nine-millimeter handgun into the open door of a home in which fifteen to twenty people were socializing. It was clearly reasonable for the jury to conclude that Jones used the handgun, undoubtedly a deadly weapon, in a manner likely to cause death or serious injury, and thus that he acted with the requisite [*mens rea*].

Jones also claims that the jury's verdict on murder cannot stand because it is wholly inconsistent with its finding of not guilty on attempted murder. Because the shots that were fired at both victims all occurred in rapid succession, Jones reasons that if the jury did not find that the defendant intentionally attempted to kill Gamble, then it could not reasonably [convict him of murder for killing] Williams.

To convict a defendant of attempted murder, the jury must find beyond a reasonable doubt that the defendant, acting with intent to kill the victim, engaged in conduct which constituted a substantial step toward commission of the crime. Spradlin v. State, 569 N.E.2d 948, 950 (Ind. 1991). Specific intent to kill is required, and a jury's determination that the defendant acted with any lesser degree of culpability requires that it find the defendant not guilty. [*See id.* at 951 ("We hold that, by definition, there can be no 'attempt' to perform an act unless there is a simultaneous 'intent' to accomplish such act.").]

To convict a defendant of murder, on the other hand, the jury must find[, as we explained above, that he "either has a conscious objective to kill another or is aware of a high probability that his conduct will result in the death of that other individual." *Burkhalter*, 397 N.E.2d at 598]. Accordingly, even if the jury does not find that the defendant acted with specific intent to kill, it may convict him of murder if it finds that he was aware of a high probability that the victim's death could result from his actions.

In the present case, Jones was charged with both murder and attempted murder based on the shots he fired which killed Williams and injured Gamble. If the jury found that Jones did not act with a specific intent to kill but that he was aware of a high probability that his actions could result in death, it could quite logically find him guilty of murder and not guilty of attempted murder. We thus cannot say that the verdicts are inconsistent.

NOTES AND QUESTIONS

1. The Specific Intent Requirement. Jones sets out the commonly accepted rule for the *mens rea* of attempt. Liability will attach only when a defendant specifically intends to commit the underlying crime—or, in the language of the Model Penal Code's *mens rea* provisions, acts with the purpose of committing that offense, the highest possible *mens rea* threshold. Only a small number of jurisdictions diverge from this rule, imposing attempt liability not only when the defendant intends to cause a prohibited harm, but also when he knows his conduct will do so. Arkansas' attempt statute, for example, provides that, "[w]hen causing a particular result is an element of the offense, a person commits the offense of criminal attempt if [she] purposely engages in conduct that constitutes a substantial step in a course of conduct intended *or known* to cause the particular result." Ark. Code Ann. §5-3-201(b) (emphasis added); *see also* Haw. Rev. Stat. §705-500(2); Ohio Rev. Code Ann. §2923.02(A); Neb. Rev. Stat. §28-201(2); People v. Krovarz, 697 P.2d. 378, 383 (Colo. 1985) (en banc). The Model Penal Code advocates this minority approach, motivating its choice with an example involving a defendant who tries (but fails) to demolish a building when he knows, but does not intend, that people inside the building will be killed. Under the Code, such a defendant would be guilty of attempted murder "based on the conclusion that the manifestation of the actor's dangerousness is just as great—or very nearly as great—as in the case of purposive conduct." Model Penal Code and Commentaries §5.01 cmt. 2 at 305; *see* Model Penal Code §5.01(1)(b).

2. Moral Luck Revisited. A stringent *mens rea* requirement necessarily constricts the scope of criminal liability. In this respect, the specific intent rule of *Jones* operates similarly to the common practice, mentioned above, of punishing attempted crimes less seriously than completed ones. Both principles temper punishment for potentially harmful conduct when the harm does not manifest.

This differential treatment can produce seemingly incongruous outcomes. Consider the facts of *Jones* itself: The defendant sprayed bullets into a crowded house and struck two people. One of them died, the other survived. Under broadly accepted principles of criminal law, this defendant could be convicted of murdering the first person on a recklessness-plus theory of liability. But he could *not* be found guilty of attempting to murder the other person — unless the prosecution could prove that he was *trying* to kill that person, rather than simply trying to send a message to a rival gang. But realize that the outcome of the defendant's actions may have been partly beyond his control. Once the bullets left the gun, the victims might have died, survived, or perhaps even emerged unscathed depending on how, exactly, their bodies were positioned, how the bullets traveled through the glass, and so on. Put another way, the defendant's liability can vary substantially even though his actions — and, seemingly, the wrongfulness of his actions — are fixed once he pulls the trigger. Observing this point recalls a tension encountered in Chapter Four (p. 228) when we explored the relationship between criminal punishment and moral luck. Returning to that debate between James Fitzjames Stephens and H.L.A. Hart, do the competing arguments seem different in the context of criminal attempts?[3]

3. Unintentional Attempts? Note an important legal implication of attempt law's specific intent requirement. "An attempt to commit criminal negligent homicide," for example, would require "proof that the defendant *intended* to perpetrate an *unintentional* killing." People v. Hernandez, 614 P.2d 900, 901 (Colo. App. 1980). To many courts, this is "a logical impossibility," which means that negligent homicide simply cannot be attempted. *Id.* "Other courts have likewise found attempted reckless homicide a logical impossibility," State v. Lyerla, 424 N.W.2d 908, 913 (S.D. 1988), because a person cannot "intentionally attempt to cause the death of another by a reckless act," People v. Perez, 437 N.Y.S.2d 46, 48 (N.Y. Sup. Ct. 1981). And for the same reason, courts have held that "attempted felony murder is not a cognizable crime," given that the felony murder rule does not require an intent to kill. State v. Nolan, 25 N.E.3d 1016, 1018 (Ohio 2014).[4]

4. Contrasting Complicity. Attempt law's specific intent requirement also departs from complicity law's approach to *mens rea* for unintended results. As we saw in Chapter Seven, in states that follow the MPC approach as discussed in *Riley v. State* (p. 547), an accomplice must intend to aid or encourage a principal's conduct but can generally be held liable for unintended results of that conduct if she acted with the level of *mens rea* required for the underlying offense, which need not be intent. Consider what this means in practice: A doctor who knows it is unsafe to reuse syringes but encourages her nurses to do so to save money could be guilty (as an accomplice) of manslaughter or perhaps even murder if a patient dies from an infectious injection. But the doctor would not be convicted of attempted manslaughter or attempted murder if the same patient survived—even if the doctor administered the dirty syringe herself.

5. Attendant Circumstances. While the application of attempt law's specific intent requirement is clear with respect to elements of a crime concerning a defendant's conduct or the results of that conduct, it is muddier with respect to attendant circumstances. What should happen, for example, in a jurisdiction with a strict liability statutory rape offense if an adult tries—but fails—to have sex with someone she believes to be eighteen years old but who is in fact only fifteen? Should the adult be guilty of attempted statutory rape because she intended to have sex with this specific person? Or should attempt liability fail because she did not specifically intend to have sex with someone she believed to be underage? Most courts would impose attempt liability in this case. *See, e.g.,* Maxwell v. State, 895 A.2d 327, 330 n.3 (Md. Ct. Spec. App. 2006) (listing cases). The Model Penal Code is in accord, providing for liability if, with respect to the victim's age, the defendant acts "with the kind of culpability otherwise required for the commission of the crime"—in this case, none at all. Model Penal Code §5.01(1); *see also* Model Penal Code and Commentaries §5.01 cmt. 2 at 301-303.[5]

6. The Reason for Specific Intent. The preceding notes highlight the potentially incongruous outcomes that can flow from attempt law's insistence on a demanding *mens rea* threshold, all of which raises a question: why does the law require a showing of intent to impose liability for attempts? For Professor Antony Duff, the answer lies in the fact that acts intended to harm—and only such acts—constitute "attacks" on another person's legally protected interests, and are thus "intrinsically" harmful.

> The paradigm or central case of wrongdoing is that in which there is a unity of subjective [intention] and objective [harm caused in the world]: an intended killing, or wounding, or damaging property. Actions that fall short of this paradigm will still count as criminal, so long as they are closely enough related to it: we can still ascribe a killing, or wounding, or damaging, to an agent as his culpably criminal action, for example, even though he did not intend it, if his action displayed a criminal recklessness as to the risk that it would cause death, or injury, or damage.
>
> When the harm which the paradigm crime involves has not actually occurred, however, the difference between intention and recklessness becomes more crucial, as marking the distinction between attacks and (mere) endangerment. One who acts with the intention of causing some legally relevant harm is attacking a legally protected interest: her action is intrinsically or essentially harmful even if the harm does not in fact ensue, since it is structured by the prospect of causing that harm; the actual occurrence of harm would simply give objective actualization to the character that the action already has. . . . An attack is thus more

intimately related to the paradigm of crime than are acts of endangerment: this gives us reason to treat failed attacks more seriously than we treat endangerments which actually cause no material harm, and to define a general law of inchoate crimes that captures attacks but not endangerments (although we might also want to criminalize some relatively serious kinds of endangerment).[6]

Again, for Duff, acts intended to harm are "intrinsically" harmful—in a metaphysical sense if not in terms of real-world damage—and thus deserve punishment as attempts. But for Professor Vincent Chiao, it is the prospect of *actual* harm in the world that matters most, which leads Chiao to distinguish between two different *types* of attempts—those in which the actor's ultimate conduct remains uncertain, and those in which he has already done everything he planned to do (but caused no harm). Chiao seems to favor requiring specific intent as a prerequisite to punishing the former, but not the latter.

> Complete attempts are attempts where the agent has taken the last step in her plan of action, but has nevertheless failed to cause harm[.] [By contrast,] incomplete attempts are those where the agent is stopped, or renounces, while there are still steps untaken. . . . [C]omplete and incomplete attempts . . . should be treated separately, as they raise distinct issues. Notably, there is a question regarding the degree of certainty with which we can predict what an incomplete attempter will do, an issue that simply does not arise from the *ex post* perspective of complete attempts. Moreover, the preparatory steps which can give rise to attempt liability may themselves be perfectly legal and, taken on their own, innocuous. It is thus likely that in some cases of incomplete attempts, it will be difficult to assess not just whether the agent will carry through with her criminal plan, but whether she has a criminal plan at all. For these reasons, it might be plausible to construe the criminal intent requirement as serving to filter out innocent agents with respect to incomplete attempts. But these concerns would of course be immaterial in the case of complete attempts . . . . So the traditional *mens rea* rule of attempts may well be intelligible with respect to one class of attempts but not the other.[7]

Chiao's emphasis on the relationship between the intent requirement and the potentially innocuous "preparatory steps" that might give rise to attempt liability highlights an important interrelationship between attempt law's *mens rea* requirement and its *actus reus* requirement. As Oliver Wendell Holmes, Jr., wrote, "[t]he importance of the intent [requirement] is not to show that the act was wicked, but to show that it was likely to be followed by hurtful consequences." Understood on these terms, the challenge is to define the point at which a person's preparatory steps toward committing a crime advance so far that this likelihood of "hurtful consequences" outweighs the risk of penalizing actions that, in Chiao's words, "may themselves be perfectly legal and, taken on their own, innocuous." As Chiao observes, a specific intent requirement can, at least for incomplete attempts, help to "filter out" the latter set of cases from the former. But so too can the *actus reus* requirement, to which we now turn.[8]

B.　*Actus Reus*

Attempt, like conspiracy, is an *inchoate crime*. It penalizes conduct that does not itself violate any preexisting criminal law and that may not ever cause any real harm. But whereas conspiracy ties criminal liability to a specific act — namely, an *agreement* between two or more people to commit some future crime — the *actus reus* of attempt is more ambiguous. That ambiguity stems in part from the general nature of attempt statutes, which typically incorporate by reference all the other substantive offenses in a jurisdiction's penal code. A typical attempt statute thus might say that a "person is guilty of an attempt to commit a crime when, with intent to commit a crime, he engages in conduct which tends to effect the commission of such crime." N.Y. Penal Law §110.00. Under this statute, the *actus reus* of attempt is any "conduct that tends to effect the commission of" any one of the potentially hundreds or thousands of substantive crimes separately codified in the jurisdiction. But to say as much raises the central *actus reus* question more than it answers it: At what point does a person's conduct "tend to effect the commission" of another offense? Or, to use terminology common to the cases, when does conduct cease to be "mere preparation," which is ordinarily not a crime, and become "sufficiently proximate" to a completed offense "to be [labeled] an attempt"? Commonwealth v. McCloskey, 341 A.2d 500, 501 (Pa. Super. Ct. 1975).

The notes and cases that follow explore the various answers to that question put forward by courts across the country. Conceptually, those answers can be organized along a temporal spectrum, ranging from the earliest contemplation of an offense at one end to the last step toward its completion at the other. The first two notes discuss the broadly accepted legal rules governing this spectrum's opposite poles. The lead case and notes that follow then explore the diverse set of approaches courts take to analyze cases between the polar extremes.

NOTES AND QUESTIONS

1. **Cogitationis Poenam:** *Culpable Thoughts.* At one end of the spectrum lie cases in which courts uniformly agree that criminal liability does *not* attach. Captured by the Latin maxim *cogitationis poenam nemo patitur,* the idea here is that culpable thoughts alone are not punished. To take a stylized example, a person cannot be prosecuted for confessing to her partner, therapist, or boss that she "can't stop thinking about killing her coworker." This remains true even if the confessed thoughts contain extensive details about how the persistently fantasized homicide would be performed.

To say that such guilty thoughts do not constitute a crime is simply to restate a core premise of criminal liability, which requires a guilty mind plus some guilty action—a *mens rea* plus some *actus reus*. But while the *cogitationis poenam* rule is ubiquitous, its underlying logic is not self-evident. After all, as William Blackstone writes in one of the excerpts below, one could reasonably think that "a fixed design or will to do an unlawful act is almost as heinous as the commission of it." Why, then, refuse to punish guilty thoughts alone? Consider the answers offered by the following authors.

Jordan Wallace-Wolf, *Think Again: The Thought Crime Doctrine and the Limits of Criminal Law*, 1 J. Free Speech L. 5, 49 (2021). [P]unishing a person's thoughts is like damming a river or putting a plant in the dark. It suppresses the activity by which persons preserve their personhood and preserve, in principle, their chance to see what is correct. No doubt, there are sobering consequences to giving persons permission to think for themselves . . . but this permission cannot be revoked, least of all by a political system. To do so would give up on persons altogether. Instead, a political community must have the courage to let its members realize the value of thinking, despite the risks.

Heidi M. Hurd, *What in the World Is Wrong?*, 5 J. Contemp. Legal Issues 157, 174 (1994). [I]t is doubtful that we can choose the motivations on which we act, and it is also dubious whether we have much capacity to choose what it is we think about or believe as we choose to act.

R.A. Duff, *Criminal Attempts* 389 (1996). [If] we intervene forcibly to prevent [someone from] advancing his criminal enterprise, we cease to treat him as a responsible agent: we deny him the freedom to decide for himself whether to desist; we pre-empt his future actions by force, and thus infringe his autonomy. If the law is to treat its citizens as responsible agents, it must leave them free to decide for themselves, not merely whether to embark on a criminal enterprise, but whether to continue with it.

4 William Blackstone, *Commentaries* *21. [A] fixed design or will to do an unlawful act is almost as heinous as the commission of it, yet, as no temporal tribunal can search the heart, or fathom the intentions of the mind, otherwise than as they are demonstrated by outward actions, it therefore cannot punish for what it cannot know. For which reason in all temporal jurisdictions an overt act, or some open evidence of an intended crime, is necessary, in order to demonstrate the depravity of the will, before the man is liable to punishment.

Douglas Husak, *Does Criminal Liability Require an Act?*, in *The Philosophy of Criminal Law: Selected Essays* 17, 49 (2010). In the absence of an act, it is barely conceivable that evidence "beyond a reasonable doubt" could be obtained to prove that a defendant performed a given mental act for which liability was to be imposed. Confessions might provide the only reliable means of gaining such evidence. Needless to say, such confessions would be exceedingly rare. Moreover, the potential for abuse would be enormous if the state were forced to rely on confessions in order to convict persons for a given offense.

Gerald Dworkin & David Blumfeld, *Punishment for Intentions*, 75 Mind 396, 401 (1966). What would a system of laws embodying a rule providing for the punishment of intentions look like? . . . Would we not be constantly worried about the nature of our mental life? Am I only wishing my mother-in-law were dead? Perhaps I have gone further. The resultant guilt would tend to impoverish and stultify the emotional life.

2 James Fitzjames Stephen, *A History of the Criminal Law of England* 78 (1883). Sinful thoughts and dispositions of mind might be the subject of confession and of penance, but they were never punished in this country. . . . The reasons for imposing this great leading restriction upon the sphere of criminal law are obvious. If it were not so restricted it would be utterly intolerable; all mankind would be criminals, and most of their lives would be passed in trying and punishing each other for offences which could never be proved.

    2. The Last Act. At the other end of the spectrum, one could imagine a rule that attaches attempt liability only when a person has "taken the last step which he was able to take along the road of his criminal intent." King v. Barker [1924] NZLR 865 (CA) at 873. Sometimes called the *last act* or *last proximate act* rule, this approach was briefly entertained in an oft-discussed English opinion from 1855, *Regina v. Eagleton* (1855) 169 Eng. Rep. 826. In that case, the court held that if "any further step on the part of the defendant" would have "been necessary" for him to complete the offense, attempt liability could not attach. *Id.* at 835. Only "the last act, depending on [the defendant] himself, towards the [commission of the offense] ought to be considered as an attempt." *Id.* at 836. As described in subsequent opinions, the *Eagleton* rule imposes attempt liability when a person has "done all that he intended to do and was able to do for the purpose of effectuating his criminal purpose," but not when "he has stopped short of this, whether because he has repented, or because he has been prevented, or because the time or occasion for going further has not arrived, or for any other reason." *Barker*, [1924] NZLR at 873. The logic of this rule is that prior to the ultimate step toward offending, a person "still has a *locus poenitentiae*," meaning space to change his mind, and might do so. *Id.*

    Note the implications of this rule. Under *Eagleton*, a person would be guilty of attempted murder if he points a gun at someone, pulls the trigger, and misses, or if the victim is struck by the bullet and survives. But he would not be guilty of attempted murder at any point prior to pulling the trigger.

Critics of *Eagleton*, including the drafters of the Model Penal Code, argue the approach is far too tolerant of wrongful behavior that can risk serious harm. More fundamentally, they say, it fails to appreciate that "the primary purpose of punishing attempts" in the first place is "to neutralize dangerous individuals." Model Penal Code and Commentaries §5.01 cmt. 5(b) at 323. With respect to the last act rule, these critics have won the day. According to the MPC's drafters, "[n]o jurisdiction operating within the framework of Anglo-American law [requires] that the last proximate act occur before an attempt can be charged." *Id.* at 321 n.97. The *Eagleton* rule, in other words, is broadly rejected across the United States today.[9]

Taken together, the *cogitationis poenam* principle and the broad rejection of the *Eagleton* rule establish two fixed points. Guilty thoughts alone are insufficient. Yet the defendant need not reach the final step on the road to committing an offense. "The dividing line between preparation and attempt is to be found somewhere between these two extremes." *Barker*, [1924] NZLR at 874. But where should that line be drawn? The following, more modern case examines this question in the context of the persistent and uniquely American problem of mass shootings.

State v. Lammers

479 S.W.3d 624 (Mo. 2016)

RUSSELL, J. Blaec Lammers (Defendant) appeals his convictions for attempted first-degree assault and armed criminal action. . . . On appeal, Defendant argues there was insufficient evidence of both elements of attempt: the intent to complete the crime and a substantial step toward completing it. . . .

Factual Background. At the time of the events leading to the convictions in this case, Defendant was 20 years old and lived at home with his parents. . . . Defendant was taking prescription drugs for depression and had been hospitalized a number of times for psychiatric problems. One of these hospitalizations occurred in 2009 after a psychotic episode at the local Walmart, in which the sheriff's office was called to intervene. Although Defendant's mother took efforts to ensure he took his medication, he did not like taking it and admitted that, in the past, he had sometimes "cheeked" his medication by hiding the pills in his mouth and pretending to swallow them.

On November 12 and 13, 2012, Defendant legally purchased two assault rifles (a .22 caliber and a .223 caliber) and ammunition from the Bolivar Walmart.[2] Defendant . . . had never shot a gun before. [His] friend showed him how to sight and load the guns, and the two practiced shooting. [The

---

2. No mental health background check is required under Missouri Law.

next day, the Defendant moved the weapons to the home of his girlfriend's father because] he knew his mother would not approve of him possessing guns. The father, who evidently was aware to some extent of Defendant's past mental health issues, hesitantly agreed to store the guns. . . . He told Defendant he would keep them in a secure location and Defendant would have to come to him to get them back. The father was suspicious of why Defendant did not want his mother to know about the guns, so he contacted Defendant's mother.

Defendant's mother was very concerned when she heard Defendant was in possession of two assault rifles. . . . The next day, Defendant's mother drove to the sheriff's office . . . and voiced her concerns about Defendant's mental illness [and gun purchase]. She was worried that he might not be taking his medication and should not be in possession of guns. She testified that it was not her intent for Defendant to be arrested but, rather, for officers to keep an eye on him. She was worried that Defendant would get access to the guns and harm himself.

Later that day, officers . . . found Defendant at the local Sonic Drive-In with his girlfriend in her vehicle. They told Defendant that his mother had contacted them because she was worried about him. They discussed his medication and the assault rifles. Defendant indicated that he had been taking his medication and that he planned to use the guns to go hunting, although he lacked a hunting license. The officers asked Defendant if he would come down to the police station to talk further. Defendant said that he would. . . .

At the police station, a Bolivar police detective interviewed Defendant. . . . The detective's primary goal throughout the interview was to ascertain why Defendant purchased the assault rifles. Defendant first stated that he intended to use them to go hunting. . . . The detective told Defendant he did not believe this story because Defendant bought the guns without telling his parents, these particular assault rifles were not typically used for hunting, and Defendant admitted that he had never been hunting before. Defendant next claimed that he had purchased the assault rifles because he thought guns were cool and just wanted to have one. He also stated that he thought owning a gun would impress his father, but that he did not tell his father because he would have said "No." The detective again said he thought Defendant was lying.

[Later in the interview, the Defendant] admitted that, prior to purchasing the weapons, he had envisioned committing a mass shooting, specifically at the Bolivar Walmart, but that he changed his mind after taking target practice.

Officer: So tell me about your thoughts you had.

Defendant: Well I was watching [this] movie called *April Showers*. It's about Columbine. . . . [M]y sister was in it. And I was like oh it's just . . . I want to see what it was about. It was a high school shooting

> and . . . these thoughts were going through my head, like, what would happen if I ever did that. So I went out and bought them [the assault rifles] and then I realized I don't want to spend the rest of my life in prison. I don't want to do that.

Officer: But here, but here's the thing. You're not in school.

Defendant: No I'm out of school.

Officer: So you wouldn't shoot up . . . . [W]here did you, where did you think about shooting up?

Defendant: Walmart.

Officer: Walmart?

Defendant: Yes sir. It was when I bought that. But then I realized when I went shooting[,] I was like this, this isn't me. I don't know why I did this.

Later in the interview, Defendant described being in the Walmart on an occasion prior to when he bought the assault rifles. He was looking through magazines and thinking about concealed weapons:

Defendant: . . . I was like oh that looks pretty cool.

Officer: And then it just came to you I'm going to shoot up Walmart?

Defendant: Yeah.

When asked about his plan specifically from start to finish, Defendant stated that he would just walk into the Walmart, start shooting people at random, and wait until police arrived. . . .

At the conclusion of the interview, the detective placed Defendant under arrest, charging him with attempted first-degree assault [and] armed criminal action. Following a court-ordered mental examination, the trial court found Defendant mentally competent to stand trial, and Defendant waived his right to a jury trial. . . . The trial court . . . found him guilty of attempted first-degree assault and armed criminal action and sentenced him to two concurrent terms of 15 years imprisonment. . . .

Legal Analysis. A person attempts to commit a crime under [our penal code] when, "with the purpose of committing the offense, he does any act which is a substantial step towards the commission of the offense." Mo. Rev. Stat. §564.011.* Accordingly, to be convicted of attempted first-degree assault, Defendant must have: (1) had the purpose to commit that offense and (2) committed some act that is a substantial step toward completing that offense. . . . "Substantial step" is defined as "conduct which is strongly corroborative of the firmness of the actor's purpose to complete the commission of the offense." *Id.*

. . . Viewing the facts in the light most favorable to the trial court's verdict, [the court as factfinder court could have concluded that Lammers]

---

* Editor's Note: After the decision in this case, §564.011 was transferred to §562.012.

watched a movie about the Columbine shootings, envisioned doing something similar, and bought two assault rifles to carry out a mass shooting, with Walmart in mind as a specific target. . . . When asked specifically about his plan "from start to finish," Defendant stated that he would have walked in the front door and started shooting. He would have shot random people until police arrived. . . .

Intent is rarely susceptible to proof by direct evidence and is most often inferred circumstantially. [Here], there was sufficient evidence to find that Defendant had the purpose to kill or cause serious physical injury to another person. Defendant's own statements offer direct evidence of such intent. His idea of emulating the Columbine shooters occurred well before he bought the guns and practiced shooting them; when questioned by police, he described in some detail how he planned to act. Further, his conduct in purchasing the guns and learning to shoot them, taken together with his repeated subterfuge regarding why he bought the guns, are probative of a criminal intent.

. . . A finding of intent, however, does not end the inquiry. It is further necessary to determine whether Defendant took a substantial step toward commission of the offense. The alleged substantial steps Defendant took were buying the assault rifles and practicing shooting them. The question this Court must answer in determining whether Defendant took a substantial step is whether this conduct was "strongly corroborative of the firmness of [Defendant's] purpose" to complete the offense.

Section 564.011, effective in 1979, lowered the threshold needed to find the offense by . . . adopting the "substantial step" test of the Model Penal Code.[7] The result was that the emphasis was shifted away from what an actor had left to accomplish and refocused, instead, on what the actor had already done. In that regard, because there was sufficient evidence of Defendant's conscious purpose to commit assault, a reasonable fact-finder could have deemed his later purchase of assault rifles and ammunition, together with extensive target practice, strongly corroborative of that purpose. The trial court did not err in finding sufficient evidence that Defendant's conduct constituted a substantial step under section 564.011.

The dissenting opinion suggests, based on the comments to section 564.011, that to be considered a substantial step, the conduct must be illegal. The statute, however, does not mandate that conduct be illegal to constitute a substantial step. All that is required under section 564.011 is that the alleged substantial step strongly corroborate the intent to complete the offense. . . .

---

7. The comments to the 1973 proposed section 564.011 highlight the reason for the change: ". . . that the law is not interested merely in punishing dangerous acts, but also in neutralizing dangerous individuals."

Defendant [next] asserts . . . that [his relinquishing the guns to his girl-friend's father] impacts the evaluation of whether he had the requisite crim-inal purpose and whether he took a substantial step. Evidence of voluntary withdrawal may be relevant to the determination of substantial step, which includes evaluating the actor's firmness of purpose. State v. Rollins, 321 S.W.3d 353, 360 (Mo. Ct. App. 2010) (an act showing a change of direction may raise doubt as to the firmness of the actor's purpose and is a factor to consider in determining whether the substantial step was strongly corrobora-tive of the firmness of the actor's purpose). [But the] father testified at trial that he did not believe Defendant was permanently giving him the guns. . . . The trial court was free to credit this testimony, disbelieve Defendant, and believe instead the State's contention that Defendant actually stored the guns at the father's home because he did not want his mother to find out, as she feared that, in Defendant's words, "a Virginia Tech is going to happen with me." Viewing the evidence in the light most favorable to the verdict and ignoring contrary inferences, Defendant's relinquishment of the guns can-not be construed as abandonment evidence. As a result, it has no impact on whether Defendant is guilty of the charged crimes.

[In sum, there] was sufficient evidence for a reasonable finder of fact to determine that Defendant had the necessary purpose to complete the crime of attempted first-degree assault and took substantial steps toward completion of that offense. The judgment of the trial court is affirmed.[14]

TEITELMAN, J., dissenting. . . . The line between thought and the crime of attempt is crossed only after one takes a "substantial step" toward the com-mission of the offense. Mr. Lammers admitted to homicidal thoughts, but he never engaged in conduct that, beyond a reasonable doubt, strongly cor-roborated a firm plan to act on those thoughts. Mr. Lammers should be receiving treatment for his mental illness rather than serving time in prison for a crime he did not commit.

Section 564.011 required the State to prove beyond a reasonable doubt that Mr. Lammers performed a "substantial step" toward committing a first-degree assault. A "substantial step" requires some act that is "strongly cor-roborative of the firmness of the actor's purpose to complete the commis-sion of the offense." Id. The 1973 comment to the proposed section 564.011 provides examples of actions constituting a substantial step:

- lying in wait, searching for or following the contemplated victim of the offense [or] enticing or seeking to entice the contemplated vic-tim of the offense to go to the place contemplated for its commission.

---

14. This Court is sympathetic to Defendant's mother's belief that her son would benefit more from mental health treatment than prison, but the Court is obligated to follow the law regarding the crime of attempt as written by the legislature.

- reconnoitering the place contemplated for the commission of the offense [or unlawfully entering] a structure, vehicle or enclosure in which it is contemplated that the offense will be committed.
- possession of materials to be employed in the commission of the offense, which are specially designed for such unlawful use or which can serve no lawful purpose of the actor under the circumstances. . . .

The foregoing list is not exhaustive, but each example shares at least two common characteristics. First, each example identifies conduct that would most likely be undertaken only as a precursor to completing the commission of the intended criminal offense. When an individual lies in wait for the intended victim, entices the victim to a certain place, . . . or gathers items specifically designed to commit the crime under circumstances that have no lawful purpose, that individual has engaged in conduct demonstrating a firm purpose to complete the intended offense. The second common characteristic is that Mr. Lammers engaged in none of this conduct. . . . If the evidence in this case constitutes an attempt, then it is also an attempt to privately entertain the idea of hitting a random person, buying a bat, swinging the bat, and then discarding the bat. The crime of attempt requires more. When the terrifying thoughts entertained by Mr. Lammers are set aside, the case against him crumbles. What remains is an expansive net of criminal liability that is not contemplated by the language of section 564.011 or prior case law. Mr. Lammers' thoughts are cause for grave concern, but his conduct was not criminal. I would reverse the judgment and vacate the conviction for attempted first-degree assault.

NOTES AND QUESTIONS

1. Mass Shootings. For readers who grew up in the United States at any point in the last quarter-century, the facts of *Lammers* will likely evoke some collective memories—of active-shooter drills conducted each year from elementary school through high school, and of the string of mass murders that have made those drills commonplace. For many, these collective memories date back to the shooting at Columbine High School in 1999 discussed in the *Lammers* opinion. From then to today an unbroken string of shootings stretches forward in time, with some of the most salient examples including the mass murders at Sandy Hook Elementary School in 2012, at the Emmanuel African Methodist Episcopal Church in Charleston in 2015, outside the Mandalay Bay Hotel in Las Vegas in 2017, at Marjory Stoneman Douglas High School in 2018, at the Tree of Life Synagogue later that same year, at a predominantly Latino-frequented Walmart in El Paso in 2019, at a predominantly Black-frequented supermarket in Buffalo in 2022, and at a pair of Lunar New Year celebrations in Asian American communities in 2023.

While these events were each widely reported in national media, they represent only a small slice of mass killings perpetrated with firearms in the United States each year. According to the FBI, between 2018 and 2022 there were 211 "active shooter" incidents across the country in which "one or more individuals actively engaged in killing or attempting to kill people in a populated area." Together, these events resulted in 429 deaths and 774 nonfatal injuries. The Congressional Research Service defines "mass shootings" more narrowly as incidents "in which four or more victims are murdered with firearms." Even so, under this definition researchers have counted 168 mass shootings between 1966 and 2019. Nearly all mass shooters in the United States are male; just over half are white, about one-fifth are Black, and around one-tenth are Latino.[10]

By all accounts, the same researchers concluded, it is clear that mass shootings "are becoming more frequent, and they are getting deadlier." It is also clear that, while isolated examples can be found in other countries, the number of mass shootings in the United States outstrips that in all other industrialized nations—as does gun possession more generally. We will return to the topic of gun possession later in this chapter.[11]

    2. Dangerous Proximity. The disagreement between the majority and dissent in *Lammers* reflects the central dispute in the law of attempt: Where along the spectrum between mere thoughts and a completed offense should criminal liability attach? In *Lammers,* the stakes of that question are clear. Erring too far in one direction increases the risk that someone intending to cause potentially massive harm might succeed in doing so before state actors can intervene to stop him. But erring too far in the other direction creates a serious risk that a person might spend years in prison based on only loosely formed thoughts that may never have materialized into criminal, let alone harmful, conduct. Each opinion in *Lammers* views the other as committing one of these errors, and thinks the mistake is serious.

Note, though, that while the two opinions disagree as to the holding of the case, both are applying the same overarching legal framework to define the *actus reus* of attempt. Each opinion applies the "substantial step" test adopted by the Model Penal Code and currently employed by a majority of jurisdictions. This is not the only framework courts use to address this issue. Among the various alternatives, the most prominent competitor is the *dangerous proximity* test, which differs from the substantial step test in its basic temporal orientation. Rather than starting at the beginning of the timeline and focusing, as *Lammers* put it, "on what the actor had already done," it examines the case from the imagined completed offense and puts the "emphasis [on] what an actor had left to accomplish." To appreciate how this alternative framing might play out in practice, consider the following two cases.[12]

People v. Warren, 489 N.E.2d 240 (N.Y. 1985). [The evidence] established that informant "JWB" met with defendants, [who] said they wanted to purchase about half a pound of cocaine [from him.] JWB and his source—an undercover police officer—met with defendants in [a] hotel. After discussing the quality of the cocaine, defendants agreed to purchase eight ounces at $2,050 per ounce. The transaction was not consummated, however, for several reasons. [The] defendants did not have with them the $16,400 required for the purchase. Moreover, [the defendants] wanted the cocaine wrapped in four two-ounce packages, while the cocaine supplied to the police officer was wrapped in six one-ounce packages. [The defendants also] did not want to receive the cocaine in the hotel room because [they] feared detection. [They said that, instead, they would meet JWB and the undercover officer] in a distant parking lot at about 8:00 p.m. to test the cocaine and effect the transaction. Before the [hotel] meeting ended, [as the] defendants were examining [the] one-ounce bags[,] police officers, who had been secretly watching the transaction, entered the room and arrested them.

. . . In addition to proof of intent to commit a specific crime, [attempt liability in our jurisdiction] requires a showing that defendant committed an act or acts that carried the project forward within dangerous proximity to the criminal end to be attained. *See* People v. Rizzo, 158 N.E. 888 (N.Y. 1927). Here, the defendants did not come very near to the accomplishment of the intended crime. The planned purchase was to take place hours later, in another part of town, after testing. At the time they were arrested, defendants did not possess sufficient funds to make the purchase, and the informant and the police officer did not have sufficient cocaine to make the sale. Thus, several contingencies stood between the agreement in the hotel room and the contemplated purchase. . . .

People v. Rizzo, 158 N.E. 888 (N.Y. 1927). The police of the city of New York did excellent work in this case by preventing the commission of a serious crime. It is a great satisfaction to realize that we have such wide-awake guardians of our peace. Whether or not the steps which the defendant had taken up to the time of his arrest amounted to the commission of a crime, as defined by our law, is, however, another matter. . . .

Charles Rizzo [and] three others . . . planned to rob one Charles Rao of a payroll valued at about $1,200 which [Rao] was to carry from [a] bank. . . . These defendants, two of whom had firearms, started out in an automobile, looking for Rao. . . . They went to the bank from which he was supposed to get the money. . . . [Though they did not know it,] they were watched and followed by two police officers. As Rizzo jumped out of the car and ran into the building all four were arrested. . . . The defendants had not found or seen the man they intended to rob[; in fact, no] person with a pay roll was at [the building] where they had stopped. . . . The four men intended to rob the pay roll man [and] were looking for him, but they had not seen or discovered him up to the time they were arrested.

Does this constitute the crime of an attempt to commit robbery in the first degree? . . . The law . . . considers those acts only as tending to the commission of the crime which are so near to its accomplishment that in all reasonable probability the crime itself would have been committed, but for timely interference. The cases which have been before the courts express this idea in different language, but the idea remains the same. The act or acts must come or advance very near to the accomplishment of the intended crime. . . . [Under this test a person would not] be guilty of an attempt to commit murder if he armed himself and started out to find the person whom he had planned to kill but could not find him. So here these defendants were not guilty of an attempt to commit robbery in the first degree when they had not found or reached the presence of the person they intended to rob.

Questions: The *Rizzo* court praises the police officers for arresting Rizzo, describing them as "wide-awake guardians of our peace" who did "excellent work." How does this statement square with the opinion's holding? If Rizzo is not guilty of attempted robbery, is he guilty of any other criminal offense?

3. Comparing the Tests in Practice. Critics of the dangerous proximity test argue that its name reveals its central flaw. By imposing liability only once a person with criminal intent is *dangerously* close to turning that intention into reality, the approach can impede law enforcement's ability "to neutralize dangerous individuals." Model Penal Code and Commentaries §5.01 cmt. 5(b) at 323. By contrast, the substantial step test, in the words of the Model Penal Code's principal author, is designed to "prove less of a hurdle for the prosecution."[13]

But does the dangerous proximity test actually make prosecutions harder in practice? Experimental research, discussed in the following excerpt, counterintuitively finds the opposite: The facially pro-defendant test may actually favor prosecutors on the ground.

Avani Mehta Sood, *Attempted Justice: Misunderstanding and Bias in Psychological Constructions of Criminal Attempt,* 71 Stan. L. Rev. 593, 616-620, 640-642 (2019). [This study] presented the participants with a hypothetical case of a defendant charged with attempted arson. The legally relevant case facts were delivered in three stages. The first set of facts pointed largely toward innocence but included some suspicious circumstances to make the charged crime credible. The second set of facts introduced a potential motive for committing arson, thereby rendering the evidence more ambiguous with respect to the defendant's culpability. Finally, the third set of facts presented additional evidence that swung the pendulum toward guilt.

All the participants received all three sets of facts in the same order and rendered judgments about the defendant's criminal liability after each set. . . . [But different groups of subjects received different instructions as to the governing law.] For the act requirement of attempted arson, the participants were randomly assigned to apply either the substantial step test or the proximity test [defined as follows]:

> *Substantial step test*: The prosecution must prove beyond a reasonable doubt that the defendant engaged in a substantial step toward committing arson—which means that the conduct was strongly corroborative of (clearly indicated) intent to commit arson.

> *Proximity test*: The prosecution must prove beyond a reasonable doubt that the defendant engaged in conduct that tended toward committing arson—which means that the conduct came dangerously close or very near to committing arson.

. . . The manipulation of the legal standard made no significant difference to lay determinations of liability when the case facts pointed toward either innocence or guilt. . . . This suggests that the theoretical contrast between where these different legal standards for attempt draw their respective lines of liability is unlikely to matter in lay applications of the law when the weight of the evidence is relatively clear in either direction. . . .

[However,] when the facts of the given case were ambiguous with regard to the defendant's culpability . . . the given law mattered markedly—but in a manner directly opposite to legal expectations. Participants . . . were significantly more likely to deliver a guilty verdict, when applying the theoretically more defense-friendly proximity test as compared with the substantial step test. [Specifically,] when participants judged the ambiguous case facts, they assigned significantly more guilty verdicts (60.6%) than acquittals (39.4%) if they were applying the proximity test, whereas there was no statistically significant difference between the number of convictions and acquittals if they were applying the substantial step test. . . .

What led to the lay-legal disconnects exhibited in these studies? [To explore this question,] the participants were presented with both the substantial step and the proximity test toward the end of the survey, and were asked to identify which test presents a lower bar for proving criminal attempt. . . . Among the approximately one-quarter of participants who flipped the conventional legal understandings of attempt law even when viewing the standards side by side (incorrectly perceiving the proximity test as presenting a lower threshold for liability), written responses revealed recurring misinterpretations of opaque concepts and terms within the language of the standards. For instance, the use of the terms "substantial" and "step" in the substantial step test, but not the proximity test, led some participants to believe that the proximity test sets a lower bar for liability because it "does not require an *actual step* in the completion of the crime"—or at least not one that has to be "substantial." . . . Such lay interpretations suggest that the MPC's chosen language for the substantial step test, which was designed "to extend the criminality of attempts" . . . may in practice have the opposite effect of signaling a *higher* threshold for liability to jurors than the common law's proximity test. [By contrast, some] lay decisionmakers erroneously construed [the proximity] test's use of the word "tending" as *lowering* the bar for prosecution by casting a broader net of criminal liability than the substantial step test.

C.   Defenses to Attempt Liability

If the *mens rea* and *actus reus* of attempt are established, criminal liability will generally attach, unless one of two potential defenses can be shown. The first, known as *abandonment*, arises in scenarios where the defendant—after crossing the *actus reus* threshold—backtracks from the completed offense. The second, known as *impossibility*, arises where the defendant argues that attempt liability should not attach because the alleged target offense never could have been committed. Both lines of defense implicate doctrinal nuances and complications, many of which vary across jurisdictions, as discussed in the two sections that follow.

1. Abandonment

The defendant in *Lammers* argued that even if he might at one point have intended to commit a mass shooting, and even if he had taken sufficient steps toward that goal, he abandoned those plans when he turned the assault rifles over to his girlfriend's father. The Missouri Supreme Court rejected this argument on factual grounds, holding that the factfinder could have reasonably concluded that Lammers was not actually relinquishing the guns but rather was hiding them at his girlfriend's father's house to prevent his mother from discovering them. On this reading of the facts, turning over the guns would have furthered Lammers' criminal purpose by helping him avoid detection. But what if the facts had more conclusively shown an effort to abandon any criminal intentions? How should such abandonment (sometimes called *renunciation*) factor into the analysis?

Courts typically analyze this question in one of three ways. Most simply, many jurisdictions conclude that abandonment is irrelevant to attempt liability on the theory that a crime, including an attempt, cannot be "uncommitted" once its elements have been satisfied. *See, e.g.,* Collins v. Commonwealth, 720 S.E.2d 530 (Va. 2012). Alternatively, some courts follow the MPC, which provides that if a person's "conduct would otherwise constitute an attempt . . . , it is an affirmative defense that he abandoned his effort to commit the crime" so long as the circumstances demonstrate "a complete and voluntary renunciation of his criminal purpose." Model Penal Code §5.01(4). Courts following this framework must first determine whether the defendant's actions before the point of abandonment would constitute an attempt; if so, "complete and voluntary" abandonment extinguishes liability. Finally, some courts fold evidence of abandonment directly into the *mens rea* and *actus reus* analyses. The *Lammers* opinion reflects this approach when it says that "an act showing a change of direction may raise doubt as to the firmness of the actor's purpose and is a factor to consider in determining whether the substantial step was strongly corroborative of the firmness of the actor's purpose."[14]

NOTES AND QUESTIONS

1. Defenses Versus Elements. Note at least two practical consequences of the distinctions among the frameworks just described. First, if abandonment is classified as an affirmative defense, the defendant may bear the burden of producing evidence supporting the claim, and perhaps the burden of persuading the jury that he in fact abandoned his criminal intentions. Second, taking the alternative approach of incorporating evidence of abandonment into the determination of *actus reus* and *mens rea* can produce some counterintuitive outcomes. Consider, for example, *Commonwealth v. McCloskey*, 341 A.2d 500 (Pa. Super. Ct. 1975). In that case, the defendant, who was incarcerated in Pennsylvania, took a number of steps toward escaping from prison. He acquired street clothes and hid them in a laundry bag, cut a hole through barbed wire leading to the prison yard, and ultimately "scaled a fence within the prison walls that led to the recreation yard and then to the prison wall." *Id.* at 502. But then he changed his mind and turned back, ultimately approaching a guard and admitting, "I was gonna make a break last night, but I changed my mind because I thought of my family, and I got scared of the consequences." *Id.* at 501.

Integrating this evidence of abandonment into its analysis of whether the defendant had ever crossed the line into committing an attempted escape, the Pennsylvania Superior Court reversed the defendant's conviction. The court first observed that McCloskey "went only as far as the yard before giving up his plan." *Id.* at 502. And because he "was thus in a position to abandon the criminal offense of attempted prison breach voluntarily," the court concluded that he was "still only contemplating a prison breach, and not yet attempting the act." *Id.* (emphasizing that he "was still within the prison"). Judge Cercone, concurring only in the result, wrote separately to disagree with the majority's reasoning:

> I would have found little difficulty . . . in affirming appellant's conviction had he been apprehended by the guards immediately after he had snipped the barbed wire and crossed the inner fence. To hold otherwise

is to require that prisoners must literally be plucked from the prison wall before their conduct may be characterized as attempted prison breach. . . . As a practical matter, it has long been recognized that plans voluntarily abandoned are less likely to be found to be attempts than are plans carried to the same point, but interrupted by the apprehension of the perpetrators. Unfortunately, in jurisdictions where voluntary abandonment or renunciation of a criminal purpose has not been recognized as an affirmative defense, the courts have sought to give effect to the defendant's abandonment, *sub silentio*, by characterizing his conduct as "preparatory." That is precisely the error which the majority has made in the instant case. . . . I have concluded that appellant had clearly gone further than preparation. Rather, I would rest the instant decision on appellant's unequivocal and undisputedly voluntary abandonment of his criminal purpose.

Id. at 503-505 (Cercone, J., concurring in the judgment).

2. Complete and Voluntary. In jurisdictions that treat abandonment as a defense, there is the question of what makes such abandonment "complete and voluntary," to quote the MPC formulation. Consider the following two cases.

State v. Riley, 123 A.3d 123 (Conn. App. Ct. 2015). . . . On March 18, 2012, the defendant drove to the Mohegan Sun Casino in Montville in order to make up an $800 gambling loss from the prior day. Upon his arrival at the casino, the defendant attempted to withdraw money from an automated teller machine, but could not do so because his wife had transferred money out of their account. After returning to his car and falling asleep for a period of time, the defendant woke up and decided to commit a robbery. The defendant thus slipped a knife up the sleeve of his sweatshirt and began to walk around the parking garage.

Louise Carty, an eighty-three year old woman, was at the casino . . . to play the penny slots. As she was entering the elevator in the [parking garage, she noticed the defendant] was following her inside. After the elevator door closed, [according to Carty, the defendant] "all of a sudden pulled a knife out of his pocket and headed toward me." In response, Carty screamed, "No, no, no," and shoved [him], causing him to jump away from her. Carty then grabbed the man's sweatshirt by the sleeve and pursued him off the elevator. The man never took or demanded money or property from Carty or verbally threatened her.

At trial, the defendant . . . [testified as follows to describe] what happened in the elevator as he began to approach Carty: "My intentions as I approached her, as I took, like, the second or third step to her, I'm, like, oh, my God, this could by my grandmother; what am I doing? . . . I immediately said I'm sorry. I basically curled the knife toward myself, and I was, like, I'm sorry, I'm sorry. She then grabbed me."

. . . The defendant first claims that the state failed to disprove beyond a reasonable doubt that he renounced his criminal purpose . . . . At common law, renunciation was not universally recognized as a defense to the crime of attempt. . . . Two main reasons have been advanced for allowing the defense of renunciation to the crime of attempt. First, an actor's renunciation of his criminal purpose prior to the completion of a substantive crime suggests that he did not have a firm purpose to commit the crime, and thus tends to negate his dangerousness. Second, the availability of the defense can provide the actor with the motivation to desist from his criminal effort, "thereby diminishing the risk that the substantive crime will be committed." Model Penal Code and Commentaries §5.01 cmt. 8 at 359. Connecticut first codified renunciation as an affirmative defense to the crime of attempt in 1969, basing it in substance on the Model Penal Code. . . .

Construing this evidence in the light most favorable to the state, we conclude . . . [the] jury reasonably could have concluded . . . that the defendant, upon hearing [Carty] scream and feeling her resist him physically, abandoned his criminal effort to rob her under circumstances that were neither voluntary nor complete. The jury reasonably could have concluded that the defendant decided that the screaming Carty would "increase the probability of [his] detection or apprehension," because her actions could draw attention to him. Conn. Gen. Stat. §53a-50 [(describing circumstances when renunciation defense is unavailable)]. Moreover, the jury reasonably could have concluded that Carty's screaming at and wrestling with the defendant—both circumstances that were not apparent at the inception of the defendant's criminal conduct—led the defendant to "postpone [his] criminal conduct or to transfer the criminal effort to another but similar objective or victim," such as a more cooperative victim. *Id.* The video evidence . . . shows the defendant turning away from Carty only *after* she sought to defend herself against him by grabbing him and shoving him away. The jury thus reasonably could have viewed the video as supporting the state's version of events—that the defendant did not abandon his criminal effort until it became clear to him that Carty would not be a passive victim.

Jones v. State, 87 N.E.3d 450 (Ind. 2017). We cherish stories about changes of heart and abandoned criminal endeavors. Take Dr. Seuss's beloved children's tale about the Grinch, whose softened heart and renounced endeavor to steal Christmas ended the story with joyful celebration. This case, too, involves an individual going from house to house overnight, stealing property from sleeping inhabitants—as well as opportunities to abandon criminal efforts and escape liability. But this story's ending gives no reason to celebrate. . . .

One night in Terre Haute, Destin Jones went to several houses and stole various items from the sleeping residents. At about 2:00 a.m., Jones and his accomplice, Stoney Johnson, decided to rob a Speedway gas station.

With dark hoods over their heads, masked faces, and what appeared to be guns in their hands, they walked toward the station from its rear. But unlike the tranquil homes, the station was bustling with a stream of customers. Jones and Johnson lurked for a while on one side of the building, crouched behind a pair of large outdoor freezers. A few times they advanced toward the front entrance before again ducking out of view. Eventually they unmasked their faces, removed their hooded sweatshirts, and entered the store with empty hands—and with a different crime in mind. While customers preoccupied the store's cashier, Jones burglarized the back office and rummaged through the manager's safe. Jones and Johnson then left, retrieving their discarded attire from behind the freezers.

. . . Jones acknowledges on appeal that [in addition to surreptitiously burglarizing the Speedway, he also] attempted . . . to rob the Speedway [and its cashier, insofar as his initial plan had been to enter the store openly and threaten the cashier with weapons. But Jones argues that no rational factfinder could convict him of attempted robbery because] the State failed to disprove his asserted abandonment defense. . . .

For abandonment to be voluntary, the decision to withdraw from the "effort to commit the underlying crime" must "originate with the accused." Ind. Code § 35-41-3-10. That decision must "in no way be attributable" to "extrinsic factors that increase the probability of detection or make more difficult the accomplishment of the criminal purpose." Smith v. State, 636 N.E.2d 124, 127 (Ind. 1994). In other words, abandonment is not voluntary unless the criminal effort was abandoned "under such circumstances as would show that there were no outside causes prompting the abandonment." Barnes v. State, 378 N.E.2d 839, 843 (Ind. 1978).

The State can disprove voluntariness in several ways. It can show that the defendant unexpectedly encountered a person at the crime scene who made the crime harder to carry out. Or that a person or object the defendant *expected* to encounter posed an *unexpected* difficulty. This unexpected difficulty can be as blatant as a stubborn door that won't break open, or as subtle as a bank teller speaking in a voice slightly louder than normal, which "fluster[s]" the defendant, Gravens v. State, 836 N.E.2d 490, 497 (Ind. Ct. App. 2005). Even if the evidence doesn't show an additional obstacle to the criminal endeavor, there is sufficient evidence to disprove voluntariness if the jury could infer that the defendant's abandonment was "due to a fear of discovery" or apprehension, Babin v. State, 609 N.E.2d 3, 5 (Ind. Ct. App. 1993), rather than wholly attributable to a "rising revulsion for the harm intended" or a "change of heart" that "originated with the accused," *Smith*, 636 N.E.2d at 127. . . .

Here, the jury could have inferred that Jones's abandonment was not voluntary because it was at least partially attributable to extrinsic factors. The evidence showed that Jones preferred to commit crimes with a minimal likelihood of detection. All six of Jones's overnight thefts, for example, took place while the victims were sleeping. Unlike those homes, the Speedway presented an obvious danger of detection. When Jones and Johnson arrived, the store was particularly busy, especially for a weekday at about 2:00 a.m. Customers streamed in to purchase snacks and lottery tickets as cars came and went in the front lot. Jones and Johnson did not empty their hands and cast aside their hooded sweatshirts and masks until after they approached the front entrance, where—the jury could infer—they saw how busy the store was and so altered their criminal plan from brash robbery to stealthy burglary. The evidence thus supports two reasonable inferences: (1) that it was the unanticipated steady stream of customers—and not a change of heart—that deterred Jones from carrying out the robbery as planned, or (2) that Jones had anticipated the busyness of the store, but realized upon seeing the parade of patrons that his detection and apprehension were more likely than he had originally appreciated. Either permissible inference is enough to support a jury finding that Jones's abandonment was not voluntary, which defeats his abandonment defense.

2. Impossibility

To this point, we have considered two general fact patterns that implicate the law of attempt. Sometimes, an attempt is *complete:* the defendant has done all she can to commit a crime but fails to effectuate a criminally proscribed result, as occurs when an attacker shoots to kill but misses or delivers only a nonfatal blow. Other times, attempts are *incomplete:* the defendant begins pursuing a criminal end but (for some reason) stops short of the intended criminal endpoint, as occurred in both *Lammers* and the dangerous proximity cases above.

There remains one additional set of cases. Sometimes, the defendant sets out to commit a crime but, for reasons not apparent to the defendant at the time, her course of conduct *cannot possibly* lead to a completed offense. Consider, for example, the case of Saira Jabr, who "drove across the country from California to the District of Columbia with an intention to meet with then-President Trump in person."

> [Jabr] believed herself to be a victim of a conspiracy between law enforcement and various casinos she visited on her trip, and she felt compelled to inform the President about it face-to-face. When her car's GPS device marked her arrival at the White House, she parked the car, exited it, scaled two fences, ran across a courtyard, and sprinted up the stairs of the building towards the entrance, where Secret Service officers intercepted her.
>
> However ill-conceived Jabr's plan to attain an audience with the President may have been in its design, it was all the more unlikely to succeed because of a significant hiccup in its implementation: Jabr, it turned out, had dashed up the stairs of the wrong building. She had tried to enter the United States Treasury Building, which sits immediately adjacent to the White House.

United States v. Jabr, 4 F.4th 97, 99-100 (D.C. Cir. 2021). In this case, the key question was whether Jabr violated a very specific federal statute that prohibits entering the "White House or its grounds" without lawful authority. The prosecution conceded that the Treasury Building lies outside the "White House grounds," which prompted the key question: Could Jabr be convicted of *attempting* to enter the White House without permission when her actual course of conduct, followed all the way through to completion, could not have violated that statute?

Courts have grappled with fact patterns of this general nature, which are referred to as *impossibility* cases, for over a century. Early courts drew fine and highly formalistic distinctions between a subset of cases that came to be called *factual impossibility* cases, in which attempt liability attached, and another subset known as *legal impossibility* cases, in which it didn't. More recently, prompted largely by the MPC's intervention, most jurisdictions have abandoned the distinction and largely abolished the so-called impossibility defense by imposing liability in both sets of cases. The following case discusses this doctrinal evolution.

People v. Thousand, 631 N.W.2d 694 (Mich. 2001). Deputy William Liczbinski was assigned by the Wayne County Sheriff's Department to conduct an undercover investigation [in which he would] pose as a minor and log onto "chat rooms" on the Internet for the purpose of identifying persons using the Internet as a means for engaging in criminal activity. [W]hile using the screen name "Bekka," Liczbinski was approached by defendant, who . . . described himself as a twenty-three-year-old male from Warren. [Posing as Bekka, Liczbinski pretended to be] a fourteen-year-old female from Detroit. . . . [T]he conversation became sexually explicit. Defendant made repeated lewd invitations to Bekka to engage in various sexual acts, despite various indications of her young age. During one of his online conversations with Bekka, after asking her whether anyone was "around there," watching her, defendant indicated that he was sending her a picture of himself. Within seconds, Liczbinski received over the Internet a photograph of male genitalia. . . .

[The defendant was charged with] attempted distribution of obscene material to a minor [and other offenses. He argued that], because the existence of a child victim was an element of each of the charged offenses, the evidence was legally insufficient to support the charges. The circuit court agreed and dismissed the case, holding that it was legally impossible for defendant to have committed the charged offenses. . . .

The doctrine of "impossibility" as it has been discussed in the context of inchoate crimes represents the conceptual dilemma that arises when, because of the defendant's mistake of fact or law, his actions could not possibly have resulted in the commission of the substantive crime underlying an attempt charge. Classic illustrations of the concept of impossibility include [cases where] the defendant is prosecuted for attempted larceny after he tries to "pick" the victim's empty pocket[;] the defendant is prosecuted for attempting to receive stolen property where the property he received was not, in fact, stolen; and the defendant is prosecuted for attempting to hunt deer out of season after he shoots at a stuffed decoy deer. In each of these examples, despite evidence of the defendant's criminal intent, he cannot be prosecuted for the *completed* offense . . . because proof of at least one element of each offense cannot be derived from his objective actions. The question, then, becomes whether the defendant can be prosecuted for the *attempted* offense, and the answer is dependent upon whether he may raise the defense of "impossibility."

Courts and legal scholars have drawn a distinction between two categories of impossibility: "factual impossibility" and "legal impossibility." [A]t common law, legal impossibility is a defense to a charge of attempt, but factual impossibility is not. . . . An example of a "factual impossibility" scenario is where the defendant is prosecuted for attempted murder after pointing an unloaded gun at someone and pulling the trigger, where the defendant believed the gun was loaded. [By contrast, courts] have recognized a defense of legal impossibility or have stated that it would exist if [a defendant] receives unstolen property believing it was stolen[;] offers a bribe to a "juror" who is not a juror; tries to hunt deer out of season by shooting a stuffed animal; shoots a corpse believing that it is alive; or shoots at a tree stump believing that it is a human. [In each of these cases, the conduct the defendant performed is (albeit unbeknownst to him) not actually a crime.] . . .

It is notable that "the great majority of jurisdictions have . . . abolished impossibility as a defense." United States v. Hsu, 155 F.3d 189, 199 (3d Cir. 1998). For example, several states have adopted statutory provisions similar to Model Penal Code §5.01(1), which provides: "A person is guilty of an attempt to commit a crime if, acting with the kind of culpability otherwise required for commission of the crime, he purposely engages in conduct which would constitute the crime if the attendant circumstances were *as he believes them to be* . . . or . . . purposely does . . . anything which, *under the circumstances as he believes them to be*, [would be] a substantial step in a course of conduct planned to culminate in his commission of the [intended] crime."[*]

---

* Editor's Note: Elsewhere in the court's opinion, the court explains that "it is generally undisputed" even in states following the MPC approach that one remaining variant of impossibility "will bar an attempt conviction." *Thousand*, 631 N.W.2d at 698. This variant occurs "when an actor engages in conduct that he believes is criminal, but is not actually prohibited by law. . . . As an example, consider the case of a man who believes that the legal age of consent is sixteen years old, and who believes that a girl with whom he had consensual sexual intercourse is fifteen years old. If the law actually fixed the age of consent at fifteen, this man would not be guilty of attempted statutory rape, despite his mistaken belief that the law prohibited his conduct." *Id.* at 699.

The Court of Appeals panel in this case . . . concluded that it was legally impossible for defendant to have committed the charged offense of attempted distribution of obscene material to a minor. The panel held that, because "Bekka" was, in fact, an adult, an essential requirement of the underlying substantive offense was not met (dissemination to a minor), and therefore it was legally impossible for defendant to have committed the crime.

[T]he concept of "impossibility," in either its "factual" or "legal" variant, has never been recognized by this Court as a valid defense to a charge of attempt. . . . We are unable to discern from the words of the attempt statute any legislative intent that the concept of "impossibility" provide any impediment to charging a defendant with, or convicting him of, an attempted crime. . . . The attempt statute carves out no exception for those who, possessing the requisite criminal intent to commit an offense prohibited by law and taking action toward the commission of that offense, have acted under an extrinsic misconception. . . . The notion that it would be "impossible" for the defendant to have committed the *completed* offense [of distributing lewd material to a minor when he actually distributed it to an adult] is simply irrelevant to the analysis. Rather, in deciding guilt on a charge of attempt, the trier of fact must examine the unique circumstances of the particular case and determine whether the prosecution has proven that the defendant possessed the requisite specific intent and that he engaged in some act "towards the commission" of the intended offense.

NOTES AND QUESTIONS

1. Factual vs. Legal Impossibility. As the *Thousand* opinion states, most jurisdictions have essentially abolished the impossibility defense. But not all. Courts in Massachusetts, for example, continue to treat legal impossibility, but not factual impossibility, as a valid defense. In *Commonwealth v. Bell,* 853 N.E.2d 563 (Mass. App. Ct. 2006), an undercover police officer posed as a sex worker willing to sell the sexual favors of a child to the defendant. *Id.* at 565. No actual child was involved in the undercover sting, so, when the officer met the defendant at a prearranged location, she was of course "unable to bring the nonexistent child." *Id.* As the court observed, "Had the police not arrested him, the defendant would have traveled to the nearby park only to discover that his expected, imminent victim was not present." *Id.* at 568.

In a jurisdiction like Massachusetts that still distinguishes between legal and factual impossibility, how should a court rule on the defendant's impossibility defense? Would the court rule the same way on the facts in *Thousand?* Recall now the facts of *Jabr.* Would the defendant's liability for attempting to enter "the White House grounds" differ under *Thousand* and *Bell?* Considering your answers to these questions, why might the MPC and courts adopting its approach be moved to abandon the distinction between legal and factual impossibility and, with it, basically abandon the impossibility defense altogether?

2. Safer Stings. Note a common feature of both the *Thousand* and *Bell* cases above: Both involve sting operations. Generally speaking, a sting operation is any undercover law enforcement tactic in which the police actively promote or manufacture criminal activity that they closely watch unfold in real time, in hopes of catching an unsuspecting target in the act of offending. The tactic inevitably involves either confidential informants, undercover officers, or both — and can raise a host of concerns discussed at length in Chapter Seven in connection with the doctrine of entrapment. The added insight here is that attempt doctrine makes stings even more attractive to law enforcement by making them safer and easier to control. The police can mitigate the risk that any actual crime will occur by arresting the target of the sting at any point after he crosses the *actus reus* threshold. And impossibility doctrine makes stings safer still. Leveraging the cases above, agents running a sting can *guarantee* the planned offense will never occur by making it impossible for the defendant to commit it. A reverse buy-and-bust operation can be conducted with shrink-wrapped kilograms of baking soda in place of cocaine. A child-molestation sting operation can be run without any children. A stash-house-robbery sting, as in Chapter Seven's *Mayfield* case, need not involve an actual house. In each case, it is impossible for the sting's targets to cause harm by committing the imagined offense. But they can be arrested and prosecuted for it all the same.

D. Attempt in Relation to Other Forms of Liability

As suggested in the introduction to this chapter, attempt liability is a central doctrinal tool with which law enforcement actors can engage in *preemptive* or *proactive* policing. It allows police officers to effectuate lawful arrests and prosecutors to obtain convictions *before* the harm implicated by a defendant's future conduct materializes. As should by now be clear, attempt liability is a robust doctrinal tool for pursuing such early intervention. But it is not the only one. In this section, we discuss some close cousins of attempt liability, before turning, in the next half of the chapter, to the law of criminal possession, another major tool of preemptive policing.

NOTES AND QUESTIONS

1. Substantive Crimes Incorporating Attempts. Nearly every jurisdiction in the United States has a general attempt statute that operates along the lines discussed in this chapter. As explained above, these laws make it a crime to attempt to commit any of the substantive offenses in the penal code. But many jurisdictions also have other, more specific penal statutes that criminalize preparatory conduct or actions that resemble criminal attempts within a narrower set of factual circumstances.[15]

Some of these statutes simply criminalize a completed offense and attempts to commit it in one fell swoop. The federal criminal code, for example, punishes anyone who "knowingly transfers obscene matter" to a minor "or attempts to do so," 18 U.S.C. §1470, or anyone who "knowingly and willfully damages or attempts or conspires to damage the property of an energy facility," 18 U.S.C. §1366. Note that one consequence of criminalizing these attempts alongside the completed substantive crime is that any distinction in statutorily authorized punishments between attempt and completion disappears, because attempts and completed offenses violate the very same statute. These statutes bear a structural similarity to the longstanding crime of assault, which dates back to the common law and which, in many places, is defined to include an attempt to commit physical battery.[16]

Separately, some substantive crimes consist of engaging in wrongful conduct en route to committing another, more serious crime—even if that more serious crime is never actually completed. Burglary, for example, is commonly defined as breaking and entering (itself a crime) with the specific intent to commit some other crime—traditionally a felony—inside the targeted property (p. 448).[17]

Finally, some statutes make stand-alone crimes of specific preparatory acts. One federal statute, for example, makes it a crime "to teach or demonstrate the making or use of an explosive . . . with the intent that the teaching . . . be used for, or in furtherance of, an activity that constitutes a Federal crime of violence." 18 U.S.C. § 842. Likewise, an Illinois statute punishes anyone who "[e]nters or remains in a place of prostitution with intent to engage in an act of sexual penetration." 720 Ill. Comp. Stat. Ann. 5/11-18. We will return to this idea of criminalizing specific acts of preparation when we discuss the law of possession later in this chapter.

2. Solicitation. How does the law of attempt interact with doctrines of group liability encountered in the preceding chapter? Consider the following true story:

> Wendy Wein . . . wanted her ex-husband dead. But she didn't want to kill him herself and didn't know anyone she trusted to do it for her. So she did what a lot of people do when they have a job they can't or don't want to do themselves—she searched for help on the Internet. On RentAHitman.com. What Wein found was presumably reassuring. The website promised her confidentiality. It boasted of industry awards. It showed off testimonials of satisfied customers. . . .
>
> The trouble for Wein was that RentAHitman.com is a fake website. It's [run] by Bob Innes, a 54-year-old Northern California man who

forwards any serious inquiries to law enforcement. Innes launched the site 16 years ago as part of an Internet security business that never went anywhere. Instead, it has served as a honeypot of sorts, attracting people who want to hire professional killers.[18]

If Innes had been a real hitman and had gone through with killing Wein's ex-husband, Wein would clearly be guilty of murder as Innes' accomplice, given that she encouraged him to commit the crime. Likewise, if Innes had *attempted* to murder Wein's ex-husband but failed—for example, by shooting and missing—Wein would be an accomplice to and thus guilty of that attempted murder. Indeed, if Innes had merely pretended to agree with Wein's plan but never followed through, Wein would still be guilty of conspiracy to commit murder in the majority of jurisdictions that recognize unilateral conspiracies.

But what if Innes instead simply forwards Wein's murder-for-hire request to the police, without ever responding to her? Precisely because Innes committed no crime, complicity liability would be off the table. And there was no conspiracy because Innes never agreed to participate in any murder. But is Wein nonetheless guilty (as a principal) of *attempting* to kill her ex-husband, by trying to get someone else to do so? Many courts would say no, either because her acts did not pass the threshold from preparation to attempt or because she never intended to commit the offense herself. In most jurisdictions, however, Wein would still be exposed to prosecution under an offense bearing a close relationship to attempt liability that covers precisely this scenario: criminal *solicitation.*[19]

In one commonplace formulation, an individual commits solicitation "if, with the intent that another person engage in conduct constituting a crime, he or she solicits, requests, commands or importunes another person to engage in such conduct." Ala. Code §13A-4-1(a)(1). As Wein's case makes clear, for solicitation liability to lie, it is not necessary that the crime solicited be completed, attempted, or even agreed to. For this reason, solicitation has been called "the most inchoate of the three anticipatory offenses." State v. Jensen, 195 P.3d 512, 517 (Wash. 2008). In the words of the Model Penal Code's primary drafters, it is a mere "attempt to conspire." And as is true of attempt, punishment for solicitation is typically keyed to, but less than, punishment for the crime solicited, though some states allow the two to be punished equally. *Compare, e.g.,* Ala. Code §13A-4-1(f) (grading solicitation one offense level below the offense solicited), *with, e.g.,* Mont. Code Ann. §45-4-101(2) (prescribing punishment for solicitation up to the maximum for the offense solicited).[20]

3. Efforts to Aid Crimes That Never Occur. Solicitation statutes are most relevant when a person importunes someone else to commit a crime but fails to persuade him to do so. But as we saw in Chapter Seven, complicity liability can also attach when an accomplice renders aid instead of encouragement. What if the crime that aid is designed to facilitate similarly never occurs? Recall from our discussion of complicity liability the case of Judge Tally, who tried to assist the Skelton brothers in killing Robert Ross by blocking a telegram that would have warned Ross he was in danger (p. 533). When the Skeltons murdered Ross, Tally's efforts made him an accomplice. Similarly, if the Skeltons had attempted but failed to murder Ross—if their bullets had missed their mark—Tally would have been an accomplice to this attempted murder. But imagine that instead Tally was mistaken about the Skeltons' intentions: they never had any plan to kill Ross—but Tally thought they did and sent his telegram in hopes of assisting them. Here, Tally is an accomplice to nothing, as the Skeltons have committed no crime. But is he guilty, as a principal, of attempting to commit a crime?

The traditional common law approach said no. But the Model Penal Code urges otherwise. Section 5.01(3) of the Code states that anyone "who engages in conduct designed to aid another to commit a crime which would establish his complicity . . . if the crime were committed by such other person, is guilty of an attempt to commit the crime, although the crime is not committed or attempted by such other person." Under this rule, Tally would be guilty of attempted murder even if the Skeltons never planned to harm Ross, because Tally's conduct was "designed to aid" the Skeltons in murdering Ross and would have established Tally's complicity in such a murder had the Skeltons committed it.[21]

Notice how this provision works hand in hand with the crime of solicitation—both provide paths to liability for people who try to facilitate crimes that never occur. Conduct that requests or commands someone else to commit a crime is punished as solicitation. Conduct designed to aid another in the commission of a crime is punished as an attempt.

II. POSSESSION

> "[T]he offense of possession—whether of drugs, of guns, or anything else—has emerged as the policing device of choice in the war on crime."
>
> Markus Dirk Dubber, *Policing Possession: The War on Crime and the End of Criminal Law*, 91 J. Crim. L. & Criminology 829, 855 (2001)

How does the law of attempt relate to the set of statutes and doctrines that criminalize the possession of prohibited items? Consider the following case.

People v. Southard

62 Cal. Rptr. 3d 48 (Cal. Ct. App. 2007)

RICHMAN, J. . . . At 12:00 noon on March 15, 2005, Crescent City Police Officer Eric Apperson was on patrol in a marked police car when he observed [an Oldsmobile] vehicle . . . speeding north on A Street at an estimated 35 to 40 miles per hour in a 25-mile per hour residential zone. . . . [B]oth driver's side windows were down, and Apperson recognized the driver as [John Southard], who he had encountered several times in the past. Through the open window, Apperson yelled for defendant to stop; rather than complying with the command, defendant accelerated, proceeding through an intersection without stopping at the stop sign and continuing to pick up speed. [The chase continued through side streets at speeds near 90 miles per hour and ended with Southard getting out of the car and running into a swamp behind a cemetery. The police] set up a perimeter around the swamp. Defendant was apprehended in the swamp area approximately 40 minutes later.

After defendant had been taken into custody and read his *Miranda* rights, he was asked by an officer why he fled. He responded that it was because his license was suspended. A search of defendant uncovered a key that operated the doors and ignition of the Oldsmobile. [The police] conducted a full inventory of the Oldsmobile after it had been towed from the scene and found a myriad of tools, including a steel pry bar, a crow bar, five pairs of pliers, a large pair of bolt cutters, a sledge hammer, an unspecified number of screwdrivers and hammers, and a tool box. [They] also found three walkie-talkie radios, two black sweatshirts (including one with a hood), a strap-on head light, a flashlight, a ski mask, a pair of binoculars, a bundle of in excess of 100 keys, and an assortment of loose keys.

At trial, [police officer Paul] Arnett opined that the items were for possible use in a burglary. While acknowledging on cross-examination that the individual items also had legitimate purposes, Arnett explained on redirect that although none of the individual items was illegal to possess, the sum of items made them suspicious because, collectively, the tools would be useful for breaking into a building. . . .

Karen Olson, a chief deputy district attorney, also testified at trial. According to Olson, some time in April 2005, she had a conversation with defendant in which he requested "his burglary tools, a release for his burglary tools." Concerning this, Olson explained at trial that "[i]t struck me as odd. I actually found it amusing. I thought he was joking."

As pertinent here, [penal code] section 466 provides, "Every person having upon him or her in his or her possession a picklock, crow, keybit, crowbar, screwdriver . . . or other instrument or tool with intent feloniously to break or enter into any building . . . is guilty of a misdemeanor."

[To convict under this statute,] the prosecution must establish three elements: (1) possession by the defendant; (2) of tools within the purview of the statute; (3) with the intent to use the tools for the felonious purposes of breaking or entering.

[Southard argues] that his conviction for possession of burglary tools in violation of section 466 must be reversed because there was insufficient evidence of the third element, namely his intent to use the tools for a felonious purpose. . . . The thrust of defendant's argument appears to be that in order to prove intent . . . the prosecution [must] establish that defendant has a history of committing burglaries, committed a burglary in the area, or had "loot" in his possession. . . .

While other jurisdictions have recognized a wide range of circumstances that evidence the requisite intent, we discuss only those circumstances present here demonstrating the substantial evidence supporting defendant's conviction.

First, cases have recognized that the possession of items commonly used by burglars to facilitate a burglary, but not themselves within the statutory definition of burglary tools, can evidence the requisite felonious intent. . . . [P]ersuasive is *Burrell v. State*, 429 So.2d 636 (Ala. Crim. App. 1982). There, the police responded to an early morning report of a suspicious vehicle but found nothing out of the ordinary and left. They were called back to the scene a short while later, where they found an individual training a gun on the defendant, who was lying on the ground with a ballpeen hammer, a nail prying tool, a broken hacksaw blade, and a screwdriver in his hand and a flashlight and a pair of gloves in his pocket. The defendant was convicted of possession of burglar's tools. . . . The court explained, "Although a flashlight is not adapted for breaking and entering and a conviction under the statute could not be based on the possession of that item alone, it is relevant to the question of intent when possessed along with other tools which are adapted for nefarious purposes. It follows that appellant's possession of the gloves would also be relevant to the question of intent."

Here, defendant was found in possession of numerous tools that clearly fall within the scope of section 466, such as a steel pry bar, a crow bar, multiple pairs of pliers, a large pair of bolt cutters, a sledge hammer, screwdrivers, and hammers. At the same time defendant was also in possession of two black sweatshirts, a ski mask, a pair of binoculars, multiple walkie-talkie radios, a flashlight, and a strap-on head light. [D]efendant's possession of these items can be considered when evaluating the purpose for which defendant possessed the tools. That evaluation strongly supports the inference that defendant possessed the "burglary tools" with a felonious intent. . . .

A second indicia of intent present here is flight from law enforcement. . . . Here, the testimony of Officers Apperson and Arnett clearly established defendant's attempt to flee from law enforcement, so much so that he was convicted of evading a peace officer. This flight was suggestive of defendant's consciousness of guilt. It, too, supports a finding of felonious intent. . . .

Last, but by no means incidentally, we have the unique evidence of defendant's intent not found in any other authority we examined: *defendant requested his "burglary tools" back from the district attorney's office.* Defendant dismisses the significance of this evidence because Olson also testified she thought defendant was "joking." . . . [But] the jury was at liberty to interpret defendant's request as it reasonably saw fit and could have disagreed with Olson that defendant was making a joke.

In sum, defendant's possession of other items outside the scope of section 466 but also used to commit burglaries, his flight from law enforcement, his transportation of the suspect items collectively in his vehicle, and his request for the return of his "burglary tools" constitute substantial evidence of defendant's felonious intent supporting the jury verdict.

NOTES AND QUESTIONS

1. Possession as Preparation. The defendant in *Southard* was convicted under a statute that made it a crime to possess burglary tools. The key question in the case concerned his intent. Was there sufficient evidence that he intended to use these items *as* burglary tools? Implicit in this question is an important observation about the different functions the law of criminal possession can serve. Typically, the criminal code of a given jurisdiction includes scores of possessory offenses, each prohibiting the possession of certain items. Some of these items, like the nerve gas sarin or the poison ricin, have virtually no legitimate use and are essentially banned without exception across the globe. Others are unlawful to possess only in certain circumstances. For example, an item might be unlawful to possess by anyone under a certain age, as is true of alcohol, or by anyone without a special license or permit, as is true of many explosives and, sometimes, firearms. In these instances, the assumption is that the item is either inherently dangerous or at least too risky to be possessed under the proscribed circumstances or by the proscribed groups of people.[22]

But sometimes the criminal law prohibits possession of seemingly inoffensive items—like the flashlights, pliers, and hammer that supported the conviction in *Southard*. Here, possession statutes are doing something fundamentally different. Rather than ban or cabin the use of inherently harmful or risky items, they prohibit possession that, in the words of one leading treatise, is "of itself harmless but which has been made criminal because it is (or is very likely to be) a step toward the doing of harm." As we saw in *Southard*, these statutes distinguish between innocuous and unlawful possession of such items by deciphering the possessor's intent. Possessing a flashlight for the purpose of telling ghost stories, navigating a blackout, or pretending to be a Jedi is thus perfectly lawful. But possessing it with the purpose of burglarizing a home is a crime.[23]

Understood in these terms, the relationship between "a host of possession-type crimes" and the law of criminal attempts becomes readily apparent. Both criminalize actions that are steps toward the commission of some other offense, and both use a specific-intent requirement to help separate innocuous conduct from criminal conduct. Indeed, when possessory offenses are used in this fashion, they are indistinguishable from the specialized attempt statutes described earlier in this chapter, which similarly criminalize discrete forms of preparatory conduct such as teaching a person how to use an explosive device with the intent that it will be used in a crime of violence. Like those statutes, possession statutes criminalize a discrete set of acts along the road to some other offense — either mirroring the law of attempt or expanding it, if simple possession would otherwise be deemed "merely preparatory in nature" and thus not "encompassed within the general law of attempts" in the jurisdiction.[24]

2. Possession as Demand-Side Market Regulation. The preceding note observes how criminal possession statutes can closely track the law of attempt and can thus function, like attempt statutes, as straightforward tools of preventive policing. But possession statutes can also operate more broadly, as second-order tools of prevention that aim to curtail future crime indirectly. One way in which this occurs is when possession laws are used to target consumers or end users of items that are harmful to *produce*. Statutes prohibiting possession of child pornography are a salient example, as the Supreme Court explained in *Ohio v. Osborne*, 495 U.S. 103 (1990), which upheld such a statute against First Amendment challenge. *Id.* at 111. In *Osborne*, the defendant attempted to invoke existing Supreme Court precedent barring states from criminalizing the private possession of obscene materials depicting adults. *Id.* at 108. As the *Osborne* Court wrote:

> The difference here is obvious: The State does not rely on a paternalistic interest in regulating Osborne's mind. Rather, Ohio has enacted [its statute] in order to protect the victims of child pornography; it hopes to destroy a market for the exploitative use of children. "It is evident beyond the need for elaboration that a State's interest in safeguarding the physical and psychological well-being of a minor is compelling." New York v. Ferber, 458 U.S. 747, 756-758 (1982). It is also surely reasonable for the State to conclude that it will decrease the production of child pornography if it penalizes those who possess and view the product, thereby decreasing demand. . . . Osborne contends that the State should use other measures, besides penalizing possession, to dry up the child pornography market. . . . [But given] the importance of the State's interest in protecting

the victims of child pornography, we cannot fault Ohio for attempting to stamp out this vice at all levels in the distribution chain. . . . [M]uch of the child pornography market has been driven underground; as a result, it is now difficult, if not impossible, to solve the child pornography problem by only attacking production and distribution. Indeed, 19 States have found it necessary to proscribe the possession of this material.

Id. at 109-111. A similar rationale can be used to explain any number of statutes criminalizing possession of items by consumers in an effort to dry up markets and prevent harms further up the distribution chain. Statutes criminalizing receipt of stolen property, for example, aim to squelch the market for stolen goods and thus prevent future thefts by making them less economically attractive. And as we will soon see, similar arguments have been advanced—not without controversy—to support statutes criminalizing the simple possession of drugs.[25]

3. Possession as Proxy, Possession as Pretext. Market regulation is not the only way the state can use possession statutes as indirect tools of preemptive policing. Two other uses are both common and controversial. First, possessory offenses sometimes operate, at least in part, as *proxies* for other types of harmful behavior. Possession of large quantities of drugs, for example, might be criminalized in part on the theory that it correlates with a distinct set of harmful conduct, such as gun violence or gang-related killings. The preventive logic here is that, in prosecuting and incapacitating large numbers of drug dealers, the state might also prevent some number of future shootings and homicides—even though it won't be able to point to any particular person as someone it knows (or even reliably predicts) would have committed such a crime if left free. Second, and even more controversially, possessory offenses can serve as a *pretextual* hook for preemptive interventions by the police. Here, widely possessed items, like marijuana cigarettes, might be criminalized not because their possession correlates with future harm, but rather to give police the power to take preemptive action against (i.e., to question, search, or arrest) any number of people they believe pose a threat or should otherwise be targeted for intervention or social control. We explore these potential uses of possessory offenses in the two remaining sections of this chapter, and will continue examining these themes in the chapter that follows, which discusses policing and law enforcement discretion.

A. Possessing Drugs

"[The] invention of the war on drugs as a political tool was cynical, but every president since—Democrat and Republican alike—has found it equally useful for one reason or another."

Dan Baum, *Legalize It All,* Harper's Mag. (Apr. 2016)

As we saw in the preceding section, an array of rationales can be invoked, alone or in combination, to support the enactment or expansion of a given possessory offense. Such a statute might be justified on the ground that possession of the item in question is inherently harmful, that it is harmful in certain discrete circumstances, that it represents preparatory action toward some other crime, that it correlates generally with some other set of behaviors, or that it is simply a useful device for allowing the police to target the people they wish to question, search, or arrest. Depending on the context, some of these justifications can raise complicated empirical and normative questions that shape the extent to which a given possession offense can or should be deemed desirable and justified.

Nowhere are these questions more salient than with respect to drugs, the possession of which is broadly criminalized and prosecuted in the United States. Roughly half the people incarcerated in federal prisons are serving time for a drug-related conviction, as are more than ten percent of the people incarcerated in state prisons. These statistics arose within living memory. A little more than a century ago, many of the drugs that can lead to decades-long prison sentences today—including cocaine and heroin—were perfectly legal to possess, and in fact were available for purchase over the counter from local pharmacies. That changed, and incarceration for drug possession exploded, due to a set of criminalization and law enforcement policies adopted in the early 1900s and intensified during the 1980s—a decade that launched what is now commonly called the War on Drugs.[26]

In this section, we will examine the laws and policies governing drug criminalization. We begin with an overview of some of the doctrinal issues related to the law of possession in this context and of the role that drug quantity plays in assessing liability and apportioning punishment. We then explore some of the empirical and normative debates that frame the decades-old and still-live controversy over the War on Drugs.

1.   The Law of Drug Possession: Constructive Possession

State v. Miller

678 S.E.2d 592 (N.C. 2009)

EDMUNDS, J. In this case, we consider whether the evidence presented at defendant's trial for possession of a controlled substance was sufficient to support a finding of guilt based upon the theory of constructive possession. . . . [O]n 8 December 2005, Winston-Salem Police Detective R.J. Paul obtained a search warrant for the residence at 1924 Dacian Street after citizen complaints and resulting surveillance revealed heavy vehicle and pedestrian traffic in the area. Later that day, a Winston-Salem Police Special Enforcement Team entered the residence, commanding everyone to get on the floor. The officers found several individuals in the living room. Defendant, who was sitting on the corner of a bed in an adjoining room, slid to the floor as officers entered. While he was on the floor, defendant's head lay between one to four feet from the bedroom door. Another individual in the bedroom remained seated in a chair about eight feet from the door.

Detective Paul entered the bedroom and recovered a small white rock-like substance from the end of the bed where defendant had been sitting[1] [and] a plastic bag containing several small white rocks from behind the open bedroom door, about two feet from where defendant had been lying on the floor. Later testing revealed that all the material recovered from the bedroom was crack cocaine weighing a total of 1.3 grams. Defendant's birth certificate and state-issued identification card were found on a television stand in the bedroom, along with several small plastic jewelry bags. An officer testified that cocaine is normally packaged in some type of plastic bag and that plastic jewelry bags are sometimes used.

Two of defendant's children lived at 1924 Dacian with their mother, Alicia Johnson. Testifying on behalf of defendant, Johnson stated that defendant did not live in the house and was there at the time of the search because he was preparing to pick up the children from school. She further testified that the furnishings in the bedroom . . . belonged to her and that the crack cocaine found in the room with defendant also was hers. However, she had not been at the residence when police executed the search warrant.

Defendant was tried for possessing cocaine with the intent to sell and deliver. . . . The jury found defendant guilty of simple possession of cocaine . . . and the trial court sentenced him to 107 to 138 months imprisonment. . . .

The State prosecuted defendant upon the theory that he constructively possessed crack cocaine. A defendant constructively possesses contraband when he or she has "the intent and capability to maintain control and dominion over" it. State v. Beaver, 346 S.E.2d 476, 480 (N.C. 1986). The defendant may have the power to control either alone or jointly with others. Unless a defendant has exclusive possession of the place where the contraband is found, the State must show other incriminating circumstances sufficient for the jury to find a defendant had constructive possession.

Our cases addressing constructive possession have tended to turn on the specific facts presented.* [T]wo factors frequently considered are the defendant's proximity to the contraband and indicia of the defendant's

---

1. The record is subject to interpretation as to whether the contraband was in plain view. . . .

* Editor's Note: Here, the majority provides a string citation to five cases with brief parenthetical descriptions; four of these cases are discussed in more detail in the opinion of Justice Brady, below.

control over the place where the contraband is found. Here, police found defendant in a bedroom of the home where two of his children lived with their mother. When first seen, defendant was sitting on the same end of the bed where cocaine was recovered. Once defendant slid to the floor, he was within reach of the package of cocaine recovered from the floor behind the bedroom door. Defendant's birth certificate and state-issued identification card were found on top of a television stand in that bedroom. The only other individual in the room was not near any of the cocaine. Even though defendant did not have exclusive possession of the premises, these incriminating circumstances permit a reasonable inference that defendant had the intent and capability to exercise control and dominion over cocaine in that room.

The Court of Appeals majority found this evidence insufficient, relying in part on the absence of evidence that defendant appeared nervous or made any observed motion to hide anything. However, proper application of the standard of review focuses our analysis on the evidence that the State did present in these highly fact-specific cases, not on evidence that a reviewing court thinks the State should have presented. In other words, absence of evidence is not evidence of absence. Viewing the evidence admitted here in the light most favorable to the State, we hold that sufficient evidence was presented from which a reasonable mind could conclude that defendant constructively possessed cocaine.

BRADY, J., dissenting. Today's majority opinion dangerously turns a blind eye to our well-established precedent setting out the law of constructive possession. The evidence the State presented against defendant was grossly insufficient. . . . Because the majority decision leads our constructive possession jurisprudence down a perilous road of guilt by mere proximity without substantial corroboration, I respectfully dissent. . . .

Upon entering the small, single family residence, law enforcement officers found at least six adults inside.[2] In a bedroom in the front left corner of the residence they discovered Andre Miller (defendant) with another adult male. The record does not contain the exact dimensions of the bedroom, but it was estimated by law enforcement that the foot of the bed was approximately three feet from the door to the room. . . . [D]efendant did not live at 1924 Dacian Street and was at [Ms. Jones's] residence on the day in question because she had asked him to pick up their children from school while she went Christmas shopping. She further stated that the controlled

---

2. Detective R.J. Paul . . . testified that there were six individuals, "give or take a few," at 1924 Dacian Street when the raid occurred. From the video footage taken that day by law enforcement . . . it appears that at least seven adults and at least two children were inside the residence. According to the Forsyth County Tax Administration Office the residence at 1924 Dacian Street has 1176 square feet of living space.

substances were found in her personal bedroom and belonged to her, not defendant. . . .

As noted by several legal scholars and this Court, the law of possession is a morass of confusion and inconsistency. Instead of clarifying existing law, or simply following this Court's well-established precedent, the majority's decision attempts to erase current jurisprudence by allowing any questionable circumstance to qualify as substantial evidence of constructive possession. . . .

While a trial court should view the evidence and every reasonable inference in the light most favorable to the State, the standard of substantial evidence requires more than "a suspicion or conjecture as to either the commission of the offense or the identity of the defendant as the perpetrator of it." In re Vinson, 260 S.E.2d 591, 602 (N.C. 1979). . . . To convict defendant of possession of cocaine under a constructive possession theory, the State is required to present substantial evidence that defendant had the "intent and capability to maintain control and dominion over the narcotics." State v. Matias, 556 S.E.2d 269, 270 (N.C. 2001). . . . In the case *sub judice*, as both the trial court and the Court of Appeals concluded, there was no substantial evidence that defendant had "exclusive possession of the place where the narcotics were found." *Id.* at 271. Therefore, any analysis of whether substantial evidence exists to support the possession charge should be limited to an inquiry of whether "other incriminating circumstances" were present and were substantial enough to tie defendant to the controlled substance to show that he had the intent and capability to maintain control and dominion over it. *Id.* . . .

The majority improvidently asserts that defendant's proximity to the drugs found at 1924 Dacian Street, coupled with the fact that his North Carolina Identification Card and birth certificate were found in the same room are sufficient to conclude he constructively possessed the cocaine. This scintilla of unconvincing evidence hardly establishes constructive possession.

First, the majority's use of proximity evidence to establish an incriminating circumstance is dangerously thin. While proximity to narcotics is always a *factor* in constructive possession cases, it has never been the *only* factor, as illustrated by the very cases the majority relies upon. Until today, evidence of more culpable conduct was always needed. . . . To consider a charge brought on this basis is to ask this Court to "sail in a sea of conjecture and surmise . . . ." State v. Minor, 224 S.E.2d 180, 185 (N.C. 1976). . . .

In every case the majority cites there is ample evidence of incriminating circumstances in addition to evidence of defendant's proximity to narcotics. In *State v. Butler*, the defendant's suspicious behavior and his concerted effort to evade law enforcement officers provided incriminating evidence along with proximity evidence showing that the defendant was observed reaching into an area where narcotics were soon discovered. 567 S.E.2d

137, 141 (N.C. 2002). In the instant case, defendant displayed no suspicious behavior and followed all instructions given to him by law enforcement. . . .

[Consider next *Matias,* where] the defendant was a passenger in a vehicle that had the distinct odor of marijuana and contained rolling papers and marijuana seeds. 556 S.E.2d at 271. [T]his Court ruled that a jury could reasonably determine the defendant at least had knowledge that narcotics were in the vehicle. This evidence was offered in addition to proximity evidence showing that the defendant was the only individual in the vehicle who was able to hide a bag of cocaine between a crease in the seat cushions where it was later discovered. [But] *Matias* is markedly different from the instant case in that it cannot be shown here that defendant even had . . . knowledge that the narcotics were in the bedroom at 1924 Dacian Street. Video footage of the crime scene, shot immediately following the raid, reveals that the narcotics were not in plain view. The small BB-sized pellet of rock cocaine was seized from among the light-colored sheets of a disheveled bed, and the small plastic bag containing cocaine was found on the floor in a dark corner behind an open door. As the trial judge perceptively stated, this bag "could have been there for weeks." Furthermore, there were at least five other adults in the residence when the items were discovered. To conclude that defendant constructively possessed these objects, let alone even knew they were in the room, is mere conjecture and speculation. . . .

Lastly, the majority attempts to use *State v. Baxter,* 208 S.E.2d 696 (N.C. 1974), and *State v. Allen,* 183 S.E.2d 680 (N.C. 1971). . . . Both are critically distinguishable from the present case. In *Baxter,* the State presented evidence, which included men's clothing found in dresser drawers containing marijuana and a man's jacket with marijuana in its pocket, that was sufficient to show the defendant occupied the bedroom in which the narcotics were seized. In *Allen,* the defendant's United States Uniform Services identification card and several other papers bearing the defendant's name were found in the residence; public utilities for the residence were listed in the defendant's name; and a sixteen year old witness testified that he had obtained heroin from the residence pursuant to the defendant's directions. No similar evidence can be found in the present record to justify a finding of incriminating circumstances. No personal effects belonging to defendant were found at the residence, and the State could offer no other proof, aside from physical presence, to suggest defendant had any control over the premises at 1924 Dacian Street.

When evidence of incriminating circumstances [is] lacking . . . , this Court has repeatedly rejected theories of constructive possession. . . . The majority offers the fact that defendant was in *someone else's* bedroom, with *another individual,* where cocaine and plastic jewelry bags were discovered to support this conviction. . . . [And b]ecause it is well established that proximity to narcotics alone cannot substantiate a finding of constructive possession, the majority uses the fact that defendant's North Carolina State

Identification Card and birth certificate were found in the bedroom with the narcotics to show indicia of his control over the room. This is not substantial evidence. There exist many innocent, plausible explanations of why defendant had two forms of identification with him while he was visiting 1924 Dacian Street and why these documents were in the room where defendant was found.[8] Additionally, these identification documents were found on top of an entertainment center near the door to the bedroom, not tucked away in a drawer or filing cabinet. In today's society who does not, as a matter of course, carry an identification card? Furthermore, how is the presence of a certificate of live birth evidence of an incriminating circumstance? . . .

The majority's decision today effectively nullifies the substantial evidence requirement in constructive possession cases, thereby giving the State free reign to prosecute anyone who happens to be at the wrong place at the wrong time. . . . This unprecedented, unjustified, and unfounded expansion of the law strains credulity and dangerously exposes our citizens to prosecutorial overreaching at the expense of personal liberty. Therefore, I respectfully dissent.

[Opinion of TIMMONS-GOODSON, J., dissenting, omitted.]

NOTES AND QUESTIONS

1. "Confusion and Inconsistency." The *Miller* opinions set out some broadly accepted precepts of the law of possession. First, possession can be either *actual*, meaning physical, or, as in *Miller, constructive.* Second, possession need not be exclusive; two or more people can possess the same item at once. Third, possession typically must be conscious; a person must know he possesses the item in question. And finally, in cases of constructive possession, mere proximity to an item will generally be insufficient. Rather, a person must have both the power and the intention to exercise control over the item, a requirement sometimes captured by the phrase "dominion and control." As the *Miller* case illustrates, such dominion and control can be, and often is, demonstrated through circumstantial evidence.

And yet, notwithstanding these shared principles, it is not uncommon for judges to declare, as Justice Brady does in *Miller*, that "the law of possession is a morass of confusion and inconsistency." This inconsistency stems from the fact that, to quote one leading treatise, the "word 'possession' is often used in the criminal law without definition," or least

---

8. In fact, the record reveals that defendant was scheduled to pick up two of his children from school on the afternoon of the raid. Identification is often required to pick up children from school. Driver's licenses, state-issued identification cards, uniform service identification cards, birth certificates, and/or passports are the forms of identification normally associated with establishing an individual's actual identity.

without a definition that is "informative in any functional manner." Rather, as Professor Charles Whitebread and Ronald Stevens put it, the "terms 'dominion' and 'control' are nothing more than labels used by courts to characterize given sets of facts," which vary from one case to another *ad infinitum*.[27]

As Justice Antonin Scalia once famously wrote, such intensely fact-bound inquiries invite inconsistent outcomes. "Today," one group of appellate judges may "decide that these nine facts" support a given outcome, but "[w]hether only eight of them will do so — or whether the addition of a tenth will change the outcome — are questions for another day. . . . To adopt such an approach . . . is effectively to conclude that uniformity is not a particularly important objective with respect to the legal question at issue." And indeed, appellate decisions attempting to navigate the law of constructive possession have "given rise to so many conflicting rulings 'that for the practitioner the problems are difficult to understand and apparently for the courts impossible to master.' "[28]

Thus, while cases like *Miller*, in which a defendant is held to have constructively possessed drugs — and is sentenced to a decade in prison as a result — are commonplace, it is also possible to find any number of cases with stronger evidence of possession in which defendants are deemed not guilty as a matter of law. *See, e.g.*, Williams v. State, 110 So.3d 59, 61 (Fla. Dist. Ct. App. 2013) (no constructive possession of marijuana found in a bag in a car even though "the car was rented in [the defendant's] name, she was driving it, and her personal belongings were in the car, [and] there was nothing on or in the black bag that tied it [to] anyone else"); Conley v. State, 433 S.W.3d 234 (Ark. 2014) (no constructive possession of marijuana found in laundry room of house owned and occupied by defendant and his family, even though marijuana also found in his bedroom).

2. Possession vs. Conspiracy. Many constructive possession cases arise in circumstances involving multiple people, as was the case in *Miller*, where at least six adults were found relatively close to the drugs. Sometimes, surrounding circumstances will give prosecutors a basis to charge people in such cases under two overlapping theories of liability: as individual constructive possessors of the drugs or as co-conspirators in drug-related crimes who are vicariously liable for each other's possession. Oftentimes, prosecutors will take a belt-and-suspenders approach, charging both theories at once, as occurred in *United States v. Hunte*, 196 F.3d 687 (7th Cir. 1999). In that case, the facts were as follows:

> In March 1997, Hunte decided to accompany her boyfriend, now co-defendant, Joseph Richards, on a trip to California with an acquaintance known as Luis Gonzalez. Richards was a known drug dealer, and there was little mystery that the purpose of the trip was to purchase and bring back a load of narcotics. . . . Richards agreed to pay Gonzalez seven pounds

of marijuana for help driving the van. . . . Hunte, on the other hand, stood to gain nothing from the deal. She apparently went along for the ride. Richards directed the trip and made all or most of the decisions. [When a van full of drugs was eventually delivered to the house where the group was staying], Hunte remained in the living room watching television. With Hunte in the other room, the . . . men weighed the bundles of marijuana. Richards cut one bundle open to make sure it was all marijuana and extracted some buds for sampling. Gonzalez testified at trial that Richards took precautions to keep Hunte out of the business aspects of the deal. Hunte helped roll the buds into a joint and closed the window blinds while the group smoked the marijuana. . . . Richards and Gonzalez re-wrapped the marijuana and loaded it into the van. [During a portion of the trip,] Hunte registered for a motel room for herself and Richards. . . . Richards paid all expenses, including the motels, throughout the trip.

Questions: On the facts above, is there sufficient evidence to sustain a conviction of Hunte on a charge of conspiracy to possess the entire van's worth of marijuana? Is there sufficient evidence to conclude that she constructively possessed all of those drugs? Which charge seems easier to prove?

3. *"Women of Circumstance."* The *Miller* and *Hunte* cases share a feature common in many drug prosecutions. Each involves a man and a woman with a familial or intimate bond who are jointly exposed to liability for drug-related crimes. In *Miller*, the mother of the defendant's children testified "that the controlled substances were found in her personal bedroom and belonged to her, not defendant." In *Hunte*, the defendant was a drug dealer's girlfriend who, to quote the opinion, "went along for the ride" as he drove across the country trafficking marijuana.

These cases raise a broader set of questions about the impact that drug policy has on "women of circumstance," a phrase Shimica Gaskins uses to refer to "women who are minimally involved in drug crime, but are disparately punished by the existing criminal justice system" because they "are the wives, mothers, sisters, daughters, girlfriends, and nieces" of "a male drug trafficker." A 2005 report by the ACLU entitled *Caught in the Net: The Impact of Drug Policies on Women and Families*, highlights the role that substantive criminal law—including the law of constructive possession—has played in exposing some of these women to criminal liability.[29]

As the terms "kingpin" and "drug lord" denote, men are almost always at the head of major drug operations, and yet the [growth] rate of imprisonment of women for drug crimes has far outpaced that of men. Families and children suffer—but why? . . .

Even when they have minimal or no involvement in the drug trade, women are increasingly caught in the ever-widening net cast by current drug laws through provisions such as conspiracy, accomplice liability, and constructive possession, which expand criminal liability to reach partners, relatives, and bystanders. . . . Current drug laws punish not just those who sell drugs, but also a wide range of people who help or merely associate with those who sell drugs. . . .

As a result, even when they have minimal or no involvement whatsoever in the drug trade, women are increasingly captured in the ever-widening net cast by the war on drugs, and subjected to the same or, in some cases, harsher sentences than the principals in the drug trade at whom the sentencing statutes are aimed. In too many cases, women are punished for the act of remaining with a boyfriend or husband engaged in drug activity. . . .

Such was the case for Leah Bundy, who was dating a man involved with drugs. Although she was aware of his drug activities, Leah denied any involvement in his crimes. Leah was arrested when the police mistakenly entered her boyfriend's apartment in response to a call about an incident in a neighboring apartment. When they searched the apartment, police found two handguns and several types of drugs. Leah was arrested, charged, and convicted of criminal possession of a controlled substance, criminal possession of a weapon, and criminal use of drug paraphernalia, all under the theory of constructive possession, through which her possession of these items was presumed by her presence in her boyfriend's apartment. At age 21, Leah was sentenced to 15 years to life.[30]

As other authors have observed, women who find themselves in the circumstances above confront an entanglement of what Professor Courtenay Daum and Holly Boux describe as "personal and familial constraints that operate individually or collectively to condition the[ir] choices." Some of these women defend their male relatives or partners out of love, or in an effort to protect the family from the man's incarceration. But as Chieko Clarke observes, it is also true that many women charged with drug offenses "come from a low socioeconomic status and have found themselves in an unhealthy relationship" with men in their lives who are involved in drug-related activity, two interrelated facts that can limit their "economic and social power to overcome their circumstances." For these women, the pressure to defend a potentially more culpable male associate—perhaps by covering up or taking the fall for his illegal behavior—can be especially strong, and can stem from a complex mix of motivations.[31]

At the same time, women on the periphery of drug transactions may be attractive targets for law enforcement actors who are trying to build a case against the men in their lives. Sometimes, law enforcement might threaten to punish the women in hopes of gaining leverage over the men. According to one report on false confessions, this tactic is not uncommon. In 8 percent of exonerations that involve false confessions, "the exoneree falsely confessed after an officer threatened to arrest a member of the exoneree's family, place one or more children in the exoneree's family in state custody, or otherwise put family members in harm's way if the exoneree did not confess." In the words of one experienced defense lawyer, "prosecutors leveraging one family member against another is a page directly out of a four-decade old prosecutorial playbook used successfully in Wall Street prosecutions," not to mention "organized crime and gang prosecutions." Alternatively, the state may threaten women on the periphery of drug-related activity in hopes of turning them into informants, deploying the same "information forcing" tactics discussed at the end of Chapter Seven. Critics of these tactics highlight their gendered dimension in the context of drug prosecutions, arguing that the women targeted in this way can find themselves "trapped by a patriarchal law enforcement system that offers a binary choice—whether or not to cooperate with authorities—where either option could ultimately result in her and/or her husband's imprisonment, the destruction of her family unit, and the confiscation of her home and family assets."[32]

Taking these various factors together, scholars and advocates have long warned that the War on Drugs "has become a war on women." As the Sentencing Project reports, while "many more men are in prison than women, the rate of growth for female imprisonment has been twice as high as that of men since 1980." And as the report goes on to observe, this "profound change in the involvement of women within the criminal justice system . . . is the result of more expansive law enforcement efforts, stiffer drug sentencing laws, and post-conviction barriers to reentry that uniquely affect women." Notably, one-quarter of all incarcerated women are serving time for narcotics-related offenses—more than double the rate of men.[33]

4. Transitory Possession. As compared to constructive possession, cases of actual possession are relatively straightforward. Typically, if the prosecution can prove "actual physical control" over an item, possession is established. State v. Daline, 30 P.3d 426, 430 (Or. Ct. App. 2001). Interestingly, this was not always the case. Courts first confronted criminal possession cases in large volumes during the Prohibition Era—and tended to be much more sympathetic to defendants than they are today. Consider, for example, the case of *State v. Lane*, 297 S.W. 708 (Mo. Ct. App. 1927), where a "constable of Pascola township" saw the defendant, Peck Lane, "with a half pint bottle of 'moonshine whisky' in his hand and . . . 'in the act of drinking.'" *Id.* at 709. Lane "had the bottle in his hand 'just long enough to take a drink and hand it back' [to] Ted Hodge [who] said the whisky was his." *Id.* On these facts, the court accepted as true that Lane "did have the liquor in his hand and took a drink therefrom," but nonetheless held that he "was not in actual possession or control of the bottle of whisky" given that his "possession was 'fleeting and shadowy'" and that the bottle apparently "belonged to another." *Id.* at 710.

Within a few decades, as government enforcement turned from alcohol to narcotics, courts adopted the opposite approach. The Supreme Court of Hawai'i's 1971 opinion, *State v. Hogue*, 486 P.2d 403 (Haw. 1971), is emblematic of the shift:

> [T]he State is able to prove by the testimony of the three arresting officers that . . . they observed Charles Glagolich turn over a pipe containing marihuana in hashish form to one Stephanie Kay Stearns, who after a couple of puffs turned it over to one Johnny Ray Griffith, who after a couple of puffs turned it over to defendant Gregory Dale Hogue. [According to the officers, Hogue] was observed . . . with a hashish pipe in his hands, no one else was holding it, and [he took] two puffs from said pipe knowing it to contain marihuana in hashish form. [T]he State's contention is that the offense committed by the defendant Gregory Dale Hogue is the knowingly taking of two puffs from a pipe containing marihuana. . . . [A] motion for dismissal was made on the ground that the mere passing and puffing from a marihuana pipe owned and supplied by another was insufficient as a matter of law to constitute possession of marihuana proscribed [in our statute. But the] facts stipulated, as having been observed by the officers, show conscious and substantial possession, not a mere involuntary or superficial possession, and much more than a passing control, fleeting and shadowy in nature.

Id. at 404-406.

Today, *Hogue* has won out over *Lane*. Holding drugs in order to use them, even if just "two puffs" (or one), counts as actual possession. Indeed, as we will see in a moment, the simple act of *passing* drugs from one person to another typically satisfies the elements of the separate and more severely punished crime of *distribution*. The sole modern remnant of *Lane*'s fleeting-possession doctrine is a narrower rule, available in only some jurisdictions, that shields a defendant from liability if he "takes temporary possession of contraband for the sole purpose of turning it in to the authorities" or disposing of it. Stanton v. State, 746 So. 2d 1229, 1230 (Fla. Dist. Ct. App. 1999); *see also* People v. Martin, 25 P.3d 1081, 1088-1089 (Cal. 2001) (holding that "the defense of transitory possession . . . applies only to momentary or transitory possession of contraband for the purpose of disposal").

5. Intoxication as Possession. It is generally difficult to ingest drugs without physically holding them. Indeed, some states hold that a drug is criminally "possessed" even as it is being metabolized, on the theory that "an altered state" of the drug is being carried around inside "the human body." State v. Schroeder, 674 N.W.2d 827, 830-831 (S.D. 2004) (quoting statutory language). But the majority of states take the opposite view, holding that evidence of intoxication alone is insufficient to prove possession of a controlled substance because the crime of possession requires a showing of *knowledge*. Consider the following example.

State v. Harris, 646 S.E.2d 526 (N.C. 2007). [D]efendant's probation officer . . . obtained a urine sample to determine whether defendant had used controlled substances in violation of his probation. The urine sample was analyzed twice by personnel in the North Carolina Department of Correction Substance Abuse and Intervention Program, and both analyses of the sample confirmed the presence of marijuana . . . metabolites in defendant's urine. At trial, Dr. Robert McClelland, who was tendered without objection as an expert in general pharmacology, testified that . . . marijuana remains detectable [in the body] for a . . . period of approximately 40 to 45 days. . . .

The *only* evidence presented at trial pertaining to marijuana was the presence of marijuana metabolites in the urine sample obtained from defendant on 24 August 2004. . . . From this test result, the jury can know that the metabolites were present, but is left to speculate as to how the substance resulting in those metabolites entered defendant's system. . . . The State asserted both in its brief and at oral argument that a positive drug test gives rise to an inference that defendant knowingly possessed marijuana. However, the only reasonable inference that may be drawn from these test results is that marijuana was somehow introduced into defendant's system. This inference, in itself, is insufficient to permit a jury to find that defendant had the power and intent to control the substance. . . . [A] positive urinalysis indicating the presence of marijuana metabolites alone is not substantial evidence sufficient to prove that defendant knowingly and intentionally possessed marijuana. . . .

6. Knowing Possession. As the preceding note underscores, criminal possession of an item, whether actual or constructive, typically requires the defendant's awareness of his control over the item. This awareness is (counterintuitively) a component of the *actus reus* of a possessory offense, because possession qualifies as a voluntary act only when coupled with awareness. *See, e.g.*, Tex. Penal Code Ann. §6.01(b) ("Possession is a voluntary act if the possessor knowingly obtains or receives the thing possessed or is aware of his control of the thing for a sufficient time to permit him to terminate his control."). A separate *mens rea* issue can arise as to whether the defendant knows *what the item is. See, e.g.*, Ramirez-Memije v. State, 444 S.W.3d 624, 628 (Tex. Crim. App. 2014) ("[K]nowingly receiving an object is [the] voluntary act[;] knowing the forbidden nature of the object that is knowingly possessed is the culpable mental state. . . .").

A prosecution under a statute criminalizing the "knowing possession of cocaine" could thus fail in two different ways. The defendant might not have known that *any* substance was present, and thus have no *actus reus*. Or the defendant might have known something was present but not that it was cocaine, and thus have no *mens rea*. Note though that if the statute instead created a strict-liability offense — criminalizing possession of cocaine even if the defendant had no way of knowing what the substance was — the *mens rea* argument about the nature of the item would fall away. The defendant would, however, still be able to argue that he had not known any substance was present at all, because in that case he would not have "possessed" it.

7. Willful Blindness.   A related set of questions can and frequently does arise in prosecutions for drug possession. How can a prosecutor prove that a defendant actually knew the drugs were present? And what should happen if the defendant does not know about the drugs only because she went out of her way to remain ignorant about them — to be, in the language of the cases, *willfully blind?* As noted in Chapter Four (p. 225), these questions can arise in any number of contexts where a defendant is alleged to have intentionally avoided learning facts the knowledge of which is an element of criminal liability. The issue commonly arises in cases related to smuggling, including the smuggling of drugs, as in the following case.

United States v. Heredia, 483 F.3d 913 (9th Cir. 2007) (en banc).   Defendant Carmen Heredia was stopped at an inland Border Patrol checkpoint while driving from Nogales to Tucson, Arizona. Heredia was at the wheel and her two children [and mother] were passengers. The border agent at the scene noticed what he described as a "very strong perfume odor" emanating from the car. A second agent searched the trunk and found 349.2 pounds of marijuana surrounded by dryer sheets, apparently used to mask the odor. . . .

At trial, Heredia testified that on the day of her arrest she had accompanied her mother on a bus trip from Tucson to Nogales, where her mother had a dentist's appointment. After the appointment, she borrowed her Aunt Belia's car to transport her mother back to Tucson. Heredia told DEA Agent Travis Birney at the time of her arrest that, while still in Nogales, she had noticed a "detergent" smell in the car as she prepared for the trip and asked Belia to explain. Belia told her that she had spilled Downey fabric softener in the car a few days earlier, but Heredia found this explanation incredible.

Heredia admitted on the stand that she suspected there might be drugs in the car, based on the fact that her mother was visibly nervous during the trip and carried a large amount of cash, even though she wasn't working at the time. However, Heredia claimed that her suspicions were not aroused until she had passed the last freeway exit before the checkpoint, by which time it was too dangerous to pull over and investigate. . . .

[In a seminal case on the concept of willful blindness, *United States v. Jewell,* 532 F.2d 697 (9th Cir. 1976) (en banc), we held that when Congress criminalized drug possession] it meant to punish not only those who know they possess a controlled substance, but also those who don't know because they don't want to know.[4] . . . Since *Jewell* was decided in 1976, every

---

4. As our cases have recognized, deliberate ignorance, otherwise known as willful blindness, is categorically different from negligence or recklessness. A willfully blind defendant is one who took *deliberate* actions to avoid confirming suspicions of criminality. A reckless defendant is one who merely knew of a substantial and unjustifiable risk that his conduct was criminal; a negligent defendant is one who should have had similar suspicions but, in fact, did not.

regional circuit—with the exception of the D.C. Circuit—has adopted its central holding. Indeed, many colloquially refer to the deliberate ignorance instruction as the "*Jewell* instruction." . . . [As commonly stated, the instruction informs a jury that in order to find the knowledge requirement satisfied based on deliberate ignorance, it must determine that two things have been established. First, that the defendant was aware of the high probability of the fact in question, and second, that she consciously and deliberately avoided learning of that fact.] A deliberate action is one that is "intentional; premeditated; fully considered." *Black's Law Dictionary* 459 (8th ed. 2004). A decision influenced by coercion, exigent circumstances or lack of meaningful choice is, perforce, not deliberate. A defendant who fails to investigate for these reasons has not deliberately chosen to avoid learning the truth. . . .

Defendant . . . claims there was insufficient foundation to give the *Jewell* instruction [based on the facts of this case]. . . . When knowledge is at issue in a criminal case, the court must first determine whether the evidence of defendant's mental state, if viewed in the light most favorable to the government, will support a finding of actual knowledge.[13] If so, the court must instruct the jury on this theory. Actual knowledge, of course, is inconsistent with willful blindness. The deliberate ignorance instruction only comes into play, therefore, if the jury rejects the government's case as to actual knowledge. In deciding whether to give a willful blindness instruction, in addition to an actual knowledge instruction, the district court must determine whether the jury could rationally find willful blindness even though it has rejected the government's evidence of actual knowledge. If so, the court may also give a *Jewell* instruction.

This case well illustrates the point. Taking the evidence in the light most favorable to the government, a reasonable jury could certainly have found that Heredia actually knew about the drugs. Not only was she driving a car with several hundred pounds of marijuana in the trunk, but everyone else who might have put the drugs there—her mother, her aunt, her husband—had a close personal relationship with Heredia. Moreover, there was evidence that Heredia and her husband had sole possession of the car for about an hour prior to setting out on the trip to Tucson. Based on this evidence, a jury could easily have inferred that Heredia actually knew about the drugs in the car because she was involved in putting them there.

The analysis in the foregoing paragraph presupposes that the jury believed the government's case in its entirety, and disbelieved all of Heredia's exculpatory statements. While this would have been *a* rational

---

13. As previously noted, willful blindness is tantamount to knowledge. We use the phrase "actual knowledge" to describe the state of mind when defendant, in fact, knows of the existence of the contraband rather than being willfully blind to its existence.

course for the jury to take, it was not the only one. For example, a rational jury might have bought Heredia's basic claim that she didn't know about the drugs in the trunk, yet disbelieved other aspects of her story.[14] The jury could, for example, have disbelieved Heredia's story about *when* she first began to suspect she was transporting drugs. The jury could have found that her suspicions were aroused when Belia gave her the unsatisfactory explanation for the "detergent" scent, or while she drove to Tucson but before the last exit preceding the checkpoint. Or, the jury might have believed Heredia that she became suspicious only after she had passed the last exit before the checkpoint but disbelieved that concerns about safety motivated her failure to stop [and investigate. Under any of these alternative factual premises, a jury could conclude that Heredia was aware of the high probability that drugs were present (a fact she essentially concedes) and could further conclude that she consciously and deliberately avoided learning whether drugs were actually in the car.] . . .

The government has no way of knowing which version of the facts the jury will believe, and it is entitled (like any other litigant) to have the jury instructed in conformity with each of these rational possibilities. That these possibilities are mutually exclusive is of no consequence. A party may present alternative factual theories, and is entitled to instructions supporting all rational inferences the jury might draw from the evidence. . . . For [these reasons], the district court did not abuse its discretion by giving the *Jewell* instruction here.

8. Attempt and Impossibility Revisited. Suppose someone unwittingly purchases a bag of baking soda, believing it to be cocaine. He cannot be convicted of possessing cocaine, as the white powder in his bag was not, in fact, cocaine. But in most jurisdictions, he could still be guilty of *attempting* to possess cocaine because, as the Model Penal Code's attempt provision puts it, he "purposely engage[d] in conduct which would constitute the crime if the attendant circumstances were as he believe[d] them to be." Model Penal Code §5.01(1)(a). To put the point differently, the argument that it's not a crime to possess baking soda is an appeal to the doctrine of legal impossibility, which (as we saw earlier in this chapter, p. 641) has been widely rejected as a defense to attempt liability.

The government can benefit from this ability to prosecute drug crimes as attempts in a few ways. First, as noted in Chapter Seven, attempt liability facilitates sting operations, and impossibility doctrine reduces the risk involved in those stings—in this instance, by allowing the state to use fake drugs in place of real ones. Second, the ability to substitute an attempt

---

14. We have long held that juries are not bound to believe or disbelieve all of a witness's testimony. "The jury may conclude a witness is not telling the truth as to one point, is mistaken as to another, but is truthful and accurate as to a third." Elwert v. United States, 231 F.2d 928, 934 (9th Cir. 1956).

charge for a possession charge allows the prosecution to avoid calling a laboratory analyst to verify the nature of seized evidence in cases involving *actual* controlled substances. In practice, that escape valve can be important. In a case called *Melendez-Diaz v. Massachusetts*, 557 U.S. 305 (2009), the Supreme Court held that prosecutors cannot simply rely on certificates from drug-lab analysts to verify that the substance seized in a given case has been tested and confirmed to be drugs. *Id.* at 312. Those certificates, the Court held, are "testimonial statements, and the analysts" who made them are therefore " 'witnesses' for purposes of the Sixth Amendment" who must appear in court and be subject to cross-examination by the defendant's lawyer. *Id.* This means that a potentially small number of analysts in a given jurisdiction's drug lab must be available to testify in potentially hundreds of cases every year, each one of which could involve hours of waiting in a courtroom hallway before taking the stand. If an analyst is not available when the government needs her on the stand, the prosecution for possession of a controlled substance will fail, because the state will not be able to prove that the item in question *is* a controlled substance. *See id.* at 340-341 (Kennedy, J., dissenting) (cautioning that requiring analysts to testify in person could impose a "crushing burden" and "put prosecutions nationwide at risk of dismissal based on erratic, all-too-frequent instances when a particular laboratory technician . . . simply does not or cannot appear").[34]

Attempt law lets the prosecution off the hook. In *Lesher v. United States*, 149 A.3d 519 (D.C. 2016), for example, the defendant was convicted of attempted possession of marijuana even though "the government presented no evidence that the green weed-like substance" found in the defendant's possession "actually was marijuana." *Id.* at 525. It was sufficient that the government put on testimony that the substance "both smelled like and was packaged like marijuana, and that the bags of the substance were found stuffed behind a radiator, an out-of-sight location supporting an inference that they had been hidden or secreted because what they contained was *thought to be* illegal to possess." *Id.* (emphasis added). At least in the federal system, moreover, the prosecution sacrifices nothing by bringing attempt charges, as the penalties for attempted drug crimes are the same as for the underlying crimes. *See* 21 U.S.C. §846.

2. The Law of Drug Possession: Possession with Intent to Distribute

Cotton v. State

686 S.E.2d 805 (Ga. Ct. App. 2009)

SMITH, J. Omali Cotton [argues that] insufficient evidence exists to support his felony conviction for possessing marijuana with the intent to distribute. . . . Viewed in the light most favorable to the verdict, the record shows that in a search incident to Cotton's arrest for driving without a license, police officers found three identical small plastic "nickel bags" of marijuana and $60 (two $5 bills, one $10 bill, and two $20 bills) in the same pocket, as well as another identical small bag of marijuana on the ground near his feet. All of the marijuana in the four bags combined weighed 2.7 grams.

The officer who arrested Cotton testified that he spent a lot of time helping a canine officer with "drug enforcement." In his duties as a patrol officer, he would come into contact with drugs at least once a week. The officer testified that he suspected that Cotton was distributing marijuana because he was arrested in an area well-known for drug activity (Ridgecrest Apartments), he did not have a smoking device, he was driving a car that did not belong to him in an apartment complex in which he did not live, personal users normally have all of their marijuana in one bag instead of separate baggies, distributors sell marijuana in small bags like the ones found on Cotton for approximately $10-$20, and the denominations of the cash found in his pocket lent themselves to giving change. The combination of all these facts led the officer to believe that Cotton possessed marijuana with the intent to distribute. The officer acknowledged that his testimony was based upon his experience and information he learned from other officers and people he had previously arrested.

Another officer who assisted with the arrest testified that, based upon his experience patrolling apartments known for being a "high-drug area" where a lot of drugs are bought and sold, as well as his experience with street-level dealers, the drugs and money found on Cotton

> were consistent with a—basically a street level dealer. There were four bags of marijuana separately packaged. The money was in the same location that the drugs were found. There was no wallet. It was easy access for somebody to distribute and take money during a transaction. The money was consistent with the amount of drugs that was on his person.
>
> The amount of the bags was consistent with—like basically a dime bag or a $10 bag would be consistent with the amount of money that he had. He had four bags on him, which isn't a lot of bags, but he had the corresponding money with that.
>
> And my prior experience is if somebody's standing outside of an apartment or something along those lines, they're not going to keep, you know they're not going to keep all 20, 30 on them. They're going to stash them either in a bush or inside an apartment or inside a car and keep them—you know, a minimum amount on their person. And then when they get low, they go back and restock, and then they sell what they have and they conduct business that way.

The officer also found it significant that Cotton did not have a pipe, rolling papers or other smoking device with him which "indicates he wasn't a user, that he was more of a distributor."

Cotton's girlfriend, who lived at Ridgecrest Apartments, testified that Cotton was unemployed at the time of his arrest, that he stayed with her the night before his arrest, that she gave him $80 the day before he was arrested, that he smoked marijuana every day in a blunt made from tobacco cigars, that it was not uncommon for Cotton to possess four $5 bags for his personal use, that he would obtain his marijuana somewhere within Ridgecrest Apartments, and that she had never known him to sell marijuana. . . .

"No bright line rule exists regarding the amount or type of evidence sufficient to support a conviction for possession with intent to distribute." Harper v. State, 645 S.E.2d 741, 744 (Ga. Ct. App. 2007). We have previously held that possession of four individual packages of crack cocaine provided sufficient evidence of intent to distribute. In this case, the State also submitted unobjected-to opinion testimony by both officers that the packaging of the marijuana in combination with the denominations of cash found together in Cotton's pants pocket, as well as the absence of a smoking device, demonstrated an intent to distribute. We find this evidence sufficient to support Cotton's intent to distribute conviction. . . .

NOTES AND QUESTIONS

1. The Stakes. Omali Cotton clearly possessed the 2.7 grams of marijuana recovered from his pocket. He did not argue otherwise. Rather, his claim was that there was insufficient evidence to prove that he possessed the drugs *with the intent to distribute them.* Possession with intent to distribute, sometimes shorthanded as PWID, is a standalone criminal offense that is punished much more severely than simple possession. Under Georgia law, for example, a person charged with simple possession of less than one ounce of marijuana would be guilty of a misdemeanor and exposed to no more than one year of incarceration. *See* Ga. Code Ann. §16-13-2(b). One ounce is equivalent to 28 grams, which is more than ten times the amount of marijuana Cotton had in his pocket. But because Cotton was charged with and convicted of possession with intent to distribute that marijuana, he was guilty of a felony punishable by "not less than one year nor more than ten years" in prison. Ga. Code Ann. §16-13-30(j)(2). And in fact, the judge in Cotton's case sentenced him to the maximum ten years, four of which Cotton was ordered to serve in prison immediately with the remaining six years suspended during a term of probation following his release.[35]

2. Attempted Distribution. Possession with intent to distribute is a central criminal offense in the prosecutorial arsenal of the War on Drugs. The reason is straightforward. Whereas drug *users* might be (and are) prosecuted for the misdemeanor offense of simple possession when police officers find small amounts of drugs on or near their person, these small-time folks are generally not the focal point of major narcotics investigations and prosecutions. The high-value targets of the War on Drugs are the people who profit off the drug trade: manufacturers, importers, and distributors.

Of these three groups of actors, manufacturers and importers can—and typically must—hide their operations from law enforcement to avoid detection and disruption. Police officers might try to infiltrate such clandestine operations by using the information-forcing tools at their disposal, including the conspiracy laws and informant tactics discussed in the preceding chapter. But that is difficult.

Distributors, by contrast, do not have the luxury of operating in secret. To make money selling drugs, a distribution network needs customers, typically a lot of them. And that requires a presence in the community. The act of distribution, when drugs move from one person to another, is thus a key moment for law enforcement intervention. The crime of distribution is accordingly punished very severely—often as severely as manufacturing or importation—with sentences commonly escalating tenfold or more above simple possession, depending on the type and quantity of the drug at issue.*

But distribution itself can also be hard to prosecute. Indeed, precisely because distribution is such a focal point for law enforcement, people who sell drugs generally try to keep these transactions secret, conducting them indoors or using furtive hand-to-hand exchanges that can be difficult for law enforcement officers to discern from a distance. One way the police can overcome this challenge is to try to get eyes "inside" the exchange, via the undercover buy-and-bust and "reverse buy" tactics described in the preceding chapter (p. 578). But another option is to lean on a now-familiar tool of preemptive policing. The state can criminalize actions taken in *preparation* for distribution, such as the possession of drugs with the intent to distribute them. Here again, we see a possession offense operating as a specialized attempt statute, combining preparatory conduct with a specific-intent requirement, all in hopes of making it easier to stop the targeted conduct—drug distribution—before it occurs.

And importantly, of all the moments along the drug distribution chain, from manufacture to consumption, the period in which a person possesses drugs in preparation for distribution is the most exposed to detection and prosecution. It is simply not practical for a street-level dealer to carry around only a single sale's worth of product at a time. Economies

---

* While the paradigmatic distribution case involves sales, federal case law makes clear that "sharing of narcotics on a social basis" also counts as distribution. United States v. Wallace, 532 F.3d 126, 127 (2d Cir. 2008); *see also* United States v. Cormier, 468 F.3d 63, 70 n.3 (1st Cir. 2006) ("It is well accepted that drugs may be distributed by giving them away for free. . . ."). "Thus a defendant who holds narcotics solely for personal use is in possession; one who delivers or transfers narcotics to another—for consideration or gratis—is distributing." *Wallace*, 532 F.3d at 129.

of scale will compel him to pursue quick repeat transactions. As a result, a street-level dealer will typically keep moderate amounts of drugs on or near his person, separately packaged for individual sale, along with small bills—either receipts of past trades, or for easy change in new ones. And, as the decision in *Cotton* makes clear, the criminal law treats precisely such conduct as strong circumstantial evidence of PWID—even if, in so doing, it might also expose simple *consumers* to prosecution and lengthy prison sentences because they happen to purchase three nickel bags at once (as may have been true of Mr. Cotton).

3. Police Expertise. Given the small quantity of marijuana he possessed, it's safe to say the government's case against Omali Cotton rested heavily on the testimony of the police officers—specifically, their assertion that "the packaging of the marijuana in combination with the denominations of cash found together in Cotton's pants pocket, as well as the absence of a smoking device, demonstrated an intent to distribute." Cotton's case was not unusual in this sense. Drug prosecutions routinely entail similar testimony from beat officers whom courts and juries treat as experts in the drug trade.

As Professor Anna Lvovsky describes, this idea "that trained, experienced officers develop rarefied and reliable insight into crime," including drug crime, has both a long and a contested history.

> Beginning in the early 1960s, police experts increasingly testified regarding whether the drugs found on a defendant were more consistent with personal or commercial use, based on such factors as quantity, packaging, and other contextual clues. Policemen informed juries about the common doses of particular drugs and popular methods of packaging sales. They explained the use of "stash house[s]" to store contraband and described counter-surveillance techniques used by dealers. . . .

As Lvovsky continues, defense lawyers initially objected that "such testimony exceeded the police's professional knowledge . . . or was either too commonsensical or speculative to qualify as 'expertise.'" But these objections did not prevail, and before long "police witnesses on criminal intent assumed a central role in narcotics litigation."[36]

The objections, however, remain. As Lvovsky notes, "most research into police practices since the 1960s has been deeply critical of police expertise, both as an empirical matter and as a factor in the courts' [legal] analysis." Part of the criticism is institutional, Lvovsky explains, with scholars contending that treating the police as experts allows "policemen to define the legal limits" of civilian behavior. But another set of critics, Lvovsky observes, "question the *merits* of police judgment, emphasizing the absence of hard evidence that officers develop any systematic codes for crime" or actually "rely on distinct patterns in evaluating suspects." Rather, these critical scholars contend, officers really just deploy "narratives of suspicion" or "scripts" that cloak untested and unsupported officer intuitions in a veil of expert authority. Indeed, when researchers have attempted to assess the validity of such scripts, they have frequently found not only that the scripts fail to map underlying realities, but also that the police deploy them inconsistently, and sometimes even contradictorily, across cases.[37]

4. Drug Quantity. Part of what makes the *Cotton* case striking is that the amount of drugs Cotton possessed was extremely low. At 2.7 grams, Cotton possessed roughly the equivalent of three to five joints or a single cigarillo-sized blunt, quantities commonly associated with personal use. When the amount of drugs in a case is that low, prosecutors typically must lean heavily on circumstantial evidence of intent to distribute, such as the presence of scales or packaging used to parcel out consumer-sized amounts of product, of currency indicative of dealing, or of suspicious or furtive behavior suggesting transactions. Conversely, when a person is found with a *large* amount of drugs, that fact alone can play an important role in the assignment of both liability and punishment, in a number of different respects.

First, quantity is frequently used as *evidence of intent to distribute.* The idea is straightforward: the greater the quantity, the stronger the inference that the defendant "possessed a quantity which was more than he would possess for his own use." United States v. Lopez, 42 F.3d 463, 467 (8th Cir. 1994). Indeed, in some cases, drug quantity is the *only* evidence of intent to distribute. *See, e.g.,* United States v. Jones, 600 F.3d 985, 989 (8th Cir. 2010) (235 grams of cocaine).

Second, quantity can be used to prove *knowledge of possession* when the contested issue is not whether the defendants intended to distribute the drugs, but rather whether they knew they possessed the drugs at all. In *United States v. Serrano-Lopez,* 366 F.3d 628 (8th Cir. 2004), for example, Nebraska state troopers discovered more than five kilograms of cocaine hidden inside the body of the car the defendants were driving. *Id.* at 632. Critically, the drugs "were not visible from anywhere in the car until the car was dismantled," *id.*, and the defendants denied any knowledge that the drugs were there. Affirming the defendants' convictions for possession with intent to distribute, the Eighth Circuit wrote that "[t]he large quantity of drugs involved is evidence of the defendants' knowledge." *Id.* at 635. "Even if the drugs were not owned by the defendants," the court reasoned, "it is unlikely that the owner would place approximately $130,000 worth of cocaine in the hands of people who do not even know it is there." *Id.*

Finally, drug quantity is, along with drug type, the principal determinant of drug *sentencing.* In the federal system, for example, Congress has prescribed mandatory minimum sentences for trafficking particular quantities of particular drugs. *See* 21 U.S.C. §841(b). Possession with intent to distribute methamphetamine, for example, carries a mandatory minimum sentence of five years if the defendant had 5 grams of the drug, with the mandatory sentence climbing to 10 years if the defendant had 50 grams or more. Within these statutory bounds, moreover, sentences are heavily influenced by a set of tables in the U.S. Sentencing Guidelines that tie the weight of each drug type to a base offense level that, when combined with the defendant's criminal history, gives judges a recommended sentencing range that can be adjusted upwards or downwards based on aggravating or mitigating circumstances. The higher the amount of drugs, the higher the base offense and the recommended range. *See* U.S. Sentencing Guidelines Manual §2D1.1 (U.S. Sent'g Comm'n 2021).

Precisely because drug sentencing works this way, the methods for assessing quantity—for weighing drugs—are significantly contested. As one example, in *Chapman v. United States*, 500 U.S. 453 (1991), the U.S. Supreme Court divided over how to weigh the hallucinogenic LSD for sentencing purposes. A pure dose of LSD, the Court explained, "is such an infinitesimal amount that it must be sold to retail customers in a 'carrier,'" such as a sugar cube or a small piece of absorbent blotter paper. *Id.* at 457. The Court held that, in determining eligibility for mandatory minimum sentences, the weight of the carrier—in Chapman's case, blotter paper weighing 100 times more than the LSD itself—must be included. *See id.* at 455-456. The dissent bemoaned the "absurdity and inequity" of this rule, which, it said, meant that "[i]f 100 doses of LSD were sold on sugar cubes, the sentence would range from 188-235 months, whereas if the same dosage were sold in its pure liquid form, the sentence would range only from 10-16 months." *Id.* at 473-474 (Stevens, J., dissenting).[38]

3. The War on Drugs

It should be clear by this point that the government strongly disapproves of drugs. But why?

For readers who have grown up knowing little but the War on Drugs, criminalizing drug possession may seem natural or inevitable. But for most of U.S. history, drugs were legal. As Professor Paul Butler writes, "In the nineteenth century you could walk into your local apothecary and purchase opium, cocaine, or marijuana." And in fact, according to Professor Steven Duke, "tens of millions of Americans consumed cocaine and opiates in the nineteenth century," with cocaine serving as an active "ingredient in Coca Cola until 1905" and opium "fed to colicky babies." Heroin, Dukes notes, "was originally sold as a cough suppressant." Notably, Duke continues, dependence on these now-illegal drugs "was never as serious a problem as alcoholism" and "problems associated with their use were less serious than they are today."[39]

Still, as Professor Erik Luna recounts, by the early 1900s "American drug anxiety" began to set in among national policymakers, driven in part by racially stoked fears suggesting a link between drugs and violence—themes we will return to shortly. In 1914, Congress enacted the Harrison Anti-Narcotics Act, the first piece of federal legislation constraining drug usage in the states. The statute's text technically only limited physicians' ability to prescribe narcotics, but federal law enforcement actors deployed it as a de facto ban on drugs, and federal judges acquiesced. "As a result," Professor Shima Baradaran Baughman writes, drug users for the first time "became subversive and connected to a culture of crime."[40]

Incarceration for drug-related offenses followed. Within roughly a decade, by the late 1920s, almost one third of the roughly 8,000 people incarcerated in federal prisons were serving time for Harrison Act violations. In subsequent decades, from the late 1930s through the 1970s, drug-prohibition laws proliferated in the states and at the federal level, with states uniformly outlawing drugs like cocaine, heroin, and marijuana and the federal government enacting the first mandatory minimum penalties for drug offenses.[41]

And then came the War on Drugs. While that phrase is often associated with President Richard Nixon, his use of the phrase was, according to Professor Michelle Alexander, "largely rhetorical," insofar as he called "drugs 'public enemy number one' without proposing dramatic shifts in drug policy." In fact, Nixon was not even the first president to announce such a war, which President Eisenhower had similarly done a decade prior. It was under President Ronald Reagan, though, that the War on Drugs truly took shape. As Alexander describes:

> In October 1982, President Reagan officially announced his administration's War on Drugs. . . . Practically overnight the budgets of federal law enforcement agencies soared. Between 1980 and 1984, FBI antidrug funding increased from $8 million to $95 million. Department of Defense antidrug allocations increased from $33 million in 1981 to [$1.04 billion] in 1991. During that same period, DEA antidrug spending grew from [$86 million to $1.02 billion]. By contrast, funding for agencies responsible for drug treatment, prevention, and education was dramatically reduced. The budget of the National Institute for Drug Abuse, for example, was reduced from $274 million to $57 million from 1981 to 1984. . . .[42]

As Alexander goes on to note, Reagan's strategy also included a successful "media offensive to justify the War on Drugs." When Reagan took office, only 2 percent of the American public saw drugs as the most important issue facing the nation. But within just a few years, following his relentless focus on crack cocaine, both *Newsweek* and *Time Magazine* declared crack to be the biggest national issue to hit the country since Vietnam and Watergate. "Between October 1988 and October 1989," Alexander reports, "the *Washington Post* alone ran 1,565 stories about the 'drug scourge,'" an emphasis the paper's ombudsman would later criticize as a failure of journalistic judgment. By the end of the 1980s, a national poll conducted by *The New York Times* and CBS found that a record 64 percent of the public described drugs as "the most significant problem in the United States."[43]

With the national conversation thus reframed, subsequent presidents followed in Reagan's footsteps. Reagan's vice president, George H.W. Bush, who succeeded Reagan in office, called drug use "the most pressing problem facing the nation." A few years later, President Bill Clinton put tough-on-crime and anti-drug policies at the center of his political brand. As Alexander writes:

> [I]n 1992, presidential candidate Bill Clinton vowed that he would never permit any Republican to be perceived as tougher on crime than he. . . . Once elected, Clinton endorsed the idea of a federal 'three strikes and you're out law' [and championed to passage a] $30 billion crime bill [that was] hailed as a victory for the Democrats, "who were able to wrest the crime issue from the Republicans and make it their own." The bill created dozens of new federal capital crimes, mandated life sentences for some three-time offenders, and authorized more than $16 billion for state prison grants and expansion of state and local police forces. Far from resisting [it], Clinton escalated the drug war beyond what conservatives had imagined possible a decade earlier.[44]

As the chart below indicates, President George W. Bush followed the path set by his predecessors, cementing in place a three-decade War on Drugs that in turn helped fuel the most massive and sustained spike in the federal prison population in history.

Figure 8.1.   Federal Prison Population Over Time

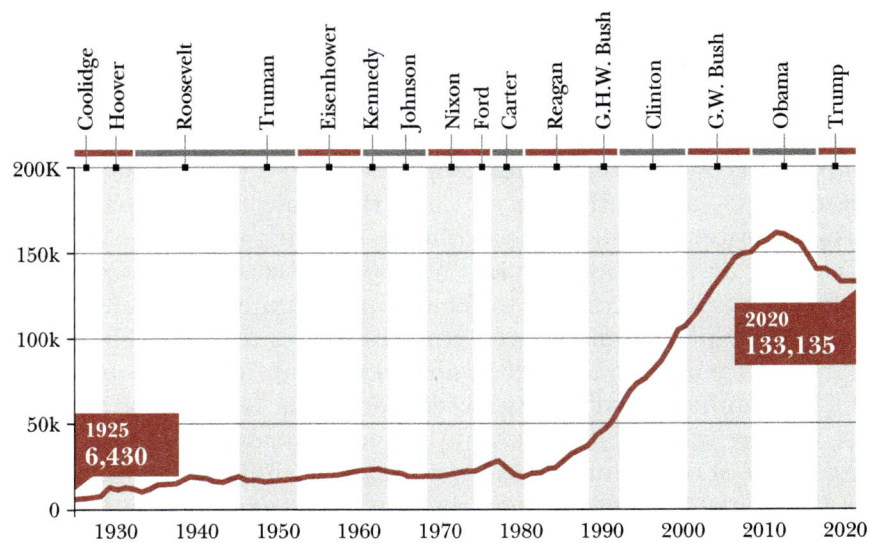

Niall McCarthy, *The Evolution of America's Federal Prison Population*, Statista (Feb. 25, 2021)

As noted earlier, half the people in federal prison today are serving sentences for drug-related crimes. (The percentage is considerably smaller, about 12.5 percent, in state prisons.) All told, estimates suggest the War on Drugs has cost the federal government over a trillion dollars. And that figure does not include any of the costs, financial and personal, borne by the people serving time in prison and the families and communities they have left behind.[45]

All of which raises the question: Has the War on Drugs been worth it? And relatedly, why did it happen? Should it have happened? Should something change?

In the remainder of this section, we explore these central questions. We begin by examining some of the empirical and normative questions related to drug control and penal paternalism, asking when if ever it might be appropriate to punish people "for their own good." Next, we turn to a set of empirical and normative questions related to the potential externalities associated with drug addiction, asking when if ever it might be appropriate to punish drug users and dealers for harms they impose on others—and whether criminalization itself might be to blame for those harms. We then explore a comparative policy question, asking what it might mean to craft an approach to drugs that mirrors the government's approach to other potentially harmful substances, like alcohol and tobacco. Finally, in the chapter's next section, we conclude our discussion of the War on Drugs with a series of notes examining its racial dynamics and history, confronting directly the question whether the war is in truth, as many of its critics argue, a war on Black people.

NOTES AND QUESTIONS

1. The Impacts of Drugs on Users: Some Evidence. One argument often marshaled in defense of criminalizing drugs is that drugs harm the people who use them, and that criminal sanctions could reduce those harms by deterring drug use and making drugs harder to acquire. To begin assessing this argument, one needs to know some facts about the impact drugs have on their users—and perhaps about how those impacts compare to other harmful behaviors, like drinking alcohol or smoking tobacco.

Consider first the most extreme form of self-harm associated with drug use: fatal overdoses. According to the National Center on Health Statistics, nearly 107,000 people died from drug overdoses in 2021. That figure is more than twice as high as in 2011 and more than five times as high as in 2001. The number of fatal drug overdoses in the United States, in other words, is large and rapidly growing. Today, overdoses are the seventh-leading cause of death, and possibly *the* leading cause of death for people under 45 years old. Opioids, primarily fentanyl, currently claim the largest share of lives, followed by methamphetamine and cocaine.[46]

Moreover, as recent research has shown, "the drug mortality crisis extends beyond individuals lost to overdoses," given that drug use can also lead to fatal diseases and accidents. In recent years, these drug-implicated fatalities have accounted for 4,670 additional deaths per year (as of 2019). Taking the data together, there were likely close to 115,000 drug-related deaths in the United States in 2021. That is a large number—almost three times as large, for example, as the number of people who died in fatal car crashes that year (42,939).[47]

But notably, the number of drug-related deaths pales in comparison to deaths caused by two other intoxicating substances: alcohol and tobacco. According to a Surgeon General's Report issued in 2014, tobacco alone kills around 480,000 smokers each year, primarily by causing heart disease, lung cancer, and other chronic illnesses. Cigarettes, in other words, appear to kill more than *three times* more Americans each year than cocaine, heroin, and all other illegal drugs combined. Alcohol, by comparison, is considerably less deadly than tobacco. But even it accounts for more deaths per year than illegal drugs, with almost 180,000 people dying from alcohol-attributable deaths annually in 2020 and 2021.[48]

Short of death, there are other harms associated with drug use. Research shows that even marijuana, legal now in many states, can impair attention, reaction time, and psychomotor performance—doubling, for example, the risk of a car accident. In the longer run, persistent marijuana use beginning in adolescence is associated with neuropsychological decline (including a decline in IQ), and some evidence links it to psychotic symptoms and mental illness. Harder drugs pose additional risks. Long-term cocaine use, for example, may negatively impact the heart and cardiovascular system as well as cognitive functions and may also increase the risk for movement disorders such as Parkinson's Disease. Persistent use of methamphetamine and heroin may similarly damage vital organs and cause other vexing symptoms such as insomnia, paranoia, and hallucinations. Chronic drug use more generally can cause sleep disturbances and malnutrition that have multiple adverse health effects. Finally, injected drugs can be vectors for disease transmission. CDC data suggest, for example, that about 10 percent of all HIV diagnoses are attributable to intravenous drug use.[49]

And yet, here too, the adverse health effects of alcohol and tobacco are larger in scale than those associated with illegal drugs. For example, the CDC reports that for "every person who dies because of smoking, at least 30 people live with a serious smoking-related illness," which means that more than "16 million Americans are living with at least one serious smoking-related disease" at any given time. Likewise, the elevated fatality rate associated with alcohol tracks additional, nonfatal health risks.[50]

To be sure, the comparison to alcohol and tobacco is not perfect. For one thing, drugs tend to kill people earlier in life, with overdose rates highest for adults ages 35 to 44 and lowest for adults over 65. By contrast, smoking causes fatal illnesses over time, shortening the lives of heavy smokers by at least 10 years on average. A quarter of these smokers die before turning 65, but the majority live past that milestone. Drugs, in other words, take away more years of life from the people they kill, even though they kill fewer people. Separately, any comparison of illegal drugs to alcohol and tobacco is of course comparing illegal substances to legal ones. It is possible, though not certain, that the overall use of illegal drugs and any accompanying harms could increase if drugs were decriminalized—a question we'll return to shortly.[51]

Finally, it bears emphasizing that most of the substance-related harms described thus far, for both illegal drugs and for alcohol and tobacco, are concentrated among chronic users. But as research confirms, "a large majority" of people "who have used drugs do not proceed to develop drug dependence" or otherwise become "problematic drug use[rs]." Most people who have used drugs at some point in their lifetimes have not done so in the past year, and even fewer have done so in the past month. As researcher Anne Schlag reports, "rather than being problematic, drug use is often transient, with many people 'growing out of it' and stopping use in their late 30s." Indeed, even drugs "known for their dependence liability," such as heroin and cocaine, have relatively low addiction rates, as reflected in the tables below. In short, Schlag concludes, "most people who use drugs do so only experimentally or moderately."[52]

Figure 8.2. Percentage of U.S. Respondents Who Have Used Drugs

Drug	Lifetime	Past year	Past month
Cannabis	45.2	15.0	9.6
Cocaine	14.9	2.2	0.8
Crack	3.5	0.3	0.2
Heroin	1.9	0.3	0.2
Hallucinogens	15.5	1.9	0.5
LSD	9.6	0.8	0.2
PCP	2.2	0.0	0.0
Ecstasy	7.0	0.9	0.2
Methamphetamine	5.4	0.6	0.3

Anne Katrin Schlag, *Percentages of Problem Drug Use and Their Implications for Policy Making: A Review of the Literature*, 6 Drug Sci., Pol'y & L. tbl.1 (2020)

Figure 8.3. Percentage of U.S. Drug Users Who Develop Dependence

Substance	Dependency Rate
Tobacco	33%
Alcohol	10-15%
Cannabis	9%
Cocaine	15-20%
Heroin	23-30%
Methamphetamine	5-10%
Psychedelics	9%

Anne Katrin Schlag, *Percentages of Problem Drug Use and Their Implications for Policy Making: A Review of the Literature*, 6 Drug Sci., Pol'y & L. tbl.2 (2020)

2. The Impacts of Drugs on Users: Some More Evidence.

As the preceding note makes clear, psychoactive substances—including alcohol, tobacco, and illegal drugs—can cause serious adverse health effects, especially in chronic users. Public policy discussions tend to center these harms. But as in all cost-benefit analyses, there is another side to the equation: the benefits of drug use. Professor Carl Hart, a neuroscientist and psychologist, summarizes some of these, reporting that many currently illegal drugs "can enhance pleasure, openness, intimacy, energy, sexual satisfaction, and a range of other experiences normal people routinely seek." Paul Butler, a law professor and former federal prosecutor, puts the point more succinctly. "Some drugs," he writes, "are big fun." Butler goes on:

> Some of my fondest memories of Yale and Harvard involve being drunk or stoned, or trying to get that way. In my third year of law school, when I was supposed to be in Administrative Law, I instead looked for Ecstasy. . . . What a fantastic name for a consumer product! How could you not want to find Ecstasy?
>
> Any honest consideration of drugs ought to acknowledge the pleasures of intoxication. I remember Amsterdam, with Susan: we had space cakes, and then took the tram, which turned into a flying carpet. We laughed so hard; we were stupid happy. It is one of the top ten memories of my life, a memory made even sweeter now that Susan is gone. I remember [taking] some magic mushrooms . . . [and listening with others] to Nina Simone's "Lilac Wine." After she sang the last wistful note, we opened our eyes and looked at each other in wonder: can you believe all this beauty in the world?[53]

To some, Butler's passage may seem a rhapsodic ode to hedonism, a celebration of pleasure for pleasure's sake. It bears remembering, though, that at least for classic utilitarians, "happiness" (including pleasure) is the "final good" that all laws and social policies are supposed to maximize. There is, in other words, some resonance between Jeremy Bentham's insistence that "all laws" should "augment total happiness in the community" and Hart's argument in favor of drug decriminalization that "[p]leasure is a good thing, something that should be embraced."[54]

Nor is simple pleasure the only benefit associated with drugs. Popular writing and scientific studies alike highlight some of the positive mental health outcomes associated with responsible drug use. Consider, for example, author Michael Pollan's widely read observations, based on his personal experimentation with psychedelics, that drug use can help people learn many of "the kinds of things one might learn in the course of psychotherapy: insights into important relationships; the outlines of fears and desires ordinarily kept out of view; repressed memories and emotions; and, perhaps most interesting and useful, a new perspective on how one's mind works." In a similar vein, multiple scientific reports confirm that both Ecstasy and LSD—commonly known as "acid" and illegal across the country—can be used to treat depression and other mental illnesses. Both drugs reportedly encourage the "growth of new connections between neurons in the brain" and thus mitigate neurological dysregulation. LSD has also been found effective as a treatment for alcoholism. Perhaps more surprisingly, Hart reports that even "the effects produced by crack cocaine are predominantly positive," with his "research participants consistently report[ing] feelings of well-being" after using the drug.[55]

Taking these data and personal anecdotes together, "the bottom line" for Hart is that illegal drugs "can and do improve day-to-day living" for many people. Generalizing to the societal level, he concludes that "most drug-use scenarios are actually beneficial for human health and functioning."[56]

3. Penal Paternalism: A Libertarian Critique. Hart may be right about the benefits of drugs outweighing the costs. Or he might be wrong. A more fundamental question, though, is whether it matters. As Professor Thomas Szasz observes, the government regularly allows adults to engage in any number of concededly dangerous activities "not because we do not believe [they] are dangerous, but because we believe even more strongly that civil liberties are precious." Yet when it comes to drugs, Szasz notes, that presumption disappears; here, the state seems to value "paternalism more highly." This paternalism draws forceful critiques, not only from the political left but also from the libertarian right, with prominent conservatives such as economist Milton Friedman and legal scholar Randy Barnett arguing in favor of drug decriminalization. Consider Barnett's position in the following excerpt, and the personal counterpoint from Professor Michael Clune that follows.[57]

Randy E. Barnett, *The Harmful Side Effects of Drug Prohibition*, 2009 Utah L. Rev. 11, 13, 15-18, 21, 32, 34. Drug laws reflect the decision of some persons that other persons who wish to consume certain substances should not be permitted to act on their preferences. . . . The prime motivation for the drug user's behavior is to alter his state of mind to get "high." . . . One can argue that such persons must be "self-destructive"—that is, out to harm themselves in some way. It is doubtful, however, that such generalizations are any truer for drug users than they are for alcohol users or cigarette smokers . . . or for skydivers, skiers, or bicyclers on city streets. . . . We can conclude then that the *end* or purpose of drug laws is to discourage people from engaging in risky activity in which they wish to engage[, often] because they desire the intoxicating effects they associate with the consumption of a drug. . . . The *means* that drug laws employ to accomplish this end is using force against those who would engage in such activities, either to prevent them from doing so or to punish those who nonetheless succeed in doing so. . . .

Imprisonment must generally be considered a harm to the person imprisoned. . . . [N]ormally such punishment is deliberately imposed on the lawbreaker to protect *someone else* who we consider to be completely innocent—like the victim, or potential victim, of a rape, robbery, or murder. . . . Drug laws are different in this respect from many other criminal laws. With drug prohibition we are supposed to be concerned with the well-being of prospective drug users. So the object of drug laws—the persons whom drug laws are supposed to "protect"—are often the same persons who are the subject of drug laws. . . . While law enforcement efforts typically cause harm to criminals who victimize others, such effects are far more problematic with laws that seriously harm the very people for whom these laws are enacted to help.

. . . The only practical way of facilitating the pursuit of happiness for each individual who chooses to live in a social setting is to recognize the rights of individuals to control their external possessions and their bodies—traditionally known as property rights—free from the forcible interference of any other person. . . . To deny these rights is to act unjustly. . . . Drug laws undermine this control by seeking . . . forcibly to prevent persons from using their bodies in ways that they desire and that do not interfere with the equal liberty of others. . . .

. . . Legal institutions are not capable of correcting every ill in the world. On this point most would agree. . . . If the rights of individuals to choose how to use their person and possessions are fully respected, there is no guaranty that people will exercise their rights wisely. Some may mistakenly choose the path of finding happiness in a bottle or in a vial. Others may wish to help these people by persuading them of their folly and supporting them when they seek to wean themselves from their dependency. We must not, however, give in to the powerful temptation to grant some the power to impose their consumptive preferences on others by force.

Michael W. Clune, Opinion, *Why Decriminalizing Drugs Is a Bad Idea*, Wash. Post (Apr. 10, 2023). The movement to decriminalize drugs keeps gaining momentum. . . . This is a mistake. I know from my own experience with addiction that legal consequences can play an essential role in pushing people toward a path to recovery. . . . Treatment for addiction is not as effective as proponents say it is. . . . For me and for nearly every other person I know recovering from addiction, it took arrest and prosecution.

When I was arrested in Chicago in 2002 and charged with felony possession of heroin, my first feeling was an enormous sense of relief. Over the previous years, I tried everything to stop using. I'd taken buprenorphine, anti-depressants, anti-anxiety drugs. I'd tried therapy, exercise, meditation. I'd tried moving, changing friends, switching drugs. I'd checked myself into at least a dozen rehabs. I knew everything there was to know about the 12 steps, peer support and abstinence.

Nothing worked. When I was high, all I could think about was getting clean. As soon as the drugs wore off, all I could think about was how to get more drugs. With enormous effort, I sometimes won periods of freedom from heroin—a month, six weeks, six months. But I always ended up strung-out again. Nothing could stop me from using.

Nothing but the law. I believe that my arrest saved my life. Through a court-mandated treatment program, I began my road to recovery. I recently celebrated 21 years of being clean.

What was missing from my earlier attempts at recovery was motivation. Sooner or later, I'd say, "to hell with this recovery crap." And I'd get high again. My legal consequences gave me the motivation to recover. Even while kicking heroin on the jail cell floor, I felt relieved. No more hiding. I had to try something new.

This doesn't necessarily mean putting drug users in prison. I never went to prison, as is the case for most people with addiction. In fact, contrary to what many proponents of decriminalization suggest, fewer than 15 percent of inmates of state prisons are incarcerated because of nonviolent drug crimes. For many users who have a brush with the law, court-mandated treatment and the threat of worse outcomes in the future are enough to set them on the right track.

People who haven't experienced the unbelievable compulsion to use drugs find it easy to accept the assumption that if we shift the resources we pour into enforcement into treatment, addiction will become manageable. But in many cases—such as mine—treatment becomes effective only when the addict faces the cataclysmic shock of arrest.

4. The Impact of Drugs on Others: Some Evidence on Externalities. The libertarian argument for drug decriminalization depends in part on the empirical premise that drugs mainly harm users, not others. Absent that premise, the charge of paternalism largely fades away. After all, as John Stuart Mill writes, when "there is a definite damage, or a definite risk of damage, either to an[other] individual or to the public, the case is taken out of the province of liberty and placed in that of morality or law." In fact, while Mill is often celebrated by libertarians, he defended laws that regulated and in some cases prohibited "drunkenness" and "intemperance," on the theory that such intoxication entails negative externalities. By contrast, contemporary theorists like Barnett, who bemoan the way drug laws "seek forcibly to prevent persons from using their bodies in ways that they desire," often pair their protestation with the assertion that drug users "do not interfere with the equal liberty of others."[58]

The evidence on the negative externalities of drugs, though, is more complicated. For starters, the broad claim that substance abuse entails almost no negative externalities is hard to defend. As Mill observed, even harms "which a person does to himself may seriously affect, both through their sympathies and their interests, those nearly connected with him," including his loved ones. Indeed, contemporary research indicates that children of individuals suffering from drug abuse disorders are impacted in myriad ways, "including but not limited to having unmet developmental needs, impaired attachment, economic hardship, legal problems, [and] emotional distress." More broadly, society at large bears some of the financial cost of caring for individuals impacted by drug abuse. Taxpayers fund billions in drug-related health care costs, for example.[59]

Of course, alcohol and tobacco abuse can generate the same kinds of externalities. Excessive drinking alone reportedly cost the government nearly $17 billion in health care costs in 2010. Second-hand cigarette smoke, a negative externality of smoking, causes 41,000 deaths every year. Yet alcohol and tobacco are legal, which suggests these sorts of externalities are insufficient to justify criminal prohibition.[60]

Proponents of the War on Drugs have long relied instead on what they assert is a unique and uniquely severe externality of illegal narcotics: the role they purportedly play in fomenting crime—violent crime, especially. But the truth of this assertion is hotly contested. Extensive research demonstrates a *correlation* between drugs and crime. The fighting issue is whether drugs actually *cause* crime.[61]

Thinking on both sides of this debate has for decades been structured by a tripartite conceptual framework proposed by Paul Goldstein, which posits three ways drugs might cause crime: *pharmacological, economic,* and *systemic.* These three pathways are independent but may operate simultaneously to explain the same crime. As Justice Kennedy once summarized the idea:

> (1) A drug user may commit crime because of drug-induced changes in physiological functions, cognitive ability, and mood; (2) A drug user may commit crime in order to obtain money to buy drugs; and (3) A violent crime may occur as part of the drug business or culture.

Harmelin v. Michigan, 501 U.S. 957, 1002 (1991) (Kennedy, J., concurring in part).[62]

Note that with respect to each of these hypotheses, it can be hard to identify causal effects. Randomized controlled trials are not an option, leaving researchers to rely on observational data. But even when drugs are shown to correlate with crime, there may be some third factor, such as poverty or a "risk-loving" personality, driving both drug use and criminal behavior. Causation might even run in the opposite direction—from crime to drugs—if economic crimes like theft give people more money to buy drugs. Given these challenges, it is unsurprising that there is no expert consensus on the question whether drugs cause crime.

Consider the pharmacological pathway. Roughly half of the people currently serving time in state prisons for property offenses and a third serving time for violent offenses report using drugs at the time of their offense. But these statistics don't tell us the percentage of all drug users who engage in crime while intoxicated, which may be very small, nor do they tell us whether these same people would have committed the same crimes absent the use of drugs. Meanwhile, studies that make progress on those questions by analyzing crime rates in the wake of group-level changes in drug consumption find competing evidence. One found that higher cocaine prices were followed by decreases in violent and property crime, while another found no reduction in crime when consumption of methamphetamine temporarily plummeted due to an enforcement crackdown.[63]

There is somewhat stronger evidence for the idea that drug users may commit crimes to obtain money to purchase drugs. Around 30 percent of people in state prisons for property offenses self-report that drug money was a motive for their crimes. The numbers are largest among those who use drugs daily and those who lack a source of legal income. A recent national study also found that property-crime rates (but not violent-crime rates) are strongly associated with rates of nonmedical use of opioids in ways that suggest a causal relationship.[64]

Finally, there is robust evidence that crime results from the illicit drug trade itself. Frank Zimring and Gordon Hawkins estimate, for example, that between 10 percent and 25 percent of all U.S. homicides have some connection to the illegal drug trade, with figures sometimes as high as 50 percent in heavily impacted cities. Yet this connection, Zimring and Hawkins hasten to add, seems to be contingent on other socioeconomic conditions. Other countries, they note, have large illegal drug markets but "extensive drug-related lethal violence is not in evidence." Nevertheless, in the United States, a significant portion of homicides and violence do appear to arise from conflicts related to the illegal drug trade.[65]

5. The Impact of Drug Prohibition on Crime. The observation that violence often arises from conflicts associated with illegal drug markets raises an important related question. Might it be that drug *prohibition*, rather than drugs, explains the drug-crime connection? Nobel laureate Milton Friedman believed the answer is yes. "The harm that is done by drugs," he argued, "is predominantly caused by the fact that they are illegal." Thinking back to Goldstein's framework, one can imagine multiple ways in which Friedman's claim could be true. Pharmacologically, unsafe adulterated drugs might be more common in unregulated illicit markets. Economically, criminalization could drive up drug prices and thus increase pressure to commit crimes that can finance an addiction. Finally and most obviously, the violent nature of the drug business could arise from the fact that the business is illegal. To quote Professor Paul Butler, "Al Capone and his ilk disappeared when Prohibition was repealed . . . . Budweiser and Heineken battle [each other today] with cute commercials during the Super Bowl, not drive-by shootings."[66]

Substantial scholarship and research examine and debate the role prohibition itself plays in fostering drug-related crime. The following excerpt develops the argument in detail, focusing on violent crime, in particular.[67]

Jeffrey A. Miron, *Drug Prohibition and Violence,* in 1 *Reforming Criminal Justice: Introduction and Criminalization* 99 (Erik Luna ed., 2017). Prohibitions do not typically eliminate the market for the prohibited good. Instead, prohibitions drive markets underground. In these markets, participants cannot easily resolve disputes via standard, nonviolent mechanisms. For example, black-market producers of a good cannot use the legal system to adjudicate commercial disputes such as non-payment of debts. . . . Buyers of black-market goods cannot sue for product liability, nor can sellers use the courts to enforce payment. Along a different line, rival firms cannot compete via advertising and thus might wage violent turf battles instead. Thus, in black markets, disagreements are more likely to be resolved with violence. . . .

[P]articipants in black markets are likely to develop mechanisms for avoiding violence, but [robust law] enforcement makes this more difficult. For example, rival suppliers might agree to cartelize a market, [dividing territory and] thus reducing the need for advertising [and direct competition]. The arrest of one of these suppliers, however, can generate violence among the remaining suppliers, who attempt to capture new market share. Alternatively, black-market suppliers might create private, nonviolent mechanisms for resolving disputes, but enforcement that creates turnover among suppliers destroys reputational capital and makes such arrangements difficult to maintain. . . . Likewise, consumers of the prohibited commodity might purchase repeatedly from a reliable supplier, but enforcement that generates turnover among suppliers makes this harder, increasing the scope for disagreements. . . .

[Meanwhile,] increased enforcement of a prohibition might be accompanied by a redistribution of criminal justice resources away from other violence-reducing government policies. . . . For example, increased enforcement of drug prohibition for a given sized police budget implies reduced enforcement of laws against homicide, robbery, assault, and the like. . . .

[Prohibitions also] often raise the price of the prohibited commodity. Elevated prices . . . can encourage increased income-generating crime to finance purchases of the good. This mechanism does not necessarily imply violence directly, since many income-generating crimes are nonviolent (e.g., theft, shoplifting, prostitution). Some income-generating crimes are violent, however (e.g., robbery), and violence can occur incidentally as a result of otherwise nonviolent crimes. . . .

Prohibition might also encourage violence by making consumers or producers of the prohibited commodity less likely to use the official dispute-resolution system for disputes not related to the prohibited commodity. For example, a drug user or seller who has been robbed of non-drug items might not report this to the police — since this could risk penalties related to possession or sale of drugs — and instead attempt to punish the perpetrator of the robbery himself, possibly using violence. Higher enforcement is likely to increase this effect. If police routinely overlook small quantities of prohibited substances, the effect is likely to be small; if police routinely hassle anyone thought to be associated with the prohibited good, the effect is likely to be large.

6. Decriminalization and Harm Reduction. If one believes that legal prohibitions on drugs are the problem, or that they do more harm than good, the obvious policy response is decriminalization. Note that decriminalization does not imply agnosticism or surrender on the state's part when it comes to reducing the harms associated with problematic drug use. As Paul Butler writes, "If you think that designated drivers are a good idea when people are going out for a night on the town, you are already a fan of the public health policy known as 'harm reduction.' This philosophy accepts that people will engage in certain kinds of risky conduct, and seeks to minimize the danger" associated with that conduct by deploying tools other than penal sanctions.[68]

In other contexts, the approach has proven successful. The percentage of people who smoke cigarettes, for example, has fallen precipitously and continuously for decades. Over 40 percent of Americans smoked in the mid-1960s. By 2005, that number was cut in half and by 2022 it was halved again, to a record low of 11 percent. All of this was done without resort to penal sanctions, with experts instead crediting "a variety of efforts" including "anti-smoking campaigns, programs that educate children about the danger of smoking, laws that severely restrict where people could smoke and where cigarette companies could advertise, as well as better access to smoking cessation programs and higher taxes that make cigarettes expensive."[69]

To some extent, federal and state governments engage in harm reduction with respect to drugs as well. At the federal level, for example, the government spends significant resources attempting to reduce the incidence of overdose deaths, with the Department of Health and Human Services adopting a multi-pronged approach focused on prevention, evidence-based treatment, and recovery support. In a similar vein, the Food and Drug Administration took steps in 2023 to widen access to opioid overdose reversal treatments, making naloxone nasal sprays (often referred to as Narcan) available over the counter. This move was accompanied by the Center for Disease Control's "Stop Overdose" messaging campaign, which, among other things, educates drug users about the lifesaving power of naloxone. Within weeks of Narcan becoming available, municipalities and nonprofits spread the message to the public at large, posting billboards encouraging everyone to carry naloxone, which could help save a person in distress.[70]

With the widespread decriminalization of marijuana, the last few decades have also seen the largest move toward drug legalization in the United States since the end of Prohibition. In 1996, California became the first state to legalize marijuana for medical purposes. As of 2023, marijuana is now legal for medical use in nearly 40 states and is legal for adult recreational use in 24 states and the District of Columbia. In October 2022, President Biden issued a blanket pardon to everyone who had ever been federally convicted of simple possession of marijuana and directed the Attorney General to consider reclassifying marijuana under federal law.[71]

Evidence regarding the impact of these decriminalization efforts is mixed. According to several recent systematic reviews, many researchers have concluded that marijuana decriminalization in the United States has not led to changes in drug usage patterns. Others, however, have found that decriminalization may have increased marijuana usage to a degree, especially in adults. Evidence about the follow-on effects of use is likewise mixed. Some studies, for example, show an increase in marijuana-related health care visits. Yet others demonstrate *decreased* opioid prescription activity and opioid-related fatalities.[72]

7. Debating Decriminalization. As marijuana legalization becomes increasingly normalized, advocates and policymakers have begun to consider extending the harm-reduction philosophy more broadly. In 2022, for example, Harvard University professor Danielle Allen ran for governor of Massachusetts with a promise "to decriminalize all controlled substances" if elected, while at the same time promising "an expansion of treatment resources such as access to treatment beds, low-barrier supportive housing, and 'community-based, trauma-centered health recovery programs.'"[73]

Allen's proposal was expressly modeled after Measure 110, which decriminalized simple possession of all illicit drugs in Oregon in 2020. Before the measure, simple possession was a misdemeanor offense punishable by up to a year in jail. Under the new law, people who possessed less than one gram of heroin or two grams of methamphetamine would be issued a citation that carries a $100 fine, which they could avoid paying by calling a treatment referral number and agreeing to participate in a health assessment. Adopted by a popular ballot initiative, Measure 110 was supported by 58 percent of the electorate. But in the four years following its enactment, it sparked ongoing debate, in Oregon and nationally, ultimately ending in its repeal. The following excerpts give a sampling of that debate.[74]

Bret Stephens, Opinion, *The Hard-Drug Decriminalization Disaster,* N.Y. Times (Aug. 1, 2023). How soon is too soon to call a progressive and libertarian policy obsession a public policy fiasco? In the case of . . . Measure 110, the moment can't come soon enough. . . . Supporters of the measure called it a huge first step and a paradigm-shifting win that would bring down overdose rates, lessen the spread of disease, reduce racial inequities and make it easier for addicts to seek out treatment. . . . Now comes the reality check.

"On her walk to work at Forte Portland, a coffee shop and wine bar that she operates with her brother in the sunken lobby of a commercial building, Jennifer Myrle sidesteps needles, shattered glass and human feces," *The Times*'s Jan Hoffman [recently] reported. . . . Other scenes the piece describes and depicts: A woman who, according to Myrle, performed oral sex on a man at 11:30 in the morning on a block between Target and Nordstrom. A police officer handing out toothless citations to addicts shooting up in public, sometimes, the officer said, on playgrounds. . . . [A] fentanyl and meth addict named Noah Nethers [tells Hoffman he] likes Portland [because]: "He can do drugs wherever he wants, and the cops no longer harass him. There are more dealers, scouting for fresh customers moving to paradise. That means drugs are plentiful and cheap." (Not as idyllic: "Folks in nearby tents, high on meth, hit him with baseball bats.")

What these anecdotes suggest, the data confirms. In 2019 there were 280 unintentional opioid overdose deaths in Oregon. In 2021 there were 745. In 2019 there were 413 shooting incidents in Portland. In 2022 there were 1,309. (Numbers have abated a bit this year.) Of the 4,000 drug use citations issued in Oregon during the first two years of Measure 110, *The Economist* found, only 40 people called the hotline and were interested in treatment. "It has cost taxpayers $7,000 a call," *The Economist* reported. The number of people living on the street in Multnomah County, which includes Portland, rose by 29 percent from January 2022 to January 2023.

In their defense, proponents of Measure 110 — support for which has plummeted — argue that decriminalization is still in its early days and funds for harm reduction, housing and other services have been slow to arrive. . . . But the sticky fact that proponents of decriminalization rarely confront is that addicts are not merely sick people trying to get well, like cancer sufferers in need of chemotherapy. They are people who often will do just about anything to get high, however irrational, self-destructive or, in some cases, criminal their behavior becomes. Addiction may be a disease, but it's also a lifestyle — one that decriminalization does a lot to facilitate. It's easier to get high wherever and however you want when the cops are powerless to stop you.

Jacob Sullum, *Did Drug Decriminalization Cause a "Catastrophe" in Oregon?*, Reason (Aug. 3, 2023).[*] Stephens' assessment [above] . . . combines legitimate concerns about drug addiction and public order with misleading implications based on out-of-context statistics. And because Stephens ignores the main argument for decriminalization — that it is unjust to treat drug use as a crime — he never grapples with the morality of the policy it replaced. . . .

Stephens thinks the fact that drug-related deaths continued to rise in Oregon shows that decriminalization has failed. [But] Stephens neglects to mention that drug-related deaths rose nationwide during that period,

---

* Editor's Note: Portions of this excerpt have been reordered from the original.

from about 71,000 in 2019 to more than 107,000 in 2021. The number of deaths involving opioids rose from about 50,000 to about 81,000 — a 62 percent increase.

To be sure, the increase in Oregon that Stephens notes was much larger. But how does it compare to trends in other jurisdictions that did not decriminalize drug use? Between 2019 and 2021, Oregon's age-adjusted opioid overdose death rate rose from 7.6 to 18.1 per 100,000 residents. California saw a similar increase . . . [and in Washington the] rate likewise nearly doubled. . . . And even in 2021, Oregon's rate was lower than the national rate (24.7) and much lower than the rates in states such as Connecticut (38.3), Delaware (48.1), Kentucky (44.8), Maine (42.4), Maryland (38.5), Tennessee (45.5), Vermont (37.4), and West Virginia (77.2). On its face, this does not look like evidence that decriminalization is responsible for Oregon's continuing rise in opioid-related deaths. . . .

[More fundamentally, Stephens] seems confused about how to classify the conduct of people with drug problems. . . . Viewing addiction as a disease that overrides free will is convenient for drug warriors, because it justifies forcible intervention. . . . At the same time, however, it seems patently unjust to punish people for behavior they purportedly cannot control. . . . Stephens tries to square that circle by selectively applying the disease model. Addicts are sick, he says, but they are also bad, because they have chosen a destructive and antisocial "lifestyle." . . . Their "disease" means they should not be treated as autonomous moral agents, except when it comes to holding them criminally liable for their actions.

. . . [As for Stephens' focus on crimes other than drug use, there is nothing] unfair about holding [addicts] responsible for [choices that] impinge on other people's rights. That means a heavy drug user who steals to support his habit is not immune from criminal penalties. It also means the government can justifiably regulate what drug users do in public, where their actions might offend, incommode, or alarm people who have an equal right to use sidewalks, parks, and other taxpayer-funded facilities. Although Stephens implies otherwise, eliminating criminal penalties for drug possession does not require tolerating public drug use, defecation, or blowjobs.

[Finally, it] is important to keep in mind that Oregon's Measure 110 did nothing to address the supply of illegal drugs, which remain just as iffy and potentially deadly as they were before the initiative was approved. Decriminalization was limited to drug *users*. . . . This distinction between drug users and drug suppliers is similar to the policy enacted during Prohibition, when bootleggers were treated as criminals but drinkers [generally] were not. . . . Decriminalizing drug possession, in short, is a half-way measure that reduces but by no means eliminates the harm caused by prohibition.

Jordan Bollag, *Drug Decriminalization Policies Work — With Properly Funded Treatment Services,* Jacobin (Aug. 12, 2023). Recent articles from the New York Times and the Washington Post have depicted serious problems with overdoses and public drug use in [Oregon, which] has led conservatives like Bret Stephens to decry "The Hard-Drug Decriminalization Disaster." . . . [Stephens] is not alone in taking aim at decriminalization policies. Not even three years after Oregon's decriminalization measure passed with 58 percent of the vote, an even greater percentage of Oregonians — 63 percent — support recriminalizing drug possession.

Oregon's Measure 110 has in fact been a failure, but not because it decriminalized drugs. Its failure lies in an underfunded and inadequate addiction treatment and recovery system. Even before Measure 110, the state had the second-highest addiction rate in the nation and ranked very last in access to addiction treatment services. While Measure 110 promised to fund recovery and improve the situation, that funding has been woefully inadequate. . . . Medicaid patients wait months for a treatment bed, so those leaving hospital detox are thrown back into the world without access to inpatient services and only limited access to outpatient ones — a clear recipe for relapse. Last year, the state had fewer than thirty youth residential treatment beds that accepted Medicaid. But if addicts cannot get help at the moment they are ready, they may be dead or no longer ready for treatment by the time it arrives. . . . While [Stephens] cites data showing most addicts in Oregon don't seek treatment, it is likely that many aren't trying to get treatment precisely because they already know that the treatment system is inadequate and unlikely to help them. . . .

Jacob Sullum writing in the free-market libertarian *Reason* magazine, has defended Oregon['s] decriminalization efforts against Stephens's attacks while calling for full legalization. But *Reason* ignores the real culprit behind the drug problems in Oregon . . . and everywhere else: an underfunded and privatized treatment and recovery system.

While drug-warrior conservatives like Stephens want to solve addiction by locking addicts in cages, libertarians would let addicts die on the street without access to treatment. Both of these approaches are an affront to human dignity. We need a left alternative to drug policy that works alongside decriminalization: robust state-provided treatment at every step of the way, along with a social safety net that would give people the stability that can help stop them from relapsing or from becoming addicted in the first place. If the decriminalization movement does not demand this, it is more likely to fail, and we may well see the fruitless, destructive war on drugs return as a result.

8. Criminalizing Downstream Consequences of Drug Use. Even though alcohol is legal, a drunk driver who kills a pedestrian can still be prosecuted for criminal homicide, as we saw in Chapter Four. Indeed, we frequently punish people who engage in risky alcohol-related behavior like driving while intoxicated even when no harm ultimately occurs. Along similar lines, some states make it a crime for bartenders to overserve patrons who are visibly drunk.

As Jacob Sullum notes in the excerpt above, legalizing drugs does not prevent the state from taking similar approaches when drug users or purveyors cause or create the risk of similar harms. Many states already include illegal drugs alongside alcohol in statutes that criminalize driving while intoxicated or vehicular homicide. Likewise, as recent high-profile examples demonstrate, it is not uncommon for drug sellers to be prosecuted when their customers die from overdose. The man who sold fentanyl to actor Michael K. Williams was sentenced to 10 years in prison; the man who sold fentanyl to rapper Mac Miller was sentenced to 17.[75]

In some states, these cases can be charged under existing murder statutes, on the theory that drug sales entail "conscious indifference" to the possibility of fatal overdose and thus "evince malice." State v. Randolph, 676 S.W.2d 943, 947 (Tenn. 1984). More commonly, sellers in fatal overdose cases are prosecuted under specialized state and federal statutes that penalize "drug-induced homicide" or "distribution resulting in death." *See, e.g.,* 21 U.S.C. §841(b)(1)(C). As Leo Beletsky, Emma Rock, and Sunyou Kang report, prosecution under these statutes "has exploded" since they first emerged in 1975. "Between 2012 and 2018 alone, the recorded number of [such] prosecutions jumped from 109 to 696. As of 2019, 25 states have implemented legislation empowering prosecutors and judges to impose and adjudicate these and related charges." Notably, at least at the federal level, the offense is a strict liability crime. The statute "does not require . . . that death resulting from the use of a drug distributed by a defendant was a reasonably foreseeable event." United States v. Patterson, 38 F. 3d 139, 145 (4th Cir. 1994).[76]

Questions: How should statutes criminalizing drug users' risky behavior or the downstream harms of their conduct factor into the debate over drug decriminalization? For those concerned about the negative impacts of drug use, are such prosecutions sufficient substitutes for criminalizing drugs outright? For those who believe drugs should be fully legal, is it fair to punish sellers who inadvertently facilitate fatal overdoses? If some punishment is warranted, should it be 17 years, as in the case of the man who sold drugs to Mac Miller? Or should it be a misdemeanor, as in the case of a Texas bartender who overserved a patron whose subsequent drunk driving proved fatal?[77]

4. "A War on Blacks"

To this point, we have examined drug criminalization with tools commonly used to generate or assess laws and social policy. We've assembled and analyzed available evidence, put that evidence in conversation with underlying and contested normative principles, and explored different ways that legal and social policy could be crafted in response.

But for many critics, it is a mistake to treat the War on Drugs as if it were an effort to craft sound social policy. Rather, a central critique of the War on Drugs, echoed by scholars and activists over decades, is that American drug policy is in truth an instrument of racial subordination and oppression — that it is and was always designed to be, in the words of Professor Kenneth Nunn, "a [w]ar on Blacks."[78]

In this section, we explore this critique, presenting evidence of the disparate impact the War of Drugs has had on people of color and examining some of the possible causes of those disparities.

NOTES AND QUESTIONS

1. The Disparate Impact of Drug Criminalization on People of Color. There can be no dispute that the War on Drugs disproportionately impacts people of color. As a baseline, a variety of sources, including the federal government's National Survey on Drug Use and Health, report that white, Black, and Hispanic people in the United States use drugs and suffer from substance use disorders at generally similar rates. Data on drug dealing, as opposed to use, are scarcer, but two different federal government surveys of youth involvement in distribution again report similar rates among white, Black, and Hispanic populations.[79]

Yet while rates of drug use and sales are apparently equal across races, Black and Hispanic people are arrested, charged, and incarcerated for drug-related crimes at far higher rates than white people. Black people are approximately 13 percent of the U.S. population, for example, but represent 26 percent of people arrested for drug crimes nationwide. This translates to a drug-arrest rate twice as high as the rate for white people. The disparity is larger for some drugs and in some localities. With respect to marijuana offenses, Black people across the country are more than 3.5 times as likely as white people to be arrested notwithstanding evidence of equal usage rates. In New York City, they're eight times as likely; in Manhattan, fifteen times.[80]

These disparities only increase as cases move through the penal system's pipeline. At the charging stage, 45 percent of felony drug defendants in the 75 largest U.S. counties were Black as of 2009, the last year for which such data are available. In Cook County, Illinois, where roughly a quarter of residents are Black, nearly two-thirds of simple-possession charges between 2011 and 2021 were filed against Black people. For distribution and possession with intent to distribute, the number spikes to over 90 percent. As for sentencing, studies find that these disparities are compounded once again. Black defendants receive longer sentences for drug crimes than white defendants after controlling for a variety of case- and defendant-specific characteristics, including drug type and criminal history. In 2017, for example, a report by the U.S. Sentencing Commission found that Black male defendants convicted of drug crimes in federal court were given sentences almost 18 percent longer than those imposed on similarly situated white defendants. A 2023 update found that the disparity in incarceration length had shrunk, but that Black male defendants were far less likely than their white counterparts to receive probation-only sentences.[81]

The upshot is that Black people bear the brunt of incarceration from the War on Drugs. That fact remains true even as the war shows some early signs of abating. Thus, while both prison admissions for Black people convicted of drug offenses and the total number of Black adults in prison for drug convictions have declined since 2009—when the national prison population reached its peak—racial disparities in imprisonment "continue, with Black individuals comprising 28 percent and 36 percent of people admitted to or serving time in prison for drug offenses, respectively" as of 2019, according to the Pew Charitable Trust. And again, these disparities are even sharper in some jurisdictions. In the State of Illinois, for example, which is about 15 percent Black, Black defendants made up well over half of all prison admissions for drug crimes in 2018.[82]

2. The Impact of (Racialized) Poverty on Drug Enforcement. In Chapter Three, we studied how ongoing legacies of racial discrimination yield systemic inequalities along racial lines. Racialized inequalities in poverty rates are one major example of these structural effects. In the words of sociologists Robert Sampson and William Julius Wilson, decades of government policy and private discrimination have "combined to concentrate urban black poverty" in inner cities to the point that "blacks and whites face vastly different environments in which to live, work, and raise their children."[83]

How might racially concentrated poverty impact, and perhaps partially explain, the disparate rates of drug enforcement described in the preceding note? Consider the following pair of excerpts.

William J. Stuntz, *Race, Class, and Drugs*, 98 Colum. L. Rev. 1795, 1819-1824 (1998). Because [drug] crimes are consensual, the police do not receive reports of crimes when they happen. In order to catch the criminals, the police must seek them out; they must look for the crime, not merely respond to it. Because the criminal transactions involve goods or services that many people want . . . there are [also] a lot of [these] crimes. . . . So not only must the police look for the crimes, they must decide *where* to look, in a world where the crimes are happening everywhere. . . .

This is worth emphasizing, because it is very different from the ordinary posture of criminal law enforcement. Criminal *investigation*—the process of catching people who have committed offenses in the past, and building an evidentiary case that allows the state to prosecute them—tends by its nature to be reactive. Crime *prevention*—establishing a public police presence in areas where crimes are likely to occur—has the opposite tendency. . . . [W]hen the police are seeking to solve past crimes, the geographic allocation is done by the criminals, not by the police, for the police must go where the crimes happened. . . . Drug investigations are much more commonly police-initiated than other sorts of criminal investigations, since there is no crime victim to initiate them. And initiating investigations means targeting either particular places or particular people. [W]hom the police catch depends on where, or at whom, they look.

Michael Tonry, *Malign Neglect: Race, Crime, and Punishment in America* 105-106 (1995). For a variety of reasons it is easier to make arrests in socially disorganized neighborhoods, as contrasted with urban blue-collar and urban or suburban white-collar neighborhoods. First, more of the routine activities of life, including retail drug dealing, occur on the streets and alleys in poor neighborhoods. In working-class and middle-class neighborhoods, many activities, including drug deals, are likelier to occur indoors. This makes it much easier to find dealers from whom to make an undercover buy in a disadvantaged urban neighborhood than elsewhere.

Second, it is easier for narcotics officers to penetrate networks of friends and acquaintances in poor urban minority neighborhoods than in more stable and closely knit working-class and middle-class neighborhoods. The stranger buying drugs on the urban street corner or in an alley or overcoming local suspicions by hanging around for a few days and then buying drugs, is commonplace. . . .

Both these differences between socially disorganized urban neighborhoods and other neighborhoods make extensive drug-law enforcement operations in the inner city more likely and, by police standards, more successful. [Moreover, because] urban drug dealing is often visible, individual citizens, the media, and elected officials more often pressure police to take action against drugs in poor urban neighborhoods than in other kinds of neighborhoods.[84]

3. "Race-Neutral" Defenses of Racial Disparities: The Case of Crack Cocaine. The preceding note describes a dynamic between poverty and drug enforcement that, in a constitutional law class, would be called a *race-neutral* explanation for racially disparate law enforcement practices. The basic idea is that it might be poverty, not race, that drives the Drug War's enforcement priorities; racial disparities, on this view, are incidental. Of course, as already noted, poverty disparities themselves derive from legacies of overt racial discrimination. But as a lawyerly term of art, calling an explanation for racial disparities "race-neutral" captures the possibility that the policymakers who adopted it might not have *intended* to discriminate against Black people *because* they are Black. Indeed, one could imagine a hypothetical legislator or prosecutor who championed the War on Drugs but who failed to predict how poverty might skew drug-enforcement patterns. Such a person might be surprised—perhaps even horrified—to learn of the massive racial disparities created by the policies they helped adopt or enforce.

The actual history of the War on Drugs does not track this hypothetical. Policymakers were generally aware that the laws they adopted would disproportionately burden Black people. Consider for example the federal government's decision to punish possession of a single gram of crack cocaine as severely as possession of 100 grams of powder cocaine. As Professor David Sklansky and others have demonstrated, the legislators who supported this policy seemed to know it would create racial disparities, given that the crack users marked for severe sentences were disproportionately Black. Legislators were also aware, in the wake of the policy's adoption, that it produced massive racial disparities in incarceration rates. As early as 1995, the United States Sentencing Commission sent a report to Congress that said "[t]he 100-to-1 crack cocaine to powder cocaine disparity is a primary cause of the growing disparity between sentences for Black and White federal defendants." In the words of sociologist Devah Pager, "No single offense type has more directly contributed to contemporary racial disparities in imprisonment than drug crimes."[85]

But as students of both criminal law and constitutional law can appreciate, knowledge is not the same thing as intent. Indeed, one could imagine legislators who *knew* that severely punishing crack possession would disproportionately incarcerate Black people, but who nonetheless supported the policy on the (race-neutral) ground that crack is uniquely harmful, or perhaps on the ground that it is uniquely harmful *to poor communities of color.* Consider, for example, an argument put forward by Professor Bill Stuntz, which he suggested could explain how legislators "might end up punishing crack much more harshly than powder."

> [C]onduct that causes more harm is worse than conduct that causes less harm, all else being equal. . . . [And drug sales] in street markets in poor neighborhoods are worse than [sales] in other, better hidden illegal markets. . . . The violence and social injury that attends illegal street markets is real. . . . [P]ublic criminality (which is what street markets represent) causes fear and retreat by law-abiding citizens, which in turn causes more criminality. . . . And a poor buyer's greater susceptibility to a range of harms—joblessness, inability to care for one's children, a need to steal to support the illegal habit—means that the provision of goods like drugs in poor neighborhoods will likely cause more human tragedy than the provision of those same goods to wealthier customers. . . . [If these observations are true, then] there are entirely plausible reasons why many decent, not-at-all-bigoted people would wish the legal system to work especially hard at stamping out illegal markets in poor neighborhoods.

Many of the legislators who pushed to adopt the 100:1 crack-powder disparity advanced arguments along the lines Stuntz suggests. As it turns out, many of those arguments have not stood the test of time, as described in the following Supreme Court opinion and as reflected in subsequent congressional action.[86]

Kimbrough v. United States, 552 U.S. 85 (2007). Crack and powder cocaine are two forms of the same drug. Powder cocaine, or cocaine hydrochloride, is generally inhaled through the nose; it may also be mixed with water and injected. Crack cocaine, a type of cocaine base, is formed by dissolving powder cocaine and baking soda in boiling water. The resulting solid is divided into single-dose "rocks" that users smoke. The active ingredient in powder and crack cocaine is the same. The two forms of the drug also have the same physiological and psychotropic effects, but smoking crack cocaine allows the body to absorb the drug much faster than inhaling powder cocaine, and thus produces a shorter, more intense high.

. . . Crack cocaine was a relatively new drug when the 1986 Act [creating the crack/powder sentencing disparity] was signed into law, but it was already a matter of great public concern: "Drug abuse in general, and crack cocaine in particular, had become in public opinion and in members' minds a problem of overwhelming dimensions." *See United States Sentencing Commission, Special Report to Congress: Cocaine and Federal Sentencing Policy* 121 (Feb. 1995). Congress apparently believed that crack was significantly more dangerous than powder cocaine in that: (1) crack was highly addictive; (2) crack users and dealers were more likely to be violent than users and dealers of other drugs; (3) crack was more harmful to users than powder, particularly for children who had been exposed by their mothers' drug use during pregnancy; (4) crack use was especially prevalent among teenagers; and (5) crack's potency and low cost were making it increasingly popular.

Based on these assumptions, the 1986 Act adopted a "100-to-1 ratio" that treated every gram of crack cocaine as the equivalent of 100 grams of powder cocaine. . . .

While Congress was considering adoption of the 1986 Act, the [federal] Sentencing Commission was engaged in formulating the Sentencing Guidelines[, which serve as a reference point for judges deciding how to sentence a defendant within the often-broad sentencing ranges authorized by statute]. . . . In setting offense levels for crack and powder cocaine, the Commission, in line with the 1986 Act, adopted the 100-to-1 ratio. . . . [But over the ensuing decades, the Commission] determined that the crack/powder sentencing disparity is generally unwarranted. . . . In a series of reports, the Commission identified three problems with the crack/powder disparity.

First, the Commission reported, the 100-to-1 ratio rested on assumptions about "the relative harmfulness of the two drugs and the relative prevalence of certain harmful conduct associated with their use and distribution that more recent research and data no longer support." United States Sentencing Commission, *Report to Congress: Cocaine and Federal Sentencing Policy* 91 (May 2002); *see* United States Sentencing Commission, *Report to Congress: Cocaine and Federal Sentencing Policy* 8 (May 2007) (ratio Congress embedded in the statute far "overstate[s]" both "the relative harmfulness" of crack cocaine, and the "seriousness of most crack cocaine offenses"). For example, the Commission found that crack is associated with "significantly less trafficking-related violence than previously assumed." 2002 Report 100. It also observed that "the negative effects of prenatal crack cocaine exposure are identical to the negative effects of prenatal powder cocaine exposure." *Id.* at 94. The Commission furthermore noted that "the epidemic of crack cocaine use by youth never materialized to the extent feared." *Id.* at 96.

Second, the Commission concluded that the crack/powder disparity is inconsistent with the 1986 Act's goal of punishing major drug traffickers more severely than low-level dealers. Drug importers and major traffickers generally deal in powder cocaine, which is then converted into crack by street-level sellers. But the 100-to-1 ratio can lead to the "anomalous" result that "retail crack dealers get longer sentences than the wholesale drug distributors who supply them the powder cocaine from which their crack is produced." 1995 Report 174.

Finally, the Commission stated that the crack/powder sentencing differential "fosters disrespect for and lack of confidence in the criminal justice system" because of a "widely-held perception" that it "promotes unwarranted disparity based on race." 2002 Report 103. Approximately 85 percent of defendants convicted of crack offenses in federal court are black; thus the severe sentences required by the 100-to-1 ratio are imposed "primarily upon black offenders." *Id.*

Despite these observations, the Commission's most recent reports do not urge identical treatment of crack and powder cocaine. In the Commission's view, "some differential in the quantity-based penalties" for the two drugs is warranted, *id.* at 102, because crack is more addictive than powder, crack offenses are more likely to involve weapons or bodily injury, and crack distribution is associated with higher levels of crime. But the 100-to-1 crack/powder ratio, the Commission concluded, significantly overstates the differences between the two forms of the drug. Accordingly, the Commission recommended that the ratio be "substantially" reduced. *Id.* at viii. . . .

————————

Shortly after the *Kimbrough* decision, Congress took action to address the crack-powder disparity. The Fair Sentencing Act of 2010 eliminated the five-year mandatory minimum for simple possession of crack and reduced the crack-powder disparity from 100:1 to 18:1. Eight years later, in 2018,

Congress made these changes retroactive to anyone still in prison and sentenced before the 2010 act's adoption. In the wake of these laws, federal sentences for crack offenses have fallen and are now closer to those doled out for powder cocaine, though a meaningful disparity remains.[87]

Notably, many states have gone further than Congress. According to the advocacy group Families Against Mandatory Minimums, only eight states have any crack-powder disparity in their penal code. Of those that retain the distinction, ratios of 3:1 or 2:1 are most common. At 18:1, the federal government's current ratio is the third highest, behind New Hampshire and Missouri. As recently as 2021, the Department of Justice informed Congress that it supports full elimination of the disparity. It described the disparity as "not supported by science," a source of "unwarranted racial disparities," and "not necessary to achieve . . . law enforcement priorities," which the Department says the disparity "actually undermine[s]." When Congress took no action, Attorney General Merrick Garland instructed all federal prosecutors to "advocate for a sentence consistent with the guidelines for powder cocaine, rather than crack cocaine," in cases where defendants are convicted of possessing the latter.[88]

4. Knowledge vs. Intent: Evidence of Overt Racism in the War on Drugs. Speaking on the floor of the Senate in support of the Fair Sentencing Act of 2010, Senator Richard Durbin, who had initially voted for the 1986 crack-powder disparity, offered a *mea culpa.* Crack cocaine "had just appeared on the scene" when the earlier legislation was enacted, he said, "and it scared us, because it was cheap and it was addictive. We thought it was more dangerous than many narcotics. . . ." Durbin quoted former Senator and then-Vice President Joe Biden, "one of the authors of the legislation creating this disparity," who supported the 2010 reforms. "Each of the myths upon which we based the disparity," Biden said, "has since been dispelled or altered." Representative Daniel Lungren, who had also voted for the initial disparity, offered an even sharper confession of error.

> We initially came out of committee with a 20-to-1 ratio. By the time we finished on the floor, it was 100-to-1. We didn't really have an evidentiary basis for it, but that's what we did, thinking we were doing the right thing at the time.

For his part, Representative Bobby Scott, who was not a member of Congress in 1986 and who is Black and Filipino, accepted his colleagues' claims that the racial disparities engendered by the laws were unintended. "We are not blaming anybody for what happened in 1986," he said, "but we have had years of experience and have determined that there is no justification for the 100-to-1 ratio."[89]

To many critics, though, the suggestion that the policymakers who mounted the War on Drugs thought they were "doing the right thing"

is hard to accept. To these critics, American drug policy has never been
"race neutral" even as that term is defined by lawyers. Instead, they argue,
policymakers over a span of decades promoted American drug policy not
only with knowledge of its predictable racial impacts but also *because* of
those impacts. The claim, bluntly stated, is that the War on Drugs is and
has always been a "war on Blacks," waged to perpetuate racial subordination and to bolster white supremacy. In this line of critique, the War on
Drugs is cast as the culmination of a sequence of racially motivated drug
battles spanning back more than a century. The excerpts that follow offer
a sampling of these criticisms and the historical evidence marshaled to
support them.[90]

Erik Grant Luna, *Our Vietnam: The Prohibition Apocalypse*, 46 DePaul
L. Rev. 483, 490-502 (1997). [In the late 1800s,] Chinese laborers . . .
had been brought to the western United States for railroad construction.
The harsh conditions and intense work lured the Chinese workers into
"opium dens" to escape local abuse and suppress their longings for home.
Antagonistic Caucasian leaders, however, vilified Chinese laborers as the
cause of high unemployment and ascribed all social and economic ills to
Asians and their culture. . . . [I]n 1875, San Francisco banned the operation of opium dens, allegedly to prevent the spread of opium smoking to
the Caucasian population. . . . Within a decade, eighteen other states had
passed similar legislation . . . [and] Chinese immigrants became the scape-
goat for increased crime, squalor and uncleanliness. A report to the governor of California, for example, bordered on the genocidal: "[A] marked
decrease has been noted in the number of Asiatic immigrants . . . because
of their inability to secure the opium necessary to satisfy their cravings.
Hence we are in this manner instrumental in ridding the community of this
class of undesirable citizens."

African-Americans were the brunt of similar racial propaganda.
Addiction among African-Americans during the nineteenth century was
rare and led one southern doctor to declare that "the colored man is not
as susceptible to the habit as the white." However, as antidrug evangelism
spread, so did the myths of rampant addiction among African-Americans.
For example, a 1903 report by the American Pharmaceutical Association
stated that "[t]he negroes, the lower and immoral classes, are naturally
most readily influenced, and therefore among them we have the greater
number [of addicts]."

Of particular concern to the early twentieth-century bigot was the
effect of cocaine on African-Americans. . . . One racist delusion held that
African-Americans on cocaine were impervious to .32 caliber bullets.
The malevolently gullible police departments of the South responded by
switching to .38 caliber firearms and redoubling efforts to subdue African-
American society. . . . [And when federal legislators began to consider

national anti-drug legislation in the early 1900s, a leading anti-drug advocate, Dr. Hamilton Wright, explicitly invoked racist tropes] to secure the votes of southern legislators:

> It has been stated on very high authority that the use of cocaine by the negroes of the South is one of the most elusive and troublesome questions which confront the enforcement of the law in most of the Southern States. . . . In the South the drug is commonly sold in whisky dives. . . . The combination of low-grade spirits and cocaine makes a maddening compound. . . . It has been authoritatively stated that cocaine is often the direct incentive to the crime of rape by the negroes of the South and other sections of the country.

. . . [W]hen expressed in terms of African-American uprisings and the rape of Caucasian women, all states' rights concerns [about federal legislation] were abandoned.

Ta-Nehisi Coates, *The Black Family in the Age of Mass Incarceration*, Atlantic (Oct. 2015). The American response to crime cannot be divorced from a history of equating black struggle — individual and collective — with black villainy. . . . In 1966, Richard Nixon picked up the charge, linking rising crime rates to Martin Luther King's campaign of civil disobedience. . . . The cure, as Nixon saw it, was not addressing criminogenic conditions, but locking up more people. "Doubling the conviction rate in this country would do far more to cure crime in America than quadrupling the funds for [the] War on Poverty," he said in 1968. . . . Drugs in particular attracted Nixon's ire. Heroin dealers were "literally the slave traders of our time," he said, "traffickers in living death. They must be hunted to the end of the earth."

Nixon's war on crime was more rhetoric than substance. "I was cranking out that bullshit on Nixon's crime policy before he was elected," wrote White House counsel John Dean, in his memoir of his time in the administration. "And it was bullshit, too. We knew it." . . . The true target of Nixon's war on crime lay elsewhere. Describing the Nixon campaign's strategy for assembling enough votes to win the 1972 election, Nixon's aide John Ehrlichman later wrote, "We'll go after the racists. . . . That subliminal appeal to the antiblack voter was always in Nixon's statements and speeches on schools and housing." According to H.R. Haldeman, another Nixon aide, the president believed that when it came to welfare, the "*whole* problem [was] really the blacks." Of course, the civil-rights movement had made it unacceptable to say this directly. "The key is to devise a system that recognizes this while not appearing to," Haldeman wrote in his diary. But there was no need to devise new systems from scratch: When Nixon proclaimed drugs "public enemy No. 1" . . . he didn't need to name the threat. A centuries-long legacy of equating blacks with criminals and moral degenerates did the work for him.

Dam Baum, *Legalize It All*, Harper's Mag. (Apr. 2016). In 1994, John Ehrlichman, [who had been Richard Nixon's domestic-policy advisor,] unlocked for me one of the great mysteries of modern American history: How did the United States entangle itself in a policy of drug prohibition that has yielded so much misery and so few good results? . . . At the time, I was writing a book about the politics of drug prohibition. I started to ask Ehrlichman a series of earnest, wonky questions that he impatiently waved away. "You want to know what this was really all about?" he asked with the bluntness of a man who, after public disgrace and a stretch in federal prison, had little left to protect. "The Nixon campaign in 1968, and the Nixon White House after that, had two enemies: the antiwar left and black people. You understand what I'm saying? We knew we couldn't make it illegal to be either against the war or black, but by getting the public to associate the hippies with marijuana and blacks with heroin, and then criminalizing both heavily, we could disrupt those communities. We could arrest their leaders, raid their homes, break up their meetings, and vilify them night after night on the evening news. Did we know we were lying about the drugs? Of course we did."

David A. Sklansky, *Cocaine, Race, and Equal Protection*, 47 Stan. L. Rev. 1283, 1292-1297 (1995). [Throughout the twentieth century, as American drug criminalization policies developed], the drug of primary concern was strongly associated in the white public mind with a particular racial minority: opium in the late nineteenth century with Chinese immigrants on the west coast, powder cocaine in the early twentieth century with southern blacks, marijuana in the 1920s and 1930s with Mexican Americans in the southwest, and heroin in the 1950s with urban blacks. In each case, moreover, much of the public anxiety about the feared narcotic stemmed from a concern that use of the drug was spreading beyond the confines of the minority group with which it traditionally had been associated.

To a notable extent, the crack scare of 1986 followed a similar pattern. Whites strongly associated crack with the same minority group they linked with heroin — inner city blacks — and there was widespread fear that use of the drug was expanding beyond the ghetto into suburbia. The association between crack and urban blacks was twofold. Not only did crack do most of its damage in the ghetto, or at least most of its visible damage, but crack vendors were widely understood to be, for the most part, black men. This second association gave a particular tinge to media reports that crack was entering "middle class" neighborhoods. For example, a relatively early series of articles about crack in the *Palm Beach Post and Evening Times*, commended and inserted into the *Congressional Record* by Senator Lawton Chiles [during debate over the 1986 act that created the crack-powder disparity], noted that "[l]ess than a block from where unsuspecting white retirees play tennis, bands of young black men push their rocks on passing motorists, interested or not." And when a *Newsweek* cover story, also reprinted and applauded in the *Congressional Record,* warned of "ominous signs that crack and rock dealers are expanding well beyond the inner city," it accompanied that warning with photographs of two crack dealers, both black males, and offered the following description of a third:

> One of the boldest dealers on the street is 'Eare,' a big-shouldered Trinidadian wearing gold chains and a diamond-studded bracelet with his name engraved in it. . . . Eare operates as brazenly as a three-card-monte dealer, waving fistfuls of bills around as he deals his drugs at the corner of 42nd and Seventh.

What was coming was not just a drug — it was a black drug, sold by black men. That was not the only reason crack was frightening to white Americans, but it was one of the reasons.

5. "Locking Up Our Own": Black Voters and Elected Leaders in the War on Drugs. The excerpts above quote politicians across decades who expressed open or veiled racist sentiments as motivations for American drug policy. But might it be possible to view the Drug War's focus on Black communities as a form of racial justice? Consider, for example, an argument put forward by Professor Kate Stith:

> While it appears true that the enhanced penalties for crack cocaine more often fall upon black defendants, the legislature's action might also have been viewed as a laudatory attempt to provide enhanced protection to those communities — largely black . . . who are ravaged by abuse of this potent drug.[91]

In *Race, Crime, and the Law,* Professor Randall Kennedy endorses Stith's argument, adding that it is important when assessing the racial motivations behind legislation not to ignore "the positions and statements of *black* members of Congress," their constituents, and other leaders of the Black community. In the words of Professor James Forman, taking those views into account offers a more nuanced and more complicated account of "the role that blacks have played in shaping criminal justice policy over the past forty years." Consider the following two excerpts from Kennedy and Forman, which expand on these themes.[92]

Randall Kennedy, *Race, Crime, and the Law* 370-372 (1997). [V]irtually all of the . . . critics who have condemned as racist the crack-powder distinction have failed to take into account the opinions of the members of Congress who concerned themselves most intently and consistently with elevating the fortunes of African-Americans, namely the black members of Congress. . . . This is not to say that the opinions of black members of Congress should be viewed as dispositive. Persons of any hue can be wrong, opportunistic, or racially prejudiced even with respect to people of their own racial background. Still, it would be useful to some extent to know where the black members of Congress have stood on the matter. The claim that illicit racial beliefs and perceptions animated the enactment of the crack-powder distinction would surely be strengthened if all or even most of the black members of Congress had objected to the statute on racial grounds.

The fact is, however, that eleven of the twenty-one blacks who were then members of the House of Representatives voted in favor of the law which created the 100-to-1 crack-powder differential. It is difficult to interpret precisely the meaning of a vote. A representative might be against certain portions of a bill but favor others sufficiently to support the legislation overall. Or one might even vote in favor of a bill while inwardly opposing it. Still, in light of charges that the crack-powder distinction was enacted partly because of conscious or unconscious racism, it is noteworthy that *none* of the black members of Congress made that claim at the time the bill was initially discussed. Still more striking is that some of the black members of Congress who did vote for the bill [at various times] expressed views regarding crack cocaine that strongly support the logic of the crack-powder differential.

Charles Rangel, an African-American liberal Democratic representative from Harlem, New York, chaired the House Select Committee on Narcotics Abuse and Control when the federal crack-powder differential was enacted. In March 1986, he became the first person in Congress to draw attention to crack as a new and special danger, noting that "what is most frightening about crack is that it has made cocaine widely available and affordable for abuse among our youth."

Five months later, Major Owens, a liberal Democratic representative from the predominantly black Bedford-Stuyvesant section of Brooklyn, New York, introduced legislation to increase punishment for trafficking in cocaine. . . . At that time, trafficking in cocaine was punished much less harshly than trafficking in heroin. Owens's proposed legislation lowered the amount of cocaine presumed to signal that a person is a distributor and raised the penalties substantially. . . . "We must make it perfectly clear," Owens declared, "that we view this drug as highly dangerous and that we will not tolerate its importation, possession, or sale." . . . [He then said,] "None of the press accounts really have exaggerated what is actually going on. It is as bad as any articles have stated. It is as bad as anything you have read about. It is as bad as anything you have seen on television or heard on radio." . . . [Owens concluded,] "Current law does not take cocaine seriously. It is not surprising [therefore] that we have an epidemic now which is heightened by the appearance of a purified form of cocaine which is called crack. . . ."

Representative Owens was followed on the floor of the House by Alton Waldon, another African-American liberal Democratic representative from a predominantly black district in New York. His message was much the same as Owens's but with a bit more punitive bite and a more focused attention on crack:

> The madness which is crack has no respect for social, professional or economic status. Crack usage is the evidence that our society may in fact be losing control of itself. For those of us who are black this self-inflicted pain is the worst oppression we have known since slavery. . . . Let us . . . pledge to crack down on crack.

The comments of Rangel, Owens, and Waldon were made before the 100-to-1 crack-powder differential was proposed as legislation. They are, however, consistent with that legislation and helped to prepare the ground for it. After all, if crack trafficking represents, in Waldon's words, "the worst oppression we have known since slavery," one reasonable response might well be to impose severe mandatory minimum sentences on those guilty of such antisocial conduct.

The absence of any charge by black members of Congress that the crack-powder differential was racially unfair speaks volumes; after all, several of these representatives had long histories of distinguished opposition to any public policy that smacked of racial injustice. That several of these representatives demanded a crackdown on crack is also significant. It suggests that the initiative for what became the crack-powder distinction originated to some extent *within* the ranks of African-American congressional officials. All of these facts are relevant in evaluating whether the crack-powder distinction should be prohibited on racial justice grounds. . . .

James Forman Jr., *Locking Up Our Own: Crime and Punishment in Black America* 10-11 (2017). [A] portion of African American social, political, and intellectual history . . . gets ignored or elided when we fail to appreciate the role that blacks have played in shaping criminal justice policy over the past forty years. African Americans performed this role as citizens, voters, mayors, legislators, prosecutors, police officers, police chiefs, corrections officials, and community activists. Their influence grew as a result of black progress in attaining political power, especially after the passage of the Voting Rights Act in 1965. And to a significant extent, the new black leaders and their constituents supported tough-on-crime measures.

To understand why, we must start with a profound social fact: in the years preceding and during our punishment binge, black communities were devastated by historically unprecedented levels of crime and violence. Spurred by a heroin epidemic, homicides doubled and tripled in D.C. and many other American cities throughout the 1960s. Two decades later, heroin would be eclipsed by crack, a terrifying drug whose addictive qualities and violent marketplace caused some contemporaries to label it "the worst thing to hit us since slavery."

Letters from black citizens, neighborhood association newsletters, and the pages of the black press from the past forty years reveal astonishing levels of pain, fear, and anger. In 1968, a group of black nationalists in D.C. called drug dealers "black-face traitors of our people who sell dope to our young boys and girls and make whores and thieves of them." . . . By the 1980s and 1990s, the files of D.C. Council members were crammed with letters from scared constituents, complaining that "we feel like prisoners in our homes, strangers on our own streets," and begging for more police action.

As they confronted this devastating crime wave, black officials exhibited a complicated and sometimes overlapping mix of impulses. Some displayed tremendous hostility toward perpetrators of crime, describing them as a "cancer" that had to be cut away from the rest of the black community. Others pushed for harsher penalties but acknowledged that these measures would not solve the crisis at hand. Some even expressed sympathy for the plight of criminal defendants, who they knew were disproportionately black. But that sympathy was rarely sufficient to overcome the claims of black crime victims, who often argued that a punitive approach was necessary to protect the African American community—including many of its most impoverished members—from the ravages of crime.[93]

6. Equal Protection of the Laws. One might imagine, in view of some of the excerpts above, that American drug laws would be exposed to constitutional challenge under the Equal Protection Clause of the Fourteenth Amendment, which prohibits state actors from discriminating on the basis of race. And in fact, as Professor David Sklansky reports, "Black defendants have mounted equal protection challenges to the federal crack sentences in each of the regional federal courts of appeals." But as he goes on to report, the outcomes of those challenges "have been remarkably consistent: the defendants always have lost, and the opinions generally have been both unanimous and short." In essence, the courts uniformly concluded, in the words of one representative opinion, "that Congress clearly had rational motives for creating the distinction between crack and powder cocaine," including rational beliefs about "the potency of the drug, the ease with which drug dealers can carry and conceal it, the highly addictive nature of the drug, and the violence which often accompanies trade in it." United States v. Clary, 34 F.3d 709, 712 (8th Cir. 1994). In other words, the courts "concluded that there was no evidence that Congress . . . had a racially discriminatory motive when it crafted the . . . extended sentences for crack cocaine felonies." *Id.*[94]

7. Drug Warriors: The War on Drugs and Police Power. The preceding notes have examined the direct racial impacts of the War on Drugs, as measured in arrests, prosecutions, convictions, and sentences. But there is a broader way in which the War on Drugs can create racial disparities in the penal system. In the words of Professor Randy Barnett, the police officers and prosecutors charged with the war's execution will predictably seek expanded law enforcement powers to bolster the war's success. They will, in other words, seek to "stretch the outer boundaries of legal searches" and arrests, in ways that "can be expected, over time, to contribute to the eventual loosening up of the rules by the courts." According to many critics, these efforts have been successful. Professor Michelle Alexander, for example, argues that the Supreme Court has "seized every opportunity to facilitate the drug war, primarily by eviscerating Fourth Amendment protections against unreasonable searches and seizures by the police. The rollback has been so pronounced that some commentators charge that a virtual 'drug exception' now exists to the Bill of Rights." Justice John Paul Stevens shared the critique, writing once in dissent that "No impartial observer could criticize this Court for hindering the progress of the war on drugs. On the contrary, [our] decisions . . . support the conclusion that this Court has become a loyal foot soldier in the Executive's fight against crime." California v. Acevedo, 500 U.S. 565, 601 (1991) (Stevens, J. dissenting). As Alexander goes on to observe, the impacts of this expanded police power are felt most acutely in communities of color. "Black and brown youth are the primary targets. It is not uncommon for a young black teenager living in a ghetto community to be stopped, interrogated, and frisked numerous times in the course of a month, or even a single week, often by paramilitary units."[95]

We will return to the interplay between substantive criminal laws and police enforcement powers and practices more generally in the next chapter. With respect to policing the War on Drugs in particular, consider the following excerpt.[96]

Trevor Burrus, *How the Drug War Broke Policing*, Cato Inst.: Cato at Liberty Blog (June 15, 2020). With drug use, the purported victim and the criminal are the same person . . . . Police must therefore adopt strategies to catch unwilling "victims" and to interdict the drugs at their source.

Catching unwilling victims is difficult. Anyone could be a criminal/victim, after all, hiding illicit drugs on their body, car, or property. . . . [C]asual interactions with citizens become riddled with suspicion. Is this driver hiding something? Perhaps if I search that random person on the street, I'll find drugs. . . .

If drug users are out in the street, it's relatively easy. But what if they're in their homes, carrying out their crimes in private? . . . Helicopters can be flown over the house or, now, more likely drones. Heat-sensitive cameras can test for "grow rooms," and there are always informants who are more than willing to fess up for leniency or a small cash payment. There's a drug dealer in there, they tell the cops, and now police can go after the source.

But the criminals/victims still won't invite the police into the house, so it is time to suit up and go in with force. . . . A modern police officer can don the accoutrements of a soldier fighting in Fallujah and arrive at the "scene of the crime" in an armored personnel carrier designed for military use. They can also request permission from a magistrate judge (nearly always given) to carry out a "no-knock" raid—such as the raid that killed a young black woman named Breonna Taylor—and go in with full force. The door is violently busted open, flash bang grenades are thrown in, and armed men come rushing in throwing the occupants to the ground threatening to shoot them, if not actually pulling the trigger.

What else could they do? After all, *drugs* were in there.

B. Possessing Guns

Early in this chapter, when reading *State v. Lammers* (p. 626), we paused to observe the substantial harms caused by mass shootings in the United States, and to note the extent to which the U.S. is a global outlier with respect to these large-scale acts of violence. The impact of U.S. gun violence is even more pronounced when one considers not just mass shootings but all gun-related killings and assaults. In 2021, almost 50,000 people in the U.S. were killed by firearms. Slightly more than half of these deaths were suicides; slightly fewer than half were homicides, which account for 80 percent of all homicides in the country. In 2020, firearm homicides were the single leading cause of death for Americans ages 1 to 19.[97]

Compared to other similarly situated countries, people in the United States are 25 times more likely to be shot to death by an assailant with a gun—49 times more likely for young people between ages 15 and 24. Nor is gun violence limited to fatal shootings. According to victims surveyed in 1993, nearly one third of people who commit sexual assault, robbery, or aggravated assault carried a gun while perpetrating their crime. Similarly, surveys indicate that 15 to 20 percent of all people imprisoned for crimes say they used or possessed a gun during their offense. For violent crimes, the number rises to 30 to 35 percent.[98]

As we saw in Chapters Three and Four, violent crime is concentrated in poor communities of color—a predictable consequence of structural inequality and systemic racism. The same concentrated disparities are apparent with respect to gun violence. Black people in the United States are more than ten times as likely as white people to be victims of firearm homicides; Latinos are twice as likely as whites. Beyond fatalities, between 2001 and 2017, over 400,000 Black people went to emergency rooms across the country for gunshot injuries, compared to 122,000 white people. In some states, these disparities are even more striking. Black males between 15 and 34 years old in California are 17 times more likely to be hospitalized with a gunshot wound than white males the same age. In New Jersey, the disparity climbs to 98 to 1.[99]

At the same time, just as debates over drug policy can be skewed by focusing only on harms, neglecting the benefits that many Americans associate with gun possession and use can distort conversations about guns. Gun ownership in the United States is widespread. Nearly half of all adults live in a household with at least one gun. Many people own multiple guns, with the sum total of civilian-owned firearms in the country exceeding 300 million. Roughly half of these are owned by suburbanites, 30 percent by those in rural areas, and 20 percent by city dwellers. Handguns compose about half of this national stock.[100]

Gun owners commonly identify two primary benefits of gun possession. First, guns have aesthetic, emotional, and hedonic value. They are objects their owners might collect and admire, pass down through generations, and use for recreational or family bonding experiences such as hunting or sport shooting. To borrow from Professor Paul Butler, one might say that guns, like drugs, can be "big fun."[101]

Second, gun owners often cite the importance of firearm possession for self-defense. It is hard to measure the related psychological benefit of gun possession; people might feel more secure with a gun in their home even if it is never used. As for actual instances of defensive gun use, reliable data is "elusive," with Professors Phil Cook and Kristin Goss concluding that the true "answer is unknown, and in a sense unknowable." Estimates from different studies range wildly, from 70,000 defensive uses of firearms per year to 2.5 million.[102]

Importantly, the defensive potential of firearms points to one way in which the debate over criminalizing possession in this context differs from many others. In the United States, gun possession is a constitutional right. The U.S. Supreme Court first recognized that right in 2008, holding that the Second Amendment guarantees individuals the right to possess handguns within the home. *See* District of Columbia v. Heller, 554 U.S. 570 (2008). That ruling was expanded in 2022 to "protect an individual's right to carry a handgun for self-defense outside the home." N.Y. State Rifle & Pistol Ass'n v. Bruen, 142 S. Ct. 2111, 2122 (2022). The Court has summarized the core rationale for the right this way:

> [I]n *Heller,* we held that individual self-defense is "the *central component*" of the Second Amendment right. . . . Thus, we concluded, citizens must be permitted "to use [handguns] for the core lawful purpose of self-defense." *Heller* makes it clear that this right is "deeply rooted in this Nation's history and tradition. . . . " [T]he 1689 English Bill of Rights explicitly protected a right to keep arms for self-defense, and . . . by 1765, Blackstone was able to assert that the right to keep and bear arms was "one of the fundamental rights of Englishmen."

McDonald v. City of Chicago, 561 U.S. 742, 767-768 (2010).

In the wake of the Supreme Court's rulings, national debates over gun control, gun violence, and the Second Amendment are often cast in straightforwardly partisan terms. Those toward the political left are generally taken to oppose the Court's rulings and to favor more aggressive gun control policies—including more aggressive efforts to prosecute illegal gun possession. Their counterparts on the right meanwhile are generally taken to embrace the right to bear arms and to oppose legal restrictions on gun purchases, sales, and possession.

On closer inspection, however, the ideological fault lines surrounding these contentious issues are not so clear cut. As noted in Chapter Four (p. 343), there have always been strong advocates of the right to bear arms on the political left, stretching from Ida B. Wells's declaration that a "Winchester rifle should have a place in every black home" as a guard against racist oppression and continuing up through calls by the Black Panthers, the Pink Pistols, and Jews for the Preservation of Firearm Ownership to embrace firearms as tools of liberation in the face of oppression.[103]

More recently, academics and advocates approaching the issue from the ideological left have begun to attack criminalization of gun possession by leveraging arguments that parallel critiques of the War on Drugs. As these critics observe, the Supreme Court's Second Amendment jurisprudence has so far left in place "longstanding prohibitions on the possession of firearms by felons and the mentally ill" as well as other criminal "laws forbidding the carrying of firearms in sensitive places such as schools and government buildings." *Heller*, 554 U.S. at 626. Due to these exceptions, gun prosecutions remain common in the United States. In federal prisons, drugs are the largest driver of incarceration, but guns are second, with about thirty percent of all federal prisoners serving time for an offense involving a weapon. Those prison terms arise in large part from statutes that punish gun possession by people with prior criminal records and people who carry guns while possessing drugs. As one might expect given the racial disparities in both drug criminalization and in criminal enforcement writ large, this approach to firearm criminalization has large and disparate racial impacts. Over half of the people sentenced in federal court for firearm-possession offenses are Black.[104]

Joining cause with conservative groups like the National Rifle Association and leveraging the Supreme Court's recent precedents, critics of gun criminalization on the political left have begun to challenge gun control laws in the courts. And they have had early success, including in the *Bruen* case cited above. To some on the political left, the fact that arguments supporting such rulings came from ideological fellow travelers gave cause for concern. For others, it forced an increasingly pointed question. Should those who oppose the War on Drugs join with the NRA and others on the political right in resisting the so-called War on Guns? Or are there principled lines of distinction that permit one to argue for drug decriminalization while supporting firearm criminalization? The excerpts in the remainder of this section present arguments in this emerging and continuing debate.

Benjamin Levin, *Guns and Drugs*, 84 Fordham L. Rev. 2173, 2175-2177, 2192-2207, 2213-2216, 2221-2225 (2016). If we find compelling the critiques of criminal law as a blunt instrument for social change that has wrought undue collateral damage in the context of the War on Drugs, can we reconcile these concerns with a drive to criminalize other social problems? . . . [I]f widespread incarceration of particular demographic groups under criminal drug statutes is a cause for public concern, why should widespread incarceration of the same groups under other criminal statutes be accepted without inquiry? . . .

[Consider] a regulatory paradigm of choice and in which many of the same pathologies appear: gun possession. . . . At first blush, the legal treatment of, and political attitudes toward, gun possession and drugs may appear wholly distinct and unrelated. . . . [But] the criminal regulation of gun possession should be viewed in the context of the trenchant critiques leveled against the failed War on Drugs. Both criminalization projects have grown out of public concern about social scourges that have wreaked havoc in communities of color and lower-income urban communities, but both have also contributed to the mass incarceration of members of those same communities. Additionally, the two legal areas are deeply intertwined — drug convictions often serve as predicates for a range of felon-in-possession gun crimes, and policing of guns and drugs are often closely tied. . . .

Gun control proponents have long sought to advance legal measures that make it harder for individuals to own guns; gun rights advocates have strongly opposed these measures. But this easy story misses a crucial point of consensus. Both sides of the gun control debate have occasionally compromised, and these compromises have generally yielded criminal statutes designed to impose harsh punishments on unlawful gun owners. That is, in a polarized political climate, there is occasionally a space for consensus gun control — criminal law. . . . [Let's] explore the potential costs of this compromise. . . .

Demographics: Different Crimes, Same Defendants. . . . One consequence of the political Right's support for gun rights is the popularization of the image of the gun owner as a rural white male. This idealized gun owner has become a symbol of sorts in a wide variety of political debates and, indeed, in a range of scholarly debates regarding the legal treatment of firearms and self-defense. If we are concerned about the effects of criminal regulation, however, this framing may be inaccurate and terribly deceptive. Even if the stereotypical white male NRA member were the prototypical gun owner, this does not mean that he would be the prototypical defendant in a criminal weapons case. . . . In 2000, 54 percent of the state court defendants convicted for weapons crimes were black, as compared to 44 percent white. . . . [T]he data for New York City paint an even starker picture. In 2012, only 4.2 percent of the 3287 individuals arrested for firearms charges were white; 73.2 percent were black, and 21.5 percent were Hispanic. . . .

[T]he prevalence of felon-in-possession statutes and the close relationship between antigun and antidrug initiatives suggests that criminal regulation of gun possession may well reinscribe the inequalities of the drug war. . . . [T]o the extent that the War on Drugs has led to more people of color with felony convictions, a system of gun control that requires mandatory minimum prison terms for felons risks sending the same individuals to prison for extended sentences. . . . The War on Drugs has helped to drive home the significance of the race-based costs of widespread criminalization and criminal enforcement. In order to conclude . . . that these costs are justified in the gun possession context, we must address the racial costs of the current regime and of further criminal regulation of gun possession. . . .

Police Power. From a policing standpoint, possessory drug crimes allow for . . . aggressive and interventionist preventative policing. . . . Gun control proponents might conclude . . . that the benefits of an aggressive criminal regulatory approach to gun possession trump any costs. . . . But a theory of criminal law and law enforcement consistent with the civil libertarian critiques raised in the drug context should require a much more nuanced cost-benefit analysis that takes seriously the growing power of police and the potential risks to individual liberties. . . . [M]any of the erosions and carve-outs in Fourth Amendment jurisprudence, which are frequently attributed to the War on Drugs, are actually traceable directly to the criminal regulation and policing of firearms. The judicially created "drug exception to the Constitution" finds root in a set of assumptions about drugs and violence. More specifically (but perhaps less explicitly), it relies on assumptions about the relationship between guns and the drug trade and about the sorts of people who use and deal drugs. The operative concern that has shaped the judicial expansion of police powers in the drug context is not only deference to legislative determinations about drugs and their danger, but also fear for officer safety in communities and contexts in which guns might be ubiquitous. . . .

The same elements of drug possession that make it a crime that invites intrusive policing—difficulty to detect, prevalence of offense, and lack of easily identifiable victim—are similarly present in the case of gun possession. . . . [And just] as police in the drug context have been empowered to fight a war against the citizenry, in the gun context, officers now operate in a space in which they are trained to view citizens as armed—potential threats not only to the public, but also to the officers' personal safety. . . . [G]uns clearly possess a closer tie to violence and immediate third-party harms. But if we were concerned about the escalation of a war mentality and a proliferation of potentially violent confrontations between police and civilians in the drug context, then we cannot discount possessory gun crime as a space that has yielded both massive judicial deference to officers and also a normalization of officer force. . . .

Driving Mass Incarceration. Like criminal drug statutes, existing and proposed criminal gun possession statutes should also trigger skepticism from critics of mass incarceration. If we are concerned about mass incarceration because of its social or economic costs, we should subject to close scrutiny any legislation that further ramps up punishment or potentially increases the number of individuals serving extended sentences. . . . In this respect, the parallel to criminal drug statutes is compelling. In the drug context, the use of criminal law to handle a public health crisis ultimately merged with a strong punitive streak, yielding a regulatory regime undergirded with violent moralism. Shaped by this preference for incarceration, the criminal gun statutes in the federal system and in many states advance a web of exponentially [increasing] sentences. Like drug crime offenses, possessory [gun] offenses quickly multiply, allowing prosecutors to stack charges and to extend significantly the prison term that a defendant faces. The end result is a legal regime that—much like drug prohibition—feeds into a growing carceral population. . . .

Different Crimes, Same Critiques? . . . Support for stringent gun control has become deeply embedded in the contemporary liberal/progressive worldview. . . . Additionally, support for gun control as a means of curtailing gun violence remains strong in black communities that have borne the brunt of the nation's gun violence. While support for the War on Drugs has waned, and while those on the political Left have been some of the most vociferous critics of criminal drug policies, any argument that cuts against the grain of these deeply held beliefs about guns will presumably face strong opposition. . . .

In his work on "cultural cognition," Dan Kahan has focused on the gun control debate and argued that the political divide on gun regulation cannot be understood on purely rational terms. "Whatever they say in public," contends Kahan, "those involved in the gun control debate are not really motivated by beliefs about guns and crime. . . . What *does* motivate them, a wealth of sociological and historical literature suggests, is their attachment to competing cultural styles that assign social meanings to guns." According to Kahan and other scholars of gun law and policy, attitudes toward guns are articles of faith, often deeply embedded in views of self and society. . . .

Past experience has shown us the realities of criminal intervention in social problems. And past experience has led to a range of recognized critiques. So why pretend that there could be a magic wand when we are presented with a social problem that we find particularly pressing or an item, substance, or behavior that we find particularly reprehensible? Given that there will still be gun regulation after *Heller* and *McDonald*, we must determine what such regulation should look like and which legal institutions should shape U.S. gun policy. "What will improve the gun debate . . . ," argues Franklin Zimring, one of the nation's preeminent gun law scholars, "is careful attention to the differences between types and intensities of firearm regulation." . . . If we are to learn from the War on Drugs and avoid repeating past mistakes, it means internalizing the critiques of criminal law, not only in the drug context but in other "hard cases."

Brief of the Black Attorneys of Legal Aid, The Bronx Defenders, Brooklyn Defender Services, et al., in N.Y. Rifle Ass'n v. Bruen, 142 S. Ct. 2111 (2022). [E]ach year, we represent hundreds of indigent people whom New York criminally charges for exercising their right to keep and bear arms. For our clients, New York's [handgun] licensing regime renders the Second Amendment a legal fiction. Worse, virtually all our clients whom New York prosecutes for exercising their Second Amendment right are Black or Hispanic. And that is no accident. New York enacted its firearm licensing requirements to criminalize gun ownership by racial and ethnic minorities. That remains the effect of its enforcement by police and prosecutors today.

The consequences for our clients are brutal. New York police have stopped, questioned, and frisked our clients on the streets. They have invaded our clients' homes with guns drawn, terrifying them, their families, and their children. They have forcibly removed our clients from their homes and communities and abandoned them in dirty and violent jails and prisons for days, weeks, months, and years. They have deprived our clients of their jobs, children, livelihoods, and ability to live in this country. And they have branded our clients as "criminals" and "violent felons" for life. They have done all of this only because our clients exercised a constitutional right. . . .

New York violates our clients' rights to keep and bear arms by arresting, jailing, and prosecuting them for possessing a firearm—anywhere—unless they have applied to and survived the state's expensive and onerous discretionary licensing process. . . . [B]ut securing such a license is no easy feat—especially for those who are indigent. For example, the New York City Police Department . . . requires that applicants submit over $400 in fees [to obtain a license,] pricing out indigent people, like those living in the most impoverished Congressional district in the country, which is in the Bronx. . . .

New York's firearm licensing requirement originated with the 1911 Sullivan Law . . . [which] made it unlawful to possess any firearm, anywhere, without a license, and gave local police broad discretion to decide who could obtain one. The bill was one of the "early Northern controls" that was passed in response to post-Reconstruction "concerns about organized labor, the huge number of immigrants, and race riots in which some blacks defended themselves with firearms." . . .

The Second Amendment is a right held by all the people. . . . Our experience illustrates that New York effectively deprives its people of the Second Amendment right by requiring that they successfully obtain a license from the police before exercising it. As a result, we urge this Court to enforce the Second Amendment by issuing a clear and durable rule. The Court should hold that . . . New York cannot condition Second Amendment rights on a person first obtaining a license.

[W]e are mindful that the right to keep and bear arms has "controversial public safety implications." McDonald v. City of Chicago, 561 U.S. 742, 783 (2010). . . . But . . . New York's licensing requirements . . . [also] have controversial public safety implications. It is not safe to be approached by police on suspicion that you possess a gun without a license. It is not safe to have a search warrant executed on your home. It is not safe to be caged pretrial at Rikers Island. It is not safe to lose your job. It is not safe to lose your children. It is not safe to be sentenced to prison. And it is not safe to forever be branded as a "criminal," or worse, as a "violent felon." In sum, New York's licensing requirements are not safe.

The Court must not "stand by idly" while New York denies its people the right to keep and bear arms, "particularly when their very lives may depend on it." Peruta v. California, 137 S. Ct. 1995, 2000 (2017) (Thomas, J., dissenting from the denial of certiorari).[105]

Elie Mystal, *Why Are Public Defenders Backing a Major Assault on Gun Control?*, Nation (July 26, 2021). The argument public defenders make against gun laws is exactly the same as the argument I and others have made against drug laws. . . . According to the public defenders, the solution to all of these (entirely legitimate) concerns is to . . . allow gun owners to walk the state with their firearms without a permit. Unfortunately, that solution is misguided and destined to lead to more gun deaths . . . . [O]ne recent study indicates that a loosening of permit laws leads to increased Black homicide rates, not lower ones. . . . The government must have some authority to regulate private arsenals in order to carry out its essential function of keeping people safe. . . . I completely support forcing the state to exercise its authority fairly and without racial bias, but doing away with the authority altogether is just going to get more people, *specifically Black people*, killed. I want racial justice, but I also don't want to be shot to death in a crossfire of "liberty."

PART 3

THE PENAL SYSTEM: CONSTRAINTS, REFORMS, AND ALTERNATIVES

The last two chapters of this book explore the ramifications of substantive criminal law's expansion, with a focus on the attendant pathologies and the potential alternative pathways that critics have identified.

We begin, in Chapter Nine, with a study of the relationship between substantive criminal law and the institutional power of two key law enforcement actors: police officers and prosecutors. The chapter's first part, on the police, examines the history and modern-day manifestations of what is sometimes called order-maintenance or broken-windows policing, identifies the linkage between substantive criminal law and those and related police practices, and examines the extent to which the constitutional law of the Fourth Amendment and the Equal Protection Clause may or may not operate as meaningful checks on police power. The chapter then moves on to study a phenomenon often described as "overcriminalization," and explores how various constitutional doctrines—including vagueness, the Eighth Amendment's ban on cruel and unusual punishment, and substantive due process—might constrain, or fail to constrain, the state's power to enact a broad criminal code. Finally, the chapter concludes with a study of prosecutorial discretion and the central practice driving the criminal adjudication process: plea bargaining. Here, we study plea bargaining's essential characteristics and dynamics, and observe once again how constitutional law might constrain, or fail to constrain, prosecutors' ability to shape or dictate the outcome of criminal cases through their charging and plea-bargaining practices.

Finally, the book concludes with Chapter Ten, which examines a set of ideas and interventions advanced by scholars, policymakers, activists, and organizers working to address many of the issues identified in Chapter Nine and throughout this book. The chapter begins with a study of some overarching ideas, exploring tensions between sweeping social movements working toward fundamental societal change—as in the case of the prison abolition movement—and more incremental efforts to achieve pragmatic reforms in the near term. The chapter then concludes with an examination of a series of concrete interventions—ranging from the election of progressive prosecutors, to investments in public defense and restorative justice, to efforts to organize collective action within criminal courtrooms—that have been attempted or proposed as part of the broader effort to end mass incarceration.

CHAPTER 9

THE CONSTITUTION OF MASS INCARCERATION:
Policing, Overcriminalization, and Plea Bargaining

"[There is] a basic irony about criminal law: the more it expands, the less it matters."

William J. Stuntz, *Plea Bargaining and Criminal Law's Disappearing Shadow*, 117 Harv. L. Rev. 2548, 2550 (2004)

INTRODUCTION

Criminal law is often framed as a backwards-looking enterprise. In the words of Professor Bill Stuntz, it is a law that focuses on "people who have [allegedly] committed offenses in the past" and asks whether police and prosecutors have assembled "an evidentiary case that allows the state to prosecute them" and convict them. And yet, as we saw in the last two chapters, society often views law enforcement—and law enforcement actors often view themselves—as serving a different, forward-looking function. The job of law enforcement on this account is to *prevent* crimes before they happen. As Stuntz observes, the state can do this by establishing a "police presence in areas where crimes are likely to occur" and by projecting power into those spaces. Such power can take various forms, including surveillance of civilian activity and direct engagement with people in the community—either through conversations or through coercive tactics like stops, frisks, searches, arrests, and ultimately prosecutions and convictions.[1]

These manifestations of state power—on the street, where stops, frisks, and arrests occur, and in courtrooms, where arrests progress into prosecutions, convictions, and prison sentences—are essential to understanding how substantive criminal law actually works. As Stuntz famously observed, "Anyone who reads criminal codes" and appellate opinions "in search of a picture of what conduct leads to a prison term . . . will be seriously misled," because "criminal law *does not drive criminal punishment*." Rather, Stuntz argues, substantive criminal law today operates mainly as a tool "to empower prosecutors" and police officers, "who are the criminal justice system's real lawmakers."[2]

Put more simply, and as prior chapters of this book have begun to show, criminal law does not just define crimes and punishments. It is an *instrument* of law enforcement power. The decision to criminalize certain conduct empowers police officers to investigate that conduct and to arrest people suspected of engaging in it. The more conduct that is criminalized, the more power police officers have in the world. Expanding the scope and severity of substantive criminal law also empowers prosecutors. A sweeping and severe criminal code allows prosecutors to threaten more criminal charges and longer prison sentences in any given case. It also lets them ensure more cases will end in convictions — by letting them trade away higher charges and longer sentences for defendants' guilty pleas.

These two relationships, between substantive criminal law and policing and between substantive criminal law and plea bargaining, are the focus of this chapter. As the chapter will make clear, these relationships are shaped by another body of law grounded in the Bill of Rights to the U.S. Constitution, which intersects with policing, criminalization, and plea bargaining in myriad ways. Four of the Constitution's first ten amendments speak directly to, and purport to constrain, the state's power to police and punish its people. Over a span of more than two centuries, courts have interpreted those constitutional provisions and, through their opinions, have defined the Constitution's practical content. As we will see in this chapter, some of those opinions place checks on the state's penal powers. And as we will also see, on many occasions courts have opted instead to leave those powers largely unconstrained.

The chapter proceeds in three parts. The first examines police power. Here, we describe a set of practices and tactics that fall under the broad umbrella of preventive policing — tactics facilitated and made possible by the substantive criminal law. We then discuss how the law of the Fourth and Fourteenth Amendments could, but in practice largely does not, constrain those tactics. In the second part of the chapter, we turn to examine the phenomenon of overcriminalization, in which legislatures boost police and prosecutorial power by enacting an expansive criminal code. Here, we will study constitutional doctrines of vagueness, substantive due process, and status crimes that occasionally constrain — but generally do not impede — the state's ability to penalize certain conduct. Finally, in the chapter's third part, we examine plea bargaining, the process by which around ninety-five percent of criminal convictions in the United States are produced. We offer a description of the interlocking charging practices that afford prosecutors broad authority to determine the outcomes of the cases they file. And we study constitutional doctrines related to due process, sentence length, and equal protection that could, but again in practice generally do not, constrain that power.

I. THE CONSTITUTIONAL LAW OF POLICING

> "The goal of nipping every potential threat in the bud, combined with the impossibility of its achievement, sets in motion a continuing expansion of preventive measures, an infinite regress along the causal chain toward the origin of threats . . . ."
>
> Markus Dirk Dubber, *Policing Possession: The War on Crime and the End of Criminal Law*, 91 J. Crim. L. & Criminology 829, 842 (2001)

In Chapter Eight, we explored how crimes of possession sometimes function as instruments of preventive policing. Most narrowly, possessory offenses can mirror the crime of attempt, as occurs when preparatory conduct like possessing burglary tools is punished to prevent future burglaries. More broadly, and more controversially, possessory crimes can facilitate widescale preemptive tactics, particularly if the state criminalizes items that are commonly possessed and easily concealed—like drugs. According to Professor Benjamin Levin, when used in this way, possessory offenses can "function as a dragnet of sorts, granting the state a broad legal authorization for criminal social control," with police officers using possession investigations as "a proxy for some general [notion] of risk, danger, or lawlessness," or "for past, future, or ongoing criminality." Possession crimes, Levin submits, are thus "an ideal weapon in the War on Crime." By facilitating law enforcement's power "to identify and incarcerate individuals" whom the police generally "suspect[] of posing a greater risk to public safety," they are "emblematic of an expansive approach to criminalization and law enforcement."[3]

But possessory offenses are not the only example of criminal law being used this way. On the contrary, as Professor Bill Stuntz observes, the basic idea that the state can expand police power by criminalizing wide swaths of behavior helps explain all sorts of crimes, including some proscribing conduct many would consider relatively innocuous. Think of jaywalking, spitting on the sidewalk, or eating on the subway. Each of these activities could land a person under arrest or in jail in some jurisdictions. Stuntz describes one logic behind these crimes:

> To the extent that police seek to make arrests, or to exercise coercive power short of arrest, they need criminal law to enable them to do those things. The Fourth Amendment requires that arrests be supported by probable cause to believe the arrestee has committed a crime. Street stops must be supported by reasonable suspicion of crime. In both instances, the operative word is "crime." If that word includes enough behavior,

if crime is defined broadly enough, police can stop or arrest whomever they wish.

Thus, police benefit from laws that criminalize street behavior that no one wishes actually to punish, solely as a means of empowering them to seize suspects. This is the force that drives much of the current movement to expand the range of so-called "quality of life" offenses, crimes that cover low-level street behavior that will only rarely be prosecuted, but that often serve as a convenient basis for an arrest and, perhaps, a search. Such crimes make policing cheaper, because they permit searches and arrests with less investigative work.[4]

The dynamic Stuntz describes is not hypothetical. As Professor and Judge Debra Livingston has observed, jurisdictions across the country "have either passed or started enforcing ordinances prohibiting things like aggressive panhandling, unlicensed street vending, graffiti scrawling, public drinking and urinating, and loitering in the vicinity of automated teller machines," all as part of an "ongoing transformation in the philosophy of American policing" that emphasizes "the 'order maintenance' activities of police."[5]

That phrase, *order-maintenance policing,* comes from an influential article penned in 1982 by political scientist James Wilson and criminologist George Kelling. Titled *Broken Windows,* the essay became "one of the most influential articles on policing" and ultimately helped reshape police behavior nationwide. Wilson and Kelling's basic hypothesis was that small signs of social disorder, like broken windows on abandoned houses or cars, can spiral into more serious societal decay. "[O]ne unrepaired broken window," they wrote, "is a signal that no one cares, and so breaking more windows costs nothing." Extrapolating from this idea, the authors suggested that "'untended' behavior also leads to the breakdown of community controls" and can quickly transform a "stable neighborhood of families who care for their homes, mind each other's children, and confidently frown on unwanted intruders" into "an inhospitable and frightening jungle."[6]

> Teenagers gather in front of the corner store. . . . Fights occur. Litter accumulates. People start drinking in front of the grocery . . . . Pedestrians are approached by panhandlers. At this point . . . many residents will think that crime, especially violent crime, is on the rise, and they will modify their behavior accordingly. They will use the streets less often, and when on the streets will stay apart from their fellows, moving with averted eyes, silent lips, and hurried steps. . . . Though it is not inevitable, it is more likely that . . . drugs will change hands, prostitutes will solicit, and cars will be stripped. That the drunks will be robbed by boys who do it as a lark, and the prostitutes' customers will be robbed by men who do it purposefully and perhaps violently. That muggings will occur.[7]

The antidote to this presumed decay, Wilson and Kelling argued, was to send police officers into the community, patrolling on foot, with a mission "to elevate, to the extent they could, the level of public order in these neighborhoods." To do this, officers were instructed "to keep an eye on strangers, and make certain that the disreputable regulars observed some informal but widely understood rules."

> Bottles had to be in paper bags. Talking to, bothering, or begging from people waiting at the bus stop was strictly forbidden. . . . If a stranger loitered, [the officer should] ask him if he had any means of support and what his business was; if he gave unsatisfactory answers, he was [to be] sent on his way.[8]

In the decades following *Broken Windows'* publication, its basic idea gave rise to a set of interrelated practices that go by many names: preventive policing, proactive policing, broken-windows policing, community policing, order-maintenance policing, stop-question-frisk. These terms do not all describe precisely the same thing, nor do they mean the same thing to all people, especially to scholars who study policing. But they share a common thread and a common history. They are all practices the police use systematically to try to suppress crime in targeted communities. And in many jurisdictions, they have grown to be massive in scale.[9]

A lawsuit in New York City, for example, demonstrated that between 2004 and 2012, the New York City Police Department "conducted over 4.4 million [investigative] stops" of civilians, 94 percent of which did not result in arrest. Floyd v. City of New York, 959 F. Supp. 2d 540, 556-559 (S.D.N.Y. 2013). In some neighborhoods, the *New York Times* reported, individual civilians were stopped and frisked more than 60 times before they turned 18 years old. In Brownsville, a neighborhood in Brooklyn, the police conducted an average of 93 stops for every 100 residents each year. According to the district court's opinion in *Floyd*, these tactics created marked racial disparities across the city. "In 52% of the 4.4 million stops," the court wrote, "the person stopped was black," while "New York City's resident population was roughly 23% black." *Id.* at 559.[10]

As Wilson and Kelling implicitly acknowledge, and as Livingston would later emphasize, using the criminal law this way—as a largely discretionary tool of police power—can be "in tension with legal presuppositions," including principles of fair notice, equal treatment, and civil liberty. Ultimately, Livingston writes, Wilson and Kelling's essay "provocatively put what may be the ultimate question" about police authority, a question forthrightly stated in *Broken Windows* itself: "Should police activity on the street be shaped, in important ways, by . . . the rules of the state?" Put more simply, what is the role of law in shaping and potentially constraining police power?[11]

As Stuntz observes, substantive criminal law is an important part of this story. For the police to lawfully stop, frisk, search, or arrest a civilian, they must have some basis to believe that "an offense has been or is being committed" by that person or "that evidence bearing on that offense will be found in the place to be searched." Safford Unified Sch. Dist. No. 1 v. Redding, 557 U.S. 364, 370 (2009). Substantive criminal law defines what conduct is criminal in the first place, and is thus a central component of law enforcement power.

But the other part of the story turns on constitutional law, in two key ways. First, the Constitution's Fourth Amendment and, to a lesser degree, its Equal Protection Clause regulate police behavior by specifying the circumstances under which stops, frisks, searches, and arrests are lawful. Second, a smattering of constitutional provisions, including the Due Process Clause and the Eighth Amendment, speak to the state's power to criminalize conduct in the first instance — and thus to augment police power in the ways described above. In the rest of this chapter's first part, we examine the Fourth Amendment and equal protection doctrines related to these issues. In the part that follows, we turn to the relationship between the Constitution and overcriminalization.

A.   *The Power to Stop and Arrest*

The principal law regulating police power in the United States is the Fourth Amendment to the U.S. Constitution. This itself is an unusual fact. For most government actors, the Constitution sets the outer limit on permissible activity but statutes, regulations, policy documents, and norms do most of the work of shaping permissible behavior. Yet when it comes to the police, as Professors Barry Friedman and Maria Ponomarenko observe, the law of virtually every state "simply authorizes [them] to enforce the substantive criminal law," while saying "little or nothing about *what* enforcement actions [they] are permitted to take." The upshot, to quote one leading textbook, is that "Fourth Amendment law is the primary source of legal restraint; it regulates ordinary, run-of-the-mill interactions between officers and suspects."[12]

What does this regulation look like? To what extent does it cabin law enforcement power? In this section, we begin to answer these questions by examining some of the basic building blocks of Fourth Amendment regulation: the so-called "warrant requirement," the idea of probable cause, and the constitutional doctrine of stop and frisk.

1. Warrantless Arrests

The Fourth Amendment to the U.S. Constitution reads as follows:

The right of the people to be secure in their persons, houses, papers, and effects, against unreasonable searches and seizures, shall not be violated, and no Warrants shall issue, but upon probable cause, supported by Oath or affirmation, and particularly describing the place to be searched, and the persons or things to be seized.

The Amendment's second clause, sometimes called the *Warrant Clause*, has long been interpreted to entail what courts term a *warrant requirement*. The basic idea is that coercive police tactics—the Amendment's *searches and seizures*—are presumptively unconstitutional unless authorized in advance by a neutral magistrate or judge in the form of a warrant. In the words of the U.S. Supreme Court, when the requirement applies, "the Government's obligation is a familiar one—get a warrant." Carpenter v. United States, 585 U.S. 296, 317 (2018).

Note at the outset that the very existence of such a requirement is unusual. In other courses you have taken, legal rules and standards are generally enforced through after-the-fact judicial review, as occurs in lawsuits alleging a breach of contract, a tort, or a violation of a regulation or statute. As Professor Stuntz observes, "[p]otential tortfeasors do not ordinarily seek judicial permission to engage in risky conduct; they decide how to behave in light of the governing law and (if things work out badly) defend themselves in litigation later." It is possible to enforce the Fourth Amendment the same way. In fact, suppression hearings—in which criminal defendants ask judges to exclude evidence from trial that they allege the police obtained in an illegal manner—offer an easy and commonly used way to subject police behavior to judicial review after the police have acted. All of which raises a question: Why require warrants *at all?*[13]

As Professors Oren Bar-Gill and Barry Friedman observe, one potentially powerful answer is that "[r]equiring warrants can aid in preventing police perjury" about the facts used to justify a search or seizure, including most especially perjury designed to evade legal constraints on police power (p. 731). Building on Stuntz's work, they note that two "structurally inherent" aspects of after-the-fact suppression hearings create both the opportunity and incentive for police officers to lie about civilian interactions. First, suppression hearings pit the word of "the police officer against a *guilty* defendant," insofar as the defendant is usually trying to suppress inculpatory evidence (like drugs or a weapon) the police have recovered from his person. The status differential between a uniformed police officer and a "guilty" civilian creates a "credibility gap" the officer can exploit to "strain the truth." Second, as Bar-Gill and Friedman go on to write, "the timing of the suppression hearing, after all the facts are known, is conducive to police perjury," because it "is easier to lie without getting caught when all objectively provable facts are known and the lie can be tailored to avoid conflicts with these provable facts."[14]

Bar-Gill and Friedman argue that the warrant requirement addresses each of these issues:

> [In] an ex ante warrant hearing, the . . . individual against whom the warrant is to be issued may well be innocent[, which means the magistrate may] more closely scrutinize the police officer's story to protect the

potentially innocent [target]. Moreover, [as] Stuntz eloquently puts it, the ex ante nature of the warrant hearing "makes perjury somewhat harder, since the officer cannot so easily manufacture details consistent with a story he does not yet know."[15]

Given these dynamics, Bar-Gill and Friedman, along with other scholars of criminal procedure, argue that warrants should be treated "as the center-piece of the Fourth Amendment." In truth, though, the warrant require-ment has always been subject to exceptions. And while the Supreme Court sometimes describes those exceptions as "jealously and carefully drawn," Jones v. United States, 357 U.S. 493, 499 (1958), the reality, as one leading casebook observes, is quite the opposite. "Taken individually, th[e] excep-tions may seem narrow enough," but taken together, "the exceptions may be the rule—and warrants the real exception."[16]

The full doctrinal extent and configuration of the Warrant Clause's exceptions is addressed in courses on constitutional criminal procedure. For present purposes, given our focus on law enforcement power in the context of street policing, one exception in particular looms large, and is crystallized in the following case.

United States v. Watson

423 U.S. 411 (1976)

WHITE, J. This case presents questions under the Fourth Amendment as to the legality of a warrantless arrest. . . .

[A]n informant, one Khoury, telephoned a postal inspector informing him that respondent Watson was in possession of a stolen credit card and had asked Khoury to cooperate in using the card to their mutual advan-tage. . . . [T]he inspector asked Khoury to arrange to meet with Watson . . . [which Khoury did] at a restaurant. . . . Khoury had been instructed that if Watson had additional stolen credit cards, Khoury was to give a desig-nated signal. The signal was given, the officers closed in, and Watson was forthwith arrested. [Immediately subsequent to his arrest, agents searched his car and recovered] an envelop[e] containing two credit cards in the names of other persons [that became] the basis for two counts . . . charging Watson with possessing stolen mail . . . . Prior to trial, Watson moved to sup-press the cards, claiming that his arrest was illegal for want of . . . an arrest warrant. . . . The motion was denied, and Watson was convicted of illegally possessing the two cards seized from his car. . . .

Watson's arrest was not invalid because executed without a warrant. . . . "The usual rule is that a police officer may arrest without warrant one believed by the officer upon reasonable cause to have been guilty of a fel-ony." Carroll v. United States, 267 U.S. 132, 156 (1925). . . . Just last Term, while recognizing that maximum protection of individual rights could be assured by requiring a magistrate's review of the factual justification prior to any arrest, we stated that "such a requirement would constitute an intolerable handicap for legitimate law enforcement" and noted that the Court "has never invalidated an arrest supported by probable cause solely because the officers failed to secure a warrant." Gerstein v. Pugh, 420 U.S. 103, 113 (1975). The cases construing the Fourth Amendment thus reflect the ancient common-law rule that a peace officer was permitted to arrest without a warrant for a misdemeanor or felony committed in his presence as well as for a felony not committed in his presence if there was reasonable ground for making the arrest. . . .

The balance struck by the common law in generally authorizing felony arrests on probable cause, but without a warrant, has survived substantially intact. It appears in almost all of the States in the form of express statutory authorization. This is [also] the rule Congress has long directed its principal law enforcement officers to follow. . . . Law enforcement officers may find it wise to seek arrest warrants where practicable to do so, and their judgments about probable cause may be more readily accepted where backed by a warrant issued by a magistrate. But we decline to transform this judicial preference into a constitutional rule when the judgment of the Nation and Congress has for so long been to authorize warrantless public arrests on probable cause . . . .

POWELL, J. concurring. . . . Today's decision is the first square holding that the Fourth Amendment permits a duly authorized law enforcement officer to make a warrantless arrest in a public place even though he had adequate opportunity to procure a warrant after developing probable cause for arrest. On its face, our decision today creates a certain anomaly. There is no more basic constitutional rule in the Fourth Amendment area than that which makes a warrantless search unreasonable except in a few "jealously and carefully drawn" exceptional circumstances. Jones v. United States, 357 U.S. 493, 499 (1958). . . . [T]he course of judicial development of the Fourth Amendment with respect to searches has remained true to the principles so well expressed by Mr. Justice Jackson:

> Any assumption that evidence sufficient to support a magistrate's disinterested determination to issue a search warrant will justify the officers in making a search without a warrant would reduce the Amendment to a nullity. . . . When the right of privacy must reasonably yield to the right of search is, as a rule, to be decided by a judicial officer, not by a policeman or Government enforcement agent. Johnson v. United States, 333 U.S. 10, 14 (1948).

Since the Fourth Amendment speaks equally to both searches and seizures, and since an arrest, the taking hold of one's person, is quintessentially a seizure, it would seem that the constitutional provision should impose the same limitations upon arrests that it does upon searches. Indeed, as an abstract matter an argument can be made that the restrictions upon arrest perhaps should be greater. A search may cause only annoyance and temporary inconvenience to the law-abiding citizen, assuming more serious dimension only when it turns up evidence of criminality. An arrest, however, is a serious personal intrusion regardless of whether the person seized is guilty or innocent. . . .

But logic sometimes must defer to history and experience. The Court's opinion emphasizes the historical sanction accorded warrantless felony arrests. . . . Of course, no practice that is inconsistent with constitutional protections can be saved merely by appeal to previous uncritical acceptance. But the warrantless felony arrest, long preferred at common law and unimpeached at the passage of the Fourth Amendment, is not such a practice. Given the revolutionary implications of such a holding, a declaration at this late date that warrantless felony arrests are constitutionally infirm would have to rest upon reasons more substantial than a desire to harmonize the rules for arrest with those governing searches. . . .

MARSHALL, J., dissenting. By granting police broad powers to make warrantless arrests, the Court today sharply reverses the course of our modern decisions construing the Warrant Clause of the Fourth Amendment. . . . There are two serious flaws in [the majority's] approach. First, as a matter of factual analysis, the substance of the ancient common-law rule provides no support for the far-reaching modern rule that the Court fashions on its model. Second, as a matter of doctrine, the longstanding existence of a Government practice does not immunize the practice from scrutiny under the mandate of our Constitution.

The common-law rule was indeed as the Court states it: "[A] peace officer was permitted to arrest without a warrant for a misdemeanor or felony committed in his presence as well as for a felony not committed in his presence if there was reasonable grounds for making the arrest." To apply the rule blindly today, however, makes as much sense as attempting to interpret Hamlet's admonition to Ophelia, "Get thee to a nunnery, go," without understanding the meaning of Hamlet's words in the context of their age.[3] For the fact is that a felony at common law and a felony today bear only slight resemblance, with the result that the relevance of the common-law rule of arrest to the modern interpretation of our Constitution is minimal. . . . Only the most serious crimes were felonies at common law, and many crimes now classified as felonies under federal or state law were

---

3. Nunnery was Elizabethan slang for house of prostitution. 7 *Oxford English Dictionary* 264 (1933).

treated as misdemeanors. . . . To make an arrest for any of these [misde-meanors] at common law, the police officer was required to obtain a warrant, unless the crime was committed in his presence. Since many of these same crimes are commonly classified as felonies today however, under the Court's holding a warrant is no longer needed to make such arrests, a result in contravention of the common law. . . . [T]he only clear lesson of history is contrary to the one the Court draws: the common law considered the arrest warrant far more important than today's decision leaves it. . . .

The rule the Court announces today for arrests . . . simply does not provide adequate protection for the important personal privacy interests codified in the Fourth Amendment. Given "the history of the use, and not infrequent abuse, of the power to arrest," Wong Sun v. United States, 371 U.S. 471, 479 (1963), and the fact that arrests are, in terms, as fully governed by the Fourth Amendment as searches, the logical presumption is that arrests and searches should be treated equally under the Fourth Amendment. Analysis of the interests involved confirms this supposition. . . . "Being arrested and held by the police, even if for a few hours, is for most persons, awesome and frightening. Unlike other occasions on which one may be authoritatively required to be somewhere or do something, an arrest abruptly subjects a person to constraint, and removes him to unfamiliar and threatening surroundings. Moreover, this exercise of control over the person depends not just on his willingness to comply with an impersonal directive, such as a summons or subpoena, but on an order which a policeman issues on the spot and stands ready then and there to back up with force." ALI, Model Code of Pre-arraignment Procedure, Commentary 290-291 (1975).

A warrant requirement for arrests would, of course, minimize the possibility that such an intrusion into the individual's sacred sphere of personal privacy would occur on less than probable cause. Primarily for this reason, a warrant is required for searches. Surely there is no reason to place greater trust in the partisan assessment of a police officer that there is probable cause for an arrest than in his determination that probable cause exists for a search. . . .

[Opinion of STEWART, J., concurring in the result, omitted.]

NOTES AND QUESTIONS

1. The Arrest Exception. The *Watson* opinion arose from a sting operation in which police officers monitored a confidential informant who signaled that a suspect on the scene had key inculpatory evidence, namely the stolen credit cards at the heart of the investigation. Under these circumstances, one could argue that the police did not actually have, to quote Justice Powell's opinion, "adequate opportunity to procure a warrant after developing probable cause for arrest." The suspect might have left the area, and perhaps disappeared, while the police went to see a judge. Justice Marshall, who dissented in *Watson*, would have allowed warrantless arrests when the delay associated with securing a warrant "could cause the escape of the suspect or the destruction of the evidence." 423 U.S. at 435 (Marshall, J., dissenting). But he dissented from the Court's broader and more categorical ruling in *Watson*, which authorizes "warrantless public arrests on probable cause" alone. That categorical rule is the central holding and essential take-away from the opinion. In the words of Professor Akhil Amar, the Court in "*Watson* carved out an 'arrest exception' to its so-called 'warrant requirement.' "[17]

2. Consequences of Arrest. In much the same way that Bentham described all criminal punishment as a form of pain, law enforcement tactics like arrests can cause real hardship for the people directly impacted by them. Professor Rachel Harmon describes some of these consequences:

> By its nature, every arrest diminishes a citizen's freedom. It denies the arrestee — albeit briefly — the possibility of living according to his own reasons and motives. Protecting this kind of autonomy is a central goal of liberalism, and depriving a person of it is a moral and political harm. . . . But arrests also have more concrete consequences. . . . In the near term, arrests are often frightening and humiliating. Arrestees lose income during the arrest, and sometimes their jobs when they do not show up for work. They pay arrest fees, booking fees, and perhaps attorney's fees, if they hire a lawyer for their first appearance. If a suspect's car is towed because of an arrest during a traffic stop, he loses the value of the time it takes to find his car, travel to the impound lot, and secure the vehicle's release, as well as the impound fees. An arrest can affect child custody rights, it can trigger deportation, and it can get a suspect kicked out of public housing. Over the long term, individuals with arrest records may have worse employment and financial prospects. And all of these consequences can occur even if the arrestee is never convicted of a crime. . . .
>
> [R]ecent high-profile killings by police officers [further] underscore that every arrest involves a confrontation between a suspect and a police officer that can go badly awry. Once a police officer attempts an arrest, he is authorized to use force, sometimes deadly force, to enforce that decision. As a result, arrests always risk and sometimes lead to injury or death. . . .
>
> [Finally,] the harms of arrests extend far beyond the suspects who might have engaged in wrongdoing. When someone is arrested, his family and community suffer, too. His family is deprived of the housework and childcare he would have provided if he were home, and they fully feel his lost income and weaker job prospects. . . . The suspect's community experiences disruption as well, both in feelings of insecurity and alienation

and in more practical terms. Even strangers are affected by arrests. When police engage in foot pursuits, car chases, and physical struggles to complete an arrest, for instance, they risk harm to bystanders, as well as suspects.[18]

3. *Warrants as Resource Constraints.* The holding in *Watson* rests primarily on a historical analysis. But the majority also advances a functional argument for its position. Imposing a warrant requirement on street arrests, the Court says, "would constitute an intolerable handicap for legitimate law enforcement." Such a handicap would stem in part from the warrant process itself. As Professor Stuntz observes, "[w]arrants are costly to the police: they require both paperwork and hours hanging around a courthouse waiting to see the magistrate." *Watson* frees the police of that burden. Of course, in so doing, it also enables the police to conduct many more arrests, including arrests they would otherwise decline to pursue. As Professor Donald Dripps writes, "If the police view obtaining a warrant as a costly proposition" but are nonetheless required to do it, they will pursue only those arrests that "promise . . . returns to justify the expenditure of law-enforcement resources." Citing a study in which officers were interviewed directly about their resource constraints and practices, Dripps quotes one officer who said, "Actually, there are a lot of warrants that are not sought because of the hassle. You just figure it's not worth the hassle." In this respect, Professor Stuntz argues, warrants "function as a tax" on arrests, "payable in police time rather than money." A warrant requirement for street arrests, he goes on to suggest, would thus lead to a world with fewer arrests, because "anytime one raises the price of anything, one gets less of it."[19]

If this analysis is correct, the essential issue in *Watson* may boil down to a core normative question: Would the country be better off with more arrests, or fewer? For the *Watson* Court, the answer to that question is clear, even if not explicitly reasoned. Forcing the police to arrest fewer people would be "an intolerable handicap." By contrast, for the dissent, "[a]nalysis of the interests involved confirms" the opposite conclusion.[20]

4. *Warrants and Testilying.* Recall that for Professors Bar-Gill, Friedman, and Stuntz, the warrant requirement principally serves to minimize opportunities for police perjury. By removing that requirement for the large swath of arrests that occur in public, *Watson* leaves the door to such perjury open. And as Professor Morgan Cloud observes, the police sometimes walk through. "[E]mpirical studies on the subject suggest that perjured testimony is common," Cloud writes, noting "that police officers commit perjury most often to avoid suppression of evidence and to fabricate probable cause." Professor Andrew Manuel Crespo argues that such perjury, sometimes called *testilying* by the officers who commit it, stems from two features of street policing.

[First,] to quote Justice Jackson, [police officers] are "zealous[ly] . . . engaged in the often competitive enterprise of ferreting out crime." The targets of searches and seizures, in other words, are people whom the police see themselves as competing *against*—an inherent bias. . . . [Second,] if those biases are the motive for police perjury, lack of accountability creates the opportunity. As Christopher Slobogin notes, police officers are "seldom made to pay for their lying" by prosecutors, who may worry about not being able to convict all of the offending officers or about the implications of trying to do so. Officers thus tend to "think they can get away" with testilying, and they are usually right.[21]

From time to time, newspaper exposés have highlighted the scope and nature of the testilying problem. In 2018, for example, the *New York Times* identified twenty-five instances in which New York Police Department officers gave perjured testimony in court in the preceding three years. Describing the phenomenon as "an entrenched perjury problem several decades in the making," the reporters believed their tally represented "almost certainly only a fraction" of the broader problem, given that the "vast majority of cases end in plea deals before an officer is ever required to take the witness stand in open court, meaning the possibility that an officer lied is seldom aired in public." For an account of one instance that the reporters were able to capture, see the following excerpt.

Joseph Goldstein, *"Testilying" by Police: A Stubborn Problem*, N.Y. Times (Mar. 18, 2018). Officer Nector Martinez took the witness stand in a Bronx courtroom . . . and swore to tell the truth, the whole truth, and nothing but the truth, so help him God. There had been a shooting, Officer Martinez testified, and he wanted to search a nearby apartment for evidence. A woman stood in the doorway, carrying a laundry bag. Officer Martinez said she set the bag down "in the middle of the doorway"—directly in his path. "I picked it up to move it out of the way so we could get in." . . . When he put it down, he said, he heard a "clunk, a thud." . . . Officer Martinez tapped the bag with his foot and felt something hard, he testified. He opened the bag, leading to the discovery of a Ruger 9-millimeter handgun and the arrest of the woman.

But a hallway surveillance camera captured the true story: There's no laundry bag or gun in sight as Officer Martinez and other investigators . . . stride into the apartment. Inside, they did find a gun, but little to link it to the woman, Kimberly Thomas. Still, had the camera not captured the hallway scene, Officer Martinez's testimony might well have sent her to prison.

When Ms. Thomas's lawyer sought to play the video in court, prosecutors . . . dropped the case[,] hiding from view a problem so old and persistent that the criminal justice system sometimes responds with little more than a shrug. . . . "Behind closed doors, we call it testilying," a New York City police officer, Pedro Serrano, said in a recent interview, echoing a word that officers coined at least 25 years ago.

2.   Probable Cause

A warrant requirement could potentially deter or screen out some unlawful searches or seizures before they occur. But as the preceding section demonstrates, this procedural protection simply does not exist when it comes to street arrests, which constitute the vast majority of the nearly 10 million arrests conducted in the United States every year. In that setting, if the Fourth Amendment is to offer any protection, it must do so through after-the-fact enforcement of the Amendment's substantive component: the *probable cause* requirement. As Professor Andrew Manuel Crespo writes, "Doctrinally and conceptually, 'probable cause lies at the heart of the Fourth Amendment' for one simple reason: the requirement to demonstrate probable cause . . . is 'the line of distinction' between legal and illegal searches and seizures."[22]

As Crespo elsewhere observes, this dividing line is "inescapably empirical." Supreme Court precedent confirms as much, as the Court has held that searches and seizures are constitutional only if the government can point to facts that provide a basis to believe "an offense has been or is being committed" by the person searched or seized or "that evidence bearing on that offense will be found in the place to be searched." Safford Unified Sch. Dist. No. 1 v. Redding, 557 U.S. 364, 370 (2009). As Crespo explains, this requirement means that in virtually every Fourth Amendment case, the government makes an "evidentiary claim" that must "be assessed by asking [the] basic probable-cause question: [H]ow *likely is it* that the target is either a person who committed an illegal act or a place that contains evidence of such an act?"[23]

Understood on these terms, one important question embedded within the probable cause analysis relates to the *standard of proof* by which the government's claim should be assessed. How likely is likely enough? Standards of proof are common across all areas of law. In other contexts, you may have encountered some familiar ones. Sometimes, to prevail on a given issue, a party must support a claim with a preponderance of the evidence. Other times, clear and convincing evidence or even proof beyond a reasonable doubt (the standard for criminal convictions) is required. At the other end of the spectrum, a colorable claim or perhaps even a scintilla of evidence will sometimes suffice.

As Crespo writes, "the decision of where to set" the standard of proof "allocates the risk of a *wrong* decision between the parties and thus inevitably balances their competing interests."

> In the Fourth Amendment context, this competition pits the state's interest in maintaining public order, safety, and security against the individual's interest in her liberty, privacy, autonomy, dignity, reputation, and personal safety. A neutral standard of proof (whether framed in words like "preponderance of the evidence" or captured mathematically

as more than fifty percent) treats those interests as roughly coequal, whereas a higher standard puts a thumb on the scale in favor of individuals targeted for search or seizure and a lower one tips it toward the government.[24]

And yet, important as the standard of proof is to the underlying interests and analysis, when it comes to probable cause, courts have left the standard stubbornly undefined. As Crespo writes, quoting various Supreme Court opinions, the Court "defines probable cause as 'a fluid concept' [and] accordingly rejects efforts to develop 'a neat set of legal rules' in this domain, a task it deems 'not readily' attainable, 'or even usefully' pursued." In fact, the Court has gone so far as to assert that "[a]rticulating precisely" what probable cause means "is not possible." Ornelas v. United States, 517 U.S. 690, 695 (1996). Unsurprisingly, scholars describe the Court's precedents as "elusive," "hopelessly indeterminate," and "shrouded in mystery." To quote Professor Christopher Slobogin, in the law of police behavior, probable cause "is the standard with which we are most familiar — except that we don't really know what it means."[25]

Nor apparently do judges. In one well-known survey conducted in the early 1980s, 166 judges were asked to assign a numerical degree of certainty to the probable cause standard. They offered widely varying responses, with nearly equal numbers pegging the standard at 30 percent certainty and 60 percent certainty, and broad disparity across the board.[26]

Figure 9.1. Percentages Associated with Probable Cause

Probable Cause

Percentage	Number of Judges
10%	2
20%	5
30%	27
40%	44
50%	52
60%	25
70%	8
80%	2
90%	1

C.M.A. McCauliff, *Burdens of Proof: Degrees of Belief, Quanta of Evidence, or Constitutional Guarantees?*, 35 Vand. L. Rev. 1293, 1327 tbl.3 (1982)

The following excerpt from the Court's leading opinion on the topic captures well the standard's ambiguity, which the excerpt following it then critiques.

Illinois v. Gates, 462 U.S. 213 (1983). Perhaps the central teaching of our decisions bearing on the probable-cause standard is that it is a "practical, nontechnical conception." Brinegar v. United States, 338 U.S. 160, 176 (1949). "In dealing with probable cause, as the very name implies, we deal with probabilities. These are not technical; they are the factual and practical considerations of everyday life on which reasonable and prudent men, not legal technicians, act." Id. at 175. . . . "The process does not deal with hard certainties, but with probabilities. Long before the law of probabilities was articulated as such, practical people formulated certain common-sense conclusions about human behavior; jurors as factfinders are permitted to do the same—and so are law enforcement officers. Finally, the evidence . . . must be seen and weighed not in terms of library analysis by scholars, but as understood by those versed in the field of law enforcement." As these comments illustrate, probable cause is a fluid concept—turning on the assessment of probabilities in particular factual contexts—not readily, or even usefully, reduced to a neat set of legal rules. . . . The task . . . is simply to make a practical, common-sense decision whether, given all the circumstances . . . , there is a fair probability that contraband or evidence of a crime will be found in a particular place.

Andrew Manuel Crespo, *Probable Cause Pluralism,* 129 Yale L.J. 1276, 1280-1281 (2020). With striking candor, the Supreme Court has [insisted] that "articulating precisely what . . . 'probable cause' mean[s] is not possible." Rather, the most explicit guidance the Court has offered is to say that judges should consider the "totality of the circumstances" and then make "a practical, common sense decision," yea or nay. . . . This is a problem in at least two respects. For one, a jurisprudence premised wholly on raw and unstructured "common sense" will struggle to yield a predictable and consistent body of decisions. It will struggle, [to quote Justice Antonin Scalia], to produce "any law worthy of the name," let alone a body of law clear enough to guide the civilians it protects or the state actors it governs. Equally troubling, an amorphous approach to probable cause will leave judges ill equipped to stand as "guardians of the Bill of Rights," in "between the citizen and the police." After all, as [Justice Scalia] observed, judges armed with only their own gut instincts will often lack the "judicial courage" to push back against the state's constant demands for greater police authority—demands grounded in the ever-pressing and ever-urgent need to ensure the community's safety. In short, an infinitely malleable approach to probable cause raises both rule-of-law and civil-liberty concerns.

3. Stop and Frisk

The probable cause requirement may be vaguely defined, but it is still a requirement. Even warrantless arrests must be backed by probable cause to withstand Fourth Amendment scrutiny. And yet, as noted earlier in this chapter, the vast majority of coercive police tactics—including forcible seizures of people's bodies—do not rise to the level of a formal arrest. The following case, which is one of the Supreme Court's most famous decisions, describes the constraints the Fourth Amendment imposes on these most widely deployed coercive police tactics: stops and frisks.

Terry v. Ohio

392 U.S. 1 (1968)

WARREN, C.J. This case presents serious questions concerning the role of the Fourth Amendment in the confrontation on the street between the citizen and the policeman investigating suspicious circumstances.

Petitioner Terry was convicted of carrying a concealed weapon and sentenced to the statutorily prescribed term of one to three years in the penitentiary. [T]he prosecution introduced in evidence two revolvers and a number of bullets seized from Terry and a codefendant, Richard Chilton, by Cleveland Police Detective Martin McFadden. At the hearing on the motion to suppress this evidence, Officer McFadden testified that while he was patrolling in plain clothes in downtown Cleveland at approximately 2:30 in the afternoon of October 31, 1963, his attention was attracted by two men, Chilton and Terry, standing on the corner of Huron Road and Euclid Avenue. He had never seen the two men before, and he was unable to say precisely what first drew his eye to them. However, he testified that he had been a policeman for 39 years and a detective for 35 and that he had been assigned to patrol this vicinity of downtown Cleveland for shoplifters and pickpockets for 30 years. He explained that he had developed routine habits of observation over the years and that he would "stand and watch people or walk and watch people at many intervals of the day." He added: "Now, in this case when I looked over they didn't look right to me at the time."

His interest aroused, Officer McFadden took up a post of observation in the entrance to a store 300 to 400 feet away from the two men. . . . He saw one of the men leave the other one and walk southwest on Huron Road, past some stores. The man paused for a moment and looked in a store window, then walked on a short distance, turned around and walked back toward the corner, pausing once again to look in the same store window. He rejoined his companion at the corner, and the two conferred briefly. Then the second man went through the same series of motions . . . . The two men repeated this ritual alternately between five and six times apiece

. . . . At one point, while the two were standing together on the corner, a third man approached them and engaged them briefly in conversation. This man then left the two others . . . . Chilton and Terry resumed their measured pacing, peering and conferring. After this had gone on for 10 to 12 minutes, the two men walked off together . . . following the path taken earlier by the third man.

By this time Officer McFadden had become thoroughly suspicious. He testified that after observing their elaborately casual and oft-repeated reconnaissance of the store window on Huron Road, he suspected the two men of "casing a job, a stick-up," and that he considered it his duty as a police officer to investigate further. He added that he feared "they may have a gun."

Thus, Officer McFadden followed Chilton and Terry and saw them stop in front of Zucker's store to talk to the same man who had conferred with them earlier on the street corner. Deciding that the situation was ripe for direct action, Officer McFadden approached the three man, identified himself as a police officer and asked for their names. At this point his knowledge was confined to what he had observed. . . . When the men "mumbled something" in response to his inquiries, Officer McFadden grabbed petitioner Terry, spun him around so that they were facing the other two, with Terry between McFadden and the others, and patted down the outside of his clothing. In the left breast pocket of Terry's overcoat Officer McFadden felt a pistol. He reached inside the overcoat pocket, but was unable to remove the gun. At this point, keeping Terry between himself and the others, the officer ordered all three men to enter Zucker's store. As they went in, he removed Terry's overcoat completely, removed a .38-caliber revolver from the pocket and ordered all three men to face the wall with their hands raised. Officer McFadden proceeded to pat down the outer clothing of Chilton [and] discovered another revolver in the outer pocket of Chilton's overcoat . . . . The officer testified that he only patted the men down to see whether they had weapons, and that he did not put his hands beneath the outer garments of either Terry or Chilton until he felt their guns. . . . Officer McFadden seized Chilton's gun, asked the proprietor of the store to call a police wagon, and took [the] men to the station, where [they] were formally charged with carrying concealed weapons. . . .

Unquestionably petitioner was entitled to the protection of the Fourth Amendment as he walked down the street in Cleveland. The question is whether in all the circumstances of this on-the-street encounter, his right to personal security was violated by an unreasonable search and seizure.

We would be less than candid if we did not acknowledge that this question thrusts to the fore difficult and troublesome issues regarding a sensitive area of police activity — issues which have never before been squarely presented to this Court. Reflective of the tensions involved are the practical and constitutional arguments pressed with great vigor on both sides of the public debate over the power of the police to "stop and frisk"—as it is sometimes euphemistically termed—suspicious persons.

On the one hand, it is frequently argued that in dealing with the rapidly unfolding and often dangerous situations on city streets the police are in need of an escalating set of flexible responses, graduated in relation to the amount of information they possess. For this purpose it is urged that distinctions should be made between a "stop" and an "arrest" . . . and between a "frisk" and a "search." Thus, it is argued, the police should be allowed to "stop" a person and detain him briefly for questioning upon suspicion that he may be connected with criminal activity. Upon suspicion that the person may be armed, the police should have the power to "frisk" him for weapons. If the "stop" and the "frisk" give rise to probable cause to believe that the suspect has committed a crime, then the police should be empowered to make a formal "arrest," and a full incident "search" of the person. This scheme is justified in part upon the notion that a "stop" and a "frisk" amount to a mere "minor inconvenience and petty indignity," which can properly be imposed upon the citizen in the interest of effective law enforcement on the basis of a police officer's suspicion.

On the other side the argument is made that the authority of the police must be strictly circumscribed by the law of arrest and search as it has developed to date in the traditional jurisprudence of the Fourth Amendment. It is contended with some force that there is not—and cannot be—a variety of police activity which does not depend solely upon the voluntary cooperation of the citizen and yet which stops short of an arrest based upon probable cause to make such an arrest. . . . Acquiescence by the courts in the compulsion inherent in the field interrogation practices at issue here, it is urged, would constitute an abdication of judicial control over, and indeed an encouragement of, substantial interference with liberty and personal security by police officers whose judgment is necessarily colored by their primary involvement in "the often competitive enterprise of ferreting out crime." Johnson v. United States, 333 U.S. 10, 14 (1948). This, it is argued, can only serve to exacerbate police-community tensions in the crowded centers of our Nation's cities.

In this context we approach the issues in this case mindful of the limitations of the judicial function in controlling the myriad daily situations in which policemen and citizens confront each other on the street. . . . The[se] range from wholly friendly exchanges of pleasantries or mutually useful information to hostile confrontations of armed men involving arrests, or injuries, or loss of life. Moreover, hostile confrontations are not all of a piece. Some of them begin in a friendly enough manner, only to take a different turn upon the injection of some unexpected element into the conversation. Encounters are initiated by the police for a wide variety of purposes, some of which are wholly unrelated to a desire to prosecute for crime.

Doubtless some police "field interrogation" conduct violates the Fourth Amendment. But . . . the exclusionary rule . . . is powerless to deter invasions of constitutionally guaranteed rights where the police either have no interest in prosecuting or are willing to forgo successful prosecution in the interest of serving some other goal. . . . The wholesale harassment by certain elements of the police community, of which minority groups, particularly Negroes, frequently complain,[11] will not be stopped by the exclusion of any evidence from any criminal trial. Yet a rigid and unthinking application of the exclusionary rule, in futile protest against practices which it can never be used effectively to control, may exact a high toll in human injury and frustration of efforts to prevent crime. . . .

Having thus roughly sketched the perimeters of the constitutional debate over the limits on police investigative conduct in general and the background against which this case presents itself, we turn our attention to the quite narrow question posed by the facts before us: whether it is always unreasonable for a policeman to seize a person and subject him to a limited search for weapons unless there is probable cause for an arrest. . . .

It must be recognized that whenever a police officer accosts an individual and restrains his freedom to walk away, he has "seized" that person. And it is nothing less than sheer torture of the English language to suggest that a careful exploration of the outer surfaces of a person's clothing all over his or her body in an attempt to find weapons is not a "search." Moreover, it is simply fantastic to urge that such a procedure performed in public by a policeman while the citizen stands helpless, perhaps facing a wall with his hands raised, is a "petty indignity."[13] It is a serious intrusion upon the sanctity of the person, which may inflict great indignity and arouse strong resentment, and it is not to be undertaken lightly.

---

11. The President's Commission on Law Enforcement and Administration of Justice found that, "[i]n many communities, field interrogations are a major source of friction between the police and minority groups." *Task Force Report: The Police* 183 (1967). It was reported that the friction caused by "[m]isuse of field interrogations" increases "as more police departments adopt 'aggressive patrol' in which officers are encouraged routinely to stop and question persons on the street who are unknown to them, who are suspicious, or whose purpose for being abroad is not readily evident." *Id.* at 184. "[F]risking" . . . cannot help but be a severely exacerbating factor in police-community tensions. This is particularly true in situations where the "stop and frisk" of youths or minority group members is "motivated by the officers' perceived need to maintain the power image of the beat officer, an aim sometimes accomplished by humiliating anyone who attempts to undermine police control of the streets." L. Tiffany et al., *Detection of Crime: Stopping and Questioning, Search and Seizure, Encouragement and Entrapment* 47-48 (1967).

13. Consider the following apt description: "The officer must feel with sensitive fingers every portion of the prisoner's body. A thorough search must be made of the prisoner's arms and armpits, waistline and back, the groin and area about the testicles, and entire surface of the legs down to the feet." L.L. Priar & T.F. Martin, *Searching and Disarming Criminals*, 45 J. Crim. L., Criminology & Police Sci. 481 (1954).

. . . In this case there can be no question, then, that Officer McFadden "seized" petitioner and subjected him to a "search" when he took hold of him and patted down the outer surfaces of his clothing. We must decide whether at that point it was reasonable for Officer McFadden to have interfered with petitioner's personal security as he did. . . .

[I]n justifying the particular intrusion the police officer must be able to point to specific and articulable facts which, taken together with rational inferences from those facts, reasonably warrant that intrusion. . . . [I]t is imperative that the facts be judged against an objective standard: would the facts available to the officer at the moment of the seizure or the search "warrant a man of reasonable caution in the belief" that the action taken was appropriate? *Cf.* Carroll v. United States, 267 U.S. 132 (1925). Anything less would invite intrusions upon constitutionally guaranteed rights based on nothing more substantial than inarticulate hunches, a result this Court has consistently refused to sanction. . . .

Applying these principles to this case, we consider first the nature and extent of the governmental interests involved. One general interest is of course that of effective crime prevention and detection; it is this interest which underlies the recognition that a police officer may in appropriate circumstances and in an appropriate manner approach a person for purposes of investigating possibly criminal behavior even though there is no probable cause to make an arrest. It was this legitimate investigative function Officer McFadden was discharging when he decided to approach petitioner and his companions. He had observed Terry [and] Chilton . . . go through a series of acts, each of them perhaps innocent in itself, but which taken together warranted further investigation. . . . It would have been poor police work indeed for an officer of 30 years' experience in the detection of thievery from stores in this same neighborhood to have failed to investigate this behavior further.

[Further,] there was justification for McFadden's invasion of Terry's personal security by searching him for weapons in the course of that investigation. . . . Certainly it would be unreasonable to require that police officers take unnecessary risks in the performance of their duties. American criminals have a long tradition of armed violence, and every year in this country many law enforcement officers are killed in the line of duty, and thousands more are wounded. Virtually all of these deaths and a substantial portion of the injuries are inflicted with guns and knives. . . .

We conclude that the revolver seized from Terry was properly admitted in evidence against him. . . . Officer McFadden had reasonable grounds to believe that petitioner was armed and dangerous, and it was necessary for the protection of himself and others to take swift measures to discover the true facts and neutralize the threat of harm if it materialized. The policeman carefully restricted his search to what was appropriate to the discovery of the particular items which he sought. . . .

HARLAN, J., concurring. While I unreservedly agree with the Court's ultimate holding in this case, I am constrained to fill in a few gaps, as I see them, in its opinion. . . . [I]f [a] frisk is justified in order to protect the officer during an encounter with a citizen, the officer must first have constitutional grounds to insist on an encounter, to make a forcible stop. . . . [Ordinarily a person approached by the police has the] right to ignore his interrogator and walk away; he certainly need not submit to a frisk for the questioner's protection. I would make it perfectly clear that the right to frisk in this case depends upon the reasonableness of a forcible stop to investigate a suspected crime. . . .

The facts of this case are illustrative of a proper stop and an incident frisk. Officer McFadden had no probable cause to arrest Terry for anything, but he had observed circumstances that would reasonably lead an experienced, prudent policeman to suspect that Terry was about to engage in burglary or robbery. His justifiable suspicion afforded a proper constitutional basis for accosting Terry, restraining his liberty of movement briefly, and addressing questions to him, and Officer McFadden did so. . . . Officer McFadden's right to interrupt Terry's freedom of movement and invade his privacy arose only because circumstances warranted forcing an encounter with Terry in an effort to prevent or investigate a crime.

DOUGLAS, J., dissenting. I agree that petitioner was "seized" within the meaning of the Fourth Amendment. I also agree that frisking petitioner and his companions for guns was a "search." But it is a mystery how that "search" and that "seizure" can be constitutional by Fourth Amendment standards, unless there was "probable cause" to believe that (1) a crime had been committed or (2) a crime was in the process of being committed or (3) a crime was about to be committed.

. . . [T]here is no basis for concluding that the officer had "probable cause" for believing that [a] crime was being committed. Had a warrant been sought, a magistrate would, therefore, have been unauthorized to issue one, for he can act only if there is a showing of "probable cause." We hold today that the police have greater authority to make a "seizure" and conduct a "search" than a judge has to authorize such action. We have said precisely the opposite over and over again. . . .

To give the police greater power than a magistrate is to take a long step down the totalitarian path. Perhaps such a step is desirable to cope with modern forms of lawlessness. But if it is taken, it should be the deliberate choice of the people through a constitutional amendment. Until the

Fourth Amendment . . . is rewritten, the person and the effects of the individual are beyond the reach of all government agencies until there are reasonable grounds to believe (probable cause) that a criminal venture has been launched or is about to be launched.

There have been powerful hydraulic pressures throughout our history that bear heavily on the Court to water down constitutional guarantees and give the police the upper hand. That hydraulic pressure has probably never been greater than it is today. Yet if the individual is no longer to be sovereign, if the police can pick him up whenever they do not like the cut of his jib, if they can "seize" and "search" him in their discretion, we enter a new regime. The decision to enter it should be made only after a full debate by the people of this country.

[Opinion of WHITE, J., concurring, omitted.]

NOTES AND QUESTIONS

1. The Law of Stop and Frisk. In the decades since *Terry*, a well-defined legal framework has evolved that governs stops and frisks. That framework follows the two-part analysis laid out in Justice Harlan's concurring opinion, which clearly delineates between two distinct Fourth Amendment events: a *stop* and a *frisk*. In a nutshell, a police officer may stop an individual if he has *reasonable suspicion* to believe that criminal activity is afoot. That standard sets a lower threshold than probable cause but must still be more than a hunch — the officer must have, as the *Terry* Court put it, "specific and articulable facts which, taken together with rational inferences from those facts, reasonably warrant that intrusion." After a stop has occurred, the officer may then conduct a frisk for weapons if he has, in addition to the reasonable suspicion justifying the stop, reasonable suspicion to believe the individual is armed and dangerous. When people talk about "investigative stops," "*Terry* stops," "stop-and-frisk," or "stop-question-frisk," they are talking about the coercive seizures and searches authorized and governed by this body of law. Traffic stops, too, are governed by these principles. *See* Berkemer v. McCarty, 468 U.S. 420 (1984).

2. Defining a Stop: Arrests, Stops, and Contacts. *Terry* stops sit between two other types of police-civilian encounters on a spectrum of police coercion. One level more intense are full-blown arrests, which still require probable cause, even after *Terry*. Sometimes the dividing line between a stop and an arrest is clear. The police might explicitly tell someone, "You are under arrest." Or, without uttering those words, they might handcuff the person, place him in a police car, and forcibly transport him to the police station for questioning. In that scenario, the Supreme Court has held, a person is under arrest for Fourth Amendment purposes regardless of whether he has been "told he was under arrest," been formally "booked," or would have a formal "arrest record" if later released from the station. Dunaway v. New York, 442 U.S. 200, 212 (1979). Shy of a trip to the police station, however, it is not always clear when a *Terry* stop might "ripen" into a *de facto* arrest out on the street, as the test for marking when this happens is a functional and hazy one. *See, e.g.*, Florida v. Royer, 460 U.S. 491 (1983). The Court, for example, has held that "a 20-minute stop" does not necessarily rise to the level of an arrest so long as "the police diligently pursued a means of investigation that was likely to confirm or dispel their suspicions quickly." United States v. Sharpe, 470 U.S. 675, 686, 688 (1985).

On the other side of the spectrum lie what are sometimes called "contacts." Unlike stops, the law considers these encounters to be consensual police-civilian interactions that do not constitute "seizures" under the Fourth Amendment. As a result, these interactions require no suspicion at all on the part of the police. The test for distinguishing stops from contacts is again a functional one. Courts consult an array of factors to determine whether, all things considered, a reasonable person would have felt free to terminate the encounter with the police and walk away. *See, e.g.*, United States v. Mendenhall, 446 U.S. 544, 554 (1980). As this language suggests, the inquiry is an objective one, such that encounters can be—and often are—deemed "consensual" even if the civilians experiencing them wouldn't describe them that way.

3. Defining a Frisk: Full Searches and Plain Feel. As the *Terry* opinion makes clear, a frisk is a kind of search under the Fourth Amendment. But just as the law distinguishes between stops and "full-blown" arrests, it distinguishes between frisks—which do not require probable cause—and more intensive searches of a person's body, which do. In the Court's words, a frisk "must be limited to that which is necessary for the discovery of weapons . . . and may realistically be characterized as something less than a 'full' search, even though it remains a serious intrusion." *Terry*, 392 U.S. at 26. In practice, a frisk amounts to a pat-down of the exterior of an individual's clothing to feel for weapons. An officer may not reach inside an individual's clothing or pockets—which would amount to a "full" search—unless he has probable cause. But that probable cause can derive from what the officer feels *during* the frisk itself. This happens in two principal scenarios. First, if the officer develops probable cause to believe he's felt a weapon, he may retrieve it for safety, as Officer McFadden did (twice) in *Terry*. Second, if the officer "feels an object whose contour or mass makes its identity immediately apparent" and provides probable cause to believe the item is contraband, such as drugs, he may lawfully reach into the person's clothing to seize it under the Court's "plain feel" doctrine. Minnesota v. Dickerson, 508 U.S. 366, 375 (1993).

4. Failure to Stop. In many states, it is a crime for a civilian to disobey the "lawful order" of a police officer, including a lawful order to stop. The fact that disobeying such an order is a crime poses great difficulties for anyone who believes they're being stopped without good cause, as Professor Orin Kerr explains in the following excerpt.[27]

Orin Kerr, Sandra Bland and the "Lawful Order" Problem, Wash. Post: Volokh Conspiracy (July 23, 2015). [I]t's often a crime to disobey a lawful order from a police officer. But from a citizen's perspective, it's often impossible to know what is a lawful order. . . . Even if the police pulled over the world's greatest legal expert, the citizen still couldn't know what orders are lawful because the laws often hinge on facts the citizen can't know.

Here's an example. Imagine an officer walks up to you and tells you to put your hands behind your back so he can handcuff you. To do that lawfully, the officer needs at least reasonable suspicion that you are engaged in a crime and pose a threat to him and maybe probable cause that you have committed a crime. But you can't know how much cause the officer has. Maybe the officer has no cause and is flagrantly violating your constitutional rights. Or maybe ten nuns have just sworn under oath that you robbed a bank in broad daylight that morning. You're innocent, as it was a case of mistaken identity. But the officer doesn't know that. And as the citizen, you can't tell which is which. . . .

The uncertainty caused by such laws is likely a contributor to the anxiety and stress many people feel, particularly in minority communities, when interacting with the police. It's hard to know if the officer is following the law or violating your rights. And if you don't know that, you can't know what you're allowed to do legally in response to the officer or what kind of reaction is justified. The officer has all the cards.

Faced with this, a citizen's cautious strategy might be just to do everything the officer says regardless of whether the officer's command is lawful. Even if you're right that the order is unlawful, the officer may not know that. You might decide it's better just to follow the officer's illegal commands than to be arrested and spend the night in jail out of principle.

But this is America, and we didn't fight a revolution to make that the only choice. And your options, if you want to assert the rights you have, can be awfully hard to figure out.

5. *Resisting Arrest.* As the preceding note explains, failure to submit to a lawful police order can be prosecuted as a criminal offense. But the police can also force compliance with lawful orders on the street, including by resorting to physical violence. As the Supreme Court has long recognized, "the right to make an arrest," including for disobeying a lawful order, "necessarily carries with it the right to use some degree of physical coercion or threat thereof." Graham v. Connor, 490 U.S. 386, 396 (1989). Fleeing, resisting, or fighting back against such *lawful* police violence is separately prosecutable under criminal statutes that generally prohibit "resisting arrest." *See, e.g.,* N.Y. Penal Law §205.30 ("A person is guilty of resisting arrest when he intentionally prevents or attempts to prevent a police officer . . . from effecting an authorized arrest . . . ."). In such scenarios, a person could be prosecuted for failing to submit to police force, even if the police eventually overpower—and potentially seriously injure—the person. Indeed, one newspaper's review of resisting arrest prosecutions in San Jose, California found that 70 percent of the cases involved officer use of force.[28]

The rules are sometimes different if the police exert *unlawful* force, either because they did not have a lawful basis to initiate a coercive encounter in the first place or because they used more force than was reasonable under the circumstances. As discussed in Chapter Four (p. 305), at common law civilians possessed a right to resist an unjustified, and therefore illegal, arrest. The modern trend generally rejects this right, at least when the civilian knows or should have known he is dealing with a police officer. *See, e.g.,* Model Penal Code §3.04(2)(a)(i); Ariz. Rev. Stat. §13-404(B)(2). But many states retain the right for a civilian to defend against excessive force in the making of an arrest. *See, e.g.,* Alaska Stat. §11.81.400(a)(1).[29]

In practice, whether a person will be prosecuted for resisting arrest or will be able to successfully argue self-defense will turn on the underlying facts, which the officers and the civilian involved often dispute. Note, however, that officers may have an especially strong incentive to engage in the testilying practices described earlier if their use of force caused serious injuries and was potentially illegal. According to Professor Paul Chevigny, who both studied and litigated these issues, "police sometimes use resisting arrest and similar charges to 'cover' errors including false arrests and the use of excessive force." Moreover, Chevigny observes, there "is a well-known" phenomenon in which resisting arrest charges are "brought against suspects whose arrests follow defiance by the suspects" or other forms of general disrespect shown toward the officers, "which is not in itself illegal. Their real crime," Chevigny adds, "is known as 'contempt of cop.'"[30]

B. *Pretextual Policing*

The preceding section describes the Fourth Amendment's basic parameters when it comes to street policing. The police can approach an individual and initiate contact with him for any reason, or for no reason at all, so long as a reasonable person in the same circumstances would feel free to walk away. To force the person to stop, however, the police must have reasonable suspicion of a crime. To frisk him during that stop, they must have reasonable suspicion he is armed and dangerous. And to initiate an even more coercive arrest, they must have probable cause that he committed a crime, which could arise during the stop or frisk itself—but they don't need a warrant.

These rules form the backdrop law of policing. But they do not fully explain how the law facilitates *order-maintenance* policing — the broad enforcement of low-level offenses that Professor Levin says can "function as a dragnet of sorts, granting the state a broad legal authorization for criminal social control." After all, the police in *Watson* investigated and arrested Mr. Watson for stealing multiple credit cards; the police in *Terry* investigated and arrested a pair of armed men who may have been about to commit an armed robbery. These are not the low-level offenses that Wilson and Kelling put at the center of broken windows policing.[31]

To appreciate how the Fourth Amendment intersects with and helps to promote that broadscale set of preemptive police tactics, we need to return to Professor Stuntz's observation of how substantive criminal law relates to police power:

> Th[e] police benefit from laws that criminalize street behavior that no one wishes actually to punish, solely as a means of empowering them to seize suspects . . . . [These offenses] serve as a convenient basis for an arrest and, perhaps, a search [and thus] make policing cheaper, because they permit searches and arrests with less investigative work.[32]

Stuntz's analysis focuses on the substantive criminal law, but that is only half the story. The dynamic he describes is equally attributable to a trio of interlocking Fourth Amendment doctrines that Professor Donald Dripps once referred to as the Amendment's "iron triangle." Together, this trio permits the police to arrest civilians for *de minimis* nonjailable offenses, to subject arrestees to a full-blown search of their person and belongings, and to predicate such tactics on expressly pretextual justifications—invoking one alleged infraction as an excuse to investigate unrelated behavior for which they may not have any articulable suspicion at all. In other words, Dripps argues, "[t]he Iron Triangle means in practice that the police have general search power over anyone," just as Stuntz feared. Consider this claim as you read the following Supreme Court opinions, which establish each of the triangle's three legs.[33]

Atwater v. City of Lago Vista

532 U.S. 318 (2001)

SOUTER, J. . . . . In Texas, if a car is equipped with safety belts, a front-seat passenger must wear one, and the driver must secure any small child riding in front. Violation of either provision is "a misdemeanor punishable by a fine not less than $25 or more than $50." Tex. Transp. Code Ann. §545.413(d). Texas law expressly authorizes "[a]ny peace officer [to] arrest without warrant a person found committing a violation" of these seatbelt laws, §543.001, although it permits police to issue citations in lieu of arrest.

In March 1997, petitioner Gail Atwater was driving her pickup truck in Lago Vista, Texas, with her 3-year-old son and 5-year-old daughter in the front seat. None of them was wearing a seatbelt. Respondent Bart Turek, a Lago Vista police officer at the time, observed the seatbelt violations and pulled Atwater over. . . . Turek approached the truck and "yelled" something to the effect of "we've met before" and "you're going to jail." He then called for backup and asked to see Atwater's driver's license and insurance documentation, which state law required her to carry. When Atwater told Turek that she did not have the papers because her purse had been stolen the day before, Turek said that he had "heard that story two-hundred times."

Atwater asked to take her "frightened, upset, and crying" children to a friend's house nearby, but Turek told her, "you're not going anywhere." As it turned out, Atwater's friend learned what was going on and soon arrived to take charge of the children. Turek then handcuffed Atwater, placed her in his squad car, and drove her to the local police station, where booking officers had her remove her shoes, jewelry, and eyeglasses, and empty her pockets. Officers took Atwater's "mug shot" and placed her, alone, in a jail cell for about one hour, after which she was taken before a magistrate and released on $310 bond. Atwater . . . ultimately pleaded no contest to the misdemeanor seatbelt offenses and paid a $50 fine. . . .

Atwater . . . filed suit . . . under 42 U.S.C. §1983 [alleging that Turek and the City] had violated [her] Fourth Amendment "right to be free from unreasonable seizure" . . . . [S]tatutes in all 50 States and the District of Columbia permit warrantless misdemeanor arrests by at least some (if not all) peace officers . . . . Atwater [nonetheless] asks us to mint a new rule of constitutional law . . . forbidding custodial arrest, even upon probable cause, when conviction could not ultimately carry any jail time and when the government shows no compelling need for immediate detention.

If we were to derive a rule exclusively to address the uncontested facts of this case, Atwater might well prevail. She was a known and established resident of Lago Vista with no place to hide and no incentive to flee, and common sense says she would almost certainly have buckled up as a condition of driving off with a citation. In her case, the physical incidents of arrest were merely gratuitous humiliations imposed by a police officer who was (at best) exercising extremely poor judgment. Atwater's claim to live free of pointless indignity and confinement clearly outweighs anything the City can raise against it specific to her case.

But we have traditionally recognized that a responsible Fourth Amendment balance is not well served by standards requiring sensitive, case-by-case determinations of government need, lest every discretionary judgment in the field be converted into an occasion for constitutional review. . . . Courts attempting to strike a reasonable Fourth Amendment balance thus credit the government's side with an essential interest in readily administrable rules.

At first glance, Atwater's argument may seem to respect the values of clarity and simplicity . . . [by distinguishing] between "jailable" and "fine-only" offenses. . . . The trouble with this distinction, of course, is that an officer on the street might not be able to tell. It is not merely that we cannot expect every police officer to know the details of frequently complex penalty schemes, but that penalties for ostensibly identical conduct can vary on account of facts difficult (if not impossible) to know at the scene of an arrest. Is this the first offense or is the suspect a repeat offender? Is the weight of the marijuana a gram above or a gram below the fine-only line? . . . And so on. . . .

Just how easily the costs could outweigh the benefits may be shown by asking, as one Member of this Court did at oral argument, "how bad the problem is out there." The very fact that the law has never jelled the way Atwater would have it leads one to wonder whether warrantless misdemeanor arrests need constitutional attention, and there is cause to think the answer is no. . . . Indeed, when Atwater's counsel was asked at oral argument for any indications of comparably foolish, warrantless misdemeanor arrests, he could offer only one. We are sure that there are others,[24] but just as surely the country is not confronting anything like an epidemic of unnecessary minor-offense arrests. . . .

Accordingly, we confirm today what our prior cases have intimated: the standard of probable cause "applies to all arrests, without the need to 'balance' the interests and circumstances involved in particular situations." Dunaway v. New York, 442 U.S. 200, 208 (1979). If an officer has probable cause to believe that an individual has committed even a very minor criminal offense in his presence, he may, without violating the Fourth Amendment, arrest the offender. . . .

[Opinion of O'CONNOR, J., dissenting, omitted.]

United States v. Robinson

414 U.S. 218 (1973)

REHNQUIST, J. . . . . . Officer Richard Jenks, a 15-year veteran of the District of Columbia Metropolitan Police Department, observed the respondent driving . . . . [A]s a result of previous investigation following a check of respondent's operator's permit four days earlier, [Jenks] determined there was reason to believe that respondent was operating a motor vehicle after the revocation of his operator's permit. . . . Jenks signaled respondent to stop the automobile, which respondent did. . . . At that point Jenks informed

---

24. One of Atwater's *amici* described a handful in its brief. Brief for American Civil Liberties Union et al. as Amici Curiae 7-8 (reporting arrests for littering, riding a bicycle without a bell or gong, operating a business without a license, and "walking as to create a hazard").

respondent that he was under arrest for "operating after revocation and obtaining a permit by misrepresentation." It . . . is conceded by the respondent here[] that Jenks had probable cause to arrest respondent, and that he effected a full-custody arrest.

In accordance with procedures prescribed in police department instructions, Jenks then began to search respondent. He explained at a subsequent hearing that he was "face-to-face" with the respondent, and "placed (his) hands on (the respondent), my right-hand to his left breast like this (demonstrating) and proceeded to pat him down thus (with the right hand)." During this patdown, Jenks felt an object in the left breast pocket of the heavy coat respondent was wearing, but testified that he "couldn't tell what it was" and also that he "couldn't actually tell the size of it." Jenks then reached into the pocket and pulled out the object, which turned out to be a "crumpled up cigarette package." . . . "As I felt the package I could feel objects in the package but I couldn't tell what they were. . . . I knew they weren't cigarettes."

The officer then opened the cigarette pack and found 14 gelatin capsules of white powder which he thought to be, and which later analysis proved to be, heroin. . . . The heroin seized from the respondent was admitted into evidence at the trial which resulted in his conviction [for possession of a controlled substance]. . . .

In its decision of this case, the Court of Appeals decided that even after a police officer lawfully places a suspect under arrest . . . he may . . . conduct [only] a limited frisk of the outer clothing and remove [any] weapons . . . . [Essentially], the Court of Appeals felt that the principles of [*Terry v. Ohio*] should be carried over to this probable-cause arrest for driving while one's license is revoked. Since there would be no further evidence of such a crime to be obtained in a search of the arrestee, the court held that only a search for weapons could be justified. . . .

[But] *Terry v. Ohio* did not involve an arrest for probable cause [and this] Court's opinion explicitly recognized that there is a "distinction in purpose, character, and extent between a search incident to an arrest and a limited search for weapons." 392 U.S. 1, 25 (1968). . . . *Terry*, therefore, affords no basis to carry over to a probable-cause arrest the limitations this Court placed on a stop-and-frisk search permissible without probable cause. . . .

The justification or reason for the authority to search incident to a lawful arrest rests quite as much on the need to disarm the suspect in order to take him into custody as it does on the need to preserve evidence on his person for later use at trial. The standards traditionally governing a search incident to lawful arrest are not, therefore, commuted to the stricter *Terry* standards by the absence of probable fruits or further evidence of the particular crime for which the arrest is made. Nor are we inclined, on the basis of what seems to us to be a rather speculative judgment, to qualify the breadth

of the general authority to search incident to a lawful custodial arrest on
an assumption that persons arrested for the offense of driving while their
licenses have been revoked are less likely to possess dangerous weapons
than are those arrested for other crimes. It is scarcely open to doubt that
the danger to an officer is far greater in the case of the extended exposure
which follows the taking of a suspect into custody and transporting him to
the police station than in the case of the relatively fleeting contact resulting
from the typical *Terry*-type stop. This is an adequate basis for treating all custodial arrests alike for purposes of search justification.

. . . The authority to search the person incident to a lawful custodial
arrest, while based upon the need to disarm and to discover evidence, does
not depend on what a court may later decide was the probability in a particular arrest situation that weapons or evidence would in fact be found upon
the person of the suspect. A custodial arrest of a suspect based on probable
cause is a reasonable intrusion under the Fourth Amendment; that intrusion being lawful, a search incident to the arrest requires no additional justification. It is the fact of the lawful arrest which establishes the authority to
search . . . .

MARSHALL, J., dissenting. . . . The majority's approach represents a clear
and marked departure from our long tradition of case-by-case adjudication of the reasonableness of searches and seizures under the Fourth
Amendment. . . . The Government does not now contend that the search
of respondent's pocket can be justified by any need to find and seize evidence in order to prevent its concealment or destruction, for . . . there is
no evidence or fruits of the offense [for] which respondent was [arrested].
The only rationale for a search in this case, then, is the removal of weapons
which the arrestee might use to harm the officer and attempt an escape. . . .

The majority opinion fails to recognize that the search conducted by
Officer Jenks did not merely involve a search of respondent's person. It also
included a separate search of effects found on his person. . . . [But once]
Jenks had the cigarette package in his hands, there is no indication that he
had reason to believe or did in fact believe that the package contained a
weapon. More importantly, even if the crumpled-up cigarette package had
in fact contained some sort of small weapon, it would have been impossible
for respondent to have used it once the package was in the officer's hands.
Opening the package, therefore, did not further the protective purpose of
the search. . . .

The Government argues that it is difficult to see what constitutionally
protected "expectation of privacy" a prisoner has in the interior of a cigarette pack. One wonders if the result in this case would have been the same
were respondent a businessman who was lawfully taken into custody for
driving without a license and whose wallet was taken from him by the police.
Would it be reasonable for the police officer, because of the possibility that

a razor blade was hidden somewhere in the wallet, to open it, remove all the contents, and examine each item carefully? . . . The search conducted by Officer Jenks in this case went far beyond what was reasonably necessary to protect him from harm or to ensure that respondent would not effect an escape from custody. In my view, it therefore fell outside the scope of a properly drawn "search incident to arrest" exception to the Fourth Amendment's warrant requirement.

[Opinion of POWELL, J., concurring, omitted.]

Whren v. United States

517 U.S. 806 (1996)

SCALIA, J. In this case we decide whether the temporary detention of a motorist who the police have probable cause to believe has committed a civil traffic violation is inconsistent with the Fourth Amendment's prohibition against unreasonable seizures unless a reasonable officer would have been motivated to stop the car by a desire to enforce the traffic laws.

[P]lainclothes vice-squad officers of the District of Columbia Metropolitan Police Department were patrolling a "high drug area" of the city in an unmarked car. Their suspicions were aroused when they passed a dark Pathfinder truck with temporary license plates and youthful occupants waiting at a stop sign, the driver looking down into the lap of the passenger at his right. The truck remained stopped at the intersection for what seemed an unusually long time—more than 20 seconds.

When the police car executed a U-turn in order to head back toward the truck, the Pathfinder turned suddenly to its right, without signaling, and sped off at an "unreasonable" speed. The policemen followed, and in a short while overtook the Pathfinder when it stopped behind other traffic at a red light. They pulled up alongside, and Officer Ephraim Soto stepped out and approached the driver's door, identifying himself as a police officer and directing the driver, petitioner Brown, to put the vehicle in park. [Soto] immediately observed two large plastic bags of what appeared to be crack cocaine in petitioner Whren's hands. Petitioners were arrested, and quantities of several types of illegal drugs were retrieved from the vehicle. Petitioners were charged in a four-count indictment with violating various federal drug laws. . . .

. . . As a general matter, the decision to stop an automobile is reasonable where the police have probable cause to believe that a traffic violation has occurred. Petitioners accept that Officer Soto had probable cause to believe that various provisions of the District of Columbia traffic code had been violated. They argue, however, that . . . the use of automobiles is so heavily and minutely regulated that total compliance with traffic and safety rules is nearly impossible[. A] police officer will almost invariably be able to catch any given motorist in a technical violation. This creates the temptation to use traffic stops as a means of investigating other law violations, as to which no probable cause or even articulable suspicion exists. Petitioners, who are both black, further contend that police officers might decide which motorists to stop based on decidedly impermissible factors, such as the race of the car's occupants. To avoid this danger, they say, the Fourth Amendment test for traffic stops should be, not the normal one . . . of whether probable cause existed to justify the stop; but rather, whether a police officer, acting reasonably, would have made the stop for the reason given. . . .

We think [our precedents] foreclose any argument that the constitutional reasonableness of traffic stops depends on the actual motivations of the individual officers involved. We of course agree with petitioners that the Constitution prohibits selective enforcement of the law based on considerations such as race. But the constitutional basis for objecting to intentionally discriminatory application of laws is the Equal Protection Clause, not the Fourth Amendment. Subjective intentions play no role in ordinary, probable-cause Fourth Amendment analysis.

. . . Petitioners urge as an extraordinary factor in this case that the "multitude of applicable traffic and equipment regulations" is so large and so difficult to obey perfectly that virtually everyone is guilty of violation, permitting the police to single out almost whomever they wish for a stop. But we are aware of no principle that would allow us to decide at what point a code of law becomes so expansive and so commonly violated that infraction itself can no longer be the ordinary measure of the lawfulness of enforcement. And even if we could identify such exorbitant codes, we do not know by what standard (or what right) we would decide, as petitioners would have us do, which particular provisions are sufficiently important to merit enforcement.

For the run-of-the-mine case, which this surely is, we think there is no realistic alternative to the traditional common-law rule that probable cause justifies a search and seizure. Here the District Court found that the officers had probable cause to believe that petitioners had violated the traffic code. That rendered the stop reasonable under the Fourth Amendment, the evidence thereby discovered admissible.

NOTES AND QUESTIONS

1. The Iron Triangle. In *Whren*, a pair of plainclothes vice officers were patrolling the streets of Washington, D.C., looking for people selling or possessing drugs. They testified that they saw a car occupied by two young Black men stopped at a stop sign for about 20 seconds as the men looked at some item in the passenger's lap. At this point, based on these limited observations, did the officers have reasonable suspicion to think the men were involved in drug dealing or otherwise violating drug possession laws? As you know, the probable cause and reasonable suspicion standards are malleable and deferential to law enforcement. But even so, many judges would likely find these facts insufficient to support a coercive stop predicated on suspicion of a narcotics offense. Yet the central holding of *Whren* is that the police did not need such suspicion to stop the men. So long as they had grounds to believe that the men had committed *any* offense — including a minor, nonjailable traffic infraction — the Fourth Amendment authorized a stop, even if the police executed the stop solely in hopes of finding drugs.

Note, moreover, that while the drugs in *Whren* happened to be in the officer's plain view once he approached the vehicle's window, the other two legs of the iron triangle can make it easy for an officer to search for drugs inside a car or on the driver's person. Under *Atwater*, "[i]f an officer has probable cause to believe that an individual has committed even a very minor criminal offense in his presence," such as the seat-belt infraction at issue in that case, "he may, without violating the Fourth Amendment, arrest the offender." And under *Robinson,* "a search incident to the arrest requires no additional justification. It is the fact of the lawful arrest which establishes the authority to search." As *Robinson* and related precedents confirm, such "a search may be made of the person of the arrestee" and "of the area within the control of the arrestee." *Robinson*, 414 U.S. at 224. When a person is arrested near his car and "the passenger compartment is within [his] reaching distance," that automatic search authority may extend to "the entire [passenger] compartment and any containers therein [that] may be reached." Arizona v. Gant, 556 U.S. 332, 341 (2009).

Put more simply, the mere fact that a person commits a minor, nonjailable offense gives police officers constitutional authority to arrest him and to search his person and his personal effects — to look for drugs (as occurred in *Robinson*) or any other items they might hope to find. This doctrinal reality is what Professor Dripps has in mind when he argues that "[t]he Iron Triangle means in practice that the police have general search power over anyone."

Nor, it should be noted, is the issue limited to traffic violations. To be sure, the defendants in *Whren* emphasized "that the 'multitude of applicable traffic . . . regulations' is so large and so difficult to obey perfectly that virtually everyone is guilty of violation" and thus subject to being stopped. But in rejecting that argument, the Court spoke in broad terms: "[W]e are aware of no principle that would allow us to decide at what point *a code of law* becomes so expansive and so commonly violated that infraction itself can no longer be the ordinary measure of the lawfulness of enforcement." In other words, the Fourth Amendment does not bar the police from pretextually deploying any expansive criminal code to justify broadscale stops, searches, and arrests, including a code that prohibits minor offenses regularly committed by pedestrians on the street, such as jaywalking or spitting on the sidewalk. In this respect, the iron triangle makes possible the world Stuntz warned against, in which "police benefit from laws that criminalize street behavior that no one wishes actually to punish" because those laws can "serve as a convenient basis for an arrest and, perhaps, a search."[34]

2. The Hidden Epidemic. At the outset of this chapter, we observed that preemptive policing tactics are widespread and, in some jurisdictions, executed at massive scale, as demonstrated by the 4.4 million coercive stops conducted by the New York City Police Department over a span of eight years. And yet, writing for the majority in *Atwater*, Justice Souter suggests that the iron triangle has little to do with widescale policing tactics on the ground. Indeed, he rejects Ms. Atwater's attempt to place limits on officers' power to arrest for minor nonjailable offenses partly because, he asserts, "the country is not confronting anything like an epidemic of unnecessary minor-offense arrests."

But is it possible Justice Souter is looking for an epidemic in the wrong place? The world Professors Stuntz and Dripps fear and predict would not necessarily entail an epidemic of *minor-offense* arrests. Rather, the worry is that the police will use a criminal code full of minor offenses as pretext to approach thousands of civilians—without any suspicion of a serious crime—and subject them all to searches predicated on those pretextual minor crimes. Notably, the Supreme Court has separately held that it is not "particularly important" that a search incident to arrest "preceded the arrest," so long as "the police clearly had probable cause to place [the suspect] under arrest." Rawlings v. Kentucky, 448 U.S. 98, 111 (1980). Searches incident to arrest, in other words, can actually occur before an arrest—or perhaps even *without* one—so long as an arrest would have been justified.

In a world in which thousands of low-level arrests are authorized, it is thus possible for officers to put thousands of people up against the wall, reach into thousands of pockets and pull out cigarette boxes or wallets, open their book bags or rummage through their cars, all in search of guns, drugs, or any other evidence they may be hoping to find. Critically, if the police in fact find such evidence, the person will be arrested—but not for a minor offense. He will be arrested for drug possession or firearm possession or whatever other felony the recovered evidence supports. And if the police do not find anything, they will either issue a citation for whatever minor offense served as pretext for the search (a jaywalking ticket, perhaps) or will just send the person on his way. In neither instance, though, will the individual be *arrested* for a minor offense. It is thus entirely possible that *Atwater*, in combination with *Robinson* and *Whren*, is producing what critics would call an epidemic of order-maintenance policing, all without producing the "epidemic of unnecessary minor-offense arrests" that Justice Souter was comforted not to find when writing the *Atwater* opinion.

3. Nonenforcement Discretion. Note an essential component of both the theory and practice of the iron triangle. The police need—and have—broad discretion *not* to arrest a given person even when they have probable cause to do so. Absent such discretion, the dynamic Professor Stuntz describes would be unworkable; everyone would constantly be arrested for jaywalking, sidewalk spitting, and any number of other widely criminalized but rarely prosecuted behaviors. In Stuntz's words, "Enforcement discretion permits overcriminalization, which in turn encourages more discretion."[35]

In fact, discretion not to arrest is baked into the constitutional law of policing, as confirmed in *Castle Rock v. Gonzales*, 545 U.S. 748 (2005). In that case, a woman who had a restraining order against her estranged husband repeatedly called the police asking for the order to be enforced after her husband came and picked up their children in violation of the order's terms. A governing statute stated that police officers "shall use every reasonable means to enforce a restraining order," including by arresting its subject. But the officers repeatedly ignored the woman's requests. Hours later, the husband arrived at the police station and opened fire with a semiautomatic handgun he had purchased earlier that evening. Police shot back, killing him; upon searching his car, they discovered he had killed the three children. The woman, their mother, later sued the city and police department for failing to enforce the restraining order, arguing that this inaction violated her constitutional rights. The Supreme Court rejected her claim:

> We do not believe that these provisions of Colorado law truly made enforcement of restraining orders *mandatory*. A well established tradition of police discretion has long coexisted with apparently mandatory arrest statutes. "In each and every state there are long-standing statutes that, by their terms, seem to preclude nonenforcement by the police. . . . However, for a number of reasons, including their legislative history, insufficient resources, and sheer physical impossibility, it has been recognized that such statutes cannot be interpreted literally. . . . They clearly do not mean that a police officer may not lawfully decline to . . . make an arrest. . . ." 1 ABA Standards for Criminal Justice 1-4.5, commentary, pp. 1-124 to 1-125 (2d ed. 1980). . . . Against that backdrop . . . . [i]t is hard to imagine that a Colorado peace officer would not have some discretion to determine that—despite probable cause to believe a restraining order has been violated—the circumstances of the violation or the competing duties of that officer or his agency counsel decisively against enforcement in a particular instance.

4. Pretext in Practice. The street policing tactics described thus far are not hypothetical. In practice, the precedents described above—either alone or in combination with similarly police-empowering doctrines related to consensual searches, canine searches, and automobile searches — are staples of everyday police-civilian encounters. Consider the following excerpt, written by a former police officer.

Raeford Davis, *Why I Hated Being a Cop,* Marshall Project (Apr. 21, 2016). I remember very early on in my career, I was on patrol in an area where we were basically pulling people over for not using their turn signals, and then turning [the stop] into a drug search. I was with some officers who pulled over a black kid on a moped for not using a signal. There were four or five of us, big guys in uniforms with guns on our hips, all standing around him. We asked, "You don't mind if we search your vehicle do you, to see if you have any drugs?" What's this kid going to do? He's not going to say no. We stripped the moped. He didn't have anything. We sent him on his way. But I felt like we earned that kid's enmity that day.

Another time, we were doing traffic stops and I had a K-9 officer with me. We stopped a guy basically just because he was in a drug neighborhood. He was a middle-aged black guy driving a nice car. We brought the dog over. It jumped up on the side of the car and scratched the door. Then, of course, the dog jumps in the car all over his leather seats and scratches them. I can see the dog doing this, and I'm thinking, *Holy shit!* We didn't find anything in the car, which was now all scratched up. It was like, "Here's your ticket for failure to use a turn signal, and have a nice day." Brutal. All because he aroused our merest suspicion.

5. *A Triangle of Violence.* As noted earlier, granting the police authority to stop, frisk, and arrest "necessarily carries with it the right to use some degree of physical coercion." Graham v. Connor, 490 U.S. 386, 396 (1989). In Professor Rachel Harmon's words, "[t]he very thing that makes a police officer a police officer is that states authorize [violent] actions that might be criminal under different circumstances." Of course, as the criminal law expands, the situations in which such police violence is authorized will expand as well, and with it the risk of harmful encounters, as noted in the following excerpt.[36]

Stephen L. Carter, *Law Puts Us All in Same Danger as Eric Garner,* Bloomberg View (Dec. 4, 2014). On the opening day of law school, I always counsel my first-year students never to support a law they are not willing to kill to enforce. Usually they greet this advice with something between skepticism and puzzlement, until I remind them that the police go armed to enforce the will of the state, and if you resist, they might kill you.

I wish this caution were only theoretical. It isn't. Whatever your view on the refusal of a New York City grand jury to indict the police officer whose chokehold apparently led to the death of Eric Garner, it's useful to remember the crime that Garner is alleged to have committed: He was selling individual cigarettes, or loosies, in violation of New York law.

[But it's] not just cigarette tax laws that can lead to the death of those the police seek to arrest. It's every law. Libertarians argue that we have far too many laws, and the Garner case offers evidence that they're right. I often tell my students that there will never be a perfect technology of law enforcement, and therefore it is unavoidable that there will be situations where police err on the side of too much violence rather than too little. Better training won't lead to perfection. But fewer laws would mean fewer opportunities for official violence to get out of hand. . . .

[T]he legal scholar William Stuntz [warned] that we are moving toward "a world in which the law on the books makes everyone a felon." . . . Part of the problem . . . is the growing tendency of legislatures — including Congress — to toss in a criminal sanction at the end of countless bills on countless subjects. It's as though making an offense criminal shows how much we care about it.

Well, maybe so. But making an offense criminal also means that the police will go armed to enforce it. [And] as the Garner case reminds us — the police might kill you. I don't mean this as a criticism of cops, whose job after all is to carry out the legislative will. The criticism is of a political system that takes such bizarre delight in creating new crimes for the cops to enforce. It's unlikely that the New York legislature, in creating the crime of selling untaxed cigarettes, imagined that anyone would die for violating it. But a wise legislator would give the matter some thought before creating a crime. . . . Every new law requires enforcement; every act of enforcement includes the possibility of violence. There are many painful lessons to be drawn from the Garner tragedy, but one of them, sadly, is the same as the advice I give my students on the first day of classes: Don't ever fight to make something illegal unless you're willing to risk the lives of your fellow citizens to get your way.

C. Race and Equal Protection

"Stories of black men being stopped by the police for no apparent reason other than the color of their skin are so common that they are not even considered news, and often get reported only when the victims happen to be celebrities or the confrontation is captured on film."

David Cole, *No Equal Justice: Race and Class in the American Criminal Justice System* 24-25 (1999)

Order-maintenance policing has long been criticized not just for its scale and its broad authorization of discretionary coercive tactics, but for its systemically racial origins and consequences.[37]

The evidence of racial disparities in street policing is dramatic. As noted earlier in this chapter, a class action lawsuit built upon nearly a decade of stop-and-frisk data from New York City found that 52 percent of the 4.4 million people stopped were Black, even though New York City was only 23 percent Black at the time. *See* Floyd v. City of New York, 959 F. Supp. 2d 540, 556-559 (S.D.N.Y. 2013). The litigation further showed that in the vast majority of stops, no weapons or contraband were found and no arrest was made — a finding consistent with the broad use of pretextual order-maintenance tactics. But notably, when weapons or contraband were found, they were found more frequently on white people than on people of color:

> Weapons were seized in 1.0% of the stops of blacks, 1.1% of the stops of Hispanics, and 1.4% of the stops of whites. Contraband other than weapons was seized in 1.8% of the stops of blacks, 1.7% of the stops of Hispanics, and 2.3% of the stops of whites. *Id.*

And yet, in 2013, the year *Floyd* was decided, Black people accounted for approximately 70 percent of all firearm arrests in the city while Latinos accounted for another 22 percent. Black and Latino people together accounted for over 80 percent of all drug arrests, split evenly between the two groups. White people, in other words, were more likely to be found with guns or drugs on their person when stopped by the police — but people of color were *dramatically* more likely to be subjected to stops and arrests.[38]

This sharp racial disparity is hard to explain in "race neutral" terms. As a group of scholars analyzing the same data report:

> [D]ata on *Terry* stops in New York City can be used to . . . compute the likelihood that any particular stop-and-frisk will result . . . in the discovery of particular kinds of evidence, given the information available to the officer before the encounter — that is, time of day, location, suspect characteristics, and the circumstances identified by the officer as giving rise to suspicion. All of this information is recorded in what the NYPD calls a "UF-250" report, and it can be used to estimate . . . the *ex ante* probability of discovering a weapon, based on all the factors that were known to the officer before the *Terry* stop. Th[is] stop-level hit rate, or "SHR," can be thought of as a measure of the strength of the evidence supporting the suspicion that the individual to be stopped and frisked has a gun . . . a kind of numerical measure of "articulable suspicion."
>
> SHRs computed in this manner are quite revealing. It turns out that 43 percent of the *Terry* stops carried out by the NYPD based on suspicion of [criminal possession of a weapon] had less than a 1 percent chance of actually resulting in the discovery of a weapon. And these low-odds stops had a heavy racial tilt: 49 percent of the stops of blacks fell below the 1 percent probability threshold, as did 34 percent of the stops of Hispanics, compared with only 19 percent of the stops of whites. So the SHR method offers further support for the finding . . . that the stop-and-frisk practices of the NYPD have been racially discriminatory.[39]

The evidence from New York City aligns with evidence mapping the disparate racial impact of order-maintenance policing and related policies writ large. In a recent study, sociologists Vesla Weaver, Andrew Papachristos, and Michael Zanger-Tishler show that individuals who "reached adulthood under the policy and practices of broken windows policing" in the late 1990s were much more likely to have been arrested than those who came of age two decades prior, even though the earlier generation "reported engaging in substantially more offending." This "decoupling" of criminal offending and criminal justice contact was especially pronounced for Black people, creating "a cavernous disparity by racial membership" in which "black Americans' exposure to arrest is both higher than their black counterparts of one generation past and markedly different from that of their white counterparts of the same generation."[40]

To many people who have grown up in heavily policed communities, these empirical studies simply confirm a wealth of lived experience. As Professor David Cole has written, the "routine stopping of black citizens, particularly young black men, is a consistent complaint in black communities across the country, and no doubt contributes to the pervasive sense among African Americans that the criminal justice system is biased against them." Professor Charles Ogletree, one of the first Black people to teach criminal law at Harvard Law School, pointedly captured the critique. "If I'm dressed in a knit cap and hooded jacket," he said, "I'm probable cause."[41]

These sentiments would hardly surprise the Justices who wrote *Terry v. Ohio* back in 1968. Quoting a contemporaneous report from a presidential commission on law enforcement and criminal justice, the Court noted that police departments had increasingly begun using a tactic then called " 'aggressive patrol' in which officers [were] encouraged routinely to stop and question persons on the street who are unknown to them, who are suspicious, or whose purpose for being abroad is not readily evident." The Court then described how these tactics were "a major source of friction" in "many communities," especially "between the police and minority groups." That friction was only exacerbated when officers stopped and frisked "youths or minority group members" in an effort "to maintain the power image of the beat officer, an aim sometimes accomplished by humiliating anyone who attempts to undermine police control of the streets." Years later, when Wilson and Kelling penned their *Broken Windows* essay, they candidly acknowledged the risk that police officers might "become the agents of neighborhood bigotry," using proxies like "skin color or national origin" as "the basis for distinguishing the undesirable from the desirable."[42]

The young Black men stopped by the police in *Whren v. United States* clearly shared this worry. Urging the Court to cabin the use of pretextual stops, they warned that such tactics could enable "police officers [to] decide

[whom] to stop based on decidedly impermissible factors," such as race. The Supreme Court offered a straightforward response:

> We of course agree with petitioners that the Constitution prohibits selective enforcement of the law based on considerations such as race. But the constitutional basis for objecting to intentionally discriminatory application of laws is the Equal Protection Clause, not the Fourth Amendment.

But to some, the Court's promise of equal protection rings hollow. The problem, according to critics like Professor David Owens, is that the Court is really engaged in "a terrifying shell game" when "it comes to the consideration of race and the police." It "weakens constitutional protections or enforcement in one area by talking about the availability of a right or remedy in another area," Owens writes. But "then, when you get to that other area," namely, the Equal Protection Clause, "the court weakens your constitutional protection in that area" too.[43]

The Equal Protection Clause has been interpreted in countless judicial opinions and analyzed in an even greater number of books, briefs, and scholarly works. Much of this terrain is covered in depth in classes on constitutional law. The notes that follow do not summarize that large body of law and its surrounding debates. Rather, they give an overview of how equal protection doctrine in theory could — but in practice does not — meaningfully prevent discriminatory policing, and of the consequences of that reality. We begin with a rare federal district court opinion concluding that a set of broadscale order-maintenance policing tactics violated the Equal Protection Clause, before turning to notes highlighting the limits of equal protection doctrine in this context.

Floyd v. City of New York

959 F. Supp. 2d 540 (S.D.N.Y. 2013)

SCHEINDLIN, J. . . . This case is about the tension between liberty and public safety in the use of a proactive policing tool called "stop and frisk." The New York City Police Department ("NYPD") made 4.4 million stops between January 2004 and June 2012. Over 80% of these 4.4 million stops were of blacks or Hispanics. In each of these stops a person's life was interrupted. The person was detained and questioned, often on a public street. More than half of the time the police subjected the person to a frisk.

Plaintiffs — blacks and Hispanics who were stopped — argue that . . . they were targeted for stops because of their race in violation of the Fourteenth Amendment. . . . The Fourteenth Amendment's Equal Protection Clause declares that "[n]o State shall . . . deny to any person within its jurisdiction the equal protection of the laws." The Clause . . . prohibits intentional discrimination on the basis of race, but not government action that merely has a disproportionate racial impact. *See* Washington v. Davis, 426 U.S. 229, 239-240 (1976).

The Second Circuit has outlined "several ways for a plaintiff to plead intentional discrimination that violates the Equal Protection Clause." Brown v. City of Oneonta, 221 F.3d 329, 337 (2d Cir. 2000). First, "[a] plaintiff could point to a law or policy that 'expressly classifies persons on the basis of race.'" *Id.* Second, "a plaintiff could identify a facially neutral law or policy that has been applied in an intentionally discriminatory manner." *Id.* Third, "[a] plaintiff could also allege that a facially neutral statute or policy has an adverse effect and that it was motivated by discriminatory animus." *Id.* . . . In order to show intentional discrimination under the second and third models of pleading above, plaintiffs need not prove that . . . a discriminatory purpose "was the 'dominant' or 'primary' one." Village of Arlington Heights v. Metro. Hous. Dev. Corp., 429 U.S. 252, 265 (1977). Rather, plaintiffs must prove that "a discriminatory purpose has been *a* motivating factor" in the challenged action. *Id.* at 265-266 (emphasis added). . . .

As the Supreme Court and the Second Circuit have explained[,] [t]he consequences of government action are sometimes evidence of the government's intent: "proof of discriminatory intent must necessarily usually rely on objective factors. . . . The inquiry is practical. What a legislature or any official entity is 'up to' may be plain from the results its actions achieve, or the results they avoid." Personnel Adm'r of Massachusetts v. Feeney, 442 U.S. 256, 279 n.24 (1979). . . .

FINDINGS OF FACT

Expert Testimony. The crux of plaintiffs' Fourteenth Amendment claim is that blacks and Hispanics are stopped more frequently than they would be if police officers did not discriminate based on race when deciding whom to stop. Assessing this claim require[s] comparing statistics about rates of stops of blacks and Hispanics to [a] benchmark . . . meant to capture "what the racial distribution of the stopped pedestrians would have been if officers' stop decisions had been racially unbiased." Greg Ridgeway, Rand, *Analysis of Racial Disparities in the New York Police Department's Stop, Question, and Frisk Practices* xi (2007). . . . [A] valid benchmark requires estimates of the supply of individuals of each racial or ethnic group who are engaged in the targeted behaviors and who are available to the police as potential targets for the exercise of their stop authority. Since police often target resources to the places where crime rates and risks are highest, and where populations are highest, some measure of population that is conditioned on crime rates is an optimal candidate for inclusion as a benchmark. . . .

[Using such a benchmark, as analyzed by the plaintiff's expert, Professor Jeffrey Fagan,] I make the following findings. First, . . . the NYPD carries out more stops in areas with more black and Hispanic residents, even when other relevant variables are held constant. The best predictor for the rate of stops in a geographic unit—be it precinct or census tract—is the racial composition of that unit rather than the known crime rate. . . . Second, within any area, regardless of its racial composition, . . . blacks and Hispanics are more likely to be stopped than whites within precincts and census tracts, even after controlling for the racial composition, crime rate, patrol strength, and various socioeconomic characteristics of the precincts or census tracts where the stops take place. . . . Third, . . . blacks who were subject to law enforcement action following their stop were about 30% more likely than whites to be arrested (as opposed to receiving a summons) after a stop for the same suspected crime, even after controlling for other relevant variables. Fourth, . . . after controlling for suspected crime and precinct characteristics, blacks who were stopped were about 14% more likely—and Hispanics 9% more likely—than whites to be subjected to the use of force. Fifth, . . . all else being equal, the odds of a stop resulting in any further enforcement action were 8% *lower* if the person stopped was black than if the person stopped was white. In addition, the greater the black population in a precinct, the less likely that a stop would result in a sanction. These results show that blacks are likely targeted for stops based on a lesser degree of objectively founded suspicion than whites. . . .

Targeting "the Right People." [Beyond the expert statistical analyses described above, the trial in this case also included testimony from NYPD personnel. Based on that testimony, I find that] NYPD maintains two different policies related to racial profiling in the practice of stop and frisk: a written policy that prohibits racial profiling and requires reasonable suspicion for a stop—and another, unwritten policy that encourages officers to focus their reasonable-suspicion-based stops on "the right people, the right time, the right location," [to quote former Chief of Department Joseph Esposito, the highest ranking uniformed member of the NYPD throughout the relevant timeframe]. Chief Esposito . . . was especially frank about the NYPD's policy of targeting racially defined groups for stops. . . .

Q: Do you believe the disparity in stop, question and frisk among black and Latino men is evidence of racial profiling?

A: No. I don't believe that. . . . Because the stops are based on complaints that we get from the public. . . .

THE COURT: But there are many street stops that have nothing to do with complaints, right?

THE WITNESS: Correct.

THE COURT: It's observed conduct. . . . It's not based on a complaint of a victim.

THE WITNESS: It's based on the totality of, okay, who is committing the—who is getting shot in a certain area? . . . *Well who is* *doing those shootings? Well, it's young men of color in their late teens, early 20s.*

. . . New York State Senator Eric Adams' testimony provided further evidence of official acquiescence in racial profiling by NYPD leadership. Senator Adams, a former NYPD captain, testified about a small meeting he attended at the Governor's office in Manhattan in July 2010. Former New York Governor David Paterson, Senator Adams, [two other legislators,] and [NYPD] Commissioner [Raymond] Kelly were all present to discuss a bill related to stop and frisk. Senator Adams raised his concern that a disproportionate number of blacks and Hispanics were being targeted for stops. Commissioner Kelly responded that he focused on young blacks and Hispanics "because he wanted to instill fear in them, every time they leave their home, they could be stopped by the police." Senator Adams testified that he was "amazed" that Commissioner Kelly was "comfortable enough to say that in the setting."

I find Senator Adams' testimony credible, especially in light of the Senator's former affiliation with the NYPD, Commissioner Kelly's decision not to appear at trial to rebut the testimony, the City's failure to offer *any* rebuttal evidence regarding Commissioner Kelly's statement at this meeting, and the other evidence of tolerance toward racial profiling at the NYPD. In fact, the substance of Commissioner Kelly's statement is not so distant from the City's publicly announced positions. Mayor Bloomberg stated in April that the NYPD's use of stop and frisk is necessary "to *deter* people from carrying guns. . . . [I]f you end stops looking for guns, . . . there will be more guns in the hands of young people and more people will be getting killed." At the same time, the City emphasized in its opening arguments that "blacks and Hispanics account for a disproportionate share of . . . crime perpetrators," and that "90 percent of all violent crime suspects are black and Hispanic." When these premises are combined—that the purpose of stop and frisk is to deter people from carrying guns and that blacks and Hispanics are a disproportionate source of violent crime—it is only a short leap to the conclusion that blacks and Hispanics should be targeted for stops in order to deter gun violence, regardless of whether they appear objectively suspicious. Commissioner Kelly simply made explicit what is readily inferrable from the City's public positions.

CONCLUSIONS OF LAW

Racial profiling constitutes intentional discrimination in violation of the Equal Protection Clause if it involves . . . an express classification based on race that does not survive strict scrutiny; the application of facially neutral criminal laws or law enforcement policies "in an intentionally discriminatory manner"; or a facially neutral policy that has an adverse effect and was motivated by discriminatory animus. The City's policy of targeting "the right people" for stops clearly violates the Equal Protection Clause under the second method of proof, and, insofar as the use of race is explicit, the first.

Intentionally Discriminatory Application of a Facially Neutral Policy. . . . The NYPD has directed officers to target young black and Hispanic men because these groups are heavily represented in criminal suspect data — the reliability of which is questionable — in those areas where the NYPD carries out most of its stops. Under the NYPD's policy, targeting the "right people" means stopping people in part because of their race. Together with Commissioner Kelly's statement that the NYPD focuses stop and frisks on young blacks and Hispanics in order to instill in them a fear of being stopped . . . there is a sufficient basis for inferring discriminatory intent.

The fact that the targeted racial groups were identified based on crime victim complaints does not eliminate the discriminatory intent. Just as it would be impermissible for a public housing agency to adopt a facially race-neutral policy of disfavoring applications from any group that is disproportionately subject to tenant complaints, and then apply this policy to disfavor applications from a racially defined group, so it is impermissible for a police department to target its general enforcement practices against racially defined groups based on crime suspect data.

Express Classification. . . . While it is a closer call, I also conclude that the use of race is sufficiently integral to the policy of targeting "the right people" that the policy depends on express racial classifications. When an officer is directed to target "male blacks 14 to 21" for stops *in general* based on local crime suspect data — a practice that the City has defended throughout this litigation — the reference to "blacks" is an express racial classification subject to strict scrutiny. Chief Esposito's concession that the NYPD has targeted young blacks and Hispanics for stops confirms that explicit references to race are not limited to a few rogue supervisors. The City has not attempted to defend — nor could it defend — the proposition that the targeting of young black males or any other racially defined group for stops is narrowly tailored to achieve a compelling government interest. Because the use of express racial classifications in the City's policy of indirect racial profiling cannot withstand strict scrutiny, the policy violates the Equal Protection Clause.

This policy far exceeds the permissible use of race in stopping suspects as set forth in *Brown v. City of Oneonta, New York*. There, the Second Circuit held that when the police carry out stops as part of a "search[] for a particular perpetrator," the use of racial information from the victim's description of the suspect is not an express racial classification subject to strict scrutiny. The court explained that the Oneonta police department's "policy was to investigate crimes by interviewing the victim, getting a description of the assailant, and seeking out persons who matched that description" and, as such, "was race-neutral on its face."

The NYPD's policy of targeting "the right people" for stops, by contrast, is not directed toward the identification of a specific perpetrator. Rather, it is a policy of targeting expressly identified racial groups for stops *in general.* There is no dispute that it would violate equal protection for a police department to adopt an express policy of targeting members of one race for stops or other enforcement activities — such as an express policy of only pulling over speeding drivers who are Hispanic. Similarly, the following hypothetical police department policy would surely be subject to strict scrutiny, despite its failure to mention any *specific* race at the outset: "No one is to be stopped except the members of whatever race participated at the highest rate in violent crime during the previous month, based on suspect descriptions." Such a policy would be especially deserving of strict scrutiny if its drafters knew that the same race would be targeted every month, and managers implementing the policy were responsible for expressly directing officers to stop members of that race. The NYPD's policy of indirect racial profiling is closer to this hypothetical policy than it is to the race-neutral policy in *Brown.*

CONCLUSION

Whether through the use of a facially neutral policy applied in a discriminatory manner, or through express racial profiling, targeting young black and Hispanic men for stops based on the alleged criminal conduct of other young black or Hispanic men violates bedrock principles of equality. Two young men in the 81st Precinct who are similarly situated in every way, except that one is black and the other white, are similarly situated for the purposes of equal protection and must be treated alike. . . . The Equal Protection Clause does not sanction treating similarly situated members of different racial groups differently based on racial disparities in crime data. Indeed, such treatment would eviscerate the core guarantees of the Equal Protection Clause. If equal protection means anything, it means that individuals may not be punished or rewarded based on the government's views regarding their racial group, regardless of the source of those views.

NOTES AND QUESTIONS

1. The Limits of Floyd. Judge Scheindlin's decision in *Floyd* was hailed by some as a potential landmark ruling, with hopes that it would usher in new waves of litigation challenging and curtailing racialized policing tactics. Yet the opinion's reach could be far narrower, given the inherent challenges in proving racial discrimination under current equal protection doctrine.[44]

As previously noted, and as the *Floyd* opinion acknowledges, that doctrine requires a showing of discriminatory *intent* before an equal protection claim will be sustained. Discriminatory impact, alone, is not enough. In individual cases, proving such intent will often be impossible. As Professor David Cole explains, "the very nature of a 'pretext' stop makes it extremely difficult to establish such a motivation. If the officer follows a driver until there is a traffic violation, the violation itself will inevitably be advanced as the reason for the stop, and *Whren* makes any traffic violation, no matter how petty and pretextual, a legitimate rationale." Against this backdrop, Professor Michelle Alexander adds, "[d]efending against claims of racial bias in policing is easy."

> [A]ny officer with a fifth-grade education will be able to cite multiple non-racial reasons for initiating an encounter. . . . Police officers . . . are highly adept at offering race-neutral reasons for actions that consistently disad-vantage African Americans. . . . "Your honor, we didn't stop him because he's black; we stopped him because he failed to use his turn signal at the right time" . . . . Judges are . . . reluctant to second-guess an officer's motives . . . . So long as officers refrain from uttering racial epithets and so long as they show the good sense not to say "the only reason I stopped him was 'cause he's black," courts generally turn a blind eye to patterns of discrimination by the police.[45]

Indeed, on close inspection, the *Floyd* opinion emphasizes the well-documented discriminatory effects of New York's policing tactics, but the court does not treat those effects as the primary basis for its ruling. Nor could it under current equal protection doctrine. As Professor Reva Siegel explains, the Supreme Court in *Personnel Administrator v. Feeney*, 442 U.S. 256 (1979), "sharply restricted" the "use of impact evidence for proving purpose" under the Equal Protection Clause, and in so doing "changed the structure of equal protection doctrine." Prior to *Feeney*, Siegel writes, multiple federal appellate courts as well as opinions from individual Supreme Court Justices indicated "that discriminatory purpose could be inferred (perhaps exclusively) from foreseeable . . . racial impact." Courts operating in this vein "looked to a policy's foreseeable effects as evidence of the government's presumed purposes." But *Feeney* rejected this approach, holding instead that "[w]hen the basic classification" system used to treat people differently "is rationally based, uneven effects upon particular groups within a class are ordinarily of no constitutional concern" even if they fall along racial lines. 442 U.S. at 272. According to Siegel, *Feeney* thus "insulated facially neutral action with foreseeable racial disparate impact from constitutional challenge." In the words of legal scholar Guy Rubinstein, *Feeney* is thus "[o]ften referred to as a requirement for 'smoking gun' evidence" of discriminatory purpose, and "is largely considered the principal reason why equal protection claims in general, and selective prosecution or selective [law] enforcement claims in particular, nearly always fail."[46]

Against this legal backdrop, one can better understand both the significance and the limitations of the court's opinion in *Floyd*. Judge Scheindlin held that the "plaintiffs' statistical evidence of racial disparities in stops [was] sufficient to show a discriminatory *effect.*" 959 F. Supp. 2d at 661 (emphasis added). But, consistent with *Feeney,* she did not treat those statistics as sufficient to "establish discriminatory intent." *Id.* at 662. Rather, her ruling rested heavily on trial testimony describing explicitly racial statements made by police commanders, including the statement attributed to Police Commissioner Raymond Kelly in which he said he supported targeting "young blacks and Hispanics 'because he wanted to instill fear in them [that] every time they leave their home, they could be stopped by the police.'"

Floyd, in short, is arguably the rare case in which litigants produced, and a judge credited, the sort of smoking gun evidence of discriminatory intent that equal protection doctrine demands. Suffice to say, such evidence is exceedingly uncommon in civil rights litigation. As Professor Cole explains:

> Government officials do not commonly admit that their actions were motivated by prejudice. Indeed, because there is such a strong social sanction against racial prejudice, few people are even willing to admit to themselves that they have acted for racial reasons. . . . The Court's prohibition of intentional discrimination weeds out the bigots who admit they are racist, but ignores (and thereby effectively legitimates) all other discrimination.[47]

2. **Floyd's Aftermath.** As for *Floyd* itself, Judge Scheindlin's ruling was initially appealed to the U.S. Court of Appeals for the Second Circuit by Mayor Michael Bloomberg's administration. While that appeal was pending, New York City held its mayoral election, in which Bill de Blasio prevailed after openly campaigning to end the City's stop-question-and-frisk practices. Upon assuming office, Mayor de Blasio directed the City's attorneys to drop the then-pending appeal. As a result, Judge Scheindlin's opinion and the remedial order that she put in place to address the City's practices went into effect, free from appellate review.[48]

In the meantime, stop-and-frisk activity plummeted in New York City—and elsewhere. The number of pedestrian stops in New York fell by 97 percent between 2011 and 2015. An even swifter drop took place in Chicago in late 2015. Some have called the end of widespread stop and frisk "illusory," however, pointing to evidence from Chicago that the police substituted traffic stops for pedestrian stops, leaving the total number of police-civilian interactions "nearly unchanged." Others observe that in New York, stop-and-frisk was replaced by a new tactic called "omnipresence." As *New York Times* reporter Stephen Farrell describes this approach, "It is what it says. At night, in targeted projects there's a police cruiser parked at nearly every major junction. Flashing lights bounce off the walls until the early hours and powerful floodlights turn night into artificial day." The approach, Farrell continues, "is the fruit of . . . Mayor Bill de Blasio's early attempts to reduce crime without resorting to overuse of the controversial stop and frisk policing tactic favored by his predecessors."[49]

Mayor de Blasio was succeeded in office by Eric Adams in 2022. As a state senator, Adams was the source of the "smoking gun" statement from Commissioner Kelly that played a key role in Judge Scheindlin's ruling. As a mayoral candidate, however, Adams criticized de Blasio's policies on stop-question-and-frisk as soft on crime and prevailed in a crowded primary over candidates with track records as civil rights and racial justice advocates. Following his election as mayor, Adams initiated policies on policing that opponents criticized as "pushing New York into a new era of more aggressive law enforcement." According to the *New York Times,* the mayor, who is himself Black, came "under particularly harsh scrutiny" not from "white leftists" but rather from "Black leaders and [community] members."[50]

3. Procedure and Practicalities. On the rare occasion a case has legs under the demanding equal protection standards described above, a host of procedural and practical hurdles nonetheless make equal protection litigation a weak check on racialized policing. As Professor David Cole describes, the Supreme Court "has constructed a set of all-but-impassable barriers . . . [that] operate at the threshold, stopping the complaint from even being aired." These barriers, Cole maintains, help explain why "few claims are even filed, notwithstanding shocking racial disparities and widespread belief among minority groups that criminal justice is enforced in a discriminatory manner."[51]

One such barrier is the Supreme Court's standing doctrine, which blocks most would-be plaintiffs from suing for forward-looking relief—such as a court order enjoining further discriminatory policing practices. Under a case called *City of Los Angeles v. Lyons,* 461 U.S. 95 (1983), a plaintiff seeking such an order cannot point to past harms he has experienced. Rather, he must demonstrate a "real and immediate" threat that he will personally be subjected to the challenged practice again in the future, out on the street. *Id.* at 102-104. According to Professor Michelle Alexander, this is "virtually impossible" to do, given the millions of discrete and variable police-civilian interactions.*

---

* The *Floyd* litigation was a rare exception in which, due to a prior settlement that required careful documentation of NYPD's widespread stop-and-frisk activity, the plaintiffs were able to produce credible evidence suggesting that they would, indeed, be subject to police coercion again. *See* Floyd v. City of New York, 283 F.R.D. 153, 160, 169-170 (S.D.N.Y. 2012) ("[T]he frequency of alleged injuries inflicted by the practices at issue here creates a likelihood of future injury sufficient to address any standing concerns.").

Suing for monetary damages may be no easier. Sovereign immunity protects the state from liability. Meanwhile, cities and other municipalities can be sued only if they've authorized the challenged practice by law or custom. "Most cities," Alexander observes, "do not have policies specifically authorizing illegal conduct (particularly race discrimination) and 'custom' is notoriously difficult to prove." "Accordingly," she concludes, "suing a city police department for damages is generally not an option." And while individual officers can be sued for damages, they enjoy what is called "qualified immunity," which shields "all but the plainly incompetent or those who knowingly violate the law." Malley v. Briggs, 475 U.S. 335, 341 (1986).[53]

Finally, practical hurdles to damages suits abound as well, as Cole documents. For one thing, while an "illegal search motivated by race" can "be extremely intrusive and humiliating," a plaintiff might not be able "to point to harm" giving rise to meaningful damages awards if "the police do no physical damage." Without the prospect of damages and contingent legal fees, many lawyers will be unwilling to pursue a case, especially for clients who do not have the resources to pay by the hour. Moreover, Cole observes, "many such suits reduce to a swearing match between a police officer and the individual stopped," in which people who "are disproportionately poor and members of minority groups" must "convince a judge or jury to accept their word over a police officer's."[54]

The upshot of all this, says Cole, is a system that maintains "the illusion of a constitutional prohibition against discrimination in criminal justice," but in which "the avenue left open for enforcing it is so narrow and difficult that few will succeed in navigating its course."

> At one level, that may have the effect of legitimating the system; the courts can say that they abhor and forbid race discrimination, but that they simply do not see it. But . . . at a deeper level this strategy eats away at the system's legitimacy. The charade cannot be maintained forever. Ultimately members of minority groups are likely to conclude that the courts and the law cannot be counted on to guarantee equal protection.[55]

4. Policing Black Communities. The preceding cases and notes suggest that constitutional law is at best a weak check on aspects of order-maintenance policing that critics have long decried as problematic and unjust. Indeed, in *Terry v. Ohio* itself, Chief Justice Earl Warren offered a strikingly candid account of the limits of legal controls when it comes to regulating these forms of police behavior. Focusing on the power of courts to exclude unconstitutionally obtained evidence in criminal trials, which scholars and jurists consider the primary enforcement mechanism of constitutional rights in the criminal arena, Chief Justice Warren wrote:

> Doubtless some police 'field interrogation' conduct violates the [Constitution]. . . . But . . . [r]egardless of how effective the [exclusionary]

rule may be where obtaining convictions is an important objective of the police, it is powerless to deter invasions of constitutionally guaranteed rights where the police either have no interest in prosecuting or are willing to forgo successful prosecution in the interest of serving some other goal.

392 U.S. 1, 13-14 (1968). Put more simply, when the police act in their order-maintenance capacity as opposed to in their crime-solving capacity, judges are limited in their ability to protect constitutional rights, precisely because so little of this street-level policing finds its way before the courts. That is the nature of the "hidden epidemic" described above. And it renders courts—and by extension law—at best poor constraints on problems arising from the policing practices described thus far.[56]

For this reason, debates over the proper role of the police in contemporary American society frequently extend beyond courtrooms and law school classrooms. Indeed, in the aftermath of the killings of Michael Brown and Eric Garner in 2014 and of George Floyd in 2020—all unarmed Black people killed by white police officers—conversations and contestation over American policing have been central features of our national public life. In just the short time since those events, scores of books, scholarly analyses, and public essays have been written on these issues. It would be impossible to distill that wide-ranging discourse into just a few passages. Rather, the excerpts that follow are designed to reflect some prominent arguments and themes offered by individuals on various sides of this longstanding and ongoing debate over the proper role of the police in American society.

James Q. Wilson & George L. Kelling, *Broken Windows: The Police and Neighborhood Safety,* Atlantic (Mar. 1982). [In the first half of the twentieth century, the police] assisted in th[e] reassertion of [neighborhood] authority by acting, sometimes violently, on behalf of the community. Young toughs were roughed up, people were arrested "on suspicion" or for vagrancy, and prostitutes and petty thieves were routed. . . . This pattern of policing was not an aberration or the result of occasional excess. . . . [But more recently, the police have come] increasingly under the influence of legal restrictions, provoked by media complaints and enforced by court decisions and departmental orders. As a consequence, the order-maintenance functions of the police are now governed by rules developed to control police relations with suspected criminals. This is, we think, an entirely new development. For centuries, the role of the police as watchmen was judged primarily not in terms of its compliance with appropriate procedures but rather in terms of its attaining a desired objective. The objective was order, an inherently ambiguous term but a condition that people in a given community recognized when they saw it. . . . [The low-level criminal offenses that allow the police to pursue such order] exist not because society wants judges to punish vagrants or drunks but because it wants an officer to have the legal tools to remove undesirable persons from a neighborhood when informal efforts to preserve order in the streets have failed.

Once we begin to think of all aspects of police work as involving the application of universal rules under [legally grounded] procedures, we inevitably ask what constitutes an "undesirable person" and why we should "criminalize" vagrancy or drunkenness. A strong and commendable desire to see that people are treated fairly makes us worry about allowing the police to rout persons who are undesirable by some vague or parochial standard. . . . [But t]his wish to "decriminalize" disreputable behavior that "harms no one"—and thus remove the ultimate sanction the police can employ to maintain neighborhood order—is, we think, a mistake. Arresting a single drunk or a single vagrant who has harmed no identifiable person seems unjust, and in a sense it is. But failing to do anything about a score of drunks or a hundred vagrants may destroy an entire community. A particular rule that seems to make sense in the individual case makes no sense when it is made a universal rule and applied to all cases. It makes no sense because it fails to take into account the connection between one broken window left untended and a thousand broken windows. Of course, agencies other than the police could attend to the problems posed by drunks or the mentally ill, but in most communities—especially where the "deinstitutionalization" movement has been strong—they do not.

The concern about equity is more serious. We might agree that certain behavior makes one person more undesirable than another but how do we ensure that age or skin color or national origin or harmless mannerisms will not also become the basis for distinguishing the undesirable from the desirable? How do we ensure, in short, that the police do not become the agents of neighborhood bigotry?

We can offer no wholly satisfactory answer to this important question. We are not confident that there *is* a satisfactory answer except to hope that by their selection, training, and supervision, the police will be inculcated with a clear sense of the outer limit of their discretionary authority. That limit, roughly, is this—the police exist to help regulate behavior, not to maintain the racial or ethnic purity of a neighborhood.

Monica Bell, *Police Reform and the Dismantling of Legal Estrangement,* 126 Yale L.J. 2054, 2068-2070, 2087 (2017). For as long as scholars have studied the relationship between African Americans and criminal justice, they have documented deep distrust of the system. In the early twentieth century, W.E.B. Du Bois was likely the first scholar to empirically document this distrust. . . . Du Bois's research was prescient, at least with respect to the direction of research and scholarship on African Americans' relationship to the crime control system over the next century. A high watermark was the 1968 Kerner Commission Report, commissioned by the Johnson Administration in the wake of twenty-three episodes of urban unrest during the mid- and late 1960s. The Report concluded that, for many African Americans, the "police have come to symbolize white power, white racism, and white repression." Like Du Bois's . . . study, the Report documented "tension" and "hostility" between law enforcement and urban African Americans, blaming the "abrasive relationship" on a combination of increased demands for protection and service and the police practices thought necessary to provide those services. In the South and in the Northeastern and Midwestern Rust Belt cities where many African Americans relocated during the Second Great Migration, police forces often functioned to maintain the expulsion of African Americans from the center of social and political life, at times violating the law in service of racial control. Despite pervasive harsh policing that ostensibly was intended to suppress and deter crime, African Americans felt inadequately protected.

The litany of evidence confirming the existence of a tense and distrustful relationship between African Americans and law enforcement mounted steadily over the ensuing decades. John Hagan and Celesta Albonetti, for example, used data from a national survey conducted in the late 1970s to conclude that, although African Americans were more likely than whites to see all aspects of the criminal justice system as unjust, they perceived the police as the most unjust aspect of the criminal justice system. Drawing from nationally representative survey data from the late 1980s, Tracey Meares argued that many African Americans experience "dual frustration" with drugs on the one hand and with harsh courts and law enforcement on the other. More recently, Lawrence Bobo and Victor Thompson reached similar conclusions, finding that while sixty-eight percent of white respondents expressed at least "'some' or 'a lot' of confidence in the police," only eighteen percent of black respondents would say the same. Contemporary events, particularly the increased political, social, and academic attention directed at police use of force because of the Black Lives Matter movement, have shed new light on longstanding tensions between African Americans and law enforcement. . . .

Some scholarship on the legal mistrust of poor African Americans could be misread to suggest that a large subset of this group possesses values that are antithetical to law-abiding behavior, almost as if these individuals do not care what the law is and do not believe they should be bound by it. A better-supported interpretation is that many poor African Americans might see police as a legitimate authority in the ideal, and might even empathize with some police officers' plight, but they find the police as a whole too corrupt, unpredictable, or biased to deem them trustworthy. Even as they accept the ideal vision of the police as the state-authorized securers of public safety, their nonideal working theory might be, as earlier research suggests, that the police are "just another gang."

Dorothy E. Roberts, *Foreword: Abolition Constitutionalism,* 133 Harv. L. Rev. 1, 20-27 (2019). The first police forces in the United States were slave patrols. Beginning in the early 1700s, southern white men formed armed groups that entered slaveholding properties and roamed public roads to ensure that enslaved people did not escape or rebel against their enslavers. . . . Modern police forces are descendants of armed urban patrols like the Charleston City Guard and Watch, which was established as early as 1783 to constantly monitor and inspect both enslaved and free black residents to "minimize Negro fraternizing and, more especially, to prevent the growth of an organized colored community."

    . . . In the aftermath of Emancipation, when slaveholders' human property was no longer protected by slave law, "a new set of innovations and regulation[s] had to emerge, again under the rubric of policing." Like overseers and slave patrols, Jim Crow police and private citizens who abetted them used terror primarily to enforce racial subjugation, not to apprehend people culpable for crimes. Take, for example, coercive interrogation techniques, now known as "the third degree," that have become a staple of modern policing. The first stage of lynching, typically carried out with the participation or sanction of the police, was often "extract[ing] a confession by whipping or burning the accused." Prior to *Miranda v. Arizona,* which barred the admissibility of presumptively coerced confessions, southern police routinely used torture to force blacks to confess to crimes. . . .

    Even after the civil rights movement, "[p]olice torture of suspects continues to be a tolerated means of confirming the presumed criminality of blacks." For example, from the 1970s to the 1990s, white police officers in Chicago engaged in systematic torture of black residents. Under the command of Lieutenant Jon Burge, police coerced dozens of confessions from suspects by beating them, burning them with radiators and cigarettes, putting guns in their mouths, placing plastic bags over their heads, and delivering electric shocks to their ears, noses, fingers, and genitals. Burge's reign of torture was known and condoned by police officers, the State's Attorney's office, judges, and doctors at Cook County Hospital. Racialized terror that bridged slave patrols, lynchings, and police whippings remained a feature of policing in the post-Civil Rights Era criminal punishment system.

    . . . Like the Black Codes and the slave codes before them, order-maintenance policies give police wide discretion to control black people's presence on public streets. Law enforcement continues to enforce the logic of slave patrols, to view black people as a threat to the security of propertied whites, and to contain the possibility of black rebellion.[57]

Mariame Kaba & Andrea J. Ritchie, *No More Police: A Case for Abolition* 1-2, 42-43 (2022). When was the moment you first started to question the violence of policing? . . . Every generation has their flashpoints—moments when the violence of policing overwhelms, when the stories we are told about cops and safety don't add up. For many in this generation, the catalyst was the sight of Michael Brown's body lying in the street for four hours after being shot by Ferguson, Missouri, police officer Darren Wilson . . . [or] of Eric Garner saying "I can't breathe" eleven times as NYPD officer Daniel Pantaleo squeezed the life out of him using a banned chokehold. Stories of police violence continued to flood the headlines. In December 2014, the #SayHerName hashtag created by the African American Policy Forum began to increase visibility of the numerous stories of Black women, girls, and trans people killed and violated by police. In April 2015, less than a year after Garner and Brown were killed, came the news that Freddie Gray's back was broken by Baltimore police who intentionally slammed his body around a police van during what they euphemistically termed a "rough ride," following an arrest prompted solely by the fact that Gray was trying to avoid an interaction with the cops who would go on to kill him. Just three months later, in July 2015, Sandra Bland died in a Waller County, Texas, jail cell after a violent traffic stop for not using her turn signal as she attempted to get out of the way of the cop car following her.

Many of us can point to the exact moment we realized there is something profoundly wrong with equating policing with public safety. For many people and communities targeted by police, it came with our own brutalization, sexual assault, criminalization, or humiliation by a cop, or when we were forced to witness a loved one killed, assaulted, or arrested by police, or when parents, family, and friends desperate to ensure our survival taught us that police represent danger, not safety. Or when we called for help and none came; or, worse yet, when the cops did come, they came for us. . . .

. . . Even though the U.S. spends over $100 billion a year on policing, a figure that has been increasing steadily over the past half century, the U.S. continues to experience some of the highest rates of violence across all industrialized countries. . . . [G]un-related homicide rates in the U.S. are twenty-five times higher than twenty-two of the world's wealthiest nations. Longitudinal studies indicate that markers of resource deprivation — lack of sufficient income, health care, etc. — are critical factors in heightened violent crime rates. Yet, bottomless police budgets capture a growing share of our collective resources, and programs proven to reduce, prevent, intervene in, and help survivors heal from violence are starved of nutrients. . . .

In a twisted feat of logic, police trumpet claims that violence is on the rise — evidence of their own failure to prevent it in spite of the billions invested in them — as a reason that they need more cops, more cash, more laws, and, of course, *less* scrutiny and *less* accountability. And they would like to have it both ways: If officially documented rates of violence fall — as they have for the most part over the past four decades — cops claim credit, leveraging the threat of a hypothetical future increase in violence to keep increasing their budgets and power. [But p]olice failure to stop, interrupt, or transform violence is no accident. Policing has never been about preventing violence. It has always been about fabricating and maintaining "order" by using violence — directly and indirectly — to control and contain racialized and gendered populations of people . . . . Cops do not simply enforce laws, they make and use the law — and the power given to them both legally and extralegally — to maintain a raced, gendered, abled, classed, and global social order.

Tracey Meares & Dan Kahan, *When Rights Are Wrong*, Boston Rev. (Apr. 1, 1999). [In a recent class action lawsuit, the American Civil Liberties Union challenged the legality of mass building searches in Chicago's low-income housing projects.] Judge Wayne Anderson agreed that the building searches violated the residents' constitutional rights. The decision sounds like the rare case of a judge protecting a vulnerable population from police coercion, but for one important detail: an overwhelming majority of the residents [of the housing projects] opposed the ACLU's effort to block the building searches.

The Chicago Housing Authority (CHA) adopted its building-search policy as an emergency response to the deadly outbursts of gun fire associated with incessant gang warfare; in one four-day period near this time, the police recorded more than 300 gun-fire incidents in the Robert Taylor Homes and Stateway Gardens projects. When the ACLU filed suit, the elected representatives of 18 of CHA's 19 projects intervened to support the CHA. But Judge Anderson dismissed the residents' willingness to consent to building searches as evidence of the corrosive effect of poverty and crime on their own "self-respect."

Judge Anderson's ruling was certainly paradoxical. We ordinarily think of rights as belonging to individuals. Rights express the respect owed to each of us as autonomous actors whose choices about how to secure our own well-being shouldn't be second-guessed by political officials. Yet in the CHA case, Judge Anderson invoked the residents' rights [in order] to *overrule* their choices . . . .

As strange as this story seems, it is no aberration. The CHA building searches are only one of many law-enforcement policies attacked by civil libertarians and invalidated by courts on the ground that they violate the rights of the very individuals who support them. Before it derailed the CHA's building searches, for example, the ACLU sued to block the installation of metal detectors requested by project residents. It has also attacked youth curfews and gang-loitering provisions on the ground that these policies promote harassment of inner-city residents — even though residents of the inner-city have in fact been the driving political force behind many of these measures.

Albert W. Alschuler & Stephen J. Schulhofer, *Antiquated Procedures or Bedrock Rights?*, 1998 U. Chi. Legal F. 215, 215-217. Tracey Meares and Dan Kahan contend that . . . "residents of poor, minority neighborhoods favor Chicago's gang loitering ordinance" and [other order-maintenance policing tactics.] [But] no one view can be attributed to "residents of the inner city" or to "the minority community." . . . [C]itizens and courts [must] be on guard against the appealing but highly manipulable rhetoric of "community," a rhetoric that is increasingly prevalent in contemporary discourse. It is easy to appreciate the attractions of a sense of place, shared values, and neighborhood empowerment—the aspirations that communitarian arguments compellingly evoke. But before we agree with Meares and Kahan "not to second guess the inner-city community's determination . . ." we must, at a minimum, be sure that this "community" exists and that it holds the views attributed to it. At the intersection of politics, crime, police discretion, and race lie problems of enormous complexity and explosiveness. . . . Far from serving the needs of the disadvantaged, the concept of community can, in the wrong hands, become another weapon for perpetuating the disempowerment and discrimination that continue to haunt urban America.

II.   THE CONSTITUTIONAL LAW OF OVERCRIMINALIZATION

"In short, the most pressing problem with the criminal law today is that we have too much of it."

Douglas Husak, *Overcriminalization: The Limits of the Criminal Law* 3 (2007)

To this point, we have studied how substantive criminal law enhances police power. The more conduct the state criminalizes, the easier it is for law enforcement actors to intervene—preemptively, coercively, discretionarily, sometimes unjustly—in the lives of private civilians. A corollary of this insight is that we can and should expect criminal law to grow. In fact, Professor Bill Stuntz argues, we should expect a feedback loop because law enforcement actors "can tell legislatures what legislation they need." In practice, legislative committees routinely invite police and prosecutor organizations to propose and shape criminal legislation, and those actors routinely reach out to legislatures with proposals of their own for new criminal statutes. At the same time, Stuntz continues, law enforcement actors' discretionary enforcement authority "frees legislators from having to worry about criminalizing too much, since not everything that is criminalized will be prosecuted" or even lead to arrests. More likely, if a criminal statute is overused or misused, the officials responsible for enforcing it will be blamed—not the diffuse group of legislators who enacted the law at some point in the potentially distant past. The upshot, Stuntz argues, is that the "criminal law expands in different areas at different times and places, but it always expands."[58]

In his book *Overcriminalization: The Limits of Criminal Law*, Professor Douglas Husak notes that these institutional dynamics have led to "phenomenal growth in the number of offenses" in the United States over the past century. Even people "who have spent most of their careers wrestling with the intricacies of the criminal law are familiar with only a fraction of the statutes to which we are subject." The resultant overcriminalization, Husak contends, is not only a defining feature of American criminal law but also a serious problem. We "have a great deal of unjust punishment" in the United States, he argues, because a "substantial amount of contemporary punishments . . . are inflicted for conduct that should not have been criminalized at all."[59]

The first part of this chapter highlighted how an abundance of criminal law can create a glut of police power. As we will see in the final part of the chapter, too much criminal law is also associated with prosecutors wielding potentially too much power. But before turning to that issue, it is worth pausing to ask whether legal constraints—crafted and enforced by judges—might operate as a check on overcriminalization itself, or as mechanisms of decriminalization.

For Stuntz, the possibility of such judicially imposed constraints was a source of hope, because he saw judges as "a good deal less prone" to the symbiotic biases among prosecutors and legislators driving the feedback loop described above. It "is natural to see legislative crime definition as something in need of restraint," he concluded, "and it is natural to see courts as good candidates for doing the restraining." And yet, Stuntz recognized at least one major problem in counting on courts to check overcriminalization even if one assumes they are inclined to do so. Courts conventionally play important roles as *interpreters* of substantive criminal statutes, but they are subordinate to legislatures, who have the power to enact new statutes and to override judicial interpretations of existing ones. Courts, in other words, generally lack the power to force decriminalization on legislators set against it.[60]

The one exception to this rule arises in the domain of constitutional law. After all, as the Supreme Court wrote in a seminal Second Amendment opinion striking down a criminal gun-possession statute, "the enshrinement of constitutional rights necessarily takes certain policy choices off the table," moving them beyond the reach of legislatures' crime-making power. District of Columbia v. Heller, 554 U.S. 570, 636 (2008). Still, courts are often reluctant to exercise this power given the complex moral and social judgments immanent in criminal law, which judges generally prefer to leave to more democratically accountable actors. In the Supreme Court's words:

> "The doctrines of *actus reus*, *mens rea*, insanity, mistake, justification, and duress" . . . reflect both the "evolving aims of the criminal law" and the "changing religious, moral, philosophical, and medical views of the nature

of man." Or said a bit differently, crafting those doctrines involves balancing and rebalancing over time complex and oft-competing ideas about "social policy" and "moral culpability"—about the criminal law's "practical effectiveness" and its "ethical foundations." That "constantly shifting adjustment" could not proceed in the face of rigid "constitutional formulas." Within broad limits, . . . "doctrines of criminal responsibility" must [therefore] remain "the province of the States."

Kahler v. Kansas, 589 U.S. 271, 280 (2020) (quoting Powell v. Texas, 392 U.S. 514, 533 (1968) (plurality opinion) (cleaned up)).

Still, the question remains: What "broad limits" *does* the Constitution impose on democratically elected legislatures' power to promulgate crimes? And should courts be more aggressive in defining those limits in ways that promote decriminalization, striking down criminal statutes as "off the table" on the ground that they are inconsistent with "the enshrinement of constitutional rights"? In this section, we explore these questions by examining three areas in which constitutional law has been interpreted to constrain states' crime-making power. We begin with *vagueness doctrine,* turn next to the constitutional prohibition on so-called *status crimes,* and conclude with discussions of constitutionally *protected activity.* We then close with a case in which the Constitution was invoked against, but failed to block, the sort of low-level offense at the heart of order-maintenance policing, as an example of the Constitution's limits as a tool of judicially imposed decriminalization.

A. *Vagueness*

Papachristou v. City of Jacksonville

405 U.S. 156 (1972)

DOUGLAS, J. . . . Margaret Papachristou, Betty Calloway, Eugene Eddie Melton, and Leonard Johnson were all arrested early on a Sunday morning, and charged with vagrancy—"prowling by auto." . . . Papachristou and Calloway are white females. Melton and Johnson are black males. Papachristou was enrolled in a job-training program sponsored by the State Employment Service at Florida Junior College in Jacksonville. Calloway was a typing and shorthand teacher at a state mental institution located near Jacksonville. She was the owner of the automobile in which the four defendants were arrested. . . .

At the time of their arrest the four of them were riding in Calloway's car on the main thoroughfare in Jacksonville. They had left a restaurant owned by Johnson's uncle where they had eaten and were on their way to a nightclub. The arresting officers denied that the racial mixture in the car played any part in the decision to make the arrest. The arrest, they said, was made because the defendants had stopped near a used-car lot which had been broken into several times. There was, however, no evidence of any breaking and entering on the night in question.

Of these four charged with "prowling by auto" none had been previously arrested except Papachristou who had once been convicted of a municipal offense. . . .

Jacksonville's ordinance and Florida's [analogous] statute were "derived from early English law," Johnson v. State, 202 So. 2d 852, 854 (Fla. 1967), and employ "archaic language" in their definitions of vagrants.[1] The history is an often-told tale. The breakup of feudal estates in England led to labor shortages which in turn resulted in the Statutes of Laborers, designed to stabilize the labor force by prohibiting increases in wages and prohibiting the movement of workers from their home areas in search of improved conditions. Later vagrancy laws became criminal aspects of the poor laws. . . .

This ordinance is void for vagueness, both in the sense that it "fails to give a person of ordinary intelligence fair notice that his contemplated conduct is forbidden by the statute," United States v. Harriss, 347 U.S. 612, 617 (1954), and because it encourages arbitrary and erratic arrests and convictions.

Living under a rule of law entails various suppositions, one of which is that all persons "are entitled to be informed as to what the State commands or forbids." Lanzetta v. New Jersey, 306 U.S. 451, 453 (1939). *Lanzetta* is one of a well-recognized group of cases insisting that the law give fair notice of the offending conduct. In the field of regulatory statutes governing business activities, where the acts limited are in a narrow category, greater leeway is allowed. The poor among us, the minorities, the average householder are not in business and not alerted to the regulatory schemes of vagrancy laws; and we assume they would have no understanding of their meaning and impact if they read them. . . .

The Jacksonville ordinance makes criminal activities which by modern standards are normally innocent. "Nightwalking" is one. Florida construes

---

1. Jacksonville Ordinance Code §26-57 provided at the time of these arrests and convictions as follows:

> "Rogues and vagabonds, or dissolute persons who go about begging, common gamblers, persons who use juggling or unlawful games or plays, common drunkards, common night walkers, thieves, pilferers or pickpockets, traders in stolen property, lewd, wanton and lascivious persons, keepers of gambling places, common railers and brawlers, persons wandering or strolling around from place to place without any lawful purpose or object, habitual loafers, disorderly persons, persons neglecting all lawful business and habitually spending their time by frequenting houses of ill fame, gaming houses, or places where alcoholic beverages are sold or served, persons able to work but habitually living upon the earnings of their wives or minor children shall be deemed vagrants and, upon conviction in the Municipal Court shall be punished as provided for Class D offenses."

Class D offenses at the time of these arrests and convictions were punishable by 90 days' imprisonment, $500 fine, or both. . . .

the ordinance not to make criminal one night's wandering, only the "habitual" wanderer or, as the ordinance describes it, "common night walkers." We know, however, from experience that sleepless people often walk at night, perhaps hopeful that sleep-inducing relaxation will result. . . .

[As for] "persons able to work but habitually living upon the earnings of their wives or minor children" . . . [this] might implicate unemployed pillars of the community who have married rich wives [or] unemployed people out of the labor market, by reason of a recession or disemployed by reason of technological or so-called structural displacements.

Persons "wandering or strolling" from place to place have been extolled by Walt Whitman and Vachel Lindsay. The qualification "without any lawful purpose or object" may be a trap for innocent acts. Persons "neglecting all lawful business and habitually spending their time by frequenting . . . places where alcoholic beverages are sold or served" would literally embrace many members of golf clubs and city clubs.

Walkers and strollers and wanderers may be going to or coming from a burglary. Loafers or loiterers may be "casing" a place for a holdup. Letting one's wife support him is an intra-family matter, and normally of no concern to the police. Yet it may, of course, be the setting for numerous crimes.

The difficulty is that these activities are historically part of the amenities of life as we have known them. They are not mentioned in the Constitution or in the Bill of Rights. These unwritten amenities have been in part responsible for giving our people the feeling of independence and self-confidence, the feeling of creativity. These amenities have dignified the right of dissent and have honored the right to be nonconformists and the right to defy submissiveness. They have encouraged lives of high spirits rather than hushed, suffocating silence. . . .

This aspect of the vagrancy ordinance before us is suggested by what this Court said in 1876 about a broad criminal statute enacted by Congress: "It would certainly be dangerous if the legislature could set a net large enough to catch all possible offenders, and leave it to the courts to step inside and say who could be rightfully detained, and who should be set at large." United States v. Reese, 92 U.S. 214, 221 (1875).

. . . Here the net cast is large, not to give the courts the power to pick and choose but to increase the arsenal of the police. . . . "[S]tatute[s] of the type that seek to control 'vagrancy' . . . are in a class by themselves, in view of the familiar abuses to which they are put. Definiteness is designedly avoided so as to allow the net to be cast at large, to enable men to be caught who are vaguely undesirable in the eyes of police and prosecution, although not chargeable with any particular offense. In short, these 'vagrancy statutes' and laws against 'gangs' are not fenced in by the text of the statute or by the subject matter so as to give notice of conduct to be avoided." Winters v. New York, 333 U.S. 507, 540 (1948) (Frankfurter, J., dissenting).

Another aspect of the ordinance's vagueness appears when we focus, not on the lack of notice given a potential offender, but on the effect of the unfettered discretion it places in the hands of the Jacksonville police. . . . A direction by a legislature to the police to arrest all "suspicious" persons would not pass constitutional muster. A vagrancy prosecution may be merely the cloak for a conviction which could not be obtained on the real but undisclosed grounds for the arrest. . . . Those generally implicated by the imprecise terms of the ordinance—poor people, nonconformists, dissenters, idlers—may be required to comport themselves according to the life style deemed appropriate by the Jacksonville police and the courts. Where, as here, there are no standards governing the exercise of the discretion granted by the ordinance, the scheme permits and encourages an arbitrary and discriminatory enforcement of the law. It furnishes a convenient tool for "harsh and discriminatory enforcement by local prosecuting officials, against particular groups deemed to merit their displeasure." Thornhill v. Alabama, 310 U.S. 88, 97-98 (1940). It results in a regime in which the poor and the unpopular are permitted to "stand on a public sidewalk . . . only at the whim of any police officer." Shuttlesworth v. Birmingham, 382 U.S. 87, 90 (1965).

. . . The implicit presumption in these generalized vagrancy standards—that crime is being nipped in the bud—is too extravagant to deserve extended treatment. Of course, vagrancy statutes are useful to the police. Of course, they are nets making easy the roundup of so-called undesirables. But the rule of law implies equality and justice in its application. Vagrancy laws of the Jacksonville type teach that the scales of justice are so tipped that even-handed administration of the law is not possible. The rule of law, evenly applied to minorities as well as majorities, to the poor as well as the rich, is the great mucilage that holds society together.

The Jacksonville ordinance cannot be squared with our constitutional standards and is plainly unconstitutional.

NOTES AND QUESTIONS

1. Parsing **Papachristou**. A careful read of *Papachristou* reveals three distinct strands of reasoning—three different rationales for invalidating Jacksonville's vagrancy ordinance. First, the statute's wording failed "to give notice of the conduct to be avoided" because it did not make clear precisely what it prohibited. Second, by placing "unfettered discretion . . . in the hands of the Jacksonville police," the ordinance encouraged "arbitrary and discriminatory enforcement of the law." Indeed, the Court made a point of noting the "racial mixture" of the *Papachristou* defendants, a subtle but noteworthy nod to the fact that vagrancy laws have a long history of use as tools of class and race oppression. Finally, the ordinance criminalized "activities which by modern standards are normally innocent," what the Court called "the amenities of life as we have known them."[61]

As vagueness doctrine has developed, the Court's "amenities of life" rationale has largely gone by the wayside. Today, an argument that the state cannot criminalize certain "normally innocent" conduct sounds not in vagueness, but in an appeal to separate constitutional protections, such as due process or the First Amendment. As we will soon see, these pockets of constitutionally protected activity are, even in combination, more modest than *Papachristou*'s soaring language contemplates.

The relationship between *Papachristou*'s other two rationales — fair notice and arbitrary and discriminatory enforcement — is something of a puzzle. At times the Supreme Court has suggested that avoiding arbitrariness and discrimination is "the more important aspect of the vagueness doctrine," Kolender v. Lawson, 461 U.S. 352, 358 (1983), which exists, on this account, to guard against sweeping criminal statutes that allow "policemen, prosecutors, and juries to pursue their personal predilections," Smith v. Goguen, 415 U.S. 566, 575 (1974). Consistent with this view, courts have sometimes struck down criminal statutes that are not textually vague — that is, statutes that give fair notice of what they prohibit — on the ground that they confer too much discretion.

Perhaps most well-known is *City of Chicago v. Morales*, 527 U.S. 41 (1999), in which the Court invalidated a Chicago ordinance that made it a crime for "criminal street gang members" who were "remaining in any one place with no apparent purpose" to fail to "disperse and remove themselves" from the area when ordered to do so by a police officer. *Id.* at 47. As the Court summarized the statute, if "any person . . . disobeys the officer's order, that person is guilty of violating the ordinance." *Id.* Writing for three Justices in dissent, Justice Thomas argued that "[t]here is nothing 'vague' about an order to disperse." *Id.* at 112 (Thomas, J., dissenting). After all, he argued, "the vast majority of people who are ordered by the police to 'disperse and remove themselves from the area' will have little difficulty understanding how to comply." *Id.* Justices O'Connor and Breyer apparently agreed with Justice Thomas on this point. But, along with three other Justices who would have invalidated the statute on both prongs of the modern vagueness test, they voted to strike down the statute on the discretion prong alone. In Justice Breyer's words, the "ordinance is unconstitutional, not because it provides insufficient notice, but because it does not provide 'sufficient minimal standards to guide law enforcement officers.'" *Id.* at 72 (Breyer, J., concurring in part and concurring in judgment).

> [T]he ordinance violates the Constitution because it delegates too much discretion to a police officer to decide whom to order to move on, and in what circumstances. And I see no way to distinguish in the ordinance's terms between one application of that discretion and another. The

ordinance is unconstitutional, not because a policeman applied this discretion wisely or poorly in a particular case, but rather because the policeman enjoys too much discretion in *every* case.

Id. at 71; *accord id.* at 60 (Stevens, J., for the Court).

But if vagueness doctrine truly renders criminal laws unconstitutional because they give the police "too much discretion" or have a "broad sweep," *id.*, then it seems to present something of a conundrum. As we've seen in much of the material leading up to this point, discretion is endemic in criminal law. Indeed, anyone familiar with the American penal system could cite numerous examples of laws that convey nearly limitless discretion to law enforcement, as occurs any time a statute clearly criminalizes conduct in which people regularly engage. And yet, scholars broadly agree that courts would never actually strike down such statutes as unconstitutionally vague. Judge Debra Livingston elaborates the point this way:

> Traffic rules regulating speed, lane changing, and the like are among the most precise regulations to be found in state and local legal codes. These laws, by traditional standards, are simply not vague. Despite the specificity of such laws, however, no one could deny that the opportunity for their arbitrary and discriminatory enforcement is huge . . . . Low-level traffic offenses (like most laws regulating minor misconduct) are not invariably enforced, even when the evidence of their violation is clear. . . . In effect, clear and precise traffic laws empower police to pursue their own predilections in targeting people for enforcement *in precisely the manner condemned by the vagueness prohibition.*

And of course, Livingston's point carries over to any number of ordinances beyond the traffic code that are precisely worded but sweeping in scope — including many of the criminal statues at the heart of order-maintenance policing.[62]

Put more simply, a doctrine that invalidates "broad" criminal laws that entail a lot of "police discretion" would seem primed to raze much of American criminal law. Recognizing this tension, Livingston suggests that the "the substantive overtones lurking in the *[Papachristou]* opinion" may indicate "that the Court's judgment" was not really "about vagueness at all, but was an implicit judicial conclusion that police may not enforce 'middle-class virtue' in dealing with the public." In a prominent article, Professor John Jeffries elaborates on the idea that the subject matter of a given statute may determine its susceptibility to vagueness challenge. According to Jeffries, broad order-maintenance laws are particularly vulnerable to attack based on their risk of arbitrary and discriminatory enforcement "because they lend themselves to informal social control of undesirables." In contrast, he argues, when the crime at issue is more serious, "the risk of abusive enforcement is reduced." In these instances, Jeffries continues, "there is an identifiable victim" who can "keep track of police action," as well as broader "public monitoring of prosecutorial decisions," all of which work as de facto checks on arbitrary enforcement—and judges' "tolerance for indefinite standards is increased accordingly."[63]

Jeffries' account offers a way to make some sense of the internal tensions in the Court's vagueness doctrine. But it does not fully capture contemporary case law. In recent years, for example, the Supreme Court has invoked arbitrary-enforcement concerns to strike down sentencing enhancements applied by federal judges, a setting far removed from the "moment-to-moment judgment of the policeman on his beat." *Morales*, 527 U.S. at 60; *see, e.g.*, United States v. Davis, 588 U.S. 445 (2019); Johnson v. United States, 576 U.S. 591 (2015). In the end, then, we can draw only a few tentative conclusions about the current state of the law. First, statutes that are textually unclear, and thus fail to give fair notice of what they prohibit, are most likely to be declared vague, like the ordinance prohibiting "annoying" conduct struck down in *Coates v. Cincinnati*, 402 U.S. 611 (1971). A law like this is vague, the Court has said, "not in the sense that it requires a person to conform his conduct to an imprecise but comprehensible normative standard, but rather in the sense that no standard of conduct is specified at all." *Id.* at 614. Second, it's hard to say when—or why—courts will invalidate a law for authorizing arbitrary and discriminatory enforcement; this aspect of vagueness law remains undertheorized and cases in both the Supreme Court and lower courts land in unpredictable ways. Finally, for the reasons laid out above, it seems unlikely that the anti-discretion prong of the doctrine will or can be interpreted broadly, given the myriad ways in which discretion is inherent to and inextricable from the administration of criminal law.

2. Specificity vs. Breadth. Note that if the core of vagueness doctrine is a limitation on statutes that are vaguely *worded*, the doctrine will do little to constrain law enforcement discretion or to curb overcriminalization. In fact, Professor Bill Stuntz argues in the following excerpt, vagueness doctrine may exacerbate overcriminalization by encouraging legislatures to replace broad, vague statutes with a host of narrower, more specific ones.

William J. Stuntz, *The Pathological Politics of Criminal Law,* 100 Mich. L. Rev. 505, 559-561 (2001). Vagueness doctrine requires that legislatures be reasonably specific when defining crimes. . . . It thus prevents legislatures from creating all-encompassing crimes like the infamous vagrancy ordinance in *Papachristou v. Jacksonville*, or the not-so-infamous gang loitering law in *Chicago v. Morales*. The clear goal is to prevent the state from criminalizing everything, and thereby delegating the real work of defining crimes to prosecutors. But vagueness doctrine cannot accomplish that goal, for legislatures can achieve breadth and specificity at the same time. The history of the post-*Papachristou* law of street disorder proves the point. Old-style loitering and vagrancy statutes used language broad enough to encompass almost anything people (or at least people whom the police perceive as troublesome) might do in public. *Papachristou* itself is a good example; in that case the ostensibly criminal conduct consisted of two mixed-race couples driving down one of Jacksonville's main thoroughfares. [And indeed, c]ourts invalidated most of those loitering and vagrancy statutes in the late 1960s and early 1970s. Ever since, legislatures, state and local, have been replacing them with a series of more carefully defined offenses: anti-cruising ordinances, anti-noise ordinances, loitering-with-intent statutes, and youth curfew laws are all examples. At the same time, police have been reviving small-scale (and specific) prohibitions that had been dormant. A well-known case from Illinois, *People v. Kail*, involved a suspected prostitute arrested for riding a bicycle without a bell, under an explicit police department policy requiring officers to enforce any prohibitions they could find against vice suspects.

Kail and contemporary street disorder statutes show why *Papachristou* could not eliminate catch-all crimes. The real problem with old-style vagrancy and loitering laws was not their vagueness, but their breadth. Barring vague statutes does little about breadth. And breadth is much harder for courts to regulate, for it is a function not of particular criminal statutes but of the whole criminal code. The problem with *Kail* is not the unfairness of barring bell-less bicycles, but the unfairness of barring that plus a couple dozen other sorts of ordinary street behavior, which, taken together, criminalize everything and everyone the police and prosecutors might wish to punish.

[In sum, v]agueness doctrine rules out enacting all-encompassing crimes, but it permits the creation of many smaller, more tightly defined offenses. It thus pushes legislatures to expand criminal law by accumulation, by adding ever more distinct acts to the criminal code. . . . In other words, vagueness doctrine actually accents the tendency to create more crimes.

B. Status Crimes and the Eighth Amendment

In 1962, the Supreme Court held in *Robinson v. California*, 370 U.S. 660, that a statute that "makes it a criminal offense for a person to 'be addicted to the use of narcotics'" violated the Eighth Amendment to the Constitution, which prohibits "cruel and unusual punishments." As the Court wrote:

> This statute . . . is not one which punishes a person for the use of narcotics, for their purchase, sale or possession, or for antisocial or disorderly behavior resulting from their administration. . . . Rather, we deal with a statute which makes the 'status' of narcotic addiction a criminal offense, for which the offender may be prosecuted 'at any time before

he reforms.' . . . It is unlikely that any State at this moment in history would attempt to make it a criminal offense for a person to be mentally ill, or a leper, or to be afflicted with a venereal disease. . . . We cannot but consider the statute before us as of the same category. . . . We hold that a state law which imprisons a person thus afflicted as a criminal . . . inflicts a cruel and unusual punishment . . . . To be sure, imprisonment for ninety days is not, in the abstract, a punishment which is either cruel or unusual. But the question cannot be considered in the abstract. Even one day in prison would be a cruel and unusual punishment for the 'crime' of having a common cold.

Id. at 666-667.

Robinson is generally understood to hold that the Eighth Amendment prohibits so-called "status crimes." But it is also the only case in which the Supreme Court has ever invalidated a statute imposing criminal liability under the Eighth Amendment. As a result, the scope—and the continued validity—of the opinion's holding is in doubt, as the following two cases demonstrate.

Martin v. City of Boise, 920 F.3d 584 (9th Cir. 2019). The plaintiffs-appellants are six current or former residents of the City of Boise, who are homeless or have recently been homeless. Each plaintiff alleges that . . . he or she was cited by Boise police for violating one or both of two city ordinances [that make] it a misdemeanor to use "any of the streets, sidewalks, parks, or public places . . . as a temporary or permanent place of dwelling, lodging, or residence." . . .

The Eighth Amendment states: "Excessive bail shall not be required, nor excessive fines imposed, nor cruel and unusual punishments inflicted." The Cruel and Unusual Punishments Clause "circumscribes the criminal process in three ways." Ingraham v. Wright, 430 U.S. 651, 667 (1977). First, it limits the type of punishment the government may impose; second, it proscribes punishment "grossly disproportionate" to the severity of the crime; and third, it places substantive limits on what the government may criminalize. *Id.* . . . Cases construing substantive limits as to what the government may criminalize are rare, however, and for good reason—the Cruel and Unusual Punishments Clause's third limitation is "one to be applied sparingly." *Id.*

Robinson [is] the seminal case in this branch of Eighth Amendment jurisprudence . . . [but it] did not explain at length the principles underpinning its holding. In *Powell v. Texas*, 392 U.S. 514 (1968), however, the Court elaborated [on this issue when considering] the constitutionality of a Texas law making public drunkenness a criminal offense. Justice Marshall, writing for a plurality of the Court, distinguished the Texas statute from the law at issue in *Robinson* on the ground that the Texas statute made criminal not alcoholism but *conduct*—appearing in public while intoxicated. . . . The

Powell plurality opinion went on to interpret *Robinson* as precluding only the criminalization of "status," not of "involuntary" conduct. . . .

Four Justices dissented from the Court's holding in *Powell*; Justice White concurred in the result alone. Notably, Justice White noted that many chronic alcoholics are also homeless, and that for those individuals, public drunkenness may be unavoidable as a practical matter. ". . . For some of these alcoholics I would think a showing could be made that resisting drunkenness is impossible and that avoiding public places when intoxicated is also impossible. As applied to them this statute is in effect a law which bans a single act for which they may not be convicted under the Eighth Amendment—the act of getting drunk." *Id.* at 551 (White, J., concurring in the judgment). The four dissenting Justices adopted a position consistent with that taken by Justice White . . . . Thus, five Justices gleaned from *Robinson* the principle that "that the Eighth Amendment prohibits the state from punishing an involuntary act or condition if it is the unavoidable consequence of one's status or being." Jones v. City of Los Angeles, 444 F.3d 1118, 1138 (9th Cir. 2006), *vacated*, 505 F.3d 1006 (9th Cir. 2007).

This principle compels the conclusion that the Eighth Amendment prohibits the imposition of criminal penalties for sitting, sleeping, or lying outside on public property for homeless individuals who cannot obtain shelter[, as was true of the individuals in this case, given the limited capacity of Boise's homeless shelters]. "Whether sitting, lying, and sleeping are defined as acts or conditions, they are universal and unavoidable consequences of being human." *Id.* at 1136. Moreover, any "conduct at issue here is involuntary and inseparable from status—they are one and the same, given that human beings are biologically compelled to rest, whether by sitting, lying, or sleeping." *Id.* As a result, just as the state may not criminalize the state of being "homeless in public places," the state may not "criminalize conduct that is an unavoidable consequence of being homeless—namely sitting, lying, or sleeping on the streets." *Id.* at 1137. . . . [A]s long as there is no option of sleeping indoors, the government cannot criminalize indigent, homeless people for sleeping outdoors, on public property, on the false premise they had a choice in the matter. . . .

City of Grants Pass v. Johnson, 144 S. Ct. 2202 (2024). People become homeless for a variety of reasons . . . beyond their control. Some have been affected by economic conditions, rising housing costs, or natural disasters. Some have been forced from their homes to escape domestic violence and other forms of exploitation. And still others struggle with drug addiction and mental illness. . . .

Rather than focus on a single policy to meet the challenges associated with homelessness, many States and cities have pursued a range of policies and programs. Beyond expanding shelter and affordable housing opportunities, some have reinvested in mental-health and substance-abuse treatment programs. Some have trained their employees in outreach tactics designed to improve relations between governments and the homeless they serve. And still others have chosen to pair these efforts with the enforcement of laws that restrict camping in public places, like parks, streets, and sidewalks. . . .

Five years ago, the U. S. Court of Appeals for the Ninth Circuit took one of those tools off the table [i]n *Martin v. Boise*, 920 F.3d 584 (2019). . . . No other circuit has followed *Martin*'s lead with respect to public-camping laws. . . .

[O]ther constitutional provisions address what a government may criminalize and how it may go about securing a conviction, [but] the Eighth Amendment's prohibition against "cruel and unusual punishments" focuses on what happens next . . . . [T]hat would seem to make the Eighth Amendment a poor foundation on which to rest the kind of decree the plaintiffs seek in this case and the Ninth Circuit has endorsed since *Martin*. The Cruel and Unusual Punishments Clause focuses on the question what "method or kind of punishment" a government may impose after a criminal conviction, not on the question whether a government may criminalize particular behavior in the first place or how it may go about securing a conviction for that offense. Powell v. Texas, 392 U.S. 514, 531-532 (1968) (plurality opinion). . . .

Yet, echoing the Ninth Circuit in Martin, [the plaintiffs here] insist one notable exception exists[:] *Robinson v. California*. . . . [In that case,] the Court charted its own course, reading the Cruel and Unusual Punishments Clause to impose a limit . . . unprecedented in the history of the Court before 1962. . . . [Not] in the 62 years since *Robinson*, has this Court once invoked it as authority to decline the enforcement of any criminal law, leaving the Eighth Amendment instead to perform its traditional function of addressing the punishments that follow a criminal conviction.

Still, no one has asked us to reconsider *Robinson*. Nor do we see any need to do so today. Whatever its persuasive force as an interpretation of the Eighth Amendment, it cannot sustain the Ninth Circuit's course since *Martin*. . . . Rather than criminalize mere status, Grants Pass forbids actions like "occupy[ing] a campsite" on public property "for the purpose of maintaining a temporary place to live." Grants Pass Municipal Code §§5.61.030, 5.61.010. Under the city's laws, it makes no difference whether the charged defendant is homeless, a backpacker on vacation passing through town, or a student who abandons his dorm room to camp out in protest on the lawn of a municipal building. In that respect, the city's laws parallel those found in countless jurisdictions across the country. And because laws like these do not criminalize mere status, *Robinson* is not implicated. . . .

[In fact, t]his case is no different from *Powell*. Just as there, the plaintiffs here seek to expand *Robinson*'s "small" intrusion "into the substantive criminal law" [by] extend[ing] its rule beyond laws addressing "mere status" to laws addressing actions that, even if undertaken with the requisite *mens rea*, might "in some sense" qualify as " 'involuntary.' "[6] . . . *Robinson* already sits uneasily with the [Eighth] Amendment's terms, original meaning, and our precedents. . . . [W]e discern nothing in the Eighth Amendment that might provide us with lawful authority to extend *Robinson* beyond its narrow holding.

NOTES AND QUESTIONS

1. Necessity, Reprised. Note the similarity between the penal statutes targeting homelessness in the preceding cases and the statutes at issue in the opinion we read in Chapter Six, *Commonwealth v. Magadini* (p. 462). In one sense, the *Magadini* court's holding is broader even than the *Martin* holding repudiated by the Supreme Court: It permitted Magadini to trespass onto *private* property. In another sense, though, *Magadini* is narrower than *Martin:* it recognized a necessity defense only for homeless individuals who could show that sleeping outdoors would pose a serious risk of hypothermia. The opinions thus have overlapping subject matter but meaningfully different rationales. Necessity doctrine may prevent the state from punishing a homeless person who comes in from the dangerous cold. The opinions above, by contrast, ask whether the Eighth Amendment bars the state from punishing a homeless person for being homeless—or for doing basic human things, like sleeping, outdoors.

2. Robinson's Limits. Following *Grants Pass,* it is clear the Eighth Amendment's substantive prong extends no further than the holding of *Robinson*—and that *Robinson* itself may not last long. It bears noting, though, that in prohibiting states from enacting criminal statutes penalizing pure status, *Robinson* does little more than constitutionalize a longstanding common law rule. As the *Powell* plurality put the point, "The entire thrust of *Robinson*'s interpretation of the Cruel and Unusual Punishment Clause is that criminal penalties may be inflicted only if the accused has committed some act, has engaged in some behavior, which society has an interest in preventing, or perhaps in historical common law terms, has committed some actus reus." 392 U.S. at 533. But as noted in the introduction to Part II of this book (p. 161), that *actus reus* requirement is itself a core requisite of criminal liability. The Eighth Amendment's substantive prong, confined to *Robinson,* thus likely operates only at the very outermost margins

---

6. In *Martin,* the Ninth Circuit suggested Justice White's solo concurrence somehow rendered the *Powell* dissent controlling and the plurality a dissent. [T]he plaintiffs [do not] defend that theory, and for good reason: In the years since *Powell,* this Court has repeatedly relied on Justice Marshall's opinion, as we do today.

of American criminal law, barring states from criminalizing things that are almost never criminalized in the first place.

C. *Constitutionally Protected Activity*

Lawrence v. Texas
_____

539 U.S. 558 (2003)

KENNEDY, J. . . . Liberty presumes an autonomy of self that includes freedom of thought, belief, expression, and certain intimate conduct. The instant case involves liberty of the person both in its spatial and in its more transcendent dimensions. . . .

In Houston, Texas, officers of the Harris County Police Department were dispatched to a private residence in response to a reported weapons disturbance. They entered an apartment [and] observed [petitioner] Lawrence and another man, Tyron Garner, engaging in a sexual act. The two petitioners were arrested, held in custody overnight, and charged and convicted before a Justice of the Peace. The complaints described their crime as "deviate sexual intercourse, namely anal sex, with a member of the same sex (man)." . . . The petitioners were adults at the time of the alleged offense. Their conduct was in private and consensual.

We conclude the case should be resolved by determining whether the petitioners were free as adults to engage in the private conduct in the exercise of their liberty under the Due Process Clause of the Fourteenth Amendment to the Constitution. . . . In *Griswold v. Connecticut*, 381 U.S. 479 (1965), the Court invalidated a state law prohibiting the use of drugs or devices of contraception and counseling or aiding and abetting the use of contraceptives. The Court described the protected interest as a right to privacy and placed emphasis on the marriage relation and the protected space of the marital bedroom. After *Griswold* it was established that the right to make certain decisions regarding sexual conduct extends beyond the marital relationship. In *Eisenstadt v. Baird*, 405 U.S. 438 (1972), the Court invalidated a law prohibiting the distribution of contraceptives to unmarried persons. . . . The opinions in *Griswold* and *Eisenstadt* were part of the background for the decision in *Roe v. Wade*, 410 U.S. 113 (1973). As is well known, the case involved a challenge to the Texas law prohibiting abortions . . . . Although the Court held the woman's rights were not absolute, her right to elect an abortion did have real and substantial protection as an exercise of her liberty under the Due Process Clause. . . . *Roe* [thus] . . . confirmed once more that the protection of liberty under the Due Process Clause has a substantive dimension of fundamental significance in defining the rights of the person. . . .

Bowers v. Hardwick, 478 U.S. 186 (1986), [upheld] a Georgia statute making it a criminal offense to engage in sodomy. . . . The laws involved in *Bowers* and here are, to be sure, statutes that purport to do no more than prohibit a particular sexual act. Their penalties and purposes, though, have more far-reaching consequences, touching upon the most private human conduct, sexual behavior, and in the most private of places, the home. The statutes do seek to control a personal relationship that, whether or not entitled to formal recognition in the law, is within the liberty of persons to choose without being punished as criminals. . . . When sexuality finds overt expression in intimate conduct with another person, the conduct can be but one element in a personal bond that is more enduring. The liberty protected by the Constitution allows homosexual persons the right to make this choice. . . .

It must be acknowledged, of course, that the Court in *Bowers* was making the broader point that for centuries there have been powerful voices to condemn homosexual conduct as immoral. The condemnation has been shaped by religious beliefs, conceptions of right and acceptable behavior, and respect for the traditional family. . . . These considerations do not answer the question before us, however. The issue is whether the majority may use the power of the State to enforce these views on the whole society through operation of the criminal law. . . .

[The] continuance [of *Bowers*] as precedent demeans the lives of homosexual persons . . . . The offense [at issue], to be sure, is but a class C misdemeanor, a minor offense in the Texas legal system. Still, it remains a criminal offense with all that imports for the dignity of the persons charged. . . . We are advised that if Texas convicted an adult for private, consensual homosexual conduct . . . the convicted person would come within the [sex offender] registration laws of at least four States . . . . Furthermore, the Texas criminal conviction carries with it the other collateral consequences always following a conviction, such as notations on job application forms, to mention but one example. . . .

The rationale of *Bowers* does not withstand careful analysis. . . . *Bowers* was not correct when it was decided, and it is not correct today. . . . The petitioners are entitled to respect for their private lives. . . . Their right to liberty under the Due Process Clause gives them the full right to engage in their conduct without intervention of the government. . . .

SCALIA, J., dissenting. . . . [Texas's prohibition of sodomy] undoubtedly imposes constraints on liberty. So do laws prohibiting prostitution [and] recreational use of heroin . . . . But [the] Fourteenth Amendment *expressly allows* States to deprive their citizens of "liberty," *so long as "due process of law" is provided* . . . . Our opinions applying the doctrine known as "substantive due process" . . . have held repeatedly . . . that *only* fundamental rights qualify for . . . "heightened scrutiny" protection—that is, rights which are "'deeply rooted in this Nation's history and tradition.'" Washington v. Glucksberg, 521 U.S. 702, 721 (1997). All other liberty interests may be abridged or abrogated pursuant to a validly enacted state law if that law is rationally related to a legitimate state interest.

. . . Noting that . . . "sodomy was a criminal offense at common law and was forbidden by the laws of the original 13 States when they ratified the Bill of Rights," and that many States had retained their bans on sodomy, *Bowers* concluded that a right to engage in homosexual sodomy was not "'deeply rooted in this Nation's history and tradition.'" The Court today does not overrule this holding. . . . Instead, . . . the Court concludes that the application of Texas's statute to petitioners' conduct fails the rational-basis test [because it] "furthers no legitimate state interest which can justify its intrusion into the personal and private life of the individual." . . . This proposition is so out of accord with our jurisprudence—indeed, with the jurisprudence of *any* society we know—that it requires little discussion. The Texas statute undeniably seeks to further the belief of its citizens that certain forms of sexual behavior are "immoral and unacceptable"—the same interest furthered by criminal laws against fornication, bigamy, adultery, adult incest, bestiality, and obscenity. *Bowers* held that this *was* a legitimate state interest. The Court today reaches the opposite conclusion. . . . This effectively decrees the end of all morals legislation. If, as the Court asserts, the promotion of majoritarian sexual morality is not even a *legitimate* state interest, none of the above-mentioned laws can survive rational-basis review. . . .

Let me be clear that I have nothing against homosexuals, or any other group, promoting their agenda through normal democratic means. Social perceptions of sexual and other morality change over time, and every group has the right to persuade its fellow citizens that its view of such matters is the best. That homosexuals have achieved some success in that enterprise is attested to by the fact that Texas is one of the few remaining States that criminalize private, consensual homosexual acts. But persuading one's fellow citizens is one thing, and imposing one's views in absence of democratic majority will is something else. . . . What Texas has chosen to do is well within the range of traditional democratic action, and its hand should not be stayed through the invention of a brand-new "constitutional right" by a Court that is impatient of democratic change. . . .

[Additional opinions omitted.]

Dobbs v. Jackson Women's Health Org., 597 U.S. 215 (2022). Abortion presents a profound moral issue on which Americans hold sharply conflicting views. Some believe fervently that a human person comes into being at conception and that abortion ends an innocent life. Others feel just as strongly that any regulation of abortion invades a woman's right to control her own body and prevents women from achieving full equality. Still others in a third group think that abortion should be allowed under some but not all circumstances, and those within this group hold a variety of views about the particular restrictions that should be imposed.

For the first 185 years after the adoption of the Constitution, each State was permitted to address this issue in accordance with the views of its citizens. Then, in 1973, this Court decided *Roe v. Wade*, 410 U.S. 113. Even though the Constitution makes no mention of abortion, the Court held that it confers a broad right to obtain one. . . . At the time of *Roe*, 30 States still prohibited abortion at all stages. In the years prior to that decision, about a third of the States had liberalized their laws, but *Roe* abruptly ended that political process. . . . [Yet] Americans continue to hold passionate and widely divergent views on abortion, and state legislatures have acted accordingly. Some have recently enacted laws allowing abortion, with few restrictions, at all stages of pregnancy. . . . And in this case, 26 States have expressly asked this Court to overrule *Roe* . . . and allow the States to regulate or prohibit pre-viability abortions.

. . . We hold that *Roe* and [the cases reaffirming it] must be overruled. The Constitution makes no reference to abortion, and no such right is implicitly protected by any constitutional provision, including the . . . Due Process Clause of the Fourteenth Amendment. That provision has been held to guarantee some rights that are not mentioned in the Constitution, but any such right must be "deeply rooted in this Nation's history and tradition" and "implicit in the concept of ordered liberty." Washington v. Glucksberg, 521 U.S. 702, 721 (1997). The right to abortion does not fall within this category. . . . Indeed, when the Fourteenth Amendment was adopted, three quarters of the States made abortion a crime at all stages of pregnancy. . . . It is time to heed the Constitution and return the issue of abortion to the people's elected representatives. "The permissibility of abortion, and the limitations, upon it, are to be resolved like most important questions in our democracy: by citizens trying to persuade one another and then voting." Planned Parenthood of Southeastern Pa. v. Casey, 505 U.S. 833, 979 (1992) (Scalia, J., concurring in judgment in part and dissenting in part).

BREYER, SOTOMAYOR and KAGAN, JJ., dissenting. For half a century, *Roe v. Wade*, 410 U.S. 113 (1973), and *Planned Parenthood of Southeastern Pa. v. Casey*, 505 U.S. 833 (1992), have protected the liberty and equality of women. *Roe* held, and *Casey* reaffirmed, that the Constitution safeguards a woman's right to decide for herself whether to bear a child. . . . [T]he government could not make that choice for women. . . .

Roe and *Casey* well understood the difficulty and divisiveness of the abortion issue. The Court knew that Americans hold profoundly different views about the "moral[ity]" of "terminating a pregnancy, even in its earliest stage." *Casey*, 505 U.S. at 850. . . . So the Court struck a balance, as it often does when values and goals compete. . . . Today, the Court discards that balance. . . . A State can [now] impose criminal penalties on abortion providers, including lengthy prison sentences. But some States will not stop there. Perhaps, in the wake of today's decision, a state law will criminalize the woman's conduct too, incarcerating or fining her for daring to seek or obtain an abortion. . . .

Neither law nor facts nor attitudes have provided any new reasons to reach a different result than *Roe* and *Casey* did. All that has changed is this Court. [A] new and bare majority of this Court—acting at practically the first moment possible—overrules *Roe* and *Casey*. It converts a series of dissenting opinions expressing antipathy toward *Roe* and *Casey* into a decision greenlighting even total abortion bans. . . . In doing all of that, it places in jeopardy other rights, from contraception to same-sex intimacy and marriage. And finally, it undermines the Court's legitimacy.

NOTES AND QUESTIONS

1. Substantive Due Process. The doctrine of substantive due process is one of the most hotly debated areas of modern constitutional jurisprudence. You will undoubtedly spend considerable time studying and discussing the Supreme Court's opinions in this area in your constitutional law class. For present purposes, two essential points are worth noting.

First, *Lawrence v. Texas* is a criminal appeal. In this respect, it is identical in posture to virtually every case you have read in this book. Government officials, invoking a state's penal code, prosecuted individuals for criminally proscribed conduct and obtained convictions. The defendants appealed, arguing to an appellate tribunal that their convictions were unlawful and should not stand. The only difference is that, rather than argue that the convictions were unauthorized by or inconsistent with the state's substantive criminal law, the defendants in *Lawrence* argued that the state's criminal law itself was unlawful—because it violated the federal Constitution. The Supreme Court agreed and invalidated the convictions, and in so doing barred enforcement of the criminal law upon which the convictions were based.

Lawrence is hardly unique in this respect. In fact, each case in the trio of substantive due process opinions it describes—*Griswold v. Connecticut, Eisenstadt v. Baird,* and *Roe v. Wade*—invalidated a criminal statute. Likewise, in the famous case *Loving v. Virginia,* 388 U.S. 1 (1967), the Supreme Court blocked enforcement of a criminal prohibition on interracial marriage on substantive due process grounds (as well as equal protection grounds). Courts, in other words, can and do use the Due Process Clause as a direct check on legislative power to enact criminal laws—on the theory, to borrow from Professor Douglas Husak's criticism of overcriminalization more broadly, that the challenged statutes proscribe "conduct that should not have been criminalized at all."[64]

Second, and relatedly, invocations of substantive due process are controversial in part because they empower judges to strike down laws, including criminal laws, that have been democratically enacted. The doctrine, in other words, is a central exhibit in what Professor Alexander Bickel famously called the counter-majoritarian difficulty. The difficulty arises from a tension inherent in the idea of constitutional democracy itself. In such a system, legislators typically have the authority to enact laws, including criminal laws, that further the community's goals, desires, and morals, so long as those laws do not infringe on fundamental individual rights and freedoms. The courts, in turn, often define and safeguard those rights and freedoms. But the rights are not always clearly defined, as they often arise from what Professor John Hart Ely called the Constitution's "open textured" phrases — phrases like "due process." For this reason, substantive due process challenges inevitably raise a hard and important question of institutional power. Who should decide whether certain conduct can be criminalized — legislatures or courts? As the dueling opinions in *Lawrence* and *Dobbs* reflect, that question does not have a stable answer, even in a judiciary guided by principles of *stare decisis*.[65]

2. State Constitutional Law. State courts have, in recent decades, been somewhat more aggressive than their federal counterparts in invalidating criminal laws on constitutional grounds, including under due process provisions in state constitutions. The Supreme Court of Illinois, for example, has on multiple occasions struck down laws that do not, in the court's view, embody "a reasonable method of preventing the targeted conduct" or that subject "wholly innocent conduct to criminal penalty." People v. Madrigal, 948 N.E.2d 591, 594 (Ill. 2011). In *Madrigal*, the Illinois court overturned a conviction under an identity theft statute so broad as to "criminalize such innocuous conduct as someone using the internet to look up how their neighbor did in the Chicago Marathon." *Id.* at 596. According to a leading treatise, state courts are also "more likely to pass judgment on the legislative conclusion that an evil exists which calls for criminal legislation" and "more willing to pass upon the wisdom of the legislature's response to an acknowledged evil by taking account of other, less restrictive means by which the public interest might be protected."[66]

3. Other Domains of Constitutionally Protected Activity. Beyond the Due Process Clause, multiple other provisions of the federal Constitution can be, and have been, invoked to nullify the application of criminal laws. Perhaps the most robust source of such protection lies in the First Amendment's Free Speech Clause. As far back as the Alien and Sedition Acts of 1798, statutes criminalizing certain modes of speech or communicative actions have been challenged on free speech grounds. And the modern Supreme Court's speech jurisprudence is replete with examples of penal statutes the Court has deemed unenforceable, including bans on "offensive conduct," advocating violence, hate speech, labor picketing, pornography, and flag burning. Of course, as you by this point know well, it is also true that much of substantive criminal law pertains to conduct that technically consists of speech acts. An agreement to form a conspiracy is a form of speech. So too are words encouraging others to commit crimes. This "speech integral to criminal conduct" does not fall within the First Amendment's otherwise potentially robust protection against laws criminalizing expression. *See* United States v. Alvarez, 567 U.S. 709, 717 (2012). Neither do threats of violence or words instigating an assault, which have been broadly criminalized for centuries. *See id.*[67]

In addition to the First Amendment's Free Speech Clause, courts in recent years have begun to develop a body of constitutional law under the Second Amendment, which the Supreme Court held in 2008 provides an individual right to bear arms. *See* District of Columbia v. Heller, 554 U.S. 570 (2008). That right is not absolute, and courts continue to develop its contours. But as the discussion in Chapter Eight shows (p. 709), one of the most frequent targets of Second Amendment litigation is statutes criminalizing the possession of firearms and other weapons—provisions that may fall under Second Amendment scrutiny.

These two bodies of law are among the most common constitutional doctrines invoked to challenge laws carrying criminal sanctions. But in principle, any provision of the Bill of Rights, or of the Constitution more generally, could be invoked to strike down laws—including criminal laws—that contravene the Constitution's parameters. Thus, courts have invalidated criminal laws based on the First Amendment's Free Exercise Clause, Church of the Lukumi Babalu Aye, Inc. v. City of Hialeah, 508 U.S. 520 (1993); the Fourth Amendment's protection against unreasonable searches, Camara v. Municipal Court, 387 U.S. 523 (1967); the Fifth Amendment's Self-Incrimination Clause, Marchetti v. United States, 390 U.S. 39 (1968); the Fourteenth Amendment's Equal Protection Clause, Loving v. Virginia, 388 U.S. 1 (1967); and the Commerce Clause, Hughes v. Oklahoma, 441 U.S. 322 (1979).

D.   *The Constitution of Order Maintenance Policing*

The preceding sections describe three ways constitutional law might constrain criminal law. For scholars concerned about overcriminalization, these doctrines suggest a potential pathway to decriminalization. But only if the doctrines are interpreted and applied robustly. "For judges to displace [criminal] legislation," Professor Stuntz writes, "they must have some constitutional warrant," which means that broadscale judicially driven decriminalization requires robust "constitutional power over criminal law." That state of affairs, Stuntz concedes, is unlikely. "Never in our history has constitutional law taken so dramatic a step."[68]

Consider, as a final pass on the constitutional law of overcriminalization, the following newspaper article and the short opinion that follows, written by the future Chief Justice of the United States.

Martine Powers, *Metro Transit Police Arrest Teenager for Carrying Chips and Lollipop into Station,* Wash. Post (Oct. 19, 2016). Metro Transit Police are being criticized for excessive use of force after a video posted Tuesday showed an officer pushing and tripping a high school student, knocking her to the ground, after she refused to throw away a bag of potato chips and a lollipop. The three-minute video, posted by a member of the District's Black Lives Matter chapter, shows the 18-year-old in handcuffs, surrounded by three police officers, just outside the fare gates at Columbia Heights station.

"All right, sit down," one officer says. "Sit down." The handcuffed teen refuses, crying, "No!" The officer then hooks his arm behind her elbow and kicks backward against her calf, knocking her to the ground as people watching and filming the altercation gasp. The teen props herself up against the wall, and the officer pushes on her shoulder and forces her back down. "Sit down!" he yells. "Stop touching me!" she yells back.

. . . The person who posted the footage on YouTube said in the video description that the girl is 17, not 18, and a student at Bell Multicultural High School. The description also said that an officer "slammed her against the car" when she was transported to the police station. On Twitter, the Black Lives Matter chapter criticized the arrest, saying the footage shows transit police "violently interacting with Black bodies as usual."

According to the arrest report, the incident happened just after 6:30 p.m. Tuesday. Police said the teenager was on the paid side of the fare gates, holding a bag of potato chips, and an officer told her to put the food away. Metro bans customers from eating or drinking on trains and in stations.

The police report said the teenager "responded with a defiant 'No!'" Police then told her twice that she would need to leave the station if she didn't put her food way. When she refused, the arrest report said, the officer reached for her wrist and placed handcuffs on her. . . . One officer then opens her backpack and begins searching inside.

"You didn't have to put it that tight," she says, apparently talking about the handcuffs. She then demands to know why officers are searching her bag and asks a friend to remove it. The yellow bag of potato chips sits in the foreground of the shot until an officer slides it away with his foot.

A crowd is gathered around the fare gates . . . . The officer who knocked the teenager to the floor starts to shoo away the growing crowds, instructing bystanders to get on a train or leave the station. "Thanks for riding Metro," he says. "You guys have a good day."

In the video, a bystander explains to others in the crowd that the teenager had been holding a bag of chips and a lollipop. "Oh, goodness. Because she had a lollipop? That is outrageous," says one woman watching the officers search the student's backpack. "That is ridiculous." Some of the bystanders began speaking directly to the officers. "You could have told her to put it away, or [taken] the lollipop. . . that is crazy," one says.

An officer turns to the crowd, arguing back. "Well, we asked her for the lollipop, we asked her for the food, and she refused and told me she wasn't going to do it," the officer says. "That's why she's under arrest."

"It's a little girl!" says the bystander. "Little girls can break the law! Little girls can get arrested like everybody else!" the officer responds. "And she goes to juvenile detention and her mom comes and picks her up. That's how it works!"

It's not the first time Metro Transit Police have come under fire for their handling of snack scofflaws. In 2004, a 45-year-old employee of the Environmental Protection Agency was arrested at Metro Center for chewing on the last bite of a PayDay candy bar as she passed through the fare gates. She was released several hours later after paying a $10 fine. And in 2000, a 12-year-old girl made international headlines when she was arrested for eating a french fry at the Tenleytown-AU station. If she had been an adult, police would have issued her a citation and fine, but because they cannot fine minors, they charged her with a criminal offense and took her into custody. Her case was ultimately brought before the U.S. Court of Appeals.

Hedgepeth v. WMATA, 386 F.3d 1148 (D.C. Cir. 2004) (Roberts, J.). No one is very happy about the events that led to this litigation. A twelve-year-old girl was arrested, searched, and handcuffed. Her shoelaces were removed, and she was transported in the windowless rear compartment of a police vehicle to a juvenile processing center, where she was booked, fingerprinted, and detained until released to her mother some three hours later—all for eating a single french fry in a Metrorail station. The child was frightened, embarrassed, and crying throughout the ordeal. The district court described the policies that led to her arrest as "foolish" . . . . The question before us, however, is not whether these policies were a bad idea, but whether they violated the . . . Constitution. Like the district court, we conclude that they did not, and accordingly we affirm.

It was the start of another school year and the Washington Metropolitan Area Transit Authority (WMATA) was once again getting complaints about bad behavior by students using the Tenleytown/American University Metrorail station. In response WMATA embarked on a week-long undercover operation to enforce a "zero-tolerance" policy with respect to violations of certain ordinances, including one that makes it unlawful for any person to eat or drink in a Metrorail station. . . . Committing an offense under District of Columbia law, such as eating in a Metrorail station, constitutes a "delinquent act." D.C. Code §16-2301(7). The upshot of all this is that zero-tolerance enforcement . . . entailed the arrest of every offending minor . . . .

[One of those minors, twelve-year-old Ansche Hedgepeth, through her mother, filed this lawsuit against WMATA alleging that the zero-tolerance policy violated the Due Process Clause of the Fifth Amendment and the Fourth Amendment.]

[With respect to the former claim, t]he law of this land does not recognize a fundamental right to freedom of movement when there is probable cause for arrest. That is true even with respect to minor offenses. Atwater v. City of Lago Vista, 532 U.S. 318, 354 (2001). . . . Ansche has made no effort to establish that there is a fundamental right, "deeply rooted in this Nation's history and tradition," Washington v. Glucksberg, 521 U.S. 702, 720-721 (1997), to free movement when there is probable cause for arrest. . . . The district court had and we too may have thoughts on the wisdom of this policy choice . . . but it is not our place to second-guess such legislative judgments.

Ansche [separately] challenges her arrest on the ground that it was an unreasonable seizure in violation of the Fourth Amendment. This claim quickly runs into the Supreme Court's recent holding in *Atwater*. . . . While we can inquire into the reasonableness of the manner in which an arrest is conducted, the most natural reading of *Atwater* is that we cannot inquire further into the reasonableness of a decision to arrest when it is supported by probable cause. That is true whether the decision to arrest upon probable cause is made by the officer on the beat or at a more removed policy level. . . . Given the undisputed existence of probable cause, *Atwater* precludes further inquiry into the reasonableness of Ansche's arrest under the Fourth Amendment.[69]

Questions: Then-Judge John Roberts, writing for the D.C. Circuit Court of Appeals in *Hedgepeth,* holds that arresting a twelve-year-old child for eating a french fry on the subway does not violate the Fourth Amendment's bar on unreasonable searches and seizures, given *Atwater.* Likewise, whereas the *Papachristou* Court observed that "[p]ersons 'wandering or strolling' from place to place have been extolled by Walt Whitman and Vachel Lindsay" and partake "of the amenities of life as we have known them," the *Hedgepeth* court holds that the Constitution "does not recognize a fundamental right to freedom of movement when there is probable cause for arrest." *Hedgepeth,* in other words, seems to demonstrate why neither the Fourth Amendment nor the Due Process Clause will block enforcement of statutes like the one at issue here, which can be taken as stand-ins for scores of other statutes driving overcriminalization. Would a vagueness challenge have fared any better? A substantive Eighth Amendment claim? An equal protection claim?

More fundamentally, just how robust would those doctrines need to be to meaningfully curb overcriminalization and the expansive police power it produces? For a closing thought on that question, consider the following speech delivered by Professor Rachel Harmon, a leading scholar of policing, to the Institute for Humane Studies.

Rachel Harmon, *More Law, More Power? Rethinking the Impact of Criminal Laws on Policing*, Keynote Address, Fairfax, Virginia (July 30, 2021). Despite disagreements about the details, commentators largely agree about the state of criminal law: there are just too many crimes, and there are too many human activities that shouldn't be crimes but are. This is what we call overcriminalization. . . . State and city codes are filled with minor offenses that criminalize all sorts of public behavior that were once civil offenses, if they were offenses at all. Today, these activities can land you in jail, at least briefly, at the discretion of a police officer. And, indeed, people are regularly stopped, ticketed, and arrested for lying down in public, spitting on sidewalks, jaywalking, missing too many days of school, and panhandling. When you look at what the police actually do, these crimes are important. . . . In 2019, for example, police arrested as many people in this country just for drunkenness and liquor law violations as they did for all violent crimes combined.

So, what about these offenses? Is it reasonable to think, as some commentators suggest, that eliminating many of these crimes would reduce police power and the intrusions on liberty, privacy, and bodily integrity that result from it? I don't think so. . . . [I]n the end, so long as people are calling the police, the police are going to try to do something. And it just doesn't take very many crimes on the books for the police to be off and running. Right now, police are writing tickets and kicking people out of the park for littering, noise violations, and staying in the park after it closes. If we decriminalize those activities, the police will stop and arrest more people for drug possession, prostitution, theft, and assault. And when those crimes have not been committed, they will look to laws against disorderly conduct, being drunk in public, loitering, indecent exposure, and so on.

We can try to attack police power by peeling back the layers of criminalization police use to manage the streets. But I think that we will find that there are a lot of layers, and some of them have been around for centuries. That suggests that expansive police power is not so much a result of recent overcriminalization, and it is not going to be easy to reverse. . . . That is why famed criminologist Egon Bittner was able to say more than 50 years ago that "any policeman worth his salt is virtually always in a position to find a bona fide charge of some kind when he believes the situation calls for an arrest." That was after the Supreme Court had declared unconstitutional vagrancy statutes that had previously functioned as power tools for police officers.

In most circumstances, then and today, we can get rid of one crime or many. But police will still usually have substitute crimes available to them. That is why police could legally harass and arrest immigrants gathered in labor demonstrations in the 1890s, black men trying to work in the 1930s, hippies on the streets in the 1960s, squeegee men in New York in the 1980s, and people protesting police violence today. If officers could not have arrested Eric Garner for selling loose cigarettes, as Stephen Carter wishes, local business would still have called the police complaining about him. And the police would still have tried arresting him, but for loitering or obstructing the sidewalk, instead. . . . Strike some crimes from the code, and other crimes will still give the police enough power.[70]

III. PLEA BARGAINING

> "[C]riminal law and the law of sentencing define prosecutors' options, not litigation outcomes. . . . They are [like] items on a menu from which the prosecutor may order as she wishes. . . . The menu does not define the meal; the diner does."
>
> William J. Stuntz, *Plea Bargaining and Criminal Law's Disappearing Shadow*, 117 Harv. L. Rev. 2548, 2549 (2004)

Overcriminalization does not increase just criminal law's breadth. It also increases its depth: as codes expand to include multiple, overlapping crimes, a given criminal event will often implicate multiple criminal statutes at once. As Professor Rachel Harmon observes, when it comes to policing, this aspect of overcriminalization is not especially relevant. While "police power rises dramatically with the first low-level criminal statutes . . . the curve starts flattening out" after that, "because additional crimes only increase the scope of police authority a nominal amount." After all, Harmon explains, "one crime is enough for the police to stop, ticket, or arrest" someone on the street, so adding extra crimes doesn't matter all that much.[71]

For prosecutors the story is quite different. Here, Harmon notes, overlapping criminal provisions "enable prosecutors to manipulate charging decisions to get the outcomes they want." Overcriminalization, in other words, in both its breadth and its depth, increases *prosecutorial power*—in system-defining and potentially troubling ways. Indeed, the magnitude of prosecutorial power is one of the attributes of the American criminal system scholars have most widely and consistently critiqued. Surveying that literature, Professor David Sklansky writes:

The starting point for virtually every discussion of prosecutors in the United States is their tremendous clout. "The American prosecutor rules the criminal justice system," exercising "almost limitless discretion" and "virtually absolute power." The concentration of power in the hands of prosecutors has been called the "overriding evil" of American criminal justice — which is saying something, given the range and magnitude of the system's problems. Nor is this a new concern. Since at least the early twentieth century, "[t]he immense authority of the public prosecutor over criminal justice has been a universally recognized feature of American criminal prosecution." [Supreme Court Justice and former Attorney General] Robert Jackson took it as obvious in 1940 that "[t]he prosecutor has more control over life, liberty, and reputation than any other person in America." Since then, prosecutors in the United States are widely thought to have grown significantly more powerful . . . .[72]

Prosecutorial power stems from multiple sources. But among criminal law scholars, one mechanism stands out above the rest: *plea bargaining*. As Professor Rachel Barkow argues, "prosecutors control the terms of confinement in this vast penal system because they have the authority to make charging decisions, enter cooperation agreements, accept pleas, and recommend sentences." In a system "dominated by pleas instead of trials," she continues, prosecutors are "not merely law enforcers. They are the final adjudicators in the vast majority of cases."[73]

To Barkow and others, this expansive and largely unchecked power is troubling in its own right, offending principles of separation of powers and due process. But to many critics, prosecutorial power is equally if not more troubling for the world it has helped to create. According to Professor John Pfaff's empirical analysis, "prosecutorial toughness" in charging and plea bargaining has been a "primary driver of incarceration." As a result, Professor Andrew Manuel Crespo argues, "[p]lea bargaining lies at the root of American mass incarceration."

The reason is simple: the system is massively over-leveraged. It is the largest system of human incarceration in the history of the world. But it purchased its scale on the cheap, at plea bargaining rates. The system, in other words, is both an outgrowth of and *dependent upon* plea bargaining for its existence. . . .

To appreciate why this is so, one has to fully absorb the resource constraints shaping the behavior of the system's key administrators: the prosecutors and judges whose legal decisions transform free people into prisoners. In courthouses across the country, [individual] prosecutors routinely handle over one thousand felony cases each year. This translates to hundreds of open cases at any given time and multiple cases scheduled for trial *every day*. . . . No prosecutor can try multiple cases in different courtrooms at once, let alone prepare hundreds of cases for trial at the same time. It is thus impossible for the system to do what the Sixth Amendment and countless television dramas suggest should be or is the

norm: provide people charged with crimes "the right to a speedy and public trial" in "all criminal prosecutions."

    . . . Plea bargaining is how the system bridges that resource chasm.
As Bill Stuntz once explained, it is the mechanism by which the state converts millions of "potential trials into guilty pleas," which "are not simply
cheaper than trials" but "enormously cheaper." And with roughly 95 percent of all convictions arising from guilty pleas, the alchemy works. To
quote [Professor Albert] Alschuler . . . , "By lowering the price of imposing criminal punishment, plea bargaining gave America more of it."
A lot more.

The American penal system, in short, truly is as the Supreme Court describes
it: "a system of pleas." Lafler v. Cooper, 566 U.S. 156, 170 (2012).[74]

    To be sure, that system is not without defenders. Courts and schol-
ars have long argued that plea bargaining is an efficiency- and welfare-
maximizing tool that benefits prosecutors and criminal defendants alike.
Professor and Judge Frank Easterbrook captures the point well when he
writes that principles of "[a]utonomy and efficiency support" plea bargaining in much the same way they support settlement in civil cases. "Settlements
of civil cases make both sides better off; settlements of criminal cases do
too." The Supreme Court, for its part, largely agrees.

> For a defendant who sees slight possibility of acquittal, the advantages of
> pleading guilty and limiting the probable penalty are obvious — his expo-
> sure is reduced, the correctional processes can begin immediately, and
> the practical burdens of a trial are eliminated. For the State there are also
> advantages — the more promptly imposed punishment after an admission
> of guilt may more effectively attain the objectives of punishment; and
> with the avoidance of trial, scarce judicial and prosecutorial resources
> are conserved for those cases in which there is a substantial issue of the
> defendant's guilt or in which there is substantial doubt that the State can
> sustain its burden of proof. It is this mutuality of advantage that perhaps
> explains the fact that [so many] criminal convictions in this country rest
> on pleas of guilty . . . .

Brady v. United States, 397 U.S. 742, 752 (1970).[75]

    To critics, however, efforts to analogize plea bargaining to civil nego-
tiations miss a fundamental difference. As Professor and Judge Gerard
Lynch argues, plea bargaining doesn't really track an "exchange of values
based on relative bargaining strength" because the prosecutor has "virtually
unilateral power to inflict pain on the defendant." According to Professor
Tracey Meares, that power means the prosecutor has the "ability to control
the dynamics of plea bargaining" and thus "to control, essentially unilaterally, the defendant's ability to plead guilty in most cases." For Professor
Máximo Langer, the prospect that such control can become coercive makes
all the difference. If "the prosecutor unilaterally decides who is innocent and guilty, and for which offense, by using coercive plea proposals,"

Langer writes, the "coercive proposals make the defendant's guilty plea involuntary."[76]

For all of these reasons, legal historian John Langbein argued in a classic article, the proper analogy for plea bargaining is not civil settlement. Instead, he says, we should think of plea bargaining as "torture."

> In twentieth-century America we have duplicated the central experience of medieval European criminal procedure . . . . We coerce the accused against whom we find probable cause to confess his guilt. To be sure, our means are much politer; we use no rack, no thumbscrew, no Spanish boot to mash his legs. But like the Europeans of distant centuries who did employ those machines, we make it terribly costly for an accused to claim his right to the constitutional safeguard of trial. . . .
>
> There is, of course, a difference between having your limbs crushed if you refuse to confess, or suffering some extra years of imprisonment if you refuse to confess, but the difference is of degree, not kind. . . . One can test this point simply by imagining a differential so great (*e.g.*, death versus a fifty-cent fine) that any reasonable defendant would waive even the strongest defenses. Like torture, the sentencing differential in plea bargaining elicits confessions of guilt that would not be freely tendered. It is, therefore, coercive in the same sense as torture, although not in the same degree.

As Langbein's essay makes clear, one way to understand the difference between the competing sides in this debate is to focus on the size of the differential between the punishment a prosecutor threatens if the defendant goes to trial and the punishment she agrees to substitute in exchange for a guilty plea—what is often called the "trial penalty." "This sentencing differential," Langbein argues, "is what makes plea bargaining coercive," at least in cases where it is especially large.[77]

One key question thus concerns the relationship between that differential and the law. The remainder of this part explores that relationship and the role that both substantive criminal law and constitutional law play in building and defining prosecutors' plea bargaining power. We begin with an examination of how criminal and constitutional law together facilitate prosecutors' plea bargaining power. We then proceed to study a trio of constitutional provisions—the Eighth Amendment, the Due Process Clause, and the Equal Protection Clause—that might constrain prosecutorial power in this arena, and consider the Supreme Court precedents that have largely eliminated those constraints.

A. *Plea Bargaining's Mechanics and Power Dynamics*

The two excerpts below, from a pair of plea bargaining scholars, lay a conceptual foundation for this section's discussion of plea bargaining's mechanics and power dynamics. The cases and notes that follow explore how legal doctrines facilitate prosecutors' ability to build up the pile of charges and sentences criminal defendants face, as well as their power to trade that pile away in exchange for pleas of guilt.

William J. Stuntz, *The Pathological Politics of Criminal Law*, 100 Mich. L. Rev. 505, 535-537 (2001). Like most of us, line prosecutors are likely to seek to make their jobs easier, to reduce or limit their workload where possible. . . . The best way to do that is to convert potential trials into guilty pleas. . . . [L]egislatures can push toward greater efficiency by expanding criminal law, thereby making it easier for prosecutors to obtain guilty pleas. If crimes are defined in ways that make guilt hard to prove, the threat of trial will be less serious to many defendants, and the inducements to plead will be accordingly less substantial. If, on the other hand, crimes are defined so as to make conviction easy, the threat value of trial is increased. And if prosecutors are able to threaten defendants who take their cases to trial with a range of overlapping charges that produce a severe sentence, the ability to induce a plea is magnified still more. Legislators can help prosecutors pursue guilty pleas, then, both by creating new crimes and by creating overlapping crimes that allow for charge-stacking.

Andrew Manuel Crespo, *The Hidden Law of Plea Bargaining*, 118 Colum. L. Rev. 1303, 1310-1315 (2018). The ability to control a defendant's sentencing exposure by manipulating the charges against him—that is to say, the ability to charge bargain—is widely recognized by scholars as "the core of prosecutorial power in the United States." The practice itself is simple enough to describe: A criminal defendant's sentencing exposure is a function of his likelihood of conviction and his likely sentence if convicted. Those two factors, in turn, are heavily influenced by the charges he faces, which define the possible grounds for conviction, the maximum potential sentence, and frequently the minimum sentence as well. A charge bargain is thus simply an agreement to replace a higher charge with a lower one in exchange for the defendant's promise to plead guilty, which guarantees the prosecutor a conviction without the expense of trial.

   Yet while such an exchange may sound like an actual bargain, with each party gaining, to quote the Supreme Court, a "mutuality of advantage" from the deal, most knowledgeable observers describe it as something else: a fundamentally coercive practice (occasionally analogized to torture) that produces involuntary pleas, sometimes to crimes the defendant did not commit. The core problem is twofold. First, while defendants always want to minimize their potential sentences, prosecutors rarely want to maximize them, hoping instead to obtain only their *preferred* sentence, in the most efficient way possible. This asymmetry allows prosecutors to trade away "extra" years of incarceration that the defendant desperately wants to avoid but that the prosecutor doesn't particularly value.

As for the second problem: This free leverage is typically overwhelming, because most criminal codes authorize sentences much higher than what a typical prosecutor — or a typical person, for that matter — would actually want to see imposed in a given case. Thus, by threatening a seriously inflated set of charges and then offering to replace it with the charges that she truly desires, the prosecutor is able to control the defendant's incentive to plead guilty, and with it the outcome of any subsequent "negotiation." In the aggregate, prosecutors so empowered can obtain more convictions, with longer sentences, at lower costs . . . .

In practice, charge manipulation involves three interrelated moves. First, the prosecutor can inflate the quantity of charges the defendant faces, by *piling on* overlapping, largely duplicative offenses — increasing with each new charge the defendant's potential sentence, his risk of conviction, and the "sticker shock" of intimidation that accompanies a hefty charging instrument. Second, the prosecutor can achieve similar effects by inflating the substance of the charges themselves, *overreaching* beyond what the law, the evidence, or the equities of the case support. Finally, after deploying these tactics to "jack up the threat value of trial," the prosecutor can capitalize on the ensuing leverage by *sliding down* from her initial threat to the lower set of charges that she actually prefers. Indeed, it is the difference between the threat and the subsequent offer that constitutes the prosecutor's power: The larger the differential, the more likely the defendant is to plead guilty — whether he is in fact guilty or not.

To make these three moves more concrete, consider a straightforward example[:] . . . Imagine a defendant suspected of approaching someone on a street corner at night, of pointing a gun at that person, of ordering them to move a few steps to the left (out from under a streetlamp), and, finally, of taking their wallet and running off with it. To any lay observer, the crime alleged here is straightforward: armed robbery. And yet, in practice, a prosecutor could and routinely would commence a prosecution against such a defendant by *piling on* a host of additional charges, including (to list just some examples) aggravated assault, theft, threats, possession of a weapon, and using a firearm during a crime of violence. Moreover, given the defendant's alleged command to move out from under the streetlamp, the prosecutor might also *overreach*, tacking on the far more serious but questionably applicable charge of kidnapping for good measure. Finally, bringing her leverage to bear, the prosecutor would then offer to *slide down* from these inflated charges to the charge that she — and she alone — deems appropriate, based on her personal assessment of the evidence and of the defendant's culpability: Plead guilty to a single count of armed robbery, she tells the defendant — or, even more enticingly, to misdemeanor counts of theft and possession of a weapon — and everything else will go away.

As plea bargaining scholars consistently recognize, prosecutorial charging discretion exercised in this fashion "translates into power in the plea bargaining context." . . . The true scope of prosecutors' charge-bargaining power, however, [turns] on a broader set of procedural questions: With respect to piling on, *how many charges* can a prosecutor threaten and *how much* will each additional charge increase the defendant's sentencing exposure? With respect to overreaching, *what standards* must be satisfied before substantively inflated charges can proceed beyond the filing stage, and *how will those standards be enforced?* With respect to sliding down, *what restrictions, if any,* will be placed on the prosecutor's ability to replace one set of charges with another?

Missouri v. Hunter

459 U.S. 359 (1983)

BURGER, C.J. . . . On the evening of November 24, 1978, respondent and two accomplices entered an A&P supermarket in Kansas City, Missouri. Respondent entered the store manager's office and ordered the manager, at gun point, to open two safes. While the manager was complying with the demands of the robbers, respondent struck him twice with the butt of his revolver. . . . Respondent and his accomplices were apprehended . . . and . . . convicted of robbery in the first degree, armed criminal action and assault with malice.

Missouri's statute proscribing . . . armed criminal action . . . provides in pertinent part:

> Any person who commits any felony under the laws of this state by, with, or through the use, assistance, or aid of a dangerous or deadly weapon is also guilty of the crime of armed criminal action and, upon conviction, shall be punished by imprisonment by the division of corrections for a term of not less than three years. The punishment imposed pursuant to this subsection shall be in addition to any punishment provided by law for the crime committed by, with, or through the use, assistance, or aid of a dangerous or deadly weapon. . . .

[R]espondent was sentenced to concurrent terms of (a) ten years' imprisonment for the robbery; (b) 15 years for armed criminal action [predicated on the robbery]; and (c) to a consecutive term of five years' imprisonment for assault, for a total of 20 years.

On appeal to the Missouri Court of Appeals, respondent claimed that his sentence for both robbery in the first degree and armed criminal action violated the Double Jeopardy Clause of the Fifth Amendment . . . . The Missouri Court of Appeals agreed and reversed respondent's conviction and 15-year sentence for armed criminal action. The Court of Appeals relied entirely upon the [prior] holding of the Missouri Supreme Court . . . that under the test announced in *Blockburger v. United States*, 284 U.S. 299

(1932), armed criminal action and any underlying offense are the "same offense" under the Fifth Amendment's Double Jeopardy Clause. [The opinion in *Blockburger* stated: "The applicable rule is that where the same act or transaction constitutes a violation of two distinct statutory provisions, the test to be applied to determine whether there are two offenses or only one, is whether each provision requires proof of a fact which the other does not." 284 U.S. at 304. . . . Here, the Missouri court had concluded, there is only one offense because commission of the robbery offense is itself a predicate element of the armed criminal action offense, such that all of the elements of robbery are by definition subsumed within the latter crime. The Missouri Supreme Court] acknowledged that the Missouri legislature had expressed its clear intent that a defendant should be subject to conviction and sentence under the armed criminal action statute in addition to any conviction and sentence for the underlying felony. The court nevertheless held that the Double Jeopardy Clause "prohibits imposing punishment for both armed criminal action and for the underlying felony." Sours v. State, 593 S.W.2d 208, 223 (Mo. 1980).

. . . The Double Jeopardy Clause is cast explicitly in terms of being "twice put in jeopardy." We have consistently interpreted it "to protect an individual from being subjected to the hazards of trial and possible conviction more than once for an alleged offense." Burks v. United States, 437 U.S. 1, 11 (1978). Because respondent has been subjected to only one trial, it is not contended that his right to be free from multiple trials for the same offense has been violated. Rather, the Missouri court vacated respondent's conviction for armed criminal action because of the statements of this Court that the Double Jeopardy Clause also "protects against multiple punishments for the same offense." North Carolina v. Pearce, 395 U.S. 711, 717 (1969). Particularly in light of recent precedents of this Court, it is clear that the Missouri Supreme Court has misperceived the nature of the Double Jeopardy Clause's protection against multiple punishments. With respect to cumulative sentences imposed in a single trial, the Double Jeopardy Clause does no more than prevent the sentencing court from prescribing greater punishment than the legislature intended.

. . . In *Albernaz v. United States*, 450 U.S. 333 (1981), we addressed the issue whether a defendant could be cumulatively punished in a single trial for conspiracy to import marihuana and conspiracy to distribute marihuana. . . . [W]e concluded that the two statutes did not proscribe the "same" offense in the sense that "each provision requires proof of a fact that the other does not." *Id.* at 339. We might well have stopped at that point and upheld the petitioners' cumulative punishments under the challenged statutes since cumulative punishment can presumptively be assessed after conviction for two offenses that are not the "same" under *Blockburger*. However, we went on to state that because "the *Blockburger* test is a 'rule of statutory construction,' and because it serves as a means of discerning congressional purpose *the rule should not be controlling where, for example, there is a clear indication of contrary legislative intent.*" *Id.* at 340.

. . . We concluded our discussion . . . with this language:

"The question of what punishments are constitutionally permissible is no different from the question of what punishment the Legislative Branch intended to be imposed. *Where Congress intended, as it did here, to impose multiple punishments, imposition of such sentences does not violate the Constitution.*" *Id.* at 344.

Here, the Missouri Supreme Court has . . . recognized that the legislature intended that punishment for violations of the statutes be cumulative. We are bound to accept the Missouri court's construction of that State's statutes. However, we are not bound by the Missouri Supreme Court's legal conclusion that these two statutes violate the Double Jeopardy Clause, and we reject its legal conclusion.

Our analysis and reasoning in . . . *Albernaz* lead[s] inescapably to the conclusion that simply because two criminal statutes may be construed to proscribe the same conduct under the *Blockburger* test does not mean that the Double Jeopardy Clause precludes the imposition, in a single trial, of cumulative punishments pursuant to those statutes. The rule of statutory construction . . . is not a constitutional rule requiring courts to negate clearly expressed legislative intent. . . . Legislatures, not courts, prescribe the scope of punishments. Where, as here, a legislature specifically authorizes cumulative punishment under two statutes, regardless of whether those two statutes proscribe the "same" conduct under *Blockburger*, a court's task of statutory construction is at an end and the prosecutor may seek and the trial court or jury may impose cumulative punishment under such statutes in a single trial.

[Opinion of MARSHALL, J., dissenting, omitted.]

NOTES AND QUESTIONS

1. Cumulative Punishments vs. Serial Prosecutions. In *Hunter*, the defendant was charged with and convicted of two overlapping crimes — effectively, robbery and armed robbery — in a single prosecution. He was then sentenced such that the conviction for the armed offense entailed five additional years beyond the conviction for robbery alone. That outcome, the Supreme Court held, is consistent with the Constitution's Double Jeopardy Clause.

According to the Court, that Clause "affords a defendant three basic protections: It protects against a second prosecution for the same offense after acquittal. It protects against a second prosecution for the same offense after conviction. And it protects against multiple punishments for the same offense." Ohio v. Johnson, 467 U.S. 493, 498 (1984) (cleaned up). As *Hunter* makes clear, the Court views the first two of these protections — both of which guard against successive *prosecutions* — as the Amendment's core. As the Court has "explained on numerous occasions," this "bar to retrial following acquittal or conviction ensures that the State does not make repeated attempts to convict an individual, thereby exposing him to continued embarrassment, anxiety, and expense, while increasing the risk of an erroneous conviction or an impermissibly enhanced sentence." *Id.* at 498-499. Accordingly, the Court has interpreted the Constitution to prohibit a second prosecution for the "same offense" under two circumstances. First, if an initial prosecution ends in either a conviction or an acquittal, a second prosecution is barred for any offense that constitutes the same offense under the *Blockburger* test described in *Hunter.* Second and separately, if an initial prosecution ends in an acquittal, the Double Jeopardy Clause offers additional protection that bars the prosecution from relitigating "an issue of ultimate fact" that was resolved in the defendant's favor by the initial acquittal. Ashe v. Swenson, 397 U.S. 436, 443 (1970). As the Court has explained, "Where a previous judgment of acquittal was based upon a general verdict, as is usually the case, this approach requires a court to 'examine the record of a prior proceeding . . . and conclude whether a rational jury could have grounded its verdict upon an issue other than that which the defendant seeks to foreclose from consideration.'" *Id.* at 444.

As multiple scholars note, double jeopardy doctrine "has long been attacked as 'inadequate to provide meaningful protection against multiple prosecutions,'" given the ease with which both the *Blockburger* and *Ashe* tests can be overcome. The core holding of *Hunter,* however, is that even these protections do not apply to overlapping charges in the same case. As the Court has reiterated, "[i]n contrast to the double jeopardy protection against multiple trials, the final component of double jeopardy — protection against cumulative punishments — is designed to ensure that the sentencing discretion of courts is confined to the limits established by the legislature." *Johnson,* 467 U.S. at 499. The question, in other words, "is essentially one of legislative intent." *Id.* According to Professor Andrew Manuel Crespo, this means that "the Clause does not prohibit cumulative punishments at all." Rather, he says, "states are free" to enact overlapping criminal statutes and thus to empower their prosecutors to pile on multiple charges — all without running afoul of constitutional constraint.[78]

2. Charging Discretion. A clear implication of *Hunter* is that prosecutors have broad discretion to layer multiple charges on top of one another — to *charge stack* or *pile on,* as scholars describe the practice. And indeed, as Professor Josh Bowers observes, "[i]n the charging context, courts and scholars take it as something of an article of faith that the prosecutor should enjoy principal — or even exclusive — authority." Of course, *Hunter* itself addressed only the Constitution's Double Jeopardy Clause. But as the following case demonstrates, the Supreme Court has upheld broad prosecutorial charging discretion in the face of other constitutional challenges as well.[79]

United States v. Batchelder, 442 U.S. 114 (1979). At issue in this case are two overlapping provisions [that] prohibit convicted felons from receiving firearms [but that authorize] different maximum penalties. . . . [T]he substantive elements of 18 U.S.C. §922(h) and 18 U.S.C. App. §1202(a) are identical as applied to a convicted felon who unlawfully receives a firearm . . . . [But the latter statute allows no more than a 2-year maximum sentence, whereas the former permits a sentence up to 5 years]. . . .

This Court has previously noted the partial redundancy of §§922(h) and 1202(a), both as to the conduct they proscribe and the individuals they reach. However, we find nothing in the language, structure, or legislative history . . . to suggest that because of this overlap, a defendant convicted under §922(h) may be imprisoned for no more than the maximum term specified in §1202(a). As we read the Act, each substantive statute, in conjunction with its own sentencing provision, operates independently of the other. . . .

[The court] below expressed "serious doubts about the constitutionality of two statutes that provide different penalties for identical conduct." Specifically, the court suggested that the statutes might (1) be void for vagueness, (2) implicate "due process and equal protection interests in avoiding excessive prosecutorial discretion and in obtaining equal justice," and (3) constitute an impermissible delegation of congressional authority. We find no constitutional infirmities.

. . . A criminal statute is . . . invalid if it "fails to give a person of ordinary intelligence fair notice that his contemplated conduct is forbidden." United States v. Harriss, 347 U.S. 612, 617 (1954); *see* Papachristou v. Jacksonville, 405 U.S. 156, 162 (1972). So too, vague sentencing provisions may pose constitutional questions if they do not state with sufficient clarity the consequences of violating a given criminal statute. The provisions in issue here, however, unambiguously specify the activity proscribed and the penalties available upon conviction. That this particular conduct may violate both [laws] does not detract from the notice afforded by each. Although the statutes create uncertainty as to which crime may be charged and therefore what penalties may be imposed, they do so to no greater extent than would a single statute authorizing various alternative punishments. So long as overlapping criminal provisions clearly define the conduct prohibited and the punishment authorized, the notice requirements of the Due Process Clause are satisfied.

This Court has long recognized that when an act violates more than one criminal statute, the Government may prosecute under either so long as it does not discriminate against any class of defendants. Whether to prosecute and what charge to file . . . are decisions that generally rest in the prosecutor's discretion. The Court of Appeals acknowledged this "settled rule" [but believed that] . . . when two statutes prohibit "exactly the same conduct," the prosecutor's "selection of which of two penalties to apply" would be "unfettered" [and] . . . could produce "unequal justice" . . . . We find this analysis factually and legally unsound. . . . [T]here is no appreciable difference between the discretion a prosecutor exercises when deciding whether to charge under one of two statutes with different elements and the discretion he exercises when choosing one of two statutes with identical elements. In the former situation, once he determines that the proof will support conviction under either statute, his decision is indistinguishable from the one he faces in the latter context. The prosecutor may be influenced by the penalties available upon conviction, but this fact, standing alone, does not give rise to a violation of the Equal Protection or Due Process Clause. Just as a defendant has no constitutional right to elect which of two applicable . . . statutes shall be the basis of his indictment and prosecution neither is he entitled to choose the penalty scheme under which he will be sentenced.

Approaching the problem of prosecutorial discretion from a slightly different perspective, the Court of Appeals postulated that the statutes might impermissibly delegate to the Executive Branch the Legislature's responsibility to fix criminal penalties. We do not agree. The provisions at issue plainly demarcate the range of penalties that prosecutors and judges may seek and impose. In light of that specificity, the power that Congress has delegated to those officials is no broader than the authority they routinely exercise in enforcing the criminal laws. Having informed the courts, prosecutors, and defendants of the permissible punishment alternatives available under each [provision], Congress has fulfilled its duty. Accordingly, the judgment of the Court of Appeals is reversed.

3. Impacts of Charge Stacking. As the preceding notes make clear, prosecutors enjoy virtually unchecked discretion to file charges against defendants. In the words of Professor Tracey Meares, as "long as the prosecutor has probable cause to believe that the accused committed an offense, the prosecutor is entitled to bring the charge [and will] rarely [be] second-guessed by the courts." As a result, prosecutors can and often do pile on scores of crimes for a single alleged event. To take one example, *The Chicago Sun Times* reports that "prosecutors piled more than 50 felony counts" in a case against a defendant accused of fatally shooting a police officer, including "more than two dozen counts of murder, as well as a combined 32 additional counts of armed violence and related weapons charges—a total of 56 counts in all." The article goes on to observe that for prosecutors in that jurisdiction, filing "dozens of additional counts" beyond the lead charge is "not uncommon, either as a hedge against making a case in the most serious charges at trial, to send a message to the defendant, or both."[80]

The message this tactic sends to defendants is heard across multiple registers. Perhaps most obviously, filing a large pile of charges communicates to the defendant that he faces the risk of a very long sentence if convicted at trial. In some cases, additional charges automatically increase a defendant's sentencing exposure because the legislature mandates that any resulting sentences run consecutively to other sentences. These consecutive terms can quickly add up. Consider Marion Hungerford, a "52 year-old mentally disturbed woman with no prior criminal record" who was charged with "one count of conspiracy, seven counts of robbery, and seven counts of use of a firearm in relation to a crime of violence," all stemming from a quartet of robberies committed by her boyfriend in which she was accused of being an accomplice and co-conspirator. United States v. Hungerford, 465 F.3d 1113, 1119 (9th Cir. 2006) (Reinhardt, J., concurring in the judgment). "Although she never touched a gun," she was threatened with and ultimately sentenced "to over 159 years in prison" after prosecutors stacked together a series of offenses carrying 25-year sentences for gun possession that Congress mandated run consecutively. *Id.*

In many cases, however, the sentencing impacts of charge stacking are mitigated by rules, guidelines, or norms that require or encourage trial courts to run sentences concurrently or to merge convictions when they arise from nested or closely related offenses stemming from a single criminal event or course of conduct. In Georgia, for example, state law provides that a defendant "may not . . . be convicted of more than one crime if" one of them "is included in the other" as a lesser-included offense, meaning an offense whose elements are a subset of a more serious crime, as with robbery and armed robbery. Ga. Code Ann. §16-1-7(a). According to a survey conducted by Professor Crespo, state rules and practices vary considerably with respect to concurrent and consecutive sentencing; across the country, laws "require consecutive sentences in some specified subset of cases," "require concurrent sentences in certain circumstances," and in other settings allow judges "to sentence consecutively or concurrently as they see fit—perhaps nudged toward one option or the other by default rules favoring consecutive or concurrent sentences."[81]

But as Crespo goes on to observe, even "a rule requiring concurrent sentences will not eliminate all of the tactical benefits that charge-stacking affords, as a hefty indictment can still increase the likelihood of conviction and can also have psychological effects on the defendant." Scholars conducting jury experiments, for example, have found that a "'halo' effect" often causes jurors to view a defendant more negatively when he is charged with multiple offenses: increasing counts in the indictment leads the jury "to assume that the accused must be guilty of *something*." Increasing the number of charges also makes it possible for a conflicted jury to "horse-trade" one set of charges for others and thus reach a "compromise verdict of guilty." As for the defendant's psychology, Professor and Judge Stephanos Bibas argues that hefty charging documents can anchor defendants, making them "more likely to think that they are getting good deals when they are offered lower sentences." Professors Michael Seigel and Christopher Slobogin similarly maintain that "multiple charges [can] intimidate defendants" when the thud of a heavy indictment hits the table. For all these reasons and more, Professor Daniel Richman observes, there is a "tendency of prosecutors to pad indictments with as many counts as they can derive from the available facts—even when sentences will be concurrent."[82]

4. Parallel Crimes. The cases described thus far involve prosecutors piling on what one might call *nested* or *closely intertwined* offenses. In *Hunter*, a defendant who hit someone with a gun during a robbery was charged with robbery, assault, and using a firearm during a felony. All of those crimes arise from a tightly bound factual nexus—the assaultive robbery itself. As a result, if the defendant were to go to trial, all three charges could be subject to the same defense theory: If Hunter could persuade a jury that he was not actually the person at the A&P, or that he was acting under duress, he would likely defeat all three charges. And if he believed those potential defenses to be strong, he might even resist a prosecutor's plea offer, opting to take his chances at trial.

Note, however, that a prosecutor can often increase her leverage against a defendant by adding other crimes to the mix that travel in parallel to the core offenses at issue, and that might be easier to prove. Professor Stuntz describes the basic idea this way:

> Suppose a given criminal statute contains elements *ABC*; suppose further that *C* is hard to prove, but prosecutors believe they know when it exists. Legislatures can make it easier to convict offenders by adding . . . new crime *DEF*, where those elements correlate with *ABC* but are substantially easier to prove. Prosecutors can continue to enforce the original crime, but more cheaply, by enforcing the substitutes.

These parallel crimes can be added to a prosecution alongside (or perhaps even in place of) the core crimes of interest, operating in effect as an insurance policy that makes a conviction more certain—and thus a plea deal more likely. Consider, in this respect, the following case.[83]

United States v. Brogan, 522 U.S. 398 (1998). [Petitioner James Brogan, a union official,] accepted cash payments from . . . a real estate company whose employees were represented by the union. On October 4, 1993, federal agents from the Department of Labor and the Internal Revenue Service visited petitioner at his home. The agents identified themselves and . . . asked petitioner if he would answer some questions, and he agreed. One question was whether he had received any cash or gifts from [the company] when he was a union officer. Petitioner's response was "no." At that point, the agents disclosed that [they had] . . . company records showing the contrary. They also told petitioner that lying to federal agents in the course of an investigation was a crime. Petitioner did not modify his answers, and the interview ended shortly thereafter.

Petitioner was indicted for accepting unlawful cash payments from an employer in violation of 29 U.S.C. §186 and making a false statement within the jurisdiction of a federal agency in violation of 18 U.S.C. §1001. . . . At the time petitioner falsely replied "no" to the Government investigators' question, 18 U.S.C. §1001 provided:

> "Whoever, in any matter within the jurisdiction of any department or agency of the United States knowingly . . . makes any false, fictitious or fraudulent statements or representations . . . shall be fined not more than $10,000 or imprisoned not more than five years, or both."

By its terms, 18 U.S.C. §1001 covers "any" false statement — that is, a false statement "of whatever kind." The word "no" in response to a question assuredly makes a "statement," see, *e.g.,* Webster's New International Dictionary 2461 (2d ed. 1950), and petitioner does not contest that his utterance was false or that it was made "knowingly and willfully." In fact, petitioner concedes that under a "literal reading" of the statute he loses. Petitioner asks us, however, to depart from the literal text that Congress has enacted, and to [hold] that a simple denial of guilt does not come within the statute. . . . Petitioner repeats the argument made by many supporters of the "exculpatory no" [doctrine he seeks] that the doctrine is necessary to eliminate the grave risk that §1001 will become an instrument of prosecutorial abuse. The supposed danger is that overzealous prosecutors will use this provision as a means of "piling on" offenses . . . . The objectors' principal grievance on this score, however, lies not with the hypothetical prosecutors but with Congress itself, which has decreed the obstruction of a legitimate investigation to be a separate offense, and a serious one. It is not for us to revise that judgment. . . .

GINSBURG, J., concurring in the judgment. Because a false denial fits the unqualified language of 18 U.S.C. §1001, I concur in the affirmance of Brogan's conviction. I write separately, however, to call attention to the extraordinary authority Congress, perhaps unwittingly, has conferred on prosecutors to manufacture crimes . . . of a kind that only a Government officer could prompt. . . . At oral argument, the Solicitor General forthrightly observed that §1001 could even be used to "escalate completely innocent conduct into a felony." More likely to occur, "if an investigator finds it difficult to prove some elements of a crime, she can ask questions about other elements to which she already knows the answers. If the suspect lies, she can then use the crime she has prompted as leverage or can seek prosecution for the lie as a substitute for the crime she cannot prove." Comment, *False Statements to Federal Agents: Induced Lies and the Exculpatory No*, 57 U. Chi. L. Rev. 1273, 1278 (1990).

5. Pretext Crimes. In the *Brogan* case excerpted in the preceding note, the prosecution for making false statements occurred in tandem with prosecution for the underlying bribery charges. But as Justice Ginsburg noted in her separate opinion, these sorts of proxy crimes can also be used *pretextually* to charge and convict a person when a prosecutor could not actually prove the core crime at issue. In this instance, Ginsburg writes, the worry is that "an overzealous prosecutor or investigator—aware that a person has committed some suspicious acts, but unable to make a criminal case—will create a crime by surprising the suspect, asking about those acts, and receiving a false denial." 552 U.S. at 416. As Professors Daniel Richman and Bill Stuntz write, this sort of tactic is routinely employed:

> It is common in the United States and especially common in the federal justice system for law enforcers to go after a criminal defendant because they suspect him of one crime [or] . . . a set of crimes . . . and then to charge and convict him of a different crime, unrelated to and less severe than the first. That practice has generated a standard debate, and the debate has a standard resolution. The defendant claims the government is behaving arbitrarily, singling him out for different treatment than that which others receive. "Pretext" is a dirty word; it connotes something shady and underhanded. The government responds that nonpayment of income taxes (or false statements, or mail fraud, or whatever the charged offense) is a legitimate crime, something for which any ordinary citizen might be prosecuted and punished if guilty. . . . That government response almost always wins in court, and that resolution is generally tolerated in the academic literature as well. Pretextual prosecutions are a widely accepted feature of our criminal justice system, and they are widely, albeit not universally, understood to be both legally and ethically permissible.[84]

6. Inequitable Overreach. The preceding two notes describe circumstances in which prosecutors add easy-to-prove charges to their case, and thus raise the odds of conviction at trial and with them the odds of a guilty plea. Note, though, that a prosecutor can also increase the prospect of a guilty plea by raising the potential sentence a defendant faces if convicted. One straightforward way to do this is to add offenses with higher sentences. Sometimes, these *aggravated offenses* will clearly fit the core conduct at issue, as with the armed criminal action charge in *Hunter*, which increased Hunter's prison exposure beyond the robbery charge he faced. But creative prosecutors can, and sometimes do, use their discretion more aggressively—filing charges that seem odd fits for the facts at hand, but that may be legally permissible all the same. Recall Professor Crespo's example:

> Imagine a defendant suspected of approaching someone on a street corner at night, of pointing a gun at that person, of ordering them to move a few steps to the left (out from under a streetlamp), and, finally, of taking their wallet and running off with it. To any lay observer, the crime alleged here is straightforward: armed robbery. . . . [But this defendant may face] a far more serious charge of kidnapping—premised solely on the allegation that, in the course of the robbery, he told the victim to move a few steps to the left, out from under a streetlamp.
>
> Putting aside for the moment the factual question of whether the defendant ever issued such a command (or committed the robbery), the prosecutor's ability to threaten him with a hefty kidnapping charge depends on the answer to a straightforward question of law: Does this brief alleged restraint of the victim's freedom of movement constitute a kidnapping?[85]

Note that this question is fundamentally one of substantive criminal law: The elements of kidnapping, as written by legislatures and interpreted by courts, will determine whether that offense—and its more serious penalty—apply to the facts Professor Crespo imagines. In some jurisdictions, the answer is yes. The Supreme Court of Georgia, for example, has held that "[u]nlawful asportation," meaning movement of a person, "even for a short distance, is sufficient to support a conviction for kidnapping." Ellis v. State, 440 S.E.2d 235, 239 (Ga. Ct. App. 1994). And according to Melanie Prince, this statutory interpretation is not unusual, as courts in multiple states have similarly interpreted their kidnapping statutes to "allow prosecution of criminal defendants for both kidnapping and the underlying offense that involved some restraint."[86]

In these jurisdictions, Prince goes on to observe, "criminal defendants could face two convictions for essentially one action, and the severe sentences that were originally intended to punish ransom-kidnappers [c]ould be applied to those guilty of a lesser crime." Prosecutors in these jurisdictions thus have the power to threaten kidnapping charges as a matter of course—even in cases in which the defendant has barely restrained the victim and in which the prosecutor herself does not actually want to punish the defendant for kidnapping. The inflated charge, in other words, serves simply as a means of pressuring the defendant to plead guilty to the charge the prosecutor prefers. Professor Crespo describes the filing of such charges as "equitable overreaching." Even if one accepts that a defendant's "alleged conduct technically meets the legal elements of a kidnapping," he writes, "one might appropriately ask whether threatening him with such a charge—and with the decades of imprisonment it could entail—is fair, just, and equitable under the circumstances." As Professor Josh Bowers observes,

however, prosecutors in practice "enjoy almost unbridled equitable discretion" to make that decision for themselves.[87]

7. Factual Overreach. As Professor Crespo observes, prosecutors
can overreach beyond the equitable set of charges in a case in a different way: Sometimes, they can pursue charges that have a weak factual
foundation.

> [C]onsider once again our hypothetical armed robbery defendant, only
> imagine now that the sole witness against him is a blind convicted drug
> dealer with an axe to grind against the defendant. A defense attorney read-
> ing that sentence will rightly conclude that the prosecutor has a weak case,
> with significant—but, importantly, still uncertain—odds of ending in an
> acquittal. If, however, the prosecutor believes her witness, or has some
> other reason to pursue criminal charges against the defendant, she is free
> to prosecute him—and to exercise whatever attendant leverage she can to
> induce him to plead guilty, the weakness of her case notwithstanding.

As Professor Crespo goes on to explain, "the primary protection against
such overreaching is the defendant's constitutional right to a trial," the
"basic purpose" of which, the Supreme Court has said, "is the determination of truth." Tehan v. United States *ex rel.* Shott, 382 U.S. 406, 416 (1966).
But of course, those protections disappear if the prosecutor succeeds in
inducing the defendant to plead guilty.[88]
    According to Professors Ronald Wright and Marc Miller, prosecu-
tors may have a perverse incentive to overreach in weaker cases, precisely
because their desire to avoid trial on weaker charges is stronger. In these
circumstances, there may be a "temptation to file more serious charges
than the evidence can support," which raises what they call the "urgent"
and "substantial problem" of plea bargains ensnaring "the innocent defendant." According to the Innocence Project, eighteen percent of people who
have been formally exonerated initially pled guilty to offenses they did not
commit—a conservative estimate given the skew toward serious offenses in
the underlying sample.[89]

8. Sliding Down: The Importance of Nonenforcement Discretion. Note that,
just as with police power, an essential component of prosecutorial plea bargaining power relates to *nonenforcement* discretion. In order to generate plea
bargaining leverage, the prosecutor must be free to *decline* to pursue the
most serious charges authorized by the law. Indeed, without that discretion, the prosecutor could not plea bargain at all. She would be required
to charge and pursue the most serious offense available, and defendants
would have every incentive to take each case to trial in hopes of winning
an acquittal against those severe charges. For this reason, just as with police
discretion not to arrest, prosecutorial discretion not to pursue charges is
often described by courts as deeply ingrained in the system. Consider the

following example of an opinion confirming that view, in the context of an uprising at Attica prison in New York.[90]

Inmates of Attica v. Rockefeller, 477 F.2d 375 (2d Cir. 1973). This appeal raises the question of whether the federal judiciary should, at the instance of victims, compel federal and state officials to investigate and prosecute persons who allegedly have violated certain federal and state criminal statutes. Plaintiffs . . . are certain present and former inmates of New York State's Attica Correctional Facility [and] the mother of an inmate who was killed when Attica was retaken after the inmate uprising in September 1971 . . . . The complaint alleges that . . . the inmates were intentionally subjected to cruel and inhuman treatment prior to the inmate riot, that State Police, Troopers, and Correction Officers . . . intentionally killed some of the inmate victims without provocation during the recovery of Attica, [and] that state officers . . . assaulted and beat prisoners after the prison had been successfully retaken and the prisoners had surrendered . . . .

The complaint further alleges that . . . the United States Attorney for the Western District of New York . . . has not arrested, investigated, or instituted prosecutions against any of the state officers accused of criminal violation of plaintiffs' federal civil rights, and he has thereby failed to carry out [his] duty . . . . [P]laintiffs request relief in the nature of mandamus [against these prosecutors] requiring [them to pursue the] prosecution of the offenses charged against the named and unknown state officers . . . .

[O]rdinarily the courts are "not to direct or influence the exercise of discretion of the officer or agency in the making of the decision." United States *ex rel.* Schonbrun v. Commanding Officer, 403 F.2d 371, 374 (2d Cir. 1968). More particularly, federal courts have traditionally and, to our knowledge, uniformly refrained from overturning, at the instance of a private person, discretionary decisions of federal prosecuting authorities not to prosecute persons regarding whom a complaint of criminal conduct is made.

This judicial reluctance to direct federal prosecutions at the instance of a private party . . . has been applied even in cases such as the present one where, according to the allegations of the complaint, which we must accept as true for purposes of this appeal, serious questions are raised as to the protection of the civil rights and physical security of a definable class of victims of crime and as to the fair administration of the criminal justice system.

The primary ground upon which this traditional judicial aversion to compelling prosecutions has been based is the separation of powers doctrine. ". . . [I]t is as an officer of the executive department that [the U.S. Attorney] exercises a discretion as to whether or not there shall be a prosecution in a particular case. It follows, as an incident of the constitutional separation of powers, that the courts are not to interfere with the free exercise of the discretionary powers of the attorneys of the United States in their control over criminal prosecutions." United States v. Cox, 342 F.2d 167, 171 (5th Cir. 1965).

Although a leading commentator[, Kenneth Culp Davis,] has criticized this broad view as unsound and incompatible with the normal function of the judiciary in reviewing for abuse or arbitrariness administrative acts that fall within the discretion of executive officers, he has also recognized, as have most of the cases . . . , that the manifold imponderables which enter into the prosecutor's decision to prosecute or not to prosecute make the choice not readily amenable to judicial supervision.

In the absence of statutorily defined standards governing reviewability, or regulatory or statutory policies of prosecution, the problems inherent in the task of supervising prosecutorial decisions do not lend themselves to resolution by the judiciary. The reviewing courts would be placed in the undesirable and injudicious posture of becoming "superprosecutors." . . . Nor is it clear what the judiciary's role of supervision should be were it to undertake such a review. At what point would the prosecutor be entitled to call a halt to further investigation as unlikely to be productive? What evidentiary standard would be used to decide whether prosecution should be compelled? How much judgment would the United States Attorney be allowed? Would he be permitted to limit himself to a strong "test" case rather than pursue weaker cases? What collateral factors would be permissible bases for a decision not to prosecute, e.g., the pendency of another criminal proceeding elsewhere against the same parties? What sort of review should be available in cases like the present one where the conduct complained of allegedly violates state as well as federal laws? With limited personnel and facilities at his disposal, what priority would the prosecutor be required to give to cases in which investigation or prosecution was directed by the court?

These difficult questions engender serious doubts as to the judiciary's capacity to review and as to the problem of arbitrariness inherent in any judicial decision to order prosecution. On balance, we believe that substitution of a court's decision to compel prosecution for the U.S. Attorney's decision not to prosecute, even upon an abuse of discretion standard of review and even if limited to directing that a prosecution be undertaken in good faith, would be unwise.

9. Prosecutors as Judges: Separation of Powers Concerns. In addition to fears of defendant coercion, scholarly critics of prosecutors' plea bargaining power also worry that the practice can raise separation of powers concerns, effectively transforming prosecutors into judges. Consider the following excerpts.

Rachel E. Barkow, *Separation of Powers and Criminal Law,* 58 Stan. L. Rev. 989, 1025, 1026-1028 (2006). Despite the significance of prosecutorial power, prosecutors operate with little oversight or regulation. The same prosecutor who investigates a case can make the final determination about what plea to accept. There is therefore no structural separation of adjudicative and executive power, and defendants have no right to a formal process or internal appeal within the agency. In addition, in the course of bargaining with a defendant over charges, the prosecutor can engage in ex parte contacts with the police and investigators, and the defendant need not be given access to the information on which the prosecutor relies—that is, the prosecutor's evidence of the defendant's guilt. . . . Prosecutors [also] need not treat similar cases similarly for purposes of plea bargaining, and they need not explain why they agreed to reach a deal with one defendant but refused to do so with another defendant guilty of the same crime. Indeed, because prosecutors need not make the terms of their plea bargains available to the public through publication and because prosecutorial law enforcement is largely exempt from open government laws like FOIA, a defendant might not even know that another similarly situated defendant received a particular deal. Nor may defendants be aware that a prosecutor is diverging from office policy.

David Lynch, *The Impropriety of Plea Agreements: A Tale of Two Counties,* 19 Law & Soc. Inquiry 115, 125 (1994). After spending three years as a public defender[, I went to work as a prosecutor in a county I will here call Lincoln County]. I quickly learned that prosecutors in Lincoln County were the real judges when it came to sentencing decisions. By allowing plea bargaining, . . . Lincoln County judges successfully dumped the burdens of sentencing most criminal defendants onto prosecutors. How did prosecutors in Lincoln County handle this sentencing burden? The answer, I soon learned, was "any way they wanted to." There were no official rules that bound me or my fellow prosecutors in the making of plea-bargaining offers. . . . Prosecutors . . . had nearly complete discretion in deciding what offers to make to defense counsel. . . . If their "gut" told them that [a given sentence within the locally published sentencing guidelines wasn't] appropriate, they could ignore them entirely, or else relabel one crime as something else, so that it would fit neatly into the sentence guideline range they desired. . . . This is not to say that prosecutors spent long periods of time agonizing over appropriate sentences. A prosecutor would often work through a pile of cases in machine-gun fashion, making snap decisions as to appropriate punishments in just a few minutes per case.

10. Fact Bargaining. The lack of meaningful judicial oversight of plea bargaining raises related concerns over the transparency of prosecutorial decisionmaking, and of the accuracy of the underlying convictions. In part, this is a concern that coercive tactics can lead to innocent people pleading guilty, as discussed above (p. 818). But there is a related worry that convictions produced through plea bargains will simply not reflect the reality of what the parties know to be the true facts of the case. Consider the following excerpts.

Gerard E. Lynch, *Our Administrative System of Criminal Justice*, 66 Fordham L. Rev. 2117, 2120 (1998). Formally, of course, any determination of culpability occurs in court, even in cases disposed of without trial. The court enters a judgment based on the defendant's judicial admission of guilt in a plea of guilty. Sometimes this plea follows a fairly extensive course of judicial proceedings—indictment, discovery, motion practice, even evidentiary hearings by the court—but in many cases it occurs at the very outset of the formal process. In [that] substantial number of cases, the judicial "process" consists of the simultaneous filing of a criminal charge by the prosecutor . . . and admission of guilt by the defendant. The charging document may be quite skeletal, the defendant's account of his guilty actions brief, and the judicial inquiry concerned more with whether the defendant is of sound mind and understands the consequences of what he is doing than with the accuracy of the facts to which he is attesting.

Thea Johnson, *Lying at Plea Bargaining*, 38 Ga. St. U. L. Rev. 673, 690-693 (2022). In [some] pleas, the parties manipulate the facts to achieve a desired result. . . . There are many examples of these pleas. For instance, [there is the] defendant who transformed a single felony sex offense into three separate misdemeanor sex offenses that each corresponded to a separate "act." Even though all parties (including the judge) agreed there was only one criminal act, the three misdemeanor pleas proceeded. In this way, the defendant avoided sex offender registration and other onerous burdens accompanying a felony sex offense. Plus, the prosecutor still achieved a long sentence by running three misdemeanor sentences consecutive to one another, while avoiding the time and expense of a trial. . . . Fictional pleas like this allow a defendant to escape some penalty associated with the crime that he did commit, including immigration consequences, sex offender registration, a higher charge or sentence, or points on one's driver's license. Prosecutors consent to these pleas because they benefit from the plea—namely, the certainty of a criminal conviction—and they may not have a strong interest in seeing the defendant suffer the non-criminal penalty. . . . [T]he result is a plea that does not reflect, and sometimes does not even relate to, the underlying factual allegations that the parties believe to be the truth.[91]

B.　Cruel and Unusual Punishment: The Proportionality Principle and the Constitution

As the preceding section makes clear, one major component of prosecutors' plea bargaining power comes from their ability to exploit defendants' fear of lengthy prison sentences. As Professor Stuntz observes, "[r]aising the threatened sentence raises the cost of going to trial just as effectively as raising the likelihood of conviction," and thus "increases the incentive for the defendant to plead guilty." In the United States, prosecutors' power is exceptional in this regard, because criminal sentences authorized by statute and credibly threatened by prosecutors are extremely high, as discussed in Chapter One (p. 18).[92]

Here again, substantive criminal law is a major part of the story. Over the past few decades, state and federal legislatures have frequently enacted criminal statutes with higher maximum sentences and often higher mandatory-minimum sentences as well. As the Congressional Research Service reports,

> When the first Congress assembled, it enacted several mandatory minimums, each of them a capital offense. The 19th century, however, witnessed the appearance of a host of discretionary schemes designed to ease the harshness of criminal law in individual cases. The courts could suspend sentence and were vested with broad authority in the selection of those sentences they chose to impose. Probation and parole were born and became prominent. By late in the century . . . most federal criminal statutes merely established a maximum penalty and left to the discretion of the courts the sentences to be imposed within the maximum. The 1909 federal criminal code revision eliminated most mandatory minimums. . . .
>
> [But the tough-on-crime policies of the 20th century saw a turn in approach.] Driven by concerns that broad discretion had led to rootless sentencing, unjustifiable in its leniency in some instances and in its severity in others, legislative bodies moved to curtail discretionary sentencing on several fronts. Determinate sentencing, sentencing commissions and guidelines, and mandatory minimum sentences became more prevalent. Parole and probation were abolished or greatly restricted in several jurisdictions. . . . The armed career criminal, three strikes, and several of the other prominent drug, child pornography, and gun related mandatory minimums followed in the ensuing years.[93]

These trends were observable across the states, most notably in jurisdictions that adopted "three strikes" laws with mandatory life sentences for people convicted of a third felony offense, even if that offense was relatively minor. As noted in Chapter One, the Pew Center on the States found that time served on state prison sentences increased on average 36 percent between 1990 and 2009. In some of the most populous states, the explosion was dramatic, with sentence lengths increasing 51 percent in California, 91 percent in Virginia, and 166 percent in Florida.[94]

As these severe sentencing laws and policies came into effect, litigation over their constitutionality began to make its way into the courts. The focal point of that litigation was the Eighth Amendment's ban on "cruel and unusual punishments." Beginning in the early 1970s, that Amendment was used, with varying success, to establish limits on capital punishment, which the Supreme Court briefly ruled unconstitutional in *Furman v. Georgia*, 408 U.S. 238 (1972), but later permitted within a set of constitutionally defined parameters developed over the ensuing decades. The jurisprudence setting those constitutional limits on the death penalty is intricate enough to support a full class. Compared to the American penal system as whole, however, the death penalty represents a minuscule proportion of sentences meted out. With respect to the constitutional limitations on plea bargaining and mass incarceration, one key question thus becomes what restrictions, if any, the Eighth Amendment imposes on prison sentences, as opposed to death sentences. Consider the following cases.[95]

Graham v. Florida

560 U.S. 48 (2010)

KENNEDY, J. The issue before the Court is whether the Constitution permits a juvenile offender to be sentenced to life in prison without parole for a non-homicide crime. . . . Petitioner challenges the sentence under the Eighth Amendment's Cruel and Unusual Punishments Clause. . . . Petitioner is Terrance Jamar Graham. He was born on January 6, 1987. Graham's parents were addicted to crack cocaine, and their drug use persisted in his early years. Graham was diagnosed with attention deficit hyperactivity disorder in elementary school. He began drinking alcohol and using tobacco at age 9 and smoked marijuana at age 13.

In July 2003, when Graham was age 16, he and three other school-age youths attempted to rob a barbeque restaurant in Jacksonville, Florida. . . . Graham's masked accomplice twice struck the restaurant manager in the back of the head with a metal bar. . . . The restaurant manager required stitches for his head injury. No money was taken. [Graham pled guilty to armed burglary and attempted armed robbery for this incident. He was sentenced to a three-year term of probation. Under the terms of that probation, the court reserved the right to impose any term of imprisonment authorized for the two charges of conviction if Graham were ever to violate his probation conditions.] Less than six months later, on the night of December 2, 2004, Graham again was arrested [and charged with an armed home-invasion burglary in which he] forcibly entered the home and held a pistol to [the victim's] chest. For the next 30 minutes, [he held the victim] at gunpoint while [he] ransacked the home searching for money. . . .

Graham's probation officer [sought to revoke his probation. The trial court held a hearing at which it considered the new allegations of wrongdoing in order to determine what sentence to impose on the original charges of conviction]. Under Florida law the minimum sentence Graham could receive absent a downward departure by the judge was 5 years' imprisonment. The maximum was life imprisonment. Graham's attorney requested the minimum nondeparture sentence of 5 years. A presentence report prepared by the Florida Department of Corrections recommended that Graham receive an even lower sentence — at most 4 years' imprisonment. The State recommended that Graham receive 30 years on the armed burglary count and 15 years on the attempted armed robbery count.

After hearing Graham's testimony, the trial court explained the sentence it was about to pronounce:

> Mr. Graham, as I look back on your case, yours is really candidly a sad situation. You had, as far as I can tell, you have quite a family structure. You had a lot of people who wanted to try and help you get your life turned around including the court system, and you had a judge who took the step to try and give you direction through his probation order to give you a chance to get back onto track. . . . I don't know why it is that you threw your life away. . . . [T]his is an escalating pattern of criminal conduct on your part and . . . we can't help you any further. We can't do anything to deter you. . . . So then it becomes a focus, if I can't do anything to help you, if I can't do anything to get you back on the right path, then I have to start focusing on the community and trying to protect the community from your actions. . . .

The trial court . . . sentenced him to the maximum sentence authorized by law on each charge: life imprisonment for the armed burglary and 15 years for the attempted armed robbery. Because Florida has abolished its parole system, a life sentence gives a defendant no possibility of release unless he is granted executive clemency.

. . . The Eighth Amendment states: "Excessive bail shall not be required, nor excessive fines imposed, nor cruel and unusual punishments inflicted." . . . The concept of proportionality is central to the Eighth Amendment. Embodied in the Constitution's ban on cruel and unusual punishments is the "precept of justice that punishment for crime should be graduated and proportioned to the offense." Weems v. United States, 217 U.S. 349, 367 (1910). The Court's cases addressing the proportionality of sentences fall within two general classifications. The first involves challenges to the length of term-of-years sentences given all the circumstances in a particular case. The second comprises cases in which the Court implements the proportionality standard by certain categorical restrictions on the death penalty. . . .

The [latter cases have] used categorical rules to define Eighth Amendment standards [regarding] the death penalty [that consist] of two subsets, one considering the nature of the offense, the other considering the characteristics of the offender. With respect to the nature of the offense, the Court has concluded that capital punishment is impermissible for nonhomicide crimes against individuals. [See Kennedy v. Louisiana, 554 U.S. 407, 419 (2008) (prohibiting the death penalty for a person convicted of sexually assaulting a child).] In cases turning on the characteristics of the offender, the Court has adopted categorical rules prohibiting the death penalty for defendants who committed their crimes before the age of 18, *Roper v. Simmons*, 543 U.S. 551 (2005), or whose intellectual functioning is in a low range, *Atkins v. Virginia*, 536 U.S. 304 (2002).

In the cases adopting categorical rules the Court . . . first considers "objective indicia of society's standards, as expressed in legislative enactments and state practice," to determine whether there is a national consensus against the sentencing practice at issue. *Roper*, 543 U.S. at 572. Next, guided by "the standards elaborated by controlling precedents and by the Court's own understanding and interpretation of the Eighth Amendment's text, history, meaning, and purpose," *Kennedy*, 554 U.S. at 421, the Court must determine in the exercise of its own independent judgment whether the punishment in question violates the Constitution.

The present case involves an issue the Court has not considered previously: a categorical challenge to a term-of-years sentence. . . . This case implicates a particular type of sentence as it applies to an entire class of offenders who have committed a range of crimes. As a result, a threshold comparison between the severity of the penalty and the gravity of the crime does not advance the analysis. [T]he appropriate analysis is the one used in cases that involved the categorical approach, specifically *Atkins*, *Roper*, and *Kennedy*.

The analysis begins with objective indicia of national consensus. . . . Six jurisdictions do not allow life without parole sentences for any juvenile offenders. Seven jurisdictions permit life without parole for juvenile offenders, but only for homicide crimes. Thirty-seven States as well as the District of Columbia permit sentences of life without parole for a juvenile nonhomicide offender in some circumstances. [But] "[t]here are measures of consensus other than legislation." *Id.* at 433. . . . Here, an examination of actual sentencing practices in jurisdictions where the sentence in question is permitted by statute discloses a consensus against its use. Although these statutory schemes contain no explicit prohibition on sentences of life without parole for juvenile nonhomicide offenders, those sentences are most infrequent. . . . [T]here are 124 juvenile nonhomicide offenders serving life without parole sentences. A significant majority of those, 77 in total, are serving sentences imposed in Florida. The other 46 are imprisoned in just 10 States . . . . Thus, only 11 jurisdictions nationwide in fact impose life without parole sentences on juvenile nonhomicide offenders—and most of those do so quite rarely. . . .

Community consensus, while "entitled to great weight," is not itself determinative of whether a punishment is cruel and unusual. *Id.* at 434. In accordance with the constitutional design, "the task of interpreting the Eighth Amendment remains our responsibility." *Roper*, 543 U.S. at 575. The judicial exercise of independent judgment requires consideration of the culpability of the offenders at issue in light of their crimes and characteristics, along with the severity of the punishment in question. In this inquiry the Court also considers whether the challenged sentencing practice serves legitimate penological goals.

Roper established that because juveniles have lessened culpability they are less deserving of the most severe punishments. As compared to adults, juveniles have a "lack of maturity and an underdeveloped sense of responsibility"; they "are more vulnerable or susceptible to negative influences and outside pressures, including peer pressure"; and their characters are "not as well formed." *Id.* at 569-570. . . . Accordingly, "juvenile offenders cannot with reliability be classified among the worst offenders." *Id.* at 569. . . .

[I]t is relevant to consider next the nature of the offenses to which this harsh penalty might apply. The Court has recognized that defendants who do not kill, intend to kill, or foresee that life will be taken are categorically less deserving of the most serious forms of punishment than are murderers. . . . This is because "life is over for the victim of the murderer," but for the victim of even a very serious nonhomicide crime, "life is not over and normally is not beyond repair." Coker v. Georgia, 433 U.S. 584, 598 (1977) (plurality opinion). . . . It follows that, when compared to an adult murderer, a juvenile offender who did not kill or intend to kill has a twice diminished moral culpability. The age of the offender and the nature of the crime each bear on the analysis.

As for the punishment, life without parole . . . deprives the convict of the most basic liberties without giving hope of restoration, except perhaps by executive clemency—the remote possibility of which does not mitigate the harshness of the sentence. . . . Life without parole is an especially harsh punishment for a juvenile. Under this sentence a juvenile offender will on average serve more years and a greater percentage of his life in prison than an adult offender. A 16-year-old and a 75-year-old each sentenced to life without parole receive the same punishment in name only.

. . . Criminal punishment can have different goals, and choosing among them is within a legislature's discretion. [But a] sentence lacking any legitimate penological justification is by its nature disproportionate to the offense. With respect to life without parole for juvenile nonhomicide offenders, none of the goals of penal sanctions that have been recognized as legitimate—retribution, deterrence, incapacitation, and rehabilitation—provides an adequate justification.

Retribution is a legitimate reason to punish, but it cannot support the sentence at issue here. . . . [A]s *Roper* observed, "whether viewed as an attempt to express the community's moral outrage or as an attempt to right the balance for the wrong to the victim, the case for retribution is not as strong with a minor as with an adult." 543 U.S. at 571. The case becomes even weaker with respect to a juvenile who did not commit homicide. *Roper* found that "retribution is not proportional if the law's most severe penalty is imposed" on the juvenile murderer. [Likewise,] retribution does not justify imposing the second most severe penalty on the less culpable juvenile nonhomicide offender.

Deterrence does not suffice to justify the sentence either. . . . Because juveniles' "lack of maturity and an underdeveloped sense of responsibility . . . often result in impetuous and ill-considered actions and decisions," Johnson v. Texas, 509 U.S. 350, 367 (1993), they are less likely to take a possible punishment into consideration when making decisions. This is particularly so when that punishment is rarely imposed. That the sentence deters in a few cases is perhaps plausible, but "this argument does not overcome other objections." Kennedy, 554 U.S. at 441. . . . [I]n light of juvenile nonhomicide offenders' diminished moral responsibility, any limited deterrent effect provided by life without parole is not enough to justify the sentence.

Incapacitation, a third legitimate reason for imprisonment, does not justify the life without parole sentence in question here. Recidivism is a serious risk to public safety, and so incapacitation is an important goal. But [to argue] that the juvenile offender forever will be a danger to society requires the sentencer to make a judgment that the juvenile is incorrigible. The characteristics of juveniles make that judgment questionable. "It is difficult even for expert psychologists to differentiate between the juvenile offender whose crime reflects unfortunate yet transient immaturity, and the rare juvenile offender whose crime reflects irreparable corruption." Roper, 543 U.S. at 572. . . .

Finally there is rehabilitation, a penological goal that forms the basis of parole systems. The concept of rehabilitation is imprecise; and [it] . . . is for legislatures to determine what rehabilitative techniques are appropriate and effective. A sentence of life imprisonment without parole, however, cannot be justified by the goal of rehabilitation. The penalty forswears altogether the rehabilitative ideal . . . .

In sum, penological theory is not adequate to justify life without parole for juvenile nonhomicide offenders. This determination; the limited culpability of juvenile nonhomicide offenders; and the severity of life without parole sentences all lead to the conclusion that the sentencing practice under consideration is cruel and unusual. . . .

THOMAS, J., dissenting. The Court holds today that it is "grossly disproportionate" and hence unconstitutional for any judge or jury to impose a sentence of life without parole on an offender less than 18 years old, unless he has committed a homicide. [In so doing, the Court] rejects the judgments of those legislatures, judges, and juries [that have authorized such sentences] regarding what the Court describes as the "moral" question whether this sentence can ever be "proportionate" when applied to the category of offenders at issue here. I am unwilling to assume that we, as Members of this Court, are any more capable of making such moral judgments than our fellow citizens. Nothing in our training as judges qualifies us for that task, and nothing in Article III gives us that authority. . . .

The Court's decision today is significant because it does not merely apply [our proportionality] standard — it remarkably expands its reach. For the first time in its history, the Court declares an entire class of offenders immune from a noncapital sentence using the categorical approach it previously reserved for death penalty cases alone. . . . The Court now claims . . . the power . . . to declare that "less culpable" persons are categorically exempt from the "*second* most severe penalty." No reliable limiting principle remains to prevent the Court from immunizing any class of offenders from the law's third, fourth, fifth, or fiftieth most severe penalties as well. . . .

[In reaching its judgment,] the Court acknowledges that, at a minimum, the imposition of life-without-parole sentences on juvenile nonhomicide offenders serves two "legitimate" penological goals: incapacitation and deterrence. By definition, such sentences serve the goal of incapacitation by ensuring that juvenile offenders who commit armed burglaries, or those who commit . . . grievous sex crimes . . . no longer threaten their communities. That should settle the matter, since the Court acknowledges that incapacitation is an "important" penological goal. Yet, the Court finds this goal "*inadequate*" to justify the life-without-parole sentences here. A similar fate befalls deterrence. . . .

. . . Ultimately, however, the Court's "independent judgment" and the proportionality rule itself center on retribution — the notion that a criminal sentence should be proportioned to "the personal culpability of the criminal offender." . . . [But the] question of what acts are "deserving" of what punishments is bound so tightly with questions of morality and social conditions as to make it, almost by definition, a question for legislative resolution. It is true that the Court previously has relied on the notion of proportionality in holding certain classes of offenses categorically exempt from capital punishment. But never before today has the Court relied on its own view of just deserts to impose a categorical limit on the imposition of a lesser punishment. Its willingness to cross that well-established boundary raises the question whether any democratic choice regarding appropriate punishment is safe from the Court's ever-expanding constitutional veto.

[Additional opinions omitted.]

Ewing v. California

538 U.S. 11 (2003)

O'CONNOR, J., announced the judgment of the Court and delivered an opinion, in which THE CHIEF JUSTICE and Justice KENNEDY join. In this case, we decide whether the Eighth Amendment prohibits the State of California from sentencing a repeat felon to a prison term of 25 years to life under the State's "Three Strikes and You're Out" law.

California's three strikes law reflects a shift in the State's sentencing policies toward incapacitating and deterring repeat offenders who threaten the public safety. . . . [California legislators introduced a version of the law in 1993, but the Assembly Committee on Public Safety quickly defeated the bill.] Public outrage over the defeat sparked a voter initiative to add Proposition 184, based loosely on the bill, to the ballot in the November 1994 general election. On October 1, 1993, while Proposition 184 was circulating, 12-year-old Polly Klaas was kidnaped from her home in Petaluma, California. Her admitted killer, Richard Allen Davis, had a long criminal history that included two prior kidnaping convictions. Davis had served only half of his most recent sentence . . . . Had Davis served his entire sentence, he would still have been in prison on the day that Polly Klaas was kidnaped.

Polly Klaas' murder galvanized support for the three strikes initiative [which] voters approved . . . by a margin of 72 to 28 percent. . . . California thus became the second State to enact a three strikes law. . . . Between 1993 and 1995, twenty-four States and the Federal Government enacted three strikes laws. Though the three strikes laws vary from State to State, they share a common goal of protecting the public safety by providing lengthy prison terms for habitual felons.

[Under Proposition 184, if a] defendant has two or more prior "serious" or "violent" felony convictions, he must receive "an indeterminate term of life imprisonment." Defendants sentenced to life under the three strikes law become eligible for parole [after at least 25 years, and sometimes more depending on the underlying crime of conviction]. . . .

On parole from a 9-year prison term, petitioner Gary Ewing walked into the pro shop of the El Segundo Golf Course . . . . He walked out with three golf clubs, priced at $399 apiece, concealed in his pants leg. A shop employee . . . telephoned the police[, who] apprehended Ewing in the parking lot.

Ewing is no stranger to the criminal justice system. [Between 1984 and 1993, he was convicted of multiple theft offenses, misdemeanor battery, burglary, possession of a firearm, and possession of drug paraphernalia, as well as] three burglaries and one robbery at a Long Beach, California, apartment complex over a 5-week period. . . . [In the robbery,] Ewing accosted a victim in the mailroom of the apartment complex[,] claimed to have a gun and ordered the victim to hand over his wallet. When the victim resisted, Ewing produced a knife and forced the victim back to the apartment itself. . . . Ewing absconded with the victim's money and credit cards.

. . . Only 10 months [after he was paroled for the Long Beach offenses], Ewing stole the golf clubs at issue in this case. He was charged with, and ultimately convicted of, one count of felony grand theft . . . . [T]he trial court . . . found[] that Ewing had been convicted previously of four serious or violent felonies for the three burglaries and the robbery . . . . As a newly convicted felon with two or more "serious" or "violent" felony convictions in his past, Ewing was sentenced under the three strikes law to 25 years to life.

. . . The Eighth Amendment, which forbids cruel and unusual punishments, contains a "narrow proportionality principle" that "applies to noncapital sentences." Harmelin v. Michigan, 501 U.S. 957, 996-997 (1991) (Kennedy, J., concurring in part and concurring in judgment). . . . In *Rummel v. Estelle*, 445 U.S. 263 (1980), we held that it did not violate the Eighth Amendment for a State to sentence a three-time offender to life in prison with the possibility of parole. . . . Rummel's two prior offenses were a 1964 felony for "fraudulent use of a credit card to obtain $80 worth of goods or services," and a 1969 felony conviction for "passing a forged check in the amount of $28.36." His triggering offense was a conviction for felony theft—"obtaining $120.75 by false pretenses." *Id.* at 266. . . . Although we stated that the [Eighth Amendment's] proportionality principle "would . . . come into play in the extreme example . . . if a legislature made overtime parking a felony punishable by life imprisonment," *id.* at 274 n.11, we held that "the mandatory life sentence imposed upon this petitioner does not constitute cruel and unusual punishment . . . ," *id.* at 285.

. . . Three years after *Rummel*, in *Solem v. Helm*, 463 U.S. 277, 279 (1983), we held that the Eighth Amendment prohibited "a life sentence without possibility of parole for a seventh nonviolent felony." The triggering offense in *Solem* was "uttering a 'no account' check for $100." *Id.* at 281. We . . . explained that three factors may be relevant to a determination of whether a sentence is so disproportionate that it violates the Eighth Amendment: "(i) the gravity of the offense and the harshness of the penalty; (ii) the sentences imposed on other criminals in the same jurisdiction; and (iii) the sentences imposed for commission of the same crime in other jurisdictions." *Id.* at 292. Applying these factors in *Solem*, we struck down the defendant's sentence of life without parole[, noting] the contrast between that sentence and the sentence in *Rummel*, pursuant to which the defendant was eligible for parole. . . .

Eight years after *Solem*, we grappled with the proportionality issue again in *Harmelin*. *Harmelin* was not a recidivism case, but rather involved a first-time offender convicted of possessing 672 grams of cocaine. He was sentenced to life in prison without possibility of parole. A majority of the Court rejected Harmelin's claim that his sentence was so grossly disproportionate that it violated the Eighth Amendment [but] could not agree on why his proportionality argument failed. Justice Scalia, joined by the Chief Justice, [would] have declined to apply gross disproportionality principles except in reviewing capital sentences. Justice Kennedy, [by contrast,] specifically recognized that "the Eighth Amendment proportionality principle also applies to noncapital sentences." 501 U.S. at 997 (concurring in part and concurring in judgment). He then identified four principles of proportionality

review — "the primacy of the legislature, the variety of legitimate penological schemes, the nature of our federal system, and the requirement that
proportionality review be guided by objective factors" — that "inform the
final one: The Eighth Amendment does not require strict proportionality
between crime and sentence. Rather, it forbids only extreme sentences that
are 'grossly disproportionate' to the crime." *Id.* at 1001. [We adopt the] proportionality principles . . . distilled in Justice Kennedy's concurrence [to]
guide our application of the Eighth Amendment in the new context that we
are called upon to consider.

[B]etween 1993 and 1995, three strikes laws effected a sea change in
criminal sentencing throughout the Nation. These laws responded to widespread public concerns about crime . . . . Throughout the States, legislatures
enacting three strikes laws made a deliberate policy choice that individuals
who have repeatedly engaged in serious or violent criminal behavior . . .
must be isolated from society in order to protect the public safety. Though
three strikes laws may be relatively new, our tradition of deferring to state
legislatures in making and implementing such important policy decisions is
longstanding.

Our traditional deference to legislative policy choices finds a corollary
in the principle that the Constitution "does not mandate adoption of any
one penological theory." *Id.* at 999. A sentence can have a variety of justifications, such as incapacitation, deterrence, retribution, or rehabilitation. . . .
When the California Legislature enacted the three strikes law, it made a
judgment that protecting the public safety requires incapacitating criminals
who have already been convicted of . . . serious or violent crime. Nothing in
the Eighth Amendment prohibits California from making that choice. . . .
The State's interest in deterring crime also lends some support to the three
strikes law. . . . Four years after the passage of California's three strikes law,
the recidivism rate of parolees returned to prison for the commission of a
new crime dropped by nearly 25 percent. Even more dramatically, [accord-
ing to the California Office of the Attorney General,] "An unintended but
positive consequence of 'Three Strikes' has been the impact on parolees
leaving the state. More California parolees are now leaving the state than
parolees from other jurisdictions entering California. . . ."

To be sure, California's three strikes law has sparked controversy.
Critics have doubted the law's wisdom, cost-efficiency, and effectiveness in
reaching its goals. This criticism is appropriately directed at the legislature,
which has primary responsibility for making the difficult policy choices that
underlie any criminal sentencing scheme. We do not sit as a "superlegis-
lature" to second-guess these policy choices. It is enough that the State of
California has a reasonable basis for believing that dramatically enhanced
sentences for habitual felons "advances the goals of its criminal justice system in any substantial way." *See Solem,* 463 U.S. at 297 n.22. . . .

Ewing's sentence is justified by the State's public-safety interest in incapacitating and deterring recidivist felons, and amply supported by his own long, serious criminal record. . . . To be sure, Ewing's sentence is a long one. But it reflects a rational legislative judgment, entitled to deference, that offenders who have committed serious or violent felonies and who continue to commit felonies must be incapacitated. The State of California "was entitled to place upon [Ewing] the onus of one who is simply unable to bring his conduct within the social norms prescribed by the criminal law of the State." *Rummel*, 445 U.S. at 284. Ewing's is not "the rare case in which a threshold comparison of the crime committed and the sentence imposed leads to an inference of gross disproportionality." *Harmelin*, 501 U.S. at 1005 (Kennedy, J.). . . .

BREYER, J., dissenting. . . . The sentence [at issue here] amounts to a real prison term of at least 25 years. The sentence-triggering criminal conduct consists of the theft of three golf clubs priced at a total of $1,197. The offender has a criminal history that includes four felony convictions arising out of three separate burglaries (one armed). In *Solem v. Helm*, 463 U.S. 277 (1983), the Court found grossly disproportionate a somewhat longer sentence imposed on a recidivist offender for triggering criminal conduct that was somewhat less severe. In my view, the differences are not determinative, and the Court should reach the same ultimate conclusion here.

. . . [C]ourts faced with a "gross disproportionality" claim must first make "a threshold comparison of the crime committed and the sentence imposed." Harmelin v. Michigan, 501 U.S. 957, 1005 (1991) (Kennedy, J., concurring in part and concurring in judgment). If a claim crosses that threshold—itself a *rare* occurrence—then the court should compare the sentence at issue to other sentences . . . in the same, or in other, jurisdictions [to] "validate" or invalidate "an initial judgment that a sentence is grossly disproportionate to a crime." *Solem*, 463 U.S. at 290-291.

. . . I believe that the case before us is a "rare" case—one in which a court can say with reasonable confidence that the punishment is "grossly disproportionate" to the crime. . . . In *Rummel*, the Court held constitutional a sentence of life imprisonment *with parole available within 10 to 12 years*, for the offense of obtaining $120 by false pretenses, committed by an offender with two prior felony convictions . . . . In *Solem*, the Court held unconstitutional a sentence of life imprisonment *without parole*, for the crime of writing a $100 check on a nonexistent bank account, committed by an offender with six prior felony convictions (including three for burglary). . . . Now consider the present case. [Ewing's] prior record[] does not differ significantly . . . from that in *Solem*. [As to his offense behavior, it] would be difficult to say that the actual behavior itself here (shoplifting) differs significantly from that at issue in *Solem* . . . or in *Rummel* . . . . Rather the difference lies in the *value* of the goods obtained. That difference . . . comes down (in 1979 values) to about $379 here compared with $100 in *Solem*, or (in 1973 values) to $232 here compared with $120.75 in *Rummel*. . . .

The difference in *length* of the real prison term—the first, and critical, factor in *Solem* and *Rummel*—is considerably more important. Ewing's sentence here amounts, in real terms, to at least 25 years without parole or good-time credits. That sentence is considerably shorter than [the] sentence in *Solem*, which amounted, in real terms, to life in prison. Nonetheless Ewing's real prison term is more than twice as long as the term at issue in *Rummel*, which amounted, in real terms, to at least 10 or 12 years. And, Ewing's sentence, unlike Rummel's (but like [the] sentence in *Solem*), is long enough to consume the productive remainder of almost any offender's life. (It means that Ewing himself, seriously ill when sentenced at age 38, will likely die in prison.) The upshot is that the length of the real prison term . . . places Ewing closer to *Solem* than to *Rummel*, though the greater value of the golf clubs that Ewing stole moves Ewing's case back slightly in *Rummel*'s direction. Overall, the comparison places Ewing's sentence well within the twilight zone between *Solem* and *Rummel* . . . .

Believing Ewing's argument a strong one, sufficient to pass the threshold, I turn to the comparative analysis. . . . [B]etween the end of World War II and 1994 (when California enacted the three strikes law), no one like Ewing could have served more than *10* years in prison [based on then-governing statutes. And] statistics suggest that recidivists *of all sorts* convicted during that same time period in California served a small fraction of Ewing's real-time sentence. . . . [We also] know that California has reserved, and still reserves, Ewing-type prison time, *i.e.*, at least 25 real years in prison, for criminals convicted of crimes far worse than Ewing's. . . . As to other jurisdictions, we know the [federal government, applying] the federal Sentencing Guidelines, would impose upon a recidivist, such as Ewing, a sentence that, in any ordinary case, would not exceed 18 months in prison. . . . We also know that California, the United States, and other States supporting California in this case, despite every incentive to find someone else like Ewing . . . have come up with . . . a single instance of a similar sentence imposed outside the context of California's three strikes law, out of a prison population now approaching two million individuals. The upshot is that comparison of other sentencing practices . . . validates what an initial threshold examination suggested[, such that] we can assume for constitutional purposes that the following statement is true: Outside the California three strikes context, Ewing's recidivist sentence is virtually unique in its harshness for his offense of conviction, and by a considerable degree. . . .

. . . In sum, . . . Ewing's sentence . . . is grossly disproportionate to the triggering offense conduct—stealing three golf clubs—Ewing's recidivism notwithstanding. For these reasons, I dissent.

[Additional opinions omitted.]

NOTES AND QUESTIONS

1. Term-of-Years Proportionality Review. The Supreme Court issued *Ewing* the same day as another Eighth Amendment proportionality decision, *Lockyer v. Andrade,* 538 U.S. 63 (2003). In that case, Leandro Andrade was convicted of shoplifting from two separate stores over a span of two weeks. According to Professor Erwin Chemerinsky, who represented Andrade before the Supreme Court, Andrade was "a nine-year Army veteran and father of three" who was caught shoplifting nine children's videotapes. Combining the two separate incidents, he stole videos worth $153.54.[96]

As the Supreme Court observed, these "were not Andrade's first or only encounters with law enforcement." *Id.* at 66. Over the preceding decade, he had been convicted twice of misdemeanor theft, once for a trio of burglary offenses, and, separately, of two marijuana offenses and a parole-related offense. With respect to the most serious of these crimes, the burglaries, Professor Chemerinsky notes that Andrade "committed the three residential burglaries on the same day. He was unarmed, and nobody was home when he did this."[97]

As for the videotapes, "each of Andrade's convictions for theft . . . triggered a separate application of the three strikes law." *Id.* at 68. As a result, "[p]ursuant to California law, the judge sentenced Andrade to two consecutive terms of 25 years to life in prison," *id.,* meaning that he would be incarcerated for at least fifty years, and would likely die in prison.[98]

In a five-to-four decision, the Supreme Court upheld the sentence against Andrade's Eighth Amendment challenge, which he filed via a habeas corpus petition. Applying the standard of review governing such a challenge, the Court held that the California courts' decisions upholding Andrade's sentence were not "an unreasonable application of" the Supreme Court's Eighth Amendment precedents, as summarized in *Ewing. Id.* at 77.

Dissenting from the Court's opinion, Justice Souter said that he would have held Andrade's sentence unconstitutional "for the reasons set forth in Justice Breyer's dissent in *Ewing.*" *Id.* (Souter, J., dissenting). "This is the rare sentence of demonstrable gross disproportionality," he wrote. Indeed, he went on, "[i]f Andrade's sentence is not grossly disproportionate, the principle has no meaning." *Id.* at 83. Reflecting on and agreeing with Justice Souter, Professors Carol and Jordan Steiker, leading experts of the Court's Eighth Amendment and capital punishment jurisprudence, concluded that "[i]n the aftermath of these decisions . . . there seemed to be little remaining hope that any sentences of incarceration would be deemed disproportionate under the Eighth Amendment."[99]

2. **Whither Graham?** Seven years after deciding *Ewing* and *Lockyer,* the Supreme Court issued its decision in *Graham.* Another five-to-four opinion, this case went the other way. The Court held unconstitutional a specific type of prison sentence (life without parole) for a specific category of defendants (juveniles) with respect to a specific class of offenses (nonhomicides). Reading *Graham* and *Ewing* together, it is possible to observe some meaningful tension in the Court's reasoning across the two cases—and to detect a different overall valence with respect to its Eighth Amendment proportionality review.

Notably, the opinions are the work product of the same person. Justice Anthony Kennedy wrote the concurring opinion in *Harmelin,* which became the anchor for the Court's opinions in *Ewing* and *Lockyer* constraining proportionality review. He also wrote the Court's opinion in *Graham,* which, according to Justice Thomas' dissent, threatened to "remarkably" expand proportionality review as a tool for "immunizing any class of offenders from" criminal penalties of even moderate severity. Examining these opinions together with some of Justice Kennedy's subsequent writings and comments opposing solitary confinement, some commentators saw a trend in which he "increasingly invoked the [Eighth] [A]mendment" as a tool to limit harsh sentences of incarceration. And indeed, in 2012, two years after writing *Graham,* Justice Kennedy joined another five-to-four majority opinion extending the logic of that case to juveniles convicted of murder. *See* Miller v. Alabama, 567 U.S. 460 (2012). Concluding that everything *Graham* "said about children . . . [is] evident in the same way, and to the same degree" with respect to homicide offenses, the Court struck down a Florida statute mandating life without parole for all juveniles convicted of murder. *Id.* at 473, 479. And once again, Justice Thomas feared a slippery slope, writing in dissent that the Court's holding laid "the groundwork for future incursions on the States' authority to sentence criminals." *Id.* at 508 (Thomas, J., dissenting).[100]

But then, in 2018, Justice Kennedy retired. And by the time the Court decided its next case in this line of precedent three years later, three new Justices—Justices Gorsuch, Kavanaugh, and Barrett—had joined its ranks. In that case, *Jones v. Mississippi*, 593 U.S. 98 (2021), those Justices joined the three Justices who disagreed with Justice Kennedy's approach in *Graham*—Justices Roberts, Thomas, and Alito—to form a new Eighth Amendment majority, which tacked sharply away from the trendline *Graham* and *Miller* had charted. Specifically, in *Jones,* the Court held that juveniles convicted of homicide could be sentenced to life without parole so long as sentencing judges had discretion to consider less serious penalties. Moreover, the Court held that trial courts could impose such sentences as a matter of course, without making any findings as to a juvenile's likelihood of future dangerousness.

Justice Sotomayor dissented on behalf of herself and the two other Justices still on the Court who had joined the *Miller* majority. She opened, "Today, the Court guts *Miller v. Alabama.*" *Id.* at 129 (Sotomayor, J., dissenting). To observers like Professor Dora Klein, the writing was on the wall. "[T]he ideological shift in the makeup of the Supreme Court," Klein concludes, "undoubtedly affected the decision in *Jones,*" suggesting that any momentum toward more robust Eighth Amendment proportionality review Justice Kennedy had generated at the end of his career is unlikely to continue.[101]

3. *Long Sentences by the Numbers.* In 2022, the Council on Criminal Justice published an analysis of long prison sentences across the country. According to the report, half the people sentenced to state prison in 2020 received sentences less than five years long. By contrast, 16 percent of people sent to state prison were sentenced to 10 or more years. Of those, 83 percent were sentenced to terms between 10 and 25 years, with the remaining 17 percent receiving sentences longer than 25 years, including 4 percent sentenced to life, life without parole, or death. But as the report notes, while people serving "long sentences account for a relatively small share of state prison admissions" each year, the number of such individuals "stack[s] up over time" given that they "serve long periods." Thus, at the end of 2020, "63 percent of people in prison were serving a long prison sentence," meaning a sentence 10 years or longer.[102]

With respect to offense types, the Council reports that "[m]ore than half (56 percent) of the people admitted to prison with a long sentence in 2020 were convicted of a violent offense, while 18 percent were convicted of drug crimes." Another 11 percent were sentenced for a wide variety of offenses termed "public order" crimes, which include firearms offenses, "habitual driving under the influence, prostitution, and disorderly conduct." As for the portion of individuals convicted of certain offenses who are sentenced to long terms of incarceration, the Council provides the following graph:[103]

Figure 9.2.   Share of Newly Admitted People Sentenced to 10+ Years, 2020

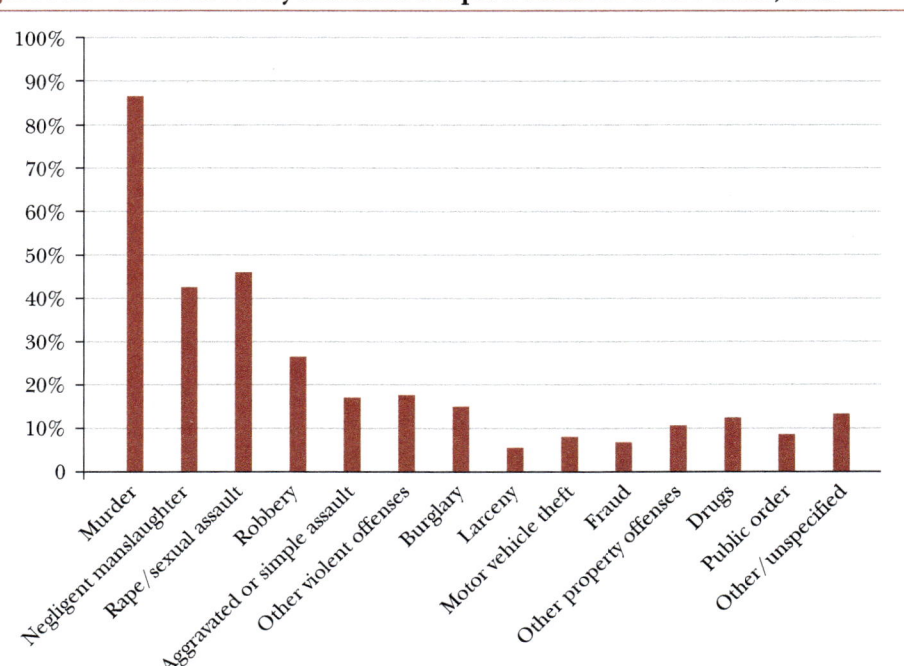

Long Sentences by the Numbers, Council on Crim. Just.

4. *Reckoning with Recidivism.* In *Ewing*, the Court held that Ewing's sentence was "justified by the State's public-safety interest in incapacitating and deterring recidivist felons." According to the Bureau of Justice Statistics, recidivism is extremely common. In an analysis of people released from state prisons across twenty-four states in 2008, researchers found that 69 percent had been convicted of a new offense by the end of 2018, half within their first two years out of prison. As noted in Chapter Two (p. 74), however, it is not clear that the fault for such high recidivism rates should be laid entirely at the feet of the individuals returning to prison, given the "growing body of work" showing that incarceration itself can "increase recidivism" by disrupting prosocial familial and community ties and by impeding economic opportunities.[104]

In view of this empirical evidence, legal philosophers offer competing thoughts on how recidivism should be counted when assessing sentence proportionality. Echoing the conventional account, Professor Youngjae Lee argues "that repeat offenders are more culpable and that sentencing enhancements for prior convictions are [thus] justifiable on retributivist grounds" because punishment should not only "fit the crime" but also "fit the person." Specifically, Lee asserts that

> we should think of the recidivist premium as stemming not from . . . repeat offenders' bad characters or allegedly defiant attitudes, but from what the repeat offenders have failed to do between the time of the previous conviction and the time of the new offense. . . . [T]he relationship between an offender and the state is altered when the first conviction and punishment occur. The offender then has an obligation to organize his life in a way that reduces the risk of his reoffending, and it is the failure to fulfill that obligation that justifies the additional punishment.[105]

By contrast, Professor Christopher Lewis argues that the widespread practice of punishing recidivists more harshly than first-time offenders gets things precisely backwards. Given the collateral consequences of criminal convictions and incarceration "and the social conditions they engender," Lewis writes, "judges and sentencing commissions" should "treat prior criminal convictions as a presumptive mitigating factor, rather than an aggravating one — imposing a recidivist sentencing *discount*, rather than a premium." As Lewis explains:

> [T]he wide range of barriers that people with prior criminal convictions face to finding employment; beginning careers; getting welfare, housing, and education; and to achieving a basic level of social status or esteem in their communities . . . give people with prior convictions stronger "incentives" than first-time offenders to commit just about any kind of crime — with the possible exception of sexual violence. So, we cannot justifiably blame or punish them for reoffending as severely as we could do for the same crime, if it were a first offense.[106]

5. Charge Bargaining vs. Sentence Bargaining. As the cases and materials thus far make clear, mandatory-minimum sentencing statutes are a prevalent feature of the American penal system—and, in the vast majority of cases, easily pass constitutional muster. To prosecutors, these statutes are an immensely powerful tool. Because while the statutes make certain sentences mandatory for a judge to impose, they are *optional* for the prosecutor to charge. A prosecutor can thus charge someone like Ewing under a recidivist statute carrying a mandatory twenty-five-year prison term, but if the defendant agrees to plead guilty, the prosecutor can offer to replace that charge with a simple theft charge, which may carry only a year or two of prison exposure. It is this basic dynamic, critics argue, that turns prosecutors into de facto adjudicators, with the power not only to ensure a case ends in conviction, but to determine the sentence as well.

A better approach, some of these critics contend, would be to move away from *charge* bargaining and toward *sentence* bargaining. As Professor Andrew Manuel Crespo describes the practice, sentence bargaining occurs when "the prosecutor negotiates with the defendant over the sentence that she will recommend to the judge if the defendant pleads guilty." Because judges often weigh prosecutors' recommendations heavily, the prosecutor maintains real leverage in sentence bargaining. But, as Professor Tracey Meares observes, the practice "necessarily limits the prosecutor's power because . . . she must share her power with judges." For this reason, Professors Ronald Wright and Marc Miller argue, "[s]entence bargains do less harm than charge bargains."[107]

Still, Professor Crespo argues, "[w]hile the judge's involvement generally renders this practice less prone to abuse than charge bargaining, prosecutors can still obtain undue leverage when engaging in sentence bargaining." As Crespo continues, prosecutors can exploit both "defendants' uncertainty about judges' future sentencing decisions" and "judges' comparative lack of access to facts about the underlying criminal conduct, which can cause judges to defer too much to prosecutors' sentencing recommendations." To mitigate such leverage, Professors Wright and Miller observe, "a growing number of states encourage . . . judicial involvement in plea discussions," in hopes of giving "defendants more complete and reliable information" about how their case might be resolved. Indeed, Crespo reports, some jurisdictions go so far as to limit, or even eliminate, prosecutors' ability to recommend specific sentences at all.[108]

6. State Constitutional Law. Some state supreme courts, interpreting their own states' constitutions, have gone further than *Graham* and *Miller* in enforcing constitutional limits on sentencing. Consider the following example.

Commonwealth v. Mattis, 224 N.E.3d 410 (Mass. 2024). When it comes to determining whether a punishment is constitutional under either the

Eighth Amendment to the United States Constitution or art. 26 of the
Massachusetts Declaration of Rights, youth matters. In *Miller v. Alabama,* the
United States Supreme Court struck down mandatory life imprisonment
without the possibility of parole for juveniles based in part on the "mitigating qualities of youth." Approximately one and one-half years later, this
court went further than *Miller* and concluded that sentencing a juvenile to
life without parole in any circumstance would violate art. 26. See Diatchenko
v. District Attorney for the Suffolk Dist., 466 Mass. 655 (2013). . . . Here, we
consider whether our holding in *Diatchenko* should be extended to apply
to emerging adults, that is, those who were eighteen, nineteen, and twenty
years of age when they committed the crime. Based on precedent and contemporary standards of decency in the Commonwealth and elsewhere, we
conclude that the answer is yes. . . .

An assessment of a punishment's proportionality occurs "in light of
contemporary standards of decency which mark the progress of society."
Id. at 669. . . . [W]here modern scientific consensus regarding a particular
class exists, it can be useful in determining the contemporary standards of
decency as they relate to that class. Advancements in scientific research have
confirmed what many know well through experience: the brains of emerging adults are not fully mature. Specifically, the scientific record strongly
supports the contention that emerging adults have the same core neurological characteristics as juveniles have. . . . [E]merging adults have a lack
of impulse control similar to sixteen and seventeen year olds in emotionally
arousing situations, are more prone to risk taking in pursuit of rewards than
those under eighteen years and those over twenty-one years, are more susceptible to peer influence than individuals over twenty-one years, and have
a greater capacity for change than older individuals due to the plasticity of
their brains. . . .

Massachusetts, like most States, distinguishes emerging adults from
older adults on a range of issues, granting rights and imposing responsibilities in a graduated manner. For example, one must be eighteen years of
age to enter binding and enforceable contracts, to sit on a jury, to purchase
lottery tickets, and to drive a common carrier motor vehicle. However, one
must be twenty-one years of age to purchase and sell alcoholic beverages, to
purchase tobacco products, to obtain a license to carry a handgun, to be a
police officer, and to gamble. These statutes reflect the commonly held view
that emerging adults generally are not equipped to assume all the responsibilities of adulthood, especially with respect to high risk activities.

We are not the first State Supreme Court to appreciate the distinct
ways in which our laws bear on emerging adults. Recently, the high courts
in Washington and Michigan prohibited the mandatory imposition of life
without the possibility of parole for those who are from eighteen to twenty
years of age, and for those who are eighteen years of age, respectively. . . .

Our comprehensive review informs us that Supreme Court precedent, as well as our own, dictates that youthful characteristics must be considered in sentencing, that the brains of emerging adults are not fully developed and are more similar to those of juveniles than older adults, and that our contemporary standards of decency in the Commonwealth and elsewhere disfavor imposing the Commonwealth's harshest sentence on this cohort. . . . As such, [emerging adult offenders] must be granted a "meaningful opportunity to obtain release based on demonstrated maturity and rehabilitation" before the Massachusetts parole board, who will "evaluate the circumstances surrounding the commission of the crime, including the age of the offender, together with all relevant information pertaining to the offender's character and actions during the intervening years since conviction." *Id.* at 674.

C. Plea Bargaining and Due Process

To this point, we have observed how substantive criminal law permits prosecutors to generate plea bargaining leverage by piling on charges and inflating sentences, and thus to threaten defendants with consequences beyond what even the prosecutor would deem fair or just—all in hopes of inducing the defendant to plead guilty. But as Professor Andrew Manuel Crespo observes, "for the prosecutor to capitalize on that leverage," she needs to be able to do more than just threaten severe consequences. She "needs to be able to replace her inflated charges with some lower set of charges that can be offered to the defendant as an inducement to plead guilty." Because remember, "[i]t is the differential between the threat and the offer that creates the leverage."[109]

For this reason, Crespo continues, "plea bargaining scholars have long noted that restricting a prosecutor's ability to *reduce* a defendant's sentencing exposure can make it more 'costly to choose unrealistically high charges' at the outset of the negotiations." Indeed, if the prosecutor can offer only a small discount from an inflated set of charges, the defendant's incentives could flip. As the costs of going to trial shrink, it is increasingly rational to try one's luck with a jury and hope for an acquittal, which, as Crespo observes, the jury has "unreviewable and plenary power" to grant. Put more simply, it is at least conceptually possible to regulate prosecutors' plea bargaining power by regulating the *size* of the differentials between the charges they threaten and the plea deals they offer. Indeed, Professor James Vorenberg once predicted that a "prescribed sentencing concession of ten or twenty percent . . . for a guilty plea" would "avoid much of the injustice" involved in plea bargaining. A cap along such lines, Professor Russel Covey later argued, would "reduce prosecutorial incentives to overcharge criminal defendants by eliminating the bargaining leverage that can be obtained through strategic overcharging."[110]

Consider these arguments as you read the next two cases.

Brady v. United States

397 U.S. 742 (1970)

WHITE, J. In 1959, petitioner was charged with kidnaping in violation of 18 U.S.C. §1201(a). [Under that statute, a convicted defendant could be sentenced to death only upon a jury's recommendation after trial; a defendant who pleaded guilty thus insulated himself from a death sentence. Petitioner pleaded guilty and was sentenced to 50 years' imprisonment, later reduced to 30. A decade after petitioner's conviction, this Court decided in *United States v. Jackson*, 390 U.S. 570 (1968), that the statutory framework at issue "impose[d] an impermissible burden upon the exercise of a constitutional right," namely, the Sixth Amendment right to demand a jury trial, insofar as the death penalty was "applicable only to those defendants who assert[ed] the right to contest their guilt before a jury." *Id.* at 581. As a result, the *Jackson* Court held, a death sentence could not be imposed under the statute as written.]

[Following our decision in *Jackson*, petitioner sought to undo his plea, arguing that it was not voluntarily given. Specifically, he argues that the statutory scheme] operated to coerce his plea, [that] his counsel exerted impermissible pressure upon him, and [that] his plea was induced by representations with respect to reduction of sentence and clemency. . . . Since the "inevitable effect" of the death penalty provision of §1201(a) was said by the [*Jackson*] Court to be the needless encouragement of pleas of guilty and waivers of jury trial, Brady contends that *Jackson* requires the invalidation of every plea of guilty entered under that section, at least when the fear of death is shown to have been a factor in the plea. Petitioner, however, has read far too much into the *Jackson* opinion. . . . Plainly, it seems to us, *Jackson* ruled neither that all pleas of guilty encouraged by the fear of a possible death sentence are involuntary pleas nor that such encouraged pleas are invalid whether involuntary or not. . . .

[A] plea . . . is the defendant's . . . waiver of his right to trial before a jury or a judge. Waivers of constitutional rights not only must be voluntary but must be knowing, intelligent acts done with sufficient awareness of the relevant circumstances and likely consequences. On neither score was Brady's plea of guilty invalid. The trial judge in 1959 found the plea voluntary before accepting it [and,] after an evidentiary hearing [on Brady's current challenge, a district court judge once again] found that the plea was voluntarily made . . . . We see no reason on this record to disturb the judgment of those courts. Petitioner, advised by competent counsel, tendered his plea after his codefendant, who had already given a confession, determined to plead guilty and became available to testify against petitioner. It was this development that the District Court found to have triggered Brady's guilty plea. . . .

But even if we assume that Brady would not have pleaded guilty except for the death penalty provision of §1201(a), this assumption merely identifies the penalty provision as a "but for" cause of his plea. . . . The State to some degree encourages pleas of guilty at every important step in the criminal process. For some people, . . . apprehension and charge, both threatening acts by the Government, jar them into admitting their guilt. In still other cases, the post-indictment accumulation of evidence may convince the defendant and his counsel that a trial is not worth the agony and expense to the defendant and his family. All these pleas of guilty are valid in spite of the State's responsibility for some of the factors motivating the pleas . . . .

Of course, the agents of the State may not produce a plea by actual or threatened physical harm or by mental coercion overbearing the will of the defendant. But nothing of the sort is claimed in this case; nor is there evidence that Brady was so gripped by fear of the death penalty or hope of leniency that he did not or could not, with the help of counsel, rationally weigh the advantages of going to trial against the advantages of pleading guilty. . . . Insofar as the voluntariness of his plea is concerned, there is [thus] little to differentiate Brady from [a] defendant . . . who is advised by counsel that the judge is normally more lenient with defendants who plead guilty than with those who go to trial [or a] defendant who pleads guilty to certain counts with the understanding that other charges will be dropped. In each of these situations,[8] as in Brady's case, the defendant might never plead guilty absent the possibility or certainty that the plea will result in a lesser penalty than the sentence that could be imposed after a trial and a verdict of guilty. We decline to hold, however, that a guilty plea is compelled and invalid under the Fifth Amendment whenever motivated by the defendant's desire to accept the certainty or probability of a lesser penalty rather than face a wider range of possibilities extending from acquittal to conviction and a higher penalty authorized by law for the crime charged.

The issue we deal with is inherent in the criminal law and its administration because . . . both the State and the defendant often find it advantageous to preclude the possibility of the maximum penalty authorized by law. For a defendant who sees slight possibility of acquittal, the advantages

---

8. We here make no reference to the situation where the prosecutor or judge, or both, deliberately employ their charging and sentencing powers to induce a particular defendant to tender a plea of guilty. In Brady's case there is no claim that the prosecutor threatened prosecution on a charge not justified by the evidence or that the trial judge threatened Brady with a harsher sentence if convicted after trial in order to induce him to plead guilty.

of pleading guilty and limiting the probable penalty are obvious — his exposure is reduced, the correctional processes can begin immediately, and
the practical burdens of a trial are eliminated. For the State there are also
advantages — the more promptly imposed punishment after an admission
of guilt may more effectively attain the objectives of punishment; and with
the avoidance of trial, scarce judicial and prosecutorial resources are con-
served . . . . It is this mutuality of advantage that perhaps explains the fact
that at present well over three-fourths of the criminal convictions in this
country rest on pleas of guilty, a great many of them no doubt motivated
at least in part by the hope or assurance of a lesser penalty than might be
imposed if there were a guilty verdict after a trial to judge or jury. . . . A contrary holding would require the States and Federal Government to forbid
guilty pleas altogether. . . . The Fifth Amendment does not reach so far. . . .

The record before us [shows that Brady] was advised by competent
counsel, he was made aware of the nature of the charge against him, and
there was nothing to indicate that he was incompetent or otherwise not in
control of his mental faculties. . . . [He] was aware of precisely what he was
doing. . . . A defendant is not entitled to withdraw his plea merely because
he discovers long after the plea has been accepted that his calculus misap-
prehended the quality of the State's case or the likely penalties attached to
alternative courses of action. More particularly, absent misrepresentation
or other impermissible conduct by state agents, a voluntary plea of guilty
intelligently made in the light of the then applicable law does not become
vulnerable because later judicial decisions indicate that the plea rested on a
faulty premise. . . .

[Additional opinions omitted.]

Bordenkircher v. Hayes

434 U.S. 357 (1978)

STEWART, J. The question in this case is whether the Due Process Clause of
the Fourteenth Amendment is violated when a state prosecutor carries out
a threat made during plea negotiations to reindict the accused on more
serious charges if he does not plead guilty to the offense with which he was
originally charged.

The respondent, Paul Lewis Hayes, was indicted . . . on a charge of
uttering a forged instrument in the amount of $88.30, an offense then pun-
ishable by a term of 2 to 10 years in prison. After arraignment, Hayes, his
retained counsel, and the Commonwealth's Attorney met . . . to discuss a
possible plea agreement. During these conferences the prosecutor offered
to recommend a sentence of five years in prison if Hayes would plead guilty
to the indictment. He also said that if Hayes did not plead guilty and "save[]
the court the inconvenience and necessity of a trial," he would return to the

grand jury to seek an indictment under the Kentucky Habitual Criminal Act, which would subject Hayes to a mandatory sentence of life imprisonment by reason of his two prior felony convictions. Hayes chose not to plead guilty, and the prosecutor did obtain an indictment charging him under the Habitual Criminal Act. It is not disputed that the recidivist charge was fully justified by the evidence, that the prosecutor was in possession of this evidence at the time of the original indictment, and that Hayes' refusal to plead guilty to the original charge was what led to his indictment under the habitual criminal statute. A jury found Hayes guilty [and, as] required by the habitual offender statute, he was sentenced to a life term in the penitentiary. . . .

"Whatever might be the situation in an ideal world, the fact is that the guilty plea and the often concomitant plea bargain are important components of this country's criminal justice system. Properly administered, they can benefit all concerned." Blackledge v. Allison, 431 U.S. 63, 71 (1977). The open acknowledgment of this previously clandestine practice has led this Court to recognize the importance of counsel during plea negotiations, the need for a public record indicating that a plea was knowingly and voluntarily made, and the requirement that a prosecutor's plea-bargaining promise must be kept. The decision of the Court of Appeals in the present case, however, did not deal with considerations such as these, but held that the substance of the plea offer itself violated the limitations imposed by the Due Process Clause of the Fourteenth Amendment. *Cf.* Brady v. United States, 397 U.S. 742, 751 n.8 (1970). For the reasons that follow, we have concluded that the Court of Appeals was mistaken in so ruling.

This Court [has held] that the Due Process Clause of the Fourteenth Amendment . . . prohibit[s] a prosecutor from reindicting a convicted misdemeanant on a felony charge after the defendant had invoked an appellate remedy[.] [Such a] situation [entails] a "realistic likelihood of 'vindictiveness'" [and is thus unconstitutional]. Blackledge v. Perry, 417 U.S. 21, 27 (1974). [In that case,] the Court was dealing with the State's unilateral imposition of a penalty upon a defendant who had chosen to exercise a legal right to attack his original conviction—a situation "very different from the give-and-take negotiation common in plea bargaining between the prosecution and defense, which arguably possess relatively equal bargaining power." Parker v. North Carolina, 397 U.S. 790, 809 (1970) (opinion of Brennan, J.). . . . To punish a person because he has done what the law plainly allows him to do is a due process violation of the most basic sort, and for an agent of the State to pursue a course of action whose objective is to penalize a person's reliance on his legal rights is "patently unconstitutional." Chaffin v. Stynchcombe, 412 U.S. 17, 32-33 n.20 (1973). But in the "give-and-take" of plea bargaining, there is no such element of punishment or retaliation so long as the accused is free to accept or reject the prosecution's offer.

Plea bargaining flows from "the mutuality of advantage" to defendants and prosecutors, each with his own reasons for wanting to avoid trial. *Brady*, 397 U.S. at 752. Defendants advised by competent counsel and protected by other procedural safeguards are presumptively capable of intelligent choice in response to prosecutorial persuasion, and unlikely to be driven to false self-condemnation. . . . While confronting a defendant with the risk of more severe punishment clearly may have a "discouraging effect on the defendant's assertion of his trial rights, the imposition of these difficult choices is an inevitable"—and permissible—"attribute of any legitimate system which tolerates and encourages the negotiation of pleas." *Chaffin*, 412 U.S. at 31. It follows that, by tolerating and encouraging the negotiation of pleas, this Court has necessarily accepted as constitutionally legitimate the simple reality that the prosecutor's interest at the bargaining table is to persuade the defendant to forgo his right to plead not guilty.

. . . [S]o long as the prosecutor has probable cause to believe that the accused committed an offense defined by statute, the decision whether or not to prosecute, and what charge to file or bring before a grand jury, generally rests entirely in his discretion. Within the limits set by the legislature's constitutionally valid definition of chargeable offenses, "the conscious exercise of some selectivity in enforcement is not in itself a federal constitutional violation" so long as "the selection was not deliberately based upon an unjustifiable standard such as race, religion, or other arbitrary classification." Oyler v. Boles, 368 U.S. 448, 456 (1962). . . .

There is no doubt that the breadth of discretion that our country's legal system vests in prosecuting attorneys carries with it the potential for both individual and institutional abuse. And broad though that discretion may be, there are undoubtedly constitutional limits upon its exercise. We hold only that the course of conduct engaged in by the prosecutor in this case, which no more than openly presented the defendant with the unpleasant alternatives of forgoing trial or facing charges on which he was plainly subject to prosecution, did not violate the Due Process Clause of the Fourteenth Amendment.

BLACKMUN, J., dissenting. . . . [I]n this case vindictiveness is present to the same extent as it was thought to be in . . . *Perry*; the prosecutor here admitted that the sole reason for the new indictment was to discourage the respondent from exercising his right to a trial. Even had such an admission not been made, when plea negotiations, conducted in the face of the less serious charge under the first indictment, fail, charging by a second indictment a more serious crime for the same conduct creates "a strong inference" of vindictiveness. . . . I therefore do not understand why . . . due process does not require that the prosecution justify its action on some basis other than discouraging respondent from the exercise of his right to a trial. . . .

[I would therefore not permit a prosecutor to replace an initial charge with a substantially more severe one to induce a guilty plea. Of course, such a holding might merely] prompt the aggressive prosecutor to bring the greater charge initially in every case, and only thereafter to bargain. The consequences to the accused would still be adverse, for then he would bargain against a greater charge, face the likelihood of increased bail, and run the risk that the court would be less inclined to accept a bargained plea. Nonetheless, it is far preferable to hold the prosecution to the charge it was originally content to bring and to justify in the eyes of its public.[2]

POWELL, J. dissenting. . . . It seems to me that the question to be asked . . . is whether the prosecutor reasonably might have charged respondent under the Habitual Criminal Act in the first place. The deference that courts properly accord the exercise of a prosecutor's discretion perhaps would foreclose judicial criticism if the prosecutor originally had sought an indictment under that Act, as unreasonable as it would have seemed. But here the prosecutor evidently made a reasonable, responsible judgment not to subject an individual to a mandatory life sentence when his only new offense had societal implications as limited as those accompanying the uttering of a single $88 forged check . . . . I think it may be inferred that the prosecutor himself deemed it unreasonable and not in the public interest to put this defendant in jeopardy of a sentence of life imprisonment.

There may be situations in which a prosecutor would be fully justified in seeking a fresh indictment for a more serious offense. . . . In most cases a court could not know why the harsher indictment was sought, and an inquiry into the prosecutor's motive would neither be indicated nor likely to be fruitful. In those cases, I would agree with the majority that the situation would not differ materially from one in which the higher charge was brought at the outset.

But this is not such a case. Here, any inquiry into the prosecutor's purpose is made unnecessary by his candid acknowledgment that he threatened to procure and in fact procured the habitual criminal indictment because of respondent's insistence on exercising his constitutional rights. We have stated in unequivocal terms, [that] "if the only objective of a state practice is to discourage the assertion of constitutional rights it is 'patently

---

2. That prosecutors, without saying so, may sometimes bring charges more serious than they think appropriate for the ultimate disposition of a case, in order to gain bargaining leverage with a defendant, does not add support to today's decision, for this Court, in its approval of the advantages to be gained from plea negotiations, has never openly sanctioned such deliberate overcharging or taken such a cynical view of the bargaining process. [This is so even though, in practice,] it is impossible to show that this is what the prosecutor is doing, and the courts necessarily have deferred to the prosecutor's exercise of discretion in initial charging decisions. . . .

unconstitutional.'" Chaffin v. Stynchcombe, 412 U.S. 17, 32 n.20 (1973). And in *Brady v. United States*, 397 U.S. 742 (1970), we drew a distinction between the situation there approved and the "situation where the prosecutor or judge, or both, deliberately employ their charging and sentencing powers to induce a particular defendant to tender a plea of guilty." *Id.* at 751 n.8.

The plea-bargaining process, as recognized by this Court, is essential to the functioning of the criminal-justice system. It normally affords genuine benefits to defendants as well as to society. And if the system is to work effectively, prosecutors must be accorded the widest discretion, within constitutional limits, in conducting bargaining. This is especially true when a defendant is represented by counsel and presumably is fully advised of his rights. Only in the most exceptional case should a court conclude that the scales of the bargaining are so unevenly balanced as to arouse suspicion. In this case, the prosecutor's actions denied respondent due process because their admitted purpose was to discourage and then to penalize with unique severity his exercise of constitutional rights[, which] is not a constitutionally permissible exercise of discretion.

NOTES AND QUESTIONS

1. The Defense Attorney's Role in Plea Bargaining. The opinions in *Brady* and *Bordenkircher* hold that the plea deals in those cases satisfied the Constitution's due process requirements because, to quote the *Brady* Court, the defendant "was advised by competent counsel," who helped ensure he was fully "aware of the nature of the charge against him." And in fact, the Supreme Court has separately held that the Sixth Amendment guarantees every criminal defendant a right to an effective attorney, regardless of his ability to pay. *See* Gideon v. Wainwright, 372 U.S. 335 (1963); Strickland v. Washington, 466 U.S. 668 (1984). This right extends to the plea bargaining process, such that "[b]efore deciding whether to plead guilty, a defendant is entitled to 'the effective assistance of competent counsel'" who must give him reasonable advice as to the "direct and collateral consequences" of pleading guilty. Padilla v. Kentucky, 559 U.S. 356, 364-365 (2010). But to what extent should advice from a defense attorney render a plea deal constitutional? Consider the following excerpts describing and critiquing the role of defense counsel in the plea bargaining process.

Albert W. Alschuler, *The Supreme Court, the Defense Attorney, and the Guilty Plea,* 47 U. Colo. L. Rev. 1, 55-58 (1975): If a defendant has been fully advised by his attorney, his guilty plea will inevitably reflect a knowing abandonment of his rights. In Brady, however, the Supreme Court seemed to conclude that a competently counseled guilty plea would ordinarily be, not only a knowing plea, but a voluntary plea as well. [But] the presence of counsel has little relevance to the question of voluntariness. A guilty plea entered at gunpoint is no less involuntary because an attorney is present to explain how the gun works.

Under today's guilty-plea system, the basic function of the defense attorney is indeed to explain "how the gun works"—something that was illustrated by the record in *Brady.* . . . For several months of pretrial detention, the defendant . . . insisted that he was innocent and that he wanted a jury trial. After a conscientious investigation of the facts and the law, however, the defendant's attorney . . . informed the defendant that he "just couldn't go to a jury . . . because it would be almost sure conviction and possibly a death penalty." The attorney told the defendant that "he would be convicted beyond a shadow of a doubt."

. . . When [Brady eventually] agreed to plead guilty [the] defense attorney was, I think, entitled to feel gratified; he had done a capable job and may indeed have saved the defendant from a death sentence. The defendant's principal complaint did not, however, concern his attorney's performance; it was directed to the fact that exercise of the right to trial might have incurred an awesome penalty. This underlying reality was beyond the defense attorney's control but not beyond the control of the Supreme Court.

Andrew Manuel Crespo, *No Justice, No Pleas,* Inquest (Apr. 20, 2023). When I was a public defender, I advised scores of individuals—almost all of them Black men—as they considered plea deals placed before them by the state. Each time that I conveyed a plea offer, I watched their eyes fall as they wrestled with the cruelty of it all. The oppressive weight of prison, masquerading behind the façade of a supposedly welfare-maximizing choice. A "bargain."

It was obvious from the start that what was happening here was anything but. Nor did it take long for me to question my role in it all. . . . As a lawyer, I could calculate and compare the sentencing ranges associated with any given plea deal. I could offer careful advice about the pros and cons of the different options. But the people confronting these choices needed more than information and advice. They needed power.

Paul D. Butler, *Poor People Lose: Gideon and the Critique of Rights,* 122 Yale L.J. 2176, 2178 (2013). The reason that prisons are filled with poor people, and that rich people rarely go to prison, is not because the rich have better lawyers than the poor. It is because prison is for the poor, and not the rich. In criminal cases poor people lose most of the time, not because indigent defense is inadequately funded, although it is, and not because defense attorneys for poor people are ineffective, although some are. Poor people lose, most of the time, because in American criminal justice, poor people are losers. Prison is designed for them. This is the real crisis of indigent defense.

2. Plea Bargaining Caps and Bans. As the foregoing materials make clear, federal constitutional law does not limit a prosecutor's ability to replace one set of charges with another in the course of plea bargaining. Under *Bordenkircher,* a prosecutor can charge a person accused of passing an $88 forged check with an offense triggering a mandatory life sentence—and offer to replace that charge with one carrying a sentence as low as two years if the defendant were to plead guilty. That differential is arguably not so different from "death versus a fifty-cent fine," the differential Professor John Langbein imagined when arguing that plea bargaining is "coercive in the same sense as torture."

In view of the Supreme Court's rulings, critics who believe plea bargaining practices are fundamentally coercive have looked to state laws and internal prosecutorial policies in hopes of regulating—or even ending—such tactics. With respect to internal prosecutorial policies, Professors Ronald Wright and Marc Miller urge district attorneys and other head prosecutors to embrace what they call "the screening/bargaining tradeoff." Specifically, they say, prosecutors should gather "sufficient information" about a given case "before the initial charge is filed" and "make an early and careful assessment" of the case's merits. Then, they should "file only appropriate charges," meaning charges "the office would generally want to result in a criminal conviction and sanction" and that it "can very likely prove in court." Finally, "and critically," they argue, "the office must severely restrict all plea bargaining, and most especially charge bargaining."[111]

Importantly, Wright and Miller go on to observe, their proposed ban on plea bargaining is not hypothetical.

> We know this practice is viable because it is now operating in a few American jurisdictions, without much controversy and without attracting the attention it deserves. For instance, over the last three decades New Orleans District Attorney Harry Connick has emphasized early screening of cases and has actively discouraged any changes of criminal charges as a result of negotiations after the charges are filed. [Data] containing detailed information on more than ten years' worth of felony cases [in] New Orleans . . . confirms that . . . [t]his screening leads to relatively high rates of declination (that is, refusals to prosecute a case after the police recommend charges). When combined with policies discouraging reductions in charges once they are filed, the results are lower levels of negotiated pleas, slightly higher rates of trial, and notably higher rates of open guilty pleas than in typical American jurisdictions. . . .
>
> [These results track one of] the most famous American plea bargaining bans [which] occurred in Alaska during the 1970s and 1980s [when] Attorney General Avrum Gross declared that prosecutors would no longer engage in charge bargaining or sentence bargaining. . . . Major studies [of the policy's implementation showed that] both charge bargaining and sentence bargaining became rare events . . . . For a few years, the trial rate increased modestly. Seven percent of charged cases went to trial before

the ban, and the rate moved to 10% before returning to 7% by the end of the 1980s. Since the cases were not ending in negotiated pleas or trials, what was happening to them? The answer was a combination of aggressive screening and open guilty pleas. Before the ban, prosecutors in Fairbanks refused to prosecute about 4% of the felonies referred to them by the police or other investigators. After the ban, the proportion of felonies that prosecutors declined to prosecute increased to about 44%. A large portion of the case load (about 23%) was disposed of through open pleas of guilt.[112]

The plea bargaining policies described above were self-imposed. Prosecutors opted to restrain themselves voluntarily. But as Professor Andrew Manuel Crespo argues, plea bargaining differentials can also "be regulated directly" by the rules of criminal procedure. As he writes, a "prosecutor's ability to trade charges for guilty pleas is a direct function of the law of amendment and dismissal, which . . . determine when and whether one set of charges can be replaced with another—a necessary component of any bargain." According to a survey Crespo conducted of the various states, procedural rules governing this issue vary across jurisdictions: "Thirteen states afford prosecutors the full range of flexibility in charge sliding," but "the majority (thirty-three) require judicial approval before charges can be amended or dismissed—with fifteen of those expressly granting judges the authority to reject charge bargains that they deem inappropriate."[113]

3. The Shadow of Trial. As the preceding note indicates, rules and practices restricting plea bargaining can and have had substantial decarceral impacts, in some instances causing prosecutorial declination rates to increase tenfold. Notably, though, trial rates did not increase very much—and large numbers of people still pled guilty. On one view, this is a sign of the system working well. The people who pled guilty under "open pleas" without any promise of leniency must have thought that doing so was in their best interest, and we should treat their decisions as both welfare-enhancing and fair. Or so the argument goes. But according to Professor Daniel Harawa, before we can conclude that such open pleas are fair, we need to examine the fairness of the backdrop against which they are made: the trial system.

Daniel Harawa, *Trials Without Justice,* Inquest (Sept. 21, 2021). In theory, I believe in the power of juries to help advance justice . . . . I was a public defender in a well-resourced office where lawyers were unafraid to take cases to trial and would often win. It was also a jurisdiction where juries were diverse, the white people were mostly "progressive," and the public defenders and their investigators were unrelenting. If I were a defendant in that jurisdiction (or a similar jurisdiction), depending on the strength of my case, I may readily take my chances and go to trial (although my colleagues were also very skilled at extracting client-centered pleas).

I also know that Keith Tharpe was condemned to death in Georgia by a white juror who called him a "n****r*" and wondered if Black people even have souls. I know that Andre Thomas, who just appealed his case to the Supreme Court, was condemned to death in Texas by white jurors who openly opposed interracial relationships for fear of diluting the white race. That Curtis Flowers was tried for a murder that he did not commit *six* times in Mississippi, and, every time the jury was all white or mostly white, it returned a guilty verdict and condemned him to death, but when the jury was diverse, it could not reach a verdict. These are just a few fairly recent examples. Race can color all aspects of trial. It can determine whether you believe a police officer or the alibi witness. Whether you are whipped up or disgusted by a prosecutor's dog whistle language. And even whether you think a person deserves punishment in the first place. Because I am Black, if I were a defendant in many places across the country and the prosecutor presented me with a decent plea offer, I might take it, no matter how strong my case or how firm my innocence. I may use whatever agency I have to extract the best plea possible, out of the belief that this may be the closest thing to "justice" I could hope to attain.

The truth is that race affects trials. Indeed, race and racism can distort what one even believes is *true.* Thus, race can, does, and (unfortunately) should weigh into a Black or Brown defendant's decision on whether to accept a plea or risk trial. Race is a stubbornly complicating dynamic in the plea-bargaining process. This is important to remember when criticizing plea bargaining and billing trial as the best alternative. . . . After all, there is no justice in replacing one unfair system with another. If we have a plea problem in jurisdictions across the country, we have a trial problem, too. One reinforces the other. Until we fix both, defendants, especially Black and Brown defendants, will lose out no matter which route they choose.

D. Race and Equal Protection

Throughout this book, we have examined the ways in which race shapes the American penal system. And given that the system is in large part "a system of pleas," Lafler v. Cooper, 566 U.S. 156, 168 (2012), we should not be surprised if race shapes prosecutors' charging practices and, as a result, the outcomes of criminal prosecutions. The following excerpts describe the salient role prosecutors play in a complex system of actors and institutions that, together, produce racially disparate criminal case outcomes. And the second excerpt attempts to measure prosecutors' contribution to those disparities. Following these excerpts, you will read two Supreme Court opinions from the equal protection context. The first addresses prosecutors' charging decisions, while the second steps back to situate those decisions within the broader criminal process.

Byungbae Kim et al., *Federal Sentencing as a Complex Collaborative Process: Judges, Prosecutors, Judge-Prosecutor Dyads, and Disparity in Sentencing*, 53 Criminology 597, 597-598 (2015). [R]esearch examining sentencing decisions typically has focused on the role played by the judge in determining whether to sentence the offender to prison and, if so, for how long. . . . This focus on the judge is understandable but misleading. . . . The sentences defendants eventually receive are produced by a collaborative exercise involving legislators, prosecutors, jurors, probation officials, trial court judges, corrections officials, and possibly appellate court judges. . . . The role played by the prosecutor is particularly salient. The prosecutor decides whether to file charges, what charges to file, and whether to engage in plea bargaining as the case moves toward trial. The prosecutor also may recommend a sentence or, in the federal court system, file a motion for a downward departure . . . from the guidelines . . . . The highly discretionary and consequential decisions made by prosecutors clearly affect sentence severity. They also have the potential to introduce disparity into the sentencing process. One of the important goals of the sentencing reform movement—in which indeterminate sentencing schemes were replaced with sentencing guidelines and mandatory minimum sentences—was to increase uniformity and reduce unwarranted disparity in sentencing by constraining judicial discretion. These reforms, however, did not restrain prosecutorial discretion. In fact, several scholars have contended that the reforms did not reduce overall discretion in sentencing; rather, they simply shifted discretion from the judge at sentencing to the prosecutor at charging and during plea negotiations. . . .

M. Marit Rehavi & Sonja B. Starr, *Racial Disparity in Federal Criminal Sentences*, 122 J. Polit. Econ. 1320, 1320-1323 (2014). Black men constitute 6 percent of the US adult population but are approximately 35 percent of the prison population and are incarcerated at a rate six times that of white males. One in three black men will be incarcerated at some point in his life. The federal prison system is the largest and fastest-growing in the United States. Black male defendants in federal criminal cases receive much longer prison sentences than white men do. In federal courts, the average sentence during 2008 and 2009 was 55 months for whites and 90 months for blacks. The extent to which these disparities reflect differences in criminal conduct as opposed to differential treatment is a long-standing question in law and economics. That is, do otherwise similar black and white arrestees caught engaging in the same criminal conduct receive different prison sentences? . . .

[Our] data allow us to compare the sentencing outcomes for black and white men who are arrested for the same offenses and appear comparable when they enter the federal justice system. We thus estimate the extent to which observed racial disparities in federal sentences can be explained by differences in arrest offense characteristics and preexisting defendant characteristics such as criminal history. . . . We find that the majority of the disparity between black and white sentences can be explained by differences in legally permitted characteristics, in particular, the arrest offense and the defendant's criminal history. Black arrestees are also disproportionately concentrated in federal districts that have higher sentences in general.

Yet even after we control for these and other prior characteristics, an unexplained black-white sentence disparity of approximately 9 percent remains . . . . There are approximately 95,000 black men in federal prisons. Eliminating the "black premium" that we identify would reduce the steady-state level of black men in federal prison by 8,000-11,000 men and save $230-$320 million per year in direct costs.

Observing each case from arrest through to sentencing makes it possible to pinpoint where unexplained disparities emerge in the judicial process. We identify an important procedural mechanism that appears to give rise to the majority of the otherwise-unexplained disparity in sentences: how prosecutors initially choose to handle the case, in particular, the decision to bring charges carrying "mandatory minimum" sentences. The racial disparities in this decision are stark: ceteris paribus, black men have 1.75 times the odds of facing such charges . . . . The initial mandatory minimum charging decision alone is capable of explaining more than half of the black-white sentence disparities not otherwise explained by pre-charge characteristics. . . .

United States v. Armstrong

517 U.S. 456 (1996)

REHNQUIST, C.J. . . . In April 1992, respondents were indicted in the United States District Court for the Central District of California on charges of conspiring to possess with intent to distribute more than 50 grams of cocaine base (crack) and conspiring to distribute the same, in violation of 21 U.S.C. §§841 and 846, and [on] federal firearms offenses. . . . In response to the indictment, respondents filed a motion for discovery or for dismissal of the indictment, alleging that they were selected for federal prosecution because they are black. In support of their motion, they offered . . . an affidavit by a "Paralegal Specialist," employed by the Office of the Federal Public Defender representing one of the respondents. The only allegation in the affidavit was that, in every one of the [twenty-four] §841 or §846 cases closed by the office during 1991, the defendant was black. Accompanying the affidavit was a "study" listing the 24 defendants, their race, whether they were prosecuted for dealing cocaine as well as crack, and the status of each case.

The Government opposed the discovery motion, arguing, among other things, that there was no evidence or allegation "that the Government has acted unfairly or has prosecuted non-black defendants or failed to prosecute them." The District Court granted the motion. It ordered the Government (1) to provide a list of all cases from the last three years in which the Government charged both cocaine and firearms offenses, (2) to identify the race of the defendants in those cases, (3) to identify what levels of law enforcement were involved in the investigations of those cases, and (4) to explain its criteria for deciding to prosecute those defendants for federal cocaine offenses.

The Government moved for reconsideration of the District Court's discovery order [and attached] affidavits and other evidence to explain why it had chosen to prosecute respondents and why respondents' study did not support the inference that the Government was singling out blacks for cocaine prosecution. The federal and local agents participating in the case alleged in affidavits that race played no role in their investigation. . . .

In response, one of respondents' attorneys submitted an affidavit alleging that an intake coordinator at a drug treatment center had told her that there are "an equal number of caucasian users and dealers to minority users and dealers." Respondents also submitted an affidavit from a criminal defense attorney alleging that in his experience many nonblacks are prosecuted in state court for crack offenses, and a newspaper article reporting that federal "crack criminals . . . are being punished far more severely than if they had been caught with powder cocaine, and almost every single one of them is black." Newton, *Harsher Crack Sentences Criticized as Racial Inequity*, Los Angeles Times, Nov. 23, 1992.

. . . A selective-prosecution claim is not a defense on the merits to the criminal charge itself, but an independent assertion that the prosecutor has brought the charge for reasons forbidden by the Constitution. Our cases delineating the necessary elements to prove a claim of selective prosecution have taken great pains to explain that the standard is a demanding one. These cases afford a background presumption that the showing necessary to obtain discovery should itself be a significant barrier to the litigation of insubstantial claims.

A selective-prosecution claim asks a court to exercise judicial power over a "special province" of the Executive. Heckler v. Chaney, 470 U.S. 821, 832 (1985). The Attorney General and United States Attorneys retain "broad discretion" to enforce the Nation's criminal laws. Wayte v. United States, 470 U.S. 598, 607 (1985). . . . As a result, "the presumption of regularity supports" their prosecutorial decisions and, "in the absence of clear evidence to the contrary, courts presume that they have properly discharged their official duties." United States v. Chemical Foundation, Inc., 272 U.S. 1, 14-15 (1926). In the ordinary case, "so long as the prosecutor has probable cause to believe that the accused committed an offense defined by statute, the decision whether or not to prosecute, and what charge to file or bring before a grand jury, generally rests entirely in his discretion." Bordenkircher v. Hayes, 434 U.S. 357, 364 (1978).

Of course, a prosecutor's discretion is "subject to constitutional constraints." United States v. Batchelder, 442 U.S. 114, 125, (1979). One of these constraints . . . is that the decision whether to prosecute may not be based on "an unjustifiable standard such as race, religion, or other arbitrary classification." Oyler v. Boles, 368 U.S. 448, 456 (1962). . . . The requirements for a selective-prosecution claim draw on ordinary equal protection standards. The claimant must demonstrate that the federal prosecutorial policy had a discriminatory effect and that it was motivated by a discriminatory purpose. To establish a discriminatory effect in a race case, the claimant must show that similarly situated individuals of a different race were not prosecuted. . . .

Having reviewed the requirements to prove a selective-prosecution claim, we turn to the showing necessary to obtain discovery in support of such a claim. If discovery is ordered, the Government must assemble from its own files documents which might corroborate or refute the defendant's claim. . . . It will divert prosecutors' resources and may disclose the Government's prosecutorial strategy. The justifications for a rigorous standard for the elements of a selective-prosecution claim thus require a correspondingly rigorous standard for discovery in aid of such a claim.

. . . The Court of Appeals [ruled in favor of the respondents] in part because it started "with the presumption that people of *all* races commit *all* types of crimes — not with the premise that any type of crime is the exclusive province of any particular racial or ethnic group." 48 F.3d 1508, 1516-1517 (9th Cir. 1995). It cited no authority for this proposition, which seems contradicted by the most recent statistics of the United States Sentencing Commission. Those statistics show: More than 90% of the persons sentenced in 1994 for crack cocaine trafficking were black; 93.4% of convicted LSD dealers were white; and 91% of those convicted for pornography or prostitution were white. Presumptions at war with presumably reliable statistics have no proper place in the analysis of this issue.

. . . In the present case, if the claim of selective prosecution were well founded, it should not have been an insuperable task to prove that persons of other races were being treated differently than respondents. For instance, respondents could have investigated whether similarly situated persons of other races were prosecuted by the State of California and were known to federal law enforcement officers, but were not prosecuted in federal court. We think the required threshold — a credible showing of different treatment of similarly situated persons — adequately balances the Government's interest in vigorous prosecution and the defendant's interest in avoiding selective prosecution.

[R]espondents' "study" . . . failed to identify individuals who were not black and could have been prosecuted for the offenses for which respondents were charged, but were not so prosecuted. . . . The newspaper article, which discussed the discriminatory effect of federal drug sentencing laws, was not relevant to an allegation of discrimination in decisions to prosecute. Respondents' affidavits, which recounted one attorney's conversation with a drug treatment center employee and the experience of another attorney defending drug prosecutions in state court, recounted hearsay and reported personal conclusions based on anecdotal evidence. The judgment of the Court of Appeals is therefore reversed . . . .

STEVENS, J., dissenting. . . . The United States Attorney for the Central District of California is a member and an officer of the bar of that District Court. As such, she has a duty to the judges of that Court to maintain the standards of the profession in the performance of her official functions. If a District Judge has reason to suspect that she, or a member of her staff, has singled out particular defendants for prosecution on the basis of their race, it is surely appropriate for the judge to determine whether there is a factual basis for such a concern. . . .

[T]he Anti-Drug Abuse Act of 1986 and subsequent legislation established a regime of extremely high penalties for the possession and distribution of so-called "crack" cocaine. . . . [T]he disparity between the treatment of crack cocaine and powder cocaine is matched by the disparity between the severity of the punishment imposed by federal law and that imposed by state law for the same conduct. . . . For example, if respondent Hampton is found guilty, his federal sentence might be as long as a mandatory life term. Had he been tried in state court, his sentence could have been as short as 12 years, less worktime credits of half that amount. Finally, it is undisputed that the brunt of the elevated federal penalties falls heavily on blacks. . . . [These] troubling racial patterns of enforcement give rise to a special concern about the fairness of charging practices for crack offenses. . . . In my view, the District Judge . . . acted well within her discretion to call for the development of facts that would demonstrate what standards, if any, governed the choice of forum where similarly situated offenders are prosecuted.

. . . The . . . affidavit [submitted by the respondents from the local attorney] plainly contained more than mere hearsay; [he] offered information based on his own extensive experience in both federal and state courts. . . . The criticism that the affidavits were based on "anecdotal evidence" is also unpersuasive. [D]efendants do not need to prepare sophisticated statistical studies in order to receive mere discovery in cases like this one. Certainly evidence based on a drug counselor's personal observations or on an attorney's practice in two sets of courts, state and federal, can "tend to show the existence" of a selective prosecution. . . . The presumption that some whites are prosecuted in state court is not "contradicted" by the statistics the majority cites, which show only that high percentages of blacks are *convicted* of certain federal crimes, while high percentages of whites are convicted of other federal crimes. Those figures are entirely consistent with the allegation of selective prosecution. . . .[6]

I cannot accept the majority's conclusion that the District Judge either exceeded her power or abused her discretion when she [ordered discovery]. I therefore respectfully dissent.

[Additional opinions omitted.]

McCleskey v. Kemp

481 U.S. 279 (1987)

POWELL, J. This case presents the question whether a complex statistical study that indicates a risk that racial considerations enter into capital sentencing determinations proves that petitioner McCleskey's capital sentence is unconstitutional under the Eighth or Fourteenth Amendment.

McCleskey, a black man, was convicted of two counts of armed robbery and one count of murder in the Superior Court of Fulton County, Georgia, on October 12, 1978. McCleskey's convictions arose out of the robbery of a furniture store and the killing of a white police officer during the course of the robbery. . . . Under Georgia law, the jury could not consider imposing the death penalty unless it found beyond a reasonable doubt that the murder was accompanied by one of the statutory aggravating circumstances. The jury in this case found two aggravating circumstances to exist beyond a reasonable doubt: the murder was committed during the course of an armed robbery, and the murder was committed upon a peace officer engaged in the performance of his duties. . . . The jury recommended that [McCleskey] be sentenced to death on the murder charge and to consecutive life sentences on the armed robbery charges. . . .

McCleskey [argues] that the Georgia capital sentencing process is administered in a racially discriminatory manner . . . . In support of his claim, McCleskey proffered a statistical study performed by Professors David

---

6. Also telling was the Government's response to respondents' evidentiary showing. It submitted a list of more than 3,500 defendants who had been charged with federal narcotics violations over the previous three years. It also offered the names of 11 nonblack defendants whom it had prosecuted for crack offenses. All 11, however, were members of other racial or ethnic minorities. The District Court was authorized to draw adverse inferences from the Government's inability to produce a single example of a white defendant, especially when the very purpose of its exercise was to allay the court's concerns about the evidence of racially selective prosecutions. As another court has said: "Statistics are not, of course, the whole answer, but nothing is as emphatic as zero. . . ." United States v. Hinds County School Bd., 417 F.2d 852, 858 (C.A.5 1969) (per curiam).

C. Baldus, Charles Pulaski, and George Woodworth (the Baldus study) that purports to show a disparity in the imposition of the death sentence in Georgia based on the race of the murder victim and, to a lesser extent, the race of the defendant. The Baldus study is actually two sophisticated statistical studies that examine over 2,000 murder cases that occurred in Georgia during the 1970's. The raw numbers collected by Professor Baldus indicate that defendants charged with killing white persons received the death penalty in 11% of the cases, but defendants charged with killing blacks received the death penalty in only 1% of the cases. The raw numbers also indicate a reverse racial disparity according to the race of the defendant: 4% of the black defendants received the death penalty, as opposed to 7% of the white defendants.

Baldus also divided the cases according to the combination of the race of the defendant and the race of the victim. He found that the death penalty was assessed in 22% of the cases involving black defendants and white victims; 8% of the cases involving white defendants and white victims; 1% of the cases involving black defendants and black victims; and 3% of the cases involving white defendants and black victims. Similarly, Baldus found that prosecutors sought the death penalty in 70% of the cases involving black defendants and white victims; 32% of the cases involving white defendants and white victims; 15% of the cases involving black defendants and black victims; and 19% of the cases involving white defendants and black victims.

Baldus subjected his data to an extensive analysis, taking account of 230 variables that could have explained the disparities on nonracial grounds. One of his models concludes that, even after taking account of 39 nonracial variables, defendants charged with killing white victims were 4.3 times as likely to receive a death sentence as defendants charged with killing blacks. According to this model, black defendants were 1.1 times as likely to receive a death sentence as other defendants. . . .

[McCleskey thus] argues that race has infected the administration of Georgia's statute in two ways: persons who murder whites are more likely to be sentenced to death than persons who murder blacks, and black murderers are more likely to be sentenced to death than white murderers. As a black defendant who killed a white victim, McCleskey claims that the Baldus study demonstrates that he was discriminated against because of his race and because of the race of his victim. In its broadest form, McCleskey's claim of discrimination extends to every actor in the Georgia capital sentencing process, from the prosecutor who sought the death penalty and the jury that imposed the sentence, to the State itself that enacted the capital punishment statute and allows it to remain in effect despite its allegedly discriminatory application. We agree with the Court of Appeals, and every other court that has considered such a challenge, that this claim must fail. . . .

[T]o prevail under the Equal Protection Clause, McCleskey must prove that the decisionmakers in *his* case acted with discriminatory purpose. He offers no evidence specific to his own case that would support an inference that racial considerations played a part in his sentence. Instead, he . . . argues that the Baldus study compels an inference that his sentence rests on purposeful discrimination. McCleskey's claim that these statistics are sufficient proof of discrimination, without regard to the facts of a particular case, would extend to all capital cases in Georgia, at least where the victim was white and the defendant is black.

The Court has accepted statistics as proof of intent to discriminate in certain limited contexts. . . .[12] . . . But the nature of the capital sentencing decision, and the relationship of the statistics to that decision, are fundamentally different . . . . Most importantly, each particular decision to impose the death penalty is made by a petit jury selected from a properly constituted venire. Each jury is unique in its composition, and the Constitution requires that its decision rest on consideration of innumerable factors that vary according to the characteristics of the individual defendant and the facts of the particular capital offense. Thus, the application of an inference drawn from the general statistics to a specific decision in a trial and sentencing simply is not comparable to . . . cases [in which] the statistics relate to fewer entities, and fewer variables are relevant to the challenged decisions.[15]

[Additionally,] the policy considerations behind a prosecutor's traditionally "wide discretion" suggest the impropriety of our requiring prosecutors

---

12. *Gomillion v. Lightfoot*, 364 U.S. 339 (1960), and *Yick Wo v. Hopkins*, 118 U.S. 356 (1886), are examples of those rare cases in which a statistical pattern of discriminatory impact demonstrated a constitutional violation. In *Gomillion*, a state legislature [altered] the boundaries of a particular city "from a square to an uncouth twenty-eight-sided figure" [and thereby] excluded 395 of 400 black voters without excluding a single white voter. In *Yick Wo*, an ordinance prohibited operation of 310 laundries that were housed in wooden buildings, but allowed such laundries to resume operations if the operator secured a permit from the government. When laundry operators applied for permits to resume operation, all but one of the white applicants received permits, but none of the over 200 Chinese applicants were successful. In those cases, the Court found the statistical disparities "to warrant and require," *Yick Wo*, 118 U.S. at 373, a "conclusion that was irresistible, tantamount for all practical purposes to a mathematical demonstration," *Gomillion*, 364 U.S., at 341, that the State acted with a discriminatory purpose.

15. . . . It is also questionable whether any consistent policy can be derived by studying the decisions of prosecutors. The District Attorney is elected by the voters in a particular county. Since decisions whether to prosecute and what to charge necessarily are individualized and involve infinite factual variations, coordination among district attorney offices across a State would be relatively meaningless. Thus, any inference from statewide statistics to a prosecutorial "policy" is of doubtful relevance. Moreover, the statistics in Fulton County alone represent the disposition of far fewer cases than the statewide statistics. Even assuming the statistical validity of the Baldus study as a whole, the weight to be given the results gleaned from this small sample is limited.

to defend their decisions to seek death penalties, "often years after they were made." . . . McCleskey challenges decisions at the heart of the State's criminal justice system. "[O]ne of society's most basic tasks is that of protecting the lives of its citizens and one of the most basic ways in which it achieves the task is through criminal laws against murder." Gregg v. Georgia, 428 U.S. 153, 226 (1976) (White, J., concurring). Implementation of these laws necessarily requires discretionary judgments. Because discretion is essential to the criminal justice process, we would demand exceptionally clear proof before we would infer that the discretion has been abused. . . . Accordingly, we hold that the Baldus study is clearly insufficient to support an inference that any of the decisionmakers in McCleskey's case acted with discriminatory purpose.

McCleskey also suggests that the Baldus study proves that the State as a whole has acted with a discriminatory purpose. . . . For this claim to prevail, McCleskey would have to prove that the Georgia Legislature enacted or maintained the death penalty statute *because of* an anticipated racially discriminatory effect. In *Gregg v. Georgia*, this Court found that the Georgia capital sentencing system could operate in a fair and neutral manner. There was no evidence then, and there is none now, that the Georgia Legislature enacted the capital punishment statute to further a racially discriminatory purpose. . . .

At most, the Baldus study indicates a discrepancy that appears to correlate with race. Apparent disparities in sentencing are an inevitable part of our criminal justice system. . . . As this Court has recognized, any mode for determining guilt or punishment "has its weaknesses and the potential for misuse." Singer v. United States, 380 U.S. 24, 35 (1965). *See* Bordenkircher v. Hayes, 434 U.S. 357, 365 (1978). . . . In light of the safeguards designed to minimize racial bias in the process, the fundamental value of jury trial in our criminal justice system, and the benefits that discretion provides to criminal defendants, we hold that the Baldus study does not demonstrate a constitutionally significant risk of racial bias affecting the Georgia capital sentencing process.

. . . McCleskey's claim, taken to its logical conclusion, throws into serious question the principles that underlie our entire criminal justice system. The Eighth Amendment is not limited in application to capital punishment, but applies to all penalties. Solem v. Helm, 463 U.S. 277, 289-290 (1983). Thus, if we accepted McCleskey's claim that racial bias has impermissibly tainted the capital sentencing decision, we could soon be faced with similar claims as to other types of penalty. Moreover, the claim that his sentence rests on the irrelevant factor of race easily could be extended to apply to claims based on unexplained discrepancies that correlate to membership in other minority groups, and even to gender. . . . As these examples illustrate, there is no limiting principle to the type of challenge brought by McCleskey. . . .

BRENNAN, J., dissenting. . . . At some point in this case, Warren McCleskey doubtless asked his lawyer whether a jury was likely to sentence him to die.

A candid reply to this question would have been disturbing. . . . [T]here was a significant chance that race would play a prominent role in determining if he lived or died. The Court today . . . finds no fault in [such] a system [because] the Baldus study cannot "*prove* that race enters into any capital sentencing decisions or that race was a factor in McCleskey's particular case." . . .

The statistical evidence in this case . . . relentlessly documents the risk that McCleskey's sentence was influenced by racial considerations. . . . [But evaluation] of McCleskey's evidence cannot rest solely on the numbers themselves. . . . For many years, Georgia operated openly and formally precisely the type of dual system the evidence shows is still effectively in place. The criminal law expressly differentiated between crimes committed by and against blacks and whites, distinctions whose lineage traced back to the time of slavery. During the colonial period, black slaves who killed whites in Georgia, regardless of whether in self-defense or in defense of another, were automatically executed. By the time of the Civil War, [the] state criminal code [provided] for an automatic death sentence for murder committed by blacks, but declared that anyone else convicted of murder might receive life imprisonment if the . . . the jury so recommended. . . . A black convicted of assaulting a free white person with intent to murder could be put to death at the discretion of the court, but the same offense committed against a black, slave or free, was classified as a "minor" offense. . . . In more recent times, some 40 years ago, Gunnar Myrdal's epochal study of American race relations produced findings mirroring McCleskey's evidence: "For offenses which involve any actual or potential danger to whites . . . Negroes are punished more severely than whites." G. Myrdal, *An American Dilemma* 551-553 (1944).

. . . History and its continuing legacy thus buttress the probative force of McCleskey's statistics. Formal dual criminal laws may no longer be in effect, and intentional discrimination may no longer be prominent. Nonetheless, as we acknowledged in *Turner [v. Murray]*, "subtle, less consciously held racial attitudes" continue to be of concern, 476 U.S. 28, 35 (1986), and the Georgia system gives such attitudes considerable room to operate. . . . Professor Baldus and his colleagues have compiled data on almost 2,500 homicides committed during the period 1973–1979. They have taken into account the influence of 230 nonracial variables, using a multitude of data from the State itself, and have produced striking evidence that the odds of being sentenced to death are significantly greater than average if a defendant is black or his or her victim is white. The challenge to the Georgia system is not speculative or theoretical; it is empirical. . . .

The Court [says] that its unwillingness to regard petitioner's evidence as sufficient is based in part on the fear that recognition of McCleskey's claim would open the door to widespread challenges to all aspects of criminal sentencing. Taken on its face, such a statement seems to suggest a fear of too much justice. . . . The prospect that there may be more widespread abuse than McCleskey documents may be dismaying, but it does not justify complete abdication of our judicial role. The Constitution was framed fundamentally as a bulwark against governmental power, and preventing the arbitrary administration of punishment is a basic ideal of any society that purports to be governed by the rule of law.

. . . McCleskey presents evidence that is far and away the most refined data ever assembled on any system of punishment, data not readily replicated through casual effort. Moreover, that evidence depicts not merely arguable tendencies, but striking correlations, all the more powerful because nonracial explanations have been eliminated. . . . [I]t has been scarcely a generation since this Court's first decision striking down racial segregation, and barely two decades since the legislative prohibition of racial discrimination in major domains of national life. These have been honorable steps, but we cannot pretend that in three decades we have completely escaped the grip of a historical legacy spanning centuries. Warren McCleskey's evidence confronts us with the subtle and persistent influence of the past. His message is a disturbing one to a society that has formally repudiated racism, and a frustrating one to a Nation accustomed to regarding its destiny as the product of its own will. Nonetheless, we ignore him at our peril, for we remain imprisoned by the past as long as we deny its influence in the present. . . .

[Additional opinions omitted.]

NOTES AND QUESTIONS

1. Justice Powell's Regret. The Supreme Court upheld Warren McCleskey's death sentence by a vote of five to four. The opinion's author, Justice Lewis Powell, retired from the Court a few months later. Four years after that, Justice Powell was interviewed by his biographer, Professor John Jeffries, Jr., who asked him if he would change any of the votes he had made in the course of his judicial career. "Yes," Powell replied, "McCleskey v. Kemp." He went on to say, "I have come to think that capital punishment should be abolished. [It] brings discredit on the whole legal system." A few months after Powell gave that interview, on September 25, 1991, Warren McCleskey was executed.[114]

2. McCleskey's Critics. As Professor Randall Kennedy has observed, the "Court's decision in *McCleskey v. Kemp* was immediately beset by sharp criticism and, in some instances, outright denunciation," with numerous scholars comparing it "to such notorious holdings as *Dred Scott v. Sandford*, *Plessy v. Ferguson*, and *Korematsu v. United States*." Looking back on the case decades later, Professor Scott Sundby describes it "as a resident in the exclusive but not so desirable neighborhood of Notorious Cases." Particularly "in the criminal law area," he goes on, "a legal scholar can invoke *McCleskey* confident that the reader will understand that the case is being used as shorthand for 'cases in which the Supreme Court failed the Constitution's most basic values.'" Consider the following illustrative, elaborating excerpts.[115]

Anthony G. Amsterdam, *Opening Remarks: Race and the Death Penalty Before and After* McCleskey, 39 Colum. Hum. Rts. L. Rev. 34, 47 (2007). *McCleskey* is the *Dred Scott* decision of our time. It is a declaration that African-American life has no value which white men are bound to respect. It is a decision for which our children's children will reproach our generation and abhor the legal legacy we leave them. One inherent evil of the death penalty is that it extends the boundaries of permissible inhumanity so far that every lesser offense against humanity seems inoffensive by comparison, leading us to tolerate them relatively easily. *McCleskey* extends the boundaries of permissible discrimination and hypocrisy in that same measure. Accept *McCleskey*, and race discrimination in matters less momentous than life or death can be shrugged off. Accept *McCleskey*, and any hypocrisy with less than lethal consequences can be viewed as trivial in a legal system where the highest tribunal sits in a building bearing the proud motto "Equal Justice Under Law" on its west facade and ignores it.

Paul Butler, *Equal Protection and White Supremacy,* 112 Nw. U. L. Rev. 1457, 1460-1461 (2018). The [*McCleskey*] Court is as forthright as the Supreme Court is ever going to be about establishing white supremacy. The Court says if we recognize the kind of harm of race discrimination in capital cases, well, then we will have to recognize it in other kinds of criminal cases too. And that would undermine the entire criminal justice system.

Justice Scalia kept it even more real. He wrote a bench memo while the case was pending, and the Court was wrestling with how it should deal with the Baldus study. Scalia said, essentially, "I don't need no stinking social science. We already know everything that the Baldus study purports [to show]." But, Scalia wrote, racism is "ineradicable" from the U.S. criminal legal process, and thus, not a good reason to reverse Mr. McCleskey's death sentence. *McCleskey* is a worse case than *Plessy*, because at least *Plessy* requires formal equality. *McCleskey* is okay with a good-enough-for-black-people kind of justice.

3. Deciphering the Data on Discrimination. As Justice Brennan's dissent observes, the Baldus study was regarded in its time as one of the most careful and methodical analyses ever conducted of racism's impact on the administration of the American death penalty, if not on the American penal system writ large. As Professor Ben Cohen reports, the Supreme Court's refusal to heed the study's findings has received "near universal condemnation" from scholars. Much of that criticism takes issue with the Court's conclusion that evidence of *systemic* racism is insufficient to render a criminal sentence, including a sentence of death, unconstitutional unless a defendant can isolate *individual* actors within the system and prove they acted with *racist intent.*[116]

In the view of some scholars, however, it is important not to over-read *McCleskey* as foreclosing data-driven efforts to mount precisely such a challenge. "Although some scholars have concluded understandably that *McCleskey* precludes all statistically based attacks involving racial bias," Professors John Blume, Theodore Eisenberg and Sheri Lynn Johnson write, "*McCleskey* does not hold on its face that [such] selective-prosecution claims are not cognizable." On the contrary, they continue, using statistical analyses to challenge charging practices that are "prosecutor-specific" would be "consistent with *McCleskey.*" Elaborating on this point, Professor Andrew Manuel Crespo argues that the Court's rejection of the Baldus study "could well be limited to the specific circumstances at issue" in the case.

> For example, the evidence presented . . . was criticized by the Court for failing to isolate causal effect among the large number of entities involved in the process (including not only discrete district attorneys, but also a countless and constantly changing array of independent and uncoordinated jury panels). The Court further rejected the specific statistics before it because it believed the "inference from *statewide* statistics" was "of doubtful relevance" when evaluating a practice implemented at the local level, and because it additionally believed that the statistics at the individual county level "represent[ed] the disposition of far fewer cases than the statewide statistics" and were thus insufficiently reliable. [T]he Court did *not* say that such county-level data, if robust, would lack constitutional weight [but rather] reaffirmed that "an unexplained statistical discrepancy *can* be said to indicate a consistent policy of the decisionmaker," if the statistics are robust and if a single decisionmaker or institution is indeed responsible for the decision.

In view of these caveats, Professor Erica Hashimoto argues that while selective prosecution claims "continue to be very difficult to prove even with data, it is possible that more sophisticated data collection may ultimately make the claims more readily provable." In a similar vein, a team of legal academics and data scientists recently predicted that "as statistical proof of racial bias becomes more and more convincing, courts will—and should—be more comfortable relying on it."[117]

4. Systemic Facts. Of course, even if *McCleskey* leaves open the possibility that statistically based challenges to discrimination might succeed with better data, defendants still need to acquire such data in the first place. It is in this context that *United States v. Armstrong* looms large, eclipsing perhaps even *McCleskey* in scholarly condemnation. The problem, according to Professor Bill Stuntz, is that *Armstrong* creates a "classic legal Catch-22." Armstrong's claim "couldn't win without more information, yet Armstrong could get that information only if he had a winning claim without it."

Echoing Stuntz and summarizing a large body of academic literature, Guy Rubinstein reports that in the wake of *Armstrong*, scholars "have described selective prosecution and selective enforcement claims as 'impossible' or 'virtually impossible' to prove, and the [doctrinal] requirements [as] nearly 'insurmountable.'"[118]

Professor Andrew Manuel Crespo, however, has a different view. "*Armstrong* is fairly criticized for impeding efforts to discover, and thus to counteract, racially biased charging decisions," he writes.

> And yet, the barrier that *Armstrong* erects may increasingly become a vestige of a bygone technological age, given that contemporary criminal courts' own [internal administrative data, what we can call their] systemic facts[,] often reveal precisely the information that *Armstrong* permits prosecutorial offices to withhold. In the District of Columbia, for example, case-processing software . . . generates within the court's own records a digital catalog of virtually every charging decision local prosecutors make—including the decision not to prosecute. And for each such decision, it also collects important data on the dependent and independent variables that would be necessary to construct a rich statistical analysis of the office's charging practices. On the dependent variable side, this includes records of the initial charging or declination decision, as well as records of subsequent charge amendments, plea offers, diversion offers, safety-valve or cooperation reductions, and sentences sought at allocution—in short, a record of virtually every enforcement decision made by the office in every case. As for independent variables, the court records key data concerning factors that ought *not* to be influencing the charging decision—such as the race, gender, and income of the defendant—as well as factors that *should* be taken into account, such as the defendant's criminal history, the alleged offense, any acceptance by the defendant of responsibility, any cooperation on his part with law enforcement, and any positive or negative experience he may have had with prior judicial supervision.
>
> [In short, by] leveraging its systemic facts, the court can . . . come substantially closer to understanding whether race is influencing prosecutorial charging decisions in a constitutionally suspect manner. And indeed, academics have begun to engage in precisely such analyses. Professor Crystal Yang, for example, has constructed a massive dataset comprising over 400,000 federal prosecutions, and, through multivariate analysis, has demonstrated that "[b]lack offenders are generally more likely to be charged with mandatory minimum sentences than are similar white offenders" after controlling for other variables of interest, a reality that she reports ultimately contributes to racially disparate incarceration rates. [And notably,] all of the data that Yang relied upon in her robust and powerful analysis was data that came from *within the judiciary*

itself. . . . [L]everaged properly, [such data] can enhance not only judges' institutional awareness and comprehension of institutional law enforcement practices, but also their ability to regulate and oversee such practices at a systemic level.[119]

Professor Paul Butler, by contrast, has a more pessimistic account. Speaking to those "interested in using social science to win equal protection claims, including in criminal justice," Butler cautions: "That project is doomed." More specifically, he says, it rests on the false premise that "there is not enough evidence of discrimination or not the right kind of evidence, and if we could just get that good evidence, then the Court would be persuaded." In reality, Butler insists, "we already know that discrimination is endemic in the criminal justice system," and so do the courts. "That's how the system works. And if it's not broke, then you can't fix it."[120]

CHAPTER 10

THE END OF MASS INCARCERATION:

Ideas and Interventions

"You have to act as if it were possible to radically transform the world. And you have to do it all the time."

Angela Y. Davis, Lecture at Southern Illinois
University Carbondale (Feb. 13, 2014)

"[R]eforms that could make life better for people currently suffering in prisons and jails might fail . . . if too many advocates opt to hold out for bolder options . . . that are unlikely to ever materialize."

Rachel E. Barkow, *Promise or Peril? The Political Path of Prison
Abolition in America*, 58 Wake Forest L. Rev. 245, 319 (2023)

INTRODUCTION

Throughout this book, we have examined the interrelationship between criminal law and the American penal system. Over the span of the most recent chapters, that examination has focused on the role law and legal actors have played in constituting American mass incarceration.

Most people who have lived in the United States over the past decade will be broadly familiar with some of the contentious debates surrounding this topic. Beginning with the Ferguson uprising in the wake of Michael Brown's killing at the hands of police officer Darren Wilson and continuing through nationwide protests following the murder of George Floyd by police officer Derek Chauvin, the Black Lives Matter movement has put systemic injustices related to American policing and incarceration at the center of our national discourse. According to the *New York Times*, it is likely "the largest movement in U.S. history."[1]

As a result of that movement, once-fringe ideas like prison abolition and defunding the police are now familiar to millions of Americans. Indeed, you are studying criminal law at a time unlike any other in history, a moment when many see a new political landscape within reach. It is a time when the conservative Koch Foundation and the liberal ACLU some-times join cause on legislative initiatives to limit criminal liability (p. 509). A time when drug decriminalization and alternative treatment measures can and have been enacted into law (p. 689). A time when the prison pop-ulation modestly but markedly declined for over a decade (p. 15). And a time when politicians ranging from Donald Trump to Kamala Harris to numerous local district attorneys have run for office touting, at least at times, proposals and prior accomplishments that curtail incarceration rather than expand it.[2]

At the same time, backlash to this movement has been undeniable. As we have seen, some decriminalization efforts have been reversed (p. 689). The year 2022 saw the prison population increase for the first time in roughly a decade. And the rhetoric of leading presidential candidates in the 2024 election was noticeably less oriented toward penal system reforms than was true in 2020. More broadly, criticism and skepticism of anti-carceral efforts are apparent in multiple quarters. Some of these responses come from defenders of the status quo who see calls for change or reform as attacks on law enforcement or as embracing, defending, or promoting criminality. But there is also backlash from progressive scholars, advocates, and policymakers, many of whom embrace deep structural critiques of the status quo but urge more incrementalist interventions than are sought in some of the most prominent calls for change.[3]

In part, these latter disagreements capture divergences over fundamen-tal and age-old ideas, including ideas about the tradeoffs between radical and pragmatic approaches to change. In part they capture divergent ideas about who might be the most effective changemakers: grassroots movement actors, local democratic constituencies and civic leaders, elected policymak-ers, subject-matter experts with specialized training, lawyers and judges, survivors of criminal violence and their loved ones, formerly incarcerated people and their loved ones. Finally, disagreements about the path forward sometimes arise over specific policy proposals or interventions.

Our goal in this concluding chapter is to offer an overview of some of these key questions and debates. We have divided the chapter into two parts, one focused on big-picture ideas and the other on more specific interven-tions. In the first part, we begin by examining a tension between efforts to end mass incarceration by pursuing fundamental societal change—includ-ing, most notably, efforts in the words of Professor Angela Y. Davis "to abolish the prison system in its present form"—and contrasting efforts to pursue more incrementalist, pragmatic, and near-term-achievable reforms. We then turn to examine debates over where the center of gravity in the decarceral political struggle should be situated, focusing on competing ideas over whether and how to democratize the effort. Next, in the second part of the chapter, we focus on a series of specific interventions that form a constellation of decarceral approaches—including efforts to downgrade criminal offenses and release some groups of people from prison; to elect progressive prosecutors; to better fund public defenders; to adopt and transition to restorative justice practices; to defund carceral actors; and to build and deploy collective power within the courtroom.[4]

Throughout the chapter, our goal is to present something of a reader on these topics, highlighting passages from leading thinkers and actors who are working to mitigate, reform, or end mass incarceration as it currently exists. There are volumes beyond what these concluding pages contain. We invite students interested in learning more about these topics to consult additional sources and guides collected in the endnotes.

I.   COMPETING DECARCERAL IDEAS

In this part, we examine two major fault lines in debates over how to end mass incarceration — one between abolition and reform, and another between populist- and professional-driven efforts.

A.   Abolition and Its Skeptics

In a foreword to the *Harvard Law Review* written in 2019, law professor and abolitionist scholar Dorothy Roberts describes prison abolitionism as "a coherent, though amorphous, set of theories, principles, and strategies" that have been articulated over a span of decades "in numerous books, articles in scholarly journals and mass media, conference presentations, speeches, video interviews, and blogs, as well as on social media." Roberts, like many others, traces the modern origin of the American prison abolition movement to the formation, in 1997, of an organization called Critical Resistance by a group of scholars and activists including Angela Y. Davis, Ruth Wilson Gilmore, Rose Braz, Rachel Herzing, and Dylan Rodríguez. In their collected bodies of work, these writers and many others have offered some of the leading accounts of abolition as a political ideology. The sections that follow give an overview of abolitionist ideology, an overview of abolitionist practice, and a set of contemporary critiques and concerns — including from writers who agree with much of what abolitionism says is wrong with the modern American penal system.[5]

1.   Abolitionist Ideology

Angela Y. Davis, *Political Prisoners, Prisons, and Black Liberation* (1971). In the heat of our pursuit of fundamental human rights, black people have been continually cautioned to be patient. We are advised that as long as we remain faithful to the existing democratic order, the glorious moment will eventually arrive when we will come into our own as full-fledged human beings. But having been taught by bitter experience, we know that . . . the people are not the ultimate matrix of the laws and the system which govern them — certainly not black people and other nationally oppressed people, but not even the mass of whites. . . . Needless to say, the history of the Unites States has been marred from its inception by an enormous quantity of unjust laws, far too many expressly bolstering the oppression of black people. . . .

The prison is a key component of the state's coercive apparatus, the overriding function of which is to ensure social control. . . . While cloaking itself with the bourgeois aura of universality — imprisonment was supposed to cut across all class lines, as crimes were to be defined by the act, not the perpetrator — the prison has actually operated as an instrument of class domination, a means of prohibiting the have-nots from encroaching upon the haves. . . .

Prisoners — especially blacks, Chicanos and Puerto Ricans — are increasingly advancing the proposition that they are *political* prisoners. They contend that they are political prisoners in the sense that they are largely the victims of an oppressive politico-economic order, swiftly becoming conscious of the causes underlying their victimization. . . . In black communities, wherever they are located, there exists an ever-present reminder that our universe must remain stable in its drabness, its poverty, its brutality. From Birmingham to Harlem to Watts, black ghettos are occupied, patrolled and often attacked by massive deployments of police. The police, domestic caretakers of violence, are the oppressor's emissaries, charged with the task of containing us within the boundaries of our oppression. . . . The vicious circle linking poverty, police, courts, and prison is an integral element of ghetto existence. Unlike the mass of whites, the path which leads to jails and prisons is deeply rooted in the imposed patterns of black existence. For this very reason, an almost instinctive affinity binds the mass of black people to the political prisoners. . . .

One of the fundamental historical lessons to be learned from past failures to prevent the rise of fascism is the decisive and indispensable character of the fight against fascism in its incipient phases. . . . Although the most unbridled expressions of the fascist menace are still tied to the racist domination of blacks, Chicanos, Puerto Ricans, Indians, it lurks under the surface wherever there is potential resistance . . . . Potentially it can profoundly worsen the conditions of existence for the average American citizen. Consequently, the masses of people in this country have a real, direct, and material stake in the struggle to free political prisoners, the struggle to abolish the prison system in its present form, the struggle against all dimensions of racism.

Dylan Rodríguez, *Abolition as Praxis of Human Being: A Foreword*, 132 Harv. L. Rev. 1575, 1576-1578 (2019). The long historical praxis of abolition is grounded in a Black radical genealogy of revolt and transformative insurgency against racial chattel enslavement and the transatlantic trafficking of captive Africans. Understood as part of the *historical present tense*, abolitionist critique, organizing, and collective movement . . . honor and extend this tradition [of] struggle against the continuities of *carceral state violence*, including but not limited to imprisonment, jailing, detention, and policing. In this sense, abolition is not merely a practice of negation — a collective attempt to eliminate institutionalized dominance over targeted peoples and populations — but also a radically imaginative, generative, and socially productive communal (and community-building) practice. . . .

. . . [A]n abolitionist historical mandate provides a useful and necessary departure from the liberal assumption that either the carceral state or carceral power is an inevitable and permanent feature of the social formation. This historical mandate animates abolition as a creative, imaginative, and speculative collective labor: while liberal-to-progressive reformism attempts to protect and sustain the institutional and cultural-political coherence of an existing system by adjusting and/or refurbishing it, abolitionism addresses the historical roots of that system in relations of oppressive, continuous, and asymmetrical violence and raises the radical question of whether those relations must be uprooted and transformed (rather than reformed or "fixed") for the sake of particular peoples' existence and survival as such.

Consider abolition as both a long accumulation and future planning of acts, performed by and in the name of peoples and communities relentlessly laboring for their own *physiological and cultural integrity as such.* Embrace the obligation that accompanies the term abolition — a complex, dynamic, and deeply historical shorthand, if you will — in the work of constantly remaking sociality, politics, ecology, place, and (human) being against the duress that some call dehumanization, others name colonialism, and still others identify as slavery and incarceration. . . . Now and long before, abolition is and was a practice, an analytical method, a present-tense visioning, an infrastructure in the making, a creative project, a performance, a counterwar, an ideological struggle, a pedagogy and curriculum, an alleged impossibility that is furtively present, pulsing, produced in the persistent insurgencies of human being that undermine the totalizing logics of empire, chattel, occupation, heteropatriarchy, racial-colonial genocide, and Civilization as a juridical-narrative epoch.

Dorothy E. Roberts, *Foreword: Abolition Constitutionalism*, 133 Harv. L. Rev. 1, 7 (2019). It is hard to pin down what prison abolition means. Activists engaged in the movement have resisted "closed definitions of prison abolitionism" and have instead suggested a variety of terms to capture what prison abolitionists think and do — abolition is "a form of consciousness," "a theory of change," "a long-term political vision," and "a spiritual journey." . . . For purposes of my analysis, I find especially useful three central tenets that are common to formulations of abolitionist philosophy. First, today's carceral punishment system can be traced back to slavery and the racial capitalist regime it relied on and sustained. Second, the expanding criminal punishment system functions to oppress black people and other politically marginalized groups in order to maintain a racial capitalist regime. Third, we can imagine and build a more humane and democratic society that no longer relies on caging people to meet human needs and solve social problems. These tenets lead to the conclusion that the only way to transform our society from a slavery-based one to a free one is to abolish the prison industrial complex.

Michael J. Coyle & David Scott, *The Six Hues of Penal Abolitionism*, in *The Routledge International Handbook of Penal Abolition* 1, 1-2 (Michael J. Coyle & David Scott eds., 2021). In short, penal abolitionists question the legitimacy of the penal rationale, arguing that rather than effectively handling or solving social problems, interpersonal disputes, conflicts and harms, much less holding transgressors responsible, the result of law, policing, courts, prisons and their numerous tentacles is to actually increase individual and societal problems, interpersonal violence and troubles. In addition, for penal abolitionists, centuries of observation demonstrate that punishments are not just intolerable, but also counterproductive and frequently dehumanising. The task of the penal abolitionist is thus to be a public intellectual deploying moral and political arguments to challenge hegemonic norms and standards which ask us to accept penal institutions that can never be separated from their heritage and ongoing dependence on white supremacy, colonialism and racial capitalism. Further, the task of the penal abolitionist is to be an activist working to awaken the mass populace to the abject failure of the penal system as a systematic response to transgression ("crime"), which is ubiquitous in human relationships and social living and not the purview of some "criminal" classes or individuals. . . .

[T]he abolitionist imagines how greater access to opportunities and rights—such as healthcare, housing, work and education—will always create better outcomes than the use of criminalisation to solve the social, economic, behavioural and interpersonal problems we face. The abolitionist imagines a state that goes beyond what Ruth Wilson Gilmore calls the organised state abandonment of entire populations within communities (such as the working class or the homeless). The abolitionist imagines a state that goes beyond concentrating on targeted, vengeful, punitive responses to problematic conduct and harms. Opposite to these, the abolitionist imagines a state that calls for an end to the penal sanction and the creation of a more equitable society.

A penal abolitionist wants to see an end to the deployment of the penal rationale and a true levelling in the social and economic distributions of rights, opportunities, wealth and power. The abolitionist wants these not only because they see the emergence of the penal rationale and inequalities as lying in white supremacy, colonialism, racial capitalism, gender oppression, racism/ethnocentrism, classism, sexism and the like but because they also understand that if an individual's needs are not being met, then they are not going to have time for other people's needs or have the inclination to show compassion and care about how people (including themselves) step into transgressive acts ("crimes"). Penal abolitionists all around the world have consistently argued that all forms of state-inflicted suffering and harm are morally and politically unjustified and that nonviolent, needs-based social organising and interventions must be promoted in their place.

Mariame Kaba, *We Do This 'Til We Free Us* 4-5 (2021). None of us has all of the answers, or we would have ended oppression already. But if we keep building the world we want, trying new things, and learning from our mistakes, new possibilities emerge. . . . [W]hen we set about trying to transform society, we must remember that we ourselves will also need to transform. Our imagination of what a different world can be is limited. We are deeply entangled in the very systems we are organizing to change. White supremacy, misogyny, ableism, classism, homophobia, and transphobia exist everywhere. We have all so thoroughly internalized these logics of oppression that if oppression were to end tomorrow, we would be likely to reproduce previous structures. Being intentionally in relation to one another, a part of a collective, helps to not only imagine new worlds, but also to imagine ourselves differently. . . . [A]s scholar and activist Ruth Wilson Gilmore notes, building a different world requires that we not only change how we address harm but also that we change everything. The [prison industrial complex] is linked in its logics and operation with all other systems—from how students are pushed out of schools when they don't perform as expected to how people with disabilities are excluded from our communities and the ways in which workers are treated as expendable in our capitalist system. Changing everything might sound daunting, but it also means there are many places to start, infinite opportunities to collaborate, and endless imaginative interventions and experiments to create.

2. Abolition as a Practice

Ruth Wilson Gilmore & James Kilgore, *The Case for Abolition*, Marshall Project (June 19, 2019). While we value philosophy, we . . . prefer to talk about what we do. Ultimately, abolition is a practical program of change rooted in how people sustain and improve their lives, cobbling together insights and strategies from disparate, connected struggles. We know we won't bulldoze prisons and jails tomorrow, but as long as they continue to be advanced as the solution, all of the inequalities displaced to crime and punishment will persist. We're in a long game. . . . [F]or decades abolitionists have been doing everything we can imagine to bring about change. We stand on the frontlines to oppose all forms of state violence. We work with communities sited for prisons to fight expansion, while organizing to secure decent wages and housing in the regional economy. We work with Republican ranchers worried about the water table, and with undocumented agricultural workers vulnerable to pesticides and Immigration and Customs Enforcement. We work with city managers and residents of prison towns disappointed in lockups touted for economic development that never deliver. . . . In other words, we work the entire ecology of precarious existence that shapes, but is not bounded by, the aggrandizing "criminal justice system," including housing, jobs, education, income, faith, environment, status. Far from being starry-eyed idealists, we are specialists in the daily grind of the deliberate, patient and persistent work necessary for what we want—freedom and justice.

Rachel Herzing, *Abolition Is Practical*, Inquest (July 11, 2023). Prison-industrial complex (PIC) abolition is the political praxis that seeks to eliminate the use of surveillance, policing, sentencing, imprisonment, and execution *and* to build healthy, stable, self-determined societies that do not rely on coercion and vengeance to address harm. . . . Some of the most conspicuous PIC abolitionist organizing of the past few years has been around defunding policing . . . as one of a set of steps toward eliminating policing altogether. . . . Defund campaigns are just a small portion of all abolitionist organizing, however. . . . [Abolitionist organizers] won moratoriums on prison construction and executions in the 1970s, and in more recent decades have prevented the construction and expansion of prisons and jails across the United States. They have also eliminated the use of sets of policing practices such as civil gang injunctions. These wins haven't eliminated the PIC yet, but they have struck definitive blows that are still being leveraged for additional gains on the path to its complete abolition. Just like all transformational change-making, power structures come back and attempt to regain what they have lost. This back and forth is not unique to the movement for PIC abolition and should not be used as an indication that this praxis is not realistic or viable, but rather a sign that, as the old civil rights song reminds us, freedom is a constant struggle.

Dean Spade, *Solidarity Not Charity*, 38 Soc. Text 131, 136 (2020). Mutual aid is a form of political participation in which people take responsibility for caring for one another and changing political conditions, not just through symbolic acts or putting pressure on their representatives in government but by actually building new social relations that are more survivable. There is nothing new about mutual aid—people have worked together to survive for all of human history. The framework of mutual aid is significant in the context of social movements resisting capitalist and colonial domination, in which wealth and resources are extracted and concentrated and most people can survive only by participating in various extractive relationships. Providing for one another through coordinated collective care is radical and generative.

Effective social movements always include elements of mutual aid. The most famous example on the left in the United States is the Black Panther Party's survival programs, including the free breakfast program, the free ambulance program, free medical clinics, a program offering rides to elderly people doing errands, and a school aimed at providing a liberating and rigorous curriculum to children. The Black Panthers' programs mobilized people by creating spaces where they could access basic needs and build shared analysis about the conditions they were facing. . . .

The Black Panthers' survival programs have inspired many other organizations to organize mutual aid efforts to attract people to movements and to build shared analysis of problems as collective rather than individual. People often come to social movement organizations because they need something, such as eviction defense, child care, social connection, health care, or advocacy. . . . It is hard to be part of organizing when you are struggling with a barrier to survival. Getting support through a mutual aid project that has a political analysis of the conditions that produced your crisis also helps break stigma and isolation. . . . Mutual aid exposes the failures of the current system and shows an alternative.

It . . . is [also] antiauthoritarian, demonstrating how to do things together in ways that we were told not to imagine and how to organize human activity without coercion. . . . For example, in Occupy encampments that emerged in 2011, people . . . committed to police abolition and antiracism cultivated conversations about not calling the police. This was inconsistent and imperfect, but it introduced many people to new skills about responding to harm, which they took with them in their work after Occupy encampments were dismantled by the police. Mutual aid lets people learn and practice the skills and capacities we need to live in the world we are trying to create—a world shaped by practices of collective self-determination.

Cristian Farias, *On Both Sides of the Gun,* Inquest (July 13, 2023). At its core, community violence intervention centers the community, relying on its members—that is, the people closest to the problem and the needs of the community—to serve as street-level interventionists, intermediaries, interrupters, and even innovators. Many of them have been criminalized or spent time in prison, lending them credibility to deescalate or intervene in interpersonal conflicts. But they may also be mothers or concerned adults who have lost or fear losing loved ones to gun violence; self-described peacemakers who walk designated city streets at hours where violence may be more prevalent; advocates in hospital settings who provide trauma-informed services to survivors of violence; or mentors who give direct cash assistance and other forms of support to young people on the brink of committing harm or being harmed themselves. . . .

Stick Talk, a [gun-violence intervention] group based in Chicago, . . . takes young people as it finds them. . . . If a person owns an illicit firearm or they're carrying without a permit, Stick Talk doesn't judge. At these neighborhood-level firearm harm reduction "hubs," participants find a space to learn about safer, responsible gun ownership and use; to understand the history and present of racialized gun control and criminalization; and to gain critical skills such as emergency first responder training and first-aid practices for treating gunshot injuries. . . . One of its partners, Ujimaa Medics (UMedics, for short) — a Black-led group of organizers, community members, and health professionals — trains bystanders throughout Chicago on how to keep gun violence victims alive during those critical moments before the ambulance arrives. These lifesaving techniques include the treatment of gunshot wounds, securing people's airways, and controlling heavy bleeding.

These first-aid trainings, which UMedics has offered to high school students and community groups where gun violence is most prevalent, don't fit the mold of community violence prevention as the practice has been popularized in today's nonprofit world. Yet in talking about their work, group leaders have been clear that police do not keep the community safe and aren't equipped to provide healing and care, so bystanders must be empowered to step in. "I don't know that we're a solution to gun violence," Martine Caverl, a UMedics cofounder, told ABC30. "But I know that we're a solution for communities that need to build power. That's what I know."

3. Non-Reformist Reform

Daniel Farbman, *A Commons in the Master's House,* 90 Fordham L. Rev. 2061, 2062-2065 (2022). In the late summer of 1853, white abolitionists in Cincinnati had a tragic fight about how far to take political purity. [A] federal marshal [had arrested an enslaved man named] George "Wash" McQuerry in Ohio. A Kentuckian named Henry Miller claimed that McQuerry was his property and sought to use the mechanics of the Fugitive Slave Act of 1850 to re-enslave McQuerry and bring him back to Kentucky. [The ensuing] trial became a public spectacle that drew national attention. . . . But when the trial ended with the tragic conclusion that McQuerry was to be re-enslaved, a fight broke out among the abolitionists over what measures they should take to free him. Under public pressure, Miller had promised to sell McQuerry into freedom if his supporters could raise $1,200. Some abolitionist leaders in the city organized an effort to capitalize on public outrage and raise the money to free McQuerry. Others opposed this effort on the grounds that participating in the monstrous economy of slavery was a ratification of the institution. The disagreement was such that, despite their best efforts, the collection fell short.

The proximate result of this intramovement disagreement was a human tragedy. Wash McQuerry was enslaved, torn from his family and life, and relegated to the status of property. From our perspective today, this looks like an avoidable tragedy—a catastrophic consequence of short-sighted purity politics in the face of a moral cataclysm. . . . But this tidy presentist moral calculus makes matters too easy. In the brutal reality of slavery, McQuerry's tragedy was just one among thousands of moral horrors occurring every day. To radical purists, any compromise or complicity with slavery was an endorsement and perpetuation of the system itself, and such an endorsement was too steep a price to pay to save McQuerry. The radical pragmatists who sought to purchase McQuerry's freedom had to make peace with the fact that they were willing to participate within a system of property and capitalism that was murderous, oppressive, and fundamentally horrific.

. . . Questions of purity and pragmatism battle at the heart of most movement strategies. In our fallen world, situated as we are within overlapping imperfect (and often overtly oppressive) systems, those of us who seek to change or overhaul those systems often face the question of how to situate our struggles within and against these systems. Should we reject the systems altogether? Should we participate in them in good faith? Should we participate in them with the goal of undermining them? How do we balance pragmatism and strategy against purism and moral clarity?

Angela Y. Davis, *Are Prisons Obsolete?* 20 (2003). Over the last few years the previous absence of critical positions on prison expansion in the political arena has given way to proposals for prison reform. While public discourse has become more flexible, the emphasis is almost inevitably on generating the changes that will produce a better prison system. In other words, the increased flexibility that has allowed for critical discussion of the problems associated with the expansion of prisons also restricts this discussion to the question of prison reform. As important as some reforms may be — the elimination of sexual abuse and medical neglect in women's prison, for example—frameworks that rely exclusively on reforms help to produce the stultifying idea that nothing lies beyond the prison. Debates about strategies of decarceration, which should be the focal point of our conversations on the prison crisis, tend to be marginalized when reform takes the center stage.

Amna A. Akbar, *Non-Reformist Reforms and Struggles Over Life, Death, and Democracy*, 132 Yale L.J. 2497, 2518-2520 (2023). On the left, the term "reformism" is used pejoratively. . . . The primary concern is that to focus on reformism is to orient action toward entrenching, rather than overthrowing or substituting, a fundamentally corrupt system, institution, or set of relations. As Rosa Luxemburg explained in *Reform or Revolution*, "Instead of taking a stand for the establishment of a new society[, people who pronounce themselves in favor of reform] take a stand for surface modification of the old society." . . . Reformism telegraphs to the public that the system, institution, or set of relations it seeks to tweak are here to stay; that the problem is not structural or symptomatic but stray. . . . In form and substance, reformism shields the status quo and its protectorate from ongoing challenges necessary to contest their power and build another world. In so doing, reformism consolidates the hand of those in power and deepen[s] preexisting inequalities. Reformism [thus] becomes an essential strategy of the ruling class to reestablish its rule; to do as little as possible to quell revolt that might force deeper changes and self-rule[; to] coopt the energy from the streets to reassert their own power and make excuses for or divert attention away from their inability to act.

Prison Rsch. Educ. Action Project, *Instead of Prisons* 62-63 (1976). As prison abolitionists, it is important that we examine whether our actions move us toward our goals. . . . The prospect of changing a system as massive, complex and powerful as the prison system could overwhelm and paralyze us if we were unable to design our work into a series of manageable parts. Visualizing our long range goal of prison abolition as a chain of shorter campaigns around specific issues provides us with the "handles" we need on the overall problem. . . . We have structured an attrition model as one example of a long range process for abolition. "Attrition," which means the rubbing away or wearing down by friction, reflects the *persistent and continuing* strategy necessary to diminish the function and power of prisons in our society. . . . [T]he reforms we recommend are "abolishing-type" reforms: those that do not add improvement to or legitimize the prevailing system. . . . We can test the model's consistency with abolitionist goals by asking the following questions:

- Do the actions we advocate make possible the development of the caring community?
- Do we move toward empowering the persons most adversely affected by the present system, the prisoners themselves?
- Does our advocacy reflect and support the values of economic and social justice thruout society, concern for all victims and reconciliation?
- Do the actions we advocate avoid improving or legitimizing the prevailing system?
- Do our suggested campaigns move us closer to our long range goal of abolition?

Critical Resistance, *Reformist Reform vs. Abolitionist Steps to End Imprisonment* (2021).

DOES THIS…	reduce the number of people imprisoned, under surveillance, or under other forms of state control?	reduce the reach of jails, prisons, and surveillance in our everyday lives?	create resources and infrastructures that are steady, preventative, and accessible without police and prison guard contact?	strengthen capacities to prevent or address harm and create processes for community accountability?
Building jails or prisons to address overcrowding or rising numbers of "new" prisoners (for example, migrants)	*NO.* If they build it, they will fill it! Building more jails and prisons creates more cages, period!	*NO.* Building more jails and prisons increases the reach of the PIC and prison and jail infrastructures. Creating more cages means building something we have to tear down later.	*NO.* Adding cages takes away state and local funding and resources that could be directed to community-led infrastructures.	*NO.* Building more prisons and jails entrenches the carceral logic of accountability. They are sites that perpetuate violence and harm.
Building "closer to home," or "nicer," "modern," "rehabilitative" alternatives to existing jails or prisons	*NO.* The history of the prison is a history of reform. New jails and prisons that are proposed as improvements on existing sites or buildings expand the arguments for and lengthen the life of imprisonment.	*NO.* There is no such thing as a "humane" cage. Construction under the pretense of addressing the harms [of] imprisonment reinforces the logics of using cages as a solution for social, economic, and political issues.	*NO.* Arguments for jails "closer to home" reinforce the idea that jails and police create "safety" and take away the capacity to build resources that can create well-being.	*NO.* Prisons and jails do not enable accountability. They are sites that perpetuate violence and harm.
Building jails / prisons that focus on "providing services" to address the needs of specific "populations"	*NO.* Life-affirming resources cannot be provided in spaces of imprisonment. These "services" do not decrease numbers of imprisoned people – they keep specific populations of people imprisoned.	*NO.* Building jails and prisons that lock up specific populations expands the reach of imprisonment by normalizing the idea that care can and should be coupled with policing and imprisonment.	*NO.* The argument for these jails and prisons is that they provide specialized services through policing, imprisonment, and control. Environments of control and violence cannot provide care.	*NO.* Prisons and jails do not enable accountability. They are sites that perpetuate violence and harm, and solidify oppressive social expectations around gender, sexuality, and mental health.
Legislative and other efforts to single out some conviction categories as "exceptions"	*NO.* This strategy entrenches the idea that anybody "deserves" or "needs" to be locked up. Prioritizing only some people for release justifies expansion.	*NO.* By doubling-down on the "need" for some people to be locked up, these efforts strengthen and expand the reach of prisons, jails, and the PIC.	*NO.* Manufacturing divisions between imprisoned people, as more or less dangerous," limits our ability to create real supports and resources that sustain all people.	*NO.* These efforts reinscribe the idea that some people are "risks" to society and others "deserve another chance," strengthening logics of punishment without engaging the context of how harms happen.
Use of electronic monitoring (home-arrest) and other law enforcement-led "alternatives" to jails and prisons	*NO.* Electronic monitoring is a form of state control. It escalates the frequency of contact with the PIC for all members of a household, increasing the vulnerability of people already subject to policing and surveillance.	*NO.* Monitoring brings the prison, jail, or detention center into a person's home, turning it into a space of incarceration, which takes both a psychological and a financial toll.	*NO.* E-carceration means that regular daily movements are constantly linked to threats of arrest. This does not allow people to build and maintain community.	*NO.* E-carceration extends the violence and harm of imprisonment into people's homes and everyday lives. Nothing about electronic monitoring creates systems of accountability or healing.
Public / private "partnerships" to contract services that replicate conditions of imprisonment	*NO.* These services move people from one locked facility into another facility often with similar rules and with the threat of jail or prison looming.	*NO.* This expands the reach of imprisonment, by adding to the larger case system. This is particularly the case where the partnerships replicate and expand logics and rules of jails and prisons, as opposed to intentionally challenging them.	*NO.* These programs require moving through the policing and court systems to access any services that might be available there.	*NO.* Court mandated / police-run "justice" processes hold similar threats for participants as the broader PIC. They do not necessarily include meaningful processes for creating accountability or tools for preventing future harm.

DOES THIS...	*reduce the number of people imprisoned, under surveillance, or under other forms of state control?*	*reduce the reach of jails, prisons, and surveillance in our everyday lives?*	*create resources and infrastructures that are steady, preventative, and accessible without police and prison guard contact?*	*strengthen capacities to prevent or address harm and create processes for community accountability?*
Decarceration or reducing the number of people in prisons and jails	YES. Decarceration takes people out of prisons and jails, and out of direct state control, with the aim of supporting people to stay outside.	YES. By de-prioritizing and de-legitimizing jails, prisons, and related systems we reduce the common-sense idea that they are necessary and/or "effective."	YES. As part of abolitionist organizing we must focus on getting people out while building strong infrastructures of support.	YES. When we work to diminish carceral logic, we can pair our work toward decarceration with other ways of responding to preventing harm. Investing in one will grow our capacities for the other.
Shutting down existing jails and prisons and not replacing them	YES. By reducing the number of cages, we can reduce the number of people inside.	YES. When we close a jail or prison and do not replace it with other carceral systems, we chip away at the idea that cages address social, political, and economic problems.	YES, when we organize for it. When we fight to close jails and prisons we can open the way to defund imprisonment and invest in infrastructures locally that support and sustain people. Abolition is also a BUILDING strategy.	YES. Our work to close prisons and jails and keep them closed is one step toward shifting the focus to addressing and preventing harm without violence and putting resources into that work.
Rejecting government spending for jail and prison construction, renovation, expansion	YES. Nearly all spending projects include enhancements that support arguments for the "benefits" of incarceration.	YES. By rejecting spending on jails and prisons, we counter the common-sense argument that they are necessary and reduce the system's reach.	YES. When we reject funding for jails and prisons this can create opportunities to defund imprisonment and invest in infrastructures locally that support and sustain people.	YES. When we reject funding for jails and prisons this can create opportunities to defund imprisonment and invest in infrastructures locally that support and sustain people.
Reducing policing and police contact in general and "quality of life" policing, specifically	YES. Policing feeds imprisonment, and is an important part of systems of control. Reducing police contact reduces the number of people caught in the criminal legal system.	YES. Policing is a justification for imprisonment. By reducing police contact, the legitimacy and power of jails and prisons can be reduced.	YES. When we fight to reduce police contact and funding, we can organize allocation to community-led infrastructures that are decoupled from policing. We must eliminate all forms of policing from social and community services.	YES. Policing does not prevent harm, but actually causes it. Fighting to reduce policing provides opportunities for communities to invest in systems that prevent harm and create accountability.
Creating voluntary, accessible, community-run services and infrastructures	YES. Access to services that address needs people articulate for themselves can reduce vulnerability to police contact and prevent harm, while building sites for self-determination.	YES. Voluntary services that are community-led and -informed take power away from jails and prisons by removing the focus on imprisonment as a solution to social, economic, and political issues.	YES. When we crate services and infrastructures that are de-coupled from policing and imprisonment we develop systems with the potential to engage with people's complex needs in consistent and trust-building ways.	YES. People getting their needs met in community-determined and -led ways prevents harm. By bolstering resources that address harm, without replicating harm, we create opportunities for community accountability, not punishment and isolation.

Rachel Herzing, *Abolitionist Practices, Reformist Moments*, Upping the Anti (Aug. 2, 2017). [S]ome abolitionists take the rigid stance that working with legal or policy realms is anti-abolitionist by its very nature, [but] it's possible to imagine legal strategies that increase imprisoned people's ability to fight the PIC from the inside out and chip away at prison regimes in a way that erodes them and their power. . . . The campaign against the use of civil gang injunctions in Oakland, for instance, was successful because it integrated grassroots organizing, legal defense, policy advocacy, and cultural work. [W]ithout legal defense of people named, or continued pressure on local lawmakers, the organizing strategy would have failed. That said, neither legal nor policy remedies alone will move us towards abolishing the PIC. Those strategies are only useful abolitionist tools when used in service of meeting organizing goals.

Jamelia Morgan, *Abolition in the Interstices*, Law & Pol. Econ. Project Blog (Dec. 14, 2023). Over the past decade, non-reformist reforms have taken hold of abolitionist movements and discourse. For many, the idea serves as a kind of litmus test for assessing campaign goals and strategies: interventions that qualify as a non-reformist reform are to be pursued, while reformist reforms are to be avoided. The appeal of the concept in this domain is not hard to understand. Non-reformist reforms—which aim to undermine the prevailing political, economic, social order, and construct an essentially different one—provide a clear response to the oft-posed question of "what is abolition" or "what do abolitionists want" in particular cases. . . .

But like with most things, the devil is in the details. Even if the ultimate goals are clear, and even if one is clear about what does and does not count as a non-reformist reform, should the pathways to achieving those goals include non-reformist and reformist strategies? As a theoretical matter, pursuing reformist strategies as an abolitionist would be blasphemous, but while engaged in the day-to-day activities of abolition on the ground—the million experiments, as Mariame Kaba has called it—the answer is much less straightforward.

Take abolitionist[] groups that have supported electoral campaigns or worked to elect . . . so-called progressive prosecutors. In some cases, these activities might themselves be a non-reformist reform—if, for instance, there is an effort to expand power [and] democratize power . . . within and across the campaign and importantly, after the electoral victory or loss. But how should abolitionists groups relate to electoral politics in cases where this isn't plausibly the case? On the one hand, working to elect "progressive prosecutors" can be seen as providing support for, and thereby legitimizing, the existing carceral structure. Yet, on the other hand, sitting on the sidelines can result in significant harm to members of the community, if a more aggressive prosecutor is installed in office.

Or what about groups that litigate cases seeking relief in the form of access to accommodations or medical and mental health treatment for incarcerated people? These are reformists strategies, since they leave untouched the structure of the prison, but in many cases like this one, the imperatives of harm reduction — a life-saving strategy within communities facing imminent harms due to police violence, environmental degradation, housing instability, etc. — require pursuing reformist, piecemeal strategies. . . .

[Ultimately, abolitionists] working within and alongside movements constantly have to grapple with one important reality: that the radically reconfigured world abolitionists seek is not the world abolitionists have now. This in-between state leads to difficult and complicated questions regarding how to dismantle systems and structures that cause harm today, while simultaneously working to build systems and structures for the abolitionist horizon. That in-between state is abolition in the interstices . . . . Non-reformist reforms provide a guidepost for how abolitionists can and should shape their strategies for radical social change. They invite deliberation and thus clarity about whether to engage with a particular strategy, how to engage, and whether and when to disengage. Yet recognizing that the work of abolition is largely work done in the interstices, non-reformist reforms take on new meaning for abolitionist movements.

4. Criticisms and Concerns

Randall Kennedy, *Say It Loud* 444-446 (2021). If the abolitionist literature displays certain virtues, it also manifests certain vices. [T]he term "abolition" is in itself a problem. . . . [A]nti-slavery abolitionists demanded the immediate and unconditional cessation of enslavement . . . because slavery was unequivocally evil and served no good social function. The same cannot be said of prisons or the police. . . . Prisons house convicted inmates who have hurt society by injuring victims absent justification or excuse. They are confined to prevent further criminality, to deter others who might be inclined to transgress the boundaries of criminal law, and to impose punishment.

Now, it is true that far too many people are imprisoned in the United States . . . and that cruel, inhumane, and dangerous conditions are far too prevalent in American prisons. . . . But it is not improper for a society to protect itself from individuals who rape, murder, assault, or rob others in violation of laws that set bounds that, if crossed, make one vulnerable to imprisonment. To the contrary, it is morally imperative for a polity to maintain agencies of collective self-defense, including police and prisons. Justice requires that arbitrariness, prejudice, and cruelty be removed from such agencies. But that is a project of reform, not abolition.

Some abolitionists insist that the number of people who can properly be confined against their will for the safety of the community is much smaller than is usually realized. [That] proves only that some fraction of the incarcerated population is unjustifiably imprisoned. What about the rest—the several thousand (probably the tens of thousands) of prisoners who did in fact engage in serious, violent criminal encroachments—murder, robbery, assault, rape? . . . Many prison abolitionists . . . awkwardly admit that they do not actually favor unlocking all prison gates right away. Rather they want to shrink, dramatically, the overblown presence of incarceration in American life. Fine. But if massive shrinkage is what they really seek, as opposed to total erasure, as opposed to abolition, why not say so? . . .

Some [abolitionists] adamantly insist that they *really* do seek the complete removal of all carceral institutions. . . . This aspiration is so far-fetched that it lacks the plausibility needed to gain substantial political traction. No political movement can do away with human evil and thus moot the necessity for protection against it. I, for one, am repulsed by the prospect of a polity in which serious criminality . . . faces no credible threat of containment, deterrence, and punishment. I am not claiming that police and prisons can ensure our safety. . . . There are limits to what any system of criminal law enforcement can accomplish. . . . But by seeking to apprehend, detain, deter, and punish lawbreakers, society at least signals a profound disapproval of criminal encroachment upon others. That signal is rendered all too indistinct by abolitionist theorists.

Tommie Shelby, *The Idea of Prison Abolition* 54-55, 165, 181-182 (2022). Few would deny that actions that are wrong and cause harm should sometimes be penalized to reduce the incidence of such actions. . . . So why prison? After all, there are less harmful penalties available. [T]he first thing to say is that imprisonment is likely the harshest penalty a society can impose that also plausibly satisfies human rights requirements. Some penalties . . . are too harsh and inhumane, for example, maiming and death. . . . Other penalties are too mild to deter serious crimes. A fine or community service is unlikely to be severe enough to discourage murder or rape. . . . The public owes the disincentive of imprisonment to people who are vulnerable to victimization. We should maintain a penal regime for purposes of public safety, to discourage and prevent criminal conduct within the general population. These penalties are a prudent concession to the unfortunate reality that some among us—not just monsters or predators but ordinary people—can be expected to act wrongly in the absence of sanctions. . . .

With serious crime a rare occurrence, it could be argued that the practice of imprisonment is indefensible. A just and good society would simply live with this small risk of harmful wrongs (perhaps making use of noncarceral penalties . . .) rather than impose the suffering that prison causes. This approach to serious crime is even more plausible when we keep in mind that imprisonment harms not only prisoners but also those who care about or depend on them. . . . But in those remaining occurrences of serious crime in the imagined prison-less society, what could the public say to victims? They could complain that had we established a credible general threat of imprisonment, their assailants may have refrained from attacking them. Or where an aggressor has seriously harmed others before, any new victims could rightly complain that the state should have incapacitated the individual . . . to prevent harm to anyone else. The public could have taken perfectly permissible measures to avert this harmful wrongdoing but chose not to. Given that a primary responsibility of a legitimate state is to protect residents within its jurisdiction from unjust harm to their person, the state would be correctly seen as wronging the victims of crime.

Máximo Langer, *Penal Abolitionism and Criminal Law Minimalism: Here and There, Now and Then*, 134 Harv. L. Rev. F. 42, 61, 63-64 (2020). [T]he lack of criminal law enforcement and criminal punishment may promote racial inequality. For instance, Jill Leovy's book *Ghettoside* suggests the abysmally low homicide clearance rate in South Central L.A. promotes vigilantism and self-help in the minority communities there. . . . It is also important to highlight that punishment of harmful conduct has been a long-standing demand of many Black leaders and the civil rights movement in the United States. Both have seen criminal law and criminal punishment, including prison, as important tools to fight against white rule and white supremacy and to have the rights of Blacks protected. . . . This is a defense neither of anything close to mass incarceration, nor of overspending on and overusing penal responses to social problems, nor of current policing and prisons in the United States, which should be radically different and more humane. This is also not an argument against combining punishment with nonpunitive approaches to justice in response to harmful conduct, nor against fully replacing punishment with nonpunitive approaches when certain conditions are met. Rather, it is an argument for why fully discarding criminal law enforcement, involuntary confinement, and punishment as social responses to harm may be unfair, inhumane, and unprotective of individuals and communities, including individuals and communities of color.

Christopher Lewis & Adaner Usmani, *Abolition of What?*, 114 J. Crim. L. & Criminology __ (2024). [A]bolitionists propose to solve the social problems to which the criminal law purports to respond by abolishing prisons and police, and reinvesting the resources saved in social programs. This is commonly referred to as "justice reinvestment." . . . Abolitionism today, like abolitionism yesterday, is [thus] a positive vision of a more equal society, rather than a movement focused solely on the negative goal of eliminating prisons . . . . [But] the kinds of programs that would be the most efficient tools for eliminating [structural] disadvantage—namely, hyper-targeted programs specifically designed for the least-well off—tend to be the least politically feasible. This is true in any capitalist society, where the disadvantaged tend to be politically disempowered. But it is especially true in a society like the United States, where the legacy of slavery has hampered solidarity [among] poor [social classes of different races]. . . .

The result is that all capitalist countries spend much more on social than penal policy. . . . [T]he United States government spends about $375 billion dollars a year on the largest carceral state ever built by a developed country, yet around $6 trillion dollars on one of the least generous public welfare states in the advanced capitalist world. Consider what this implies. If all the resources currently tied up in the carceral state were reinvested in social programs, it would amount to no more than a 6% expansion of the welfare state. Imagine distributing these $375 billion dollars in a cash transfer directly to each of the 124 million households in America. Each household would receive around $3,000. This would not be insignificant, but it is a far cry from fundamental social transformation.

Rachel E. Barkow, *Promise or Peril? The Political Path of Prison Abolition in America*, 58 Wake Forest L. Rev. 245, 252-255 (2023). Instead of helping the cause of decarceration and improving the lives of those under the control and supervision of the state's punitive apparatus, there is the possibility that abolitionist arguments could, perversely, make things worse. This risk exists for two main reasons.

First, the rhetoric of abolition may worry segments of the public who would otherwise support decarceration, perhaps even radical decarceration, but who are not prepared to rule out the possibility of incarceration entirely, at least not until there are satisfactory, concrete alternatives presented to them. . . . Many members of the public may not want to associate with a movement that does not seem to sufficiently condemn [severe] cases [of criminality] with adequate punishment. They may also be concerned that abolitionists do not have adequate deterrents or means of incapacitating people who will engage in harmful conduct.

That fear, in turn, could fuel a backlash, not only to abolition but to criminal justice reform more generally, because politicians will take steps to avoid being associated with an abolitionist framing that is politically unpopular and thus bend over backward to show that they support tougher responses to crime. . . . Politicians may respond to abolitionist calls by perversely clinging to and celebrating prisons in the same way we are seeing them recommit to policing in response to calls for defunding the police. Language and messaging matter in politics, and the abolition message may prove to be politically costly even if it is a valuable organizing strategy at the community and individual level. . . . To be sure, reformers can try to distinguish themselves and their arguments from more extreme calls for abolition, but the associational risks cannot be ignored and may chill people who would otherwise support meaningful criminal justice reforms from doing so. . . .

The second reason an abolitionist framing may ultimately produce more harm than good . . . is that some abolitionists call for opposition to reforms that could bring benefits to those currently harmed by incarceration. Many abolitionists reject what they call "reformist reforms" that do not contribute to dismantling the existing legal order. For example, some abolitionists reject calls to invest in improvements to prisons or to put in place greater staffing, even if doing so would improve the lives of currently incarcerated people, on the view that this additional funding ultimately expands the role of prisons in society and leads to incarceration being more entrenched overall. Other abolitionists have rejected proposals that would release certain groups of incarcerated people—such as those serving offenses that do not involve violence—because of a concern that excluding others "entrenches the idea that anybody 'deserves' or 'needs' to be locked up."

The question of whether to support a political compromise is always difficult because one has to balance the gains the reform brings with the risk that it will kill the prospects for bigger changes that could otherwise be possible without the compromise. In that sense, abolitionists are engaging in the same strategic calculations that all political actors do. The end sought by abolitionists, however, is unlikely to materialize because they seek the total elimination of prisons and state detention, which they concede would require enormous societal changes to obviate the harms that prisons are created to address. Abolitionists are playing for a utopian endgame that is unlikely ever to occur and certainly not for generations. The abolitionist framing therefore runs the risk of sacrificing too many reforms in the here and now that would benefit people currently suffering from incarceration.

Tomas Keen, *A 'Warm' Closure,* Inquest (June 26, 2021). Responding to an average daily population that has fallen 20 percent since January 2020, the Washington State Department of Corrections announced a plan on May 25, 2021, to close 18 living units and to redirect saved funds to expand a home-detention program. . . . As 13 of the 18 units selected for closure lie on the western side of Washington State, where the majority of people live, the closures would force many more prisoners to the rural eastern side, far away from their communities. . . . From the prisoner perspective, I can tell you what closing the 13 western-lying units would mean: a return to cramped living, reduced visits from loved ones, and fewer units that foster pro-social environments. All of this is antithetical to decarceration, which has to be about more than just shrinking the number of people in prison. A true decarceral movement has to remember those of us who are on the inside now, and will remain here for years to come. And it has to realize that our quality of life isn't binary—in or out. What happens within prison walls has an enormous impact on us and those around us, including when prisons close.

5. Public Safety and "the Dangerous Few"

Allegra M. McLeod, *Prison Abolition and Grounded Justice*, 62 U.C.L.A. L. Rev. 1156, 1168-1171 (2015). [I]t bears noting that there may be, in the end, some people who are so dangerous to others that they cannot live safely among us, those rare persons referred to in abolitionist writings as "the dangerous few." Who and how many are the dangerous few? The answer to this question is by no means self-evident but its complete and final resolution ought not to interfere with serious engagement with abolitionist analysis . . . .

[Some people] convicted of crimes of violence are not especially dangerous and would not perpetrate such violence if they had a means of self-support or means of mental health care or other necessary care that would enable them to avoid criminal process contact in the future. This point is powerfully conveyed by the experience of those who committed heinous, violent crimes as young people — including murders, carjackings, beheadings, and torture — after which these individuals moved on to full, productive, even altruistic lives of service to others through contributions to social justice, culture, business, and the arts. . . . [U]nder circumstances of social coexistence enabled by positive abolition, [these individuals] would pose no threat of harm to themselves or others. . . .

If there are indeed some small subset of people properly denominated the dangerous few, they are [thus] only those who are intent on perpetrating acts of vicious harm against others such that they are an imminent threat to all those around them regardless of their circumstances. An abolitionist framework is not necessarily committed to denying the existence of these dangerous few persons. . . . [But because] any such dangerous few persons constitute at most only a small minority of the many millions of people under criminal supervision in the United States . . . the question of the danger these few may pose can be deferred for some time as decarceration could by political necessity only proceed gradually.

[Ultimately,] the question of the dangerous few ought not to eclipse or overwhelm the urgency of a thorough consideration of abolitionist analyses and reformist projects of displacement of criminal regulation by other regulatory approaches. [Moreover], an abolitionist ethic recognizes that even if a person is so awful in her violence that the threat she poses must be forcibly contained, this course of action ought to be undertaken with moral conflict, circumspection, and even shame, as a choice of the lesser of two evils, rather than as an achievement of justice. . . . Even when confronting the dangerous few, on an abolitionist account, justice is not meaningfully achieved by caging, degrading, or even more humanely confining, the person who assaulted the vulnerable among us.

Thomas Ward Frampton, *The Dangerous Few: Taking Seriously Prison Abolition and Its Skeptics*, 135 Harv. L. Rev. 2013, 2017-2021, 2038, 2044, 2048-2051 (2022). [C]onversations about prison abolition seem to begin and end with some version of the following exchange:

Skeptic: Wait, so no more prisons?
Abolitionist: Yes, that's the basic idea.
Skeptic: None?
Abolitionist: Pretty much.
Skeptic: But you don't really mean you intend to set loose the axe murderers and serial rapists? That's a terrible idea.

. . . Abolitionists typically have several different answers they might then offer [that are generally] less than satisfactory to the skeptic: they either offer too few assurances or present watered-down versions of abolitionism that recast the project in decidedly reformist terms. Even those firmly within the abolitionist camp have acknowledged that this issue (the problem of "the dangerous few") constitutes a "spectral force haunting abolitionist thought," a topic that inevitably arises "as soon as abolitionist discourses navigate towards the programmatic and enter the public arena." . . .

One of the most common abolitionist responses to the question of "the dangerous few" is to concede that for a very limited class of dangerous persons, some form of restraint will remain necessary. . . . There is significant appeal to this position, particularly given the vast number of individuals presently incarcerated with no discernible benefit to "public safety" as traditionally conceived. . . . But in ceding this ground to our skeptical interlocutor, the abolitionist ventures down a slippery slope, blurring the lines between prison abolition and other species of less ambitious criminal justice reform (on both the political left and right). Indeed, Professor Máximo Langer argues that those "penal abolitionists that do not take the ideal of 'a society without prisons' all the way down . . . can be understood not actually as penal abolitionists, but as embracing some version of criminal law minimalism." . . .

[But crucially, the] category of "the dangerous few" has utility as an organizing principle only to the extent that we have reliable mechanisms for identifying who is, and who is not, a member. And, on this score, even a rudimentary survey of how criminal law has functioned throughout United States history paints a bleak picture. . . . [P]erhaps it is worth emphasizing that it is the skeptical interlocutor who — in imagining or assuming some perfect mechanism by which our criminal justice system could identify "the dangerous few" — is [the one who is truly engaged in] utopian thinking. . . . The hypercarceral politics of the United States have always been profoundly racialized . . . . [C]andor requires the skeptic to confront the following point (particularly if we are committed to shunning utopian thinking in this discussion): any system that continues to cage "the dangerous few" in the United States will also necessarily cage many people who do *not* need to be caged, and those individuals will overwhelmingly be poor and nonwhite. . . .

Also implicit in the skeptic's question . . . is the assumption that, were "the dangerous few" at liberty to walk amongst us, free society would become an unrecognizably dangerous and scary place. . . . But this is not really true [either]: despite the massive number of people we imprison, the skeptic's nightmare scenario is not far from the status quo. . . . As Professor Shima Baradaran Baughman's recent study of "clearance rates" over the past fifty years demonstrates, most of those who commit murder and the vast majority of those who commit rape "get away with their crimes." "[W]e live in a world," she writes, "where, much more often than not, crimes go unsolved and unaccounted for." . . . [And clearance] rates drop precipitously (despite being far easier to manipulate) when we examine serious crimes other than killings. According to Bureau of Justice Statistics data, there are between "15 to 20 million felony victimizations annually in the United States, and fewer than 1 million of these cases end in conviction." . . .

None of the foregoing is intended to minimize or denigrate the fear of interpersonal violence that animates the skeptic's question, or downplay the differential exposure to such harm that exists along axes of race, gender, class, sexuality, and more. But here it's worth returning again to the realist critique often leveraged against the abolitionist: "[T]here is reason [to] be leery of utopian hopes [regarding crime prevention, abolition skeptics say,] because crime . . . seems to be a normal aspect of human life . . . [and] is found in varying degrees in all modern nations." The likely permanence of deviance certainly doesn't take the issue off the table, but I think it does alleviate some of the burden on the abolitionist: in all likelihood, we have all already shared a bus, a classroom, a pew, or an office with a member of "the dangerous few."[6]

Monica Bell, *Safety, Friendship, and Dreams*, 54 Harv. C.R.-C.L. L. Rev. 703, 719-720 (2019). We need a movement that advocates for safety as a universal value that the government is obligated to proactively respect. Respecting the entitlement to safety requires laser-sharp focus on eradicating criminogenic social conditions — poverty, residential segregation by race and wealth, virulent discrimination based on race and criminal justice involvement. It also requires a commitment to reining in state violence alongside interpersonal violence. Violence, in all its forms, threatens safety. White middle-class communities, "law-and-order" politicians, and some police leaders have appropriated "safety" and made it inaccessible as a claim for communities of color, especially those who live in marginalized communities. This should end. In order for a universal safety entitlement to have the desired effects, the legal and policy response to this movement must take a different path than it did in the late twentieth century, when the "solutions" to un-safety became heavy policing and incarceration. They must finally take the bold, holistic approach that many leaders then were calling for by meeting demands for safety with strategies that will end criminogenic conditions in black communities, such as expansion of the social safety net. They must do this because safety is a positive precondition for individual and collective freedom, perhaps especially for those to whom it has been long denied.[7]

Tewkunzi Green, *Surviving Everywhere,* Inquest (Nov. 16, 2021). [There is] a truth I've been made to feel the courts do not want to hear, especially having gone through a sentencing hearing that led to a sentence of 34 years. . . . My truth is that I was in hardship for years. And now I understand where I need to get to in life. But the system didn't give me that chance when it had the chance to. It just slapped cuffs on me. It just took me away. It just made me invisible. . . . When you're a survivor of harm and violence—when you're still surviving—sometimes you deny yourself. There's a lot of shame . . . . So many of us are surviving—domestic abuse, harm in our families, relationships and communities, rejection, abandonment, and then also surviving mass incarceration. We are surviving everywhere. . . . You know, the word victim is so interesting. Take a murder case, for example, [like mine, for killing my abusive partner]. We talk about how the victim passed away. But then do we ever consider that the suspect may have been a victim as well? The criminal system doesn't know how many suspects are victims—actually victims—in that situation. It does not get to define that I cannot be a victim. I'm not going to be invisible any longer. I've been invisible all my life.

B.   *Democratization vs. Professionalization*

Related to the preceding discussion of what the end of mass incarceration looks like and how it might come about is a set of questions about *who* ought to be the central actors in such efforts. Do some voices or perspectives deserve more attention or deference than others? Are some methods of seeking change—such as grassroots community organizing, research-backed policy advocacy, or lawyer-driven law reform efforts—more worthwhile or more likely to yield success than others?

These questions are interrelated with but also distinct from those considered in the preceding section. And as Professor Joshua Kleinfeld writes, they present a "foundational, enormously important . . . line of disagreement" among those working to dismantle mass incarceration. "On one side," he continues

> are those who think the root of the present crisis is the outsized influence of the American public—a violent, vengeful, stupid, uninformed, racist, indifferent, or otherwise wrongheaded American public—and the

solution is to place control over criminal justice in the hands of officials and experts. On the other side are those who think the root of the present crisis is a set of bureaucratic attitudes, structures, and incentives divorced from the American public's concerns and sense of justice, and the solution is to make criminal justice more community focused and responsive to lay influences.

In this debate, Kleinfeld goes on, the first camp "flies the banners of professionalization, instrumental rationality, and bureaucratic control," while the second "flies the banners of community, value rationality, and — the watchword of the movement — *democracy*. The two views, *bureaucratic professionalization* versus *democratization*, represent a conflict of visions."[8]

The excerpts that follow represent some of these competing views.

1. Democratization

William J. Stuntz, *Unequal Justice*, 121 Harv. L. Rev. 1969, 1973-1974 (2008). In the late nineteenth and early twentieth centuries, when local politics governed the amount and distribution of criminal punishment, the justice system was stable, reasonably lenient, and surprisingly egalitarian. Prison populations were much smaller than today's, and varied little across place and time. Outside the South, the groups most likely to be the targets of discriminatory punishment . . . achieved results as favorable as native-born white men, or nearly so. No legal rules commanded those results; rather, political equilibrium produced them. In the twentieth century's second half, that equilibrium unraveled. Suburban populations mushroomed, diluting poor city neighborhoods' electoral power; big-city police forces grew more professionalized, hence more detached from the streets they patrol. Crime became a live issue in state and national elections, shifting political power from high-crime cities to the safer suburbs and countryside. The constitutional law of criminal procedure expanded dramatically, shifting legal authority from locally elected trial judges to state and federal appellate courts.

As local control faded, variation of all kinds — across place, time, and demographic category — exploded. In the 1950s, 1960s, and early 1970s, Northern prison populations fell sharply, in the midst of an unprecedented crime wave. The balance of the twentieth century saw an unprecedented punishment wave, while urban crime remained stubbornly high. Both the lenient turn of the century's third quarter and the punitive turn of its last quarter struck high-crime cities, and black neighborhoods within those cities, especially hard. So did the rise of massive, racially disparate drug enforcement. And so did the underpunishment of urban violence . . . . These varied trends are linked: all flow, in large measure, from the decline of locally self-governing justice systems in high-crime cities. . . .

To the suburban voters, state legislators, and state and federal appellate judges whose decisions shape policing and punishment on city streets, criminal justice policies are mostly political symbols or legal abstractions, not questions the answers to which define neighborhood life. Decisionmakers who neither reap the benefit of good decisions nor bear the cost of bad ones tend to make bad ones. Those sad propositions explain much of the inequality in American criminal justice. How are the relevant trends to be reversed? [P]lace more power in the hands of residents of high-crime city neighborhoods—for they feel the effects of rising and falling rates of crime and punishment . . . . Make criminal justice more locally democratic, and justice will be both more moderate and more egalitarian.

Jocelyn Simonson, *Radical Acts of Justice* 1-11 (2023). I referred to the prosecution as "the People" on the record on more than one occasion when I was a defense attorney . . . . The language of "the People" seeps into everyday courtroom practices, written motions, and case law [until the] term comes to seem ordinary. And it comes to seem true: prosecutors are elected officials, and so they must represent the people. People accused of crimes are not part of "the People," part of the public that matters. . . . In many ways, our approach to public safety depends for survival on this limited notion of which "people" matter. . . . The idea of "the People" assumes that all victims of harm want to prosecute and incarcerate those who harmed them [when in fact] surveys of survivors show that many prefer to hold those who harm them accountable through options other than prison. . . .

Now imagine that instead of prosecutors having the only claim to defining justice, other representatives of "the People" emerge. A group of people pays bail for a stranger after a judge has set bail . . . . Another group gathers outside a courthouse with the names of people who have died inside the local jail, holding banners that say, "Not in Our Name." A coalition of many groups spends hundreds of hours collectively bringing forth a "People's Budget" with its own definitions of how the state can provide justice and safety. . . .

When done collectively, by traditionally excluded groups and in opposition to the system's dominant ideals, these communal acts raise foundational questions that call into doubt the legitimacy of the system itself. [P]eople who ordinarily are not in charge of legal interpretation work within the system to live out a new definition of "the people," recasting the concepts of justice and safety so that those ideas can no longer support the status quo. . . . [T]hese collective tactics are most powerful, and most radical, when they are done as contestation—what in democratic theory is known as agonism. People engaging in agonistic acts take an adversarial stance toward practices and ideologies of institutions in power, but do so through engagement with those institutions. . . . Groups that engage in this kind of collective contestation of the criminal system set up a new ideological struggle—the people v. the people—where the collective stakes of criminal punishment are on the table.

Alicia Garza, *The Purpose of Power* 141-142, 212-218 (2020). Movements bring people together to change laws and to change culture. Successful movements know how to use the tools of media and culture to communicate what they are for, and to help paint a picture of what an alternative world can look like, feel like, be like. . . . The real story behind any successful movement is many people coming together to create the change they want to see in the world. This truth has been obscured by popular narratives of successful social change that tend to revolve around the courageous actions and moral clarity of one person. . . . [I]n order to stay sturdy, [movements] need a base — people who keep the movements anchored in the needs, dreams, and lived experiences of those who are directly impacted by the problem at hand. . . . Today, there are some powerful organizations building a base of directly impacted people, who are coming together to change their conditions and transform how power operates . . . . These organizations are able to mobilize, activate, and engage millions of people on the issues that impact their lives . . . because they are intentional about building a political community around and with their base . . . . These successful organizations give people a sense of their own power.

Raj Jayadev & Pilar Weiss, *Organizing Towards a New Vision of Community Justice*, Law & Pol. Econ. Project Blog (May 9, 2019). Mainstream political candidates openly claim they are progressive [while offering] reformist reforms in the name of "the community." The experiences of people of color, the poor, the LGBTQ community, and immigrants in the criminal legal system have of course been that these claims of action and reform in the name of "the community" are not reflective of their actual needs or priorities. In contrast, all across the country, activists and organizers are building a grassroots movement that is seeking to realize a different vision of justice, one that is based on a radical repositioning of "the community" and its power. This is a fight based on survival but also one seeking to shift power from those who have historically held it to those who have been historically disempowered, under-resourced, targeted by the system, and most impacted by structural inequalities. . . . This repositioning . . . situates the community as the drivers of what the ultimate realization of a new vision of justice, healing, and power will look like. . . . When we, as organizers, refer to "the community," we are referring to individuals and their families, neighborhood, and those with a common interest and/or shared identity who are all directly impacted by structural inequalities. . . . The constantly growing movement to end incarceration is a complex effort with no single defining campaign. It is hundreds of formal and informal organizational formations of different size and orientation tackling the numerous drivers of the carceral state. . . . Organizing tactics and practices that contest power and the place of community may be the devices we use to win local and immediate struggles, but they are also the vehicles pushing us towards an answer to the question of what we will build after we win, how do we realize the larger vision of abolition. . . . The world we are building, the one without incarceration and with true community power, will not contain the formations we had to try out to dismantle the system, but rather will be at the end of the path we built together.

Erin Collins, *The Evidence-Based Trap*, Inquest (July 22, 2022). [A]n evidence-based, data-driven . . . paradigm [for reform] is neither neutral nor inevitable. It is the result of a choice, and a deeply political one at that. And that choice — along with the subsequent decisions about what we measure, why we measure, and how we measure — favors the status quo. . . . [E]vidence-based methodology itself participates in the reproduction of epistemic biases and white supremacy. It sends a clear message about what (and who) counts. [T]he paradigm valorizes quantitative data, ideally gathered from randomized controlled trials, to guide and assess reforms. It thus centers reform initiatives and assessments in institutes, academies, and organizations with the credentials and resources to conduct rigorous, large-scale studies. Individual or collective accounts of personal experience with a certain reform or procedure explicitly and intentionally do not qualify as evidence under the evidence-based paradigm. As a result, the paradigm reinforces a hierarchy of knowledge and promotes epistemic injustice: only the findings of the researchers matter, while those whose experiences are often the subject of such studies will not be heard. Taken to its logical conclusion, this evidence-based orientation suggests we should not take bold action to redress problems until, or unless, we can show such actions are necessary and effective through quantitative empirical testing.

2. Professionalization

Edward L. Rubin & Malcolm M. Feeley, *Criminal Justice Through Management: From Police, Prosecutors, Courts, and Prisons to a Modern Administrative Agency*, 100 Or. L. Rev. 261, 347-348 (2022). [T]he organizing principle of [democratization] is that criminal justice is and should be a local, community-based institution, democratically organized and operated, and administered to the extent possible by lay-leaders selected from within the affected community. There are several fairly obvious empirical arguments against this proposal. One argument is that it suffers from [a] pastoral nostalgia that . . . draws its inspiration from images of small, rustic towns — often fantasy images of ingrown societies that were in fact seething with misery, inequality, and petty hatreds. Such nostalgia, whether justified or not, is inapplicable and thus dysfunctional in this era of High Modernity. Today's big cities are not comprised of a multiplicity of urban villages, each with its own cultural coherence and accepted norms, but rather are interconnected sprawls of residential properties whose inhabitants travel long distances to work or shop and socialize in cyberspace. Second, managing any basic function of modern society, whether it is education, public health, environmental protection, or criminal justice is a complex task, requiring specialized knowledge and full-time attention. Untrained volunteers can certainly provide valuable advice and information, but they are not likely to function effectively in a managerial role. . . . Third, delegating authority to small communities does not necessarily solve the abiding problem of democracy, which is the tyranny of the majority. The majority within that community, even if it is a minority within the nation as a whole, is fully capable of mistreating those in its midst whom it regards as Other.

John Rappaport, *Some Doubts About "Democratizing" Criminal Justice*, 87 U. Chi. L. Rev. 711, 775-777 (2020). A growing comparative literature . . . suggests that populism makes criminal justice more, not less, severe. This may explain why the United States is widely regarded as having both the most punitive and the most popularly democratic criminal justice system, at least in the developed world.

Professor James Whitman frames the basic inquiry this way: "Why has American politics turned to the kind of retributivism that both French and German politics generally resists?" . . . "It is surely the case," Whitman reasons, "that Americans punish more harshly because the management of the punishment system in the United States is more given over to democratic politics." Professor David Garland agrees, observing that "explicit attempts to express public anger and resentment have become a recurring theme of the rhetoric that accompanies penal legislation and decision-making" in the United States.

"Conversely," says Whitman, "it is manifest that part of the reason that the retributive temper has not established itself in France and Germany is that democratic politics has much less impact on criminal justice in Europe than it does in the United States." In continental Western Europe, "state apparatuses remain highly autonomous, largely steered by bureaucracies that are far more insulated from democratic pressures." "Tepid bureaucratic routinization of criminal law," the argument goes, "is an important barrier to the kind of overheated democratic retributivism that has come to America." Garland, again, is in accord, crediting the rise of "professional bureaucracies" with the marginalization of "punitive sentiments," which are "replaced by more utilitarian objectives and expectations." The same distinction explains how European elites abolished the death penalty notwithstanding popular support for its retention.

Subsequent studies examining a larger number of countries, across a broader array of variables, have enriched Whitman and Garland's observations. Surveying the literature a decade ago, Professor Michael Tonry identified "risk" and "protective" factors that make it more or less likely, respectively, that a society will adopt punitive policies. "Prominent risk factors," Tonry explains, "include 'conflict' political systems, elected judges and prosecutors, sensationalist journalism, . . . and a populist view that criminal justice policy should be strongly influenced by public sentiment and partisan politics." "Prominent protective factors," in contrast, "include consensus political systems, nonpartisan judges and prosecutors, . . . and a predominant view that criminal justice policy falls appropriately within the province of expert knowledge and professional experience."

Rachel E. Barkow, *Prisoners of Politics: Breaking the Cycle of Mass Incarceration* **2-4 (2019).** If we want better outcomes that will improve public safety, we need to change the institutional framework we currently use to make criminal justice policy. Instead of policies designed to appeal to the emotions of voters who lack basic information about crime, we need to create an institutional structure that creates a space for experts who look at facts and data to set policies that will improve public safety outcomes, even if they are not easily reduced to sound bites or fail to provide emotional appeal.

This institutional model is a well-traveled path for better outcomes. Indeed, this is the model we use in most other areas of governance, from fiscal policy to environmental regulation. We do not have our elected officials set policies based on their intuitive reactions to outlier stories that make the news and arouse the public. . . . Instead, we rely on expert agencies to set policies based on the best data available to minimize risks and achieve the greatest benefits at the lowest costs. But all too often crime policy in America is based on a reaction to a single crime without any evaluation of overall programs or approaches. People who care about reducing mass incarceration and want to improve criminal justice thus need to push for a model of criminal justice decision-making that looks more like the way we make policy in other regulatory areas where expertise plays a more significant role.

This is not to say that a shift from policy by populism to expertise will be easy or completely transformative. [L]arge segments of the public are likely to be particularly resistant to the idea that crime policy is something for experts . . . . If criminal justice were just a matter of achieving retributive justice or determining what someone morally deserves as punishment for a crime, then a model that relies on the public's emotional reaction might make more sense. But that is not the only goal of criminal punishment. The public and policymakers often emphasize that the aim of criminal justice policy is the utilitarian goal of maximizing public safety and making the most of limited resources; to the extent that is the goal, we could be doing much better. We have data and evidence about better approaches that would give us better safety outcomes with our limited resources and that would result in less human suffering by individuals currently facing excess punishments. . . . The key to making better decisions about public safety and the use of our limited resources is to create a decision-making structure where we no longer ignore evidence about what does and does not work and at what cost.

II. INTERVENTIONS

Efforts to end mass incarceration grow from the myriad and sometimes competing ideas set forth above to yield concrete, systemic interventions. Proposals and projects run the gamut, from reducing the number of crimes, prosecutions, and lengthy sentences, to emphasizing the role of progressive prosecutors and public defenders, to building nonpunitive alternative forms of accountability, to divesting from carceral institutions, to building collective power within and outside of courtrooms. As in the first part of this chapter, our goal in the sections that follow is to provide a high-level overview of work in these various domains, drawing on selected writings from those closely engaged in or studying such efforts.[9]

A. *Depopulating Prisons: Legislative Reform, Litigation, and Clemency*

Ending mass incarceration, of course, requires reducing the number of people sent to and detained within prisons and jails. As noted in Chapter One, those numbers have been in decline for much of the past decade and a half. According to a report published by the Sentencing Project, while the prison population grew at an average rate of 5.8 percent every year between 1972 and 2009, it has been declining at an average rate of approximately 1.9 percent since then (not counting an anomalous 14.1 percent drop during the COVID-19 pandemic). This decline is visible across multiple states, although some have had enormous declines while others have seen only modest changes. Others still have seen post-pandemic increases, and in 2022, the national prison population increased by 2 percent—its first rise after roughly a decade of decline.[10]

In this section, we examine some of the actions by legislatures, voters, courts, and governors that have helped to reduce the prison population. In the section that follows, we examine prosecutorial discretion to decline charges for certain offenses.

1. Decarceral Mechanisms

Jacob Kang-Brown et al., Vera Inst. of Just., *The New Dynamics of Mass Incarceration* 9-11 (2018). Since 2000, state and local governments have been under increasing pressure to address overcrowding in prisons and jails, and several have passed legislation aimed directly at reducing the number of incarcerated people. . . . A handful of states led the way . . . . Michigan, for example, overhauled its sentencing statutes and practices over a nearly 10-year span, beginning in 1998. This legislative reform is estimated to have reduced the number of people committed to prison between 2002 and 2004 by 1,366, and increased parole approval rates so that an average of 900 additional people were paroled each year. At the time, it was the only state to have made significant progress in repealing mandatory minimums. Comprehensive reform packages followed in other jurisdictions, lowering prison populations in states like Connecticut (2003-04) and Texas (2007). Gradually, more states adopted legislation aimed at reducing incarceration, and rhetoric from policymakers also began to shift from "tough on crime" to "smart on crime." . . . Between 2013 and 2015, 286 bills, executive orders, or ballot initiatives targeting sentencing or corrections reform were advanced across 46 states. Vital change has been made via voter-driven initiatives as well. Voters in California and Oklahoma passed ballot initiatives in 2014 and 2016 respectively that reduced punishment for certain crimes by classifying them as misdemeanors rather than felonies.

Brown v. Plata, 563 U.S. 493 (2011). This case arises from serious constitutional violations in California's prison system. . . . At the time of trial, California's correctional facilities held some 156,000 persons. This is nearly double the number that California's prisons were designed to hold, and California has been ordered [by the trial court below] to reduce its prison population to 137.5% of design capacity. By the [lower] court's own estimate, the required population reduction could be as high as 46,000 persons. . . . The population reduction potentially required is . . . of unprecedented sweep and extent. Yet so too is the continuing injury and harm resulting from these serious constitutional violations. For years the medical and mental health care provided by California's prisons has fallen short of minimum constitutional requirements and has failed to meet prisoners' basic health needs. Needless suffering and death have been the well-documented result. Over the whole course of years during which this litigation has been pending, no other remedies have been found to be sufficient. Efforts to remedy the violation have been frustrated by severe overcrowding . . . .

Establishing the population at which the State could begin to provide constitutionally adequate medical and mental health care, and the appropriate timeframe within which to achieve the necessary reduction, requires a degree of judgment. The inquiry involves uncertain predictions regarding the effects of population reductions, as well as difficult determinations regarding the capacity of prison officials to provide adequate care at various population levels. . . . The [lower] court concluded that the population of California's prisons should be capped at 137.5% of design capacity. This conclusion is supported by the record. Indeed, some evidence supported a limit as low as 100% of design capacity. . . . The [lower] court [further] ordered the State to achieve this reduction within two years. . . . The medical and mental health care provided by California's prisons falls below the standard of decency that inheres in the Eighth Amendment. This extensive and ongoing constitutional violation requires a remedy, and a remedy will not be achieved without a reduction in overcrowding. The relief ordered by the [lower] court is required by the Constitution and was authorized by Congress in the [Prison Litigation Reform Act]. The State shall implement the order without further delay.

Mia Bird et al., Pub. Pol'y Inst. of Cal., *The Impact of Proposition 47 on Crime and Recidivism* 4-7 (2018). The court-mandated [prison population reduction affirmed in *Brown v. Plata*] prompted significant legislative reforms. First, in October 2011, California enacted public safety realignment (AB 109), which shifted responsibility for many non-serious, non-violent, and non-sexual offenders to county jail and probation systems. The reform cut the prison population by about 27,400 in its first year—but not by enough to meet the court mandate. The prison population declined further as a result of Proposition 36 in 2012, which revised California's three-strikes law, but the mandated target still was not met.

In November 2014, another major reform, Proposition 47 (Prop 47), passed with the support of almost 60 percent of voters. Prop 47 reduced the penalties associated with a set of lower-level drug and property offenses. These offenses were reclassified from felonies or wobblers—which could be charged as either felonies or misdemeanors at the prosecutor's discretion—to misdemeanors that carry a maximum sentence of one year in jail. The law also applied retroactively, meaning that individuals already serving prison or jail sentences at the time of passage could petition to be released or to have their sentences shortened. . . . Importantly, the law also aims to reduce California's stubbornly high recidivism rates by requiring that 65 percent of the net state savings from the measure go toward grants and programs for mental health and substance-use disorder treatment. . . .

Both state prisons and county jails saw reduced populations under Prop 47. One year after the reform's passage, the prison population declined by a total of 8,100 inmates (or 6.0%), with the biggest drop occurring in the first six months. . . . The jail population also decreased sharply following Prop 47. One year after passage, jails held about 7,000 (or 8.5%) fewer inmates, easing population pressure in crowded jail systems. . . . [These lower] incarceration levels stem from changes to both releases and admissions . . . . Early releases from jails and prisons took place as individuals already serving time for Prop 47 offenses qualified for resentencing from a felony to a misdemeanor. . . . Incarceration levels were also affected by changes in arrests. The monthly number of arrests decreased after Prop 47, while the monthly number of cite and releases in the field increased—especially when measured as a share of total arrests—in the first year following the reform.

Leah Sakala et al., Urban Inst., How Governors Can Use Categorical Clemency as a Corrective Tool 1-3 (2020). If someone is in prison, clemency can result in their release, a sentence reduction leading to earlier release, or a sentence modification (e.g., commuting a death penalty sentence to life without parole, or granting or expediting eligibility to be considered for parole). Many states' governors have authority to use executive clemency to address problems in the justice system and advance state reform goals, and categorical clemency is one way they can exercise this power. Categorical clemency refers to clemency eligibility or grants issued to certain groups based on shared circumstances, as opposed to eligibility or grants issued on an individualized case-by-case basis. Governors can offer eligibility or grants to groups based on various criteria, including their offenses, personal characteristics, and experiences. They can also base categorical clemency eligibility on determinations about systemic policy issues. . . .

Recently, several governors have exercised their executive clemency power to apply reforms and other legal changes retroactively. Such actions are designed to ensure that people do not continue to be imprisoned for convictions that are no longer eligible for prison sentences, or carry criminal records for behavior that is no longer criminalized. [For example, a 2016 referendum] asked Oklahoma voters whether they would approve of recategorizing certain felonies, such as drug possession and minor property crimes, as misdemeanors, and it passed by a 16 percent margin. [Subsequent clemency actions] allowed 527 people to have their sentences commuted and 462 people to be released from state prisons in 2019. . . . [In similar fashion, in] October 2020, Colorado governor Jared Polis issued an executive order that pardoned more than 2,700 convictions of possession of an ounce or less of marijuana that were issued before the state legalized personal marijuana use in 2012 . . . . The executive order followed legislation passed in June 2020 designed to make Colorado's cannabis industry more equitable, including by granting streamlined pardon powers to the governor for people convicted of possession of up to two ounces of marijuana.[11]

2. Tradeoffs and Challenges

Ben Grunwald, Data-Driven Decarceration, Inquest (Jan. 12, 2023). How, exactly, should we shrink, unwind, or close prisons? . . . The options are numerous, and even those that would achieve the same numeric target—whether it's reducing the prison population by 10, 50, or 100%—can have vastly different social consequences. Some approaches, for example, might be structured to divert as many people as possible from ending up in prison in the first place. Others might try to minimize the risk that decarceration could increase crime on the outside. Still others might seek to reduce the prison population as quickly as possible. And still more might focus on limiting racial disparities among those still incarcerated.

No one path to decarceration can achieve all these goals at once. That's in part because decarceration . . . would likely occur against a backdrop of familiar constraints, including the composition of today's prison population and the political reality of our current social order. Even when decarceral reforms are in reach, in other words, we may need to consider the tradeoffs of competing decarceral pathways and make choices that reflect deep value judgments about our priorities.

To make these choices more concrete . . . I used prison data from 39 states to forecast the effects of hundreds of decarceral strategies. My goal was to answer a few key questions: What would happen if we cut prison admissions—by decreasing the number of convictions or carceral sentences—by 25, 50, 75, or 100%? What would happen if we shortened the time prisoners serve—by cutting sentences or granting clemency—either retroactively to current prisoners or prospectively to future ones? And what if we combined these strategies or applied them to some offenses but not others? . . . To keep things simple, [I] assume the goal is cutting the prison population in half, but the same basic insights apply to other goals too—even shuttering every prison in the country. . . .

[Take first timing.] With the right political will, some strategies could happen almost overnight. Universal clemency, for example, could bring the prison population to zero immediately. By contrast, [even] if we stop convicting people entirely or slash sentences for all future cases, the prison population will remain large for years because many people are already serving long sentences. These polar examples highlight how the structure of a decarceration strategy impacts its timeline. The same lessons apply to less sweeping reforms. For example, if we cut sentences by 75% for future prisoners convicted of nonviolent or less-serious violent offenses (such as robbery and assault), we could reduce the prison population to half its current level—but it would take *more than a decade*. By contrast, applying similar reductions to both future and current prisoners would achieve the same goal immediately.

Given the fickle dynamics of U.S. politics, . . . slower decarceration strategies [might] allow more time for political pushback . . . . That said, quicker decarceration also has its own political costs [because] some government officials may be unwilling to support a strategy that they perceive provides insufficient insulation against political backlash . . . . Slower decarceration can push the risk of high-profile crimes to the future, sometimes after the relevant decisionmakers will have already retired or left office.

[Next consider crime.] In seeking to reduce one form of harm—civilian-on-civilian crime—prisons inflict other serious harms on the same communities they purport to protect. . . . Fortunately, there are ways to reduce crime without the same social harms. As abolitionists have argued for decades, the best approach is likely large-scale investment in communities and infrastructure. . . . Critically, however, these community interventions require time both to implement and take effect. Their impacts on crime will therefore lag. Based on the available empirical evidence, many scholars believe that some carceral approaches that are already in place—like policing and incarceration—decrease civilian-on-civilian crime, at least under certain circumstances. In the short term, then, a shift from carceral to non-carceral crime-reduction policy risks increasing crime. Efforts to reduce the prison population thus face a near-term tradeoff between two types of harms—those caused by crime and those caused by prison.

Strategies that shrink prison while seeking to minimize crime tend to focus on people convicted of low-level offenses, presumably because they are thought to commit less crime upon release. [But crucially, we] cannot shrink the prison population, even by half, by decarcerating non-violent offenses alone. Only 14 and 28% of people in state prisons are serving time for drug and other nonviolent crimes, respectively. Thus, to make large-scale inroads on mass incarceration, we need to include violent offenses, too—a statistical reality that highlights the danger of focusing decarceral efforts exclusively on nonviolent offenses and thus reinforcing the perception that violent offenses are too dangerous for decarceration. . . .

[Finally, consider race.] Ending racial disparity is a central aim of many decarceral efforts. My forecasts, though, highlight a dilemma: Virtually all plausible pathways would exacerbate or leave unchanged current levels of disparity. This finding stems from the fact that, relative to white prisoners, Black prisoners are admitted at heightened and roughly constant rates per capita across offense types—with the exception of violent offenses, for which they are admitted at even higher rates. It also stems from Black prisoners serving, on average, a similar length of time as other prisoners for nonviolent offenses but more time for violent ones. The upshot is that decarcerating nonviolent offenses alone would likely *increase* racial dispari-ties among those left behind—by up to 13% . . . . Out of all the decarcera-tion strategies I tested, the only ones that reduce racial disparity are those that decarcerate violent offenses far more than nonviolent ones—an unlikely policy reform. And, even then, they never reduce Black overrepre-sentation dramatically.

To be clear, this is not an argument against decarceration, nor is it an argument that decarceration is inconsistent with racial justice. After all, Black prisoners would disproportionately benefit from nearly all decarcera-tion strategies precisely because they are so overrepresented in prison. But the fact remains that virtually all plausible efforts to shrink the prison pop-ulation would leave us with similar or even starker racial disparities among those who remain.

Magnus Lofstrom & Steven Raphael, *Incarceration and Crime: Evidence from California's Public Safety Realignment Reform*, 664 Annals Am. Acad. Pol. & Soc. Sci. 196, 197, 216-218 (2016). A key question of interest to both policymakers and criminal justice researchers concerns the effects of [decarceral] reforms on crime rates. Existing research finds that incarcerating a convicted criminal offender does on average reduce crime through incapacitation and deterrence, with the lion's share of the reduction operating through incapacitation. However, these effects exhibit diminishing returns to scale that set in at quite low levels of incarceration and very small incapacitation/deterrence effects at the incarceration rates that currently characterize most U.S. states.

[W]e assess the effects of a recent reform in California that caused a sharp and permanent reduction in the state's incarceration rate. . . . We exploit the large variation across California counties in the effect of this reform on county-specific prison incarceration rates. . . . We find that the reduction in California's prison population . . . modestly increased property crime primarily through motor vehicle thefts but had little effect on violent crime. . . . Our estimates suggest that at California's pre-[reform] incarceration rate, for an additional offender serving one year in prison, roughly one to two property crimes per year and little to no violent crime are prevented.

Are these effects large? There are a number of ways to answer this question. First, we can compare our results to those from previous research. . . . Our review of . . . research in the United States using different methods and different time periods of analysis suggests that the amount of crime prevented per prison year served during the 1970s and 1980s is many multiples the effect sizes that we document here. . . .

An alternative manner of characterizing these results would be to ask whether the returns in terms of crimes prevented outweigh the budgetary or, better yet, the complete social costs of incarcerating these marginal offenders. . . . Our . . . results suggest that each prison year served prevents 1.2 auto thefts. [Other research] implies that each auto theft costs on average $9,533 (in 2013 dollars). This suggests that each prison year served for those who as a result of [the decarceral reforms] are no longer incarcerated prevents $11,783 in crime related costs. [California] estimates that the annual cost of incarcerating a prison inmate in California is $51,889. This suggests a return of 23 cents on the dollar. Incorporating some of the more difficult to price social costs in the calculation would certainly lower the return even further.

Nazgol Ghandnoosh & Kristen M. Budd, Sent'g Project, *Incarceration & Crime: A Weak Relationship* 9, 12 (2024). As some lawmakers pivot to widen the reach of the criminal legal system in response to public concern, recent state trends illustrate that less imprisonment often happens alongside improvements to community safety. Over a nine year period (2013-2022), 46 states reduced the footprint of their prison population while experiencing crime declines. In some states, these declines were substantial. But experiencing declines in crime and incarceration has not prevented some states from returning to a punitive playbook in the face of crime upticks. Louisiana, for example, reduced its prison population by 30% while experiencing an 18% decrease in its crime rate from 2013 to 2022. While some Louisiana cities in 2022 and 2023 saw sharp increases in homicides, preliminary data suggests many of these trends are reversing. For example, preliminary 2024 data from New Orleans suggest that most violent crime, including homicide, is trending down. Yet, in response to these temporary spikes in violent crime, Louisiana lawmakers increased sentences for certain crime types in a special session in 2024, requiring 85% of sentences to be served prior to possible release for "good time" credit, eliminating parole with very few exceptions, and automatically sending 17-year-olds to adult criminal court. Instead of investing in evidence-based, localized responses to crime, particularly in communities experiencing sharp increases in violence, lawmakers took a broad state-wide approach which is anticipated to balloon the state's prison and jail populations, while contributing little to community safety.

William J. Stuntz, *The Pathological Politics of Criminal Law*, 100 Mich. L. Rev. 505, 527-528, 577, 600 (2001). [P]ublic opinion and ideological commitments . . . are likely to push in different directions on different issues at different times and places. If ordinary politics drives criminal law, it will drive it toward more liability here and less there, more liability now but less then. One sees some of that variability in the history of American criminal law, but not much. . . . [B]eneath the currents of ordinary politics, other, deeper forces are at work. Criminal law is not just the product of politics; it is the product of a political system, a set of institutional arrangements by which power over the law and its application is dispersed among a set of actors . . . . Police and prosecutors can choose whom to target from among the universe of potential offenders. That reduces the cost to legislatures of expanding criminal law's scope. . . . It would no doubt be a good thing if legislatures were to improve their drafting, even more so if they would make better normative judgments. But there is no reason to assume they will do so, given that it is in their interest to behave as they do now.

B.   Progressive Prosecution

Statutes that authorize severe levels of incarceration can be mitigated, or perhaps even neutralized, if prosecutors decide not to invoke them when filing charges — or if they decline to prosecute certain offenses altogether.

As discussed in Chapter Nine, prosecutors have traditionally enjoyed broad discretion when deciding whether to file charges in a given case. In recent years, a movement to elect progressive prosecutors who will use that discretion toward decarceral ends has successfully elected dozens of prosecutors across the country, many of whom made good on campaign promises to stop prosecuting certain low-level crimes. Some of these prosecutors—most famously, San Francisco District Attorney Chesa Boudin—were subsequently defeated at the polls. But others—most famously, Philadelphia District Attorney Larry Krasner—have beaten back political opponents and secured reelection. The excerpts that follow give an overview of this movement and, in the eyes of some critics, its limitations. We then turn to a more focused debate on the legitimacy and legality of broadscale prosecutorial declination policies.

1. Promise and Pitfalls

Emily Bazelon, *Charged* xxv-xxx, 296 (2019). Over the last forty years, prosecutors have amassed more power than our system was designed for. And they have mostly used it to put more people in prison, contributing to the scourge of mass incarceration . . . . [But] prosecutors also hold the key to change. They can protect the innocent. They can guard against racial bias. They can curtail mass incarceration. Change who occupies the prosecutor's office, and you can make the system begin to operate differently. The power of the D.A. makes him or her the actor—the only actor—who can start to fix what's broken without changing a single law.

A movement of organizers and activists and local leaders and defense lawyers and professors and students and donors is fighting for that change. This movement is working to elect a new type of D.A. in city after city and county after county. . . . The candidates the movement embraces see ensuring fairness as integral to public safety. . . . The movement to transform American prosecution is bipartisan. It has roots in civil rights history, the Black Lives Matter campaign against violence and racism, libertarian skepticism of government overreach, and conservative concerns about waste and spending. So far, the newly elected D.A.s represent a small fraction of the more than twenty-four hundred prosecutors who hold elected office nationwide. But they include Democrats and Republicans, in red states as well as purple and blue ones . . . . [And because] campaigns to reform D.A.'s offices are local, they show how urban strongholds can control their destinies without waiting for state legislatures to get on board. . . .

It's not clear yet whether the movement to transform American prosecution will be equal to the challenge—whether it will spread beyond a few dozen D.A.'s offices, and thus impact incarceration on a national scale. In much of the country, prosecutors still lean hard toward punitive outcomes and toward retribution . . . . [But t]he movement to elect a new kind of prosecutor is the most promising means of reform I see on the political landscape. . . . We have to fix the broken parts of America's criminal justice system. And we the people have the power to do it, with our votes.

Larry Krasner, *Power to the Voters,* Inquest (June 25, 2024). In January 2018 I became the first reform district attorney in Philadelphia's history. That election was won by a grassroots movement for criminal justice reform that, like all great social justice movements, needed some lawyers. Along with Kim Foxx in Chicago and George Gascon in San Francisco (then Los Angeles), among many other reform chief prosecutors who now represent almost 20 percent of the U.S. population, that movement elected me—a political newcomer—to be one of its lawyers. My election came after a thirty-year career trying cases almost daily in state and federal court as a public defender, as a private criminal defense attorney, and as a civil rights attorney specializing in police abuse cases. Having watched Philly prosecutors use their discretion and power in the Philadelphia District Attorney's Office (DAO) to drive up mass incarceration for three decades, I theorized that a reform prosecutor could help that grassroots movement to drive mass incarceration down. . . .

Please consider the below, partial inventory of decarceration achieved by that movement, with the help of the Philadelphia DAO:

- Future mass incarceration has been cut in half [meaning that the sentences to] jail and prison generated in Philly criminal courts are down about 50 percent annually, as compared to prior (traditional) Philly prosecutors' administrations. Soon enough, this reduction will total nearly 50,000 total years of custody. . . .

- Half of Pennsylvania state prison population declines come from Philadelphia (which supplies about 20 percent of all people incarcerated in state prisons). Pennsylvania contains 67 counties, of which Philadelphia is only one. . . .

- The number of Philly juveniles in carceral facilities is massively down, having been reduced by roughly 80 percent . . . .

- One major on-ramp to reincarceration—mass supervision by means of excessive periods of probation and parole—has been reduced by about 65 percent. . . .

- The number of criminal matters prosecuted in Philadelphia has declined by 50 percent, from a high of about 70,000 to about 35,000 over the last 10 years, with most of the sustained decline owing to the current administration. Certain offenses are seldom prosecuted now (unlike prior administrations), including certain drug possession offenses, sex work, and nonviolent protest activity sans property destruction.

- The Philly DAO has not sought the death penalty in six-plus years. Just one prior Philly DA sought it routinely and got it every two months of her term. . . .

- Unprecedented resources are now dedicated to a trauma-based approach to addressing the needs of victims, survivors, and witnesses . . . .

- Anti-carceral forms of accountability (e.g., diversion and restorative justice, specifically tailored to the needs of juveniles, young adults, and older adults) have been radically expanded.

Benjamin Levin, *Imagining the Progressive Prosecutor*, 105 Minn. L. Rev. 1415, 1425-1446 (2021). The popular embrace of the "progressive prosecutor" moniker certainly might . . . suggest that the Overton window for prosecutorial politics has shifted. . . . [But] the success of the movement might actually highlight its shortcomings—if everyone can claim to be a progressive prosecutor, then what good does the categorization do? As John Pfaff (a proponent of progressive prosecution) has observed:

> It is increasingly easy for district attorney candidates to *sound* progressive or reform-leaning, but there is a growing risk that commonly-invoked words . . . could mean very different things to different people, and that ambiguity could allow candidates who lack a serious commitment to reform to avoid accountability if they win their elections but implement few real changes.

Frustratingly, the slipperiness of the progressive prosecutor categorization and its increasing popularity in the media and advocacy circle invites greater uncertainty about prosecutorial elections and—perhaps more provocatively—about whether progressive prosecution even is a worthwhile goal. . . . [Consider the different types of prosecutors who currently march under the progressive prosecutor banner.]

The Progressive Who Prosecutes. The first ideal type is . . . progressive in the sense of her general politics. That is, her voting patterns, endorsements, political beliefs, and so forth might be identified as "progressive" or falling somewhere left of center on the political spectrum. . . . But . . . the progressive who prosecutes doesn't necessarily bring her politics to her job or to the administration of criminal law. Regardless of her views on a host of other divisive left/right issues (e.g., reproductive rights, affirmative action, health care), she views her function as prosecutor to be a role in and of itself, divorced from other political battlegrounds. Maybe she "adopts vaguely critical buzz words about mass incarceration that are trendy in liberal elite circles," but this familiarity with reformist rhetoric doesn't necessarily translate to policy or specific goals. . . .

The Proceduralist Prosecutor. The second ideal type . . . brings a sort-of good government liberalism to the DA's office. Viewed through this frame, the social function of the prosecutor is important and the work of the DA's office is fundamentally good. But, the mission has been clouded or subverted by bad apples or perhaps even by a culture of disinterest or lawlessness. The proceduralist prosecutor brings a focus on procedural justice[, which usually] means: complying with *Brady* obligations, not encouraging or relying on problematic police behavior (e.g., "testilying," unconstitutional stops and searches), and guarding against cognitive biases and practices that might lead to wrongful convictions . . . .

The Prosecutorial Progressive. Unlike the proceduralist prosecutor, the prosecutorial progressive's political commitments are explicitly left. . . . [She] embraces her role as prosecutor and the power of state violence, but she does so with an eye towards advancing political ends favored by progressives and the political left (broadly conceived). There are different flavors of prosecutorial progressivism and different sets of prosecutorial progressive priorities: those focused on crimes committed by powerful defendants (e.g., white-collar crime, political corruption, or police violence), those focused on crimes that further historical inequality or subordination (e.g., intimate partner violence, sexual assault, or hate crimes) . . . . Regardless of which class of marginalized victims or relatively powerful defendants the prosecutorial progressive chooses to prioritize, her mission or approach accepts the fundamental legitimacy and desirability of the criminal system and carceral state violence. To the prosecutorial progressive, many aspects of mass incarceration and the contemporary construction of criminal policy might be objectionable. But, those objections rest on a belief that resources and energies have been misdirected and that the objectionable corners of the criminal system are aberrations. Rather than rejecting prosecutorial politics or embracing a skeptical view of the prosecutorial credential in the political sphere, this approach remains firmly rooted in a vision of the heroic or crusading prosecutor. . . .

The Anti-Carceral Prosecutor. . . . [T]he anti-carceral prosecutor harbors no illusions about criminal law as a vehicle for positive change. Instead, to the anti-carceral prosecutor, criminal law and the carceral state are fundamentally flawed. The anti-carceral prosecutor's job is not to repurpose the existing institutional structures for good (as the prosecutorial progressive would wish) but rather to shrink those institutions, or perhaps do away with them altogether. . . . Rather than arguing for more investment in DAs offices so that they can do their jobs better, the anti-carceral prosecutor advocates for a divestment from prosecution and the criminal system. Similarly, where the prosecutorial progressive might prioritize enforcing certain types of crimes, the anti-carceral prosecutor seeks to enact policies of declination—i.e., formally refusing to bring charges. . . . "Doing justice" to this prosecutor entails not prosecuting at all. A growing number of former defense attorneys and civil rights lawyers have run for DA with a stated mission of changing the system from a position of power. The anti-carceral prosecutor stands at the extreme pole of this posture—a sort of double-agent committed to destroying the system from within. To the anti-carceral prosecutor, the problem isn't that the wrong people are incarcerated, it's that people are incarcerated.

Bennett Capers, *Maybe, If . . .*, Inquest (June 25, 2024). *Can* progressive prosecutors . . . make a difference? A partial answer might look something like this:

- Maybe, if the prosecutor is committed not only to charging fewer low-level crimes, but also to reckoning with why some conduct is made criminal in the first place.

- Maybe, if the prosecutor not only creates a conviction integrity unit and practices open-file discovery, but also advocates for equal funding of public defenders, which is what is needed to really level the playing field, and advocates for the empowerment of victims, including victims who want mercy instead of cages.

- Maybe, if the prosecutor is committed not only to reducing racial disparities and holding police accountable for excessive force, but also to acknowledging that, for many, racial disparities and excessive force are a feature, not a bug. Or, as Paul Butler puts it in the title of one of his articles, "the system is working the way it is supposed to."

- Maybe, if the prosecutor not only requires line assistants to acknowledge the financial costs of incarceration, but also to acknowledge the costs, financial and otherwise, to their families. . . .

- Maybe, if the prosecutor is not only committed to keeping "us" on the outside safe, but also to keeping safe those whom we lock up in jails and prisons.

- Maybe, if the prosecutor is willing not only to use their power wisely, but also to cede power.

In short, believing that prosecutors can play a role in ending mass incarceration requires imagining a reform-minded prosecutor whose goal is not merely reformist reforms, but non-reformist reforms.

Hana Yamahiro & Luna Garzón-Montano, *A Mirage Not a Movement: The Misguided Enterprise of Progressive Prosecution*, 46 Harbinger 130, 135-138 (2022). Even if an elected prosecutor were able to reform the culture of an office to the point where . . . the metric of success is not securing convictions, prosecution is structurally incompatible with a radical revisioning of our society's approach to assessing and repairing harm for three reasons.

First, prosecutors rely on the police to choose their cases. . . . We know that poor Black and brown communities are more heavily surveilled and policed, which necessarily means that Black and brown people are arrested at disproportionate rates. In addition, the police also frame cases for prosecutors: they write the reports prosecutors rely on to make important decisions.

Second, prosecution — even so-called progressive prosecution — is guided by and reinforces respectability politics. Elected prosecutors . . . must make judgment calls about which people deserve leniency. That leniency will likely be afforded to the "deserving poor," those deemed non-violent offenders: the drug offenders, the petty thieves. People who commit acts of sexual or physical violence, arguably the people who would benefit most from support and mercy and who, in any event, populate our prisons and jails in great numbers, will remain in the carceral system. . . .

Finally, and, most importantly, being a prosecutor requires prosecuting. In this country, that means sending poor people to prison, most of them Black and brown. There is no dearth of evidence about how violent—both physically and sexually—prisons are. There is nothing progressive about deciding that nonviolent people should be spared that violence and abuse, but people who commit more serious harm deserve it. . . .

In our adversarial system, prosecutors may be able to decide whether or not to drop drug charges, or seek the death penalty, but prosecution can *never*—and does not purport to—address the conditions that lead to crime or meaningfully break cycles of violence that contribute to crime and poverty. Additionally, any prosecutor with a cursory understanding of prison conditions and dynamics knowingly seeks the incarceration of human beings in physically and sexually violent institutions. Therefore, any investment in criminal prosecution—whether "progressive" or not—only serves to legitimize our current system.

Brooks Holland & Steven Zeidman, *Progressive Prosecutors or Zealous Defenders, from Coast-to-Coast*, 60 Am. Crim. L. Rev. 1467, 1477-1479 (2023). We question the logic of looking for solutions and meaningful redress in the very position of authority that is responsible for the problem in the first place. Scholars . . . argue that prosecutors were the main drivers of the blight of mass incarceration. As Paul Butler has written:

> Becoming a prosecutor to help resolve unfairness in the criminal justice system is like . . . working as an oil refiner because you want to help the environment. Yes, you get to choose the toxic chemicals. True, the boss might allow you to leave one or two pristine bays untouched. Maybe, if you do really good work as a low-level polluter, they might make you the head polluter. But rather than calling yourself an "environmentalist," you should think of yourself as a polluter with a conscience.

Despite promises of significant change, . . . [t]he aspirations of the progressive prosecutor have not materialized for several reasons, beginning with the vehement opposition expressed by local law enforcement and police unions. The newly elected district attorney also inherits a staff that might not share the new, progressive agenda. Veteran line prosecutors are likely to bristle at top-down changes to the way they operated for years. . . . In some cases, the election of a self-proclaimed progressive prosecutor led to mass resignations of staff prosecutors.

While some might attribute these challenges and resignations to disagreement and displeasure with a progressive agenda, they highlight that for many prosecutors the essential purpose of the job is . . . to investigate, charge, convict, and punish. Further, an entrenched culture quickly culturizes even new prosecutors who purport to share progressive ideals. . . . And even when new policies are implemented, strong resistance can come from judges, many of whom were themselves prosecutors who, as institutional actors in the criminal legal system, can cling tightly to the status quo.

In addition to opposition from office staff, local police, and the judiciary, progressive prosecutors have faced an onslaught of hostility from elected officials. [G]overnors from Florida to New York have taken drastic action ranging from replacing or threatening to replace a progressive district attorney, taking cases away from prosecutors, and putting prosecutors on notice that they are being closely watched and are subject to removal.

2.   Debating Declination

Prerna Jagadeesh et al., Data for Progress, *A New Generation of Prosecutors Is Leading the Charge to Reimagine Public Safety* 1-4 (2021). Dozens of prosecutors have been elected across the country by campaigning on the transformation of their criminal legal systems, including in Los Angeles, Chicago, Philadelphia, San Francisco, St. Louis, Boston, Austin, and many other jurisdictions. Many were recently elected or even re-elected by robust margins, reflecting the popular enthusiasm for substantial criminal legal system reform. In the summer of 2021, Data for Progress surveyed 19 of these reform-minded prosecutors to identify their approaches to community safety, key policy changes, goals for the future, and obstacles impeding their efforts to achieve transformational change. . . .

[R]educing the use of jails and prisons proved a top-of-mind concern for respondents. . . . Every single one of the respondent prosecutors has implemented policies or practices . . . that are designed to reduce the number of people they send to jail and prison, and an overwhelming majority—95 percent—indicated that these policies have in fact led to a decrease in their local jail or prison populations. . . . The prosecutors we surveyed indicated that declining to prosecute various types of cases is a key element of their efforts to improve safety and implement fair and proportionate criminal legal policies. An overwhelming majority, 89 percent, have declined to prosecute some categories of cases. The vast majority of respondents, 80 percent, do not prosecute low-level misdemeanor and felony drug offenses, particularly those related to marijuana (in states where the use of marijuana is still illegal). Other categories of offenses that respondents have declined to prosecute include those related to sex work, trespass where the underlying driver is homelessness, and minor traffic offenses.

Rachael Rollins, *The Rachael Rollins Policy Memo* 25-26 & Appx. C (2019). I made a promise to the residents of Suffolk County that for low-level, non-violent offenses, I would emphasize declination or diversion whenever possible. That decision was part of a strategy to achieve two important goals: first, to reduce the footprint of the criminal justice system where it served no public safety interest, and second, to allocate more of our prosecution resources to the serious offenses that harm people, families, and the community as a whole. Based on my in-depth consultation with representatives from law enforcement, the criminal defense bar, the judiciary, and the neighborhoods we serve, I identified 15 charges that in most cases are best addressed through diversion or declined for prosecution entirely. In addition to being low-level, non-violent offenses with minimal long-term impact, they are most commonly driven by poverty, substance use disorder, mental health issues, trauma histories, housing or food insecurity, and other social problems rather than specific malicious intent. . . .

The list of 15 offenses identified for declination and diversion are included in the chart [below].* Charges on the list of 15 should be declined or dismissed pre-arraignment without conditions. . . . The line ADA always retains discretion to seek a deviation from this policy when a person poses an identifiable threat to another individual or other circumstances of similar gravity. In that instance, the ADA should consult with their supervisor, and place their justification in writing, along with the supervisor's determination, in the case file. . . . Deviation such as these should be the exception rather than the rule. . . .

Charge	Exceptions or Factors for Consideration
Trespass	If there are repeat, recent issues on public or private property, or a verifiable imminent safety risk, the ADA may escalate this to a pre- or post-arraignment continuance with a stay away order as a condition. Pre-arraignment or pre-plea diversion should be the next resort, with consultation from the property owner. . . .
Breaking and Entering	When there are repeat issues on public or private property, the ADA may escalate this to a pre-arraignment dismissal with a stay away order as a condition. Pre-arraignment diversion should then be the next resort. If these preliminary options are not working, and the individual continues engaging in the behavior, the ADA should consult their supervisor to come up with alternative solutions such as assistance with shelter or housing (if based on homelessness), and supportive treatment (if it is based on a mental health or substance use condition). If prosecution is considered, it requires supervisory approval and should be a last resort.

---

* Editor's Note: For ease of reading, the table below reorders and consolidates some of the rows as compared to the original source.

Charge	Exceptions or Factors for Consideration
Shoplifting, Larceny, Receiving Stolen Property	When the item taken is recovered and returned, the individual appears to have substance use issues, mental health issues, and/or the item is taken out of necessity (e.g. food, diapers, child care related items, etc.) due to a lack of employment or resources, the policy is for the ADA to presumptively decline the charge(s). When the items taken are NOT out of necessity, AND there is a pattern of this type of conduct within the past three years OR the item was unrecovered or damaged, the ADA can move to a pre-arraignment restitution agreement that takes the individual's ability to pay into account. . . .
Destruction of Property	The ADA will work with the individual to develop a prearraignment restitution agreement that is obtainable given the individual's means and abilities. Restorative justice may also be an alternative to financial restitution.
Threats	Where there is a credible risk of violence toward an identifiable individual, shown by clear evidence, or where the individual charged has a history of threats toward that person, the ADA can proceed to arraignment. . . .
Resisting Arrest	Resisting involves the actual use of physical force against a police officer. If there is actual physical force used, then the case can proceed to arraignment.
Disorderly Conduct	[This charge may be filed, with supervisor approval, only in circumstances involving crowd control operations before, during, or after] a sporting event, rally, protest, parade, or other event involving large numbers of people. . . .
Driving with a Suspended License	[This charge may not be filed unless the person's license was suspended for an underlying criminal driving suspension, such as vehicular homicide, leaving the scene of an accident, or DUI.]
Minor in Possession of Alcohol	No exceptions.

Amanda Agan et al., *Misdemeanor Prosecution*, 138 Q.J. Econ. 1453, 1455, 1496, 1500-1501 (2023). District attorneys around the country . . . have implemented presumptions of nonprosecution for certain nonviolent misdemeanor offenses . . . . [To test the net causal effect of these policies on crime, we] explore the impacts of the inauguration of Rachael Rollins as district attorney of Suffolk County on January 2, 2019. . . . [Our] estimates suggest that policies introducing a presumption of nonprosecution for nonviolent misdemeanor offenses may have social benefits. The increases in nonprosecution of nonviolent misdemeanor offenses induced by the Rollins inauguration appear to have decreased the rates at which defendants were issued new criminal complaints within one year of the current case. [More broadly, examining any potential drop in general deterrence for the offenses slated for nonprosecution,] we find significant reductions in reports of property damage and reports of theft/fraud [following the adoption of the Rollins memo]. There is no evidence of an increase in any of these crime types.

Overall, we interpret these effects of Rollins's inauguration and implementation of policies that reduced the prosecution of nonviolent misdemeanors as suggestive evidence that this policy shift, a relatively large expansion in leniency, reduced the subsequent average criminal justice involvement of the broader pool of defendants now experiencing leniency. Effects on reported crime are noisy, but there is no evidence that this policy change had detrimental effects on public safety.[12]

Ass'n of Deputy Dist. Att'ys for L.A. Cnty. v. Gascón, 295 Cal. Rptr. 3d 1 (Cal. Ct. App. 2022). [O]n November 3, 2020 . . . the voters of Los Angeles County [elected] George Gascón as their district attorney. In December 2020 the new district attorney adopted several "Special Directives" concerning sentencing [that] prohibited deputy district attorneys in most cases from alleging prior serious or violent felony convictions (commonly referred to as "strikes") under the three strikes law or sentence enhancements and required deputy district attorneys in pending cases to move to dismiss or seek leave to remove from the charging document allegations of strikes and sentence enhancements. The Special Directives' stated objectives, through these policies, were to promote the "interests of justice and public safety" by reducing "long sentences" that "do little" to deter crime.

The Association of Deputy District Attorneys for Los Angeles County (ADDA) is the certified [union that] consists of approximately 800 deputy district attorneys in Los Angeles County. ADDA sought a writ of mandate and a preliminary injunction to prevent the district attorney from enforcing the Special Directives, arguing they violated a prosecutor's duties to "plead and prove" prior strikes under the three strikes law [and] to exercise prosecutorial discretion in alleging and moving to dismiss [under the governing statutes any] prior strikes and sentence enhancements on a case-by-case basis. . . . The trial court largely agreed with ADDA and issued a preliminary injunction enjoining the district attorney from enforcing certain aspects of the Special Directives.

. . . Fundamentally, the district attorney argues his unreviewable prosecutorial discretion includes [the authority to determine] whether to allege prior convictions under the three strikes law and whether to continue prosecuting existing allegations of prior convictions and sentence enhancements in pending cases. The district attorney overstates his authority. He is an elected official who must comply with the law, not a sovereign with absolute, unreviewable discretion. . . . "The purpose of the Three Strikes law is 'to ensure longer prison sentences and greater punishment for those who commit a felony and have been previously convicted of serious and/or violent felony offenses.'" *In re* Young, 87 P.3d 797, 801 (Cal. 2004). . . . [The statute] provides: "Notwithstanding any other law, [the three strikes law] *shall be applied in every case* in which a defendant has one or more prior serious or violent felony convictions . . . . The prosecuting attorney *shall plead and prove* each prior serious or violent felony conviction except as provided in paragraph (2)." (Italics added.) The exception in [paragraph (2) then] states: "The prosecuting attorney may move to dismiss or strike a prior serious or violent felony conviction allegation in the furtherance of justice . . . or if there is insufficient evidence to prove the prior serious or violent felony conviction. If upon the satisfaction of the court that there is insufficient evidence to prove the prior serious or violent felony conviction, the court may dismiss or strike the allegation. . . ."

[T]he district attorney argues that interpreting the "shall plead and prove" language as creating a mandatory duty would infringe on the separation of powers doctrine by limiting prosecutorial discretion "to plead a criminal charge or sentencing enhancement." . . . [But] imposing a duty to plead and prove prior serious and felony convictions is consistent with the Legislature's stated intent of "ensuring" longer sentences and greater punishment for repeat felons. . . . [N]othing in the plain language of the statute suggests a prosecutor has any discretion not to plead or prove known strikes. The Legislature could have allowed for prosecutorial discretion by, for example, including language permitting a prosecutor to plead and prove prior strikes "when warranted" or "if deemed appropriate," by using the permissive "may" instead of the mandatory "shall," or by simply not including the "shall plead and prove" language. . . . That "prosecutors across California have exercised prosecutorial discretion" not to plead known strikes in the past, as the district attorney asserts, is not relevant to the interpretation of the statute. . . .

There is "no doubt that the initiation of criminal proceedings is a core, inherent function of the executive branch" and that the public prosecutor "ordinarily has sole discretion to determine whom to charge, what charges to file and pursue, and what punishment to seek." Steen v. App. Div. of Superior Ct., 331 P.3d 136, 141 (Cal. 2014). But "[i]t is the function of the legislative branch to define crimes and prescribe punishments." People v. Anderson, 211 P.3d 584, 602 (Cal. 2009). . . . Under this authority, the Legislature regularly limits the discretion a prosecutor has in charging and a court has in sentencing. . . .

[T]he Legislature (and the voters) enacted the three strikes law to create an alternative sentencing scheme when the defendant has qualifying prior felony convictions. To ensure the alternative sentencing scheme applies "in every case," Cal. Penal Code §667(f)(1), to which it should apply, the Legislature (and the voters) required prosecutors to plead the necessary preconditions to its application. That requirement does not violate the separation of powers doctrine because it does not materially impair a prosecutor's discretion to choose whom or what to charge. Instead, like the determinate sentencing scheme, the three strikes law establishes the punishment for persons convicted of charges a prosecutor chooses to bring. The prosecutor retains sole discretion over whom to charge, what to charge, what punishment to seek from among available alternatives, and how to conduct a trial to prove the charges brought. . . . Of course, because a prosecutor may and often does determine whether a prior strike exists before filing a charging document, the act of alleging a prior strike could be viewed as part of a prosecutor's unreviewable pre-charging discretion. But giving a prosecutor the discretion to decide whether to allege prior serious or violent felony convictions, in light of the Legislature's and the voters' clear intent to eliminate any such discretion, would violate the separation of powers doctrine, not honor it. . . . The district attorney's blanket policy not to plead prior strikes except in limited circumstances "completely frustrates" the purpose and mandate of the three strikes law. Esteybar v. Mun. Ct., 485 P.2d 1140, 1144 n.3 (Cal. 1971). . . . Therefore, mandamus is available to compel the district attorney to plead qualifying prior felony convictions "in every case" in which the district attorney has probable cause to believe a defendant has suffered a prior strike.

We reach a different conclusion regarding [the Special Directive's requirement that deputy district attorneys ask trial courts to dismiss strikes after those strikes have been filed]. Section 667, subdivision (f)(2), makes clear [that] a prosecutor "may" move to dismiss or strike an allegation of a prior serious or violent felony conviction, either [in the interest of justice] or if there is insufficient evidence to prove the allegation. Thus, the decision whether to "prove" a prior strike allegation or move to dismiss or strike it is discretionary. . . . [T]he criminal justice concerns expressed in the Special Directives, including whether lengthy sentences create an effective deterrent, are legitimate bases for motions to dismiss [in the interest of justice]. . . . [Our prior case law's directive] to consider only defendant-specific factors [when considering such a motion] applies to trial courts dismissing prior strikes on their own motion, not to prosecutors in their representation of the "interests of society." The Supreme Court [has not addressed], and we need not decide, the range of factors that would support dismissal of a prior serious or violent felony conviction "in furtherance of justice" on the motion of a prosecutor.

[Finally, our penal code] allows a prosecutor to "amend an information without leave of court prior to entry of a defendant's plea" and a trial court to "permit an amendment of an information at any stage of the proceedings." People v. Hamernik, 204 Cal. Rptr. 3d 649, 659 (Cal. Ct. App. 2016). . . . [In theory, this statute might be read to permit prosecutors to dismiss unilaterally any strikes that have been charged. But] nothing in the Special Directives suggests the district attorney has required or will require deputy district attorneys to abandon a [filed charge. A]t the hearing on the application for a preliminary injunction, counsel for the district attorney conceded the Special Directives intended to refer only to seeking leave to amend a charging document, not to unilaterally withdrawing existing allegations. In seeking such leave to amend, prosecutors have discretion to make whatever arguments they believe, in their professional judgment and under the laws of the United States and California, will promote the interests of the People. . . . [N]either the Legislature nor a court can control the arguments a prosecutor makes in good faith.

Bruce A. Green & Rebecca Roiphe, *A Fiduciary Theory of Progressive Prosecution*, 60 Am. Crim. L. Rev. 1431, 1442, 1444-1445, 1447 (2023). [T]he very nature of categorical decision making invites criticism. This is especially true of categorical policies that involve the wholesale, or virtually wholesale, refusal to enforce or implement certain criminal laws or to pursue certain sentences for which the laws provide. . . . Legislatures generally expect prosecutors to exercise discretion in enforcing the laws, which sometimes means declining to pursue eligible cases but also means being open to enforcing the law in some cases. Legislatures rarely adopt criminal laws solely to condemn certain conduct by criminalizing it without expecting prosecutors ever to enforce the laws. When traditional prosecutors go through the process of scrutinizing the evidence and weighing a host of relevant considerations before making a discretionary decision [in an individual case], they are, by all appearances, paying respect to the underlying legislative judgments. In contrast, a progressive prosecutor's promise never to prosecute someone for marijuana possession or for another category of offense is perceived as a rejection of the legislature's judgment that the proscribed conduct is bad or harmful enough to deserve punishment at least sometimes. Little wonder that legislatures push back.

But it is not only legislatures that are offended by categorical declination policies. Many judges view prosecutors' case-by-case exercise of discretion as a defining feature of criminal prosecution, one deeply embedded in the professional culture. In general, judges have limited authority to second guess prosecutors' decisions, and even to the extent that judges might do so, they tend to be highly deferential in dealing with traditional prosecutors. But judges have been less deferential to progressive prosecutors. . . .

Finally, subordinate prosecutors are likely to disfavor categorical policies that restrict their ability to participate in the office's exercise of professional judgment. . . . Subordinate prosecutors understand that the elected prosecutor has ultimate responsibility for the office's charging decisions and other decisions and that such choices should reflect the elected prosecutor's criminal law philosophy and public policy preferences. But they generally believe they have a role to play because the facts of a case matter and they are most familiar with the facts of their cases. The conventional approach allows room for dialogue between those with different views and, often, compromise among those who assess a case differently. . . . In contrast, progressive prosecutors' political commitments, expressed in categorical charging policies, may foment discontent among current subordinate prosecutors while also limiting the pool of lawyers interested in joining the office.

The practical problems that progressive prosecutors have faced are not merely a product of political disagreement. . . . The tenor of the pushback is not simply that some members of the public would prefer a different prosecutor who better reflects their goals and priorities but rather that the prosecutor has abdicated the role and no longer deserves the public trust.

W. Kerrel Murray, *Populist Prosecutorial Nullification*, 96 N.Y.U. L. Rev. 173, 176, 179-181, 221-222 (2021). At least on the retail level, most agree that [prosecutorial] declinations are not only inevitable but optimal. They facilitate deserved mercy and oil the gears of criminal justice. Not only are resources limited, but some cases of factual guilt would simply be wrong to pursue. Either way, no one doubts that prosecutors sometimes may thwart the law's application where, by its letter, it would govern. The question is how far "sometimes" goes . . . . [In answering that question, we must place due] emphasis on these prosecutors' *elected* status. . . . When fettered to localized popular will, programmatic prosecutorial nullification acts as a hydraulic descendant of jury nullification: It facilitates wholesale the species of democratic local control that jury nullification permits retail. Thus, far from lawless novelty, this *populist* prosecutorial nullification grows from longstanding democratic thought. . . . [The] issue is about where power resides. Who, that is, should decide whether a community permits sex work, or recreational drug possession, unlicensed cosmetology, or a host of other possible legal declarations of what ought or ought not happen? Even under the (perhaps unwarranted) assumption of representative legislatures, nonrandom geographic ideological sorting may mean legislative views on a law may not align with the views within a given locality. . . . [By] facilitating local control over the state's most coercive domestic activity—criminal law enforcement—populist prosecutorial nullification can return a measure of autonomy to groups and individuals.

C.   Public Defense

For a number of decades, from roughly the constitutionalization of the right to counsel in *Gideon v. Wainwright*, 372 U.S. 335 (1963), up through the turn of the millennium, lawyers eager to combat rising incarceration turned to one line of work: public defense. The primary critique leveled by progressives of that era was that public defender offices lacked the resources necessary to fulfill *Gideon*'s promise. Today, public defender offices across the country continue to attract talented lawyers fiercely committed to helping those most directly impacted by incarceration and policing. And they continue to be under-resourced, even as some other segments of the criminal defense bar lag further behind in providing the ideal of zealous, state-funded representation. But as abolitionist critiques of mass incarceration have gained sway, public defense has increasingly become the subject of a separate line of inquiry—one that asks whether public defense is itself part of the machinery that lends mass incarceration legitimacy and that thus makes mass incarceration possible. Consider the excerpts that follow.[13]

Gideon v. Wainwright, 372 U.S. 335 (1963). The Sixth Amendment provides, "In all criminal prosecutions, the accused shall enjoy the right . . . to have the Assistance of Counsel for his defence." . . . [R]eason and reflection require us to recognize that in our adversary system of criminal justice, any person haled into court, who is too poor to hire a lawyer, cannot be assured a fair trial unless counsel is provided for him. This seems to us to be an obvious truth. Governments, both state and federal, quite properly spend vast sums of money to establish machinery to try defendants accused of crime. Lawyers to prosecute are everywhere deemed essential to protect the public's interest in an orderly society. Similarly, there are few defendants charged with crime, few indeed, who fail to hire the best lawyers they can get to prepare and present their defenses. That government hires lawyers to prosecute and defendants who have the money hire lawyers to defend are the strongest indications of the wide-spread belief that lawyers in criminal courts are necessities, not luxuries. . . . A defendant's need for a lawyer is nowhere better stated than in the moving words of Mr. Justice Sutherland in *Powell v. Alabama*, 287 U.S. 45, 68-69 (1932):

> The right to be heard would be, in many cases, of little avail if it did not comprehend the right to be heard by counsel. Even the intelligent and educated layman has small and sometimes no skill in the science of law. If charged with crime, he is incapable, generally, of determining for himself whether the indictment is good or bad. He is unfamiliar with the rules of evidence. Left without the aid of counsel he may be put on trial without a proper charge, and convicted upon incompetent evidence, or evidence irrelevant to the issue or otherwise inadmissible. He lacks both the skill and knowledge adequately to prepare his defense, even though he have a perfect one. He requires the guiding hand of counsel at every step in the proceedings against him. Without it, though he be not guilty, he faces the danger of conviction because he does not know how to establish his innocence.

Eric Holder, U.S. Att'y Gen., Speech at the U.S. Department of Justice's 50th Anniversary Celebration of *Gideon v. Wainwright* (Mar. 15, 2013). Fifty years ago this Monday, writing for a unanimous Supreme Court, Justice

Black observed that it "seems to us to be an obvious truth" that "in our adversary system, any person haled into court, who is too poor to hire a lawyer, cannot be assured of a fair trial unless counsel is provided to him." This constituted a watershed moment—and a critical step forward—in our nation's enduring pursuit of equal justice for all. . . . And it paved the way for the expansion of the right to counsel in the years that followed. . . .

Of course, the progress heralded by the Court's opinion and the sweeping changes it demanded from coast to coast would not happen overnight. And they could never be handed down from the bench. In many ways, this decision would have to be put into action by the American people and their state and local leaders. In the decades since this remarkable case—and Gideon's retrial, at which he was found not guilty—public defender systems have been established in some states and strengthened in others. . . .

Yet, despite half a century of progress, even today, in 2013, far too many Americans struggle to gain access to the legal assistance they need. And far too many children and adults routinely enter our juvenile and criminal justice systems with little understanding of the rights to which they're entitled, the charges against them, or the potential sentences they may face. In short, America's indigent defense systems exist in a state of crisis.

Like many of you, this is something I've seen firsthand. As a judge on the District of Columbia Superior Court and, later, as United States Attorney for the District of Columbia, I frequently witnessed the devastating consequences of inadequate representation. I saw that wrongful convictions and unjust sentences carry a moral cost that's impossible to measure—and undermine the strength, integrity, and public trust in our legal system. I also recognize that, in purely economic terms, they drain precious taxpayer resources and constitute an outrageous waste of court funds on new filings, retrials, and appeals just because the system failed to get it right the first time.

Today, together, it's time to declare, once again, that this is unacceptable—and unworthy of a legal system that stands as an example for all the world. It's time to reclaim Gideon's petition, and resolve to confront the obstacles facing indigent defense providers. Most of all, it's time to speak out—with one voice—to rally our peers and partners at every level of government and the private sector to this important cause.

Eve Brensike Primus, *Culture as a Structural Problem in Indigent Defense*, 100 Minn. L. Rev. 1769, 1769, 1771-1772 (2016). There is a serious cultural problem in many indigent defense delivery systems nationwide: too many lawyers appointed to represent poor criminal defendants do not perform their intended role in the system, because they have been conditioned not to fight for their clients. As a result, many indigent defendants who go through the criminal justice system (as well as the friends and families of defendants who suffer through these ordeals with them) feel confused, angry, and ignored. They have no faith in the system or in the legitimacy of their convictions. Rather, they experience the criminal justice system as an assembly line to prison, mostly for poor people of color. . . .

It comes as no surprise to close observers of indigent defense delivery systems that this culture of indifference exists. Consider the environment in which we ask indigent defense attorneys to work. . . . The American Bar Association guidelines recommend that no defender handle more than 150 felonies or 400 misdemeanor cases in a year, but a 2009 report found that defenders in New Orleans Parish were handling the equivalent of 19,000 misdemeanor cases per attorney annually. That means an average of about seven minutes per case. In Florida's Miami-Dade County, public defenders have been forced to handle more than 700 felony cases per year. In Chicago, Miami, and Atlanta, defenders had more than 2,000 misdemeanor cases a year. With so many cases, defenders are unable even to meet with each client before trial. By necessity, defendants are depersonalized and their cases are triaged according to the charges. . . .

The judges, most of whom are former prosecutors, are impatiently waiting for the defender to hurry up and dispose of her cases so they can clear their heavily-congested dockets. As one Ohio judge bluntly stated as he held a public defender in contempt for indicating that he could not represent a man he had only just met, "public defenders often plead their clients guilty only minutes after meeting them. [You] spent 20 minutes with him, which is probably all the time you're going to spend with a client." Given these circumstances, it is remarkable that so many criminal defenders do continue to show high levels of commitment to giving their clients the best possible representation. And it is not at all remarkable that many defenders compromise, or become worn down, and deliver considerably less.

Noah Berlatsky, *Want to Reduce Mass Incarceration? Fund Public Defenders,* Medium (Sept. 11, 2018). Public defenders aren't senators or presidents; they don't get a lot of time in the media spotlight. As a result, it can be easy to forget them when thinking about criminal justice policy. But while mass incarceration is a national problem, it is fueled by local decisions and actions. The nitty gritty, small-scale effective administration of justice for individuals can add up over time and be just as effective as sweeping policy changes. . . . In theory, public defenders are supposed to provide a counterweight to prosecutors. Public defenders work to make sure that indigent defendants have advocates who work to reduce their sentences, or to find evidence suggesting they shouldn't be sentenced at all.

When defendants don't get adequate representation, they receive longer sentences. Even before trial, without adequate defense the accused may be hit with high bail, which means they end up sitting in jail before they've even been convicted of crime; 500,000 pre-trial detainees spend time in jail every year. In contrast, [attorney Colleen] Cullen told me, during her own time in the well-funded Georgetown legal clinic, not a single one of her clients was sentenced. "Just looking at my own personal anecdotal experience, the more time and effort you're able to put into your case, the better outcomes you'll see for your clients."

. . . . [N]ational spending on indigent defense is somewhere around $4.5 billion dollars. Congress could double that by spending $9 billion a year—a fraction of the roughly $200 billion spent on criminal justice each year. . . . Adequately funded public defender offices could reduce sentences across the country, and start to roll back some of the worst excesses of mass incarceration. Just as important, [Professor John] Pfaff says, public defenders with adequate resources could hold prosecutors accountable when they say they want to reduce sentencing. If a reform prosecutor says she wants to stop prosecuting cannabis cases, public defenders are in a position to report on whether such a policy actually goes into effect. At the moment, public defenders can't even provide adequate defense for their clients. But if their offices were actually funded and fully staffed, they could start serving as a check on prosecutors in the political arena as well as in the courts. . . . If we want to reduce mass incarceration, we should make sure they have the resources to do their jobs.

Andrew Manuel Crespo, *Root and Branch: Lawyers, Movements, and the End of Mass Incarceration*, 60 Harv. C.R.-C.L. L. Rev. (forthcoming 2025). I still remember the first time I ever saw the handwritten petition for certiorari, written in a prison cell by Clarence Earl Gideon. . . . I remember feeling inspired by the case—by the idea that everyone should have the right to a lawyer. It was not until law school, though, that this inspiration would become something I felt more as a calling, in the almost religious sense of the word, a calling to a vocation. My first year criminal law class was taught by one of the most famous public defenders in the country's history, a man named Charles Ogletree. If you ever heard "Tree," as we all lovingly called him, talk about being a public defender, which he had been before becoming a law professor, it was hard not to feel called to that work. . . . He had written about it in a famous *Harvard Law Review* article, where he said that, for him, being called to public defense was about two things: "empathy and heroism." When Tree talked about the heroism, it was stirring. "I saw myself," he wrote, "as a hero of the oppressed. The one who fights against all odds, a sort of Robin Hood figure who can conquer what others cannot." But when he talked about the empathy it would touch you right in your soul. "I did not think about what my client had done," Tree said, "nor did I feel responsible for what he might do if released. I knew that at that moment I was my client's only friend, and that my friend wanted to go home."

Still today, when I read those words, I feel called. And yet, if I am being honest with myself, while I was practicing as a public defender, I also felt an uneasiness—a dissonance—that at the beginning was hard to place.

Although, if I had really read *Gideon* more closely perhaps I would have seen at least some of the discordant notes right there in the opinion. When the Court, for example, explains that one of the reasons the right to counsel is so important is to protect those who are *innocent* . . . . [Or when the] Court goes on to emphasize fairness exclusively in procedural terms [without indicating] concern over whether the imprisonment itself was substantively unfair. In fact, quite to the contrary, the Court writes that "governments, both state and federal, quite properly, spend vast sums of money to *establish machinery* to try defendants accused of crime." . . . Played that way, the song sounded less heroic.

Matthew Caldwell, *The End of Public Defenders,* Inquest (Sept. 9, 2024). A little more than 15 years ago, I began my career as a public defender. Propelled by outrage, I was encouraged to see my work as a crucial check on law enforcement — and I did. [But after a] few years in, working in Miami and then various offices in New York City, I began to question the role of public defenders. Are we a check or a collaborator? . . . As Sara Mayeux recounts in her excellent *Free Justice: A History of the Public Defender in Twentieth-Century America,* what we call our public defender system wasn't created by Progressive Era lawyers, or socialists, or by a man named Gideon holding the line against injustice. Rather, as Mayeux tells the story, it was the result of many years of behind-the-curtain work by white, wealthy attorneys. . . . Voices of the poor, and anyone who was not an elite attorney, were excluded from any meaningful input in the design of the public defender system. By the middle of the 20th century, the Cold War was all-consuming for these attorneys, and a motivating interest for their concept of the public defender became positioning "democratic justice" over communism. In this context, defense counsel in a purely adversarial legal system was "elevated into an essential element of what made trials not only fair, but also democratic," Mayeux writes. In other words, the real problem was not actual racial and economic injustice, but the appearance of procedural injustice. It wasn't that there were too many unlawful arrests, but that we had too few lawyers ready to process them all. . . . One of the things that's most confounding about being a public defender is our bifurcated awareness: that the work is critical and useful on an individual scale, even as it directly supports a violent system of racist control of the poor. It is impossible to do the former without the latter, overwhelmingly so considering that so much of our work ends in standing next to a client as they plead guilty.

Paul Butler, *Poor People Lose:* Gideon *and the Critique of Rights,* 122 Yale. L.J. 2176, 2178-2179, 2197, 2202 (2013). *Gideon v. Wainwright* is widely regarded as a milestone in American criminal justice. When it was decided in 1963, it was seen as a major step forward in assuring fairness to poor people and racial minorities. Yet, fifty years later, low-income and African-American people in the criminal justice system are considerably worse off. It would be preferable to be a poor black charged with a crime in 1962 than now, if one's objective is to avoid prison or serve as little time as possible. . . . Arguably, *Gideon* has not improved the situation of accused persons, and may even have worsened their plight. . . .

In criminal cases poor people lose most of the time, not because indigent defense is inadequately funded, although it is, and not because defense attorneys for poor people are ineffective, although some are. Poor people lose, most of the time, because in American criminal justice, poor people are losers. Prison is designed for them. This is the real crisis of indigent defense. *Gideon* obscures this reality, and in this sense stands in the way of the political mobilization that will be required to transform criminal justice. . . . It invests the criminal justice system with a veneer of impartiality and respectability that it does not deserve. . . . If more poor people are represented by lawyers because of *Gideon*, arguably their trials or plea bargains are fairer than before *Gideon*, when they did not have lawyers. Thus, the poor have simultaneously received a fairer process and more punishment. *Gideon* makes it more work — and thus more difficult — to make economic and racial critiques of criminal justice. This is not to say people cannot and do not make those claims, but rather that *Gideon* makes their arguments less persuasive. . . .

I want to be especially clear on one point. People should still become criminal defense attorneys. The most important good that defense attorneys do is helping individual clients. Reducing potential sentences by six months, as one study suggests that effective defense counsel can, makes an enormous difference in the lives of incarcerated people and their families. Effective defense attorneys can also increase the cost of prosecution, and, in theory, this has the potential to reduce mass incarceration on a macro level. . . . [But] *Gideon* has not, and will not, change the fact that in American criminal justice, poor people are losers.

D.   *Restorative Justice and Transformative Justice*

How might a society moving away from prisons deal with antisocial, harmful, and potentially even violent transgressions when they occur? In the words of abolitionists Mariame Kaba and Andrea Ritchie, "elimination of policing and punishment doesn't mean that there will be no consequences for violence or harm." Rather, they continue, "abolition focuses on accountability rather than punishment," with accountability defined as a "voluntary process of stepping into responsibility for causing harm and committing to repair the harm."[14]

This practice is generally known as restorative justice. As Professor Adriaan Lanni writes, while "there is no authoritative theory or agreed-upon definition" of the phrase, various restorative justice practices "share the view that the proper response to an offense should focus not on punishment, but on meeting the needs of the victim, holding the offender accountable for the harm caused, taking steps to repair as much as possible the harm suffered by the victim and the community, and addressing the offender's needs to prevent reoffending and promote reintegration." And as Lanni goes on to observe, between 2010 and 2015, fifteen states passed new statutes promoting restorative justice practices as components of their penal systems—evidence that the practice is embraced beyond abolitionist circles.[15]

The excerpts that follow give an overview of restorative justice's motivations, approaches, successes, and potential limitations.

Terrell Carter, Rachel López & Kempis Songster, *Redeeming Justice*, 116 Nw. U. L. Rev. 315, 325-330 (2021). In order to redeem yourself, you must first acknowledge that you have done something wrong. This seemingly simple idea turned out not to be so simple at all. Through our dialogue of discovery [while incarcerated], we would find that we were tainted by an adversarial system of "justice" that made accepting responsibility and trying to make amends feel like a liability. Like all things American, the criminal legal system is highly competitive. It is an "us versus them" system in which you either win or lose. The flaw in this way of operating is that winning becomes the sole objective, leaving "justice" broken, bloody, and bruised by the wayside. . . . [W]e discovered that, at the moment of arrest, we became players in a game of life or death in which the stakes could not be higher. To win meant living, getting our lives back, while to lose meant hopelessness and death, because to live a life without hope is to live a life with the kind of emptiness that can only be found in a grave.

So we denied [our wrongs]. We imagined narratives that gave us the best chance of winning, convinced that, when we entered those hallowed halls of justice, our lies disguised as the truth would save us and carry us to victory. The process was so highly competitive that there was no space for nuance, regret, reconciliation, or healing. It was either guilt or innocence, death or life. You either lost or you won. . . . We realized that there existed within the process a pernicious, deliberate indifference to fairness and equality that was so all-consuming that it made it hard for us to see ourselves and the parts we played in these human tragedies. What we had done became invisible, caught in a game of winning and losing. Atonement was not a conscious thought at all. . . .

Yet with time . . . we developed a greater understanding of the impact that this flawed hypercompetitive system of "justice," this us versus them dynamic, had on us. We were able to come to grips with the realization that the criminal legal system had embedded within us a selfishness—a sense of entitlement—that only allowed us to see how we were wronged. We [came] to see—to realize—that we did not live in a world populated only by ourselves and that our actions had consequences reaching far beyond what had happened to us. [W]e strived to make right what we had done wrong and make amends to the communities and, if possible, to the families that we had harmed.

Danielle Sered, *Until We Reckon* **132-138 (2019).** Communities have long had the capacity to address the pain that arises within them. When we combine the inherent ability of human beings to participate in transforming harm with some of the centuries-old tools for doing so, we open pathways to safety and justice that are otherwise unavailable. Restorative justice is one such pathway. . . . Restorative justice will not fully replace incarceration; it is not a panacea. But for an enormous number of cases in the criminal justice system, its existence does mean that we can no longer pretend we do not know what else to do. . . .

Restorative justice is a decision-making process that involves those most directly impacted by a given harm in identifying the pathway toward repair—and then carrying out the actions to get there. . . . In most restorative justice approaches, the central method of that involvement is a dialogue process, often called a circle, that includes the responsible party, the harmed party, and support people. . . . [T]he circle provides a framework and opportunity for accountability on the part of the responsible parties and healing on the part of those harmed. . . .

In the circle, all parties decide on agreements other than incarceration to hold the responsible party accountable in ways meaningful to the person harmed. These may include responsible parties providing community service at places significant to those harmed, pursuing their education, completing job training and/or obtaining employment, paying financial restitution, making apologies, learning about their own culture and the culture of the harmed parties, becoming positive role models to younger people in their lives and communities, addressing any harmful reliance on alcohol or other drugs, developing their skill sets as parents, or any number of other creative commitments particular to each case and the needs of the people affected by it. . . .

Th[e] emphasis on repair reflects restorative justice's primary concern with harm rather than with broken rules. Restorative justice contends that crime causes harm to people, relationships, and community—and this is different from thinking of crime primarily as a violation of the law. If the primary understanding of crime is about a legal infraction, then the most urgent concern is to reassert the power of the state through the enforcement of the law. But if the core concern is that people have been harmed, the priority is to repair that harm.

Michelle Alexander, *Reckoning with Violence,* **N.Y. Times (Mar. 3, 2019).** [F]ully 90 percent of survivors in New York City, when given the chance to choose whether they want the person who harmed them incarcerated or in a restorative justice process . . . choose the latter. . . . The people who choose to participate are victims of serious violent felonies—people who have been shot, stabbed or robbed. . . . [These] survivors, as a group, are [not] especially merciful. To the contrary, they're pragmatic. They know the criminal justice system will almost certainly fail to deliver what they want and need most to overcome their pain and trauma. . . . [They] know the system cannot be trusted to validate their suffering, give them answers or even a meaningful opportunity to be heard.

Yotam Shem-Tov et al., *Can Restorative Justice Conferencing Reduce Recidivism? Evidence from the Make-it-Right Program,* 92 Econometrica 61, 62 (2024). This paper studies the "Make-it-Right" (MIR) program, a restorative justice conferencing intervention implemented by the San Francisco District Attorney (SFDA). The program targets teenagers who would otherwise face felony charges [for medium-severity offenses such as vehicle theft, grand theft, burglary, or assault]. Eligible cases were randomly assigned to either a treatment group where they were given the opportunity to participate in MIR, or a control group subjected to regular prosecution. Successful completion of the program results in formal charges never being filed. . . . The program's target population is high-risk youth: 43 percent of control group members are rearrested within six months, and 83 percent are rearrested within four years . . . .

We find that MIR substantially reduced future arrests. Youths assigned to MIR were 19 percentage points less likely to be rearrested within six months . . . (a 44 percent reduction). Moreover, the effects persisted [for] years . . . . Those assigned to MIR were 15 percentage points (20 percent) less likely to be rearrested within three years and 27 percentage points (32 percent) less likely after four years. Juveniles assigned to MIR were also less likely to be subsequently arrested for both new misdemeanor as well as new felony offenses. MIR youth were also less likely to be convicted for a future offense.

Adriaan Lanni, *Taking Restorative Justice Seriously,* 69 Buff. L. Rev. 635, 658-661, 681 (2021). To have a meaningful impact on incarceration rates, restorative justice would have to be expanded enormously—which raises the vital question of whether these programs can be scaled up without losing their effectiveness. . . . A large-scale shift toward a restorative approach . . . would likely require the use of professional facilitators rather than volunteers [because t]he caseload would be far too large for unpaid volunteers to handle. Some restorative justice proponents resist any move toward professionalism . . . . But there may be some advantages[:] Recruiting and training paid facilitators from the local community would promote diversity, continuity, experience, and quality in the facilitator pool, and encourage consistent treatment of cases without sacrificing attention to local circumstances. . . .

[T]here is a [related] danger that programs run by government employees may dilute the sense that the process is a community response to harm, thereby jeopardizing a program's support and legitimacy within the community. Community support is crucial to encourage victim and offender participation and referrals from prosecutors and judges [so it] would be preferable to scale up restorative justice through independent community organizations rather than creating state-run restorative justice programs. . . .

Can restorative justice be scaled up enough to make a difference in mass incarceration? It is a difficult, but not insurmountable task. . . . [Any] expansion has to strike the right balance between centralized quality control and preserving a personal touch, local knowledge, and high morale and motivation among facilitators. All this is a tall order. But New Zealand's juvenile justice system provides an example of a relatively successful approach to mainstreaming restorative justice, with enormous benefits to society—particularly when compared to the United States, where the existing criminal legal system provides such a bleak alternative. . . . As we consider expanding restorative justice, we would do well to remember this basic fact: the perfect should not be the enemy of the good.

Cameron Rasmussen & Sonya Shah, *Growing Justice,* **Inquest (Sept. 9, 2022).** Like [restorative justice (RJ)], transformative justice (TJ) has multiple origins stories. [It] grew out of anti-violence movements in the late 1990s and early 2000s, initiated primarily by Black women, women of color, domestic and sexual violence survivors, and queer communities, many of whom were survivors of violence. Together, they sought non-dominating, non-punitive approaches to justice entirely outside of the criminal legal system. TJ was conceived as both a relational and political approach to justice that understood punishment and the criminal legal system itself as inherently harmful. TJ's approach thus necessitated responding to harm between people without relying on the state—the police and incarceration especially. . . . While TJ has taken some of its ideology and practices from RJ, what makes it most distinct is its emphasis on non-state response and focus on structural and state violence. [By contrast, some critics believe that] RJ has a muddied and often contradictory relationship to the criminal legal system, leading many to see RJ as co-opted, colonized, or misaligned with the aims of social movements seeking liberation. The oft-repeated line regarding the limits of professionalized RJ—"It is not possible to restore justice to people and communities where justice never existed"—points to a real understanding of history and oppression in the U.S. and around the world.

Yet all of this misses the nuanced and deeply relational beliefs and practices that RJ is grounded in and has helped to spread. While TJ holds deep political commitments to systemic change, at times it has been less grounded in the relational transformation that RJ at its best prioritizes. We believe it's possible to hold and grapple with these gifts and contradictions while honoring and valuing the current and historical contributions of both RJ and TJ. We believe that RJ and TJ at their best are complementary and often intersecting, and that our movements and collective work are stronger with this understanding and orientation.

Tommie Shelby, *The Idea of Prison Abolition* 175-176 (2022). The main limitation of [restorative or] transformative justice is that it depends on the willing participation of persons who have experienced harm and persons who harm. That it is a voluntary and nonviolent strategy to address harm is a great virtue. But we cannot always expect willing cooperation from the relevant parties. Sometimes a survivor will decline to participate in these reparative and restorative processes . . . . Often survivors won't feel safe, and in fact won't be safe, if those who harmed them are effectively free to attack them again, particularly if the aggressors show no signs of remorse. Survivors and the broader public still need an effective mechanism to stop or inhibit those who mean others harm. Criminal justice procedures, though far from ideal, should be available to survivors whose assailants refuse to be accountable and to survivors who are unwilling to participate in [restorative or] transformative justice practices.[16]

E. Defunding the System

Ending mass incarceration means, at a minimum, making the American penal system dramatically smaller. For abolitionists like Rachel Herzing, one major part of the movement's "end game" is "to substantially decrease the size, scope, and legitimacy of the system." In this vein, Herzing and others highlight campaigns to defund police departments and deny resources to other carceral institutions as central components of abolitionist practice. But the idea that resource constraints can and should be leveraged — or manufactured — to force decarceration is not limited to abolitionists, as demonstrated by the first excerpt below, written by then-professor, now-Judge Stephanos Bibas, who was appointed to the U.S. Court of Appeals for the Third Circuit by President Donald Trump. The excerpts in this section explore these resource-oriented decarceral efforts, including calls to defund the police and reactions to that proposal.[17]

Stephanos Bibas, *Sacrificing Quantity for Quality: Better Focusing Prosecutors' Scarce Resources*, 106 Nw. U. L. Rev. Colloquy 138, 139 (2011). In a world of overcriminalization, limited budgets are not all bad. The silver lining is that prosecutors cannot possibly pursue all of the new crimes that their legislative allies have created. Resource constraints and scarcity can force prosecutors to rank priorities, mitigating in practice the problem of overcriminalization on the books. Limited funds thus are not a bug but a design feature: they check prosecutors from prosecuting the entire universe of people who are technically guilty of something but do not especially deserve conviction and full punishment. The value of pursuing crimes is a declining curve, and at some point the costs of extra enforcement will exceed the benefits. . . . [T]he optimal funding level is much less than would be required to try every single alleged crime. That is particularly true because an extra dollar spent on criminal justice is a dollar less for other programs. At some point, criminal justice's bottomless appetite must give way to other needs.

Richard A. Bierschbach & Stephanos Bibas, *Rationing Criminal Justice*, 116 Mich. L. Rev. 187, 193-194, 227-229, 232-233 (2017). While many criminal justice institutions are desperately underfunded and overworked, in some respects scarcity is a feature, not a bug: it can force police, prosecutors, judges, and other actors to do triage, focusing their efforts on the most socially beneficial interventions. By creating beneficial scarcity and related constraints, [we] can promote similar effects. . . . Prosecutors might [for example be given] a limited pretrial-detention budget . . . calibrated to detention's average daily costs. To reflect the more severe social costs of longer detentions, that price might increase along with the length of detentions. This scheme could force prosecutors to better ration detention by screening cases early, before detainees languish in jail, and by efficiently moving along cases for which they believed detention was justified. It could also encourage them to use less restrictive alternatives to detention . . . . Analogous regimes could inform prison or parole, with judges or parole boards working with sentencing or detention budgets that better reflected the costs of their decisions. . . .

Where actual monetary payments or even notional accounts might be too expensive or administratively burdensome, caps could accomplish much the same budgeting and incentivizing effects. . . . [A] capping scheme [could] limit the number of prison beds that local prosecutors can use in generating personal, political, and social gains. . . . Prosecutors and judges could use those prison beds however they pleased; once they hit their cap, however, their local taxpayers would be forced to pay the state directly for further imprisonments. That would enhance accountability for use of criminal justice dollars. So too would making the cap a hard-and-fast one, with no option to purchase additional beds, which would further encourage prosecutors to use prison sparingly in favor of other, less costly sanctions. . . .

At bottom, caps are just a special kind of budgeting mechanism. . . . The conventional wisdom decries scarcity and underfunding in criminal justice. . . . But some institutions, such as prisons, do too little with too much. . . . Scarcity, then, should not always be thought of as a problem.

Amna A. Akbar, *An Abolitionist Horizon for (Police) Reform*, 108 Calif. L. Rev. 1781, 1826-1831 (2020). From #FreeThemAll campaigns to empty jails in the face of COVID-19 to campaigns to defund the police, there are a range of campaigns aimed at shrinking the material footprint of police and prisons. In the wake of the George Floyd uprisings, a growing number of campaigns are demanding that cities cut their police budgets, and that school districts and universities cut their ties with police departments—undermining the school-to-prison pipeline by removing police in schools. These campaigns are having some success, leading to city councils exploring budget cuts, and school districts and universities allowing their contracts with local police to expire and others diminishing police within schools and exploring additional investments in counselors. . . .

Chicago's #NoCopAcademy campaign is a prominent example of a campaign focused on shrinking police infrastructure. After the DOJ found a pattern and practice of unconstitutional violence within the Chicago Police Department in the wake of the police killing of Laquan McDonald, former Chicago Mayor Rahm Emanuel announced his intentions to spend $95 million to build a second police training facility. . . . The #NoCopAcademy campaign argued that a police training facility cannot "address the structural violence of policing." The campaign contrasted Chicago's daily spending of $4 million on police and $642 million on police misconduct settlements over twelve years with Emanuel's 2012 closure of six mental health clinics—which required $2.2 million to remain open—and the 2013 closure of fifty-four majority Black schools. #NoCopAcademy rejected the idea that increased police spending reduces harm, and argued that "investing in things like mental health, education, jobs, housing" are the sorts of investments "that can actually cut back on the trauma, poverty, and pain that often leads to violence in our communities." . . . By demanding investments, these campaigns suggest alternate modes that the state can take to respond to all manner of currently criminalized social problems [and] aim to reshape the material infrastructure of our cities.

Jason Johnson, *"Defund the Police" Led to Lower Standards*, Wall St. J. (Feb. 22, 2023). The post-George Floyd rise in antipolice sentiment and policies are dissuading young people from pursuing law-enforcement careers and driving experienced cops out of the job. Data compiled by the Police Executive Research Forum show that resignations increased 42.7% from 2019 to 2021 and retirements increased 23.6%. According to a 2022 survey of law enforcement officers in eight states, 51% of cops have considered quitting because of antipolice attitudes while 59% personally knew a colleague who left because of public hostility. To fill vacancies, most large police agencies have lowered their standards.

In 2020 Chicago Police Superintendent David Brown announced that certain applicants would no longer be required to obtain 60 college credits. The department received 400 applications the day of the announcement. Philadelphia dropped its residency and age requirements in 2017 and applications jumped 20%. But it didn't work for long, as poor recruitment and high attrition have since returned to those departments.

The longer the staffing crisis goes on, the worse community-police tensions will become as faith in the competence and trustworthiness of law enforcement erodes. A four-year college degree may not be necessary to perform the duties of a police officer, but applicants with sketchy employment and education résumés are unlikely to possess the communication skills and self-control necessary to do well as cops. A history of drug and alcohol abuse or criminal activity has been shown to increase the risk that an officer will use excessive force or engage in serious misconduct on the job. Officers who are in poor physical shape can't credibly protect the public from crime. . . . The deprofessionalization of policing is a danger to public safety. Waiving or eliminating standards exacerbates the staffing problem by demoralizing veteran officers and turning off high-quality candidates. Excellence attracts excellence.

Ethan Lowens, *Resource Attacks on the Criminal Legal System*, 47 N.Y.U. Rev. L. & Soc. Change. 479 (2025). Defund the police. No new jails. . . . [T]hese slogans share something in common. They are *indirect* attacks on the criminal legal system, aiming to limit its capacity to cause harm—in contrast to direct attacks that abolish or restrict its harmful practices outright. . . . Resource attacks are a coherent and distinct approach to decreasing the footprint of the criminal legal system. . . . [They] can materialize quickly, have tremendous impact potential, and offer unique political advantages. . . .

[But they may also] backfire, causing a net *increase* in harm. Resource constraints necessitate resource reallocation, which can put discretion in the hands of the very actors whose conduct was objectionable in the first place. They may reallocate resources in a way that increases, rather than decreases, the harm the institution causes relative to the pre-constraint status quo. . . . [Moreover,] in a resource crunch, institutions may redirect resources away from programs and practices that are helpful, or, at the very least, not the most harmful, and concentrate them in those that are more harmful. In order to keep the number of arrests and prosecutions flowing at status quo rates, police and prosecutors could cut programs such as victims' services and compensation, community outreach, community violence interrupters, mentorships, trainings in cultural sensitivity or mental health crisis response, or efforts to promote diversity in hiring.

[Resource constraints may also increase racial injustice.] In *Systemic Triage: Implicit Racial Bias in the Criminal Courtroom*, L. Song Richardson describes how racist implicit biases influence every actor in the criminal system, and, critically, how the effects of these implicit biases are exacerbated by resource constraints. Evidence indicates that law enforcement officers lean into racist heuristics and stereotypes to save time and maintain arrest volume. Law enforcement and prosecutors draw on implicit perceptions that Black defendants are more deserving of punishment and race-correlated criteria such as history of prior convictions to decide which cases to prioritize and which to let go. . . .

[Finally, the] effects of resource constraints are inherently reversible. Police, courts, and prosecutors are powerful lobbies: they may successfully appeal for more funds, undoing the harm reduction created by a resource constraint, or, worse, undoing these effects while expanding the monetary footprint of the criminal system. Most, if not every, police department whose funding was cut following the summer of 2020 ultimately had it restored.

F. Collective Action in the Courtroom

Ultimately, efforts to end mass incarceration must contend with questions of power. Who has the power to make changes in society? How do groups of people without such power generate it to bring about the change they want to see in the world? Lawyers often have access to conventional forms of power. They engage with the institutional actors who hold formal decisionmaking authority within the state and they are trained to speak persuasively to those empowered actors about key decisions, from the outcome of a given case to the shape of broadly sweeping laws and policies. Oftentimes, lawyers are the decisionmakers themselves — on the bench, in prosecutors' offices, in legislatures, and in other key governmental agencies.

Social movements and organizers, by contrast, often work to build power outside of existing formal structures, and to deploy it against or within those structures to force changes decisionmakers might otherwise resist. In the words of organizing scholar Professor Marshall Ganz, they ask "how can people work together to turn the resources they have into the power they need to win that change?" And how can they "make it more costly for you to resist the change than accept it?"[18]

As Professor Jocelyn Simonson writes when describing the anticarceral movement, efforts to build the power Ganz describes sometimes take the form of "collective resistance within the courtroom," as organizers engage in "grassroots forms of participation in and disruption of everyday criminal justice." These organized forms of contestation, Simonson argues, "are not only powerful and important, but also crucial for *democratic* criminal justice."

> Collective mechanisms of resistance and contestation build agency, remedy power imbalances, bring aggregate structural harms into view, and shift deeply entrenched legal and constitutional meanings. Many of these forms of contestation display a faith in local democracy as a tool of responsive criminal justice, while simultaneously maintaining a healthy skepticism of the law and existing legal institutions that maintain the status quo. These forms of resistance and contestation are not antagonistic, but agonistic . . . . [They represent] a politics that respects conflict and adversarialism, but seeks to channel it through democratic channels.[19]

In this concluding section of this chapter, we examine different forms of collective action and resistance that take place within the formal structures of the criminal process. We begin by exploring efforts to engage organized members of the surrounding community in key stages of the process, through practices such as court watching, community bail funds, and participatory defense. We then examine the special role of the jury in the criminal process and efforts to organize jurors to act as a check on carceral actors. Finally, we consider efforts to organize criminal defendants themselves, exploring how collective action with respect to plea bargaining might operate as a form of organized resistance to mass incarceration.

1. Court Watching, Bail Funds, and Participatory Defense

Jocelyn Simonson, *The Criminal Court Audience in a Post-Trial World*, 127 Harv. L. Rev. 2173, 2181-2183 (2014). Consider the effects that an audience can have on a routine criminal proceeding—for example, an arraignment or a plea allocution—at which no jurors are present. When community members gain access to a nontrial courtroom, their presence in court does not just affect the case that they are there to see. The effect of their presence in the courtroom can be to change the nature of the nontrial proceedings as well. Audience members watch the players in the courtroom; they react to what they see and hear through facial expressions, laughs, and grumbles. Most of all, they sit, look, and listen. Their presence can have a palpable effect on the speakers in the courtroom. . . .

The audience's power, born from its physical presence in the courtroom, is bolstered by its ability to act based on what it hears: not only through voting for district attorneys, sheriffs, and sometimes judges, but also by contributing to public discourse at local gatherings, protests, or even in casual conversations with neighbors. Witnessing local criminal justice policies at play in routine cases informs audience members' opinions about the efficacy and fairness of those policies. Those audience members can then engage in conversation and debate in informal settings—with family members, neighbors, co-workers, and even while waiting in line at the courthouse—that contribute to the flow of opinion in the "wild" (that is, unregulated) public sphere. These informal methods of political participation are crucial if "affected locals" are to have input into more formal political decisionmaking. Indeed, modern courtrooms are often the sole sites in which the public can witness the adjudication of disputes and thereby hold the state accountable for the ways in which it administers that adjudication. In these ways, the potential for audience empowerment through observation contributes to both the legitimacy and the overall fairness of proceedings.

The act of observing can also connect audience members to outside movements for social and legal change, including those movements that focus explicitly on local issues of policing, prosecution, and punishment. Some local movements recognize the political power that comes from courtroom observation; these movements include organizing initiatives that gather community members to attend court in support of young people accused of crimes and "courtwatch" programs, volunteer networks that promote the prosecution of specific categories of crimes—often domestic violence—by following specific cases and attending court when those cases are on the calendar.

Jocelyn Simonson, *Bail Nullification*, 115 Mich. L. Rev. 585, 587-592 (2017). In recent years, community groups in jurisdictions across the United States have increasingly begun to use bail funds to post bail on behalf of strangers, using a revolving pool of money. These funds include new charities set up in partnership with public defender offices in Massachusetts, the Bronx, Brooklyn, and Nashville as well as identity-based bail funds that range from a bail fund for transgender sex workers of color in Queens, New York to a bail fund supporting communities of color targeted by policing in Chicago, and bail funds formed by activists within the Movement for Black Lives, who have used crowd-sourced funding to post bail for hundreds of protesters and allies in Ferguson, Baltimore, Cleveland, Oakland, and Baton Rouge. Each time a community bail fund pays bail for a stranger, the people in control of the fund reject a judge's determination that a certain amount of the defendant's personal money was necessary for the defendant's release. . . .

Community bail funds inject community input into a critical moment in the public adjudication of a criminal case. For most indigent defendants, bail is the ballgame: if a judge sets bail in an amount that they can afford, then they are able to fight their case from a position of freedom, without losing jobs, housing, or custody of their children. On the other hand, if bail is set in an amount higher than a defendant can pay, that defendant is incentivized to plead guilty early in the process, without the benefit of extended discussions with counsel, case investigation, or discovery from the prosecution. Studies have shown time and time again that pretrial detention increases the chances of a conviction, extends the probable length of a sentence, and decreases the chance that the charges will be dismissed altogether. Moreover, as the public learned in the summer of 2015 with the deaths of Kalief Browder in New York City and Sandra Bland in Texas—both of whom had been in jail because they could not pay bail—jail is often a violent and damaging place. When community bail funds post bail, they are not only facilitating the liberty of a defendant, they may also be changing the eventual outcome of that criminal case.

Over time, as community bail funds post bail for multiple defendants, these individual acts can add up to a larger statement about the fairness of money bail. Literal action—the posting of bail—itself becomes a form of on-the-ground resistance to the workings of the criminal justice system. The result is a powerful form of popular input into criminal justice from outsiders who rarely have a say in how their local justice systems are administered.

Raj Jayadev, *Protect Your People* 3-4, 6-7, 10-11 (2024). Participatory defense is a strategic practice for families and communities to intervene in and ultimately positively impact the outcome of court cases, transforming the landscape of power in the courts. Family here goes beyond blood to include the friends, neighbors, partners, coaches, and others who care about the person about to walk through [the] courthouse doors. . . . [At Silicon Valley De-Bug, organized families] have built up participatory defense and used this approach to impact the cases of their loved ones since 2006. [The approach abandoned] the limiting perspective that courts were only for lawyers. . . . At the De-Bug office, on a whiteboard, beneath the names of each person who had an active court case, we took an inventory of what we already knew and listed any possible actions we could take to impact the case. What are the charges? Is there a defense attorney involved? Has bail been set? Do we have the police report? When is the next court date? These questions helped identify what the action steps could be. For instance, if someone had a court date coming up that week, we would offer to show up, letting the judge and prosecutor know that the person facing charges was part of a supportive community that was invested in the person's future and well-being. Or it might be a session to review the police report and identify the falsehoods and inconsistencies. A family's action step might be collecting letters of future employment opportunities for a person to get to the defense attorney before they went to their next hearing. . . .

The direct impact on cases was undeniable. We saw charges get dismissed. We saw sentencing enhancements which would have committed a person to die in prison get removed. We saw people who had substance or mental health needs get treatment and care rather than fall deeper into a criminal punishment system that would have only harmed them further. . . . Participatory defense was effective even after a conviction occurred, when a family made a compelling argument that their loved one deserved to be resentenced and returned to the community. . . . Over time, we developed a collective, cumulative intelligence. With every meeting, we learned about different charges, defense strategies, prosecutorial theories, individual judges' biases, the best ways to talk to different types of attorneys, and so much more.

2. Juries and Nullification

a. The Right to a Jury of One's Peers

Duncan v. Louisiana, 391 U.S. 145 (1968). Appellant, Gary Duncan, was [prosecuted for misdemeanor simple battery, a crime punishable by up to two years in prison. He] sought trial by jury, but because the Louisiana

Constitution grants jury trials only in cases in which capital punishment or imprisonment at hard labor may be imposed, the trial judge denied the request. Appellant was convicted and sentenced to serve 60 days in the parish prison . . . .

Appellant was 19 years of age when tried. While driving on Highway 23 in Plaquemines Parish on October 18, 1966, he saw two younger cousins engaged in a conversation by the side of the road with four white boys. Knowing his cousins, Negroes who had recently transferred to a formerly all-white high school, had reported the occurrence of racial incidents at the school, Duncan stopped the car, got out, and approached the six boys. . . . [A]ppellant encouraged his cousins to break off the encounter and enter his car. . . . The whites testified that just before getting in the car appellant slapped Herman Landry, one of the white boys, on the elbow. The Negroes testified that appellant had not slapped Landry, but had merely touched him. The trial judge concluded that the State had proved beyond a reasonable doubt that Duncan had committed simple battery, and found him guilty. . . .

The history of trial by jury in criminal cases has been frequently told. It is sufficient for present purposes to say that by the time our Constitution was written, jury trial in criminal cases had been in existence in England for several centuries and carried impressive credentials traced by many to Magna Carta. . . . The Declaration of Independence stated solemn objections to the King's . . . "depriving us in many cases, of the benefits of Trial by Jury" . . . . [The Constitution, in provisions applicable only to the federal government when enacted, twice states that criminal prosecutions must be by jury.] The constitutions adopted by the original States guaranteed jury trial [as did] the constitution of every State entering the Union thereafter in one form or another . . . .

Even such skeletal history is impressive support for considering the right to jury trial in criminal cases to be fundamental to our system of justice . . . . The guarantees of jury trial in the Federal and State Constitutions reflect a profound judgment about the way in which law should be enforced and justice administered. A right to jury trial is granted to criminal defendants in order to prevent oppression by the Government. Those who wrote our constitutions knew from history and experience that it was necessary to protect against unfounded criminal charges brought to eliminate enemies and against judges too responsive to the voice of higher authority. The framers of the constitutions strove to create an independent judiciary but insisted upon further protection against arbitrary action. Providing an accused with the right to be tried by a jury of his peers gave him an inestimable safeguard against the corrupt or overzealous prosecutor and against the compliant, biased, or eccentric judge. If the defendant preferred the common-sense judgment of a jury to the more tutored but perhaps less sympathetic reaction of the single judge, he was to have it. Beyond this, the jury trial provisions in the Federal and State Constitutions reflect a fundamental decision about the exercise of official power—a reluctance to entrust plenary powers over the life and liberty of the citizen to one judge or to a group of judges. Fear of unchecked power, so typical of our State and Federal Governments in other respects, found expression in the criminal law in this insistence upon community participation in the determination of guilt or innocence. The deep commitment of the Nation to the right of jury trial in serious criminal cases as a defense against arbitrary law enforcement qualifies for protection under the Due Process Clause of the Fourteenth Amendment, and must therefore be respected by the States.

Of course jury trial has "its weaknesses and the potential for misuse." Singer v. United States, 380 U.S. 24, 35 (1965). We are aware of the long debate, especially in this century, among those who write about the administration of justice, as to the wisdom of permitting untrained laymen to determine the facts in civil and criminal proceedings. Although the debate has been intense, with powerful voices on either side, most of the controversy has centered on the jury in civil cases. Indeed, some of the severest critics of civil juries acknowledge that the arguments for criminal juries are much stronger. In addition, at the heart of the dispute have been express or implicit assertions that juries are incapable of adequately understanding evidence or determining issues of fact, and that they are unpredictable, quixotic, and little better than a roll of dice. Yet, the most recent and exhaustive study of the jury in criminal cases concluded that juries do understand the evidence and come to sound conclusions in most of the cases presented to them and that when juries differ with the result at which the judge would have arrived, it is usually because they are serving some of the very purposes for which they were created and for which they are now employed. . . .

We would not assert, however, that every criminal trial—or any particular trial—held before a judge alone is unfair or that a defendant may never be as fairly treated by a judge as he would be by a jury. Thus we hold no constitutional doubts about the practices, common in both federal and state courts, of accepting waivers of jury trial and prosecuting petty crimes without extending a right to jury trial. . . . [Louisiana argues that] the conviction before us is valid and constitutional because here the petitioner was tried for simple battery and was sentenced to only 60 days in the parish prison. We are not persuaded. . . . [A] crime punishable by two years in prison is, based on past and contemporary standards in this country, a serious crime and not a petty offense. Consequently, appellant was entitled to a jury trial and it was error to deny it.

Lewis v. United States, 518 U.S. 322 (1996). [T]o determine whether an offense is petty, we consider the maximum penalty attached to the offense. . . . An offense carrying a maximum prison term of six months or less is presumed petty, unless the legislature has authorized additional statutory penalties so severe as to indicate that the legislature considered the offense serious. . . . [In this case], the maximum authorized penalty for [the charged offense] is six months' imprisonment—a penalty that presumptively places the offense in the "petty" category. We face the question whether petitioner is nevertheless entitled to a jury trial, because he was tried in a single proceeding for two counts of the petty offense so that the potential aggregated penalty is 12 months' imprisonment. . . . The fact that the petitioner was charged with two counts of a petty offense does not revise the legislative judgment as to the gravity of that particular offense, nor does it transform the petty offense into a serious one, to which the jury trial right would apply. . . . Certainly the aggregate potential penalty faced by petitioner is of serious importance to him. But . . . we look to the legislature's judgment . . . . [Where] the deprivation of liberty exceeds six months only as a result of the aggregation of charges, the jury trial right does not apply.

Jeffrey Abramson, *Two Ideals of Jury Deliberation*, 1998 U. Chi. Legal F. 125, 125-129, 131, 133-134. [D]eliberative democracy theorists often cite the jury as an institution that embodies the ideal of using collective reasoned discussion to attain a common verdict. [But] even in the jury setting we are confused about exactly what the deliberative ideal is . . . . Two theories compete. One theory demands that each juror be as impartial as possible. . . . The alternative . . . renounces the search for individually impartial jurors and aims instead at the impartiality of deliberations achievable when a jury represents a cross-section of the community. The more closely the jury mirrors the community makeup, it is argued, the more impartial its deliberations will be. . . .

Those who make impartiality the crux of the deliberative ideal prod jurors to bracket or to put aside their personal preconceptions, perspectives, and prejudices about the case. [On this view,] impartiality is achieved only to the extent that jurors pull up the anchors of their own identity, take new bearings from evidence considered impersonally, and then guide themselves toward a "verdict," which is Latin for "spoken truth." . . .

How do we select jurors able to render truthful verdicts and not just deliver opinions? . . . Since impartiality requires uncommon virtue, the impartialist has historically not sought to recruit jurors from the general population but preferred to screen for people "esteemed in the community for their integrity, good character, and sound judgment." Carter v. Jury Commission, 396 U.S. 320, 331 (1970). Even today, when jury selection by law must start from a list representative of the community at large, the impartialist defends lawyers' remaining rights to eliminate any or all potential jurors suspected of bias, regardless of the ultimate effect on jury diversity.

By contrast, those who treat representation as the key to jury deliberation [argue that few] if any people can live up to an ideal that requires them to suppress the influence of their station in life, let alone the force of their deeply held moral commitments. But even if jurors could conform to the bracketing ideal, such a norm would still be undesirable because . . . jurors are not simply judges by another name. Their unique mission is to expose adjudication to the experiences of ordinary people drawn from different walks of life, not to insulate adjudication from such perspectives. Deliberation should therefore invite and embrace, not exclude and bracket, expressions of what one differently knows as a woman, a person of color, a taxicab driver, or a victim of crime. Under this model, jurors seek the truth, but it is a "whole truth" best knowable when diversity prods jurors to consider all relevant information and perspectives. . . . Moreover, when juries are representative, the group bias of some jurors checks the group bias of others, silencing the most blatant expressions of prejudice and encouraging a consensus-driven mode of conversation. The very diversity of jury membership helps bring out arguments capable of moving a divergent group of people toward a mutually acceptable verdict. . . .

[Imagine on this view, in the case of Bernhard Goetz,] a jury room echoing with the arguments of both those mugged on subways and black kids tired of getting suspicious looks every time they ride the cars. Imagine jurors who themselves carry guns for protection arguing the issues with those who feel more threatened by armed vigilantes in the subway than by African American youths. That would be a jury room with loud and angry exchanges. It certainly would not be a jury ready to decide the issue in a flash and it might even be a jury unable to agree on a verdict in the end. But if the jury could reach a verdict, it would be because power ultimately flowed to those arguments capable of moving minds across the usual fault lines. This is the ideal of representative deliberation, where conversation informed by diversity allows the behavior of the so-called reasonable person to be studied from competing angles and different perspectives until the jury achieves the impartiality that the impartialists . . . search for in isolated individuals.

Impartialists remain skeptical about all of this. They ask why anyone should believe a victim of a subway mugging is capable of serving impartially on the Goetz jury, any more than a card-carrying member of the National Rifle Association or the mother of an African American teenager assaulted by skinheads. [U]nless we whittle [the jury] pool down by throwing out those whose minds cannot be changed by deliberation, we make a fetish of diversity for diversity's sake, in ways that will produce hung juries at best, and openly political compromises among partisan jurors at worst. . . .

. . . [Ultimately, the view] that I find persuasive, concludes [that] jury selection should randomly draw people from a representative cross-section of the population . . . . [D]eliberation among diverse people [could] awaken all jurors to the blinders of their own demographics, exposing each juror to community diversity more fully in the jury room than almost anywhere else. That experience, one hopes, is awakening and liberating. So awakened, jurors ideally will not serve as representatives of the political sort, as if they owed allegiance to the mere preferences popular in their section of town. Certainly jurors should insist that the views of "their sort of people" be heard and afforded equal consideration with the views of any other group. Merely articulating this desire is an important democratic moment in jury deliberations, a moment where the quotidian hierarchies of power and respect give way to true equality. But if and when this insurgence occurs, jurors should represent their differences only as a way to enrich the capacity of an egalitarian, collective jury to reason beyond its differences toward a mutually acceptable, unanimous verdict.

Hernandez v. New York, 500 U.S. 352 (1991). Petitioner Dionisio Hernandez asks us to review the New York state courts' rejection of his claim that the prosecutor in his criminal trial exercised peremptory challenges to exclude Latinos from the jury by reason of their ethnicity. . . . We concern ourselves here only with the jury selection process and the proper application of *Batson v. Kentucky*, 476 U.S. 79 (1986). . . .

After 63 potential jurors had been questioned and 9 had been empaneled, defense counsel objected that the prosecutor [used his] peremptory challenges to exclude [two] Latino potential jurors . . . . [The prosecutor explained the strikes as follows]:

> "Your honor, my reason for rejecting . . . these two jurors . . . is I feel very uncertain that they would be able to listen and follow the interpreter. . . . We talked to them for a long time . . . . I believe that in their heart they will try to follow [the interpreter regarding] Spanish-speaking witnesses . . . . [But when I asked, they] each looked away from me and said with some hesitancy that they would try, not that they could, but that they would try . . . . I feel that in a case where the interpreter will be for the main witnesses, they would have an undue impact upon the jury."

. . . In *Batson*, we outlined a three-step process for evaluating claims that a prosecutor has used peremptory challenges in a manner violating the Equal Protection Clause. . . . First, the defendant must make a prima facie showing that the prosecutor has exercised peremptory challenges on the basis of race. Second, if the requisite showing has been made, the burden shifts to the prosecutor to articulate a race-neutral explanation for striking the jurors in question. Finally, the trial court must determine whether the defendant has carried his burden of proving purposeful discrimination.

[Here, because the prosecutor volunteered an explanation for his strikes immediately after being challenged by the defense, we can assume a prima facie showing has been established and proceed to step two of the analysis.] The prosecutor's articulated basis for these challenges divided potential jurors into two classes: those whose conduct during *voir dire* would persuade him they might have difficulty in accepting the translator's rendition of Spanish-language testimony and those potential jurors who gave no such reason for doubt. Each category would include both Latinos and non-Latinos. While the prosecutor's criterion might well result in the disproportionate removal of prospective Latino jurors, that disproportionate impact does not turn the prosecutor's actions into a *per se* violation of the Equal Protection Clause.

Petitioner contends that despite the prosecutor's focus on the individual responses of these jurors, his reason for the peremptory strikes has the effect of a pure, language-based reason because "any honest bilingual juror would have answered the prosecutor in the exact same way." . . . But even if we knew that a high percentage of bilingual jurors would hesitate in answering questions like these and, as a consequence, would be excluded under the prosecutor's criterion, that fact alone would not cause the criterion to fail the race-neutrality test. . . . Equal protection analysis turns on the *intended* consequences of government classifications. Unless the government actor adopted a criterion with the intent of causing the [disparate] impact asserted, that impact itself does not violate the principle of race neutrality. Nothing in the prosecutor's explanation shows that he chose to exclude jurors who hesitated in answering questions about following the interpreter *because* he wanted to prevent bilingual Latinos from serving on the jury. . . .

In the context of this trial, the prosecutor's frank admission . . . raised a plausible, though not a necessary, inference that language might be a pretext for what in fact were race-based peremptory challenges. . . . [T]his trial took place in a community with a substantial Latino population, and petitioner and other interested parties were members of that ethnic group. It would be common knowledge in the locality that a significant percentage of the Latino population speaks fluent Spanish, and that many consider it their preferred language, the one chosen for personal communication, the one selected for speaking with the most precision and power, the one used to define the self. The trial judge can consider these and other factors when deciding whether a prosecutor intended to discriminate. . . . [But the] trial judge in this case chose to believe the prosecutor's race-neutral explanation for striking the two jurors in question, rejecting petitioner's assertion that the reasons were pretextual. . . . Deference to trial court findings on the issue of discriminatory intent makes particular sense in this context because, as we noted in *Batson*, the finding "largely will turn on evaluation of credibility." *Id.* at 98 n.21. In the typical peremptory challenge inquiry, the decisive question will be whether counsel's race-neutral explanation for a peremptory challenge should be believed. There will seldom be much evidence bearing on that issue, and the best evidence often will be the demeanor of the attorney who exercises the challenge. . . . We discern no clear error in the state trial court's determination that the prosecutor did not discriminate on the basis of the ethnicity of Latino jurors.

b. "The Prerogative of Lenity"

Harry Kalven & Hans Ziesel, *The American Jury* 8-9 (1966). [One] group of issues about the jury goes to what is perhaps the most interesting point. The critics complain that the jury will not follow the law, either because it does not understand it or because it does not like it, and that thus only a very uneven and unequal administration of justice can result from reliance on the jury; indeed, it is said that the jury is likely to produce that government by man, and not by rule of law, against which Anglo-American political tradition is so steadfastly set. This same flexibility of the jury is offered by its champions as its most endearing and most important characteristic. The jury, it is said, is a remarkable device for insuring that we are governed by the spirit of the law and not by its letter; for insuring that rigidity of any general rule of law can be shaped to justice in the particular case. One is tempted to say that what is one man's equity is another man's anarchy.

United States v. Dougherty, 473 F.2d 1113 (D.C. Cir. 1972). Seven of the so-called "D.C. Nine" bring this joint appeal from convictions arising out of their unconsented entry into the Washington offices of the Dow Chemical Company, and their destruction of certain property therein. . . . The undisputed evidence showed that on Saturday, March 22, 1969, appellants broke into the locked fourth floor Dow offices at 1030-15th Street, N.W., Washington, D.C., threw papers and documents about the office and into the street below, vandalized office furniture and equipment, and defaced the premises by spilling about a bloodlike substance [all as] an attack on the role of Dow Chemical Company and other unspecified corporations in supporting American military efforts in the Vietnam War. . . . [At the close of the trial the judge] instructed the jury on the three counts of each indictment as well as on the lesser-included offense of unlawful entry under the burglary count. He refused to instruct the jury that it could disregard the law as he gave it to them, and refused to instruct the jury that "moral compulsion" or "choice of the lesser evil" constituted a legal defense [to the charged offenses]. . . .

[Appellants argue] the jury has a well-recognized prerogative to disregard the instructions of the court even as to matters of law, and that they accordingly have the legal right that the jury be informed of its power. There has evolved in the Anglo-American system an undoubted jury prerogative-in-fact, derived from its power to bring in a general verdict of not guilty in a criminal case, that is not reversible by the court. . . . The pages of history shine on instances of the jury's exercise of its prerogative to disregard uncontradicted evidence and instructions of the judge. Most often commended are . . . the 19th century acquittals in prosecutions under the fugitive slave law. The values involved drop a notch when the liberty vindicated by the verdict relates to the defendant's shooting of his wife's paramour, or purchase during Prohibition of alcoholic beverages.

. . . The existence of an unreviewable and unreversible power in the jury, to acquit in disregard of the instructions on the law given by the trial judge, has for many years co-existed with legal practice and precedent upholding instructions to the jury that they are required to follow the instructions of the court on all matters of law. There were different soundings in colonial days and the early days of our Republic. We are aware of the number and variety of expressions at that time from respected sources—John Adams; Alexander Hamilton; prominent judges—that jurors had a duty to find a verdict according to their own conscience, though in opposition to the direction of the court; that their power signified a right; that they were judges both of law and of fact in a criminal case, and not bound by the opinion of the court. . . . [But as] the distrust of judges appointed and removable by the king receded, there came increasing acceptance that under a republic the protection of citizens lay not in recognizing the right of each jury to make its own law, but in following democratic processes for changing the law. . . .

Since the jury's prerogative of lenity, . . . in Learned Hand's words[,] introduces a "slack into the enforcement of law, tempering its rigor by the mollifying influence of current ethical conventions," it is only just, say appellants, that the jurors be so told. It is unjust to withhold information on the jury power of "nullification," since conscientious jurors may come, ironically, to abide by their oath as jurors to render verdicts offensive to their individual conscience, to defer to an assumption of necessity that is contrary to reality.

This so-called right of jury nullification is put forward in the name of liberty and democracy, but its explicit avowal risks the ultimate logic of anarchy. . . . "No legal system could long survive if it gave every individual the option of disregarding with impunity any law which by his personal standard was judged morally untenable." United States v. Moylan, 417 F.2d 1002, 1009 (4th Cir. 1969). . . . [T]he advocates of jury "nullification" apparently assume that the articulation of the jury's power will not extend its use or extent, or will not do so significantly or obnoxiously. [But can] this assumption fairly be made? . . .

The jury system has worked out reasonably well overall, providing "play in the joints" that imparts flexibility and avoid[s] undue rigidity. An equilibrium has evolved—an often marvelous balance—with the jury acting as a "safety valve" for exceptional cases, without being a wildcat or runaway institution. There is reason to believe that the simultaneous achievement of modest jury equity and avoidance of intolerable caprice depends on formal instructions that do not expressly delineate a jury charter to carve out its own rules of law. . . . The way the jury operates may be radically altered if there is alteration in the way it is told to operate. The jury knows well enough that its prerogative is not limited to the choices articulated in the formal instructions of the court. The jury gets its understanding as to the arrangements in the legal system from more than one voice. There is the formal communication from the judge. There is the informal communication from the total culture—literature (novel, drama, film, and television); current comment (newspapers, magazines and television); conversation; and, of course, history and tradition. The totality of input generally convey adequately enough the idea of prerogative, of freedom in an occasional case to depart from what the judge says. . . .

. . . Moreover, to compel a juror involuntarily assigned to jury duty to assume the burdens of mini-legislator or judge, as is implicit in the doctrine of nullification, is to put untoward strains on the jury system. It is one thing for a juror to know that the law condemns, but he has a factual power of lenity. To tell him expressly of a nullification prerogative, however, is to inform him, in effect, that it is he who fashions the rule that condemns. That is an overwhelming responsibility, an extreme burden for the jurors' psyche. And it is not inappropriate to add that a juror called upon for an involuntary public service is entitled to the protection, when he takes action that he knows is right, but also knows is unpopular, either in the community at large or in his own particular grouping, that he can fairly put it to friends and neighbors that he was merely following the instructions of the court.

BAZELON, C.J., dissenting. [T]he Court apparently concedes—although in somewhat grudging terms—that the power of nullification is a "necessary counter to case-hardened judges and arbitrary prosecutors" . . . . We could not withhold that concession without scoffing at the rationale that underlies the right to jury trial in criminal cases, and belittling some of the most legendary episodes in our political and jurisprudential history. The sticking point, however, is whether or not the jury should be told of its power to nullify the law in a particular case. Here, the trial judge not only denied a requested instruction on nullification, but also barred defense counsel from raising the issue in argument before the jury. The majority affirms that ruling. I see no justification for, and considerable harm in, this deliberate lack of candor. . . .

[I]f it were true that nullification which arises out of ignorance is in some sense more worthy than nullification which arises out of knowledge, the Court would have to go much further. For under the Court's assumption, the harm does not arise because a jury is *told* of its power to disregard the law, but because it *knows* of its power. Logically construed, the Court's opinion would seem to require the disqualification at voir dire of any prospective juror who admitted to knowledge of the doctrine. By excluding jurors with knowledge of the doctrine the Court could insure that its invocation would be spontaneous. And yet, far from requiring the exclusion of jurors who are aware of the power, the Court takes comfort in the fact that informal communication to the jury "generally convey[s] adequately enough the idea of prerogative, of freedom in an occasional case to depart from what the judge says." One cannot, it seems to me, have the argument both ways. . . .

D.C. Bar, Legal Ethics Committee, Opinion 320 (2003). [A] lawyer may not, consistent with the rules of professional conduct, expressly urge a jury to disregard the law. Nor may a lawyer disregard a ruling of the tribunal limiting the scope of permissible argument. The legal system continues, however, to permit juries to exercise the power to nullify. A lawyer may, therefore, within the bounds of zealous advocacy, advance arguments that have a good faith evidentiary basis even though those same arguments may also heighten the jury's awareness of its capacity to nullify . . . . [T]here are many variant forms that a jury nullification argument made by a zealous advocate can take—forms that may range from explicit requests to ignore the law to far more nuanced arguments that arguably have the same effect (and about which reasonable minds may differ). Consider the following hypothetical: Counsel wishes to argue that the police investigation of and testimony about a crime is not credible because it is biased by animus toward the political viewpoint of the defendant. At one level this is a straightforward argument based upon reasonable inferences from the evidence—officers with political bias might, indeed, fabricate evidence. At another level, however, the same argument may also be characterized as a call for the jury to acquit based not on the evidence but on the political viewpoint of the defendant.

It is in practice often impossible to distinguish between these two forms of argument. Counsel may often be able to make good-faith evidentiary arguments that have the collateral effect of heightening the jury's awareness of its capacity to nullify. . . . Thus, there is an obvious tension . . . . We think . . . the correct balance in the context of jury nullification arguments [calls for the following approach:] unless the advocate expressly urges nullification (an expression likely prohibited by the substantive law of this jurisdiction) or has been prohibited by the presiding officer from making a particular argument, a criminal defense counsel may zealously represent his client and may offer any argument for which he has a good faith evidentiary basis. Such arguments should not be deemed a violation of the Rules of Professional Conduct. Indeed, we can imagine situations in which it "may be possible for a defense lawyer to satisfy [the effective assistance of counsel requirement imposed by the Sixth Amendment through] a reasonable strategy of seeking jury nullification when no valid or practicable defense exists." United States v. Sams, 104 F.3d 1407 (D.C. Cir. 1996). . . . So long as the power to acquit in disregard of the evidence exists, we do not believe that the Rules of Professional Conduct prohibit zealous advocacy by a criminal defense lawyer that appeals indirectly to that power.

Benjamin Weiser, *Prosecution Explains Jury Tampering Charge*, N.Y. Times (Nov. 28, 2011). Julian P. Heicklen, a 79-year-old retired chemistry professor, has often stood on a plaza outside the United States Courthouse in Manhattan, holding a "Jury Info" sign and handing out brochures that advocate jury nullification. . . . Then, last year, federal prosecutors had Mr. Heicklen indicted, charging that his activity violated the law against jury tampering. . . . Reached by telephone on Friday, Mr. Heicklen said, "Since when is telling the truth a crime?" . . . [His advocacy is] part of a larger effort that has taken him to dozens of courthouses [where he] distributes his own materials and pamphlets produced by a national group called the Fully Informed Jury Association. . . . Mr. Heicklen, who could face a six-month sentence if convicted, has asked for a jury trial. [But prosecutor Rebecca] Mermelstein, opposing that demand, cited as one reason Mr. Heicklen's ardent stance that juries should nullify. He would probably "urge a jury to do so in a case against him," she wrote.

Paul Butler, *Racially Based Jury Nullification: Black Power in the Criminal Justice System*, 105 Yale L.J. 677, 690-694, 700-706, 711-715, 724-725 (1995). Imagine a country in which more than half of the young male citizens are under the supervision of the criminal justice system, either awaiting trial, in prison, or on probation or parole. Imagine a country in which two-thirds of the men can anticipate being arrested before they reach age thirty. Imagine a country in which there are more young men in prison than in college. Now give the citizens of the country the key to the prison. Should they use it?

Such a country bears some resemblance to a police state. When we criticize a police state, we think that the problem lies not with the citizens of the state, but rather with the form of government or law, or with the powerful elites and petty bureaucrats whose interests the state serves. Similarly, racial critics of American criminal justice locate the problem not so much with the black prisoners as with the state and its actors and beneficiaries. . . . Most white Americans, especially liberals, would . . . probably concede that racism, historical and current, plays a major role in creating an environment that breeds criminal conduct. From this premise, the radical critic deduces that but for the (racist) environment, the African-American criminal would not be a criminal. In other words, racism creates and sustains the criminal breeding ground, which produces the black criminal. Thus, when many African-Americans are locked up, it is because of a situation that white supremacy created. Obviously, most blacks are not criminals, even if every black is exposed to racism. To the radical critics, however, the law-abiding conduct of the majority of African-Americans does not mean that racism does not create black criminals. Not everyone exposed to a virus will become sick, but that does not mean that the virus does not cause the illness of the people who do. . . .

African-American jurors who endorse these critiques are in a unique position to act on their beliefs when they sit in judgment of a black defendant. As jurors, they have the power to convict the defendant or to set him free. May the responsible exercise of that power include voting to free a black defendant who the juror believes is guilty? . . .

Any juror legally may vote for nullification in any case, but, certainly, jurors should not do so without some principled basis. The reason [that juries in the 1850s who refused to convict escaped slaves under the Fugitive Slave Act] are viewed approvingly is that most of us now believe that the jurors in those cases did the morally right thing. . . . It is true that nullification later would be used as a means of racial subordination by some Southern jurors, but that does not mean that nullification in the approved cases was wrong. It only means that those Southern jurors erred in their calculus of justice. . . .

There is no question that jury nullification is subversive of the rule of law. . . . To borrow a phrase from the D.C. Circuit, jury nullification "betrays rather than furthers the assumptions of viable democracy." [But] "democracy," as practiced in the United States, has betrayed African-Americans far more than they could ever betray it. . . . If African-Americans believe that democratic domination exists . . . , they should not back away from lawful self-help measures, like jury nullification, on the ground that the self-help is antidemocratic. . . . [Rather,] African-Americans[, who] wield little influence over criminal law, state or federal[,] . . . should embrace the antidemocratic nature of jury nullification because it provides them with the power to determine justice in a way that majority rule does not. . . . At this point, every African-American should ask herself whether the operation of the criminal law in the United States advances the interests of black people. If it does not, the doctrine of jury nullification affords African-American jurors the opportunity to control the authority of the law over some African-American criminal defendants. In essence, black people can "opt out" of American criminal law. . . .

To allow African-American jurors to exercise their responsibility in a principled way, I make the following proposal. . . . In cases involving violent *malum in se* crimes like murder, rape, and assault, [black] jurors should consider the case strictly on the evidence presented, and, if they have no reasonable doubt that the defendant is guilty, they should convict. For nonviolent *malum in se* crimes such as theft or perjury, nullification is an option that the juror should consider, although there should be no presumption in favor of it. A juror might vote for acquittal, for example, when a poor woman steals from Tiffany's, but not when the same woman steals from her next-door neighbor. Finally, in cases involving nonviolent, *malum prohibitum* offenses, including "victimless" crimes like narcotics offenses, there should be a presumption in favor of nullification. . . .

I hope that all African-American jurors will follow my proposal . . . . I note, however, that even with limited participation by African-Americans, my proposal could have a significant impact. In most American jurisdictions, jury verdicts in criminal cases must be unanimous. One juror could prevent the conviction of a defendant. The prosecution would then have to retry the case, and risk facing another African-American juror with emancipation tendencies. I hope that there are enough of us out there, fed up with prison as the answer to black desperation . . . to cause retrial after retrial, until, finally, the United States "retries" its idea of justice.

Randall Kennedy, *Race, Crime, and the Law* 301-303, 310 (1997). [J]ury nullification is an exceedingly poor means for advancing the goal of a racially fair administration of criminal law. . . . If a large number of blacks clearly engage in "guerrilla warfare" as jurors, their action might call into question the right of blacks to be selected for jury service on precisely the same terms as others. . . . [More fundamentally, calls for racially selective jury nullification should be opposed because they are] based on a sentiment that is regrettably widespread in American culture: an ultimately destructive sentiment of racial kinship that prompts individuals of a given race to care more about "their own" than people of another race. . . . [The proposal] assumes that it is proper for prospective black jurors to care more about black communities than white communities, that it is proper for black jurors to be more concerned with the fate of black defendants than white defendants, and that it is proper for black jurors to be more protective of the property (and perhaps the lives?) of black people than white people. Along that road lies moral and political disaster. The disaster includes not only increasing but, worse, legitimizing the tendency of people to privilege in racial terms "their own." Some will say that this racial privileging has already happened and is, in any event, inevitable. The situation can and will get worse, however, if Butler's plan and the thinking behind it gains adherents. His program, although animated by a desire to challenge racial injustice, would demolish the moral framework upon which an effective, attractive, and compelling alternative can and must be built.

3. Collective Defense

Christopher W. Schmidt, *Divided by Law: The Sit-ins and the Role of the Courts in the Civil Rights Movement*, 3 Law & Hist. Rev. 93, 93-99 (2015). A central goal of the lunch counter sit-ins of 1960, the protests that launched the direct-action phase of the Civil Rights Movement, was to give new meaning to the very idea of "civil rights." . . . The sit-in movement began on the afternoon of Monday, February 1, 1960, when four African American students from the Agricultural and Technical College in Greensboro, North Carolina, sat down at the lunch counter of their local Woolworth store and asked to be served. The Greensboro Woolworth's, like most department stores in the South, had a policy of serving only whites at the lunch counter. . . . By the end of the week an estimated 200 students had taken part in the Greensboro protests [and] the sit-ins spread to other North Carolina cities. . . . Nashville, Tennessee, soon joined the movement, as did Tallahassee, Florida. Both cities had student groups that had been carefully planning their own sit-in protests months before the one in Greensboro. On being arrested and convicted, Nashville and Tallahassee protesters chose to serve jail sentences rather than pay a fine. . . . By the end of the spring, sit-ins had taken place in all thirteen Southern states and, according to one estimate, involved approximately 50,000 protesters.

Martin Luther King, Jr., *A Creative Protest* (1960). Victor Hugo once said that there is nothing in all the world more powerful than an idea whose time has come. The dynamic idea whose time has come today is the quest for freedom and human dignity. Men are tired of being trampled over by the iron feet of oppression. They are tired of being plunged into the abyss of exploitation where they experience the bleakness of nagging despair. . . . You students of North Carolina have captured this dynamic idea in a marvelous manner. You have taken the undying and passionate yearning for freedom and filtered it in your own soul and fashioned it into a creative protest that is destined to be one of the glowing epics of our time. . . .

May I say to you as you continue your protest, you will confront moments of difficulty. But let us realize that no great and lasting gain comes in history without suffering and sacrifice. . . . To suffer in a righteous cause is to grow to our humanity's full stature. . . . Let us not fear going to jail. If the officials threaten to arrest us for standing up for our rights, we must answer by saying that we are willing and prepared to fill up the jails of the South.

Kris Hermes, *Collective Action Behind Bars: A History of Jail Solidarity and Its Importance for Today's Social Movements*, Upping the Anti (June 28, 2016). With the intensified use of militaristic, violent, and repressive domestic policing methods, activists are increasingly forced to spend time in jail and endure criminal prosecution for their actions. But, by using certain tactics collectively, activists have mitigated harm in jail and achieved objectives that would have been impossible through individual action. . . . Jail solidarity, as it has become known, has a rich history in the US through its periodic use over the past hundred years by many different social movements. . . . Integral to the success of jail solidarity is the ability to exploit vulnerabilities in the legal system through collective action and non-cooperation. This is achieved because the authorities need the cooperation of arrestees to process them, it's expensive to detain large numbers of people, and many jails are near or beyond capacity and unable to deal with heavy influxes. . . . By refusing bail, arrestees can stay in jail together and place greater strain on the state. But this can sometimes involve a serious time commitment. And, while effective negotiations can eliminate the need for arrestees to defend themselves later in court, it can also take several days to achieve that goal. Therefore, such tactics are often only used by those who can endure the real-world consequences of spending days in jail, like missing out on work and other economic, social or family obligations.

Non-cooperation tactics can vary dramatically and are often as creative as the arrestees employing them. The mass refusal to provide identification is the foundation of contemporary jail solidarity and the tactic most familiar in the activist milieu. By agreeing not to carry identification, to use aliases or "action names," and refusing to cooperate during processing, arrestees can severely hamper the efforts of jail authorities and create a singular, collective identity that builds strength and fosters selflessness. This unified approach, which can be understood as an extension of collective political action in the streets, stands as a human bulwark against the jail system's efforts to atomize and incapacitate those under its control.

Andrew Manuel Crespo, *No Justice, No Pleas*, Inquest (April 20, 2023). The very idea of plea bargaining . . . gestures tantalizingly at a powerful set of related ideas. Ideas like collective bargaining. And, not far behind that, the idea of unions. Maybe even the idea of a strike. . . . As far back as 1937, Massachusetts Supreme Court justice Henry Lummus observed that if "all the defendants should combine to refuse to plead guilty, and should dare to hold out, they could break down the administration of criminal justice in any state in the Union." . . . The U.S. penal system is astonishingly vulnerable to the real and serious threat of [such] collective action [because it] is massively over-leveraged. It is the largest system of human incarceration in the history of the world. But it purchased its scale on the cheap, at plea bargaining rates. The system, in other words, is both an outgrowth of and dependent upon plea bargaining for its existence. To quote the Supreme Court, it is "a system of pleas."

To appreciate why this is so, one has to fully absorb the resource constraints shaping the behavior of the system's key administrators: the prosecutors and judges whose legal decisions transform free people into prisoners. In courthouses across the country, prosecutors routinely handle over a thousand felony cases each year. This translates to hundreds of open cases at any given time and multiple cases scheduled for trial every day. That is not a tenable equation for the carceral state. No prosecutor can try multiple cases in different courtrooms at once, let alone prepare hundreds of cases for trial at the same time. It is thus impossible for the system to do what the Sixth Amendment and countless television dramas suggest should be or is the norm: provide people charged with crimes "the right to a speedy and public trial" in "all criminal prosecutions."

In fact, decades of constitutional doctrine ensure that every single criminal trial will be an almost inescapably expensive undertaking for the state. Defendants have a constitutional entitlement not only to a trial but also to summon and assemble a jury; to cross-examine every prosecution witness about every element of every offense; to subpoena witnesses and to put on a defense of their own; to compel the prosecutor to produce certain labor-intensive forms of pretrial discovery; and to litigate pretrial motions related to a range of issues, some of which require evidentiary hearings to resolve. On top of all of that, they are entitled to a lawyer, *paid for by the state*, who can litigate all these rights aggressively in court.

To be clear, the United States currently sinks hundreds of billions of dollars each year into the penal system, money the federal government itself has said would be far better spent on welfare-enhancing social programs. But even still, the state allocates nowhere close to the resources that would be needed to sustain mass incarceration's endless convictions while adhering to the basic constitutional processes outlined above. Nowhere close.

Plea bargaining is how the system bridges that resource chasm. As Bill Stuntz once explained, it is the mechanism by which the state converts millions of "potential trials into guilty pleas," which "are not simply cheaper than trials" but "enormously cheaper." . . . Of course, prosecutors know this. And sometimes they even admit it. Here, [the] words [of Seattle's Chief Prosecutor Dan Satterberg] echo in my ears:

> Prosecutors cling to plea bargaining as a survival instinct. . . . My office files about 7,000 felony cases a year. We do four to five hundred trials. And we are packed. Our people can't do more than that. . . . We've settled on an equilibrium in major city court systems where about a 3 percent trial rate is considered a healthy trial rate. And it's really about all we can do.

This is a jaw-dropping statistic. . . . [It means that a] mere 3 percent of criminal defendants in a given courthouse could bring their local penal system to its knees. If that many defendants banded together and refused to plead guilty, they could immediately double the trial rate in that courthouse (from 3 percent to 6 percent). This would massively expand the resource demands on a system that is already operating at full capacity. There is not a major court system in the country that could absorb such a shock.

Three percent. And the whole thing could come grinding to a halt.

Of course, there's another side to the story. . . . Prosecutors can send people to prison, potentially for a very long time. And they could use that power to try to crush a plea strike before it ever starts. Lummus, the Massachusetts justice writing back in 1937, captured this dynamic. "The prosecutor," he wrote, "is like a man armed with a revolver who is cornered by a mob. A concerted rush would overwhelm him, but each individual in the mob fears that he might be one of those shot during the rush." As economists have modeled, prosecutors could leverage this fear to maximal effect by strategically focusing their attention on the strike's leading edge, threatening the first wave of defendants with massive sentences (or offering them irresistible deals) all in hopes of unraveling the strike before it starts. . . . No responsible discussion of collective plea bargaining can minimize this risk.

At the same time, it is important not to presume how people facing the systemic harms of mass incarceration can, will, or should respond to that risk. Likewise, it is important to bear in mind two truths. First, the status quo of mass incarceration imposes its own risks and harms, every day, on tens of millions of people. Second, there is no historical example of collective action undertaken in the face of systemic oppression that did not involve risk. On the contrary, as labor scholars Benjamin Sachs and Kate Andrias observe, "fear of retaliation" can always "jeopardize collective action," particularly when people attempt acts of solidarity in high-risk environments. Workers, renters, people in debt—all of them risk lost jobs, lost homes, and other frightening harms if targeted by their employers, landlords, or whomever else they might be organizing against. To be sure, imprisonment is a unique form of harm. But even that harm is not unfamiliar to labor and civil rights organizers who have faced threats of incarceration and violence throughout history.

And yet, as Sachs and Andrias go on to note, "retaliation and repression do not always defeat organization." On the contrary, effective organizing aims precisely to overcome such threats, [by deploying concrete and] strategic action that turns community resources into tactical wins. . . . We ought not assume that people facing prosecution lack the same capacity to form and deploy the solidarity, resources, and brave strategic action that social movements throughout time have used to challenge oppression. On the contrary, just like labor and community organizers before them, striking defendants and their communities could find sources of inspiration and solidarity in their shared experiences. Coming together to fight the collective oppression of mass incarceration, they could support one another not only spiritually but materially, through strike funds and other forms of mutual aid that promise financial assistance and robust community support to anyone harmed by a strike—before, during, and after any periods of incarceration. They could also coordinate their actions strategically to minimize the risk of harm to strike participants, including by starting the strike in sectors of the courthouse where the risks are the least serious, or by leveraging their insider knowledge about the strengths and weaknesses of their cases to try to sequence their proceedings in ways that are maximally disruptive while mitigating risk. Most of all, they could build enduring structures of solidarity that enable them to cultivate intra-community leadership, to marshal collective resources, to develop effective strategy, and to coordinate inspirational and effective action.

In short, people facing prosecution could form a union. And through it, they could pursue a wide range of emancipatory ends by leveraging their collective power—including the power to withhold that essential shared resource that the carceral state needs so desperately to survive: their pleas.[20]

CHAPTER 1

1. Max Weber, *Politics as a Vocation*, in *From Max Weber: Essays in Sociology* 77, 78 (Hans H. Gerth & C. Wright Mills trans., 2013) (1919).

2. *The Oxford History of the Prison: The Practice of Punishment in Western Society* vii (Norval Morris & David J. Rothman eds., 1995). As historian Lawrence Friedman observes, "[t]here is more to know about crime and punishment in this society than any human being can possibly know" and "no way to tell it all." Lawrence M. Friedman, *Crime and Punishment in American History* ix (1993). For an overview of the history presented in this section, see Friedman, *supra*, and also David J. Rothman, *The Discovery of the Asylum: Social Order and Disorder in the New Republic* (1971); Samuel Walker, *Popular Justice: A History of American Criminal Justice* (1980); Adam J. Hirsch, *The Rise of the Penitentiary: Prisons and Punishment in Early America* (1992); *The Oxford History of the Prison, supra*; Rebecca M. McLennan, *The Crisis of Imprisonment: Protest, Politics, and the Making of the American Penal State, 1776–1941* (2008); and, for a considerably earlier account, Gustave de Beaumont & Alexis de Tocqueville, *On the Penitentiary System in the United States and Its Application to France* (Emily Katherine Ferkaluk trans., 2018) (1833).

3. Kathryn Preyer, *Crime, the Criminal Law & Reform in Post-Revolutionary Virginia*, 1 Law & Hist. Rev. 53, 57-59 (1983).

4. Preyer, *supra* note 3, at 56-57 ("revolting," "sanguinary hue"); Friedman, *supra* note 2, at 37-40. On the use of executions in England and the colonies, see Friedman, *supra* note 2, at 41-44; McLennan, *supra* note 2, at 18.

5. Friedman, *supra* note 2, at 74. To some, the shift away from sanguinary punishment was not unrelated to the Revolution itself. For example, Benjamin Rush, who signed the Declaration of Independence, argued that sanguinary punishments are "the natural off-spring of monarchical governments," where Kings "consider their subjects as their property" and shed their "blood with as little emotion as men shed the blood of their sheep or cattle." By contrast, Rush continued, "republican governments speak a very different language," one that views sanguinary punishment as "offensive to the sovereignty of the people" and "to the majesty of heaven" alike. Benjamin Rush, *Considerations on the Injustice and Impolicy of Punishing Murder by Death* 18 (1792).

6. Beaumont & Tocqueville, *supra* note 2, at 4; Rothman, *supra* note 2, at 62. For a contrasting account offering contemporaneous ideological foundations for incarceration, see Hirsch, *supra* note 2, at 13-31.

7. Friedman, *supra* note 2, at 77.

8. Friedman, *supra* note 2, at 79-80 ("of penitence," "committed to silence"); Beaumont & Tocqueville, *supra* note 2, at 59. Historians of the early American prisons distinguish between the New York and Pennsylvania models. As Dana McKinney White and Lisa Haber-Thomson write,

> Two important U.S. models—Auburn Prison (1816) in Auburn, New York, and Eastern State Penitentiary (1829) in Philadelphia—refined ideas regarding how to manage their respective populations of what was then widely spoken of as 'criminal characters.' At Auburn (now known as the

Auburn Correctional Facility and still in use today as a maximum-security state prison), incarcerated people were housed in individual cells, and made to work collectively under enforced silence. This so-called Auburn System (sometimes known as the Congregate System) contrasted with the Philadelphia System, which was based on Quaker ideals. At Eastern State, where the Philadelphia System was fully implemented to widespread admiration, imprisoned people were held in near-total isolation throughout their sentence, with the idea that solitary reflection would lead to repentance and reform.

Building Carcerality, Inquest (May 23, 2024).

9. Beaumont & Tocqueville, *supra* note 2, at 58 ("remedy," "monomania"); James B. Finley, *Memorials of Prison Life* 41-42 (1850), quoted in Rothman, *supra* note 2, at 84. For early examples of "carceral enthusiasm," see Hirsch, *supra* note 2, at 66-67.

10. Friedman, *supra* note 2, at 155; McLennan, *supra* note 2, at 51.

11. Friedman, *supra* note 2, at 156; Rothman, *supra* note 2, at 125 ("overcrowding," "by their thumbs"); *id.* at 124 (quoting Charles Dickens, *American Notes* 142 (1850)); Edgardo Rotman, *The Failure of Reform,* in *The Oxford History of the Prison, supra* note 2, at 172 ("shower bath"). For a description of a broad array of physical abuses, see Friedman, *supra* note 2, at 158.

12. Enoch Wines & Theodore Dwight, *Report on the Prisons and Reformatories of the United States and Canada* 62, 287 (1867); Friedman, *supra* note 2, at 159; Rotman, *supra* note 11, at 194 ("so strongly built").

13. Rotman, *supra* note 11, at 175, 170.

14. The quotations in this paragraph are from Rotman, *supra* note 11, at 178-185.

15. *The Challenge of Crime in a Free Society: A Report by the President's Commission on Law Enforcement and Administration of Justice* 159 (1967); Rotman, *supra* note 11, at 170 ("persistent but ultimately unsuccessful"); David J. Rothman, *Perfecting the Prison,* in *The Oxford History of the Prison, supra* note 2, at 125 ("mantle of legitimacy"); Hirsch, *supra* note 2, at 117 ("monument to failure").

16. Hirsch, *supra* note 2, at xiv (citing Georg Rusche & Otto Kirchheimer, *Punishment and Social Structure* (1939); Michel Foucault, *Discipline and Punish* (1978); Dario Melossi & Massimo Pavarini, *The Prison and the Factory* (1981); and Michael Ignatieff, *A Just Measure of Pain* (1978)).

17. The quotations in the text are from McLennan, *supra* note 2, at 53-68. Alexis de Tocqueville similarly observed, back in 1833, that "the labor of the criminal is . . . necessary" in part because "his imprisonment, expensive for society when he is idle, becomes less onerous when he works." Beaumont & Tocqueville, *supra* note 2, at 28.

18. On prisoner wages, see McLennan, *supra* note 2, at 193-238; Wendy Sawyer, *How Much Do Incarcerated People Earn in Each State?,* Prison Pol'y Initiative (Apr. 10, 2017) (reporting prison wages under one dollar per hour in most states). On the interaction between the private sector and prisons, see Heather Ann Thompson, *Rethinking Working-Class Struggle Through the Lens of the Carceral State: Toward a Labor History of Inmates and Guards,* 8 Labor 15, 34-40 (2011), and George E. Sexton, Nat'l Inst. of Just., *Work in American Prisons: Joint Ventures with the Private Sector* (1995). For more on prison labor, see Chapter Six (p. 458).

19. Douglas A. Blackmon, *Slavery by Another Name* 52 (2008). For further discussion of the role Southern prisons played in promoting white supremacy, see Alex Lichtenstein, *Twice the Work of Free Labor: The Political Economy of Convict Labor in the New South* (1999); David Oshinsky, *Worse Than Slavery: Parchman Farm and the Ordeal of Jim Crow Justice* (1996). For the

argument that prison labor of the nineteenth century should not be confounded with chattel slavery, see McLennan, *supra* note 2, at 9.

20. U.S. Const. amend. XIII; Loïc Wacquant, *The New "Peculiar Institution": On the Prison as a Surrogate Ghetto*, 4 Theoretical Criminology 377, 379-380 (2000) [hereinafter Wacquant, *Peculiar Institution*]. On the demographic shift in Southern prisons, see Friedman, *supra* note 2, at 156 ("Before the Civil War, most prisoners in the South were white, not black[.]").

21. U.S. Const. amend. XIII (emphasis added); Wacquant, *Peculiar Institution*, *supra* note 20, at 384 (noting that Southern prisons "turned black overnight" on the "morrow of Emancipation"). For data on the racial composition of prisons in Virginia and Georgia in the late nineteenth century, see Friedman, *supra* note 2, at 156. According to historian Eric Foner, "the members of Congress who voted on the 13th Amendment did not anticipate" that "cunning rebels" would exploit the Amendment's crime-exception clause "to reduce freed persons to slavery." Eric Foner, *We Are Not Done with Abolition*, N.Y. Times (Dec. 15, 2020) (describing Southern abuse of the clause as an "unanticipated consequence[]"). As Foner further reports, "a group of Democratic members of Congress introduced an Abolition Amendment to the U.S. Constitution" in December 2020 to eliminate the exception. *Id.*; *see also* H.R. Res. 104, 116th Cong. (2020); S. Res. 81, 116th Cong. (2020). The proposals did not receive a vote.

22. Blackmon, *supra* note 19, at 55; Wacquant, *Peculiar Institution*, *supra* note 20, at 384-385.

23. Blackmon, *supra* note 19, at 56-57.

24. Rotman, *supra* note 11, at 157; Friedman, *supra* note 2, at 95; Blackmon, *supra* note 19, at 57.

25. Wacquant, *Peculiar Institution*, *supra* note 20, at 385 (quoting Lichtenstein, *supra* note 19, at 195); Blackmon, *supra* note 19, at 9. For more context, see Oshinsky, *supra* note 19, at 46-47 (noting that a quarter of the Black people subjected to Southern convict leasing were "an adolescent or a child").

26. Whitney Benns, *American Slavery, Reinvented*, Atlantic (Sept. 21, 2015).

27. Compare Bureau of Just. Stat., *Prisoners 1925–81* (1982), with Allen J. Beck & Christopher J. Mumola, Bureau of Just. Stat., *Prisoners in 1998* (1999), and Heather C. West et al., Bureau of Just. Stat., *Prisoners in 2009* (2010).

28. E. Ann Carson, Bureau of Just. Stat., *Prisoners in 2019* (2020). On local jail populations increasing, see Emma Kaufman, *The Prisoner Trade*, 133 Harv. L. Rev. 1815, 1842 n.169 (2020) (citing Jacob Kang-Brown et al., Vera Inst. of Just., *The New Dynamics of Mass Incarceration* 5 (2018)).

29. Wacquant, *Peculiar Institution*, *supra* note 20, at 386-387.

30. David Garland, *The Culture of Control* 2 (2001).

31. The notes that follow draw heavily on BJS reports as well as reports produced by The Prison Policy Initiative, The Sentencing Project, and by Professor Ben Grunwald in his article *Toward an Optimal Decarceration Strategy*, 33 Stan. L. & Pol'y Rev. 1 (2022).

32. Laura M. Maruschak & Todd D. Minton, Bureau of Just. Stat., *Correctional Populations in the United States, 2017–2018*, at 2 tbl.1 (2020) (2018 average daily population); John Pfaff, *The War on Drugs and Prison Growth: Limited Importance, Limited Legislative Options*, 52 Harv. J. Legis. 173, 191 (2015) (emphasis added); Grunwald, *supra* note 31, at 6, 16; Zhen Zeng, Bureau of Just. Stat., *Jail Inmates in 2018*, at 2 tbl.1 & 8 tbl.8 (2020) (annual admissions in 2018 and weekly turnover).

33. *See* Peter K. Enns et al., *What Percentage of Americans Have Ever Had a Family Member Incarcerated?: Evidence from the Family History of Incarceration Survey (FamHIS)*, 5 Socius 1, 5, 10

(2019); *id.* at 6 (noting that 14% of Americans have an immediate family member who has spent a year or more incarcerated); *see also* Keith Finlay et al., *Children's Indirect Exposure to the U.S. Justice System: Evidence from Longitudinal Links Between Survey and Administrative Data*, 138 Q.J. Econ. 2181 (2023).

34. Helen Fair & Roy Walmsley, World Prison Brief, *World Prison Population List* (14th ed. 2024) (comparative data). For the most current global incarceration rates, see World Prison Brief Data, http://www.prisonstudies.org/world-prison-brief-data.

35. Holger Spamann, *The U.S. Crime Puzzle: A Comparative Perspective on U.S. Crime and Punishment*, 18 Am. L. & Econ. Rev. 33, 41-43 & tbl.1 (2015) (emphasis added); Franklin E. Zimring & Gordon Hawkins, *Crime Is Not the Problem: Lethal Violence in America* 7, 113 (1997). For more background, see James P. Lynch & William Alex Pridemore, *Crime in International Perspective*, in *Crime and Public Policy* 25 (James Q. Wilson & Joan Petersilia eds., 2011).

36. Alfred Blumstein et al., *Cross-National Measures of Punitiveness*, 33 Crime & Just. 347, 348 (2005). For further analysis, see Spamann, *supra* note 35, at 34, 48 (concluding that the U.S. incarceration rate is four times higher than what one would predict based on "known cross-country determinants of crime and incarceration"). For data on homicide convictions as a proportion of prison population, see Carson, *supra* note 28, at 21 tbl.14.

37. Council of Economic Advisers, *Economic Perspectives on Incarceration and the Criminal Justice System* 12 (2016). On the overall crime rate, see Peter K. Enns, *Incarceration Nation* 104 fig.5.2 (2016).

38. Spamann, *supra* note 35, at 35-36 (emphasis added). For analysis that suggests that moderate incarceration reduces crime outside prison, see Aaron Chalfin & Justin McCrary, *Criminal Deterrence: A Review of the Literature*, 55 J. Econ. Lit. 5, 25-26 (2017).

39. On imprisonment rates and the composition of the prison population, see Carson, *supra* note 28, at 6 tbl.3, 9 tbl.5 (reporting, among other things, that 23% of people in prison are Latinos, compared to a national population of 16.7%). For similar figures for jails, see Zeng, *supra* note 32, at 4-5 tbls.2 & 3. On the reliability of data about Hispanics, see Sarah Eppler-Epstein, Urban Inst., *We Don't Know How Many Latinos Are Affected by the Criminal Justice System* (Oct. 16, 2016), which notes that only 67 percent of states regularly publish "statistics on race and ethnicity that include a 'Hispanic' or 'Latino' category."

40. For statistics on the sex of sentenced prisoners in federal and state correctional authorities, see Carson, *supra* note 28, at 6 tbl.3. On LGBTQ individuals, see Ilan H. Meyer et al., *Incarceration Rates and Traits of Sexual Minorities in the United States: National Inmate Survey, 2011–2012*, 107 Am. J. Pub. Health 267, 267 (2016), which reports that 9.3% of men and 42.1% of women in prison identify as lesbian, gay, or bisexual or report a same-sex sexual experience prior to being incarcerated, corresponding to an incarceration rate triple the national adult baseline. On income, see Bernadette Rabuy & Daniel Kopf, Prison Pol'y Initiative, *Prisons of Poverty: Uncovering the Pre-Incarceration Incomes of the Imprisoned* fig.3 (2015), which finds that 57% of incarcerated men make less than $22,500 per year and that incarcerated men are "concentrated at the lowest ends of the national income distribution." As for age, one quarter of all people in prison are twenty-nine years old or younger and more than half are thirty-nine years old or younger, with the Black and Hispanic prison populations trending younger than the white prison population. See Carson, *supra* note 28, at 15 tbl.9. By comparison, 20.9% of the broader national population is between 15 and 29 years old and 33.9% is between 15 and 39 years old. See Lindsay M. Howden & Julie A. Meyer, U.S. Census Bureau, *Age and Sex Composition: 2010*, at 4 tbl.2 (2011).

41. Bruce Western, *Mass Incarceration, Visualized*, Atlantic (Sept. 11, 2015). For differences in incarceration rates among Black, Hispanic, and white men, see Thomas P. Bonzcar, Bureau of Just. Stat., *Prevalence of Imprisonment in the U.S. Population, 1974–2001*, at 1 (2003). On the lifetime incarceration rate for Black men, see Glenn Kessler, *The Stale Statistic That*

One in Three Black Males "Born Today" Will End Up in Jail, Wash. Post (June 16, 2015). And for an estimate of the incarceration rate for Black men without a high school degree born between 1975–1979, see Bruce Western & Christopher Wildeman, *The Black Family and Mass Incarceration*, 621 Annals Am. Acad. Pol. & Soc. Sci. 221, 231 tbl.1 (2009).

42. John Pfaff, *Locked In* 13 (2017). For incarceration numbers and rates, see Carson, *supra* note 28, at 7 tbl.4, 11-12 tbl.7, which offers a breakdown of sentenced persons in federal prisons compared to each state that shows a high of 887 people per 100,000 in Louisiana, a low of 165 per 100,000 in Massachusetts, and wide variation between the poles. In recent years, some states have cut their prison populations by nearly 40% while others have increased theirs by as much as 23% over the same time horizon. Nazgol Ghandnoosh, Sent'g Project, *U.S. Prison Population Trends: Massive Buildup and Modest Decline* 4 fig.3 (2019).

43. German Lopez, *Want to End Mass Incarceration? This Poll Should Worry You.*, Vox (Sept. 7, 2016) (polling data); Carson, *supra* note 28, at 20 & tbl.13, 22 tbl.15 (incarceration data).

44. Carson, *supra* note 28, at 20 tbl.13.

45. Pew Ctr. on the States, *Time Served: The High Cost, Low Return of Longer Prison Terms* 13 tbl.1 (2012). For the view that the move to "more punitive sentencing rules" explains why "prison populations grew in the United States," see Derek Neal & Armin Rick, *The Prison Boom and Sentencing Policy*, 45 J. Legal Stud. 1, 13-14 (2016). For a contrary view, arguing that charging practices, not sentencing, drove prison growth, see John F. Pfaff, *The Myths and Realities of Correctional Severity: Evidence from the National Corrections Reporting Program on Sentencing Practices*, 13 Am. L. & Econ. Rev. 491 (2011).

46. Loïc Wacquant, *The Curious Eclipse of Prison Ethnography in the Age of Mass Incarceration*, 3 Ethnography 371, 381 (2002) [hereinafter Wacquant, *Prison Ethnography*].

47. Wacquant, *Prison Ethnography*, *supra* note 46, at 381-382. As Wacquant goes on to observe, prison ethnography, which attempted to provide a systematic and scholarly account of life inside of penal institutions, "all but vanished just as the United States was settling into mass incarceration," mainly because prison officials began limiting access. *Id.* at 385-387. As a result, Wacquant argues, scholars lost this window into life on the inside "at the very moment when it was most urgently needed on both scientific and political grounds." *Id.* Notably, the Supreme Court held in 1978 that there is no First Amendment right of access to prisons for the media or the public. Houchins v. KQED, 438 U.S. 1 (1978). The upshot, sociologist Bruce Western writes, is that "much of the ethical talk about incarceration, in law and philosophy, is naïve about the empirical reality in which [punishment] is administered." Bruce Western, *Homeward: Life in the Year After Prison* 4 (2018). For examples of prison ethnographies from earlier eras, see Donald Clemmer, *The Prison Community* (1940) (describing the social organization of prisons); Gresham M. Sykes, *The Society of Captives* (1958) (same, in the setting of a maximum security prison); James B. Jacobs, *Stateville: The Penitentiary in Mass Society* (1977) (examining prison organization in Stateville Prison).

48. For a discussion situating the qualitative experience of American incarceration on a spectrum that includes international examples, see Jacob Bronsther, *Long-Term Incarceration and the Moral Limits of Punishment*, 41 Cardozo L. Rev. 2369, 2387-2398 (2020). Bronsther discusses Rwanda's Gitarama prison, where 7,000 people were crammed into a facility built for 400 such that most "had no option but to stand" or squat "in filth" and one of every eight people incarcerated died in a nine-month span, as well as "Norway's minimum-security Bastøy Prison" that incarcerates 115 people at a time, "many of whom have been convicted of serious and violent crimes," who live in communal group homes on an island where they work from 8:30am to 3:30pm "tending to sheep, cows, and chickens, looking after fruit and vegetable gardens." For more on Norwegian prisons, see Ashley Kilmer & Sami Abdel-Salam, *Pretty & Punitive*, Inquest (Oct. 20, 2022).

49. Issa Kohler-Hausmann, *Misdemeanorland* 2 (2018).

50. Alexandra Natapoff, *The Penal Pyramid*, in *The New Criminal Justice Thinking* 71, 79 (Sharon Dolovich & Alexandra Natapoff eds., 2017).

51. For general trends in lengths of probation, see Alexis Lee Watts, Robina Inst., *Probation In-Depth: The Length of Probation Sentences* 1-2 tbls.1 & 2 (2016), which reports that most states cap probation at five years or less but that some allow it to extend to a decade or, for some underlying crimes, indefinitely. For a more detailed account of probation regimes across the country, see generally Ronald P. Corbett et al., Robina Inst., *Profiles in Probation Revocation: Examining the Legal Framework in 21 States* (2015); Fiona Doherty, *Obey All Laws and Be Good: Probation and the Meaning of Recidivism*, 104 Geo. L.J. 291 (2016).

52. For the relevant statistics, see Danielle Kaeble & Mariel Alper, Bureau of Just. Stat., *Probation and Parole in the United States, 2017–2018*, at 1-3 & tbl.2 (2020). Determinate sentencing systems use fixed terms of incarceration but create an analog to parole in the form of a post-release period of supervised release. *See* Fiona Doherty, *Indeterminate Sentencing Returns: The Invention of Supervised Release*, 88 N.Y.U. L. Rev. 958 (2013). For general trends in probation and parole from the 1970s to 2010s, see generally Bureau of Just. Stat., *Adults on Probation, Federal and State-By-State, 1977–2012* (2013); Bureau of Just. Stat., *Adults on Parole in the United States, 1975–2012* (2013). And for demographic trends in community supervision, see Kaeble & Alper, *supra*, at 20, app'x tbl.4 (reporting that 75% of people on probation are men and that 30% are Black); *id.* at 27, app'x tbl.8 (reporting that 87% of people on parole are men and that 37% are Black).

53. For examples of scholarly commentary on the shift in the character of community supervision, see Joel M. Caplan, *Parole System Anomie: Conflicting Models of Casework and Surveillance*, 70 Fed. Prob. 32, 34 (2006); Lloyd E. Ohlin et al., *Major Dilemmas of the Social Worker in Probation and Parole*, 2 Crime & Delinq. 211 (1956) (distinguishing between the "welfare worker" and "punitive officer" models of community supervision). For a comparison between the impact of rehabilitative programming versus pure surveillance programs lacking counseling services, see Joan Petersilia & Susan Turner, *Intensive Supervision for High-Risk Probationers: Findings from Three California Experiments* (1990); Joan Petersilia & Susan Turner, Nat'l Inst. of Just., *Evaluating Intensive Supervision Probation/Parole: Results of a Nationwide Experiment* (1993). For an overview of studies indicating that intensive supervision of low-level offenders can lead to more crime, see Haci Duru et al., *Does Reducing Supervision for Low-Risk Probationers Jeopardize Community Safety?*, 84 Fed. Prob. 21, 22 (2020). For background on blended forms of supervision, see Joel Miller, *Contemporary Modes of Probation Officer Supervision: The Triumph of the "Synthetic" Officer?*, 32 Just. Q. 314 (2015), and Carl B. Klockars, Jr., *A Theory of Probation Supervision*, 64 J. Crim. L. & Criminology 549, 550-552 (1972) (describing "synthetic officers").

54. On the variability of supervision in practice, see Miller, *supra* note 53, at 314. For an example of the high caseloads assigned to probation officers, see Joan Petersilia, *Probation in the United States*, 22 Crime & Just. 149, 150 (1997), describing officers with "100-plus caseloads" who can only meet with their assigned probationers or parolees "at most once a month." For an example of high-intensity probation programs, see Avlana K. Eisenberg, *Mass Monitoring*, 90 S. Cal. L. Rev. 123, 125 (2017), which observes that use of electronic monitoring in the United States "expanded from fewer than one hundred people in 1984 to more than 200,000 by 2009"; as well as M.M., *Living with an Ankle Bracelet*, Marshall Project (July 16, 2015), which offers a first-hand account of electronic surveillance. For an overview of the different supervision levels and the research on their effectiveness, see Edward J. Latessa & Myrinda Schweitzer, *Community Supervision and Violent Offenders: What the Research Tells Us and How to Improve Outcomes*, 103 Marq. L. Rev. 911 (2019).

55. Corbett et al., *supra* note 51, at 3. For background on the constitutional standards governing probation and parole revocation processes, see *Morrissey v. Brener*, 408 U.S. 471 (1972), and *Gagnon v. Scarpelli*, 411 U.S. 778 (1973).

56. Richard P. Seiter, *Prisoner Reentry and the Role of Parole Officers*, 66 Fed. Prob. 50, 51 (2002).

57. Corbett et al., *supra* note 51, at 4.

58. Sarah Stillman, *Get Out of Jail, Inc.*, New Yorker (June 16, 2014).

59. Friedman, *supra* note 2, at 38.

60. U.S. Dep't of Just., Civil Rights Div., *Investigation of the Ferguson Police Department* 2 (2015).

61. Alexes Harris et al., *Drawing Blood from a Stone: Legal Debt and Social Inequality in the Contemporary United States*, 115 Am. J. Socio. 1753, 1756 (2010); Katherine Beckett & Alexes Harris, *On Cash and Conviction: Monetary Sanctions as Misguided Policy*, 10 Criminology & Pub. Pol'y 509, 518 (2011).

62. See Collateral Consequences Inventory, Nat'l Inventory of Collateral Consequences of Conviction, https://niccc.nationalreentryresourcecenter.org.

63. For an overview of the interrelationship between state penal systems and federal immigration enforcement, see Jennifer M. Chácon, *Overcriminalizing Immigration*, 102 J. Crim. L. & Criminology 613 (2012). For background on the role of state court actors in immigration, see Margaret H. Taylor & Ronald F. Wright, *The Sentencing Judge as Immigration Judge*, 51 Emory L.J. 1131 (2002) (judges), and Paul Crane, *Charging on the Margin*, 57 Wm. & Mary L. Rev. 775 (2016) (prosecutors). For background on the role federal criminal law plays in regulating and punishing immigration, see Ingrid Eagly, *Prosecuting Immigration*, 104 Nw. U. L. Rev. 1281 (2010), and Juliet Stumpf, *The Crimmigration Crisis: Immigrants, Crime, and Sovereign Power*, 56 Am. U. L. Rev. 367, 383 (2006).

64. President William Clinton, Remarks by the President at the One Strike Symposium (Mar. 28, 1996); Human Rights Watch, *No Second Chance: People with Criminal Records Denied Access to Public Housing* 46 (2004). For an example of a statute banning access to federally funded public housing based on drug offenses, see 42 U.S.C. §13661(b). For an example of a law granting increased discretion to deny housing based on a criminal record of any kind, see Housing Opportunity Program Extension Act of 1996, Pub. L. No. 104-120, 110 Stat. 834 (1996). For more on how criminal convictions lead to discrimination in the private housing market, see Hensleigh Crowell, Note, *A Home of One's Own: The Fight Against Illegal Housing Discrimination Based on Criminal Convictions, and Those Who Are Still Left Behind*, 95 Tex. L. Rev. 1103, 1105 (2017), which notes that discrimination against people with criminal records is "[e]nabled by easy and increasingly inexpensive access to criminal-record data" and "has long been considered legal because it is not based on a protected status—race, sex, national origin, or religion."

65. Valerie Schneider, *The Prison to Homelessness Pipeline: Criminal Record Checks, Race, and Disparate Impact*, 93 Ind. L.J. 421, 432-433 (2018).

66. For background on how criminal convictions bar participation in civic life, see Amy E. Lerman & Vesla Weaver, *Arresting Citizenship* (2014). For specific examples, see Tex. Elec. Code Ann. §141.001 (barring anyone with a felony conviction from elected office), and Brian C. Kalt, *The Exclusion of Felons from Jury Service*, 53 Am. U. L. Rev. 65 (2003) (reporting that the majority of states permanently ban anyone with a felony conviction from serving on a jury). For background on the historical development of the term "civil death," see Gabriel J. Chin, *The New Civil Death: Rethinking Punishment in the Era of Mass Incarceration*, 160 U. Pa. L. Rev. 1789 (2012), and Alec C. Ewald, *"Civil Death": The Ideological Paradox of Criminal Disenfranchisement Law in the United States*, 2002 Wis. L. Rev. 1045. The U.S. Supreme Court upheld the constitutionality of felon disenfranchisement laws in *Richardson v. Ramirez*, 418 U.S. 24 (1974).

67. Jeff Manza & Christopher Uggen, *Locked Out: Felon Disenfranchisement and American Democracy* 41, 49-51, 57, 67 (2006).

68. Manza & Uggen, *supra* note 67, at 191-198. As the authors further observe, "the 'average' felon [leans] toward the Democratic Party in any given electoral contest." *Id.* at 183. For the opposite argument that disenfranchisement laws actually hurt Bush in Florida in 2000, see Traci Burch, *Did Disfranchisement Laws Help Elect President Bush? New Evidence on the Turnout Rates and Candidate Preferences of Florida's Ex-Felons*, 34 Pol. Behav. 1, 3 (2012), which relies on survey data to conclude that "the ex-felon population in Florida most likely would have favored President Bush in 2000." See also Marc Meredith & Michael Morse, *Why Letting Ex-Felons Vote Probably Won't Swing Florida*, Vox (Nov. 2, 2018). Prisons can further distort the electoral landscape because the Census counts incarcerated people as residents of the district in which they are incarcerated. For more on this phenomenon, sometimes called prison gerrymandering, see Taylor King & Gabriela Limón, Brennan Ctr. for Just., *Prison Gerrymandering Undermines Our Democracy* (2021), https://www.brennancenter.org/our -work/research-reports/prison-gerrymandering-undermines-our-democracy.

69. Pamela S. Karlan, *Convictions and Doubts: Retribution, Representation, and the Debate over Felon Disenfranchisement*, 56 Stan. L. Rev. 1147, 1169-1170 (2004).

70. *See* Prison Pol'y Initiative, *Mass Incarceration: The Whole Pie 2020* (2020), https://www.prisonpolicy.org/reports/pie2020.html.

71. For statistics on jail populations, see Zeng, *supra* note 32, at 5 tbl.3. The case of Kalief Browder is often cited as an example of the potential injustices of pretrial detention. Browder was a teenager accused of stealing a backpack. He spent three years in pretrial detention on Rikers Island, was never convicted of any crime, and later took his own life due to the ongoing trauma caused by his pretrial detention. *See* Jennifer Gonnerman, *Three Years on Rikers Without Trial*, New Yorker (Sept. 29, 2014).

72. For statistics on immigration detention, see U.S. Immigr. & Customs Enf't, *U.S. Immigration and Customs Enforcement Fiscal Year 2019 Enforcement and Removal Operations Report* 5 (2019). For the argument that the U.S. immigration system operates in practice as a system of punishment, see César Cuauhtémoc García Hernández, *Immigration Detention as Punishment*, 61 U.C.L.A. L. Rev. 1348, 1349 (2014). The U.S. Supreme Court has long deemed immigration detention to be civil in nature. *See* Carlson v. Landon, 342 U.S. 524, 537-538 (1952) ("Deportation is not a criminal proceeding and has never been held to be punishment. . . . Detention is necessarily a part of this deportation procedure. Otherwise aliens arrested for deportation would have opportunities to hurt the United States during the pendency of deportation proceedings.").

On conditions in immigration detention facilities, see, for example, Caitlin Dickerson, *'There is a Stench': Soiled Clothes and No Baths for Migrant Children at a Texas Center*, N.Y. Times (June 21, 2019) ("A chaotic scene of sickness and filth is unfolding in an overcrowded border station . . . where hundreds of young people who have recently crossed the border are being held . . . . Some of the children have been there for nearly a month."); Madeline Joung, *What Is Happening at Migrant Detention Centers? Here's What to Know*, Time (July 12, 2019) ("Adults and children have been held for days, weeks, or even months in cramped cells, sometimes with no access to soap, toothpaste, or places to wash their hands or shower. Some reports have emerged of children sleeping on concrete floors; others of adults having to stand for days due to lack of space. A May report . . . found 900 people crammed into a space designed to accommodate 125 at most.").

73. Prison Pol'y Initiative, *supra* note 70. On the dearth of available data on civil commitment, see Nathaniel P. Morris, *Detention Without Data: Public Tracking of Civil Commitment*, 71 Law & Psychiatry 741, 741 (2020). On state power to quarantine, see David P. Fidler et al.,

Through the Quarantine Looking Glass: Drug-Resistant Tuberculosis and Public Health Governance, Law, and Ethics, 35 J.L. Med. & Ethics 616, 620 (2007). For more on civil detention in cases involving mental insanity, see Chapter Three (p. 141).

74. For one example, see Carol Marbin Miller, *Busted Toilets, Peeling Paint, Sewage Backups, Lice: A Peek Inside Juvenile Lockups,* Miami Herald (Nov. 30, 2017), which reports that lawmakers who made a surprise inspection of juvenile facilities in Miami-Dade and Broward counties found the conditions to be "horrible, horrific, deplorable."

75. *See* The Guantánamo Docket, N.Y. Times (Aug. 7, 2024) (recounting the number of people detained in Guantánamo over the last two decades). On the legality of detention of "enemy combatants," see *Hamdi v. Rumsfeld,* 542 U.S. 507 (2004). For an argument linking the current law of executive detention applicable in Guantánamo Bay to the Supreme Court's legitimation of Japanese internment camps during World War II, see Aya Gruber, *Raising the Red Flag: The Continued Relevance of the Japanese Internment in the Post-*Hamdi *World,* 54 U. Kan. L. Rev. 307, 373-374 (2006).

76. Henry M. Hart, Jr., *The Aims of the Criminal Law,* 23 Law & Contemp. Probs. 401, 404 (1958).

77. Hart, *supra* note 76, at 404-405.

78. Herbert Wechsler, *The Challenge of a Model Penal Code,* 65 Harv. L. Rev. 1097, 1098 (1952); Hart, *supra* note 76, at 402.

CHAPTER 2

1. J.L. Mackie, *Morality and the Retributive Emotions,* 1 Crim. Just. Ethics 3, 4 (1982). On internal heterogeneity among retributivists, see Douglas Husak, *Retributivism in Extremis,* 32 Law & Phil. 3, 4 (2013), which describes retributivism as "the name of a tradition or group of theories that share some loose similarities" and notes that retributivists "can and do disagree" with each other on various aspects of the theory.

2. Mitchell N. Berman, *Modest Retributivism,* in *Legal, Moral, and Metaphysical Truths* 35, 36 (Kimberly Kessler Ferzan & Stephen J. Morse eds., 2016) ("the core of retributivism"); David O. Brink, *Fair Opportunity and Responsibility* 139 (2021) ("desert") (emphasis added); Mackie, *supra* note 1, at 4.

3. Alice Ristroph, *Desert, Democracy, and Sentencing Reform,* 96 J. Crim. L. & Criminology 1293, 1334 n.161 (2006); Jean Hampton, *Correcting Harms vs. Righting Wrongs: The Goal of Retribution,* 39 UCLA L. Rev. 1659, 1659 (1992) ("steady rise in the popularity"); James Q. Whitman, *A Plea Against Retributivism,* 7 Buff. Crim. L. Rev. 85, 89 (2003) ("impact at all"). For an additional argument that retributivism, and in particular the principle known as *lex talionis* or "an eye for an eye," would require massive decarceration of the United States if actually applied as a touchstone of American punishment, see Christopher Lewis, *Unlocking Lex Talionis* (working paper).

4. Jeremy Bentham, *An Introduction to the Principles of Morals and Legislation* 170 (Oxford 1907) (1789) [hereinafter Bentham, *An Introduction*]. For more on utilitarian justifications for punishment, see Cesare Beccaria, *On Crimes and Punishments* (1764).

5. Göran Duus-Otterström, *Why Retributivists Should Endorse Leniency in Punishment,* 32 Law & Phil. 459, 463 (2012); *see also* Ristroph, *supra* note 3, at 1327 ("The simple claim that an offender deserves a given punishment is opaque: it does not reveal what factors were used to assess desert.").

6. Dale Whittington & Duncan MacRae, Jr., *The Issue of Standing in Cost-Benefit Analysis*, 5 J. Pol'y Analysis & Mgmt. 665, 665-666 (1986). For more on the latent value judgments embedded within criminal adjudication, see Benjamin Levin, *Values and Assumptions in Criminal Adjudication*, 129 Harv. L. Rev. F. 379 (2016).

7. Bentham, *An Introduction, supra* note 4, at 170; R.A. Duff, *Punishment, Communication, and Community* 3-4 (2001) ("final good").

8. Council of Economic Advisers, *Economic Perspectives on Incarceration and the Criminal Justice System* 34 (2016) (emphases added) [hereinafter *CEA Perspectives*].

9. Immanuel Kant, *The Philosophy of Law* 194 (William Hastie trans., Clark 1887); *see also* Youngjae Lee, *Desert and the Eighth Amendment*, 11 U. Pa. J. Const. L. 101, 113 (2008) (defining punishment as the "intentional infliction of pain"). For an overview of the principle of less eligibility, see Edward W. Sieh, *Less Eligibility: The Upper Limits of Penal Policy*, 3 Crim. Just. Pol'y Rev. 159 (1989), which discusses Bentham's views on the subject as well as accounts from other leading scholars, including Georg Rusche & Otto Kirchheimer, *Punishment and Social Structure* (1968). For a contemporary application of the argument, see Christopher Lewis & Adaner Usmani, *Abolition of What?*, 114 J. Crim. L. & Criminology ___ (forthcoming).

10. Todd Clear, *The Effects of High Imprisonment Rates on Communities*, 37 Crime & Just. 97, 103-104 (2004). For more on harms within prisons, see Ben Gifford, *Prison Crime and the Economics of Incarceration*, 71 Stan. L. Rev. 71, 76-77 (2019); *Inside This Place, Not of It: Narratives from Women's Prisons* (Robin Levi & Ayelet Waldman eds., 2011). For more data on the impacts incarceration has on families, see Peter K. Enns et al., *What Percentage of Americans Have Ever Had a Family Member Incarcerated?: Evidence from the Family History of Incarceration Survey (FamHIS)*, 5 Socius 1, 5, 10 (2019) (noting that nearly half of all Americans will see a parent, sibling, partner, or child incarcerated); *CEA Perspectives, supra* note 8, at 50 ("Over half of all prisoners are parents . . . . In a reflection of the demographics of the incarcerated population, 1 percent of White children have a parent in prison compared to 7 percent of Black children and 2 percent of Hispanic children."); *see also* Keith Finlay et al., *Children's Indirect Exposure to the U.S. Justice System: Evidence from Longitudinal Links Between Survey and Administrative Data*, 138 Q.J. Econ. 2181 (2023).

11. Associated Press, *At $75,560, Housing a Prisoner in California Now Costs More Than a Year at Harvard*, L.A. Times (June 4, 2017). For data on operational costs per prisoner by state, see Chris Mai & Ram Subramanian, Vera Inst. of Just., *The Price of Prisons: Examining State Spending Trends 2010–2015*, at 8 tbl.1 (2017). For trends in prison spending compared to trends in education spending, see Stephanie Stullich et al., U.S. Dep't of Educ., *State and Local Expenditures on Corrections and Education* 1 (2016), which reports that between 1979 and 2013, state and local expenditures on prisons grew three times faster than investments in pre-kindergarten through twelfth grade public education.

12. For more on penal system expenditures, see *CEA Perspectives, supra* note 8, at 43-44 (observing that with respect to all criminal justice expenditures, "[a]pproximately 50 percent . . . is attributable to local governments, 30 percent is spent by States and 20 percent is spent by the Federal Government"). Beyond *public* spending on punishment and policing, private actors also spend quite a bit of money on crime prevention. "When crime increases, more resources are devoted to the production of goods such as burglar alarms, protective firearms, security cameras, locks, and safes." David A. Anderson, *The Aggregate Cost of Crime in the United States*, 64 J.L. & Econ. 857, 862 (2021); *see id.* at 874 tbl.2 (estimating the cost of security systems alone at approximately $55 billion per year).

13. *CEA Perspectives, supra* note 8, at 45.

14. *CEA Perspectives, supra* note 8, at 39-40 ("increase recidivism"); Todd Clear et al., *Coercive Mobility and Crime: A Preliminary Examination of Concentrated Incarceration and Social*

Disorganization, 20 Just. Q. 33, 34-35 (2003) ("incarceration"). For evidence on criminogenic "peer effects" in carceral facilities, see Patrick Bayer et al., *Building Criminal Capital Behind Bars: Peer Effects in Juvenile Corrections*, 124 Q.J. Econ. 105 (2009); Megan Stevenson, *Breaking Bad: Mechanisms of Social Influence and the Path to Criminality in Juvenile Jails*, 99 Rev. Econ. & Stat. 824 (2017); Anna Piil Damm & Cédric Gorinas, *Prison as a Criminal School: Peer Effects and Criminal Learning Behind Bars*, 63 J.L. & Econ. 149 (2020). For the argument that social interactions among incarcerated people are *not* criminogenic, see Heather M. Harris et al., *Do Cellmates Matter? A Causal Test of the Schools of Crime Hypothesis with Implications for Differential Association and Deterrence Theories*, 56 Criminology 87 (2018). For more on the impact of incarceration on social networks, see Jeffrey D. Morenoff & David J. Harding, *Incarceration, Prisoner Reentry, and Communities*, 40 Ann. Rev. Socio. 411 (2014).

15. Duff, *supra* note 7, at 4.

16. Patricio Domínguez & Steven Raphael, *The Role of the Cost-of-Crime Literature in Bridging the Gap Between Social Science Research and Policy Making*, 14 Criminology & Pub. Pol'y 589, 590 (2015) ("bang-per-buck"). On the bottom-up approach, see, for example, Madison Armstrong & Jennifer Carlson, *We've Spent Over a Decade Researching Guns in America. This Is What We Learned.*, N.Y. Times (Mar. 26, 2021), which collects studies showing "that surviving or being exposed to gun violence survival is associated with an increased risk of symptoms linked to PTSD (including anxiety and depression) in both urban and rural contexts; short-term decreases in reading ability, vocabulary and impulse control; unemployment and substance use; and even shifts in friendship formation — toward protection-seeking and avoidance."

17. Domínguez & Raphael, *supra* note 16, at 605 ("buy and sell victimization"); *id.* at 594-597 ("welfare of the wealthy"). For overviews of the competing methods, see *id.* at 604-625.

18. For examples of varying estimates of the costs of crime, see Leigh Linden & Jonah E. Rockoff, *Estimates of the Impact of Crime Risk on Property Values from Megan's Laws*, 98 Am. Econ. Rev. 1103, 1121 tbl.6 (2008) (using changes in housing prices following a registered sex offender's moving into a neighborhood to estimate that people would spend between $90,000 and $2.5 million to avoid sex-offense victimization); Aaron Chalfin, *Economic Costs of Crime*, in *The Encyclopedia of Crime and Punishment* 7-11 (Wesley G. Jennings ed., 2016) (noting that different studies place the statistical value of a single life between $0.7 million and $26.4 million, with some convergence on a range of $3 million to $8 million). For a collection of estimated costs of individual criminal events from different studies, see Chalfin, *supra*, at 8 tbl.1.

19. Anderson, *supra* note 12, at 876 tbl.4. For discussion of the human costs of crime for individuals and communities, see Thomas Abt, *Bleeding Out* (2019); Elliott Currie, *A Peculiar Indifference* (2020); Patrick Sharkey, *Uneasy Peace* (2018). For a quantitative study on the labor market effects of criminal victimization, see Anna Bindler & Nadine Ketel, *Scaring or Scarring? Labor Market Effects of Criminal Victimization*, 40 J. Labor Econ. 939 (2022).

20. Duff, *supra* note 7, at 4.

21. *CEA Perspectives*, *supra* note 8, at 5, 41. For more examples on the superior cost effectiveness of some noncarceral interventions, see John J. Donohue III & Peter Siegelman, *Allocating Resources Among Prisons and Social Programs in the Battle Against Crime*, 27 J. Legal Stud. 1 (1998). For further discussion of the distinction between cost-benefit analysis and cost-effectiveness analysis, see Domínguez & Raphael, *supra* note 17, at 597-598.

22. *The Collected Dialogues of Plato* 321 (Edith Hamilton & Huntington Cairns eds., 1963).

23. Jeremy Bentham, *Principles of Penal Law*, in 1 *The Works of Jeremy Bentham* 396, 402 (John Bowring ed., Russell & Russell 1962) (1843) [hereinafter Bentham, *Principles of Penal Law*]. For more on Bentham's account of deterrence, see Jeremy Bentham, *The Rationale of Punishment* 61 (James T. McHugh ed., Prometheus Books 2009) (1830).

24. Gary Becker, *Crime and Punishment: An Economic Approach*, 76 J. Pol. Econ. 169, 176 (1968). For a collection of seminal works applying rational choice theory to criminal law, see *Essays in the Economics of Crime and Punishment* (Gary S. Becker & William M. Landes eds., 1974).

25. Henry N. Butler et al., *Economic Analysis for Lawyers* 385 (3d ed. 2014).

26. Butler et al., *supra* note 25, at 385.

27. Butler et al., *supra* note 25, at 385.

28. On misapprehending odds of getting caught, see Aaron Chalfin & Justin McCrary, *Criminal Deterrence: A Review of the Literature*, 55 J. Econ. Literature 5, 10-12 (2017); Kenneth D. Tunnell, *Choosing Crime: Close Your Eyes and Take Your Chances*, 7 Just. Q. 673, 680-681 (1990). On discounting future pain of punishment, see Christine Jolls et al., *A Behavioral Approach to Law and Economics*, 50 Stan. L. Rev. 1471, 1538-1541 (1998). On expressive and emotional crimes, see William J. Chambliss, *Types of Deviance and the Effectiveness of Legal Sanctions*, 1967 Wisc. L. Rev. 703, 712.

29. Paul H. Robinson & John M. Darley, *The Role of Deterrence in the Formulation of Criminal Law Rules: At Its Worst When Doing Its Best*, 91 Geo. L.J. 949, 951 (2003) (emphasis removed). The concept of bounded rationality is no longer controversial in economic or criminological circles, though commentators continue to debate the extent to which it undermines the basic premise of rational choice theory. *See* Ronald V. Clarke & Derek B. Cornish, *Rational Choice*, in *Explaining Criminals and Crime: Essays in Contemporary Criminological Theory* 23 (Raymond Paternoster & Ronet Bachman eds., 2001).

30. Butler et al., *supra* note 25, at 385. The emphasis on opportunity costs in rational choice theory resonates with a theory in the field of criminology known (similarly) as *opportunity theory*. This theory posits that "[e]verybody could do at least some crime at some time" if given the opportunity. Marcus Felson, *Crime and Everyday Life* 11 (2d ed. 1998). For more on the theory, see Lawrence E. Cohen & Marcus Felson, *Social Change and Crime Rate Trends: A Routine Activity Approach*, 44 Am. Socio. Rev. 588 (1979). What explains crime, on this view, is the confluence of the right set of circumstances — in particular, a motivated offender, a vulnerable target, and the absence of a capable guardian, such as a friend or neighbor. One oft-replicated study, for example, found that young adults commit more crimes when they engage in more unstructured socializing, even when their peers are not generally prone to deviant behavior. *See* D. Wayne Osgood et al., *Routine Activities and Individual Deviant Behavior*, 61 Am. Socio. Rev. 635 (1996); Dana L. Haynie & D. Wayne Osgood, *Reconsidering Peers and Delinquency: How Do Peers Matter?*, 84 Soc. Forces 1109 (2005).

31. Butler et al., *supra* note 25, at 385.

32. Tommie Shelby, *Dark Ghettos* 205 (2016); Becker, *supra* note 24, at 176; Butler et al., *supra* note 25, at 385 ("region, rate of unemployment").

33. *The Collected Dialogues of Plato*, *supra* note 22, at 321 (emphasis added); Bentham, *Principles of Penal Law*, *supra* note 23, at 396.

34. For a study isolating a specific deterrence effect, see Benjamin Hansen, *Punishment and Deterrence: Evidence from Drunk Driving*, 105 Am. Econ. Rev. 1581, 1604 (2015). See the same source for discussion of potential mechanisms behind the effect, including that specific deterrence could be a function of "bounded rationality, learning due to incomplete information, or perhaps salience." See also Chalfin & McCrary, *supra* note 28, at 6, who describe specific deterrence "as a change in information or, perhaps more exotically, a change in

preferences themselves." On the interaction between specific deterrence and the criminogenic nature of incarceration, see Jennifer L. Doleac, *Encouraging Desistance from Crime*, 61 J. Econ. Literature 383 (2023).

35. Those interested in exploring the empirical literature assessing rational choice theory and the criminal law more generally might start with Chalfin & McCrary, *supra* note 28. For further reading, see *Deterrence, Choice, and Crime: Contemporary Perspectives* (Daniel S. Nagin et al. eds., 2018); Anthony N. Doob & Cheryl Marie Webster, *Sentence Severity and Crime: Accepting the Null Hypothesis*, 30 Crime & Just. 143 (2003); Steven N. Durlauf & Daniel S. Nagin, *Imprisonment and Crime: Can Both Be Reduced?*, 10 Criminology & Pub. Pol'y 13 (2011); Steven D. Levitt & Thomas J. Miles, *Empirical Study of Criminal Punishment*, in *Handbook of Law and Economics* 455 (A. Mitchell Polinsky & Steven Shavell eds., 2007); Daniel S. Nagin, *Deterrence: A Review of the Evidence by a Criminologist for Economists*, 5 Ann. Rev. Econ. 83 (2013); Travis C. Pratt et al., *The Empirical Status of Deterrence Theory: A Meta-Analysis*, in *Taking Stock: The Status of Criminological Theory* 367 (Francis T. Cullen et al. eds., 2006); Michael Tonry, *Learning from the Limitations of Deterrence Research*, 37 Crime & Just. 279 (2008).

36. Jane Jacobs, *The Death and Life of Great American Cities* 45 (Modern Library 2011) (1961).

37. Paul F. Cromwell et al., *Breaking and Entering: An Ethnographic Analysis of Burglary* 45-46 (1991).

38. Steven Mello, *More COPS, Less Crime*, 172 J. Pub. Econ. 174 (2019). For more evidence, see Sebastian Blesse & André Diegmann, *The Place-Based Effects of Police Stations on Crime: Evidence from Station Closures*, 207 J. Pub. Econ. 104605 (2022); Anthony A. Braga et al., *Hot Spots Policing and Crime Reduction: Update of an Ongoing Systematic Review and Meta-Analysis*, 15 J. Experimental Criminology 289 (2019); Aaron Chalfin et al., *Police Force Size and Civilian Race*, 4 Am. Econ. Rev.: Insights 139 (2022); William N. Evans & Emily G. Owens, *COPS and Crime*, 91 J. Pub. Econ. 181 (2007); Sarit Weisburd, *Police Presence, Rapid Response Rates, and Crime Prevention*, 103 Rev. Econ. & Stat. 280 (2021); Emily K. Weisburst, *Safety in Police Numbers: Evidence of Police Effectiveness from Federal COPS Grant Applications*, 21 Am. L. & Econ. Rev. 81 (2019).

39. On community monitors, see Robert Gonzalez & Sarah Komisarow, *Community Monitoring and Crime: Evidence from Chicago's Safe Passage Program*, 191 J. Pub. Econ. 104250 (2020); *see also* Daniel McMillen et al., *Do More Eyes on the Street Reduce Crime? Evidence from Chicago's Safe Passage Program*, 110 J. Urban Econ. 1 (2019). On outdoor lighting, see, for example, Jennifer L. Doleac & Nicholas J. Sanders, *Under the Cover of Darkness: How Ambient Light Influences Criminal Activity*, 97 Rev. Econ. & Stat. 1093 (2015), and for a review, see Brandon C. Welsh et al., *The Impact and Policy Relevance of Street Lighting for Crime Prevention: A Systematic Review Based on a Half-Century of Evaluation Research*, 21 Criminology & Pub. Pol'y 739 (2022). For an overview of the broader literature on the deterrent effects of apprehension risk, see Chalfin & McCrary, *supra* note 28, at 13-23. For a discussion of private security officers and their relationship to public policing, see Ben Grunwald, John Rappaport & Michael Berg, *Private Security and Public Police*, 21 J. Empirical Legal Stud. 428 (2024).

40. Beccaria, *supra* note 4, at 93; Chalfin & McCrary, *supra* note 28, at 32. The challenge of distinguishing deterrence from incapacitation (discussed later in this chapter, p. 87) is acute for researchers studying this question: Longer prison terms could reduce crime because rational actors are refraining from crime to avoid increased punishment *or* because people who would otherwise be committing crime are being incarcerated for longer stretches and are thus disabled from offending outside prison. Only evidence of the former dynamic would tend to support a deterrence-based rational choice theory of offending.

41. Cromwell et al., *supra* note 37, at 86-87. For additional studies on the effects of drastic punishments, see Franklin E. Zimring et al., *Punishment and Democracy: Three Strikes*

and You're Out in California 103-105 (2001); Eric Helland & Alexander Tabarrok, *Does Three Strikes Deter? A Nonparametric Estimation*, 42 J. Hum. Res. 309 (2007); Francesco Drago et al., *The Deterrent Effects of Prison: Evidence from a Natural Experiment*, 117 J. Pol. Econ. 257 (2009).

42. Chalfin & McCrary, *supra* note 28, at 27, 32 (emphasis added). For studies finding little evidence of deterrence when comparing people just above and below the age of majority, see, for example, Randi Hjalmarsson, *Crime and Expected Punishment: Changes in Perceptions at the Age of Criminal Majority*, 11 Am. L. & Econ. Rev. 209 (2009), and David S. Lee & Justin McCrary, *The Deterrence Effect of Prison: Dynamic Theory and Evidence*, in *Regression Discontinuity Designs: Theory and Applications* 73 (Mattias D. Cattaneo & Juan Carlos Escanciano eds., 2017). For a contrary finding in states with the largest jump in sanction severity at the age of criminal majority, see Steven D. Levitt, *Juvenile Crime and Punishment*, 106 J. Pol. Econ. 1156 (1998). On the failure of punishments to deter when people doubt their imposition, see, for example, Shona A. Morrison & Ian O'Donnell, *An Analysis of the Decision-Making Practices of Armed Robbers*, in *The Politics and Practice of Situational Crime Prevention* 160, 178-180 (Ross Homel ed., 1996).

43. Duff, *supra* note 7, at 5; *The Collected Dialogues of Plato*, *supra* note 22, at 1415; Jean-Jacques Rousseau, *The Social Contract*, in *The Greatest Works of Jean-Jacques Rousseau* (Barbara Foxley et al. trans., 2018). A seminal work on the rehabilitative ideal is Francis A. Allen, *Criminal Justice, Legal Values and the Rehabilitative Ideal*, 50 J. Crim. L. & Criminology 226 (1959).

44. Michael S. Moore, *Law and Psychiatry: Rethinking the Relationship* 234-235 (1984). For an example drawing a distinction between punishment and rehabilitation, see Herbert Morris, *Persons and Punishment*, 52 Monist 475, 480-485 (1968) (contrasting "a system of just punishment" with "a thoroughgoing system of treatment").

45. Joan Petersilia, *Beyond the Prison Bubble*, Nat'l Inst. of Just. J., Oct. 2011, at 26, 29-30; Mark W. Lipsey & Francis T. Cullen, *The Effectiveness of Correctional Rehabilitation: A Review of Systematic Reviews*, 3 Ann. Rev. L. & Soc. Sci. 297, 314 (2007). For an example of a meta-analysis of rehabilitative efforts involving education, see Robert Bozick et al., *Does Providing Inmates with Education Improve Postrelease Outcomes? A Meta-Analysis of Correctional Education Programs in the United States*, 14 J. Experimental Criminology 389 (2018), which finds a 28% decrease in recidivism for incarcerated persons who participated in correctional educational programs. For an empirical analysis isolating the causal effects of one rehabilitation program and pegging them at a three-month reduction in recidivism on the order of 25%, with effects growing over time, see Marcella Alsan et al., *"Something Works" In U.S. Jails: Misconduct and Recidivism Effects of the IGNITE Program*, NBER Working Paper 32282 (2024).

46. Petersilia, *supra* note 45, at 29; David Garland, *The Culture of Control* 8 (2001). For the full Martinson Report, see Robert Martinson, *What Works? Questions and Answers About Prison Reform*, 35 Pub. Interest 22, 25 (1974) (arguing that rehabilitative programs have "no appreciable effect on recidivism"). For an example of a contemporaneous critique of the Martinson Report, see Ted Palmer, *Martinson Revisited*, 12 J. Rsch. Crime & Delinq. 133 (1975). For Martinson's walkback of his claims in the Martinson Report, see Robert Martinson, *New Findings, New Views: A Note of Caution Regarding Sentencing Reform*, 7 Hofstra L. Rev. 243 (1979). On the reasons for declining support for rehabilitation, see Francis A. Allen, *The Decline of the Rehabilitative Ideal: Penal Policy and Social Purpose* (1981).

47. Franklin E. Zimring & Gordon Hawkins, *Incapacitation* v (1995) ("least complicated"); James Q. Wilson, *Thinking About Crime* 235 (1975); Ben Wattenberg, *Crime Solution—Lock 'em Up*, Wall St. J. (Dec. 17, 1993).

48. On the word "thug," see, for example, NPR, *The Racially Charged Meaning Behind The Word 'Thug'* (Apr. 30, 2015) (interviewing John McWhorter, who observes that the word "thug" has become "a nominally polite way of using the N-word").

49. Markus Dirk Dubber, *Recidivist Statutes as Arational Punishment*, 43 Buff. L. Rev. 689, 709 (1995) ("locus of crime"); Guyora Binder & Ben Notterman, *Penal Incapacitation: A Situationist Critique*, 54 Am. Crim. L. Rev. 1, 46 (2017).

50. Gifford, *supra* note 10, at 76, 77, 124-126 (cleaned up); Christopher Lewis, *The Paradox of Recidivism*, 70 Emory L.J. 1209, 1221 (2021). For a critique of the failure to count crime within prisons in analyses of recidivism, see Lewis, *supra*, at 1221 (measurements of incapacitation effects "almost always treat crime within prisons as non-existent"), and Shawn D. Bushway, *Incapacitation*, in 4 *Reforming Criminal Justice* 38 n.3 (Erika Luna ed., 2017) (noting that "most researchers assume" that incarceration produces less crime in prison than it prevents outside). For further discussion, see David Alan Sklansky, *A Pattern of Violence* 182 (2021), which observes that violence in jails and prisons "often seems tacitly accepted, if not actively encouraged."

51. For data on reentry rates, see Nathan James, Cong. Rsch. Serv., *Offender Reentry: Correctional Statistics, Reintegration into the Community, and Recidivism* 1 (2015) (reporting that "[s]ince 1990, an average of 590,400 inmates have been released annually from state and federal prisons"), and also Danielle Kaeble, Bureau Just. Stat., *Time Served in State Prison, 2016*, at 3 tbl.2 (2018) (reporting that forty percent of state prisoners serve less than one year in prison and that 99% serve less than 20). For a discussion of the effect aging has on criminal behavior, see Ilyana Kuziemko, *How Should Inmates Be Released from Prison? An Assessment of Parole Versus Fixed-Sentence Regimes*, 128 Q.J. Econ. 371, 379, 382 (2013), and Robert J. Sampson & John H. Laub, *Life-Course Desisters? Trajectories of Crime Among Delinquent Boys Followed to Age 70*, 41 Criminology 555, 565 (2004) (describing an age-crime curve that "peak[s] in adolescence followed by a less sharp decline through middle adulthood, with eventual disappearance in the sixties").

52. For more on replacement effects, see Isaac Ehrlich, *On the Usefulness of Controlling Individuals: An Economic Analysis of Rehabilitation, Incapacitation, and Deterrence*, 71 Am. Econ. Rev. 307 (2001).

53. Bushway, *supra* note 50, at 41, 51, 52. On the difficulty of measuring replacement effects, see *id.* at 40.

54. H.J. McCloskey, *A Non-Utilitarian Approach to Punishment*, 8 Inquiry 249, 255 (1965); *see also* Carol S. Steiker & Jordan M. Steiker, *Courting Death: The Supreme Court and Capital Punishment* 25 (2016) (observing that Kentucky "brought back public hanging for rape [in the 1920s] after a lynch mob sparked a riot in which five died and 17 were wounded in the mob's unsuccessful attempt to snatch a black [man accused of rape] from custody").

55. Duff, *supra* note 7, at 8.

56. Duff, *supra* note 7, at 10, 11 ("*intrinsic* wrong," "punish only those who have voluntarily broken the law"); J.L. Mackie, *Morality and the Retributive Emotions*, 1 Crim. Just. Ethics 3, 4 (1982) ("not guilty must not be punished"); H.L.A. Hart, *Punishment and Responsibility* 9 (1968).

57. *CEA Perspectives*, *supra* note 8, at 5, 52 (emphases added).

58. Bushway, *supra* note 50, at 47; *CEA Perspectives*, *supra* note 8, at 36 ("incarceration rates are high"); Rucker Johnson & Steven Raphael, *How Much Crime Reduction Does the Marginal Prisoner Buy?*, 55 J.L. & Econ. 275, 302-303 (2012)

59. *CEA Perspectives*, *supra* note 8, at 36.

60. Bentham, *Principles of Penal Law*, *supra* note 23, at 401.

61. Paul H. Robinson & John M. Darley, *The Role of Deterrence in the Formulation of Criminal Law Rules*, 91 Geo. L.J. 949, 951 (2003); J. Robert Lilly et al., *Criminological Theory: Context and Consequences* 359 (7th ed. 2019) ("crass and simplistic rational choice theory").

62. Émile Durkheim, *The Division of Labor in Society* 63 (W.D. Halls trans., 1984) (1893).

63. Erin I. Kelly & Göran Duus-Otterström, *Injustice and the Right to Punish*, Phil. Compass, Feb. 2019, at 1.

64. Dorothy Roberts, *Foreword: Abolition Constitutionalism*, 133 Harv. L. Rev. 1, 6-8, 11 (2019).

65. Máximo Langer, *Penal Abolitionism and Criminal Law Minimalism: Here and There, Now and Then*, 134 Harv. L. Rev. F. 42, 57 (2020) (noting that in Argentina in the 1990s, "penal abolitionism was a common theme in criminal law and criminology discussions," but that "to this day, prison abolitionism is not even mentioned in most if not all of the main American criminal law casebooks").

66. Allegra McLeod, *Prison Abolition and Grounded Justice*, 62 UCLA L. Rev. 1156, 1210 (2015); Derecka Purnell, *How I Became a Police Abolitionist*, Atlantic (July 6, 2020).

67. Victor Tadros, *Poverty and Criminal Responsibility*, 43 J. Value Inquiry 391, 393, 412-413 (2009).

68. Shelby, *supra* note 32, at 247. For example, abolitionist scholar Allegra McLeod writes that "an abolitionist ethic does not necessarily deny that in some instances there may be people so violent that they cannot be permitted to live among others." McLeod, *supra* note 66, at 1210. For more on an abolitionist account of violence itself, see Allegra McLeod, *An Abolitionist Critique of Violence*, 89 U. Chi. L. Rev. 525 (2022).

CHAPTER 3

1. R.A. Duff, *Blame, Moral Standing and the Legitimacy of the Criminal Trial*, 23 Ratio 123, 136 (2010).

2. See, for example, Victor Tadros, *Poverty and Criminal Responsibility*, 43 J. Value Inquiry 391, 412 (2009).

3. Bryan Stevenson, *Just Mercy* 290 (2014); Immanuel Kant, *The Philosophy of Law* 195 (William Hastie trans., Edinburgh, T.&T. Clark 1887) ("inborn personality"); Michael S. Moore, *The Moral Worth of Retribution*, in *Responsibility, Character, and the Emotions* 179, 215 (Ferdinand Schoeman ed., 1988) ("more of a person"); Erin I. Kelly, *The Limits of Blame: Rethinking Punishment and Responsibility* 168-169 (2018).

4. *See Diagnostic and Statistical Manual of Mental Disorders* 697 (5th ed. 2013) ("pedophilic disorder").

5. For a summary of medical research on how experiences of sexual abuse as a child relate to the chance of an individual developing pedophilic disorder in what is known as the "victim-to-abuser cycle" or "abused-abusers phenomenon," as well as potential theories to explain this cycle, see Ryan C.W. Hall & Richard C.W. Hall, *A Profile of Pedophilia: Definition, Characteristics of Offenders, Recidivism, Treatment Outcomes, and Forensic Issues*, 82 Mayo Clinic Proc. 457, 464 (2007). For an example of empirical studies that have documented this cycle, see Christopher Bagley et al., *Victim to Abuser: Mental Health and Behavioral Sequels of Child Sexual Abuse in a Community Survey of Young Adult Males*, 18 Child Abuse & Neglect 683 (1994).

6. Gary Becker, *Crime and Punishment: An Economic Approach*, 76 J. Pol. Econ. 169, 176 (1968).

7. Travis C. Pratt et al., *Key Ideas in Criminology and Criminal Justice* 46 (2011) ("stop looking"); J. Robert Lilly et al., *Criminological Theory: Context and Consequence* 360 (7th ed. 2019) ("larger cultural and structural context").

8. Rachel Barkow, *Promise or Peril? The Political Path of Prison Abolition in America*, 58 Wake Forest L. Rev. 245, 273-274 (2023).

9. Pratt et al., *supra* note 7, at 42.

10. For the original study, see Clifford R. Shaw & Henry D. McKay, *Juvenile Delinquency and Urban Areas* (rev. ed. 1969) (1942). More recently, one quasi-experimental study found that moving children out of disadvantaged neighborhoods leads them to commit fewer violent offenses during young adulthood. The study examined public-housing demolitions in Chicago, which relocated some low-income households to less-disadvantaged neighborhoods. Compared to children who lived in nearby public housing that was not demolished, those who moved experienced fewer violent crime arrests. *See* Eric Chyn, *Moved to Opportunity: The Long-Run Effect of Public Housing Demolition on Children*, 108 Am. Econ. Rev. 3028 (2018). For examples of similar findings in an earlier line of research based on a voluntary, voucher-based relocation program called Moving to Opportunity, see Lawrence F. Katz et al., *Moving to Opportunity in Boston: Early Results of a Randomized Mobility Experiment*, 116 Q.J. Econ. 607 (2001); Jeffrey R. Kling et al., *Neighborhood Effects on Crime for Female and Male Youth: Evidence from a Randomized Housing Voucher Experiment*, 120 Q.J. Econ. 87 (2005); Jens Ludwig et al., *Urban Poverty and Juvenile Crime: Evidence from a Randomized Housing-Mobility Experiment*, 116 Q.J. Econ. 655 (2001); Matthew Sciandra et al., *Long-Term Effects of the Moving to Opportunity Residential Mobility Experiment on Crime and Delinquency*, 9 J. Experimental Criminology 451 (2013).

11. Robert J. Sampson et al., *Neighborhoods and Violent Crime: A Multilevel Study of Collective Efficacy*, 277 Science 918, 918 (1997); Ruth Rosner Kornhauser, *Social Sources of Delinquency: An Appraisal of Analytical Models* 77-78 (1978). For a similar account to Kornhauser's, see Robert J. Sampson & Dawn Jeglum Bartusch, *Legal Cynicism and (Subcultural?) Tolerance of Deviance: The Neighborhood Context of Racial Differences*, 32 Law & Soc'y Rev. 777 (1998), which develops a related concept of "legal cynicism" that can arise in marginalized communities.

12. On how nonprofit organizations reduce violent crime, see Patrick Sharkey et al., *Community and the Crime Decline: The Causal Effect of Local Nonprofits on Violent Crime*, 82 Am. Socio. Rev. 1214 (2017). On religious institutions, see Elizabeth P. Kelly et al., *Religion, Delinquency, and Drug Use: A Meta-Analysis*, 40 Crim. Just. Rev. 505 (2015). And on the Great Migration, see Bryan A. Stuart & Evan J. Taylor, *The Effect of Social Connectedness on Crime: Evidence from the Great Migration*, 103 Rev. Econ. & Stat. 18 (2021).

On empirical support for social disorganization theory and the importance of collective efficacy more generally, see Lilly et al., *supra* note 7, at 42-44; Travis C. Pratt & Francis T. Cullen, *Assessing Macro-Level Predictors and Theories of Crime: A Meta-Analysis*, 32 Crime & Just. 373 (2005); Robert J. Sampson & W. Byron Groves, *Community Structure and Crime: Testing Social-Disorganization Theory*, 94 Am. J. Socio. 774 (1989); Barbara D. Warner, *The Role of Attenuated Culture in Social Disorganization Theory*, 41 Criminology 73, 75 (2003).

13. Elijah Anderson, *Code of the Street: Decency, Violence, and the Moral Life of the Inner City* 136 (1999). For background on how deviant behavior is learned from and reinforced by interactions with deviant actors, typically peers, see Ronald L. Akers, *Deviant Behavior: A Social Learning Approach* (1973). For the seminal version of the theory, called *differential association*, see Edwin H. Sutherland, *Principles of Criminology* 6-8 (4th ed. 1947). For a meta-analysis of 133 studies supporting the finding that an individual's number of delinquent friends strongly predicts criminal involvement, see Travis C. Pratt et al., *The Empirical Status of Social Learning Theory: A Meta-Analysis*, 27 Just. Q. 765 (2010). For evidence that social learning among individuals can increase total deviance, see Stephen B. Billings et al., *Partners in Crime*, 11 Am. Econ. J.: Applied Econ. 126, 126 (2019) (concentrating "disadvantaged youth together in the same environment leads to more total crime"); David J. Deming, *Better*

Schools, Less Crime?, 126 Q.J. Econ. 2063 (2011) (similar). Similarly, a natural experiment studying the displacement of people on parole following Hurricane Katrina found that "neighborhoods inundated with formerly incarcerated individuals [may] become characterized by the contagious spread of criminogenic influences" and that "cynicism and distrust of the law may spread through social networks." David S. Kirk, *A Natural Experiment of the Consequences of Concentrating Former Prisoners in the Same Neighborhoods*, 112 Proc. Nat'l Acad. Sci. 6943, 6948 (2015).

Note that proving causation in this context is challenging. Critics argue that, "rather than delinquent friends causing wayward behavior, this really is a case of 'birds of a feather flocking together' — of delinquent kids hanging around with one another because they share the common trait of being delinquent." Lilly et al., *supra* note 7, at 56. For examples of how economists have made strides toward proving the causal nature of "peer effects," see Patrick Bayer et al., *Building Criminal Capital Behind Bars: Peer Effects in Juvenile Corrections*, 124 Q.J. Econ. 105 (2009); Stephen B. Billings & Kevin T. Schnepel, *Hanging Out with the Usual Suspects: Neighborhood Peer Effects and Recidivism*, 57 J. Hum. Res. 1758 (2022); Lucia Corno, *Homelessness and Crime: Do Your Friends Matter?*, 127 Econ. J. 959, 992 (2015); Anna Piil Damm & Christian Dustmann, *Does Growing Up in a High Crime Neighborhood Affect Youth Criminal Behavior?*, 104 Am. Econ. Rev. 1806 (2014); Anna Piil Damm & Cédric Gorinas, *Prison as a Criminal School: Peer Effects and Criminal Learning Behind Bars*, 63 J.L. & Econ. 149 (2020). For a contrary finding, see Heather M. Harris et al., *Do Cellmates Matter? A Causal Test of the Schools of Crime Hypothesis with Implications for Differential Association and Deterrence Theories*, 56 Criminology 87 (2018). Studies are often unable to identify the precise mechanism behind peer effects, however — it could be social learning, but it could also be things like gaining new skills or connections to criminal opportunities from delinquent friends. A rare exception is Megan Stevenson, *Breaking Bad: Mechanisms of Social Influence and the Path to Criminality in Juvenile Jails*, 99 Rev. Econ. & Stat. 824 (2017)

14. Travis Hirschi, *Causes of Delinquency* 19 (1969); Barbara J. Costello & John H. Laub, *Social Control Theory: The Legacy of Travis Hirschi's* Causes of Delinquency, 3 Ann. Rev. Criminology 21, 25 (2020) ("something to lose").

15. Pratt et al., *supra* note 7, at 49 ("emotional states"). The canonical account of this general strain theory is Robert Agnew, *Foundation for a General Strain Theory of Crime and Delinquency*, 30 Criminology 47 (1992).

16. Robert Agnew, *A General Strain Theory of Community Differences in Crime Rates*, 36 J. Rsch. Crime & Delinq. 123, 126 (1999). For more on the conditions in which maladaptive coping is likely, see Agnew, *supra* note 15, at 72-73; Sherod Thaxton & Robert Agnew, *When Criminal Coping Is Likely: An Examination of Conditioning Effects in General Strain Theory*, 34 J. Quantitative Criminology 887 (2018). For studies demonstrating the empirical foundations for general strain theory, see the review at Lilly et al., *supra* note 7, at 72-75.

17. Richard H. McAdams, *The Economic Costs of Inequality*, 2010 U. Chi. Legal F. 23, 37; Morgan Kelly, *Inequality and Crime*, 82 Rev. Econ. & Stat. 530, 530 (2000). For a similar take, see Daniel L. Hicks & Joan Hamory Hicks, *Jealous of the Joneses: Conspicuous Consumption, Inequality, and Crime*, 66 Oxford Econ. Papers 1090 (2014).

18. Bruce A. Jacobs & Richard Wright, *Stick-Up, Street Culture, and Offender Motivation*, 37 Criminology 149, 158 (1999).

19. On the impact of leaving school during a recession, see Brian Bell et al., *Crime Scars: Recessions and the Making of Career Criminals*, 100 Rev. Econ. & Stat. 392 (2018). On labor market conditions for prison release, see Kevin T. Schnepel, *Good Jobs and Recidivism*, 128 Econ. J. 44 (2016); Crystal S. Yang, *Local Labor Markets and Criminal Recidivism*, 147 J. Pub. Econ. 16 (2017). For more on the intersection of labor market conditions and recidivism, see Roberto Galbiati et al., *Jobs, News and Reoffending After Incarceration*, 131 Econ. J. 247

(2021) (increased media coverage of job opportunities at the time of prison release reduces recidivism even further).

On job loss, see Diogo G.C. Britto et al., *Effect of Job Loss and Unemployment Insurance on Crime in Brazil*, 90 Econometrica 1393 (2022) (job loss increases violent and especially property crime and spills over to cohabiting sons); Gaura Khanna et al., *Job Loss, Credit, and Crime in Colombia*, 3 Am. Econ. Rev.: Insights 97 (2021) (job loss increases violent and especially property crime for displaced worker and family members); Mari Rege et al., *Job Displacement and Crime: Evidence from Norwegian Register Data*, 61 Labour Econ. 101761 (2019) (job loss increases violent and especially property crime); Evan K. Rose, *The Effects of Job Loss on Crime: Evidence from Administrative Data* (working paper) (job loss increases property crime and domestic violence).

On the minimum wage and recidivism, see Amanda Y. Agan & Michael D. Makowsky, *The Minimum Wage, EITC, and Criminal Recidivism*, 58 J. Hum. Res. 1712 (2023). For more on how higher wages and lower unemployment can both reduce crime, see Eric D. Gould et al., *Crime Rates and Local Labor Market Opportunities in the United States: 1979–1997*, 84 Rev. Econ. & Stat. 45 (2002); Jeff Grogger, *Market Wages and Youth Crime*, 16 J. Labor Econ. 756 (1998); Stephen Machin & Costas Meghir, *Crime and Economic Incentives*, 39 J. Hum. Res. 958 (2004). For a contrary take, finding that minimum-wage increases can increase property crime, possibly by inducing job loss, see Zachary S. Fone et al., *The Unintended Effects of Minimum Wage Increases on Crime*, 219 J. Pub. Econ. 104780 (2023).

20. For evidence on the effects of public assistance on crime, see Britto et al., *supra* note 19; Jillian B. Carr & Analisa Packham, *SNAP Benefits and Crime: Evidence from Changing Disbursement Schedules*, 101 Rev. Econ. & Stat. 310 (2019); Manasi Deshpande & Michael Mueller-Smith, *Does Welfare Prevent Crime? The Criminal Justice Outcomes of Youth Removed from SSI*, 137 Q.J. Econ. 1 (2022); Price V. Fishback et al., *Striking at the Roots of Crime: The Impact of Welfare Spending on Crime During the Great Depression*, 53 J.L. & Econ. 715 (2010); C. Fritz Foley, *Welfare Payments and Crime*, 93 Rev. Econ. & Stat. 97 (2011); Qiwei He & Scott Barkowski, *The Effect of Health Insurance on Crime: Evidence from the Affordable Care Act Medicaid Expansion*, 29 Health Econ. 261 (2020); Caroline Palmer et al., *Does Emergency Financial Assistance Reduce Crime?*, 169 J. Pub. Econ. 34 (2019); Cody Tuttle, *Snapping Back: Food Stamp Bans and Criminal Recidivism*, 11 Am. Econ. J.: Econ. Pol'y 301 (2019); Jacob Vogler, *Access to Healthcare and Criminal Behavior: Evidence from the ACA Medicaid Expansions*, 39 J. Pol'y Analysis & Mgmt. 1166 (2020); Crystal S. Yang, *Does Public Assistance Reduce Recidivism?*, 107 Am. Econ. Rev.: Papers & Proc. 551 (2017).

21. On early childhood education, see John Anders et al., *The Effect of Early Childhood Education on Adult Criminality: Evidence from the 1960s Through 1990s*, 15 Am. Econ. J.: Econ. Pol'y 37 (2023). For more, see Pedro Carneiro & Rita Ginja, *Long-Term Impacts of Compensatory Preschool on Health and Behavior: Evidence from Head Start*, 6 Am. Econ. J.: Econ. Pol'y 135 (2014). On educational attainment, see Lance Lochner & Enrico Moretti, *The Effect of Education on Crime: Evidence from Prison Inmates, Arrests, and Self-Reports*, 94 Am. Econ. Rev. 155 (2004). See also Randi Hjalmarsson et al., *The Effect of Education on Criminal Convictions and Incarceration: Causal Evidence from Micro-Data*, 125 Econ. J. 1290 (2015); Stephen Machin et al., *The Crime-Reducing Effects of Education*, 121 Econ. J. 463 (2011). On school and teacher quality, see Julie Berry Cullen et al., *The Effect of School Choice on Participants: Evidence from Randomized Lotteries*, 74 Econometrica 1191 (2006); Evan K. Rose et al., *The Effects of Teacher Quality on Adult Criminal Justice Contact*, NBER Working Paper 30274 (2022). For more on school quality, see Deming, *supra* note 13; E. Jason Baron et al., *Public School Funding, School Quality, and Adult Crime*, NBER Working Paper 29855 (2022). On intergenerational effects, see Aaron Chalfin & Monica Deza, *The Intergenerational Effects of Education on Delinquency*, 159 J. Econ. Behav. & Org. 553 (2019); Andrew Barr & Chloe R. Gibbs, *Breaking the Cycle? Intergenerational Effects of an Anti-Poverty Program in Early Childhood*, 130 J. Pol. Econ. 3253

(2022). For background on education and crime, see Lance Lochner, *Education and Crime*, in *The Economics of Education* 109 (Steve Bradley & Colin Green eds., 2d ed. 2020).

22. On the contemporaneous effects of school attendance, which can either reduce or increase crime, see D. Mark Anderson, *In School and Out of Trouble? The Minimum Dropout Age and Juvenile Crime*, 96 Rev. Econ. & Stat. 318 (2014); Billings et al., *supra* note 13; Brian A. Jacob & Lars Lefgren, *Are Idle Hands the Devil's Workshop? Incapacitation, Concentration, and Juvenile Crime*, 93 Am. Econ. Rev. 1560 (2003); Jeremy Luallen, *School's Out . . . Forever: A Study of Juvenile Crime, At-Risk Youths and Teacher Strikes*, 59 J. Urb. Econ. 75 (2006).

23. Jane Jacobs, *The Death and Life of Great American Cities* 54 (1961) ("eyes upon the street"). For a review of the theory and evidence, see John MacDonald, *Community Design and Crime: The Impact of Housing and the Built Environment*, 44 Crime & Just. 333 (2015).

24. The lighting experiment is Aaron Chalfin et al., *Reducing Crime Through Environmental Design: Evidence from a Randomized Experiment of Street Lighting in New York City*, 38 J. Quantitative Criminology 127 (2022). For a review of evidence on lighting, see Brandon C. Welsh et al., *The Impact and Policy Relevance of Street Lighting for Crime Prevention: A Systematic Review Based on a Half-Century of Evaluation Research*, 21 Criminology & Pub. Pol'y 739 (2022). The "cleaning and greening" experiment is Charles C. Branas et al., *Citywide Cluster Randomized Trial to Restore Blighted Vacant Land and Its Effects on Violence, Crime, and Fear*, 115 Proc. Nat'l Acad. Sci. 2946, 2947 (2018). For more on the impact of "cleaning and greening" on crime, see Charles C. Branas et al., *Urban Blight Remediation as a Cost-Beneficial Solution to Firearm Violence*, 106 Am. J. Pub. Health 2158 (2016); Jesse Cui et al., *The Effects of Vacant Lot Greening and the Impact of Land Use and Business Presence on Crime*, 49 Env't & Plan. B: Urb. Analytics & City Sci. 1147 (2022); Michelle C. Kondo et al., *The Association Between Urban Trees and Crime: Evidence from the Spread of the Emerald Ash Borer in Cincinnati*, 157 Landscape & Urb. Plan. 193 (2017); Jesenia M. Pizarro et al., *Community-Driven Disorder Reduction: Crime Prevention Through a Clean and Green Initiative in a Legacy City*, 57 Urb. Stud. 2956 (2020); Austin Troy et al., *The Relationship Between Residential Yard Management and Neighborhood Crime: An Analysis from Baltimore City and County*, 147 Landscape & Urb. Plan. 78 (2016). For evidence that residential vacancy increases crime, see Lin Cui & Randall Walsh, *Foreclosure, Vacancy and Crime*, 87 J. Urb. Econ. 72 (2015); Ingrid G. Ellen et al., *Do Foreclosures Cause Crime?*, 74 J. Urb. Econ. 59 (2013); Lauren C. Porter et al., *Understanding the Criminogenic Properties of Vacant Housing: A Mixed Methods Approach*, 56 J. Rsch. Crime & Delinq. 378 (2019).

25. Jeffrey B. Bingenheimer et al., *Firearm Violence Exposure and Serious Violent Behavior*, 308 Science 1323, 1326 (2005) ("approximately doubles"); Nancy G. Guerra et al., *Community Violence Exposure, Social Cognition, and Aggression Among Urban Elementary School Children*, 74 Child Dev. 1561 (2003) (social learning); Kathryn C. Monaghan et al., *The Effects of Violence Exposure on the Development of Impulse Control and Future Orientation Across Adolescence and Early Adulthood: Time-Specific and Generalized Effects in a Sample of Juvenile Offenders*, 27 Dev. & Psychopathology 1267 (2015) (future orientation). For further studies on the criminogenic nature of exposure to violence see, for example, Tina D. Wall Myers et al., *Understanding the Link Between Exposure to Violence and Aggression in Justice-Involved Adolescents*, 30 Dev. & Psychopathology 593 (2018).

26. Adrian Raine, *The Criminal Mind*, Wall St. J. (Apr. 26, 2013). For more on biosocial criminology and race, see Julien Larregue & Oliver Rollins, *Biosocial Criminology and the Mismeasure of Race*, 42 Ethnic & Racial Stud. 1990 (2018).

27. Pratt et al., *supra* note 7, at 27 ("physical markers"). "At the sight of that skull," Lombroso later related, "I seemed to see all at once, standing out clearly illumined as in a vast plain under a flaming sky, the problem of the nature of the criminal, who reproduces in civilized times characteristics, not only of primitive savages, but of still lower [animals] as far

back as the carnivora." Gina Lombroso Ferrero, *Criminal Man: According to the Classification of Cesare Lombroso* 6-7 (1911). For more background on Cesare Lombroso, see Paolo Mazzarello, *Cesare Lombroso: An Anthropologist Between Evolution and Degeneration,* 26 Functional Neurology 97, 97-101 (2011).

28. Pratt et al., *supra* note 7, at 30 ("illustrations," "flamboyant"); A. Conan Doyle, *Memoirs of Sherlock Holmes* 242 (1894). For a similar example, see Émile Zola, *The Beast Within* 346-347, 352 (Roger Whitehouse trans., 2007) (1890), in which a person who commits a homicide is described as having a "jaw . . . pushed forward" and "a savage grimace that made him appear almost deformed," evidence, the author writes, of his "inherited streak of violence . . . the same killer instinct that in the primeval forests drove one animal to slay another."

29. Pratt et al., *supra* note 7, at 31-32.

30. Ronald L. Akers et al., *Criminological Theories: Introduction, Evaluation, and Application* 47-48 (8th ed. 2021). The English study is Charles Goring, *The English Convict: A Statistical Study* (1913).

31. For the Hooton quotations, see 1 Earnest A. Hooton, *Crime and the Man* 329 (1939); Earnest A. Hooton, *Plain Statements About Race,* 83 Science 511, 513 (1936). For similar work by prominent sociologists of the time, see William H. Sheldon, *Varieties of Delinquent Youth: An Introduction to Constitutional Psychiatry* (1949); Sheldon Glueck & Eleanor Glueck, *Unraveling Juvenile Delinquency* (1950).

32. Akers et al., *supra* note 30, at 49; Pratt et al., *supra* note 7, at 34-35 ("efforts to incorporate," "breed out"); Paolo Mazzarello, *Lombroso and Tolstoy: An Anthropologists' Unwitting Gift to Literature,* 409 Nature 983, 983 (2001) ("born lambs"). On the invalidity of Hooton's work and related scholarship, see Ernest Sutherland, *Critique of Sheldon's* Varieties of Delinquent Youth, 16 Am. Socio. Rev. 10 (1951). For more on eugenics, see *Buck v. Bell,* 274 U.S. 200, 207 (1927) (upholding lawfulness of forced sterilization, with the ignominious assertion that "[t]hree generations of imbeciles are enough"); Adam Cohen, *Imbeciles: The Supreme Court, American Eugenics and the Sterilization of Carrie Buck* (2016). On harsh punishments for "born criminals," see Mary Gibson & Nicole Hahn Rafter, *Introduction,* in Cesare Lombroso, *Criminal Man* 18-19 (Mary Gibson & Nicole Hahn Rafter trans., 2006) (1876).

33. For examples of social scientists viewing Lombroso's work as discredited and wrong, see Akers et al., *supra* note 30, at 49-50; Pratt et al., *supra* note 7, at 24.

34. Nicole Rafter, *Shots in the Dark: Crime Films and Society* 64-65 (2d ed. 2006) ("criminal by nature"); Gibson & Rafter, *supra* note 32, at 17-18 ("injected racism"). On modern lay associations between physical appearance and deviance, see for example Heather D. Flowe, *Do Characteristics of Faces That Convey Trustworthiness and Dominance Underlie Perceptions of Criminality?,* 7 PLoS ONE e37253 (2012) (collecting sources finding that "[p]eople who commit crime are thought to have long or shaggy dark hair, tattoos, beady eyes, pock marks and scars"). On skin tones and Afrocentric facial features, see Ryan D. King & Brian D. Johnson, *A Punishing Look: Skin Tone and Afrocentric Features in the Halls of Justice,* 122 Am. J. Socio. 90 (2016).

35. Randall Kennedy, *Race, Crime, and the Law* 13 (1997).

36. Khalil Gibran Muhammad, *The Condemnation of Blackness* 3-4, 51 (2011); Charles Richmond Henderson, *Introduction to the Study of the Dependent, Defective, and Delinquent Classes and of Their Social Treatment* 246-247 (2d ed. rev. 1906) ("racial inheritance"). For Hoffman's work, see Frederick L. Hoffman, *Race Traits and Tendencies of the American Negro* (1896).

37. Muhammad, *supra* note 36, at 23 ("slowly recognized"); 1 Gunnar Myrdal, *An American Dilemma: The Negro Problem and Modern Democracy* 541 (1944).

38. Lilly et al., *supra* note 7, at 328 ("early 1990s"). For examples of social scientists promoting theories of criminality grounded in supposed racial differences in intelligence, see, for example, James Q. Wilson & Richard J. Herrnstein, *Crime and Human Nature* (1985); Richard J. Herrnstein & Charles Murray, *The Bell Curve: Intelligence and Class Structure in American Life* (1994); Robert A. Gordon, *SES Versus IQ in the Race-IQ-Delinquency Model*, 7 Int'l J. Socio. & Soc. Pol'y 30, 30 (1987).

39. Francis T. Cullen et al., *Crime and the Bell Curve: Lessons from Intelligent Criminology*, 43 Crime & Delinq. 387, 388 (1997); Robert J. Sampson et al., *Social Anatomy of Racial and Ethnic Disparities in Violence*, 95 Am. J. Pub. Health 224 (2005) [hereinafter Sampson et al., *Social Anatomy*].

40. Paul Butler, *Chokehold: Policing Black Men* 120-124 (2017) [hereinafter Butler, *Chokehold*].

41. Raine, *supra* note 26.

42. Raine, *supra* note 26 ("mounting evidence"); Lilly et al., *supra* note 7, at 394 ("rising popularity").

43. Andrea L. Glenn & Adrian Raine, *Neurocriminology: Implications for the Punishment, Prediction, and Prevention of Criminal Behaviour*, 15 Nature Revs.: Neuroscience 54, 54-56 (2014) ("Estimates of the variance that is attributable to genetics vary, but several meta-analyses place the level at between 40-60%.").

44. Glenn & Raine, *supra* note 43, at 55 (discussing lead studies). On the lasting effect of childhood stress on the body's hormonal stress-response system, see Stephanie H.M. van Goozen, *The Evidence for a Neurobiological Model of Childhood Antisocial Behavior*, 133 Psych. Bull. 149, 153-154 (2007).

45. Lilly et al., *supra* note 7, at 288-289.

46. Glenn & Raine, *supra* note 43, at 57 (emphasis added) ("multiple complex psychological processes"); Lilly et al., *supra* note 7, at 288-289 ("different individuals"). On buffering, see for example Avshalom Caspi et al., *Role of Genotype in the Cycle of Violence in Maltreated Children*, 297 Science 851, 851 (2002) (finding that "genotypes can moderate children's sensitivity to environmental insults" such as maltreatment).

47. Robert J. Sampson & John H. Laub, *Life-Course Desisters? Trajectories of Crime Among Delinquent Boys Followed to Age 70*, 41 Criminology 555, 565 (2004) ("peak"); Travis Hirschi & Michael Gottfredson, *Age and the Explanation of Crime*, 89 Am. J. Socio. 552, 552 (1983) ("brute facts"); Alfred Blumstein & Richard Rosenfeld, *Factors Contributing to U.S. Crime Trends*, in *Understanding Crime Trends: Workshop Report* 15 (2008) (baby boom). Interestingly, recent crime data suggests that the age-crime curve in the U.S. may be flattening — that "more people are now being arrested at later ages." Rachael Bedard et al., *Elderly, Detained, and Justice-Involved: The Most Incarcerated Generation*, 25 CUNY L. Rev. 161, 171 (2022). This shift may be attributable largely to members of the birth cohort that reached adolescence in the 1980s and 90s, during a period of high crime and rapidly rising incarceration, who have had trouble stabilizing ever since. *See id.* at 164-165.

48. *See* Emily Buss, *Kids Are Not So Different: The Path from Juvenile Exceptionalism to Prison Abolition*, 89 U. Chi. L. Rev. 843 (2022) (collecting evidence and discussing legal implications); *id.* at 845 (persistence of psychosocial immaturity). For more on age and crime, see Michael Rocque et al., *Age and Crime*, in *The Encyclopedia of Crime and Punishment* (Wesley G. Jennings ed., 2016).

49. *See* Rachel E. Morgan & Alexandra Thompson, Bureau of Just. Stat., *Criminal Victimization, 2020 — Supplemental Statistical Tables* 6 (2022) (4-1 male-female violent crime ratio); Emma E. Fridel & James Alan Fox, *Gender Differences in Patterns and Trends in U.S. Homicide, 1976–2017*, 6 Violence & Gender 27, 29 (2019) (10-1 ratio for homicides).

50. On biosocial theories of sex, gender, and crime, see Olivia Choy et al., *Explaining the Gender Gap in Crime: The Role of Heart Rate*, 55 Criminology 465, 466-476 (2017) (heart rate); Jill Portnoy et al., *Biological Perspectives on Sex Differences in Crime and Antisocial Behavior*, in *The Oxford Handbook of Gender, Sex, and Crime* 260, 272-273 (Rosemary Gartner & Bill McCarthy eds., 2014) (heart rate and testosterone); Raymond H. Baillargeon et al., *Gender Differences in Physical Aggression: A Prospective Population-Based Survey of Children Before and After 2 Years of Age*, 43 Dev. Psych. 13 (2007) (infancy).

51. For Lombroso's evolutionary perspective, see Cesare Lombroso & Gugliemo Ferrero, *Criminal Woman, the Prostitute, and the Normal Woman* 109-134 (Nicole Hahn Rafter & Mary Gibson trans., Duke Univ. Press 2004) (1893). On feminism's possible implications for criminology, see Kathleen Daly & Meda Chesney-Lind, *Feminism and Criminology*, 5 Just. Q. 497 (1988). For the prediction that greater equality would lead to convergence of offending between men and women, see Freda Adler, *Sisters in Crime* (1975); Rita James Simon, *Women and Crime* (1975). For examples of work demonstrating gender differences in pathways to offending, including intimate partner violence, see Robbin S. Ogle et al., *A Theory of Homicidal Behavior Among Women*, 33 Criminology 173 (1995); Kathleen Daly, *Women's Pathways to Felony Court: Feminist Theories of Lawbreaking and Problems of Representation*, 2 S. Cal. Rev. L. & Women's Stud. 11 (1992). For calls for a gendered theory of crime, see Darrell Steffensmeier & Emilie Allan, *Gender and Crime: Toward a Gendered Theory of Female Offending*, 22 Ann. Rev. Socio. 459 (1996); Jennifer Schwartz & Darrell Steffensmeier, *Gendered Opportunities and Risk Preferences for Offending Across the Life Course*, 2 J. Dev. & Life-Course Criminology 126 (2016). Debate over the need for, and content of, such gendered theories continues. For example, see Leah E. Daigle et al., *Gender Differences in the Predictors of Juvenile Delinquency: Assessing the Generality-Specificity Debate*, 5 Youth Violence & Juv. Just. 254 (2007). Readers interested in learning more may consult Lilly et al., *supra* note 7, at 233-271; Jody Miller & Christopher W. Mullins, *The Status of Feminist Theories of Criminology*, in *Taking Stock: The Status of Criminological Theory* 217 (Francis T. Cullen et al. eds., 2008); Sisters in Crime *Revisited: Bringing Gender into Criminology* (Francis T. Cullen et al. eds., 2015).

52. *See* Jessica W. Reyes, *Environmental Policy as Social Policy? The Impact of Childhood Lead Exposure on Crime*, 7 B.E. J. Econ. Analysis & Pol'y 1 (2007) (crime drop). For examples of research on lead exposure and crime more generally, see Jacqueline MacDonald Gibson et al., *Early Life Lead Exposure from Private Well Water Increases Juvenile Delinquency Risk Among US Teens*, 119 Proc. Nat'l Acad. Sci. e2110694119 (2022); Hans Grönqvist et al., *Understanding How Low Levels of Early Lead Exposure Affect Children's Life Trajectories*, 128 J. Pol. Econ. 3376 (2020). For an example of research on air pollution, see Evan Herrnstadt et al., *Air Pollution and Criminal Activity: Microgeographic Evidence from Chicago*, 13 Am. Econ. J.: Applied Econ. 70 (2021).

53. *See* Glenn & Raine, *supra* note 43, at 54-55 (fetal and infant development); Terrie E. Moffitt, *Adolescence-Limited and Life-Course-Persistent Antisocial Behavior: A Developmental Taxonomy*, 100 Psych. Rev. 674, 694-695 (1993) (individuals who never "age out").

54. Michael R. Gottfredson & Travis Hirschi, *A General Theory of Crime* 177 (1990) ("pursue short-term gratification"). For an overview of the literature on self-control theory, see Callie H. Burt, *Self-Control and Crime: Beyond Gottfredson & Hirschi's Theory*, 3 Ann. Rev. Criminology 43 (2020). On the importance of early childhood in the formation of "non-cognitive" skills such as self-control, see James J. Heckman, *Skill Formation and the Economics of Investing in Disadvantaged Children*, 312 Science 1900, 1900 (2006). On low socioeconomic status impacting prefrontal brain function, see Mark M. Kishiyama et al., *Socioeconomic Disparities Affect Prefrontal Function in Children*, 21 J. Cognitive Neurosci. 1106 (2009), and also Michael Rocque et al., *The Role of the Brain in Urban Violent Offending: Integrating Biology with Structural Theories of "The Streets,"* 28 Crim. Just. Stud. 84, 89-93 (2015). For a more general analysis, see Olivia Choy et al., *The Mediating Role of Heart Rate on the Social Adversity-Antisocial*

Behavior Relationship: A Social Neurocriminology Perspective, 52 J. Rsch. Crime & Delinq. 303, 320 (2015), which posits and provides evidence of adverse "social influences that sculpt biological functions in a way to shape antisocial and criminal behavior." On the effects of exposure to violence on self-control, see Monaghan et al., *supra* note 25; Patrick Sharkey et al., *The Effect of Local Violence on Children's Attention and Impulse Control*, 102 Am. J. Pub. Health 2287 (2012).

55. *See* Terrie E. Moffitt et al., *A Gradient of Childhood Self-Control Predicts Health, Wealth, and Public Safety*, 108 Proc. Nat'l Acad. Sci. 2693 (2011). Literature reviews and meta-analyses reflect widespread agreement on the link between self-control and crime. *See* Travis C. Pratt & Francis T. Cullen, *The Empirical Status of Gottfredson and Hirschi's General Theory of Crime: A Meta-Analysis*, 38 Criminology 931 (2000); Alexander T. Vazsonyi et al., *It's Time: A Meta-Analysis on the Self-Control-Deviance Link*, 48 J. Crim. Just. 48 (2017).

56. W.E.B. Du Bois, *The Philadelphia Negro: A Social Study* 242 (reprt. 1996) (1899).

57. David Alan Sklansky, *A Pattern of Violence* 8-9 (2021).

58. In *Kahler v. Kansas*, 589 U.S. 271 (2020), the Court upheld against federal constitutional challenge a statute that limited insanity to cognitive incapacity. In *Clark v. Arizona*, 548 U.S. 735 (2006), it upheld a law that recognized only moral incapacity instead. And long ago, the Court had held that, while states are free to recognize volitional incapacity, the federal Constitution does not compel them to do so. *See* Leland v. Oregon, 343 U.S. 790 (1952).

59. On PTSD as a "disease of the mind," see *United States v. Rezaq*, 918 F. Supp. 463 (D.D.C. 1996). On multiple personality disorder, see *United States v. Denny-Shaffer*, 2 F.3d 999 (10th Cir. 1993). In contrast, intoxication from hallucinogenic mushrooms did not qualify as a disease of the mind in *State v. Hotz*, 795 N.W.2d 645 (Neb. 2011). Nor did heroin withdrawal in *State v. White*, 142 A.2d 65 (N.J. 1958).

60. *See* Mac McClelland, *When "Not Guilty" Is a Life Sentence*, N.Y. Times Mag. (Sept. 27, 2017).

61. David J. Rothman, *The Discovery of the Asylum* (1971). For an account of Rothman's role in helping launch the field of prison history, see Ashley T. Rubin, *Early US Prison History Beyond Rothman: Revisiting* The Discovery of the Asylum, 15 Ann. Rev. L. & Soc'y 137 (2019). For more on the history and law of civil detention, see Paulina Arnold, *How Immigration Detention Became Exceptional*, 75 Stan. L. Rev. 261 (2023).

62. Lionel S. Penrose, *Mental Disease and Crime: Outline of a Comparative Study of European Statistics*, 18 Brit. J. Med. Psychol. 1 (1939). For empirical analysis of the relationship between institutionalization and incarceration rates, see Steven Raphael & Michael A. Stoll, *Assessing the Contribution of Deinstitutionalization of the Mentally Ill to Growth in the U.S. Incarceration Rate*, 42 J. Legal Stud. 187 (2013).

63. Raphael & Stoll, *supra* note 62, at 190.

64. For general figures, see Raphael & Stoll, *supra* note 62, at 187. On Cook County Jail, see Matt Ford, *America's Largest Mental Hospital Is a Jail*, Atlantic (June 8, 2015).

65. On mental illness and violence, see McClelland, *supra* note 60. On victimization, see Bernard E. Harcourt, *An Institutionalization Effect: The Impact of Mental Hospitalization and Imprisonment on Homicide in the United States, 1934–2001*, 40 J. Legal Stud. 39 (2011).

66. On the connections among mental illness, drug use, and incarceration, see Gregory G. Grecco & Andrew Chambers, *The Penrose Effect and Its Acceleration by the War on Drugs: A Crisis of Untranslated Neuroscience and Untreated Addiction and Mental Illness*, 9 Translational Psych. art. 320 (2019). For the causal effect of health care access on crime, see Samuel R. Bondurant et al., *Substance Abuse Treatment Centers and Local Crime*, 104 J. Urb. Econ. 124 (2018); Monica Deza et al., *Local Access to Mental Health Care and Crime*, 129 J. Urb.

Econ. 103410 (2022; Elisa Jácome, *Mental Health and Criminal Involvement: Evidence from Losing Medicaid Eligibility* (working paper); Vogler, *supra* note 20; Hefei Wen et al., *The Effect of Medicaid Expansion on Crime Reduction: Evidence from HIFA-Waiver Expansions*, 154 J. Pub. Econ. 67 (2017). The conditions of incarceration, too, can cause mental illness to develop in previously healthy individuals. *See* Christine Montross, *Waiting for an Echo* 119, 137, 161, 189 (2020).

67. McClelland, *supra* note 60. For more on the rarity of insanity verdicts, see Lisa A. Callahan et al., *The Volume and Characteristics of Insanity Defense Pleas: An Eight-State Study*, 19 Bull. Am. Acad. Psychiatry L. 331 (1991); Stephen G. Valdes, *Frequency and Success: An Empirical Study of Criminal Law Defenses, Federal Constitutional Evidentiary Claims, and Plea Negotiations*, 153 U. Pa. L. Rev. 1709 (2005) (citing sources and presenting survey results). The low rate of success is partly a function of the demanding legal definitions for insanity, but it may also stem partly from the discretion the law affords the factfinder. No matter how many mental health experts testify to a defendant's insanity, at the end of the day, the jury (or judge, in a bench trial) is free to reject the defense. In *Barcroft v. State*, 111 N.E.3d 997 (Ind. 2018), for example, three mental health experts — one hired by the defense and two appointed by the court — agreed that the defendant was insane at the time of offense. But the trial judge (sitting as factfinder) rejected the expert consensus, relying on lay descriptions of the defendant's demeanor before, during, and just after the crime. The Indiana Supreme Court upheld the trial court's decision.

68. On Gigante, see Selwyn Raab, *Vincent Gigante, Mob Boss Who Feigned Incompetence to Avoid Jail, Dies at 77*, N.Y. Times (Dec. 20, 2005). A related fear is that clever defense lawyers will dupe judges or jurors with evidence about phony mental disorders. In one notorious case, lawyers for teenager Ethan Crouch successfully argued that he should receive a sentence of probation following his conviction of multiple counts of vehicular manslaughter (for driving while drunk) on the ground that he suffered from "affluenza." Summarizing the argument, press reports observed that the psychologist who testified on Couch's behalf at his sentencing hearing told the judge that Couch's wealth and privilege should be mitigating factors because he "received whatever he asked for as a child and was constantly rewarded with gifts, wreaking havoc on his ability to perceive the consequences of his actions." Alex Horton, *'Affluenza' Drunk Driver Who Killed Four Now Free After Serving Two Years*, Wash. Post (Apr. 2, 2018).

69. For pertinent statistics on mental illness, see *Mental Illness*, Nat'l Inst. of Mental Health, https://www.nimh.nih.gov/health/statistics/mental-illness (last visited Nov. 23, 2022); Ronald C. Kessler et al., *The Prevalence and Correlates of Untreated Serious Mental Illness*, 36 Health Servs. Rsch. 987 (2001); Ford, *supra* note 64.

70. For Tapia's quotation, see Ford, *supra* note 64.

71. 2 Wayne R. LaFave, *Substantive Criminal Law* §9.5 (3d ed. 2017 & Supp. 2023).

72. For additional examples of courts applying the rule from *F.D.L.*, see *Brancaccio v. State*, 698 So. 2d 597 (Fla. Dist. Ct. App. 1997); *Heyward v. State*, 470 N.E.2d 63 (Ind. 1984); *State v. Pittman*, 647 S.E.2d 144 (S.C. 2007).

73. For examples of how state statutes treat pathological intoxication as an affirmative defense, see Haw. Rev. Stat. §702-230 (pathological intoxication "will constitute an excusing condition if it results in the same type of incapacitation to appreciate wrongfulness of conduct or to control conduct that precludes responsibility"); N.J. Stat. §2C:2-8 (same). For examples of how state courts have come down on mixing involuntarily and voluntarily ingested substances, see *State v. McClenton*, 781 N.W.2d 181 (Minn. Ct. App. 2010); *State v. Sette*, 611 A.2d 1129 (N.J. Super. Ct. App. Div. 1992).

74. On genetic vulnerability to addiction, see George R. Uhl & Robert W. Grow, *The Burden of Complex Genetics in Brain Disorders*, 61 Archives Gen. Psychiatry 223 (2004). On the

role of prescription opioids, see Theodore J. Cicero et al., *The Changing Face of Heroin Use in the United States: A Retrospective Analysis of the Past 50 Years*, 71 JAMA Psychiatry 821 (2014).

75. People in state prison sentenced for a violent offense were more likely (34 percent) to report drinking alcohol at the time of the offense than those sentenced for a property (24 percent) or drug (22 percent) offense and less likely (35 percent) to report using drugs than those serving time for a property (49 percent) or drug (55 percent) offense. Laura M. Maruschak & Jennifer Bronson, Bureau of Just. Stat., *Alcohol and Drug Use and Treatment Reported by Prisoners* 2 (2021).

76. For examples of states that forbid any defensive use of evidence of voluntary intoxication, see Ariz. Rev. Stat. §13-503; Del. Code tit. 11, §421; Fla. Stat. §775.051. For states that limit such evidence to offenses that require an especially elevated showing of *mens rea*, see, for example, Cal. Penal Code §29.4; Colo. Rev. Stat. §18-1-804; La. Rev. Stat. §14:15. For a historical discussion of the expansion and retrenchment of the intoxication defense alongside changing understandings of addiction and crime, see Mitchell Keiter, *Just Say No Excuse: The Rise and Fall of the Intoxication Defense*, 87 J. Crim. L. & Criminology 482 (1997).

77. For examples of the common-law-style, tripartite framework, see S.D. Stat. §22-3-1 (excepting from criminal liability any child under ten and "[a]ny child of the age of ten years, but under the age of fourteen years, in the absence of proof that at the time of the committing the act or neglect charged, the child knew its wrongfulness"); Wash. Rev. Stat. §9A.04.050 (excepting children under eight and presuming incapacity for children between eight and twelve, "but this presumption may be removed by proof that they have sufficient capacity to understand the act or neglect, and to know that it was wrong").

78. Some states have rejected the tripartite common law framework but retained the basic "age of capacity" construct from the infancy defense using a single, conclusive capacity cutoff. For example, see Colo. Rev. Stat. §18-1-801 (10 years old); Ga. Stat. §16-3-1 (13 years old); Minn. Stat. Ann. §609.055 (14 years old). For examples of states that implement the infancy defense through the statutory allocation of jurisdiction between the juvenile and criminal courts, as described in the text, see Ala. Code §13A-3-3 (14 years old); Haw. Rev. Stat. §§571-11, -22 (18 years old but with exceptions). For background on conditions of confinement in juvenile detention facilities, see Lilah Wolf, *Purgatorio: The Enduring Impact of Juvenile Incarceration and a Proposed Eighth Amendment Solution to Hell on Earth*, 14 Stan. J. C.R. & C.L. 89 (2018). For an overview of how different jurisdictions define the permissible length of detention for juveniles, see Samuel M. Davis, *Rights of Juveniles: The Juvenile Justice System* §7.6 (2022) (collecting statutes). For a critique of blended sentencing, see Shelly S. Schaefer & Christopher Uggen, *Blended Sentencing Laws and the Punitive Turn in Juvenile Justice*, 41 Law & Soc. Inquiry 435 (2016).

79. For examples of minimum ages for juvenile delinquency charges, or lack thereof, see Fla. Stat. §985.031 (minimum of 7 years old); 705 Ill. Comp. Stat. §405/5-120 (no minimum age). For examples of upward shifts in minimum age, see Jason Grant, *Hochul Signs Law Raising Minimum Age for Nonhomicide Arrest and Prosecution*, N.Y.L.J. (Jan. 4, 2022); *Juvenile Justice Implements New "Minimum Age" Law*, N.C. Dep't Pub. Safety (Dec. 1, 2021), https://www .ncdps.gov/news/press-releases/2021/12/01/juvenile-justice-implements-new-'minimum -age'-law.

For critical commentary on the juvenile system, see Edward Humes, *No Matter How Loud I Shout: A Year in the Life of Juvenile Court* (1996); Barry C. Feld & Perry L. Moriearty, *Race, Rights, and the Representation of Children*, 69 Am. U. L. Rev. 743 (2020); Thalia Gonzalez, *Youth Incarceration, Health, and Length of Stay*, 45 Fordham Urb. L.J. 45 (2017); Kristin Henning, *Criminalizing Normal Adolescent Behavior in Communities of Color: The Role of Prosecutors in Juvenile Justice Reform*, 98 Cornell L. Rev. 383 (2013); Nancy Rodriguez, *Juvenile Court Context and Detention Decisions: Reconsidering the Role of Race, Ethnicity, and Community*

Characteristics in Juvenile Court Process, 24 Just. Q. 629, 648 (2007); Barry Holman & Jason Ziedenberg, Just. Pol'y Inst., *The Dangers of Detention: The Impact of Incarcerating Youth in Detention and Other Secure Facilities* (2006).

80. On rebutting the common law presumption of incapacity in cases involving atrocious acts, see 4 William Blackstone, *Commentaries* *24. For examples of criticism of the long-term trend toward trying more children in criminal court, see David O. Brink, *Immaturity, Normative Competence, and Juvenile Transfer: How (Not) to Punish Minors for Major Crimes*, 82 Tex. L. Rev. 1555 (2004); Barry C. Feld, *Competence and Culpability: Delinquents in Juvenile Courts, Youths in Criminal Courts*, 102 Minn. L. Rev. 473 (2017); Christopher Slobogin, *Treating Juveniles Like Juveniles: Getting Rid of Transfer and Expanded Adult Court Jurisdiction*, 46 Tex. Tech. L. Rev. 103 (2013); Kim Taylor-Thompson, *Minority Rule: Redefining the Age of Criminality*, 38 N.Y.U. Rev. L. & Soc. Change 143 (2014). For an account of different philosophical rationales for exculpating children, see Gideon Yaffe, *The Age of Culpability: Children and the Nature of Responsibility* (2018).

81. N.Y. Penal Law §30.00. For examples of other state schemes allowing for the criminal prosecution of children, see Ky. Rev. Stat. §635.020 (allowing for the prosecution of children as young as 14 for capital offenses); N.H. Rev. Stat. §628:1 (allowing children aged 13 and older to be charged as adults). On charging very young children as adults for murder, see Steven Boes, *Charging 10-Year-Old as Adult in Death of Infant Is Not Only Wrong, But Damaging*, USA Today (May 29, 2019); Keith Bradsher, *Michigan Boy Who Killed at 11 Is Convicted of Murder as Adult*, N.Y. Times (Nov. 17, 1999); Mensah M. Dean, *At 11, She Became City's Youngest "Adult,"* Phil. Inquirer (Nov. 23, 2011). For an example of violent-crime carve-outs from recent raise-the-age statutes, see Raise the Age, Off. for Just. Initiatives, N.Y. State Unified Ct. Sys., https://ww2.nycourts.gov/ip/oji/raisetheage.shtml (raising the age of criminal responsibility to 18 years old only for non-violent offenses).

82. Michele Estrin Gilman, *The Poverty Defense*, 47 U. Rich. L. Rev. 495, 499 (2013); Norval Morris, *Psychiatry and the Dangerous Criminal*, 41 S. Cal. L. Rev. 514, 520 (1968).

83. Gilman, *supra* note 82, at 499; David L. Bazelon, *The Morality of the Criminal Law*, 49 S. Cal. L. Rev. 385, 388, 401-402 (1976). For more on the rationale for a severe environmental deprivation defense, see Richard Delgado, *Rotten Social Background: Should the Criminal Law Recognize a Defense of Severe Environmental Deprivation*, 3 Law & Ineq. 9 (1985).

84. Stephen J. Morse, *The Twilight of Welfare Criminology: A Reply to Judge Bazelon*, 49 S. Cal. L. Rev. 1247, 1251-1254 (1976) [hereinafter Morse, *Twilight*].

85. Morse, *Twilight*, *supra* note 84, at 1253.

86. Stephen J. Morse, *Severe Environmental Deprivation (AKA RSB): A Tragedy, Not a Defense*, 2 Ala. C.R. & C.L. L. Rev. 147, 150 (2011) [hereinafter Morse, *SED*] ("no reason to believe," "sufficiently impaired"); Morse, *Twilight*, *supra* note 84, at 1253 ("simply not convinced").

87. Morse, *SED*, *supra* note 86, at 150.

88. Morse, *SED*, *supra* note 86, at 158.

89. Tadros, *supra* note 2, at 393.

90. Elliott Currie, *A Peculiar Indifference* 9-10 (2020); Robert J. Sampson & William J. Wilson, *Toward a Theory of Race, Crime, and Urban Inequality*, in *Crime and Inequality* 37-38 (John Hagan & Ruth D. Peterson eds., 1995) ("police bias").

91. For official statistics, see FBI, *Uniform Crime Reporting Program* tbl.43A (2019). For a small sampling of studies demonstrating racial biases in policing, see for example, Scott Abrahams, *Officer Differences in Traffic Stops of Minority Drivers*, 67 Labour Econ. 101912 (2020) (finding that 30-40 percent of officers exhibit a higher propensity to stop Black drivers);

William C. Horrace & Shawn M. Rohlin, *How Dark Is Dark? Bright Lights, Big City, Racial Profiling*, 98 Rev. Econ. & Stat. 226, 231 (2016) (finding that "the odds of a black driver being stopped (relative to nonblack drivers) increase 15% in daylight," when skin tone is more apparent); Emma Pierson et al., *A Large-Scale Analysis of Racial Disparities in Police Stops Across the United States*, 4 Nature: Hum. Behav. 736 (2020) (finding, based on analysis of nearly 100 million traffic stops, that police stop and search decisions suffer from persistent racial bias). Compare also data showing that 13 percent of drug users are black, while 26 percent of drug-abuse arrestees are Black. Substance Abuse & Mental Health Servs. Admin., *National Survey on Drug Use and Health* tbl.1.23A (2019); FBI, *Uniform Crime Reporting Program* tbl.43A (2019). For a direct test of racial bias in arrest records, see Ben Grunwald, *Racial Bias in Criminal Records*, 40 J. Quantitative Criminology 489 (2024).

92. Sampson & Wilson, *supra* note 90, at 38 ("subterfuge"); Paul Butler, *Racially Based Jury Nullification: Black Power in the Criminal Justice System*, 105 Yale L.J. 677, 692 (1995) [hereinafter Butler, *Black Power*] ("strain credulity"); Butler, *Chokehold, supra* note 40, at 50 ("disproportionate share"). For studies substantiating the point, see for example Allen J. Beck & Alfred Blumstein, *Racial Disproportionality in U.S. State Prisons: Accounting for the Effects of Racial and Ethnic Differences in Criminal Involvement, Arrests, Sentencing, and Time Served*, 34 J. Quantitative Criminology 853, 875-876 (2018) (finding a strong correlation between the percentage of Black offenders in arrest data and in victim reports for non-fatal violent crimes); Sampson et al., *Social Anatomy, supra* note 39, at 228 (finding, based on self-reported data, that Black respondents commit violent offenses 1.85 times more frequently than white respondents); Robert J. Sampson et al., *Reassessing "Toward a Theory of Race, Crime, and Urban Inequality,"* 15 Du Bois Rev. 1, 18 (2018) [hereinafter Sampson et al., *Reassessing*] ("Despite the significant and unexpected crime drop in America [following the 1990s], racial disparities in violent offending and victimization continue."). As these scholars make clear, the point is not that "many police officers are not racist, but [rather that] there is no evidence that there is a crisis of [a] magnitude" sufficient to erase the race-crime differential reflected in official data. Butler, *Black Power, supra*, at 692; *see also* Sampson & Wilson, *supra* note 90, at 38 (noting that "evidence not only from death records but also from survey reports" confirms race differentials among "people victimized by, and involved in, criminal violence"). For a contrary take, finding that "evidence of a compelling association between race and self-reported offending [is] lacking," see Tracy WP Sohoni et al., *Understanding the Gap in Self-Reported Offending by Race: A Meta-Analysis*, 46 Am. J. Crim. Just. 770, 783 (2021).

93. W.E.B. Du Bois, *The Philadelphia Negro: A Social Study* (reprt. 1996) (1899); Clifford R. Shaw & Henry D. McKay, *Rejoinder*, 14 Am. Socio. Rev. 614, 617 (1949) (emphasis added).

94. Sampson & Wilson, *supra* note 90, at, 42-43. For a thorough accounting of how law and policy promoted racial segregation, see Richard Rothstein, *The Color of Law: A Forgotten History of How Our Government Segregated America* (2017).

95. Currie, *supra* note 90, at 159; Butler, *Chokehold, supra* note 40, at 140 ("when white men," "black masculinity"). Economist Stephen Billings argues that "neighborhood and school segregation itself may be partially responsible for high crime rates in disadvantaged urban areas" because "concentrating disadvantaged youth together increases total crime" due to social-interaction effects. Billings et al., *supra* note 13, at 126, 128. For more on black masculinity as a protective factor, see Graham C. Ousey, *Homicide, Structural Factors, and the Racial Invariance Assumption*, 37 Criminology 405 (1999); Darrell Steffensmeier et al., *Scope and Conceptual Issues in Testing the Race-Crime Invariance Thesis: Black, White, and Hispanic Comparisons*, 48 Criminology 1133 (2010) (presenting mixed evidence).

For empirical research showing that racial discrimination predicts criminal involvement, see for example Gene H. Brody et al., *Perceived Discrimination and the Adjustment of African American Youths: A Five-Year Longitudinal Analysis with Contextual Moderation Effects*,

77 Child Dev. 1170 (2006); Callie Harbin Burt et al., *Racial Discrimination, Ethnic-Racial Socialization, and Crime: A Micro-Sociological Model of Risk and Resilience*, 77 Am. Socio. Rev. 648 (2012); Ronald L. Simons et al., *Incidents of Discrimination and Risk for Delinquency: A Longitudinal Test of Strain Theory with an African American Sample*, 20 Just. Q. 827 (2003).

For studies analyzing the criminogenic impact of systemic racism through the lens of social disorganization theory, see Paul E. Bellair & Thomas L. McNulty, *Beyond the Bell Curve: Community Disadvantage and the Explanation of Black-White Differences in Adolescent Violence*, 43 Criminology 1135, 1158 (2005) ("the relative exposure of blacks over whites to disadvantaged community structures," rather than individual differences, "explains the greater involvement in violence among black adolescents"); Sampson et al., *Social Anatomy, supra* note 39, at 231 (analyzing data collected over seven years from roughly 3,000 participants in 180 Chicago neighborhoods to conclude that neighborhood context is the most important driver of the racial gap in violent offending and that individual differences like literacy and impulsivity are the least).

For studies applying a strain theory lens, see Robert Agnew, *Pressured into Crime: An Overview of General Strain Theory* 148 (2006) (racial discrimination is a "major source of strain in and of itself"), and David Eitle & R. Jay Turner, *Stress Exposure, Race, and Young Adult Male Crime*, 44 Socio. Q. 243, 258 (2003) (race is "a marker of increased risk for stress exposure"); *see also* Currie, *supra* note 90, at 133 (scholars long have observed the ever-present "awareness" in Black communities "that deprivation and restricted opportunities [a]re conditions imposed from the outside by white institutions").

For a biosocial perspective, consider studies reporting that the blood lead level of young children in Chicago is higher in neighborhoods of color — especially Black neighborhoods — even after controlling for "socioeconomic factors, such as poverty and education" and for "housing-related factors, such as unit age, vacancy, and dilapidation." Robert J. Sampson & Alix S. Winter, *The Racial Ecology of Lead Poisoning: Toxic Inequality in Chicago Neighborhoods, 1995–2013*, 13 Du Bois Rev. 261, 279 (2016). "[L]ead toxicity," the authors conclude, "is a source of ecological inequity by race and a pathway through which racial inequality literally gets into the body." *Id.*; *see also* Christopher W. Tessum et al., *Inequity in Consumption of Goods and Services Adds to Racial-Ethnic Disparities in Air Pollution Exposure*, 116 Proc. Nat'l Acad. Sci. 6001 (2019) (whites experience 17 percent less air pollution exposure than they produce, while Black and Hispanic people experience 56 percent and 63 percent more exposure than they produce). Statistical analyses suggest that the harms of these biosocial disadvantages help to explain observed racial disparities in rates of deviant behavior. *See, e.g.*, J.C. Barnes et al., *Exposure to Pre- and Perinatal Risk Factors Partially Explains Mean Differences in Self-Regulation Between Races*, 11 PLoS ONE e0141954 (2016) (racial differences in exposure to pre- and perinatal risk factors at least partly explain racial differences in child self-regulation as measured by parent interviews); Rebecca Umbach et al., *Neighborhood Disadvantage and Neuropsychological Functioning as Part Mediators of the Race-Antisocial Relationship: A Serial Mediation Model*, 34 J. Quantitative Criminology 481 (2018) (the effects of neighborhood adversity on neuropsychological functioning help explain racial differences in offending).

Finally, some argue that it is too simple to say only that Black Americans "simply experience more factors conducive to crime than Whites." Deena A. Isom Scott & Jessica M. Grosholz, *Unpacking the Racial Disparity in Crime from a Racialized General Strain Theory Perspective*, 40 Deviant Behav. 1445, 1445 (2019). Rather, these scholars contend, a truly race-conscious theory of criminology would recognize the "peerless worldview" of Black Americans. James D. Unnever & Shaun L. Gabbidon, *A Theory of African American Offending: Race, Racism, and Crime* 27 (2011). Racism, on this view, is "not just one strain that Blacks experience" but something qualitatively unique and "central to their lived experiences in American society." Lilly et al., *supra* note 7, at 76. Consistent with this race-centric account, studies have found, for example, that discrimination at the hands of the police negatively impacts the behavior of Black youths more than that of other youths, including Latinos. *See* James D. Unnever et al., *The Racial Invariance Thesis Revisited: Testing an African American Theory of Offending*, 32 J. Contemp. Crim. Just. 7 (2016). For more on race-centric criminology, see, for example, *Building a Black Criminology: Race, Theory and Crime* (James D. Unnever et al. eds., 2019); Joanne M. Kaufman et al., *A General Strain Theory of Racial Differences in Criminal Offending*, 41 Austrl. & N.Z. J. Criminology 421, 422 (2008); Ruth D. Peterson et al., *Race, Ethnicity, Crime, and Justice in Uncertain Times*, 15 Du Bois Rev. 1 (2018).

96. Sampson et al., *Reassessing, supra* note 92, at 28; Currie, *supra* note 90, at 10.

CHAPTER 4

1. David Alan Sklansky, *A Pattern of Violence* 45, 52 (2021); Alice Ristroph, *The Curriculum of the Carceral State*, 120 Colum. L. Rev. 1631, 1645-1646 (2020).

2. Ristroph, *supra* note 1, at 1667; Sklansky, *supra* note 1, at 7.

3. Patrick Sharkey, *Uneasy Peace* 7 (2018). For the pertinent crime statistics, see Fed. Bureau of Investigation, *Crime in the United States, 2019* tbl.1 (2020), and James Alan Fox & Marianne W. Zawitz, Bureau of Just. Stat., *Homicide Trends in the United States* (2007).

4. Ristroph, *supra* note 1, at 1635-1636, 1664, 1668 (emphasis added). For more on the role of law school education in criminal law reform, see Shaun Ossei-Owusu, *Criminal Legal Education*, 58 Am. Crim. L. Rev. 413 (2021); Shaun Ossei-Owusu, *Making Penal Bureaucrats*, Inquest (Aug. 23, 2021).

5. Herbert Wechsler, *The Challenge of a Model Penal Code*, 65 Harv. L. Rev. 1097, 1098 (1952).

6. Amna A. Akbar, *Toward a Radical Imagination of Law*, 93 N.Y.U. L. Rev. 405, 410 (2018). For examples of calls to prosecute police from Black Lives Matter activists, see, for example, Press Release, Black Lives Matter, Statement by Black Lives Matter Global Network Foundation in Response to Grand Jury Verdict in the Breonna Taylor Case (Sept. 23, 2020) ("Here we are, yet again . . . . There is no question that Breonna Taylor was murdered inside of her apartment and there is also no question that there are three officers who walk free—with not one charge being brought against them. Today's decision [by the prosecuting attorney] is completely disgraceful and unjustifiable."); Paul Butler, Opinion, *This Is What Derek Chauvin's Sentence Should Be*, Wash. Post (June 24, 2021) (abolitionist law professor urging eighteen-year sentence for officer who killed George Floyd). See also Akbar, *supra*, at 408 & n.5, which notes that "organizations and individuals functioning in the movement ecosystem have pushed for" reforms, including "indictments for police killings [and] independent prosecutors to investigate police shootings."

7. Sklansky, *supra* note 1, at 27. On violent crime driving mass incarceration, see John Pfaff, *Locked In* 187-190 (2017). On racial and ethnic skew in sentencing, see, for example, Brian D. Johnson et al., *Life Lessons: Examining Sources of Racial and Ethnic Disparity in Federal Life Without Parole Sentences*, 59 Criminology 704 (2021); Catherine M. Grosso et al., *Race Discrimination and the Death Penalty: An Empirical and Legal Overview*, in *America's Experiment with Capital Punishment* 525, 533-545 (James R. Acker et al. eds., 3d ed. 2014).

8. Patrick Sharkey & Robert J. Sampson, *Violence, Cognition, and Neighborhood Inequality in America*, in *Social Neuroscience* 320, 320 (Russell K. Schutt et al. ed., 2015); Elliott Currie, *A Peculiar Indifference* 6-7 (2020) ("years of life from black men"). On societal consequences of violence, see Patrick Sharkey, *The Long Reach of Violence: A Broader Perspective on Data, Theory, and Evidence on the Prevalence and Consequences of Exposure to Violence*, 1 Ann. Rev. Criminology

85 (2018); Sharkey, *supra* note 3, at 76-95. For example, in "communities with high rates of violent crime, babies are more likely to be born early, children are more likely to struggle in school and adults are more likely to report being depressed, as well as face increased risk of heart disease." Eugenia C. South, Opinion, *To Combat Gun Violence, Clean Up the Neighborhood*, N.Y. Times (Oct. 8, 2021).

9. John Clegg & Adaner Usmani, *The Economic Origins of Mass Incarceration*, 3 Catalyst no. 3, 2019; Currie, *supra* note 8, at 10.

10. Wesley Lowery et al., *Murder with Impunity: An Unequal Justice*, Wash. Post (July 25, 2018). Echoing a problem with contemporary criminal justice data more generally, a lack of data concerning "the race and ethnicity of Hispanic victims" makes it difficult to assess clearance rates when Latinos are killed. *Id.* In at least one large city "where police reliably tracked Hispanic victims, officers were least likely to make an arrest in a homicide if the victim was Hispanic." *Id.* (describing Houston).

11. Lowery et al., *supra* note 10.

12. Lowery et al., *supra* note 10 (quoting Ibram X. Kendi). For other examples of Black leaders calling attention to violence in Black communities, see *id.* (noting that civil rights leader Rev. William Barber "called the failure by police to solve black homicides a civil rights crisis on par with questionable police shootings of minorities and wrongful convictions of black men"); James Forman Jr., *Locking Up Our Own* 47-77 (2017) (documenting the history of Black community leaders describing racialized gun violence as a civil rights issue); Randall Kennedy, *Race, Crime, and the Law* 19 (1997) (arguing that "the principal injury suffered by African-Americans in relation to criminal matters is not overenforcement but underenforcement").

13. Alexandra Natapoff, *Underenforcement*, 75 Fordham L. Rev. 1715, 1719 (2006).

14. Currie, *supra* note 8, at 8.

15. 4 William Blackstone, *Commentaries* *21.

16. Francis Bowes Sayre, *Mens Rea*, 45 Harv. L. Rev. 974, 988 (1932).

17. Wechsler, *supra* note 5, at 1130. For background on the Code's adoption, see Sanford H. Kadish, *Fifty Years of Criminal Law: An Opinionated Review*, 87 Cal. L. Rev. 943, 947 (1999) [hereinafter Kadish, *Opinionated Review*]; Sanford H. Kadish, *Codifiers of the Criminal Law: Wechsler's Predecessors*, 78 Colum. L. Rev. 1098 (1978); Herbert Wechsler & Jerome Michael, *A Rationale of the Law of Homicide: I*, 37 Colum. L. Rev. 701, 701 n.1 (1937).

18. Wechsler, *supra* note 5, at 1130. Sanford Kadish observes that "[s]tate and federal courts commonly [treat the MPC] and commentary as persuasive, if not authoritative, even in the absence of legislative reform." Kadish, *Opinionated Review, supra* note 17, at 949.

19. For examples of state statutes, see Minn. Stat. §609.185(a)(4) (classifying as first-degree murder any intentional killing of a police officer, prosecuting attorney, judge, or prison guard); N.Y. Penal Law §125.27(1)(a)(iv) (classifying as first-degree murder an intentional homicide committed by a person who is already serving a lengthy prison sentence); Cal. Penal Code §189(a) (classifying as first-degree murder "[a]ll murder that is perpetrated by means of a destructive device or explosive, a weapon of mass destruction, [or] knowing use of ammunition designed primarily to penetrate metal or armor").

20. Elizabeth Papp Kamali, Felonia Felonice Facta: *Felony and Intentionality in Medieval England*, 9 Crim. L. & Phil. 397, 417 (2015). As Professor Kamali further explains, in addition to "thousands of silent acquittals" marking the medieval scrolls, English law also developed a set of parallel practices such as sanctuary, abjuring the realm, and benefit of clergy to mitigate sentence severity in cases of homicide. *Id.* at 417 & n.72. As Professor Kaye explains, "Manslaughter, though a felony and therefore capital, was clergyable: for a first offence a

convicted person was punished by imprisonment not exceeding one year and by branding, intended to prevent his pleading clergy on any subsequent occasion." J.M. Kaye, *The Early History of Murder and Manslaughter: Part I*, 83 Law Q. Rev. 365, 365 (1967). The benefit of clergy was a medieval doctrine by which priests and other religious clerics could escape capital punishment. Over time, the process for identifying a cleric eligible for the benefit was formalized first into a simple literacy test (on the theory that only clerics knew how to read) and eventually into a "test" that asked every accused person to read the same commonly known verse, which even an illiterate person could memorize in advance. In this fashion, the benefit evolved into a widely used and largely *pro forma* device that converted manslaughter and other clergyable offenses into noncapital crimes. For more on the benefit of clergy, see generally J.M. Beattie, *Crime and the Courts in England: 1660-1800* (1986).

21. Model Penal Code and Commentaries §210.2 cmt. at 16.

22. J.L. Mackie, *Morality and the Retributive Emotions*, 1 Crim. Just. Ethics, Winter/Spring 1982, at 3, 4.

23. Jeremy Bentham, *Principles of Penal Law*, in 1 *The Works of Jeremy Bentham* 365, 400 (John Bowring ed., Edinburgh, William Tait 1893) (footnote omitted).

24. Mr. Forrest's sentence was ultimately commuted and he was released from prison in 1992. *See* John Forrest, Offender No. 0132974, *North Carolina Department of Public Safety: Offender Public Information.* For the presumptive minimums at the time of Mr. Forrest's conviction, see *State v. Melton*, 298 S.E.2d 673, 676 (1983) (citing N.C. Gen. Stat. §14-17 (1981); N.C. Gen. Stat. §15A-1340.4 (Cum. Supp. 1981)); Valerie B. Spalding, *Using the Fair Sentencing Act to Protect the Criminal Defendant*, 9 Campbell L. Rev. 127, 130 n.24 (1986) (citing N.C. Gen. Stat. §15A-1340.4(f) (1983)).

25. Benjamin N. Cardozo, *What Medicine Can Do for Law*, in *Law and Literature and Other Essays and Addresses* 99-101 (1931); Kimberly Kessler Ferzan, *Plotting Premeditation's Demise*, 75 Law & Contemp. Probs. 83, 87 (2012). For an overview of jurisdictional approaches on this issue, see 2 Wayne R. LaFave, *Substantive Criminal Law* §14.7(a) (3d ed. 2017 & Supp. 2023).

26. The Nevada court in *Byford* defined premeditation as "a design, a determination to kill, distinctly formed in the mind by the time of the killing" and deliberation as "the process of determining upon a course of action to kill as a result of thought, including weighing the reasons for and against the action and considering the consequences of the action." Byford v. State, 994 P.2d 700, 714 (Nev. 2000).

27. Cardozo, *supra* note 25, at 100; Ferzan, *supra* note 25, at 84-85.

28. Ferzan, *supra* note 25, at 90-91 (quoting Samuel H. Pillsbury, *Judging Evil: Rethinking the Law of Murder and Manslaughter* 104 (1998)).

29. Professor Michael Zydney Mannheimer offers a different but still deterrence-driven defense of the premeditation doctrine: "[B]ecause the value of punishment as a deterrent depends in large measure on the likelihood of swift punishment, crimes that are harder to detect and prosecute, all other things being equal, ought to be punished more severely. . . . Given two equally dangerous and culpable intentional murderers, the theory goes, we are justified in punishing more severely the one who, by virtue of better planning beforehand, is more likely to escape or delay detection." Michael J. Zydney Mannheimer, *Not the Crime but the Cover-Up: A Deterrence-Based Rationale for the Premeditation-Deliberation Formula*, 86 Ind. L.J. 879, 881 (2011). For an opposing perspective, see Ferzan, *supra* note 25, at 91 ("As a matter of consequentialist theory, the bottom line is that premeditation's justification is empirically contingent. That is, its efficacy will depend on whether the benefits . . . obtain. Indeed, the question will ultimately turn on whether deterring cold, calculating, premeditating actors with more-severe punishment is more advisable than incapacitating hot-blooded, rash defendants.").

30. Cardozo, *supra* note 25, at 100; Mannheimer, *supra* note 29, at 889.

31. Stephen J. Morse, *Undiminished Confusion in Diminished Capacity*, 75 J. Crim. L. & Criminology 1, 33 (1984).

32. Jonathan Witmer-Rich, *The Heat of Passion and Blameworthy Reasons to Be Angry*, 55 Am. Crim. L. Rev. 409, 409, 411, 412 (2018).

33. V.F. Nourse, *Reconceptualizing Criminal Law Defenses*, 151 U. Pa. L. Rev. 1691, 1718, 1728 (2003); Witmer-Rich, *supra* note 32, at 412.

34. Dan M. Kahan & Martha C. Nussbaum, *Two Conceptions of Emotion in Criminal Law*, 96 Colum. L. Rev. 269, 297 (1996).

35. Emily L. Miller, Comment, *(Wo)manslaughter: Voluntary Manslaughter, Gender, and the Model Penal Code*, 50 Emory L.J. 665, 692 (2001) ("cultural values"). For statistics on intimate-partner violence, see Sharon G. Smith et al., Ctrs. for Disease Control & Prevention, *The National Intimate Partner and Sexual Violence Survey: 2015 Data Brief — Updated Release* 8-9, 20-22 (2018); Shannan Catalano, Bureau of Just. Stat., *Intimate Partner Violence: Attributes of Victimization, 1993–2011*, at 3 tbl.2 (2013).

36. Elizabeth Rapaport, *Capital Murder and the Domestic Discount: A Study of Capital Domestic Murder in the Post-Furman Era*, 49 S.M.U. L. Rev. 1507, 1546 (1996). For more on patriarchal violence, see generally Jeremy Horder, *Provocation and Responsibility* (1992); Reva B. Siegel, *"The Rule of Love": Wife Beating as Prerogative and Privacy*, 105 Yale L.J. 2117, 2122-2123 (1996).

37. Cynthia Lee, *Murder and the Reasonable Man* 20, 22 (2003) [hereinafter Lee, *Murder*].

38. Lee, *Murder*, *supra* note 37, at 20.

39. Miller, *supra* note 35, at 668-669, 671.

40. Victoria Nourse, *Passion's Progress: Modern Law Reform and the Provocation Defense*, 106 Yale L.J. 1331, 1332-1334 (1997). Cynthia Lee observes that the "subjective Model Penal Code approach has led to some shocking verdicts," including multiple cases in which juries "rejected murder charges in favor of manslaughter when the provocation consisted of a female partner dancing with another man." Lee, *Murder*, *supra* note 37, at 35.

41. Catharine A. MacKinnon, Viewpoint, *Feminism, Marxism, Method, and the State: Toward Feminist Jurisprudence*, 8 Signs 635, 658 (1983).

42. Miller, *supra* note 35, at 693; *see also* Rapaport, *supra* note 36, at 1547 ("In contemporary society, patriarchal values have no more legitimate place in criminal law than they do in [other areas of law]. . . . It is the work of the criminal law in this period of social transition to delegitimate and transcend this patriarchal moral framework.").

43. Aya Gruber, *A Provocative Defense*, 103 Calif. L. Rev. 273, 313-314, 319 (2015). Gruber cites Laurie L. Ragatz & Brenda Russell, *Sex, Sexual Orientation, and Sexism: What Influence Do These Factors Have on Verdicts in a Crime-of-Passion Case?*, 150 J. Soc. Psych. 341 (2010), which attributes lenient sentences for women to "benevolent sexism." For more on leniency toward women in intimate homicides, see Gruber, *supra*, at 310, asserting that the "scant evidence" that exists indicates that the "sexist defendants who concern feminists" do not actually prevail on provocation arguments and citing Stuart M. Kirschner et al., *The Defense of Extreme Emotional Disturbance: A Qualitative Analysis of Cases in New York County*, 10 Psych. Pub. Pol'y & L. 102, 126 (2004), and Amy Farrell et al., *Intersections of Gender and Race in Federal Sentencing: Examining Court Contexts and the Effects of Representative Court Authorities*, 14 J. Gender Race & Just. 85, 85-86 (2010), observing that "leniency toward women has become an almost accepted phenomenon among scholars studying criminal case processing."

44. Martha Minow, *Between Vengeance and Forgiveness: Feminist Responses to Violent Injustice*, 32 New Eng. L. Rev. 967, 972 (1998); Gruber, *supra* note 43, at 318.

45. Gruber, *supra* note 43, at 312 (quoting Aya Gruber, *Murder, Minority Victims, and Mercy*, 85 U. Colo. L. Rev. 129, 185 (2014)).

46. Gruber, *supra* note 43, at 309.

47. Cynthia Lee, *The Trans Panic Defense Revisited*, 57 Am. Crim. L. Rev. 1411, 1412-1413 (2020) (quoting Kenrya Rankin, *James Dixon to Serve 12 Years for Killing Islan Nettles*, Colorlines (Apr. 20, 2016); Yanan Wang, *The Islan Nettles Killing: What the Trial Means to a Transgender Community Anxious for a Reckoning*, Wash. Post. (Apr. 4, 2016)). For other sources analyzing the gay panic defense, see Lee, *Murder, supra* note 37, at 83; Edward J. Kempf, *Psychopathology* 477-480 (1920); *Developments in the Law — Sexual Orientation and the Law*, 102 Harv. L. Rev. 1508, 1542 (1989).

48. *See* Christy Mallory et al., Williams Inst., *Banning the Use of Gay and Trans Panic Defenses* 2-13 (2021) (victimization data); *id.* at 21-22 (statutory interventions). For a judicial opinion barring the gay panic defense, see *Commonwealth v. Pierce*, 642 N.E.2d 579, 582 (Mass. 1994), holding that "the victim's invitation, 'You know you want it,' and the grabbing of the defendant's testicles, was not provocation warranting a voluntary manslaughter instruction." Other scholars argue against such limitations, at least in cases where a person kills in response to an unwelcome sexual advance. Joshua Dressler, Commentary, *When "Heterosexual" Men Kill "Homosexual" Men: Reflections on Provocation Law, Sexual Advances, and the "Reasonable Man" Standard*, 85 J. Crim. L. & Criminology 726, 754-755 (1995).

49. *See* 2 LaFave, *supra* note 25, §15.2(b)(6).

50. Randall Kennedy, *Nigger: The Strange Career of a Troublesome Word* 28 (2003) ("nuclear bomb") (quoting Farai Chideya, *The Color of Our Future* 9 (1999)); Jenna Wortham, *Still Processing, The N-Word*, N.Y. Times Podcast (Mar. 18, 2021).

51. Richard Delgado, *Words That Wound: A Tort Action for Racial Insults, Epithets, and Name-Calling*, 17 Harv. C.R.-C.L. L. Rev. 133, 143, 157 (1982). For a similar perspective, see Mari J. Matsuda, *Public Response to Racist Speech: Considering the Victim's Story*, 87 Mich. L. Rev. 2320, 2338 (1989), observing that racist speech "hits right at the emotional place where we feel the most pain."

52. Kennedy, *supra* note 50, at 74; Lee, *Murder, supra* note 37, at 61. *Compare* People v. Green, 519 N.W.2d 853 (Mich. 1994) (refusing manslaughter instruction), *and* State v. Watson, 214 S.E.2d 85 (N.C. 1975) (same), *with* Lee, *Murder, supra* note 37, at 63 (describing the jury's decisionmaking in the trial of a Black incarcerated person found guilty of stabbing a white prison guard after the "guard made anti-gay comments and racial insults").

53. Francis X. Shen et al., *Sorting Guilty Minds*, 86 N.Y.U. L. Rev. 1306, 1309 (2011).

54. William Prosser, *Handbook of the Law of Torts* §34, at 185 (4th ed. 1971).

55. Restatement (Second) of Torts §282. For cases applying the ordinary negligence standard, see *Cornella v. Justice Court*, 377 P.3d 97, 102-103 (Nev. 2016) (holding that the phrase "simple negligence" in misdemeanor vehicular manslaughter statute requires only ordinary negligence); *State v. Hazelwood*, 946 P.2d 875, 884 n.17 (Alaska 1997) (reporting that the "overwhelming majority of jurisdictions allow [some] crimes based on ordinary negligence"). But note that "the legislatures and the courts have often made it clear that criminal liability generally requires more fault than the ordinary negligence which will do for tort liability." 1 LaFave, *supra* note 25, §5.4(b).

56. 4 William Blackstone, *Commentaries* *199.

57. Shen et. al., *supra* note 53, at 1309 (mock juror study); Sherry F. Colb, *Why Can't Jurors Distinguish "Knowing" from "Reckless" Misconduct?*, Justia: Verdict (Jan. 11, 2012) (emphases added).

58. Brief for Respondent at 2, State v. Herrera, 364 P.3d 1180 (Idaho 2015) (No. 41494), 2014 WL 6710645.

59. 3 James Fitzjames Stephen, *A History of the Criminal Law of England* 311-312 (London, MacMillan & Co. 1883).

60. H.L.A. Hart, *The Morality of the Criminal Law* 53 (1965).

61. For Congress's investigation, see H.R. Rep. No. 95-1386, 95th Cong. 2d Sess. (1978), as reprinted in 1978 U.S.C.C.A.N. 7530, 7531. For more on the forced removal of Native American children, including federal funding of state agencies, see William Byler, *Removing Children: The Destruction of American Indian Families*, Civ. Rts. Dig., Summer 1977, at 19, 24. For critiques of child welfare agencies more generally, see Dorothy Roberts, *Torn Apart: How the Child Welfare System Destroys Black Families—And How Abolition Can Build a Safer World* (2022); Dorothy Roberts, *A Veneer of Benevolence*, Inquest (Apr. 29, 2022). For contemporary news accounts, see, for example, Caitlin Gibson, *They Brought Their Sick Baby to the Hospital. Three Days Later, the State Took Their Kids Away.*, Wash. Post (Dec. 7, 2022); Jonathan E. Bromwich & Andy Newman, *Child Abuse Investigators Traumatize Families, Lawsuit Charges*, N.Y. Times (Feb. 20, 2024).

62. Oliver Wendell Holmes, *The Common Law* 50-51 (1881).

63. Nourse, *Reconceptualizing, supra* note 33, at 1693-1695, 1729.

64. Guyora Binder, *The Culpability of Felony Murder*, 83 Notre Dame L. Rev. 965, 979-981 (2008) [hereinafter Binder, *Culpability*].

65. *See* Guyora Binder, *The Origins of American Felony Murder Rules*, 57 Stan. L. Rev. 59, 69 (2004) [hereinafter Binder, *Origins*]. On criticism of felony murder, see David Crump, *Reconsidering the Felony Murder Rule in Light of Modern Criticisms: Doesn't the Conclusion Depend Upon the Particular Rule at Issue?*, 32 Harv. J.L. & Pub. Pol'y 1155, 1158 (2009) ("[W]hen evaluating the criticisms, a great deal depends upon which version of the felony murder doctrine the critics choose to denounce. The better versions are responsive to, and can withstand, the critics' assaults, whereas the less acceptable formulations give ammunition to the rule's opponents."). On state-level variation, see Paul H. Robinson & Tyler Scot Williams, *Mapping American Criminal Law* 53-58 (2018).

66. Restatement (Second) of Torts §519 cmt. d. Professor Binder notes that "[l]egal scholars are almost unanimous in condemning felony murder as a morally indefensible form of strict liability." Binder, *Culpability, supra* note 64, at 966.

67. Crump, *supra* note 65, at 1157. For examples of "troubling cases," see Binder, *Culpability, supra* note 64, at 980 n.59 (citing State v. Colenburg, 773 S.W.2d 184, 185-186 (Mo. Ct. App. 1989) (nonreckless car collision occurred months after felonious theft of car); People v. Matos, 634 N.E.2d 157, 157 (N.Y. 1994) (police officer fell down airshaft while chasing suspect)); Guyora Binder, *Making the Best of Felony Murder*, 91 B.U. L. Rev. 403, 405-407 (2011) [hereinafter Binder, *Making the Best*] (citing eleven examples of "troubling cases" from ten different jurisdictions).

68. Professor Binder analogizes felony murder doctrine to a rule that bases "murder liability on criminal negligence with respect to death, aggravated by a felonious motive independent of that negligence." Binder, *Culpability, supra* note 64, at 970.

69. Binder, *Origins, supra* note 65, at 67. "[M]any states" apply the inherently dangerous felony limitation, and others still require "that the felony be one of the few which were felonies at common law (i.e., rape, sodomy, robbery, burglary, arson, mayhem, larceny)," which frequently "involve a danger to life." 2 LaFave, *supra* note 25, §14.5(b). On the prevalence of the inherently dangerous felony limitation, see also Guyora Binder, *Felony Murder* 17-18 (2012) [hereinafter Binder, *Felony Murder*].

70. Binder, *Origins, supra* note 65, at 67 (citing Mark Kelman, *Strict Liability: An Unorthodox View*, in 4 *Encyclopedia of Crime and Justice* 1512, 1516-1518 (Sanford H. Kadish ed., 1983)). As Professor Binder elaborates: "[A] legislature may impose deserved punishment for carelessly causing harm by two different means: by conditioning punishment on aware-ness of risk, or by conditioning it on particularly dangerous conduct that the legislature regards as culpable per se. The second approach does not require proof of a culpable men-tal state with respect to the proscribed harm, and adds an additional objective element—the dangerous conduct—without a corresponding culpable mental state. As such, it imposes strict liability in the formal sense, but not in the substantive sense." Binder, *Culpability, supra* note 64, at 987-988 (footnotes omitted). On the classic predicate crimes, see 2 LaFave, *supra* note 25, §14.5(b); Binder, *Making the Best, supra* note 67, at 436.

71. Herbert Wechsler, *Codification of Criminal Law in the United States: The Model Penal Code*, 68 Colum. L. Rev. 1425, 1446 (1968). For more on the politics underlying the MPC reforms, see Franklin E. Zimring & Gordon Hawkins, *Murder, the Model Code, and the Multiple Agendas of Reform*, 19 Rutgers L.J. 773, 777-778 (1988).

72. On the prevalence of the proximate cause limitation on felony murder, see Binder, *Felony Murder, supra* note 69, at 18.

73. 2 LaFave, *supra* note 25, §14.5(d). On proximate causation in tort law, see *Restatement (Third) of Torts: Liability for Physical and Emotional Harm* ch. 6 special note (Am. L. Inst. 2010) ("Although the term 'proximate cause' has been in widespread use in judicial opinions, treatises, casebooks, and scholarship, the term is . . . an especially poor one to describe the idea to which it is connected.").

74. Binder, *Origins, supra* note 65, at 67-68.

75. For more on the mechanics of the proximate cause requirement, see 1 LaFave, *supra* note 25, §6.4, which describes some of the common fact patterns in which the doc-trine can have meaningful impact, including cases in which the harm intended or risked by a defendant's action differs from the harm actually caused with respect to (1) the person harmed, (2) the manner in which the harm occurred, or (3) the degree of harm.

76. For a list of statutes, see 2 LaFave, *supra* note 25, §14.5(c) n.31.

77. For a survey of different jurisdictions' approaches to this issue, see Maria T. Kolar, *Felony Murder Liability for Homicides by Police: Too Unfair and Too Much to Bear*, 113 J. Crim. L. & Criminology 241 (2023).

78. Nelson E. Roth & Scott E. Sundby, *The Felony-Murder Rule: A Doctrine at Constitutional Crossroads*, 70 Cornell L. Rev. 446, 491 (1985).

79. Binder, *Origins, supra* note 65, at 67.

80. Dahleen Glanton, *A Kid Charged with His Friend's Murder During a Botched Burglary in 2008 Got a Second Chance. The Teens Charged in Lake County Deserve One Too.*, Chi. Trib. (Aug. 26, 2019).

81. Dua Eldeib, *Controversial Law Charges People with Murder for Death at Other's Hand*, Chi. Trib. (Feb. 20, 2016).

82. Sklansky, *supra* note 1, at 32; H.L.A. Hart, *Punishment and Responsibility* 14 (2d ed. 2008) [hereinafter Hart, *Punishment*].

83. For the Chicago jury study, see Harry Kalven, Jr. & Hans Zeisel, *The American Jury* 221 n.1 (1966). For examples of related defenses, see Model Penal Code §3.05 (defense of others); *id.* §3.06 (defense of property); 2 LaFave, *supra* note 25, §10.5 (defense of others); *id.* §10.6 (defense of property).

84. 3 William Blackstone, *Commentaries* *4. For similar perspectives, see *Runyan v. State*, 57 Ind. 80, 84 (1877); Thomas Hobbes, *Leviathan* 91 (Michael Oakeshott ed., Basil Blackwell 1946) (1651) ("A covenant not to defend myself from force, by force, is always void.").

85. Ristroph, *supra* note 1, at 1674. For an argument that self-defense doctrine reflects and constructs the relationship between the individual and the state, see Nourse, *Reconceptualizing, supra* note 33, at 1703-1710.

86. 3 William Blackstone, *Commentaries* *4.

87. Hart, *Punishment, supra* note 82, at 13-14 ("what is done," "is deplored," "public condemnation"); 4 William Blackstone, *Commentaries* *182 ("commendation").

88. 2 LaFave, *supra* note 25, §10.4(d). Richard Rosen describes imminence as a " 'translator' of the underlying principle of necessity." Richard A. Rosen, *On Self-Defense, Imminence, and Women Who Kill Their Batterers*, 71 N.C. L. Rev. 371, 380 (1993).

89. Cynthia K. Gillespie, *Justifiable Homicide: Battered Women, Self-Defense, and the Law* xi (1989).

90. Fiona Leverick, *Killing in Self-Defence* 89 (2006) (emphasis added).

91. George P. Fletcher, *Domination in the Theory of Justification and Excuse*, 57 U. Pitt. L. Rev. 553, 567 (1996). For some contrasting viewpoints in that debate, compare Rosen, *supra* note 88, at 405 (arguing that imminence should not be required where a killing is otherwise necessary), with Kimberly Kessler Ferzan, *Defending Imminence: From Battered Women to Iraq*, 46 Ariz. L. Rev. 213, 217 (2004) (arguing that imminence appropriately separates genuine threats "from mere inchoate and potential" ones).

92. For a detailed overview of the relevant literature, as well as a critical review of additional perspectives, see Chapter 3 of Leverick, *supra* note 90, and Shlomit Wallerstein, *Justifying the Right to Self-Defense: A Theory of Forced Consequences*, 91 Va. L. Rev. 999 (2005).

93. Leverick, *supra* note 90, at 60. On the "fundamental interest in [one's] own life," see *Tennessee v. Garner*, 471 U.S. 1, 9 (1985). For more on the forfeiture theory of self-defense, see Suzanne Uniacke, *Permissible Killing: The Self-Defence Justification of Homicide* 26 (1994); Judith Jarvis Thomson, *Self-Defense*, 20 Phil. & Pub. Affs. 283 (1991).

94. R.B. Brandt, *Conscience (Rule) Utilitarianism and the Criminal Law*, 14 Law & Phil. 65, 88 (1995).

95. Leverick, *supra* note 90, at 64. On the question of the child aggressor, see Tziporah Kasachkoff, *Killing in Self-Defense: An Unquestionable or Problematic Defense?*, 17 Law & Phil. 509, 518 (1998); Lawrence A. Alexander, *Justification and Innocent Aggressors*, 33 Wayne L. Rev. 1177, 1187 (1987) ("[S]elf-defense in the context of innocent aggressors is almost always excusable, but less frequently and perhaps rarely justified").

96. On rape as a denial of humanity, see Leverick, *supra* note 90, at 143; Jean Hampton, *Defining Wrong and Defining Rape*, in *A Most Detestable Crime: New Philosophical Essays on Rape* 118, 135 (Keith Burgess-Jackson ed. 1999); Jonathan Quong, *The Morality of Defensive Force* 5 (2020); Kasachkoff, *supra* note 95, at 511. One might also argue that acts of rape entail a serious risk of danger *to the victim's life* and are thus inherently assimilated into actual threats of death. Leverick, *supra* note 90, at 148-149.

97. Margaret Raymond, *Looking for Trouble: Framing and the Dignitary Interest in the Law of Self-Defense*, 71 Ohio St. L.J. 287, 293-294 (2010).

98. Compare, for example, states allowing the initial aggressor to defend against disproportionate response, Kan. Stat. Ann. §21-5226(c)(1); N.D. Cent. Code §12.1-05-03(2)(b), with statutes that make no such allowances, Ariz. Rev. Stat. §13-404(B)(3); N.Y. Penal Law §35.15(1)(b).

99. Raymond, *supra* note 97, at 293-294; Leverick, *supra* note 90, at 123. For examples of withdrawal standards, see *Behenna, supra* p. 270; Mo. Rev. Stat. §563.031.1(1)(a). As the Supreme Court explained in *Rowe v. United States*, 164 U.S. 546, 557 (1896), the requirement that withdrawal be in good faith prevents an initial aggressor from recovering the right by feigning withdrawal as "a mere device . . . to obtain some advantage of his adversary."

100. Kristin Henning, *The Rage of Innocence* 191 (2021); President Barack Obama, *Remarks by the President on Trayvon Martin* (July 19, 2013); Lowery et al., *supra* note 10 ("planted the seeds"). For more on the response to Martin's death, see Henning, *supra*, at 180 ("In the days and weeks after Trayvon's death, public reaction divided along racial lines, with more Blacks than Whites believing that Zimmerman was guilty of murder and had acted with racial bias.").

101. Henning, *supra* note 100, at 181.

102. For further factual background on the case, see Henning, *supra* note 100, at 180-196, 267-273; Greg Botelho, *What Happened the Night Trayvon Martin Died*, CNN (May 23, 2012); All Things Considered, *Prosecution's Star Witness Cross-Examined in Zimmerman Case*, NPR (June 27, 2013).

103. Alafair Burke, *What You May Not Know About the Zimmerman Verdict: The Evolution of a Jury Instruction*, Huffington Post (Sept. 14, 2013).

104. *See* Kimberly Kessler Ferzan, *Provocateurs*, 7 Crim. L. & Phil. 597, 615 (2013).

105. For example statutes, see Ark. Code Ann. §5-2-606(b)(1); Or. Rev. Stat. §161.215(1)(a).

106. For statutes permitting the use of nondeadly force, see Del. Code Ann. tit. 11, §464(e)(1); Haw. Rev. Stat. §703-304(5)(a); *see also* Model Penal Code §3.04(2)(b)(i). For examples of states withholding the right of self-defense when the defendant provokes the respondent with the purpose of causing an affray, see Ind. Code §35-41-3-2(g)(2); Iowa Code §704.6(2).

107. Randall Kennedy & Eugene Volokh, *The New Taboo: Quoting Epithets in the Classroom and Beyond*, 49 Cap. U. L. Rev. 1, 12-19 (2021) ("liberal luminaries"); Wesley Morris, Still Processing, *The N-Word*, N.Y. Times Podcast (Mar. 18, 2020) ("much different to say it"). One opinion stated: "The Court recognizes that some of the language that Plaintiffs allege to have been directed against them is undeniably offensive and may be painful for some readers. Nonetheless, the Court does not see fit to censor or euphemize Plaintiffs' allegations in this Opinion. As Plaintiffs' counsel stated at oral argument, 'the language matters in this case, and there's a way in which, by not articulating some of these things, they lose their force.'" T.E. v. Pine Bush Cent. Sch. Dist., 58 F. Supp. 3d 332, 339 n.5 (S.D.N.Y. 2014).

108. Ronald S. Sullivan, Jr., *The Rittenhouse Trial: A Legal Scholar Responds*, Quillette (Nov. 23, 2021). For perspectives arguing in favor of a duty to avoid violent and potentially deadly conflict, see, for example, Andrew Ashworth, *Principles of Criminal Law* 144-145 (5th ed. 2006); Alexander, *supra* note 95, at 1183-1184; Model Penal Code §3.04(2)(b)(ii) (prohibiting deadly defensive force if "the actor knows that he can avoid the necessity of using such force with complete safety . . . by complying with a demand that he abstain from any action which he has no duty to take").

109. Ferzan, *Provocateurs, supra* note 104, at 609.

110. On the prevalence of felony convictions, see Christopher Uggen et al., *Citizenship, Democracy, and the Civic Reintegration of Criminal Offenders*, 605 Annals Am. Acad. Pol. & Soc. Sci. 281, 304 (2006).

111. Oklahoma's highest court for criminal cases likewise advises that mere "possession of illegal drugs" would forfeit the right to self-defense. Dawkins v. State, 252 P.3d 214,

218 (Okla. Crim. App. 2011). Consider how far this theory reaches. Roughly $150 billion worth of illicit drugs are purchased in the U.S. each year, consumed by roughly 20 percent of the population. Gregory Midgette et al., Rand Corp., *What America's Users Spend on Illegal Drugs, 2006-2016* xi (2019); Substance Abuse & Mental Health Servs. Admin., U.S. Dep't of Health & Hum. Servs., *Key Substance Use and Mental Health Indicators in the United States: Results from the 2020 National Survey on Drug Use and Health* 2 (2021). Likewise, around 15 percent of American men have paid for sex. Nikolas Westerhoff, *Why Do Men Buy Sex?*, Sci. Am. (Oct. 1, 2012). More broadly, the "shadow" or "underground" economy in the U.S.—encompassing all forms of "off the books," and thus illegal, work—is vast. Estimates put its annual value at around $2 trillion; California estimates that more than 15 percent of the state's labor force participates in it. These workers are drawn disproportionately from impoverished and immigrant communities whose members face barriers to participation in the formal economy. Rick Newman, *The New Underground Economy*, U.S. News (Mar. 18, 2013); Claire Goldstene, *The Rise of the Underground Economy*, Inequality.org (July 16, 2015).

112. 4 William Blackstone, *Commentaries* *184-185.

113. For sample statutes, see Del. Code Ann. tit. 11, §464(e); Haw. Rev. Stat. §703-304(5); *accord* Model Penal Code §3.04(2)(b).

114. 4 William Blackstone, *Commentaries* *185 ("to the wall"). On early exceptions to the duty to retreat, see Cynthia V. Ward, *"Stand Your Ground" and Self-Defense*, 42 Am. J. Crim. L. 89, 97-99 (2015). Professor Eugene Volokh recently tallied the split as 35 states opposed to the duty, with only 15 embracing it. Eugene Volokh, *Stand Your Ground (35 States) vs. Duty to Retreat (15 States)*, Volokh Conspiracy (Dec. 21, 2020). On states that weigh the untaken opportunity to retreat against the defendant, see Raymond, *supra* note 97, at 313-317.

115. Richard Maxwell Brown, *No Duty to Retreat: Violence and Values in American History and Society* 17 (1991) ("values of masculine bravery"); Caroline E. Light, *Stand Your Ground: A History of America's Love Affair with Lethal Self-Defense* 59 (2017). On the spread of firearms, see David B. Kopel, *The Self-Defense Cases: How the United States Supreme Court Confronted a Hanging Judge in the Nineteenth Century and Taught Some Lessons for Jurisprudence in the Twenty-First*, 27 Am. J. Crim. L. 293, 307 (2000). The phrase "true man," as initially used by English jurist Sir Matthew Hale and later the *Erwin* court, referred to a man who was honest and scrupulous. Over time, however, the term came to reflect ideas about machismo and masculinity. Jeannie Suk, *The True Woman: Scenes from the Law of Self-Defense*, 31 Harv. J.L. & Gender 237, 244, 250-252 (2008).

116. Model Penal Code and Commentaries §3.04 cmt. 4(c) at 54. Blackstone states: "[I]t may be cowardice, in time of war between two independent nations, to flee from an enemy; yet between two fellow subjects the law countenances no such point of honour: because the king and his courts are the *vindices injuriarum*, and will give to the party wronged all the satisfaction he deserves." 4 William Blackstone, *Commentaries* *185.

117. *See* Lowery et al., *supra* note 10.

118. 2 LaFave, *supra* note 25, §10.4(a). On the take-up of Stand Your Ground laws, see Alexa R. Yakubovich et al., *Effects of Laws Expanding Civilian Rights to Use Deadly Force in Self-Defense of Violence and Crime: A Systematic Review*, 111 Am. J. Pub. Health e1, e2 (2021). For examples of Stand Your Ground laws, see Fla. Stat. §776.012(2) ("does not have a duty to retreat and has the right to stand his or her ground"); *id.* §776.032 (immunity); Ga. Code Ann. §16-3-23.1 ("has no duty to retreat and has the right to stand his or her ground"). On the elimination of the duty to retreat over time, compare Judith E. Koons, *Gunsmoke and Legal Mirrors: Women Surviving Intimate Battery and Deadly Legal Doctrines*, 14 J.L. & Pol'y 617, 630 n.41 (2006) (counting 23 duty-to-retreat states including Florida), with Volokh, *supra* note 114 (counting 15 duty-to-retreat states in 2020).

119. Obama, *supra* note 100.

120. Yakubovich et al., *supra* note 118, at e2, e6 (reviewing 32 studies); *Fortifying the Right to Self-Defense* NRA-ILA, (Feb. 6, 2006) (NRA advocacy for Stand Your Ground laws). For studies finding that unjustified homicides accounted for most of the increase in homicides after enactment of Stand Your Ground Laws, see David K. Humphreys et al., Research Letter, *Association Between Enactment of a "Stand Your Ground" Self-Defense Law and Unlawful Homicides in Florida*, 177 JAMA Internal Med. 1523, 1523 (2017); Chandler McClellan & Erdal Tekin, *Stand Your Ground Laws, Homicides, and Injuries*, 52 J. Hum. Res. 621, 644 (2017).

121. Light, *supra* note 115, at 13. For additional analysis of white male privilege in self-defense, see *id.* at 63-85, 99-100; Gillespie, *supra* note 89, at 182. For racial disparities, see Michelle Degli Esposti et al., *Increasing Adolescent Firearm Homicides and Racial Disparities Following Florida's "Stand Your Ground" Self-Defense Law*, 26 Injury Prevention 187 (2020) (victimization); Yakubovich et al., *supra* note 118, at e11 (enforcement).

122. Adam Liptak, *15 States Expand Right to Shoot in Self-Defense*, N.Y. Times (Aug. 7, 2006).

123. Jarvis DeBerry, *Does "Standing Your Ground" in Louisiana Mean You Can Shoot a Fleeing Suspect?*, NOLA.com (Mar. 25, 2012). On the Zimmerman deliberations, see Nicole Flatow, *Zimmerman Juror Says Panel Considered Stand Your Ground in Deliberations: "He Had a Right to Defend Himself,"* ThinkProgress (July 16, 2013).

124. For an incisive discussion of these issues, see Sklansky, *supra* note 1, at 221-227.

125. For the old adage, see Edward Coke, *The Third Part of the Institute of the Laws of England* *162 (1648).

126. Leverick, *supra* note 90, at 85. One court stated: "He is not bound to flee and become a fugitive from his own home, for, if that were required, there would, theoretically, be no refuge for him anywhere in the world." Barton v. State, 420 A.2d 1009, 1010 (Md. Ct. Spec. App. 1980).

127. Curt Brown, *Little Falls Teen Shooting Deaths Called "Cold-Blooded,"* StarTribune (Dec. 22, 2012). For sources asserting that one shot would have been justified, see *id.* (quoting Professor Joseph Olson as saying "I think the first shot is justified"); Patrick Thornton, *In Morrison County Shooting Case, Minnesota State Law on Trial*, Minn. Law. (Dec. 7, 2012).

128. For similar statutes, see Cal. Penal Code §198.5; Fla. Stat. §776.013(2).

129. For accounts of this incident, see Bruce Vielmetti, *Party, Call to Police Preceded Fatal Shooting in Slinger*, Milwaukee J. Sentinel (Mar. 24, 2012); *Rally Held at UW-Madison over Martin, Morrison Shootings*, Channel3000 (Mar. 27, 2012); Maria Rohde, *Wisconsin Shooting Puts "Castle" Law Under Scrutiny*, Reuters (Mar. 26, 2012).

130. Light, *supra* note 115, at 12; Benjamin Levin, Note, *A Defensible Defense? Reexamining Castle Doctrine Statutes*, 47 Harv. J. Legis. 523, 548 (2010).

131. 2 LaFave, *supra* note 25, §10.4(f).

132. Suk, *supra* note 115, at 251-252, 258-259.

133. Quong, *supra* note 96, at 12.

134. Rachel Harmon, *The Law of the Police* 14 (2021).

135. Jamiles Lartey, *Why It's Not So Simple to Arrest the Cops Who Shot Breonna Taylor*, Marshall Project (Aug. 8, 2020) ("police have the unique power"); Cynthia Lee, *Reforming the Law on Police Use of Deadly Force: De-Escalation, Preseizure Conduct, and Imperfect Self-Defense*, 2018 U. Ill. L. Rev. 629, 661 [hereinafter Lee, *Reforming*].

136. On Breonna Taylor's death, see Richard A. Oppel, Jr. et al., *What to Know About Breonna Taylor's Death*, N.Y. Times (Apr. 26, 2021) ("A New York Times examination of video

footage from the scene, witness accounts, statements by the police officers and forensics reports showed that the raid was compromised by poor planning and reckless execution. It found that the only support for the grand jury's conclusion that the officers had announced themselves before bursting into Ms. Taylor's apartment . . . was the account of a single witness who had given inconsistent statements."). For other, lesser-known cases of deadly home invasions by police, including ones in which the officers conducted a raid at the wrong address or submitted falsified information to obtain the warrant authorizing the raid, see Jim Fisher, *SWAT Madness and the Militarization of the American Police* 150 (2010) (mistaken raid on Kenneth Jamar's home in which SWAT officers found Jamar standing in his bedroom holding a gun and opened fire); Peter Jamison, *Confidential Informant Blows Whistle in Fatal Tampa SWAT Raid*, Tampa Bay Times (Dec. 28, 2014) (fatal raid on Jason Westcott's home premised on a warrant tainted by false information).

137. For the turn away from a right to resist, see Darrell A.H. Miller, *Retail Rebellion and the Second Amendment*, 86 Ind. L.J. 939, 953 (2011); Model Penal Code §3.04(2)(a)(i) (stating that defensive force "is not justifiable . . . to resist an arrest that the actor knows is being made by a peace officer, although the arrest is unlawful").

138. Unlike civilians, police officers "are often not *permitted* to retreat." Rachel A. Harmon, *When Is Police Violence Justified?*, 102 Nw. U. L. Rev. 1119, 1120 (2008) (emphasis added).

139. President's Task Force on 21st Century Policing, *Final Report of the President's Task Force on 21st Century Policing* 20 (2015) (quoting testimony of Chuck Wexler) (second emphasis added).

140. For accounts of the Schultz case, see Liam Stack, *Georgia Tech Student Leader Is Shot Dead by Campus Police*, N.Y. Times (Sept. 18, 2017); *Georgia Tech Officer Who Killed Student Won't Face Charges*, AP News (Mar. 13, 2020). For a divided opinion from the U.S. Supreme Court immunizing a police officer from civil liability for a shooting under comparable circumstances, see *Kisela v. Hughes*, 584 U.S. 100 (2018) (per curiam).

141. Franklin E. Zimring, *When Police Kill* 78-83, 89, 97 (2017) (emphasis added).

142. U.S. Dep't of Just., *Department of Justice Report Regarding the Criminal Investigation into the Shooting Death of Michael Brown by Ferguson, Missouri Police Officer Darren Wilson* (2015). For a detailed account of the evidence in the case, organized by witness, see Laura Santhanam, *What Do the Newly Released Witness Statements Tell Us About the Michael Brown Shooting?*, PBS (Nov. 24, 2014).

143. U.S. Dep't of Just., *supra* note 142, at 6.

144. Steven Salky et al., *Lawful Use of Deadly Force by the Police: What's Wrong in Ferguson and Elsewhere*, Champion, May 2015, at 20, 22.

145. For a history of police violence and protests by Black Americans, see Elizabeth Hinton, *America on Fire: The Untold History of Police Violence and Black Rebellion Since the 1960s* (2021).

146. Matt Farber et al., *What Happened in the Chaotic Moments Before George Floyd Died*, N.Y. Times (June 10, 2020) (documenting the events of Floyd's murder). For reporting on the Black Lives Matter movement, see Larry Buchanan et al., *Black Lives Matter May Be the Largest Movement in U.S. History*, N.Y. Times (July 3, 2020); *Protestors Around the World Rally for George Floyd and Against Police Brutality*, France 24 (July 6, 2020).

147. Paul Butler, *Chokehold: Policing Black Men* 2 (2017).

148. Bureau of Just. Stat., *National Sources of Law Enforcement Employment Data* 2-3 tbls.1 & 2 (2016) (law enforcement employment data); Tom Jackman, *For a Second Year, Most U.S. Police Departments Decline to Share Information on Their Use of Force*, Wash. Post (June 9,

2021) (failed FBI data collection initiative). On the underreporting of police violence, see Zimring, *supra* note 141, at 39-40; GBD 2019 Police Violence US Subnational Collaborators, *Fatal Police Violence by Race and State in the USA, 1980–2019: A Network Meta-Regression*, 398 Lancet 1239, 1239 (2021).

149. In direct response to the killing of Michael Brown, the *Washington Post* began logging every deadly police shooting in the United States. As of 2024, the effort had recorded more than 10,000 such shootings. The statistic given in the text is drawn from this database, which is available at: https://www.washingtonpost.com/graphics/investigations/police-shootings-database/. For other statistics on U.S. police violence, see Frank Edwards et al., *Risk of Being Killed by Police Use of Force in the United States by Age, Race-Ethnicity, and Sex*, 116 Proc. Nat'l Acad. Sci. 16,793 (2019) (leading cause of death for young men); Zimring, *supra* note 141, at 74-90 (international comparison).

150. For estimates of the proportion of police shootings that are fatal, see Justin Nix & John A. Shjarback, *Factors Associated with Police Shooting Mortality: A Focus on Race and a Plea for More Comprehensive Data*, 16 PLoS ONE e0259024, at 3 (2021) (55 percent); Allison McCann et al., *Police Shoot Far More People Than Anyone Realized, a VICE News Investigation Reveals*, Vice News (Dec. 12, 2017) (one-third); Jolie McCullough et al., *Unholstered: When Texas Police Pull the Trigger*, Tex. Trib. (Aug. 30, 2016) (38 percent); Ben Montgomery, *Why Cops Shoot*, Tampa Bay Times (Apr. 5, 2017) (over 50 percent).

151. Ted R. Miller et al., *Perils of Police Action: A Cautionary Tale from US Data Sets*, 23 Injury Prevention 27, 28-29 (2016) (data from hospital admissions). For the argument that police behavior is not worsening, but rather societal responses are intensifying, see Aurélie Ouss & John Rappaport, *Is Police Behavior Getting Worse? Data Selection and the Measurement of Policing Harms*, 49 J. Legal Stud. 153 (2020).

152. Edwards et al., *supra* note 149, at 16,793 (1-in-1,000 odds); Cody T. Ross, *A Multi-Level Bayesian Analysis of Racial Bias in Police Shootings at the County-Level in the United States, 2011-2014*, 10 PLoS ONE e0141854, at 12 (2015) ("higher median probability of being *unarmed* black individuals"). For racial disparities in the use of lethal force, see Gabriel L. Schwartz & Jaquelyn L. Jahn, *Mapping Fatal Police Violence Across U.S. Metropolitan Areas: Overall Rates and Racial/Ethnic Inequities, 2013-2017*, 15 PLoS ONE e0229686, at 5 (2020) (finding that Black people are 3.23 times as likely as white people to be killed by police); Justin Nix et al., *A Bird's Eye View of Civilians Killed by Police in 2015*, 16 Criminology & Pub. Pol'y 309, 325-326 (2017) (finding that Black civilians killed by the police in 2015 were more than twice as likely as white civilians to have been unarmed). For racial disparities in the use of less-lethal force, see Roland G. Fryer, Jr., *An Empirical Analysis of Racial Differences in Police Use of Force*, 127 J. Pol. Econ. 1210, 1213 (2019); Miller et al., *supra* note 151, at 29-31; Nix & Shjarback, *supra* note 150, at 5; McCann et al., *supra* note 150.

153. For evidence tending to suggest that racial animus, fear, and bias drive police use of force against Black people, see Fryer, *supra* note 152, at 1216; Mark Hoekstra & CarlyWill Sloan, *Does Race Matter for Police Use of Force? Evidence from 911 Calls*, 112 Am. Econ. Rev. 827 (2022); Lee, *Murder, supra* note 37, at 179 ("Racial stereotypes may alter the officer's perception of danger, threat, and resistance to authority."). For data on the proportional relationship between police force incidents involving Black civilians and police encounters with Black civilians, see Miller et al., *supra* note 151, at 29; Emily K. Weisburst, *Police Use of Force as an Extension of Arrests: Examining Disparities Across Civilian and Officer Race*, 109 AEA Papers & Proc. 152, 152 (2019); Sendhil Mullainathan, *Police Killings of Blacks: Here Is What the Data Say*, N.Y. Times (Oct. 16, 2015).

154. For sources discussing evidence of racial bias in the decision to use force, see generally Steven N. Durlauf & James J. Heckman, *An Empirical Analysis of Racial Differences in Police Use of Force: A Comment*, 128 J. Pol. Econ. 3398 (2020); Dean Knox et al., *Administrative*

Records Mask Racially Biased Policing, 114 Am. Pol. Sci. Rev. 619 (2020); Cody T. Ross et al., *Resolution of Apparent Paradoxes in the Race-Specific Frequency of Use-of-Force by Police*, 4 Palgrave Commc'ns 61 (2018).

155. For studies on the effects of police violence on students, see Desmond Ang, *The Effects of Police Violence on Inner-City Students*, 136 Q.J. Econ. 115, 117-118 (2021); Joscha Legewie & Jeffrey Fagan, *Aggressive Policing and the Educational Performance of Minority Youth*, 84 Am. Socio. Rev. 220, 220 (2019) ("We find that exposure to police surges significantly reduced test scores for African American boys, consistent with their greater exposure to policing."). For evidence of the effect of police killings of unarmed Black people on Black mental health, see Jacob Bor et al., *Police Killings and Their Spillover Effects on the Mental Health of Black Americans: A Population-Based, Quasi-Experimental Study*, 392 Lancet 302, 303 (2018); Abhery Das et al., *Emergency Department Visits for Depression Following Police Killings of Unarmed African Americans*, 269 Soc. Sci. & Med. 113561 (2021); Melissa N. McLeod et al., *Police Interactions and the Mental Health of Black Americans: A Systematic Review*, 7 J. Racial & Ethnic Health Disparities 10 (2020). For an account of how police violence and mistreatment can cause community-wide distrust of law enforcement, including through the "vicarious marginalization" that occurs when people experience or become aware of "police maltreatment that is targeted toward others," see Monica C. Bell, *Police Reform and the Dismantling of Legal Estrangement*, 126 Yale L.J. 2054, 2104 (2017).

156. Shaila Dewan, *Few Police Officers Who Cause Deaths Are Charged or Convicted*, N.Y. Times (Nov. 30, 2021).

157. For discussion of these issues, see Radley Balko, Opinion, *Boston's First Black Woman Prosecutor Has Yet to Take Office, but She's Already Facing an Ethics Complaint*, Wash. Post (Dec. 28, 2018); Kate Levine, *Who Shouldn't Prosecute the Police?*, 101 Iowa L. Rev. 1447 (2016).

158. N.J. Stat. Ann. §52:17B-107.

159. Paul J. Watford, *Hallows Lecture:* Screws v. United States *and the Birth of Federal Civil Rights Enforcement*, 98 Marquette L. Rev. 465, 482 (2014); George Floyd Justice and Policing Act of 2020, H.R. 7120, 116th Cong. §101. On the federal criminal charges against the officers involved in George Floyd's death, see Katie Benner & Nicholas Bogel-Burroughs, *Former Police Officers Indicted on Civil Rights Charges in George Floyd's Death*, N.Y. Times (Jan. 24, 2022). For more analysis of the paucity of federal prosecutions, see Harmon, *Law of the Police, supra* note 134, at 691-715. It bears noting that Judge Watford's assessment of *Screws*'s legacy is nuanced. "[V]iewing the decision with the benefit of almost seventy years of hindsight," he writes, "[t]he most important legacy of *Screws* is that Section 242 survived" constitutional challenge. And "in the aftermath of *Screws*," he goes on, "lawyers in the Civil Rights Section noted that even when Section 242 prosecutions in the South did not result in convictions, they still had a noticeable deterrent effect on the local police forces involved." Ultimately, he concludes, "Section 242 has been used to prosecute police misconduct in many different settings over the years, and not just in the South." Watford, *supra*, at 483-484.

160. On procedural protections that make it more difficult to prosecute police officers, see Kate Levine, *Police Suspects*, 116 Colum. L. Rev. 1197 (2016) [hereinafter Levine, *Police Suspects*]. On the blue wall of silence, see Jerome Skolnick, *Corruption and the Blue Code of Silence*, 3 Police Prac. & Rsch 7 (2002).

161. 2021 Md. Laws ch. 59 (repealing Maryland's Law Enforcement Officer Bill of Rights). For more on substantive law as an obstacle to law enforcement reform, see Seth W. Stoughton et al., *Evaluating Police Uses of Force* 60-61 (2020) ("[I]t is likely that most uses of force simply do not meet the criteria for a criminal act."); Paul Butler, *The System Is Working the Way It Is Supposed to: The Limits of Criminal Justice Reform*, 104 Geo. L.J. 1419, 1425 (2016).

162. On contract protections and indemnification, see Stephen Rushin, *Police Union Contracts*, 66 Duke L.J. 1191 (2017); Aziz Z. Huq & Richard H. McAdams, *Litigating the*

Blue Wall of Silence: How to Challenge the Police Privilege to Delay Investigation, 2016 U. Chi. Legal F. 213; Joanna C. Schwartz, *Police Indemnification*, 89 N.Y.U. L. Rev. 885 (2014). For reinstatement or rehiring after firing, see Stephen Rushin, *Police Disciplinary Appeals*, 167 U. Pa. L. Rev. 545 (2019); Ben Grunwald & John Rappaport, *The Wandering Officer*, 129 Yale L.J. 1676 (2020). For statistics on the distribution of misconduct, see Kyle Rozema & Max Schanzenbach, *Good Cop, Bad Cop: Using Civilian Allegations to Predict Police Misconduct*, 11 Am. Econ. J.: Econ. Pol'y 225 (2019). For calls to prosecute officers for their misconduct, see for example Lolis Eric Elie, *It's Not Just Police Shootings That Spark Protests. It's the Denial of Justice*, Wash. Post (July 14, 2016); Zimring, *supra* note 141, at 169 ("Any less drastic countermeasures [than criminal sanctions] would seem to diminish the seriousness of the killing and the blameworthiness of the killers.").

163. Zimring, *supra* note 141, at 87. For statistics on assaults of officers, see Michael Sierra-Arévalo & Justin Nix, *Gun Victimization in the Line of Duty: Fatal and Nonfatal Firearm Assaults on Police Officers in the United States, 2014–2019*, 19 Criminology & Pub. Pol'y 1041, 1046 (2020); Michael D. White et al., *Assessing Dangerousness in Policing: An Analysis of Officer Deaths in the United States, 1970–2016*, 18 Criminology & Pub. Pol'y 11, 12 (2019).

164. On difficulties recruiting new officers, see Int'l Ass'n of Chiefs of Police, *The State of Recruitment: A Crisis for Law Enforcement* (2019).

165. For an argument to prosecute fewer ordinary people rather than more police, see Kate Levine, *Police Prosecutions and Punitive Instincts*, 98 Wash. U. L. Rev. 997 (2021). On giving to civilians the procedural protections police enjoy, see Levine, *Police Suspects*, *supra* note 160.

166. Barbara E. Armacost, *Organizational Culture and Police Misconduct*, 72 Geo. Wash. L. Rev. 453, 457, 459, 476, 494, 512 (2004). As a statistical matter, "identifying and surgically incapacitating the 'bad apples' is unlikely to have a large and direct impact on use of force." Aaron Chalfin & Jacob Kaplan, *How Many Complaints Against Police Officers Can Be Abated by Incapacitating a Few "Bad Apples?"*, 20 Criminology & Pub. Pol'y 351, 364 (2021).

167. George P. Fletcher, *Rethinking Criminal Law* 759 (Oxford Univ. Press 2000) (1978); *see also* Leverick, *supra* note 90, at 17 (describing excuse as arising when a person says "that, although what she did was unacceptable, there is a reason why she should not be blamed for it").

168. 2 LaFave, *supra* note 25, §10.4 (emphasis added).

169. John Gardner, *The Gist of Excuses*, 1 Buff. Crim. L. Rev. 575, 590 (1998).

170. Hart, *Punishment*, *supra* note 82, at 43-49; *see* Jeremy Bentham, *The Principles of Morals and Legislation* 172-175 (Prometheus Books 1988) (1789). For a perspective opposing Hart's, see Donald A. Dripps, *Rehabilitating Bentham's Theory of Excuses*, 42 Tex. Tech. L. Rev. 383 (2009).

171. Lillian B. Rubin, *Quiet Rage: Bernie Goetz in a Time of Madness* 104 (1986) (quoting James Q. Wilson). Rubin's book gives a thorough account of the *Goetz* case and—along with Mark Lesly, *Subway Gunman: A Juror's Account of the Bernhard Goetz Trial* (1988), and George P. Fletcher, *A Crime of Self-Defense: Bernhard Goetz and the Law on Trial* (1988) [hereinafter Fletcher, *Self-Defense*] — is the source of a number of details in this note. Lesly served as a juror in the case. For background on frustration with crime and policing in New York City at the time, see for example Franklin E. Zimring, *The City That Became Safe* (2011), and Fletcher, *Self-Defense*, *supra*, at 199-201.

172. Rubin, *supra* note 171, at 10. For polling statistics, see Robert D. McFadden, *Poll Indicates Half of New Yorkers See Crime as City's Chief Problem*, N.Y. Times (Jan. 14, 1985).

173. Rubin, *supra* note 171, at 78-79 ("talk-show hosts"); Esther B. Fein, *Angry Citizens in Many Cities Supporting Goetz*, N.Y. Times (Jan. 7, 1985) ("less concerned with the

exact events") (emphasis added); Rubin, *supra* note 171, at 42, 44 ("certain sympathetic understanding").

174. Louis Harris, *Public Reacts to the Goetz Case*, Harris Survey, Feb. 7, 1985 (polling). On Goetz's strategic use of the media, see Rubin, *supra* note 171, at 149, 168-180.

175. Sarah Lyall, *N.A.A.C.P. Leader Seeks Federal Case on Goetz*, N.Y. Times (June 20, 1987) ("fear, not race"). For the shift in public opinion, see *id.*; Marcia Chambers, *Goetz Spoke to One Youth, Then Shot Again, Police Say*, N.Y. Times (Feb. 28, 1985).

176. For the demographics of the jurors, see Lesly, *supra* note 171, at 15; Otto Friedrich et al., *Not Guilty*, Time (June 29, 1987).

177. Fletcher, *Self-Defense*, *supra* note 171, at 105. The prosecution argued that Goetz shot Cabey "execution-style." Lesly, *supra* note 171, at 38.

178. Lesly, *supra* note 171, at 286, 291.

179. Lesly, *supra* note 171, at 309-310 ("frightened, confused, bitter man"); Fletcher, *Self-Defense*, *supra* note 171, at 175, 196 ("[i]n all probability") (quoting Assistant District Attorney Gregory Waples). The *New York Times* reported that "jurors said . . . they had rejected the account because there were too many inconsistencies in it." David E. Pitt, *Blacks See Goetz Verdict as Blow to Race Relations*, N.Y. Times (June 18, 1987).

180. Fletcher, *Self-Defense*, *supra* note 171, at 100-102 (emphasis added).

181. Fletcher, *Self-Defense*, *supra* note 171, at 199 (Gallup statistics); Ronald Sullivan, *Goetz Released After Spending 8 Months in Jail*, N.Y. Times (Sept. 21, 1989) (reporting on Goetz's release); Adam Nossiter, *Bronx Jury Orders Goetz to Pay Man He Paralyzed $43 Million*, N.Y. Times (Apr. 24, 1996) (civil jury's verdict); *Larry King Live* (CNN television broadcast Dec. 17, 2004) ("I don't think I've paid a penny").

182. Richard Restak, *The Fiction of the "Reasonable Man,"* Wash. Post. (May 17, 1987) ("no reasonable people," "neurologically unrealistic"); Fletcher, *Self-Defense*, *supra* note 171, at 59-60 ("simply unjust," "state of consciousness").

183. For examples requiring objective reasonableness, see Ala. Code §13A-3-23(a); Colo. Rev. Stat. §18-1-704(1). On the historical roots of the objective-reasonableness requirement, see for example 1 David Hume, *Commentaries on the Law of Scotland Respecting Crimes* 219 (Edinburgh, Bell & Bradfute 2d ed. 1819) ("It is not sufficient that the [defendant] have killed out of an apprehension, though ever so serious on his part, of danger to his life, if it was not also a reasonable apprehension, and well grounded in the circumstances of the situation.").

184. *See* Holly Maguigan, *Battered Women and Self-Defense: Myths and Misconceptions in Current Reform Proposals*, 140 U. Pa. L. Rev. 379, 410-412 (1991).

185. For cases permitting the defendant to demonstrate his knowledge of the decedent's prior acts, see *People v. Davis*, 408 P.2d 129 (Cal. 1965) (en banc); *People v. Minifie*, 920 P.2d 1337 (Cal. 1996) (evidence about the decedent's associates).

186. Diana Serpe, *Inside the Jury Room*, N.Y. Daily News (June 18, 1987) ("might not be reasonable for me"); *see* Lesly, *supra* note 171, at 35, 149-50; Fletcher, *Self-Defense*, *supra* note 171, at 12.

187. Lesly, *supra* note 171, at 291.

188. Model Penal Code §§3.04(1), 3.09(2). For states following the MPC, see Ky. Rev. Stat. Ann. §§503.050(1), 503.120(1); Neb. Rev. Stat. §§28-1409(1), 28-1414(2).

189. Sklansky, *supra* note 1, at 27.

190. For other examples rejecting cultural background as a factor in the reasonableness analysis, see *People v. Romero*, 81 Cal. Rptr. 2d. 823, 824 (Cal. Ct. App. 1999); Donna

Coker & Lindsay C. Harrison, *The Story of* Wanrow: *The Reasonable Woman and the Law of Self-Defense*, in *Criminal Law Stories* 213, 253-255 (Donna Coker & Robert Weisberg eds., 2013) (describing the Washington courts' exclusion of expert testimony on how the defendant's "Native American culture" informed her perception and behavior).

191. Jonathan Markovitz, *"A Spectacle of Slavery Unwilling to Die": Curbing Reliance on Racial Stereotyping in Self-Defense Cases*, 5 U.C. Irvine L. Rev. 873, 927 (2015) ("Goetz's legal team"); Fletcher, *Self-Defense, supra* note 171, at 127, 207 ("blown-up pictures," "fit and muscular").

192. Nat'l Task Force on Stand Your Ground Laws, Am. Bar Ass'n, *Report and Recommendations* 15 (2015) ("stereotypical association"); Lee, *Murder, supra* note 37, at 137, 139, 155-174.

193. Lee, *Murder, supra* note 37, at 148; Butler, *Chokehold, supra* note 147, at 25; Jody D. Armour, *Race Ipsa Loquitor: Of Reasonable Racists, Intelligent Bayesians, and Involuntary Negrophobes*, 46 Stan. L. Rev. 781, 796 (1994). In the aftermath of the *Goetz* case, commentators explicitly made the argument that racial inferences are rational. See for example Joseph Berger, *Goetz Case: Commentary on Nature of Urban Life*, N.Y. Times (June 18, 1987) (quoting criminologist Marvin Wolfgang, who argued that "rates of crime for . . . homicide, rape, robbery and aggravated assault" were, at the time, "at least ten times as high for blacks as they [were] for whites," and who further said that " '[t]he expectation that four young black males are going to do you harm is indeed greater than four young whites"). For more discussion of the fallacy of race-based inferences of violence, see Armour, *supra*, at 791 ("[E]mploying race as the dominant index of dangerousness cannot be statistically justified; blacks arrested for violent crimes comprised less than 1 percent of the black population in 1991, and less than 1.7 percent of the black male population, making the odds that any particular black person will commit a violent crime very long indeed."); Butler, *Chokehold, supra*, note 147, at 24 ("The person who is at most risk from a black man is another black man, and even this risk is relatively low.").

194. Lee, *Murder, supra* note 37, at 137. For discussion of how lynching was used to perpetuate "racial terror," see Light, *supra* note 115, at 86-107. For the story of John White, see *People v. White*, 901 N.Y.S.2d 346 (App. Div. 2010) (upholding jury conviction for manslaughter); Jacob Gershman & Tamer El-Ghobashy, *Father Who Killed Is Freed*, Wall St. J. (Dec. 24, 2010) (early release from prison).

195. Elizabeth M. Schneider, *Equal Rights to Trial for Women: Sex Bias in the Law of Self-Defense*, 15 Harv. C.R.-C.L. L. Rev. 623, 623 (1980).

196. Coker & Harrison, *supra* note 190, at 215, 241-242 (quoting Elizabeth M. Schneider, *Battered Women and Feminist Lawmaking* 33 (2000)).

197. For the argument that traditional criminal law standards can fairly resolve women's self-defense claims, see Maguigan, *supra* note 184, at 381-382. For evidence of leniency toward women, see Kalven & Zeisel, *supra* note 83, at 231-234.

198. Coker & Harrison, *supra* note 190, at 213-216.

199. Anne M. Coughlin, *Excusing Women*, 82 Calif. L. Rev. 1, 6 (1994). For a review of the literature on battered woman syndrome, see Regina A. Schuller & Neil Vidmar, *BWS Evidence in the Courtroom: A Review of the Literature*, 16 Law & Hum. Behav. 273 (1992). For a history of the legal system's treatment of spousal abuse, see Siegel, *supra* note 36. For an example opinion, see *State v. Gartland*, 694 A.2d 564, 575 (N.J. 1997) (per curiam), which held that, "[a]t a minimum, the jury . . . should have been asked to consider whether, if it found such to be the case, a reasonable woman who had been the victim of years of domestic violence would have reasonably perceived on this occasion that the use of deadly force was necessary to protect herself from serious bodily injury."

200. Ida B. Wells, *Southern Horrors: Lynch Law in All Its Phases* (1892), reprinted in Ida B. Wells-Barnett, *On Lynchings* 23 (1969).

201. Light, *supra* note 115, at 108-109. On lynchings and Black access to firearms, see Michael D. Makowsky & Patrick L. Warren, *Firearms and Lynching*, 66 J.L. & Econ. 259 (2023).

202. Light, *supra* note 115, at 108-109.

203. Light, *supra* note 115, at 8-9. On the officer's acquittal, see Mitch Smith, *Minnesota Officer Acquitted in Killing of Philando Castile*, N.Y. Times (June 16, 2017).

204. For statistics on shootings of unarmed victims, see McCullough et al., *supra* note 150 (17 percent); Montgomery, *supra* note 150 (19 percent); McCann et al., *supra*, note 150 (20 percent). For fatal shootings, one source reports a lower proportion, around 11 percent. Zimring, *supra* note 171, at 57 fig.3.6. For statistics on people shot who were armed with something other than a firearm, see *id.*; McCann et al., *supra* note 150. On the "effective monopoly" of firearms as a death risk for police, see Zimring, *supra* note 171, at 96-97.

205. On racial disparities in victims shot by the police, see Montgomery, *supra* note 150 (unarmed Black people are eight times more likely to be shot by police); Nix et al., *supra* note 152, at 325-326 (Black civilians killed by police were more than twice as likely to be unarmed as whites); Zimring, *supra* note 171, at 59 (police twice as likely to inaccurately assume firearm possession for people of color versus whites).

206. Lee, *Reforming*, *supra* note 135, at 655, 661-664. For an argument for strict misdemeanor liability for officers who kill unarmed civilians, see Kelly M. Hogue, Note, *When an Officer Kills: Turning Legal Police Conduct into Illegal Police Misconduct*, 98 Tex. L. Rev. 601 (2020).

CHAPTER 5

1. Tarana Burke (@TaranaBurke), X (Oct. 15, 2017, 6:19PM), https://x.com/Tarana Burke/status/919704393934614528; Alyssa Milano (@Alyssa_Milano), X (Oct. 15, 2017, 3:21PM), https://x.com/alyssa_milano/status/919659438700670976. Burke is widely credited as originating both the "Me Too" phrase and an organizing campaign that draws on the phrase's power. The phrase moved into widespread national usage in 2017, spurred by numerous sexual assault allegations against Hollywood producer Harvey Weinstein. For background, see Abby Ohlheiser, *The Woman Behind "Me Too" Knew the Power of the Phrase When She Created It—10 Years Ago*, Wash. Post. (Oct. 19, 2017).

2. Kathleen C. Basile et al., Ctrs. for Disease Control & Prevention, *The National Intimate Partner and Sexual Violence Survey: 2016/2017 Report on Sexual Violence* 22 tbl.1, 33 tbl.9 (2022). The phrase "sexual violence" as used in the cited survey encompasses four categories of conduct: *rape, sexual coercion, unwanted sexual contact,* and (for male respondents only) *forced penetration.* For purposes of the survey, "rape" and "sexual coercion" both refer to instances of unwanted sexual penetration (vaginal, oral, or anal), with a distinction drawn between instances involving force, threat of force, or incapacitation (defined in the survey as "rape") and instances involving nonphysical pressure (defined in the survey as "sexual coercion"). As will be clear later in this chapter, the definition of the term "rape" as used in this survey is not necessarily synonymous with the term's definition in the criminal law, which varies across jurisdictions and does not always require physical force or threats of force. The term "unwanted sexual contact" is defined in the survey as "unwanted sexual experiences involving touch but not sexual penetration, such as being kissed in a sexual way or having sexual body parts fondled, groped, or grabbed." Respondents of all genders were asked if they had been subjected to the three categories of sexual violence just described.

For male respondents only, the survey also asked whether they had ever been made to penetrate another person against their will by force or threatened force (defined in the survey as "being made to penetrate").

For more on the prevalence of male rape victimization, see Bennett Capers, *Real Rape Too*, 99 Calif. L. Rev. 1259 (2011). For more on sexual violence in prison, see Laura M. Maruschak & Emily D. Buehle, Bureau of Just. Stat., *Survey of Sexual Victimization in Adult Correctional Facilities, 2012–2018 – Statistical Tables* (2021) and also discussion *supra* Chapter 2 at pp. 87-88.

3. On reporting to law enforcement, see Rachel E. Morgan & Alexandra Thompson, Bureau of Just. Stat., *Criminal Victimization, 2020*, at 7 tbl.4 (2021), documenting that, in 2020, 22.9% of rapes and sexual assaults were reported to police, compared to 54.3% of robberies and 57% of aggravated assaults. On attrition within the law enforcement and prosecution processes, see, for example, Rebecca Campbell, *The Psychological Impact of Rape Victims' Experiences with the Legal, Medical, and Mental Health Systems*, 63 Am. Psych. 702, 704 (2008), and Majority Staff of S. Comm. on the Judiciary, 103d Cong., *The Response to Rape: Detours on the Road to Equal Justice* 2 (Comm. Print 1993). For an argument that attrition statistics alone do not demonstrate systemic bias against rape victims, see David P. Bryden & Sonja Lengnick, *Rape in the Criminal Justice System*, 87 J. Crim. L. & Criminology 1194, 1211-1212 (1997), in which the authors write:

> For the sake of illustration, suppose that of every 100 rapes, thirty are not reported for personal reasons that have nothing to do with anticipated official bias. In another fifteen cases the perpetrator was a stranger who cannot be identified. Assume that two false rape reports have been made, and that in twenty cases the complainant, though honest, ultimately decided not to press charges. Finally, suppose that in twenty-eight cases the rapist could not be proved guilty beyond a reasonable doubt to the satisfaction of an impartial factfinder. In that event, if only five of every 100 rapes lead to criminal convictions, the justice system may be working perfectly, screening out false reports plus a much larger number of cases in which either the victim does not cooperate, or the perpetrator's identity is unknown, or his guilt cannot be proven.
>
> But, of course, attrition statistics also are amenable to less sanguine interpretations. For example, rape victims might have decided to remain silent about the crime because they feared official mistreatment. Also, the system might have screened out some of the truthful complaints rather than the false ones. Detectives might have persuaded truthful complainants that it would not be in their interest to undergo the rigors of a trial. Police or prosecutors might have brushed aside truthful accusations by women of whom they disapproved, or against ex-husbands or boyfriends, while perhaps mistakenly believing some honest misidentifications in stranger rape cases. And, of course, cases in which officials or juries decided that the crime did not occur, or was not proven beyond a reasonable doubt, may have been real rapes, amply proven. By themselves, rape attrition statistics do not provide a basis for excluding any of these hypotheses.

For more on the interaction between these various sociolegal dynamics, see pp. 441-445 of this chapter.

4. Michelle Bowdler, *Is Rape a Crime?* (2020). For national prison statistics, see E. Ann Carson, Bureau of Just. Stat., *Prisoners in 2020 — Statistical Tables* 22 tbl.14 (2021). On the historical use of capital punishment in rape cases, see, for example, Estelle B. Freedman,

Redefining Rape 13 (2013), which reports that of "the seventy-three guilty verdicts for rape between 1700 and 1776 throughout the British colonies, all but five resulted in a death sentence."

5. Freedman, *supra* note 4, at 3.

6. Amia Srinivasan, *The Right to Sex* 146 (2021).

7. Jeannie Suk Gersen, *The Trouble with Teaching Rape Law*, New Yorker (Dec. 15, 2014); *see also* Jennifer M. Denbow, *The Pedagogy of Rape Law: Objectivity, Identity, and Emotion*, 64 J. Legal Educ. 16, 29 (2014) ("Since the law school classroom is one place where future legal professionals, many of whom will have substantial power, form their ideas about rape, discussion is crucial.").

8. James J. Tomkovicz, *On Teaching Rape: Reasons, Risks, and Rewards*, 102 Yale L.J. 481, 504 (1992). For an important counterpoint to Tomkovicz's concern that classroom discussion might cause personal anguish to survivors, see, for example, Conor Friedersdorf, *At Law School, Is Insensitivity Grounds for an Objection?*, Atlantic (Dec. 19, 2014) (arguing that "many bygone victims of violent crimes find that the hard experience of dispassionately analyzing the law ultimately leaves them feeling empowered"); Suk Gersen, *supra* note 7 ("If the topic of sexual assault were to leave the law-school classroom, it would be a tremendous loss—above all to victims of sexual assault."). On statistics regarding sexual assault on college campuses in particular, see Christopher P. Krebs et al., *Campus Climate Survey Validation Study: Final Technical Report*, Bureau of Just. Stat. Rsch. & Dev. Series (2016); Christopher P. Krebs et al., *The Campus Sexual Assault (CSA) Study: Final Report* (2007). For a critical appraisal of these statistics, see Aya Gruber, *Anti-Rape Culture*, 64 U. Kan. L. Rev. 1027, 1031-1039 (2016) [hereinafter Gruber, *Anti-Rape Culture*].

9. Suk Gersen, *supra* note 7 ("was not taught," "became a major part"); Denbow, *supra* note 7 ("too hysterical"). For a personal perspective, see Susan Estrich, *Real Rape* 6-7 (1987) [hereinafter Estrich, *Real Rape*] ("When I began law school, a few months after being raped, I expected to learn the law of rape. I was wrong. Rape was, I discovered, just not taught. . . . When I asked why, I was told that it was not interesting enough, or complicated enough, or important enough to merit a chapter in a criminal law casebook or a week in a course."). For reports of contemporary calls to remove sexual assault from the curriculum, see Suk Gersen, *supra* note 7 ("Some students have . . . suggested that rape law should not be taught because of its potential to cause distress"); *id.* (reporting that "a dozen new teachers of criminal law at multiple institutions" told the author "that they are not including rape law in their courses, arguing that it's not worth the risk of complaints of discomfort by students").

10. Susan Estrich, *Teaching Rape Law*, 102 Yale L.J. 509, 515 (1992); *see also* Denbow, *supra* note 7, at 29 ("Precisely because people have such different and charged views of rape, it is important that future lawyers at least have the opportunity to discuss it.").

11. Aviva Orenstein, *No Bad Men: A Feminist Analysis of Character Evidence in Rape Trials*, 49 Hastings L.J. 663, 677-678 (1998).

12. Stephen Schulhofer, *Unwanted Sex* ix-x (1998). For statistics on acquaintance and stranger rapes, see Basile et al., *supra* note 2, at 7, 9 fig.3. For more on the prevalence of "rape myths" that treat violent stranger rapes as prototypical examples of sexual violence, see Christina E. Wells & Erin Elliott Motley, *Reinforcing the Myth of the Crazed Rapist: A Feminist Critique of Recent Rape Legislation*, 81 B.U. L. Rev. 127, 153-161 (2001) (collecting sources). For a groundbreaking treatment of this issue, see Estrich, *Real Rape, supra* note 9.

13. David P. Bryden, *Redefining Rape*, 3 Buff. Crim. L. Rev. 317, 356 (2000). Bryden elaborates: "In most cases involving acquaintances the force element is, in effect, a resistance requirement. This is because an unarmed acquaintance rapist typically does not employ force unless he meets resistance. If the woman does not resist, he will simply have

intercourse with her, and the great majority of courts do not regard the sexual act itself as inherently forcible." *Id.*; *see also* Estrich, *Real Rape, supra* note 9, at 60 ("The prohibition of 'force' or 'forcible compulsion' ends up being defined in terms of a woman's resistance.").

14. Estrich, *Real Rape, supra* note 9, at 63; Lauren Kelly, *America Has a Rape Problem — and Kate Harding Wants to Fix It,* Rolling Stone (Aug. 24, 2015) (quoting Harding). For more from Harding, see Kate Harding, *Asking for It: The Alarming Rise of Rape Culture – And What We Can Do About It* (2015). The phrase "rape culture" (or "rape-supportive culture") dates back to the 1970s. For an overview of the term's history and evolution, see Joyce E. Williams, *Rape Culture,* in *The Blackwell Encyclopedia of Sociology* (George Ritzer ed., 2015), and Patricia Donat & John D'Emilio, *A Feminist Redefinition of Rape and Sexual Assault: Historical Foundations and Change,* 48 J. Soc. Issues 9 (1992), which traces the phrase to the groundbreaking work of Susan Brownmiller, *Against Our Will* (1975). For a critique that the phrase has become "so discursively prolific as to be banal," see Gruber, *Anti-Rape Culture, supra* note 8, at 1028 (arguing that the phrase "is said to include everything from brutal sexual assaults to jokes about sex, women's general inequality, casual sex, catcalling, child beauty contests" and more, and contending further that "[t]he term's expansiveness and slippery nature renders it unhelpful in identifying how law and policy should specifically address violent or otherwise harmful sex").

15.   *See* Nancy E. Roman, *Scales of Justice Weigh Tiers of Sexual Assault; State May Reform Rape Law,* Wash. Times (June 16, 1994) ("Camille Paglia, a professor of humanities at the University of the Arts in Philadelphia who has written and lectured about date rape, said the Berkowitz case 'isn't even remotely about rape.' 'Oh, please, she goes into the room of a man who's in bed and sits on the floor with her breasts sticking up: What are we teaching our girls?' she said. 'When you go into a man's room and stretch on the floor, you are sending a signal.'"). Professor David Bryden argues that while it would be wrong "to focus too much on aspects of the victim's behavior that have little or no probative value," it is impossible to ignore the behavior of both people involved in a sexual encounter when assessing an accusation of rape: the factfinder will always "have to determine whether" the person alleging a rape "consented," and "that inquiry would require scrutiny of her words and behavior as well as his." Bryden, *supra* note 13, at 370.

16. Schulhofer, *supra* note 12, at 15; Martha Chamallas, *Consent, Equality, and the Legal Control of Sexual Conduct,* 61 S. Cal. L. Rev. 777, 842 (1988).

17. Elisa Glick, *Sex Positive: Feminism, Queer Theory, and the Politics of Transgression,* 64 Feminist Rev. 19, 20 (2000); Carole S. Vance, *More Danger, More Pleasure: A Decade After the Barnard Sexuality Conference,* 38 N.Y.L. Sch. L. Rev. 289, 290-291 (1993); Srinivasan, *supra* note 6, at 36. Sex-positive feminism is not, however, the only mode of feminism. On the contrary, it is in part a reaction to an earlier and still extant view that "sex as we know it [is] a patriarchal construct — an eroticization of gender inequality — from which there can be no true liberation without revolution in relations between men and women. Short of this, separatism, lesbianism, or abstinence [a]re (at best) the only emancipatory options." Srinivasan, *supra* note 6, at 36. We will discuss this mode of feminism later in the chapter. For some of the canonical work in the sex-positive tradition, see, for example, *Pleasure and Danger: Exploring Female Sexuality* (Carol Vance ed., 1992); *Powers of Desire: The Politics of Sexuality* (Ann Snitow et al. eds., 1983). For work linking sex-positivity to queer theory, see, for example, Judith Butler, *Gender Trouble* 30 (1990); Gayle Rubin, *Thinking Sex: Notes for a Radical Theory of the Politics of Sexuality,* in *Pleasure and Danger, supra,* at 302-303.

18. Michelle J. Anderson, *All-American Rape,* 79 St. John's L. Rev. 625, 627 (2005).

19. Dorothy Roberts, *Rape, Violence, and Women's Autonomy,* 69 Chi.-Kent L. Rev. 359, 362 (1993).

20. *Patriarchy, Oxford English Dictionary* (2023).

21. 1 William Blackstone, *Commentaries* *430.

22. Leigh Bienen, *Rape III - National Developments in Rape Reform Legislation*, 6 Women's Rts. L. Rep. 170, 184 (1980); Michelle J. Anderson, *Marital Immunity, Intimate Relationships, and Improper Inferences: A New Law on Sexual Offenses by Intimates*, 54 Hastings L.J. 1465, 1478 (2000) [hereinafter Anderson, *Marital Immunity*]. For a historical analysis documenting how feminists as early as the mid-1800s "waged a vigorous, public, and extraordinarily frank campaign against a man's right to forced sex in marriage," see Jill Elaine Hasday, *Contest and Consent: A Legal History of Marital Rape*, 88 Cal. L. Rev. 1373, 1377 (2000).

23. Freedman, *supra* note 4, at 22 ("female chastity," "prospective husbands," "appropriation"); *id.* at 35 ("sullied"); *id.* at 14 ("accused of fornication"); Anderson, *Marital Immunity, supra* note 22, at 1478. For more on these points, see Brownmiller, *supra* note 14, at 18 (describing rape of this era as "a property crime of man against man"); Michelle J. Anderson, *From Chastity Requirement to Sexuality License: Sexual Consent and a New Rape Shield Law*, 70 Geo. Wash. L. Rev. 51, 54 (2002) ("The law often required a woman to be sexually virtuous, engaging in no significant sexual behavior outside the scope of marriage . . . ."). For a thorough analysis of the interplay between the crime of fornication and the crime of rape, see Anne M. Coughlin, *Sex and Guilt*, 84 Va. L. Rev. 1 (1998), and also Bryden, *supra* note 13, at 363.

24. Freedman, *supra* note 4, at 14 (noting "the subtitle of an eighteenth-century poem" that read "The Agreeable Rape" and "insinuated that women wished to be taken by force"); Christina M. Tchen, *Rape Reform and a Statutory Consent Defense*, 74 J. Crim. L. & Criminology 1518, 1522 (1983) ("love play"); *id.* at 1523 ("forceful sexual intercourse").

25. George G. Byron (Lord Byron), *Don Juan: Canto I* (1819), reprinted in 2 *The Norton Anthology of English Literature* 621, 637 (M.H. Abrams & Stephen Greenblatt eds., 7th ed. 2000). For an analysis of the persistence of internalized sexual hierarchies, see LeeAnn Kahlor & Matthew S. Eastin, *Television's Role in the Culture of Violence Toward Women: A Study of Television Viewing and the Cultivation of Rape Myth Acceptance in the United States*, 55 J. Broad. & Elec. Media 215, 216 (2011) (discussing how " 'dominant-submissive, competitive, sex-role stereotyped culture' not only leads to disproportionate crimes against women, but also may lead men and women to internalize related norms" and noting that "both men and women exhibit attitudes consistent with the objectification of women"); Corey Rayburn Yung, *Sex Panic and Denial*, 21 New Crim. L. Rev. 458, 471 (2018) ("Although men are more likely to support myths about sexual violence, studies have shown significant support of myths by women as well."). For more on internalized social hierarchies more generally, in which oppressed groups may come to acquiesce in or even embrace frameworks of their own oppression, see Cass R. Sunstein, *Preferences and Politics*, 20 Phil. & Pub. Affs. 3 (1991); Olga Popov, *Towards A Theory of Underclass Review*, 43 Stan. L. Rev. 1095 (1991).

26. Richard Klein, *An Analysis of Thirty-Five Years of Rape Reform: A Frustrating Search for Fundamental Fairness*, 41 Akron L. Rev. 981, 987 (2008).

27. Estrich, *Real Rape, supra* note 9, at 5; Patricia J. Falk, *Rape by Fraud and Rape by Coercion*, 64 Brooklyn L. Rev. 39, 155 (1998) [hereinafter Falk, *Rape by Fraud*].

28. Coughlin, *supra* note 23, at 6-8. "[A] woman who claimed to have been raped was not only accusing a man of rape," Professor Bryden explains: "She was also offering a defense to her own potentially criminal conduct, saying in effect that she committed fornication or adultery only under duress." Bryden, *supra* note 13, at 363.

29. Coughlin, *supra* note 23, at 9; Klein, *supra* note 26, at 1050-1051.

30. Bryden, *supra* note 13, at 322; John F. Decker & Peter G. Baroni, *"No" Still Means "Yes": The Failure of the "Nonconsent" Reform Movement in American Rape and Sexual Assault Law,* 101 J. Crim. L. & Criminology 1081, 1084 (2011).

31. Am. L. Inst., Model Penal Code: Sexual Assault and Related Offenses, Tent. Draft No. 5, at 111-113 (May. 4, 2021).

32. Am. L. Inst., Model Penal Code: Sexual Assault and Related Offenses, Tent. Draft No. 5, at 111-116 & nn.40 & 61, 268 & n.15 (May. 4, 2021). For the most current tally, including the report of the number of states with consent-only felony and misdemeanor offenses as stated in the text, see Stephen J. Schulhofer & Erin Murphy, Reporters - Model Penal Code: Sexual Assault and Related Offenses, American Law Institute, *Current State of the Law—Consent Only Offenses* 1-4 (May 13, 2016).

33. 2 Wayne R. LaFave, *Substantive Criminal Law* §17.3(b) (3d ed. 2017 & Supp. 2023).

34. For further discussion of these issues, see Falk, *Rape by Fraud, supra* note 27; Kimberly Kessler Ferzan, *Consent and Coercion,* 50 Ariz. St. L. Rev. 951 (2018); Stephen J. Schulhofer, *Taking Sexual Autonomy Seriously: Rape Law and Beyond,* 11 Law & Phil. 35 (1992).

35. N.J. S. L. & Pub. Safety Comm., Statement to Assembly, No. 2767 (Dec. 9, 2019). As Stephen Schulhofer reports, two additional states (Washington and Wisconsin) enacted statutes "punishing any act of intercourse without 'freely given' consent" in the 1970s. Schulhofer, *supra* note 34, at 40. For more recent examples, see Schulhofer & Murphy, *supra* note 32.

36. For a synoptic account of the ALI's process from the project's associate reporter, see Erin Murphy, *Writing on an Unclean Slate: Challenges in Substantive Reform of a Penal Code,* 76 N.Y.U. Ann. Surv. Am. L. 473, 476 (2021). As Professor Murphy summarizes, "the most salient objections" to the original 1962 sexual assault provisions included:

> Its highly gendered character [insofar as it] restricts the most serious penalties for vaginal penetration and does not contemplate that a man might be sexually assaulted by a woman; it further labels anal and oral penetration as "deviate" sexual intercourse.
>
>   Its procedural and evidentiary rules [insofar as it] retains a marital exemption; permits a defense if the complainant is "promiscuous" or a "voluntary social companion" of the actor; and broadly requires prompt complaint, corroboration, and "special care" jury instructions [(see p. 442)].
>
>   Its substantive scope [insofar as it] effectively requires force and resistance for liability; its child-offenses are also fairly restrictive relative to current law.

37. Am. L. Inst., Model Penal Code: Sexual Assault and Related Offenses, Tent. Draft No. 6, at 99 (April 15, 2022), *as revised* July 2022.

38. Am. L. Inst., Model Penal Code: Sexual Assault and Related Offenses, Tent. Draft No. 6, at 98 (April 15, 2022).

39. Am. L. Inst., Model Penal Code: Sexual Assault and Related Offenses, Tent. Draft No. 6, at 106-107 (April 15, 2022).

40. Schulhofer & Murphy, *supra* note 32, at 1-4.

41. For an overview of the state of the law on this topic, see Am. L. Inst., Model Penal Code: Sexual Assault and Related Offenses, Tent. Draft No. 5, at 243-248 (May 4, 2021).

42. According to Alexandra Brodsky, "the law is largely silent" with respect to one "widespread" form of sexual deception that is at least arguably a form of fraud in the factum: the practice, sometimes called "stealthing," of removing a condom during intercourse

without the other person's consent. Alexandra Brodsky, *"Rape-Adjacent": Imagining Legal Responses to Nonconsensual Condom Removal,* 32.2 J. Law & Gender 183, 184 (2017). Reacting in part to Brodsky's scholarship, published while she was a law student, some legislators have proposed or enacted reforms that would create at least civil liability for such conduct. *See* Helen Rosner, *The Meaning of California's Bill Against Nonconsensual Condom Removal,* New Yorker (Sept. 16, 2021); Anne Branigin, *Condom "Stealthing" Is Sexual Violence, Bill Says. Here's What to Know.,* Wash. Post (June 15, 2022).

43. Patricia J. Falk, *Not Logic, But Experience: Drawing on Lessons from the Real World in Thinking About the Riddle of Rape-by-Fraud,* 123 Yale L.J. Online 353, 361 (2013); Roseanna Sommers, *Commonsense Consent,* 129 Yale L.J. 2232, 2242-2243 (2020).

44. Sommers, *supra* note 43, at 2239, 2246 (quoting and citing Joan McGregor, *Why When She Says No She Doesn't Mean Maybe and Doesn't Mean Yes: A Critical Reconstruction of Consent, Sex, and the Law,* 2 Legal Theory 175, 202 (1996); Martha Chamallas, *Consent, Equality, and the Legal Control of Sexual Conduct,* 61 S. Cal. L. Rev. 777, 832 & n.227 (1988); Brodsky, *supra* note 42, at 194); Estrich, *Real Rape, supra* note 9, at 103. For additional argument that "rape-by-deception is an unjustified exception [that] can be solved simply by criminalizing it," see Corey Rayburn Yung, *Rape Law Fundamentals,* 27 Yale J.L. & Feminism 1, 9 (2015) (noting that "[m]any feminists and rape law reformers have argued as such" and citing sources).

45. Deborah Tuerkheimer, *Sex Without Consent,* 123 Yale L.J. Online 335, 344-345 (2013); Sommers, *supra* note 43, at 2236-2238.

46. Sommers, *supra* note 43, at 2237-2238; Am. L. Inst., Model Penal Code: Sexual Assault and Related Offenses, Tent. Draft No. 5, at 243-245 (May 4, 2021). Under the proposed MPC revisions, the offense of "Sexual Assault by Prohibited Deception" contains an *actus reus* element that is satisfied whenever a person pretends that a sexual act has "diagnostic, curative, or preventive medical properties" or causes a person "to believe falsely that the [defendant] was someone else who was personally known to" the victim. For more on the question of deception in the context of sex and sexual assault, see the sources cited in the preceding notes and also Schulhofer, *supra* note 34, at 152-159; Joel Feinberg, *Victim's Excuses: The Case of Fraudulently Procured Consent,* 96 Ethics 330 (1986).

47. For a well-cited treatment, see Patricia J. Falk, *Rape by Drugs: A Statutory Overview and Proposals for Reform,* 44 Ariz. L. Rev. 131 (2002) [hereinafter Falk, *Rape by Drugs*]. For further discussion, see Michal Buchhandler-Raphael, *The Conundrum of Voluntary Intoxication and Sex,* 82 Brook. L. Rev. 1031 (2017); Allison C. Nichols, Note, *Out of the Haze: A Clearer Path for Prosecution of Alcohol-Facilitated Sexual Assault,* 71 N.Y.U. Ann. Surv. Am. L. 213 (2015); Erin Price, *The Model Penal Code's New Approach to Rape and Intoxication,* 48 U. Pac. L. Rev. 423 (2017).

48. For a contemporary analysis of this question and survey of the law across states, see 2 LaFave, *supra* note 33, §17.4(b). On unconsciousness and the force requirement, see Falk, *Rape by Drugs, supra* note 47, at 137.

49. On the breakdown of rules among the states, see 2 LaFave, *supra* note 33, §17.4(b); Falk, *Rape by Drugs, supra* note 47, at 173. Note that here, again, some states adhering to the force requirement nonetheless impose criminal liability when a defendant surreptitiously drugs his victim — with some courts reading the physical act of spiking a drink or secretly administering drugs as the "forcible" act. *See* Falk, *Rape by Drugs, supra* note 47, at 135-136.

50. 2 LaFave, *supra* note 33, §17.4(b) (citing sources).

51. For an analysis of the role of the defendant's intoxication, see Valerie M. Ryan, Comment, *Intoxicating Encounters: Allocating Responsibility in the Law of Rape,* 40 Cal. W. L. Rev. 407, 416-420 (2004).

52. Am. L. Inst., Model Penal Code: Sexual Assault and Related Offenses, Tent. Draft No. 5, at 60-61 (May 4, 2021).

53. 2 LaFave, *supra* note 33, §17.4(c) ("range of age differences"). For a survey of state statutory rape provisions, see Paul H. Robinson & Tyler Scot Williams, *Mapping American Criminal Law* 207-211 (2018).

54. On the prevalence of the mistake-of-age defense, see 2 LaFave, *supra* note 33, §17.4(c).

55. Am. L. Inst., Model Penal Code: Sexual Assault and Related Offenses, Tent. Draft No. 5, at 146-147, 155-156 (May. 4, 2021). In a study of over 170 appellate cases where a defendant was charged with a sexual offense under a mental disability statute, Professor Jasmine Harris found that the defendant was described as nondisabled 97.7% of the time. *See* Jasmine E. Harris, *Sexual Consent and Disability*, 93 N.Y.U. L. Rev. 480, 542 tbl.3 (2018).

Sex with a physically disabled person can also constitute rape, regardless of apparent consent, when the individual's physical condition renders her unaware that a sex act is occurring or "physically helpless" and thus unable to resist or to communicate nonconsent. *See, e.g.*, N.H. Rev. Stat. §632-A:2(I)(b). In *United States v. James*, 810 F.3d 674 (9th Cir. 2016), for example, the Ninth Circuit upheld a conviction for sexual abuse where the victim's "cerebral palsy was sufficiently severe that it rendered her incapable of being understood by others, and thereby incapable of communicating to [the defendant] her unwillingness to participate in the sexual act." *Id.* at 682. But the bar for establishing such inability to communicate can be high. In *State v. Fourtin*, 52 A.3d 674 (Conn. 2012), the Connecticut Supreme Court overturned a conviction under a statute criminalizing sex with a person "physically unable to communicate unwillingness to an act" where the intellectually disabled victim suffered from cerebral palsy and lacked the ability to communicate verbally but could still "communicat[e] with others by gesturing and vocalizing" and could "kick, bite and scratch" to "manifest her displeasure." *Id.* at 676-677. The availability of those "nonverbal methods of communication," the court held, defeated the prosecution's argument "that she was physically incapable of manifesting . . . her lack of consent to sexual intercourse at the time of the alleged sexual assault." *Id.* at 689-690.

56. 2 LaFave, *supra* note 33, §17.4(b) ("legislative purpose"). For the 2011 survey, see Decker & Baroni, *supra* note 30, at 1126-1132, which collects a wealth of additional examples of "position-of-authority" statutes.

57. Schulhofer, *supra* note 34, at 14.

58. The sentence beginning "[I]f sexual interaction is ruled legally out of bounds" and the sentence that follows appear in the introduction to *Unwanted Sex* and are excerpted here out of order, interpolated into an excerpt from later in the book.

59. Srinivasan, *supra* note 6, at 82, 127.

60. Srinivasan, *supra* note 6, at 127.

61. Jody Miller & Martin D. Schwartz, *Rape Myths and Violence Against Street Prostitutes*, 16 Deviant Behav. 1, 9 (1995) (quoting in part Ralph Weisheit & Susan Mahan, *Women, Crime, and Criminal Justice* (1998) ("impunity")); Noël Bridget Busch et al., *Male Customers of Prostituted Women*, 8 Violence Against Women 1093, 1093 (2002) ("consistently documents"). Miller and Schwartz's study, which was based on interviews with sixteen women incarcerated for prostitution, found that fifteen of them (93.8%) experienced some form of sexual assault with three quarters having been raped by a customer. On violence against trans women who are sex workers, see, for example, Deborah Cohan et al., *Sex Worker Health: San Francisco Style*, 82 Sexually Transmitted Infections 418, 419 tbl. 1 (2006).

62. Srinivasan, *supra* note 6, at 82. For 2011 prosecution statistics, see Lara Gerassi, *From Exploitation to Industry: Definitions, Risks, and Consequences of Domestic Sexual Exploitation and Sex Work Among Women and Girls*, 25 J. Hum. Behav. Soc. Env't 591 (2015).

63. Portions of this excerpt are reproduced in a different order from in the original source.

64. Schulhofer, *supra* note 34, at 17; Klein, *supra* note 9, at 1031. For additional studies, see Cassia Spohn & Julie Horney, *Rape Law Reform: A Grassroots Revolution and Its Impact* (1992); Ronet Bachman & Raymond Paternoster, *A Contemporary Look at the Effects of Rape Law Reform: How Far Have We Really Come?*, 84 J. Crim. L. & Criminology 554 (1993); Bryden & Lengnick, *supra* note 3, at 1199 (reviewing research).

65. Vicki McNickle Rose, *Rape as a Social Problem: A Byproduct of the Feminist Movement*, 25 Soc. Probs. 75 (1977); Rose Corrigan, *Up Against a Wall: Rape Reform and the Failure of Success* 27 (2013).

66. Aya Gruber, *Consent Confusion*, 38 Cardozo L. Rev. 415, 419 (2016); Am. L. Inst., Model Penal Code: Sexual Assault and Related Offenses, Prelim. Draft No. 5, at 15 (Sept. 8, 2015).

67. Aya Gruber, *The Feminist War on Crime* 7, 45 (2020) [hereinafter Gruber, *Feminist War*]; Elizabeth Bernstein, *The Sexual Politics of the "New Abolitionism,"* 18 Differences 128 (2007).

68. Lynne Henderson, *Rape and Responsibility*, 11 Law & Phil. 127, 175-176 (1992); Nat'l Org. Women, Resolution 20 (1974) (archived in the Schlessinger Library of the Radcliffe Institute at Harvard University, *Records of the National Organization of Women, 1959–2002*, Series III, Subseries B, Carton 23).

69. For detailed overviews of these events, see *California Judge Recalled for Sentence in Sexual Assault Case*, 132 Harv. L. Rev. 1369 (2019), and Gruber, *supra* note 67, at 178-190.

70. Lawyer and filmmaker Rebecca Richman Cohen produced a short documentary film about the case called *The Recall: Reframed*. Describing her motivation for that project, Cohen writes that for her Turner's case captures conflicting moral outrages and poses vexing questions. "How can we imagine a form of justice for survivors of sexual violence that does not also perpetuate the harms of mass incarceration? How can we investigate, understand, and respond to perpetrators of sexual and gender violence in a way that restores and rebalances their debt to society, without also stocking our jails and prisons in this, the most incarcerated nation in the world?" Rebecca Richman Cohen, *The Recall: Reframed*, Inquest (June 8, 2023). Cohen's film can be viewed at: https://inquest.org/the-recall-reframed/.

71. See Srinivasan, *supra* note 6, at 5 (citing Ida B. Wells, *A Red Record: Tabulated Statistics and Alleged Causes of Lynchings in the United States, 1892-1893-1894* (1895), in *The Light of Truth: The Writings of an Anti-Lynching Crusader* 220-312 (Mia Bay ed., 2014)).

72. Angela Y. Davis, *Women, Race & Class* 182 (1981); Srinivasan, *supra* note 6, at 12.

73. Sharon Block, *Rape and Sexual Power in Early America* 163-164 (2006).

74. Gruber, *Feminist War*, *supra* note 67, at 34-35; Crystal N. Feimster, *Southern Horrors: Women and the Politics of Rape and Lynching* 4-5 (2011). For statistics on capital punishment for rape in Virginia, see Eric W. Rise, *The Martinsville Seven: Race, Rape, and Capital Punishment* 102 (1995).

75. Angela P. Harris, *Race and Essentialism in Feminist Legal Theory*, 42 Stan. L. Rev. 581, 599 (1990); A. Leon Higginbotham, Jr. & Anne F. Jacobs, *The "Law Only as an Enemy": The Legitimization of Racial Powerlessness Through the Colonial and Antebellum Criminal Laws of Virginia*, 70 N.C. L. Rev. 969, 1056 (1992) ("no reported cases"); Jeffrey J. Pokorak, *Rape as a Badge of*

Slavery: The Legal History of, and Remedies for, Prosecutorial Race-of-Victim Charging Disparities, 7 Nev. L.J. 1, 6 (2006).

76. Jessica Shaw & HaeNim Lee, *Race and the Criminal Justice System Response to Sexual Assault: A Systemic Review,* 64 Am. J. Cmty. Psych. 256, 274 (2019).

77. Shaw & Lee, *supra* note 76, at 274; Christopher D. Maxwell et al., *The Impact of Race on the Adjudication of Sexual Assault and Other Violent Crimes,* 31 J. Crim. Just. 523, 534-535 (2003). For the equivalence in lifetime sexual assault victimization between Black and white women, see Basile et al., *supra* note 2, at 5. For evidence that most sexual assault is intraracial, see Maxwell et al., *supra,* at 534. Consistent with the finding of Bryden & Lengnick, *supra* note 3, that underreporting is the major driver of underenforcement, Maxwell et al., *supra,* posits that "[l]ower levels of victim cooperation and participation in the prosecution of sexual assault cases may also explain some of the findings regarding race."

78. The last two sentences of this excerpt appear earlier in the source material.

79. Estrich, *Real Rape, supra* note 9, at 97-98 (quoting Model Penal Code and Commentaries §2.02 cmt. 4 at 243).

80. Srinivasan, *supra* note 6, at 2; Samuel R. Gross, et al., National Registry of Exonerations, *Race and Wrongful Convictions in the United States* 18 (2022) ("Fifty-nine percent"). For a dashboard showing exonerations by year and by crime of conviction, see The National Registry of Exonerations, https://www.law.umich.edu/special/exoneration/Pages/Exonerations-in-the-United-States-Map.aspx. Note an important but often overlooked aspect of these exonerations, as conveyed by Professor Srinivasan:

> When we think of a false rape accusation we picture a scorned or greedy woman, lying to authorities. But many, perhaps most, wrongful convictions of rape result from false accusations levied against men by other men: by cops and prosecutors, overwhelmingly male, intent on pinning an actual rape on the wrong suspect. In the U.S. . . . . [f]ewer than half of [men exonerated] were deliberately framed by their alleged victims. Meanwhile, over half of their cases involved "official misconduct": a category that applies when the police coach false victim or witness identifications, charge a suspect despite the victim's failure to identify him as the attacker, suppress evidence or induce false confessions.

Srinivasan, *supra* note 6, at 4. As to the incidence of actual false reporting, Professor Aya Gruber reports the following:

> False rape statistics range from Susan Brownmiller's famous 2 percent to criminologist Eugene Kanin's infamous 41 percent rate from his examination of rape cases in one small town. Most studies over the last few decades put the false reporting rate somewhere between 5 and 10 percent.

Gruber, *Feminist War, supra* note 67, at 140 (citing Brownmiller, *supra* note 14, at 387; Eugene J. Kanin, *False Rape Allegations,* 23 Archives Sexual Behav. 84 (1994); David Lisak et al., *False Allegations of Sexual Assault: An Analysis of Ten Years of Reported Cases,* 16 Violence Against Women 1318 (2010) (citing further studies putting rate at 2 to 10 percent)).

81. Srinivasan, *supra* note 6, at 2.

82. For more on rape shield laws, see Michelle J. Anderson, *From Chastity Requirement to Sexuality License: Sexual Consent and a New Rape Shield Law,* 70 Geo. Wash. L. Rev. 51 (2002). On secondary victimization, see Vivian D. Berge, *Man's Trial, Woman's Tribulation: Rape Cases in the Courtroom,* 77 Colum. L. Rev. 1 (1977).

83. 4 William Blackstone, *Commentaries* *352.

84. Am. L. Inst., Model Penal Code: Sexual Assault and Related Offenses, Discussion Draft No. 2, at 166-171 (April 28, 2015). For more on the history of evidentiary rules in rape cases, see Michelle J. Anderson, *Diminishing the Legal Impact of Negative Social Attitudes Toward Acquaintance Rape Victims*, 13 New Crim. L. Rev. 644, 646-652 (2010).

CHAPTER 6

1. Caroline Wolf Harlow, Bureau of Just. Stat., *Defense Counsel in Criminal Cases* 1 (2000). For prison population by offense, see Wendy Sawyer & Peter Wagner, Prison Pol'y Initiative, *Mass Incarceration: The Whole Pie 2024* (2024). For data on income levels, see Bernadette Rabuy & Daniel Kopf, Prison Pol'y Initiative, *Prisons of Poverty: Uncovering the Pre-Incarceration Incomes of the Imprisoned* (2015); the $38,000 in the text reflects the value reported in this source adjusted for inflation to its 2024 value.

2. Susan Konig, *Helping Shoplifters to Reform*, N.Y. Times (Sept. 29, 1996). On store closures and declining profits, see Alina Selyukh, *Retailers Howled About Theft Last Year. Why Not Now?*, NPR (Mar. 11, 2024).

3. On Target, see Gabrielle Fonrouge, *Target Blamed Theft and Violence for Store Closures. Crime Is Higher at Locations It Kept Open Nearby*, CNBC (Dec. 19, 2023). On the William Blair report, see Megan Cerullo, *Lobbying Group Overstated How Much "Organized" Shoplifting Hurt Retailers*, CBS News (Dec. 8, 2023).

4. John Rappaport, *Criminal Justice, Inc.*, 118 Colum. L. Rev. 2251, 2261 (2018); Selyukh, *supra* note 2.

5. The sentence discussing the "optimal damages that would be required for deterrence" appears earlier in this source than its placement in the excerpt. The sentence beginning "The car might, of course, confer more utility" appears in a footnote in the original text.

6. A contrary line of research finds little long-term effect of incarceration on labor market outcomes, partly because people who end up going to prison are often on poor labor market trajectories already. See, for example, Andrew Garin et al., *The Impact of Incarceration on Employment, Earnings, and Tax Filing*, NBER Working Paper 32747 (2024); David J. Harding et al., *Imprisonment and Labor Market Outcomes: Evidence from a Natural Experiment*, 124 Am. J. Socio. 49 (2018); Jeffrey R. Kling, *Incarceration Length, Employment, and Earnings*, 96 Am. Econ. Rev. 863 (2006); Charles E. Loeffler, *Does Imprisonment Alter the Life Course? Evidence on Crime and Employment from a Natural Experiment*, 51 Criminology 137 (2013).

7. For more on prison fire camps, see Sebastian Miller, *The Phantom Prison*, Inquest (June 4, 2024).

8. Saneta deVuono-Powell et al., *Who Pays? The True Cost of Incarceration on Families* 9 (2015) ("average debt incurred"); Abby Shafroth, Nat'l Consumer Law Ctr., *Criminal Justice Debt in the South: A Primer for the Southern Partnership to Reduce Debt* 3-4 (2018). According to a recent report, the total amount of criminal justice debt nationwide is unknown because more than half the states do not collect or report adequate data; drawing just on those that do, however, the national court debt total is at least $27.6 billion. *See* Briana Hammons, Fines & Fees Justice Ctr., *Tip of the Iceberg: How Much Criminal Justice Debt Does the U.S. Really Have?* 4 (2021). For more on fines and fees, see sources cited in Chapter One (p. 37) and also Alexes Harris et al., *A Pound of Flesh*, Inquest (May 18, 2022).

9. Rappaport, *supra* note 4, at 2265 & n.71. To say that middle-class people are most likely to shoplift is not to deny that some people shoplift out of economic need. Indeed, one major review of the social scientific literature found a "slight to moderate inverse

relationship between social class and shoplifting behavior." Lloyd W. Klemke, *The Sociology of Shoplifting: Boosters and Snitches Today* 64 (1992).

10. Alex Sherman, *Netflix Estimates 100 Million Households Are Sharing Passwords and Suggests a Global Crackdown Is Coming*, CNBC (Apr. 19, 2022). For the survey reporting the rate of password sharing and average monthly savings, see DailyStoke, *Password Sharing Rebellion: 1 in 2 Americans Would Cancel Subscriptions* (May 26, 2023). For Netflix's share of the streaming market, see Ana Durrani, *Top Streaming Statistics in 2024*, Forbes (June 13, 2024).

11. Orin Kerr, *Shared Passwords and the Computer Fraud and Abuse Act*, Wash. Post (Oct. 15, 2015) ("Ann gives Bob," "Bob may be guilty"); Henry T. Casey, *Password Sharing Still Illegal, but You're Probably Safe*, Tomsguide.com (July 7, 2016) (quoting Professor Kerr) ("criminal theft of service"). For more on how the Computer Fraud and Abuse Act might apply to password sharing, see Orin Kerr, *Norms of Computer Trespass*, 116 Colum. L. Rev. 1143, 1178-1180 (2016); Orin Kerr, *The Supreme Court Reins in the CFAA in* Van Buren, Lawfare (June 9, 2021) (arguing that the U.S. Supreme Court's decision in *Van Buren v. United States*, 593 U.S. 374 (2021), "leaves to lower courts the largely interstitial work of figuring out the hard line-drawing of what exactly counts as enough of a [computer trespass] to trigger liability" under the statute). For Netflix's efforts to crackdown on password sharing and the resulting boost in subscriptions, see Samantha Delouya, *Netflix Cracked Down on Password Sharing. The Result? Millions of New Subscribers*, CNN (Apr. 19, 2024).

12. 2 Wayne R. LaFave, *Substantive Criminal Law* §10.1(b) (3d ed. 2017 & Supp. 2023) ("part of the law," "fixed rules").

13. For an account of states rejecting application of the necessity doctrine in cases of homicide, see Fern L. Kletter, *Application of Defense of Necessity to Murder*, 23 A.L.R. 7th Art. 1 (2017). For a critique of the equal-life principle as applied to cases in which doctors triage life-saving care like ventilators from sicker patients to healthier ones under conditions of scarcity, as in the case of a pandemic, see I. Glenn Cohen, Andrew M. Crespo & Douglas B. White, *Potential Legal Liability for Withdrawing or Withholding Ventilators During COVID-19: Assessing the Risks and Identifying Needed Reforms*, 323 J. Am. Med. Assoc. 1901 (2020).

14. For scholarship on the narrow judicial interpretation of necessity doctrine in cases of economic need, see Stuart P. Green, *Looting, Law, and Lawlessness*, 81 Tul. L. Rev. 1129, 1154 (2007) ("[R]eported cases in which a defendant charged with theft or trespass was acquitted by virtue of the necessity defense are virtually nonexistent, at least in modern times. . . . Victor Hugo's story of a man who steals a loaf of bread to feed his starving family is often cited as the paradigmatic example of a crime committed out of necessity. But it is worth recalling that, like almost every other modern case in which necessity has been asserted as a defense to charges of theft or trespass, [Jean] Valjean's plea was unsuccessful."); *see also* Eduardo Moisés Peñalver & Sonia K. Katyal, *Property Outlaws*, 155 U. Pa. L. Rev. 1095, 1173 (2007) (citing "[s]everal courts [that] have held that, as a categorical matter, the doctrine is not available when the evil the defendant seeks to avoid is caused by economic forces alone").

15. For a contrary view, see Jed S. Rakoff, *The Financial Crisis: Why Have No High-Level Executives Been Prosecuted?*, N.Y. Rev. Books (Jan. 9, 2024), where Judge Rakoff writes:

> I completely discount the argument sometimes made that no such prosecutions have been brought because the top prosecutors were often people who previously represented the financial institutions in question and/or were people who expected to be representing such institutions in the future: the so-called "revolving door." In my experience, most federal prosecutors, at every level, are seeking to make a name for themselves, and the best way to do that is by prosecuting some high-level person. . . .

[W]hatever small influence the "revolving door" may have in discouraging certain white-collar prosecutions is more than offset, at least in the case of prosecuting high-level individuals, by the career-making benefits such prosecutions confer on the successful prosecutor.

16. For more on the case involving Walmart's bribery, see, for example, Nathaniel Meyersohn, *Walmart Settles with US Government over International Bribery Investigation*, CNN (June 20, 2019) ("Walmart is paying nearly $283 million to settle a seven-year federal bribery investigation involving its business in Brazil, China, India and Mexico. . . . As part of the settlement, the Department of Justice won't prosecute Walmart . . . .").

17. 1 William Blackstone, *Commentaries* *455. For more on contemporary debates over corporate personhood, see, for example, Adam Winkler, *We the Corporations* (2018), and Nikolas Bowie, *Corporate Personhood v. Corporate Statehood*, 132 Harv. L. Rev. 2009 (2019).

18. Brandon Garrett, *Too Big to Jail* 3-5 (2014). As one leading treatise reports, some courts have expressed the view that certain "crimes, such as bigamy, perjury, rape or murder, are inherently human and thus not subject to commission by a corporation," though it "is now established that a corporation may be guilty of manslaughter." 2 LaFave, *supra* note 12, §13.5(a).

19. Albert W. Alschuler, *Two Ways to Think About the Punishment of Corporations*, 46 Am. Crim. L. Rev. 1359, 1367 (2009).

20. Gabriel Markoff, *Arthur Andersen and the Myth of the Corporate Death Penalty: Corporate Criminal Convictions in the Twenty-First Century*, 15 U. Pa. J. Bus. L. 797, 806 (2013). Markoff reports that three of the five companies that failed did so more than three years after being convicted; with respect to the other two, he reports based on contemporary accounts that factors other than the convictions drove the business failures.

21. U.S. Dep't of Just., Justice Manual §§9-28.200, .1100 (2023).

22. Some jurisdictions recognize an exception to this general rule that permits a corporation to be convicted of a knowledge-based crime based on the "collective knowledge" of its employees. "Under the collective knowledge doctrine," Professor Mihailis Diamantis explains, "prosecutors do not need to find a single employee with all the relevant knowledge; they can attribute to a corporation anything known by any and all of its employees." This means that "corporations can be guilty of knowledge-based crimes in jurisdictions that accept the collective knowledge doctrine even when there is no single employee with all the guilty knowledge." Mihailis E. Diamantis, *Functional Corporate Knowledge*, 61 Wm. & Mary L. Rev. 319, 344-345 (2019).

23. Benjamin Levin, *The Consensus Myth in Criminal Justice Reform*, 117 Mich. L. Rev. 259, 292 n.165, 301 (2018). For more on this topic, see Benjamin Levin, *Mens Rea Reform and Its Discontents*, 109 J. Crim. L. & Criminology 491 (2019).

24. Kimberly Kessler Ferzan, *Probing the Depths of the Responsible Corporate Officer's Duty*, 12 Crim. L. & Phil. 455, 460 (2018).

25. Ferzan, *supra* note 24, at 456. For a similar take to Ferzan's, see Todd S. Aagaard, *A Fresh Look at the Responsible Relation Doctrine*, 96 J. Crim. L. & Criminology 1245 (2006). For more critical contemporary perspectives, see, for example, Samuel W. Buell, *The Responsibility Gap in Corporate Crime*, 12 Crim. L. & Phil. 471 (2018); Craig S. Lerner, *The Trial of Joseph Dotterweich: The Origins of the "Responsible Corporate Officer" Doctrine*, 12 Crim. L. & Phil. 493 (2018); Kenneth W. Simons, *Can Strict Criminal Liability for Responsible Corporate Officers Be Justified by the Duty to Use Extraordinary Care?*, 12 Crim. L. & Phil. 439 (2018).

CHAPTER 7

1. Leo Katz, *The Story of* Tally*: Judge Tally and the Problem of the Superfluous Accomplice*, in *Criminal Law Stories* 373, 373-374 (Donna Coker & Robert Weisberg eds., 2013).

2. Notice that, if *no one* had shown up, there would have been no concert for Hawkins to play. This means the audience members, collectively, *were* a but-for cause of Hawkins' offense, even though each individual's attendance was gratuitous given the attendance of all the others. The famous analogy from tort is of a lake that is materially harmed only by a certain level of pollution, where each polluter contributes less than the requisite amount. And each of these polluters is, like Wilcox, held liable. *See* Landers v. E. Tex. Salt Water Disposal Co., 248 S.W.2d 731 (Tex. 1952). For a discussion of causation in *Wilcox* and similar cases, see Eric A. Johnson, *Criminal Liability for Loss of a Chance*, 91 Iowa L. Rev. 59, 113-114 (2005).

3. Sanford Kadish, *A Theory of Complicity*, in *Issues in Contemporary Legal Philosophy: The Influence of H.L.A. Hart* 291-292 (Ruth Gavison ed., 1987) [hereinafter Kadish, *A Theory*]; Joshua Dressler, *Reforming Complicity Law: Trivial Assistance as a Lesser Offense?* 5 Ohio St. J. Crim. L. 427, 439-440 (2008). For the blackletter rule that the principal's actions break the chain of proximate causation, see Leo Katz, *Do We Need a Doctrine of Complicity?*, in *Legal, Moral, and Metaphysical Truths* 125, 126 (Kimberly Kessler Ferzan & Stephen J. Morse eds., 2016); Michael S. Moore, *Causing, Aiding, and the Superfluity of Accomplice Liability*, 156 U. Pa. L. Rev. 395, 408-409 (2007); Andrew Simester, *Fundamentals of Criminal Law* 159-160 (2021). For the argument that complicity exists to establish liability in the absence of ordinary causation, see generally Kadish, *A Theory*, *supra*. And for the position that complicity doctrine is superfluous because it is subsumed within causation, see generally Moore, *supra*.

4. On the common law standard, see Sanford Kadish, *Complicity, Cause and Blame: A Study in the Interpretation of Doctrine*, 73 Calif. L. Rev. 323, 358-359 (1985) [hereinafter Kadish, *Cause and Blame*]; Robert Weisberg, *Reappraising Complicity*, 4 Buff. Crim. L. Rev. 217, 228 (2000) ("the state [must] prove that the accomplice acted in a time and manner such that her actions *might* have played some causal role"); Kadish, *A Theory*, *supra* note 3, at 299 ("There is no accomplice liability where it can be established that the attempted contribution failed to achieve its purpose because it never reached its target."); Simester, *supra* note 3, at 162 ("The encouragement or assistance must be *received*, but [the secondary actor's] participation need not *make a difference*."). For a related argument analogizing the materiality standard for complicity liability to tort law's "lost chance" doctrine, see Johnson, *supra* note 2. For additional discussion on the relationship between causation and complicity, see John Gardner, *Complicity and Causation*, 1 Crim. L. & Phil. 127 (2007).

5. See, for example, Ariz. Rev. Stat. §13-301; Mo. Stat. §562.041; Or. Rev. Stat. §161.155.

6. Commentators have proposed various, related ways to conceptualize a noncausal basis for accomplice liability. Sanford Kadish, for example, argues that "by intentionally acting to further the criminal actions of another, the secondary party voluntarily identifies himself with the principal party," the "equivalent to manifesting consent to accountability." Kadish, *Cause and Blame*, *supra* note 4, at 354. Gideon Yaffe focuses on "the social relation" between the accomplice and principal "constituted by lending a helping hand." Gideon Yaffe, *Moore on Causing, Acting, and Complicity*, 18 Legal Theory 437, 458 (2012). A third account grounds accomplice liability in agency relations: By intentionally facilitating the principal's crime, the accomplice makes the principal her agent and is thus responsible for what the principal does. Saba Bazargan-Forward, *Complicity*, in *Routledge Handbook of Collective Intentionality* 327, 333 (Marija Jankovic & Kirk Ludwig eds., 2018). And a final take maintains that the accomplice's responsibility "rests upon her act of sufficiently *involving* or *associating* herself with that crime, rather than in her causal impact upon [the principal's] wrong." Simester, *supra* note 3, at 163.

A somewhat different perspective focuses on risk-creation. Even though some accomplices do not causally influence the principal, the argument goes, in the aggregate, acts of aiding and abetting increase the risk that crime will occur. As philosopher John Gardner writes:

> [A]ssistance and encouragement often do make all the difference between commission and non-commission of the principal wrong. Often they tip the balance. The risk that one will tip the balance in any particular case arguably justifies a general rule against providing assistance or encouragement to potential wrongdoers, a general rule that applies even to cases where the help or encouragement proves unnecessary, because the wrong will be committed anyway.

Gardner, *supra* note 4, at 138; *see* Moore, *supra* note 3, at 435 ("risk imposition is a desert basis independent of causation"). On the analogy between complicity and attempt, see Heidi M. Hurd & Michael S. Moore, *Untying the Gordian Knot of Mens Rea Requirements for Accomplices*, 32 Soc. Phil. & Pol'y 161, 166-170 (2016); Katz, *supra* note 3, at 129-137.

7. For examples of states that require only knowledge, see Ind. Code §35-41-2-4; Wyo. Stat. §6-1-201. For surveys of state law, see Paul H. Robinson & Tyler Scot Williams, *Mapping American Criminal Law* 109-114 (2018) (counting 13 states that require only knowledge); John F. Decker, *The Mental State Requirement for Accomplice Liability in American Criminal Law*, 60 S.C. L. Rev. 237 (2008). On the evolution of the doctrine as well as various compromise proposals, see 2 Wayne R. LaFave, *Substantive Criminal Law* §13.2(d) (3d ed. 2017 & Supp. 2023); Sherif Girgis, Note, *The Mens Rea of Accomplice Liability: Supporting Intentions*, 123 Yale L.J. 460, 468-471 (2013). For an argument that complicity should require only knowing, rather than intentional, aid, see Kimberly Kessler Ferzan, *Conspiracy, Complicity, and the Scope of Contemplated Crime*, 53 Ariz. St. L.J. 453 (2021).

8. Simester, *supra* note 3, at 171, 176; Kadish, *Cause and Blame*, *supra* note 4, at 353. On the tension presented, see Glanville Williams, *Criminal Law: The General Part* 369-370 (2d ed. 1961).

9. Kadish, *Cause and Blame*, *supra* note 4, at 349-350.

10. Kadish, *Cause and Blame*, *supra* note 4, at 350.

11. Kadish, *Cause and Blame*, *supra* note 4, at 350-351. For an argument that "the scope of intention is not only those factors that are motivationally significant, but also those factors that are understood by the agent to be conceptually and empirically entailed by the factors that are motivationally significant," see Ferzan, *supra* note 7, at 463. Ferzan's position suggests that the scope of intention, properly understood, encompasses the examples discussed in the text; the intention requirement is not being relaxed at all.

12. On the distinction between conduct and results, see Hurd & Moore, *supra* note 6, at 167-168 (arguing that the difference is "wholly artificial and unsustainable, because all act-types prohibited by the criminal law contain results elements").

13. See, for example, Joshua Dressler, *Understanding Criminal Law* §30.06[C], at 473-474 (9th ed. 2022); 2 LaFave, *supra* note 7, §13.3(c); Douglas N. Husak, *Justifications and the Criminal Liability of Accessories*, 80 J. Crim. L. & Criminology 491 (1989).

14. Kadish, *Cause and Blame*, *supra* note 4, at 340.

15. Note that the following sentence in this excerpt has been transposed from earlier in the article: "There is a great deal of difference between conduct that a system of norms should tolerate and not punish or condemn, as opposed to conduct that is worthy of praise and emulation."

16. On duress cases as involving innocent agents, see 2 LaFave, *supra* note 7, §9.7(e).

17. Alexandra Natapoff, *Snitching: Criminal Informants and the Erosion of American Justice* 5 (2d ed. 2022). For a helpful analysis of various modes of police participation in crime, see Elizabeth E. Joh, *Breaking the Law to Enforce It: Undercover Police Participation in Crime*, 62 Stan. L. Rev. 155 (2009).

18. Natapoff, *supra* note 17, at 33, 36.

19. Natapoff, *supra* note 17, at 31; Anna Lvovsky, *Rethinking Police Expertise*, 131 Yale L.J. 475, 481 (2021). For more on how "substantive necessity" has shaped judicial doctrine that regulates law enforcement activity, see William J. Stuntz, *O.J. Simpson, Bill Clinton, and the Transsubstantive Fourth Amendment*, 114 Harv. L. Rev. 842, 858-863 (2001) [hereinafter Stuntz, *O.J. Simpson*]. On the necessity of undercover tactics to the investigation of organized crime, see William J. Stuntz, *Local Policing After the Terror*, 111 Yale L.J. 2137, 2181 (2002) ("Tactics like wiretaps and undercover agents are not only useful; they are sometimes essential to the enterprise of cracking open organized crime networks."); *see also* Gary T. Marx, *Undercover: Police Surveillance in America* 37-40 (1988) (white-collar crime networks). For an argument that undercover tactics have not only *informational* utility, but also *behavioral* (or deterrent) effects, see Bruce Hay, *Sting Operations, Undercover Agents, and Entrapment*, 70 Mo. L. Rev. 387, 392-394 (2005).

20. Natapoff, *supra* note 17, at 2; *id.* at 19; *id.* at 1; *id.* at 122. For a related point, see Richard A. Posner, *An Economic Theory of the Criminal Law*, 85 Colum. L. Rev. 1193, 1220 (1985), arguing that "it is much cheaper to catch [a suspect] in an arranged crime than in his ordinary criminal activities." For an argument that different law enforcement tactics should be permissible in different investigative settings, see generally Stuntz, *O.J. Simpson*, *supra* note 19.

21. Richard H. McAdams, *The Political Economy of Entrapment*, 96 J. Crim. L. & Criminology 107, 112-113 (2005). For additional critiques, see Bernard W. Bell, *Theatrical Investigation: White-Collar Crime, Undercover Operations, and Privacy*, 11 Wm. & Mary Bill Rts. J. 151 (2002); Tracey Maclin, *Informants and the Fourth Amendment: A Reconsideration*, 74 Wash. U. L.Q. 573 (1996); Robert L. Misner & John H. Clough, *Arrestees as Informants: A Thirteenth Amendment Analysis*, 29 Stan. L. Rev. 713 (1977); Michael L. Rich, *Coerced Informants and Thirteenth Amendment Limitations on the Police-Informant Relationship*, 50 Santa Clara L. Rev. 681 (2010); Geoffrey R. Stone, *The Scope of the Fourth Amendment: Privacy and the Police Use of Spies, Secret Agents, and Informers*, 1 Am. Bar Found. Rsch. J. 1193 (1976); Andrew E. Taslitz, *Wrongly Accused Redux: How Race Contributes to Convicting the Innocent: The Informants Example*, 37 Sw. U. L. Rev. 1091 (2008); Ian Weinstein, *Regulating the Market for Snitches*, 47 Buffalo L. Rev. 563 (1999).

22. Andrew Manuel Crespo, *Probable Cause Pluralism*, 129 Yale L.J. 1276, 1334 (2020); Natapoff, *supra* note 17, at xiii, 87. For more on false information from informants, see *N. Mariana Islands v. Bowie*, 243 F.3d 1109, 1124 (9th Cir. 2001) ("[E]ach contract for testimony is fraught with the real peril that the proffered testimony will not be truthful, but simply factually contrived to 'get' a target of sufficient interest to induce concessions from the government."); George C. Harris, *Testimony for Sale: The Law and Ethics of Snitches and Experts*, 28 Pepp. L. Rev. 1, 49-58 (2000); Jessica A. Roth, *Informant Witnesses and the Risk of Wrongful Convictions*, 53 Am. Crim. L. Rev. 737 (2016).

23. Crespo, *supra* note 22, at 1334 n.241; Natapoff, *supra* note 17, at 91.

24. Natapoff, *supra* note 17, at 4; *id.* at 2; Crespo, *supra* note 22, at 1335.

25. Natapoff, *supra* note 17, at 2 ("official deceit"); Clifford S. Zimmerman, *Toward a New Vision of Informants: A History of Abuses and Suggestions for Reform*, 22 Hastings Const. L.Q. 81, 146 (1994).

26. Alison Siegler & William Admussen, *Discovering Racial Discrimination by the Police*, 115 Nw. U. L. Rev. 987, 988-990 (2021) (quoting Brad Heath, *Investigation: ATF Drug Stings Targeted Minorities*, USA Today (Apr. 24, 2019)).

27. Lvovsky, *supra* note 19, at 510; Elizabeth Hinton, *From the War on Poverty to the War on Crime: The Making of Mass Incarceration in America* 182-184 (2016).

28. Natapoff, *supra* note 17, at 131-132.

29. On the scarcity of other forms of regulation of undercover operations, see McAdams, *supra* note 21, at 115.

30. On the total number of post-9/11 terrorism prosecutions, see *Trial and Terror*, Intercept (June 14, 2023). On the prevalence of entrapment indicators, see Jesse J. Norris & Hanna Grol-Prokopczyk, *Estimating the Prevalence of Entrapment in Post-9/11 Terrorism Cases*, 105 J. Crim. L. & Criminology 609, 655-656 (2016). On the failure of the entrapment defense in terrorism prosecutions, see Jesse J. Norris, *Accounting for the (Almost Complete) Failure of the Entrapment Defense in Post-9/11 US Terrorism Cases*, 45 Law & Soc. Inquiry 194 (2020); Erin Luibrand, *The Death of the Entrapment Defense: How the Entrapment Defense Has Evolved in Federal Terrorism Cases to the Point of Extinction in the Post-9/11 Era*, 9 Va. J. Crim. L. 33 (2020). For further reading, see Sahar F. Aziz, *Race, Entrapment, and Manufacturing "Homegrown Terrorism,"* 111 Geo. L.J. 381 (2023); Rozina Ali, *The "Herald Square Bomber" Who Wasn't*, N.Y. Times (June 15, 2023); Matt Ford, *The Case of the Fitness Instructor Who Spied on California Muslims—Then Helped Them Sue the FBI*, New Republic (Nov. 8, 2021); Janet Reitman, *"I Helped Destroy People,"* N.Y. Times Mag. (Sept. 9, 2021).

31. 2 LaFave, *supra* note 7, §9.8(a) ("no limits").

32. Rebecca Roiphe, *The Serpent Beguiled Me: A History of the Entrapment Defense*, 33 Seton Hall L. Rev. 257, 269 (2003). On the basic stability of formal entrapment doctrine since *Sorrells*, see Jessica A. Roth, *The Anomaly of Entrapment*, 91 Wash. U. L. Rev. 979, 1033 (2014). For more historical and conceptual background, see T. Ward Frampton, *Predisposition and Positivism: The Forgotten Foundations of the Entrapment Doctrine*, 103 J. Crim. L. & Criminology 111 (2013); Paul Marcus, *The Development of Entrapment Law*, 33 Wayne L. Rev. 5 (1986).

33. Louis Michael Seidman, *The Supreme Court, Entrapment, and Our Criminal Justice Dilemma*, 1981 Sup. Ct. Rev. 111, 114 ("There are few entrapment defenses mounted, and fewer still that are successful."); Dru Stevenson, *Entrapment by Numbers*, 16 U. Fla. J.L. & Pub. Pol'y 1 (2005); Stephen G. Valdes, Comment, *Frequency and Success: An Empirical Study of Criminal Law Defenses, Federal Constitutional Evidentiary Claims, and Plea Negotiations*, 153 U. Pa. L. Rev. 1709 (2005).

34. Ronald J. Allen et al., *Clarifying Entrapment*, 89 J. Crim. L. & Criminology 407, 415 (1999); *see also* McAdams, *supra* note 21, at 176-179 (refining Allen et al.'s analysis).

35. Seidman, *supra* note 33, at 120; *see also* Allen et al., *supra* note 34, at 410-413 (refining Seidman's analysis). On the popularity of the different doctrinal tests, see 2 LaFave, *supra* note 7, §9.8(b). There is, however, some experimental evidence suggesting the two tests function differently in practice—in particular, that jurors may be more likely to reject the defense based on a defendant's prior conviction when applying the dominant, two-pronged test (predisposition plus inducement) than when applying the test of inducement alone. *See* Eugene Borgida & Roger Park, *The Entrapment Defense: Juror Comprehension and Decision Making*, 12 Law & Hum. Behav. 19 (1988).

36. For early cases originating the doctrine, see 2 LaFave, *supra* note 7, §9.8(a) (citing Saunders v. People, 38 Mich. 219 (1878); O'Brien v. State, 6 Tex. App. 665 (1879); William E. Mikell, *The Doctrine of Entrapment in the Federal Courts*, 90 U. Pa. L. Rev. 245 (1942)). For an example of statutory codification of the doctrine, see 18 Pa. Cons. Stat. §313.

37. 2 LaFave, *supra* note 7, §9.8(g).

38. 2 LaFave, *supra* note 7, §12.3(b)(2).

39. On federal conspiracy law, see Charles Doyle, Cong. Rsch. Serv., R41223, *Federal Conspiracy Law: A Brief Overview* 4 (2020).

40. For examples of conspiracy punishment exceeding punishment for the object crime, see Cal. Penal Code §182; Clune v. United States, 159 U.S. 590 (1895) (upholding eighteen-month sentence where object crime could be punished only by a $100 fine). For discussion of jurisdictions that cap conspiracy sentences, see 2 LaFave, *supra* note 7, §12.4(d); *see also* Model Penal Code §5.05. Federal sentencing guidelines also discourage consecutive sentences for conspiracy charges and their object crimes. U.S. Sentencing Guidelines Manual §2X1.1 (U.S. Sent'g Comm'n 2023).

41. For discussion of this view, see Mark Noferi, *Towards Attenuation: A "New" Due Process Limit on* Pinkerton *Conspiracy Liability*, 33 Am. J. Crim. L. 91, 131 (2006) ("Courts generally upheld the *Alvarez* court's extension of *Pinkerton* to unintended but foreseeable crimes, while conducting a perfunctory 'attenuation' analysis to satisfy due process.").

42. Decker, *supra* note 7 (state survey). For scholarly comparison of *Luparello* liability to *Pinkerton* liability, see Ferzan, *supra* note 7, at 457.

43. Matthew A. Pauley, *The* Pinkerton *Doctrine and Murder*, 4 Pierce L. Rev. 1, 24-25 (2005).

44. For more on *Pinkerton* and due process, see, for example, Alex Kreit, *Vicarious Criminal Liability and the Constitutional Dimensions of* Pinkerton, 57 Am. U. L. Rev. 585 (2008); Noferi, *supra* note 41.

45. Andrew Ingram, *Pinkerton Short-Circuits the Model Penal Code*, 64 Vill. L. Rev. 71, 80 (2019). For a sampling of scholarly critiques of the doctrine, see George Fletcher, *Rethinking Criminal Law* 659-664 (1978); Donald A. Dripps, *Fundamental Retribution Error: Criminal Justice and the Social Psychology of Blame*, 56 Vand. L. Rev. 1383, 1386, 1406 (2003); Moore, *supra* note 3, at 447-448; Paul H. Robinson, *Imputed Criminal Liability*, 93 Yale L.J. 609, 657-658 (1984); Jens David Ohlin, *Group Think: The Law of Conspiracy and Collective Reason*, 98 J. Crim. L. & Criminology 147 (2007).

CHAPTER 8

1. Cesare Bonesana Beccaria, *An Essay on Crimes and Punishments* 148 (1793).

2. For examples of attempt statutes carrying lower sentences than prescribed for the completed crimes, see Fla. Stat. §777.04(4); Ky. Rev. Stat. Ann. §506.010(4); Or. Rev. Stat. §161.405(2). Some states specify that punishment for attempt may be as great as that for the completed offense. See, for example, Del. Code Ann. tit. 11, §531; Haw. Rev. Stat. §705-502; Pa. Cons. Stat. tit. 18, §905(a).

3. For further discussion of the role of moral luck in attempt and beyond, see Larry Alexander et al., *Crime and Culpability: A Theory of Criminal Law* 171-187, 192-193 (2009); Michael S. Moore, *Placing Blame: A Theory of the Criminal Law* 192-247 (1997); Arthur Ripstein, *Equality, Responsibility, and the Law* 133-245 (1999); Gideon Yaffe, *Attempts* 310-334 (2010); Joel Feinberg, *Equal Punishment for Failed Attempts: Some Bad but Instructive Arguments Against It*, 37 Ariz. L. Rev. 117 (1995); Barbara Herman, *Feinberg on Luck and Failed Attempts*, 37 Ariz. L. Rev. 143 (1995); Sanford H. Kadish, *The Criminal Law and the Luck of the Draw*, 84 J. Crim. L. & Criminology 679 (1994); David Lewis, *The Punishment That Leaves Something to Chance*, 18 Phil. & Pub. Affs. 53, 55-56 (1989); Michael S. Moore, *Causation and Responsibility: An Essay*

in Law, Morals, and Metaphysics 20-33 (2009). On moral luck and the law more generally, see David Enoch, *Moral Luck and the Law,* 5 Phil. Compass 42 (2010).

4. Extending the logic of these opinions, one leading treatise says that it is not possible to convict a person of attempting to commit any strict liability crime, with a possible exception for cases in which the facts show "that the defendant acted with an intent to bring about the proscribed result." 2 Wayne R. LaFave, *Substantive Criminal Law* §11.3(c) (3d ed. 2017 & Supp. 2023). This is true for crimes that impose strict liability with respect to prohibited conduct or results; strict liability with respect to attendant circumstances of the crime is often treated differently. For a discussion of attempt and attendant circumstances, see *infra* Note 5 in the main text.

5. For further discussion, see Larry Alexander & Kimberly D. Kessler, Mens Rea *and Inchoate Crimes,* 87 J. Crim. L. & Criminology 1138, 1176-1178 (1997); R.A. Duff, *The Circumstances of an Attempt,* 50 Cambridge L.J. 100, 104-111 (1991); Arnold N. Enker, Mens Rea *and Criminal Attempt,* 1977 Am. Bar Found. Rsch. J. 845, 866-871; George P. Fletcher, *Constructing a Theory of Impossible Attempts,* 5 Crim. Just. Ethics 53, 59-61 (1986); Paul H. Robinson & Jane A. Grall, *Element Analysis in Defining Criminal Liability: The Model Penal Code and Beyond,* 35 Stan. L. Rev. 681, 744-751 (1983); J.C. Smith, *Two Problems in Criminal Attempts Reexamined,* 1962 Crim. L. Rev. 135.

6. R.A. Duff, *Subjectivism, Objectivism and Criminal Attempts,* in *Harm and Culpability* 19, 40-41 (A.P. Simester & A.T.H. Smith eds., 1996).

7. Vincent Chiao, *Intention and Attempt,* 4 Crim. L. & Phil. 37, 38-39 (2010).

8. Oliver Wendell Holmes, Jr., *The Common Law* 68 (Little, Brown & Co. 1923) (1881). For further discussion, see Frederick Schauer, *On the Distinction Between Speech and Action,* 65 Emory L.J. 427, 443-444 (2015).

9. According to the Model Penal Code drafters, while courts and commentators have sometimes treated *Eagleton* "as the law of England," the opinion was short-lived even in its own time: the same court that wrote *Eagleton* defined the *actus reus* of attempt differently in an opinion issued later the same year. *See* Regina v. Roberts (1855) 7 Cox Crim. Cases 39 (Crim. App.). As for the United States, at least one jurisdiction (Pennsylvania) appears to have employed the last act rule for a few decades in the mid-twentieth century, as evidenced by *Commonwealth v. Willard,* 116 A.2d 751 (Pa. Super. Ct. 1955). In that case, undercover police officers conducted a sting operation targeting a doctor who performed abortions, which were criminal in the state at the time. The doctor accepted $160 in payment for the procedure from an undercover police agent posing as a patient, told her to undress and lie on the operation bed, and then briefly left the room before returning with surgical instruments. At that point he was arrested and charged with attempted abortion. These acts were held not to be "sufficiently close or proximate to the completed crime so that it could be said that they were done in pursuance of the intent to commit the crime as distinguished from mere preparation to commit the crime." *Id.* at 753. As Professor Welsh White argues, this holding "seemed to approximate the last act doctrine." Welsh S. White, *The Inchoate Crimes Provisions of the New Pennsylvania Penal Code,* 35 Pitt. L. Rev. 235, 237-238 (1973). But as he further notes, the Pennsylvania legislature expressly overruled *Willard* when it adopted a revised penal code in 1972, which tracks the Model Penal Code's "substantial step" test discussed in this chapter's main text. *Id.* at 238.

10. For the FBI's active shooter data, see Fed. Bureau of Investigation, *Active Shooter Incidents in the United States in 2022,* at 1, 3, 8, 9 (2023). For research using the Congressional Research Service's definition and including demographic information on shooters, see Jillian Peterson et al., *A Multi-Level, Multi-Method Investigation of the Psycho-Social Life Histories of Mass Shooters* 2-3, 11 (2021). On the relationship between mass shootings and "strained

masculinity," see Skyler Morgan et al., *Strained Masculinity and Mass Shootings: Toward a Theoretically Integrated Approach to Assessing the Gender Gap in Mass Violence*, 28 Homicide Stud. 441 (2024). On differential media portrayals of mass shooters based on race and mental illness, see Scott W. Duxbury et al., *Mental Illness, the Media, and the Moral Politics of Mass Violence: The Role of Race in Mass Shootings Coverage*, 55 J. Rsch. Crime & Delinq. 766 (2018). On the role of the media in promoting "copycat" shootings, see James N. Meindl & Jonathan W. Ivy, *Mass Shootings: The Role of the Media in Promoting Generalized Imitation*, 107 Am. J. Pub. Health 368 (2017).

11. Peterson et al., *supra* note 10, at 10. For international comparisons, see Frederic Lemieux, *Effect of Gun Culture and Firearm Laws on Gun Violence and Mass Shootings in the United States: A Multi-Level Quantitative Analysis*, 9 Int'l J. Crim. Just. Scis. 74 (2014); Max Fisher & Josh Keller, *Why Does the U.S. Have So Many Mass Shootings? Research Is Clear: Guns.*, N.Y. Times (Nov. 7, 2017). On gun ownership, see John Berrigan et al., *The Number and Type of Private Firearms in the United States*, 704 Annals Am. Acad. Pol. & Soc. Sci. 70 (2023).

12. While the substantial step and dangerous proximity tests appear to be the two dominant modes of defining the *actus reus* of attempt, courts have employed other models. Examples discussed by the Model Penal Code drafters and a leading treatise include the physical proximity test, the indispensable element approach, the probable desistance test, the abnormal step approach, the *res ipsa loquitur* test, and the equivocality approach. For further discussion of these competing frameworks, see Model Penal Code §5.01 cmt. 5 at 321-329; 2 LaFave, *supra* note 4, §11.4. On the breakdown of doctrinal tests across the states, see Paul H. Robinson & Tyler Scot Williams, *Mapping American Criminal Law* 101-102 (2018).

13. Herbert Wechsler et al., *The Treatment of Inchoate Crimes in the Model Penal Code of the American Law Institute: Attempt, Solicitation, and Conspiracy*, 61 Colum. L. Rev. 571, 593-595 (1961). For an argument that "Charles Rizzo . . . would not have fared well" under the MPC's substantial step approach, see Robert Weisberg, *The Story of* Rizzo*: The Shifting Landscape of Attempt*, in *Criminal Law Stories* 329, 370 (Donna Coker & Robert Weisberg eds., 2013).

14. For an overview of how different states approach the law of abandonment, and a consequentialist analysis of the optimally deterrent legal framework, see Murat C. Mungan, *Abandoned Criminal Attempts: An Economic Analysis*, 67 Ala. L. Rev. 1 (2015).

15. Unlike in most states, "[t]here is no general federal 'attempt' statute. A defendant therefore can only be found guilty of an attempt to commit a federal offense if the statute defining the offense also expressly proscribes an attempt." United States v. Hopkins, 703 F.2d 1102, 1104 (9th Cir. 1983). The Congressional Research Service adds:

> The absence of a general prohibition, however, can be deceptive. Federal prosecution is the likely result for anyone who attempts to commit any of the most common federal crimes [because] Congress has elected to pro-scribe attempt on a case-by-case basis, outlawing attempt to commit a par-ticular crime or group of crimes, such as attempted murder and attempted drug trafficking. In those instances, the statute outlaws attempt, sets the penalty, and implicitly delegates to the courts the task of developing the federal law of attempt on a case-by-case basis . . . . Over the years, proposals have surfaced that would establish attempt as a federal crime of general application, codify federal common law of attempt, and perhaps adopt some of the adjustments recommended by the Model Penal Code and found in the states. Thus far, however, Congress has preferred to maintain the federal law of attempt in its current state and to expand the number of federal attempt offenses on a selective basis.

Cong. Rsch. Serv., *Attempt: An Overview of Federal Criminal Law* 1 (2020).

16. For examples of statutes defining assault as an attempted battery, see N.J. Stat. Ann. §2C:12-1(a) ("A person is guilty of assault if the person . . . [a]ttempts to cause or . . . causes bodily injury to another"); Ohio Rev. Code Ann. §2903.13(A) ("No person shall knowingly cause or attempt to cause physical harm to another or to another's unborn."). Assault is also frequently defined to include placing another person in reasonable apprehension of battery. *See, e.g.*, Kan. Stat. Ann. §21-5412(a); Fla. Stat. §784.011(1).

17. For examples of burglary statutes employing this definition, see Ala. Code §13A-7-7; N.J. Stat. Ann. §2C:18-2.

18. All of the facts about Wendy Wein's case, as well as the quoted text, are from Jonathan Edwards, *A Michigan Woman Tried to Hire an Assassin Online at RentAHitman.com. Now She's Going to Prison*, Wash. Post (Nov. 22, 2021).

19. For a nuanced argument about when solicitation should constitute attempt, see Gideon Yaffe, *Criminal Attempts*, 124 Yale L.J. 92, 122 (2014) ("[I]f the defendant has asked another person to bring about an event that is a result element of the completed crime, then the defendant may have thereby attempted the crime; if, however, the event that the defendant has asked another person to bring about figures into the definition of an act element of the completed crime, then the defendant has not attempted through his solicitation.").

20. Wechsler et al., *supra* note 13, at 621 ("attempt to conspire").

21. For an interesting and modern application of MPC §5.01(3), see *United States v. Washington*, 106 F.3d 983 (D.C. Cir. 1997), which upheld attempt convictions of three D.C. police officers who aided undercover FBI agents they believed were trafficking in drugs.

22. On bans of chemical weapons like the nerve gas sarin and the poison ricin, see the Chemical Weapons Convention (CWC), a treaty administered by the Organisation for the Prohibition of Chemical Weapons, which 193 countries have ratified. The United States implemented the CWC by enacting 22 U.S.C. §§6701-6771. On bans of other inherently dangerous items, such as alcohol, explosives, and firearms, see, for example, Mass. Gen. Laws 138 §34C (alcohol); N.Y. Penal Law §265.04(1) ("any explosive substance"); Cal. Penal Code §30600 ("assault weapons").

23. 2 LaFave, *supra* note 4, §11.2(a).

24. 2 LaFave, *supra* note 4, §11.2(a). Professor LaFave offers a sampling of specific-intent possessory offenses fitting this model: "possession of obscene material with intent to disseminate it, possession of a forged instrument with intent to issue or deliver same, possession of burglary tools with intent to commit a burglary, possession of explosives or incendiary devices with intent to use them in committing an offense, possession of any instrument adapted for the use of narcotics by subcutaneous injection, possession of weapons with intent to use same against another unlawfully." *Id.*

25. On the rationale for criminalizing receipt of stolen property, see Wayne R. LaFave & Austin W. Scott, Jr., *Handbook on Criminal Law* 682 (1972).

26. On the pre-criminalization period, see Steven B. Duke, *Drug Prohibition: An Unnatural Disaster*, 27 Conn. L. Rev. 571 (1995). On the origins and growth of the War on Drugs, see Michelle Alexander, *The New Jim Crow* 49-58 (2012). On drug convictions as proportions of federal and state prison sentences, see Bureau of Just. Stat., *Prisoners in 2021 – Statistical Tables* 31 tbl.16, 35 tbl. 19 (2022).

27. 1 LaFave, *supra* note 4, §6.1(e); Charles H. Whitebread & Ronald Stevens, *Constructive Possession in Narcotics Cases: To Have and Have Not*, 58 Va. L. Rev. 751, 759-760 (1972).

28. Antonin Scalia, *The Rule of Law as a Law of Rules*, 56 U. Chi. L. Rev. 1175, 1177-1179 (1989); Whitebread & Stevens, *supra* note 27, at 751 (quoting United States v. Holland, 445 F.2d 701, 704 n.1 (D.C. Cir. 1971) (Tamm, J., concurring)) ("given rise").

29. Shimica Gaskins, *"Women of Circumstance"— The Effects of Mandatory Minimum Sentencing on Women Minimally Involved in Drug Crimes*, 41 Am. Crim. L. Rev. 1533, 1533 (2004).

30. American Civil Liberties Union, *Caught in the Net: The Impact of Drug Policies on Women and Families* 35-37 (2005).

31. Holly Jeanine Boux & Courtenay W. Daum, *Stuck Between a Rock and a Meth Cooking Husband: What* Breaking Bad*'s Skyler White Teaches Us About How the War on Drugs and Public Antipathy Constrain Women of Circumstance's Choices*, 45 N.M. L. Rev. 567, 589 (2015); Chieko M. Clarke, *Maternal Justice Restored: Redressing the Ramifications of Mandatory Sentencing Minimums on Women and Their Children*, 50 How. L.J. 263, 270 (2006). For additional discussion, see Marylyn Harrell, Note, *Serving Time for Falling in Love: How the War on Drugs Operates to the Detriment of Women of Circumstance in Poor Urban Communities of Color*, 11 Geo. J.L. & Mod. Critical Race Persps. 139 (2019); Eda Katharine Tinto, *The Role of Gender and Relationship in Reforming the Rockefeller Drug Laws*, 76 N.Y.U. L. Rev. 906 (2001).

32. *See* Samuel R. Gross et al., *Government Misconduct and Convicting the Innocent: The Role of Prosecutors, Police and Other Law Enforcement* 55 (2020) ("the exoneree"); Jacob Frenkel, *Will Michael Flynn Plead Guilty and Cooperate to Protect His Son?*, Forbes (Nov. 27, 2017) ("prosecutors leveraging"); Boux & Daum, *supra* note 31, at 586 ("binary choice"). For one high-profile example where this tactic may have been used, consider former National Security Advisor and Army general Michael Flynn, who pled guilty to a federal crime of lying to federal investigators in connection with Special Counsel Robert Mueller's inquiry into potential foreign interference in the 2016 presidential election. Flynn's lawyers argued that he was "was coerced into pleading guilty . . . by special counsel Robert Mueller's team [who] threaten[ed] that if he refused to plead, they would prosecute his son" for failing to register under the Foreign Agents Registration Act, 22 U.S.C. §611. Andrew C. McCarthy, *Something Seems Rotten in Flynn's Case—And Maybe Others, Too*, Hill (April 30, 2020); *see also* Jim Sciutto & Marshall Cohen, *Flynn Worries About Son in Special Counsel Probe*, CNN (Nov. 9, 2017). Attorney General William Barr subsequently directed prosecutors to seek dismissal of the case, notwithstanding Flynn's guilty plea. *See* Josh Gerstein & Kyle Cheney, *DOJ Drops Criminal Case Against Michael Flynn*, Politico (May 7, 2020). The matter was ultimately resolved when President Donald Trump pardoned Flynn. Charles Savage, *Trump Pardons Michael Flynn, Ending Case His Justice Dept. Sought to Shut Down*, N.Y. Times (Nov. 26, 2020).

33. Meda Chesney-Lind, *The Female Offender* 147 (1997) ("war on women"); Niki Monazzam & Kristen M. Budd, Sent'g Project, *Incarcerated Women and Girls* 1, 4 (2023).

34. On the increase in time forensic analysts spent in court after *Melendez-Diaz*, see Tom Jackman, *Va. Rushes to Address Ruling on Analysts; Drug-Case Demands Have Strained State Lab*, Wash. Post (Aug. 18, 2009). On the extent to which the dissent's concerns were borne out in the longer run, see Andrew Hamm, *Looking Back at Predictions in* Melendez-Diaz v. Massachusetts, SCOTUSBlog (Sept. 7, 2017, 10:33 AM), https://www.scotusblog.com/2017/09/looking-back-predictions-melendez-diaz-v-massachusetts/. For an example of a prosecution that failed because no forensic analyst was available, see Rebecca Waters, *Supreme Court Requires Lab Analysts to Testify: Now What?*, Forensic Mag. (July 24, 2009) (describing DUI case reduced to reckless driving).

35. *See* Judgment and Sentence, Georgia v. Cotton, 2007 CR 1678C (Ga. Sup. Ct., Hall County Aug. 13, 2008).

36. Anna Lvovsky, *The Judicial Presumption of Police Expertise*, 130 Harv. L. Rev. 1995, 1999, 2021 (2017).

37. Lvovsky, *supra* note 36, at 2068-2069; Jeffrey Fagan & Amanda Geller, *Following the Script: Narratives of Suspicion in* Terry *Stops in Street Policing*, 82 U. Chi. L. Rev. 51, 62, 63 (2015) ("narratives of suspicion," "scripts"). For more on police officer uses of scripts, including criticism of such practices, see Andrew Manuel Crespo, *Systemic Facts: Toward Institutional Awareness in Criminal Courts*, 129 Harv. L. Rev. 2049, 2070-2086 (2016); Andrew Manuel Crespo, *Probable Cause Pluralism*, 129 Yale L.J. 1276, 1288-1320 (2020). For additional critical perspectives on police expertise, see Lvovsky, *supra* note 36, at 1998 nn.3, 5-7 (collecting sources); Anna Lvovsky, *Rethinking Police Expertise*, 131 Yale L.J. 475, 495-497 (2021). And for empirical research demonstrating the invalidity of commonly used scripts, see, for example, Ben Grunwald & Jeffrey Fagan, *The End of Intuition-Based High-Crime Areas*, 107 Cal. L. Rev. 345 (2019); Sharad Goel et al., *Combatting Police Discrimination in the Age of Big Data*, 20 New Crim. L. Rev. 181 (2017).

38. For further criticism of using drug quantity as a proxy for culpability, see Lex A. Coleman, *Crack 2.0: Federal Methamphetamine Sentencing Policy, the Crack/Meth Sentencing Disparity, and the Meth/Meth-Mixture Ratio — Why Drug Type, Quantity, and Purity Remain "Incredibly Poor Proxies" for Sentencing Culpability Under 21 U.S.C. §841(b) and U.S.S.G. §2D1.1*, 34 Fed. Sent'g Rep. 29 (2021).

39. Paul Butler, *Let's Get Free: A Hip-Hop Theory of Justice* 43 (2009); Duke, *supra* note 26, at 571-572. For more detail on the history of narcotics control, see the canonical account in David F. Musto, *The American Disease: Origins of Narcotic Control* (3d ed. 1999).

40. Erik Luna, *Our Vietnam: The Prohibition Apocalypse*, 46 DePaul L. Rev. 483, 486-489 (1997); Shima Baradaran, *Drugs and Violence*, 88 S. Cal. L. Rev. 227, 241 (2015).

41. On the federal prison population, see Rufus G. King, *The Narcotics Bureau and the Harrison Act: Jailing the Healers and the Sick*, 62 Yale L.J. 736, 738 n.12 (1953) ("As of June 30, 1928, of the 7,738 prisoners in federal penitentiaries, 2,529 were sentenced for narcotics offenses, 1,156 for prohibition law violations, and 1,148 for stolen-vehicle transactions."). On the proliferation of drug prohibition laws at the state and federal level, see Baradaran, *supra* note 40, at 243-246.

42. Alexander, *supra* note 26, at 47-50, 62-63. In 1954, the *New York Times* described President Dwight Eisenhower's call "for a new war on narcotic addiction" and his creation of a task force to launch "a campaign against illegal narcotics," efforts that eventually spurred a new federal drug prohibition statute in 1956. W.H. Lawrence, *President Launches Drive on Narcotics*, N.Y. Times (Nov. 28, 1954).

43. Alexander, *supra* note 26, at 63, 67-69 (collecting and discussing sources).

44. Alexander, *supra* note 26, at 71.

45. Dante Chinni, *Costs in the War on Drugs Continue to Soar*, NBC News (July 2, 2023). One empirical study found that, while increased incarceration associated with the War on Drugs appears to have led to small reductions in violent and property crime, it is unlikely to have been cost-effective overall. Ilyana Kuziemko & Steven D. Levitt, *An Empirical Analysis of Imprisoning Drug Offenders*, 88 J. Pub. Econ. 2043 (2004). For the percentage of people in state prison for drug offenses, see E. Ann Carson, Bureau of Just. Stat., *Prisoners in 2022 — Statistical Tables* 29 tbl.16 (2023).

46. For statistics on total overdose deaths and overdoses by drug type, see *Drug Overdose Death Rates*, Nat'l Inst. on Drug Abuse (2024), https://nida.nih.gov/research-topics /trends-statistics/overdose-death-rates. To see how the rate of overdose deaths compares to other causes of death, compare data downloaded from *id.*, which show an age-adjusted overdose death rate of 32.4 in 2021, with Jiaquan Xu et al., Ctrs. for Disease Control &

Prevention, NCHS Data Brief No. 456, *Mortality in the United States, 2021*, at 4 fig.4 (2022). For causes of death among younger Americans, see *Injuries and Violence Are Leading Causes of Death*, Ctrs. for Disease Control & Prevention (2024), https://www.cdc.gov/injury/wisq ars/animated-leading-causes.html. In 2022, "unintentional injury" was the leading cause of death among this group; most of these are poisonings, and most poisonings, we suspect, are drug overdoses. See, for example, *Poisoning and Drug Overdose*, Wash. State Dep't Health (2023), https://doh.wa.gov/you-and-your-family/poisoning-and-drug-overdose (explaining that 90% of poisoning deaths in Washington are from drug overdoses).

47. For drug-implicated deaths beyond overdoses, see Mike Vuolo et al., *Trends in Psychotropic-Drug-Implicated Mortality: Psychotropic Drugs as a Contributing but Non-Underlying Cause of Death*, 226 Drug & Alcohol Dependence 108843 (2021). On traffic fatalities, see Nat'l Highway Traffic Safety Admin., U.S. Dep't Transp., *2021 State Traffic Data* (2023).

48. Surgeon General's Report, *The Health Consequences of Smoking — 50 Years of Progress: A Report of the Surgeon General*, U.S. Dep't Health & Human Servs. 11 (2014). For alcohol-related deaths, see *Alcohol and Public Health: Alcohol-Related Disease Impact (ARDI)*, Ctrs. for Disease Control & Prevention (2024), https://nccd.cdc.gov/DPH_ARDI/default/ default.aspx. For an additional point of comparison, see Susan A. Carlson et al., *Percentage of Deaths Associated with Inadequate Physical Activity in the United States*, 15 Preventing Chronic Disease: Pub. Health Rsch., Practice & Pol'y 1, 4 (2018), which finds that inadequate levels of physical activity are significantly associated with an increased risk of premature death. The authors conclude that 8.3% of adult deaths among nondisabled people in the United States can be "attributed to inadequate levels of physical activity."

49. On the short-term effects of marijuana, including increased risk of accidents, as well as the link between marijuana use and mental illness, see Jonathan P. Caulkins et al., RAND Corp., *Considering Marijuana Legalization: Insights for Vermont and Other Jurisdictions* 33-38 (2015), which gathers relevant literature. On the effects of persistent marijuana use on neuropsychological functioning, see Madeline H. Meier et al., *Persistent Cannabis Users Show Neuropsychological Decline from Childhood to Midlife*, 109 Proc. Nat'l Acad. Sci. E2657 (2012). On cocaine, see Nat'l Inst. on Drug Abuse, *Cocaine Research Report* 15-16 (2016). On meth-amphetamine, see *Know the Risks of Meth*, Substance Abuse & Mental Health Servs. Admin (2023), https://www.samhsa.gov/meth. On drugs and sleep disturbance, see Gustavo A. Angarita et al., *Sleep Abnormalities Associated with Alcohol, Cannabis, Cocaine, and Opiate Use: A Comprehensive Review*, 11 Addiction Sci. & Clinical Prac. 1 (2016); on the harms of sleep deprivation, see *What Are Sleep Deprivation and Deficiency?*, Nat'l Heart, Lung, and Blood Inst. (2022), https://www.nhlbi.nih.gov/health/sleep-deprivation. On malnutrition, see Nadine Mahboub et al., *Nutritional Status and Eating Habits of People Who Use Drugs and/or Are Undergoing Treatment for Recovery: A Narrative Review*, 79 Nutrition Revs. 627 (2021). On the link between drug use and viral infections including HIV, see *HIV*, Nat'l Inst. on Drug Abuse (2021), https://nida.nih.gov/research-topics/hiv; *Viral Hepatitis*, Nat'l Inst. on Drug Abuse, https://nida.nih.gov/research-topics/viral-hepatitis. For additional data on HIV and intravenous drug use, see *Injection Drug Use*, Ctrs. for Disease Control & Prevention (2022), https://www.cdc.gov/hiv/risk/drugs/index.html.

50. *Tips from Former Smokers: About the Campaign*, Ctrs. for Disease Control & Prevention (2024), https://www.cdc.gov/tobacco/campaign/tips/about/index.html ("30 peo-ple," "16 million"). For additional information on smoking-related diseases, see Surgeon General's Report, *supra* note 48; Farhad Islami et al., *Proportion and Number of Cancer Cases and Deaths Attributable to Potentially Modifiable Risk Factors in the United States*, 68 CA: Cancer J. for Clinicians 31 (2018). On alcohol-related diseases, see *Alcohol Use and Your Health*, Ctrs. for Disease Control & Prevention (2024), https://www.cdc.gov/alcohol/about-alcohol-use/; Kevin D. Shield, *Chronic Diseases and Conditions Related to Alcohol Use*, 35 Alcohol Rsch. 155

(2014); Islami et al., *supra*; Silvia Di Federico et al., *Alcohol Intake and Blood Pressure Level: A Dose-Response Meta-Analysis of Nonexperimental Cohort Studies*, 80 Hypertension 1961 (2023).

51. For overdose death rates differentiated by age cohort, see Merianne Rose Spencer et al., Ctrs. for Disease Control & Prevention, NCHS Data Brief No. 457, *Drug Overdose Deaths in the United States, 2001-2021* (2022). For research on smoking shortening lifespans, see Prabhat Jha et al., *21st-Century Hazards of Smoking and Benefits of Cessation in the United States*, 368 N. Eng. J. Med. 341 (2013).

52. Anne Katrin Schlag, *Percentages of Problem Drug Use and Their Implications for Policy Making: A Review of the Literature*, 6 Drug Sci., Pol'y & L. 1, 4-6 (2020). Note that estimates of the prevalence of marijuana use disorder vary. For a study finding that nearly 3 of 10 marijuana users manifest a marijuana use disorder, see Deborah S. Hasin et al., *Prevalence of Marijuana Use Disorder in the United States Between 2001-2002 and 2012-2013*, 72 JAMA Psychiatry 1235 (2015).

53. Carl L. Hart, *Drug Use for Grown-Ups: Chasing Liberty in the Land of Fear* 105 (2021); Butler, *supra* note 39, at 41-42.

54. R.A. Duff, *Punishment, Communication, and Community* 3-4 (2001) ("final good"); Jeremy Bentham, *An Introduction to the Principles of Morals and Legislation* 170 (Oxford 1907) (1789); Hart, *supra* note 53, at 173.

55. Michael Pollan, *How to Change Your Mind* 406 (2018); *How Psychedelic Drugs May Help with Depression*, Nat'l Insts. of Health (2023), https://www.nih.gov/news-events/nih-research-matters/how-psychedelic-drugs-may-help-depression ("new connections"); Hart, *supra* note 53, at 173. On LSD and alcoholism, see Juan José Fuentes et al., *Therapeutic Use of LSD in Psychiatry: A Systematic Review of Randomized-Controlled Clinical Trials*, 10 Frontiers Psychiatry 1 (2020).

56. Hart, *supra* note 53, at 23-24.

57. Thomas S. Szasz, *The Ethics of Addiction*, 128 Am. J. Psychiatry 541, 542 (1971). For Milton Friedman's position, see Milton Friedman, *Prohibition and Drugs*, Newsweek (May 1, 1972). For more on the classic debate between libertarianism and paternalism, including a discussion of leading works by John Stuart Mill, James Fitzjames Stephen, Patrick Devlin, and HLA Hart, see Bernard E. Harcourt, *Mill's* On Liberty *and the Modern "Harm to Others" Principle*, in *Foundational Texts in Modern Criminal Law* 163 (Markus D. Dubber ed., 2014).

58. John Stuart Mill, *On Liberty* 78-80 (Elizabeth Rapaport ed., 1978); Randy E. Barnett, *The Harmful Side Effects of Drug Prohibition*, 2009 Utah L. Rev. 11, 32; Gary Gutting & Douglas Husak, *Why Punish Drug Users at All?*, N.Y. Times (Nov. 24, 2015). For a full discussion of Mill's acceptance of morals legislation, see Harcourt, *supra* note 57.

59. Mill, *supra* note 58, at 79; Laura Lander et al., *The Impact of Substance Use Disorders on Families and Children: From Theory to Practice*, 28 Soc. Work Pub. Health 194, 194 (2013) ("including but not limited to"). On taxpayer-funded health care costs, see Jessica L. Ryan & Veronica R. Rosa, *Healthcare Cost Associations of Patients Who Use Illicit Drugs in Florida: A Retrospective Analysis*, 15 Substance Abuse Treatment, Prevention & Pol'y 1 (2020). For more on family impacts of substance abuse, see Marina Barnard, *Drug Addiction and Families* 87 (2007); Eva Tedgård et al., *An Upbringing with Substance-Abusing Parents: Experiences of Parentification and Dysfunctional Communication*, 36 Nordic Stud. Alcohol & Drugs 223 (2019).

60. On family effects of alcohol abuse, see Lander et al., *supra* note 59. On public costs of excessive drinking, see Jeffrey J. Sacks et al., *2010 National and State Costs of Excessive Alcohol Consumption*, 49 Am. J. Prev. Med. e73, e75 tbl. 1 (2015). On second-hand smoke, see *Health Problems Caused by Secondhand Smoke*, Ctrs. for Disease Control & Prevention (2024), https://www.cdc.gov/tobacco/secondhand-smoke/health.html. For data on the scale of impact, see *Alcohol's Effect on Health: Consequences for Families in the United States*, Nat'l Inst.

on Alcohol Abuse & Alcoholism (2023), https://www.niaaa.nih.gov/alcohols-effects-health /alcohol-topics/alcohol-facts-and-statistics/consequences-families-united-states (reporting that "Approximately 10.5% (7.5 million) of U.S. children ages 17 and younger live with a parent who has alcohol use disorder. . . .").

61. On the importance of the drug-crime connection in motivating the War on Drugs, see Baradaran, *supra* note 40, at 246-251.

62. On the tripartite framework, see Paul J. Goldstein, *The Drugs/Violence Nexus: A Tripartite Conceptual Framework*, 15 J. Drug Issues 493 (1985). For an example of research positing simultaneous operation of all three pathways, see Dhaval Dave et al., *Prescription Drug Monitoring Programs, Opioid Abuse, and Crime*, 87 S. Econ. J. 808 (2021), which found that restrictions on opioid prescription practices reduced both violent and property crime.

63. On the share of offenders who report drug use at the time of the offense, see Laura M. Maruschak et al., Bureau of Just. Stat., *Survey of Prison Inmates, 2016: Alcohol and Drug Use and Treatment Reported by Prisoners* (2021). On the effects of cocaine prices on crime, see Jeff Desimone, *The Effect of Cocaine Prices on Crime*, 39 Econ. Inquiry 627 (2001). On methamphetamine, see Carlos Dobkin & Nancy Nicosia, *The War on Drugs: Methamphetamine, Public Health, and Crime*, 99 Am. Econ. Rev. 324 (2009). For the overall state of the evidence, see Jeffrey A. Miron, *Drug Prohibition and Violence*, in 1 *Reforming Criminal Justice: Introduction and Criminalization* 99, 106-112 (Erik Luna ed., 2017); Emma E. McGinty et al., *The Relationship Between Controlled Substances and Violence*, 38 Epidemiologic Revs. 5 (2016); Baradaran, *supra* note 40, at 278-279.

64. On the share of offenders who report having committed crimes to obtain money to purchase drugs, see Christopher J. Mumola & Jennifer C. Karberg, Bureau of Just. Stat., *Drug Use and Dependence, State and Federal Prisoners, 2004* (2007); Richard B. Felson & Jeremy Staff, *Committing Economic Crime for Drug Money*, 63 Crime & Delinq. 375 (2017). On the relationship between property-crime rates and rates of opioid misuse, see McCaslin Giles & Michael Malcolm, *Prescription Opioid Misuse and Property Crime*, 102 Soc. Sci. Q. 663 (2021). For a classic study finding mixed evidence on Goldstein's economic pathway, see Jan M. Chaiken & Marcia R. Chaiken, *Drugs and Predatory Crime*, 13 Crime & Just. 203 (1990).

65. Franklin E. Zimring & Gordon Hawkins, *Crime Is Not the Problem: Lethal Violence in America* 141-145, 148 & appx. 6 (1997). For a review of epidemiological evidence of systemic crime, see McGinty et al., *supra* note 63, at 5-8.

66. For Friedman's quote, see George Church et al., *Thinking the Unthinkable*, Time (May 30, 1988). For Butler's quote, see Butler, *supra* note 39, at 53. On prohibition impacting the safety of drugs, see Ethan A. Nadelmann, *Drug Prohibition in the United States: Costs, Consequences, and Alternatives*, 245 Science 939, 942 (1989); Luna, *supra* note 40, at 529. On drug prices, see Barnett, *supra* note 58, at 18-19.

67. For empirical evidence relevant to Miron's claims, see Bruce L. Benson, *Is Property Crime Caused by Drug Use or by Drug Enforcement Policy?*, 24 Applied Econ. 679 (1992); for a review, see Dan Werb et al., *Effect of Drug Law Enforcement on Drug Market Violence: A Systematic Review*, 22 Int'l J. Drug Pol'y 87 (2011).

68. Butler, *supra* note 39, at 52.

69. Jen Christensen, *US Cigarette Smoking Rate Falls to Historic Low, But E-Cigarette Use Keeps Climbing*, CNN: Health (Apr. 27, 2023) ("variety of efforts"). On tobacco usage rates, see *U.S. Adult Cigarette Smoking Hits New All-Time Low*, PBS NewsHour (Apr. 27, 2023); *Current Cigarette Smoking Among Adults in the United States*, Ctrs. for Disease Control & Prevention (2023), https://www.cdc.gov/tobacco/data_statistics/fact_sheets/adult_data/cig_smoking /index.htm.

70. On HHS's four-pronged campaign, see *Overdose Prevention Strategy*, U.S. Dep't of Health & Human Servs., https://www.hhs.gov/overdose-prevention/. On the FDA's approvals, see *Information about Naloxone and Nalmefene*, U.S. Food & Drug Admin. (2024), https://www.fda.gov/drugs/postmarket-drug-safety-information-patients-and-providers/information-about-naloxone-and-nalmefene; *FDA Approves Second Over-the-Counter Naloxone Nasal Product*, U.S. Food & Drug Admin. (2023), https://www.fda.gov/news-events/press-announcements/fda-approves-second-over-counter-naloxone-nasal-spray-product. On the CDC's "Stop Overdose" campaign, see *About Stop Overdose*, Ctrs. for Disease Control & Prevention (2024), https://www.cdc.gov/stopoverdose/index.html.

71. On state marijuana laws, see *State Medical Cannabis Laws*, Nat'l Conf. of State Legislatures (2024), https://www.ncsl.org/health/state-medical-cannabis-laws. On Biden's pardon, see *A Proclamation on Granting Pardon for the Offense of Simple Possession of Marijuana*, White House (2022).

72. For systematic reviews, see Ayden I. Scheim et al., *Impact Evaluations of Drug Decriminalisation and Legal Regulation on Drug Use, Health and Social Harms: A Systematic Review*, 10 BMJ Open 1 (2020); Maria Athanassiou et al., *The Clouded Debate: A Systematic Review of Comparative Longitudinal Studies Examining the Impact of Recreational Cannabis Legalization on Key Public Health Outcomes*, 13 Frontiers Psychiatry 1 (2023); Kyra N. Farrelly et al., *The Impact of Recreational Cannabis Legalization on Cannabis Use and Associated Outcomes: A Systematic Review*, 17 Substance Abuse: Rsch. & Treatment 1 (2023). On opioid-related mortalities, see Joseph J. Sabia et al., *The Effects of Recreational Marijuana Laws on Drug Use and Crime*, 234 J. Pub. Econ. 105075 (2024); David Powell et al., *Do Medical Marijuana Laws Reduce Addictions and Deaths Related to Pain Killers?*, 58 J. Health Econ. 29 (2018). *But see* Neil K. Mathur & Christopher J. Ruhm, *Marijuana Legalization and Opioid Deaths*, 88 J. Health Econ. 102728 (2023).

73. Christopher Gavin, *Danielle Allen Wants Mass. to Take a New Approach to the Opioid Crisis: Decriminalization*, Boston.com (Feb. 2, 2022); *see also Reimagining Justice and Safety For All*, Danielle Allen for Mass., https://allenforma.com/justice-and-safety-agenda.

74. On Oregon's recriminalization of drug possession, see, for example, Mike Baker, *Oregon Is Recriminalizing Drugs, Dealing Setback to Reform Movement*, N.Y. Times (Mar. 5, 2024).

75. Hurubie Meko, *Man Who Sold Michael K. Williams Drugs That Killed Him Is Sentenced*, N.Y. Times (Aug. 18, 2023) ; Rachel Treisman, *A Dealer is Sentenced to 17.5 Years for His Role in Mac Miller's Fatal Overdose*, NPR (May 17, 2022).

76. Leo Beletsky et al., *Drug-Induced Panic*, Inquest (Apr. 14, 2022) ("drug-induced homicide," "distribution 'result[ing]' in death").

77. *Bartender Charged with Overserving Man Convicted in Drunken Crash That Killed Euless Detective*, NBC 5 Dall. Fort Worth (Feb. 3, 2023).

78. Kenneth B. Nunn, *Race, Crime and the Pool of Surplus Criminality: Or Why the "War on Drugs" Was a "War on Blacks,"* 6 J. Gender Race & Just. 381 (2002).

79. On drug use and substance use disorder, see Substance Abuse & Mental Health Servs. Admin., *Highlights by Race/Ethnicity for the 2021 National Survey on Drug Use and Health*. On drug dealing, see Leah J. Floyd et al., *Adolescent Drug Dealing and Race/Ethnicity: A Population-Based Study of the Differential Impact of Substance Use on Involvement in Drug Trade*, 36 Am. J. Drug & Alcohol Abuse 87 (2010); Howard N. Snyder & Melissa Sickmund, Nat'l Center Juvenile Just., *Juvenile Offenders and Victims: 2006 National Report* 70 (2006).

80. For national arrest data, see Fed. Bureau of Investigation, *2019 Crime in the United States* tbl.43A, https://ucr.fbi.gov/crime-in-the-u.s/2019/crime-in-the-u.s.-2019/topic-pages/tables/table-43. For disparate arrest rates, see *Drug Arrests Stayed High Even*

as Imprisonment Fell from 2009 to 2019, Pew (2022), https://www.pewtrusts.org/en/research-and-analysis/issue-briefs/2022/02/drug-arrests-stayed-high-even-as-imprisonment-fell-from-2009-to-2019. For marijuana arrests nationally, see Ezekiel Edwards et al., ACLU, *A Tale of Two Countries: Racially Targeted Arrests in the Era of Marijuana Reform* 5 (2020). On New York City, specifically, see Benjamin Mueller et al., *Surest Way to Face Marijuana Charges in New York: Be Black or Hispanic*, N.Y. Times (May 13, 2018).

81. For national charging data, see Brian A. Reaves, Bureau of Just. Stat., *Felony Defendants in Large Urban Counties, 2009 – Statistical Tables* (2013). On Cook County, see Sarah Staudt, *Dynamics of Drug Possession Charges in Illinois, From Investigatory Stops to Sentences*, Chi. Appleseed Center for Fair Courts (June 15, 2022), https://www.chicagoappleseed.org/2022/06/15/dynamics-of-drug-possession-charges-in-illinois/. On sentencing, see U.S. Sent'g Comm'n, *Demographic Differences in Federal Sentencing* 27-28 (2023); U.S. Sent'g Comm'n, *Demographic Differences in Sentencing: An Update to the 2012* Booker *Report* 26 (2017). For earlier, consistent studies, see, for example, Celesta A. Albonetti, *Sentencing Under the Federal Sentencing Guidelines: Effects of Defendant Characteristics, Guilty Pleas, and Departures on Sentence Outcomes for Drug Offenses, 1991-1992*, 31 Law & Soc'y Rev. 789 (1997); James D. Unnever, *Direct and Organizational Discrimination in the Sentencing of Drug Offenders*, 30 Soc. Probs. 212 (1982).

82. *Drug Arrests Stayed High, supra* note 80. On Illinois demographics, see *QuickFacts: Illinois*, U.S. Census Bureau, https://www.census.gov/quickfacts/fact/table/IL/PST045222. On Illinois prison admissions, see Justin Escamilla & Sharyn Adams, *Illinois Arrests and Prison Admissions for Drug Offenses: Interactive Data*, Ill. Crim. Just. Auth. (2018), https://icjia.illinois.gov/researchhub/articles/illinois-arrests-and-prison-admissions-for-drug-offenses-interactive-data. For additional evidence of racially disparate drug enforcement, see Deborah J. Vagins & Jesselyn McCurdy, ACLU, *Cracks in the System: Twenty Years of the Unjust Federal Crack Cocaine Law* (2006); Samuel R. Gross et al., Nat'l Registry of Exonerations, *Race and Wrongful Convictions in the United States* 16 (2017); Drug Policy Alliance, *The Drug War, Mass Incarceration and Race* (2015); Radley Balko, *There's Overwhelming Evidence That the Criminal Justice System Is Racist. Here's the Proof*, Wash. Post (June 10, 2020) (collecting sources).

83. Robert J. Sampson & William J. Wilson, *Toward a Theory of Race, Crime, and Urban Inequality*, in *Crime and Inequality* 37, 42-43 (John Hagan & Ruth D. Peterson eds., 1995).

84. For empirical studies supporting Tonry's analysis, see Leonard Saxe et al., *The Visibility of Illicit Drugs: Implications for Community-Based Drug Control Strategies*, 91 Am. J. Pub. Health 1987, 1987 (2001), which reports that visible drug sales were 6.3 times more likely to be reported in the most disadvantaged neighborhoods than in the least disadvantaged (while illicit drug use was only 1.3 times more likely). A similar relationship exists between the proportion of minority residents and the rate of visible drug sales. A separate study finds that a focus on outdoor drug venues contributes to racial disparities in drug arrests, as white people comprised a larger share of those arrested for distribution indoors than outdoors, while Black people comprised a larger share of those arrested outdoors than indoors. This study, however, finds that even when controlling for these "race neutral," poverty-based differentials, there remains a residual racial disparity, which suggests race may be playing a direct role in driving disparate arrest rates. Katherine Beckett et al., *Race, Drugs, and Policing: Understanding Disparities in Drug Delivery Arrests*, 44 Criminology 105 (2006).

85. U.S. Sent'g Comm'n, *Cocaine and Federal Sentencing Policy* (1995); Devah Pager, *Marked: Race, Crime, and Finding Work in an Era of Mass Incarceration* 20 (2007). On passage of the 100:1 crack-powder disparity, see David A. Sklansky, *Cocaine, Race, and Equal Protection*, 47 Stan. L. Rev. 1283, 1290-1297 (1995).

86. William J. Stuntz, *Race, Class, and Drugs*, 98 Colum. L. Rev. 1795, 1816-1819 (1998).

87. On the effects of the Fair Sentencing Act, see U.S. Sent'g Comm'n, *Report to the Congress: Impact of the Fair Sentencing Act of 2010*, at 23 (2015); David Bjerk, *Mandatory Minimum Policy Reform and the Sentencing of Crack Cocaine Defendants: An Analysis of the Fair Sentencing Act*, 14 J. Empirical Legal Stud. 370 (2017).

88. On crack-powder disparities in the states, see FAMM, *Crack-Cocaine Disparity Reform in the States* (2021). For the DOJ's position, see *Examining Federal Sentencing for Crack and Powder Cocaine: Hearing Before the Sen. Comm. on the Judiciary* (statement of Regina M. LaBelle, Acting Director, Office Nat'l Drug Control Pol'y) (June 22, 2021). For Attorney General Garland's instructions, see Memorandum, Additional Department Policies Regarding Charging, Pleas, and Sentencing in Drug Cases (Dec. 16, 2022), https://www.justice.gov/media/1265321/dl?inline.

89. 156 Cong. Rec. S1680 (daily ed. March 17, 2010) (statement of Sen. Durbin) ("just appeared"); 155 Cong. Rec. S10491 (daily ed. Oct. 15, 2009) (statement of Sen. Durbin) ("one of the authors"); 156 Cong. Rec. H6202 (daily ed. July 28, 2010) (statement of Rep. Lungren); 156 Cong. Rec. H6202 (daily ed. July 28, 2010) (statement of Rep. Scott).

90. For a contrary perspective, arguing that American drug laws have been driven by concerns about the moral integrity of white youth, see George Fisher, *Beware Euphoria: The Moral Roots and Racial Myths of America's War on Drugs* (2024); George Fisher, *Racial Myths of the Cannabis War*, 101 B.U. L. Rev. 933 (2021). See also Matthew D. Lassiter, *The Suburban Crisis: White America and the War on Drugs* (2023).

91. Kate Stith, *The Government Interest in Criminal Law: Whose Interest Is It, Anyway?*, in *Public Values in Constitutional Law* 137, 153 (Stephen E. Gottlieb ed., 1993).

92. Randall Kennedy, *Race, Crime, and the Law* 370 (1997); James Forman Jr., *Locking Up Our Own: Crime and Punishment in Black America* 10 (2017). For additional discussion, see Vanessa Barker, *The Politics of Imprisonment: How the Democratic Process Shapes the Way America Punishes Offenders* 149-152 (2009); John Rappaport, *Some Doubts About "Democratizing" Criminal Justice*, 87 U. Chi. L. Rev. 711, 787-794 (2020).

93. For empirical evidence substantiating concerns about the toll of drugs, and crack cocaine specifically, on Black communities, see, for example, Roland G. Fryer Jr et al., *Measuring Crack Cocaine and Its Impact*, 51 Econ. Inquiry 1651, 1651 (2013), finding that violence attending the spread of crack cocaine explains much of the rise in Black youth homicide in the 1980s, including a doubling of homicide victimization among Black males aged 14 to 17 years. Overdose death rates are positively correlated with income inequality, especially for Black and Hispanic populations—the fatal overdose rate in counties with the highest income inequality was, for both these groups, more than twice that of counties with the lowest income inequality. *See* Mbabazi Kariisa et al., *Vital Signs: Drug Overdose Deaths, by Selected Sociodemographic and Social Determinants of Health Characteristics—25 States and the District of Columbia, 2019-2020*, 71 Morbidity & Mortality Wkly. Rep. 940 (2022).

94. Sklansky, *supra* note 85, 1302-1303. For competing views on the equal protection question, see Randall Kennedy, *The State, Criminal Law, and Racial Discrimination: A Comment*, 107 Harv. L. Rev. 1255, 1270-1277 (1994), and Sklansky, *supra* note 85, at 1298-1302.

95. Barnett, *supra* note 58, at 28; Alexander, *supra* note 26, at 61, 124-125.

96. For further argument about how the War on Drugs reduced judicial oversight of the police, see Paul Finkleman, *The Second Casualty of War: Civil Liberties and the War on Drugs*, 66 S. Cal. L. Rev. 1389 (1993).

97. On the breakdown of deaths by firearm in the U.S., including by homicide and by suicide, see *Web-Based Injury Statistics Query and Reporting System (WISQARS) Fatal Injury Data*, Ctrs. for Disease Control and Prevention (2023), https://wisqars.cdc.gov/explore/. On firearms as the leading cause of death for ages 1 to 19, see Jason E. Goldstick et al.,

Correspondence, *Current Causes of Death in Children and Adolescents in the United States*, 386 New Eng. J. Med. 1955 (2022).

98. For international comparisons, see Erin Grinshteyn & David Hemenway, *Violent Death Rates: The US Compared with Other High-Income OECD Countries, 2010*, 129 Am. J. Med. 266, 270-271 (2016). On gun use in crime, see Marianne W. Zawitz, Bureau of Just. Stat., *Guns Used in Crime* 1, 2 (1995); Caroline Wolf Harlow, Bureau of Just. Stat., *Firearm Use by Offenders* 1, 7 (2002).

99. On homicide rates by race, see Julie A. Ward et al., *Differences in Perceptions of Gun-Related Safety by Race and Gun Ownership in the United States*, 51 J.L. Med. & Ethics 14, 14 (2023). On hospital visits, see Elliott Currie, *A Peculiar Indifference: The Neglected Toll of Violence on Black America* 34-37 (2020).

100. For statistics on gun ownership, see Berrigan et al., *supra* note 11; Press Release, *One in Five American Households Purchased a Gun During the Pandemic*, NORC at Univ. of Chi. (Mar. 24, 2022), https://www.norc.org/research/library/one-in-five-american-households-purchased-a-gun-during-the-pande.html.

101. On reasons for gun ownership, see, for example, Ruth Igielnik & Anna Brown, *Key Takeaways on Americans' Views of Guns and Gun Ownership*, Pew Rsch. Ctr. (June 22, 2017), https://www.pewresearch.org/short-reads/2017/06/22/key-takeaways-on-americans-views -of-guns-and-gun-ownership/.

102. Philip J. Cook & Kristin A. Goss, *The Gun Debate: What Everyone Needs to Know* 20-22 (2d ed. 2020). On the potential psychological utility of gun ownership, see Nicholas Buttrick, *Protecting Gun Ownership as a Coping Mechanism*, 15 Persps. Psych. Sci. 835 (2020); Roni Caryn Rabin, *Why Some Americans Buy Guns*, N.Y. Times (July 26, 2023).

103. Ida B. Wells, *Southern Horrors: Lynch Law in All Its Phases* 21 (1892). On the common racial origins of drug and gun criminalization, see Douglas N. Husak, *Guns and Drugs: Case Studies on the Principled Limits of the Criminal Sanction*, 23 Law & Phil. 437, 455 n.58 (2004) ("[B]oth gun and drug controls have racist roots. Drug prohibitions were first enacted against the substances used by disfavored immigrant groups. Similarly, guns were largely unregulated until whites became worried about the arms carried by militant groups like the Black Panthers."); *see also* Clayton E. Cramer, *The Racist Roots of Gun Control*, 4 Kan. J.L. & Pub. Pol'y 17 (1995).

104. On the proportion of federal prisoners serving time for an offense involving a weapon, see U.S. Sent'g Comm'n, *Quick Facts: Federal Offenders in Prison* (2023). For a discussion of the general structure of criminal gun regulation, including its focus on banning gun possession by members of certain ineligible groups, see Husak, *supra* note 103, at 447-448. On racial demographics in federal firearm sentencing, see Matthew J. Iaconetti et al., U.S. Sent'g Comm'n, *What Do Federal Firearms Offenses Really Look Like?* (2022).

105. For an interview of the public defenders who authored this brief, in which they describe their motivations for doing so, see Avinash Samarth et al., *Second Class*, Inquest (Nov. 5, 2021).

CHAPTER 9

1. William J. Stuntz, *Race, Class, and Drugs*, 98 Colum. L. Rev. 1795, 1820 (1998).

2. William J. Stuntz, *The Pathological Politics of Criminal Law*, 100 Mich. L. Rev. 505, 506-507 (2001) [hereinafter Stuntz, *Pathological Politics*] (emphasis added).

3. Benjamin Levin, *Guns and Drugs*, 84 Fordham L. Rev. 2173, 2205-2206 (2016). In making this argument, Levin draws and builds on Markus Dirk Dubber, *Policing Possession: The War on Crime and the End of Criminal Law*, 91 J. Crim. L. & Criminology 829 (2001).

4. Stuntz, *Pathological Politics*, *supra* note 2, at 539.

5. Debra Livingston, *Police Discretion and the Quality of Life in Public Places: Courts, Communities, and the New Policing*, 97 Colum. L. Rev. 551, 556, 558 (1997) [hereinafter Livingston, *Police Discretion*].

6. Samuel Walker, *The Police in America* 28 (2d ed. 1992) ("most influential"); James Q. Wilson & George L. Kelling, *Broken Windows: The Police and Neighborhood Safety*, Atlantic (Mar. 1982).

7. Wilson & Kelling, *supra* note 6.

8. Wilson & Kelling, *supra* note 6.

9. For a discussion of the overlap and differences between order-maintenance policing and community policing, see Dorothy E. Roberts, *Foreword: Race, Vagueness, and the Social Meaning of Order-Maintenance Policing*, 89 J. Crim. L. & Criminology 775, 776-777 (1999).

10. For a short documentary film on Tyquan Brehon, a young man in Brooklyn who says he was stopped more than 60 times between the ages of 15 and 18, see Julie Dressner & Edwin Martinez, *The Scars of Stop-and-Frisk*, N.Y. Times (June 13, 2013). For a short documentary film on the use of stop and frisk in Brownsville, Brooklyn, see Matthew Orr et al., *Stop & Frisk in Brownsville*, N.Y. Times (July 11, 2010).

11. Livingston, *Police Discretion*, *supra* note 5, at 584 ("in tension"); *id.* at 560 (quoting Wilson & Kelling, *supra* note 6) ("ultimate question").

12. Barry Friedman & Maria Ponomarenko, *Democratic Policing*, 90 N.Y.U. L. Rev. 1827, 1844 (2015); Ronald Allen et al., *Criminal Procedure: Investigation and Right to Counsel* 322 (3d ed. 2016).

13. William J. Stuntz, *Warrants and Fourth Amendment Remedies*, 77 Va. L. Rev. 881, 881 (1991) [hereinafter Stuntz, *Warrants*].

14. Oren Bar-Gill & Barry Friedman, *Taking Warrants Seriously*, 106 Nw. U. L. Rev. 1609, 1651-1652 (2012) (quoting Stuntz, *Warrants*, *supra* note 13, at 914).

15. Bar-Gill & Friedman, *supra* note 14, at 1652 (quoting Stuntz, *Warrants*, *supra* note 13, at 915).

16. Bar-Gill & Friedman, *supra* note 14, at 1609; Allen et al., *supra* note 12, at 449.

17. Akhil Reed Amar, *Fourth Amendment First Principles*, 107 Harv. L. Rev. 757, 764 (1994).

18. Rachel A. Harmon, *Why Arrest?*, 115 Mich. L. Rev. 307, 313-315, 317 (2016) [hereinafter Harmon, *Why Arrest*]. For additional accountings of the personal and social costs of arrest, see Eisha Jain, *Arrests as Regulation*, 67 Stan. L. Rev. 809 (2015); John Rappaport, *Criminal Justice, Inc.*, 118 Colum. L. Rev. 2251, 2279-2281 & nn.176-183 (2018).

19. William J. Stuntz, *The Distribution of Fourth Amendment Privacy*, 67 Geo. Wash. L. Rev. 1265, 1274-1275 (1999); Donald Dripps, *Living with Leon*, 95 Yale L.J. 906, 926-927 (1986).

20. For an academic analysis consistent with the dissent's position, see Harmon, *Why Arrest*, *supra* note 18.

21. Morgan Cloud, *The Dirty Little Secret*, 43 Emory L.J. 1311, 1312 (1994); Andrew Manuel Crespo, *Probable Cause Pluralism*, 129 Yale L.J. 1276, 1330-1331 (2020) [hereinafter Crespo, *Probable Cause*]. For more on barriers to holding police officers accountable for misconduct, including perjury, see Kate Levine, *How We Prosecute the Police*, 104 Geo. L.J. 745

(2016); Kate Levine, *Who Shouldn't Prosecute the Police*, 101 Iowa L. Rev. 1447 (2016); Somil Trivedi & Nicole Gonzalez Van Cleve, *To Serve and Protect Each Other: How Police-Prosecutor Codependence Enables Police Misconduct*, 100 B.U. L. Rev. 895 (2020).

22. Crespo, *Probable Cause, supra* note 21, at 1279. For the number of arrests, see *Arrest: How Many Arrests Are Made Annually, and for What?*, Vera, https://arresttrends.vera .org/arrests (summarizing data from the FBI's Uniform Crime Report).

23. Andrew Manuel Crespo, *The Unavoidably Empirical Fourth Amendment: A Case Study of* Kansas v. Glover, 1 Cts. & Just. L.J. 217, 231 (2019) ("inescapably empirical"); Crespo, *Probable Cause, supra* note 21, at 1288 ("evidentiary claim").

24. Crespo, *Probable Cause, supra* note 21, at 1341.

25. Crespo, *Probable Cause, supra* note 21, at 1282; Craig S. Lerner, *The Reasonableness of Probable Cause*, 81 Tex. L. Rev. 951, 953, 957 (2003) ("elusive," "hopelessly indeterminate," "shrouded in mystery"); Christopher Slobogin, *Let's Not Bury* Terry: *A Call for Rejuvenation of the Proportionality Principle*, 72 St. John's L. Rev. 1053, 1082 (1998).

26. For an argument that the default probable cause standard should be defined as a preponderance of the evidence standard, and an analysis of existing Supreme Court precedent on the point, see Crespo, *Probable Cause, supra* note 21, at 1345-1350.

27. On the prevalence of lawful-order statutes, as well as variation among state regimes, see James Mooney, Comment, *The Power of Police Officers to Give "Lawful Orders,"* 129 Yale L.J. 1568 (2020).

28. Sean Webby, *San Jose Police Often Use Force in Resisting-Arrest Cases*, San Jose Mercury News (Oct. 31, 2009).

29. *See* Darrell A.H. Miller, *Retail Rebellion and the Second Amendment*, 86 Ind. L.J. 939, 953-954 (2011). For a classic treatment of the right to resist an unlawful arrest, see Paul G. Chevigny, *The Right to Resist an Unlawful Arrest*, 78 Yale L.J. 1128 (1969).

30. Chevigny, *supra* note 29, at 1128 ("police sometimes use"); Webby, *supra* note 28 (quoting Chevigny) ("well-known," "contempt of cop"). For further discussion of the strategic use of resisting arrest charges, see Webby, *supra* note 28 ("Across the country, resisting arrest charges have raised concerns inside and outside police departments, because of allegations that they have been misused by officers to justify unwarranted force.").

31. Levin, *supra* note 3, at 2205.

32. Stuntz, *Pathological Politics, supra* note 2, at 539.

33. Donald A. Dripps, *The Fourth Amendment and the Fallacy of Composition: Determinacy Versus Legitimacy in a Regime of Bright-Line Rules*, 74 Miss. L.J. 341, 393 (2004). Professor Dripps introduced the idea of the iron triangle in the context of discussing stops, arrests, and searches of automobiles. As a result, he identifies *New York v. Belton*, 453 U.S. 454 (1981), an automobile-search case, as one of the three main precedents in the trio. *Belton*, however, is an application of the broader search-incident-to-arrest doctrine, for which, Dripps observes, "[t]he watershed decision was *United States v. Robinson*." Dripps, *supra*, at 363. We treat *Robinson* as one of the iron triangle's sides, alongside the other two precedents Dripps identified: *Atwater* and *Whren*.

34. Stuntz, *Pathological Politics, supra* note 2, at 539.

35. Stuntz, *Pathological Politics, supra* note 2, at 579.

36. Rachel Harmon, *The Law of the Police* 659 (2021).

37. For an excellent example of such criticism, see Roberts, *supra* note 9.

38. N.Y. Police Dep't, *Crime and Enforcement Activity in New York City* 18-19 (2013).

39. Sharad Goel et al., *Combatting Police Discrimination in the Age of Big Data*, 20 New Crim. L. Rev. 181, 187-188 (2017).

40. Vesla M. Weaver et al., *The Great Decoupling: The Disconnect Between Criminal Offending and Experience of Arrest Across Two Cohorts*, 5 RSF: Russell Sage Found. J. Soc. Scis. 89, 91, 110 (2019).

41. David Cole, *No Equal Justice: Race and Class in the American Criminal Justice System* 46-47 (1999); Ellen Goodman, *Simpson Case Divides Us by Race*, Boston Globe (July 10, 1994) (quoting Professor Charles Ogletree).

42. Wilson & Kelling, *supra* note 6.

43. David B. Owens, *The Equal Protection-Fourth Amendment Shell Game: An Essay on the Limited Reach of the 2023 Affirmative Action Cases, the Fourth Amendment, and Race Beyond Skin Color*, 47 N.Y.U. Rev. L. & Soc. Change __ (forthcoming 2024).

44. On *Floyd* as a landmark case, see, for example, Jonathan Oberman & Kendea Johnson, *The Never Ending Tale: Racism and Inequality in the Era of Broken Windows*, 37 Cardozo L. Rev. 1075, 1089 (2016); Ryan Devereaux, *New York's Stop-and-Frisk Trial Comes to a Close with Landmark Ruling*, Guardian (Aug. 12, 2013).

45. Cole, *supra* note 41, at 39-40; Michelle Alexander, *The New Jim Crow: Mass Incarceration in the Age of Colorblindness* 132-133 (2010).

46. Reva B. Siegel, *Foreword: Equality Divided*, 127 Harv. L. Rev. 1, 14-20, 17 n.77 (2012); Guy Rubinstein, *Selective Prosecution, Selective Enforcement, and Remedial Vagueness*, 2022 Wis. L. Rev. 825, 831. In the *Floyd* opinion, Judge Scheindlin quotes a footnote in *Feeney* that leaves the door open to impact evidence operating as one factor in the intent analysis: "What a legislature or any official entity is 'up to' may be plain from the results its actions achieve, or the results they avoid." See also *Feeney*, 442 U.S. at 279 n.25 (noting that the Court's opinion "is not [meant] to say that the inevitability or foreseeability of consequences of a neutral rule has no bearing upon the existence of discriminatory intent"). For an argument that the *Feeney* footnotes should be read broadly to treat evidence of "disparate impact" as "potentially a powerful" factor "in determining discriminatory purpose," as some lower courts did prior to *Feeney* itself, see Noam Biale et al., *The Discriminatory Purpose of the 1994 Crime Bill*, 16 Harv. L. & Pol'y Rev. 115, 118-125 (2021).

47. Cole, *supra* note 41, at 167.

48. Ligon v. City of New York, 743 F.3d 362, 364 (2d Cir. 2014); *see also* Floyd v. City of New York, 302 F.R.D. 69, 81 (S.D.N.Y. 2014); Benjamin Weiser & Joseph Goldstein, *Mayor Says New York City Will Settle Suits on Stop-and-Frisk Tactics*, N.Y. Times (Jan. 30, 2014).

49. David Hausman & Dorothy Kronick, *The Illusory End of Stop and Frisk in Chicago?*, 9 Sci. Advances No. 39 DOI:10.1126/SciAdv.adh3017 (2023) ("illusory"); Stephen Farrell, *Omnipresence: New Stop-and-Frisk?*, N.Y. Times (Sept. 19, 2014).

50. Katie Glueck & Ashley Southall, *As Adams Toughens on Crime, Some Fear a Return to '90s Era Policing*, N.Y. Times (Mar. 26, 2022); Jeffrey C. Mays, *Black Leaders Are Conveying the Far Left's Unease with Eric Adams*, N.Y. Times (July 21, 2022).

51. Cole, *supra* note 41, at 161, 167.

52. Alexander, *supra* note 45, at 126.

53. Alexander, *supra* note 45, at 127.

54. Cole, *supra* note 41, at 167.

55. Cole, *supra* note 41, at 167-168. Countless works discuss the legal system's failure to hold police accountable for misconduct, including racially biased policing. For one thorough, recent take, see Joanna Schwartz, *Shielded: How the Police Became Untouchable* (2023).

56. In addition to the practical obstacles to accountability outlined in the text, it is unclear whether the exclusionary rule applies at all to violations of equal protection by the police. *See* Rubinstein, *supra* note 46, at 833-842 (documenting the Supreme Court's "remedial vagueness" on this question).

57. For more on the historical linkages between policing and slave patrols, as well as other forms of class and racial control, see Simon Balto & Max Felker-Kantor, *Police and Crime in the American City, 1800—2020* (2022), in *Oxford Research Encyclopedia of American History*, where the authors write:

> In general, there are three central frames through which to understand the raisons d'être and role of police in early American urban history. One is police as a form of class control, especially in Northern cities like New York and Chicago, where modern policing began out of concern with the growing number of immigrants deemed unruly by the forces of law and order, and quickly morphed into a broader apparatus for controlling the working class. A second is policing in cities in the slaveholding South and "middle-ground" cities like Baltimore, where policing through slave patrols, legally sanctioned white vigilante groups, and nascent formalized police departments served the broader racial structures of society, targeting Black people and communities for control and surveillance, and aiding and abetting the expropriation of profit and power via control of them. The third is the settler colonial model described by Kelly Lytle Hernández, who shows how in Western cities like Los Angeles, early policing and jailing was aimed at regulating the behavior of the city's Indigenous populations. It should go without saying that these frameworks frequently overlapped with one another. Class control and racial control in the United States, after all, are deeply entangled historically, and there are plenty of examples of early police officers acting in direct service of white supremacy while still operating within a system more generally ordered around protecting capital and controlling European immigrants. (Consider, as just one case, Jonathan Daniel Wells's research on pre-Civil War New York's "kidnapping club"—a network of white men centered around New York police officers, who made a profit by capturing African Americans and sending them into slavery in the South.)

See as well Jill Lepore, *The Invention of the Police*, New Yorker (July 13, 2020), for additional discussion of historical linkages between policing and slavery, in the South and also in Northern cities such as Boston.

58. Stuntz, *Pathological Politics, supra* note 2, at 535 ("can tell legislatures"); *id.* at 527-528 ("frees legislators," "criminal law expands"). On police and prosecutor lobbying regarding the criminal law and more, see Carissa Byrne Hessick et al., *The Prosecutor Lobby*, 80 Wash. & Lee. L. Rev. 143 (2023); Zoë Robinson & Stephen Rushin, *The Law Enforcement Lobby*, 107 Minn. L. Rev. 1965 (2023); Brenner Fissell, *Police-Made Law*, 108 Minn. L. Rev. 2561 (2024).

59. Douglas Husak, *Overcriminalization: The Limits of the Criminal Law* 12 (2007) ("phenomenal growth," "only a fraction"); *id.* at 3 ("great deal," "substantial amount").

60. Stuntz, *Pathological Politics, supra* note 2, at 557-558.

61. On the history of vagrancy enforcement, see Dubber, *supra* note 3, at 911-914, and especially Risa Goluboff, *Vagrant Nation: Police Power, Constitutional Change, and the Making of the 1960s* (2016).

62. Debra Livingston, *Gang Loitering, the Court and Some Realism About Police Patrol*, 1999 Sup. Ct. Rev. 141, 173. For a related argument—that "[o]rdinary criminal prosecutions often raise the same problems as vague statutes"—see Carissa Byrne Hessick, *Vagueness Principles*, 48 Ariz. St. L.J. 1137, 1138 (2016).

63. Livingston, *Police Discretion, supra* note 5, at 604-605; John Calvin Jeffries, Jr., *Legality, Vagueness, and the Construction of Penal Statutes*, 71 Va. L. Rev. 189, 216 (1985). On the "substantive overtones" point, see also Robert C. Post, *Reconceptualizing Vagueness: Legal Rules and Social Orders*, 82 Cal. L. Rev. 491 (1994).

64. Husak, *supra* note 59, at 3.

65. John Hart Ely, *Democracy and Distrust: A Theory of Judicial Review* 13 (1980). On the counter-majoritarian difficulty, see Alexander Bickel, *The Least Dangerous Branch* (1962).

66. 1 Wayne R. LaFave, *Substantive Criminal Law* §3.3(b) (3d ed. 2017 & Supp. 2023).

67. For examples of cases blocking the application of penal statutes on free speech grounds, see Cohen v. California, 403 U.S. 15, 16 (1971) ("offensive conduct"); Brandenburg v. Ohio, 395 U.S. 444, 444-445 (1969) (advocating violence); R.A.V. v. City of St. Paul, 505 U.S. 377, 380 (1992) (hate speech); Thornhill v. Alabama, 310 U.S. 88, 91 (1940) (labor picketing); Jenkins v. Georgia, 418 U.S. 153, 154 (1974) (pornography); Texas v. Johnson, 491 U.S. 397, 397 (1989) (flag burning).

68. Stuntz, *Pathological Politics, supra* note 2, at 588 ("For judges to displace"); *id.* at 600 ("Never in our history").

69. The *Hedgepeth* court technically addressed the "fundamental right" issue not in the context of a substantive due process claim but rather an equal protection claim. That doctrine requires heightened scrutiny not only when challenged state action treats people differently based on a suspect classification, like race, but also when it treats people differently with respect to the exercise of a fundamental right. *See* Griffin v. Illinois, 351 U.S. 12 (1956). As the Supreme Court has explained, in this analysis "[d]ue process and equal protection principles converge." Bearden v. Georgia, 461 U.S. 660, 665 (1983). In *Hedgepeth*, the equal protection analysis is formally grounded not in the Equal Protection Clause of the Fourteenth Amendment, which applies only to the states, but rather under what is known as the "equal protection component" of the Fifth Amendment's Due Process Clause—which governs the federal and D.C. governments, and which doctrinally mirrors the Fourteenth Amendment's Equal Protection Clause. *See* Bolling v. Sharpe, 347 U.S. 497 (1954).

70. There is another reason decriminalization may not effectively curb police power: At least in some jurisdictions, courts have held that the police may arrest for civil infractions, including for offenses the legislature has explicitly decriminalized. *See* Wayne A. Logan, *After the Cheering Stopped: Decriminalization and Legalism's Limits*, 24 Cornell J.L. & Pub. Pol'y 319, 335-339 (2014).

71. Rachel Harmon, *More Law, More Power? Rethinking the Impact of Criminal Laws on Policing*, Keynote Address, Fairfax, Virginia (July 30, 2021) [hereinafter Harmon, *More Law*].

72. Harmon, *More Law, supra* note 71; David Alan Sklansky, *The Nature and Function of Prosecutorial Power*, 106 J. Crim. L. & Criminology 473, 480-481 (2016) (quoting additional sources).

73. Rachel E. Barkow, *Institutional Design and the Policing of Prosecutors: Lessons from Administrative Law*, 61 Stan. L. Rev. 869, 871 (2009).

74. John F. Pfaff, *Locked In* 6 (2017) ("The primary driver of incarceration is increased prosecutorial toughness when it comes to charging people . . . ."); Andrew Manuel Crespo, *No Justice, No Pleas: Subverting Mass Incarceration Through Defendant Collective Action*, 90 Fordham L. Rev. 1999, 2004 (2022) ("root"); Andrew Manuel Crespo, *Defendants, United,*

Could Strike the State Blindsided, Law & Pol. Econ. Project Blog (Apr. 17, 2023), https://lpe project.org/blog/defendants-united-could-strike-the-state-blindsided/ ("reason is simple").

75. Frank H. Easterbrook, *Plea Bargaining as Compromise,* 101 Yale L.J. 1969, 1978 (1992).

76. Gerard E. Lynch, *Our Administrative System of Criminal Justice,* 66 Fordham L. Rev. 2117, 2132 (1998); Tracey L. Meares, *Rewards for Good Behavior: Influencing Prosecutorial Discretion and Conduct with Financial Incentives,* 64 Fordham L. Rev. 851, 873, 886 (1995); Máximo Langer, *Rethinking Plea Bargaining: The Practice and Reform of Prosecutorial Adjudication in American Criminal Procedure,* 33 Am. J. Crim. L. 223, 224 (2006).

77. John H. Langbein, *Torture and Plea Bargaining,* 46 U. Chi. L. Rev. 3, 12-13 & n.24 (1978).

78. Daniel C. Richman, *Bargaining About Future Jeopardy,* 49 Vand. L. Rev. 1181, 1188 n.23 (1996) (quoting George C. Thomas III, *The Prohibition of Successive Prosecutions for the Same Offense: In Search of a Definition,* 71 Iowa L. Rev. 323, 370 (1986)) ("long been attacked"); Andrew Manuel Crespo, *The Hidden Law of Plea Bargaining,* 118 Colum. L. Rev. 1303, 1333 (2018) [hereinafter Crespo, *Hidden Law*]. As Crespo explains, current double jeopardy doctrine is criticized as a weak protection against serial prosecutions because *Blockburger* "bars serial prosecutions only if *all* of the elements in *all* of the charges of a proposed second prosecution contain, or are contained within, the elements of a prior offense from the same factual episode for which the defendant was already acquitted or convicted—a test rarely satisfied in a world where criminal codes are full of only partially overlapping offenses." *Id.* at 1329. Meanwhile, the "added layer of protection" in cases of acquittal "bars subsequent prosecutions only if a conviction in the second case would require a jury to accept facts that the first jury *definitively* rejected—a thin reed that 'will not often be available,' given that multi-element offenses and general jury verdicts often make it too difficult 'to determine with precision' just how the first 'jury has decided any particular issue.' " *Id.* (quoting 5 Wayne R. LaFave et al., *Criminal Procedure* §17.4(a) (4th ed. 2015)).

79. Josh Bowers, *Legal Guilt, Normative Innocence, and the Equitable Decision Not to Prosecute,* 110 Colum. L. Rev. 1655, 1686 (2010).

80. Meares, *supra* note 76, at 862; Andy Grimm, *Shomari Legghette Formally Indicted for Cmdr. Paul Bauer's Murder,* Chi. Sun Times (Mar. 9, 2018).

81. Crespo, *Hidden Law, supra* note 78, at 1335-1337.

82. Crespo, *Hidden Law, supra* note 78, at 1333 n.84 ("a rule"); Edith Greene & Elizabeth F. Loftus, *When Crimes Are Joined at Trial,* 9 Law & Hum. Behav. 193, 194 (1985) ("halo effect"); Michael L. Seigel & Christopher Slobogin, *Prosecuting Martha: Federal Prosecutorial Power and the Need for a Law of Counts,* 109 Penn St. L. Rev. 1107, 1125-1126 (2005) ("horse-trade," "multiple charges"); Stephanos Bibas, *Plea Bargaining Outside the Shadow of Trial,* 117 Harv. L. Rev. 2463, 2518-2519 (2004) ("more likely"); Richman, *supra* note 78, at 1195 ("tendency of prosecutors").

83. Stuntz, *Pathological Politics, supra* note 2, at 519.

84. Daniel C. Richman & William J. Stuntz, *Al Capone's Revenge: An Essay on the Political Economy of Pretextual Prosecution,* 105 Colum. L. Rev 583, 584-585 (2005).

85. Crespo, *Hidden Law, supra* note 78, at 1314, 1352-1353.

86. Melanie A. Prince, Comment, *Two Crimes for the Price of One: The Problem with Kidnapping Statutes in Tennessee and Beyond,* 76 Tenn. L. Rev. 789, 789 (2009).

87. Prince, *supra* note 86, at 789; Crespo, *Hidden Law, supra* note 78, at 1357-1358; Bowers, *supra* note 79, at 1659. As Professors Crespo and Anna Roberts separately note, some jurisdictions permit judges to dismiss charges the judges deem unfair—what Crespo

calls "equitable dismissal." Crespo, *Hidden Law, supra* note 78, at 1357-1360; Anna Roberts, *Dismissals as Justice,* 69 Ala. L. Rev. 327, 330-332 (2017) (describing practical and institutional "constraints that limit this remedy" as a meaningful check on prosecutorial discretion).

88. Crespo, *Hidden Law, supra* note 78, at 1338-1339. As Professor Crespo writes, "long-standing precedent hold[s] that there is no constitutional right to pretrial judicial review of the evidence supporting 'the formal accusation [filed] by the district attorney' " in a given case, although, as he goes on to observe, state rules often do create mechanisms for some form of pretrial evidentiary review by judges, "executed in strikingly different ways across jurisdictions." *Id.* at 1341 (quoting Woon v. Oregon, 229 U.S. 586, 590 (1913)).

89. Ronald Wright & Marc Miller, *The Screening/Bargaining Tradeoff,* 55 Stan. L. Rev. 29, 85, 94 (2002); *Why Do Innocent People Plead Guilty to Crimes They Didn't Commit?,* Innocence Project (2018), https://www.guiltypleaproblem.org.

90. For more on the Attica prison uprising, see *"We Are Men,"* Inquest (Sept. 28, 2021); Luca Falciola, *Defending Attica,* Inquest (Jan. 26, 2023); Orisanmi Burton, *The Long Revolt,* Inquest (Oct. 31, 2023).

91. For more on bargaining over collateral consequences, see Paul T. Crane, *Charging on the Margin,* 57 Wm. & Mary L. Rev. 775 (2016).

92. Stuntz, *Pathological Politics, supra* note 2, at 531.

93. Cong. Rsch. Serv., *Federal Mandatory Minimum Sentencing* 5-7 (2013).

94. Pew Ctr. on the States, *Time Served: The High Cost, Low Return of Longer Prison Terms* 13 tbl.1 (2012).

95. The United States has not executed more than 35 people in a given year since 2013 and has never executed more than 100 people in a given year since the Supreme Court reinstated the death penalty in *Gregg v. Georgia,* 428 U.S. 153 (1976). Death Penalty Info. Ctr., *Facts About the Death Penalty* 1 (2024).

96. Erwin Chemerinsky, *Cruel and Unusual: The Story of Leandro Andrade,* 52 Drake L. Rev. 1, 1-2 (2003).

97. Chemerinsky, *supra* note 96, at 2.

98. Chemerinsky, *supra* note 96, at 3. According to one media account, "In 2012, California voters passed Proposition 36, an initiative that softened the law's impact by, among other things, limiting life sentences to people whose third strike is a 'serious or violent' felony. People sentenced for minor offenses were allowed to petition the court for new sentences; Leandro Andrade did so successfully and was released shortly after Prop 36's passage." Jay Willis, *How Two Supreme Court Cases Made "Cruel and Unusual Punishment" Meaningless,* Balls & Strikes (Mar. 30, 2023).

99. Carol S. Steiker & Jordan M. Steiker, *Courting Death: The Supreme Court and Capital Punishment* 307-308 (2016).

100. Editorial, *Justice Kennedy's Plea to Congress,* N.Y. Times (Apr. 4, 2015).

101. Dora W. Klein, *Taking Corrigibility Seriously,* 28 Berkeley J. Crim. L. 35, 64 (2023).

102. *Long Sentences by the Numbers,* Council on Crim. Just., https://counciloncj .foleon.com/tfls/long-sentences-by-the-numbers/.

103. *Long Sentences by the Numbers, supra* note 102.

104. Leonardo Antenangeli & Matthew R. Durose, Bureau of Just. Stat., *Recidivism of Prisoners Released in 24 States in 2008: A 10-Year Follow-Up Period (2008–2018),* at 7 tbl.7 (2021); Council of Economic Advisers, *Economic Perspectives on Incarceration and the Criminal Justice System* 39-40 (2016) ("increase recidivism").

105. Youngjae Lee, *Recidivism as Omission: A Relational Account*, 87 Tex. L. Rev. 571, 577-578 (2009) (emphasis omitted).

106. Christopher Lewis, *The Paradox of Recidivism*, 70 Emory L.J. 1209, 1212-1214 (2021). For a similar argument, see Benjamin Ewing, *Prior Convictions as Moral Opportunities*, 46 Am. J. Crim. L. 283 (2019).

107. Crespo, *Hidden Law, supra* note 78, at 1368 n.198; Meares, *supra* note 76, at 888; Wright & Miller, *supra* note 89, at 111-112.

108. Crespo, *Hidden Law, supra* note 78, at 1368 n.198; Wright & Miller, *supra* note 89, at 89.

109. Crespo, *Hidden Law, supra* note 78, at 1360-1361.

110. Crespo, *Hidden Law, supra* note 78, at 1360; James Vorenberg, *Decent Restraint of Prosecutorial Power*, 94 Harv. L. Rev. 1521, 1560-1561 (1981); Russell D. Covey, *Fixed Justice: Reforming Plea Bargaining with Plea-Based Ceilings*, 82 Tul. L. Rev. 1237, 1243-1256 (2008). For more on plea bargaining caps, see sources cited *infra* note 113.

111. Wright & Miller, *supra* note 89, at 32.

112. Wright & Miller, *supra* note 89, at 34, 44.

113. Crespo, *Hidden Law, supra* note 78, at 1362-1364. For more on plea bargaining bans and restrictions, see Oren Gazal-Ayal, *Partial Ban on Plea Bargains*, 27 Cardozo L. Rev. 2295 (2006); Oren Bar-Gill & Oren Gazal-Ayal, *Plea Bargains Only for the Guilty*, 49 J.L. & Econ. 353 (2006); Covey, *supra* note 110.

114. David Von Drehle, *Retired Justice Changes Stand on Death Penalty*, Wash. Post (June 9, 1994) (describing Jeffries' interview of Justice Powell); *The Legacy of* McCleskey v. Kemp, Equal Just. Initiative (Apr. 22, 2022), https://eji.org/news/the-legacy-of-mccleskey-v-kemp/.

115. Randall L. Kennedy, McCleskey v. Kemp*: Race, Capital Punishment, and the Supreme Court*, 101 Harv. L. Rev. 1388, 1388-1389 (1988); Scott E. Sundby, *The Loss of Constitutional Faith:* McCleskey v. Kemp *and the Dark Side of Procedure*, 10 Ohio St. J. Crim. L. 5, 5 (2012).

116. G. Ben Cohen, McCleskey*'s Omission: The Racial Geography of Retribution*, 10 Ohio St. J. Crim. L. 65, 67 (2012).

117. John H. Blume et al., *Post-*McCleskey *Racial Discrimination Claims in Capital Cases*, 83 Cornell L. Rev. 1771, 1773-1774 (1998); Andrew Manuel Crespo, *Systemic Facts: Toward Institutional Awareness in Criminal Courts*, 129 Harv. L. Rev. 2049, 2097 n.210 (2016) [hereinafter Crespo, *Systemic Facts*]; Erica J. Hashimoto, *Class Matters*, 101 J. Crim. L. & Criminology 31, 49 (2013); Goel et al., *supra* note 39, at 187 ("as statistical proof"). For further analysis, see Marc Price Wolf, Note, *Proving Race Discrimination in Criminal Cases Using Statistical Evidence*, 4 Hastings Race & Poverty L.J. 395, 395 (2007), discussing "ways in which criminal defendants might attempt to prove racial discrimination in their case by using statistical studies to support their claim even after *McCleskey*." For an argument from the authors of the original Baldus study pushing back on the Court's dismissal of the study's findings, see David C. Baldus et al., McCleskey v. Kemp*: Denial, Avoidance, and the Legitimization of Racial Discrimination in the Administration of the Death Penalty*, in *Death Penalty Stories* 229 (John H. Blume & Jordan Steiker eds., 2009).

118. William J. Stuntz, *The Collapse of the American Criminal Justice System* 120 (2011); Rubinstein, *supra* note 46, at 832.

119. Crespo, *Systemic Facts, supra* note 117, at 2098-2101.

120. Paul Butler, *Equal Protection and White Supremacy*, 112 Nw. U. L. Rev. 1457, 1461 (2018).

CHAPTER 10

1. Larry Buchanan et al., *Black Lives Matter May Be the Largest Movement in U.S. History*, N.Y. Times (July 3, 2020).

2. For examples of sources discussing national presidential campaigns, see *Biden vs. Trump: Who's the Actual Criminal Justice Reformer?*, Politico (Apr. 23, 2020); Ayesha Rascoe, *Touting Law to Help Prisoners, Trump Says Knows What It's Like to Be Treated Unfairly*, NPR (Oct. 25, 2019); Katie Park & Jamiles Lartey, *2020: The Democrats on Justice*, Marshall Project (Apr. 8, 2020). For discussion of elected district attorneys, see later in this chapter, p. 906-913.

3. On the prison population increase in 2022, see Ashley Nellis, Sent'g Project, *Mass Incarceration Trends* 1 (2024). For some examples of the rhetoric in the 2024 presidential campaign, see Shaila Dewan, *Kamala Harris and the Return of 'Tough on Crime,'* N.Y. Times (Aug. 17, 2024); Helen Coster & Nathan Layne, *Trump Pushes Tough-on-Crime Agenda in Town with Historic Links to White Extremism*, Reuters (Aug. 20, 2024).

4. Angela Y. Davis, *Political Prisoners, Prisons, and Black Liberation* (1971).

5. Dorothy E. Roberts, *Foreword: Abolition Constitutionalism*, 133 Harv. L. Rev. 1, 11-12 (2019). For a reading list on abolition, see Critical Resistance, *Resource Guide for Teaching and Learning Abolition* (2021), and Abolitionist Futures, *Introduction to Abolition: 2022 Reading List*. For an anthology of original essays discussing abolition across the globe, see *The Routledge International Handbook of Penal Abolition* (Michael J. Coyle & David Scott eds., 2021). For a collection of essays on abolitionist practices see the *Inquest* series, *Abolition in Action*. For a detailed study of various abolitionist practices, including bail funds, court watching, and participatory defense, see Jocelyn Simonson, *Radical Acts of Justice* (2023). For some leading recent works on the subject, see Angela Y. Davis, *Abolition: Politics, Practices, Promises* (2024), Rachel Herzing & Justin Piché, *How to Abolish Prisons* (2024), Ruth Wilson Gilmore, *Abolitionist Geography* (2022), Derecka Purnell, *Becoming Abolitionists* (2021), and Mariame Kaba, *We Do This 'Til We Free Us* (2021).

6. As Professor Frampton goes on to observe (at pp. 2032-2037 of his article), the question of who counts as "dangerous," much like the definition of "crime," is in part socially constructed and thus — to different audiences — could encompass different "contested bogeymen," ranging from corporate polluters to abortion providers. For further exploration of this idea, see Purnell, *supra* note 5, at 8 ("People often ask me, 'What will we do with murderers and rapists?' Which ones? The police kill about a thousand people every year, and potentially assault, threaten, and harm hundreds of thousands more.").

7. For more on public safety from an abolitionist perspective, see Mariame Kaba & Andrea Ritchie, *No More Police: A Case for Abolition* 187 (2022) ("Contrary to assumptions that abolitionists don't care about safety, we care a great deal about it. We recognize that safety is a basic human need. We think, talk, and strategize about it constantly in order to bring more of us closer to it.").

8. Joshua Kleinfeld, *Manifesto of Democratic Criminal Justice*, 111 Nw. U. L. Rev. 1367, 1376 (2017).

9. For an anthology collecting previously written works and new materials exploring different decarceral interventions across a spectrum of approaches, organized by legal system actors including police, prosecutors, judges, public defenders, and prisons, see *Dismantling Mass Incarceration: A Handbook for Change* (Premal Dharia, James Forman Jr., Maria Hawilo eds., 2024).

10. On the average rates of prison population growth and decline, nationally and across the states, see Nazgol Ghandnoosh, Sent'g Project, *Ending 50 Years of Mass*

Incarceration: Urgent Reform Needed to Protect Future Generations 2-3 (2023). On the uptick in 2022, see Nellis, *supra* note 3, at 1.

11. For two firsthand accounts of the experience of applying for, eventually receiving, and alternatively being denied clemency, see Daryl Waters, *Hope Against Hope*, Inquest (Feb. 8, 2024), and the film *Calls from Home* (Sawdust Productions 2024).

12. For more on changes in aggregate crime rates following the election of progressive prosecutors, see the literature review and original analysis in Nick Petersen et al., *Do Progressive Prosecutors Increase Crime? A Quasi-Experimental Analysis of Crime Rates in the 100 Largest Counties, 2000-2020*, 23 Criminology & Pub. Pol'y 459 (2024).

13. For more on this debate, see the series *Beyond Gideon* published by *Inquest* in 2023. For some firsthand accounts of public defense and the motivations driving lawyers to such work, see Charles J. Ogletree, Jr., *Beyond Justifications: Seeking Motivations to Sustain Public Defenders*, 106 Harv. L. Rev. 1239 (1993); Abbe Smith, *Too Much Heart, Not Enough Heat: The Short Life and Fractured Ego of the Empathic, Heroic Public Defender*, 37 U.C. Davis L. Rev. 1203 (2004); *How Can You Represent Those People?* (Abbe Smith & Monroe H. Freedman eds., 2013).

14. Kaba & Ritchie, *supra* note 7, at 179.

15. Adriaan Lanni, *Taking Restorative Justice Seriously*, 69 Buff. L. Rev. 635, 638-640 (2021).

16. For an additional skeptical take on restorative justice as a systemic intervention, see Christopher Slobogin, *The Minimalist Alternative to Abolitionism: Focusing on the Non-Dangerous Many*, 77 Vand. L. Rev. 531, 541-543 (2024).

17. Victoria Law, *The Work of Abolishing Prisons: A Q&A with Rachel Herzing and Justin Piché*, Nation (May 9, 2024).

18. Marshall Ganz, *People, Power, Change* 19-21 (2024).

19. Jocelyn Simonson, *Democratizing Criminal Justice Through Contestation and Resistance*, 111 Nw. U. L. Rev. 1609, 1612-1617 (2017).

20. For further discussion of plea bargaining strikes, see Andrew Manuel Crespo, *No Justice, No Pleas: Subverting Mass Incarceration through Defendant Collective Action*, 90 Fordham L. Rev. 1999 (2022); Michelle Alexander, *Go to Trial: Crash the System*, N.Y. Times (Mar. 11, 2012); Jenny Roberts, *Crashing the Misdemeanor System*, 70 Wash. & Lee L. Rev. 1089 (2014); Albert W. Alschuler, *The Defense Attorney's Role in Plea Bargaining*, 84 Yale L.J. 1179, 1248-1255 (1979). For a game theoretic analysis of the challenges facing plea bargaining strikes, see Oren Bar-Gill & Omri Ben-Shahar, *The Prisoners' (Plea Bargain) Dilemma*, 1 J. Legal Analysis 737 (2009).

To locate pages in the main text discussing authors listed below by name, please consult that author's entry in the index (p. 1115)

A

Aagaard, Todd S., A Fresh Look at the Responsible Relation Doctrine, 96 J. Crim. L. & Criminology 1245 (2006), 1015n25

Abbott, Jack Henry, In the Belly of the Beast: Letters From Prison (1981, reprint 1991), 23, 28, 32

Abrahams, Scott, Officer Differences in Traffic Stops of Minority Drivers, 67 Labour Econ. 101912 (2020), 983n91

Abramson, Jeffrey, Two Ideals of Jury Deliberation, 1998 U. Chi. Legal F. 125, 941

Abt, Thomas, Bleeding Out (2019), 967n19

Adler, Freda, Sisters in Crime (1975), 979n51

Agan, Amanda Y. & Makowsky, Michael D., The Minimum Wage, EITC, and Criminal Recidivism, 58 J. Hum. Res. 1712 (2023), 975n19

Agan, Amanda Y. & Starr, Sonya, Ban the Box, Criminal Records, and Racial Discrimination: A Field Experiment, 133 Q.J. Econ. 195 (2018), 46

Agan, Amanda Y., et al., Misdemeanor Prosecution, 138 Q.J. Econ. 1453 (2023), 915

Agnew, Robert, Foundation for a General Strain Theory of Crime and Delinquency, 30 Criminology 47 (1992), 974nn15–16

Agnew, Robert, A General Strain Theory of Community Differences in Crime Rates, 36 J. Rsch. Crime & Delinq. 123 (1999), 974n16

Agnew, Robert, Pressured into Crime: An Overview of General Strain Theory (2006), 985n95

Akbar, Amna A., An Abolitionist Horizon for (Police) Reform, 108 Calif. L. Rev. 1781 (2020), 932

Akbar, Amna A., Non-Reformist Reforms and Struggles Over Life, Death, and Democracy, 132 Yale L.J. 2497 (2023), 879

Akbar, Amna A., Toward a Radical Imagination of Law, 93 N.Y.U. L. Rev. 405 (2018), 986n6

Akers, Ronald L., Deviant Behavior: A Social Learning Approach (1973), 973n13

Akers, Ronald L., et al., Criminological Theories: Introduction, Evaluation, and Application (8th ed. 2021), 977n30, 977nn32–33

Albonetti, Celesta A., Sentencing Under the Federal Sentencing Guidelines: Effects of Defendant Characteristics, Guilty Pleas, and Departures on Sentence Outcomes for Drug Offenses, 1991–1992, 31 Law & Soc'y Rev. 789 (1997), 1030n81

Alexander, Larry A., Justification and Innocent Aggressors, 33 Wayne L. Rev. 1177 (1987), 993n95, 994n108

Alexander, Larry & Kessler, Kimberly D., Mens Rea and Inchoate Crimes, 87 J. Crim. L. & Criminology 1138 (1997), 1021n5

Alexander, Larry, et al., Crime and Culpability: A Theory of Criminal Law (2009), 1020n3

Alexander, Michelle, The New Jim Crow: Mass Incarceration in the Age of Colorblindness (2010), 1023n26, 1025nn42–44, 1031n95, 1035n45, 1035nn52–53

Allen, Francis A., Criminal Justice, Legal Values and the Rehabilitative Ideal, 50 J. Crim. L. & Criminology 226 (1959), 970n43

Allen, Francis A., The Decline of the Rehabilitative Ideal: Penal Policy and Social Purpose (1981), 970n46

Allen, Ronald J., et al., Clarifying Entrapment, 89 J. Crim. L. & Criminology 407 (1999), 1019n34

Allen, Ronald J., et al., Criminal Procedure: Investigation and Right to Counsel (3d ed. 2016), 1033n12, 1033n16

Alsan, Marcella, et al., "Something Works" In U.S. Jails: Misconduct and Recidivism Effects of the IGNITE Program, NBER Working Paper 32282 (2024), 970n45

Alschuler, Albert W., The Defense Attorney's Role in Plea Bargaining, 84 Yale L.J. 1179 (1979), 1042n20

Alschuler, Albert W., The Supreme Court, the Defense Attorney, and the Guilty Plea, 47 U. Colo. L. Rev. 1 (1975), 848

Alschuler, Albert W., Two Ways to Think About the Punishment of Corporations, 46 Am. Crim. L. Rev. 1359 (2009), 1015n19

Alschuler, Albert W. & Schulhofer, Stephen J., Antiquated Procedures or Bedrock Rights?, 1998 U. Chi. Legal F. 215, 775

Amar, Akhil Reed, Fourth Amendment First Principles, 107 Harv. L. Rev. 757 (1994), 1033n17

American Bar Ass'n, Criminal Justice Mental Health Standards (1989), 134

American Bar Ass'n, National Task Force on Stand Your Ground Laws, Report and Recommendations (2015), 1002n192

American Civil Liberties Union, Caught in the Net: The Impact of Drug Policies on Women and Families (2005), 661, 1024n30

Amsterdam, Anthony G., Opening Remarks: Race and the Death Penalty Before and After *McCleskey*, 39 Colum. Hum. Rts. L. Rev. 34 (2007), 864

Anders, John, et al., The Effect of Early Childhood Education on Adult Criminality: Evidence from the 1960s Through 1990s, 15 Am. Econ. J.: Econ. Pol'y 37 (2023), 975n21

Anderson, D. Mark, In School and Out of Trouble? The Minimum Dropout Age and Juvenile Crime, 96 Rev. Econ. & Stat. 318 (2014), 976n22

Anderson, David A., The Aggregate Cost of Crime in the United States, 64 J.L. & Econ. 857 (2021), 966n12, 967n19

Anderson, Elijah, Code of the Street: Decency, Violence, and the Moral Life of the Inner City (1999), 973n13

Anderson, José Felipé, The Criminal Justice Principles of Charles Hamilton Houston: Lessons in Innovation, 35 Balt. L. Rev. 313 (2006), 280

Anderson, Michelle J., All-American Rape, 79 St. John's L. Rev. 625 (2005), 1006n18

Anderson, Michelle J., Diminishing the Legal Impact of Negative Social Attitudes Toward Acquaintance Rape Victims, 13 New Crim. L. Rev. 644 (2010), 442, 1013n84

B

Baldus, David C., et al., *McCleskey v. Kemp:* Denial, Avoidance, and the Legitimization of Racial Discrimination in the Administration of the Death Penalty, in Death Penalty Stories (John H. Blume & Jordan Steiker eds., 2009), 1040n117

Balto, Simon & Felker-Kantor, Max, Police and Crime in the American City, 1800–2020 (2022), in Oxford Research Encyclopedia of American History, 1036n57

Baradaran, Shima, Drugs & Violence, 88 S. Cal. L. Rev. 227 (2015), 1025nn40–41, 1028n61, 1028n63

Barber, Refusals to Deal Under the Federal Antitrust Laws, 103 U. Pa. L. Rev. 847 (1955), 488

Bar-Gill, Oren & Ben-Shahar, Omri, The Prisoners' (Plea Bargain) Dilemma, 1 J. Legal Analysis 737 (2009), 1042n20

Bar-Gill, Oren & Friedman, Barry, Taking Warrants Seriously, 106 Nw. U. L. Rev. 1609 (2012), 1033nn14–16

Bar-Gill, Oren & Gazal-Ayal, Oren, Plea Bargains Only for the Guilty, 49 J.L. & Econ. 353 (2006), 1040n113

Barker, David A., Note, Environmental Crimes, Prosecutorial Discretion, and the Civil/Criminal Line, 88 Va. L. Rev. 1387 (2002), 54

Barker, Vanessa, The Politics of Imprisonment: How the Democratic Process Shapes the Way America Punishes Offenders (2009), 1031n92

Barkow, Rachel E., Institutional Design and the Policing of Prosecutors: Lessons from Administrative Law, 61 Stan. L. Rev. 869 (2009), 1037n73

Barkow, Rachel E., Prisoners of Politics: Breaking the Cycle of Mass Incarceration (2019), 898

Barkow, Rachel E., Promise or Peril? The Political Path of Prison Abolition in America, 58 Wake Forest L. Rev. 245 (2023), 869, 887, 973n8

Barkow, Rachel E., Separation of Powers and Criminal Law, 58 Stan. L. Rev. 989 (2006), 820

Barnard, Marina, Drug Addiction and Families (2007), 1027n59

Barnes, J.C., et al., Exposure to Pre-and Perinatal Risk Factors Partially Explains Mean Differences in Self-Regulation Between Races, 11 PLoS ONE e0141954 (2016), 985n95

Barnett, Randy E., The Harmful Side Effects of Drug Prohibition, 2009 Utah L. Rev. 11, 682, 1027n58, 1028n66, 1031n95

Baron, Jason, et al., Public School Funding, School Quality, and Adult Crime, NBER Working Paper 29855 (2022), 975n21

Barr, Andrew & Gibbs, Chloe R., Breaking the Cycle? Intergenerational Effects of an Anti-Poverty Program in Early Childhood, 130 J. Pol. Econ. 3253 (2022), 975–976n21

Basile, Kathleen C., et al., The National Intimate Partner and Sexual Violence Survey: 2016/2017 Report on Sexual Violence, Centers for Disease Control & Prevention (2022), 1003n2, 1005n12, 1012n77

Bauer, Shane, American Prison (2018), 31

Baum, Dan, Legalize It All, Harper's Mag. (Apr. 2016), 653, 703

Bayer, Patrick, et al., Building Criminal Capital Behind Bars: Peer Effects in Juvenile Corrections, 124 Q.J. Econ. 105 (2009), 967n14, 974n13

Bazargan-Forward, Saba, Complicity, in Routledge Handbook of Collective Intentionality (Marija Jankovic & Kirk Ludwig eds., 2018), 1016n6

Bazelon, David L., The Morality of the Criminal Law, 49 S. Cal. L. Rev. 385 (1976), 983n83

Bazelon, Emily, Charged (2019), 907

Beale, Joseph H., Jr., Retreat from a Murderous Assault, 16 Harv. L. Rev. 567 (1903), 287

Beale, Sara Sun, Is Corporate Criminal Liability Unique?, 44 Am. Crim. L. Rev. 1503 (2007), 495

Beattie, J.M., Crime and the Courts in England: 1660-1800 (1986), 988n20

Beaumont, Gustave de & Tocqueville, Alexis de, On the Penitentiary System in the United States and Its Application to France (Emily Katherine Ferkaluk trans., 2018) (1833), 957n2, 957n6, 957n8, 958n9, 958n17

Beccaria, Cesare Bonesana, An Essay on Crimes and Punishments (1793), 1020n1

Beccaria, Cesare Bonesana, On Crimes and Punishments (1764), 965n4, 969n40

Beck, Allen J. & Blumstein, Alfred, Racial Disproportionality in U.S. State Prisons: Accounting for the Effects of Racial and Ethnic Differences in Criminal Involvement, Arrests, Sentencing, and Time Served, 34 J. Quantitative Criminology 853 (2018), 984n92

Beck, Allen J. & Mumola, Christopher J., Prisoners in 1998, Bureau of Justice Statistics (1999), 959n27

Becker, Gary S., Crime and Punishment: An Economic Approach, 76 J. Pol. Econ. 169 (1968), 968n24, 968n32, 972n6

Becker, Gary S. & Landes, William M. eds., Essays in the Economics of Crime and Punishment (1974), 968n24

Beckett, Katherine & Harris, Alexes, On Cash and Conviction: Monetary Sanctions as Misguided Policy, 10 Criminology & Pub. Pol'y 509 (2011), 40, 963n61

Beckett, Katherine, et al., Race, Drugs, and Policing: Understanding Disparities in Drug Delivery Arrests, 44 Criminology 105 (2006), 1030n84

Bedard, Rachael, et al., Elderly, Detained, and Justice-Involved: The Most Incarcerated Generation, 25 CUNY L. Rev. 161 (2022), 978n47

Beletsky, Leo, et al., Drug-Induced Panic, Inquest (Apr. 14, 2022), 1029n76

Bell, Bernard W., Theatrical Investigation: White-Collar Crime, Undercover Operations, and Privacy, 11 Wm. & Mary Bill Rts. J. 151 (2002), 1018n21

Bell, Brian, et al., Crime Scars: Recessions and the Making of Career Criminals, 100 Rev. Econ. & Stat. 392 (2018), 974n19

Bell, Monica, Police Reform and the Dismantling of Legal Estrangement, 126 Yale L.J. 2054 (2017), 771, 999n155

Bell, Monica, Safety, Friendship, and Dreams, 54 Harv. C.R.-C.L. L. Rev. 703 (2019), 891

Bellair, Paul E. & McNulty, Thomas L., Beyond the Bell Curve: Community Disadvantage and the Explanation of Black-White Differences in Adolescent Violence, 43 Criminology 1135 (2005), 985n95

Benns, Whitney, American Slavery, Reinvented, Atlantic (Sept. 21, 2015), 959n26

Benson, Bruce L., Is Property Crime Caused by Drug Use or by Drug Enforcement Policy?, 24 Applied Econ. 679 (1992), 1028n67

Bentham, Jeremy, An Introduction to the Principles of Morals and Legislation (1789), 965n4, 966n7, 1000n170, 1027n54

F

G

H

J

L

M

Manza, Jeff & Uggen, Christopher, Locked Out: Felon Disenfranchisement and American Democracy (2006), 964nn67–68

Marcus, Paul, The Development of Entrapment Law, 33 Wayne L. Rev. 5 (1986), 1019n32

Markoff, Gabriel, Arthur Andersen and the Myth of the Corporate Death Penalty: Corporate Criminal Convictions in the Twenty-First Century, 15 U. Pa. J. Bus. L. 797 (2013), 497, 1015n20

Markovitz, Jonathan, "A Spectacle of Slavery Unwilling to Die": Curbing Reliance on Racial Stereotyping in Self-Defense Cases, 5 U.C. Irvine L. Rev. 873 (2015), 1002n191

Martinson, Robert, New Findings, New Views: A Note of Caution Regarding Sentencing Reform, 7 Hofstra L. Rev. 243 (1979), 970n46

Martinson, Robert, What Works? Questions and Answers About Prison Reform, 35 Pub. Interest 22 (1974), 970n46

Maruschak, Laura M. & Bronson, Jennifer, Alcohol and Drug Use and Treatment Reported by Prisoners, Bureau of Justice Statistics (2021), 982n75

Maruschak, Laura M. & Buehle, Emily D., Survey of Sexual Victimization in Adult Correctional Facilities, 2012–2018 — Statistical Tables, Bureau of Justice Statistics (2021), 1004n2

Maruschak, Laura M. & Minton, Todd D., Correctional Populations in the United States, 2017–2018, Bureau of Justice Statistics (2020), 959n32

Maruschak, Laura M., et al., Survey of Prison Inmates, 2016: Alcohol and Drug Use and Treatment Reported by Prisoners, Bureau of Justice Statistics (2021), 1028n63

Marx, Gary T., Undercover: Police Surveillance in America (1988), 1018n19

Mathur, Neil K. & Ruhm, Christopher J., Marijuana Legalization and Opioid Deaths, 88 J. Health Econ. 102728 (2023), 1029n72

Matsuda, Mari J., Public Response to Racist Speech: Considering the Victim's Story, 87 Mich. L. Rev. 2320 (1989), 990n51

Maxwell, Christopher D., et al., The Impact of Race on the Adjudication of Sexual Assault and Other Violent Crimes, 31 J. Crim. Just. 523 (2003), 1012n77

Mazzarello, Paolo, Cesare Lombroso: An Anthropologist Between Evolution and Degeneration, 26 Functional Neurology 97 (2011), 977n27

Mazzarello, Paolo, Lombroso and Tolstoy: An Anthropologists' Unwitting Gift to Literature, 409 Nature 983 (2001), 977n32

McAdams, Richard H., The Economic Costs of Inequality, 2010 U. Chi. Legal F. 23, 974n17

McAdams, Richard H., The Political Economy of Entrapment, 96 J. Crim. L. & Criminology 107 (2005), 1018n21, 1019n29, 1019n34

McClellan, Chandler & Tekin, Erdal, Stand Your Ground Laws, Homicides, and Injuries, 52 J. Hum. Res. 621 (2017), 996n120

McCloskey, H.J., A Non-Utilitarian Approach to Punishment, 8 Inquiry 249 (1965), 971n54

McGinty, Emma E., et al., The Relationship Between Controlled Substances and Violence, 38 Epidemiologic Revs. 5 (2016), 1028n63, 1028n65

McGregor, Joan, Why When She Says No She Doesn't Mean Maybe and Doesn't Mean Yes: A Critical Reconstruction of Consent, Sex, and the Law, 2 Legal Theory 175 (1996), 1009n44

O

P

S

Sampson, Robert J. & Wilson, William J., Toward a Theory of Race, Crime, and Urban Inequality, in Crime and Inequality (John Hagan & Ruth D. Peterson eds., 1995), 983n90, 984n92, 984n94, 1030n83

Sampson, Robert J. & Winter, Alix S., The Racial Ecology of Lead Poisoning: Toxic Inequality in Chicago Neighborhoods, 1995–2013, 13 DuBois Rev. 261 (2016), 985n95

Sampson, Robert J., et al., Neighborhoods and Violent Crime: A Multilevel Study of Collective Efficacy, 277 Science 918 (1997), 973n11

Sampson, Robert J., et al., Reassessing "Toward a Theory of Race, Crime, and Urban Inequality," 15 Du Bois Rev. 1 (2018), 984n92, 986n96

Sampson, Robert J., et al., Social Anatomy of Racial and Ethnic Disparities in Violence, 95 Am. J. Pub. Health 224 (2005), 978n39, 984n92, 985n95

Sanderson, Marilyn, I Wonder If the Staff Consider Us Human at All, in Inside This Place, Not of It (Robin Levi & Ayelet Waldman eds., 2011), 29

Sawyer, Wendy, How Much Do Incarcerated People Earn in Each State?, Prison Pol'y Initiative (Apr. 10, 2017), 958n18

Sawyer, Wendy & Wagner, Peter, Mass Incarceration: The Whole Pie 2024, Prison Pol'y Initiative (2024), 1013n1

Saxe, Leonard, et al., The Visibility of Illicit Drugs: Implications for Community-Based Drug Control Strategies, 91 Am. J. Pub. Health 1987 (2001), 1030n84

Sayre, Francis Bowes, Mens Rea, 45 Harv. L. Rev. 974 (1932), 170, 987n16

Scalia, Antonin, The Rule of Law as a Law of Rules, 56 U. Chi. L. Rev. 1175 (1989), 1024n28

Schaefer, Shelly S. & Uggen, Christopher, Blended Sentencing Laws and the Punitive Turn in Juvenile Justice, 41 Law & Soc. Inquiry 435 (2016), 982n78

Schauer, Frederick, On the Distinction Between Speech and Action, 65 Emory L.J. 427 (2015), 1021n8

Scheim, Ayden I., et al., Impact Evaluations of Drug Decriminalisation and Legal Regulation on Drug Use, Health and Social Harms: A Systematic Review, 10 BMJ Open 1 (2020), 1029n72

Schlag, Ann Katrin, Percentages of Problem Drug Use and Their Implications for Policy Making: A Review of the Literature, 6 Drug Sci., Pol'y & L. 1 (2020), 1027n52

Schmidt, Christopher W., Divided by Law: The Sit-ins and the Role of the Courts in the Civil Rights Movement, 3 Law & Hist. Rev. 93 (2015), 951

Schneider, Elizabeth M., Battered Women and Feminist Lawmaking (2000), 1002n196

Schneider, Elizabeth M., Equal Rights to Trial for Women: Sex Bias in the Law of Self-Defense, 15 Harv. C.R.-C.L. L. Rev. 623 (1980), 1002n195

Schneider, Valerie, The Prison to Homelessness Pipeline: Criminal Record Checks, Race, and Disparate Impact, 93 Ind. L.J. 421 (2018), 963n65

Schnepel, Kevin T., Good Jobs and Recidivism, 128 Econ. J. 44 (2016), 974n19

Schulhofer, Stephen J., Taking Sexual Autonomy Seriously: Rape Law and Beyond, 11 Law & Phil. 35 (1992), 1008nn34–35, 1009n46, 1010n57, 1011n64

Schulhofer, Stephen J., Unwanted Sex (1998), 351, 391, 395, 405, 432, 1005n12, 1006n16

Schuller, Regina A. & Vidmar, Neil, BWS Evidence in the Courtroom: A Review of the Literature, 16 Law & Hum. Behav. 273 (1992), 1002n199

T

Principal cases (including lead cases, squib cases, and "red-font" cases) are indicated by italics.